THE ROUTLEDGE HANDBOOK OF INCLUSIVE EDUCATION FOR TEACHER EDUCATORS

This handbook provides foundational, conceptual, and practical knowledge and understanding of inclusive education and special needs education. It highlights the need for preparing special educators and teachers for inclusive classrooms to effectively cater to the needs of students with diverse needs in various low-, middle-, and high-income countries globally. It demonstrates various evidence-based and practice-based strategies required to create classrooms inclusive of diverse learners. While tracing the historical trajectory of the foundational underpinnings, philosophical bases, and crucial issues associated with inclusive education, this book presents a future roadmap and pathways through case instances and in-depth discussions to share with educators how they can strengthen their bases and make learning more inclusive in their context. It also provides an overview of the different models of assessment and their applications in the analysis of children in inclusive classroom settings.

Comprehensive, accessible, and nuanced, this handbook will be of immense interest and benefit to teachers, educators, special educators, students, scholars, and researchers in the areas of social inclusion, education, special needs education, educational psychology, technology for inclusion, disability studies, among other related disciplines. It will be extremely beneficial for academicians, teacher educators, special educators, and those interested in professional teacher training courses.

Santoshi Halder is a Professor at the Department of Education, University of Calcutta, India. She has a B.Ed. in Special Education, Post-graduation in Education, and Ph.D. in Applied Psychology. She is also a Board-Certified Behaviour Analyst (BACB, USA) and Special Educator licensure (Rehabilitation Council of India, RCI). Her research interests are in the area of Inclusion, Disability Studies, Educational Technology, Educational Psychology, Diversity, Cross-Cultural Comparative Studies, etc.

Shakila Dada is a Professor at the Centre for Augmentative and Alternative Communication (CAAC) at the University of Pretoria. She is currently the Director of the CAAC. She is a speech-language therapist with extensive experience in research and teaching in the field of AAC and Early Childhood Intervention.

Rashida Banerjee is a Professor and Chair of the Department of Teaching and Learning Sciences at the University of Denver. Her research areas are effective community, family, and professional partnerships; appropriate assessment of young children; especially issues around diversity; inclusive intervention for young children; and interdisciplinary early childhood workforce development.

THE ROUTLEDGE HANDBOOK OF INCLUSIVE EDUCATION FOR TEACHER EDUCATORS

Issues, Considerations, and Strategies

Edited by Santoshi Halder, Shakila Dada and Rashida Banerjee

LONDON AND NEW YORK

Cover image: Getty Images

First published 2023
by Routledge
4 Park Square, Milton Park, Abingdon, Oxon OX14 4RN

and by Routledge
605 Third Avenue, New York, NY 10158

Routledge is an imprint of the Taylor & Francis Group, an informa business

© 2023 selection and editorial matter, Santoshi Halder; individual chapters, the contributors

The right of Santoshi Halder to be identified as the author of the editorial material, and of the authors for their individual chapters, has been asserted in accordance with sections 77 and 78 of the Copyright, Designs and Patents Act 1988.

All rights reserved. No part of this book may be reprinted or reproduced or utilised in any form or by any electronic, mechanical, or other means, now known or hereafter invented, including photocopying and recording, or in any information storage or retrieval system, without permission in writing from the publishers.

Reasonable efforts have been made to publish reliable data and information, but the authors and publisher cannot assume responsibility for the validity of all materials or the consequences of their use. The authors and publishers have attempted to trace the copyright holders of all material reproduced in this publication and apologise to copyright holders if permission to publish in this form has not been obtained. If any copyright material has not been acknowledged, please write and let us know so we may rectify in any future reprint.

Trademark notice: Product or corporate names may be trademarks or registered trademarks, and are used only for identification and explanation without intent to infringe.

British Library Cataloguing-in-Publication Data
A catalogue record for this book is available from the British Library

ISBN: 978-1-032-12987-7 (hbk)
ISBN: 978-1-032-20950-0 (pbk)
ISBN: 978-1-003-26606-8 (ebk)

DOI: 10.4324/9781003266068

Typeset in Bembo
by Deanta Global Publishing Services, Chennai, India

CONTENTS

List of Figures   *x*
List of Tables   *xiii*
Foreword: Inclusion: Progress Made but We Should Not Narrow Our Focus by
Richard Rose   *xvi*
Preface by Santoshi Halder   *xxi*
Acknowledgments   *xxv*
Contributors   *xxviii*

Introduction   1

1 Preparing Teacher Educators for Inclusive Classroom: Challenges, Lacuna and Future Direction   3
 Santoshi Halder

PART I
Foundational and Conceptual Considerations   25

2 Foundational and Legal Basis of Inclusive Education and Future Directions   27
 Todd Sundeen and Rashida Banerjee

3 Universal Design and Inclusive Participation   45
 Gala Korniyenko

4 Parent Perspectives and Beliefs on Inclusive Education for Students with Intellectual Disability   58
 Jordan C. Shurr and Alexandra Minuk

5 Attitudes of Students without Disabilities towards People with
   Disabilities: Perspectives of Higher Education students 72
   Shazia Hasnain and Santoshi Halder

6 Translating Statutory Guidance into Inclusive Practice in the Classroom:
   The Case of England 92
   Susana Castro-Kemp

7 Attitudes Towards an Unfamiliar Peer with Complex Communication
   Needs Using an iPad™ with AAC Software and a Communication
   Board: Perspectives of Adolescents with Physical Disabilities 105
   Shakila Dada, Cathy Flores, Kerstin Tönsing and Jenny Wilder

PART II
Cross-Cultural and Global Perspectives **121**

8 Right to Inclusive Education for Children with Disabilities: Exploring
   the Gap through the Indian and Canadian Legal Prism 123
   Shruti Bedi and Sébastien Lafrance

9 Paradoxes of Inclusion and Segregation Dilemma Explored through the
   Lenses of Students with Disabilities and Teachers: Perspectives from Japan 139
   Santoshi Halder and Rumi Hiraga

10 Participation of Children with Disabilities and Their Peers in Low- and
   Middle-Income Countries: Comparison of Children with and without
   Disabilities 157
   *Shakila Dada, Kirsty Bastable, Alecia Samuels, Mats Granlund,
   Liezl Schlebusch, and Karina Huus*

11 Perceived Strengths of Autistic People and Roadmap for Intervention:
   Parents and Practitioners' Perspectives 191
   Santoshi Halder, Susanne Marie Bruyere, and Wendy Strobel Gower

12 Inclusive Classrooms as Thinking Spaces for Teachers and Students 206
   Sharon Moonsamy

PART III
Identification and Assessment **217**

13 Conceptual, Identification and Assessment of Students with Diverse Needs 219
   Shakila Dada

14 Issues and Trends in Assessment in Early Childhood Intervention for Diverse Populations   227
Angi Stone-MacDonald, Serra Acar, Zachary Price, and Ozden Pinar-Irmak

15 Paradigm Shift in Identification and Assessment of Neurodiverse People: Towards a Strength Focus Lens   242
Santoshi Halder, Susanne Marie Bruyere, and Wendy Strobel Gower

16 Identification of Possible Learning Problems in Children with Intellectual Disabilities   256
Patrik Arvidsson, Tom Storfors and Jenny Wilder

17 Brain–Behaviour Relationship in Attention-Deficit/Hyperactivity Disorder: A Microanalysis   266
Pritha Mukhopadhyay and Piya Saha

18 Prenatal, Perinatal and Postnatal Maternal Risk Factor for Autism Spectrum Disorder: Need to Understand the Genetic–Environment Intersect   280
Bappaditya Adak and Santoshi Halder

19 Utilizing Assessment to Build Partnership Between Students with ID, Families, and Educators   308
Devadrita Talapatra, Laurel A. Snider, and Gloria E. Miller

PART IV
Evidence-Based Intervention and Strategies   325

20 Applied Behaviour Analysis Based Interventions for Application by Teachers in Addressing the Behavioural Needs of Diverse Learners   327
Santoshi Halder

21 Augmentative and Alternative Communication for the Classroom   361
Kerstin Tönsing and Shakila Dada

22 Interventions for the Remediation of Dyslexia: A Systematic Review of Evidence-Based Practices   378
Suparna Nag and Santoshi Halder

23 The Efficacy of Literacy Interventions for Students who Use Augmentative and Alternative Communication   412
Cissy (Cheng) Cheng and Tiffany Chavers

24 Music Puzzle: A Game to Support the Sound Environment of the Deaf and Hard of Hearing Students   426
Rumi Hiraga

25 Video Modeling Interventions at Schools: A Guide for Teachers and Practitioners   438
Christos K. Nikopoulos

26 Inclusion of Children with Physical Restrictions in Out-of-the-Classroom Activities   456
Karin Bertills

27 Getting the Word Out: How Teachers Can Recognise and Support Children with Developmental Language Disorder in an Inclusive Classroom   467
Duana Quigley and Martine Smith

28 A Framework for the Selection of Assistive Technology for the Classroom   483
Karin van Niekerk, Shakila Dada, and Kerstin Tönsing

PART V
Practice-Based Consideration   493

29 Strategies for Implementing Augmentative and Alternative Communication in Classroom Settings in Low- and Middle-Income Countries   495
Nimisha Muttiah, Kathryn D.R. Drager and Inoka S. Samarasingha

30 Suicide Ideation and Prevention in Students with Intellectual Disabilities   508
Amy K. McDiarmid, Jillian Talley and Devadrita Talapatra

31 Functional Positioning for Classroom Participation   524
Kitty Uys

32 The Role of Inclusive Teaching and Creating Learning Experiences for Children with Visual Impairments and Multiple Disabilities   538
Andrea Hathazi and Vassilios Argyropoulos

33 The Use of Telepractice to Support Teachers in Facilitating Learning for Children with Communication Disorders: A South African Proposal   551
Khetsiwe Masuku, Ben Sebothoma, Nomfundo Moroe, Munyane Mophosho and Katijah Khoza-Shangase

34 Inclusion of Students with a Hearing Loss in the Classroom   561
Faheema Mahomed Asmail, Estienne Havanga, and Lidia Pottas

35 Communication Intervention Strategies for Children with Profound
    Intellectual Disabilities: What Do We Know and How Can We Use It?   577
    Juliet Goldbart

PART VI
Transitions, Vocation, and Independent Living Support   **591**

36 School-Based Transition Programming to Improve Employment
    Outcomes for Youth with Disabilities   593
    Andrew R. Scheef

37 Empowering Inclusion in Higher Education: The Case of a
    Multidimensional Peer Support Model for Students with Disabilities   608
    Magda Nikolaraizi, Maria Papazafiri and Vassilios Argyropoulos

38 Educational Environment for Students with Visual Impairment in
    Computer Science Department at Japanese University   618
    Makoto Kobayashi

39 Persons with Cerebral Palsy and Workforce Participation   626
    Shanti Raghavan and Jeeja Ghosh

40 Inclusion of individuals with disabilities in vocational training in South
    Africa?   638
    Refilwe Elizabeth Morwane

Conclusion   **651**

41 Being Pushed and Pulled: Making Sense of Inclusive and Exclusive Forces 653
    Garry Squires

Index   *673*

FIGURES

1.1	Essential components of a comprehensive teacher education programme	12
3.1	Campus wayfinding	49
3.2	Knowlton School's accessible ramp from the ground floor to the lecture hall (left) and Ed Roberts Campus building in Berkeley, California (right)	50
3.3	Flyer about a quiet room created inside Knowlton School to accommodate sensory and religious needs of students	51
3.4	Accessible app for coding on the tablet from Assistive Technology and Accessible Educational Materials Center	52
3.5	Participation in the Design Process on Campus	52
6.1	Suggested route for statutory documentation of children's needs and strengths, from the development of the child's narrative of functioning to translation in the classroom	101
9.1	Impediments of inclusive setting	145
10.1	PRISMA flow chart of the scoping review process	160
12.1	Flow map of cognitive management of information	208
12.2	Contributing aspects of cognitive instruction	211
12.3	Flow diagram illustrating a cognitive instruction	214
13.1	A zoom lens approach to assessment for children with disabilities in the school environment	223
17.1	Analytic signal representation in the complex plane for both ADHD and HP is shown (ADHD – blue signals, HP – red signals)	273
17.2	Depicting analytic signal representation in the Fp1 and Fp2 channels in the complex plane (pre-intervention – red signals; post-intervention – blue signals)	273
20.1	Defining characteristics of ABA	330
20.2	Three-term contingencies of behaviour	332
20.3	Application of behaviour interventions	332
20.4	Step-by-step assessment process comprising seven crucial aspects	333

20.5	Behaviour assessment process as funnel shaped	334
20.6	Main components for pre-intervention assessment	334
20.7	Reviewing medical records	335
20.8	Major behaviour assessment methods	336
20.9	Results of trial-based FA on a 7 years child with self-injurious head hitting behaviour shown through percentage of trials during control and test conditions	338
20.10	Environmental consideration as per the ecological theory	340
20.11	Diagrammatic representation of a Model of Ecological Assessment consisting of six steps	342
20.12	Common broad strategies of behaviour interventions	350
20.13	Findings of function-based phase by phase, personalized, individualized intervention package of a 7-year-old child with developmental disability targeting self-injurious or inappropriate behaviour	350
21.1	An overview of AAC symbols, strategies, aids, displays, and devices	363
22.1	Systematic review flow diagram specifying stages of inclusion of the papers	381
22.2	Graphical representation of intervention strategies/programs implemented for the remediation of reading difficulty or dyslexia	382
23.1	An example of a grid display on Tobii Dynavox I-13®	414
23.2	An example of a visual scene display (VSD) on Tobii Dynavox I-13®	414
24.1	Playing Taiko with Miburi	430
24.2	Original sound with the interface of a large ball	434
24.3	Sound particles	434
28.1	Adapted framework	486
29.1	A VSD showing 1 large hotspot	497
29.2	A VSD showing multiple hotspots	498
29.3	Cut-out elements	500
29.4	Showing action verb flying	501
29.5	Training for paraprofessionals	503
29.6	Example VSD	504
29.7	Example VSD	504
30.1	Overview of increased suicide risk factors for individuals with any severity ID	511
30.2	Overview lower protective against suicide factors in individuals with ID for all severity levels	512
30.3	Model of suicide prevention for students with ID	519
30.4	Model of suicide risk assessment for students with ID	520
31.1	ICF related to cerebral palsy	525
31.2	Position of the pelvis	528
31.3	Measuring the seat to fit the child	530
31.4	Tilt in space	531
34.1	ICF framework of a child with a Hearing Loss	562
34.2	Causes and type of hearing loss	564
34.3	Proposed service delivery model	568

35.1	The development of early communication	579
37.1	The interactive sectors of the PROSVASI's volunteer network	610
38.1	Braille display equipped with forty-six cells	620
38.2	Refreshable tactile display, DV-2 shows a bar graph of Microsoft Excel	622
39.1	(Enable India, 2016) Employability Framework	634
39.2	(Enable India, 2018) Includability™ Framework	634
40.1	Government department responsible for vocational training programmes in South Africa	642
41.1	Simple force field analysis	655
41.2	Pupils achieving aspirational standards in English in primary schools	663
41.3	Pupils achieving good grades in secondary schools	663
41.4	Force Field analysis to identify actions (forces) that lead to greater inclusion	667

TABLES

1.1	Challenges of teacher educators in inclusive classroom	8
2.1	Comparison of major models	37
3.1	Comparison of universal design and policies addressing barriers	46
3.2	Universal design principles addressing physical and cognitive/sensory needs	48
5.1	Means, standard deviations, and independent samples t-test for the CBAD survey scores with respect to age groups	78
5.2	Means, standard deviations, and independent samples t-test comparing the male and female scores on the CBAD scale	79
5.3	Means, standard deviations, and independent samples t-test comparing the CBAD scores with respect to students' prior familiarity with people with disabilities	80
5.4	Means, standard deviations, one-way ANOVA, and independent samples t-test comparing the scores on the CBAD scale with respect to Income groups	81
5.5	Means, standard deviations, one-way ANOVA, and independent samples t-test results comparing CBAD scores with respect to Area of Residency	83
5.6	Means, standard deviations, one-way ANOVA, and independent samples t-test results comparing the scores on the CBAD scale with respect to academic disciplines	84
5.7	Correlation Matrix of the CBAD scale (total scores and dimension-wise scores) and demographic factors (income, socio-economic status, mother's qualifications, father's qualifications, mother's occupation, father's occupation)	85
7.1	Group characteristics	109
7.2	Frequency of responses on the CADAQ: Component Affective/Behaviour	112
7.3	Frequency of responses on the CADAQ: Component B: Cognitive/Belief	113
7.4	Frequency of responses on the CADAQ: Component C: Communication Competence	114

7.5	Mean and standard deviation of Groups A and B across three components of the CADAQ	114
9.1	Demographic and personal information or details of the participants (N = 11)	143
9.2	The sub-themes extracted from the interviews (n = 11)	144
10.1	Studies included in the scoping review	161
10.2	Differences between the participation of children with developmental disabilities and children with typical development	168
10.3	Description of adaptations to measures and the participation and related constructs measured	179
11.1	Demographic details of the participants	194
12.1	Creating thinking spaces	212
12.2	Cognitive Map: Analyses of Instruction (COMAN)	213
14.1	Summary of the assessment tools	235
15.1	Exceptional skills with descriptors and the corresponding researchers and citations	244
18.1	General comparison between cases and controls as regards to some demographic factors	285
18.2	Distributions, unadjusted Odd Ratio, and 95% CI for prenatal, perinatal, and postnatal risk factors and family history	286
18.3	Adjusted association between autism and risk Factor	292
18.4	Binary logistic regression model for autism spectrum disorder	293
18.5	Hosmer and Lemeshow test	294
18.6	Omnibus tests of model coefficients	294
20.1	Sample behaviour checklist	337
20.2	Important considerations in ecological assessment (Source: Bronfenbrenner, 1979)	341
20.3	Some widely used ABA-based techniques and strategies	343
20.4	Summary of step-by-step process of ABA-based Intervention Model	351
22.1	Summary of intervention studies followed by Process Training approach	383
22.2	Studies following interventions based on an educational software-based approach	390
22.3	Intervention studies based on the Cognitive Training Approach	394
22.4	Studies following interventions based on the Multisensory Approach	396
22.5	Studies following interventions based on the Visual Reception Training Approach	398
23.1	Description of the researcher, participants, and training materials during the first read-through	420
23.2	Description of the researchers, participants, and training materials during the second read-through	421
25.1	Data collection Form for video modeling	449
26.1	The five A's applied to prerequisites for the participation of students with physical disability in out-of-the-classroom activities	460
27.1	Examples of child-focused language enrichment interventions	476

30.1	Definitions of terminology related to suicide risk assessment	509
30.2	ID adaptation of a selected suicide prevention curriculum for middle school and high school students (Gül, 2016; Jacobs, 2013; Talapatra et al., 2020)	514
30.3	Possible manifestations of warning signs for students with ID (Bardon, 2020; Lieberman et al., 2014)	515
30.4	Proposed adaptations to suicide risk assessment based on information from Bardon, 2020; Masi et al., 2012; Talapatra et al., 2020	516
31.1	Screening for functional seating	527
31.2	Checklist of criteria for each position	532
34.1	Hearing loss and associated characteristics observable in the classroom	566
34.2	Questionnaires for educators or caregivers to utilize in school or home settings	570
34.3	Facilitating strategies suggested for the inclusive classroom	572
34.4	Website resources for educators	573
36.1	No-cost toolkits developed by NTACT to support employment-related services for youth with disabilities	599
36.2	Benefits of hiring people with disabilities (as identified by Lindsay et al., 2018)	602
37.1	A representative list of PROSVASI's services	611
37.2	The diverse characteristics of volunteers	612
41.1	Percentage of children with SEND over time derived from government statistics (DfE, 2021)	657

FOREWORD

Inclusion: Progress Made but We Should Not Narrow Our Focus

Richard Rose

Issues surrounding equity and inclusion have provided a focus for educational debate and research for more than 40 years. Those of us working in the field of education have tended to consider 1994 and the signing of The Salamanca Statement and Framework for Action (UNESCO, 1994) as a pivotal moment, leading to the development of policies and interrogation of provisions for children who had previously been marginalised in our schooling systems. The influence of this and subsequent international agreements (UNESCO, 2000; UNESCO, 2015) cannot be denied, but I would suggest that while assisting in moving the equity debate forward, the narrow focus on children usually described as having special or additional educational needs has not always been an aid to progress.

Thomas (2013) emphasised that the move towards inclusive education must be regarded within a wider struggle for the respect of diversity and social justice that has challenged the ethics of separation and exclusion in all of its forms. Throughout the past two centuries, disenfranchised and marginalised groups have found it necessary to campaign and demand the rights that have been denied to them. This necessity to challenge existing systems continues today with different emphasis and priorities according to the socio-political and economic situation in each nation.

In many respects, the term inclusive education has come to represent a movement towards ensuring that learners with disabilities have an opportunity to be educated alongside their typically developing peers. This is most certainly a critical issue, having recognised that for too long individuals defined solely by their physical, sensory, cognitive, or emotional needs have been expected to receive their schooling separate from their brothers and sisters. But this simplistic interpretation, one that ignores the many struggles experienced by groups discriminated against because of the colour of their skin, their gender, sexual orientation, religion, caste, tribal status, or class, stands in danger of factionalising the very persons that campaigners, researchers, and teachers suggest that they would wish to represent.

In 1954 The US Supreme Court landmark judgment in the case of Brown versus the Board of Education ruled that segregation by racial characteristics deprived children in minority communities of equal educational opportunities, and violated the Fourteenth Amendment of the US Constitution (Bell, 2004). In 1878 The University of London became the first in the UK to award degrees to women; parallels can be drawn here with the campaign for women's suffrage to give women the vote. In 1989, The States and the Commonwealth Government initiated a National Aboriginal and Torres Strait Islander Education Policy (NATSIEP) in Australia. This established a series of goals with the aims of involving Aboriginal people in educational decision-making, equity of education access, and participation, thus working towards equitable and appropriate outcomes (Gray & Beresford, 2008). I present these historical examples not as a means of singling out specific groups that have endured significant discrimination but rather to demonstrate how equality of access to education has been and remains an issue that has demanded constant attention from those who wish to challenge inequity and marginalisation.

Two common factors can be observed in situations where educational opportunities have been limited or denied. The first is the identification of individuals or groups according to certain characteristics that are different from those of the majority of policy and decision-makers. In the examples provided, the colour of skin, the perception of women, and specific cultural identities have each challenged the understanding of those in positions of authority and either through fear or the need to exert control have resulted in discrimination and exclusion. The second factor relates to the rate of progress. Policies at both international and local levels have been instituted with the honourable intention of challenging discrimination and increasing equality of opportunity. Yet still, we see that the characteristics of minorities are used as a means of accepting low expectations and a failure to provide quality education. Furthermore, in many instances, we have seen an increase in exclusion and discrimination as for example the maltreatment of members of the Uyghur population and denial of their cultural and religious practices in Xinjiang Province China (Holder 2019), refusal to provide access to education for refugees from the Rohingya community (Human Rights Watch, 2019) and attacks against girls accessing education in Nigeria and Pakistan (OHCHR, 2015).

The issues discussed above may be far from the parameters within which many researchers currently working in the field have operated. However, I would suggest that the motivations and urgency with which educators have challenged the exclusion of children with special educational needs and/or disabilities have similar origins to those who have worked in other areas of discrimination. As Thomas (op. cit.) reminds us, many parents of children with disabilities were campaigning for the rights of their sons and daughters to attend education alongside their peers long before what has become fashionably known as the inclusion movement began. It is therefore important that we take every opportunity to learn from other professionals working in education or other allied disciplines who continue to confront policies and practices that are exclusionary and pervasive.

It is, of course, necessary that we should celebrate what has already been achieved. In much of the world educational opportunities have increased, literacy levels have risen, and school attendance has been afforded to children who were previously denied regular access (UNESCO, 2020). However, in some countries, progress remains slow and, in some instances, the situation has worsened. Because of the efforts of teachers, policymakers, parents, and researchers working in partnership, we now have a far greater understanding of teaching strategies, curriculum adaptations, and specialist approaches and resources that have enabled children to become more effective learners (Ashman, 2012; Florian & Beaton, 2018). The challenge remains to see this learning translated into effective action.

The gap between theory, knowledge, and action is currently the greatest obstacle to the effective implementation of inclusion policy. Tremendous efforts have been made by researchers to ascertain the attitudes of teachers and other professionals toward the promotion of inclusion (Srivastava et al., 2017; Ewing et al., 2018). A similar plethora of investigations has considered policy development (Hardy & Woodcock 2015; Duke et al., 2016). Far less focus has been given to an understanding of the efficacy of teaching practices for the promotion of inclusion

(Florian, 2014; Molbaek, 2018). We do know some of the characteristics of learning environments that are conducive to inclusion. For example, Watkins and Meijer (2010) present a series of approaches to classroom management and instruction that have been seen to have benefits when addressing classes with diverse needs. These include co-operative teaching, heterogeneous grouping, and collaborative problem-solving. Others (Grantham & Primrose, 2017; Shah & Rajanahally, 2019; van Geel et al., 2019) have considered the use of specific teaching approaches which may benefit all children within an inclusive learning environment. However, despite an increase in knowledge about what might work effectively in an inclusive classroom, practice across schools remains inconsistent and is often dependent upon the enthusiasm of the school's leadership and the commitment of individual teachers.

If progress towards achieving truly inclusive education is to be made, it will necessitate the closing of the gap between what is known to work effectively in providing education for classes with diverse learning needs and a greater commitment to put this into practice. This, I would suggest, requires a shift of focus away from researching attitudes and obstacles to giving greater attention to understanding how some schools have become far more effective in addressing diverse needs. Studies such as that conducted by Black-Hawkins, Florian, and Rouse (2007) have indicated that the effective management of classes of students with diverse needs can be beneficial for all concerned. Further empirical investigations of what works in schools and the incorporation of successful pedagogical practices identified in such studies into the professional development of teachers are essential if the current static nature of progress toward inclusion is to be addressed.

To return to my earlier theme, that of understanding the wider causes of exclusion, I believe that there is much that we can learn from the many interest groups that have worked to overcome discrimination. By addressing single issues, such as disability, racial discrimination, or exclusion on the basis of tribal status, we dilute our resources and, in some instances, are in danger of working against each other. The relationship between poverty and disability has been clearly established (Mousavi, 2019; Pinilla-Roncancio & Alkire, 2020). Those who live in poverty are more likely to have a child with a disability as a result of poor housing, inadequate access to health care, and poor diet. Families who have a child with a disability accrue greater expenses and are more likely to devote time to child care rather than income generation and are therefore at risk of falling into poverty. Families living as refugees are generally driven into poverty with the consequential risk of having a child with a disability. In many countries, people from ethnic, religious, or racial minorities live in poorer conditions than the majority population (Cassells & Evans, 2017) and are more likely to be labelled as problematic (Morgan et al., 2017). In some societies, girls have limited access to education or are expected to enter into early marriage arrangements with additional risk factors (Osadan, 2014; Mitra, 2015). Those living in remote rural communities are less likely to have access to good quality health care or schooling than their counterparts in metropolitan cities (Rose et al., 2021).

The symbiotic relationship between these factors indicates the importance of viewing the conditions that lead to exclusion holistically rather than addressing only the surface indicators associated with disability and special educational needs. Inclusion is many-faceted, and our understanding of the ways in which it may be achieved requires an analysis that recognises all of these influential factors. In our efforts to address the causes of exclusion, we must consider not only the ways in which we can change classrooms and prepare teachers and other professionals but rather work in partnership with colleagues across disciplines to improve our own understanding and ensure the effective deployment of our resources.

Research in inclusive education has made a significant contribution to our understanding of the ways in which the teaching and learning environment may be changed to address the needs of a diverse school population. However, until such time as we adopt a broader remit and work alongside colleagues from other disciplines, we will continue to limit our opportunities to succeed in enabling all children to gain fair access and opportunity to schools that welcome them without fear of failure free from discrimination. The research reported in this volume is certainly important and has made a major contribution toward bringing greater equity to schools. Perhaps now is a good time to reflect upon the ways in which we may intensify our efforts and partnerships, to work for a much more inclusive and equitable society.

References

Ashman, A. F. (2012) Facilitating inclusion through responsive teaching. In, C, Boyle, & K. Topping. (Eds.) *What Works in Inclusion?* Maidenhead McGraw Hill.

Bell, D. (2004) *Silent Covenants: Brown v. Board of Education and the Unfulfilled Hopes for Racial Reform*. Oxford: Oxford University Press.

Black-Hawkins, K., Florian, L, & Rouse, M. (2007) *Achievement and Inclusion in Schools*. London: Routledge.

Cassells R. C., & Evans, G.W. (2017) Ethnic variation in poverty and parenting stress. In Deater-Deckard, K. & Panneton, R. (Eds.), *Parental Stress and Early Child Development*. Cham: Springer.

Duke, J., Pillay, H., Tones, M., Nickerson, J., Carrington, S, & Ioelu, A. (2016) A case for rethinking inclusive education policy creation in developing countries, *Compare: A Journal of Comparative and International Education*, 46 (6), 906–928,

Ewing, D. L., Monsen, J., & Kielblock, S. (2018) Teachers' attitudes towards inclusive education: a critical review of published questionnaires, *Educational Psychology in Practice*, 34(2), 150–165

Florian (2014) What counts as evidence of inclusive education?, *European Journal of Special Needs Education*, 29(3), 286–294.

Florian, L, & Beaton, M. C. (2018) Inclusive pedagogy in action: getting it right for every child. *International Journal of Inclusive Education*, 22 (8) 870–884.

Grantham, R, & Primrose, F. (2017) Investigating the fidelity and effectiveness of Nurture Groups in the secondary school context. *Emotional and Behavioural Difficulties*, 22 (3), 219–236

Gray, J, & Beresford, Q. (2008) A 'formidable challenge': Australia's quest for equity in indigenous education. *Australian Journal of Education* 52 (2), 197–223.

Hardy, I. & Woodcock, S. (2015) Inclusive education policies: discourses of difference, diversity and deficit, *International Journal of Inclusive Education*, 19 (2), 141–164.

Holder, R. (2019) On the intersectionality of religious and racial discrimination: A case study on the applicability of ICERD with respect to China's Uyghur Muslim minority. *Religion and Human Rights*, 14(1), 1–30.

Human Rights Watch (2019) *"Are We Not Human?" Denial of Education for Rohingya Refugee Children in Bangladesh*. Available at www.hrw.org/report/2019/12/03/are-we-not-human/denial-education-rohingya-refugee-children-bangladesh accessed 16/6/21

Mitra, A. (2015) Son preference in India: Implications for gender development. *Journal of Economic Issues*. 48 (4), 1021–1037.

Molbaek, M. (2018) Inclusive teaching strategies: Dimensions and agendas, *International Journal of Inclusive Education*, 22 (10), 1048–1061.

Morgan, P.L., Farkas, M., Hillemeier, M, & Maczuga, S. (2017) Replicated evidence of racial and ethnic disparities in disability identification in U.S. schools. Educational Researcher 46 (6) 305 –322

Mousavi, T., (2019) Relationship between poverty and disability in OIC countries. *Disability, CBR & Inclusive Development*, 29 (3), 120–122.

Osadan, N. (2014) Gender equality in primary schools in Sub-Saharan Africa: Review and analysis. *Journal of Transnational Women's and Gender Studies*, 12(2), 215–231.

Pinilla-Roncancio, M, & Alkire, S. (2020) How poor are people with disabilities? evidence based on the global multidimensional poverty index. *Journal of Disability Policy Studies*, 31 (4), 206–216

Rose, R., Narayan, J., Matam, S, & Reddy Sambram, P. (2021) A comparison of provision and access to inclusive education for children with disabilities in a metropolitan city and a rural district in Telangana State, India. *Educational Sciences* 11 (3).

Shah, S., & Rajanahally, J. (2019) Peer mediated support strategies for children with disabilities. In P.Verma, A. Panshikar, & Y. Gupta (Eds.), *Be the Difference; Equality and Equity in Education*. New Delhi: S.R. Publishers.

Srivastava, M., de Boer, A.A, & Pijl, S.J. (2017) Preparing for the inclusive classroom: changing teachers' attitudes and knowledge. *Teacher Development*, 21 (4), 561–579.

Thomas, G. (2013) A review of thinking and research about inclusive education policy, with suggestions for a new kind of inclusive thinking. *British Educational Research Journal*. 39 (3), 473 –490

United Nations Educational, Scientific and Cultural Organisation. (1994). *The Salamanca Statement and Framework for Action on Special Needs Education*. Paris: UNESCO.

United Nations Educational, Scientific and Cultural Organisation. (2000). *The Dakar Framework for Action, Education for All*. Meeting our Collective Commitments. Paris: UNESCO.

United Nations Educational, Scientific and Cultural Organisation. (2015). *Incheon Declaration and Framework for Action for the implementation of Sustainable Development Goal 4*. Paris: UNESCO.

United Nations Educational, Scientific and Cultural Organisation. (2020). *Inclusion and Education: All Means All*. Paris: UNESCO.

United Nations Human Rights Office of the High Commissioner. (2015) *Background Paper on Attacks Against Girls Seeking to Access Education*. Geneva: OHCHR.

van Geel, M., Keuning, T., Frèrejean, J., Dolmans, D., van Merriënboer, J, & Visscher, A. J., (2019) Capturing the complexity of differentiated instruction. *School Effectiveness and School Improvement*, 30 (1), 51–67.

Watkins, A, & Meijer, C. (2010) The development of inclusive teaching and learning: A European perspective. In R. Rose (Ed.) *Confronting Obstacles to Inclusion*. London: Routledge.

PREFACE

Santoshi Halder

Inclusive Education as a human right is enshrined in several international legislation and conventions (CRC 1989; Salamanca Statement, 1994; UNCRPD, 2006; Warnock, 1979) that aim to ensure the development of a more equitable and inclusive society where each and every individual has an equal right to education and can lead a self-determined life and live with dignity on an equal footing with the people without disabilities. Such legislation proclaims that every person has the right to full participation in society. Living a quality life and enjoying a fulfilled human existence is the right of each and every individual. However, we all are not born having the same attributes; personal or social/ context-driven. Differences and diversity are a natural phenomenon of human existence, and the wide range of diversities need to be accepted, respected, and their inherent potentialities need to be facilitated in a positive, conducive environment for a sustainable quality of life.

Individuals with disabilities for long have been discriminated against and marginalized almost universally since time immemorial and even today. However, in spite of inclusion being identified as a priority at the international and national levels, there still remains an interlude in its true implementation due to the multiple challenges. Challenges are widely and extremely diverse, varying with respect to the contextual or environmental factors: country, culture, on the one hand, and also based on the level, intensity, nature, or type of disability on the other hand. These challenges need to be understood in-depth to ameliorate an effective intervention plan that can bring out the best in the individual.

The 2030 Agenda for Sustainable Development clearly proclaims one of the Sustainable Development Goal 4 (SDG 4) as to "*ensure inclusive and equitable quality education and promote lifelong learning opportunities for all*" for a global society (UNESCO, 2015). Education for Sustainable Development Goals: Learning Objectives (UNESCO 2017) stresses the need for the desired knowledge and skills needed to fulfill these aims. Equality of educational opportunity includes the provision of education for all, irrespective of religion, caste, creed, sex, and location and is the basis for forming an inclusive society.

The current human global population is approaching 8 billion (UN DESA 2017); each and every individual has a set of different abilities and strengths as well as a set of traits that might need special attention or interventions. The idea of a truly inclusive society is to find out creative ways to facilitate the potentialities of each and every individual matched to their learning patterns or styles. The role and responsibilities of the various stakeholders, parents, teachers, practitioners, specialists, professionals, etc. who are engaged in the task of bringing out the best in their child or adult with diverse needs, are extremely crucial and immense. The task begins with accepting and believing at the outset that each individual has potential irrespective of their inner or contextual diversities and that needs to be recognized, embraced, respected, and facilitated through necessary strategic and proactive actions. Our abilities lie in finding creative ways to navigate the best pathways that ensure good quality of life, independent living, and full participation for the successful inclusion of people with disabilities in society.

This book opens up a wide range of successful inclusive models and practices drawn from a variety of cultures, and countries through the lenses of experts, practitioners, educators, specialists, and researchers from all over the world. The primary objective of the book is to present and debate those perspectives together in a form that is accessible to a much broader audience not only limited to the academics but also including parents, practitioners, policymakers, administrators, and special educators who can be informed of state of the art in the various aspects of inclusive education and possibly disseminate and also implement some of what has been learned from the work of the authors within these pages, with necessary modification as appropriate to their own culture and context for effective outcomes. This book brings forth crucial perspectives and aspects of inclusion from authors from various disciplines, renowned universities, institutes, and organizations from various countries such as India, United States, United Kingdom, Australia, U.K, Canada, Sweden, Romania, South Africa, Japan, Italy, Hungary, Moscow, Greece who are specialists in their respective fields and have shared their knowledge that has been earned through years of experience of working with the people with disabilities in various settings. Studies from around the world together as a comprehensive whole will provide pivotal and critical elements and raw materials for building fertile grounds for facilitating the broader objective and aim of inclusion all over the world.

Book Objectives

The book serves the following learning objectives:

i) Provide foundational knowledge and conceptual understanding of the inclusion of learners with diverse needs.
ii) Shed light on the need for cross-cultural understanding of the challenges and addressal through relevant excerpts.
iii) Elucidate evidence-based strategies and inclusive practices by researchers, educators, and practitioners to cater to the needs of students with diverse needs.
iv) Provide an overview of related issues on various identifications and assessments.
v) Overview of after-school transitions including vocation, rehabilitation, and independent living.

The book is divided into the following six broad sections and the Introductory and Concluding Chapters:

Introductory Chapter

PART I: Foundational and Conceptual Considerations
PART II: Cross-Cultural and Global Perspectives
PART III: Identification and Assessment
PART IV: Evidence-Based Intervention and Strategies

PART V: Practice-Based Consideration
PART VI: Transitions, Vocation, and Independent Living Support

Concluding Chapter

PART 1: Foundational and Conceptual Considerations

Understanding the fundamental, philosophical, legislative, and conceptual bases of inclusive education is crucial for effective teaching-learning in inclusive classrooms and inclusion in general. **This section covers various foundational and conceptual aspects and issues of teaching and learning in inclusive classrooms.**

PART II: Cross-Cultural and Global Perspectives

Review of cross-cultural and global trends and issues on inclusion is important to understand the world perspectives and state of the art in the field. The collective synthesis and analysis of research, policy, and practices in diverse and unique contexts can inform future directions and individualized and indigenized implementation of inclusive practices across the globe. **This section discusses issues on cross-cultural, comparative research, and practice highlighting the global perspectives on crucial areas for consideration to support inclusive education.**

PART III: Identification and Assessment

Identification and assessment of students with disabilities is pivotal for successful and positive outcomes in an inclusive setting. Important aspects and methods of assessment of diverse needs of learners must be examined and implemented so that successful and effective intervention can be ameliorated. **This section discusses the various important aspects of identification and assessment that are considered potent pre-requisites of successful intervention programs.**

PART IV: Evidence-Based Interventions and Strategies

Over the years, evidence-based interventions have been developed through rigorous and sustained research and have been documented through research reports, policy briefs, and practice in diverse settings. **This section covers interventions that demonstrate treatment integrity and positive outcomes for students with disabilities in inclusive settings.**

PART V: Practice-Based Considerations

Developing and implementing educational programs is an extremely important and crucial aspect of an inclusive classroom/educational institution. Important consideration needs to be undertaken and considered while implementing interventions to increase their effectiveness. **The section covers some of the most important practice-based considerations for teachers in inclusive classrooms or educational settings.**

PART VI: Transition after School, Vocation, and Independent Living Support

Transition after education to vocational life or to community and independent living is a crucial aspect of a successful inclusive education program. The overall aim or goal is to ensure healthy wellbeing, good quality of life, adaptability, and independent living of people with diverse needs in the community. However, independent living can be extremely challenging for people with diverse needs. The important aspects of independent living are successful transitions from various settings and training and orientation accordingly beforehand for developing the utmost adaptability for a well-contented independent community life. ***This section covers the various issues and aspects of successful and effective transitions, vocations, rehabilitation, and independent living for people with diverse needs.***

Audience
General Teachers, Special Teachers, Educators, Researchers, Professionals, Practitioners, Policy Makers, Specialists, Administrators, Parents, etc.

Training courses:
In- service training for teachers and allied health professionals working in inclusive education.

References

The United Nations. (1989). Convention on the rights of the child. *Treaty Series*, *1577*, 3.

The United Nations. (2006). Convention on the rights of persons with disabilities. *Treaty Series*, *2515*, 3.

UN. (2015). Transforming our world. The 2030 agenda for sustainable development. New York: UN. Retrieved February 6, 2019, from https://sustainabledevelopment.un.org/content/documents/21252 030%20Agenda%20for%20Sustainable%20Development%20web.pdf.

UN DESA. (2017). World population projected to reach 9.8 billion in 2050, and 11.2 billion in 2100 [webnews 21 June 2017]. New York: United Nations Department of Economic and Social Affairs, Population Division. Retrieved February 7, 2019, from https://www.un.org/development/desa/en/news/population/world-population-prospects-2017.html.

UNESCO (2017a). *Education for Sustainable Development Goals: Learning objectives*. Paris: UNESCO. Retrieved February 7, 2019, from https://www.unesco.de/sites/default/fles/2018-08/unesco_education_for_sustainable_development_goals.pdf.

United Nations Education, Scientific and Cultural Organization (UNESCO). (1994). *The Salamanca Statement and Framework for Action on Special Needs Education*. Paris: UNESCO.

Warnock Report (1979). Comments on the report of the committee of enquiry into the education of handicapped children and young people- 'Special Educational Needs'. (Summary), July 1979. https://10.1192/S0140078900004788

ACKNOWLEDGMENTS

The purpose and the thought process for the book evolved eventually through the course of the journey while visiting multiple educational and research institutes in various countries and meeting various scholars and stakeholders all over the world over the last few decades. The content of the book is an accumulation of thoughts over the years through multiple exposures and engagement with varied research and teaching opportunities in the field of disability studies, inclusive education, special needs education in India and across various countries of the world (low, middle, and high income). It has been an amazing journey of nearly twenty years in the field of disability and working closely in various capacities in various locations and regions that went beyond the narrow boundaries of state, nations, or cultures. The path to inclusion is about the willingness to listen to others and being flexible and welcoming in adopting the needful elements for modification and refining of the existing thought process for the wellbeing of all and for a better tomorrow for a global sustainable world. The raw ideas gathered over the years across countries crystallized towards direction and got refined and shaped through the discussions and discourses with many significant scholars, parents, specialists, practitioners, administrators, policymakers, experts, and people with disabilities worldwide during the academic and personal visits, conferences, collaborative research projects, etc. Perhaps naming one would be missing out on so many who directly or indirectly, consciously or unconsciously have influenced the thought process further to materialize in the form of the present book in a concrete and comprehensive form.

First and foremost, I am thankful to the University of Calcutta for providing me the scope, platform, opportunities, and continuous support to flourish my multifarious research and academic endeavor most strategically and significantly.

I would like to acknowledge the support of various organizations namely, European Union, Erasmus, *United States India Education Foundation (USIEF), New Delhi and International Institute of Education (IIE), USA, Rockefeller Foundation, USA, Shastri Indo-Canadian Institute (SICI), Japan Society for Promotion of Science (JSPS), Australian Government, Department of Education and Training, Australian High Commission, Endeavour Australia India Council, Indian Institute of Social Science Research (ICSSR), New Delhi, University Grants Commission (UGC), New Delhi, National Institute for Humanities and Social Sciences (NIHSS), South Africa* for trusting me and for providing me the means through multiple academic and research opportunities to explore the unexplored through the multiple, enlightening, opportunities and networking with some of the most amazing group of scholars who stimulated and kindled my zeal and passion further through the interchange of thoughts towards addressing some of the most crucial global sustainable goal of inclusive education and inclusive participation.

I would also like to thank my wonderful group of young vibrant spectrum of scholars and students for their ever-inquisitive quest for driving me every day towards ushering the thirst for knowledge for knowing the unknown, exploring the unexplored, and energizing me even more toward significant and contributory work for the community and its people.

My sincere thanks to my co-editors Prof. Shakila Dada, University of Pretoria, South Africa, and Rashida Banerjee, University of Denver, the USA, for accepting my invitation and joining hands with their agreeableness, time, and efforts for collaborating and assisting me in the book project with the needful inputs, valuable suggestions, and contribution in all phases and stages of this book. I am glad to be able to continue our long-lasting connection with both my research colleagues through significant academic contributions.

I acknowledge the support and assistance of the Publisher Routledge India for supporting us with this book project and for providing us the needful assistance at every phase.

Finally, I would like to thank my husband Dr. Arindam Talukdar, Principal Scientist, Indian Institute of Chemical Biology, India; my daughter Mihika; my son Kiaan; my parents; and almighty God for instilling me the inspiration, drive, and energy and throughout support without which the book would not have been possible.

The book is the product of the cumulative efforts of so many people around the world in various countries who trusted to share their valuable perspectives and agreed to extend their expert arguments, innovative ideas, models, evidence-based research findings, etc. for a global audience for facilitating the pathway for creating an inclusive society. Special thanks are due to all those people whom I may have missed out.

Finally, I can't resist conveying that this is just the beginning of an amazing long journey of making the world a better place to live for all and each step of this amazing journey is a learning experience, extremely refreshing, and the foundation for the next future endeavor!

Santoshi Halder

I would like to express my gratitude to my colleagues at the Centre for Augmentative and Alternative Communication for their support and encouragement. In addition,

the Dean of the Faculty of Humanities Prof. Vasu Reddy for always emphasizing the value of "the book" in enhancing the academic project. Finally, I am grateful to the University of Pretoria for creating an enabling environment for ideas.

I am grateful to colleagues from across the globe who contributed their insights, expertise and research encompassed in the chapters in this book. It has been wonderful walking this journey with you.

I would also like to express my gratitude to the co-editors Prof. Santoshi Halder and Prof. Rashida Banerjee. Prof Santoshi Halder, it was an absolute pleasure working with you. Your enthusiasm, vision, and passion for inclusion are contagious. Prof. Rashida Banerjee, thank you for your enthusiasm, reflections, and critical questions in preparing this handbook. It was a delight working with you.

I am thankful to the Publishers Routledge India and specifically Lubna Irfan for her guidance, patience, and support in bringing this book to fruition.

I am deeply grateful to my husband Professor Naushad Emmambux for his encouragement, support, love, and kindness. To my precious children Hadia and Mohammad Iyaad for allowing me time to do what I love. Also, thank you for the endless supply of entertainment breaks and laughter.

Acknowledgments

I am grateful to the many mentors, families, and children in schools who have shared their learnings and lived experiences with me.

Finally, I am grateful to my Creator.

The right to education is a basic human right denied to many including girls and children with disabilities. I hope that this book will contribute towards ensuring this basic human right is met regardless of age, gender, ability, and any "otherism".

Shakila Dada

I am grateful to the many individuals with disabilities and their families with whom I have had the privilege of engaging over the years – as a special education teacher, as a college professor, as a community member, and as a friend. They have challenged me and continue to impress upon me the importance of mutually respectful, collaborative partnerships to improve the outcomes for students with disabilities, their families, and the professionals who serve them.

It has been such a pleasure to work with the chapter contributors who have worked tirelessly to produce, what I would call, such masterpieces that provide useful resources for educators. I am in awe of your dedication to the field and to the wide dissemination of knowledge and information to improve practice.

We are thankful to everyone on the Routledge team who has helped us so much. Special thanks to Lubna Irfan, the Associate Commissioning Editor, who has continuously and patiently answered multiple questions and provided us with valuable guidelines and feedback to improve our book. I am especially appreciative of the extensive feedback from anonymous field reviewers.

My family has been a source of sustenance for me – my parents who supported my dream of becoming a special education teacher despite all odds; my dear husband, Deb Banerjee, who, without question has stood by me and humored my obsessions with work. Papa, thank you for your wisdom – I miss you today more than ever.

Finally, thank you to my co-editors without whom I would not have entertained writing this book: Santoshi for leading this enormous effort and working tireless hours, and keeping us all on track to develop this book into an endeavor we can be proud of. Shakila, your calm, generous, and persistent personality has impressed and guided me. Thank you both!

Rashida Banerjee

CONTRIBUTORS

About the Editors

Santoshi Halder, Ph.D., is a Professor at the Department of Education, University of Calcutta, India. She has a Post-graduation in Education and Ph.D. in Applied Psychology. She is a Board-Certified Behaviour Analyst (BACB, USA) and Special Educator licensure (Rehabilitation Council of India, RCI). Her research interests are in the area of disability studies, special needs education, educational technology, inclusion, diversity, cross-cultural comparative studies, etc. She has been actively involved internationally and nationally in multifarious ways for the inclusion of people with diverse needs since 2000. She has been an international fellow and recipient of various prestigious competitive international awards and fellowships; Credit Mobility Fellowship, EU, Erasmus, *Shastri-Indo-Canadian Fellow (2022), Fulbright Academic and Professional Excellence fellow, USA (2020), Rockefeller Fellow, Italy (2019), Japan Society for Promotion of Science/ JSPS fellow, (2019), Endeavour Australia-India Education Council Research Fellow and Honorary Visiting Fellow at Olga Tennison Autism Research Centre (OTARC), La Trobe University, Australia (2015-2016), Endeavour Awards Ambassador (2018) and Fulbright Nehru Senior Research Fellow, USA (2011–2012).*

She received the *Governor's Medal (West Bengal, India)* in 2001 for her contribution to the community and people as a National Cadet Corps (N.C.C). Nine Ph.D.'s and eighteen M. Phil Dissertations have been successfully awarded under her supervision. She is passionate about the inclusion of people with diverse needs. She has edited international books on inclusion/inclusive pedagogy, research methodology, and authored a book on Education Technology (Routledge Springer, Palgrave Macmillan etc). She is currently working on various research and book projects on areas of global importance. She has completed nine projects; five international and four national on various areas funded by UGC, ICSSR, NIHSS, USIEF, IIE, JSPS, Rockefeller, SICI, etc. Dr. Halder has authored more than 20 book chapters in international books and published more than 60 papers in peer-reviewed national and international journals. She teaches BACB-approved behavior analysis courses to students from various countries including training teachers for inclusive classroom from various countries. Dr. Halder provides behavior intervention services, especially to people with autism spectrum disorder including training the parents and practitioners. She has delivered more than ninety lectures/invited presentations/talks in various institutions/universities in various low-middle-high income countries that include India, South Africa, the USA, Austria, Italy, Singapore, Japan, and Canada.

On another front she is engaged in multiple adventurous activities as an N.C.C cadet and is a nationally trained mountaineer, Basic and Advanced from leading mountaineering Institutes (NIM, Uttarkashi, and WHMI, Manali) in the country. She was selected for the All-India Women Mountaineering expedition in the year 2002. She is also an amateur painter and artist.

Shakila Dada, Ph.D., is a Professor at the Centre for Augmentative and Alternative Communication (CAAC) at the University of Pretoria. She is currently the Director of the CAAC. She is a speech language therapist with extensive experience in research and teaching in the field of AAC and Early Childhood Intervention. She has published widely in the field of Augmentative and Alternative Communication (AAC) and Early Childhood Intervention (ECI). She has co-authored over 40 papers in peer-reviewed journals and a number of book chapters. She has successfully supervised 11 PhD students and 26 Master's students. She utilizes a zoom lens approach to implementing AAC interventions focusing on the person and the AAC system but also a zooming out to take broader, systemic issues into account. For example, the involvement of the child in the family and the role of professionals (health care professionals and teachers) and policies in selecting and implementing AAC, thereby enhancing the participation and inclusion of children that require AAC.

Rashida Banerjee, Ph.D., is a Professor and Chair for the Department of Teaching and Learning Sciences at the University of Denver. Her research areas are effective community, family and professional partnerships, appropriate assessment of young children, especially issues around diversity, inclusive intervention for young children, and interdisciplinary early childhood workforce development. Dr. Banerjee has published articles, book chapters, and books, received grants, and presented at numerous national and international conferences on these topics. Her research and funded projects focus on preparing well-qualified early childhood and early childhood special educators. She has served on the board of national organizations such as Division for Early Childhood and Divisions for International Special Education Services. She served on the DEC Recommended Practices Committee responsible for ensuring the development and use of evidence-based practices in early childhood. Dr. Banerjee was the Editor of *Journal for International Special Needs Education*. She is a recipient of the International Ford Foundation Fellowship Program.

About the Authors

Serra Acar, Ph.D., is an assistant professor of early childhood education and care at the University of Massachusetts, Boston. She has worked in the field for more than 10 years. Her research includes assessment, personnel preparation in early intervention/early childhood special education, and global EI/ECSE.

Bappaditya Adak, Ph.D., is an Assistant Professor, Education, and Departmental Head, Vidyasagar Mahavidyalaya affiliated with the University of Calcutta. Dr. Adak was born in the State of West Bengal, India, and completed his Ph.D. and Masters at the University of Calcutta. His research interests lie in the area of the diverse needs of the child, psychology, abnormal psychology, and educational Management. Dr. Adak recently completed a book on Educational Management as a single author in the regional language (Bengali).

Vassilios Argyropoulos, Ph.D., is an Associate Professor at the University of Thessaly (Greece) in the field of vision disability. He has acted as coordinator and research fellow in many national, Erasmus+ and Horizon projects relevant to special education and serves the International Council for Education of People with Visual Impairments (ICEVI) as the contact person in the Balkan Countries. He has more than 100 publications, and his research areas include haptic apprehension, braille literacy skills, and issues of access and inclusion of individuals with visual impairments and multiple disabilities in learning environments

Patrik Arvidsson is a Ph.D. in Disability Research, Clinical Psychologist, and Senior Lecturer. His research focuses on participation, inclusive processes, and psychological health in people with disability, specifically people with intellectual disabilities. He is interested in research in exploring factors related to participation and psychological health, both individual and contextual factors such as societal support. Patrik Arvidsson is affiliated with the Centre for Research & Development, Region Gävleborg in Sweden, and CHILD, Swedish Institute for Disability Research at Jönköping University. He is also a Research Associate at the Centre for Augmentative and Alternative Communication, University of Pretoria, South Africa.

Rashida Banerjee, Ph.D., is a professor and Chair in the Department of Teaching and Learning Sciences at the University of Denver. Her research areas are effective community, family, and professional partnerships, appropriate assessment of young children, especially issues around diversity, inclusive intervention for young children, and early childhood workforce development. She has served on the Division for Early Childhood Board and the DEC Recommended Practices Committee, responsible for ensuring the development and use of evidence-based practices in early childhood. She is a Ford Foundation Fellow Alum and currently serves as the Editor of the *Journal for International Special Needs Education*.

Kirsty Bastable, Ph.D., is a speech, language pathologist and audiologist. She has a keen clinical interest in individuals with communication vulnerability and their participation in society. She is currently engaged in a post-doctoral fellowship at the Centre for Augmentative and Alternative Communication, the University of Pretoria, which has focused on the participation of children with disabilities from middle- and low-income countries, as well as the use of augmentative and alternative communication in health settings for communication with individuals who have communication vulnerability.

Shruti Bedi, Ph.D., is a Professor of Law at the University Institute of Legal Studies (UILS), Punjab University (PU), Chandigarh; International Fellow, National Institute of Military Justice, Washington DC, USA Co-ordinator, Department of Law, University School of Open Learning, PU; Director, Centre for Constitution and Public Policy, UILS, PU; and a TED-x speaker. Her areas of research are constitutional law, internal security law, and comparative public law. She has authored two books; co-edited four books; and has published numerous articles in reputed international and national legal journals, books, blogs, and newspapers. She has lectured at international and national forums including universities in England, Canada, Brazil, Indonesia, and Vietnam.

Karin Bertills, Ph.D., has extensive teaching experience in school-based Physical Education and Health (PEH) and teacher training at Jönköping University. She holds a Ph.D. degree in disability research and is a member of the CHILD research group, focusing on participation in everyday life for children with disabilities. She is a lecturer in Physical Education and Health (PEH) and inclusive teaching strategies in teacher training at Jönköping University and Linköping University. Research interests concern positive educational outcomes of self-efficacy and participation in PEH for students in need of special support.

Susanne M. Bruyere, Ph.D., CRC, is currently a Professor of Disability Studies, Director of the Employment and Disability Institute, and Associate Dean of Outreach at the Cornell University

ILR (Industrial and Labor Relations) School in Ithaca, New York. Prof. Bruyere is currently Project Director and Co-Principal Investigator of numerous federally sponsored research, dissemination, and technical assistance efforts focused on employment and disability policy and effective workplace practices for people with disabilities, including the U.S. Department of Labor Office of Disability and Employment Policy National Technical Assistance, Policy, and Research Center for Employers on Employment of People with Disabilities; the Rehabilitation Research and Training Center on Employer Practices to Improve Employment Outcomes for Persons with Disabilities; Organizational Practices to Increase Employment Opportunities for People with Disabilities: The Power of Social Networks. Prof. Bruyere holds a doctoral degree in Rehabilitation Psychology from the University of Wisconsin-Madison.

Susana Castro-Kemp, Ph.D., is a Reader (Associate Professor) of Education at Roehampton University, London, United Kingdom. With a background in Psychology and Early Childhood Intervention, she has published extensively on education policy in England, provision for young children with special educational needs and disabilities, mental health, wellbeing, and positive functioning in childhood. She has particular expertise in using the International Classification of Functioning Disability and Health to support the documentation of children's needs and the translation of policy into practice in inclusive settings.

Tiffany Chavers, CCC-SLP, is a doctoral student in the Speech, Language, and Hearing Sciences Department at the University of Texas at Austin. Her primary research interest is intervention and evaluation protocols for individuals with developmental disabilities who rely on augmentative and alternative communication.

Cissy Cheng is a doctoral student at the University of Texas at Austin studying under the mentorship of Dr. Rajinder Koul. Cissy earned her BA in Linguistics from Fudan University and her MS in Speech, Language, and Hearing Sciences from Boston University. She has experience working with clients with aphasia, autism spectrum disorders (ASD), and voice disorders. Her research interests include speech production training using visual support and treatment efficacy of AAC intervention for people with developmental disorders. Additionally, she is devoted to promoting communication in intensive care settings between nonspeaking patients and healthcare providers.

Shakila Dada, Ph.D., is a Professor at the Centre for Augmentative and Alternative Communication (CAAC) at the University of Pretoria. She is currently the Director of the CAAC. She is a speech-language therapist with experience in research and teaching in the field of AAC and Early Childhood Intervention. Her research seeks to systematically describe, understand and address the communication and participation patterns of persons who have complex communication needs.

Kathryn Drager, Ph.D., is the Associate Dean for Research and Graduate Education in the College of Health and Human Development and Professor of Communication Sciences and Disorders at Penn State University. She received her Ph.D. in Speech-Language Pathology from the University of Minnesota, Twin Cities, in 1999. She has significant experience in research in augmentative and alternative communication (AAC) for children and adults with severe disabilities. Her research interests include AAC for individuals with severe expressive communication disorders, especially for children, adolescents, and adults with severe disabilities who are at the beginning stages of communication, including children with autism. She is also interested in issues faced by the global community in AAC.

Cathy Flores graduated as a speech-language therapist and audiologist from the University of Pretoria in 2007. She completed her Master's degree in Augmentative and Alternative Communication through the Centre for AAC at the University of Pretoria in 2017. She has experience in both the public and private sectors in education. Her most recent work has been with learners with severe to profound intellectual disabilities within the public education sector.

Jeeja Ghosh has been involved in the social sector for more than two decades. She has been a part of the disabled people's movement and is connected with disabled rights activists pan India. Her special interest is women with disabilities. She was part of the global advocacy team which represented the Indian civil society delegation at the hearing of the India Country Report on the UNCRPD at the United Nations in Geneva in September 2019. She holds post-graduate degrees in Social Work and Disability Studies from Delhi and Leeds Universities. She has lived experience of cerebral palsy. Jeeja worked as the Head of Advocacy and Disability Studies at the Indian Institute of Cerebral Palsy in Kolkata. At present she is an independent consultant on gender and disability.

Juliet Goldbart, Ph.D., is a Professor at Manchester Metropolitan University, UK. Her research addresses communication challenges experienced by people with profound intellectual disabilities or complex physical disabilities. She has been involved in establishing the evidence base for communication interventions for children and adults with a range of difficulties and was part of the rewriting of Routes for Learning, a free online assessment for children with profound intellectual disabilities. She has a particular interest in appropriate service delivery for families with a child or adult with complex needs across the globe.

Wendy Strobel Gower is a project director at the Yang-Tan Institute. She leads the Northeast ADA Center, the Diversity Partners Project, and fee-for-service work to educate managers and supervisors about including people with disabilities. Wendy holds a Master's degree in Rehabilitation Counseling from the Medical College of Virginia at Virginia Commonwealth University (VCU). She has worked extensively in the application and training of issues around employment and reasonable accommodation in the workplace for people with disabilities. She has gained valuable experience in project management and project direction over the past ten years. Other areas of interest include person-centered planning philosophy and tools, disability legislation and its impact on services, and the identification and accommodation of the functional limitations of disabilities across the lifespan.

Mats Granlund, Ph.D., is a Professor and researcher in the field of childhood disability and a licensed clinical psychologist. Granlund's work has focused on participation outcomes, learning, health, and everyday living of children and adolescents with impairments or long-term health conditions. Professor Granlund is a lead member of the Swedish CHILD research environment, an initiative of Jönköping, which involves researchers from education, health psychology, health care sciences, and disability research. CHILD is also a part of the Swedish Institute of Disability Research involving the universities in Jönköping, and Linköping. Granlund is also an extraordinary professor at CAAC at Pretoria University.

Santoshi Halder, Ph.D., is a Board-Certified Behaviour Analyst (BACB, USA) and a Professor in the Department of Education, University of Calcutta, India. She is the recipient of various prestigious international fellowships; Shastri-Indo-Canadian Fellow (2020-22), Fulbright Academic and Professional Excellence fellow, USA (2020), Rockefeller Fellow, Italy (2019), JSPS (2019), Endeavour Australia-India Education Council Research Fellow and Honorary Visiting Fellow at Olga Tennison Autism Research Centre (OTARC), La Trobe University,

Australia (2015–2016), Endeavour Awards Ambassador (2018), and Fulbright Nehru Senior Research Fellow, USA (2011–2012). She received the Governor's Medal (West Bengal, India) in 2001 for her contribution to the community and people as a National Cadet Corps (N.C.C). Nine Ph.D.s and 18 M.Phil. dissertations have been successfully awarded under her supervision. She is passionate about the inclusion of people with diverse needs and has published more than 200 peer-reviewed journal articles and or book chapters.

Shazia Hasnain is working as an Assistant Professor in the Department of Education, Aliah University, Kolkata, West Bengal. She is pursuing her Ph.D. from the University of Calcutta under the guidance of Dr. Santoshi Halder. Her areas of academic interest include Pedagogy of English Language teaching and Educational Psychology.

Andrea Hathazi, Ph.D., is an Associate Professor at the Special Education Department, Faculty of Psychology and Educational Sciences, Babes-Bolyai University in Cluj-Napoca, Romania. She has published in the domain of multiple disabilities *Development of communication skills in deaf-blindness* (Presa Universitara Clujeana, 2014), she is the coordinator of the volume *Communication in the context of multiple disabilities*, and she is responsible for the collection of *Education of people with multiple disabilities* at Presa Universitară Clujeană publishing house. She is the coordinator of three Summer Schools regarding Multiple Disabilities that were organized at Babeş-Bolyai University. She has participated in numerous international conferences such as the 6th European Conference on Psychology and Visual Impairment, Budapest, Hungary, 2016 or the 9th ICEVI European Conference in Bruge, Belgium, 2017. Andrea Hathazi is Vice-President and member of the Board of ICEVI Europe, representing the Balkan Countries.

Estienne Havenga graduated from the University of Pretoria in 2010 and has served as a Speech-language therapist and Audiologist in the public and private sectors for the past ten years. In 2015, she completed her Master's degree in tele-intervention for children with hearing loss, which was published in the International Journal of Telemedicine and Telecare. She joined the Pretoria Cochlear Implant Team in 2017 as an adult aural rehabilitation specialist. She currently works in private practice in Pretoria and provides intervention/therapy services to children and adults with hearing loss. She also lectures part-time at the University of Pretoria.

Rumi Hiraga, Ph.D., is a professor at the Tsukuba University of Technology (NTUT), Japan. She has been teaching computer science to deaf and hard of hearing (DHH) students at NTUT for about 15 years. Both her musical abilities and the knowledge that there are many DHH people who enjoy music led her to research how DHH people listen to music. She is building a music information recommendation system for DHH people to widen their music experiences. She is also building a music training system for DHH people that can enable them to hear music and environmental sounds.

Karina Huus, Ph.D., is a Pediatric Nurse and Professor. She has worked with children at the pediatric clinic; her doctoral studies were conducted at Linköping University focused on weight gain in children. She has since worked at the School of Health Welfare, and her research continued within the research group CHILD, Jönköping University. She is one of the leaders in the interdisciplinary research group CHILD where her research focuses on children with disability and participation in everyday activities from a global perspective. She is also an active researcher within the Institute for Disability Science, which is a collaboration between Jönköping University and Linköping University.

Contributors

Katijah Khoza-Shangase, Ph.D., is the 2017 Business Women Association of South Africa's Finalist – Academic Category. She is an Associate Professor and former Head of the Speech Pathology and Audiology Department at the University of the Witwatersrand. Khoza-Shangase has won numerous awards including for her contributions to the field of audiology. She has published a number of peer-reviewed journal articles, technical and research reports, book chapters, and co-edited books. *Black Academic Voices: The South African Experience*, published in 2019, is her most current contribution to the transformation and decolonization project, which is the winner of the 2020 Humanities and Social Sciences Award.

Makoto Kobayashi, Ph.D., is Professor in the Department of Computer Science, Tsukuba University of Technology, Japan. He received an M.S. degree in Engineering in 1995 and a Doctor's degree in Engineering in 2002 both from the University of Tsukuba. His research interests are developing a support system for the daily life of blind, low vision, and deaf/hard of hearing people. Education, entertainment, and adopted sports are the main research fields. One example is the blind bowling support system which speaks the positions of remaining pins automatically. He found that blind players can enjoy not only their own game but also other sighted players' game using this system, because the system speaks all games as opposed to a human supporter who speaks only blind player's game. Through developing such a supporting system, he hopes to realize a happy life for sensory-impaired people in the world.

Gala Korniyenko has a Ph.D. in City and Regional Planning at the Knowlton School of Architecture at the Ohio State University (USA), whose research focuses on planning with autistic and neurodiverse communities. In addition to her doctoral research, Gala is actively engaged in governance, advocacy, and community-building in the wider university community. As an educator and researcher, she strives to move planning, education, and practice forward toward a more inclusive environment. As one of the founding members of Planning with Underserved Populations, a new American Planning Association Special Interest Group, which was inspired by work on the topic of autism, she dedicates her time to the mission of advancing planning around issues of urban equality and acceptance of differences.

Sébastien Lafrance is Crown Counsel (Prosecutor) at the Public Prosecution Service of Canada. Fellow of the Central Asian Legal Research centre at Tashkent State University of Law, Uzbekistan. Adjunct Professor at Universitas Airlangga, Indonesia. Adjunct Lecturer at Ho Chi Minh City University of Law, Vietnam. Former part-time professor of law at the University of Ottawa, Canada; LL.M. (Laval University); LL.B. Université du Québec à Montréal); B.Sc. (University of Montreal). He is a former clerk at the Supreme Court of Canada and at the Quebec Court of Appeal. He also was Counsel at the Law Branch of the Supreme Court of Canada.

Faheema Mahomed Asmail, Ph.D., is a senior lecturer in the Department of Speech-Language Pathology and Audiology at the University of Pretoria. Her research interests focus on improving access to person-centered ear and hearing health care as well as investigating the biopsychosocial approach in Patient/Relationship-Centered Care. She has growing national and international recognition with numerous articles published in Clarivate Analytics Web of Science accredited journals and has presented on a national and international level. Over the years Dr. Mahomed Asmail has won a number of research prizes and has received an NRF Y1 rating for the period 2020-2025.

Khetsiwe Masuku, Ph.D., is a Lecturer in the Department of Speech Pathology at the University of the Witwatersrand. She teaches and supervises Speech Pathology students at both undergraduate and postgraduate levels. She has a Master's degree in Public Health and a Ph.D. in Augmentative and Alternative Communication (Severe Disability). Her research focuses on disability, specifically access for persons with disabilities, caregivers of persons with disabilities, and the implementation of disability policies within the African context. Her other research interests include research in Aphasia and Deaf-blindness. She has published several articles in peer-reviewed journals and written book chapters.

Amy K. McDiarmid, Ph.D., NCSP, is a Clinical Assistant Professor and Director of Field Experiences in the School Psychology Program within the University of Denver's Morgridge College of Education. Her research interests include crisis prevention and intervention in schools, addiction in schools, and supervision for graduate students in school psychology.

Gloria E. Miller, Ph.D., is the Morgridge Endowed Professor in Literacy & School Psychology. Her work focuses on early language and literacy development, social-emotional learning, and elevating all families' voices as collaborators in their children's education through a multi-dimensional process of shared cultural caring and family-school-community partnering that promotes each student's school and life success.

Alexandra Minuk is a Ph.D. student at Queen's University in Ontario, Canada, in the Faculty of Education. Alexandra has worked as a special education teacher for students with autism spectrum disorder as well as a consultant for special education teacher recruitment, training, and retention. Alexandra's research focuses on the inclusion of elementary and secondary students with autism spectrum disorder within public schools and the factors that influence placement decisions.

Sharon Moonsamy, Ph.D., is an Associate Professor in Speech-Language Pathology and a Remedial-Education Consultant at Wits University. She is the Head of the School of Human & Community Development. Her teaching and research, including child language, literacy, and cognition, are centered on social justice, creating access to services for those from marginalized populations. Teacher-therapist workshops, conference presentations, and journal and book publications contribute to her scholarly profile.

Munyane Mophosho, Ph.D., is a senior lecturer at Wits University's School of Human and Community Development. She received for her research which included guest lecturing at the University of Ghana. In 2017, she was invited to be a guest lecturer at St John's University in the United States. She was a member of the JET Education Services' Consortia of Inclusive Education Experts. She served as a lecturer at the University of Pretoria's Centre for Augmentative and Alternative Communication (CAAC) before coming to Wits in February 2004. She has published extensively in peer-reviewed journal articles, technical and research reports, book chapters, and co-edited books.

Nomfundo F. Moroe, Ph.D., is a senior lecturer and current Head of Discipline (Audiology) at the University of the Witwatersrand. She is a passionate researcher with an interest in Occupational Audiology, Complex Interventions, Deaf culture, and Deaf-blindness. She is a CARTA Fellow (Consortium for Advanced Research Training in Africa) and is funded to do post-doctoral research. She has published several peer-reviewed articles and book chapters; and has presented at conferences. She has co-edited a Special Issue Journal for the South African Journal of Communication Disorders (2020). Her upcoming outputs include a co-edited book *Occupational Noise-Induced Hearing Loss: An African Perspective*.

Refilwe Elizabeth Morwane is a lecturer and Ph.D. candidate at the Centre for Augmentative and Alternative Communication (AAC) at the University of Pretoria. She is a qualified Speech-language therapist and Audiologist with a Master's degree in AAC, both completed at the University of Pretoria. She has worked in the field of severe disability with a keen interest in research in the employment of persons with severe disabilities. In addition to her involvement in academic and research activities, she also trains professionals such as caregivers, teachers, and therapists working with individuals with severe communication disabilities in AAC implementation.

Pritha Mukhopadhyay, Ph.D., Professor at the Department of Psychology, University of Calcutta (CU), India and the Coordinator of the UGC-funded project, Centre with Potential for Excellence in a Particular Area (CPEPA), CU, since 2011, is the recipient of the gold medal at the post-graduation level at the Department of Psychology, CU, in 1980. For her postdoctoral work, she received the J. William Fulbright Scholarship in 1994. She has around 66 journal publications to her credit, both at national and international levels journals and has authored one book and 19 book chapters with various reputed publication houses.

Nimisha Muttiah, Ph.D., is a Senior Lecturer in the Department of Disability Studies, Faculty of Medicine, University of Kelaniya, Sri Lanka. She received her Ph.D. in Speech-Language Pathology from The Pennsylvania State University in 2015. She has 15 years of clinical and research experience working with children with significant communication difficulties. Her primary research interests are in augmentative and alternative communication (AAC) for children. The focus of her research has been looking at individuals with complex communication needs living in low-and middle-income (LAMI) contexts and effective service delivery in such places.

Suparna Nag, M.A., MPhil., is currently working as an Assistant Professor at East Calcutta Girls' College, Kolkata, India. She has seven years of experience in the field of teaching. She is from an Education Discipline and completed her Post graduation in Education. Her special paper was Education of the Children with Special Needs.

Karin van Niekerk, Ph.D., is a lecturer at the Occupational Therapy Department of the University of Pretoria, Pretoria, South Africa. She is involved in training undergraduate occupational therapy students as well as supervising postgraduate research. The research for her Ph.D. focused on identifying the factors that influence professionals in their selection of AT for young children. She is particularly interested in the influence of the preferences, priorities, knowledge, and experiences of the recommending professional themselves on the professional reasoning process involved in AT selection.

Magda Nikolaraizi, Ph.D., is Associate Professor in the area of inclusive education and education of the deaf and a coordinator of the accessibility center at the University of Thessaly, Greece. Dr Nikolaraizi has participated in many projects as a research fellow and has many publications in international journals, conference proceedings and volumes. Her research interests lie within the area of inclusive and accessible learning for individuals with disabilities, with a special emphasis on persons who are deaf or hard of hearing. Also, she acts as an executive editor for the region of Europe and the Middle East for the journal *Deafness and Education International*.

Christos Nikopoulos, Ph.D., is a Board-Certified Behaviour Analyst® - D (Doctoral Level; BCBA-D), a former member of the Board of Directors of the (BACB®) and of the European Association of Behaviour Analysis (EABA). He has served as a clinician, a university lecturer, an educator, a consultant, a researcher, and an author in the areas of Autism Spectrum Disorder (ASD), intellectual and other developmental disabilities, as well as neurological and behavioral interventions in special education for more than 23 years. He is currently the founder and CEO of Autism Consultancy Services in London (UK) and Riyadh (KSA).

Maria Papazafiri, Ph.D., is an adjunct lecturer at the University of Thessaly, Greece, and also belongs to the scientific staff of the accessibility center at the University of Thessaly. She has participated in many research projects. Also, she has publications in international journals, conference proceedings and volumes. Her research interests include educational assessment, educational intervention and inclusive education for individuals with vision impairment and multiple disabilities or deafblindness.

Ozden Pinar-Irmak is a Ph.D. candidate in the Early Childhood Education and Care program at the University of Massachusetts, Boston. Her research includes early education and intervention programs for refugee and immigrant children and international inclusive education.

Lidia Pottas, Ph.D., is an Associate-Professor at the Department of Speech-Language Pathology and Audiology at the University of Pretoria. Her Ph.D. focused on the challenges posed to the teacher of the child with a hearing loss in inclusive education. She has a specific research interest in educational audiology, aural rehabilitation, and auditory processing disorders. She has published various articles in national and international accredited journals.

Duana Quigley, Ph.D., is a speech and language therapist with extensive clinical experience in assessing, diagnosing, and providing intervention for children with a range of communication disorders across health, education, community, and family systems. Her research explores the benefits of and overcoming the potential challenges of inter-professional practice between speech and language therapists and teachers. Other research interests lie in the areas of language enrichment, both preventative and targeted, especially supporting the language development of children growing up in areas of low socioeconomic status. Duana also examines the quality enhancement of teaching, learning, assessment, and practice education in third-level education.

Shanti Raghavan is the Co-founder of Enable India along with her husband Dipesh Sutariya. She is a social entrepreneur who celebrates the human spirit every day through the work done by Enable India. Shanti's experience started with her brother becoming blind at a young age leading to a 20-year journey with rich grassroots experience. She is a governing council member of the Skills Council for Persons with Disability (SCPwD) & Board of Workability International. She holds an MS in Computer Science, USA, and has 12 years of experience in the software industry.

Richard Rose is an Emeritus Professor in Inclusive Education at the University of Northampton, UK. He has conducted research into the education of marginalized children and children's rights in many parts of the world, including Ireland, India, Cambodia, Bhutan, and Georgia. His most recent book *Establishing Pathways to Inclusion*, co-authored with Michael Shevlin, was published by Routledge.

Piya Saha is a State Aided College Teacher in the Department of Psychology, Nabagram Hiralal Paul College, University of Calcutta (CU), India and also a Ph.D. Research Scholar at the Department of Psychology, CU, since 2017. She was the former Research Scholar in UGC funded project, Centre with Potential for Excellence in a Particular Area (CPEPA), CU. She has completed her post-graduation with a specialization in Counseling Psychology from West Bengal State University. She has received best paper award in various national and international conferences for her research work and she has four publications in reputed national and international journals.

Inoka Samarasinghe, B.Sc., is a Speech and Language Therapist with three years of clinical experience both in hospital and educational settings. She received her undergraduate degree in Speech and Language Therapy from The University of Kelaniya, Sri Lanka, in 2018. She is currently working at the Colombo South Teaching Hospital, Kalubowila, Sri Lanka. Her primary research interests are children with significant communication difficulties who would require low-tech augmentative and alternative communication (AAC) methods to communicate.

Alecia Samuels, Ph.D., is a speech-language therapist and audiologist by profession and is a senior lecturer in the Centre for Augmentative and Alternative Communication at the University of Pretoria as well as a Research Affiliate of the research group, CHILD at Jönköping University in Sweden. She has a special interest in the field of Early Childhood Intervention (ECI) and disability research. Her current research focus is on the participation and engagement of children with disabilities and their families in rehabilitation, community, and educational environments.

Andrew Scheef, Ph.D., is an Assistant Professor of Special Education at the University of Idaho (Moscow, ID). He has extensive experience teaching special education in public schools and earned his Ph.D. in Special Education at Washington State University. Dr. Scheef's research interests focus on supporting the post-school transition for students with disabilities. As a teacher, he received a Fulbright Distinguished Award in Teaching (2013-2014) that allowed him to study special education programs in Singapore designed to increase the employability of youth with disabilities.

Liezl Schlebusch, Ph.D., is a social scientist with a mission to drive positive social change. She is a committed, creative scholar who is passionate about human development, disability, and well-being, and in particular, the intersection of these three issues in resource-limited contexts. She is part of the global movement to develop and implement sustainable and scalable evidence-based care services to ensure that children with developmental disabilities and their families can flourish, regardless of where they live in the world. She completed degrees in sports science, accountancy, augmentative and alternative communication, and early childhood intervention.

Ben Sebothoma, MA (Audiology), is a clinical audiologist and an Associate Lecturer in the Department of Speech Pathology and Audiology at the University of the Witwatersrand. He has lectured and supervised students at both undergraduate and postgraduate levels. He completed his undergraduate training at the University of Cape Town. He completed his Master of Arts Degree in Audiology and is currently a Ph.D. fellow (Audiology), with a research focus on middle ear pathologies in HIV/AIDS at the University of the Witwatersrand. He has published several scientific papers in accredited journals and chapters; and has presented at local and international conferences.

Jordan Shurr, Ph.D., is an associate professor of special education at Queen's University in Ontario, Canada. Previously, Dr. Shurr worked as a special education teacher and an assistive technology consultant and has recently served as president of the Division on Autism and Developmental Disabilities of the Council for Exceptional Children. His research focuses on instruction and inclusion for students with significant support needs including both the support and training of teachers and evidence-based instructional practices.

Martine Smith, Ph.D., is a speech and language therapist with a particular interest in severe communication impairment, complex disability, and communication participation. Her research explores the relationships between spoken and written language impairments, the impact of communication difficulties on interaction and participation in society, and the life experiences of individuals with significant communication difficulties. Much of her research explores the impact of introducing augmentative and alternative communication methods on the language, learning, and interaction experiences of children and adults, in order to better understand the areas for assessment that can guide the development of robust interventions.

Laurel A. Snider, Ph.D., is a postdoctoral fellow with the Emory Autism Center's Education and Transition Services program. She received her doctoral degree in School Psychology from the University of Denver. Her research centers on leveraging collaborative relationships to improve psychosocial outcomes for individuals with intellectual and developmental disabilities.

Garry Squires, DEdPsy., is a professor in educational psychology, special educational needs and inclusion at the University of Manchester, UK. He previously worked as an educational psychologist in a large local authority in England and was the lead psychologist on the development of dyslexia-friendly schools and led on local authority policy for inclusion. He has been active in the British Psychological Society since 1995 and is currently a Fellow and the Chair of the National Awarding Committee for the EuroPsy. From 2017 to 2021, he has been a consultant to the European Agency for Special Needs and Inclusive Education. His research interests are around special educational needs; mental health; inclusion; professional educational psychology practice; the use of data in educational systems; dyslexia; cognitive behavioral therapy; therapeutic approaches in education; and evaluating school-based interventions and programs.

Dr. Angi Stone-MacDonald, is a Professor and Department Chair in Special Education, Rehabilitation, and Counseling at California State University, San Bernardino. Dr. Stone-MacDonald has worked with children and adults with disabilities for the last two decades as a paraprofessional, teacher, consultant, and researcher, including most recently as a faculty member and associate dean at the University of Massachusetts, Boston in the College of Education and Human Development. Her areas of research include early intervention, young children with autism, international inclusive education, and educator preparation for early intervention and early childhood special education.

Tom Storfors is a Lecturer in Special Education and Teacher Education for Upper Compulsory Education. He has been teaching at Mälardalen University since 2003 at all levels containing a diversity of courses. His teaching focuses on systems theory, didactics (the art and science of teaching), and philosophy of education. His research focuses on Participatory Action Research concerning teachers in special education schools. His studies are published in two book chapters, and the aim of his studies was to examine the dilemma of scientific literacy and reflective practices in praxis from a Bildung perspective.

Todd Sundeen, Ph.D., is an Associate Professor at the University of Northern Colorado. His areas of specialization include inclusive practices and co-teaching, especially in rural settings. He also focuses his research on instructional interventions for students with intellectual and developmental disabilities, with a specific emphasis on classroom learning strategies, interventions, and assessments for expressive writing.

Devadrita Talapatra, Ph.D., is an Associate Professor of School Psychology at the University of Denver. Her research is grounded in Dis/Crit and focuses on two strands: Strategies that promote inclusion in educational, vocational, and social settings for youth with intellectual disabilities; and frameworks that support equitable graduate training practices.

Contributors

Jillian Talley, PhD, is an Assistant Professor in the School Psychology program within the Education and Leadership Department at the California State University, Monterey Bay. Her research focuses on enhancing post-school outcomes for students with disabilities and training school psychologists to be leaders.

Kerstin Monika Tönsing, Ph.D., is an associate professor at the Centre for Augmentative and Alternative Communication at the University of Pretoria. Her research interests are in severe communication disability, augmentative and alternative communication (AAC), and language diversity, with a specific focus on AAC for preliterate individuals and AAC implementation in educational and other contexts.

Kitty Uys, Ph.D., is an occupational therapist with 30 years of lecturing experience for undergraduate and postgraduate students at the Department of Occupational Therapy and the Centre for Augmentative and Alternative Communication at the University of Pretoria. She is currently the head of the Department of Occupational Therapy at the University of Pretoria. Her clinical interventions focus on providing access for optimal participation for individuals with severe and multiple disabilities. Trans-disciplinary training and interprofessional education and practice inform her teaching pedagogy. Her research interests are childhood disabilities, the impact of early intervention, and interprofessional education.

Jenny Wilder, Ph.D., is a Professor of Special Education and Director of Research Studies in Special Education, Department of Special Education, Stockholm University. In her department, she is the co-leader of the research group Participation and Learning with a thematic focus on Intellectual Disabilities. Jenny Wilder has many years of experience in research and education related to children and young people with disabilities with a focus on participation, learning, interaction, and communication. Jenny Wilder is a Guest Professor at Kristianstad University, Sweden, and a Research Associate at the Centre for Augmentative and Alternative Communication, University of Pretoria, South Africa.

INTRODUCTION

1
PREPARING TEACHER EDUCATORS FOR INCLUSIVE CLASSROOM

Challenges, Lacuna and Future Direction

*Santoshi Halder**

Introduction

About 93 to 150 million children worldwide and one in three out-of-school children is reported to have a disability (Hartley, 2011; Lewis, 2019; World Bank, 2021). Status in low- and middle-income countries is even worse as around 33 million children with disabilities are reported to be out of school (Lewis, 2019). Despite having enormous potentials, strengths, and abilities children with disabilities are less likely to attend school, retain or complete education (be it primary, secondary, or higher education), drop out early and have a staggering performance gap as compared to their peers without disabilities (World Bank, 2021). Hence children and adults with disabilities continue to remain one of the most vulnerable and excluded populations worldwide. Children and adults with disabilities have been excluded from the sphere of education for time immemorial and their participation is extremely limited irrespective of their abilities in all walks of life as compared to their non-disabled counterparts (Humanity & Inclusion, 2015; Peter, 2007). The right to education has been inscribed as a basic human right and one of the most powerful instruments of change (Education Development Trust and UNICEF, 2016; Universal Declaration on Human Rights, 1948), unfortunately, there are multiple barriers to its true manifestation. Many of the barriers to education are visible in the real classroom situation where the learning needs of people with diverse needs are not understood well by many teachers and mostly remain unmet.

The current global trend witnesses a drastic shift of children and adults with disabilities from special to regular educational settings. Approximately 95% of students with disabilities were served in regular schools as compared to only 3% in special schools for those aged 6 to 21 years in the year 2018 (Forlin & Chambers, 2011; National Centre for Education Statistics, NCES, 2021). Students with disabilities continue to score below their counterparts in all competent areas across all education levels as reported by the National Assessment of Educational Progress, (NAEP) (National Centre for Education Statistics, NCES, 2011, 2021). Furthermore, what is most alarming is that these gaps remain and even increase as students progress through different levels of education (Forlin & Chambers, 2011; García & Weiss, 2017).

---

* santoshi_halder@yahoo.com; shedu@caluniv.ac.in
DOI: 10.4324/9781003266068-2

The fast-changing society has led to new emerging needs and drastic changes in all spheres of education (Stanovich & Jordan, 1998).)., and the existing teacher education has been constantly debated and questioned about addressing the new demands appropriately. Providing a quality inclusive education and meeting the diverse needs of the learners with disabilities has become one of the primary focus areas most recently. United Nations Sustainable Development Goals (SDG4) target the inclusion of all people with disabilities by 2030 and hence lay stress on removing the existing barriers to inclusive education and participation. One of the most predominant barriers impacting the quality of education and addressing the growing demands of the diverse need of students in an inclusive classroom is improving the capacity building of teachers by developing the needful skills (Forlin & Chambers, 2011; Andrew & Danladi, 2016; United Nations, 2015; UN High Commissioner for Refugees, UNHCR, 2017; UNDP, 2015a; b).

Legislative Impetus and the Increasing Number of Students with Disabilities in the Inclusive Classroom

Inclusive education has been emphasized from time to time through the various declarations and conventions that highlight the importance of education for people with disabilities; UNCRC (CRC, 1989), the Salamanca Statement (UNESCO, 1994), No Child Left Behind (No Child Left Behind [NCLB], 2002), IDEA (IDEA, 2004), United Nations Convention on the Rights of Persons with Disabilities (UNCRPD, 2006), SDG4 (UNESCO, 2015), Incheon Declaration (WEF, 2015), etc. *The Salamanca Statement* envisaged that all pupils should have a fundamental right and equal opportunity to experience education in mainstream schools (UNESCO, 1994). The IDEA (Individuals with Disabilities Education Act, IDEA) regulation states that inclusion is a human rights issue and is not a special privilege for a select few, and advocated the education of children with disabilities in the least restrictive environment (Education Week, 2001) along with their peers without disabilities in regular education environments to the greatest extent possible (IDEA, 2004). The IDEA regulation emphasized the appropriate placement of children and adults with disabilities; children with disabilities should only be placed in a separate or special educational setting if the nature or severity of the disability is such that education in regular classes is not possible or is not satisfactory even with the use of supplementary aids and services (IDEA, 1992, 2004). The No Child Left Behind (No Child Left Behind [NCLB], 2002) has fuelled the inclusive agenda even further along with the latest International Convention on the rights of persons with disabilities (UNCRPD, 2006) which has been ratified and signed by 182 and 164 countries respectively worldwide and played a significant role in creating an international spur in making inclusion a global agenda and a human rights issue for all. The Incheon Declaration (2015) at the world education forum (WEF, 2015) aimed at ensuring inclusive and equitable quality education and lifelong learning opportunities for all and mobilizing all countries and partners striving for Sustainable Development Goals (SDG4) on education, and proposes ways of implementing, coordinating, financing, monitoring and including strategies for Education by 2030 (UNESCO, 2015).

Following the various legislative impetus worldwide more students are getting enrolled than ever before in inclusive schools; hence, the trend is towards people with disabilities spending more time with people without disabilities in the regular education program (National Centre for Education Statistics NCES, 2021). As the inclusive movement has gained momentum many students previously educated in segregated special schools are now being included in general education classes (Ashman & Elkins, 2012; Forlin, 2006), leading to a dramatic increase over the past few decades and creating new needs and challenges for the education system, and teachers are among the most impacted (Ainscow & César, 2006; Cook, Cameron, & Tankersley, 2007). This shift from special to general education has been identified as one of the most challenging, controversial, and confusing issues in the sphere of education (Shaddock, MacDonald, Hook, Giorcelli, & Arthur-Kelly, 2009; Whitworth, 1999).

Defining Inclusive Education

With time inclusion has now gained significant ground worldwide in order to cater to the needs of all students per their diverse needs including those with disabilities (Bhroin & King, 2020; Education Week, 2001; European Agency for Special Needs and Inclusive Education, 2017). However, despite 'inclusion' becoming a global slogan, it is perplexed by much debate and discussion regarding its true meaning and manifestation (Miles & Singal, 2010). Inclusion envisages that students with special needs must be exposed to their typical peers and the general education setting as much as possible. Inclusive education, a much-argued concept, yet to have a universal definition (Bhroin & King, 2020), witnesses multifarious challenges constantly and demonstrates significant variation when it comes to implementation within and across countries and a huge gap persists in terms of theories and their practice (Artiles et al., 2011; Florian, 2014; Slee, 2018; Loreman et al., 2014).

Inclusive Education makes provision for services to the whole range of students with disabilities: mild, moderate, and severe, in the neighbourhood school, in age-appropriate classes along with learners without disabilities, with the needful supports and aids that may be required for the child or the teacher for facilitating the inherent potentialities to the maximum, ensuring the child's success in all walks of life - academic, behavioural, and social - and to prepare the child for independent living in order to participate and contribute as a full member of the society (Reyes et al., 2017). UNESCO (2005) defined inclusive education as responding to the diverse needs of all learners by increasing participation and reducing exclusion within education (Andrew & Danladi, 2016). Hence, inclusive education means all children have an equal right to quality education, and hence the needs of all students are crucial and should be addressed with personalized support so that they can contribute to and participate in all aspects of life in the school. The mere co-habitation of general education students with disabilities has not essentially transcended the true manifestation of the parameters of inclusion, and neither has it ensured equal or full participation of people with disabilities in the mainstream society. The foundational philosophy of inclusive education is equity, justice, and equality in education for all, regardless of their context or personal characteristics, or differentiation due to disabilities (Christopher & Elizabeth, 2012; Winter, 2020). Perhaps it is the foundation and philosophy to accommodate/include all human beings, thus the full spectrum of diverse abilities, in one system, in such a manner that all are involved and assured successful, equality, equity, and ensured quality participation in all walks of life from birth till death (Burden, 2006).

Literature is replete with debate and discussion on the concept, meaning, and various aspects of the implementation of inclusion (Acedo et al., 2009; Acedo, 2008; Ainscow, 2005; Ainscow et al., 2006; Artiles et al., 2011; Booth & Ainscow, 2002; Boyle et al., 2020; Bhroin & King, 2020; Florian, 2014; Slee, 2018; Loreman et al., 2014; Miles & Singal, 2010; OECD, 2007; Papastephanou, 2019; Parrilla, 2002; Rambla et al., 2008; UNESCO, 2005). Regardless of whether inclusion is accepted or not, the fact is inclusion is the new way of life and will prevail and predominate in the years to come and the necessity is to navigate and map the pathway of an inclusive educational community and to facilitate the process of inclusion successfully so that it results in qualitative educational experiences for all students (Mont, 2018). We need to understand that future schools will be characterized by inclusivity rather than exclusivity and hence there is a pertinent need to have the needful resources and preparedness beforehand (Acedo, 2008; Ainscow et al., 2006; Whitworth, 1999). *Inclusive schooling* includes all students, regardless of ability, under the common umbrella along with peers without disabilities (Bui et al., 2010; Alquraini & Gut, 2012) and extends far beyond mere physical proximity to provide learners with disabilities the required personalized support to have a feeling of belongingness so that they can achieve as per their abilities and strengths irrespective of their challenges along with students without disabilities. Inclusion is both a process for and outcome of understanding, acceptance, and valuing of differences among our children and youth for social justice, equity, and sustainability in our society.

Practices in many schools demonstrate that teaching all students together in general education settings can be done successfully only if appropriate practices and methods are used by the teachers (Banerji & Daily, 1995; Bishop, 1995; Male & Wodon, 2018). The need is not only to identify the evidence-based multifarious ways of teaching-learning, personalized and tailor-made with needful adaptation to cater to the needs of individuals with disabilities in inclusive classrooms, but also to find new ways of teaching-learning including alternative and updated ones that are successful instances and evidence based on various parts of the world that will prove to be significant and beneficial in supporting the needs of the increasingly heterogeneous group of students with disabilities in inclusive classrooms. Hence the need is not only to meet the demand of the present but also to get prepared for the future. The traditional typical models of special education including the existing gaps need to be replaced with evidence-based practices and components identified and collated through a global network of scholars from various disciplines and cultures for a comprehensive understanding and manifestation of inclusion and wide dissemination for successful implementation worldwide. The concept of inclusion emphasizes changing the education system rather than the child, and hence the need is to shift from the rigid, narrow structural approaches to more flexible collaborative, inclusive and innovative approaches, an educational system that is better able to accommodate the learning differences.

Role of Teacher Educators in the Inclusive Classroom

Teachers are the foundation and the most powerful resource of the entire educational systems who are continuously engaged in building the knowledge and skills of their learners and facilitating the inner potentials and abilities in the best possible way. Teachers are facing multifarious challenges in the inclusive classroom while providing instruction as they are facing skills deficits in meeting the demands of the extremely wide diversities of their classroom as never before. One of the most challenging tasks for teachers in recent times is to address the heterogenous and diverse learners in the classroom and ensure full participation in the various activities of the classroom most strategically (Australian Agency for International Development, Ministry of Education, 2017; Grimes et al., 2015). The increasing numbers of students in general inclusive schools emphasizes the need for teacher educators to be well prepared, skilled and trained to cater to the needs of a much wider range of student abilities for better adapting to the academic and social demands under one common umbrella (US Dept. of Education, 2000). The role of teacher has been posited as a critical component of creating inclusive classrooms and is perhaps the primary driving force for enhancing the quality of inclusive education in real practice upon which the success of inclusive education relies (Forlin & Lian, 2008; Lewis, 2018; UNESCO, 2017; Winter, 2006).

Concurrently, the role of the *general education teacher* in an inclusive setting has also been transformed with additional tasks and hence their role is also crucial for the success of inclusive education practice, where they can contribute through a cohesive, collaborative and cooperative partnership with the entire team (specialist, regular teacher, special educator, administrators, parents etc.) for a common goal of bringing out the best in each child (Stanovich & Jordan, 2002). It is essential that both special and general education teachers are willing and are comfortable, competent, creative and flexible at adapting and modifying curriculum and instruction as per the needs of their students. Unfortunately, many general teachers who are currently teaching in inclusive classrooms are not well prepared, lack positive attitudes towards inclusion, and are rigid about meeting the day-to-day challenges and needs of an inclusive classroom (Paula & Jordan, 2002). Managing an inclusive classroom with a heterogeneous, wide range of various categories and levels of disabilities is a complex task that surely needs proper training and orientation in a structured way with positive attitudes.

Challenges of Teachers and Skill Gap in the Existing Teacher Education Courses

There is a plethora of studies highlighting the wide range of challenges faced by teachers to address the needs of people with diverse needs in inclusive classrooms worldwide (Ferguson, 2008). There *are concerns over the effectiveness of teacher preparation courses* as 25% of newly graduated teachers considered their pre-service training to be unsatisfactory (Department of Education, Science and Training [DEST, 2006]; House of Representatives Standing Committee on Education and Vocational Training, 2007). Forlin & Chambers (2011) stated that teacher preparation courses for inclusive education are increasing the knowledge of the trainee teachers to a certain extent but raising alarming concerns for various reasons that needs immediate attention. Savolainen (2009) reported that teachers play a crucial role in what to teach and how best to facilitate learning in their learners hence, the quality of an education system cannot be increased or enhanced without enhancing the quality of its teachers. Loreman and Harvey (2005) argue that inclusion failed partly because teachers were unable to adapt and update themselves to meet the demands of delivering an appropriate curriculum to children with diverse needs due to their incapacity and skill deficits. Some of the major challenges of teachers of inclusive education are presented in Table 1.1.

The majority of newly graduated teachers, not only pre-service but also experienced in-service teachers, considered themselves to be *inadequately prepared* (Winter, 2006) as they report concerns in regard to their own abilities to effectively address the needs of their students (Forlin & Chambers, 2011). In a study by Forlin et al. (2008) 93% of 228 teachers felt their training to be insufficient to cater to the needs of students with disability in an inclusive setting. Pre-service teachers for inclusion, despite showing positive views towards inclusive education, indicated the need for further training for acquiring the teaching-learning strategies to support students with special needs as also endorsed by other researchers too (Mahlo, 2011; Richards & Clough, 2004).

About 25% to 40% of newly graduate teachers *resign or burn out* during their first few years of teaching (Ewing & Smith, 2003) or *leave the profession early* due to unpreparedness or lack of professional training in inclusive techniques and practices (Burke & Sutherland, 2004). The national enquiry into teacher education in Australia reported a concerning attrition rate of graduate teachers due to inadequacies in either the quality of teacher preparation or support provided to teachers (The Top of The Class report, House of Representatives Standing Committee on Education and Vocational Training, 2007). Teachers displayed frustration, burden, fear, and inadequacies as they didn't believe that they had the required abilities and that their professional skills were not developed properly to meet the individual needs of their learners with special needs in an inclusive setting (Shade & Stewart, 2001).

Table 1.1 Challenges of teacher educators in inclusive classroom

Barriers	Description	Citations
Concern over psycho-social wellbeing	Low self-esteem, anxiety, depressed, etc.	For e.g., Singal, 2015; Woodon et al., 2018
Over stressed and Overburdened	Burnout due to inability to cope with the demands, leaving the profession/resign from service, etc.	For e.g., Ewing & Smith, 2003
Difficulty in meeting the needs of diverse learners	Lack professional skills, specialists' skills, specific strategies, insufficient inclusive techniques, and practices, dealing with challenging behaviour, etc.	For e.g., Cooper et al., 2008
Lack of theoretical and foundational knowledge	Limited knowledge of the foundation and philosophy of inclusion etc.	For e.g., Burke & Sutherland, 2004; Forlin & Chambers, 2011
Lack practical skills of implementation	Unsatisfactory preparation, lacks proper mentoring or guidance of experts or specialists, lack of hands-on and real-life practice, insufficient practical training to hone skills, etc.	For e.g., EDT & UNICEF, 2016
Concern over qualitative parameters	Concerns over factors resulting in teacher effectiveness.	For e.g., Forlin & Chambers, 2011; Richards & Clough, 2004
Inadequate needful teaching-learning material and methods	Teachers lack appropriate materials or resources for teaching, insufficient resources	For e.g., Le Fanu, 2005; Mukhopadhyay et al., 2013; Najjingo, 2009
Lack of support from administration or lack of cooperative environment	Non-supportive environment, non-cooperative and non-flexible administrative bodies, cohesive teamwork, etc.	For e.g., Calitz, 2000; Zimba, 2011
Prejudices, stereotypy and lack of positive attitude and agreeableness	Myths, beliefs, stereotypy, conventional, inflexible, or rigid and even negative attitudes, lack of collaborative approaches	For e.g., Loreman et al., 2007; Forlin et al., 2008

Teachers in many countries *expressed lack of confidence* in delivering inclusive education *for lack of various necessary skills* and resources (Singal, 2015; Wodon et al., 2018). Teachers reported a lack of sufficient accurate instructional materials and course content to teach in inclusive classrooms (Andrew & Danladi, 2016). About 37% teachers rated their own knowledge and skill to work with students with disabilities in inclusive settings as "somewhat or extremely" limited (Cooper et al., 2008). Most teacher education programmes only include a small component of inclusive education, and that too theoretical, which is insufficient to train or hone the skills needed and also lacks proper evaluation and assessment (EDT & UNICEF, 2016).

Non-supportive, and rigid, inflexible environments have been reported by most of the teachers as one of the greatest barriers to inclusive education. Administrative rigidity, inflexibility and uncooperative attitudes were reported by studies as impediments to teachers in implementing many facets of inclusive education. Zimba (2011) reported in their study that neither the administrator nor teachers were found to be competent to adapt to an inclusive curriculum. Teachers reported a lack of funding and needful resources for the manifestation of inclusive education programmes and provisions (Fakudze, 2012).

The situation in *low- and middle-income countries* (LMI) is even worse (Mariga et al., 2014; Price, 2018; Rose et al., 2018) and more so with the ever-increasing enrolments of people with disabilities in general or inclusive set up as the teachers struggle and suffer more significantly due to overcrowded classes, limited funding or resources and the required skill deficits. As the number of students is increasing in inclusive classrooms, the educational system is facing a severe shortage of teachers capable of effectively catering to and/or supporting the needs of students with disabilities (WHO, 2011). Without addressing these skill deficits including instilling positive attitudes among teachers towards disability, true inclusive education will perhaps either take a long time or will remain a dream. Ahmed et al. (2001) posit that in Nigeria, despite genuine efforts to educate children with disabilities in public schools, a substantial number are still neglected due to societal misconception, insufficient resources, manpower and funding, as also endorsed by others (Andrew & Danladi, 2016; Bulat et al., 2017; Hayes & Bulat, 2017; Piper et al., 2019). One of the major concerns in front of the teachers in LMI countries is how to be available or attend to every student in overcrowded classes.

Prejudices against those with differences lead to discrimination and seclusion, inhibiting access to education for all and impeding quality educational process. Apart from the insufficient and inadequate teacher education programme there are also other factors *responsible for the failure* in the manifestation of inclusive education, which also indirectly influences teachers' roles and responsibilities, such as negative attitude and lack of agreeableness for collaborative, cohesive teamwork among the teachers, practitioners, specialists and other stakeholders who are the primary agents of change (Annemaree & Anne, 2003). Positive *teacher attitudes have been identified as one of the main prerequisites of inclusive education* (European Agency for Development in Special Needs Education [EADSNE] 2003, 2012a; Saloviita, 2020; UNESCO, 2009). Attitudes of teachers are an extensively researched area of all time all over the world. Most researches revealed teachers in inclusive classrooms expressing either neutral or negative attitudes regarding the existing inclusive education programmes (Bagree & Lewis, 2013; de Boer & Minnaert, 2010; Woodcock & Woolfson, 2019). It has been said that "inclusion largely depends on teachers' attitudes towards students with disabilities, their view of differences in classrooms and their willingness to respond positively and effectively to those differences" (EADSNE, 2003, p. 15; Saloviita, 2020). The attitudes are directly and indirectly impacted by the conventional, inflexible or rigid approaches prevailing in many educational systems of various countries which delays the entire process of inclusion; hence drastic visible changes of inclusion are still not very common in many countries. Many teachers may not be even prepared to interact with students with disabilities in appropriate ways and hence unconsciously or consciously may impact the inclusive environment. Frequent physical and emotional bullying has also been observed in many cases. There are repeated documentations of students with disabilities being ridiculed or ostracized in school and community, and the teachers can play an active role in instilling the right actions. The teachers with their proficiency and progressive outlook can be one of the most significant human resources for advancing the attitude and flavour of inclusive education but unfortunately teachers in many cases have been found to lack such progressive attitudes either due to lack of knowledge or exposure to various diversities or due to the contextual or environmental intersecting factors.

Inappropriate and insufficient teaching and learning methods, support material and resources were reported as prime barriers of the teachers that impacted inclusive education (Le Fanu, 2005; Zwane & Malale, 2018). Inappropriate teaching-learning methods such as the conventional teacher-centred approaches were also observed as barriers of teaching-learning (Mukhopadhyay et al., 2013) that did not cater to the needs of individual differences of learners. Teachers endorsed that the lack of instructional materials, teacher-learning materials, affects access to inclusive education (Najjingo, 2009; Zwane & Malale, 2018). As rightly pointed out by Estrada, Ignacio, 'Children should be taught as they learn rather than how we teach' (Kumar, 2018).

The *quality of teacher education programmes* is an essential requirement for the teachers to efficiently facilitate the role and responsibility of teaching tasks be they inclusive or special setting (Andrew & Danladi, 2016). The *lack of proper teacher training for inclusive settings*, as cited by numerous studies, is an important consideration for teacher training providers (Forlin & Chambers, 2011). Every year a voluminous amount of funding is spent on training and preparing millions of teachers through the in-service and pre-service teacher education programmes in the various countries for developing the requisite instructional skills to teach students with diverse needs but the result seems to be unsatisfactory as there remains a lacuna. The constant debate on the effectiveness of teacher preparation programmes in various circles has resulted in many positive outcomes surely but is not sufficient to develop and manifest a successful effective teacher education programme with all desired components (Mock & Kauffman, 2002). Despite the efforts to prepare teachers appropriately, the literature is filled with extensive evidences of failures indicating that both in-service and pre-service teachers are not prepared as needed to meet the needs of students with disabilities (DeSimone & Parmar, 2006; Gokdere, 2012; Hodkinson, 2005; Pavri, 2004). Researchers report specific areas of concern that need deliberation where additional training is required such as dealing with challenging behaviours, teaching social skills, bullying etc. in a diverse classroom setting (Omede & Sam, 2013; Pavri, 2004).

Key Components of a Comprehensive Teacher Education Programme for Inclusive Classroom

The *teacher education programme is a potent tool* that if framed properly is the key to successful implementation of effective inclusive education (Amwe, 2012). Good teachers form the foundation of good schools, and a well conceptualized teacher education programme that includes the essentials can improve teachers' skill and knowledge to a large extent (Omede & Sani, 2013). Christopher and Elizabeth (2012) stated the educational programmes of a country can only materialize if the teachers are adequately trained and prepared to carry out this responsibility efficiently, as per the needs of the society and its constantly changing needs. The effectiveness of teacher preparation courses in catering to the diversities of the classroom has become a key focus in many policy frameworks in recent times (e.g., Department of Education, Science and Training [DEST], 2006; House of Representatives Standing Committee on Education and Vocational Training, 2007; Nilholm, 2020). Despite teacher education programmes undergoing repeated revisions to meet the demands of the classroom and society from time to time there still remains a huge gap as many areas still remain unaddressed (Kearns & Shevlin, 2006).

Literature review evidences that countries are facing the *challenges in the existing teacher education programme* for not being able to effectively address the needs of the constantly changing classroom and hence there is a great impetus on revising the different aspects of the existing teacher education programme. The current teacher education courses in many countries are not able to fulfil the required needs of students with disabilities at all levels of education. Most teacher training courses are primarily focused for school teachers leaving many in-service teachers including the prospective teachers of colleges and or universities in the higher education sector in a complete dilemma. Moreover, there are variations in aspects of teacher education programmes worldwide for e.g., course content, course duration, syllabus etc. and the courses are on a constant and continuous verge of revisions over and over again in the quest to improve them. Teacher training courses vary from country to country ranging from a 1-month training course to a 3-year degree (Global Campaign for Education, 2012). On the threshold of the twenty-first century UNESCO necessitates that all teachers be trained in inclusive practices so that they are well equipped and prepared way ahead of time to cater their students' needs and that each and every teacher at some point in time would surely have one or more student with disability in their classroom. Furthermore, existing teacher education programmes in many countries lack comprehensiveness; they don't often include in-depth training on the nature and types of disabilities and necessary strategies and approaches to cater for the specific needs of diverse learners. Teacher education preparation courses, both pre-service and in-service in many countries, need comprehensive revisions from the existing ones; curriculum and modalities and crucial potent elements and aspects of inclusive education are to be incorporated within the courses in order to attune the course content to the existing needs and demands of learners with diverse needs in inclusive classrooms. The demand is to prepare future teachers as agents of change who are skilled and confident to teach in inclusive settings and this *requires a comprehensive model of teacher education* programme (Laarhoven et al., 2007; Whitworth, 1999).

However, despite many efforts taken by respective countries to upgrade the course structure, curriculum, syllabus there remains a gap as it is not yet sufficient as reflected by the parameters or indicators of inclusion reported in various literature. A teacher education programme with a comprehensive practical aspect with proper mentoring has been proved to be effective (Ackers, 2018). Teachers need to be empowered and feel confident and that will come only with a positive cohesive collaboration of scholars worldwide who can work together hand-in-hand in identifying the key components of a comprehensive teacher education programme that will prepare well trained, skilled and equipped teachers to impart quality education. Hence the role of a well conceptualized teacher education programme is a must for successful inclusion of people with disabilities (European Agency for Special Needs and Inclusive Education, 2015; EDT and UNICEF, 2016; Global Partnership for Education; GPE, 2018). Teacher preparation programmes, be they for school, college or universities should be developed based on current research outcomes and should mirror the evidence-based practices that are key to successful inclusion of students with disabilities in an inclusive classroom (Paula & Jordan, 2002). There is a need for amendment of the existing teacher education programme in many countries; a programme that includes all the required aspects for inclusive teaching learning.

There has been much debate, discussion and dialogue from time to time about the essential skills and competencies needed for teachers in an inclusive classroom (e.g., Andrews & Lupart, 2000; Competency Framework for teachers; Department of Education and Training, 2004; Forlin, 2010; Pearce, 2008; Pearce & Forlin, 2005). Recent reports in many countries are filled with important essential components needed to ameliorate effective teacher preparation courses (e.g., Andrews & Lupart, 2000; Department of Education, Science and Training [DEST], 2006; Forlin, 2010; House of Representatives Standing Committee on Education and Vocational Training, 2007; Smith & Tyler, 2011; Pearce, 2008; Pearce & Forlin, 2005). Literature reviews on challenges of teacher educators in an inclusive classroom provide a comprehensive lead for identifying the crucial elements of an effective teacher preparation programme. A range of innovative models (van Laarhoven et al., 2007) have been developed to prepare teachers for inclusive education. A good comprehensive teacher education preparation programme should cover all needful aspects of coursework namely inclusive pedagogy (Cara, 2007; Florian, 2015; Shade & Stewart, 2001), information about diversity throughout the curriculum (Jung, 2007; Romi & Leyser, 2006; Winter, 2006), direct contact, interaction and meet-ups with people of different types of disabilities (Chambers & Forlin, 2010; Forlin et al., 2007; Miller, 2008), engagements

a) Promote teacher training for inclusion at all levels of education.

b) Ensure and promote quality and quantity both.

c) Remove attitudinal barriers and promote positive attitudes.

d) Deliberate on foundational knowledge of inclusive pedagogy.

e) Emphasize training and evaluation based on practical hands-on.

f) Need for specialization; developing diverse skill sets.

g) Develop necessary advanced future skills.

h) Need for collaborative, supportive and flexible working environment

i) Paradigm shift from deficit focus to strength focus approach.

Figure 1.1 Essential components of a comprehensive teacher education programme

in inclusive activities in a real class (Stella et al., 2007) etc. Figure 1.1 outlines certain essential features of a comprehensive teacher education programme.

Promoting Teacher Training for Inclusion at all levels of Education

One of the most essential requirements of inclusive education is capacity building of teachers at all levels through incorporating the specific components of teaching students with disabilities at all levels of education; school, college and university level (European Agency for Special Needs and Inclusive Education. 2015, 2017). A comprehensive teacher education programme should comprise aspects that can enhance the teaching capabilities and ensure skills needs of teaching at all levels. At the same time crucial elements need to be covered for both in-service and pre-service teachers through a well-conceived teacher education programme consisting of in-service training for those teachers who are already in service and pre-service teacher training for fresh graduates and would-be future teachers after training. *In-Service and pre-service teacher training programmes* should emphasize honing, refining the existing skills and also on developing new twenty-first-century skills that might be needed for an inclusive school/ classroom.

Ensure and Promote both Quality and Quantity

The quality and quantity of teacher education both need substantial improvement. UNESCO recommends the need for a multitude of teachers currently and even more in the years to come to meet the needs of the increasing number of students with disabilities in inclusive classrooms and schools as the number would increase substantially in the years to come. One of the foremost challenges of LMI countries is the lack of well trained and appropriately skilled teachers. Furthermore, providing a quality education for all students in inclusive settings has been identified as perhaps another concerning, yet most important need of an inclusive classroom at the present time which needs immediate action globally. Most importantly for enhancing the quality of inclusive education is to instil an understanding, appreciation and acceptance of diversity at the outset as the foundation. It is imperative to accept, respect and embrace the differences and diversities existing in society and understand and realize its need and vice versa benefits for all for diminishing the existing discrimination and marginalization, for ensuring equality of all and for promoting quality of inclusive education.

Remove Attitudinal Barriers and Promote Positive Attitudes among Teachers

There is stupendous research worldwide recognizing the importance of positive attitudes of teachers as prerequisites of the inclusive classroom and its sizeable impact on the inclusion of people with disabilities in inclusive settings (Forlin et al., 2007, 2008; Loreman et al., 2014; Sharma et al., 2007). Prejudicial beliefs impact all aspects of inclusion and can even have adverse outcomes on the wellbeing of the students with disabilities.

However, teachers can be trained to develop positive attitudes through comprehensive debates, discussion and strategic action on the topic. Attitudes can be channelized and streamlined by creating opportunities for direct interactions with students with and without disabilities together as a part of the teacher training programme; organizing training workshops for educators integrating awareness about the benefits and values of inclusive education through regular professional development activities that may dispel the many existing negative prejudices, beliefs or myths about people with disabilities and inclusion. Instances of greater contact with people with disabilities during training (Richards & Clough, 2004; Romi & Leyser, 2006) or through course experiences (Forlin, 2003; Lancaster & Bain, 2007), have promoted teachers' positive attitudes towards inclusion. Literature reflects that teacher preparation courses that have focused on attitude change towards inclusive education have resulted in teachers who are more supportive of students with special needs (Carroll et al., 2003; Lancaster & Bain, 2007; Shade & Stewart, 2001), positive attitudes toward inclusion are most important prerequisites for creating an inclusive classroom (Savage & Erten, 2015). Sensitization training on various aspects of inclusion can help in capacity building of mainstream teachers, increase the knowledge about disability and develop positive attitude towards people with disabilities (Ahmad, 2012; Nanda & Nanda, 2007).

Deliberate on Foundational Knowledge of Inclusive Pedagogy

Teachers need to have a comprehensive understanding of the theories and foundational knowledge and philosophy of inclusive pedagogy on the one hand and need to have the knowledge of the various evidence-based practices of the successful inclusive teaching-learning models from various parts of the world on the other hand (for e.g., Burke & Sutherland, 2004; Forlin & Chambers, 2011). Crucial elements of well-conceived teacher education programmes are a good balance of rich foundational knowledge of psychology and educational theories and also the knowledge of applied or real classroom field experiences (Alquraini, & Gut, 2012; Morningstar et al., 2015; United Nations Educational Scientific and Cultural Organization, UNESCO, 2017). Concurrently, teachers who will impart inclusive education should also have a comprehensive understanding of the different forms of diversities (such as gender difference, linguistic, cultural and ethnic diversity, social–emotional diversity, cognitive and academic diversity and sensory and physical diversity) found in society (Le Fanu, 2005) as many of these diversities might be interconnected, embedded or intersected in various contexts impacting the success of inclusive education to a large extent (Zwane & Malale, 2018). Having an understanding of the background context and environment can be beneficial and aid in the implementation of the goals of inclusive education.

Emphasize Training and Evaluation Based on Practical Hands-on

There is a need to create sufficient opportunities for practical hands-on training and internship for developing skills of trainee teachers during the training period and also follow up post training so that there is sufficient practice in real-life situations under expert mentors who would guide them through the process and provide required feedback to address their errors and refine their skills (Florian & Spratt, 2013). Mandatory training, assessment and internship through practical hands-on in real classroom situations should form a part of the training completion and certification just as in any other professional degree. Hence a well-conceptualized teacher education programme must include multiple opportunities and exposures for the prospective teacher to observe and work in actual classrooms where inclusive practices are being implemented. An internship in a real inclusive classroom assisting the regular teachers in teaching students with diverse needs should form a mandatory requirement of the teacher education programme. To complete the practical aspect each trainee teacher should develop an innovative project manifesting an inclusive practice or attempt to address any of the challenges of inclusive education under the supervision of an experienced teacher or mentor having extensive experiences working in inclusive classrooms or other specialists. Such a practical requirement would flourish and facilitate the practical abilities and problem-solving skills of the trainee teachers and prepare them well for a real future classroom and its challenges. Such practical hand-on experiences will strengthen their learned skills and further refine mastery and proficiency for practical implementation confidently in the real classroom to address the challenges of the learners in an inclusive classroom most confidently.

Need for Specialization; Developing Diverse Skill Sets

There is a need for teachers who are specialized in specific areas of disabilities including crucial aspects of support so that they are able to cater to the needs of a wide range (i.e., different types) and level of disabilities (mild, moderate and severe). Specialization in most common learning disabilities needs to be developed with a higher level of expertise to cater to the diverse challenges of the classroom in collaboration with an interdisciplinary team. The diversity of contents both in theory and practice needs to be infused across all curricular areas (Kearns & Shevlin, 2006; Winter, 2006). A good comprehensive teacher education preparation programme should explicitly address the current challenges that include but are not limited to varied ways of instruction, including building the supports in specific areas such as identification and assessment, interventions, assistive technologies, universal design, curriculum adaptations/modifications, individual student learning styles and needs, ability to provide individualised programs (IEP), various strategies of teaching including alternative strategies, specialized teaching-learning aids and materials, necessary psychological, educational and inclusive principles, assistive technologies, personalization etc. There is also a pertinent need for gaining knowledge and understanding of the wide range of diversities of people in society and building an acceptance for each other (van Laarhoven et al., 2007).

Develop Necessary Advanced Future Skills

Teacher education goes through various revisions from time to time as per the drastically changing society and its needs; as rightly said education mirrors societal needs. Hence it is essential to constantly upgrade the skills and the training aspects through continuous research in various aspects of teacher education. Teacher education departments should be encouraged to do extensive and rigorous research through multiple partnerships with various stakeholders within and across countries to identify crucial areas of teacher education based on empirical research findings. Initiatives should be generated for an international network of teacher educators with allied disciplines and various stakeholders to identify new futuristic core areas of teacher education to enhance teaching-learning and promote quality education and for bringing in new potential evidence-based strategies and effective pathways.

Need for Collaborative, Supportive and Flexible Working Environment

Support involves a group of people coming together to assist learners experiencing barriers to learning and includes all activities that increase the capacity of a school to respond to diversity (Mahlo, 2011). A supportive environment that comprises a well-organized support system assigning specific roles clearly stated to each member with collaboration among teachers, district officials, principals and parents is crucial to implement the goals of inclusive education most successfully (Calitz, 2000). Collaboration is defined as '*an interactive process where a number of people with particular expertise come together as equals to generate an appropriate programme or process or find solutions to problems*' (Bhroin & King, 2020; NCSE, 2006; Bhroin et al., 2016). Healthy collaboration is one of the essential prerequisites of inclusive education as a good outcome can only be achieved when each gets the flexibility and scope to contribute to achieve the target overall goal of bringing out the best in each and every individual through cohesive partnership. Collaborative decision-making and problem solving are at the core of inclusive education (Clarke, 2000). A good partnership between the general and special teachers in an inclusive classroom is a must for effective outcomes (Lakkala et al., 2021; Oriana & Fling, 2020).

Paradigm Shift from the Deficit Focus to Strength Focus Approach

The recent decades have witnessed a paradigm shift with a strength-focused approach that begins with identifying the '*strengths of the child*' and '*what the child can do*' and '*to finding the right support for the child*' instead of focusing and beginning with '*what the child cannot do*' or '*what are the weaknesses of the child*' (Schreiner, 2013; Spiteri, 2016). The origin of the strengths-based approaches can be traced back to the 'strengths' perspective', originated from the social work educators during civil and human rights movements in the US (1960s and 1970s), positive psychology (Dweck, 2008; Jones-Smith, 2011; Kirschman et al., 2012; Rawana et al., 2009; Seligman, 1990) and social-service research (Saleebey, 1996).

Strengths-based approaches are the new trend ignited and voiced most predominantly by the advocates of the neurodiverse movement (McCashen, 2005), and it is based on the philosophy of drawing upon strengths as a basis for intervention, assisting people to identify and appreciate the existing strengths and resources and their maximum utilization (Elder et al., 2018; Halder & Bruyere, 2021), facilitating positive changes through collaborative team work and positive attitudes towards the differences, diversities and uniqueness and potentialities of human being (McCashen, 2005). The strength-based perspective is based upon principles of respect, self-determination, empowerment, social justice and the sharing of power (McCashen. 2005) and demands '*a different way of looking at individuals, families, and communities*' (Garwood, & Ampuja, 2019; Saleeby, 1996, p. 297). Making the teachers understand the philosophy and benefits of the strength-based perspective so that they can value the strengths that each child or student has is extremely crucial (Halder & Bruyere, 2021; Rod et al., 2020).

A strength-based approach is a positive psychology perspective that emphasizes the strengths, capabilities and resources of a person and allows one to see opportunities, hope and solutions rather than just problems and hopelessness (Resiliency Initiatives 2011; Zacarian et al., 2017). There is sufficient evidence that labelling students based on deficits or limitations limits the opportunities for facilitating their inner potentials and obscures the natural possibilities in the children (Sharry, 2004). Teachers need to continuously look for ways to identify and acknowledge the assets and capacities of students, understand, value and embrace their differences and support and create opportunities for learning. Effective teaching should start with the belief that each and every person has inherent assets and capacities that need to be recognized and facilitated through an appropriate environment (Zacarian et al., 2017). A comprehensive teacher education programme must incorporate the various strategies to implement such strength-focused approaches in the classroom (Brownlee et al., 2012). The various steps of strength-focused approaches are: (a) identify the inherent potentialities of students, (b) value, embrace and acknowledge the strengths, (c) make students aware of their own strengths, (d) build instructional programmes by drawing from students' strengths (Zacarian et al., 2017). There is ample empirically validated literature that focuses on people's inherent strengths leads to better outcomes than focusing on their weaknesses (Biswas-Dienera et al., 2011; Seligman et al., 2006; Zacarian et al., 2017). Hence the latest state of the art is to consider and facilitate the strength-focused approach as the base of teaching-learning in an inclusion classroom.

Future Directions

Inclusion is a process and its true manifestation may only be achieved through a step-by-step process of understanding individual needs at the outset to identify meaningful learning experiences (Florian & Spratt, 2013) through mutual learning, knowing, informing, disseminating and contributing that would come through healthy collaboration and cohesiveness among all. Developing a teacher preparation programme for teachers who would be teaching in an inclusive classroom is an extremely crucial activity upon which the entire foundation of teacher education will be based. Instead of any hasty decisions, time should be taken for deep thinking, critical reflection and a dialogue among various stakeholders who are directly or indirectly involved with the learners; educators, psychologists, clinicians, special educators, general teachers, practitioners across countries globally. The present book is the means to achieve that end by presenting various significant thoughts, ideas, foundational philosophies, critical reviews, and various evidence-based practices and strategies covering some of the most crucial aspects of the teacher education programme for manifesting effective inclusive teaching-learning. The important broad areas and specific topics presented in this book will bring forth key components of a comprehensive teacher education model and will prompt and assist the various stakeholders of teacher education including policy makers to review the existing teacher education course and curriculum in order to bridge the existing lacuna for laying the foundation of streamlining effective teacher education programmes worldwide for imparting quality teaching-learning in inclusive classroom.

Bibliography

Acedo, C. (2008). Inclusive education: Pushing the boundaries. *Prospects*, *38*(1), 5–13.
Acedo, C., Ferrer, F., & Pa`mies, J. (2009). Inclusive education: Open debates and the road ahead. *Prospects*, *39*, 227–238. https://10.1007/s11125-009-9129-7

Ackers, J. (2018). Teacher education and inclusive education. *The IIEP Letter, 34*(2). http://www.iiep.unesco.org/en/teacher-education-and-inclusive-education-4789

Ahmed, M. M., El Hag, F. M., Wahab, F. S., & Salih, S. F. (2001). Feeding strategies during dry summer for lactating desert goats in a rainfed area under tropical conditions. *Small Ruminant Research, 39*, 161–166.

Ahmed, L. (2012). Attitude of teachers, administrators and policy makers towards inclusive education. (PhD thesis), University of the Punjab, Retrieved from http://prr.hec.gov.pk/Thesis/2853S.pdf

Ainscow, M. (2005). Developing inclusive education systems: What are the levers for change? *Journal of Educational Change, 6*(2), 109–124.

Ainscow, M., & César, M. (2006). Inclusive education ten years after Salamanca: Setting the agenda. *European Journal of Psychology of Education, 21*, 23. https://doi.org/10.1007/BF03173412

Ainscow, M., et al. (2006). *Improving schools, developing inclusion*. London: Routledge.

Alquraini, T., & Gut, D. 2012. Critical components of successful inclusion of students with severe disabilities, *International Journal of Special Education, 27*(1), 42, 59.

Andrew, A. O., & Danladi, M. (2016). Teacher preparation for inclusive education of persons with special needs in Nigeria: The challenges and solutions. *European Journal of Educational and Development Psychology, 4*(1), 34–40.

Andrew, A. O., & Danladi, M. (2016). Teacher preparation for inclusive education of persons with special needs in Nigeria: The challenges and solutions. *European Journal of Educational and Development Psychology, 4*(1), 34–40.

Andrews, J., & Lupart, J. L. (2000). *The inclusive classroom: Educating exceptional children* (2nd ed.). Scarborough: Nelson.

Annemaree, C., Chris, F., & Anne, J. (2003). The impact of teacher training in special education on the attitudes of Australian preservice general educators towards people with disabilities. *Teacher Education Quarterly, 30*(3), 65–79.

Anwe, R. A. (2012). Quality teacher education: Implication for implementation inclusive education in Nigeria. *The Journal of the National Centre for Exceptional Children, 14*(2).

Artiles, A. J., Kozleski, E. B., & Gonzalez, T. (2011). Para além da sedução da educação inclusiva nos Estados Unidos: Confrontando o poder, construindo uma agenda histórico-cultural [Beyond the seduction of inclusive education in the United States: Confronting power, building a cultural-historical agenda]. *Revista Teias, 12*(24). Retrieved from http://www.periodicos.proped.pro.br/index.php?journal=revistateias&page=article&op=view&path[]=820

Ashman, A., & Elkins, J. (2012). *Education for inclusion & diversity* (4th ed.). Frenchs Forest, NSW: Pearson.

Australia Parliament House of Representatives Standing Committee on Education and Vocational Training. (2007). *Top of the class: Report on the inquiry into teacher education, House of Representatives Standing Committee on Education and Vocational Training*. Canberra: House of Representatives Publishing Unit, 228 pages. http://www.aph.gov.au/Parliamentary_Business/Committees/House_of_Representatives_Committees?url=evt/teachereduc/report.htm.

Bagree, S., & Lewis, I. (2013). *Teachers for all: Inclusive teaching for children with disabilities*. Washington, DC: International Disability and Development Consortium.

Banerji, M., & Dailey, R. A. (1995). A study of the effects of an inclusion model on students with specific learning disabilities. *J Learn Disabil., 28*(8), 511–22. https://10.1177/002221949502800806. PMID: 7595042

Bhroin, O. N., & King, F. (2020). Teacher education for inclusive education: A framework for developing collaboration for the inclusion of students with support plans. *European Journal of teacher Education, 43*(1), 38–63. https://doi.org/10.1080/02619768.2019.1691993

Bhroin, O. N., King, F., & Prunty, A. (2016). Leading inclusion: Refocusing on the collaborative process and the purpose of IEPs. Conference: ECER 2016 Network: Inclusive Education, Session: Inclusive Schools, European Education Research Association (EERA), Germany.

Bishop, M. (1995). Inclusion: Balancing the ups and downs. *Momentum, 26*(3), 28–30.

Biswas-Diener, R., Kashdan, T.B., Minhas, G. (2011). A dynamic approach to psychological strength development and intervention. *The Journal of Positive Psychology, 6*(2), 106–118

Boer, A. de, Pijl, S. J., & Minnaert, A. (2010). Regular primary school teachers' attitudes towards inclusive education: A review of the literature'. *International Journal of Inclusive Education*, 1–23. https://10.1080/13603110903030089

Booth, T., & Ainscow, M. (2002). *The index for inclusion*. Bristol, UK: Centre for studies on inclusive education.

Brownlee, K., Rawana, E. P., & MacArthur, J. M. (2012). Implementation of a strengths-based approach to teaching in an elementary school. *Journal of teaching and* learning, 8(1). https://://DOI.ORG/10.22329/JTL.V8I1.3069

Bui, X., Quirk, C., Almazan, S., & Valenti, M. (2010). Inclusive education, research and practice: Inclusion works. Retrieved March 7, 2018. http://www.mcie.org/site/usermedia/application/11/inclusion-works-(2010).pdf

Bulat, J., Macon, W., Ticha, R., & Abery, B. (2017). *School and classroom disabilities inclusion guide for low- and middle-income countries.* Research Triangle Park, NC: RTI Press.

Burden, A. (2006). Inclusive Education: Back to the future with commitment and common sense-case studies. *Educate*, 29(1&2), 28–39.

Burke, K., & Sutherland, C. (2004). Attitudes toward inclusion: Knowledge vs. experience. *Education*, 125, 163–172.

Boyle, C., Koutsouris, G., Mateu, A. S., & Anderson, J. (2020). The matter of 'evidence' in the inclusive education debate, In book: *The Oxford research encyclopedia of education.* Oxford University Press, Project: Inclusive Education. https://10.1093/acrefore/9780190264093.013.ORE_EDU-01019.R1

Calitz, M. (2000). *Guidelines for the training content of teacher support teams* (MEd dissertation, University of Stellenbosch, Stellenbosch).

Cara, C. (2007). Musical chairs: A case and commentary about creating inclusive educational practices. *The International Journal of the Humanities*, 5(7), 215–222.

Chambers, D., & Forlin, C. (2010). Initial teacher education and inclusion: A triad of inclusive experiences. In C. Forlin (Ed.), *Teacher education for inclusion: Changing paradigms and innovative approaches* (pp. 74–83). Abingdon, UK: Routledge.

Christopher, M. V., & Elizabeth, A. U. (2012). Teacher preparation for sustainable inclusive education for persons with special needs in Nigeria. *The Journal of the National Centre for Exceptional Children*, 14(2).

Clark, S. G. (2000). The IEP process as a tool for collaboration. *Teaching Exceptional Children*, 33(2), 56–66.

Cook, B. G., Cameron, D. L., & Tankersley, M. (2007). Inclusive teachers' attitudinal ratings of their students with disabilities. *The Journal of Special Education*, 40(4), 230–238. https://10.1177/00224669070400040401

Cooper, J. E., Stephanie, K., Ceola Ross, B., & Ada, V. (2008). A model for examining teacher preparation curricula for inclusion. *Teacher Education Quarterly*, 35(4), 155–176.

Department of Education, Science and Training. (2006). *Survey of former teacher education students: A follow-up to the survey of final year teacher education students.* Canberra, Australia: Author.

Department of Education and Training. (2003). *Building inclusive schools.* Perth, Australia: Author.

Department of Education and Training. (2004). *Competency framework for teachers.* Perth, Australia: Author.

DeSimone, J. R., & Parmar, R. S. (2006). Middle school math teachers' beliefs about inclusion of students with learning disabilities. *Learning Disabilities Research & Practice*, 21(2), 98–110

Diener, E. (2009). Positive psychology: Past, present, and future. In S. J. Lopez & C. R. Snyder (Eds.), *Oxford handbook of positive psychology* (pp. 7–11). New York: Oxford University Press.

Dweck, C. S. (2008). *Mindset: The new psychology of success.* Random House Digital, Inc.

Education Week. (2001). *Inclusion.* Education Week: Hot Topics. Retrieved from: http://www.edweek.org/context/topics/issuespage.cfm?id=47

Education Development Trust, UNICEF. (2016). *Eastern and Southern Africa regional study on the fulfilment of the right to education of children with disabilities.* Reading: EDT.

Ethiopia. Ministry of Education. (2015). Guideline for establishing and managing inclusive education resource/support centers (RCs). Addis Ababa: Federal Ministry of Education.

European Agency for Development in Special Needs Education (EADSNE). (2003). *Key principles for special needs education. Recommendations for policy makers.* Odense: Author.

European Agency for Development in Special Needs Education (EADSNE). (2012). *Teacher education for inclusion: Project recommendation linked to sources of evidence.* Odense: Author.

European Agency for Special Needs and Inclusive Education. (2015). *Empowering teachers to promote inclusive education: A case study of approaches to training and support for inclusive teacher practice.* Odense: European Agency for Special Needs and Inclusive Education.

European Agency for Special Needs and Inclusive Education. (2017). *Inclusive education for learners with disabilities. Study for the Peti committee.* Brussels: European Union.

Elder, B. C., Rood, C. E., & Damiani, M. L. (2018). Writing strength-based IEPs for students with disabilities in inclusive classrooms. *International Journal of Whole Schooling*, 14(1), 116–153.

Ewing, R., & Smith, D. (2003). Retaining quality beginning teachers in the profession. *English Teaching: Practice and Critique*, 2(1), 15–32.

Fakudze, S., 2012, *Supporting teachers to implement inclusive education in Kwaluseni District, Swaziland* (MEd thesis, UNISA, Pretoria).

Ferguson, D. L. (2008). International trends in inclusive education: The continuing challenge to teach each one and everyone, *European Journal of Special Needs Education, 23*(2), 109–120. https://10.1080/08856250801946236

Florian, L. (2014). What counts as evidence of inclusive education? *European Journal of Special Needs Education, 29*,3, 286–294. https://10.1080/08856257.2014.933551

Florian, L. (2015). Inclusive Pedagogy: A transformative approach to individual differences but can it help reduce educational inequalities? *Scottish Educational Review, 47*(1), 5, 14.

Florian, L., & Spratt, J. (2013) Enacting inclusion: A framework for interrogating inclusive practice, *European Journal of Special Needs Education, 28*, 2, 119–135. https://10.1080/08856257.2013.778111

Forlin. C. (2010). *Teacher Education for Inclusion Changing Paradigms and Innovative Approaches*. New York: Routledge Publishers.

Forlin. C., & Chambers, D. (2011). Teacher preparation for inclusive education: Increasing knowledge but raising concerns, *Asia-Pacific Journal of Teacher Education, 39*(1), 17–32. http://dx.doi.org/10.1080/1359866X.2010.540850

Forlin, C., & Lian, M-G. J. (Eds.). (2008). *Reform, inclusion and teacher education: Towards a new era of special education in the Asia-Pacific region*. Abingdon: Routledge.

Forlin, C., Loreman, T., Sharma, U., & Earle, C. (2007). Demographic differences in changing pre-service teachers' attitudes, sentiments and concerns about inclusive education. *International Journal of Inclusive Education, 13*(2), 195–209.

Forlin, C., Keen, M., & Barrett, E. (2008). The concerns of mainstream teachers: Coping with inclusivity in an Australian context. *International Journal of Disability, Development and Education, 55*(3), 251–264.

Forlin, C. (2006). Inclusive education in Australia ten years after Salamanca. *Eur J Psychol Educ. 21*, 265. https://doi.org/10.1007/BF03173415

Fiji. Australian Agency for International Development, Fiji. Ministry of Education. (2017). *Fiji Education Management Information System (FEMIS): Disability disaggregation package. Guidelines and forms*.

Fox, J. (2008). *Your child's strengths: Discover them, develop them, use them*. London: Penguin Books.

Galloway, R., Reynolds, B., & Williamson, J. (2016). Strengths-Based Teaching and Learning Approaches for Children. In Fan, S., Fielding-Wells, J. (Eds.), *What is next in educational research?* Rotterdam: Sense Publishers. https://doi.org/10.1007/978-94-6300-524-1_19

Garwood, J. D., & Ampuja, A. A. (2019). Inclusion of students with learning, emotional, and behavioral disabilities through strength-based approaches. *Intervention in School and Clinic. 55*(1), 46–51. https://10.1177/1053451218767918

Gardner, M., & Toope, D. (2011). A social justice perspective on strengths-based approaches: Exploring educators' perspectives and practices. *Canadian Journal of Education, 34*(3), 86–102. Google Scholar

George Street Normal School. (2014). *What is strengths-based learning?* Retrieved from http://www.georgestreet.school.nz/about-us/what-strength-based-education

Global Partnership for Education (GPE). (2018). *Disability and inclusive education: A stocktake of education sector plans and GPE-funded grants*. Washington, DC: GPE.

García, E., & Weiss, E. (2017). *Reducing and averting achievement gaps Key findings from the report 'Education inequalities at the school starting gate' and comprehensive strategies to mitigate early skills gaps Report*. https://epi.org/130888

Global Partnership for Education (GPE). (2018). *Disability and inclusive education: A stocktake of education sector plans and GPE-funded grants*. Washington, DC: GPE.

Gokdere, M. (2012). A comparative study of the attitude, concern, and interaction levels of elementary school teachers and teacher candidates towards inclusive education. *Educational Sciences: Theory and Practice, 12*(4), 2800–2806.

Grimes, P., Stevens, M., Kumar, K. (2015). An examination of the evolution of policies and strategies to improve access to education for children with disabilities with a focus on inclusive education approaches, the success and challenges. Background paper prepared for the Education for All Global Monitoring Report 2015, Education for All 2000–2015: Achievements and Challenges.

Halder, S., & Bruyere, S. M., (2021). Self-reported impediments at home, school, and community: Autistic adults' first-person accounts of their life trajectories and derived pathways, *International Journal of developmental disabilities (IJDD)*, 1–13. https://10.1080/20473869.2021.1917111

Hartley, S. D. (2011). World report on Disability. https://www.researchgate.net/publication/282877201

Hayes, A. M., and Bulat, J. (2017). *Disabilities inclusive education systems and policies guide for low- and middle-income countries*. RTI Press Publication No. OP-0043-1707. Research Triangle Park, NC: RTI Press. https://doi.org/10.3768/rtipress.2017.op.0043.1707

Hodkinson, A. (2005). Conceptions and misconceptions of inclusive education: A critical examination of final-year teacher trainees' knowledge and understanding of inclusion. *Research in Education*, 73(1), 15–28. https://10.7227/RIE.73.2

Humanity & Inclusion. 2015. 'Education for all? This is still not a reality for most children with disabilities'. Humanity & Inclusion. Last accessed 13 April 2021: https://hi.org/sn_uploads/document/Education-pour-tous_un-mythe-pour-la-plupart-des-enfants-handicapes_en_1.pdf.

IDEA—Individuals with Disabilities Education Act. (1992). Pub. L. No. 101-476. Retrieved from: http://frwebgate.access.gpo.gov/cgi-bin/getdoc.cgi?dbname=105_cong_public_la

Individuals with Disabilities Education Improvement Act of 2004, 20 U.S.C. § 1400 et seq. (2004) (reauthorization of the Individuals with Disabilities Education Act of 1990).

Jones-Smith, E. (2011). *Spotlighting the strengths of every single student: Why US schools need a new, strengths-based approach*. Santa Barbara, CA: ABC-CLIO. Google Scholar

Jung, W. S. (2007). Preservice teacher training for successful inclusion. *Education*, 128(1), 106–113.

Kearns, H., & Shevlin, M. (2006). Initial teacher preparation for special educational needs: Policy and practice in the North and South of Ireland. *Teacher Development*, 10(1), 25–42. https://10.1080/13664530600587287

Kirschman, K., Johnson, R., Bender, J., & Roberts, M. (2012). Positive psychology for children and adolescents: Development, prevention, and promotion. *Oxford Handbooks Online*. Retrieved from http://www.oxfordhandbooks.com/view/10.1093/oxfordhb/9780195187243.001.0001/oxfordhb-9780195187243-e-013

Kumar, B. (2018). Inclusive education-new challenges and strategies. *International Journal of Technical Research & Science*, 3, 304. https:// 10.30780/IJTRS.V3. I10.2018.005

Laarhoven, V., Toni R., Dennis D. M., Kathleen, L., Julie, B., & Joanne, R. (2007). A model for preparing special and general education preservice teachers for inclusive education. *Journal of Teacher Education*, 8(5), 440–455.

Lancaster, J., & Bain, A. (2007). The design of inclusive education courses and the self-efficacy of preservice teacher education students year. *International Journal of Disability, Development and Education*, 52(2), 245–256. http://dx.doi.org/10.1080/10349120701330610

Lakkala, S., Galkiene, A., Navaitiene, J., Cierpiałowska, T., Tomecek, S., & Satu Uusiautti, S. (2021). Teachers supporting students in collaborative ways: An analysis of collaborative work creating supportive learning environments for every student in a school: Cases from Austria, Finland, Lithuania, and Poland. *Sustainability*, 13, 2804. https://doi.org/10.3390/su13052804

Le Fanu, G. (2005). *The inclusion of inclusive education in teacher-training: Issues of curriculum, Pedagogy and Staffing*. Bristol: University of Goroka.

Lewis, S. G. (2019). Opinion: The urgent need to plan for disability-inclusive education. *Devex*. https://www.devex.com/news/opinion-the-urgent-need-to-plan-for-disability-inclusive-education-94059

Lewis, C. L. (2018). The Open Access Citation Advantage: Does It Exist and What Does It Mean for Libraries? *Information Technology and Libraries*, 37(3), 50–65. https://doi.org/10.6017/ital.v37i3.10604

Lopez, S. J., & Louis, M. C. (2009). The principles of strengths-based education. *Journal of College and Character*, 10(4).

Loreman, T., & Harvey, D. (2005). *Inclusive education. A practical guide to supporting diversity in the classroom*. Abingdon: Routledge.

Loreman, T., Forlin, C., & Sharma, U. (2014), Measuring Indicators of Inclusive Education: A Systematic Review of the Literature. *Measuring Inclusive Education (International Perspectives on Inclusive Education*, 3, Emerald Group Publishing Limited, Bingley, 165–187.

Mahlo, F. D. (2011). *Experiences of learning support teachers in the foundation phase, with reference to the implementation of inclusive education in Gauteng*. Pretoria: University of South Africa.

Male, C., & Wodon, Q. (2018). *Disability gaps in educational attainment and literacy. The price of exclusion: Disability and education*. Washington, DC: World Bank; GPE.

Mariga, L., McConkey, R., & Myezwa, H. (2014). *Inclusive education in low-income countries: A resource for teacher educators, parent trainers and community development workers*. Cape Town: Atlas Alliance and Disability Innovations Africa.

McCashen, W. (2005). *The strengths approach*. Bendigo: St. Lukes Innovative Resources.

Miles, S., & Singal, N. (2010). The education for all and inclusive education debate: Conflict, contradiction or opportunity? *International Journal of Inclusive Education 14*(1). https://10.1080/13603110802265125

Miller, M. (2008). What do students think about inclusion? *Phi Delta Kappan, 89*(5), 389–391. https://10.1177/003172170808900518.

Mock, D. R., & Kauffman, J. M. (2002). Preparing teacher for Full inclusion: Is it possible? *The Teacher Educator, 37*(3), 202–215.

Mont, D. (2018). Collecting data for inclusive education. *IIEP Learning Portal* (blog).

Morningstar, M. E., Shogren, K., & Born, K. (2015). Preliminary lessons about supporting participation and learning in inclusive classrooms. *Research and Practice for Persons with Severe Disabilities, 40*(3), 192–210. https://10.1177/1540796915594158

Mukhopadhyay, S., Molosiwa, M., & Moswela, E. (2013). Teacher trainees' level of preparedness for inclusive education in Botswana schools: Need for change. *International Journal of Scientific Research, 2*(2), 51–58.

Najjingo, H. (2009). *Challenges of accessing all-inclusive education services by children with disabilities (cwds): A case of Mijwala sub-county ssembabule district*. Sembabule: Makerere University.

National Center for Education Statistics. (2011). *The nation's report card: Mathematics 2011 (NCES 2012-458)*. Washington, DC: Institute of Education Sciences, U.S. Department of Education.

National Center for Education Statistics. (2021). *Digest of Education Statistics*, 2019 (NCES 2021-009), Table 204.60.

Nanda, B. P., & Nanda, S. (2007). Efficacy of mainstream teachers sensitization training on inclusive education under Sarva Siksha Abhiyan. Paper Presented in National Seminor on Inclusion of the Excluded. Agenda of Education for Social Leveling and Empowerment. University of Kalyani.

NCSE (National Council for Special Education). (2006). *Guidelines on the individual education plan process*. Dublin: The Stationery Office.

No Child Left Behind Act of 2001, P.L. 107-110, 20 U.S.C. § 6319 (2002).

Nilholm, C. (2020) Research about inclusive education in 2020: How can we improve our theories in order to change practice? *European Journal of Special Needs Education*. https://10.1080/08856257.2020.1754547

OECD. (2007). *No more failures: Ten steps to equity in education*. Paris: OECD.

Omede, A. A., & Sam, T. (2013). Improving Teacher Professionalism. As an access for effective attainment of qualitative education for national development. *The Journal of Pristine 8*(1).

Papastephanou, M. (2019). Inclusion in Education and in Public Debates on Education, The Global Partnership for Education (GPE) emphasized the inclusion of students with disabilities in education (GPE, 2018). *Beijing International Review of Education, 1*(2019), 303–323. https://10.1163/25902539-00102019

Parrilla, M. A. (2002). Acerca del origen y sentido de la educación inclusiva [Concerning the origin and meaning of inclusive education]. *Revista de educación, 327*, 11–30.

Paula, J. S., & Jordan, A. J. (2002). Preparing general educators to teach in inclusive classrooms: Some food for thought. *The Teacher Educators*, Winter, 37(3), Education collection, 173.

Pavri, S. (2004). General and special education teachers' preparation needs in providing social support: A needs assessment. *Teacher Education and Special Education, 27*(4), 433–443. https://10.1177/088840640402700410

Pearce, M. (2008). The inclusive secondary school teacher. In C. Forlin & M.-G. J. Lian (Eds.), *Reform, inclusion and teacher education: Towards a new era of special education in the Asia Pacific region* (pp. 142–152). Abingdon, UK: Routledge.

Pearce, M., & Forlin, C. (2005). Challenges and potential solutions for enabling inclusion in secondary schools. *Australasian Journal of Special Education, 29*(2), 93–105.

Peter, S. J. (2007). Education for All? A historical analysis of international inclusive education policy and individuals with disabilities. *J Disabil Policy Stud., 18*(2), 98–108.

Piper, B., Bulat, J., Kwayumba, D., Oketch, J., & Gangla, L. (2019). Measuring literacy outcomes for the blind and for the deaf: Nationally representative results from Kenya. *International Journal of Educational Development, 69*(September). 1-8. https://doi.org/10.1016/j.ijedudev.2019.05.002

Price, R. (2018). *Inclusive and special education approaches in developing countries*. K4D Helpdesk Report.

Rambla, X., Ferrer, F., Tarabini, A., & Verger, A. (2008). Inclusive education and social inequality: An update of the question and some geographical considerations. *Prospects, 38*(1), 65–76.

Rawana, E., Latimer, K., Whitley, J., & Probizanski, M. (2009). Strength-based classroom strategies for teachers. *Canadian Teacher Magazine*. BC Canada: Pasific Edge Publishing. Retrieved from http://www.canadianteachermagazine.com/archives/ctm_teaching_ideas/nov09_strength-based_classroom_strategies.shtml

Resiliency Initiatives. (2011). *Embracing a strength-based perspective and practice in education resiliency initiative, 403.274.7706.* www.resiliencyinitiatives.ca

Reyes, M. E., Hutchinson, C. J., & Little, M. (2017). Preparing educators to teach effectively in inclusive settings. *SRATE Journal, 26*(1), 21–29.

Richards, G., & Clough, P. (2004). ITE students' attitudes to inclusion. *Research in Education, 72*(1), 77–86. https://10.7227/RIE.72.6

Rod, G., Bronwyn, R., John, W. (2020). Strengths-based teaching and learning approaches for children: Perceptions and practices. *Journal of Pedagogical Research, 4*(1), 31–45. https://doi.org/10.33902/JPR.2020058178

Romi, S., & Leyser, Y. (2006). Exploring inclusion preservice training needs: A study of variables associated with attitudes and self-efficacy beliefs. *European Journal of Special Needs Education, 21*(1), 85–105. https://10.1080/08856250500491880.

Rose, P., Singal, N., Bari, F., Malik, R., & Kamran, S. (2018). *Identifying disability in household surveys: Evidence on education access and learning for children with disabilities in Pakistan.* Policy Paper, 18/1. Cambridge: REAL Centre. University of Cambridge.

Saleebey, D. (1996). *The strengths perspective in social work practice* (2nd ed.). New York: Longman Publishing.

Saloviita, T. (2020) Attitudes of teachers towards inclusive education in Finland, *Scandinavian Journal of Educational Research, 64*(2), 270–282. https://doi.org/10.1080/00313831.2018.1541819

Savage, R. S. S., & Erten, O. (2015). Teaching in inclusive classrooms: The link between teachers' attitudes, practices and student outcomes. *Journal of Psychology and Psychotherapy, 5*(6). https://10.4172/2161-0487.1000219

Savolainen, H. (2009). Responding to diversity and striving for excellence: The case for Finland. In C. Acedo (Ed.), *Prospects quarterly review of comparative education* (vol. 39, pp. 281–292). Joensuu, Finland: UNESCO IBE.

Schreiner, L. A. (2013). *Strengths-based advising. Academic advising approaches: Strategies that teach students to make the most of college* (pp. 105–120). San Francisco, CA: Jossey Bass.

Seligman, M., Ernst, R., Gillham, J., Reivich, K., & Linkins, M. (2009). Positive education: Positive psychology and classroom interventions. *Oxford Review of Education, 35*(3), 293–311. Retrieved June 29, 2021, from http://www.jstor.org/stable/27784563

Seligman, M. E. P. (1990). *Learned optimism.* NY, NY: Alfred A. Knopf

Seligman, M. E. P., Rashid, T., & Parks, A. C. (2006). Positive psychotherapy. *American Psychologist, 61*, 774–788. https://10.1037/0003-066X.61.8.774

Shaddock, A., MacDonald, N., Hook, J., Giorcelli, L., & Arthur-Kelly, M. (2009). *Disability, diversity and tides that lift all boats: Review of special education in the ACT.* https://www.researchgate.net/publication/265494993_Disability_Diversity_and_Tides_that_Lift_All_Boats_Review_of_Special_Education_in_the_ACT

Shade, R. A., & Stewart, R. (2001) General education and special education preservice teachers' attitudes toward inclusion. *Preventing School Failure: Alternative Education for Children and Youth, 46*(1), 37–41. https://10.1080/10459880109603342

Sharma, U., Loreman, T., & Forlin, C. (2007). What concerns pre-service teachers about inclusive education: An international viewpoint. *KEDI Journal of Educational Policy, 4*(2), 95–114.

Sharry, J. (2004). *Counselling children, adolescents and families: A strength-based approach.* London: Sage Publications.

Singal, N. 2015. Education of children with disabilities in India and Pakistan: An analysis of developments since 2000. Background paper prepared for the Education for All Global Monitoring Report 2015, Education for All 2000–2015: Achievements and Challenges.

Slee, R. (2018). Defining the scope of inclusive education. Paper commissioned for the 2020 global education monitoring report, inclusion and education. http://repositorio.minedu.gob.pe/bitstream/handle/MINEDU/5977/Defining%20the%20scope%20of%20inclusive%20education.pdf?sequence=1&isAllowed=y. Accessed 15 Sept 2018.

Smith, D. D., & Tyler, N. C. (2011) Effective inclusive education: Equipping education professionals with necessary skills and knowledge. *Prospects 41*, 323–339. https://doi.org/10.1007/s11125-011-9207-5

Spiteri, D. (2016). *Multiculturalism, higher education and intercultural communication: Developing strengths-based narratives for teaching and learning.* Cham: Springer.

Stanovich, P. J., & Jordan, A. (2002). Preparing general educators to teach in inclusive classrooms: Some food for thought. *The Teacher Educator, 37*(3), 173–185.

Stanovich, P. J., & Jordan, A. (1998). Canadian Teachers' and Principals' Beliefs about Inclusive Education as Predictors of Effective Teaching in Heterogeneous Classrooms. *The Elementary School Journal, 98*(3), 221–238. http://www.jstor.org/stable/1002258

Stella, C. S. C., Forlin, C., & Lan, A. M. (2007). The influence of an inclusive education course on attitude change of pre-service secondary teachers in Hong Kong. *Asia-Pacific Journal of Teacher Education*, *35*(2), 161–179. https://10.1080/13598660701268585

U.S. Department of Education. (2000). *National Center for Education Statistics, the condition of education 2000, NCES 2000–062*. Washington, DC: U.S. Government Printing Office.

UN General Assembly. (1989). Convention on the rights of the child. *United Nations, Treaty Series*, *1577*(3). http://www.refworld.org/docid/3ae6b38f0.html

UN High Commissioner for Refugees (UNHCR) (2017). *The sustainable development goals and addressing statelessness*, available at: https://www.refworld.org/docid/58b6e3364.html. Accessed 25 June 2021.

United Nations Educational Scientific and Cultural Organization (UNESCO). (1994). The Salamanca statement and framework for action on special needs education. http://www.unesco.org/education/pdf/SALAMA_E.PDF. Accessed 17 Nov 2018.

UNDP. (2015a). The millennium development goals report 2015. Retrieved November 23, 2016, from: http://www.undp.org/content/undp/en/home/librarypage/mdg/the-millennium-development-goals-report-2015.html

UNDP. (2015b). Sustainable development goals. Goal 4: Quality education. Retrieved November 23, 2016, from: http://www.undp.org/content/undp/en/home/sustainable-development-goals/goal-4-quality-education.html

UNESCO. (1994). The Salamanca statement and framework for action on special needs education. In World Conference on Special Needs Education: Access and Quality, Salamanca, Spain, 7–10 June 1994. Paris: UNESCO.

UNESCO. (2005). *Guidelines for inclusion: Ensuring access to education for all*. Paris: UNESCO.

UNESCO. (2009). *Policy guidelines on inclusion in education*. Paris: Author.

UNESCO. (2015). SDG4-education 2030, incheon declaration (ID) and framework for action for the implementation of sustainable development goal 4: Ensure inclusive and equitable quality education and promote lifelong learning opportunities for all, ED-2016/WS/28.

UNESCO. (2016). Incheon declaration and framework for action for the implementation of sustainable development goal: Ensure inclusive and equitable quality education and promote lifelong learning for all. Document of program or meeting. 02/2019- Extract from: http://www.unesco.org/new/fileadmin/MULTIMEDIA/FIELD/Santiago/pdf/ESP-Marco-de-Accion-E2030-aprobado.pdf

UNESCO. (2017). *A Guide for ensuring inclusion and equity in education*. Paris: UNESCO.

United Nations. (2006). *Convention on the rights of persons with disabilities and optional protocol*. New York: United Nations.

UNESCO (2015). SDG4-Education 2030, Incheon Declaration (ID) and Framework for Action. For the Implementation of Sustainable Development Goal 4, Ensure Inclusive and Equitable Quality Education and Promote Lifelong Learning Opportunities for All, ED-2016/WS/28

United Nations. (2015). *Transforming our world: The 2030 agenda for sustainable development*. New York: UN Publishing.

The United Nations. (1948). *Universal declaration of human rights*. California USA

Van Laarhoven, T. R., Munk, D. D., Lynch, K., Bosma, J., & Rouse, J. (2007). A model for preparing special and general education preservice teachers for inclusive education. *Journal of Teacher Education*, *58*(5), 440–455. https://10.1177/0022487107306803

Whitworth, J. W. (1999). A model for inclusive teacher preparation. *Electronic Journal for Inclusive Education*, *1*(2). 3–9

Winter, E. C. (2006). Preparing new teachers for inclusive schools and classrooms. *Support for Learning*, *1*(2), 85–91. https://doi.org/10.1111/j.1467-9604.2006.00409.x

Winter, S. (2020). Inclusive and exclusive education for diverse learning needs. In Leal Filho, W., Azul, A. M., Brandli, L., Özuyar, P. G., & Wall, T. (eds.), *Quality education. Encyclopedia of the UN sustainable development goals*. Cham: Springer. https://doi.org/10.1007/978-3-319-95870-5_24

Wodon, Q., Male, C., Montenegro, C., & Nayihouba, A. (2018). *The challenge of inclusive education in Sub-Saharan Africa*. Washington, DC: World Bank.

Wood, A. M., & Tarrier, N. (2010). Positive clinical psychology: A new vision and strategy for integrated research and practice. *Clinical Psychology Review*, *30*(7), 819–829. CrossRefGoogle Scholar.

Wood, A. M., Linley, P. A., Maltby, J., Kashdan, T. B., & Hurling, R. (2011). Using personal and psychological strengths leads to increases in well-being over time: A longitudinal study and the development of the strengths use questionnaires. *Personality and Individual Differences*, *50*(1), 15–19.

Woodcock, S., & Woolfson, L. (2019) Are leaders leading the way with inclusion? Teachers' perceptions of systemic support and barriers towards inclusion. *International Journal of Educational Research, 93*, 232–242. https://doi.org/10.1016/j.ijer.2018.11.004

World Health Organization. (2011). World report on disability. *World Report on Disability, xxiii*(1), 325p. https://apps.who.int/iris/handle/10665/44575

World Bank. (2019). *Every learner matters: Unpacking the learning crisis for children with disabilities.* Washington, DC: World Bank.

World Economic Forum (WEF) (2015). The Travel and Tourism Competitiveness Report: Growth through Shocks. http://www3.weforum.org/docs/TT15/WEF_Global_Travel&Tourism_Report_2015.pdf

World Bank. (2021). *Global economic prospects.* Washington, DC: World Bank. https://openknowledge.worldbank.org/handle/10986/34710. License: CC BY 3.0 IGO.

Zacarian, D., Alvarez-Ortiz, L., & Haynes, J. (2017). *Teaching to strengths.* ASCD Publishers.

Zimba, Z. (2011). *Managing an inclusive school in Swaziland*, Research report. Grahamstown: Rhodes University.

Zwane, S. L., & Malale, M. M. (2018). Investigating barriers teachers face in the implementation of inclusive education in high schools in Gege branch, Swaziland. *African Journal of Disability, 7*, a391. https://doi.org/10.4102/ajod.v7i0.391

PART I

Foundational and Conceptual Considerations

Understanding the fundamental, philosophical, and conceptual policies, research, and practices are crucial for successful inclusion and effective teaching and learning in inclusive classrooms. This section covers various foundational and conceptual aspects and issues of teaching and learning for inclusive classrooms.

2
FOUNDATIONAL AND LEGAL BASIS OF INCLUSIVE EDUCATION AND FUTURE DIRECTIONS

Todd Sundeen* and Rashida Banerjee

The World Health Organization (Cieza et al., 2021) estimates that about one billion people globally have disabilities, with approximately 110-190 million individuals experiencing very significant disabilities. The number of people with disabilities has grown from approximately 10% in the 1970s to a current estimate of 15%. Currently, the global estimate for disability prevalence due to epilepsy, intellectual disabilities, or sensory impairments among children and adolescents is about 291 million globally (Olusanya et al., 2020). Of this estimate, 25.2% were children from birth to 9 years old. However, these rates are often unreliable and often underreported due to (a) the lack of a common global definition of "disability" and (b) the limited and unequal availability of reliable and valid screening and assessment instruments around the world (Vargas-Barón et al., 2019). This is particularly true for infants and very young children. Developing countries often use census and household surveys to document disability rates, frequently resulting in substantially lower rates of disability than in countries applying measures that document restrictions in participation and activity limitations (World Report on Disability, 2011). In this chapter, we provide foundational knowledge necessary for educators in inclusive classrooms who support young children and youth with disabilities. We cover topics such as historical and theoretical models of disability, world policies, and statutes, the legislative basis of inclusive education. We conclude with the current issues and trends in research and evidence-based practices to support inclusion.

Historical Context

For centuries, people with disabilities have been subjected to irrational fears and injurious stereotyping. The Anti-Defamation League (2018) in the U.S. describe some of the history:

> In the 1800s, people with disabilities were considered meager, tragic, pitiful individuals unfit and unable to contribute to society, except to serve as ridiculed objects of entertainment in circuses and exhibitions. They were assumed to be abnormal and fee-

---

* Todd.sundeen@unco.edu

ble-minded, and numerous persons were forced to undergo sterilization. People with disabilities were also forced to enter institutions and asylums, where many spent their entire lives. The "purification" and segregation of persons with disability were considered merciful actions, but ultimately served to keep people with disabilities invisible and hidden from a fearful and biased society.

(p. 1)

Historically, inclusive education was based on a separate and special curriculum. Most often, the specialized curriculum included concepts not explicitly taught in general settings such as social skills, communication skills, life-skills, and functional reading skills. Moreover, students with identified disabilities were educated in separate schools or separate classes within a regular school. Students with disabilities were most often grouped by disability in smaller classes where student learning could be individualized to the greatest extent possible by teachers trained to deliver a specialized curriculum.

Processes and Policies Driving Inclusion Practices around the World

Guiding Policies in the United States

Inclusive education is a multi-faceted concept that has been interpreted differently across the years (e.g., Fuchs & Fuchs, 1994; Kauffman et al., 2018; Nilholm & Göransson, 2017). Actually, inclusive education has been a contentious issue in the U.S. for decades (Kauffman et al., 2018). Yet ideological and political support for inclusive education has been increasing over recent decades (e.g., Ainscow, 2020; Mundy, 2016; UNESCO, 2020c). As recently as 1975, the U.S. passed the first iteration of the education law that is currently known as the Individuals with Disabilities Education Act (IDEA, 2004). IDEA formalized the concept of free and appropriate public education (FAPE) and the concept of an individual education program (IEP) for children and youth with disabilities. The IEP is a written, legally binding document that addresses the unique educational needs of each child identified with a disability. One requirement of IDEA is that the IEP describes the placement of the student in the least restrictive environment (LRE). Note that the LRE is not determined prior to the development of the IEP (Yell, 2019). Rather, the IEP team (e.g., parents, students, administrators, service providers, etc.) is assembled to make educational decisions for the student and collectively decides on the most ideal LRE for the student. It is noteworthy that full student participation in general education must be the first choice for the IEP team. Justification must be written into the IEP that explains the student's ability or inability to participate in the general education program and the need for a more restrictive environment.

Parents and advocacy groups in the U.S. have been among the most potent change agents for children and youth with disabilities. Through the focused efforts of parents and advocacy groups engaging with courts, legislatures, and policy makers, the educational and inclusion rights of children and youth with disabilities have continued to be improved through the years (Yell, 2019). One of the most substantial opportunities for improving the educational situation for children and youth with disabilities in the U.S. came in 1954. The landmark case *Brown v. Board of Education* (1954) outlawed racial segregation in public education. This legal case mandated that education must be provided to all children and youth on an equal basis. In the U.S. during the 1950s and 1960s, the civil rights movement began to gain momentum (Yell, 2019). Disability advocates recognized the opportunities, initiated by the civil rights movement, to assert their own agenda and demand equal opportunities, equal access, and equal treatment under the law and in society (Anti-Defamation League, 2018). Case law has played an important role in improving inclusive education for children and youth with disabilities. Based upon the U.S. Supreme Court findings of *Brown v. Board of Education* (1954), parents and advocacy groups argued that the exclusion of students with disabilities was a denial of equal educational opportunity. The results of these efforts and the precedents set in *Brown v. Board of Education* (1954) became the basis for significant changes in school policies and approaches to the education of students with disabilities allowing for substantially more inclusive education in school settings with their nondisabled peers (Katsiyannis et al., 2001).

Guiding Global Policies and Processes

Similar to the leverage for change applied by parents and advocacy groups in the U.S., grassroots inclusive education efforts in other countries too have been propelled by family members and advocacy groups. International changes in inclusive education have also occurred as a result of the efforts of organizations and governments dedicated to making quality basic education available to all learners (UNESCO, 2020c). The United Nations Educational, Scientific and Cultural Organization (UNESCO) was established post-World War II in 1946. The UNESCO constitution made it exceptionally clear that inclusive education globally would be an ongoing mission "by instituting collaboration among the nations to advance the ideal of equality of educational opportunity without regard to race, sex or any distinctions, economic or social" (UNESCO, 2020a, p. 7).

In 1990, 150 governments adopted the *World Declaration on Education for All* statement at Jomtien, Thailand (UNESCO, 2020c). This statement supported a movement initiated by UNESCO to further the mission to promote equality of education internationally (Mundy, 2016). The document resulting from the Jomtien meeting provided a foundation towards promoting the right to education for the world's citizenry. Another foundational document for globally improving inclusivity for students with disabilities came about in 1994 with the signing of the UNESCO *Salamanca Statement on Principles, Policy and Practice in Special Needs Education* (UNESCO, 2020c). Participants in the conference included 92 governments and 25 international organizations that met in Salamanca, Spain. The resulting Salamanca Statement endorsed the idea of inclusive education, a concept that has had a major global influence in advancing the inclusive education of children and youth with disabilities. The Salamanca Statement concluded that:

> Regular schools with [an] inclusive orientation are the most effective means of combating discriminatory attitudes, creating welcoming communities, building an inclusive society and achieving education for all; moreover, they provide an effective education to the majority of children and improve the efficiency and ultimately the cost-effectiveness of the entire education system.
>
> *(UNESCO, 2020c, p. 10)*

The importance of this statement lies in the fact that it provides undergirding to the concept of inclusive schools for children and youth with disabilities. In other words, inclusive schools can be justified through three key foci (Ainscow, 2020). First, *educational justification* provides for inclusive schools to educate all children and youth in the same settings. It also means that inclusive schools must apply teaching methods that respond to individual learning differences. *Social justification* indicates that inclusive schools contribute to building a more inclusive society and reducing discrimination by educating all students together. The opportunity for *economic justification* is also supported due to the cost efficiency of educating children together rather than developing a stratified system that separates differing groups of children (Ainscow, 2020).

Following the Salamanca Statement, the *World Education Forum* in Dakar, Senegal, in the year 2000 further reaffirmed the international commitment to educational equality by adopting six Education for All (EFA) goals intended to be accomplished by 2015. The EFA goals helped focus attention on children with disabilities who may have previously been excluded from educational settings. The importance of the EFA also lies in its codification of a set of universal norms to support an architecture for improving educational rights around the world:

> Basic education for all requires assuring access, permanence, quality learning, and full participation and integration of all children and adolescents, particularly for members of indigenous groups, those with disabilities, those who are homeless, those who are workers, those living with HIV/AIDS.
>
> *(UNESCO, 2000, p. 39)*

In 2015, the UNESCO General Assembly extended the work done on the EFA agenda by adopting a new resolution called Transforming our world: The 2030 Agenda for Sustainable Development. This is a wide-ranging resolution that addresses 17 Sustainable Development Goals (SDGs), key areas for improving the world for all people. The SDGs will be implemented and monitored for success over 15 years, ending in 2030. SDG Number 4 (SDG 4) provides a specific emphasis on how inclusion and equity play a foundational role in quality education. The international commitment is for education at all levels (e.g., early childhood, primary, secondary, tertiary, technical, and vocational training) to be accessible to all people. The UNESCO General Assembly specifically addressed the importance of providing a quality inclusive education for children and youth with disabilities that allows them to fully participate in society.

It is essential to note that, as important as the actions of UNESCO are in their efforts to improve inclusive education globally, the documents and initiatives that have been adopted (e.g., *Jomtien Statement*, *Salamanca Statement*, Education for All (EFA) goals, etc.) are not legally binding on the entities that have signed them. Rather, these documents and initiatives provide a foundation, guidance, and initiative for improving inclusive education on a global scale. Essentially, forward movement has been realized in proactively identifying barriers and opportunities for improving inclusive education.

United Nations Conventions. International mandates such as the United Nations Convention on the Rights of the Child (CRC, 1989) and The United Nations Convention on the Rights of Persons with Disabilities (CRPD, 2006) have been globally adopted by countries. These Conventions firmly acknowledge the rights of all children and youth to access educational services and learn together in non-discriminating settings with reasonable accommodations. Developed through the active participation of organizations of and by people with disabilities, the CRPD is the first comprehensive human rights treaty of the 21st century that recognizes that disability is a human rights concern that requires a deep understanding of its issues and misconceptions and strong and specific action. One of the purposes of this treaty was to "ensure an inclusive education system at all levels and lifelong learning" (Art. 24, para. 1). As of July 2021, the CRC has been ratified by 193 countries and 182 countries have been signatories to the CRPD and over 164 countries have ratified the Convention. By ratifying the Convention, States takes a concrete step which signals the intention to undertake legal rights and obligations contained in the Convention or the Optional Protocol. Regional integration organizations express their consent to be bound by the Convention or Optional Protocol through "formal confirmation" – an act which has the same effect as ratification.

Through 50 Articles, CRPD sets out the human rights of persons with disabilities and the obligations of these countries to promote, protect, and ensure those rights, as well as mechanisms to support implementation and monitoring. Recognizing that disability is an evolving concept and a result of the interaction between negative attitudes or an unwelcoming environment with the condition of particular persons, the CRPD does not provide a definition of "disability" or "persons with disability". Further, the Convention uses the term "inclusive education systems" at all levels instead of "special education" in an attempt to shift from the implications of the narrow, hierarchical, and pathological paradigm of special education (Nguyen, 2013). Additionally, because the Convention celebrates human diversity and the contributions of people with disabilities, it does not argue for the prevention of disabilities (Banerjee, 2014). For more information on the CRPD, please refer to https://www.un.org/development/desa/disabilities/convention-on-the-rights-of-persons-with-disabilities.html.

Progress in improving inclusive education for more children and youth has been made in recent years as the global number of out-of-school children and youth has declined from 376 million in 2000 to 258 million in 2018 (UNESCO Institute for Statistics, 2019). Note that while these metrics do not provide specific information on children and youth with disabilities, logic would indicate that more students with disabilities are being included in regular schools. Yet the COVID-19 pandemic has jeopardized the progress made towards improving inclusive education worldwide. Prior to the pandemic, the percentage of children and youth not regularly attending school declined from 26% in 2000 to 17% in 2018 (UNESCO, 2020b). The long-term impacts of the COVID-19 pandemic on the SDGs remain to be seen. At this writing, however, it appears that progress towards achieving the SDGs by 2030 has been severely impacted.

Inclusion: Conceptualization and Definition

The concepts of inclusive education and inclusionary practices continue to vary internationally (e.g., Kauffman et al., 2018; UNESCO, 2020c; UNICEF, 2017). Scholars, policy makers, parents, advocacy groups, and other stakeholders have been engaged in an ongoing debate about the meaning and principles related to inclusion for decades (e.g., Dunn, 1968; Kauffman et al., 2018; Zigmond et al., 2009). The inconclusive definition and varying implementation models leave district administrators, school principals, and teachers to interpret how to implement inclusionary practices around the world. Yet inclusion is not simply the opposite of exclusion. Some agreement exists that inclusive education has some basic tenets. These often include the principles that everyone has the right to education and educational opportunities for students should occur in general education classrooms with typical peers, and access to the general education curriculum is essential to achieve inclusive education. Broadly, UNESCO (2009, pp. 8–9) sees inclusive education as a

> process of addressing and responding to the diversity in needs of all learners through increasing participation in learning, cultures and communities, and reducing exclusion in education. It involves changes and modifications in content, approaches, structures and strategies, with a common vision which covers all and a conviction that it is the responsibility of the regular system to educate all.

In the U.S. the concept of inclusion is reinforced by law (IDEA, 2004) through the principle of least restrictive environment (LRE). An individual education program (IEP) is developed for each student which describes, among other elements, how much time the student will spend in the general education classroom. A continuum of placement options based on the percentage of time in the general education classroom is considered by the IEP team that consists of parents, the student, school administrators, related service providers, and other relevant individuals. However, as placement decisions are made for children and youth with disabilities, the first choice must be the general education setting with their nondisabled peers. While students may not always be placed full time in general education classrooms, the decision for alternative placement must be supported by assessment data and an IEP team decision. A recent U.S. Supreme Court ruling (*Endrew F. v. Douglas County School District RE-1*, 2017) has changed the prevalent interpretation of LRE. The prevailing court case prior to *Endrew F.* was *Board of Education of the Hendrick Hudson School District v. Rowley* (1982), which interpreted appropriate LRE within IDEA (2004) as students having "access" to the general education curriculum and classroom. Under *Rowley* (1982) children and youth with disabilities were entitled to a *de minimis* education. Schools interpreted *Rowley* (1982) to mean that the LRE decision was legally compliant if students were simply provided general education access (Yell, 2019). The U.S. Supreme Court unanimous ruling for *Endrew F.* changed the interpretation of LRE to mean that IEPs must result in a "plan" focused on "student progress". The IEP team must now consider the student's "potential for growth" concurrently relative to the student's individual capabilities. Moreover, each student's educational program must be "appropriately ambitious" in light of their capacity for progress.

The international perspectives on inclusive education for children and youth with disabilities are varied (e.g., Kauffman et al., 2018; Qu, 2020). For example, Rix (2020) describes a "continuum view" of inclusive education based upon his research (Rix et al., 2013) of 55 special education school administrations in 10 countries across the world. The "continuum view" encompassed 194 concepts related to the application of the concept of inclusive education through a variety of supports, strategies, and systems. Yet, the continuum described by education administrators aligned closely with traditional placement options: inclusive classrooms, special classrooms, special schools, institutional settings, and home support. Often, administrators described placing students with disabilities in separate classrooms with their peers and utilizing a curriculum not aligned with general education.

International inclusive education has also recently been described as a basic human right which underpins a more socially just society (Ainscow, 2020). From this perspective, inclusive education is a principle that has the potential to eliminate or reduce the social exclusion in education that has typically been the result of differences in race, social class, ethnicity, religion, gender, and ability. Ainscow (2020) also emphasizes that inclusive education, from an international interpretation, must be concerned with the supporting of students who are at risk of becoming marginalized or excluded and who may experience underachievement as a result of exclusion from learning with their nondisabled peers. Similarly, inclusive education has also been broadly viewed as an ethical stance (Hernández-Torrano et al., 2020). The ethical stance provides that educational systems must empower stakeholders while taking into account individual differences. When interpreting inclusive education through an ethical lens, accountability and the building of inclusive communities must be incorporated into the inclusive approach.

Bulat and colleagues (2017) addressed the needs of Sub-Saharan African countries in their guide for implementing inclusive education. Bulat et al. (2017) describe inclusion as a process rather than a single definitive goal. The process should be developed to identify the most promising evidence-based practices for supporting children and youth in inclusive settings. Inclusion should also be considerate of human differences in terms of learning; everyone learns differently. Thus, instruction must be designed to meet the unique learning needs of each student. Bulat et al. (2017) also emphasize that effective inclusive education requires that barriers to education must be identified and removed through the applied use of classroom data to identify what works for individual students and what does not. Inclusive education must be tailored to the learning needs of each child to ensure that they are fully engaged in the learning process.

Global inclusive education must take into account the variability in cultural influences. Low-income countries have participated in the development and ratification of the CRPD while subscribing to the SDGs and have been incorporating the tenets of inclusive education into their own schools (Bannink et al., 2020). However, it is often not possible to fully integrate the proscriptive elements of these international agreements into the education systems and cultural norms of some countries. In their Ugandan study, Bannink and colleagues found that the child-centered pedagogy emphasized by international organizations was not culturally acceptable in their schools. An inclusive child-centered pedagogy reverses the power structure in classrooms. Children are empowered to express themselves and are allowed to pose questions and challenge conventional thinking. Bannink et al. found that since children in Uganda are raised to demonstrate respect for adults by not questioning their thinking, child-centered methods of instruction contradicted the culture of Uganda. Similarly, Rajab and Wright (2020) describe the disconnect between the conservative belief system in Saudi Arabia and the "individualist, rationalist" educational approaches delineated by the 2030 Agenda for Sustainable Development (SDG 4). The reciprocal relationship, described by SDG 4, between teacher and student in which both are valued as equal contributors to the knowledge creation process is in conflict with the Saudi ideological framework.

Certainly, there is no single interpretation of inclusive education and no universal application of the principles described in international agreements (e.g., *Education for All, Jomtien Statement, Salamanca Statement, SDG 4*, etc.). Though there are a wide range of interpretations of inclusive education implementation, there seems to be an overall global intention to apply the concepts in a manner designed to provide educational opportunities for the most positive outcomes for children and youth with disabilities as is humanly possible, however, varied the local interpretation and implementation.

Theoretical Foundations/Models

The primary objective for inclusive education globally is the commitment to provide a quality education for all children and youth while not excluding those with disabilities or diverse learning needs from general education classrooms or general education curriculum. It is essential to recall that inclusive education is not simply a question about *where* education is delivered. Inclusive education is also defined by *how* instruction is delivered related to students' access to participating in the general education curriculum. Hornby (2015) encapsulated a description of inclusive education in the literature into a clear summary:

> Inclusive education is generally considered to be a multi-dimensional concept that includes the celebration and valuing of difference and diversity, consideration of human rights, social justice and equity issues, as well as of a social model of disability and a socio-political model of education. It also encompasses the process of school transformation and a focus on children's entitlement and access to education.
>
> *(p. 235)*

Article 24 of the CRPD provides the first explicit mention of "inclusive education" in international treaty form. This legally binding document between international States who have ratified the Convention provides a normative framework intended to guide states in their implementation of inclusive education. The core elements described by the CRPD include:

- A 'whole systems' approach
- A 'whole educational environment'
- A 'whole person' approach
- Supported teachers
- Respect for and value of diversity
- A learning-friendly environment
- Effective transitions
- Recognition of partnerships
- Monitoring

By examining the descriptions of inclusive education in the literature and the policy documents such as CRPD, it becomes clear that how inclusive education is conceptualized is inconsistent. So, it is helpful to turn to the foundations of inclusive education described in fundamental models. These models have contributed to the development of the various interpretations and implementations of inclusive education as we know it today. Models of disability are ways of interpreting and defining disability. Not all theoretical models are value neutral. Rather, models of disability can affect how people perceive individuals with disabilities and models have the potential to cause prejudice and discrimination based on how the model is defined. Furthermore, consider that not all disabilities are visible. Certain cognitive disabilities may only manifest themselves under certain conditions or circumstances. So, it is important to remember that *how* disabilities are described has the potential to affect how individuals with disabilities are treated and regarded by others. The models and the language they use to describe students with disabilities can also affect the perceptions, interactions, and expectations of their teachers and the resources provided to support students with disabilities in educational settings. Moreover, models of disability are also influential in how persons with disabilities see themselves. Below we describe some of the prevalent models of disability. This list is by no means an exhaustive description but an attempt to give a broad and foundational overview.

Medical Model of Disability

One of the most commonly cited, and long known, models related to the foundations of inclusive education found in the extant literature includes the medical model. Historically, the medical model has been acknowledged since the 1700s as a way to describe persons with disabilities as individuals with "biological defects" (Shakespeare, 2006). The medical model of disability addresses a person's disability as a medical phenomenon that must be cured, treated, or rehabilitated. Essentially, the medical model treats disability as a biological impairment or deficit that requires medical intervention. Emphasis is placed on describing disabilities in terms of issues, diagnosis, supports, and interventions. Disability is seen as a deficit that limits the functioning of the individual. When a disability is suspected, a medical professional provides a diagnosis for their patient. If a person is medically affected, they must be medically cured, healed, or fixed in some manner so that they can better participate in society. When a person with a disability is excluded from society, the issue is considered to be an individual problem based on the disability itself. In other words, the medical model describes disability as the problem of individuals rather than a societal issue. While the medical model of disability is useful from a personal health-related standpoint, difficulties arise when this model is applied to disabilities that are not necessarily medically defined. For example, a person with a specific cognitive disability may have no outward signs of disability until they are asked to read a passage or write a letter. The medical model may refer to a person without a disability as 'normal', a term which defaults to the description of someone with a disability to not be considered normal. Moreover, the medical model of disability ascribes disability as a person's defining characteristic, thus affecting the overall views that others have towards them. Essentially, the perception of disability under the medical model is generally negative; it is something that must be corrected.

Social Model of Disability

The social model of disability is another commonly used approach to describing disability. Inclusive education finds its roots in the social model of disability as initially described by Oliver (1983). The social model of disability defines disability as a social construct where disabling barriers are the issue rather than the traits of any one person. Since disability can be considered a social construct, society itself should be responsible for correcting disabling features. Societal obstacles are issues rather than individual deficits. Consider a person in a wheelchair trying to access a building with only stairs for ingress. If the person cannot enter the building, is it the person that is disabled, or is it the building itself that needs to be adapted for the individual? Isolation and exclusion, under the social model of disability, are imposed by society and its inability to remove environmental barriers or perceptual barricades that cause others to view persons with disabilities as unable to participate in society. Additionally, any solutions to improve the lives of individuals with disabilities should be the responsibility of society through political action and social change. In fact, disability might be considered a form of diversity that should be valued and celebrated for its potential for its unique perspectives (Watson et al., 2020).

There are points of critique for the social model of disability. Critics have suggested that there is a need for a more comprehensive and inclusive model (Palmer & Harley, 2012). The social model of disability has been criticized for not fully addressing the complexities of disability experiences across a wide range of social and cultural contexts (Naraian & Schlessinger, 2017). Some researchers and advocates argue that the social model of disability does not address both impairment and disability. In this case, the term impairment would align more with the medical model of disability where factors *internal* to individuals create the disabling condition. Whereas the current view of the social model considers individuals to be disabled by society rather than their own bodies. Some critics would prefer a model that acknowledges the disabling factors of both impairment and disability rather than separating them. Yet, the social model is essentially aligned with the goal of achieving social changes benefitting individuals with disabilities.

Capabilities Model

The capabilities approach was originally proposed by Amartya Sen (1992) to describe a model that focused on an individual's internal capabilities while allowing for external circumstances that arise as part of diverse human experiences (Lim, 2020). Sen described capabilities as freedoms that individuals have for achieving their personal potential. This type of freedom means that each person has the intrinsic capabilities to achieve their internal and external goals. A person's overall capabilities are related to, but are not limited by, external influences that might impede or support their quest for personal successes. Thus, the capabilities approach is seen as how a person's quality of life relates to what they are actually capable of becoming in their lives to achieve their personal well-being (Lim, 2020). Personal freedom of choice is an essential element in this model. Robeyns and Morten (2020) provide this description:

> The capability approach changes the focus from means (the resources people have and the public goods they can access) to ends (what they are able to do and be with those resources and goods). This shift in focus is justified because resources and goods alone do not ensure that people are able to convert them into actual doings and beings. Two persons with similar sets of goods and resources may nevertheless be able to achieve very different ends depending on their circumstances.
>
> *(p. 2)*

The capabilities approach relates to inclusive education since the educational environment should be responsive to a student's capabilities and characteristics by providing each student with opportunities necessary to achieve the educational outcomes that are most meaningful to themselves (Lim, 2020). Physical presence in a general education classroom is not adequate. Children and youth with disabilities in inclusive settings should be afforded opportunities for self-determined learning coupled with full participation in social interactions and the general education curriculum. The capabilities approach "shifts our focus on achievements from the mastery of skill sets to children's flourishing as equal human beings" (Lim, 2020, p. 580). The capabilities approach also emphasizes that personal well-being is influenced by the freedom to choose the kind of lives we desire (Sen, 1992). Thus, inclusive education must also provide each student with a variety of opportunities to be successful within the bounds of their own capabilities. See Table 2.1 for a comparison of the medical model, the social model, and the capabilities model.

While there is no one model that fully encapsulates the concept of inclusive education, having an understanding of the primary models can help educators best support children in inclusive settings. Overall, inclusive education, and current international policies, are more fully aligned with the concepts associated with the social model of disability and the capabilities model approach. In contrast to the medical model of disability, students in inclusive classrooms do not expect to have their disabilities cured or fixed. Rather, the environment of inclusive settings is adapted to better meet the needs of children and youth with disabilities. Accommodations or modifications are provided for individuals so that they can better access the general education curriculum through opportunities for self-determination.

Trends in Inclusion Practices

Internationally, two of the leading proponents for educational reform that has led to the current state of inclusive education internationally have been UNICEF and UNESCO. According to Waltham (2018) reporting for UNICEF, data and research indicate that there is still little data available regarding inclusive education worldwide. Lack of data limits the probability of systemic changes to the educational system of any country (*Education Sector Analysis Methodological Guidelines Volume III*, 2021). Additionally, current indicators still show that "without exception, children with disabilities are more likely to be excluded from school than their peers without disabilities – in some countries, up to four times more likely" (Waltham, 2018, p. 2). In fact, a survey of 15 countries found that disability is one of the most frequently contributing factors for whether students will actually attend school at all (Waltham, 2018). Yet, there has been a positive global shift in attitudes towards persons with disabilities in recent decades (*Education Sector Analysis Methodological Guidelines Volume III*, 2021). Rather than the historical view of persons with disabilities as simply recipients of welfare, international law now recognizes that they have specific rights, including the right to education.

Table 2.1 Comparison of major models

Focus	Medical Model	Social Model	Capabilities Model
Origins	1700s	1983	1992
Disability definition	Disability is health-related; a person is defective or impaired	Disabilities are a construct of society	Model is focused on capabilities rather than disabilities
Societal perception of disability	Disabilities are negative or abnormal	Individuals are limited by society	Individuals are able to achieve what is most meaningful to themselves
Who is responsible for improving the lives of individuals with disabilities?	Medical professionals or the individual	Society: Through political action or social change	Society: Through the allocation of appropriate resources to persons with disabilities
Goals of interventions	Cure or treat the disability	Change the environment and remove barriers so that the individual can access and participate in all activities	Provide access equal to that of persons without disabilities to attain personal freedoms
Persons applying interventions	Medical professionals	Society, advocates, policy makers, educators, and other stakeholders	Individuals and others who can influence opportunities for self-determination
Criticisms for the approach	Deficit model of disability	Does not fully address the complexities of disabilities	Some persons with disabilities will not reach a minimum threshold for a dignified life

Recently, UNESCO (2020c) indicated that there are three main justifications for countries moving towards inclusive schools. An educational justification is a placement requirement for schools to educate students with and without disabilities in the same setting; a social justification whereby students who are educated together will help to form the basis for a "just and non-discriminatory society"; and an economic justification whose focus is to reduce the costs of educating children by reducing the need for complex systems of various types of schools when children are educated inclusively. The UNESCO approach towards increasing and improving inclusive education has been primarily an emphasis on changes in culture, policy, and implementation. However, only about half of the children in the world currently receive early childhood education (UNICEF, 2019). Most of these children live in socioeconomically disadvantaged countries. Yet, in wealthier countries one in five students do not receive the education necessary to allow them to reach the basic minimum skills to function in society today (OECD, 2020). Clearly, there is still much work to be done to provide access for all children, including those with disabilities, to experience inclusive education.

In the U.S., inclusive education is guided by the LRE mandate in IDEA (2004). Essentially, all students must be provided access to the general education curriculum in general education settings unless the individual needs of students are better met in an alternative setting

(IDEA, 2004). There are two major requirements for educating students with disabilities with their nondisabled peers. The first IDEA (2004) mandate is that children with disabilities must receive specially designed instruction in regular education classrooms in order to make progress in the general education curriculum. Secondly, students with disabilities should only be removed from general education settings if, after receiving specially designed instruction and supplementary aids and services, they are not successful in such settings (Yell, 2019). In recent years, inclusion of students with disabilities in general education settings has increased. The U.S. Department of Education reports that the percentage of students with disabilities receiving their education in general education settings has increased from 57% to 64% between 2007 and 2018 (Hussar et al., 2020), a 7% improvement over 11 years. The trend for reducing time in alternative settings has been apparent for decades (Williamson et al., 2020). In fact, Williamson and colleagues (2020) found in their analysis of data from the U.S. Department of Education and the U.S. Census Bureau that inclusive education has been improving for students with high-incidence disabilities (i.e., specific learning disabilities, emotional disturbance, speech language impairments, autism). They also found that students in secondary schools were more likely to be placed in restrictive settings than their elementary school counterparts.

Yet, students with more severe disabilities continue to be substantially less likely to be included in inclusive settings (e.g., Jackson et al., 2018; Kauffman et al., 2018; Wehmeyer et al., 2021). Recall that IDEA (2004) requires that all students with disabilities be educated in general education settings unless students' needs cannot be met even with specially designed instruction and supplementary aids and services. Within IDEA, supplementary aids and services can mean instructional supports, behavioral supports, and supports for social, communication, and physical accessibility. Receiving education in settings apart from general education has several negative consequences. These include less access to the general education curriculum and activities with nondisabled peers. Students in more restrictive settings may also receive less access to standards-based instruction and IEP goal that are written with less rigor (Kurth et al., 2019). Reasons for alternative placement decisions by IEP teams have been examined and found to be frequently justified based on "perceived incapacities" for students to benefit from general education settings or standards-based instruction (Kurth et al., 2019). In other words, IEP teams feel that students with more severe disabilities will not derive benefit from learning with their nondisabled peers. Kurth et al. also found that, despite IDEA (2004) requirements to the contrary, IEP teams rationalized removing students from general education settings based on them having a disability and requiring specially designed instruction. Since the results of the *Endrew F. v. Douglas County School District RE-1* (2017) U.S. Supreme Court decision now requires more than the prior *de minimis* education for students with disabilities, the future of inclusive education for students with severe disabilities may soon improve (Kauffman et al., 2021).

Supporting Students in Inclusive Classrooms

In the U.S. and elsewhere, the education research and policy are designed to develop practices that can effectively educate our children so that they can achieve desired learning outcomes and later become successful adults and citizens (Jackson et al., 2008). A growing body of research is developed and implemented on supporting instructional practices for providing students with meaningful access to the general education curriculum, professional and family teaming and collaboration, peer involvement, guidelines for supporting adults and practices for selecting and adapting age- and grade-appropriate curriculum content. While by no means an exhaustive list, below we present some of the contemporary discussions and research on supporting children and youth in inclusive classrooms.

Evidence-based Practices

In the past two decades, evidence-based practices (EBP) have become part of the lexicon and mindset in the field of special education. EBPs have been operationally defined as "practices that are informed by research, in which the characteristics and consequences of environmental variables are empirically established and the relationship directly informs what a practitioner can do to produce a desired outcome" (Dunst et al., 2002, p. 3). EBPs are particularly important for children with or at risk for disabilities as they require the most effective, efficient and intensive instruction to accelerate learning (Fuchs & Fuchs, 2014).

Hornby et al. (2013) examined international literature from Australia, England, Hong Kong, New Zealand, and the U.S. to analyze similarities and differences in the ways international locations approach the definition of EBPs within education. Researchers contend that there are several factors that have led to underutilization and less dissemination of EBPs beyond cultural, language, political, and/or geographic borders. Among the factors influencing limited EBP utilization and dissemination are studies with small sample sizes, limited replications and scale up, fragmented disseminations, and limited professional development for educators on EBPs. Policy makers, practitioners, researchers, and families increasingly tend to agree that the sheer pursuit of knowledge in a knowledge-based inquiry, without addressing the political, personal, and social problems we encounter, is not enough to provide effective and meaningful services to children and youth with disabilities and their families. The value-driven, wisdom-based inquiry that leads to wisdom-based evidence is also needed.

The Council for Exceptional Children (CEC), the largest U.S.-based, international professional organization of educators dedicated to advancing the success of children with exceptionalities, recently commissioned a workgroup to identify and describe indicators of evidence-based practices and operationally define them. The CEC (2014) Standards for EBPs consist of two sections: (a) quality indicators to examine the methodological soundness of studies and (b) standards for classifying the evidence base of practices on the basis of sound studies. These standards establish criteria for five evidence-based classifications: evidence-based practices, potentially evidence-based practices, mixed effects, insufficient evidence, or negative effects. For more information on these indicators, please see *Council for Exceptional Children: Standards for Evidence-Based Practices in Special Education* (CEC, 2014).

High-leverage Practices

One of the more recent changes in the guidance for delivering special education instruction, services, and supports was developed by the CEC jointly with the Collaboration for Effective Educator Development, Accountability, and Reform Center (CEEDAR). Together, these organizations identified high-leverage practices (HLPs) in special education (McLeskey et al., 2017). The HLPs were developed to address the "evolving understanding of the complexity of why learners struggle" (*About the HLPs*, 2021). These guidelines can be used for students with disabilities across multiple settings, curricular areas, and ages. The HLPs are organized into broad categories that include (a) collaboration, (b) assessment, (c) social and emotional behavior, and (d) instruction (McLeskey et al., 2017). The high-leverage practices website has a bounty of excellent free resources that can be accessed at this website: https://highleverag epractices.org.

Universal Design for Learning

Learners come to schools and classrooms possessing a wide range of skills and abilities. To address the variety of learners and learning types, a research-based framework for supporting all students, including students with disabilities, was developed. Universal Design for Learning (UDL) is based on the premise of planned variability in students. UDL is a research-based framework that can guide educators in designing classrooms, developing curriculum, and delivering instruction (CAST, 2021). In fact, UDL is anchored in the fields of both education and neuroscience. The basis in neuroscience provides insights on how the brain works so that learning environments and instructional options can be optimized (CAST, 2021). The UDL instructional framework is student-centered and was designed to help reduce barriers to student learning by providing a variety of ways that information is presented and in the way students demonstrate their learning. The UDL approach is also flexible enough to provide opportunities, accommodations, and supports for students with disabilities. The UDL framework is based on three main principles that can be applied in inclusive settings. The principles guide educators to (a) provide multiple means of engagement, (b) provide multiple means of representation, and (c) provide multiple means of action and expression (CAST, 2021). In other words, the UDL principles correlate with how educators consider ways to promote student interest while sustaining student effort, provide a variety of ways that learning material is presented, and give students options for how they demonstrate their learning (Basham et al., 2020). One of the strongest features of UDL is that it promotes proactive planning for engagement, representation, and action and expression. Research has shown that UDL is an effective approach in inclusive settings since the UDL framework is also effective for students with disabilities (Basham et al., 2020).

Peer-mediated Instruction and Intervention

The practice of peer-mediated instruction and intervention (PMII) is a powerful, evidence-based approach for teaching in inclusive classrooms. Simply put, PMII are support strategies for struggling students and students with disabilities where their peers take the role of instructional assistants. PMII is flexible enough to be applied to tutoring, modeling, and encouraging with either academic or social/interpersonal foci. During the application of PMII in classrooms, the teacher becomes a facilitator rather than the primary source of instruction. PMII begins with the recruitment and training of peers without disabilities to support the learning of their struggling peers through prompting, social interactions, and response-based opportunities (Mahoney, 2019). Student tutors provide feedback and support for their peer counterparts after they have been trained to model behaviors and provide specific feedback (Mahoney, 2019). The use of PMII has been extended to frequently include students identified with autism spectrum disorder (ASD) for social skills (Krier & Lambros, 2021) and behavioral instruction (Zagona & Mastergeorge, 2018). The use of PMII has been shown to be effective for specific content area instruction such as literacy (Simpson & Bui, 2017), mathematics (Schaefer Whitby, 2013), etc. The practices of PMII have been used effectively globally for both social skills and academic advancement (dos Santos et al., 2018).

Conclusion

Multiple historical and theoretical perspectives and models, policies, and procedural context exist that frame the current conversation surrounding inclusive education for school-aged students. Similarly, an increasing number of countries have also adopted and promoted an array of inclusive early childhood policies and developed and expanded many early childhood development programs in response to a growing awareness of the importance of providing all children with supportive and nurturing care across home and learning environments (Vargas-Baaron et al., 2019).

Despite ample evidence that inclusive education is cost effective and increases social and academic and future employment opportunities and life outcomes for children both with and without disabilities (Schuelka, 2018) barriers – such as inadequate funding, lack of intentional national policies and implementation plans with options for due process, limited professional development for teachers, flexible curricula, cultural attitudes – to inclusive education remain. Additionally, responsibility for implementation of inclusive services to fidelity rests at the local level. Often less economically developed countries target their programs towards meeting basic needs associated with poverty and lack of economic development, broader education initiatives, and the civil and human rights of larger segments of the populations related to gender or cultural practices. Thus, although these countries may adopt policies that appear to advance inclusive practices for students with disabilities, the enactment of these policies is often not their priority in practice (Banerjee, 2014).

According to the Committee on the Rights of Persons with Disabilities (United Nations, 2016), inclusive education involves a fundamental right to education, a principle that values students' well-being, dignity, autonomy, and contribution to society, a continuing process to eliminate barriers to education and promote reform in the culture, policy, and practice in schools to include all students. Schuelka (2018), in their report, discusses successful implementation strategies at the school and classroom level (e.g., school structure and culture, teachers, and school leadership) and at the policy and national level (e.g., appropriate legislation and collaboration with stakeholders, strengthening Education Management Information Systems, encouraging curricular flexibility and strengthening learning outcomes, promoting inclusive societies and economies). Thus, all stakeholders – policy makers, researchers, teacher education programs, educators, family members, and community partners – will need to collaborate and take responsibility to develop streamlined initiatives for inclusion to achieve the intended outcomes for children and youth with disabilities in inclusive communities.

References

About the HLPs. (2021). High-Leverage Practices for Students with Disabilities. https://highleveragepractices.org/about-hlps

Ainscow, M. (2020). Promoting inclusion and equity in education: Lessons from international experiences. *Nordic Journal of Studies in Educational Policy, 6*(1), 7–16. https://doi.org/10.1080/20020317.2020.1729587

Anti-Defamation League. (2018). *A brief history of the disability rights movement.* www.adl.org/education/resources/backgrounders/disability-rights-movement

Banerjee, R. (2014). Towards inclusive education in India: Implementation of the Convention on the Rights of Persons with Disabilities. *TASH Connections, 40*(3), 9–13.

Bannink, F., Nalugya, R., & van Hove, G. (2020). 'They give him a chance'- Parents' perspectives on disability and inclusive primary education in Uganda. *International Journal of Disability, Development and Education, 67*(4), 357–375. https://doi.org/10.1080/1034912X.2019.1593326

Basham, J. D., Blackorby, J., & Marino, M. T. (2020a). Opportunity in crisis: The role of universal design for learning in educational redesign. *Learning Disabilities: A Contemporary Journal, 18*(1), 71–91.

Basham, J. D., Gardner, J. E., & Smith, S. J. (2020b). Measuring the implementation of UDL in classrooms and schools: Initial field test results. *Remedial and Special Education, 41*(4), 231–243. https://doi.org/10.1177/0741932520908015

Board of Education of the Hendrick Hudson School District v. Rowley, 458 U.S. 176. (1982). Cook, B. G., & Odom, S. L. (2013). Evidence-based practices and implementation science in special education. *Exceptional Children, 79*(2), 135–144.

Bulat, J., Hayes, A. M., Macon, W., Tichá, R., & Abery, B. H. (2017). *School and classroom disabilities inclusion guide for low-and middle-income countries* (OP-0031-1701). RTI Press. https://doi.org/10.3768/rtipress.2017.op.0031.1701

CAST. (2021). *Universal design for learning guidelines*. CAST. https://udlguidelines.cast.org/?utm_source=castsite&lutm_medium=web&utm_campaign=none&utm_content=aboutudl

Cieza, A., Kamenov, K., Sanchez, M. G., Chatterji, S., Balasegaram, M., Lincetto, O., Servili, C., Bermejo, R., & Ross, D. A. (2021). Disability in children and adolescents must be integrated into the global health agenda. *BMJ*, n9. https://doi.org/10.1136/bmj.n9

Council for Exceptional Children: Standards for Evidence-Based Practices in Special Education. (2014). *Teaching Exceptional Children*, 46(6), 206–212. https://doi.org/10.1177/0040059914531389

dos Santos, R., de Bittencourt, D., Carmogo, S., & Schmidt, C. (2018). Peer-mediated intervention: Concept and implications for research and pedagogical practice of teachers of students with autism. *Arquivos Analíticos de Políticas Educativas*, 26(23), 1–23. https://doi.org/10.14507/epaa.26.3367

Dunn, L. M. (1968). Special education for the mildly retarded: Is much of it justifiable? *Exceptional Children*, 35(1), 5–22. https://doi.org/10.1177/001440296803500101

Dunst, C. J., Trivette, C. M., & Cutspec, P. A. (2002). Toward an operational definition of evidence-based practice. *Centerscope*, 1, 1–10.

Education sector analysis methodological guidelines volume III (No. 978-92-806-5214-7; Education Sector Analysis Guidelines). (2021). UNESCO International Institute for Educational Planning, UNICEF, Global Partnership for Education, Foreign & Commonwealth Development Office. https://www.unicef.org/reports/education-sector-analysis

Endrew F. v. Douglas County School District RE-1, (U.S. Supreme Court 2017).

Fuchs, D., & Fuchs, L. S. (1994). Inclusive schools movement and the radicalization of special education reform. *Exceptional Children*, 60(4), 294–309. https://doi.org/10.1177/001440299406000402

Fuchs, D., & Fuchs, L. S. (2014). Rethinking service delivery for students with significant learning problems: Developing and implementing intensive instruction. *Remedial and Special Education*, 36, 05–111. https://doi.org/doi:10.1177/0741932514558337

Hernández-Torrano, D., Somerton, M., & Helmer, J. (2020). Mapping research on inclusive education since Salamanca Statement: A bibliometric review of the literature over 25 years. *International Journal of Inclusive Education*, 1–20. https://doi.org/10.1080/13603116.2020.1747555

Hornby, G. (2015). Inclusive special education: Development of a new theory for the education of children with special educational needs and disabilities. *British Journal of Special Education*, 42(3), 234–256. https://doi.org/10.1111/1467-8578.12101

Hornby, G., Gable, R. A., & Evans, W. (2013). Implementing evidence-based practice in education: What international literature reviews tell us and what they don't. *Preventing School Failure: Alternative Education for Children and Youth*, 57(3), 119–123. https://doi.org/10.1080/1045988X.2013.794326

Hussar, B., Zhang, J., Hein, S., Wang, K., Roberts, A., Cui, J., Bullock Mann, F., Barmer, A., & Dilig, R. (2020). *The condition of education 2020 (No. 2020-144)*. Institute of Education Sciences, U.S. Department of Education. https://nces.ed.gov/programs/coe/indicator_cgg.asp

IDEA, U.S.C. § 1400 (2004).

Jackson, L. B., Fitzpatrick, H., Alazemi, B., & Rude, H. (2018). Shifting gears: Re-framing the international discussion about inclusive education. *Journal of International Special Needs Education*, 21(2), 11–22. https://doi.org/10.9782/2159-4341-21.2.01

Jackson, L. B., Ryndak, D. L., & Wehmeyer, M. L. (2008). The dynamic relationship between context, curriculum, and student learning: A case for inclusive education as a research-based practice. *Research and Practice for Persons with Severe Disabilities*, 33(4)/34(1), 175–195. doi:10.2511/rpsd.33.4.175

Katsiyannis, A., Yell, M. L., & Bradley, R. (2001). Reflections on the 25th anniversary of the individuals with disabilities education act. *Remedial and Special Education*, 22(6), 324–334. https://doi.org/10.1177/074193250102200602

Kauffman, J. M., Felder, M., Ahrbeck, B., Badar, J., & Schneiders, K. (2018). Inclusion of all students in general education? International appeal for a more temperate approach to inclusion. *Journal of International Special Needs Education*, 21(2), 1–10. https://doi.org/10.9782/17-00009

Kauffman, J. M., Wiley, A. L., Travers, J. C., Badar, J., & Anastasiou, D. (2021). Endrew and FAPE: Concepts and implications for all students with disabilities. *Behavior Modification*, 45(1), 177–198. https://doi.org/10.1177/0145445519832990

Krier, J., & Lambros, K. M. (2021). Increasing joint attention and social play through peer-mediated intervention: A single case design. *Psychology in the Schools*, 58(3), 494–514. https://doi.org/10.1002/pits.22460

Kurth, J. A., Ruppar, A. L., Toews, S. G., McCabe, K. M., McQueston, J. A., & Johnston, R. (2019). Considerations in placement decisions for students with extensive support needs: An analysis of lre statements. *Research and Practice for Persons with Severe Disabilities, 44*(1), 3–19. https://doi.org/10.1177/1540796918825479

Lim, S. (2020). The capabilities approach to inclusive education: Re-envisioning the individuals with disabilities education act's least restrictive environment. *Disability & Society, 35*(4), 570–588. https://doi.org/10.1080/09687599.2019.1649119

Mahoney, M. W. M. (2019). Peer-mediated instruction and activity schedules: Tools for providing academic support for students with ASD. *TEACHING Exceptional Children, 51*(5), 350–360. https://doi.org/10.1177/0040059919835816

McLeskey, J., Barringer, M., Billingsley, B., Brownell, M., Jackson, D., Kennedy, M., Lewis, T., Maheady, L., Rodriguez, J., Scheeler, M., Winn, J., & Ziegler, D. (2017). *High-leverage practices in special education.* Arlington, VA: Council for Exceptional Children & CEEDAR Center.

Mundy, K. (2016). "Leaning in" on Education for All. *Comparative Education Review, 60*(1), 1–26. https://doi.org/10.1086/684434

Naraian, S., & Schlessinger, S. (2017). When theory meets the "reality of reality": Reviewing the sufficiency of the social model of disability as a foundation for teacher preparation for inclusive education. *Teacher Education Quarterly, 44*(1), 81–100.

Nguyen, X. T. (2013, May). Rethinking the politics of inclusion/exclusion within the rights-based agenda of disability and education: The implications of the United Nations' Disability Convention for inclusive education. In Proceedings from paper presented at American Education Research Association (AERA), San Francisco.

Nilholm, C., & Göransson, K. (2017). What is meant by inclusion? An analysis of European and North American journal articles with high impact. *European Journal of Special Needs Education, 32*(3), 437–451. https://doi.org/10.1080/08856257.2017.1295638

OECD. (2020). *Education at a Glance 2020: OECD Indicators.* Paris: OECD. https://doi.org/10.1787/69096873-en

Oliver, M. (1983). *Social work with disabled people.* London: Macmillan.

Olusanya, B. O., Wright, S. M., Nair, M. K. C., Boo, N.-Y., Halpern, R., Kuper, H., Abubakar, A. A., Almasri, N. A., Arabloo, J., Arora, N. K., Backhaus, S., Berman, B. D., Breinbauer, C., Carr, G., de Vries, P. J., del Castillo-Hegyi, C., Eftekhari, A., Gladstone, M. J., Hoekstra, R. A., … & on behalf of the Global Research on Developmental Disabilities Collaborators (GRDDC). (2020). Global burden of childhood epilepsy, intellectual disability, and sensory impairments. *Pediatrics, 146*(1), e20192623. https://doi.org/10.1542/peds.2019-2623

Palmer, M., & Harley, D. (2012). Models and measurement in disability: An international review. *Health Policy and Planning, 27*(5), 357–364. https://doi.org/10.1093/heapol/czr047

Qu, X. (2020). A critical realist model of inclusive education for children with special educational needs and/or disabilities. *International Journal of Inclusive Education*, 1–15. https://doi.org/10.1080/13603116.2020.1760366

Rajab, A., & Wright, N. (2020). The idea of autonomy and its interplay with culture in child-centered education: Evidence from practitioners in preschools in Saudi Arabia. *Early Years, 40*(2), 174–187. https://doi.org/10.1080/09575146.2018.1434134

Rix, J. (2020). Our need for certainty in an uncertain world: The difference between special education and inclusion? *British Journal of Special Education, 47*(3), 283–307. https://doi.org/10.1111/1467-8578.12326

Rix, J., Sheehy, K., Fletcher-Campbell, F., Crisp, M., & Harper, A. (2013). Exploring provision for children identified with special educational needs: An international review of policy and practice. *European Journal of Special Needs Education, 28*(4), 375–391. https://doi.org/10.1080/08856257.2013.812403

Robeyns, I., & Morten, B. (2020). The capability approach. In E. Zalta (Ed.), *The Stanford Encyclopedia of Philosophy* (Winter). Stanford University. https://plato.stanford.edu/archives/win2020/entries/capability-approach

Schaefer Whitby, P. J. (2013). The effects of Solve it! On the mathematical word problem solving ability of adolescents with autism spectrum disorders. *Focus on Autism and Other Developmental Disabilities, 28*(2), 78–88. https://doi.org/10.1177/1088357612468764

Schuelka, M. J. (2018). *Implementing inclusive education. K4D helpdesk report.* Brighton, UK: Institute of Development Studies.

Sen, A. (1992). *Inequality reexamined.* Cambridge, MA: Harvard University Press.

Shakespeare, T. (2006). The social model of disability. In L. J. Davis (Ed.), *The disability studies reader* (2nd ed.). London: Routledge.

Simpson, L. A., & Bui, Y. (2017). Reading buddies: A strategy to increase peer interaction in students with autism. *Intervention in School and Clinic, 53*(1), 44–49. https://doi.org/10.1177/1053451217692570

UNESCO. (2000). *Education for all: Meeting our collective commitments*. https://healtheducationresources.unesco.org/sites/default/files/resources/Framework%20for%20Action_Dakar.pdf

UNESCO. (2009). *Policy guidelines on inclusion in education*. http://unesdoc.unesco.org/images/0017/001778/177849e.pdf

UNESCO. (2020a). *Basic texts: 2020 edition (revised edition)*. United Nations Educational, Scientific and Cultural Organization. https://unesdoc.unesco.org/ark:/48223/pf0000372956/PDF/372956eng.pdf.multi.page=6

UNESCO. (2020b). *The sustainable development goals report 2020*. https://unstats.un.org/sdgs/report/2020/#

UNESCO. (2020c). *Towards inclusion in education: Status, trends and challenges: The UNESCO Salamanca Statement 25 years on* (p. 43). United Nations. https://unesdoc.unesco.org/ark:/48223/pf0000374246

UNESCO Institute for Statistics. (2019). *New methodology shows that 258 million children, adolescents and youth are out of school* (Fact Sheet No. 56). UNESCO UIS. http://uis.unesco.org/sites/default/files/documents/new-methodology-shows-258- million-children-adolescents-and-youth-are-out-school.pdf

UNICEF. (2017). *Inclusive education: Understanding Article 24 of the Convention on the Rights of Persons with Disabilities*. https://www.google.com/url?sa=t&rct=j&q=&esrc=s&source=web&cd=&cad=rja&uact=8&ved=2ahUKEwjj0bLlkNvwAhUEs54KHXi4Ca0QFjAOegQIAhAD&url=https%3A%2F%2Fwww.unicef.org%2Feca%2Fsites%2Funicef.org.eca%2Ffiles%2FIE_summary_accessible_220917_0.pdf&usg=AOvVaw3aiHrWeh3mHs-ImgdnSzWL

UNICEF. (2019). *A world ready to learn: Prioritizing quality early childhood education*. https://www.unicef.org/reports/a-world-ready-to-learn-2019

United Nations. (1989). *United Nations Convention on the Rights of the Child*. Adopted by the UN General Assembly. New York: United Nations. https://www.unicef.org/crc/

United Nations. (2016). *United Nations Convention on the Rights of Persons with Disabilities, Committee on the Rights of Persons with Disabilities*. CRPD/C/GC/4. Geneva, Switzerland: https://www.ohchr.org/en/press-releases/2016/09/inclusive-education-vital-all-including-persons-disabilities-un-experts

United Nations. (2006). *United Nations Convention on the Rights of Persons with Disabilities*. Adopted by the United Nations General Assembly. New York: United Nations. https://www.un.org/development/desa/disabilities/convention-on-the-rights-of-persons-with-disabilities.html

Vargas-Barón, E., Small, J., Wertlieb, D., Hix-Small, H., Gómez Botero, R., Diehl, K., Vergara, P., & Lynch, P. (2019). *Global survey of inclusive early childhood development and early childhood intervention programs*. Washington, DC: RISE Institute.

Waltham, M. (2018, July 23). Inclusive education for children with disabilities. *UNICEF Connect*. https://blogs.unicef.org/blog/inclusive-education-children-with-disabilities/

Watson, J., Anderson, K., Frawley, P., & Balandin, S. (2020). Human rights for people with a disability. In F. H. McKay & A. Taket (Eds.), *Health Equity, Social Justice, and Human Rights* (2nd ed.). London: Routledge. https://doi.org/10.4324/9780429299841

Wehmeyer, M. L., Shogren, K. A., & Kurth, J. (2021). The state of inclusion with students with intellectual and developmental disabilities in the United States. *Journal of Policy and Practice in Intellectual Disabilities, 18*(1), 36–43. https://doi.org/10.1111/jppi.12332

Williamson, P., Hoppey, D., McLeskey, J., Bergmann, E., & Moore, H. (2020). Trends in LRE placement rates over the past 25 years. *The Journal of Special Education, 53*(4), 236–244. https://doi.org/10.1177/0022466919855052

World Health Organization, & World Bank. (2011). *World report on disability*. Geneva, Switzerland: World Health Organization. https://www.who.int/disabilities/world_report/2011/report.pdf

Yell, M. L. (2019). *The law and special education* (5th ed.). London: Pearson.

Zagona, A. L., & Mastergeorge, A. M. (2018). An empirical review of peer-mediated interventions: Implications for young children with autism spectrum disorders. *Focus on Autism and Other Developmental Disabilities, 33*(3), 131–141. https://doi.org/10.1177/1088357616671295

Zigmond, N., Kloo, A., & Volonino, V. (2009). What, where, and how? Special education in the climate of full inclusion. *Exceptionality, 17*(4), 189–204. https://doi.org/10.1080/09362830903231986

3
UNIVERSAL DESIGN AND INCLUSIVE PARTICIPATION

*Gala Korniyenko**

Introduction

The philosophical foundations of universality are reflected in the principles of universal design, which were developed by architects, designers, and engineers at North Carolina State University[1] in the late 1980s. According to Ron Mace,[2] an architect from North Carolina, universal design refers to "the design of products and environments to be usable by all people, to the greatest extent possible, without the need for adaptation or specialized design".[3] This is where universality and specificity converge.

As Rob Imrie, a geographer who studies disability and cities, highlights in his article, the challenges with universal design are at the core of the philosophical concept of universalism and the specificity or particularity of human bodies: "UD [universal design] cannot be universal unless it is embedded into the specificities of corporeality, and the differences that different bodies make in their everyday interactions with designed artefacts" (Imrie, 2012, p. 880). It is up to community practitioners, policymakers, educators, and benefactors of UD to define the scope of its principles and solutions for possible conflicting needs due to the specificity of different human experiences. The universal design's main principle is to create products and places that are accessible for all people, regardless of their age, ability, gender, or socioeconomic status. Initially, the majority of universal design solutions were directed toward the accommodation of the needs of those with physical disabilities. Ronald Mace, who contracted polio at the age of nine, had to use a wheelchair at a time when principles of accessibility, curb cuts, and ramps were not considered by designers. The social justice aspect of UD is reflected in the Convention on the Rights of Persons with Disabilities (CRPD), which was adopted by the United Nations in 2006.[4] Universal design principles were adapted by educators, websites, and software developers; they now include the sphere of public engagement and participation in the design process (Biglieri, 2021).

Universal Design Typology

Universal design implies that the design process goes beyond minimum accommodation or access standards (Nasar & Evans-Cowley, 2007). In contrast to UD, which relies on the goodwill of people who implement it or take it as guiding principles, policies, and laws require enforce-

---

* gallynart@gmail.com

Table 3.1 Comparison of universal design and policies addressing barriers

Design Recommendations	Legal Acts
Universal Design for Physical Spaces	The Architectural Barriers Act of 1968, Section 504 of the Rehabilitation Act of 1973, the Americans with Disabilities Act of 1990, and the Americans with Disabilities Act Amendments of 2008, Air Carrier Access Act of 1986 and 2009, Fair Housing Act amendment of 1988
Universal Design for Learning (UDL)	Individuals with Disabilities Education Act (IDEA) of 2004, The Higher Education Opportunity Act of 2008 (HEOA), The Assistive Technology Act of 2004
Universal Design for Web Development and Technology	Section 504 and 508 of the Rehabilitation Act of 1973

ment and responsible agents to implement them. Major laws and policies that address issues of access for people with disabilities in different spheres of human life in the US include the Architectural Barriers Act of 1968, Rehabilitation Act of 1973, Individuals with Disabilities Education Act (IDEA) of 1975, Air Carrier Access Act of 1986 and 2009, Fair Housing Act amendment of 1988, Section 508 of the Rehabilitation Act, and the key legislation: Americans with Disabilities Act (ADA) of the 1990s (Table 3.1).[5]

It is common knowledge that the ADA as a piece of legislation was designed by lawyers and policymakers who did not care much about aesthetics. In contrast, designers who were inspired to create UD principles cared about aesthetics and had an aspiration to create an environment that could be both accessible from a design perspective and aesthetically pleasing.

In contrast to physical disabilities accommodation, which emphasizes accessible physical and built environments, Universal Design principles accommodating cognitive or sensory needs are often limited to the learning environment, mainly focusing on redesigning instructions, tests, and exams, using assistive technology, closed captioning, image narration, and braille for the blind, and allowing extra time to complete assignments (Table 3.2). UD is interpreted as providing multiple ways of conveying information to students, flexible ways students can demonstrate their knowledge, understanding, and engagement (Capp, 2017). Less attention is paid to sensory accommodation in university or school classrooms and adjustment of the physical environment to sensory needs. Research on the topic of inclusive instructional and curriculum design and pedagogy is mainly focused on educators' perspectives and expert opinions on Universal Design in Learning (UDL) (Baglieri, S, 2020).

Certain barriers, such as attitudinal or cultural, are not captured by UD, but they play an important role in addressing inaccessibility through policy changes. The World Health Organization includes such barriers as negative attitudes towards people with disabilities, stereotyping, stigma, and prejudice, which lead to discrimination.[6] In college environment awareness and acceptance campaigns, diversity and inclusion training sessions are key tools to address negative stereotypes and attitudes towards disabled students. Visibility of disabled students on campus, in the classroom, in student organizations, at the decision-making table, and in the students' government helps create an inclusive environment and provides the opportunity to define what Universal Design is.

Barriers to participation in decision-making and the design process limit the opportunities to influence changes in policies, programs, and services. UD principles cannot and should not stop at the services and programs provided for disabled people. Such a limited understanding of UD identifies disabled individuals as passive receivers of services. UD principles applied to participation should extend to creating procedures where disabled students, employees, faculty, and community members are free to participate in the decision-making process, civic life, and decisions about learning and engagement. UD is two-fold: focusing on specific needs for accommodation and universality of access to policies, services, and active participation regardless of disability.

> Unlike rehabilitation experts who sought accessibility as a tool for normalization, and unlike mainstream architects and designers who understood accessibility as antithetical to creative and aesthetic choices, disability activists claimed their expertise as users of built environments to justify their authority to redefine "good design". (Hamraie, 2016, p. 8)

In addition, experiences are not limited to struggles with inaccessible learning materials, tests, and classrooms but also with policies that do not address accessibility and inclusivity for a variety of disabled lives.

Although UD principles do not differentiate cognitive/sensory needs and physical needs in their principles, those are not the same and are very specific for different disabled users or participants. Different and sometimes conflicting needs require different strategies to tackle them, which is not possible if we do not differentiate what "all people" mean specifically.

Universal Design on Campus and in the Classroom: Physical Space

The UD principle of equitable use in the university or college context means that every student, faculty, or staff member, regardless of their ability, should have access to offices, classrooms, recreation, public green spaces, facilities, dining, restrooms, library, and learning materials, including accessible transportation to get to the place of study, exercise, play, or work.

Accessibility in this case is not limited to accessible and well-maintained sidewalks and crossings but also includes the absence of obstacles on the pathway and easy wayfinding. For example, sudden changes in the environment due to construction might create unexpected barriers for someone who is blind; and readjustment of the route might require extra time to figure out how to reach the destination, especially if someone is new to the environment, has not planned for that obstacle, or was not informed ahead of time. Suddenly, what was simple and intuitive in use became complicated and confusing.

The UD principle of perceptible information is not accomplished if a user is not able to see the sign or understand the wayfinding system, which is not accessible to their particular sensory needs. With sudden changes due to construction, a common occurrence on campus, the user can get easily disoriented and feel distressed. In this case, tactile clues will not be very helpful. Accessibility works when it is done with intention, when users' opinions are considered not only prior to the creation of an accessible place or artifact but during the process of designing it and while using it. UD principles are not a static thing; it's a set of guidelines for an iterative process of adjustment.

US campuses have compliance officers and teams of specialists and experts in the application of Title II of the ADA, which covers publicly funded universities, community colleges, and vocational schools, and Title III, which covers privately funded schools.[7] The work of compliance officers is limited to classroom or campus settings. It is important to think about university/college campuses and education accessibility in terms of a holistic education environment and how it is connected to the rest of the city or community where students live. With the global

Table 3.2 Universal design principles addressing physical and cognitive/sensory needs

Principle	Physical Needs	Cognitive/Sensory Needs
1. Equitable use	Applicable to a diverse range of physical abilities; avoiding segregation and stigmatization	Easy to understand regardless of the user's experience, knowledge, language skills, or concentration level
2. Flexibility in use	Range of physical abilities, right- or left-handed access and use; adaptable to user's pace	Choice of methods or individual preferences; facilitate user's accuracy and precision
3. Simple and intuitive	Free of complexity	Easy to understand regardless of user's experience, knowledge, language skills, or concentration level; effective prompting and feedback during and after task completion
4. Perceptible information	-----//-----	Communicate information regardless of sensory abilities; application of different modes: verbal, pictorial, tactile, audio; the contrast between essential information and surroundings; easy instructions, directions; compatible with a variety of techniques and devices for sensory needs
5. Tolerance for error	Minimizes hazards and accidental or unintended actions; has fail-safe features	Creates the feeling of safety; provides warnings of hazard and error; discourages unconscious action in the task
6. Low physical effort	Minimum physical effort; reasonable operating force; minimize repetitive action	Creates minimum fatigue
7. Size and space for approach and use	Appropriate size and space regardless of body size, posture, mobility, assistive devices	Adequate space to feel free and accommodate sensory needs

Source. Adopted from The Center for Universal Design (1997). *The Principles of Universal Design, Version 2.0.* Raleigh, NC: North Carolina State University.

pandemic, when bedrooms and personal spaces at home became classrooms, it became more obvious that boundaries blurred. Similarly, if a student lives off-campus, the educational environment is wider than just a campus setting. With a change of understanding about a broader educational environment, compliance officers would require more coordination efforts and time for the provision of accessibility.

The design of the environment that requires minimum fatigue (Principle of Low Physical Effort) can be illustrated through the efforts disabled students have to deal with compared to non-disabled peers. For example, students with disabilities who want to live off-campus have to start their search for housing much earlier than students without disabilities, as not all properties are accessible. Landlords of older buildings are not required to provide accommodation, and in this case, the burden to modify housing falls on the student with disabilities who should pay for those changes themselves.[8]

In 2020, due to the pandemic, all classes transitioned to an online format entirely, which resulted in some students losing their access to note-taking assistance and creating additional anxiety.[9] Students in this situation had to figure out how to deal with the lack of accessibility post-factum, as universities were not prepared for such a fast transition in their services; this created extra burdens for students with disabilities.

In addition, students lost access to accessible classrooms, stable and reliable internet connection, and peer support in-between classes, which are much harder to establish during the structured and very formal nature of online classroom interaction.

When students are on campus, they have the opportunity to participate in accessibility audits of campus buildings, advocate for disability accommodations, and participate in the university planning and design decision-making process that addresses their needs for an accessible and inclusive environment for learning and engagement (Lissner, 2007).

Another UD principle "size and space for approach and use" mentions accommodation of sensory needs, which creates the feeling of freedom. One of the solutions to address such needs can be the creation of quiet spaces. For instance, research done in educational settings confirms the positive effect of escape spaces for autistic users, as it provides a neutral sensory environment with minimal stimulations (Mostafa, 2014).

The creation of such space does not require a lot of investment or modification of existing building structures. It can be as simple as a designated room or a quiet corner where the light can be adjusted with the curtains, soft seating, and the absence of any electronic devices or computer screens. (Please refer to Figure 3.1, 3.2, 3.3, 3.4, and 3.5 for examples of UD).

Figure 3.1 Campus wayfinding *Note.* The photo on the left shows students walking on the sidewalk, one of the students has a white cane and is holding the other student by the hand. There is a sign on the ground that says, "Share the road". The photo on the right shows the sign that the sidewalk is closed, and a metal fence is in front of it. Photo by the author

Figure 3.2 Knowlton School's accessible ramp from the ground floor to the lecture hall (left) and Ed Roberts Campus building in Berkeley, California (right) *Note.* The photo on the left shows the ramp. The ramp from the first floor to the lecture hall is at a shallower pitch than the rest of the ramp. The photo on the right shows the ramp and people sitting at the table talking. Photos by the author

Universal Design in Learning: Instructions

UDL is implemented through the provision of universal access to education through specific instructional strategies, materials, and systems, which consider a wide variety of learners (Preiser et al., 2020). Some of the recommendations provided for teachers are directed towards the school environment rather than the university.

Very often, professors are unaware of students' individual needs for accommodation in university settings due to the number of students present at the lecture. Big classrooms with up to 150 students present at the lecture create a distance between the professor and the individual student. Practical classes or rehearsals are conducted by the teaching associates, who are graduate students themselves and are not well trained to be UDL specialists. Thus, accommodation in the learning settings very often ends up being the responsibility of the office of disability services, a centralized agency that exclusively focuses on issues of student access to services on campus.[10] These might include exam accommodation, note-taking assistance, modifications in the attendance of classes, use of assistive technology, accessible media, sign language interpreting and transcribing, assistive listening devices, and a reduced course load. Accommodation for graduate or professional students is mostly focused on time extension (exams, dissertation/thesis defense, and so on). It is up to the instructor to provide supplemental notes, outlines, or comprehensive PowerPoint slides. In such cases, the student has to rely on the instructor's goodwill.

It is important to mention that some students prefer not to disclose their disability to the instructor for different reasons. Some of those reasons are being reluctant, not feeling comfortable or not establishing the level of trust to allow talking about it with the teacher, or even having internal ableism. Some teachers are strict and do not want to provide supplemental notes for some students and not for others, being afraid to be judged for favoritism or giving someone special treatment. Still, some professors do not take mental or cognitive disabilities seriously and blame students for being lazy or lying to get time extensions for submitting assignments.

During the 2020 global pandemic, a lot of universities decided to become more flexible in terms of grading policies. Thus, on a world scale, we have witnessed the application of the UD

Figure 3.3 Flyer about a quiet room created inside Knowlton School to accommodate sensory and religious needs of students *Note.* A colorful flyer on the wall informs about a quiet room created inside Knowlton School to accommodate the sensory and religious needs of students. Photo by the author

principle of flexibility in use, when universities changed their policies to accommodate a wide range of individual preferences and abilities (Edyburn, 2021). Such policies were eagerly supported by student governments. The reasoning behind it was the focus on the well-being of students and recognition of the effect of the global pandemic on academic performance. "By offering flexibility with our grading system, we are prioritizing students' well-being and recognizing that the pandemic has created new burdens for students who are juggling home, work, and educational responsibilities."[11]

The UD principle of "tolerance for error", a design that minimizes consequences of accidental or unintended actions, can be illustrated in Figure 3.4, where the instructions on the tablet screen have the option "mistake", represented by the eraser image. Opportunities for feedback prior to grading could also be an example of tolerance for error (Lissner, 2007).

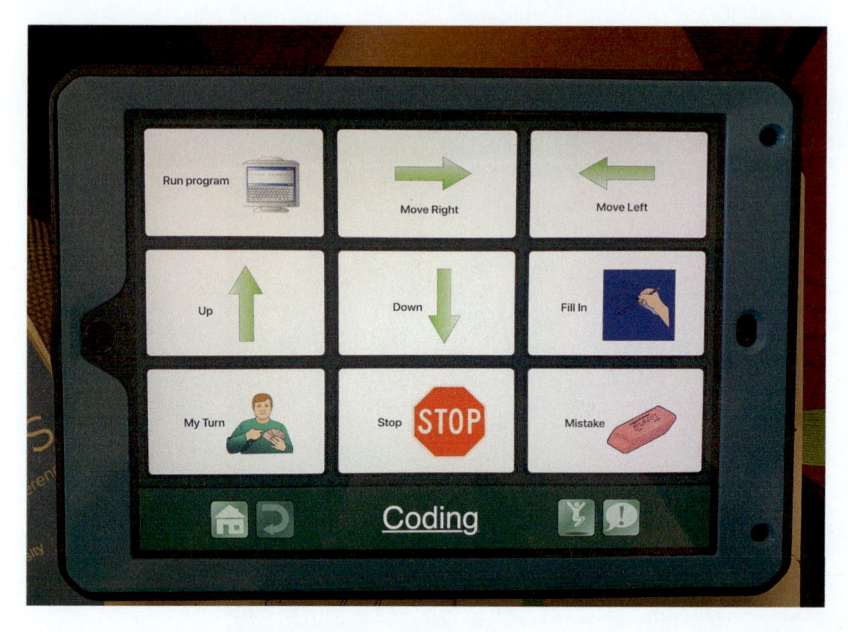

Figure 3.4 Accessible app for coding on the tablet from Assistive Technology and Accessible Educational Materials Center *Note*. The tablet screen with instructions and images: run the program, move right, move left, up, down, fill in, my turn, stop, mistake. Photo by the author.
[a]https://ataem.org

Figure 3.5 Participation in the Design Process on Campus *Note*. Participants of the Autism Design Studio and autistic adults are participating in the design process, testing design features on campus. Photo by the author

Online Accessibility: Web and Zoom

The global pandemic has radically changed the course of learning, work, and participation: society has turned to online technologies to continue conducting meetings, classroom engagement, and social interaction. The digital divide (a gap between access to technology, digital infrastructure, and knowledge about applications and technology) has affected the level of engagement.

Students with different abilities (e.g., visual, sensory, hearing, neurodivergent, ADHD) and needs communicate in different ways, and their access to technology varies as well. Educators apply different sets of tools for learning and engagement depending on the end goal, and, while the number of disabled students is increasing, instruction and support are not as easily transferable to a complete zoom learning environment with the same level of accommodation available prior to the pandemic.[12] Meeting ADA accommodations shouldn't be an afterthought that causes distress.

While Zoom promises to improve accessibility and add automatic closed captioning to free accounts, called "live transcription", students with disabilities still have to require turning on closed captioning, as the facilitators do not always consider or think about accommodation.[13] Educators exposed to different tools and approaches based on common needs that are universal technology engagement practices hopefully learned about the benefits of online accommodation, and as we turn toward in-person meetings, will continue to address inclusivity in a more systematic way.

Online learning, which entirely replaced face-to-face interaction with classmates and teachers during the pandemic, is lagging behind due to the absence of a stable social environment in some cases. Not all students are fully able to engage from home for synchronous learning: some lack a reliable internet connection, dedicated learning space, or adequate technology. Disabled students are particularly affected. Although race, class, and gender are commonly considered in the research on the accessibility of college courses, disability is not (Edyburn, 2015; Gillis & Krull, 2020). In some cases, online platforms and technologies like Zoom, Slack, and Microsoft Teams have created opportunities for engagement for those who do not enjoy social contact (Samuel, 2021).

Universal Design Principles Limitations and Holistic Application

Similar to legislative acts and amendments, UD principles are more focused on addressing physical disabilities than on cognitive and mental health needs, which are part of the human experience. In addition, probably due to the origins and history of the movement, UD is more recognizable in the literature on the built environment, web design, learning materials: actual artifacts, and outcomes, and not so much on the inclusivity of the design process or the actual process of making design decisions about accessibility and inclusivity (Buffel et al., 2018; Goodsmith, 2001). As was mentioned above, specific users and specific disabilities are not mentioned in the UD principles themselves (Hamraie, 2017).

The implementation of UD principles is also happening on the micro scale or in isolated environments, which do not address issues of accessibility to a broader landscape or community. For example, cities implementing UD principles of adapting physical infrastructure for an aging population through residential guidelines or design suggestions geographically and locally limit them to the places of congregations of the aging population (Buffel et al., 2018).

Universal design principles are applicable to the living environment as a whole: physical, online, cultural, and social spaces. Interconnected structures, such as websites and mobile applications, educational institutions, housing, public spaces, and different means of transportation, provide access to a variety of life activities: learning, work, leisure activities, and shelter. When research is focused on one particular environment, for example, design and cognitive differences, that environment is treated as a separately situated structure, such as a classroom, school garden, or home (Bates et al., 2017; Gaines et al., 2016; Hegde, 2015; Smith & Preiser, 2011; Steele & Ahrentzen, 2015). Sensory sensitivity to certain triggers, that can exist or appear in the physical environment, can have an effect on one's social and communicative environment as well. Someone who is overly sensitive to loud noises or fluorescent light may withdraw from interaction with others if light or noise becomes over-stimulating. Similarly, we can observe "interconnections between the materialities of urban space and the socialities of urban life" (Dovey & Pafka, 2016, p. 9).

Physical space and physical design both influence social environments and communication. When the elements of UD principles are applied to physical or material objects (classrooms, websites, instructional materials, tests, streets, sidewalks, etc.), we create non-physical outcomes, such as certain feelings that users experience through interactions with those objects. Through the alliteration of material objects that consider a wide variety of users and their different physical or cognitive abilities, we can create feelings of clarity, calmness, inclusivity, autonomy, safety, privacy, or sensitivity (Ezell et al., 2018).

In research on architecture and transportation, universal design is still more often associated with physical or visible disabilities (Audirac, 2008; Bayless & Davidson, 2019; Hamraie, 2017). Universal design in learning environments is often associated with assistive technology, with the main goal of improving learning opportunities and help with teaching methods or classroom accommodation (Edyburn, 2015; Metcalf, 2011; Oslund, 2014).

Cognitive or sensory needs require different approaches for accommodation in physical or online spaces. The absence of accommodation that reduces sensory overload and psychological tension can prevent the full enjoyment of one's environment (Suarez, 2012). Predictable elements of physical or online environments, such as wayfinding features, landmarks, or clear study guides or explanations, help situate one in the space and reduce stress (not only for people with sensory needs but also for those who are new to the learning environment or feel overwhelmed in an unknown area). For instance, children with sensory over-responsivity appear to be excessively cautious, become upset with changes in routine, and have difficulty with transitions between activities (Suarez, 2012). Not knowing what to expect or rapid changes without preparation for such situations might create an unnecessarily stressful situation and affect student performance or the user's ability to use public transportation next time.

Accommodation of sensory needs with universal design principles in mind is still under development (Silva et al., 2019). "Standards for Universal Design have begun to reflect the need to design for more than physical access, and to consider the needs of users with sensory impairments, intellectual disability, and cognitive impairment associated with aging and dementia" (Dalton, 2016, p. 315).

The wide practice of applying the minimum of ADA accommodation (Americans with Disabilities Act, 1990) frequently means the installment of ramps, widened entrances, and parking spaces for the main reason: not being sued for non-compliance.

Conclusion

It is important to consult with students and users on designing and implementing UD principles on campus and in the classroom. The application of UD principles does not end in the classroom or in the school/university building. When a student leaves an ADA-accessible campus or a classroom, assistive technology or accessible sidewalks might suddenly end; that is why UD principles should be applied more holistically and include a broader understanding of what it entails.

In *Creating the Universally Designed City* article, Weisman argues that the movement for universal design "must go beyond the 'letter of the law' to the 'spirit of the law'"; that is why it is important "to shift … focus from redressing human and environmental problems through remedial design to preventing problems through holistic, equitable design" (Weisman, 2000, p. 165).

Notes

1 The principles of Universal design https://projects.ncsu.edu/ncsu/design/cud/about_ud/udprinciplestext.htm
2 https://www.britannica.com/biography/Ronald-L-Mace
3 https://projects.ncsu.edu/ncsu/design/cud/about_ud/udprinciplestext.htm
4 Definitions of Convention on the Rights of Persons with Disabilities (CRPD) https://www.un.org/development/desa/disabilities/convention-on-the-rights-of-persons-with-disabilities/article-2-definitions.html
5 Timeline of Disability Rights in the United States https://www.accessibility.com/resources/timeline-of-disability-rights
6 World Health Organization, International classification of functioning, disability, and health. Geneva: 2001, WHO. p. 214.
7 https://adata.org/faq/what-are-public-or-private-college-universitys-responsibilities-students-disabilities
8 https://www.thelantern.com/2020/10/students-encouraged-to-start-search-for-accessible-housing-early/
9 https://www.thelantern.com/2020/03/student-life-disability-services-offers-class-accommodations-during-online-transition/
10 https://slds.osu.edu
11 https://oaa.osu.edu/emergency-grading-system-offers-flexibility-spring-2021
12 https://www.pewresearch.org/fact-tank/2020/04/23/as-schools-shift-to-online-learning-amid-pandemic-heres-what-we-know-about-disabled-students-in-the-u-s/
13 https://www.disabilityscoop.com/2021/03/05/zoom-commits-to-improving-accessibility/29225/

References

Audirac, I. (January 01, 2008). Accessing transit as universal design. *Journal of Planning Literature, 23*(1), 4–16.
Americans With Disabilities Act of 1990, 42 U.S.C. § 12101 *et seq.* (1990). https://www.ada.gov/pubs/adastatute08.htm
Baglieri, S. (2020). Toward Inclusive Education? Focusing a Critical Lens on Universal Design for Learning. *Canadian Journal of Disability Studies, 9*(5), 42–74. https://doi.org/10.15353/cjds.v9i5.690
Bates, C., Imrie, R., & Kullman, K. (2017). *Care and design: Bodies, buildings, cities*. (Chapter The Sensory City: Autism, Design and Care / Joyce Davidson and Victoria L. Henderson). Wiley-Blackwell
Bayless, S. H., & Davidson, S. (2019). Driverless cars and accessibility: Designing the future of transportation for people with disabilities. *The Intelligent Transportation Society of America, 4*, 1–43. https://rosap.ntl.bts.gov/view/dot/64474
Biglieri, S. (2021). The right to (re)shape the city. *Journal of the American Planning Association, 87*(3), 311–325.
Buffel, T., Handler, S., & Phillipson, C. (Eds.). (2018). *Age-friendly cities and communities: A global perspective* (Ser. Ageing in a global context). Policy Press.
Capp, M. J. (2017). The effectiveness of universal design for learning: A meta-analysis of literature between 2013 and 2016. *International Journal of Inclusive Education, 21*(8), 791–807.
Dalton, C. (January 01, 2016). Interaction design in the built environment: Designing for the 'Universal User'. *Studies in Health Technology and Informatics, 229*, 314–323.
Dovey, K., & Pafka, E. (January 23, 2016). The science of urban design? *Urban Design International, 21*, 1, 1–10.
Edyburn, D. L. (Ed.). (2015). *Accessible instructional design* (First, Ser. Advances in special education technology, volume 2). Emerald Group Publishing Limited.

Edyburn, D. L. (2021). Transforming student engagement in COVID-19 remote instruction: A research perspective. *Educational Technology Research and Development, 69*, 113–116.

Ezell, K., Stein R., & Korniyenko G. (October 1, 2018). When everyday is sensory overload. *Planning*.

Gaines, K., Bourne, A., Pearson, M., & Kleibrink, M. (2016). *Designing for autism spectrum disorders*. Routledge

Gillis, A., & Krull, L. M. (2020). Covid-19 remote learning transition in spring 2020: Class structures, student perceptions, and inequality in college courses. *Teaching Sociology, 48*(4), 283–299.

Goodsmith S. (2001). The bottom-up methodology of universal design. In Preiser, W. F. E., & Ostroff, E. (Eds.), *Universal design handbook*. McGraw-Hill.

Hamraie, A. (2016). Universal design and the problem of "post-disability" ideology. *Design and Culture, 8*(3), 1–25.

Hamraie, A. (2017). *Building access: Universal design and the politics of disability*. University of Minnesota Press.

Hegde, A. (2015). Sensory sensitivity and the built environment. *Lighting Design + Application, 45*, 56–60.

Imrie, R. (2012). Universalism, universal design and equitable access to the built environment. *Disability and Rehabilitation, 34*(10), 873–882.

Lissner S. L. (2007). Universal design in the institutional settings: Weaving a philosophy into campus planning (159–169). In Nasar, J. L., & Evans-Cowley, J. (Ed.), *Universal design and visitability: From accessibility to zoning*. The John Glenn School of Public Affairs.

Metcalf, D. J. (2011). *Succeeding in the inclusive classroom: K-12 lesson plans using universal design for learning*. SAGE.

Mostafa, M. (March 04, 2014). Architecture for autism: Autism ASPECTSS™ in School Design. *International Journal of Architectural Research: Archnet-Ijar, 8,* 1, 143–158.

Nasar, J. L., & Evans-Cowley, J. (2007). *Universal design and visitability: From accessibility to zoning*. The John Glenn School of Public Affairs.

Oslund, C. 2014. *Supporting College and University students with invisible disabilities: A guide for faculty and staff working with students with autism, AD/HD, language processing disorders, anxiety, and mental illness*. Jessica Kingsley.

Samuel, A. (March 08, 2021). As remote work becomes the norm, vast new possibilities open for autistic people. *Wall Street Journal* (Online); New York.

Silva, R. F., Costa, A., & Thomann, G. (2019). Design tool based on sensory perception, usability and universal design. *Procedia CIRP, 84*, 618–623.

Smith, K. H., & Preiser, W. F. E. (2011). *Universal design handbook*. McGraw-Hill.

Steele, K., & Ahrentzen, S. (2015). *At home with autism: Designing housing for the spectrum*. Policy Press

Suarez, M. A. (January 01, 2012). Sensory processing in children with autism spectrum disorders and impact on functioning. *Pediatric Clinics of North America, 59*(1), 203–214.

Weisman, L. K. (November 01, 2000). Creating the universally designed city: Prospects for the New Century. *Architectural Theory Review, 5*(2), 156–173.

Appendix

Resources and Examples of Universal Design Application

1. Universal Design Living Laboratory, Columbus, Ohio

National Demonstration Home in Columbus is built using universal design principles
    https://www.udll.com/media-room/articles/book-review-residential-design-for-aging-in-place/index.html
    Virtual tour inside the house
    https://www.udll.com/virtual-tour/
    General Application of Universal Design
    https://www.washington.edu/doit/resources/popular-resource-collections/applications-universal-design

2. Universal Design in Learning

https://www.umassd.edu/dss/resources/faculty--staff/universal-design/

UDL framework in face-to-face and online courses https://files.eric.ed.gov/fulltext/EJ1201588.pdf

Universal Design of Instruction (UDI)

https://www.washington.edu/doit/sites/default/files/atoms/files/UD_Instruction_06_15_20.pdf

UDL: a teacher's guide

https://www.understood.org/en/school-learning/for-educators/universal-design-for-learning/understanding-universal-design-for-learning

Accessible University (AU) is a fictional university home page designed to demonstrate a variety of common web design problems that result in visitors with disabilities being unable to access content or features.

http://www.washington.edu/accesscomputing/AU/

Assistive Technology and Accessible Educational Materials Center https://ataem.org

Multisensory instruction

https://www.understood.org/en/school-learning/partnering-with-childs-school/instructional-strategies/multisensory-instruction-what-you-need-to-know

3. Universal Design and Information Technology

Access Computing's informational brochures provide guidance on making IT, online resources, and educational opportunities accessible to individuals with disabilities.

https://www.washington.edu/accesscomputing/resources/brochures

Free Web Design & Development Curriculum

http://www.washington.edu/accesscomputing/webd2/

Web Design Standards

https://www.w3.org/

4
PARENT PERSPECTIVES AND BELIEFS ON INCLUSIVE EDUCATION FOR STUDENTS WITH INTELLECTUAL DISABILITY

Jordan C. Shurr* and Alexandra Minuk

The topic of inclusive education (IE) has developed over the past five decades from a focus on the location of instruction, to that of instructional strategy, to one centered on increased learning expectations, specifically in the area of academic content (Ryndak et al., 2013; Wehmeyer et al., 2006). While much of the research attention, policy, and advancement have been centered on including students with high-incidence disabilities (e.g., learning disabilities, ADHD, Emotional and Behavior Disorders; Gage et al., 2012), the research centered on students with intellectual disability (ID) and other low incidence disabilities is less established (Dukes & Berlingo, 2020; Norwich, 2014).

Students with ID account for roughly 1% of the population worldwide (Matson et al., 2019). Diagnosis includes deficits in both intellectual functioning and adaptive behavior, and characteristics of individuals with ID include difficulty retaining, recalling, and applying knowledge and skills without extensive support and practice (Matson et al., 2019). Within education, this often means that students with ID do best when given varied and ample support such as visual, verbal, and physical reminders, assistive technology tools, as well as frequent opportunities to practice skills and receive performance-related feedback (Shurr & Taber-Doughty, 2017). Like many disabilities, early intervention, appropriate educational supports, family involvement, and high-quality instruction are key to ensuring positive outcomes, such as academic achievement, employment, and the ability to achieve one's life goals (Matson et al., 2019).

For several decades, specialized educational settings, including separate programs, classes, and schools specifically geared toward students with disabilities have been the norm for students with ID. However, there has been a gradual increase in the placement of students with ID in inclusive environments (e.g., Brock, 2018), including the placement of students with ID in classrooms, schools, or programs alongside students without disabilities. Beyond a focus on social justice and equity in educational opportunity, IE for this population of students has been attributed to improved academic achievement and social connections as well as improved post-school outcomes, such as employment and independent living (McDonnell & Hunt, 2014). While the

---

* j.shurr@queensu.ca

benefits of IE for this population have garnered some attention, there is still considerable debate surrounding the location of education as well as other IE topics, such as educational content and support.

To date, the focus of IE research related to students with ID has largely been related to academic content, placement, and support for students, and often focused on educational staff and the students themselves (Becht et al., 2020; Shurr & Bouck, 2013). While these are undoubtedly key stakeholders in IE, the existing reviews often neglect the parent perspective. While the role of the parent in educational placement and other decision-making processes in school varies globally, there is solid evidence that family engagement and active involvement in educational planning and operation significantly impact student learning and, ultimately, student outcomes (Bouck, 2017; Castro et al., 2015). Parent input matters in the educational endeavor, and parent perspectives and experiences matter in building an understanding of the current status of parent involvement in IE.

Recently, Shurr et al. (2021) conducted a systematic review to describe the parent-related research on IE for students with ID published between 1994, to coincide with the initiation of the Salamanca Statement related to IE, and 2019. Both a database and ancestry search revealed a total of 63 articles that met the inclusion criteria. In addition to the examination of the basic article characteristics, the authors analyzed the primary aims of the included articles through inductive open-coding. Findings revealed three main categories, with some overlap, related to the experience and perspective of parents with children with ID on IE including experiences in IE (30%), relevant factors (51%), and perspectives and beliefs on IE (67%). And finally, the largest category, perspectives and beliefs on IE, included information on the perception and evaluation of the placement decision-making process, educational services and supports, and child needs and family desires and expectations.

Due to the prominence of the final category in the review and its importance in moving the field forward, it is the focus of this chapter. We have closely re-examined the 42 included articles to glean important findings from the three sub-categories. This discussion is critical as researchers and practitioners continue to work with and attempt to better understand the perspectives and insights of parents and caregivers, the often overlooked but important figures in determining and supporting the most appropriate educational placement for individuals with ID.

Placement Decision-Making Process

Research on parent perspectives and beliefs related to the placement decision-making process included focus on areas such as parent desires and goals, shifting expectations, and advocacy efforts related to the process. The six studies included in this section of the review originated in the USA ($n = 3$), Australia ($n = 2$), and Brazil ($n = 1$). In terms of the publication date, two articles were published in 1995 and four between 2013 and 2019. Two of the studies used quantitative measures including surveys, questionnaires, or rating scales, and the other four utilized qualitative interviews. Mothers were the primary sources of data, with the addition of fathers, grandparents, siblings, and other family members in three studies. This set of studies focused primarily on students from grades K–8, with three extending to Grade 12 and one with unspecified grades.

Parent Desires and Goals

In this set of studies, parents expressed a desire for education and particularly IE to serve as a means for belonging and full participation for their children (Erwin & Soodak, 1995).

Additionally, parents wanted an education that included both a safe and happy environment as well as appropriately challenging learning expectations for their children (Mann et al., 2016; Maturana et al., 2019). While many viewed IE as the most appropriate venue to achieve these goals, some parents believed that they could also be achieved in specialized settings (Lalvani, 2013). Furthermore, beyond creating opportunities for their child, parents viewed the educational placement decision as one along with the broad themes of social justice and equal opportunity with a preference toward IE (Erwin & Soodak, 1995). In short, the studies in this section highlighted the delicate balance and often overlap between parents' goals of learning and achievement and those of safety and care in making educational placement decisions.

While parents associated IE with social and academic opportunities, many also focused on the perceived quality of student support and services within their placement decisions (Lalvani, 2013; Mann et al., 2018). In Lalvani's (2013) interview with 19 parents of children with Down syndrome, it was found that specialized educational settings were viewed as more able to offer professionalized services and support when compared to IE. Similar findings were reported in Maturana and colleagues' interview study (2019) as well as Mann and colleagues' (2018) survey. This indicated that parents' views on the support provided in particular educational placements can have a significant effect on their understanding of IE and ultimately their decision-making.

Shifting Expectations

Collins (1995) found a shift in the perceptions of parents interviewed after their children moved from specialized to IE placements. While many parents worried about a lack of access to extra-curriculars and increased isolation when moving to IE, their perspectives changed after experiencing the new placement. Many who had previously expressed apprehension in the move toward inclusion shifted to finding IE more desirable. However, parents did often note a decrease in satisfaction with services and supports provided in the new setting. Mediators, or factors, that were noted that influenced parent perspectives and beliefs regarding the placement decision-making process included characteristics of the programs offered, past educational experiences, external sources of information, personal philosophies, student age, and extent of student support needs (Collins, 1995; Erwin & Soodak, 1995; Lalvani, 2013; Mann et al., 2018; Maturana et al., 2019). In brief, parents often expressed feelings outside of the decision-making process and noted how it was unfamiliar and often a struggle to fully participate (Erwin & Soodak, 1995; Lalvani, 2013; Mann et al., 2018). This in part can explain the shift many parents felt in considering inclusive placements both before and after experiencing them.

Advocacy Efforts

Even while IE placements have been on the rise for students with ID, the research focused on parent perspectives echoes that of other studies indicating that IE for this population is not yet a regular expectation within schools (e.g., Buchner et al., 2021). Therefore, the decision-making process in the case of inclusive placements often required significant time, effort, and strategy by parents (Erwin & Soodak, 1995; Lalvani, 2013; Mann et al., 2016). And while some parents indicated that their participation in the process was life-changing and highly impactful (Erwin & Soodak, 1995), others noted the considerable toll of fully engaging in the process of advocating for IE on behalf of their children (Mann et al., 2016, 2018).

It is clear that parents should and do play a key role in the placement decision-making process for their children with ID. Their role is both complex and challenging regardless of their desired setting, however often more so for those who push for IE placement, especially since parents are typically the only non-educators in this process. This outsider orientation often leads to feelings of powerlessness as well as an impetus toward advocacy to ensure that the needs and strengths of their child are fully considered in determining the location of educational services (Bacon & Causton-Theoharis, 2013).

Educational Services and Supports

Research in the area of parent perspectives and beliefs on educational services and supports included focus on teacher preparation and school climate, educational content, educational supports and resources, parental satisfaction and relevant influencing factors, as well as parental efforts and advocacy. The collection of 31 studies included a near majority from the USA ($n = 15$), as well as studies from Europe ($n = 9$), Australia ($n = 4$), and Canada, Egypt, and Malaysia ($n = 1$, each). The majority of articles were published in 2010 and beyond ($n = 13$), with the remaining between 2000 and 2009 ($n = 8$) and a substantial portion between 1994 and 1999 ($n = 10$). Most studies used qualitative methods ($n = 13$), primarily interviews, with one focus group and one observation. The remaining articles used quantitative (i.e., survey, questionnaires, or rating scales; $n = 10$), mixed ($n = 7$), and systematic review methodologies ($n = 1$). Similar to the other research sets, mothers were again the primary source of data with the addition of fathers, siblings, and other family members. The focus on student age spanned the spectrum with six studies focused on grades K–8, 19 focused on K–12 and beyond, two focused on grades 9-12 and beyond, and four without a specified school-age focus.

Teacher Preparation and School Climate

The majority of studies in this area indicated that parents were concerned that general education teachers were not sufficiently prepared for IE or to support students with ID in IE. This included parent reports of negative teacher perspectives toward inclusion and insufficient training and knowledge in inclusion and disability in general (Abdelhameed, 2015; Fisher et al., 1998; Gallagher et al., 2000; Gasteiger-Klicpera et al., 2013; Hodapp et al., 1998; Palmer et al., 2001; Reilly et al., 2015; Ryndak et al., 1996; Starr et al., 2006; Tait & Hussain, 2017). One study did find general parental satisfaction with teacher preparation; however, participants also noted a desire for training to be extended across all school personnel and not only those directly involved in inclusive roles (Batanero et al., 2019). This seems to indicate consistency around the desire for more attention to school-wide preparation in IE. While Kendall (2019) noted that parents surveyed had positive attitudes toward the staff in their inclusive placements, in this study, many of the parents described the time and effort spent on comparing and finally selecting their preferred school. In contrast, Kasari et al. (1999) found that teacher specialization and knowledge were seen as an advantage of specialized educational settings. Together, these findings seem to indicate consistency around parents' desire for additional attention to both individual teacher and school-wide preparation in IE.

The consequences of insufficient training of general education teachers in IE as reported by parents were both student difficulty in inclusive placements and parental stress (Kendall, 2019; Tait & Hussain, 2017). Furthermore, parents generally agreed that the success of IE placements rested on the school itself and not solely on individual teachers. Relatedly, the general school climate and culture around inclusivity for students with ID was viewed as a barrier to IE and a critical area in need of change (Abdelhameed, 2015; Robinson & Graham, 2019). As a potential means of addressing this issue in a more school-wide manner, Storgilos and colleagues (2015) noted parent satisfaction and support for a co-teaching model in which general and special education teachers shared instructional responsibilities and expertise as an educational team (Friend et al., 2010) to provide quality inclusive opportunities and supports. These findings on the importance of school climate, cooperation, and individual teacher attitudes for successful IE are echoed in the extant literature (e.g., McCollow et al., 2015; Woodcock & Woolfson, 2019).

Related to the importance of teacher preparation and involvement in IE, several studies also noted the significance of communication and reciprocal trust between families and their schools and teachers. Parents viewed ongoing communication about their child's needs and progress in school as vital to success in inclusive environments (Downing & Peckham-Hardin, 2007; Kendall, 2019; Mortier et al., 2010). However, in reality, many parents reported poor communication and cooperation with their school and teachers (Tryfon et al., 2019). Batanero et al. (2019) found that families with children in inclusive settings relied more on special education staff than general education staff members for information and communication, once again indicating the importance of a school-wide effort to IE.

Educational Content

In general terms, research related to educational content in the review mirrored the ongoing debate regarding educational content for students with ID (e.g., Ballard & Dymond, 2017). While some parents seemed to favor a focus on social and other functionally oriented content in educational placement, others preferred an academic focus (Fisher et al., 1998; Palmer et al., 2001; Palmer Borthwick-Duffy, & Widaman, 1998; Strogilos et al., 2015). For many parents, discussions on educational placement largely hinged on the topic of educational content. In terms of IE placements, parents noted an increase in options, opportunities, and progress especially as related to their children's socialization goals (Fisher et al., 1998; Palmer Borthwick-Duffy, & Widaman, 1998; Strogilos et al., 2015; Tryfon et al., 2019). While inclusive settings were often viewed in a positive light in terms of content, parents often expressed a desire for more instruction in social skills (Downing & Peckham-Hardin, 2007) and others did not consider academic content as the primary focus (Gallagher et al., 2000; Jelas, 2000). Palmer Borthwick-Duffy, Widaman, & Best (1998) found a link between parents with high regard for life skills-focused content and a preference for specialized settings. In contrast, critique of specialized settings often included mention of low academic rigor and opportunities to learn social skills in natural settings when compared to inclusive environments (Alnahdi & Elhadi, 2019; Hodapp et al., 1998; Palmer et al., 2001).

The research on the content of instruction clearly indicates that parent perspectives on IE are closely linked to their expectations and goals in functional life skills and academics. And parents' experiences and perspectives of the educational setting will naturally be influenced by these content goals and expectations.

Educational Supports and Resources

In addition to instructional content, parents also noted educational support and resources as important considerations for the placement of students with ID. Studies found that parents viewed instructional materials in general education settings as superior to those available in specialized settings (Ryndak et al., 1996) and that they were in favor of the co-teaching model of instruction (Strogilos et al., 2015; Tryfon et al., 2019). However, many expressed concerns about instructional practices, related services, and personnel support available within inclusive settings. For instance, Downing and Peckham-Hardin (2007) found that parents desired more explicit instruction, ample opportunities to practice skills, and sufficient modification of activities and goals than provided in IE. There was also significant parent anxiety around the loss of specific and intensive related services such as speech-language or occupational therapy when moving from specialized to inclusive settings (Fidler et al., 2003; Kasari et al., 1999). This concern is not unfounded as the prevalence of push-in-related services is on the rise (Hernandez, 2012). Experts in this area, however, would argue that despite the appearance of fewer services, this newer, transdisciplinary model can allow for deeper and more contextualized learning and therapy offering greater generalization into daily life (Rausch et al., 2021). In terms of personnel-related support, parents were interested in accessing teacher aides and increasing opportunities for teacher attention through smaller class sizes and tutoring (Fidler et al., 2003; Hodapp et al., 1998; Kasari et al., 1999). Relatedly, parents in favor of IE stressed the importance of access for their children with ID to peers without disabilities for modeling academic and social behaviors (Gallagher et al., 2000; Kasari et al., 1999).

Satisfaction

Parents mostly expressed support for their inclusive placements, while those in specialized settings were generally less satisfied with their placement (Freeman et al., 1999; Jelas, 2000; Kasari et al., 1999; Westling & Plaute, 1999; Zanobini et al., 2018). And, of those who considered a change in placement, most expressed interest in moving from specialized to inclusive placements (Westling & Plaute, 1999). For those in inclusive settings, some mentioned concerns around medical and social safety support available in IE (Gasteiger-Klicpera et al., 2013; Hodapp et al., 1998). Parents not in favor of IE also cited concerns related to student medical needs and characteristics, the need for specialized care and attention for health and safety, and independent skill acquisition, which they deemed to be outside of the scope of IE (Palmer et al., 2001). For some parents, specialized schooling environments were chosen as means of protecting their children from the perceived potential of abuse or other hardships anticipated from inclusive placements such as disability-focused bullying (Robinson & Graham, 2019). The potential of increased vulnerability to bullying for included students with ID has been echoed in more recent research (Nambiar et al., 2020), indicating that this concern may persist. However, the majority of studies in this set reported specific benefits including parent satisfaction with academic and behavioral outcomes, increased student motivation to learn, as well as more friendships and social opportunities (Fisher et al., 1998; Francis et al., 2018; Gasteiger-Klicpera et al., 2013; Ryndak et al., 1995).

Influencing Factors

Research included in this area noted several factors that impact parent perspectives and beliefs of IE. While the focus of parents is often what is best for their child, this notion is complex and often entangled with several internal and external variables specific to the individuals involved and the context in which they operate (e.g., school, community; Mann et al., 2015). Key influencing factors noted in the research included school variables (e.g., available resources and opportunities and school location), family variables (e.g., references of professionals or other families and current and future expectations for the student), and student variables (e.g., educational history, and student characteristics such as age and extent of support needs).

Parents associated the availability of resources, including personnel, support, and materials, with the quality of IE. Resource-related school variables that influenced parents' opinions on IE included personnel and material resources (Batanero et al., 2019; Elkins et al., 2003). This implied that factors such as high staff-to-student ratios or access to relevant curricular materials can help to improve parent perception of inclusive environments. Additionally, parents reported that the physical location of the school was important in their evaluation of IE (Batanero et al., 2019; Tryfon et al., 2019). In these cases, parents showed a preference for neighborhood schools rather than IE in schools outside of their typical school boundary map.

Families in some studies indicated feelings of pressure toward accepting specialized schooling by school professionals (Mann et al., 2015; Ryndak et al., 1996). Also, some parents described their reliance on other parents of children with disabilities to understand educational placements (Mann et al., 2015). In addition to outside family influences, parents were also guided by their own expectations of their children both currently and in the future, in adulthood (Francis et al., 2018; Freeman et al., 1999).

In terms of student-related variables, it was found that past educational experiences, student age, and the extent of support needs influenced parental perceptions of IE for their children. While parents of students in specialized settings often noted apprehension about moving to inclusive settings, many who made such a move were positive in their appraisal (Kasari et al., 1999; Ryndak et al., 1996). Additionally, Westling (1996) found that concerns about IE were often not shared between parents with children in specialized settings and those that moved to inclusive settings. This indicates that, in some cases, apprehension of IE could be related to fears of the unknown. In terms of student age, multiple studies found that parents' support for IE often waned as students advanced through school (Freeman et al., 1999; Hanson, 2003; Kasari et al., 1999; Reilly et al., 2015; Starr et al., 2006). An additional student variable of note was the extent of support needs. Parents of students with more significant support needs (SSN) were often less supportive of IE than those who were less significant (Abdelhameed, 2015; Palmer, Borthwick-Duffy, Widaman, & Best, 1998; Tryfon et al., 2019; Zanobini et al., 2018). However, the curriculum also played a mediating role in that parents of children in more inclusive settings reported less stress when their children were primarily accessing an alternate or modified curriculum (Gasteiger-Klicpera et al., 2013). Regardless, the research highlighted here reflects parents' reliance on specialized programs despite the current support in research and policy (Wehmeyer et al., 2020).

Parent Efforts and Advocacy

As noted earlier, parents often described their involvement in the educational process as cumbersome and exhausting. While this was noted in parents' description of the decision-making process, a need for parent advocacy and attention was also apparent in research related to ongoing services and support. The research here points to the burden that parents feel to initiate educational improvements, serve in many unfamiliar roles, and navigate complicated bureaucracy (Gallagher et al., 2000; Hanson, 2003; Tryfon et al., 2019). Not only were these efforts reported as time-consuming, but parents also expressed feelings of powerlessness, stress, and anxiety (Mann et al., 2015; Tait & Hussain, 2017).

Child Needs and Family Desires and Expectations

Research related to child needs and family desires and expectations focused on factors associated with parents' attitudes toward IE, perceptions of challenges, priorities for children's learning, satisfaction with specific placements, and participation in the IE process. Of the eight studies included in this section of the review, more than half ($n = 5$) were conducted in the USA, with Austria ($n = 1$), Israel ($n = 1$), and Jordan ($n = 1$) also being represented. The articles were published between 1996 and 2018, with half of the articles ($n = 4$) published before 2002 and half after 2003. A majority of the studies ($n = 4$) used qualitative methodologies, specifically, interviews with parents and family members. Following in prominence were studies that used quantitative methodologies ($n = 3$), which used surveys, questionnaires, and rating scales, and the remaining article was a literature review. In more than half of the studies ($n = 5$), mothers were the main source of data; however, fathers were also featured as participants in half of the articles ($n = 4$), though the number of fathers in the sample was not always specified. The full spectrum of student age was represented in the articles; half of the studies ($n = 4$) focused on K–12, two studies focused on grades 9–12, and one study each focused on K–8 and the post-secondary years.

Factors Associated with Parents' Attitudes toward Inclusive Education

While influencing factors were described in the section of the review that focused on educational supports and services, research related to child needs and family expectations and desires also identified factors that were associated with parents' attitudes toward IE, which were often specific to the parents themselves. In one study, while both Jewish and Muslim Israeli mothers' attitudes about IE for their children with Down syndrome were positive, religion was found to play a role in parents' attitudes toward inclusion (Barnoy et al., 2017). Similarly, mothers' educational level was also found to correlate with involvement in their children's past education. It was found that high educational attainment correlated with parent confidence in the ability to provide general information about their children, suggest appropriate learning objectives, and be involved in school activities (Westling & Plaute, 1999).

In addition to parent characteristics, parents' experiences with IE also appeared to be associated with their attitudes toward it. The research indicated that parents who had positive experiences with both inclusive and specialized placements were more likely to continue to choose those placements in the future (Westling, 1996; Yuan et al., 2018). Moreover, parents who had positive experiences with IE in their child's high school were also more critical of elements of inclusion in a college program, whereas parents who had fewer positive experiences with IE reported being pleased with the same program (Yuan et al., 2018). Thus, parent characteristics (e.g., religion and education) and experiences with their children's schooling, both positive and negative, can color their perceptions of IE and potentially influence their preferences for classroom placement.

School-level factors were also found to be important determinants of parents' attitudes toward IE relative to their children's needs. Similar to the research focusing on educational support and services, parents of children with ID attending IE expressed that the availability of effective support and services in schools was essential in supporting their children in regular classroom environments (Al Dababneh et al., 2017). School-wide commitment to IE was also a consideration, and parents credited schools for adapting curriculum to meet their children's needs (Lehman & Roberto, 1996). At the university level, one study found that parents of children with disabilities attending an inclusive college program believed that school-level factors such as the involvement of mentors and special education teachers were integral to their children's success (Yuan et al., 2018), serving as an example of how schools that meet students' diverse needs can shape parents' attitudes toward IE. The mothers in one study, however, viewed schools as less willing to work with their children with disabilities, describing the school as a "place their children visited every day" (p. 33) rather than an environment that ensured their academic and social development (Lehman & Roberto, 1996). Taken together, the parent and school-related variables that are associated with attitudes toward IE in terms of children's needs can have implications for classroom placement and, in turn, the children themselves.

Perceived Challenges of Inclusive Education

In addition to general attitudes about child needs and family desires and expectations, research in this area has also focused on parents' perceived challenges associated with IE. Specifically, some studies focused on older students and how the structure of secondary schools can create difficulties for adolescents in IE. In one study, half of the children with ID started their education in fully inclusive Kindergarten environments and remained in elementary classes that were either fully or partially inclusive; however, most were moved to self-contained placements by the time they entered junior high school (Hanson, 2003). In another study of adolescents with SSN, not only were most students (60%) educated in special education classes with no integration but also three-quarters spent the entire day without interacting with typically developing peers (Kraemer et al., 1997). The social networks of children with ID were described as more limited by the time they reached junior high school and adolescence, and adulthood was found to further limit students' social opportunities (Hanson, 2003).

Related to the issue of IE during adolescence was the timing of some studies relative to the passage of landmark legislation (Hanson, 2003). Despite parents' desires for their children to be socially included, many families were reluctant to make changes to their child's classroom placement during adolescence if they had attended specialized settings throughout their education, creating a cohort effect for these students (Kraemer et al., 1997). Some parents expressed awareness that their children were part of the first wave to make changes to their schooling and recognized that schools were learning about inclusion at the same time that they were, though as a result of this timing, the school years were turbulent in terms of the amount of support and number of options that were provided to parents (Hanson, 2003).

Parents' Priorities for Their Children

In general, parents' priorities for their children's needs can be described in the research in terms of the present and the future, and perspectives and beliefs varied based on whether children attended inclusive or specialized settings. In one study, parents of children with ID in inclusive placements believed that their children needed to enhance their basic academic, communication, independence, and language skills; participation in sports programming; and managing money and daily life skills, whereas more than half of parents of children attending specialized settings emphasized the need for a focus on language, academic, and self-care skills only (Al Dababneh et al., 2017). Another study found that several parents wanted their children to attend IE but preferred specialized classes due to concerns over physical and emotional safety as well as the perceived ability of inclusive environments to meet their children's unique needs (Westling, 1996).

Families' priorities for their children's futures were generally broad and tended to involve a deficit discourse; that is, they focused on what their children were missing at school rather than what they were learning. In one study, mothers reported feeling that they had to make difficult decisions for their children in adolescence, choosing between classes their children would enjoy (e.g., choir) and those that were seen as beneficial to their futures (Lehman & Roberto, 1996). Another study found that half of the parents of children with ID in inclusive schools believed that their children were likely to graduate, live independently, and have a career; however, half of the parents of children in specialized settings expressed concerns for the future and their children's ability to live independently and support themselves (Al Dababneh et al., 2017). Moreover, in discussing the effects of their children's education on their futures, mothers of adolescents with SSN emphasized the importance of social inclusion (Lehman & Roberto, 1996), demonstrating the role of schools in creating inclusive and accepting societies.

Parent Satisfaction with Classroom and School Placement

Though parent satisfaction was addressed in this review as it pertained to educational services and supports, it is also relevant in the context of child needs and family expectations and desires. While some studies have found parents' satisfaction with classroom placement for their child's particular needs to be mixed (Kraemer et al., 1997), and making decisions about classroom placement to be difficult and dependent on professional support, parent satisfaction was found to be generally high (Westling, 1996).

Similar to the research regarding the placement decision-making process, parent satisfaction was associated with the belief that a placement could meet their child's individual needs. In one study, most parents of children with ID in inclusive settings expressed positive expectations about their child's progress but felt it was happening slowly, whereas parents of children in specialized settings acknowledged that their children were making gradual progress but also believed that their lack of progress was due to low motivation (Al Dababneh et al., 2017).

Parents' Participation in Inclusive Education as a Process

While parent participation and involvement can be seen as an important theme throughout this review, it must also be considered in the context of child needs and family expectations and desires. In terms of IE as a process, some parents felt that their needs were not met by inclusive public-school programs, such as access to information about special education law, parent and student rights, disciplinary practices, classroom placement criteria, and information about parent groups, related services, medical diagnosis, respite care, and their children's future needs (Westling, 1996). While some parents reported that they were satisfied with their involvement in the planning process, parents of minority backgrounds tended to be less satisfied, suggesting that schools must make extra efforts to maximize engagement for all parents (Westling, 1996). Other factors acted as barriers to parents' participation in IE, such as distance to the educational placement and length of the program, as well as the need for parents to provide academic assistance on an ongoing basis (Yuan et al., 2018). One study found, however, that parents most often participated in their child's education by conferencing with teachers, care providers, or therapists (Westling & Plaute, 1999), highlighting the importance of parent-teacher communication in IE.

Conclusion

Inclusive education is an increasingly relevant topic in regard to students with intellectual disability. Due to the necessity and importance of family involvement in educational decisions and progress, understanding the perspectives and beliefs of parents is of critical importance for both current practice and future research. While this review encompassed a 26-year range of studies, it is apparent in both the slow progress of IE for students with ID (Wehmeyer et al., 2020) as well as the consistency of findings across decades that much has remained consistent over time. The research indicates that parents, while critical stakeholders in the educational process, often feel like outsiders forced into an advocacy role. Additional findings reveal that there are many families, school, and student-related variables that influence parent perspectives on inclusive education. Given the various mitigating factors that shape perspectives on inclusive education, it seems that experience in high-quality inclusive placements, as well as access to necessary services and supports, are of high importance.

References

★denotes included study

★Abdelhameed, H. (2015). Teachers' and parents' attitudes toward the inclusion of students with intellectual disabilities in general education schools in Egypt. *Journal of the International Association of Special Education, 16*(1), 23–32.

★Al-Dababneh, K. A., Al-Zboon, E. K., & Baibers, H. (2017). Jordanian parents' beliefs about the causes of disability and the progress of their children with disabilities: Insights on mainstream schools and segregated centres. *European Journal of Special Needs Education, 32*(3), 362–376. https://doi.org/10.1080/08856257.2016.1240341.

★Alnahdi, G. H., & Elhadi, A. (2019). Outcomes of special education programs for students with intellectual disabilities: Family members' perspectives. *International Journal of Special Education, 34*(1), 83–94.

Bacon, J. K., & Causton-Theoharis, J. (2013). 'It should be teamwork': A critical investigation of school practices and parent advocacy in special education. *International Journal of Inclusive Education, 17*(7), 682–699. https://doi.org/10.1080/13603116.2012.708060.

Ballard, S. L., & Dymond, S. K. (2017). Addressing the general education curriculum in general education settings with students with severe disabilities. *Research and Practice for Persons with Severe Disabilities, 42*(3), 155–170. https://doi.org/10.1177/1540796917698832.

★Barnoy, S., Biton, A., & Itzhaki, M. (2017). Social inclusion of children with Down Syndrome: Jewish and Muslim mothers' knowledge, attitudes, beliefs, and behavioral intentions. *Journal of Pediatric Nursing, 35*, 50–56. https://doi.org/10.1016/j.pedn.2017.02.035.

★Batanero, J. M. F., Jaén, A. M. B., Rueda, M. M., & Martínez, I. G. (2019). Do regular schools in Spain respond to the educational needs of students with down syndrome?. *Journal of Child and Family Studies*, 1–9. https://doi.org/10.1007/s10826-019-01587-2.

Becht, K., Blades, C., Agarwal, R., & Burke, S. (2020). Academic access and progress for students with intellectual disability in inclusive postsecondary education: A systematic review of research. *Inclusion, 8*(2), 90–104. https://doi.org/10.1352/2326-6988-8.2.90

Bouck, E. C. (2017). Educational outcomes for secondary students with mild intellectual disability. *Education and Training in Autism and Developmental Disabilities, 52*(4), 369–382.

Brock, M. E. (2018). Trends in the educational placement of students with intellectual disability in the United States over the past 40 years. *American Journal on Intellectual and Developmental Disabilities, 123*(4), 305–314. https://doi.org/10.1352/1944-7558-123.4.305.

Buchner, T., Shevlin, M., Donovan, M. A., Gercke, M., Goll, H., Šiška, J., ... & Corby, D. (2021). Same progress for all? Inclusive education, the United Nations Convention on the rights of persons with disabilities and students with intellectual disability in European countries. *Journal of Policy and Practice in Intellectual Disabilities, 18*(1), 7–22. https://doi.org/10.1111/jppi.12368.

Castro, M., Expósito-Casas, E., López-Martín, E., Lizasoain, L., Navarro-Asencio, E., & Gaviria, J. L. (2015). Parental involvement on student academic achievement: A meta-analysis. *Educational Research Review, 14*, 33–46. https://doi.org/10.1016/j.edurev.2015.01.002.

★Collins, B. C. (1995). The integration of students with severe or profound disabilities from segregated schools into regular public schools: An analysis of changes in parent perceptions. *Journal of Developmental and Physical Disabilities, 7*(1), 51–65. https://doi.org/10.1007/BF02578714.

★Downing, J. E., & Peckham-Hardin, K. D. (2007). Inclusive education: What makes it a good education for students with moderate to severe disabilities?. *Research and Practice for Persons with Severe Disabilities, 32*(1), 16–30. https://doi.org/10.2511/rpsd.32.1.16.

Dukes, C., & Berlingo, L. (2020). Fissuring barriers to inclusive education for students with severe disabilities. *Research and Practice for Persons with Severe Disabilities, 45*(1), 14–17. https://doi.org/10.1177/1540796919895968.

★Elkins, J., Van Kraayenoord, C. E., & Jobling, A. (2003). Parents' attitudes to inclusion of their children with special needs. *Journal of Research in Special Educational Needs, 3*(2), 122–129. https://doi.org/10.1111/1471-3802.00005.

★Erwin, E. J., & Soodak, L. C. (1995). I never knew I could stand up to the system: Families' perspectives on pursuing inclusive education. *Journal of the Association for Persons with Severe Handicaps, 20*(2), 136–146.

*Fidler, D. J., Lawson, J. E., & Hodapp, R. M. (2003). What do parents want?: An analysis of education-related comments made by parents of children with different genetic syndromes. *Journal of Intellectual & Developmental Disability, 28*(2), 196–204. https://doi.org/10.1080/1366825031000147120.

*Fisher, D., Pumpian, I., & Sax, C. (1998). Parent and caregiver impressions of different educational models. *Remedial and Special Education, 19*(3), 173–180. https://doi.org/10.1177/074193259801900305.

*Francis, G. L., Stride, A., & Reed, S. (2018). Transition strategies and recommendations: Perspectives of parents of young adults with disabilities. *British Journal of Special Education, 45*(3), 277–301. https://doi.org/10.1111/1467-8578.12232.

*Freeman, S. F., Alkin, M. C., & Kasari, C. L. (1999). Satisfaction and desire for change in educational placement for children with Down syndrome: Perceptions of parents. *Remedial and Special Education, 20*(3), 143–151. https://doi.org/10.1177/074193259902000304.

Friend, M., Cook, L., Hurley-Chamberlain, D., & Shamberger, C. (2010). Co-teaching: An illustration of the complexity of collaboration in special education. *Journal of Educational and Psychological Consultation, 20*(1), 9–27. https://doi.org/10.1080/10474410903535380.

*Gallagher, P. A., Floyd, J. H., Stafford, A. M., Taber, T. A., Brozovic, S. A., & Alberto, P. A. (2000). Inclusion of students with moderate or severe disabilities in educational and community settings: Perspectives from parents and siblings. *Education and Training in Mental Retardation and Developmental Disabilities, 35*(2), 135–147.

Gage, N. A., Lierheimer, K. S., & Goran, L. G. (2012). Characteristics of students with high-incidence disabilities broadly defined. *Journal of Disability Policy Studies, 23*(3), 168–178. https://doi.org/10.1177/1044207311425385.

*Gasteiger-Klicpera, B., Klicpera, C., Gebhardt, M., & Schwab, S. (2013). Attitudes and experiences of parents regarding inclusive and special school education for children with learning and intellectual disabilities. *International Journal of Inclusive Education, 17*(7), 663–681. https://doi.org/10.1080/13603116.2012.706321.

*Hanson, M. J. (2003). Twenty-five years after early intervention: A follow-up of children with Down syndrome and their families. *Infants & Young Children, 16*(4), 354–365. https://doi.org/10.1097/00001163-200310000-00008.

Hernandez, S. J. (2012). Evaluation of push-in/integrated therapy in a collaborative preschool for children with special needs. *Journal of the American Academy of Special Education Professionals*, Spring/Summer, 47–77. Retrieved from: https://files.eric.ed.gov/fulltext/EJ1135696.pdf

*Hodapp, R. M., Freeman, S. F., & Kasari, C. L. (1998). Parental educational preferences for students with mental retardation: Effects of etiology and current placement. *Education and Training in Mental Retardation and Developmental Disabilities, 33*(4) 342–349.

*Jelas, Z. M. (2000). Perceptions of inclusive practices: The Malaysian perspective. *Educational Review, 52*(2), 187–196. https://doi.org/10.1080/713664037.

*Kasari, C., Freeman, S. F., Bauminger, N., & Alkin, M. C. (1999). Parental perspectives on inclusion: Effects of autism and Down syndrome. *Journal of Autism and Developmental Disorders, 29*(4), 297–305. https://doi.org/10.1017/S136064170022248X.

*Kendall, L. (2019). Supporting children with Down syndrome within mainstream education settings: Parental reflections. *Education 3-13, 47*(2), 135–147. https://doi.org/10.1080/03004279.2017.1412488.

*Kraemer, B. R., Blacher, J., & Marshal, M. P. (1997). Adolescents with severe disabilities: Family, school, and community integration. *Journal of the Association for Persons with Severe Handicaps, 22*(4), 224–234. https://doi.org/10.1177/154079699702200410.

Lalvani, P. (2013). Land of misfit toys: Mothers' perceptions of educational environments for their children with Down syndrome. *International Journal of Inclusive Education, 17*(5), 435–448. https://doi.org/10.1080/13603116.2012.683047.

*Lehmann, J. P., & Roberto, K. A. (1996). Comparison of factors influencing mothers' perceptions about the futures of. *Mental Retardation, 34*(1), 27–38.

*Mann, G., Cuskelly, M., & Moni, K. (2015). Choosing a school: Parental decision-making when special schools are an option. *Disability & Society, 30*(9), 1413–1427.

*Mann, G., Cuskelly, M., & Moni, K. (2018). An investigation of parents' decisions to transfer children from regular to special schools. *Journal of Policy and Practice in Intellectual Disabilities, 15*(3), 183–192. https://doi.org/10.1111/jppi.12238.

*Mann, G., Moni, K., & Cuskelly, M. (2016). Parents' views of an optimal school life: Using social role valorization to explore differences in parental perspectives when children have intellectual disability.

International Journal of Qualitative Studies in Education, 29(7), 964–979. https://doi.org/10.1080/09518398.2016.1174893.

Matson, J. L., Matheis, M., Estabillo, J. A., Issarraras, A., Peters, W. J., & Jiang, X. (2019). Intellectual disability. In M. J. Prinstein, E. A. Youngstrom, E. J. Mash, & R. A. Barkley (Eds.), *Treatment of disorders in childhood and adolescence* (4th ed., pp. 416–447). Guilford Press.

★Maturana, A. P. P. M., Mendes, E. G., & Capellini, V. L. M. F. (2019). Schooling of students with intellectual disabilities: Family and school perspectives. *Paidéia (Ribeirão Preto), 29*. https://doi.org/10.1590/1982-4327e2925.

McCollow, M. M., Shurr, J., & Jasper, A. D. (2015). Best practices in teacher training and professional development for including learners with low-incidence disabilities. In E. A. West (Ed.), *Including learners with low-incidence disabilities*. Emerald.

McDonnell, J., & Hunt, P. (2014). Inclusive education and meaningful school outcomes. In M. Agran, F. Brown, C. Hughes, C. Quirk, & D. L. Ryndak (Eds.), *Equity and full participation for individuals with severe disabilities: A vision for the future* (pp. 155–176). Brookes Publishing

★Mortier, K., Hunt, P., Leroy, M., Van De Putte, I., & Van Hove, G. (2010). Communities of practice in inclusive education. *Educational Studies, 36*(3), 345–355. https://doi.org/10.1080/03055690903424816.

Nambiar, P., Jangam, K., Roopesh, B. N., & Bhaskar, A. (2020). Peer victimization and its relationship to self-esteem in children with mild intellectual disability and borderline intellectual functioning in regular and special schools: An exploratory study in urban Bengaluru. *Journal of Intellectual Disabilities, 24*(4), 474–488. https://doi.org/10.1177/1744629519831573.

Norwich, B. (2014). Recognising value tensions that underlie problems in inclusive education. *Cambridge Journal of Education, 44*(4), 495–510. https://doi.org/10.1080/0305764X.2014.963027

★Palmer, D. S., Borthwick-Duffy, S. A., & Widaman, K. (1998). Parent perceptions of inclusive practices for their children with significant cognitive disabilities. *Exceptional Children, 64*(2), 271–282. https://doi.org/10.1177/001440299806400209.

★Palmer, D. S., Borthwick-Duffy, S. A., Widaman, K., & Best, S. J. (1998). Influences on parent perceptions of inclusive practices for their children with mental retardation. *American Journal on Mental Retardation, 103*(3), 272–287.

★Palmer, D. S., Fuller, K., Arora, T., & Nelson, M. (2001). Taking sides: Parent views on inclusion for their children with severe disabilities. *Exceptional Children, 67*(4), 467–484. https://doi.org/10.1177/001440290106700403.

Rausch, A., Bold, E., & Strain, P. (2021). The more the merrier: Using collaborative transdisciplinary services to maximize inclusion and child outcomes. *Young Exceptional Children, 24*(2), 59–69. https://doi.org/10.1177/1096250620922206.

★Reilly, C., Senior, J., & Murtagh, L. (2015). A comparative study of educational provision for children with neurogenetic syndromes: Parent and teacher survey. *Journal of Intellectual Disability Research, 59*(12), 1094–1107.

★Robinson, S., & Graham, A. (2019). Promoting the safety of children and young people with intellectual disability: Perspectives and actions of families and professionals. *Children and Youth Services Review, 104*, 104404. https://doi.org/10.1016/j.childyouth.2019.104404.

★Ryndak, D. L., Downing, J. E., Jacqueline, L. R., & Morrison, A. P. (1995). Parents' perceptions after inclusion of their children with moderate or severe disabilities. *Journal of the Association for Persons with Severe Handicaps, 20*(2), 147–157. https://doi.org/10.1177/074193259601700206.

★Ryndak, D. L., Downing, J. E., Morrison, A. P., & Williams, L. J. (1996). Parents' perceptions of educational settings and services for children with moderate or severe disabilities. *Remedial and Special Education, 17*(2), 106–118. https://doi.org/10.1177/074193259601700206.

Ryndak, D., Jackson, L. B. and White, J. M. 2013. Involvement and progress in the general curriculum for students with extensive support needs: K–12 inclusive-education research and implications for the future. *Inclusion, 1*, 28–49.

Shurr, J., & Bouck, E. C. (2013). Research on curriculum for students with moderate and severe intellectual disability: A systematic review. *Education and Training in Autism and Developmental Disabilities, 48*(1) 76–87.

Shurr, J., & Taber-Doughty, T (2017). Teaching academic skills to secondary students with intellectual disability. In R. M. Garguilo & E. Bouck (Eds.), *Instructional strategies for students with mild, moderate, and severe intellectual disability*. SAGE.

Shurr, J., Minuk, A., Östlund, D., Holmqvist, M., Ghaith, N., & Reed, B. (2021). Inclusive education and intellectual disability: A systematic review of parent perspectives. *International Journal of Developmental Disabilities*. https://doi.org/10.1080/20473869.2021.2003612

★Starr, E. M., Foy, J. B., Cramer, K. M., & Singh, H. (2006). How are schools doing? Parental perceptions of children with autism spectrum disorders, Down syndrome and learning disabilities: A comparative analysis. *Education and Training in Developmental Disabilities*, *41*(4) 315–332.

★Strogilos, V., Tragoulia, E., & Kaila, M. (2015). Curriculum issues and benefits in supportive co-taught classes for students with intellectual disabilities. *International Journal of Developmental Disabilities*, *61*(1), 32–40. https://doi.org/10.1179/2047387713Y.0000000031.

★Tait, K., & Hussain, R. (2017). Using quality of family life factors to explore parents' experience of educational provision for children with developmental disabilities in rural Australia. *International Journal of Disability, Development and Education*, *64*(3), 328–344. https://doi.org/10.1080/1034912X.2016.1223280.

★Tryfon, M., Anastasia, A., & Eleni, R. (2019). Parental perspectives on inclusive education for children with intellectual disabilities in Greece. *International Journal of Developmental Disabilities*, 1–9. https://doi.org/10.1080/20473869.2019.1675429.

Wehmeyer, M. L., Shogren, K. A., & Kurth, J. (2020). The state of inclusion with students with intellectual and developmental disabilities in the United States. *Journal of Policy and Practice in Intellectual Disabilities*, *18*(1), 36–43. https://doi.org/10.1111/jppi.12332.

★Westling, D. L. (1996). What do parents of children with moderate and severe mental disabilities want?. *Education and Training in Mental Retardation and Developmental Disabilities*, *31*(2) 86–114.

★Westling, D. L., & Plaute, W. (1999). Views of Austrian parents about special education services for their children with mental disabilities. *Education and Training in Mental Retardation and Developmental Disabilities*, 34(1) 43–57.

Wehmeyer, M. L. 2006. Beyond access: Ensuring progress in the general education curriculum for students with severe disabilities. *Research and Practice for Persons with Severe Disabilities, 31*, 322–326

Woodcock, S., & Woolfson, L. M. (2019). Are leaders leading the way with inclusion? Teachers' perceptions of systemic support and barriers towards inclusion. *International Journal of Educational Research*, *93*, 232–242. https://doi.org/10.1016/j.ijer.2018.11.004.

★Yuan, S. J., Ryan, S. M., & Dague, E. B. (2018). From the parents' perspective: The think college experience in rural Vermont. *Rural Special Education Quarterly*, *37*(2), 113–121. https://doi.org/10.1177/8756870518761878.

★Zanobini, M., Viterbori, P., Garello, V., & Camba, R. (2018). Parental satisfaction with disabled children's school inclusion in Italy. *European Journal of Special Needs Education*, *33*(5), 597–614. https://doi.org/10.1080/08856257.2017.1386318.

5

ATTITUDES OF STUDENTS WITHOUT DISABILITIES TOWARDS PEOPLE WITH DISABILITIES

Perspectives of Higher Education students

Shazia Hasnain and Santoshi Halder*

Introduction

According to the World report on disability (2011) produced jointly by the World Health Organization and the World Bank (2011), 15% of the world's population experiences some form of disability, and the figures are even more for developing countries. Every year the number of students enrolled for special education services is increasing by leaps and bounds worldwide, particularly in developed countries. For instance, in the year 2015-16, 13% of the students (or 6.7 million) received special education services (McFarland et al., 2018), and in 2019–20, 7.3 million (or 14 percent) of all public school students (U.S. Department of Education, Office of Special Education Programs) in the USA between the ages of 3 and 21 received special education services under the "Individuals with Disabilities Education Act" (IDEA). Comparatively in India, according to the 2011 Census, the differently-abled population was 26.8 million (2.21%), with the highest disabilities being in the age group 10-19 years (46.2 lakhs, i.e., 17%) and 16% were in the age group 20-29 years. Specific disabilities (such as difficulty in reading, writing, and use of language) in India range from 5% to 15% among school children, according to the research conducted by Singh et al. (2017). With the prevalence of disabilities worldwide, the concept of inclusion emphasized the need to bring together neurotypical and children with disabilities under the same roof (Singh, 2016) and meet the needs of the students with disabilities by providing adequate support (Pingle & Garg, 2015). The principle of inclusive education was adopted at the "World Conference on Special Needs Education: Access and Quality" (Salamanca, Spain, 1994) and was restated at the World Education Forum (Dakar, Senegal, 2000). Inclusion and inclusive education have been extensively researched for a long time worldwide; however, it is fraught with multifarious challenges. According to UNESCO's report (2020 Global Education Monitoring Report: Inclusion and education-All means all), fewer than 10%

---

* santoshi_halder@yahoo.com; shedu@caluniv.ac.in

of the countries have laws to ensure inclusion in education. It has also specified reasons that lead to the exclusion of students, which include beliefs and attitudes.

Beliefs and attitudes of people towards the population with disabilities play a vital role in inclusion. Children with disabilities are exposed to negative attitudes (Nowicki & Sandieson, 2002), leading to a negative self-concept (Pijl & Frostad, 2010). Also, it has been suggested by Bates et al. (2015) that inclusive education can be successful only when "typically-developing" students embrace the idea of inclusive education. WHO (2011) has recommended that there is a need to improve the attitudes towards disability as "mutual respect and understanding contribute to an inclusive society" (World Report on Disability, 2011). There have been ample studies on the perception and attitude of teachers and trainee teachers towards students with disabilities (e.g. Dupoux et al., 2006; Hammond & Ingalls, 2003; Kumar, 2016; Sharma et al., 2017; Smith et al., 2004; Parasuram, 2006) underlining that positive attitude and inclusion may be helpful with certain strategies (MacFarlane & Woolfson, 2013; Pit-ten Cate et al., 2018; Shippen et al., 2005). Apart from studies on teachers, there are also studies on attitudes of students without disabilities towards students with disabilities (Álvarez-Delgado et al., 2020; Alqarni et al., 2019; Visse, 2016), which is currently a much-probed area, considering that there is a need to bring a change in the mindset of students to make them more accepting towards inclusion. Studies have indicated that students with disabilities in regular schools face problems being accepted by other students without disabilities (Bramston et al., 2002; Kuhne & Wiener, 2000; Pijl et al., 2008). The present study complements the knowledge in the existing area by determining the attitudes of higher education students in India towards people with disabilities. As there are barely any studies in the Indian context on the attitude of students without disabilities, the current topic was designed.

Defining Disability

Disability is "not only an individual impairment but a social phenomenon" so that individuals with disabilities have difficulty in performing "daily activities" as there are obstacles in the process of interaction with self, environmental factors as well as social factors (Kasthuri et al., 2010). WHO (2011, p. 4) defines "Disability as the umbrella term for impairments, activity limitations, and participation restrictions, referring to the negative aspects of the interaction between an individual (with a health condition) and that individual's contextual factors (environmental and personal factors)." The International Classification of Functioning, Disability, and Health (ICF) described disability as "difficulties encountered in the form of alteration in body structure and function, limitations in activity and/or restriction of participation or involvement in any area of life" (WHO, 2011). Disability has been prevalent from time immemorial, and there has been discrimination against people with disabilities "ranging from minor embarrassment and inconvenience to relegation to a life of limited experience and reduced social opportunity and civil rights" (Smart, 2001, p. 72).

Attitudes towards People with Disabilities

There is a need for a change in attitudes towards people with disabilities to promote inclusion, as inclusion alone may not foster a positive attitude towards disability (Goncalves & Lemos, 2014). Studies have found that negative attitudes towards people with disabilities constitute a major hurdle to complete inclusion and equality (Fisher & Purcal, 2017; Goncalves & Lemos, 2014). Eagly and Chaiken (1993, p. 1) define attitude as "a psychological tendency that is expressed by evaluating a particular entity with some degree of favor or disfavor". Attitudes may contain cognitive, affective, and behavioral components and often influence judgments or guide social behavior. The cognitive component of attitudes refers to beliefs, thoughts, and attributes we associate with a particular object; the affective component of attitudes refers to feelings or emotions associated with an attitude object, and the behavioral component of attitudes refers to past behaviors with respect to an attitude object (Haddock & Maio, 2008). Studies have dealt with attitudes towards people with disabilities with different attitude tools that have assessed the three components of attitude, giving an insight into how different age groups think and have certain beliefs in the context of people with disabilities.

Studies on Higher Education Students' Perceptions towards Disability

Several studies in western countries have addressed the importance of a positive attitude among students for successful inclusion. Alqarni et al. (2019) conducted the study on graduate and undergraduate students of Saint Louis University in Missouri, and the findings indicated that knowledge of disabilities was positively correlated with attitudes towards inclusion though it was not statistically significant. Westling et al. (2013) investigated university students' perceptions (in West Carolina, US) toward inclusion of students and reported positive attitudes of students. Seo and Chen (2009) conducted a study on college students from a university in Midwest where a positive attitude was obtained. Visse's (2016) study on students of Eastern Kentucky University showed positive perceptions towards those with intellectual and developmental disabilities (IDD) included in the classroom. They revealed a positive belief in the aspect of inclusion. Masci (2018) conducted a study on undergraduate college students whereby a disability awareness class was provided to one group as an intervention and the other group was not given any intervention. Significant differences were not found in terms of students' attitudes; however, there was a positive attitude in the group that was a part of the awareness class compared to the group not part of the awareness class.

Students' Attitude towards People with Disabilities in European and Asian Countries

Among the studies conducted in European countries, Dibra et al. (2013) collected data on attitudes towards people with disabilities from students of the Department of Economics and Department of Educational Sciences in Albania. It was found that students expressed their belief that people with disabilities should have equal opportunities. However, they did not have a positive attitude towards integrating them into school. Falanga et al. (2011) conducted the study at the University of Catania, Sicily, and explored the changes in social attitudes towards disability as a result of exposure to contact with subjects with disabilities housed in a rehabilitation center. The experimental group showed significant changes in social attitudes toward disability, while the control group showed no significant differences.

Li et al. (2021) focused on how exclusion affects university students with disabilities in China and found positive strategies being used by most students to cope. The authors suggest a need to make students without disabilities more aware of people with disabilities so that both the abled and students with disabilities feel comfortable in each other's company. Another study on Chinese students was conducted by Malinen & Savolainen (2008) on the attitude of university students in China towards people with disabilities. The general attitude towards inclusion was not positive, though the participants expressed positive views on certain individual items in the questionnaire. The study pointed out that more favorable attitudes have been reported in western cultures compared to Eastern countries.

Alnahdi et al. (2020) conducted a study on the college students of two countries, Saudi Arabia and Egypt, examining undergraduate students' attitudes towards people with intellectual disability (PWID) in relation to their frequency of contact with people with intellectual disability, the quality of this contact, and their knowledge of intellectual disability (ID). No differences were found between participants from the two countries.

In the Indian context, the attitude of students toward disability was found in the medical field such as a study on the attitude of physiotherapists towards persons with disability (Ghagare et al., 2015), where a moderately positive attitude was found among the participants. Another study on professional courses (Hilalulla & Selvaraj, 2021) was conducted on students studying Master of Social Work, Bachelor of Education, and Bachelor of Nursing at three different educational institutions in Puducherry. Students of all three professional courses expressed a negative attitude towards people with disabilities. No significant differences were found in gender, locality, and course of study.

Previous studies generated varied results related to attitudes towards disabilities and inclusion, with a considerably positive attitude towards people with disabilities being prevalent in the studies from western countries, particularly the United States. Comparatively, European and Asian countries indicate mixed results, as in the study by Dibra et al. (2013), where students expressed a positive attitude towards people with disabilities, yet, they were not in favor of including them in regular classrooms. This indicates that apart from positive attitudes towards people with disabilities, awareness about their rights and opportunities should also be inculcated among all the students. Among the Asian studies, Malinen & Savolainen (2008) pointed out that the students had a slightly pessimistic attitude towards people with disabilities, and yet it was positive in some items. This ambiguity in attitudes was found in other studies conducted in Eastern countries (Avramidis & Norwich 2002; Wan & Huang 2005; Wei et al. 2001).

Interventions for Developing Positive Attitudes towards People with Disabilities

Intervention and training-related studies were conducted whereby the effectiveness of the training programs has been reported. Lawson et al. (2017) administered intervention to students who had no prior contact with persons with disabilities, and at the end of the community service-learning course, they had a better positive attitude than before. This indicates that a well-designed intervention can help raise awareness regarding attitudes towards disabilities. Álvarez-Delgado et al. (2021) conducted an experimental study whereby an intervention was provided for improving students' attitudes towards disability, and it proved fruitful in improving the attitudes scores. Falanga et al. (2020) provided training to university students based on virtual contact with people with disabilities. After the training, the students showed a positive attitude towards people with disabilities. Interventions were less successful in a few studies, such as by Masci (2018), who administered disability awareness classes with two groups, one having prior contact and the other not having prior contact with people with disabilities. There were insignificant results for both groups. Reasons for the non-effectiveness of intervention could be due to prior knowledge and contact with people with disabilities. Even Tast (2017) reported insignificant results between the control and experimental group after providing disability inclusion training.

Attitudes of Students towards People with Disabilities in Relation to Demographic Variables

One of the variables frequently studied is the prior contact of participants with people with disabilities. Contact with people or peers with disabilities is considered to make a person without disabilities sensitive towards people with disabilities. Studies have reported a positive impact on attitudes when there is prior contact with people with disabilities (Lawson et al. 2017; Masci, 2018; Seo & Chen 2009; Westling et al., 2013; Phillips et al., 2019). The studies explored prior contact as it makes a person understand and develop empathy for people with disabilities. However, Alnahdi et al. (2020) reported that frequency of contact and having relatives with a disability were not significant predictors of attitudes. This discrepancy in findings needs to be delved into further in different contexts.

There have been studies exploring the variables such as gender, location, and major subjects. Malinen and Savolainen (2008) studied the demographic variables and gender, education related to inclusive teaching, hometown's location, or hometown's population and none of the variables significantly affected the attitudes. However, the same study reported that behavioral science students had negative attitudes and social science students had positive attitudes towards disability. Contrary to the findings of Malinen and Savolainen (2008), it was reported by Dibra et al. (2013) that type of study program does not affect attitudes, and participants of three different major subjects showed positive attitudes in the study. Alqarni et al. (2019) found low attitude scores for both the professionals and freshmen, compared to other levels.

Gender as a variable is frequently studied in relation to attitudes towards people with disabilities. Alqarni et al. (2019), Seo and Chen (2009) claimed in their study that females showed more positive attitudes than males towards people with disabilities. Alnahdi et al. (2020) stressed that gender was a significant predictor of attitudes. However, Gonen & Grinberg (2016) and Palmer et al. (2000) found no significant results related to gender and attitudes towards people with disabilities.

Abundant research was reported from various parts of the world, and the findings from the studies are mixed and disparate. With impetus from various national and international legislation and conventions, inclusion has become the slogan worldwide in recent times. Hence, it may be assumed that there might be some attitudinal changes in the community and people towards PwD. Attitudes are one of the crucial aspects of successful inclusion in society and community, and it is essential to know the attitude of young students towards people with disabilities. Considering India has the world's second-largest education system (Cheney et al., 2005; Soni et al., 2014) and in terms of higher education it is the third-largest, next to China and United States (Sheikh, 2017), there is an increasing number of students migrating to different countries for higher studies. Indian students' mobility has increased manifold from 2000 to 2013, according to the reports of UNESCO–UIS (2015, as cited Hercog & Van de Laar, 2017). It is undoubtedly imperative for them to understand disabilities and develop a positive attitude towards people with disabilities so that their broad outlook can enable them to adjust to different societies and cultural groups. Hence, the researchers intended to explore this pertinent area to understand the current status of attitudes towards people with disabilities through one of the important groups in society, i.e., the higher education students from India.

Objectives of the Study

The study focused on the following objectives:

1) Whether there is any significant difference in attitudes of students without disabilities (SwD) towards People with Disabilities (PwD) with respect to gender.
2) Whether there is any significant difference in attitudes of students without disabilities towards People with Disabilities with respect to age.

3) Whether there is any significant difference in attitudes of SwD towards PwD with respect to students who have prior familiarity with disability and with students with no familiarity.
4) Whether there is any significant difference in attitudes of SwD towards PwD with respect to the area of residence (urban, semi-urban, and rural).
5) Whether there is any significant difference in the attitudes of SwD towards PwD with respect to income groups (high, moderate, and low).
6) Whether there is any significant difference in the attitudes of SwD towards PwD with respect to academic disciplines (Social Science, Arts, and Humanities, Natural and Life Sciences).

Methodology

Participants

The participants in this study were 105 undergraduates, and postgraduate students (24.76% males and 75.24% females) who were pooled from the various disciplines' higher education institutions (viz., three colleges and six universities) spread across three different states: West Bengal, Punjab, and Gujarat in India. In the age group 22-23 years and above were 73.33%, while 26.67% of the participants were in the age group of 19-21 years. Out of the 105 participants, 53.33% were from the Arts and Commerce background, 34.29% from the Social Science discipline, and 12.38% from the Natural and Life Science discipline. The participants were distributed between high-, moderate- and low-income groups, with 35.24% of them belonging to the high-income group, 40% of them from a moderate-income group, and 24.76% from the low-income group. Participants from a rural background accounted for 49.52%, while 36.19% were from an urban background, and 14.29% of participants belonged to a semi-urban area. While 89.52% of the participants had no familiarity with people with disabilities in the family or the extended family, 10.48% of participants had prior familiarity.

Instrumentation

The questionnaire used for assessing the attitude of students without disability (SwD) towards people with disability (PwD) was a "Brief Questionnaire for Adolescents on Attitudes towards Persons with a Disability" (CBAD-12A). It is a five-point Likert scale designed by Álvarez-Delgado et al. (2020) where 1 is "totally disagree", and 5 is "totally agree". The questionnaire has 12 items, grouped into three factors or dimensions, with four items in each factor. The first factor, "acceptance/rejection" evaluates the students' prejudices and their possible behavioral acceptance and rejection of people with disabilities. The second factor, "competence/limitation", analyzes the social constructs based on generalizations derived from incomplete information that curtails the possibilities of developing the capabilities of people with disabilities. The third factor is "equal opportunities", which evaluates the attitudes of students that may include stereotypical beliefs about certain rights that people with disabilities should or should not achieve in society. A high score in the questionnaire indicates a negative attitude towards disability.

Álvarez-Delgado et al. (2020) conducted the study with a sample of 1282 in the age group of 12-16 years. The samples were divided equally into two sub-samples, an exploratory factorial analysis and confirmatory factorial analysis (CFA) was carried out. The Cronbach Alpha calculated for the three separate factors were acceptable and the values were: F1 = acceptance/rejection (α=0.79); F2 = competence/limitation (α = 0.73); F3 equal opportunities (α = 0.70).

The CBAD-12A questionnaire was used in the Indian context as the study intended to find the attitude of students without disabilities towards people with disability, and there were hardly any validated tools for the purpose. Therefore, this tool was apt for assessing the said construct.

Analysis

The data obtained were analyzed using the Statistical Package for Social Sciences (SPSS Version 15.0). Initially, descriptive statistics such as mean and standard deviation were computed. For inferential statistics, independent samples t-tests, One-Way ANOVA, and Pearson's correlation coefficient were performed to see whether there were statistically significant differences between the total scores, factor-wise scores of the CBAD scale, and the demographic characteristics of the sample such as age, gender, academic disciplines, income level, area of residency and prior familiarity with people with disabilities.

Results and Interpretation

The findings related to the CBAD-12 A scale evaluating the attitudes of college and university students towards disability, with respect to gender, age, income level, academic disciplines, area of residency, and familiarity with people with disabilities, are presented in the following section.

Table 5.1 indicates CBAD total scores in terms of age groups, and it shows a greater mean for the age group 19 to 21 years (M = 34.57, SD = 4.92) than the age group of 22 to 23 years and above (M = 31.48, SD = 5.04). Factor-wise scores indicated a greater mean in the first factor among the 19 to 21 years age group (M = 8.79, SD = 2.85) than the 22 to 23 years age group and above (M = 6.77, SD = 2.38). The second factor indicated a greater mean among the 19 to 21 years age group (M = 13.18, SD = 2.09) than the 22 to 23 years age group and above (M = 11.51, SD = 2.95). The third-factor scores indicated a greater mean for the 22 to 23 years and above-age group (M = 13.20, SD = 2.00) than the 19 to 21 years of age group (M = 12.60, SD = 2.63).

Table 5.1 Means, standard deviations, and independent samples t-test for the CBAD survey scores with respect to age groups

Variables	Mean and SD of CBAD scale total scores and dimension-wise scores		't' values for sources of variation due to
	22–23 years and above (N = 77)	19–21 years (N = 28)	Two age groups (22–23 years and above; 19–21 years)
CBAD - Total scores	M = 31.48 SD = 5.04	M = 34.57 SD = 4.92	2.797**
CBAD - Acceptance/Rejection	M = 6.77 SD = 2.38	M = 8.79 SD = 2.85	−3.636**
CBAD - Competence/Limitations	M = 11.51 SD = 2.95	M = 13.18 SD = 2.09	−3.225**
CBAD - Equal opportunities	M = 13.20 SD = 2.00	M = 12.60 SD = 2.63	1.244

Note. **Correlation is significant at the 0.01 level (two-tailed).
*Correlation is significant at the 0.05 level (two-tailed).

Table 5.2 Means, standard deviations, and independent samples t-test comparing the male and female scores on the CBAD scale

Variables	Mean and SD of CBAD scale (total scores and dimension-wise scores)		't' values for sources of variation due to
	Male (n = 26)	Female (n = 79)	Gender (male and female)
CBAD - Total scores	M = 32.04 SD = 4.13	M = 32.39 SD = 5.49	−.302
CBAD - Acceptance/Rejection	M = 7.19 SD = 2.81	M = 7.34 SD = 2.62	−.247
CBAD - Competence/Limitations	M = 12.04 SD = 2.56	M = 11.92 SD = 2.92	.178
CBAD - Equal opportunities	M = 12.81 SD = 2.13	M = 13.13 SD = 2.22	−.641

Note. **Correlation is significant at the 0.01 level (two-tailed).
*Correlation is significant at the 0.05 level (two-tailed).

Independent samples t-test was performed to find the differences in the total scores and factor-wise scores based on two categories of age groups. Table 5.1 indicates a significant difference in the total CBAD scores between the two age categories, t (103) = 2.797, p < 0.01. Significant differences were found between the two age categories in the first factor of CBAD (acceptance/rejection), t (103) = −3.636, p < 0.01 and also in the second factor (Competence/Limitations), t (103) = −3.225, p < 0.01. The third dimension (Equal opportunities) showed no significant results.

Table 5.2 indicates the total CBAD mean scores based on gender. Mean scores were greater for females (M = 32.39, SD = 5.49) than males (M = 32.04, SD = 4.13). The factor-wise scores indicated that the female scores were greater in the first factor, 'acceptance/rejection' (M = 7.34, SD = 2.62), than the male scores (M = 7.19, SD = 2.81). In the second factor, male scores were greater (M = 12.04, SD = 2.56) than female scores (M = 11.92, SD = 2.92); and for the third factor, the female scores were greater (M = 13.13, SD = 2.22) than the male scores (M = 12.81, SD = 2.13).

Independent samples t-test was run with respect to gender (Table 5.2), and the results were insignificant for CBAD total score and factor-wise scores.

Table 5.3 indicates that the total CBAD mean scores are greater for students with no familiarity with people with disabilities (M = 32.6, SD = 5.23) than those having familiarity (M = 29.09, SD = 3.24). The first factor of CBAD indicates a greater mean score for students with no contact with people with disabilities in the family and distant family (M = 7.58, SD = 2.62) compared to those who had familiarity with people with disabilities in the family (M = 4.90, SD = 1.58). The mean score for the second factor was greater for students who had no familiarity with people with disabilities (M = 12.05, SD = 2.89) compared to those who had familiarity (M = 11.09, SD = 2.16). The mean scores for the third factor of CBAD were greater for students who were familiar with people with disability (M = 13.09, SD = 2.16) than for students who had no familiarity with people with disabilities (M = 13.04, SD = 2.21).

An independent samples t-test was conducted to find the differences in the total scores and factor-wise scores based on participants' prior familiarity with people with disabilities. Table 5.3 indicates there was a significant difference in the total CBAD scores between those who had

Table 5.3 Means, standard deviations, and independent samples t-test comparing the CBAD scores with respect to students' prior familiarity with people with disabilities

Variables	Mean and SD of CBAD scale (total scores and dimension-wise scores)		't' values for sources of variation due to
	Whether anyone is disabled in the family or extended family – Yes (n = 11)	Whether anyone is disabled in the family or extended family – No (n = 94)	Whether anyone disabled in the family or extended family
CBAD - Total scores	M = 29.09 SD = 3.24	M = 32.68 SD = 5.23	−2.220★
CBAD - Acceptance/Rejection	M = 4.90 SD = 1.58	M = 7.58 SD = 2.62	−3.303★★
CBAD - Competence/Limitations	M = 11.09 SD = 2.16	M = 12.05 SD = 2.89	−1.067
CBAD - Equal opportunities	M = 13.09 SD = 2.16	M = 13.04 SD = 2.21	.069

Note. ★★Correlation is significant at the 0.01 level (two-tailed).
★Correlation is significant at the 0.05 level (two-tailed).

prior familiarity and those who did not have familiarity with people with disabilities, t (103) = −2.220, p < 0.05. The first factor of CBAD (acceptance/rejection) showed significant differences between those who had prior familiarity and those who did not have familiarity with people with disabilities, t (103) = −3.303, p < 0.01. The second and third factors showed insignificant results.

In Table 5.4, CBAD total mean scores in relation to income level indicate that the mean is greater in the low-income group (M = 34.46, SD = 4.46), followed by the moderate-income group (M = 32.86, SD = 5.33) and high-income group (M = 30.16, SD = 4.76). The first factor of CBAD indicates that mean scores were greater for the low-income group (M = 8.27, SD = 2.73), followed by moderate (M = 7.33, SD = 2.69) and high-income group (M = 6.59, SD = 2.41). The mean scores for the second factor indicated a greater mean for the low-income group (M = 12.81, SD = 2.47), followed by the moderate-income group (M = 12.55, SD = 2.90), and the high-income group (M = 10.67, SD = 2.60). The mean scores of the third factor indicate a greater mean for the low-income group (M = 13.38, SD = 1.92) followed by the moderate-income group (M = 12.97, SD = 1.96) and the high-income group (M = 12.89, SD = 2.62).

Results of the one-way ANOVA test on CBAD total scores indicated significant differences among the three income levels, F (2, 102) = 6.257, p < 0.01, whereby independent samples t-test indicated statistically significant differences between high- and moderate-income levels, t (77) = −2.358, p < 0.05; and high- and low-income level, t (61) = −3.623, p < 0.01. One-way ANOVA results for the first factor of CBAD (acceptance/rejection) showed significant differences among the three income levels, F (2, 102) = 3.154, p < 0.05, and independent samples t-test indicated that significant differences existed in the high-low income group, t (61) = −2.568, p < 0.05. ANOVA test on the second factor of CBAD showed significant results F (2, 102) = 6.488, p < 0.01, and independent samples t-test indicated the differences were significant between high- and moderate-income groups t (77) = −3.003, p < 0.01, and also between high- and low-income group t (61) = −3.269, p < 0.01. The third factor in relation to income groups did not yield significant results.

Table 5.4 Means, standard deviations, one-way ANOVA, and independent samples t-test comparing the scores on the CBAD scale with respect to Income groups

Variables	Mean and SD of CBAD scale (total scores and dimension-wise scores)			F ratio for sources of variation for three different income group levels	't' values for sources of variation due to		
	High-income group (n = 37)	Moderate-income group (n = 42)	Low-income group (n = 26)	F ratio	High vs moderate (n = 79)	High vs low (n = 63)	Moderate vs low (n = 69)
CBAD - Total scores	M = 30.16 SD = 4.76	M = 32.86 SD = 5.33	M = 34.46 SD = 4.46	6.257**	-2.358*	-3.623**	-1.282
CBAD - Acceptance/Rejection	M = 6.59 SD = 2.41	M = 7.33 SD = 2.69	M = 8.27 SD = 2.73	3.154*	-1.278	-2.568*	-1.384
CBAD - Competence/Limitations	M = 10.67 SD = 2.60	M = 12.55 SD = 2.90	M = 12.81 SD = 2.47	6.488**	-3.003**	-3.269**	-.380
CBAD - Equal opportunities	M = 12.89 SD = 2.62	M = 12.97 SD = 1.96	M = 13.38 SD = 1.92	.417	-.163	-.816	-.842

Note. **Correlation is significant at the 0.01 level (two-tailed).
*Correlation is significant at the 0.05 level (two-tailed).

Table 5.5 indicates the mean of total CBAD scores related to the area of residency of students that were greater for rural students (M = 33.36, SD = 4.59) followed by semi-urban students (M = 31.27, SD = 5.84) and urban students (M = 31.26, SD = 5.48). The mean value of the first factor of CBAD, i.e., 'acceptance/rejection', indicated a greater mean for rural students (M = 8.02, SD = 2.87), followed by semi-urban students (M = 6.93, SD = 2.25) and urban students (M = 6.47, SD = 2.26). The second factor 'competence/limitation' indicated a greater mean for rural students (M = 12.65, SD = 2.51) followed by semi-urban students (M = 11.47, SD = 3.18) and urban students (M = 11.18, SD = 2.93). The third factor, 'equal opportunities', showed that the mean was greater for urban students (M = 13.61, SD = 2.34), followed by semi-urban (M = 12.87, SD = 2.44) and rural students (M = 12.69, SD = 1.95).

A one-way ANOVA test was conducted to find significant differences in the CBAD scores (total scores and factor-wise scores) among the three categories of residency, and the total CBAD scores indicated insignificant differences among the three categories of residency. The ANOVA scores for the first factor showed significant differences, $F(2, 102) = 4.106, p < 0.05$. Independent samples t-test showed significant differences were between the urban and rural categories, $t(88) = -2.750, p < 0.05$. A one-way ANOVA test indicated significant differences among the mean scores in the second factor of CBAD with respect to the three categories of residency, $F(2, 102) = 3.357, p < 0.05$, and independent samples t-test showed significant differences between the urban and rural category, $t(88) = -2.551, p < 0.01$, between the urban and rural categories, $t(88) = -2.040, p < 0.05$. ANOVA test showed insignificant results for the third factor of CBAD, i.e., 'equal opportunities'; however, the independent samples t-test showed significant results in the urban and rural group, $t(88) = 2.011, p < 0.05$.

The scores related to academic disciplines indicated greater CBAD scores for Arts and Humanities (M = 33.75, SD = 5.18), followed by Social Sciences (M = 30.89, SD = 4.41) and Natural and Life Science (M = 30.00, SD = 5.29). Factor-wise scores indicated that the first factor had a greater mean in Arts and Humanities discipline (M = 8.00, SD = 2.77), followed by Social Sciences (M = 6.67, SD = 2.31) and Natural and Life Science (M = 6.08, SD = 2.33). The second factor indicates a higher mean for Arts and Humanities (M = 12.57, SD = 2.62), followed by Social Science (M = 11.50, SD = 2.85) and Natural Science (M = 10.53, SD = 3.09). CBAD third-factor scores showed a greater mean for the Science discipline (M = 13.38, SD = 2.32), followed by Arts and Humanities (M = 13.17, SD = 2.39) and Social Science (M = 12.72, SD = 1.79) (Table 5.6).

A one-way ANOVA test was conducted to find the significant differences in the mean scores of CBAD (total scores and factor-wise scores) with respect to the academic disciplines of the participants. One-way ANOVA results indicated a significant difference in the total scores of CBAD among the three categories of academic disciplines, $F(2, 102) = 5.225, p < 0.01$; independent samples t-test indicated a significant difference between Social Science and Arts and Humanities categories, $t(90) = -2.719, p < 0.01$; between Arts and Humanities and Natural and Life Science categories, $t(67) = 2.341, p < 0.05$. ANOVA results for CBAD-first factor were significant, $F(2, 102) = 4.634, p < 0.05$, and independent samples t-test showed significant differences between Social Science and Arts and Humanities, $t(90) = -2.397, p < 0.05$; significant differences were also found between Arts and Humanities and Natural and Life Science, $t(67) = 2.312, p < 0.05$. For the second factor of CBAD and the three academic disciplines, one-way ANOVA test indicated significant results, $F(2, 102) = 3.584 < 0.05$, and the independent samples t-test showed significant differences in the mean scores between Arts and Humanities and Natural and Life Science categories, $t(67) = 2.430, p < 0.05$. No significant differences among the three academic disciplines were found in the third factor of CBAD scores.

Pearson's correlations were conducted to find variables correlation (Table 5.7). Income level was correlated with CBAD total score ($r = .327, p < 0.01$), CBAD-first factor ($r = .241, p < 0.05$),

Table 5.5 Means, standard deviations, one-way ANOVA, and independent samples t-test results comparing CBAD scores with respect to Area of Residency

Variables	Mean and SD of CBAD scale (total scores and dimension-wise scores)			F ratio for sources of variation for three areas of residency	't' values for sources of variation due to		
	Urban (n = 38)	Semi-urban (n = 15)	Rural (n = 52)	F ratio	Urban vs Semi-urban (n = 53)	Urban vs Rural (n = 90)	Semi-urban vs Rural (n = 67)
CBAD - Total scores	M = 31.26 SD = 5.48	M = 31.27 SD = 5.84	M = 33.36 SD = 4.59	2.220	-.002	-1.977	-1.466
CBAD - Acceptance/Rejection	M = 6.47 SD = 2.26	M = 6.93 SD = 2.25	M = 8.02 SD = 2.87	4.106★	-.667	-2.750★★	-1.347
CBAD - Competence/Limitations	M = 11.18 SD = 2.93	M = 11.47 SD = 3.18	M = 12.65 SD = 2.51	3.357★	-.308	-2.551★	-1.517
CBAD - Equal opportunities	M = 13.61 SD = 2.34	M = 12.87 SD = 2.44	M = 12.69 SD = 1.95	1.997	1.021	2.011★	.287

Note. ★★Correlation is significant at the 0.01 level (two-tailed).
★Correlation is significant at the 0.05 level (two-tailed).

Table 5.6 Means, standard deviations, one-way ANOVA, and independent samples t-test results comparing the scores on the CBAD scale with respect to academic disciplines

Variables	Mean and SD of CBAD scale (total scores and dimension-wise scores)			F values for sources of variation for three different Academic Disciplines	't' values for sources of variation due to		
	Social Science (n = 36)	Arts and Humanities (n = 56)	Natural and Life Sciences (n = 13)	F ratio	Social Science vs. Arts and Humanities (n = 92)	Social Science vs. Natural and Life Sciences (n = 49)	Arts and Humanities vs. Natural and Life Sciences (n = 69)
CBAD - Total scores	M = 30.89 SD = 4.41	M = 33.75 SD = 5.18	M = 30.00 SD = 5.29	5.225**	−2.719**	.584	2.341*
CBAD - Acceptance/ Rejection	M = 6.67 SD = 2.31	M = 8.00 SD = 2.77	M = 6.08 SD = 2.33	4.634*	−2.397*	.789	2.312*
CBAD - Competence/ Limitations	M = 11.50 SD = 2.85	M = 12.57 SD = 2.62	M = 10.53 SD = 3.09	3.584*	−1.846	1.018	2.430*
CBAD - Equal opportunities	M = 12.72 SD = 1.79	M = 13.17 SD = 2.39	M = 13.38 SD = 2.32	.644	−.978	−1.051	−.281

Note. **Correlation is significant at the 0.01 level (two-tailed).
*Correlation is significant at the 0.05 level (two-tailed).

Table 5.7 Correlation Matrix of the CBAD scale (total scores and dimension-wise scores) and demographic factors (income, socio-economic status, mother's qualifications, father's qualifications, mother's occupation, father's occupation)

Variables	CBAD-first factor	CBAD-second factor	CBAD-third factor	CBAD total	Income	SES total	Mother's qualifications	Father's qualifications	Mother's occupation	Father's occupation
CBAD-first factor	1.00									
CBAD-second factor	.446**	1.00								
CBAD-third factor	-.090	.090	1.00							
CBAD total	.721**	.816**	.428**	1.00						
Income	.241*	.306**	.083	.327**	1.00					
SES total	-.285**	-.234*	-.034	-.289**	-.690**	1.00				
Mother's qualifications	-.263**	-.287**	-.001	-.293**	-.429**	.722**	1.00			
Father's qualifications	-.248*	-.220*	-.037	-.264**	-.425**	.770**	.655(**)	1.00		
Mother's occupation	-.055	-.009	-.111	-.080	-.232*	.614**	.351**	.358**	1.00	
Father's occupation	-.197*	-.078	.070	-.114	-.438**	.741**	.301**	.449**	.239*	1.00

Note. **Correlation is significant at the 0.01 level (2-tailed).
* Correlation is significant at the 0.05 level (2-tailed).

CBAD-Second factor (r = .306, p < 0.01). Socio-economic status total score showed a negative correlation with CBAD total score (r = −.289, p < 0.01), CBAD-first factor (r = −.285, p < 0.01), CBAD-Second factor (r = −.234, p < 0.05). There was a negative correlation between mother's qualification and CBAD total score (r = −.293, p < 0.01), mother's qualifications, CBAD-first factor (r = −.263, p < 0.01), mother's qualifications, and CBAD-Second factor (r = −.287, p < 0.01). There was a significant negative correlation between the father's educational qualifications and CBAD total score (r = −.264, p < 0.01), father's qualifications and CBAD-first factor (r = −.248, p < 0.05), father's qualifications and CBAD-Second factor (r = −.220, p < 0.05), There were no significant correlations between mother's occupation and CBAD scores total and factor-wise scores. Significant correlations were found between the father's occupation and CBAD scores of the first factor (r = −.197, p < 0.05), but factor-wise scores indicated insignificant correlations.

Discussion

The findings of the study indicated mixed results for CBAD total scores and factor-wise scores with respect to demographic details. A high score in CBAD indicates negative attitudes of students towards people with disabilities, and the results have been interpreted accordingly.

Age, Familiarity, and Gender-related Results

Findler et al. (2007) emphasized that students displayed more positive attitudes towards people with disabilities with an increase in age. However, all studies do not support this idea, and there is a difference of views in this regard. For instance, Barr and Bracchitta (2012) found that students of 18 years and above were flexible, and their misconceptions could be removed, compared to students in the age group of 22 years and above. In the present study, the statistical analysis indicated that students in the 19 to 21 years age group had higher CBAD scores than 22 to 23 years and above students. Factor-wise scores indicated significant differences in the first and second factors, while the third factor showed insignificant results. This indicates that 19 to 21 years students had more negative attitudes towards people with disabilities compared to the 22 to 23 years and above-age group. The first factor deals with statements about the acceptance or rejection of people with disabilities in their lives, indicating more rejection and less acceptance in their attitude. The statements were related to being "uncomfortable" with people with disabilities, "not going out" with people with disabilities, and not knowing "how to treat" them. The negative attitude in these statements indicates their least interaction and familiarity with people with disabilities. The second factor in CBAD has statements related to the limitation in the life of people with disabilities. High scores were obtained by students in the age group of 19 to 21 years, which again indicates the lack of knowledge and empathy for people with disabilities. The third factor related to "beliefs" showed no significant results. As Goncalves and Lemos (2014) pointed out in their study, older students showed better results in terms of cognitive attitude (beliefs) towards people with disabilities than effective factors. In the current study, the second factor of CBAD is related to beliefs that students have about people with disabilities whereas the older students indicated a better attitude towards people with disabilities. This could be due to their prior contact or knowledge gained by them on disabilities formally or informally.

Connected with the age group is the impact of *familiarity with the people with disabilities* in the family or extended family. Allport (1954) noted that contact between social groups might decrease prejudice, and therefore, the factor of prior familiarity was taken up as a variable in this study. Studies pointed out that prior contact with people with disabilities led to a positive attitude among students towards people with disabilities (Meyers & Lester, 2016; Seo & Chen, 2009). Even Gonen and Grinberg (2016) stressed that those who had a friend with a disability showed more positive attitudes than those who had none, and the same results resonated in the study by Tast (2017) on college students. In the present study, around 94 students had no familiarity with people with disabilities, and their CBAD total scores and first-factor scores were greater, which indicates that no contact with a person with a disability may influence the attitude of students towards disability.

Gender differences related to attitudes towards disability have been reported in previous studies where females were found to have a positive attitude towards people with disabilities (Barr & Bracchitta, 2012; Seo & Chen, 2009; Alqarni et al., 2019). Contrarily Girli et al. (2016) found males to have positive attitudes. Some studies did not find any gender-related differences in the attitude towards people with disabilities (Gonen & Grinberg, 2016; Palmer et al., 2000). The present study, too, did not find any significant gender differences on the CBAD scale. The reason for insignificant results related to gender could be that most of the students, both male and female, had minimal prior contact with people with disabilities.

Income Level, Socio-economic Status, and Area of Residency

The present study investigated whether a family's income and socio-economic status are responsible for positive or negative attitudes towards people with disabilities. Statistical results were significant for the total CBAD scores among the three income groups (high, moderate, and low) and the first and second factors of CBAD. Higher scores were found in the moderate and low-income groups for total scores and the second CBAD factor. The first factor had greater scores in the low-income group. An increase in low and moderate income was found to be correlated with an increased negative attitude towards people with disabilities.

Pearson correlation coefficient indicates a significant negative correlation between the socio-economic scores of the participants and their total scores on CBAD, and also with the first and second factors' scores. So, with an increase in socio-economic status, attitudes scores may decrease, signifying better attitudes towards people with disabilities. This study thus indicates that income and socio-economic status may impact the attitudes that students develop towards people with disabilities. Lack of education and knowledge on disability among the moderate- and low-income groups may hinder the nurturing of a positive attitude towards people with disabilities. Khan and Khan (2017), in their study on the undergraduates' and illiterates' attitudes towards disability, found that students had a better attitude towards disability, indicating that education plays a role in developing positive attitudes.

In India, the opportunity for inclusive education and education, in general, is not available for all students. Therefore, the area where the students reside plays an essential role in defining their attitudes. Zama et al. (2013) conducted a study in Karnataka, India, and found that attitudes towards people with disabilities were better in urban areas than in rural areas. In this study, students were from urban, semi-urban, and rural areas, and when it was studied with respect to the CBAD scores, insignificant results were found with total CBAD scores and the area of residency. However, significant scores were found in the first and second factors of CBAD, where the scores were higher for students belonging to rural areas, indicating that students from rural areas harbored a negative attitude towards people with disabilities. This attitude may be entrenched in deep-rooted prejudices and beliefs about people with disabilities in rural areas, which is an obstacle to developing positive attitudes toward people with disabilities.

Pearson's correlation coefficient indicates that parents' qualifications were negatively correlated with the students' attitudes score (total score, first- and second-factor scores on the CBAD scale). This indicates that higher qualifications of the parents lead to lower scores and, therefore, a positive attitude towards people with disabilities. However, parents' occupation was not significantly correlated to the CBAD scores.

Academic Disciplines

Some studies focused on whether the academic backgrounds of students play a role in their attitudes towards disability. Gonen and Grinber (2016) compared attitudes towards disability between students belonging to behavioral, nursing, and industrial departments. It was expected that nursing students belonging to science backgrounds would project better results than industrial department students. However, students of the three departments had positive attitudes towards disability. The results of the present study are similar to the results of Malinen and Savolainen (2008), whose study showed that behavioral science students had a negative attitude and social science students had positive attitudes. The present study found Arts and Humanities students had higher scores, followed by Social Science and Natural and Life Science. Total CBAD scores and scores of CBAD-first and second factors showed significant results, and among the three disciplines, it was Arts and Humanities that showed higher scores implying that the students of Arts background had negative attitudes towards people with disabilities, while the lowest scores of Natural and Life Science indicated that Science students comparatively had positive attitudes towards people with disabilities. However, the results related to academic disciplines in this study are in contradiction with some studies such as Dibra et al. (2013) who posited that study programs do not affect attitudes towards people with disabilities. Even Hilalulla and Selvaraj (2021) reported that students in their study belonging to three different disciplines – Master of Social Work, Bachelor of Education, and Bachelor of Nursing – expressed a negative attitude towards people with disability.

Implications of the Study

The current study sheds light on the negative attitude that higher education students have towards people with disabilities and the prevalence of misconceptions about disability. It is a clarion call for the teachers in higher education institutes to sensitize and educate the students regarding the emotional and social needs of people with disabilities. The results of the present study indicate that certain variables such as the educational qualifications of the parents and socio-economic level have a significant role in molding students' perceptions of people with disabilities. Therefore, adequate steps are required to acquaint the parents with knowledge about disabilities. Teachers, with the help of institutes, can take the initiative to organize interventions, activities, and programs for students, parents, and caregivers from time to time to develop positive attitudes in them and enable them to focus on the potential of the people with disabilities rather than focusing on their weaknesses. Teachers should be trained in inclusive education strategies, and they should be encouraged to promulgate inclusive education with full vigor in classrooms by including students with disabilities and setting an example with nondiscriminatory behavior. Further research on knowledge, perceptions, and attitudes of higher education students towards peers and people with disabilities will help the stakeholders in preparing a roadmap for attaining inclusion in Indian society.

References

Alnahdi, G. H., Elhadi, A., & Schwab, S. (2020). The positive impact of knowledge and quality of contact on university students' attitudes towards people with intellectual disabilities in the Arab world. *Research in Developmental Disabilities*, *106*, 103765

Allport, G.W. (1954). The historical background of modem social psychology. In G. Lindzey (Ed.), *Handbook of social psychology* (p. 45). Cambridge, MA: Addison-Wesley.

Alqarni, T., Algethami, R., Alsolmi, A., & Adhabi, E. (2019). College students' knowledge and attitudes toward the inclusion of persons with disabilities in the university. *Education*, *9*(1), 9–18.

Álvarez-Delgado, J., León-del-Barco, B., Polo-del-Río, M. I., & Mendo-Lázaro, S. (2020). Questionnaire for adolescents to evaluate their attitudes towards disability. *Sustainability, 12*(21), 9007.

Álvarez-Delgado, J., León-del-Barco, B., Polo-del-Río, M. I., López-Ramos, V. M., & Mendo-Lázaro, S. (2021). Improving adolescents' attitudes towards persons with disabilities: An intervention study in secondary education. *Sustainability, 13*(8), 4545.

Avramidis, E., & Norwich, B. (2002). Teachers' attitudes towards integration/inclusion: A review of the literature. *European Journal of Special Education, 17*, 129–147.

Barr, J. J., & Bracchitta, K. (2012). Attitudes toward individuals with disabilities: The effects of age, gender, and relationship. *Journal of Relationships Research, 3*, 10.

Bates, H., McCafferty, A, Quayle, E., McKenzie, K. (2015). typically-developing students' views and experiences of inclusive education. *Disability & Rehabilitation, 37*(21), 1–11.

Bramston, P., Bruggerman, K., & Pretty, G. (2002). Community perspectives and subjective quality of life. *International Journal of Disability, Development & Education, 49*, 385–397.

Cheney, G. R., Ruzzi, B. B., & Muralidharan, K. (2005). *India education profile*. New Commission on the Skills of the American Workforce. Washington, DC: National Center on Education and the Economy (NCEE). http://www.ncee.org/wp-content/uploads/2010/04/India-Education-Report.pdf.

Dibra, G., Osmanaga, F., & Bushati, J. (2013). Students' attitudes toward disability. *European Scientific Journal, 9*(31), 214–224.

Dupoux, E., Hammond, H., Ingalls, L., & Wolman, C. (2006). Teachers' attitudes toward students with disabilities in Haiti. *International Journal of Special Education, 21*(3), 1–14.

Eagly, A. H., & Chaiken, S. (1993). *The psychology of attitudes*. Fort Worth, TX: Harcourt Brace Jovanovich College Publishers.

Falanga, R., de Caroli, M. E., & Sagone, M. E. (2011). Attitudes towards disability: The experience of "contact" in a sample of Italian college students. *International Journal of Developmental and Educational Psychology: INFAD. Revista de Psicología, 4*(1), 91–100.

Falanga, R., De Caroli, M. E., & Sagone, E. (2020). Is it possible to enhance positive attitudes towards people with disability? A training with Italian university students. *New Trends and Issues Proceedings on Humanities and Social Sciences, 7*(3), 27–33.

Findler, L., Vilchinsky, N., & Werner, S. (2007). The multidimensional attitudes scale toward persons with disabilities (MAS). *Rehabilitation Counseling Bulletin, 50*, 166–176.

Fisher, K. R., & Purcal, C. (2017). Policies to change attitudes to people with disabilities. *Scandinavian Journal of Disability Research, 19*(2), 161–174.

Ghagare, J., Oswal, A., Dabadghav, R., Bedekar, N., & Shyam, A. (2015). Attitude of physiotherapy students towards disabled persons. *International Journal of Current Research and Review, 7*(9), 71–77.

Girli, A., Sarı, H.Y., Kırkım, G., & Narin, S. (2016). University students' attitudes towards disability and their views on discrimination. *International Journal of Developmental Disabilities, 62*(2), 98–107.

Gonçalves, T., & Lemos, M. (2014). Personal and social factors influencing students' attitudes towards peers with special needs. *Procedia-Social and Behavioral Sciences, 112*, 949–955.

Gonen, A., & Grinberg, K. (2016). Academic students' attitudes toward students with learning disabilities. *Journal of Education and Training Studies, 4*(9), 240–246.

Haddock, G., & Maio, G. R. (2008). Attitudes: Content, structure and functions. Hewstone, M., Stroebe, W., & Jonas, K. (Eds.), *Introduction to social psychology: A European perspective* (pp. 112–133). London: Blackwell

Hammond, H., & Ingalls, L. (2003). Teachers' attitudes toward inclusion: Survey results from elementary school teachers in three southwestern rural school districts. *Rural Special Education Quarterly, 22*(2), 24–30.

Hercog, M., & Van de Laar, M. (2017). Motivations and constraints of moving abroad for Indian students. *Journal of International Migration and Integration, 18*(3), 749–770.

Hilalulla, K. B., & Selvaraj, P. (2021). Attitude of student professionals towards persons with disabilities. *International Journal of Social Sciences and Management, 8*(1), 306–311.

Kasthuri, P., Chandrashekar, H., Kumar, C. N., & Prashanth, N. R. (2010). Disabilities research in India. *Indian Journal of Psychiatry, 52*(7), 281.

Khan, M. A., & Khan, F. S. (2017). Evaluating the difference in attitude between students and illiterates towards disabled people. *Journal Psychology Cognition, 2*(4). 209–213

Kuhne, M., & Wiener, J. (2000). Stability of social status of children with and without learning disabilities. *Learning Disability Quarterly, 23*, 64–75.

Kumar, A. (2016). Exploring the teachers' attitudes towards inclusive education system: A study of indian teachers. *Journal of Education and Practice, 7*(34), 1–4.

Lawson, J. E., Cruz, R. A., & Knollman, G. A. (2017). Increasing positive attitudes toward individuals with disabilities through community service learning. *Research in Developmental Disabilities, 69*, 1–7.

Li, H., Lin, J., Wu, H., Li, Z., & Han, M. (2021). "How do I survive exclusion?" Voices of students with disabilities at China's top universities. *Children and Youth Services Review, 120*, 105738.

MacFarlane, K., & Woolfson, L. M. (2013). Teacher attitudes and behavior toward the inclusion of children with social, emotional and behavioral difficulties in mainstream schools: An application of the theory of planned behavior. *Teaching and Teacher Education, 29*, 46–52.

Malinen, O. P., & Savolainen, H. (2008). Inclusion in the East: Chinese students' attitudes towards inclusive education. *International Journal of Special Education, 23*(3), 101–109.

Masci, C. A. (2018). Changing attitudes: The impact of a disability awareness class. *Honors Theses and Capstones* University of New Hampshire, Scholars repository https://scholars.unh.edu/honors/382/.

McFarland, J., Hussar, B., Wang, X., Zhang, J., Wang, K., Rathbun, A., Barmer, A., Forrest Cataldi, E., & Bullock Mann, F. (2018). *The condition of education (NCES 2018–144).* Washington: U.S. Department of Education.

Meyers, S., & Lester, D. (2016). An attempt to change college students' attitudes toward individuals with disabilities. *Comprehensive Psychology, 5*, 2165222816648076.

Nowicki, E. A., & Sandieson, R. (2002). A meta-analysis of school-age children's attitudes towards persons with physical or intellectual disabilities. *International Journal of Disability, Development and Education, 49*(3):243–265.

Palmer, G. A., Redinius, P. L., & Tervo, R. C. (2000). An examination of attitudes toward disabilities among college students: Rural and urban differences. *Journal of Rural Community Psychology, E3*(1), 1–9.

Parasuram, K. (2006). Variables that affect teachers' attitudes towards disability and inclusive education in Mumbai, India. *Disability and Society, 21*, 231–242.

Phillips, A. B. P., Fortney, S., & Swafford, L. (2019). College students' social perceptions towards individuals with intellectual disability. *Journal of Disability Policy Studies, 30*(1), 3–10.

Pingle, S., & Garg, I. (2015). Effect of inclusive education awareness programme on preservice teachers. (Paper presentation) *European Conference on Education.* Brighton, United Kingdom.

Pit-ten Cate, I. M., Markova, M., Krischler, M., & Krolak-Schwerdt, S. (2018). Promoting inclusive education: The role of teachers' competence and attitudes. *Insights into Learning Disabilities, 15*(1), 49–63.

Pijl, S. J., & Frostad, P. (2010). Peer acceptance and self-concept of students with disabilities in regular education. *European Journal of Special Needs Education, 25*, 93–105.

Pijl, S. J., Frostad, P., & Flem, A. (2008). The social position of pupils with special needs in regular schools. *Scandinavian Journal of Educational Research, 52*, 387–405.

Salamanca World Conference on Special Needs Education 1994. (1994). World Conference on Special Needs Education: Access and Quality, Salamanca, Spain, 7–10 June 1994. UNESCO.

Seo, W., & Chen, R. K. (2009). Attitudes of college students toward people with disabilities. *Journal of Applied Rehabilitation Counseling, 40*(4), 3.

Sharma, A., Chunawala, S., & Chari, D. (2017). Exploring teachers' attitudes towards inclusive education in indian context using 'type of disability' Lens Homi Bhabha Centre for Science Education. *TIFR, India, 6*(2), 1134–1143.

Sheikh, Y. A. (2017). Higher education in India: Challenges and opportunities. *Journal of Education and Practice, 8*(1), 39–42.

Shippen, M. E., Crites, S. A., Houchins, D. E., Ramsey, M. L., & Simon, M. (2005). Preservice teachers' perceptions of including students with disabilities. *Teacher Education and Special Education, 28*, 92–99.

Singh, S., Sawani, V., Deokate, M., Panchal, S., Subramanyam, A. A., Shah, H. R., & Kamath, R. M. (2017). Specific learning disability: A 5year study from India. *International Journal of Contemporary Pediatrics, 4*(3), 863–868.

Singh, J. D. (2016). Inclusive education in India–concept, need and challenges. *Scholarly Research Journal for Humanity Science and English Language, 3*(13), 3222–3232.

Smart, J. F. (2001). *Disability, society, and the individual.* Austin: Pro-Ed.

Smith, T. E., Polloway, E., Patton, J. R., & Dowdy, C. A. (2004). *Teaching students with special needs in inclusive settings* (4th ed.). New Jersey: Pearson-Merrill Prentice Hall.

Soni, S., Chourasia, D. B., & Soni, A. (2014). To study effect of various parameters for quality improvement in technical education. *International Journal of Engineering Research and Applications, 4*(8), 61–69.

Tast, M. A. (2017). Exploring first-year college students' attitudes toward disability: Impacts of disability inclusion training. *Culminating Projects in Community Psychology, Counseling and Family Therapy, 35.* https://repository.stcloudstate.edu/cpcf_etds/35

UNESCO. (2020). *Global Education Monitoring Report 2020: Inclusion and Education–All Means All.*

UNESCO–UIS. (2015). *Education: Outbound internationally mobile students by host region.* UNESCO Institute for Statistics Database. http://data.uis.unesco.org/.

United Nations Educational Scientific and Cultural Organization. (2000). The Dakar framework for action, education for all: Meeting our collective commitments. In World Education Forum, Dakar, Senegal, 26–28 April, 2000. Paris: UNESCO.

Visse, M. (2016). Students perceptions of individuals with intellectual and developmental disabilities and the impact of inclusion. *Honors Theses, 347.* https://encompass.eku.edu/ honors_theses/347.

Wan, L., & Huang, Y. (2005). Benke shifansheng dui suiban jiudu taidu de diaocha [An investigation into undergraduate normal students' attitudes towards children with special needs in regular class]. *Zhongguo Teshu Jiaoyu [Chinese Journal of Special Education], 55,* 28–31.

Wei, X., Yuan, W., & Liu, Q. (2001). Beijing Xianggang liang di puxiao jiaoshi dui you teshu jiaoyu xuyao xuesheng suiban jiudu taidu de bijiao yanjiu [A comparative study on teachers' attitudes towards school pupils with special needs]. *Beijing shifandaxue xuebao [Beijing Normal University Academic Journal], 163,* 34–39.

World Report on Disability. (2011). *The way forward: Recommendations.* Geneva: World Health Organization. Chp 9. Available from: https://www.ncbi.nlm.nih.gov/books/NBK304067/

Westling, D. L., Kelley, K. R., Cain, B., & Prohn, S. (2013). College students' attitudes about an inclusive postsecondary education program for individuals with intellectual disability. *Education and Training in Autism and Developmental Disabilities, 48*(3), 306–319.

Zama, S. Y., Ashok, N. C., & Kulkarni, P. (2013). Understanding the needs of persons with disabilities in rural and urban Mysore: A step towards exploring the unreached. *International Journal of Health & Allied Sciences, 2*(2), 133. *Applied Rehabilitation Counseling, 40*(4), 3.

6
TRANSLATING STATUTORY GUIDANCE INTO INCLUSIVE PRACTICE IN THE CLASSROOM
The Case of England

Susana Castro-Kemp*

Introduction

Much has been written on conceptualisations, models of, and approaches to disability in education (e.g. Florian & McLaughlin, 2008; Brett, 2002; Bricout et al., 2004). Despite this wide availability of relevant scientific literature, countries still differ in relation to how they assess and intervene with children with special educational needs and disabilities, as well as on how they officially document children's needs and strengths. These differences are often explained by discrepancies between models of disabilities adopted at policy level and the practicalities of implementing those policies with limited budgets, limited human resources and often restricted skill sets.

In England, the Children and Families Act 2014 (CFA) implemented what has been designated as the most radical change in the Special Educational Needs and Disabilities (SEND) system of this country for decades (Norwich, 2014). This policy change is significant because it aimed to translate into educational practice a new approach to disability that is more aligned with international models of functioning and participation than with traditional medical approaches based on diagnoses. In fact, the term *participation* has been included in the CFA as a desirable outcome for children with disabilities. Special Educational Needs and Disabilities have been described as present whenever a child has a 'learning difficulty or disability that calls for special educational provision to be made for him or her' (Department of Health and Department for Education, 2014). This broad definition sits within an approach to disability provision based on children's functioning, rather than on the presence of an established diagnosis. However, in practice, this legislation has been highly controversial. Several lines of critique have been put forward, both in the scientific community but also in a myriad of social media and professional practice platforms, mentioning inconsistencies between the definition of SEND and the eligibility model in practice, the lack of human and financial resources and of adequate skill sets to fully implement the policy principles in schools.

Adequately translating policy into effective high-quality inclusive practice in the classroom is a fundamental aspect of effective provision for special educational needs and disabilities. Policies

---

* s.castro-kemp@ucl.ac.uk

should guide practice for services and professionals, particularly teachers, informed by the latest available scientific knowledge and evidence-based practices. Professional Codes of practice for teachers working in SEND provision should provide clear and feasible guidance on how to support children in a variety of situations. Similarly, and of widely recognised importance, statutory documents that officially define the needs of children and the provision to be actioned in the classroom and other settings to target those needs, should be workable, understandable by all members of the SEND provision team (including parents) and be a clear representation of an individual child's functioning and participation in their everyday lives. In England, both the SEND Code of Practice 2014 and the statutory documents implemented through the Children and Families Act 2014 – the Education Health and Care plans – have been the object of wide criticism for the lack of transparency and evidence-base for a meaningful translation into effective classroom provision (e.g. Robinson et al., 2018; Castro & Palikara, 2016). A considerable body of research has been developed since, highlighting evidence-based principles for the design of effective statutory documents for children. This is useful not only for the English context but for all settings where a functioning-based approach to disability is set as the gold standard for inclusive practice.

This chapter aims to provide evidence-based guidance on what constitutes good practice in translating official statutory documents into high-quality provision in the classroom. First, the chapter will provide an account of contemporary models of disability based on functioning and participation. Second, the chapter will deliver an overview of the evidence available in the scientific literature in relation to the implementation of the new SEND policy in England, including regarding the quality of the Education Health and Care plans (the official statutory documents in this country) and the extent to which they align with a contemporary understanding of disability based on functioning and participation; last, the chapter will use the English situation as the setting scene for delivering insights on how to develop high-quality official statutory documents that translate into effective inclusive practice in the classroom, to target children's positive functioning and participation.

Contemporary Models of Disability Based on Functioning and Participation

The last three decades of the twentieth century have seen two major changes in conceiving disability, reflecting substantial transformation in the social tissue of our communities at that period of time. The first major change happened as a consequence of the human rights movement which was particularly prominent in the western world, with enhanced visibility in England. The ratification of the United Nations Conventions on the Rights of Children (United Nations, 1989) and on the Rights of Persons with Disabilities (2006) clearly reflect the extent to which these movements were conducive to changes in how we perceive, understand and live with disabilities. The traditional medicalised approach to disability by which the source of the disability is in the *body* became no longer acceptable on its own, without a full understanding that *society* is responsible for accommodating individual variability. The new *social* model of disability was an invaluable stepping stone in the process of changing how we understand and live with a disability in a collectively responsible and socially just manner (Oliver, 2013). In the 1990s, a group of studies focusing on disability from the point of view of *holistic functioning* emerged. From this point of view, disability is not conceived as sourced in the *body* only or in *society*'s adaptations per se; disability is explained by specific configurations of the dynamic and continuous interaction between body and environment, illustrated by how the individual *functions* as a whole (Simeonsson, 2006). For instance, Bailey et al. (1995) studied reliability of team consensus when rating children's *functioning* using the *Abilities Index* (Simeonsson & Bailey, 1991), a general functioning-based assessment instrument, encompassing the domains of audition, social/behavioural skills, intellectual functioning, limbs, intentional communication, tonicity, integrity of eyes, health and structural status; it aimed to overcome the problems of inappropriate categorisation of children in special educational practice and research, by focusing on the severity of functioning, rather than on diagnosis. Functional assessment by teachers has also become more popular, as research shows substantial intra- and inter-variability of functioning profiles within the classroom against the traditional special needs categories (Simeonsson et al., 1995).

This trend has largely led to a movement aiming to expand the traditional classification systems of disability to include a functioning-based taxonomy. In 2001, the World Health Organisation (WHO) published and endorsed the International Classification of Functioning, Disability and Health (ICF) as the gold standard framework and system to classify disability from a *functioning* point of view. According to this framework, within a specific health status (which might be diagnosable or not) an individual (or a child) will have a specific combination of *body functions* and *structures*, *activities* they perform, and forms of *participation* they exhibit, all within the context of *environmental factors* that may act as facilitators or barriers. Today, the body of research around the ICF and its applications, as well as the research around functioning as the ultimate outcome of provision for children with SEND, is vast and well-regarded. Countries have adopted a functioning approach to their special educational needs policy, some using the ICF, some without mentioning the ICF. For example, Portugal has adopted the ICF system and framework extensively to support the documentation of the assessment-intervention process for young children with disabilities, with successful outcomes in terms of stakeholder satisfaction (Sanches-Ferreira et al., 2015). Statutory documents in this country included the ICF as a classification system to support both eligibility and provision of support services. Japan has also included the ICF in Health, Education and Social Care settings, becoming perhaps the best example of coordinated multi-agency working using the ICF (Okawa & Ueda, 2008). Other countries, such as England, adopted a policy discourse which is clear in that *participation* must be the ultimate goal of statutory provision for children with SEND, without adopting the ICF as a supporting taxonomy by law (Castro & Palikara, 2016; Nrowich, 2014). Nevertheless, there is a wide consensus that assessment and intervention with children (particularly in younger ages) that present with special educational needs and or disabilities should be holistic, integrated, involve various disciplines in a concerted manner, and focus on functioning in everyday life.

This chapter follows this functional approach in conceiving disability by arguing that statutory policies could and should translate into effective assessment-intervention procedures that are holistic and based on *functioning*. From this point of view, special educational needs and disabilities exist when there is a significant restriction to participation in everyday life situations, regardless of whether the source of that restriction is within the individual, the environment or, most likely, the complex interaction between both. The situation of the English policy for special educational needs and disabilities provision will be used as setting the scene to illustrate how a policy based on participation outcomes should translate into functioning-based assessment and intervention.

An Overview of the Available Evidence on the Implementation of the Children and Families Act 2014 in England

In England, the introduction of the Children and Families Act in 2014 came to replace the *statements of special educational needs* and disabilities with Education, Health and Care plans. These plans are the official statutory documents specifying the needs of the children and family and the supports that need to be put in place to target those needs. The predecessors of the Education Health and Care plans – the *statements of special educational needs* – were based on the assumption that children who were eligible for the support services have a diagnosable condition. This is one of the major differences that the Children and Families Act 2014 introduced – the new statutory plans do not require that a specific diagnostic category is described. They are supposed to be holistic documents developed by a team of professionals from a variety of disciplines, as needed for each child, and should focus on detailing the holistic needs of that child and the measures to promote his or her participation in everyday life.

When introduced, this legislation was promising for its alignment with international trends in conceiving disability: away from a purely medical approach, towards a multi-dimensional and inter-professional model that enables a new holistic form of assessment and intervention, favouring functioning and full participation. In practice, however, a gap between ideology and professional practice has been described (Castro & Palikara, 2016). Critiques of the implementation of this policy involved both the process of assessment-intervention itself, as well as the design of the Education Health and Care plans and its translation into inclusive practice.

From the point of view of the professionals involved in provision of children with special educational needs and disabilities, the new legislation fell short of true change. In a study by Palikara et al. (2019) with more than 300 English professionals working with children with SEND (the majority of which being teachers), disappointment with how the policy had translated into practice was unanimous. Professionals mentioned that the new Education Health and Care plans were not workable but mere policy documents without true usefulness for educational practice; additionally, they mentioned that true multi-agency work was still not a reality, despite the change of format of the official statutory documents, requiring the collaboration of various professionals. They reported that, in practice, the Education Health and Care plans were education-only plans. This is consistent with Boesley and Crane's (2018) qualitative study with a number of Special Educational Needs Coordinators (SENCOs) working in schools with children with disabilities, where participants claim multi-agency work was simply not happening, despite the introduction of the new model. Similarly, Sales and Vincent (2018) found that interpretations of the new legislation in professional practice were not always consistent and, consequently, its principles were not being fully met in educational settings. However, from the point of view of parents, the authors reported greater parental involvement and a more person-centred approach. This is consistent with the study by Adams et al. (2017), in which two-thirds of parents reported being satisfied with the Education Health and Care planning process, and the majority agreed that their views and wishes were included in the document. However, in most cases parents reported the process (of assessment and documentation of needs and provision in the official plan) was lengthier than the timeline specified in the legislation (20 weeks). In sum, although the new policy seems to have translated into better practice for parents, professionals felt disenfranchised, without clear guidance on how to implement the theoretical guidance into the day-to-day practice of their classrooms.

A few studies have objectively assessed the content of more than 200 Education Health and Care plans and the extent to which they match the principles regulated by the Children and Families Act 2014. It has been found that despite recommendation to do so in the new legislation, the views of the children with special educational needs and disabilities were still not being fully accounted for in the design of the plans. Although the documents included a section for the views of the child, and although the Code of Practice 2014 clearly recommends that professionals describe how the view of the child was accessed, most of the times the children's voices were hypothesised, not fully accessed (Palikara et al., 2009); this has, of course, ethical implications and reflects poor inclusive practice. Additionally, it has been found that there were regional discrepancies in relation to the level of detail in describing children's needs, with most affluent areas reporting needs more accurately than more deprived areas (Castro-Kemp et al., 2019). A similar discrepancy was found between settings, with special education (segregated) settings often describing needs in more detail than mainstream. The outcomes (goals) included in these plans were assessed following procedures similar to those adopted in other countries with their equivalent statutory documents (e.g. Rakap, 2015; Boavida et al., 2010). Here, it was found that the vast majority of plans included outcomes for children that were vague, not achievable or workable and did not meet the SMART criteria (specific, measurable, attainable, realistic and time framed) that the Code of Practice 2014 instructed as ideal (Castro et al., 2019).

At this point the reader might be questioning whether statutory documents are really needed, if they often do not comply with matching legislation, and are not workable nor useful. The next section of this chapter will illuminate reasons and ways by which statutory documents can be not only useful but also necessary for good inclusive practice in the classroom. Additionally, an approach to developing high-quality statutory documents that can be workable in educational settings will be presented.

Insights for High-quality Statutory Documents that Translate into Effective Inclusive Practice in Educational Settings

Statutory documents are fundamental tools for the assessment-intervention process. On a macro-level of development and learning, the statutory documents reflect the model of disability currently adopted in that society and the prevailing classification system for disability, thus echoing ways of thinking about and living with special educational needs. On a micro-level of development and learning, they translate the policy around provision for special educational needs and disabilities into workable practice; they describe the needs of the individual child and stipulate the services and strategies to be provided and the outcomes that should be targeted for learning and development. When of high enough quality to do so, the statutory documents empower professionals as they provide guidance for routine work with children with special educational needs and disabilities in their everyday life settings, such as the classroom.

In England, until 2014, the statutory documents were based on diagnostic categories for eligibility, reflecting a traditional, medicalised view. The objective of the Children and Families Act 2014 was to introduce a shift of paradigm and foster a view of disability compatible with international trends towards a more functional approach. With the new Education Health and Care plans, special educational needs and disabilities should be conceived as resulting from the complex and dynamic interaction between biological, psychological and environmental factors, resulting in a unique functioning profile. However, the issues around the quality of these plans mentioned in the previous section of this chapter have been substantial, with consistent reports of the plans not being workable or helpful, just mere entry tickets for support services.

This chapter aims to provide guidance on how to improve not only Education Health and Care plans but also any other statutory documents worldwide that aim to illustrate a biopsychosocial view of disability and learning and how they translate into good inclusive practice in the classroom. To achieve this, this chapter will address key areas of quality that should be an integral part of statutory documents, to effectively inform professional practice: the portrayal of children's views, the reporting of children's needs, the design of SMART outcomes and translation into the classroom. To achieve true multi-agency work, these key areas should be mastered by all stakeholders involved in the assessment-intervention process, regardless of whether they are accountable for the final statutory document or just contributors. Teachers play a crucial role across all areas, as they are the main actors in one of the most important settings of the children's everyday life – the classroom. They are the main contributors to the final statutory guidance, and therefore they need the skill set to report functioning with accuracy and legitimacy. They are also responsible for the translation of this guidance onto the classroom, through high-quality inclusive practice.

The Portrayal of Children's Views

It is widely recognised that good practice in provision for children with special educational needs and disabilities should account for the children's own perspectives and views about their strengths and needs as well as for their own aspirations, despite the challenges it may present (Lewis, 2010; Tangen, 2008; Whitehurst, 2007). A child and family-centred approach to provision has been widely regarded as a recommended practice (Tomasello et al., 2010; Prizant et al., 2003). This involves having the best interest of the child and of her family at the centre of all concerns and measures for assessment and intervention. Despite being a widely regarded recommended practice, it is still not happening in many contemporary special educational needs' services. In England, it has been shown that most of the times the views of the children are still not fully gathered to be included in their statutory plans (thus informing provision). Instead, professionals hypothesise what they identify as a reasonable aspiration of the child. Most statutory documents do not specify how the 'voice' of the child has been accessed, which would be crucial information for intervention purposes: it tells us how to communicate with the child (Palikara et al., 2018).

Any high-quality statutory document should include clear information about strengths, needs and aspirations of the child from her own point of view. Specifying how this information was obtained will give teachers, for example, clear guidance on how to communicate with the child and generate classroom strategies that target the child's own interests and motivations. This is particularly relevant in contexts where the teaching workforce tends to change quite rapidly. On the other hand, teachers have the responsibility to voice the children's views, as they spend a substantial amount of time with them. It is, therefore, important that teachers detail the skill set necessary to communicate with children effectively.

There is a growing body of evidence in the scientific literature on how to gather the 'voice' of children with SEND. In England, for example, the most common functioning need reported in the statutory documents was communication and speech difficulties. Strategies to access the children's views have been put forward by researchers in this field of knowledge. For instance, Pearlman and Michaels (2019) developed a questionnaire administered as part of a structured interview, supported by Augmentative and Alternative Communication (AAC) with 22 young people with Moderate, Severe and Profound and Multiple Learning Disability (PMLD); the interview was video recorded and played to parents, teachers/and or Speech and Language Therapists (SALT) and psychologists, enhancing multi-agency working and ensuring that all stakeholders work from a child-centred point of view. Results showed that the joint use of conversation with AAC methods enabled the majority of the young people to respond to most of the prompts. The software 'Talking Mats' has been used on an iPad to ascertain the views of young people with Autism Spectrum Disorders on their employability and post-16 education; the software includes a picture-based system to support communication (Gaona et al., 2019).

Reporting Children's Needs and Strengths

In addition to obtaining the children's own perspective, it is key to conduct an objective assessment and documentation of the children's functioning needs and strengths. *Authentic*

Assessment has been regarded in the scientific literature as the gold standard for an inclusive approach to assessment (Neisworth & Bagnato, 2004). This involves evaluating the individual way in which the child functions *within* his or her natural everyday life environment. Removing the child from their natural ecological settings will bias assessments and return results that do not reflect the child's typical participation levels. Participation is affected by environmental factors; if we remove those factors, we will not obtain an accurate picture of the child's behaviour. In England, it has been shown that the reporting of children's needs is not consistent across regions and settings, with special segregated settings and the more affluent regions in the country being more detailed and accurate in this process (Castro-Kemp et al., 2019). This reveals social inequalities and a lack of generalised skill sets and conduct embedded assessments to obtain a true depiction of how the child functions.

The International Classification of Functioning Disability and Health (ICF; WHO, 2001) can provide a common framework and taxonomical system to support a more standardised process for the description of children's needs. The ICF provides a 'dictionary' of functioning characteristics across body functions and structures, activities and participation and environmental factors. The World Health Organization has embedded the ICF categories into a web browser that can be accessed by all, free of charge. For all professionals working with children in an educational setting and needing to describe how that particular child functions, the ICF browser can be accessed and the search tool used to identify a number of dimensions that might be of relevance. To achieve high-quality, specific, individualised descriptions of need, the ICF is the gold standard system (WHO, 2001). Let us provide one example: the classroom teacher is clear that one of the child's main needs relates to 'conversation'. When typing 'conversation' in the search tool of the ICF browser, the teacher will be prompted to be more specific. Is the issue around *maintaining* conversation or *starting* conversation? Such level of detail is not only useful but rather crucial, as it informs intervention; if the child has trouble keeping up with turn-taking in a conversation, visual prompts or a communication device could be used as a supporting tool. If the child's main difficulty is starting a conversation, peer support might be more adequate. One of the main issues identified in the English Education Health and Care plans was the lack of specificity in the reports on children's needs and strengths, with most statements reported by teachers as being too vague to be helpful (Castro-Kemp et al., 2019). The ICF is, to date, the only taxonomy for functioning in disability that can help with obtaining this level of specificity, using a common language that can be shared by all stakeholders involved in the statutory process.

Additionally, with the ICF Research Branch, the WHO has promoted, supported and endorsed the development and adoption of ICF core sets for specific health conditions. The ICF is a universal classification that needs to be useful to all professionals in all contexts and circumstances around the world. However, at times, only a reduced number of ICF codes will be of relevance. To facilitate the translation of the functional approach to disability, the core sets of ICF codes for each health condition describe the functioning aspects that are absolutely essential to consider. For example, there is a core set of ICF codes for Autism Spectrum Disorders (ASD). Children with ASD will obviously differ within a significantly varied range of functioning, but these sets of functioning dimensions are the essential areas that all professionals need to consider when working with children with ASD. Several other core sets have been developed for other health conditions, including (https://www.icf-core-sets.org).

Although the ICF has not been adopted by law in England, its alignment with the current policy for special educational needs and disabilities provision has been underlined in both academic and professional settings (Castro et al., 2020; Norwich, 2016). Professionals have been trained in the ICF system, and some individual settings are using it as a supporting device for documenting children's functioning and progress and to inform the development of higher-quality statutory documents – the Education Health and Care plans (Castro et al., 2020).

Even when the ICF has not been adopted by law, individual educational settings, and teachers themselves, can use the ICF to enhance the quality of their reports, improving specificity, rigour and the quality of holistic narratives about the child. Moreover, the ICF enables the reporting of both needs and strengths, thus ensuring that positive aspects of functioning are included in the narrative about the child's behaviour, which is helpful for intervention within the classroom: if statutory documents describe both needs and strengths in a standard, participation-based language, all teachers and teaching assistants can be aware of the child's interests and motivations and use these to target the specific needs.

Designing SMART Outcomes

In England, the SEND Code of Practice 2014 is clear that good quality outcomes are those that obey the SMART principle: they are specific, measurable, attainable, realistic and time framed. However, a study analysing more than 2,000 outcomes designed for children with SEND and included in their Education Health and Care plans has concluded that the vast majority of them are of poor quality and do not meet this principle (Castro et al., 2019). The issue with not having SMART outcomes in the statutory documents is that these become unworkable. Arguably, if the needs of the children are not described with enough detail and specificity, the outcomes deriving from that description are unlikely to be SMART. Consequently, the first rule to achieve good quality outcomes is to have a good quality narrative of needs and strengths. Once that good quality and specific narrative of needs and strengths has been achieved (for example, using the ICF language or ICF core sets), the most relevant areas of intervention for the child and the family (according to a person-centred approach) should be defined as targets for the development of SMART outcomes.

Good quality outcomes are those that describe *what* is being done (usually the functioning need identified as a priority by the child and family in the needs narrative), *how* (using which strategy), *in what context* (what learning opportunities will be created) and *when/how often* (for a measurement criterion). The concept of learning opportunity is key for the development of successful *authentic* assessment and intervention procedures and can be understood as the naturalistic situations that elicit the desired behaviour (VanDerHeyden et al., 2005). Outcomes that follow these principles are more likely to be SMART. For example, if the functioning need identified in the needs narrative as a priority for intervention was *being able to count to 15*, a possible outcome would be 'Sophie will be able to count to 15 (what) using objects or fingers and following peer or adult modelling (*how*), every day, in 4 different activities (*when/how often*)'.

The Goal Functionality Scale III (McWilliam, 2009) can be a supporting tool to help professionals assess the quality of the outcomes they develop, and it has been used in studies looking at the quality of children's outcomes in statutory documents in England (Castro et al., 2019), Turkey (Rakap, 2015) and Portugal (Boavida et al., 2010). The items of the scale are well aligned with the SMART principles of outcome design and therefore can provide a useful guide for both teams of professionals and individual practitioners.

Translation of Statutory Guidance into the Classroom

Once a statutory document is in place officially defining the needs and strengths of the child, the outcomes to be targeted and the provision to target those, they can be useful tools for day-to-day practice in the classroom, provided that they have been developed with sufficient quality to be workable. In their everyday practice, teachers don't always make use of statutory documents which are often filed away in individual child folders. However, approaches have been recommended to transfer the useful material of the official statutory document into the classroom. For example, Snyder et al. (2011) have suggested the adoption of a Matrix of Learning Opportunities Embedded in Routines. Typical daily routines for each child with SEND are specified in the first column, followed by the days of the week. In each cell, specific outcomes to be targeted will be placed. For example, we will know that outcome number 1 (*Sophie will be able to count to 15 using objects or fingers and following peer or adult modelling, every day, in 4 different activities*) will be placed in four cells corresponding to 4 activities, from Monday to Friday. Such a Matrix can be turned into a classroom poster so that all teachers that come to work with Sophie, and Sophie herself, always know what to expect. Other outcomes can also be targeted simultaneously within the same activity.

Additionally, weekly monitoring reports can be filed with updated functioning information about the needs of the child using the ICF browser or ICF core sets. This will, on the one hand, enable progress monitoring and on the other hand facilitate the reporting of high-quality functioning-based information to be included in the following statutory review (usually once each year or academic term). Similar procedures, often using web-based platforms, have been utilised in various countries. The ICF Schools project (https://www.icf-school.eu/index.php/en/), for example, matched assessment currently used in schools in the partner countries to the ICF and developed a web-based tool for the whole team (including parents), continuously describing the functioning of each individual child, and using the ICF as a common language. Professionals can obtain training materials on the ICF through a number of different channels: the WHO provides a beginners' manual on how to use the system (https://www.who.int/classifications/drafticfpracticalmanual.pdf); the ICF Education platform hosts a number of videos and tutorials developed by specialists on the ICF, including some materials on how to apply it in the school context (https://icfeducation.org/).

Figure 6.1 describes a suggested route for *authentic* documentation of strengths and needs followed by translation into the classroom using the ICF as a supporting tool along the way, as well as the suggested Matrix of Learning Opportunities Embedded in Routines. The process is continuous and individualised. When outcomes are achieved, the cycle continues from either re-designing the child's narrative, or selecting alternative priorities, or developing new outcomes based on the same priorities.

Conclusion

The purpose of this chapter was to provide evidence and guidance on what constitutes good practice in relation to translating official statutory documents into high-quality provision in the classroom. First, an account of contemporary models of disability based on functioning and participation was delivered; using the English context as the setting scene for the analysis, the chapter provided an overview of the evidence available in the scientific literature on the implementation of a new policy for Special Educational Needs and Disabilities in England, which includes regulations for new statutory documents based on a *functional* approach to disability; last, insights on how to develop high-quality official statutory documents that effectively translate into inclusive practice in the classroom were presented. The International Classification of Functioning, Disability and Health (ICF; WHO, 2001) was used as the overall framework as well as the taxonomy that can support the translation from policy to classroom practice in a standard language across disciplines and contexts. The insights provided, although largely backed up by

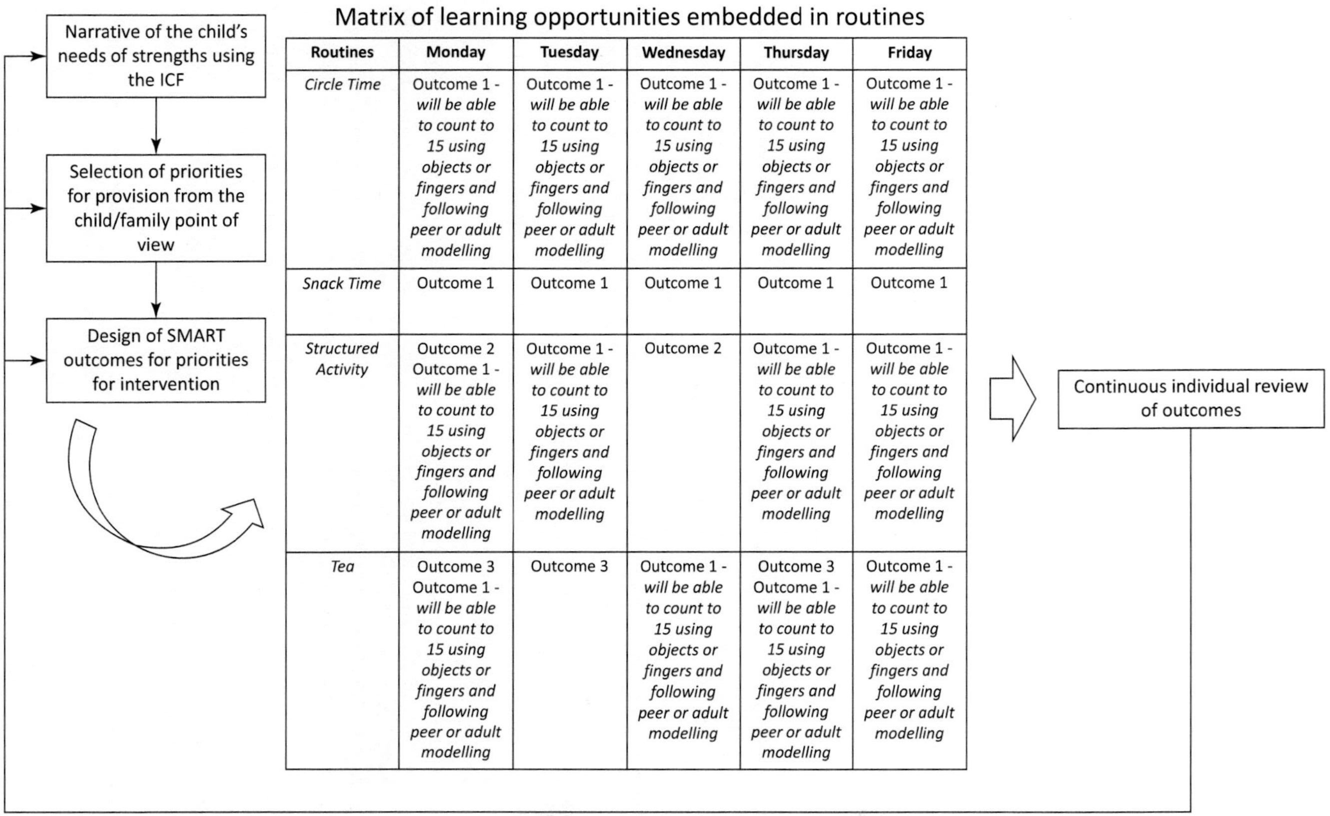

Matrix of learning opportunities embedded in routines

Routines	Monday	Tuesday	Wednesday	Thursday	Friday
Circle Time	Outcome 1 - will be able to count to 15 using objects or fingers and following peer or adult modelling	Outcome 1 - will be able to count to 15 using objects or fingers and following peer or adult modelling	Outcome 1 - will be able to count to 15 using objects or fingers and following peer or adult modelling	Outcome 1 - will be able to count to 15 using objects or fingers and following peer or adult modelling	Outcome 1 - will be able to count to 15 using objects or fingers and following peer or adult modelling
Snack Time	Outcome 1	Outcome 1	Outcome 1	Outcome 1	Outcome 1
Structured Activity	Outcome 2 Outcome 1 - will be able to count to 15 using objects or fingers and following peer or adult modelling	Outcome 1 - will be able to count to 15 using objects or fingers and following peer or adult modelling	Outcome 2	Outcome 1 - will be able to count to 15 using objects or fingers and following peer or adult modelling	Outcome 1 - will be able to count to 15 using objects or fingers and following peer or adult modelling
Tea	Outcome 3 Outcome 1 - will be able to count to 15 using objects or fingers and following peer or adult modelling	Outcome 3	Outcome 1 - will be able to count to 15 using objects or fingers and following peer or adult modelling	Outcome 3 Outcome 1 - will be able to count to 15 using objects or fingers and following peer or adult modelling	Outcome 1 - will be able to count to 15 using objects or fingers and following peer or adult modelling

Narrative of the child's needs of strengths using the ICF → Selection of priorities for provision from the child/family point of view → Design of SMART outcomes for priorities for intervention → Continuous individual review of outcomes

Figure 6.1 Suggested route for statutory documentation of children's needs and strengths, from the development of the child's narrative of functioning to translation in the classroom

evidence of the challenges encountered in England, can be useful to all professionals, worldwide, who aim to implement effective inclusive practice in the classroom that values functioning and participation as the ultimate goals of any form of provision.

What Is New for Teachers in Inclusive Classrooms

This chapter provides the conceptual background and practical strategies for teachers to consider how children in their classroom *function*. Rather than focusing on traditional and medicalised diagnostic categories, teachers are provided with the skill sets to plan interventions embedded in routines, which support how children *function* in everyday life. These are individualised rather than based on what is considered appropriate for all children with the same diagnosis. Such strategies can be used to effectively produce statutory documents to support provision, which are biopsychosocial and holistic, yet individual. Guidance is included on: (1) how to portray the children's own 'voice' or views about provision in their support documents and day-to-day intervention, (2) how to monitor children's abilities and difficulties in an individualised manner, using the ICF system, (3) how to design SMART outcomes and (4) how to translate these strategies into the classroom using embedded approaches.

List of Useful Resources

ICF Browser - https://apps.who.int/classifications/icfbrowser/
ICF research branch - https://www.icf-research-branch.org/
ICF core sets - https://www.icf-core-sets.org/
Goal Functionality Scale III - https://ectacenter.org/~pdfs/topics/families/GoalFunctionalityScaleIII_2_.pdf
ICF School - https://www.icf-school.eu/index.php/en/
ICF manual - https://www.who.int/classifications/drafticfpracticalmanual.pdf
ICF Education - https://icfeducation.org/

References

Adams, L., Tindle, A., Basran, S., Dobie, S., Thomson, D., Robinson, D., & Shepherd, C. (2017). *Experiences of education, health and care plans: A survey of parents and young people*. London: Department for Education. Url: https://derby.openrepository.com/handle/10545/622891

Bailey Jr, D. B., Buysse, V., Simeonsson, R. J., Smith, T., & Keyes, L. (1995). Individual and team consensus ratings of child functioning. *Developmental Medicine & Child Neurology, 37*(3), 246–259. DOI: 10.1111/j.1469-8749.1995.tb11999

Boavida, T., Aguiar, C., McWilliam, R. A., & Pimentel, J. S. (2010). Quality of individualized education program goals of preschoolers with disabilities. *Infants & Young Children, 23*(3), 233–243. DOI: 10.1097/IYC.0b013e3181e45925

Boesley, L., & Crane, L. (2018). 'Forget the Health and Care and just call them Education Plans': SENCOs' perspectives on Education, Health and Care plans. *Journal of Research in Special Educational Needs, 18*, 36–47. DOI: 10.1111/1471-3802.12416

Brett, J. (2002). The experience of disability from the perspective of parents of children with profound impairment: Is it time for an alternative model of disability? *Disability & Society, 17*(7), 825–843. DOI: 10.1080/0968759022000039109

Bricout, J. C., Porterfield, S. L., Tracey, C. M., & Howard, M. O. (2004). Linking models of disability for children with developmental disabilities. *Journal of Social Work in Disability & Rehabilitation, 3*(4), 45–67. DOI: 10.1300/J198v03n04_04

Castro, S., & Palikara, O. (2016, November). Mind the gap: The new special educational needs and disability legislation in England. In *Frontiers in Education* (Vol. 1, p. 4). DOI: 10.3389/feduc.2016.00004

Castro, S., Grande, C., & Palikara, O. (2019). Evaluating the quality of outcomes defined for children with Education Health and Care plans in England: A local picture with global implications. *Research in Developmental Disabilities*, *86*, 41–52. DOI: 10.1016/j.ridd.2019.01.003

Castro, S., Palikara, O., Gaona, C., & Eirinaki, V. (2020). "No policy is an island": How the ICF international classification system may support local education planning in England. *Disability and Rehabilitation*, *42*(11), 1623–1631. DOI: 10.1080/09638288.2018.1529828

Castro-Kemp, S., Palikara, O., & Grande, C. (2019). Status Quo and inequalities of the statutory provision for young children in England, 40 years on from Warnock. In *Frontiers in Education* (Vol. 4, p. 76). Frontiers. DOI: 10.3389/feduc.2019.00076

Department of Health, & Department for Education (2014). *Children and Families Act*. London: DfE. https://www.legislation.gov.uk/ukpga/2014/6/contents/enacted

Florian, L., & McLaughlin, M. J. (2008). *Disability classification in education: Issues and perspectives*. Thousand Oaks, California: Corwin Press. ISBN: 9781412938761

Gaona, C., Palikara, O., & Castro, S. (2019). 'I'm ready for a new chapter': The voices of young people with autism spectrum disorder in transition to post-16 education and employment. *British Educational Research Journal*, *45*(2), 340–355. DOI: 10.1002/berj.3497

Lewis, A. (2010). Silence in the context of 'child voice'. *Children & Society*, *24*(1), 14–23. DOI: 10.1111/j.1099-0860.2008.00200.x

McWilliam, R. A. (2009). Goal Functionality Scale III. Chattanooga. *TN: TEIDS-Plus Study, Siskin Children's Institute*.

Neisworth, J. T., & Bagnato, S. J. (2004). The mismeasure of young children: The authentic assessment alternative. *Infants & Young Children*, *17*(3), 198–212.

Norwich, B. (2014). Changing policy and legislation and its effects on inclusive and special education: A perspective from England. *British Journal of Special Education*, *41*(4), 403–425.

Norwich, B. (2016, December). Conceptualizing special educational needs using a biopsychosocial model in England: The prospects and challenges of using the international classification of functioning framework. In *Frontiers in education* (Vol. 1, p. 5). Frontiers. DOI: 10.1111/1467-8578.12079

Okawa, Y., & Ueda, S. (2008). Implementation of the International Classification of Functioning, Disability and Health in national legislation and policy in Japan. *International Journal of Rehabilitation Research*, *31*(1), 73–77. DOI: 10.1097/MRR.0b013e3282f2d972

Oliver, M. (2013). The social model of disability: Thirty years on. *Disability & Society*, *28*(7), 1024–1026. DOI: 10.1080/09687599.2013.818773

Palikara, O., Lindsay, G., & Dockrell, J. E. (2009). Voices of young people with a history of specific language impairment (SLI) in the first year of post 16 education. *International journal of language & communication disorders*, *44*(1), 56–78. doi: 10.1080/13682820801949032

Palikara, O., Castro, S., Gaona, C., & Eirinaki, V. (2018, April). Capturing the voices of children in the Education Health and Care plans: Are we there yet?. In *Frontiers in Education* (Vol. 3, p. 24). Frontiers. DOI: 10.3389/feduc.2018.00024

Palikara, O., Castro, S., Gaona, C., & Eirinaki, V. (2019). Professionals' views on the new policy for special educational needs in England: Ideology versus implementation. *European Journal of Special Needs Education*, *34*(1), 83–97. DOI: 10.1080/08856257.2018.1451310

Pearlman, S., & Michaels, D. (2019). Hearing the voice of children and young people with a learning disability during the Educational Health Care Plan (EHCP). *Support for Learning*, *34*(2), 148–161. DOI: 10.1111/1467-9604.12245

Prizant, B. M., Wetherby, A. M., Rubin, E., & Laurent, A. C. (2003). The SCERTS model: A transactional, family-centred approach to enhancing communication and socioemotional abilities of children with autism spectrum disorder. *Infants & Young Children*, *16*(4), 296–316.

Rakap, S. (2015). Quality of individualised education programme goals and objectives for pre-school children with disabilities. *European Journal of Special Needs Education*, *30*(2), 173–186. DOI: 10.1080/08856257.2014.986909

Robinson, D., Moore, N., & Hooley, T. (2018). Ensuring an independent future for young people with special educational needs and disabilities (SEND): A critical examination of the impact of education, health and care plans in England. *British Journal of Guidance & Counselling*, *46*(4), 479–491. DOI: 10.1080/03069885.2017.1413706

Sales, N., & Vincent, K. (2018). Strengths and limitations of the Education, Health and Care plan process from a range of professional and family perspectives. *British Journal of Special Education*, *45*(1), 61–80. DOI: 10.1111/1467-8578.12202

Sanches-Ferreira, M., Simeonsson, R. J., Silveira-Maia, M., & Alves, S. (2015). Evaluating implementation of the International Classification of Functioning, Disability and Health in Portugal's special education law. *International journal of inclusive education*, *19*(5), 457–468. DOI: 10.1080/13603116.2014.940067

Simeonsson, R. J. (2006). Appendix C: Defining and classifying disability in children. In M. J. Field, A. Jette, & L. Martin (Eds.), *Workshop on disability in America: A new look* (pp. 67–87). Washington, DC: National Academy Press.

Simeonsson, R. J., & Bailey, D. B. (1991). *The abilities index*. Chapel Hill: Frank Porter Graham Child Development Center. https://fpg.unc.edu/publications/abilities-index

Simeonsson, R. J., Bailey, D., Smith, T., & Buysse, V. (1995). Young children with disabilities: Functional assessment by teachers. *Journal of Developmental and Physical Disabilities*, *7*(4), 267–284. DOI: 1056-263X/95/1200-0267507.50/0

Snyder, P., McLaughlin, T., & Denney, M. (2011). Frameworks for guiding program focus and practices in early intervention. J. M. Kauffman & D. P. Hallahan (Series Eds.) & M. Conroy (Section Ed.), *Handbook of special education: Section XII early identification and intervention in exceptionality* (pp. 716–730). New York: Routledge. ISBN: 9780203837306

Tangen, R. (2008). Listening to children's voices in educational research: Some theoretical and methodological problems. *European Journal of Special Needs Education*, *23*(2), 157–166. DOI: 10.1080/08856250801945956

Tomasello, N. M., Manning, A. R., & Dulmus, C. N. (2010). Family-centered early intervention for infants and toddlers with disabilities. *Journal of Family Social Work*, *13*(2), 163–172. DOI: 10.1080/10522150903503010

United Nations (1989). *Convention on the Rights of the Child*. Geneva: Office of High Commissioner for Human Rights (OHCHR). Retrieved from https://www.ohchr.org/EN/ProfessionalInterest/Pages/CRC.aspx.

United Nations (2006). *Convention on the Rights of Persons with Disabilities*. New York: United Nations. Retrieved from: http://www.un.org/disabilities/documents/convention/convoptprot-e.pdf.

VanDerHeyden, A. M., Snyder, P., Smith, A., Sevin, B., & Longwell, J. (2005). Effects of complete learning trials on child engagement. *Topics in Early Childhood Special Education*, *25*(2), 81–94. DOI: 10.1177/02711214050250020501

Whitehurst, T. (2007). Liberating silent voices–perspectives of children with profound & complex learning needs on inclusion. *British Journal of Learning Disabilities*, *35*(1), 55–61. DOI: 10.1111/j.1468-3156.2006.00405

World Health Organization (2001). *International Classification of Functioning, Disability, and Health*. Geneva: World Health Organization.

7
ATTITUDES TOWARDS AN UNFAMILIAR PEER WITH COMPLEX COMMUNICATION NEEDS USING AN IPAD™ WITH AAC SOFTWARE AND A COMMUNICATION BOARD

Perspectives of Adolescents with Physical Disabilities[1]

Shakila Dada, Cathy Flores, Kerstin Tönsing* and Jenny Wilder

For individuals with complex communication needs (CCN), peer interactions are often limited. This is also true for the classroom context (Chung et al., 2012). The attitude that a communication partner brings to the communicative exchange is an important factor to consider as it will have an impact on interactions (Blockberger et al., 1993). According to Triandis (1971, p. 2), attitude is "an idea charged with emotion, which predisposes a class of action to a particular class of social situations". Three classes of evaluative responses are involved in the formation of an attitude: cognitive, affective and behavioural (Dada et al., 2016; Nowicki & Sandieson, 2002; Triandis, 1971). The cognitive component reflects a person's knowledge, beliefs and ideas and will determine the overall emotional reaction of an individual (Dada et al., 2016; Hyppa-Martin et al., 2016; Nowicki & Sandieson, 2002; Triandis, 1971). The affective component refers to the emotional reaction and feelings that are elicited, and the behavioural component includes the individual's behaviour, actions and responses to their beliefs (Dada et al., 2016; Hyppa-Martin et al., 2016; Nowicki & Sandieson, 2002). In this way, the cognitive component interacts with the affective component which predisposes behaviours towards a particular attitude object (Beck et al., 2010).

Individuals tend to interact with those who have similar attitudes, and these attitudes will be a predisposing factor for the way in which one acts towards another (Beck et al., 2010). In schools, classrooms tend to be social microcosms (Nowicki & Sandieson, 2002). Negative attitudes towards certain groups of learners in a classroom based on their characteristics such as (dis)

---

* kerstin.tonsing@up.ac.za

abilities or even the type of assistive technology they use have been widely reported (Estell et al., 2008; Hamovitch, 2007; Sullivan et al., 2015). In inclusive classrooms, the attitudes of peers towards children with disabilities are generally negative, which is seen as a major barrier to the social inclusion of learners with disabilities (Wyche Okpareke & Salisbury, 2017). Even amongst students who all have disabilities, social exclusion of certain groups of students may occur due to perceptions of difference and othering based on student characteristics (Davis & Watson, 2001). Attitudes towards individuals with CCN who use augmentative and alternative communication (AAC) are related to the willingness of others to interact with them (Kim et al., 2015; Radici et al., 2020). Therefore, understanding these attitudes is important to ensure successful interaction (Beck et al., 2010; Dada et al., 2016). Fortunately, negative attitudes can be shifted to a more positive attitude with the use of intervention programmes (Moore & Nettelbeck, 2013). Understanding the factors that will have an impact on attitudes will allow interventionists to influence the actions and behaviours of others in order to change negative attitudes and behaviours that exclude others (Beck et al., 2010; Dada et al., 2016; McNaughton & Light, 2005). Peer training should form a critical component of intervention in order to support interaction (Therrien & Light, 2018). This would lead to better peer acceptance and, in turn, better inclusion of learners in the school environment (Dada et al., 2016; Hyppa-Martin et al., 2016).

Understanding attitudes towards individuals who use AAC is important so that methods can be developed to change negative attitudes, thereby removing barriers and biases faced by people who use AAC (Dada et al., 2016; McNaughton & Light, 2005). According to a systematic review of the literature on attitudes towards persons using AAC (McCarthy & Light, 2005), a variety of factors have an influence on attitudes. These factors include characteristics of those who interact with a person using AAC, characteristics of the person using AAC and the AAC system itself (McNaughton & Light, 2005). Females tend to have more positive attitudes towards individuals who use AAC compared to males (Beck et al., 2010; Beck et al., 2000; Dada et al., 2016; Hyppa-Martin et al., 2016; Lilienfeld & Alant, 2002; Radici et al., 2020). More positive attitudes towards individuals who use AAC are reported by those who are more familiar with people with disabilities than those who are less familiar (Beck et al., 2000a, b, 2010; Blockberger et al., 1993). Younger children seem to have more positive attitudes, with attitudes reportedly being less positive towards those who use AAC amongst older individuals (Beck et al., 2002, 2010).

When considering the influence of the AAC system itself, findings have been varied. Earlier studies typically focused on attitudes towards so-called dedicated electronic AAC devices (i.e., devices that were designed to act exclusively as an AAC system), comparing the absence and presence of certain features on attitudes or comparing attitudes towards these electronic devices to attitudes towards non-electronic or unaided means of communication. While many studies have found that the AAC system did not seem to have an influence on the attitudes towards a person using AAC (e.g., Beck et al., 2010; Beck & Dennis, 1996; Blockberger et al., 1993), some studies found more positive attitudes towards electronic, dedicated AAC devices compared to low-tech options, such as communication boards (e.g., Bedrosian et al., 2003; Lilienfeldt & Alant, 2002).

In recent years, there have been significant developments in mobile technology with the introduction of the iPad[TM2] and other smart devices. There has also been an explosion of AAC software used on these general consumer-level technologies. These devices have therefore provided new tools for communication (McNaughton & Light, 2013), with evidence showing the effectiveness of iPad-based AAC systems as a mode of AAC (Still et al., 2014). The iPad has technology with more recent speech synthesis, is slimmer, smaller and may be more socially acceptable (Hyppa-Martin et al., 2016; McNaughton & Light, 2013) when compared to dedicated AAC devices (Hyppa-Martin et al., 2016). A few studies have explored attitudes towards such tablet- and iPad-based AAC methods, and, once again, findings were somewhat mixed. Hyppa-Martin et al. (2016) explored the attitudes of typically developing first graders towards a peer who uses an iPad-based AAC system versus a communication board to communicate. Findings showed that the type of AAC system did not have an influence on the attitudes of first graders towards the peers using AAC. Radici et al. (2020) also studied the attitudes towards a peer using an iPad-based AAC system or communication board; however they considered the attitudes of typically developing teenagers. Results showed no statistical difference in the attitudes of teenagers related to the device used. Wilder, Magnusson and Hanson (2015) studied caregivers' perceptions of attitudes about children and adolescents with severe disabilities and their use of an iPad as part of their communication. Attitudes about communication of children and adolescents with severe disabilities were discussed within blended learning networks between 36 parents and professionals. The universal design of iPads was discussed in all of the groups to be facilitative in terms of the fact that iPads could overcome boundaries between people because people of all ability levels are familiar with iPads, and iPads are a status symbol that can increase acceptance and even encourage inclusion.

However, some studies have found a more positive attitude towards tablet- and iPad-based AAC systems. Dada et al. (2016) compared the attitudes of typically developing primary school children towards an individual using a general consumer-level mobile technology device (iPad) with an AAC application and a low-tech communication board. A more positive attitude was found towards an unfamiliar peer using mobile technology with an AAC application than towards the same peer using a communication board. Schäfer et al. (2016) investigated the perceptions of adults (undergraduates and teachers) regarding three AAC modes: picture exchange, manual signing and an iPad-based AAC system. The iPad-based AAC system was nominated as the preferred AAC option. Lorah et al. (2021) investigated the perceptions of typically developing pre-schoolers regarding a pre-schooler with autism spectrum disorder (ASD) using either consumer-level mobile technology (AAC application on a tablet), a low-tech aided mode (picture exchange of printed picture symbols in a communication binder), and an unaided mode (prelinguistic communication). The results indicated the typically developing pre-schoolers perceived the use of an AAC application on a tablet by the pre-schooler with ASD as more favourable than the other communication options.

When considering the current state of research regarding attitudes towards individuals who use AAC, a few gaps emerge. First, studies have mainly concentrated on the attitudes of children and adults towards peers who use AAC. More extensive research on the attitudes of adolescents is limited (Beck et al., 2010; Radici et al., 2020). Research considering the factors that may increase the positive attitudes of adolescents towards peers who use AAC is important as adolescence is a time of transition. For children with disabilities, peer acceptance in the adolescent years would ensure successful integration into the high-school setting and later transition into the adult world (Beck et al., 2010; McDougall et al., 2004; Radici et al., 2020). Research conducted by Beck et al. (2010) regarding adolescents' attitudes towards peers who use AAC concluded that continued research regarding aspects that would increase peer acceptance of adolescents who use AAC is important; therefore further research into the attitudes of adolescents towards peers who use AAC is warranted. Second, a gap in the research exists where consideration of the attitudes of peers with disabilities regarding individuals who use AAC is limited. According to the review by McCarthy and Light (2005), and as is also evident from studies conducted later on tablet-based AAC technology, research seems to have exclusively addressed the attitudes of typically developing individuals regarding those who use AAC. However, the formation of specific attitudes towards groups of persons based on some unifying characteristic (e.g., persons with CCN) is not limited to persons without disabilities (Davis & Watson, 2001; Torrance, 2000), and persons using AAC may, by virtue of their work environment or educational placement, come into frequent contact with others who also have disabilities. Investigating the attitudes of persons with disabilities towards persons using a variety of AAC systems is therefore also warranted.

In South Africa, access to education is regulated by the principles of non-discrimination and accessibility within an inclusive and democratic political system (Blignaut et al., 2010). Policy and law such as the Education White Paper 6 (2001) and the Constitution of the country (South African Government, 1996) recognise that all children, including those with disabilities, have the right to unrestrictive school environments (Dada et al., 2016). However, reports have shown that children with disabilities are generally still placed in special schools based on their disability rather than in mainstream schools with appropriate support (Human Rights Watch, 2015). The ideals of inclusive education found in policy documents have not yet been achieved in terms of increased access to mainstream school, acceptance of learners with diverse educational needs and maximum participation of all learners in all activities (Engelbrecht et al., 2016). Most children with disabilities are still being segregated, resulting in them not being taught together with typically developing peers in the same classroom (Donohue & Bornman, 2018; Human Rights Watch, 2015). The consideration of the attitudes of peers with disabilities regarding individuals who use AAC is therefore important as these are the peers that individuals with CCN using AAC will typically be interacting with in the school environment.

Considering the gaps in the research in terms of the attitudes of adolescents with physical disabilities regarding individuals who use AAC, as well as limited research regarding general consumer-level mobile devices as a modern AAC system, this study aimed to determine and compare the attitude of adolescents with physical disabilities towards a peer with CCN using both a consumer-level mobile technology device (iPad) with AAC application and a low-technology communication board.

Method

Research Aim

This study aimed to determine and compare the attitude of adolescents with physical disabilities towards a peer with CCN using both a low-technology communication board and a consumer-level mobile technology device with an AAC application (iPad with Proloquo2Go™3).

1.1 *Sub-aims*

a) To determine the attitudes of adolescents with physical disabilities towards an unfamiliar peer with CCN who uses an iPad with Proloquo2Go.
b) To determine the attitudes of adolescents with physical disabilities towards an unfamiliar peer with CCN using a communication board.
c) To compare the attitudes of adolescents with physical disabilities towards an unfamiliar peer with CCN using either a communication board or an iPad with Proloquo2Go.

Research Design

A non-experimental descriptive survey design was used. There was paired randomisation of the participants according to age and gender, providing two equivalent groups. Two DVDs used by Dada et al. (2016) were used for the purpose of this study. Group A watched DVD-1, which depicted a peer interacting with an iPad with AAC software. Group B watched DVD-2, which depicted the same peer interacting with the use of an alphabet board. The Communication Aid/Device Attitudinal Questionnaire (CADAQ) was used as a measuring instrument (Lilienfeld & Alant, 2002).

Participants

Non-probability purposive sampling was used to select the participants for this study (McMillan & Schumacher, 2014). The participants were selected from a government school in South Africa that caters to children with physical disabilities whose home language is isiXhosa, but who are educated in English and isiXhosa. They follow the regular school curriculum and complete Grade 12 in English. The participants who met the following selection criteria were included in the study: (a) a chronological age between 13:00 (years; months) and 18:11, (b) has repeated no more than one grade, and (e) has functional or corrected vision and hearing. A total of 35 participants (17 boys and 18 girls) between the ages of 13:00 and 18:11 participated in the study.

Participant Descriptive Criteria

The participants are described in terms of their mean age, gender, previous exposure to an iPad/tablet and GMFCS-E&R in Table 7.1.

Table 7.1 illustrates that for Group A the mean age was 17.94 years. For Group B, the mean age was 18.42 years. Group A had 7 boys and 9 girls. Group B had 10 boys and 9 girls. A total of 11 and 9 participants in Groups A and B respectively had previous exposure to an iPad. Groups A and B both had a variety of levels of gross motor function as measured using the GMFCS-E&R, with an equal spread in the two groups. The diagnosis of participants included cerebral palsy, muscular dystrophy, arthrogryposis and spina bifida.

Table 7.1 Group characteristics

	Group A iPad with AAC application (N = 16)	Group B Communication Board (N = 19)
Age distribution		
Mean age (years)	17.94	18.42
Gender distribution		
Boys	7 (43.8%)	10 (52.6%)
Girls	9 (56.3%)	9 (47.4%)
Previous use of iPad™/Tablet		
Yes	11 (68.8%)	9 (47.4%)
No	5 (31.3%)	10 (52.6%)
GMFCS – E&R Level		
Level I	1 (6.3%)	7 (36.8%)
Level II	1 (6.3%)	3 (15.8%)
Level III	3 (18.8%)	2 (10.5%)
Level IV	11 (68.8%)	7 (36.8%)

Materials and Equipment

CADAQ

The CADAQ was developed by Lilienfeld and Alant (2002) to measure three components of attitudes towards peers who use AAC. The CADAQ is based on the Chedoke-McMaster Attitudes Towards Children with Handicaps (CATCH) developed by Rosenbaum et al. (1988), which measures the three dimensions of attitude (cognitive, affective and behavioural), and a questionnaire of communication competence developed by Bedrosian et al. (1992). These components include: affective/behavioural component, the cognitive component and perceptions of communicative competence. The affective and behavioural components are closely related as actions are usually motivated by feelings. For example, anxiety about one's ability to understand the person with CCN may prevent one from greeting the person. The cognitive component illustrates one's beliefs relating to the peer with CCN. For example, the belief that the individual with CCN is intellectually challenged may affect the manner in which one talks to the individual. The communication competence component will indicate one's attitude towards the individual's ability to use their communication device (Lilienfeld & Alant, 2002). The CADAQ was specifically designed to highlight differences in children's attitudes towards a person who uses AAC. It has previously been used in South Africa (Dada et al., 2016).

Originally, the CADAQ consisted of 37 statements. However, one statement was omitted as suggested by the developers (i.e. question 26, "I feel upset when I see how Alan has to talk"), as recommended by Lilienfeld and Alant (2002) as it was of the opinion that this would improve the reliability coefficient for the affective/behavioural component. Hence the CADAQ used had 36 statements. Additionally, the name of the individual was changed from Alan to Grace in order to match the young woman with CCN in the DVDs.

The CADAQ statements were kept short and simple and had a vocabulary level appropriate for Grades 6 and 7 pupils aged 11:00 to 13:00 (Lilienfeld & Alant, 2002). Although using a different age range, it seemed relevant to use this scale on the proposed adolescents as each statement appeared to be socially relevant and age appropriate. The participants had to select their responses on a Likert scale, with 'I strongly agree' scoring 5 points and 'I strongly disagree' scoring 1 point. The CADAQ was presented to the participants in the form of a booklet, together with the consent form.

Gross Motor Function Classification System; Expanded and Revised (GMFCS-E&R)

The GMFCS-E&R (Palisano et al., 2007) is a five-level classification system that describes the gross motor function of children living with cerebral palsy, with Level I indicating minimal limitations and Level V requiring maximum support. Participants had to be classified at Level IV or better. A minimum of Level IV was required and is described as "Youth use wheeled mobility in most settings. Youth require adaptive seating for pelvic and trunk control" (Palisano et al., 2007).

DVDs

Two scripted DVDs used by Dada et al. (2016) were used in this study. Both DVDs featured the same scripted conversation between a communication partner and an unfamiliar peer with CCN. The DVDs differed by the type of AAC system used. DVD-1 shows an unfamiliar adolescent peer competently using a general consumer-level mobile technology device with an AAC application (iPad with Proloquo2Go), while DVD-2 shows the same peer in the same conversation using a low-technology communication board. After an opening shot showing both communication partners, the DVDs focus on the AAC display (alphabet overlay) and the back of the unfamiliar peer as she interacts with the communication partner, who is no longer visible, in a scripted conversation. In DVD-1, the peer with CCN selects the letters on the alphabet overlay, which the device 'speaks' out loud. In DVD-2, the peer points to the letters on the communication board and the communication partner says the words/sentences as they are spelled by the peer with CCN.

Procedures

Ethical approval was obtained from the relevant higher education authorities in order to conduct the study. Permission was received from the relevant education department. Additionally, permission was obtained from the school principal where the study was conducted. Parents of potential participants, as well as the participants themselves were asked for consent/assent to participate in the study. The day before data collection all the potential participants were briefly screened and classified according to the GMFCS-E&R.

After the GMFCS-E&R classification, participants meeting the specified criteria were arranged in order from oldest to youngest for both boys and girls. Two groups were formed by placing the oldest boy in group A, then the oldest girl in group B. The second oldest boy would be placed in Group B and the second oldest girl in Group A (paired randomisation according to age and gender). This process continued until all participants had been allocated to a group using paired randomisation. A booklet was compiled for each participant, including their assent form and CADAQ form. Each participant was allocated a unique number, e.g. A01. This participant number was written on all relevant documents.

Group A was called to the test venue, a classroom at the school, where they received the letter of consent, a pencil, and a CADAQ marked with a pre-coded number allocated to each participant to ensure confidentiality. The researcher introduced herself and obtained participant assent. The researcher then read the scripted instructions to the participants before showing DVD-1 to the group. The following instructions were provided: "We are now ready to start. You are about to watch a four-minute DVD of Grace, a person with a disability who is unable to speak. Grace does use another way of communicating, which you will see in the DVD. After you have watched the DVD, I will read out some questions and you will mark your answers in the booklet".

Group A viewed DVD-1 (video of the communication interaction of an unfamiliar peer with CCN using the iPad with Proloquo2Go QWERTY display and speech output). The researcher then read each statement on the CADAQ to Group A. Before the next statement was read, a 10s pause was provided to allow the participants time to respond. Group B viewed DVD-2 (video of the communication interaction of an unfamiliar peer with CCN using the communication board). The same procedure as for Group A was followed with Group B.

Scoring

The answers to the statements in the CADAQ were scored from 1 to 5, depending on the statement. Positively worded statements were scored from 5 (*I strongly agree*) to 1 (*I strongly disagree*). Negatively worded statements were reversed-scored. Therefore, a higher score indicates a more positive attitude.

Results

Attitudes towards a peer with LNFS

The frequency with which adolescents with physical disabilities marked the five scale points on the Likert scale in response to each of the CADAQ questions is recoded in Tables 7.2 to 7.4. Frequencies are recorded for both Groups A and B, enabling a comparison of the attitudes towards a peer using a consumer-level mobile technology device (iPad) versus a low-technology communication device. Table 7.2 shows the frequency of responses on the CADAQ for the affective/behaviour component (Component A), Table 7.3 shows cognitive/belief component (Component B), and Table 7.4 shows the communication competence component (Component C).

Table 7.2 Frequency of responses on the CADAQ: Component Affective/Behaviour

Affective/Behaviour Component

No	Statement	Device	Strongly Disagree	Disagree	Uncertain	Agree	Strongly Agree
6	I would worry if Grace sat next to me in class	iPad™	25.0%	6.3%	6.3%	43.8%	18.8%
		Comm Board	10.5%	15.8%	15.8%	42.1%	15.8%
9	I would be scared to talk to Grace	iPad™	18.8%	18.8%	31.3%	25.0%	6.3%
		Comm Board	15.8%	15.8%	42.1%	15.8%	10.5%
10	I would like to talk to Grace	iPad™	37.5%	12.5%	25.0%	12.5%	12.5%
		Comm Board	31.6%	26.3%	15.8%	26.3%	0.0%
12	I would tell my secrets to Grace	iPad™	37.5%	18.8%	18.8%	6.3%	18.8%
		Comm Board	73.7%	26.3%	0.0%	0.0%	0.0%
13	I would be embarrassed to communicate like Grace does	iPad™	25.0%	18.8%	12.5%	31.3%	12.5%
		Comm Board	15.8%	5.3%	31.6%	21.1%	26.3%
15	It would be fun to talk like Grace	iPad™	6.3%	6.3%	25.0%	18.8%	43.8%
		Comm Board	15.8%	10.5%	21.1%	21.1%	31.6%
16	Grace would be unwelcome at my birthday party	iPad™	0.0%	0.0%	6.3%	37.5%	56.3%
		Comm Board	5.3%	5.3%	10.5%	10.5%	68.4%
18	If Grace was in my class I would like to do a project with her	iPad™	0.0%	18.8%	25.0%	25.0%	31.3%
		Comm Board	10.5%	10.5%	21.1%	26.3%	31.6%
21	I would try to stay away from Grace if she came to my school	iPad™	6.3%	18.8%	.6.3%	62.5%	6.3%
		Comm Board	0.0%	5.3%	0.0%	42.1%	52.6%
27	Grace would not be my best friend	iPad™	12.5%	12.5%	6.3%	37.5%	31.3%
		Comm Board	0.0%	10.5%	5.3%	47.4%	36.8%
30	I would like to go the 'The Spur' with Grace	iPad™	50.0%	37.5%	6.3%	0.0%	6.3%
		Comm Board	42.1%	36.8%	15.8%	5.3%	0.0%
36	I would like Grace to sit next to me in class	iPad™	93.8%	0.0%	0.0%	6.3%	0.0%
		Comm Board	100.0%	0.0%	0.0%	0.0%	0.0%

Table 7.3 Frequency of responses on the CADAQ: Component B: Cognitive/Belief

Cognitive/Belief Component

No	Statement	Group	Strongly Disagree	Disagree	Can't Decide	Agree	Strongly Agree
2	Our class works too quickly for Grace	iPad™	6.3%	12.5%	12.5%	43.8%	25.0%
		Comm Board	5.3%	0.0%	15.8%	36.8%	42.1%
4	Grace would find it difficult to make friends at my school	iPad™	12.5%	0.0%	18.8%	43.8%	25.0%
		Comm Board	5.3%	5.3%	15.8%	26.3%	47.4%
8	I think Grace has many friends	iPad™	12.5%	50.0%	25.0%	6.3%	6.3%
		Comm Board	63.2%	21.1%	10.5%	5.3%	0.0%
17	Grace would be teased in our class	iPad™	6.3%	0.0%	12.5%	56.3%	25.0%
		Comm Board	5.3%	0.0%	10.5%	42.1%	42.1%
20	Grace would be popular with the boys	iPad™	18.8%	12.5%	56.3%	12.5%	0.0%
		Comm Board	10.5%	57.9%	21.1%	5.3%	5.3%
25	Grace would need a lot of help in the classroom	iPad™	6.3%	6.3%	18.8%	31.3%	37.5%
		Comm Board	10.5%	5.3%	10.5%	15.8%	57.9%
28	Grace had interesting things to say	iPad™	18.8%	31.3%	12.5%	25.0%	12.5%
		Comm Board	52.6%	31.6%	10.5%	5.3%	0.0%
31	Grace most likely comes last in class	iPad™	0.0%	25.0%	6.3%	37.5%	31.3%
		Comm Board	0.0%	10.5%	15.8%	57.9%	15.8%
32	Grace should be good with computers	iPad™	12.5%	6.3%	18.8%	37.5%	25.0%
		Comm Board	10.5%	10.5%	10.5%	52.6%	15.8%
33	I do not think Grace has much fun	iPad™	6.3%	12.5%	12.5%	31.3%	37.5%
		Comm Board	0.0%	21.1%	15.8%	52.6%	10.5%
35	Grace needs a lot of help to tell a story	iPad™	12.5%	31.3%	37.5%	18.8%	0.0%
		Comm Board	5.3%	36.8%	36.8%	5.3%	15.8%

Group Comparison

Comparisons could be made between Groups A and B across the three components of the CADAQ. Table 7.5 indicates the mean, standard deviation and paired *t*-test for Group A and B respectively.

Table 7.5 shows that there are slightly higher means reported across domains for Group A, indicating that there were more positive attitudes towards an unfamiliar peer with CCN who uses an iPad with Proloquo2Go versus an unfamiliar peer with CCN who uses a low-technology communication board. A statistically significant difference was obtained in the affective/behavioural component (p = .023) and cognitive/belief component (p = .046). No statistically significant difference was evident for the communicative competence component (p = .115). This indicates that there is a statistically significant difference in peers' perceptions of the use of the iPad and communication board in the affective/behavioural and cognitive/belief components.

Table 7.4 Frequency of responses on the CADAQ: Component C: Communication Competence

Communication Competence Component

No	Statement	Group	Strongly Disagree	Disagree	Can't Decide	Agree	Strongly Agree
1	Grace took an active part in the conversation	iPad™	43.8%	43.8%	0.0%	12.5%	0.0%
		Comm Board	78.9%	15.8%	0.0%	5.3%	0.0%
3	Kim understood everything Grace said	iPad™	0.0%	25.0%	25.0%	31.3%	18.8%
		Comm Board	15.8%	10.5%	5.3%	26.3%	42.1%
5	If I couldn't speak I would like to communicate like this	iPad™	62.5%	12.5%	25.0%	0.0%	0.0%
		Comm Board	52.6%	36.8%	5.3%	0.0%	5.3%
7	I found it easy to understand what Grace meant	iPad™	18.8%	31.3%	37.5%	6.3%	6.3%
		Comm Board	52.6%	31.6%	10.5%	0.0%	5.3%
11	There must be better ways for Grace to communicate	iPad™	0.0%	6.3%	12.5%	56.3%	25.0%
		Comm Board	0.0%	5.3%	15.8%	42.1%	36.8%
14	It was easy to understand what Grace was 'saying'	iPad™	25.0%	31.3%	31.3%	6.3%	6.3%
		Comm Board	21.1%	57.9%	15.8%	5.3%	0.0%
19	Grace could not communicate quickly enough	iPad™	0.0%	6.3%	18.8%	43.8%	31.3%
		Comm Board	5.3%	0.0%	31.6%	36.8%	26.3%
22	Grace was frustrated communicating like that	iPad™	6.3%	43.8%	31.3%	12.5%	6.3%
		Comm Board	21.1%	21.1%	10.5%	36.8%	10.5%
23	Grace was unable to say what she really wanted to say	iPad™	0.0%	0.0%	18.8%	56.3%	25.0%
		Comm Board	0.0%	10.5%	10.5%	36.8%	42.1%
24	Grace could answer Kim's questions quickly enough	iPad™	56.3%	31.3%	6.3%	6.3%	0.0%
		Comm Board	63.2%	36.8%	0.0%	0.0%	0.0%
26	Kim did not always understand what Grace wanted to say	iPad™	0.0%	12.5%	37.5%	31.3%	18.8%
		Comm Board	0.0%	5.3%	5.3%	47.4%	42.1%
29	The way Grace communicated with Kim resulted in some misunderstandings	iPad™	31.3%	37.5%	12.5%	12.5%	6.3%
		Comm Board	42.1%	15.8%	21.1%	15.8%	5.3%
34	Grace could say exactly what she wanted to say	iPad™	62.5%	31.3%	6.3%	0.0%	0.0%
		Comm Board	73.7%	21.1%	5.3%	0.0%	0.0%

Table 7.5 Mean and standard deviation of Groups A and B across three components of the CADAQ

Group	Affective/Behavioural Component		Cognitive/Belief Component		Communicative Competence Component	
	Mean	SD	Mean	SD	Mean	SD
Group A	2.5833	0.42709	2.5511	0.43721	2.3269	0.32575
Group B	2.2500	0.40062	2.2344	0.46287	2.1296	0.39644
t-test p-value	0.023★		0.046★		0.115	

★$p ≤ 0.05$ indicates a statistically significant difference between the groups.

Discussion

This study aimed to determine and compare the attitude of adolescents with physical disabilities towards a peer with CCN when using two different types of AAC systems: a consumer-level mobile technology device with an AAC application (iPad with Proloquo2Go) and a low-technology communication board. The results of the study indicate that the unfamiliar peer was perceived more favourably when using the iPad with Proloquo2Go as compared to the communication board by adolescents with physical disabilities.

A statistically significant difference was found in the affective/behavioural component and cognitive/belief component, which indicates more positive attitudes towards the general consumer-level mobile technology device with an AAC application in these components. Similar results were found in previous studies investigating the attitudes of typically developing peers, with more positive attitudes towards consumer-level mobile technology compared to low-technology AAC systems. Lorah et al. (2021) found that typically developing pre-schoolers perceived the use of an AAC application on a tablet as more favourable compared to low-technology and no-technology options. Dada et al. (2016) also found that typically developing primary school children had a more positive attitude towards an unfamiliar peer using general consumer-level mobile technology (an iPad) with an AAC application (Proloquo2Go).

The revolution in mobile technology has been found to positively impact social acceptance of AAC, which has reduced attitudinal barriers regarding the use of AAC (Light & McNaughton, 2014; McNaughton & Light, 2013). This may have contributed towards the peer using the iPad with Proloquo2Go being perceived more positively compared to the peer using a communication board. For adolescents, mobile technology such as tablets and smartphones can become status symbols (Vanden Abeele & Roe, 2013). Such views may have further contributed to the more positive attitudes found towards the peers using the iPad-based application in this study. Additionally, previous studies have indicated that iPads with AAC applications are effective for individuals who use AAC (Still et al., 2014). This effectiveness, together with social validity in the eyes of important communication partners, will increase the likelihood of AAC being used in practice (Schäfer et al., 2016)

Although access to mobile technology is improving in various low- and middle-income countries (Poushter, 2016) including South Africa, access is far from universal. The digital divide in South Africa is still very much a reality, and historically and politically driven socio-economic inequalities can be seen as key contributing factors (Blignaut, 2009; Fuchs & Horak, 2008). Persons with disabilities are often economically disadvantaged (Emmett, 2005), and access to more costly iPad-based AAC solutions as compared to paper-based solutions may be problematic. Public funding models for mobile technology as a form of assistive technology need to be urgently developed, both in South Africa (Dada et al., 2017) as elsewhere (McNaughton & Light, 2013). Research showing the effectiveness and superior social acceptance of such technology is important to drive advocacy efforts in this regard.

Although the attitudes of the participants in this study were more positive towards tablet-based technology, attitudes in general were not overly positive, as indicated by the mean scores that ranged between 2.6 and 2.1 for the two groups on the three components. In a previous study also employing the CADAQ measuring tool, Dada et al. (2016) found that pre-teens without disabilities generally had more positive attitudes, with average scores of groups on the three components ranging from 3.0 to 4.1. The findings of the current study confirm previous findings that younger children tend to have more positive attitudes towards persons using AAC (Beck et al., 2002, 2010). The current findings also highlight that peers with disabilities will not necessarily 'automatically' have positive attitudes towards others with different (dis)abilities.

Adolescence is a time of transition as children integrate into the high-school setting and prepare for later transition into adulthood. Peer acceptance during these adolescent years would ensure this integration and transition (Beck et al., 2010; McDougall et al., 2004; Radici et al., 2020). More positive attitudes of adolescents with physical disabilities towards individuals using AAC will lead to a willingness to interact, leading to better peer acceptance and, in turn, better inclusion in the school environment (Dada et al., 2016; Hyppa-Martin & Reichle, 2018; Kim et al., 2015; Radici et al., 2020). The current study suggests that interventions such as peer training amongst adolescents in special educational settings may be warranted to improve attitudes towards and social acceptance of peers using AAC. Such training programmes are often only considered for peers without disabilities. However, in settings like South Africa, where the ideals of inclusive education have not yet been achieved (Engelbrecht et al., 2016; Human Rights Watch, 2015), peers with disabilities are frequent and important communication partners, who may greatly benefit from training in order to view peers using AAC more positively.

Conclusion

This study can be seen as a first step in understanding the attitudes of adolescents with physical disabilities towards the use of general consumer-level mobile technologies with AAC applications. The study found that, in various components of the CADAQ, adolescents with physical disabilities demonstrated a more positive attitude towards an unfamiliar peer with CCN who used a general consumer-level mobile device with AAC application than towards the same peer using a communication board. In order to facilitate interaction, peer acceptance and better inclusion of adolescents in the school environment, the use of general consumer-level mobile technologies with AAC applications should be considered for use by adolescents who use AAC.

The current study presents some limitations. The study did not determine the equivalence of the groups in terms of age and gender. Additionally, due to the small sample size, the generalizability of the findings is limited. The results can therefore not be generalized to all adolescents with physical disabilities. Finally, the results are limited to adolescents from within a specific geographical area (South Africa).

Acknowledgments

This study was supported by National Research Foundation (NRF) (# 150708124127) and University of Pretoria Research and Development Program. Opinions expressed and conclusions arrived at are those of the author and are not necessarily those of the funders. The authors would like to acknowledge all the participants and graduate student who assisted with this project.

Notes

1. The study was supported by the National Research Foundation. Opinions expressed are those of the authors and do not necessarily reflect the opinions of the funders. The authors would like to thank Ms Annie Jones who assisted with data collection.
2. The iPAd is a registered trademark of Apple Inc., Cupoertino, CA, USA. www.apple.com
3. Proloquo2Go is a product of Assistiveware, Amsterdam, Netherlands. www.assistiveware.com

References

Beck, A. R., & Dennis, M. (1996). Attitudes of children toward a similar-aged child who uses augmentative communication. *Augmentative and Alternative Communication, 12*(2), 78–87. https://doi.org/10.1080/07434619612331277528

Beck, A. R., Fritz, H., Keller, A., & Dennis, M. (2000a). Attitudes of school-aged children toward their peers who use augmentative and alternative communication. *Augmentative and Alternative Communication, 16*(1), 13–26. https://doi.org/10.1080/07434610012331278874

Beck, A. R., Kingsbury, K., Neft, A., & Dennis, M. (2000b). Influence of length of augmented message on children's attitudes toward peers who use augmentative and alternative communication. *Augmentative and Alternative Communication, 16*(4), 239–249. https://doi.org/10.1080/07434610012331279094

Beck, A. R., Bock, S., Thompson, J. R., & Kosuwan, K. (2002). Influence of communicative competence and augmentative and alternative communication technique on children's attitudes toward a peer who uses AAC. *Augmentative and Alternative Communication, 18*(4), 217–227. https://doi.org/10.1080/07434610212331281301

Beck, A. R., Thompson, J. R., & Prochnow, J. M. (2010). The development and utilization of a scale to measure adolescents' attitudes toward peers who use augmentative and alternative (AAC) devices. *Journal of Speech, Language and Hearing Research, 53*, 572–587.

Bedrosian, J., Hoag, L., & McCoy, K. (2003). Relevance and speed of message delivery trade-offs in augmentative and alternative communication. *Journal of Speech, Language & Hearing Research, 46*(August), 800–817. https://doi.org/10.1080/07434610600924515

Blignaut, P. (2009). A bilateral perspective on the digital divide in South Africa. *Perspectives on Global Development and Technology, 8*(4), 581–601. https://doi.org/10.1163/156915009X12583611836091

Blignaut, A. S., Hinostroza, J. E., Els, C. J., & Brun, M. (2010). ICT in education policy and practice in developing countries: South Africa and Chile compared through SITES 2006. *Computers and Education, 55*(4), 1552–1563. https://doi.org/10.1016/j.compedu.2010.06.021

Blockberger, S., Armstrong, R. W., O'Connor, A., & Freeman, R. (1993). Children's attitudes toward a non-speaking child using various augmentative and alternative communication techniques. *Augmentative and Alternative Communication, 9*(4), 243–250. https://doi.org/10.1080/07434619312331276661

Chung, Y. C., Carter, E. W., & Sisco, L. G. (2012). A systematic review of interventions to increase peer interactions for students with complex communication challenges. *Research and Practice for Persons with Severe Disabilities, 37*(4), 271–287. https://doi.org/10.2511/027494813805327304

Dada, S., Horn, T., Samuels, A., & Schlosser, R. W. (2016). Children's attitudes toward interaction with an unfamiliar peer with complex communication needs: Comparing high- and low-technology devices. *Augmentative and Alternative Communication, 32*(4), 305–311. https://doi.org/10.1080/07434618.2016.1216597

Dada, S., Kathard, H., Tönsing, K. M., & Harty, M. (2017). Severe communication difficulties in South Africa: Challenges and enablers. In S. Halder & L. Czop Assaf (Eds.), *Inclusion, disability and culture* (pp. 169–193). Springer International. https://doi.org/10.1007/978-3-319-55224-8

Davis, J. M., & Watson, N. (2001). Where are the children's experiences? Analysing social and cultural exclusion in "special" and "mainstream" schools. *Disability and Society, 16*(5), 671–687. https://doi.org/10.1080/09687590120070060

Donohue, D., & Bornman, J. (2018). The challenges of realising inclusive education in South Africa. *Learning and Teaching Around the World: Comparative and International Studies in Primary Education, 34*(2), 120–126. https://doi.org/10.4324/9780429491498-15

Education White Paper 6. (2001). *Special needs education: Building an inclusive education and system.* Pretoria, Department of Education.

Emmett, T. (2005). Disability and poverty. In E. Alant & L. L. Lloyd (Eds.), *Augmentative and alternative communication and severe disabilities: Beyond poverty* (pp. 68–94). Whurr. https://education.indiana.edu/graduate/programs/special-ed/aac/docs/Alant Chapter Four.pdf

Engelbrecht, P., Nel, M., Smit, S., & van Deventer, M. (2016). The idealism of education policies and the realities in schools: The implementation of inclusive education in South Africa. *International Journal of Inclusive Education, 20*(5), 520–535. https://doi.org/10.1080/13603116.2015.1095250

Estell, D. B., Jones, M. H., Pearl, R., Van Acker, R., Farmer, T. W., & Rodkin, P. C. (2008). Peer groups, popularity, and social preference: Trajectories of social functioning among students with and without learning disabilities. *Journal of Learning Disabilities, 41*(1), 5–14. https://doi.org/10.1177/0022219407310993

Fuchs, C., & Horak, E. (2008). Africa and the digital divide. *Telematics and Informatics, 25*(2), 99–116. https://doi.org/10.1016/j.tele.2006.06.004

Hamovitch, B. (2007). Hoping for the best: "Inclusion" and stigmatization in a middle school. In S. Books (Ed.), *Invisible children in the society and in schools* (3rd ed., pp. 263–281). Lawrence Erlbaum.

Human Rights Watch. (2015). *"Complicit in exclusion": South Africa's failure to guarantee an inclusive education for children with disabilities.* Retrieved from https://www.hrw.org/sites/default/files/report_pdf/southafricaaccessible.pdf

Hyppa-Martin, J., & Reichle, J. (2018). The effect of partner reauditorization on undergraduates' attitudes toward a peer who communicates with augmentative and alternative communication. *American Journal of Speech-Language Pathology, 27*(2), 657–671. https://doi.org/10.1044/2017_AJSLP-16-0242

Hyppa-Martin, J., Collins, D., Chen, M., Amundson, C., Timinski, K., & Mizuko, M. (2016). Comparing first graders' attitudes and preferences toward a peer using an iPad®-based speech-generating device and a non-electronic AAC system. *Augmentative and Alternative Communication, 32*(2), 94–104. https://doi.org/10.3109/07434618.2016.1146332

Kim, J. R., Kim, Y. T., Lee, H. J., & Park, E. H. (2015). Influence of message error type on Korean adults' attitudes toward an individual who uses augmentative and alternative communication. *Augmentative and Alternative Communication, 31*(2), 159–169. https://doi.org/10.3109/07434618.2015.1008569

Light, J., & McNaughton, D. (2014). Communicative competence for individuals who require augmentative and alternative communication: A new definition for a new era of communication? *Augmentative and Alternative Communication, 30*(1), 1–18. https://doi.org/10.3109/07434618.2014.885080

Lilienfeld, M., & Alant, E. (2002). Attitudes of children toward an unfamiliar peer using an AAC device with and without voice output. *Augmentative and Alternative Communication, 18*(2), 91–101. https://doi.org/10.1080/07434610212331281191

Lorah, E., Holyfield, C., & Kucharczyk, S. (2021). Typical preschoolers' perceptions of augmentative and alternative communication modes of a preschooler with autism spectrum disorder. *Augmentative and Alternative Communication, 37*(1), 52–63. https://doi.org/10.1080/07434618.2020.1864469

McCarthy, J., & Light, J. (2005). Attitudes toward individuals who use augmentative and alternative communication: Research review. *Augmentative and Alternative Communication, 21*(1), 41–55. https://doi.org/10.1080/07434610410001699753

McDougall, J., DeWit, D. J., King, G., Miller, L. T., & Killip, S. (2004). High school-aged youths' attitudes toward their peers with disabilities: The role of school and student interpersonal factors. *International Journal of Disability, Development and Education, 51*(3), 287–313. https://doi.org/10.1080/1034912042000259242

McMillan, J., & Schumacher, S. (2014). *Research in education: Evidence-based inquiry*. Pearson Education Limited.

McNaughton, D., & Light, J. (2005). Attitudes toward individuals who use augmentative and alternative communication: Research review. *Augmentative and Alternative Communication, 21*, 41–55.

McNaughton, D., & Light, J. (2013). The iPad and mobile technology revolution: Benefits and challenges for individuals who require augmentative and alternative communication. *Augmentative and Alternative Communication, 29*(2), 107–116. https://doi.org/10.3109/07434618.2013.784930

Moore, D., & Nettelbeck, T. (2013). Effects of short-term disability awareness training on attitudes of adolescent schoolboys toward persons with a disability. *Journal of Intellectual and Developmental Disability, 38*(3), 223–231. https://doi.org/10.3109/13668250.2013.790532

Nowicki, E. A., & Sandieson, R. (2002). A meta-analysis of school-age children's attitudes towards persons with physical or intellectual disabilities. *International Journal of Disability, Development and Education, 21*(1), 243–265. https://doi.org/10.1080/1034912022000007270

Palisano, R., Rosenbaum, P., Bartlett, D., & Livingston, M. H. (2007). GMFCS-R & E gross motor function classification system expanded and revised, 2007. In *CanChild Centre for Childhood Disability Research*. McMasters University.

Poushter, J. (2016). Smartphone ownership and internet usage continues to climb in emerging economies. http://assets.pewresearch.org/wp-content/uploads/sites/2/2016/02/pew_research_center_global_technology_report_final_february_22__2016.pdf

Radici, E., Heboyan, V., Mantovani, F., & de Leo, G. (2020). Attitudes and perceived communicative competence: The impact of different AAC means of communication among Italian teenagers. *International Journal of Disability, Development and Education*, 1–11. https://doi.org/10.1080/1034912X.2020.1740185

Rosenbaum, P. L., Armstrong, R. W., & King, S. M. (1988). Determinants of children's attitudes towards disability: A review of evidence. *Children's Health Care, 17*, 32–39.

Schäfer, M., Sutherland, D., Mclay, L., Achmadi, D., Meer van der, L., Sigafoos, J., Lancioni, G. E., O'Reilly, M. F., Schlosser, R. W., & Marschik, P. B. (2016). Research note: Attitudes of teachers and undergraduate students regarding three augmentative and alternative communication modalities three augmentative and alternative communication modalities. *Augmentative and Alternative Communication, 32*(4), 312–319. https://doi.org/10.1080/07434618.2016.1244561

South African Government. (1996). *The constitution of the Republic of South Africa, chapter 2: Bill of rights*. Parliament.

Still, K., Rehfeldt, R. A., Whelan, R., May, R., & Dymond, S. (2014). Facilitating requesting skills using high-tech augmentative and alternative communication devices with individuals with autism spectrum disorders: A systematic review. *Research in Autism Spectrum Disorders, 8*(9), 1184–1199. https://doi.org/10.1016/j.rasd.2014.06.003Review

Sullivan, T. N., Sutherland, K. S., Lotze, G. M., Helms, S. W., Wright, S. A., & Ulmer, L. J. (2015). Problem situations experienced by urban middle school students with high incidence disabilities that impact emotional and behavioral adjustment. *Journal of Emotional and Behavioral Disorders, 23*(2), 101–114. https://doi.org/10.1177/1063426614528243

Therrien, M., & Light, J. C. (2018). Promoting peer interaction for preschool children with complex communication needs and autism spectrum disorder. *American Journal of Speech-Language Pathology, 27*(1), 207–221. http://10.0.4.20/2017_AJSLP-17-0104%0Ahttps://search.ebscohost.com/login.aspx?direct=true&db=eue&AN=127887182&site=ehost-live

Torrance, D. A. (2000). Qualitative studies into bullying within special schools. *British Journal of Special Education, 27*(1), 16–21. https://doi.org/10.1111/1467-8527.t01-1-00151

Triandis, H. C. (1971). *Attitude and attitude change*. Wiley.

Vanden Abeele, M., & Roe, K. (2013). Adolescents' school experience and the importance of having a "cool" mobile phone: Conformity, compensation and resistance? *Poetics, 41*(3), 265–293. https://doi.org/10.1016/j.poetic.2013.03.001

Wilder, J., Magnusson, L., & Hanson, E. (2015). Professionals' and parents' shared learning in blended learning networks related to communication and augmentative and alternative communication for people with severe disabilities. *European Journal of Special Needs Education, 30*(3), 367–383.

Wyche Okpareke, A., & Salisbury, C. L. (2017). Exploring predictors of social actions by general education students towards peers with disabilities. *Journal of Education and Learning, 7*(2), 126. https://doi.org/10.5539/jel.v7n2p126

PART II

Cross-Cultural and Global Perspectives

Review of cross-cultural and global trends and issues on inclusion is important to understand the world perspectives. The collective synthesis and analysis of research, policy, and practices in diverse and unique contexts can inform future directions and individualized and indigenized implementation of inclusive practices across the globe. This section discusses issues on cross-cultural, comparative literature highlighting the global perspectives on important areas for consideration to support inclusive practices.

8
RIGHT TO INCLUSIVE EDUCATION FOR CHILDREN WITH DISABILITIES

Exploring the Gap through the Indian and Canadian Legal Prism

Shruti Bedi* and Sébastien Lafrance[1]

Introduction

A fundamental human right, education is essential for the attainment of other civil, political, social, economic and cultural rights. Education, in the true sense of the word, means creating opportunities to learn. According to Plato, education helps to evolve a matured person worthy to rule and to be ruled (Lazarus, 2009, p. 108). The practices, methods, strategies and techniques employed are parts of what teaching and learning is about. A vital ingredient of these techniques is inclusive education which has come to be accepted as a worldwide phenomenon in the recent past. Inclusive education is both a "philosophy as well as a principle and/or practice that is based on human rights and social justice" (Nagpal, 2018, p. 801). Inclusive education entails that children with special needs be educated in the same environment along with their peers at the local school. It advocates that "meaningful learning opportunities" be provided "to all students within the regular school system" with additional support as required (UNICEF Executive Summary, p. 9). Inclusion is stated to be a process that works towards the elimination of barriers that "restrict or ban the participation of children within a system" (Alkazi, 2014–15, p. 3).

The recognition that all children are different and the acknowledgment that children with disabilities (CWDs) should be able to equally be a part of the regular education system is a significant starting point (UNCHR, 2007, p. 9). The Office of the UN High Commissioner for Human Rights (OHCHR) states that inclusion is "a process that recognizes: (a) the obligation to eliminate barriers that restrict or ban participation, and (b) the need to change culture, policy and practice of the mainstream schools to accommodate the needs of all students, including those with impairments" (OHCHR, 2013, p. 5). The concept of inclusive education is a platform where legislations and policies focus on the removal of existing barriers to the participation of disabled students. Thus, it is carried out through "appropriate curricula, organizational arrange-

---

* dr.shrutibedi@gmail.com

DOI: 10.4324/9781003266068-11

ments, teaching strategies, resource use and partnerships with their communities" (Salamanca Statement, 1994, para. 9). The right to inclusive education finds a place in international law and is further strengthened by policies and legislations at the national level. However, the compliance and enforcement of this right remains a challenge in practice.

In this piece, the legal status of the right to inclusive education for CWDs is examined. The chapter is divided into three parts. The first part deals with the international perspective of this right under the United Nations Convention on the Rights of Persons with Disabilities (CRPD), specifically focussing on Article 24. The second part focusses on the policies and legislations present in India and seeks to explore the existing gaps in their effective implementation. The third part covers the Canadian legal perspective and explores the ambiguities in its legal regime and related practical issues. The objective of the article is to pinpoint the inconsistencies and irregularities in the regulation of the right to inclusive education for the CWDs in the national jurisdictions of these two countries as a lesson for other dominions.

International Perspective

The UN conventions and treaties specifically pertaining to the rights of disabled children and their education include the 1989 UN Convention on the Rights of the Child, the UN Standard Rules of 1993, the UNESCO Salamanca Statement of 1994 and the United Nations Convention on the Rights of Persons with Disabilities (CRPD). The CRPD was the culmination of decades of UN commitment to transform social attitudes towards disabled people. It was brought forth in 2006 with the objective of emphasising non-discrimination, and effective and full participation, and inclusion in society (Dias, 2013, pp. 38–39).

Article 24, CRPD

Article 24 of the CRPD consolidates the status of the right to inclusive education under international law. Clause (1) of Article 24 provides that in order to realise the right to education for persons with disabilities "without discrimination and on the basis of equal opportunity", States Parties shall guarantee an "inclusive educational system" aimed at the full development of persons with disabilities and their effective participation in society (Art. 3). Conclusively, the right to inclusive education is a non-discriminatory right and its objective is to promote the well-being of persons with disabilities.

A Non-discriminatory Right

The right to inclusive education under Article 24(1) fulfils the characteristics of a non-discriminatory right. Disability as a characteristic classifies persons into groups – such as persons with disabilities and persons without disabilities. The right to inclusive education is a universal right, which does not provide for segregated schools for different groups (Khaitan, 2015, p. 30). Members of one cognate group may experience certain disadvantages in relation to the other group (Khaitan, 2015, p. 31). The Preamble to the Convention acknowledges the presence of barriers faced by CWDs and the consequent forms of discrimination which are a violation of their human rights (Arduin, 2019, pp. 156–157). Inclusive education seeks to remove such barriers of discrimination.

Purpose of Right under Article 24(1)

Article 24 seeks to primarily promote, protect and fulfil the *well-being* of students with disabilities. Though 'well-being' is not specifically mentioned in Article 24(1), however, it can be inferred from Article 24(1)(a) and (b). Well-being, according to Sen, refers to 'wellness' of a person's state (Nussbaum & Sen, 1993, pp. 36–37; Sen, 1985, p. 169), which in turn is associated with the guarantee of essential functioning, such as being educated and the nurturing of individual talents (Nussbaum & Sen, 1993, p. 40; Collins, 2003, p. 32; Stein, 2007, p. 75).

Inclusive Education

The CRPD provides for 'inclusive education' as a principle and special education as an exception. It is evident from Article 24(1) which states that "State Parties shall ensure an inclusive education system at all levels and lifelong learning". Further Article 24(2)(a) and (b) provide that the State Parties shall ensure that "children with disabilities are not excluded from free and compulsory primary education on the basis of disability" and that "persons with disabilities can access an inclusive, quality and free primary education and secondary education on an equal basis with others in the communities in which they live". Resultantly, CWDs should not be denied access to regular school education on account of their impairments. Although 'inclusive education' is not defined, it definitely does not include education in special schools which provide for a segregated education system. Most States have adopted some form of national legislation to allow CWDs to be educated in regular schools. However, the obstacle stems from the lack of sufficient resources to implement such laws (de Beco, 2014, p. 277).

Reasonable Accommodation

Denial of reasonable accommodation is a form of discrimination (Art. 2, CRPD) and it functions as a well-established international and legal principle (Stein, 2004, p. 579). Article 2 CRPD defines "reasonable accommodation" as "necessary and appropriate modifications and adjustments not imposing a disproportionate or undue burden, where needed in a particular case, to ensure to persons with disabilities the enjoyment or exercise on an equal basis with others of all human rights and fundamental freedoms". Reasonable accommodation is an obligation which is relative to the needs of the concerned student (Waddington & Lawson, 2009, p. 52). The aim is that the CWDs should be able to attend regular schools that are close to where they live. This means that there must be easy access to buildings and classrooms, and transportation to schools must be available in addition to communication technology (Art. 9(1), CRPD).

Support Measures

CRPD also provides numerous support measures to enable CWDs to participate in the general education system. Article 24(2)(a) and (b) of the CRPD stipulate that "children with disabilities are not excluded from free and compulsory primary education on the basis of disability" and that "persons with disabilities can access an inclusive, quality and free primary education and secondary education on an equal basis with others in the communities in which they live". However, on account of the difference between theory and practice, free inclusive education has only been partially achieved (EASPD, 2011, pp. 13, 21–22).

Support measures are the general measures that aim to adapt the general education system to gradually achieve inclusive education. Even though they are general measures, they have to be specific to the special needs of the child. These may include providing personal assistance, including medical assistance, as well as the necessary equipment and material, including Braille and sign language (Art. 24(3), CRPD). The directions provided under Article 24, CRPD can be achieved by adapting both the environment and the content of education. This is the ultimate aim and objective of this extremely significant provision under the CRPD.

Inclusive Education for CWDs in India

As per the 76th National Sample Survey of 2018, 48% of people with disabilities are illiterate, while only 62.9% of people with disabilities (between the age of 3 and 35 years) have attended regular school. Only 4.1% of those who were not enrolled in regular schools had been enrolled in special schools (Rao et al., 2020, pp. 1–2). It was seen that CWDs rarely progressed beyond primary school and remain excluded from the educational system (Goyal, 2020). As per the 2011 Census there are 2.13 million CWDs, of which 28% are not in school (Bakhshi et al., 2017).

The general welfare of any society depends on ensuring education for all its citizens. The right to education is a guarantee of equality for CWDs and their inclusion. India began its journey of universalisation of elementary education with the constitutional Directive Principle of State Policy with the commencement of the Constitution of India in 1950. Directive Principles are mere directives and are accordingly non-justiciable. This position was altered in 2002 with the adoption of a right to primary education as a fundamental right under Article 21A of the Constitution. This guaranteed to all children between the ages of 6 and 14 years, the justiciable right to free, compulsory primary education.

Policies and Legislations

India ratified the CRPD in 2007. However, inclusive education for CWDs has been ransacked by "policy incongruities, lack of availability of data and dearth of assessment of achievements and quality, resulting in serious gaps in implementation and untargeted interventions" (Goyal, 2020). The right to inclusive education for CWDs has been recognised in India under the Right of Children to Free and Compulsory Education Act, 2009 (RTE Act); the Sarva Shiksha Abhiyan (SSA); Rights of Persons with Disabilities Act, 2016 (RPWD Act); and the recent National Education Policy, 2020 (NEP). However, there exist ambiguities with respect to a uniform framework for inclusive education in the country. In furtherance of the constitutional mandate and the international agreements, the RTE Act provides for free and compulsory elementary education to all children, including children belonging to 'disadvantaged groups' (s. 3, RTE Act), which includes CWDs (s. 2(d) & s. 3(3), RTE Act).

The disability laws in India have also evolved in light of the obligations imposed on India under the CRPD. The previous legislation, Persons with Disabilities (Equal Opportunities, Protection of Rights and Full Participation) Act, 1995 (PWD Act), expounded on the obligation of the government to ensure that "every child with a disability has access to free education in an appropriate environment till he attains the age of eighteen years" (s. 26). The government was also obligated to integrate CWDs into 'mainstream schools' in addition to setting up special schools. This legislation was replaced with the RPWD Act in 2016, wherein the term 'inclusive education' was given a statutory backing. Inclusive education under the Act is defined as "a system of education wherein students with and without disability learn together and the system of teaching and learning is suitably adapted to meet the learning needs of different types of students with disabilities" (s. 2(m)).

Undoubtedly, the government has taken steps to ensure inclusive education through the incorporation of new legal standards. However, the inconsistencies between the RTE Act and the RPWD Act have resulted in a contradictory and haphazard legislative framework. The RTE Act was enacted in 2009 and follows the 'integration' approach instead of 'inclusion' which is similar to the repealed PWD Act. Integrated education focusses on the "student to fit in the system rather than the system to adapt", while inclusive education stresses changes being brought in system-level practices and policies to meet the needs of the students (Sharma & Joanne, 2005, p. 1). An attempt is made to identify the existing inconsistencies between different legal frameworks and challenges in their implementation.

Sarva Shiksha Abhiyan (SSA)

The Sarva Shiksha Abhiyan (SSA) or 'Education for All' is an Indian government programme instituted in 2000–2001 to universalise primary education for children between the ages of 6 and 14 years. It commenced with the objective of establishing partnerships between the central, state and local governments wherein the states could develop their own vision of elementary education. The key interventions of this programme are the opening of new schools and alternative schooling facilities, in-service training and academic resource support for regular teachers, free textbooks, uniforms and support for improving learning achievement levels/outcome (MHRD, 2011).

The challenge faced by the SSA is the compartmentalisation of education for children with special needs (CWSN). The SSA has created a separate cadre for the education of CWSN, which is used as an excuse by teachers and administrators not to look after the CWDs. Inclusive education becomes the most neglected part of the SSA program as it is generally accepted that invited resource persons bear the responsibility of the CWDs as opposed to regular teachers. The role of teaching CWDs is delegated to special educators as regular teachers are not trained to deal with the learner needs of the CWDs. Moreover, the budget allocated for the purpose is either underspent or spent in a disorganised manner. The delay and inadequate funding with respect to CWDs is a huge hindrance to teacher training, allocation of resource persons and experts, creating awareness and community mobilisation (Rao et al., 2020, p. 6).

Regulation of School Models

Various types of schools provide elementary education. The following section examines the regulation of different types of schools from the perspective of providing the right to inclusive education for the CWDs.

Government Schools

Right to education of CWDs under RTE Act. The RTE Act is the basic law which lays down the scope and obligation of government schools with respect to primary education wherein the right to education of CWDs is recognised. The Act imposes an obligation on all 'government schools' (s. 2(n)(i)) to provide free, compulsory primary education to all children (s. 12(1)(a)) including CWDs (s. 2(ee)). Consequently, government schools are mandated to provide free and compulsory education to CWDs similar to other children. However, the manner of ensuring this mandate and creating an enabling environment is missing from the Act. The Act does not provide for any specific physical infrastructure, access to appropriate teaching techniques and pedagogical tools for inclusive education for CWDs. The Schedule to the Act provides for all-weather buildings with barrier-free access (Item 2 (ii), Schedule), but the Act nowhere mentions specific provisions for the education of CWDs.

Under the RPWD Act. Even though the RPWD Act is not the basic legislation for primary education, it contains specific duties of government educational institutions for providing inclusive education:

i) admit them without discrimination and provide education and opportunities for sports and recreation activities equally with others;
ii) make building, campus and various facilities accessible;
iii) provide reasonable accommodation according to the individual's requirements;
iv) provide necessary support individualised or otherwise in environments that maximise academic and social development consistent with the goal of full inclusion;
v) ensure that the education to persons who are blind or deaf or both is imparted in the most appropriate languages and modes and means of communication;
vi) detect specific learning disabilities in children at the earliest and take suitable pedagogical and other measures to overcome them;
vii) monitor participation, progress in terms of attainment levels and completion of education in respect of every student with disability;
viii) provide transportation facilities to the children with disabilities and also the attendant of the children with disabilities having high support needs (s. 16, RTE Act).

However, practically a lot of these rights and duties remain unrealised, a pertinent issue being the lack of awareness about the existence of such programmes and facilities amongst poor and uneducated parents.

Private Unaided Schools

Under RTE Act. The provision of free and compulsory education to the disadvantaged and weaker sections is also the responsibility of educational institutions that are not dependent on government funds (Statement of Object, RTE Bill). The definition of 'school' (s. 2(n)) under the RTE Act includes private unaided and specified category schools (s. 2(p)) as well. The responsibility of unaided educational institutions providing education is limited to the disadvantaged and weaker groups in the neighbourhood (s. 12(1)(c)). These institutions are mandated to reserve 25% of their class strength from such sections. These directions undoubtedly make provisions for the inclusion of children from weaker or disadvantaged sections, but the Act does not provide any specific benefit for the CWDs on account of the following reasons:

i) *Clubbing of CWDs with other disadvantaged groups.* Since the RTE Act does not specifically differentiate between the disadvantaged groups and the CWDs, in the 25% seats category in the private unaided institutions, the CWDs have to compete with the other disadvantaged groups for admissions. These schools also prefer to admit such students without disabilities under the 25% reserved category seats. As a result CWDs are left out of being able to use this benefit (Mehendale et al., 2015).

ii) *Restrictive Neighbourhood criteria.* Section 12(1)(c) limits the application of the provision to the neighbourhood. It is difficult for the CWDs to gain admission in private unaided institutions especially in the urban areas as such institutions may not be located within the neighbourhood (criteria follow rigid distance norms). Additionally, the neighbourhood school may not be well-equipped to accommodate the CWDs. In a path-breaking judgment, the Delhi High Court made an attempt to overcome this anomaly in the RTE Act. In *Pramod Arora v. Hon'ble Lt. Governor, Delhi* the court held that "the neighbourhood principle cannot prevail over the need to admit CWSN if, in a given case, the school is equipped to deal with or handle some or one kind of disability (blindness, speech impairment, autism etc.)" (Pramod, 2014). Though this judgment has benefitted the CWDs in Delhi, the other states continue to be restricted by the neighbourhood criteria.

iii) *Lack of enabling environment in private unaided and specified category schools.* The majority of the private unaided schools lack appropriate facilities for educating the CWDs as they do not invest in ensuring meaningful inclusion (Mehendale et al., 2015). Consequently, the CWDs drop out of school without being educated (Rao et al., 2020, p. 12).

Under RPWD Act. Under the RPWD Act, obligations are put on private aided (receiving aid from the government) educational institutions to provide inclusive education. The drawback is that there is a lack of clarity on the definition of educational institutions and its applicability to private unaided schools. Section 16 of the Act states that "the appropriate government shall endeavour that all educational institutions funded or recognised by them provide inclusive education to the children with disabilities" in the ways specified. Unlike the RTE Act, it does not provide any sanction like that of de-recognition of the school by the government, in case of non-implementations of the directions (s. 19, RTE Act). Therefore, the concept of inclusive education remains on the books on account of the lack of implementation by private schools.

Special Schools. The RPWD Act does not define special schools but includes the provision with reference to children with benchmark disabilities [equal to or greater than 40% disability (s. 2(r))]. The Act allows such children to choose between the neighbourhood school or a special school up to 18 years of age (s. 31(1))]. This provision supersedes the RTE Act (s. 31(1)). Consequently, the RPWD Act recognises the special school model in India, while the RTE Act which regulates primary education is silent on the aspect of special schools. It is therefore unclear how the model of special schools can be reconciled with that of inclusive education.

Home-based education. The RTE Act and the RPWD Act do not define the term 'home-based education'. The RTE Act provides the right to avail home-based education for children with "multiple disabilities" and "severe disability" (proviso to s. 3(3)). However, there is no explanation or clarification with respect to its meaning. It has been interpreted by experts to mean 'special training' of children with high support needs at home. Whether such training is to be carried out by regular teachers or special experts is unclear (Rao et al., 2020, p. 15). The RPWD Act replaces these terms with "high support needs" (s. 2(t)), but the fact that RTE Act remains unchanged has resulted in inconsistencies in the implementation and understanding of the legal framework.

National Education Policy, 2020 (NEP)

Teachers working in educational institutions are not trained to teach CWDs and therefore find it difficult to satisfy the specific needs of the learners. The NEP makes a special effort in this direction by making provisions for special education training as a secondary specialisation for regular teachers. The NEP aims for greater lucidity between the "National Council for Teacher Education and the Rehabilitation Council of India to ensure that special educators and teachers have the skills to implement inclusive classroom practices" (Sarkar, 2020). The NEP is examined in this part from the perspective of inclusive education for CWDs around three key aspects:

Choice of school. The NEP tries to resolve the contentions between the RTE Act and the RPWD Act. The 2012 amendment in the RTE Act provided for CWDs to be enrolled in neighbourhood schools and recognises the separate category of children with severe disabilities. The RPWD Act provides for the right of children with benchmark disabilities to enrol in either the neighbourhood schools or special schools of their choice. Therefore, the RTE is silent on the issue of special schools while the RPWD Act does not provide for home-based education. The NEP states that all three schools, i.e., neighbourhood schools, special schools and home-based education, are open as options for the education of CWDs. This attempts to resolve the ambiguities surrounding the choice of school. Nevertheless, there are some unresolved issues:

i) *Issue of home-based education* – it is essential to audit home-based education on account of concerns about the identification of children and quality of education imparted. The Block-level special educators continue to face challenges regarding home-based education, based on time and resource-based constraints, cultural norms and safety and lack of a clear curriculum, etc.

ii) *Governance of special schools* – The regulation of special schools remains unclear, which has a negative impact on CWDs as there is no clear guidance on the quality of education, curriculum, certification or infrastructure. This results in separate segregated schools instead of an inclusive schooling system (Sarkar, 2020).

Teachers and Special Educators. The NEP makes provisions for teacher education, preparation and service conditions which include short-term specialisation courses to teach CWDs within the existing programmes. Further teachers are to be trained to recognise disabilities and will no longer be required to carry out non-teaching tasks. The policy does not provide for separate special educators but incorporates the principle of special education as a specialisation for regular teachers (Gaur & Panchal, 2021, p. 24).

Standardised Assessments and Curricula. The NEP stresses achieving foundational literacy for all children by grade 3. The policy provides for changes in the curricula to be made in consultation with national institutes under the Department of Empowerment of Persons with Disabilities. Resultantly the curriculum is designed to be flexible to accommodate CWDs. It offers multiple means of engagement, assessments and representation of knowledge (Gaur & Panchal, 2021, p. 26).

To ensure that the objectives of the UNCRPD are carried out, the NEP must be effectively implemented with greater efforts towards budgetary allocation, integrating CWDs with other students and increasing coordination between government departments.

It is imperative to provide an inclusive and equitable society. The government should consequently focus on proper budgetary allocation for inclusive education for the CWDs, improve the working conditions for teachers and special educators, and take formal steps to include persons with disabilities in mainstream society (Gaur & Panchal, 2021, p. 28).

Canada

Discrimination in education affects persons with disabilities everywhere around the world (Gilmer, 2019, p. 378). Canadian citizens with disabilities are not immune from discrimination (Gilmer, 2019, p. 379) even if Canada ratified the CRPD in 2010. Canada also has "the potential to be a leader in the inclusion movement" (Timmons, 2008, p. 144) that originated both in Canada and the United States in the mid-to-late 1980s (Shevlin, 2019, p. 115). Canada has also been described as a leader in the international community with respect to the right to education of persons with disabilities (Gilmer, 2019, p. 380). Being the first country in the world to include the rights of disabled persons in its constitution, more specifically by including in 1982 the terms "physical or mental disability" under Section 15 of the *Canadian Charter of Rights and Freedoms* ('Charter') that provides for equality, is a good example of that. Interestingly, an author remarked that the majority of Canadian provincial jurisdictions use the term 'disability' in their human rights legislation, like the Charter, whereas two other provinces employ the term 'handicap'. In any event, the definition given to each term is fairly similar (1997, pp. 160–161 and pp. 165–166), and the term 'disability' "has been broadly interpreted by the Supreme Court of Canada to include a wide and evolving range of permanent, temporary or intermittent impairments, both physical and mental" (First Report of Canada, para. 26).

Canada as a Leader?

However, Canada's position as a leader or potential leader in that sector was challenged by the United Nations not so long ago. In 2017, the Concluding Observations on the Initial Report of Canada of the Committee on the Rights of Persons with Disabilities ('Committee') severely criticised Canada, including with respect to education (2017, para. 13(b)). The Committee noted, for example, that "the provisions of the [CRPD] have yet to be appropriately *incorporated into legislation* and policies across sectors and levels of government" in Canada (2017, para. 9(a)), including the adoption and implementation of policies on inclusive and quality education throughout its territory (2017, para. 44(a)). This criticism of the Committee leaves the authors of this paper perplexed. Malhotra and Hansen rightfully remarked,

> All elements of the CRPD, which are also part of customary international law, are automatically part of Canadian domestic law, *even where implementing legislation is not present*. This is because customary international law is regarded to be a part of the Canadian common law. (2011, p. 84).

This is exactly what the Supreme Court of Canada ('Court') recently recalled in the decision *Nevsun Resources Ltd. v. Araya* rendered in 2020, i.e., "customary international law is automatically adopted into domestic law without any need for legislation action" (para. 86; *R. v. Hape*, 2007, paras 36 and 39).

Historical Background

Being a country that may be considered a leader in the field, but that is also criticised, makes Canada, in our opinion, a good case study from which some lessons could be learned, which may eventually be useful for other countries. Canada, like many countries in the world, has come a long way to recognise and implement the right to inclusive education for children with disabilities. A common ground that may be shared between Canada and other countries is the fact that the history of education for children with disabilities may have followed a similar pattern (Timmons, 2008, p. 134). It is disturbing to remember that

> [p]rior to the nineteenth century, children with disabilities were considered evil or possessed and were generally excluded or hidden from society. In the late nineteenth century, Canada opened a number of institutions for people with disabilities. ... these

special schools were divorced from the general educational system and administered along with prisons, asylums, and public charities.

(Timmons, 2008, pp. 134–135)

Widespread abuse in institutions occurred throughout the country, including in "[r]esidential schools for Aboriginal children where children experienced significant isolation and abuse" (Timmons, 2008, p. 136). Over time, segregation gave way to the inclusion of persons with disabilities which led to the milestone of the 'Obstacles Report'.

The Obstacles Report

What is commonly called the 'Obstacles Report' was published in 1981 by the federal (national) Parliamentary Special Committee on the Disabled and the Handicapped. It was the first government-issued document to report issues faced by Canadians with disabilities. With respect to education, more specifically, the Obstacles Report did not make recommendations that would be considered ground-breaking nowadays, but they still outlined "practical actions which will help to overcome" (Canada, 1981, p. 1) some of these issues. For instance, Canadian provinces – because provinces have exclusive jurisdiction on education in Canada, as we will see in more detail in a moment – were encouraged to include education as a basic human right in the context where "disabled children, especially those with learning disabilities, do not have equal opportunity to education" (Canada, 1981, p. 27). This is reflected by Article 24(2)(a) of the CRPD, adopted 25 years after the Obstacles Report by the United Nations, that provides for "the customary international law right to basic education" (Malhotra and Hansen, 2011, p. 84). In addition, what was also encouraged was the development of course material on disability for teacher training, to support professional schools to learn about disabilities, and to establish a sign language department in both official languages in Canadian universities (Canada, 1981, pp. 104–105).

These last recommendations of the Obstacles Report seem to be either narrowly tailored to only address one specific item (sign language) that concerns only one disability in particular; or to be focussed on bringing awareness amongst teachers when more concrete actions to help children with disabilities were certainly called for; or to recommend a basic human right to education when such a recommendation in that context is mostly political and has no binding legal force. In spite of all the good intentions shown in the Obstacles Report, Canada certainly needed to do more to deserve being eventually called a leader in that sector. Regrettably, the recommendation regarding, for example, the sign language made in 1981 had not seemingly been properly or fully implemented in … 2017, when the Committee recommended that Canada "ensure[s] that teachers are trained in inclusive education at all levels and in sign language and other accessible format of information and communication" (para. 44(c)). A comment of a similar nature may also be formulated regarding the recommendation made in 1981 advocating for the creation of a basic human right to education. In that respect, the Committee in 2017 expressed concerns about the "persisting gaps in the exercise and enjoyment of rights by persons with disabilities, such as the rights to education" (para. 13(a)). The lack of progress shown over 40 years indicates a serious need for improvement in order to move from the theory (and non-binding promises) to the practice.

Uneven Application of the CRPD?

Some concerns identified by the Committee call for more specific comments, especially that these concerns are likely to happen elsewhere, more specifically in other federal states like India, Australia, the United States, Brazil, etc. (there are 25 federal countries in the world that cover 40% of the world's population). It is quite surprising to see that the Committee noted with concern an "uneven application of the [CRPD in Canada] by the judiciary" (2017, para. 9(b)). Indeed, it is hard to understand where an international organisation, such as the United Nations, finds its authority to criticise the proper functioning of a court system in a democratic country. In that case, the uneven application of the CRPD by the judiciary could be explained (and may be justified) by the principle that applies in Canada, providing that decisions made by provincial courts in a different provincial jurisdiction are considered persuasive and not binding. Persuasive cases are those that a court is not required to follow, but they may influence the court's decision. Therefore, the courts of a province may decide about an issue this way, while the courts of another province may decide another way, subject to potential conflicts of interpretation between the jurisprudence of each province.

While "it remains to be seen whether Canadian provinces will pass explicit implementing legislation or otherwise alter the existing relevant domestic legal framework" regarding education for children with disabilities (Malhotra and Hansen, 2011, p. 87), "it is [still] virtually impossible to determine what actual progress in support of inclusive education has been made in Canada in general" because "the individual provincial and territorial legislative policies [on education] perpetually fluctuate" (Lupart, 1998, p. 258). We shall recall that the "implementation [of the CRPD] does not need to be achieved exclusively through explicit implementing legislation" (Malhotra and Hansen, 2011, p. 86), as we discussed earlier. In practice, this would mean, if the CRPD is considered to be implemented in Canadian law via customary international law, that "persons with disabilities have the customary international right to basic education that all other individuals hold" (Malhotra and Hansen, 2011, p. 89).

CRPD and Its Legal Construction in Canada

That being said, "it is clear", as pointed out by Malhotra and Hansen, that "implementation alone is not the only method by which the [CRPD's] ratification is poised to influence Canadian law and the right to education specifically" (2011, p. 90). As the Court stated in the decision *9147-0732 Québec inc.*, "international instruments to which Canada is *not* a party [...] have only persuasive value in *Charter* interpretation" (2020, para. 35). In those situations, treaties may still be useful, at least, for example, in the interpretation of fundamental rights in Canada. Nevertheless, Canada *is* a party to the CRPD that it ratified in 2010. In a nutshell, the Committee acknowledged that the "CRPD's prohibition of discrimination on the basis of disability [could be] part of Canadian law, including as an implemented treaty obligation or an unimplemented but persuasive treaty obligation" (2017, para. 4).

CRPD and Unexpected Legal Issues

The troubling statement made by the Committee regarding an "uneven application of the [CRPD in Canada] by the judiciary" could also be deemed, if the logic was pushed to its logical end, as an attempt, more than likely if not certainly involuntary, to meddle with the independence of the judiciary in a democratic state like Canada where judges would be told by the Committee to pay lip service to this or that interpretation of international legal standards as long as an "even application" of a proper norm would be applied nationwide. Pushed a step further, this statement could even potentially defeat, at its core, the existence of the 'national importance' test of the Court (Section 40, Supreme Court Act) when applied to cases interpreting the CRPD in Canada, for example. Indeed, a 'forced' harmonization of the application of an international legal norm could have the pernicious effect of preventing at the beginning the emergence of potential conflicts of legal interpretation between the decisions rendered by different courts of several provinces (*R. v. Shea*, 2010, para. 8), which is one of the reasons why a matter is brought to the highest court.

In addition, the Committee has no authority to interfere, even indirectly, with the constitutional framework of a country, which is something that could be implied from their criticism about the "uneven application of the [CRPD in Canada] by the judiciary". As noted by Timmons, "education is a provincial responsibility, there is no national approach to inclusive education in Canada" (2008, p. 137), with the exception of Aboriginal education that is overseen by a federal (national) department (Timmons, 2008, p. 141) with the caveat that "historical treaties between Canada and Indigenous people maintained Indigenous control of education" (Gilmer, 2019, p. 388). This exception is factually grounded, summarily, in the fact that "[t]he history of education of Aboriginal children followed a different pattern from those of other Canadian children" (Timmons, 2008, p. 141), which is comprised of various traumatic events and shady institutions, such as the many infamous residential schools where children were subjected to a variety of abuses and active assimilation (Truth and Reconciliation Commission of Canada, 2015).

CRPD and Canada's Constitutional Framework

Putting that exception aside, "[t]here is no national office of education or any federal power to dictate educational policy" (Timmons, 2008, p. 134). Article 93 of the Canadian constitution also makes clear that "for each province the legislature may exclusively make laws in relation to education" (Constitution Act, 1867), then the lack of a national approach should not be understood as political negligence or nonchalance but, on the contrary, it would rather be a strict compliance with the constitutional framework that precludes the possibility for the national (federal) government to impose unilaterally a uniform approach for all provinces in the field of education.

With ten provinces in Canada that have their own *exclusive* jurisdiction over education, it makes it quite difficult, if not impossible, to have an *even* application of the CRPD by the judiciary in each province *a mari usque ad mare* in the context where "[s]ome provinces have adopted very detailed and specific legislation, whereas others have put more emphasis on changing resource allocation and philosophy" (Lupart, 1998, p. 258). This is not to say or suggest that fundamental rights, for example, that are applicable nationally, like the equality rights provided by section 15 of the Charter, should apply differently in this and that province, but we must emphasise the fact that, in Canada, the "provincial [educational] system creates considerable challenges in the development of a national picture of educational practices and policies" (Timmons, 1998, p. 134).

Along the same line of thought, the authors of this chapter must point out that one author stated erroneously that "one reason for [the] lack of impact [of the Charter in cases involving students with disabilities] is that the primary responsibility for education in Canadian schools lies within the provincial, not the federal, jurisdiction" (Lupart, 1998, p. 258), while the Charter is of federal jurisdiction. This statement is simply wrong in law. In fact, the Charter applies to the executive and legislative branches of the federal but also these branches of the *provincial* governments (*Dolphin Delivery*, 1986, para. 33; *Operation Dismantle v. The Queen*, 1985).

Relevant Canadian Jurisprudence

In light of all of the above, let us have a look into a few landmark Canadian decisions on point, even though one may acknowledge that the relevant issues litigated in Canada "in recent years [came out] with disappointing results" (Malhotra and Hansen, 2011, p. 75). Many of those issues were brought to court before Canada's ratification of the CRPD in 2010, which led an author to suggest that they "ought to be reconsidered in light of Canada's new obligations under the CRPD" (Malhotra and Hansen, 2011, p. 75).

The Eaton Case

For example, in *Eaton v. Brant County Board of Education*, a case decided by the Court in 1997, the parents of a child who suffered from cerebral palsy challenged the decision of their daughter's school board that stated she was better suited to special education classes than regular classes. The Court held, "While integration should be recognized as the norm of general application because of the benefits it generally provides, a presumption in favour of integrated schooling would work to the disadvantage of pupils who require special education in order to achieve equality" (Eaton, 1997, para. 69). This statement of the Court seems to be in contradiction with the language provided by Article 24(2)(e) of the CRPD, i.e. "Effective individualized support measures are provided in environments that maximize academic and social development, consistent with the goal of full inclusion", which supports a presumption in favour of integration.

The Auton Case

In *Auton (Guardian ad litem of) v. British Columbia (Attorney General)*, "a key decision in disability and education rights jurisprudence" rendered in 2004 (Malhotra and Hansen, 2011, p. 95), the Court held that the British Columbia government did not violate equality rights pursuant to section 15 of the Charter when it failed to fund specialised treatment required by children with autism. The Court held that *Canada Health Act* "does not promise that any Canadian will receive funding for all medically required treatment" (Auton, 2004, para. 35).

In *Moore v. British Columbia (Education)*, rendered in 2012, two years after Canada's ratification of the CRPD, Abella J., writing for a unanimous court, stated, in this case that was about a child with a severe learning disability who claimed he was discriminated against by his school, "Adequate special education ... is not a luxury. For those with severe learning disabilities, it is the ramp that provides access to the statutory commitment to education made to *all* children" (para. 5). Even though the CRPD is not relied upon by the Court, even once, in that decision, it still remains that there seems to be a shift in the language used by the court that looks more in compliance with this international instrument. As noted by a former Chief Justice of Canada, "Canada is known and is respected throughout the world for its inclusive approach to diversity" (McLachlin, 2015, p. 2). Will Canada also eventually be known worldwide for having the same approach *in practice* towards children with disabilities? We will leave the answer to be given to this question for another day.

Conclusion

Inclusive education does "not brush all children with one stroke" but engages with "specific requirements and individualized instruction and support" (Alkazi, 2014–15, p. 5). CWDs communicate differently and the CRPD emphasises that education systems have to be equipped to teach this diversity. The education systems cannot reject the CWDs on account of their disabilities. The authors have attempted to highlight the inconsistencies and irregularities in the regulation of the right to inclusive education for the CWDs in two countries, India and Canada. So many years down the line, it seems that our education systems are still battling to make it more inclusive. CWDs continue to be the most *excluded* segment of the society in both countries due to the lack of effective implementation. Despite the adoption of CRPD the tide is not changing fast enough in both countries.

Right to education has been adopted in India as a fundamental right and incorporated under various policies and legislation; however, the discourse on the education of CWDs has not changed substantively. It is worrisome to observe that in countries like Canada, deemed to be a leader in the field of inclusive education, that great advances remain to be done for inclusive education for the CWDs. These two examples of domestic application of this right should serve as a lesson for other dominions since, for example, many countries in the world, like India and Canada, have come a long way to recognise and implement the right to inclusive education for children with disabilities. Inclusive education in both countries remains narrow in scope, where the education systems fail to derive enrichment from the CRPD. In India, the education programme for the CWDs remains disjointed from the regular education system. However, despite these barriers, it has been seen that there is an effort on the part of government authorities in India to recognise such barriers and take steps towards their removal. In Canada, it is difficult, if not impossible, as we mentioned earlier, to determine the progress accomplished so far for inclusive education because "the individual provincial and territorial legislative policies [on education] perpetually fluctuate" (Lupart, 1998, p. 258). However, it is undeniable that Canada, as a whole, is still going, slowly but surely, in the right direction for the promotion of inclusive education for the CWDs, which is notably illustrated by the evolution of its jurisprudence on related issues.

Note

1 [#]This work was prepared separately from this co-author's (Sebastien Lafrance) employment responsibilities at the Public Prosecution Service of Canada. The views, opinions and conclusions expressed herein are personal to this author and should not be construed as those of the Public Prosecution Service of Canada or the Canadian federal Crown.

References

Alkazi, R. M. (2014–15). Fourth Annual report: The status of inclusive education of children with disabilities under the right to education act, 2009. *Centre for Research and Policy in Disability (CRPD)*. https://www.eenet.org.uk/resources/docs/right%20to%20education_in.pdf

Arduin, S. (2019). The expressive dimension of the right to inclusive education. In de Beco, G. (ed.), *The Right to Inclusive Education in International Human Rights Law*. Cambridge University Press.

Auton (Guardian ad litem of) v. British Columbia (Attorney General), [2004] 3 S.C.R. 657.

Bakhshi, P., Babulal, G. M., & Trani, J. F. (2017). Education of children with disabilities in New Delhi: When does exclusion occur? *Plos One*, *12*(9), e0183885. https://doi.org/10.1371/journal.pone.0183885.

Canada (1981). *House of Commons, Committees, 32nd Parliament, 1st Session: Special Committee on the Disabled and the Handicapped, Third Report.*

Collins, H. (2003). Discrimination, equality and social inclusion. *Modern Law Review*, *66*(1), 16–43.

de Beco, G. (2014). The right to inclusive education according to article 24 of the UN Convention on the rights of persons with disabilities: Background, requirements and (remaining) questions. *Netherlands Quarterly of Human Rights*, *32*(3), 263–287.

Dias, L. F. (2013). Disability and human rights: An Indian context. *Social Development Issues*, *35*(2), 38–49.

EASPD (2011). Barometer of inclusive education in selected European countries. https://includ-ed.eu/sites/default/files/good-pratice/files/dissemination-paper-english-web_0.pdf

Eaton v. Brant County Board of Education, [1997] 1 S.C.R. 241.

Gaur, G., & Panchal, A. (2021). National education Policy, 2020: Fallout from equitable and inclusive education for children with disabilities. In Kumar, B. (ed.), *Inclusivity vis-à-vis National Education Policy 2020*. NLU.

Gilmer, A. (2019). Indigenous knowledge–driven education reform as a means of achieving inclusive education in indigenous communities in Canada. In de Beco, G, Quinlivan, S. & Lord, J. E. (eds.), *The Right to Inclusive Education in International Human Rights Law*. Cambridge University Press.

Government of Canada (2014). *First Report of Canada, Convention on the Rights of Persons with Disabilities*, https://publications.gc.ca/collections/collection_2014/pc-ch/CH37-4-19-2013-eng.pdf.

Goyal, D. (2020, 7 Oct.). Assessing the level of inclusive education at the level of schools in India. Observer Research Foundation. https://www.orfonline.org/expert-speak/assessing-the-level-of-inclusive-education-at-the-school-level-in-india/

https://www.unicef.org/montenegro/media/7991/file/MNE-media-MNEpublication314.pdf

Khaitan, T. (2015). *A Theory of Discrimination Law*. Oxford University Press.

Lazarus, S. (2009, Jan.–March). Strategies to eradicate illiteracy from India in the era of globalisation. *Indian Journal of Public Administration*, 55(1), 108–118.

Lupart, J. L. (1998). Setting right the delusion of inclusion: Implications for Canadian schools. *Canadian Journal of Education*, 23(3), 251–264.

Malhotra, R. A., & Hansen, R. F. (2011). The United Nations convention on the rights of persons with disabilities and its implications for the equality rights of Canadians with disabilities: The case of education. *Windsor Yearbook on Access to Justice*, 29, 73–106.

McKenna, I. B. (1997). Legal rights for persons with disabilities in Canada: Can the impasse be resolved?. *Ottawa Law Review*, 29(1), 154–213.

McLachlin, B., The Right Honourable Beverly, Chief Justice of Canada (2015). Canadian constitutionalism and the ethic of inclusion and accommodation. *Western Journal of Legal Studies*, 6(3), 1–2.

Mehendale, A., Mukhopadhyay, R., & Namala, A. (2015). Right to education and inclusion in private unaided schools: An exploratory study in Bengaluru and Delhi. *Economic & Political Weekly*, 50(7), 45–51.

MHRD (2011). Sarva Shiksha Abhiyan: Framework for implementation: Based on the RTE act. https://dsel.education.gov.in/dsel/sites/default/files/2019-05/SSA-Frame-work_0.pdf

Moore v. British Columbia (Education), [2012] 3 S.C.R. 360.

Nagpal, R. (2018). Constitutional and government initiatives towards inclusive education in India. *International Journal of Academic Research and Development*, 3(2), 801–804.

Nevsun Resources Ltd. v. Araya, 2020 SCC 5.

Nussbaum, M., & Sen, A. (1993). *The Quality of Life*. Oxford University Press.

OHCHR (2013). *Thematic Study on the Right of Persons with Disabilities to Education: Report of the Office of the United Nations High Commissioner for Human Rights*. UN Doc A/HRC/25/29.

Operation Dismantle v. The Queen, [1985] 1 S.C.R. 441.

Persons with Disabilities (Equal Opportunities, Protection of Rights and Full Participation) Act (PWD Act) (1995). https://sjsa.maharashtra.gov.in/sites/default/files/pwd-act-1995-eng.pdf

Pramod Arora v. Lt. Governor of Delhi and Ors., W.P. (C) 1225/2014, Delhi High Court.

Quebec (Attorney General) v. 9147–0732 Québec inc., 2020 SCC 32.

R. v. Hape, [2007] 2 S.C.R. 292.

R. v. Shea, [2010] 2 S.C.R. 17.

Rao, P., Shrivastava, S., & Sarkar, T. (2020, April). *Towards an Inclusive Education Framework for India: An Analysis of the Rights of Children with Disabilities and the RTE Act*. Vidhi Centre for Legal Policy.

Right of Children to Free and Compulsory Education Act, 2009 (RTE Act). https://legislative.gov.in/sites/default/files/A2009-35_0.pdf

Rights of Persons with Disabilities Act, 2016 (RPWD Act). http://www.tezu.ernet.in/PwD/RPWD-ACT-2016.pdf

RWDSU v. Dolphin Delivery Ltd., [1986] 2 S.C.R. 573.

Salamanca Statement (1994, 7–10 June). *Salamanca Statement and Framework for Action on Special Needs Education*. Salamanca. https://www.european-agency.org/sites/default/files/salamanca-statement-and-framework.pdf

Sarkar, T. (2020, 19 Aug.). Examining disability inclusion in India's new National Education Policy. *UKFIET*. https://www.ukfiet.org/2020/examining-disability-inclusion-in-indias-new-national-education-policy/

Sen, A. (1985). Well-being, agency and freedom: The Dewey lectures 1984. *Journal of Philosophy, 82*(4), 169–221.

Sharma, U., & Joanne, D. (2005). Integrated education in India: Challenges and prospects. *Disability Studies Quarterly, 25*(1), 1–8.

Shevlin, M. (2019). Moving towards schools for all: Examining the concept of educational inclusion for disabled children and young people. In de Beco, G., Quinlivan, S., & Lord, J. E. (eds.), *The Right to Inclusive Education in International Human Rights Law*. Cambridge University Press.

Statement and Objects. Right of Children to Free and Compulsory Education Bill (2008). https://www.prsindia.org/sites/default/files/bill_files/1229341892_The_Right_of_Children_to_Free_and_Compulsory_Education_Bill__2008.pdf

Stein, M. A. (2004). Same struggle, different difference: ADA accommodations as antidiscrimination. *University of Pennsylvania Law Review, 153*(2), 579–673.

Stein, M. A. (2007). Disability human rights. *California Law Review, 95*, 75–121.

Supreme Court Act, R.S.C. 1985, c. S-2.

The Constitution Act, 1867 (UK), 30 & 31 Victoria, c. 3.

Timmons, V. (2008). Towards inclusive education in Canada. In L. Barton & F. Armstrong (eds), *Policy, Experience and Change: Cross-Cultural Reflections on Inclusive Education*. Springer.

Truth and Reconciliation Commission of Canada (2015). *Canada's Residential Schools – The Legacy: The Final Report of The Truth and Reconciliation Commission of Canada, McGill-Queen's Indigenous and Northern Studies*. McGill-Queen's University Press.

UNCHR (2007). *The Right to Education of Persons with Disabilities: Report of the Special Rapporteur on the Right to Education*. UN Doc A/HRC/4/29.

UNICEF (2019). *State of the World's Children. UNICEF Executive Summary*. UNICEF.

United Nation Convention on Rights of Persons with Disabilities (CRPD) (2006, 13 Dec.). UN Doc A/RES/61/106.

United Nations (2017, 8 May). *Convention on the Rights of Persons with Disabilities, Committee on the Rights of Persons with Disabilities, Concluding Observations on the Initial Report of Canada, CRPD/C/CAN/CO/1*.

Waddington, L., & Lawson, A. (2009). *Disability and Non-Discrimination Law in the European Union: An Analysis of Disability Discrimination Law within and beyond the Employment Field*. Publications Office of the European Union.

9
PARADOXES OF INCLUSION AND SEGREGATION DILEMMA EXPLORED THROUGH THE LENSES OF STUDENTS WITH DISABILITIES AND TEACHERS

Perspectives from Japan

Santoshi Halder* and Rumi Hiraga

Introductiond

Inclusion as a human rights issue has stirred the national and international sphere to create an all-participatory barrier-free and non-discriminatory environment for people with diverse needs. Inclusion is considered a process consisting of three dimensions; producing inclusive policies, evolving inclusive practices and creating inclusive cultures that have been widely used and validated in numerous locations around the world for manifesting inclusion and building inclusive school cultures and practices (Booth & Ainscow, 2011). Inclusion is conceptualized and understood with a myriad of thoughts ranging from the narrowest to the broadest sense of the term, encompassing beliefs, approach, practices, philosophy etc. Hence, inclusion is not merely assigning a person a place in an inclusive setting but rather extends further by manifesting successful accomplishments of the parameters of inclusion (i.e., equal rights and opportunity, participation, dignity, acceptance, decision making and choice) and participation at par with people without disabilities in society in all walks of life (Allan, 2008; Oluremi, 2012; UNESCO, 2005). Manifestation of full inclusion is possible only when the philosophy behind inclusion is deeply and rationally understood for subsequent practical implementation by fellow members of the society. In fact, inclusion per se should be as natural as human existence, as natural as development and life itself in its entirety (Hodkinson, 2010).

Emergence and Trajectory of Inclusive Education

The concept of "inclusive education" emerged at the World Education Forum in Dakar (2000) in response to a growing consensus that all children have the right to a common education in their locality regardless of their background, attainment or disability and stressed the goal of meeting

---
* santoshi_halder@yahoo.com; shedu@caluniv.ac.in

the learning needs of all young people and adults in a non-segregated educational setting (Judge, 2003; O'Brien, 2002; UNESCO, 2000, 1994). Rather than moving the child to a segregated setting to receive special services, inclusion started with the objective of bringing the needful support services to the child. Some of the most significant legislative bases that played a crucial role in bringing inclusion to the global sphere and stirred the national focus of inclusion and inclusive education as the human rights issue are: (a) United Nations Convention on the Rights of the Child (CRC, 1989); (b) Convention against Discrimination in Education of UNESCO (van Dyke, 1973); (c) Salamanca Statement (UNESCO, 1994); (d) United Nations Convention on the Rights of Persons with Disabilities (UNCRPD, 2006); and (e) Warnock Report (Warnock, 1979).

Though there has been an impetus from time to time in the implementation of inclusion worldwide, the actual process and the successes are extremely differential and gradual across countries (inter and intra). Literature in the area leaves no doubt that inclusion has become an integral aspect of our educational system, but there also exists simultaneous conflict and concerns with regard to defining inclusion in its entirety (Hodkinson, 2010; Hornby, 2002). Inclusive education involves full accommodation and participation of children with disabilities in regular classroom settings, allowing them to learn together with their peers without disabilities, laying the foundation for quality education for all children (UNESCO, 2005). As a consequence of the legislative mandates all students are guaranteed an education that is accessible, free, appropriate, timely, non-discriminatory, meaningful and measurable in the least-restrictive setting. Following the legislative mandates, a major proportion of students with disabilities switched to education in mainstream schools; however the outcome is extremely varied and differs from country to country (Snyder et al., 2016).

Inclusive education has always been controversial and is still being questioned with respect to placements and decisions of students with disabilities (inclusion vs segregation) and the extent to which inclusive practices and their philosophy has been manifested. Questions are still being raised for how much inclusion is benefitting all students with differential and diverse needs in terms of quality and meeting the needs of all learners (Agran et al., 2020; Dukes & Berlingo, 2020). Literature is replete with evidence that inclusion might not be effective or even result in negative consequences if merely led by enrolling students with certain disabilities in an inclusive setting without proper resources, facilities and support. Conversely, there is also evidence of students gaining and performing better in general education relative to special educational settings (Baker et al., 1995; Sapon-Shavin, 1996). There are also studies reporting that students with and without disabilities benefit from each other in each other's presence vis-à-vis separate settings or environments (Sapon-Shavin, 1996).

Inclusive Education in Japan

For a long time, children with disabilities in Japan were being educated in a segregated special education setting until 2006, when inclusive education came in to reform the conventional pattern of the education system and provide a new way of teaching-learning for students with disabilities (Abe, 1998). The special education reform of 2006 in Japan was the result of the combination of three intertwined political factors; (a) the international movement for school inclusion; (b) the reform of the Japanese welfare system for disabled people; and (c) the general reform of Japanese education. Meanwhile the policy and ideas of inclusive education got new impetus with the signing (2007) and ratification (2014) of the UNCRPD (2006). The outcome of such a treaty stirred the national agenda and reflected international concerns regarding the legal protection and rights of individuals with disabilities (Hayashi & Okuhira, 2001; Mithout, 2016).

Japan's inclusive education system is one of building a convivial society, where people with disabilities can fully participate and contribute to the society, where everybody respects each other's individuality, supports each other and accepts the differences (Abe, 1998; Hayashi & Okuhira, 2001). Henceforth, a complete reform of the special education system, anchored in the philosophy of "integration" (or "inclusion"), was implemented in 2006 to favour enrolment of students with disabilities into the mainstream system (Mithout, 2016). Following such reformative movement many special education settings were transformed into inclusive education settings to accommodate more and more people with diverse needs together with students without disabilities.

Rationale of the Study

In a true inclusive setting, everyone benefits from each other with dignity and respect through equal opportunities, participation and access. Henceforth the controversies related to inclusion questioned whether the services or support in an inclusive setting are able to provide an environment of equity and whether the differential needs are supported successfully and effectively. Such controversies related to teaching-learning of students with special needs still continue among the advocacy and practice groups (Hodkinson 2010) amidst the worldwide heralds of the inclusive trend. Despite the placement of students with disabilities, parents raise alarms about the gap between the needs of their children with disabilities and the inadequacies of services and support to effectively meet many of these crucial needs. Such interlude raises doubt about the inclusive education system currently flourishing in various regions or countries of the world. Hence instances of mixed outcomes stress the need to explore the educational settings (i.e., secluded and included both) to identify the areas of strengths and deficits in order to map constructive pathways for full inclusion for serving the differential needs of the students with disabilities to their fullest potential (Shapon-Shevin, 1996).

It is a matter of concern, especially for those with severe support needs, or those with a complex or severe disability who may not flourish well in the general education setting among people without disabilities due to lack of trained, competitive, willing and dedicated teachers and sometimes due to a lack of adequate infrastructure or other needful special aids or resources (O'Brien, 2002). Hence there has been strong criticism regarding the true manifestation of inclusive education that some students may be at risk of potential damage due to ineffective implementation of inclusion in real situations (Barton, 2005; Hornby, 2002).

From the existing literature it is apparent that there are major barriers to inclusion in its practical implementation. Surely mere placement of students with disabilities in inclusive mainstream settings without a meticulous understanding of the differential needs and without adequate and appropriate resources to serve the needs of all learners will not guarantee true inclusion: instead this will lead to more harm rather than benefits. There are pros and cons of the existing educational setting which need to be identified and understood beforehand for navigating an effective constructive way for benefitting the target population (people with disabilities, PwD) and manifesting inclusion in the true sense. Hence identification and understanding of the barriers are an essential prerequisite for creating an effective inclusive educational environment for people with disabilities (Anderson & Boyle, 2019).

Researchers have stressed that a successful inclusive experience involves those who are in close proximity with teaching-learning and that considering the voices of the *one who teaches preaches* and the *one who receives the teaching-learning* is very crucial as also stressed by earlier researchers (Hodkinson, 2010; Jones, 2005; Slee, 2011; UNCRC, 1989). Hence, the proposed study conducted an in-depth analysis of the existing status by deriving certain crucial elements of the educational setting from the two most important sets of people, those who offer the support or services (i.e., teachers) and those who receive the services (i.e., the students) (Hodkinson, 2010).

Study Objectives and Research Questions

a) What is "inclusion" for the students and teachers from a segregated higher education setting?
b) What are the challenges of studying in an inclusive educational setting (perspective of students and teachers)?

Sample and Participant Recruitment

The study samples (n = 11; 6 teachers and 5 special needs students) comprised 4 male and 2 female teachers, including 3 male and 2 female students with disabilities from one of the unique universities of Japan. The subjects were pooled through purposive sampling through an open recruitment process mediated by the co-author of the chapter. After the initial recruitment process only the willing and interested participants were included in the study. Informed consent was retrieved from the subjects, and a semi-structured questionnaire was filled in to acquire the demographic and desired personal details of the subjects. After the initial process of recruitment, the subjects were interviewed one to one through in-person in-depth interviews that spanned over an hour. The second author of the chapter assisted in translating and interpreting the conversations during the student interview when and where needed all through (for translation from Japanese to English and vice versa). All the interviews were recorded and transcribed with prior written consent.

The inclusion criteria for all participant recruitment were based on (a) voluntary participation, (b) having adequate skills in understanding spoken and written English, (c) being diagnosed with a disability, and (d) aged 18 years or over. Participant responses were anonymous and non-traceable, thereby ensuring confidentiality. Further details of the participants are provided in Table 9.1. The explorative approach of the interview questions intended to capture further insights for greater clarity and understanding of the responses retrieved through the semi-structured questionnaire, as it gave the participants an opportunity to freely disclose and reveal issues beyond the specific pre-selected questions. This was important for a comprehensive understanding of the area under investigation and illuminated important insights related to the aims of the study. Interviews were transcribed and analyzed to extract themes and sub-themes based on the study objectives.

Data Analysis

Qualitative methodology following a phenomenological approach extracted through thematic analysis was implemented by identifying and analyzing themes and sub-themes, as well as reporting patterns within data, by way of an independent and flexible approach to analyzing the shared lived experiences of the respondents. Qualitative research allows participants to speak in their own voices and thereby present their experiences from their perspective (O'Day & Killeen, 2002). This informs evidence-based practice (Grypdonck, 2006), which might be useful to a wide audience. Data were transcribed and analyzed following thematic analysis phenomenological approach methodology (Bogdan & Lutfiyya, 1992).

The interview was initiated by highlighting essential information about the study and its purpose before inviting the participant to talk freely about their journey or life trajectory. This was prompted by open questions such as "*Can you start by telling me about yourself, what you study currently and how you came to where you are today?*" and "*Can you let me know what challenges and*

Table 9.1 Demographic and personal information or details of the participants (N = 11)

Categories	Sub-categories	Frequency N = 11 (%)
Samples	Total	11
	Teachers	6 (55%)
	Students	5 (45%)
Age		
Teachers	41 and above	5 (45%)
	36-40	0
	30-35	1 (9%)
Students		
	22-23	3 (27%)
	20-21 yrs	2 (18%)
Gender		
Teachers	Male	4 (36%)
	Female	2 (18%)
Students	Male	2 (18%)
	Female	3 (27%)
Highest Educational qualification		
Students	Above masters	1 (9%)
	Masters	2 (18%)
	Bachelors	2 (18%)
Teachers	Above masters or Ph.D.	5 (45%)
	Masters	1 (9%)
	Bachelors	0
Experience of teaching	11 years and above	2 (18%)
	6-10 years	2 (18%)
	2-5 years	1 (9%)
	2 years and below	1 (9%)
Disability category		
Students		
	Hearing impaired	5 (45%)
Teachers	Visually impaired	0
	Hearing impaired/deaf	1 (9%)
	Non-disabled	5 (45%)
Major or core subject/course of study		
Students	Computer science	1 (9%)
	Information technology	2 (18%)
	Engineering	2 (18%)
Teachers	Computer software and hardware	1 (9%)
	Engineering	2 (18%)
	Information technology	1 (9%)
	English	1 (9%)
	Public health	1 (9%)
Course teaching	Computer software and hardware and auditory speech	2 (18%)
	Information and communication and technology	3 (27%)
	English as a language	1 (9%)
Years of teaching	12 years and above	1 (9%)
	7-12 years	2 (9%)
	3-6 years	1 (9%)
	1-2 years	2 (18%)
Teaching HI or VI students		
	Visually impaired course/students	2 (18%)
	Hearing impaired course/students	3 (27%)

benefits you experienced while studying in inclusive or mainstream education setting?" Recurrent follow-up questions were prompted such as "*Can you specify the advantages and challenges faced with certain instances?*" Students were further asked, "*Can you tell me what you mean by inclusion or what does inclusion mean to you?*" Participants were asked to specify and elaborate on each point as much as possible. Similarly, teachers were also asked to talk about the advantages and challenges of inclusive educational setting, elaborating with relevant examples wherever appropriate.

Data Saturation and Appropriateness of the Sample Size

The target was to include a small number of participants who were interested and eager to reveal the relevant and valuable information as per the study objectives (Teddlie & Yu, 2007). Data saturation was reached after 11 interviews. At this stage, the researchers decided not to include any additional participants as sufficient themes and sub-themes were already evident and were sufficient to respond to the objectives under consideration.

Findings and Discussion

The interviews were transcribed and analyzed based on themes and sub-themes, supplemented through relevant narratives and discussed further in the light of the objectives. Table 9.1 provides a complete demographic of the participants. The recorded interview responses through the semi-structured questionnaire were analyzed to extract the themes and sub-themes. Table 9.2 provides the sub-themes-wise frequencies as per the participants reporting, and Figure 9.1

Table 9.2 The sub-themes extracted from the interviews (n = 11)

Impediments	Sub-themes	Frequencies
Inclusion defined and related perspective	With and without disabilities together	9 (81%)
	Participation in all walks of life	4 (36%)
	Willingness of students with disabilities to accept non-disabled	1 (9%)
	More exposures and opportunities for creating awareness	4 (36%)
	Focusing on strengths whilst supporting weak areas	5 (45%)
	With or without disability; benefits both	5 (45%)
	Philosophy of inclusion should be instilled as early as possible	4 (36%)
	For true inclusion appropriate placement decision, a must	4 (36%)
	Majority typical people should constructively try ways	2 (18%)
	PwD can be equally be leaders and even support providers	2 (18%)
Challenges/ impediments	Enforced choice of mainstream education due to stigma	4 (36%)
	Difficult to be at par with typical students	6 (54%)
	Overcrowded class so individual attention not possible	8 (72%)
	Lack of alternative communication strategies	7 (63%)
	Limited budget	4 (36%)
	Inaccessible non-inclusive environment	6 (54%)
	Mainstream inclusive educational system still not ready	5 (45%)
	Noisy environment	2 (18%)
	Limited participation options	7 (63%)
	Mainstream inclusive educational system still not completely ready	5 (45%)

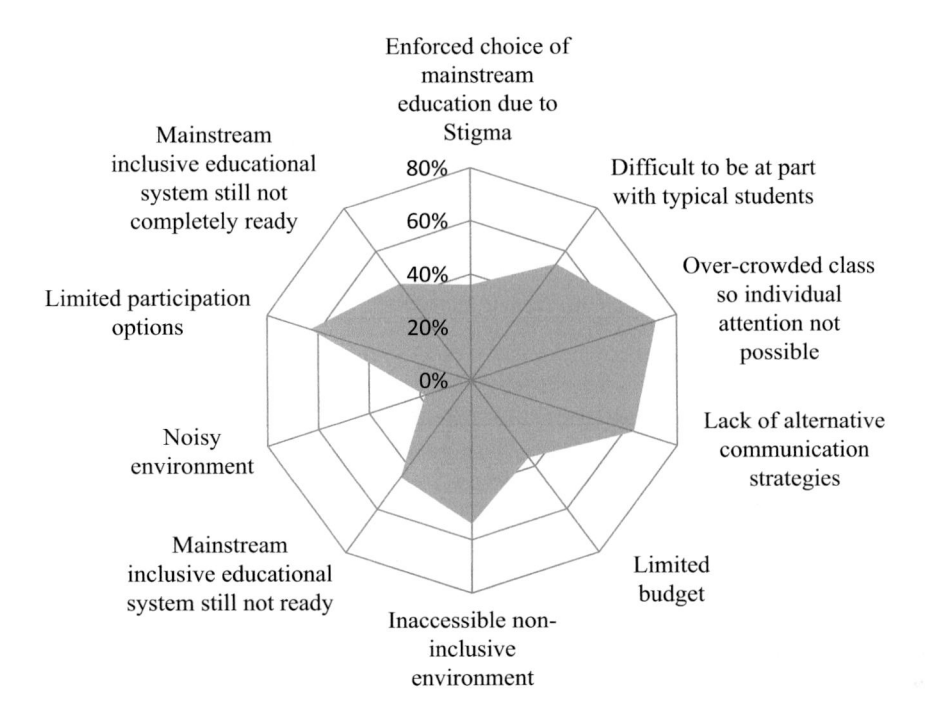

Figure 9.1 Impediments of inclusive setting

provides the details of the impediments in inclusive educational settings. The major themes extracted were;

- Perspective on Inclusion (teachers and students)
- Challenges of teaching-learning in inclusive setting (student and teacher reporting)

Perspective on Inclusion; Teachers and Students

When asked to express their understanding and perspective of the concept of inclusion, most teachers and students defined and expressed inclusion from a narrow perspective; "inclusion is students with and without disabilities educating together". It appeared all of them tried to look at inclusion from their own perspective based on their own past experience that is limited to disability. Most of them found the idea of education together, with and without disabilities, to be fascinating but expressed various impediments on its way for real implementation. Many of the students with disabilities had studied in both or either special education setting and also inclusive or mainstream educational setting during their school years (i.e., primary to high schools). Some of the most common perspectives on inclusion expressed by participants (i.e., students and teachers) are stated below.

Participants deliberated on the need for wider dissemination of inclusion in Japan as commonly most people are not aware of inclusion. Participants expressed that as they don't get opportunities or exposures to interact with people with disabilities in real life their concept remains limited. It was pointed out by some that even PwD should also be willing and shed their inhibitions to interact and mix with people without disabilities (PwoD) for inclusion to manifest. All through the findings section (^{TE}) denotes teachers and (ST) denotes students' quotes.

With and Without Disabilities Together

"Inclusion is students with and without disability studying together in the same class." (Itsuki[ST])

"Inclusion is education for everyone and that includes all. Especially those students who earlier used to have special places (blind etc.) are now having a chance to learn with students without disabilities. I just teach special needs students so my definition of inclusion may not be very broad." (Sakura[TE])

Participation in All Walks of Life

"Inclusion is when any person can take part in any activity in or outside the class irrespective of their differences. People need to know of inclusion and the basics of inclusion. In a special setting we discuss various aspects of inclusion and think of strategic actions. However, many people don't have a chance to interact with differently-abled people, especially in Japan as the topic is rarely discussed in common forums. Hence many people are not aware of inclusion as they don't get a chance to mingle with other ability groups." (Chibi[TE])

Willingness of Students with Disabilities to Accept PwoD

"Inclusion is something where people accept all other students who are different. Currently most students are joining general mainstream settings so eventually secluded settings are disappearing and in future even get extinct. There is a need for acceptance by both people with disabilities (PwD) also should have the willingness to accept people without disabilities (PwoD)." (Eiji[TE])

"I found some students with hearing impairment (H.I.) don't likely prefer talking with people who don't know sign language or do not prefer to use voice despite having voice to some extent. Living or mixing with typical people is not what they want. I think they are proud of their Japanese sign language (JSL) which they sort of consider as their 1st language and prefer that at any pretext." (Giichi[TE])

Increasing Exposures and Opportunities for Creating Awareness

"In Japan there is a culture that it's not a mandatory practice to accept people with disabilities by people without disabilities. I don't like this notion that PwD always needs to be cared for by others. I have transformed my earlier thoughts while interacting and mixing with (PwD) for a long time now. I believe they are capable of doing everything and even support others." (Eiji[TE])

Focusing on Strengths whilst Supporting Weak Areas

"Whether you have a disability or not, everybody has positive and negative traits or weaknesses. If the weaknesses are supported everybody can be included along." (Yuma[ST])

With or without Disability; Benefits Both

"Inclusion should be accepted and preferred and is necessary. One cannot go without mixing with neuro-typicals, both have to eventually live and thrive with each other. People studying in segregated settings may face challenges later in society. So, it is better if both are prepared beforehand since early years as both may benefit from each together" (Giichi[TE])

"I like studying together. I experienced inclusion earlier as I played with children with disabilities in elementary school in the USA where I studied for some time when I went with my parents. So, I am aware of their needs. Playing with them was enjoyable but I didn't get a chance to study together with them as they were in special classes." (Aito[TE])

"People without disabilities need to mix up with people with disabilities to recognize their talents and abilities." (Sakura[TE])

Philosophy of Inclusion Should Be Instilled as Early as Possible

"I would like my typical children to know various types of diversity. I expose my children to mix up with diverse people like who are in wheelchair or other disabilities. My children come up with questions and I explain them, teach them and make them understand the differences. I think the wall in between needs to be broken. I was curious to know them but didn't get scope. I have learnt about inclusion studying together in a cross cultural (during my study in a developed country) setting and liked being with them. Hence my perspective was shaped there. I don't want my children to judge others by their appearance. Especially in Japan we have all types of people, short, tall, different hair colour etc. so I want them to understand diverse perspective and differences and promote acceptance of diversities." (Aito[TE])

For True Inclusion Appropriate Placement Decision, a Must

To the question of whether they would prefer education in a segregated or inclusive setting and the reasons, there was a mixed response with valid justification based on their personalized needs driven by career choices. Some responded that they would prefer a segregated setting and expressed the reasons whilst some preferred the inclusive and or mainstream setting driven by various rationales. However, it appeared that almost all of them likely preferred teaching in an inclusive educational setting along with people without disabilities. However, the environment should have needful resources; infrastructure, facilities, accommodation, teacher attention and alternative strategies, along with a feeling of acceptance by others without feeling aloof or isolated. They also expressed that if that is not possible, they are equally happy to study in a segregated educational setting. Some teachers showed their concern regarding the difficulties that the students experience when they face mainstream society after the completion of their education. There are instances of struggles, challenges and even failures, not being able to cope well while transitioning from education to work.

"I think it depends on students' skills/preference and environment where students learn. Some students could adapt in an inclusive classroom but some may not. It is important to have careful selection of placement based on individual needs (Azuna[TE])."

"I do believe that some of our students will not be able to learn well in a mainstream inclusive setting as their needs are too unique and need personalized intervention and hence need special treatments and resources. I believe that would burden them more and create lots of struggle unnecessarily and that may interfere with their learning, performance and development (Sakura[TE])."

Majority Typical People Should Constructively Try Ways of Inclusion

"I learnt and liked sign language. Communicating using sign language helped me in understanding the students with disabilities and helped in bridging the gap (Aito[TE])."

"People without disabilities also need to be taught about inclusion and disabilities (Chibi[TE])."

"Our education system needs to be changed to fit the needs of all. We have to create opportunities to get to know others in society through constructive exchanges (Sakura[TE])."

PwD Can Equally Be Leaders and even Support Providers

"After their education here, they have to go back to their normal job so it is important for them to learn the skills needed later in life. Teaching how they can be leaders and providing them exposure is a must. The typical people also need to be taught and made aware about disability. Just receiving services should not be the end, the students with disability, if guided appropriately from the beginning, can also be leaders and support providers (Chibi[TE])."

Challenges Faced in Inclusive and/or Mainstream Settings (in Serving Needs of Students with Disabilities)

Students in the study completed their elementary and high school either in mainstream or integrated educational settings. Hence, they were able to report their experiences during their school years and their teaching-learning experiences in comparison to the later stage at the segregated educational setting during undergraduate (UG) or postgraduate (PG) studies. The most common challenges faced by students in the mainstream or integrated setting are reported below.

At the same time in some cases, it was apparent that sometimes despite the students' severe special needs the parents show their reluctance to enrol their children in a segregated setting due to the stigma attached to society. Hence in such cases it may lead to devastating results as many such personalized needs may not be served very well in mainstream or inclusive settings.

Enforced Choice of Mainstream Education due to Stigma

"Some parents are worried regarding the placements of their ward in a special educational setting. They cannot accept the fact that their children have a disability (Giichi[TE])."

Difficult to Be at Par with Typical Students

"Students coming from normal (mainstream and inclusive) high school expressed their struggle and challenges in mingling with their peers so they lacked and missed many aspects. They were happy after enrolling for a segregated higher education setting where they got all the necessary personalized support (Chibi[TE])."

Crowded Class so Individual Attention not Possible

"It is really difficult for some students in a mainstream setting to follow the class where they have numerous students (Giichi[TE])."

"I get sleepy and fatigued and tired when I have to use both ears and eyes and when the sound is very low that affects me a lot. When the environment is very noisy it's difficult as I have to concentrate more and that is too stressful (Yuma[ST])."

Lack of Alternative Communication Strategies

"In school I could not participate in debates though I found it very interesting (Itsuki[ST])."

"During one-to-one communication my friends try using finger gestures to communicate with me. But I cannot join the group when many friends are interacting together as I cannot interpret simultaneously. Some friends try to accommodate and talk to me through writing but it is always not possible. Hence I cannot participate in all activities during my school years (Mei[ST])."

"I have friends but very few. With hearing people sometimes, I communicate through voice. But sometimes I interpret wrongly due to the feeble voice (Yuma[ST])."

"In a special setting as they get to interact with their own type but in mainstream and or inclusion setting our students are not able to participate at all and rarely get students of similar need always so they feel uncomfortable and left out (Mei[ST])."

Limited Budget

It was apparent from the participants reporting that an inclusive environment calls for more budget allocation, which is most often insufficient or inadequate in a mainstream and/or inclusive education setting as fundings get divided based on the proportion of students. In a special education setting the entire budget is allocated to special needs support and services but in a mainstream or inclusive education setting there are many other priorities as well and thus many needs get overlooked, leading to limited scope for people with disabilities.

"Some students may want to learn with typical students. But hiring a language interpreter in mainstream school for just a few students may not be practical and cost effective in terms of budget or funding (Giichi[TE])."

Inaccessible Non-inclusive Environment

"Also, the campus may not be accessible or based on universal design principles and rarely equipped with safety facilities or conducive to meet their needs. Many inclusive settings lack such an inclusive framework in their campus (Eiji[TE])."

Mainstream Inclusive Educational System Still Not Completely Ready

"I think an ideal situation would be if people with and without disability can spend time together at the same place. But sometimes PwD struggles due to inadequacies of the environment. Desired accommodation is necessary. It is similar to fitting in with other forms of diversities in any society for e.g., older people, people from different cultures etc. (Azuna[TE])."

"In any mainstream or inclusive setting typically, people do not communicate in sign language. Hence students with disabilities cannot follow and understand much in a mainstream class. Inclusion is surely needed in Japan but not yet ready (Aito[TE])."

"Yes, I do believe separation is not good for anybody with or without disability. But to serve them together needs a lot of resources, time and efforts by all, also the class size needs to be small. It is not easy to serve their needs in a typical or usual general educational setting without these (Chibi[TE])."

Discussion

Participants revealed a multitude of challenges they experienced in the mainstream and inclusive educational setting during their school years. Most of the challenges are also endorsed and supported by their teachers who are currently engaged in teaching students with disabilities at a higher education level. The students with disabilities expressed the specific challenges in their everyday teaching-learning during their school years that covered specific areas related to classroom infrastructures, teaching-learning strategies, class size, time and efforts taken to understand their needs, teacher role etc. Findings are discussed as per the themes and sub-themes extracted with respect to the objectives undertaken for the study.

Challenges of Mainstream and Inclusive Educational Setting

The revelation from the participants who have themselves experienced the challenges in the inclusive and mainstream education settings provides many valuable insights about the multifarious existing inclusive and/or mainstream education systems worldwide. The first-hand experiences reflected crucial points for consideration for rectifying the same and lay constructive and strategic future directions. Participants revealed often inadequate and half-hearted ways and lack of planning and implementation of inclusion including challenges experienced by students themselves (Shapon-Shevin, 1996). The inadequacy of true inclusion has been under sharp criticism of late and has been blamed for a host of problems; overworked teachers, falling academic standards, lack of discipline and poor teacher morale (Shapon-Shevin, 1996) and some of these criticisms are consistent with the present findings.

Inclusion in the narrowest sense has been defined most commonly as the placement of special needs learners into a regular classroom along with students without disabilities (Stephane, 2010). But this is not the end of the process of inclusion as a true manifestation of inclusion entails executing multiple aspects for complete manifestation. For inclusion to be successful mainstreaming setting needs a well-adaptive, accommodating and flexible curriculum, an environment that offers architectural barrier-free accessible toilets, institutional campus, classrooms, a teaching-learning environment that provides scope for personalized approaches, alternative teaching-learning opportunities and strategies, necessary assistive technology support, aids and equipment, modified elevators, resource rooms, etc. so that the students benefit maximally when placed in inclusive or mainstream settings (Oluremi, 2012). However, it appeared from the participants' revelation that the inclusive mainstream settings were vehemently insufficient to serve the said needs which are concordant with earlier findings (Corbett, 2003; Hodkinson, 2010; Shapon-Shevin, 1996). Universal Design for Learning (UDL) needs to form a very crucial aspect of inclusion in creating an architectural barrier-free accessible environment for all. UDL is based on the notion that rather than forcing students into a one-size-fits-all learning style, educators must provide varied, personalized flexible options for teaching-learning, along with providing appropriate support and accommodations (Boroson, 2017). UDL strategies can help us acknowledge differences, differentiate instruction, and guide students to maximize their potential, while still leaving room for students' individuality to shine (Boroson, 2017).

Teachers play a crucial role in teaching-learning of the students with disabilities and their full participation and inclusion. Some of the main challenges reported are the wide teacher-student ratio as classrooms are overcrowded with few teachers to meet their unique differential needs in inclusive and mainstream educational settings. Some of the needs of some categories of disabilities like hearing and visually impaired are so unique, differentiated and individualized that one-to-one focus and attention is required which is not always possible in a mainstream classroom due to too many students (Fuchs & Fuchs, 1994/1995). Teachers in mainstream classrooms either are not willing or agreeable to serve the needs for fear of overload, and also, they find this affecting teaching general typical students (Hodkinson, 2010). Concurrently, participants also reported the lack of specialist teachers with adequate and sufficient training to understand their unique problems and serve them. Such deficits and inability to cater to the needs of their learners result in unmet needs and increasing students' struggle, as also endorsed by earlier researchers (Corbett, 2003; Hodkinson, 2010). Studies repeatedly questioned the competence of teachers who are not able to serve the needs of students with disabilities (Roach, 1995). Research posited inadequacies, teaching and non-teaching, in an inclusive setting to be devastating for students' growth (Skrtic et al., 1996).

Another important aspect of effective inclusion is budget and funding which has been reported as vastly inadequate to meet the needs of students with disabilities (Audit Commission, 2002). The software and technology support, specialist teachers, assistive devices and specialist personnel all need additional funding and that is found to be limited in many schools (Adaka, 2013). There have even been concerns raised for revising the curriculum and syllabus of teacher preparation courses, and despite such actions the gaps still persist and remain inadequate to meet the needs of teaching students with disabilities in an inclusive setting (DfES, 2004). The preparation of the educators is a primary contributor for inclusion which is severly inadquate. Most teachers are unfamiliar with many of the special strategies and methods that are so crucial and essential to break the barriers of communication between people with and without disabilities such as braille or sign language which are the essential prerequisites of communication (Adeyemi, 2013). Professional development of teachers for the inclusion classroom has been a matter of concern for a long time and is the most pertinent need worldwide, which still remains incomplete and inadequate (Adaka, 2013)

Educational institutions need to understand that people's diversity is always equivalent to enrichment as it offers everyone better learning opportunities (Stainback & Stainback, 1996). Hence difference needs to be received by the educational institutions in an effective way and the need is to think of constructive ways of creating such opportunities through real participation of various diversities together under one roof. The role of the adult mature educated coach is immense; the teacher can be a socio-pedagogical mediator who can manage personal and cultural differences that occur in the classroom constructively for inclusion to manifest (Vieira & Vieira, 2006). The teacher can bridge the gap and make fertile ground or a platform for various diversities to co-exist in a cohesive manner by creating and offering a comfortable inclusive environment of respect, acceptance and embrace (Sónia, 2012).

Some of the crucial elements from the participants' revelations are that every child is different with his own set of traits mediated by his own personal and contextual factors and those need to be considered and respected and embraced by providing a heterogeneous but inclusive classroom environment. An inclusive environment where each one feels at ease is comfortable and can thrive without any starry eyes, with a feeling of normality or not feeling deviated can manifest only when the philosophy of inclusion is enshrined in the young minds right from the growing years of life (UNESCO, 1994). Creating such a positive, cohesive environment is the prerequisite for inclusion to happen naturally all around. Young minds should be exposed to various forms of diversity in society so that eventually they are able to understand its natural existence and are better prepared and equipped to accept it with respect.

Future Directions

Enforcing inclusion superficially without implementing the true philosophy and full-fledged manifestation of the various elements of inclusion would be like seizing the essential differential individual needs of people with special needs or disabilities (Freire & Margarida 2003; Hodkinson, 2010). Surely rather than creating a path to exclusion, the goal should be prompting them back to inclusion (Rose, 1998) with the needful essential resources of an inclusive setting so as to serve their needs effectively. For a true manifestation of inclusion there is a need to understand its core values that appreciate differences by embracing and harnessing the differences and diversities (Coles & Hancock, 2002; Gee, 2020) by all people with and without disabilities so that PwD feel really included and can cast off the sense of feeling marginalized or discriminated against. Inclusion is surely a collaborative, cooperative team effort, a team that is heterogeneous and interdisciplinary with a specific role and contribution of each for making the place all-inclusive in a true sense for the diverse learners. The specialist team is required to work in cooperation with the regular teacher without any competitiveness and vice versa, without getting threatened by each other's pervasiveness (Serra, 2008). Bridging the gap between theory and practice is essential for inclusion to be successful, and that is only possible through an effective positive partnership between the regular teacher and the specialist teacher along with the entire team (Hornby, 2002; Ofsted, 2000; Booth et al., 2000).

Studies also reported that if schools are to become inclusive then they need to develop an ethos that not only enables all pupils to be supported but also provides for the needs of teachers (Hanko, 2003). These insights call for a well-designed teacher training programme for pre-service and in-service teachers that is tailor-made to develop the necessary skills to best serve the needs of students with disabilities in an inclusive setting. Earlier studies suggest that while a majority of teachers support inclusive education they do so with reservations (Croll & Moses, 2000; Hodkinson, 2005; Scruggs & Mastropieri, 1996) as they essentially may not have the necessary prerequisites for serving the needs. An effective model of teacher support that comprises collaborative, cooperative team work to cater to the needs of students with disabilities is a must for the successful inclusion of students with disabilities for true manifestation.

Important considerations for the successful manifestation of inclusion are surely based on the foundation and decision of placements based on the needs at the receiving end. The placement of students with disabilities in mainstream or inclusive education settings or segregated setting needs to be decided meticulously, based purely on regulating the severity, nature and intensity of the students' specific needs and deciding upon whether those needs could be successfully or effectively met in the proposed setting (Boroson, 2017). Earlier researchers have stressed "inclusion by choice" so that children are not forced into mainstream placements (Norwich & Kelly, 2013). Legislation certainly recommends inclusion for all, but that indeed is based on the premise of choice (Byers, 2005; Hodkinson, 2010; Warnock, 2005).

Inclusion is constructively and creatively thinking about how best to teach and learn amidst the varied nature of diversities existing in society and how best to utilize each other's strengths and address the weak areas, how best to benefit from each other and co-exist thriving together (Boroson, 2017). Hence the curriculum in inclusive classrooms must be flexible (Sapon-Shevin, 1996) so that each child is able to participate and thrive to his/her full potential as per the inherent abilities. As rightly put forth by Thousand, Villa and Nevin (1994) that inclusion invites not a watered-down curriculum but an enhanced one full of options and creative possibilities (Sapon-Shevin, 1996).

Conclusion

Interestingly the most prevalent and predominant approach for the manifestation of inclusion has been the top-down approach whilst what is needed is the bottom-up approach for inclusion to flourish successfully (Coles & Hancock, 2002). Researchers reported the top-down approach to be responsible for many of the barriers that are precluding some children from interfacing with mainstream provision (Hodkinson 2010). It is indeed high time that we realize not to repeat past errors and develop a new vision for the education of children with special educational needs that are supported by a well-coordinated and well-resourced support system to serve the needs better for realizing the dream of full inclusion all over. There is indeed a necessity to make all our schools fully inclusive with the wide range of diversities, be they gender, race and ability (Boroson, 2017) and creating opportunities for all, yielding maximum participation in the most comfortable ways.

Above all the effectiveness and success of full inclusion lies in understanding the core basics of respecting diversity in all forms, understanding that differences exist and are as normal as any other layers of development and that differences or diversities are not weakness but strengths of our survival and may be a solution to many complex intricate problems in society. Such a basic underlying philosophy of inclusion begins in the early growing years right after birth and needs to be enshrined in the child right from very beginning of their growing up in home and in school by mature adult coaches, parents and teachers who are the basic curators of the child's developmental trajectory (Vieira & Vieira, 2006). The core values and philosophy of inclusion need to be instilled in people with disabilities or without disabilities (Coles & Hancock, 2002) and most extensively among the non-disabled too so that the broader majority society attains an acceptance for any sort of deviations or differences and that comes when both strives together.

Limitation

The study has certain limitations which need to be noted. The study was a small sample study and included only those participants (teachers or students) who were willing to participate voluntarily. The students belonged to only two major departments of the University (i.e., hearing impairment and visual impairment).

Funding

Funding for the authors was supported by the Japan Society for the Promotion of Science (JSPS) Invitational Fellowship (Ref No.: S19070; 2019-23).

Acknowledgements

We would like to express our sincere gratitude to the participants of the study – students with disabilities and the teachers in Japan for their agreeableness to voluntarily participate in the study, for their willingness and for trusting us to share the first-hand account of their life experiences. We would like to thank the wonderful people who generously helped with the recruitment process.

Author Contribution

SH developed the concept, collected data, analyzed and wrote the manuscript. RH supported at every stage since the beginning and assisted in the recruitment of samples for the study and translation as an interpreter during the student interviews. All the authors read and approved the final manuscript before submission.

Conflict of Interest

Authors declare no conflict of interest.

Ethical Approval

The study was ethically approved by the National University Corporation of Tsukuba University of Technology (NTUT), Tsukuba, Japan.

Informed Consent

Written consent was undertaken from each of the participants as per the National University Corporation of Tsukuba University of Technology (NTUT), Tsukuba, Japan.

References

Abe, Y. (1998). Special education reform in Japan. *European Journal of Special Needs Education*, *13*(1), 86–97. https://10.1080/0885625980130108

Adaka, A. T. (2013). Inclusive education and systemic reform vis-a-vis national transformation. *Orient Journal of Education*, 7(1), 226–232.

Adeyemi, C. K. (2013). Challenges of providing special education services for children with visual impairment in Nigeria. In Proceedings for the Thirteenth Biennial Conference of the International Association of Special Education, Vancouver, British Columbia, Canada, July 7–11.

Agran M, Jackson L, Kurth JA, et al. (2020). Why aren't students with severe disabilities being placed in general education classrooms: Examining the relations among classroom placement, learner outcomes, and other factors. *Research and Practice for Persons with Severe Disabilities*, *45*(1), 4–13. https://10.1177/1540796919878134

Allan, J. (2008). *Rethinking Inclusive Education: The Philosophers of Difference in Practice*. (INED, volume 5), Springer. https:// 10.1007/978-1-4020-6093-9

Anderson, J., & Boyle, C. (2019). Looking in the mirror: Reflecting on 25 years of inclusive education in Australia. *International Journal of Inclusive Education*, *23*(7–8), 796–810. 10.1080/13603116.2019.1622802

Audit Commission. (2002). *Statutory Assessment and Statements of SEN: In Need of Review*, November.

Baker, E. T., Margaret C. W., & Herbert, J. W. (1994/1995). Synthesis of research: The effects of inclusion on learning. *Educational Leadership*, *52*, 33–35.

Barton, L. (2005). *Special Educational Needs: An Alternative Look. (A Response to Warnock M. 2005: Special Educational Needs - A New Look*.

Booth, A., Black-Hawkins, & Shaw, V. (2000). *The Index for Inclusion: Developing Learning and Participation in Schools*. Bristol: CSIE.

Booth, T., & Mel, Ainscow, M. (2011). *Index for Inclusion: Developing Learning and Participation in Schools*. Bristol: Centre for Studies on Inclusive Education.

Boroson, B. (2017). How has education evolved from exclusion to inclusion, from judgment to acceptance, and from disability to difference? *Educational Leadership*, April issue.

Bogdan, R., & Taylor, S. (1987, Fall). Toward a sociology of acceptance: The other side of the study of deviance. *Social Policy*, 34–39.

Byers, R. (2005). Editorial. *British Journal of Special Education 32*(3), 114–115.

Coles, C., & Hancock, R. (2002). *The Inclusion Quality Mark*. Croydon: Creative Education.

Corbett, J. (2003). Teaching approaches which support inclusive education: A connective pedagogy. *British Journal of Special Education*, *28*(2), 55–59. https://10.1111/1467-8527.00219

Croll, P., & Moses, D. (2000). Ideologies and utopias: Education professionals' views of inclusion. *European Journal of Special Needs Education*, *15*(1), 1–12. https://10.1080/088562500361664

DfES. (2004). *Removing Barriers to Achievement. The Government's Strategy for SEN*. London: DfES.

Dukes, C., & Lauren, B. (2020). Fissuring barriers to inclusive education for students with severe disabilities. *Research and Practice for Persons with Severe Disabilities*, *45*(1), 14–17.

Freire, S., & Margarida, C. (2003). "Inclusive ideals/ inclusive practices: How far is a dream from reality? Five comparative case studies." *European Journal of Special Needs Education*, *18*(3), 341–354. https://10.1080/0885625032000120224

Fuchs, D. & Fuchs, L. S. (1994/1995). Sometimes separate is better. *Educational Leadership 52*(4), 25.

Gee, K. (2020). Why indeed? Research and practice for persons with severe disabilities. *Research and Practice for Person with Severe Disabilities*, *45*(1), 18–22.

Grypdonck, M. H. (2006). Qualitative health research in the era of evidence-based practice. *Qualitative Health Research*, *16*, 1371–1385.

Hanko G. (2003), 'Towards an inclusive school culture - but what happened to Elton's affective curriculum?' *British Journal of Special Education*, *30*(3), 125–31.

Hayashi, R., & Okuhira, M. (2001). The disability rights movement in Japan: Past, present and future. *Disability & Society*, *16*(6), 855–869. https://10.1080/09687590120083994

Hodkinson, A. (2005). Inclusive and special education within the English education system: Historical perspectives. *Recent Developments and Future Challenges*, *37*(2), 61–67. https://10.1111/j.1467-8578. 2010.00462.x

Hodkinson, A. (2010). Inclusive and special education in the English educational system: Historical perspectives, recent developments and future challenges. *British Journal of Special Education*, *462*, 61–67. https://10.1111/j.1467-8578.2010.00462.x

Hornby, G. (2002). Promoting responsible inclusion: Quality education for all. In *Supporting Inclusion in the Early Years*. Jones, Maidenhead: Oxford University Press.

Judge B. (2003) Inclusive Education: Principles and practices, in Crawford K. (Ed.) *Contemporary Issues in Education*. Dereham: Peter Francis.

Jones, M. K. (2005). Is there employment discrimination against the disabled? In *WELMERC Discussion Papers*, Swansea: University of Wales.

Mithout, A.-L. (2016). Children with disabilities in the Japanese school system: A path toward social integration? *Contemporary Japan*, *28*(2), 165–184. https://10.1515/cj-2016-0009

Norwich, B., & Kelly, N. (2013). Pupils' views on inclusion: Moderate learning difficulties and bullying in mainstream and special schools. *British Educational Research Journal*, *30*(1), 43–65.

O'Brien, T. (2002). *Enabling Inclusion: Blue Skies… Dark Clouds*. London: Optimus.

O'Day, B., & Killeen, M. (2002). Research on the lives of persons with disabilities: The emerging importance of qualitative research methodologies. *Journal of Disability Policy Studies*, *13*, 9–15.

OfStEd, Office for Standards in Education. (2000). *Evaluating Educational Inclusion: Guidance for Inspectors and Schools*. London: OfStEd.

Oluremi, F. D. (2012). "Special schools and mainstreaming programme in Nigeria and lessons for 21st century. *Nigeria: Ife – Psychologia*, *21*(1), eISSN, 1117–1421.

Rose, R. (1998). O Currículo: Um veículo para a inclusão ou uma alavanca para a exclusão? In *Promover a Educação Inclusiva*. Lisboa: Porto Editora.

Roach, V. (1995). *Winning ways: Creating inclusive schools, classrooms, and communities*. Alexandria, VA: National Association of State Boards of Education.

Sapon-Shevin, M. (1996). Full inclusion as disclosing tablet: Revealing the flaws in our present system. *Theory in to Practice*, *35*(1), Inclusive Schools: The Continuing Debate (Winter, 1996), 35–41.

Scruggs, T. E., & Mastropieri, M. A. (1996). "Teacher perceptions of mainstreaming inclusion, 1958–1995: A research synthesis." *Exceptional Children*, *63*, 59–74.

Serra, H. (2008). "NEE dos alunos disléxicos e/ou sobredotados. *Revista Saber (e)" Educar*, *13*, 137–147.

Skrtic, T. M., Wayne, S. & Gee, K. (1996). Voice, collaboration, and inclusion: Democratic themes in educational and social reform initiatives. *Remedial and Special Education* 17, 142–157.

Slee, R. (2011). *The Irregular School: Exclusion, Schooling and Inclusive Education*. Abingdon: Routledge.

Snyder, T. D., de Brey, C., & Dillow, S. A. (2016). Digest of education statistics, 2014. NCES 2016006, National Center for Education Statistics, Institute of Education Sciences, US Department of Education. Available at https://nces.ed.gov/pubsearch/pubsinfo.asp?pubid= 2016006 (accessed June 1, 2016).

Sónia, L. (2012). From exclusion to inclusion going through segregation and integration: The role of the school and of the sociopedagogical mediator. *Procedia – Social and Behavioral Sciences*, *69*(24), 47–53. https://10.1016/j.sbspro.2012.11.382

Teddlie, C., & Yu, F. (2007). Mixed methods sampling: A typology with examples. *Journal of Mixed Methods Research*, *1*(1), 77–100. https://10.1177/1558689806292430

Stainback, W., Stainback, S., & Stefanich, G. (1996). Learning together in inclusive classrooms: What about the curriculum? *28*(3). https://10.1177/004005999602800303

Stephanie, T. (2010). *Special Needs: Types of Development Disabilities*. USA: Sara Malburg.

The Salamanca Statement and Framework for Action on Special Needs Education (UNESCO). (1994). Adopted by the World Conference on Special Needs Education [microform]: Access and Quality (Salamanca, Spain, June 7–10, 1994), Ref: ED-94/WS/l 8. (PDF-File, 198 KB) Retrieved from https://en.unesco.org/themes/education/

The United Nations. (1989). Convention on the Rights of the Child. *Treaty Series*, *1577*, 3.

The United Nations. (2006). Convention on the Rights of Persons with Disabilities. *Treaty Series*, *2515*, 3.

The United Nations Education, Scientific and Cultural Organization (UNESCO). (1994). *The Salamanca Statement and Framework for Action on Special Needs Education*. Paris: UNESCO.

Thousand, J. S., Villa, R. A., & Nevin, A. (1994). *Creativity and Collaborative Learning: A Practical Guide for Empowering Students and Teachers*. Baltimore: Paul H., Brookes.

United Nations Education, Scientific and Cultural Organization (UNESCO). (2000). Dakar framework for action: Education for all. In Meeting Our Collective Commitments. World Forum on Education, Dakar, Senegal, 26–28 April. Paris: UNESCO.

UNESCO. (2005). Guidelines for inclusion: Ensuring access to EFA. Retrieved from www.unesco.org/education/educprog/sne on 29/7/'09.

van Dyke. (1973 Dec.). Equality and Discrimination in Education: A Comparative and International Analysis. *International Studies Quarterly 17*(4), 375–404. https:// 10.2307/2600219

Vieira, A. M. S. N., & Vieira, R. M. N. (2006). Educação e Trabalho Social na Escola. http://www.apagina.pt/?aba=7&cat=157&doc=11623&mid=2

Warnock, M. (2005). *Special educational needs: A new look, Impact, 11.* London: The Philosophy of Education Society of Great Britain.

Warnock Report. (1979). *Comments on the Report of the Committee of Enquiry into the Education of Handicapped Children and Young People 'Special Educational Needs'.* (Summary), July. https://10.1192/S0140078900004788

10
PARTICIPATION OF CHILDREN WITH DISABILITIES AND THEIR PEERS IN LOW- AND MIDDLE-INCOME COUNTRIES

Comparison of Children with and without Disabilities

Shakila Dada*, Kirsty Bastable, Alecia Samuels, Mats Granlund, Liezl Schlebusch, and Karina Huus[1]

Participation in all aspects of life is identified as a right for all children in the Convention on the Rights of the Child (Unicef, 1999) and defined as "involvement in a life situation" (p. xvi) in the International Classification of Functioning, Disability and Health – Child and Youth Version (World Health Organisation, 2007). For children with disabilities this includes the right to involvement in education (Schuelka et al., 2020).

Inclusive education has been highlighted as a mechanism which facilitates the participation of children with disabilities in education (Sánchez et al., 2019). However, participation is a multidimensional construct which includes both attendance at (being there) and involvement in (experiencing) activities (World Health Organisation, 2007). In education, attendance at school is easily measured, but it is the involvement component of participation which captures the classroom experience of teachers and children and is ultimately responsible for the outcomes of inclusive education (Braun, 2019; Schuelka et al., 2020).

In addition, however, participation is influenced by personal constructs such as: activity competence (abilities), preferences and sense of self, as well as environmental constructs such as: activity settings, social and physical environments. Participation and its related constructs are described in the Family of Participation-Related Constructs (Imms, Granlund, et al., 2017) (fPRC) model, where participation, personal and environmental constructs are shown to have a bidirectional influence on each other (Adair et al., 2018; Granlund, 2013; Imms, Granlund, et al., 2017; G. King et al., 2004; M. King et al., 2013).

For children, who have developmental disabilities (DD), which is defined as a chronic condition that arises prior to adulthood and affects learning and development (Center for disease control and prevention & Centers for disease control and prevention, 2013), personal constructs

* shakila.dada@up.ac.za
DOI: 10.4324/9781003266068-13

relating to their disability may result in lower levels of participation in comparison to their peers who are typically developing (TD). Specifically, the diversity (attendance) of active physical, social and academic activities (G. King et al., 2010; M. King et al., 2013; Law et al., 2006) and intensity (frequency) of in- and out-of-school activities has been identified as lower for children with DD (M. King et al., 2013; Law et al., 2006). In contrast, informal and leisure activities are reported to have similar levels of participation for children with DD when compared to peers with TD (G. King et al., 2010; M. King et al., 2013; Law et al., 2006). In addition, within disabilities, children with more severe disabilities are reported to have lower diversity and intensity of participation than their peers with milder disabilities (Forsyth et al., 2007; Law et al., 2012; Longo et al., 2014; Parkes & Mccullough, 2010; Piškur et al., 2015; Shikako-thomas, Shevell, Schmitz, et al., 2013; Ullenhag et al., 2014).

Similarly, environmental factors may decrease opportunities for participation, for example lower socioeconomic status (G. King et al., 2007; Piškur et al., 2015; Shikako-thomas, Shevell, Schmitz, et al., 2013; Ullenhag et al., 2014), decreased parental education or increased parental stress (G. King et al., 2013; Law et al., 2006; Parkes & Mccullough, 2010). Furthermore children in different geographical regions have been seen to participate in different activities at different intensities (Forsyth et al., 2007; G. King et al., 2013; Ullenhag et al., 2012).

Although evidence on the participation of children is growing, this is primarily for high-income countries. A recent review (Schlebusch et al., 2020) identified only 78 studies published in a period of 18 years relating to participation in LMIC, with the majority (60%) of studies coming from four middle-income countries. Environmental factors including, poverty, low education levels and disparities in access to services and support have been highlighted as challenges to participation in LMIC (Beegle et al., 2016; Jamieson et al., 2017; Narayan et al., 2018; The World Bank, 2018b, 2018a). Involvement in activities has been identified as being particularly at risk when an accumulation of adverse environmental factors occurs (Almqvist, 2006). Hence, it may not be suitable to generalise learnings from high-income countries to LMIC countries until a better understanding of participation in LMIC is achieved (Twible & Henley, 2000).

Without understanding how participation differs between children with typical development and children with disabilities it is difficult to address the needs of children with disabilities in the classroom in order to provide them with the best possible outcomes.

Aims

This chapter aims to describe the literature related to how children in LMIC with DD are participating in comparison to their peers with TD. The review aimed to identify, compare and discuss the assessments used and participation results in line with the fPRC model of participation.

Method

A scoping review was employed in order to identify a broad range of literature from LMIC. Scoping reviews are similar to systematic reviews but provide for broader search terms and greater flexibility of inclusion criteria (Rumrill et al., 2010).

Search terms relating to children and youth, participation, disabilities or long-term health conditions and LMIC were used across six electronic databases, namely PsycINFO, MEDLINE, CINAHL, PubMed, ERIC, and Africa Wide Information. An initial search across the same search terms was conducted in 2016 (updated 2018), and the results reported by Schlebusch et al. (2020) were made available to the authors of this chapter, as the Schlebusch et al. (2020) paper reported only on the status of research in LMIC and not the outcomes of the participation of children in these countries. This search was then repeated and updated to include literature from 2018 to 2021 (May). For the full search terms refer to Schlebusch et al. (2020).

The search results were evaluated against the inclusion and exclusion criteria for this review, namely, children as study participants (0–19 years), using a standardised assessment measure and including both children with TD and children with DD. The articles were reviewed at the title and abstract level (93.7% agreement) and at the full-text level (100% agreement) by two independent reviewers.

Data Extraction

Data was extracted and described in terms of (a) author and date of publication; (b) title; (c) country of study (d) the measure defined by authors as a participation measure including a description and any adaptations; (e) sampling and source of participants; (f) participant descriptions (number of participants, age, gender, disability); (g) participation constructs (diversity and intensity, differences between children who have TD and those who had DD) and (h) related constructs (personal, e.g. activity competence – or the ability to perform an activity; and environmental e.g. cultural factors).

Data Synthesis

The extracted data was analysed and synthesised to describe the participation of the children in LMIC countries according to the components of the fPRC (Imms, Granlund, et al., 2017) and the participation measures were screened and mapped to the fPRC (Imms, Granlund, et al., 2017).

Results

A total of 1,144 articles were identified for screening at the title and abstract level and 61 at the full-text level. Twenty-two articles were initially identified for data extraction, but six of these were identified as using the same data as other articles. Where articles reported on the same data the article which most clearly reported on participation outcomes was included and the remainder were excluded, leaving 16 articles reported on in this review.

The search processes for this review are described in Figure 10.1 and Table 10.1.

Setting

The studies were conducted in urban areas in eight middle-income countries; two lower-middle-income, India (Sachdeva & Rao, 2012; Srinivasan et al., 2021) and Jordan (Almasri et al., 2019); and six upper-middle-income countries, Brazil (Amaral et al., 2014; dos Santos et al., 2013), China (Chien, Leung, et al., 2020; Chien, Li-Tsang, et al., 2020; Hu et al., 2012; Shi et al., 2021), Iran (Mehraban et al., 2016), South Africa (Samuels et al., 2020), Serbia (Milićević, 2020) and Turkey (Elbasan et al., 2013; Kara et al., 2020; Şahin et al., 2020; Tarakci et al., 2011). The studies were published between 2011 and 2021, with the majority (n = 7) published in 2020 and 2021. Children aged five to 19 years (n = 4274) were included, DD (n = 1440) and TD (n = 1934). Of the children, 2,265 were boys and 1,459 were girls, although one study (n = 100) did not report on gender. Disabilities reported included cerebral palsy, Down syndrome,

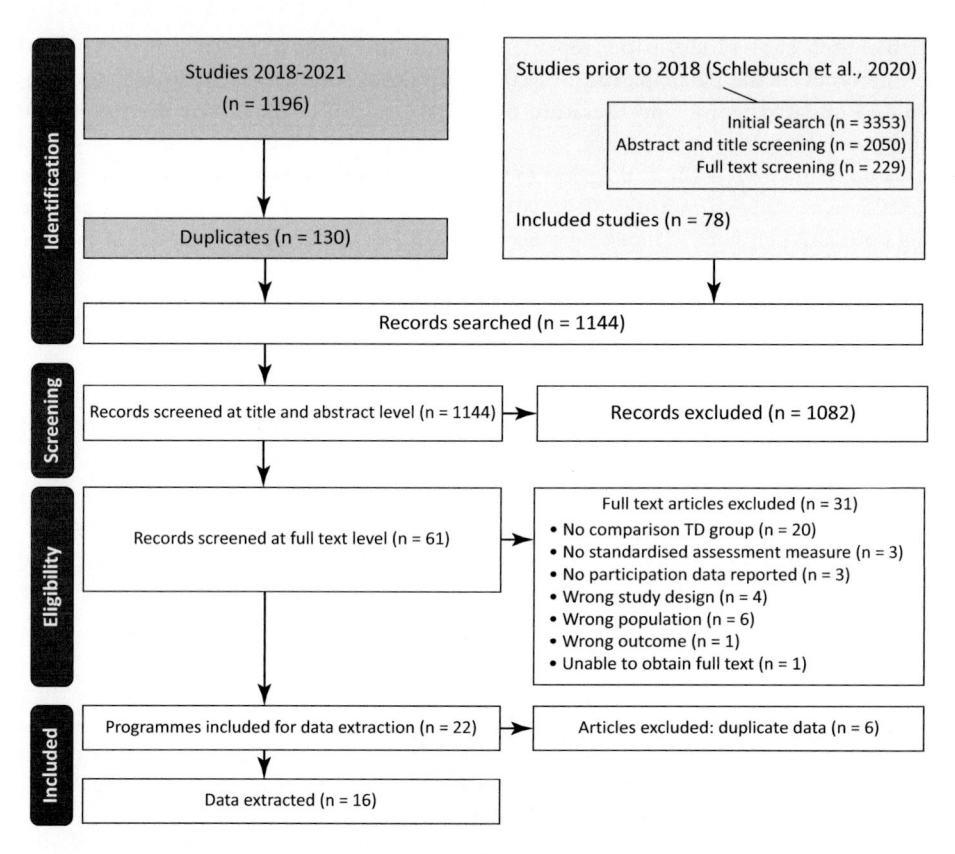

Figure 10.1 PRISMA flow chart of the scoping review process (Page et al., 2021)

hearing impairment, intellectual disabilities, learning disabilities and juvenile idiopathic arthritis. Participants were selected, and data was collected in schools, clinics, rehabilitation centres, non-profit organisations and through advertising. See Table 10.2 for the data extracted in this review.

Participation Measures Used

The studies made use of existing assessment measures administered in the language of the region. One study did not specify the language used (dos Santos et al., 2013). Information on the measures and their adaptation for use in LMIC is available in Table 10.3.

The Children's Assessment of Participation and Enjoyment (CAPE) (G. King et al., 2004) is a self-report tool that measures attendance (diversity and intensity) and involvement (enjoyment). It also measures environment/context constructs by determining with whom and where children participate (Adair et al., 2018).

The Children Helping Out: Responsibilities, Expectations and Support (CHORES) (Dunn, 2004) is a proxy report measure of the expected roles and responsibilities of children at home and the assistance required to fulfil these. The CHORES (Dunn, 2004) measures activity competence (personal construct) by determining what activities are expected of a child and the assistance required to perform that activity.

Table 10.1 Studies included in the scoping review

Author (date)	Title	Country	Participation measure	Sampling type Source	Description of Participants (N, n (TD) and n (DD), age, and gender)
Almasri, Palisano, and Kang, (2017)	Cultural adaptation and construct validation of the Arabic version of children's assessment of participation and enjoyment and preferences for activities of children measures	Jordan	CAPE (King et al., 2004) (Self-Report)	Purposeful Advertising Snowballing	$N = 150$ TD n = 75 ♂41♀34 10.7 (2.9) D n = 75 ♂46♀29 10.8 (2.7)
Amaral, Drummond, Coster, & Mancini (2014)	Household task participation of children and adolescents with cerebral palsy, Down syndrome and typical development.	Brazil	CHORES (Dunn, 2004) (Proxy report)	Purposive (D) Community health care centre Convenience (TD) Schools	$N = 75$ 9.3(2.2) TD n = 25♂15♀10 CP n = 25♂ 12♀ 13 DS n = 25♂ 12♀ 13

(Continued)

Table 10.1 (Continued)

Author (date)	Title	Country	Participation measure	Sampling type Source	Description of Participants (N, n (TD) and n (DD), age, and gender)
Chien, Leung, Schoeb, and Au (2020)	A Chinese version of the Young Children's Participation and Environment Measure: Psychometric evaluation in a Hong Kong sample	China (Hong Kong)	PEM-CY (Coster et al., 2010) (Proxy report)	Convenience and snowballing School and advertising (TD) Hospitals, Rehabilitation Centres (D)	N = 72 ♂39 ♀33 2-5 years TD n = 43 D n = 29
Chien, Li-Tsang, Cheung, Leung, Lin (2019)	Development and psychometric evaluation of the Chinese version of the Participation and Environment Measure for Children and Youth Chi-Wen	China (Hong Kong)	PEM-CY (Coster et al., 2010) (Proxy report)	Convenience Schools (TD and D)	N = 130 5.5-12.5 years TD n = 65 ♂48 ♀17 12.44 (2.89) D n = 65 ♂48 ♀17 12.75 (2.95)

Author (date)	Title	Country	Participation measure	Sampling type Source	Description of Participants (N, n (TD) and n (DD), age, and gender)
Dos Santos et al. (2013)	Sit-to-stand movement in children with hemiplegic cerebral palsy: Relationship with knee extensor torque and social participation.	Brazil	LIFE-H (Fougeyrollas et al., 1998) (Proxy report)	Purposive Rehabilitation centre	N = 25 TD n = 18 8.4 (2.3) ♂ 9 ♀ 9	CP n = 7 8.0 (2.2) ♂ 2 ♀ 5
Elbasan et al. (2013)	Is there any difference in health-related quality of life, self-care and social function in children with different disabilities living in Turkey?	Turkey	CHQ-PF50 (Ruperto et al., 2001) (Proxy report) Turkish translation (Ozdogan et al., 2001)	Purposive (TD) Schools Convenience (D) Rehab centre University clinic	N = 130 ♂82 ♀48 TD n = 285.9(0.8)	CP n = 346.0y(0.8)	ID n = 41 6.6(0.7)	HI n = 276.3(0.7)
Hu et al. (2012)	The applicability of WHODAS 2.0 in adolescents in China.	China	WHODAS 2.0 (Üstün et al., 2010) (Self-Report)	Purposive In-patients (D) Schools (TD)	N = 628 TD n = 314 10–15 years ♂ 140 ♀ 174	D n = 314 10–19 years ♂ 214 ♀ 100

(Continued)

Table 10.1 (Continued)

Author (date)	Title	Country	Participation measure	Sampling type Source	Description of Participants (N, n (TD) and n (DD), age, and gender)
Kara et al. (2020)	Psychometric properties of the Turkish version of Participation and Environment Measure for Children and Youth	Turkey	PEM-CY (Coster et al., 2010) (Proxy report)	Convenience (TD and D)	N = 410 TD n = 178 ♂93♀85 12.1 (3.9) D n = 232 ♂160♀72 11.5 (3.3)
Mehraban et al. (2016)	The comparison of participation in school-aged cerebral palsy children and normal peers: A preliminary study.	Iran	CAPE (King et al., 2004) (Self-Report)	Convenience Regular school (TD) Special schools (D)	N = 60 8–14 years TD n = 30 ♂ 15♀ 15 CP n = 30♂ 15♀ 15
Milićević (2020)	Home participation of children with and without cerebral palsy in Serbia: An exploratory study.	Serbia	PEM-CY (Coster et al., 2010) (Proxy report)	Convenience Schools (TD and D)	N = 144 TDn = 134 ♂66♀68 12.0 (3.1) CP n = 110 ♂61♀49 12.8 (3.5)

Author (date)	Title	Country	Participation measure	Sampling type Source	Description of Participants (N, n (TD) and n (DD), age, and gender)
Sachdeva & Rao (2012)	Community participation activities involving money handling skills of children with learning disability as compared to children with typical development aged 10 to 14 years.	India	Delta Screener (Morel, 2008) (Self-Report)	Purposive Inclusive public schools	N = 168 TD n = 139 ♂72 ♀67 LD n = 29 ♂18 ♀11
Şahin, Kara, Köse and Kara (2020)	Investigation on participation, supports and barriers of children with specific learning disabilities	Turkey	PEM-CY (Coster et al., 2010) (Proxy report)	Convenience Study group (D)	N = 178 TD n = 88 ♂48♀40 11.6 (3.2) LD n = 90 ♂69♀21 11.0 (2.8)

(Continued)

Table 10.1 (Continued)

Author (date)	Title	Country	Participation measure	Sampling type Source	Description of Participants (N, n (TD) and n (DD), age, and gender)
Samuels, Dada, Van Niekerk, Arvidsson and Huus (2020)	Children in South Africa with and without Intellectual Disabilities' Rating of Their Frequency of Participation in Everyday Activities.	South Africa	PMP (Arvidsson et al., 2019) (Self-report)	Purposeful Special Schools (ID)	N = 112 TD (ZA) n = 33 ♂11♀22 11.2 (1.6) ID (ZA) n = 79 ♂38♀36 12.7 (1.7)
Shi, Granlund, Zhao, Hwang, Kang, and Huus (2021)	Transcultural adaptation, content validity and reliability of the instrument 'Picture My Participation' for children and youth with and without intellectual disabilities in mainland China.	China	PMP (Arvidsson et al., 2019) (Self-report)	Convenience Hospital outpatients, special needs and mainstream schools (TD and D)	N = 762 TD n = 651 ♂423♀296 12.9 (2.3) ID n = 111 ♂355♀43 13.5 (3.8)

Author (date)	Title	Country	Participation measure	Sampling type Source	Description of Participants (N, n (TD) and n (DD), age, and gender)
Srinivasan, Roopa and Kulkarni, Vrushali and Smriti, Sana and Teplicky, Rachel and Anaby (2021)	Cross-Cultural Adaptation and Evaluation of the Participation and Environment Measure for Children and Youth to the Indian Context—A Mixed-Methods Study	India	PEM-CY (Coster et al., 2010) (Proxy report)	Convenience NPO for children with disabilities (D)	N = 130 8.7 years TD n = 65 ♂40♀25 D n = 65 ♂37♀28
Tarakci et al. (2011)	The relationship between physical activity level, anxiety, depression, and functional ability in children and adolescents with juvenile idiopathic arthritis (JIA).	Turkey	CHAQ (Ozdogan et al., 2001; Ruperto et al., 2001) (Self-Report)	Convenience Schools (TD) University clinic (D)	N = 100 TD n = 48 11.27(1.59) ♂ 17 ♀ 31 JIA n = 52 12.13(2.92) ♂ 19 ♀ 33

Note.
TD = Children with typical development DS = Children with Down Syndrome CP = Children with Cerebral Palsy
HI = Children with Hearing Impairments D = Children with disabilities ID = Children with Intellectual disabilities
LD = Children with Learning Difficulties JIA = Children with Juvenile Idiopathic Arthritis

Table 10.2 Differences between the participation of children with developmental disabilities and children with typical development

Author	Participation constructs		Related constructs			Environment
			Person			
Measure	Attendance[a]	Involvement[b]	Activity competence[c]	Sense of self[d]	Preference[e]	Environment/context[g]
Almasri, Palisano, and Kang, (2017) Assessment Measure: CAPE (King et al., 2004)	Diversity: Physical TD>D (p < 0.001) Self-improvement TD>D (p < 0.001) Social TD>D (p < 0.001) Intensity: Physical TD>D (p < 0.001) Self-improvement TD>D (p < 0.001) Social TD>D (p < 0.001)					
Amaral et al. (2014) Assessment Measure: CHORES (Amaral et al., 2012)			Performance Overall TD>CP>DS Self-care TD>CP>DS (p < 0.004) Weighted assistance Self-care TD > (CP & DS) (p < 0.001) Family care TD > DS (p < 0.022) Total TD > (CP & DS) (p < 0.001) Independence			

Chien, Leung, Schoeb, and Au (2020) Assessment Measure: PEM-CY (Coster et al., 2010)	*Frequency* School TD>D (p < 0.05)	*Involvement* Home TD>D (p < 0.05) School TD>D (p < 0.01) Community TD>D (p < 0.05)	
Chien, Li-Tsang, Cheung, Leung, Lin (2019) Assessment Measure: PEM-CY (Coster et al., 2010)	*Participation frequency* School TD>D (p < 0.01)	*Involvement:* Home TD>D (p < 0.01) School TD>D (p < 0.01)	Self-care TD > (CP & DS) (p < 0.001) Family care TD > (CP & DS) (p < 0.001) Total TD > (CP & DS) (p < 0.001)	*Desire for change:* Community D>TD (p < 0.05)
Dos Santos et al. (2013) Assessment Measure: LIFE-H (Fougeyrollas et al., 1998)			*Nutrition* TD > CP (p < 0.05) *Fitness, Mobility & Responsibilities* TD = CP (p>0.05) *Personal care* TD > CP (p < 0.05) *Recreation* TD = CP (P>0.05) *Communication & Interpersonal Relationships* TD > CP (p < 0.05)	*Home:* Environmental supports TD>D (p < 0.01) *School:* Environmental resources TD>D (p < 0.01) Housing, community, education & employment TD = CP (P>0.05)

(*Continued*)

Table 10.2 (Continued)

Author	Participation constructs		Related constructs			
			Person			Environment
Measure	Attendance[a]	Involvement[b]	Activity competence[c]	Sense of self[d]	Preference[e]	Environment/context[g]
Elbasan et al. (2013) Assessment Measure: CHQ-PF50 (Ozdogan et al., 2001)			Differences in most subsections Physical functioning TD > HI (P < 0.05) HI > CP (P < 0.05) Role physical MR > CP (P < 0.05) Self-emotional TD = HI (P>0.05) Bodily pain TD = HI = ID (P>0.05) Global general health HI > CP (P>0.05) Behaviour emotional HI > CP > ID (P>0.05) Mental health HI > ID (P<0.05) Self-care, mobility & social functioning TD < D (P>0.05) Support TD > D (P>0.05)			Socioeconomic circumstances TD = D (P>0.05) Parental education TD = D (P>0.05) Location TD = D (P>0.05) Home environment Increased stress TD < D (P>0.05) Family cohesion, Family activities & Parental time TD > D (P>0.05) Parental emotional TD = HI = ID (P>0.05) HI > CP (P>0.05) Family Functioning Understanding and communication TD > DD (p = 0.036)
Hu, Zang, & Li (2012) Assessment Measure: WHODAS 2.0 (Üstün et al., 2010)			Getting around TD > DD (p<0.001) Self-care TD > DD (p<0.001) Life activity TD > DD (p<0.001) Participation in society	Gender Life activity (p = 0.014)		Prosocial behaviours

Kara et al. (2020)		TD > DD (p<0.001) Understanding and Communication
TD > DD (p<0.001) Get along with people
TD > DD (p<0.001) Overall disability
TD < DD (p<0.001) Gender
Understanding and communication (p < 0.001)
Puberty stage
Self-care (p=0.02)
Hyperactivity (p = 0.022)
Prosocial behaviours (p =0.043)
Participation in Society
Hyperactivity/ inattention
TD < DD (p < 0.001)	TD > DD (p = 0.003)
Hyperactivity and Family function
TD > DD (p = 0.023)
PEM-CY (Coster et al., 2010)	*Participation frequency*
Home
TD>D (p < 0.0001)
School
TD>D (p < 0.0001)	*Involvement:*
home
TD>CP (p < 0.0001)
School
TD>CP (p < 0.0001)
Community
TD>CP (p < 0.0001)	*Caregiver desire for change*
Home
CP>TD (p < 0.0001)
School
CP>TD (p < 0.0001)
Community
CP>TD (p < 0.0001)	*Home:*
Barriers
CP>TD (p < 0.0001)
Helpfulness
TD>CP (p < 0.0001)
School:
Barriers
CP>TD (p < 0.0001)
Helpfulness

(*Continued*)

Table 10.2 (Continued)

Author	Participation constructs		Related constructs			
			Person			Environment
Measure	Attendance[a]	Involvement[b]	Activity competence[c]	Sense of self[d]	Preference[e]	Environment/context[g]
						TD>CP ($p < 0.0001$)
						Resources
						TD>CP ($p < 0.0001$)
						Community Barriers
						CP>TD ($p < 0.0001$)
						Helpfulness
						TD>CP ($p < 0.0001$)
Mehraban et al. (2016) Assessment Measure: CAPE (King et al., 2004)	Diversity: Physical TD>D ($p < 0.001$) Self-improvement TD>D ($p < 0.001$) Social TD>D ($p < 0.001$) Intensity: Physical		Gender Differences not significant			Overall with whom CP: individually TD: peers (strong effect) Skill-based with whom CP: individually TD: peers (medium effect)

	TD>D (p < 0.001) Self-improvement TD>D (p < 0.001) Social TD>D (p < 0.001)			
Milićević (2020) Assessment Measure: PEM-CY (Coster et al., 2010)	Computer and video games TD >CP (p < 0.001) Indoor play and games TD>CP (p < 0.001) Arts, crafts, music and hobbies TD> CP (p < 0.001) Getting together with people TD> CP (p < 0.001) Socialising using technology TD>CP (p < 0.001)	Makes participation harder: Physical demands CP>TD (p < 0.001) Cognitive demands CP>TD (p<0.001)	Caregiver desire for change: Indoor play and games CP>TD (p < 0.001) Arts, crafts, music and hobbies CP>TD (p < 0.001) Getting together with people CP>TD (p < 0.001) Socialising using technology CP>TD (p < 0.001) Personal care management	Makes participation harder: Physical layout CP>TD (p < 0.001) Adequacy of services in the home: Information CP>TD (p < 0.001) Money CP>TD (p < 0.001) Services in home not needed TD>CP> (p < 0.001)

(Continued)

Table 10.2 (Continued)

Author	Participation constructs		Related constructs			Environment
Measure	Attendance[a]	Involvement[b]	Person			Environment/context[g]
			Activity competence[c]	Sense of self[d]	Preference[e]	
		Personal care management TD>CP (p < 0.001) School preparation TD>CP (p < 0.001) Homework TD>CP (p < 0.001)			CP>TD (p < 0.001) School preparation CP>TD (p < 0.001) Homework CP>TD (p < 0.001)	
Sachdeva & Rao (2012) Assessment Measure: Delta Screener (Morel, 2008)			Communication difficulty Shopping TD: 13.6% < LD 50% Purchasing a ticket TD: 14.3% < LD 66.7% Age Difficulty making choices reported LD (younger): 68.8% > LD (older): 53.8% > TD: 0% Support required TD < LD Travelling independently TD: 64% > LD 18.8%		Difficulty making choices LD > TD: Selecting from menu independently TD: 50% > LD: 25%	Banking exposure: TD: 9.5% > LD: 0% Post-Office exposure TD: 11.1% > LD: 0%
Şahin et al. (2020) Assessment Measure: PEM-CY (Coster et al., 2010)		Involvement: Home TD>LD (p < 0.001) School TD>LD (p < 0.001)			Desire for change: School LD>TD (p < 0.001)	Environmental barriers Home LD>TD (p < 0.001) School LD>TD (p < 0.001)

Samuels et al. (2020) Assessment Measure: PMP (Arvidsson et al., 2019)	*Frequency:* Personal care Family mealtime Looking after own health Meal preparation Family time Quiet leisure Religious gatherings Social activities School	TD>ID ($p < 0.05$) TD>ID ($p < 0.05$) TD>ID ($p < 0.05$) TD>ID ($p < 0.05$) TD>ID ($p < 0.05$) TD>ID ($p < 0.05$) TD>ID ($p < 0.05$) TD>ID ($p < 0.05$) TD>ID ($p < 0.05$)
Shi et al. (2021) Assessment Measure: PMP (Arvidsson et al., 2019)	*Participation Never/ seldom* My own health Gathering supplies Meal preparation Cleaning at home	ID>TD ID>TD ID>TD ID>TD

(*Continued*)

Table 10.2 (Continued)

Author	Participation constructs			Related constructs				Environment
				Person				
Measure	Attendance[a]		Involvement[b]	Activity competence[c]	Sense of self[d]	Preference[e]		Environment[f]/context[g]
	Caring for family							
	ID>TD							
	Caring for animals							
	ID>TD							
	Family time							
	ID>TD							
	Celebrations							
	ID>TD							
	Quiet leisure							
	ID>TD							
	Social activities							
	ID>TD							
Srinivasan et al. (2021) Assessment Measure: PEM-CY (Coster et al., 2010)	*Diversity of activities:* Community TD>D ($p < 0.001$)		*Involvement:* Home TD>D ($p < 0.001$) School TD>D ($p < 0.001$) Community TD>D ($p < 0.001$)			*Desire for change:* Home D>TD ($p < 0.001$) School D>TD ($p < 0.001$) Community D>TD ($p < 0.001$)		*Home* Environmental barriers D>TD ($p < 0.001$) *School* Environmental barriers D>TD ($p < 0.001$) *Community* Environmental barriers D>TD ($p < 0.001$)

Tarakci et al. (2011)
Assessment Measure:
CHAQ (Ozdogan et al., 2001)

Physical activity TD > JIA (p=0.000)
Decreased energy expenditure TD > JIA (p=0.04)
Higher CHAQ score TD > JIA (p=0.000)
Correlation between the CHAQ and overall wellbeing

Correlation between the childhood depression inventory and the CHAQ

Note.
[a] Attendance – being there, or the range of activities attended
[b] Involvement – the experience of participation, which includes motivation, persistence, affect and social connection
[c] Activity competence – The ability to execute the activity being undertaken according to an expected standard; includes cognitive, physical and affective skills and abilities
[d] Sense of self – Intrapersonal factors related to satisfaction, self-esteem and self-determination
[e] Preference – The interests or activities that hold meaning or are valued
[f] Environment – Broad objective social and physical structures in which we live
[g] Context – Setting for activity participation that includes people, place, activity, objects and time
TD = children with typical development; DS = children with down syndrome; CP = children with cerebral palsy; HI = children with hearing Impairment; D = children with disabilities; ID = children with intellectual disabilities; LD = children with learning difficulties; JIA = children with juvenile idiopathic arthritis
GMFCS = Gross Motor Function Classification System: I = level 1 on GMFCS = mild impairment, V = level 5 on the GMFCS = severely impaired
★Significance as determined by the authors of each study. Exact p-values are provided where available; alternatively an indication of < or > p is provided.

The LIFE-Habits Questionnaire (LIFE-H) for children (Noreau et al., 2007) is a proxy report tool considering habits across 12 domains: nutrition, fitness, personal care, communication, housing, mobility, responsibility, interpersonal relationships, community, education, employment, and recreation. It determines activity competence by measuring accomplishment and type of assistance needed in activities and sense of self by measuring satisfaction (personal constructs).

The Child Health Questionnaire-Parent Form (CHQ-PF50) (Landgraf et al., 1996) was used with the Childhood Health Assessment Questionnaire (CHAQ) (Ozdogan et al., 2001; Ruperto et al., 2001; Tarakci et al., 2011). The CHQ-P50 (Landgraf et al., 1996) is a proxy questionnaire on global health; physical, social and emotional functioning; self-esteem; family functioning; and parental input. It measures activity competence by scoring the limitations in functioning due to health conditions (personal constructs) and environment/context by scoring family cohesion and activities, parental time and emotions (environmental constructs). The CHAQ (Ruperto et al., 2001) is a self-report questionnaire that considers functioning in daily life skills. This questionnaire measures activity competence by measuring the level of difficulty experienced during everyday activities (personal constructs).

The Delta Screener (Morel, 2008) was adapted from the adult version for use with children in this study and is a self-report tool which measures financial participation in activities from school to the broader community. Activities and locations were adapted to render them age appropriate. The Delta Screener measures activity competence by determining participants' independence in performing activities (personal constructs).

The Participation and Environment Measure for Children and Youth (PEM-CY) (W. Coster et al., 2011) is a parent-report tool which measures the participation of children and youth across home, school and community environments. Within each environment various activities which may be typically performed are considered according to the frequency of performance, how involved the child is in that activity and if the parent would like to see the child's level of activity change. In addition to attendance and involvement, the PEM-CY considers environmental supports and barriers which may impact participation. The PEM-CY is closely associated with the ICF-CY (World Health Organisation, 2007).

Picture My Participation (PMP) (Arvidsson et al., 2020) is a self-report tool for the measurement of participation (attendance and involvement) in 20 everyday contexts across home, social and community. The tool has been specifically developed for use in LMIC countries and has picture supports for each item.

The World Health Organization Disability Schedule 2.0 (WHODAS 2.0) (Üstün et al., 2010) is a schedule of disability levels and profiles. It is conceptually linked to the ICF-CY (World Health Organisation, 2007) and covers six domains: cognition, mobility, self-care, getting along, life activities (personal constructs) and participation. In the reported study the WHODAS 2.0 (Üstün et al., 2010) was self-administered. Each item in the questionnaire indicates the degree of difficulty experienced due to health conditions (Üstün et al., 2010) and measures activity competence by scoring the activity limitations experienced and the context in which participation restrictions are experienced.

Participation of Children with DD and TD

Attendance. Children with TD were reported to participate to a greater extent than children with disabilities at home and at school (Chien, Leung, et al., 2020; Kara et al., 2020; Milićević, 2020; Şahin et al., 2020; Samuels et al., 2020; Shi et al., 2021; Srinivasan et al., 2021). Similarly, children with TD are reported to be involved in personal care and health, household, quiet lei-

Table 10.3 Description of adaptations to measures and the participation and related constructs measured

Participation measure	Adaptations for study in LAMI country	Participation constructs		Related constructs			Environment
		Attendance[a]	*Involvement*[b]	*Person*			*Environment*
				Activity competence[c]	*Sense of Self*[d]	*Preference*[e]	*Environment/context*[g]
Childhood Health Assessment Questionnaire (CHAQ) (Ruperto et al., 2001)	Turkish version (Ozdogan et al., 2001)			Level of difficulty in daily activities			
Children Helping Out: Responsibilities, Expectations and Support (CHORES) (Dunn, 2004)	Translated into Brazilian-Portuguese Cultural adequacy and psychometric properties tested (Amaral et al., 2012)			Performance scale Assistance scale			
Life Assessment Habits for Children (LIFE-H) (Noreau et al., 2007)	None reported			Level of accomplishment Type of assistance	Level of satisfaction		

(Continued)

Table 10.3 (Continued)

Participation measure	Adaptations for study in LAMI country	Participation constructs		Related constructs				Environment
				Person				
		Attendance[a]	Involvement[b]	Activity competence[c]	Sense of Self[d]	Preference[e]		Environment/context[g]
Participation and Environment Measure for Children and Youth (PEM-CY) (Coster et al., 2011)	Turkish version: Translated into Turkish, cultural validity assessed (Kara et al, 2020). Indian version: Translated into Hindi, cultural equivalence addressed across content, administration and measurement (Srinivasan et al., 2021). Chinese version: Translated into Chinese, validity assessed (Chien et al., 2020). Serbian Version: Translated into Serbian, cultural validity assessed, psychometric properties assessed (Milićević and Nedović, 2018).	Participation frequency	Extent of involvement			Desire for change in activities		

Picture My Participation (PMP) (Arvidsson et al., 2019)	Chinese version: Translation, cultural validation, reliability assessed and simplified (Shi et al., 2021) South Africa: no modifications	Participation frequency	Level of satisfaction	Experiences outside of the home
Student Questionnaire on financial community living skills: Adapted from the Delta Screener (Morel, 2008)	The student questionnaire was adapted from the adult questionnaires. Grammar/ambiguity was addressed by two validators. Questions on communication, process knowledge, and calculation competence were included and subdivided into awareness, communication and computation. Face validity was established.		Independence in performing activities	Making choices Selecting from a menu
The Child Health Questionnaire-Parent Form (CHQ-PF50) (Landgraf, Abetz and Ware, 1996)	Turkish version (Ozdogan et al., 2001)		Limitations in functioning	Limitations in mental health	Parental and family limitations

(Continued)

Table 10.3 (Continued)

Participation measure	Adaptations for study in LAMI country	Participation constructs			Related constructs				Environment
		Attendance[a]	Involvement[b]		Person				Environment[f]/context[g]
					Activity competence[c]	Sense of Self[d]	Preference[e]		With whom Where
The Children's Assessment of Participation and Enjoyment (CAPE) (G. King et al., 2004)	Translated into Persian Content and face validity were approved qualitatively in expert panel sessions	Diversity Intensity	Enjoyment						
World Health Organization Disability Assessment Schedule (WHODAS 2.0) (Üstün et al., 2010)	Translated and validated for use in China (Hu, Zang and Li, 2012)				Activity limitations				Participation restrictions

[a] Attendance – being there, or the range of activities attended.
[b] Involvement – the experience of participation, which includes motivation, persistence, affect and social connection.
[c] Activity competence – The ability to execute the activity being undertaken according to an expected standard; includes cognitive, physical and affective skills and abilities.
[d] Sense of self – Intrapersonal factors related to satisfaction, self-esteem and self-determination.
[e] Preference – The interests or activities that hold meaning or are valued.
[f] Environment – Broad objective social and physical structures in which we live.
[g] Context – Setting for activity participation that includes people, place, activity, objects and time.

sure and social activities more frequently than their peers with disabilities (Samuels et al., 2020; Shi et al., 2021), as well as attending a greater diversity of social, self-improvement, skill-based and active physical activities (Almasri et al., 2019; Mehraban et al., 2016) than children with cerebral palsy. In turn, children with cerebral palsy were reported to engage in more activities than children with Down syndrome (Amaral et al., 2014).

Involvement. Children with TD are reported to have greater involvement in activities at home, at school and in the community than their peers with disabilities (Chien, Leung, et al., 2020; Kara et al., 2020; Şahin et al., 2020).

Participation-related Constructs Measured for Children with DD and TD

Personal constructs. The children in this review who had TD had high health-related quality of life scores for global and emotional health (dos Santos et al., 2013; Elbasan et al., 2013; Tarakci et al., 2011) and lower overall disability scores (Hu et al., 2012). Children with DD had lower 'global general health', 'role emotional behaviour', 'role physical', 'global behaviour emotional', 'mental health' and 'general health' scores (dos Santos et al., 2013; Elbasan et al., 2013).

Activity competence. Children with DD (Amaral et al., 2014; Hu et al., 2012) and juvenile idiopathic arthritis (Tarakci et al., 2011) had greater overall disability scores (Amaral et al., 2014; Hu et al., 2012) and more difficulty in daily activities (Tarakci et al., 2011) and self-care (Amaral et al., 2014; Elbasan et al., 2013; Hu et al., 2012) than children with cerebral palsy (dos Santos et al., 2013; Mancini et al., 2016) and children with TD. Similarly, children with cerebral palsy were reported to have increased difficulty participating due to physical and cognitive demands (Milićević, 2020).

Children with DD displayed significantly lower physical activity than children with TD (dos Santos et al., 2013; Elbasan et al., 2013; Hu et al., 2012; Tarakci et al., 2011) and between disabilities, children with cerebral palsy had lower physical functioning than children with hearing impairment (Elbasan et al., 2013). Significant differences were reported between the communication of children with TD and those with DD (Hu et al., 2012), intellectual disabilities (Sachdeva & Rao, 2012) and cerebral palsy (dos Santos et al., 2013).

Two studies (Hu et al., 2012; Sachdeva & Rao, 2012) reported that older children had fewer self-care difficulties than their younger peers. In addition, one study reported that gender affected understanding, communication and life activity (Hu et al., 2012).

Sense of self. One study (Tarakci et al., 2011) reported decreased scores on the childhood depression inventory correlating with decreased scores on the CHAQ (Ruperto et al., 2001) for children with juvenile idiopathic arthritis in comparison to their peers with TD. Another study reported significant differences between children of different genders in relation to life activity (Hu et al., 2012).

Preference. Caregivers of children with disabilities reported a desire for change in the participation of their children in home, school and community activities (Chien, Leung, et al., 2020; Kara et al., 2020; Şahin et al., 2020), while another indicated that children with intellectual disabilities had greater difficulty making choices independently than did their peers with TD (Sachdeva & Rao, 2012).

Environment/context constructs. Environmental barriers in the home, at school and in the community were reported to be a challenge for children with disabilities (Kara et al., 2020) and learning disabilities (Şahin et al., 2020). For children with cerebral palsy, close family interactions occurred more frequently than peer or outside interactions than for their peers with TD (Mehraban et al., 2016), but helpfulness was reported to a greater extent by caregivers of children with typical development than those with children with disabilities at home, school and in the community (Kara et al., 2020). Housing, location, community, parental education and employment were not reported to result in significant differences in participation by two studies (dos Santos et al., 2013; Elbasan et al., 2013). But increased stress, decreased family cohesion and increased demands on parental time were identified for families of children with DD in comparison to families of children with TD (Elbasan et al., 2013). Families of children with cerebral palsy, specifically, reported that parents experienced greater emotional difficulty (Elbasan et al., 2013).

Discussion

This scoping review described the differences in participation and its related constructs of children with and without disabilities in LMIC countries. However, an absence of participation studies in the most vulnerable (low-income) countries and communities was evident.

Measurement Tools

Although nine tools were used to provide information on participation, when analysed against the components of participation (Adair et al., 2018; Imms, Granlund, et al., 2017), only three tools actually measured the attendance and/or involvement components of participation, namely the CAPE (G. King et al., 2004), the PEM-CY (W. Coster et al., 2011) and the PMP (Arvidsson et al., 2020). In addition, only the PEM-CY (W. Coster et al., 2011) measures both attendance and involvement, while the CAPE (G. King et al., 2004) and the PMP (Arvidsson et al., 2020) measure attendance only. The remaining assessments measured related personal constructs including: activity competence, sense of self, preference and environment/contextual constructs. The use of tools that primarily measure related constructs has arisen in the field due to the multidimensional nature of participation; however it is positive to see that as tools focusing on the attendance and involvement elements of participation have become available, these are being used more frequently. A challenge for the education sector, also observed in high-income countries, is that the measurement tools are primarily measuring attendance with only two, the PEM-CY (W. Coster et al., 2011) and the CAPE (G. King et al., 2004) measuring involvement. As educational achievement is positively associated with involvement (Schuelka et al., 2020), a greater focus on the experience of learning needs to be developed.

A strength of most of the studies included in this review is the validation of the assessment tools for use in the languages and populations where they were applied. All but one tool (Noreau et al., 2007) was reported to be both translated and culturally validated in the countries in which they were applied.

Of the tools used, four were proxy report measures (W. Coster et al., 2011; Dunn, 2004; Landgraf et al., 1996; Noreau et al., 2007), and in line with a preference for participation to be self-reported due to the role of self-perceptions in participation, the remaining five measures made use of self-reporting, namely the WHODAS 2.0 (Üstün et al., 2010), the CHAQ (Ruperto et al., 2001), the CAPE (G. King et al., 2004), the PMP (Arvidsson et al., 2020) and the Delta Screener (Morel, 2008).

Participation

Attendance and involvement. Overall, the studies included in the review reported that children with disabilities, regardless of the type of disability, attended fewer activities than children with typical development (Amaral et al., 2014; Chien, Leung, et al., 2020; Kara et al., 2020; Mehraban et al., 2016; Samuels et al., 2020). These results are comparable to those obtained in high-income countries, both in pattern and in extent, regardless of the measurement instrument used (Dunn et al., 2009; Imms, King, et al., 2017; G. King et al., 2013; Law et al., 2013; Longo et al., 2014; Ullenhag et al., 2014).

In addition, the patterns of attendance measured using both the PEM-CY (W. J. Coster et al., 2010) and the CAPE (G. King et al., 2004) were similar to those reported for children with disabilities and their peers in high-income countries with physical, self-improvement and social activities highlighted as particular areas of difficulty (Amini et al., 2019; Dunn et al., 2009; Imms, King, et al., 2017; G. King et al., 2013; Longo et al., 2014; Ullenhag et al., 2014).

Similarly for involvement, children with disabilities were less involved than their peers with typical development at home, at school and in the community (Chien, Leung, et al., 2020; Chien, Li-Tsang, et al., 2020; Kara et al., 2020; Milićević, 2020; Şahin et al., 2020; Srinivasan et al., 2021), a pattern which has also been observed in high-income countries (Law et al., 2013).

Personal constructs. Global health and activity competence were at comparable levels in high- and LMIC countries, with global health in Turkey equal (Elbasan et al., 2013; Tarakci et al., 2011) to high-income countries including Germany and the USA (Warschburger et al., 2003). Similarly, for children with DD, the studies indicated significantly lower scores for health and activity competence than peers with TD, while different physical, social and academic participation patterns identified between children with TD and DD were comparable to those in high-income countries (G. King et al., 2013; Ullenhag et al., 2014). The differences in participation may be explained for some children by the results of Milićević (2020), who highlighted increased physical and cognitive demands, which make participation more difficult for children with CP in comparison to their peers with TD.

Changes in participation patterns relating to age were reported in high-income countries (Sachdeva & Rao, 2012). Although differences in participation according to sex were not noted in Iran (Mehraban et al., 2016), which is in contrast to evidence from high-income countries (G. King et al., 2010), they were evident in China (Hu et al., 2012).

Although no impact of the severity of disability on household tasks was reported for children with cerebral palsy in Brazil (Amaral et al., 2014), in contrast to reports from high-income countries where increases in severity have been seen to decrease participation (Forsyth et al., 2007; Shields et al., 2015), however, only mild to moderately impaired children were included in the study, which may have impacted these results.

Caregivers of children with DD indicated a greater desire for change in their participation than caregivers of children with TD, as is also seen in high-income countries.

Environmental constructs. Similar results relating to environmental constructs to those for high-income countries were indicated (Ullenhag et al., 2014) with regards to children with DD participating alone or with adults to a greater extent than children with TD, and the latter having more interaction with peers (Amaral et al., 2014; Mehraban et al., 2016).

Life experiences and family activities also affected participation in high- (Solish et al., 2010) and LMIC similarly, with children with DD having fewer life experiences (Sachdeva & Rao, 2012) and less exposure to places outside of the home than their peers with TD (Elbasan et al., 2013; Mehraban et al., 2016). In addition, increased parental stress and decreased support for the families of children with disabilities, when compared to their peers with TD, was similar in LMIC (Hu et al., 2012; Mehraban et al., 2016) and high-income countries (Dyson, 1996; Hassall, Rose, & McDonald, 2005; Majnemer et al., 2008; Shikako-Thomas, Shevell, Lach, et al., 2013).

This review provided evidence of overall decreased participation for children with DD when compared with their peers with TD in LMIC countries. For educators the results of the review emphasise various areas in which children with DD may lack experience in comparison to their peers with TD, which will need to be taken into account in the classroom in order for learning to be best directed to meet the needs of each child (Braun, 2019).

Overall no clear differences in participation of either children with TD or those with DD were noted between the results of this review of children from low- and middle-income countries and those reported in other studies from high-income countries, hence this review, although small, suggests that the participation of children may follow universal patterns across countries of various income levels.

Conclusion

Children with DD are reported to have decreased participation in comparison to their peers with TD, particularly in relation to physical, self-improvement and social activities. However, this review provided preliminary evidence of more similarities than differences in the participation and participation-related constructs of children, regardless of the income level of the country in which they live. Such differences in participation need to be taken into account in inclusive classrooms as children will have significantly different life experiences.

However, gaps in the literature are evident. First, in the details of participation. Overall scores provide evidence that children with DD are participating less than their peers with TD; however, the manifestation of these differences is mostly unknown. In particular for education the information on involvement remains sparse. Second, a lack of focus on environmental constructs that may affect participation is evident. As environmental characteristics are the primary factors that distinguish high-income and LMIC countries, their role in participation cannot be ignored, and further investigation into environmental factors influencing participation is required.

Strengths and Limitations

The current review used a search strategy covering a large area of research. However only articles that were in peer-reviewed journals and available in English were used. As LMIC countries may not have the resources to publish in peer-reviewed journals and English, some studies may have been missed. Second, the consideration of only studies which used standardised measures may have limited the studies identified.

Recommendations for Future Research

Based on this scoping review, future research on participation needs to focus on increasing the diversity of the children studied, both within and between countries. In particular low-income countries need to be represented.

Note

1 The study was supported by the NRF/STINT. Opinions expressed are those of the authors and not necessarily reflect the opinions of the funders.

References

Adair, B., Ullenhag, A., Rosenbaum, P., Granlund, M., Keen, D., & Imms, C. (2018). Measures used to quantify participation in childhood disability and their alignment with the family of participation-related constructs: A systematic review. *Developmental Medicine and Child Neurology, 60*(11), 1101–1116. https://doi.org/10.1111/dmcn.13959

Almasri, N. A., Palisano, R. J., & Kang, L.-J. (2019). Cultural adaptation and construct validation of the Arabic version of children's assessment of participation and enjoyment and preferences for activities of children measures. *Disability and Rehabilitation: An International, Multidisciplinary Journal, 41*(8), 958–965.

Almqvist, L. (2006). Patterns of engagement in young children with and without developmental delay. *Journal of Policy and Practice in Intellectual Disabilities, 3*(1), 65–75. https://doi.org/10.1111/j.1741-1130.2006.00054.x

Amaral, M., Drummond, A. de F., Coster, W. J., & Mancini, M. C. (2014). Household task participation of children and adolescents with cerebral palsy, Down syndrome and typical development. *Research in Developmental Disabilities, 35*(2), 414–422. https://doi.org/10.1016/j.ridd.2013.11.021

Amini, M., Hassani Mehraban, A., Pashmdarfard, M., & Cheraghifard, M. (2019). Reliability and validity of the children participation assessment scale in activities outside of school–parent version for children with physical disabilities. *Australian Occupational Therapy Journal, 66*(4), 482–489.

Arvidsson, P., Dada, S., Granlund, M., Imms, C., Bornman, J., Elliott, C., & Huus, K. (2020). Content validity and usefulness of picture my participation for measuring participation in children with and without intellectual disability in South Africa and Sweden. *Scandinavian Journal of Occupational Therapy, 27*(5), 336–348. https://doi.org/10.1080/11038128.2019.1645878

Beegle, K., Christiaensen, L., Dabalen, A., & Gaddis, I. (2016). *Poverty in a Rising Africa*. World Bank Publications.

Braun, A. M. B. (2019). Psychological inclusion: Considering students' feelings of belongingness and the benefits for academic achievement. In M. J. Schuelka, C. J. Johnstone, G. Thomas, & A. J. Artiles (Eds.), *The Sage Handbook of Inclusion and Diversity in Education* (pp. 66–75). Sage Publications. https://doi.org/10.4135/9781526470430.n8

Center for Disease Control and Prevention, & Centers for Disease Control and Prevention. (2013). *Developmental Disabilities*. Website. https://www.cdc.gov/ncbddd/developmentaldisabilities/facts.html

Chien, C.-W., Leung, C., Schoeb, V., & Au, A. (2020a). A Chinese version of the young children's participation and environment measure: Psychometric evaluation in a Hong Kong sample. *Disability and Rehabilitation*, 1–9. https://doi.org/10.1080/09638288.2020.1727032

Chien, C.-W., Li-Tsang, C. W. P., Cheung, P. P. P., Leung, K.-Y., & Lin, C.-Y. (2020b). Development and psychometric evaluation of the Chinese version of the participation and environment measure for children and youth. *Disability and Rehabilitation: An International, Multidisciplinary Journal, 42*(15), 2204–2214. https://doi.org/10.1080/09638288.2018.1553210

Coster, W. J., Bedell, G., Law, M., Khetani, M. A., Teplicky, R., Liljenquist, K., Gleason, K., & Kao, Y. C. (2011). Psychometric evaluation of the participation and environment measure for children and youth. *Developmental Medicine and Child Neurology, 53*(11), 1030–1037. https://doi.org/10.1111/j.1469-8749.2011.04094.x

Coster, W. J., Law, M. C., Bedell, G., & Teplicky, R. (2010). *Participation and Environment Measure for Children and Youth (PEM-CY)*. Boston University.

dos Santos, A. N., Pavão, S. L., Santiago, P. R. P., Salvini, T. de F., & Rocha, N. A. C. F. (2013). Sit-to-stand movement in children with hemiplegic cerebral palsy: Relationship with knee extensor torque and social participation. *Research in Developmental Disabilities, 34*(6), 2023–2032. https://doi.org/10.1016/j.ridd.2013.03.021

Dunn, L. (2004). Validation of the CHORES: A measure of school-aged children's participation in household tasks. *Scandinavian Journal of Occupational Therapy, 11*(4), 179–190. https://doi.org/10.1080/11038120410003673

Dunn, L., Coster, W. J., Orsmond, G. I., & Cohn, E. S. (2009). Household task participation of children with and without attentional problems. *Physical and Occupational Therapy in Pediatrics, 29*(3), 258–273. https://doi.org/10.1080/01942630903008350

Dyson, L. L. (1996). The experiences of families of children with learning disabilities: Parental stress, family functioning, and sibling self-concept. *Journal of Learning Disabilities, 29*, 280–286. https://doi.org/10.1177/002221949602900306

Elbasan, B., Duzgun, I., & Oskay, D. (2013). Is there any difference in health related quality of life, self care and social function in children with different disabilities living in Turkey? *Iranian Journal of Pediatrics, 23*(3), 281–288.

Forsyth, R. J., Colver, A., Woolley, M., & Lowe, M. (2007). Participation of young severely disabled children is influenced by their intrinsic impairments and environment. *Developmental Medicine & Child Neurology*, *49*, 345–349. https://doi.org/10.1111/j.1469-8749.2007.00345.x

Granlund, M. (2013). Participation - challenges in conceptualization, measurement and intervention. *Child: Care, Health and Development*, *39*(4), 470–473. https://doi.org/10.1111/cch.12080

Hassall, R., Rose, J., & McDonald, J. (2005). Parenting stress in mothers of children with an intellectual disability: The effects of parental cognitions in relation to child characteristics and family support. *Journal of Intellectual Disability Research : JIDR*, *49*(Pt 6), 405–418. https://doi.org/10.1111/j.1365-2788.2005.00673.x

Hu, L., Zang, Y. L., & Li, N. (2012). The applicability of WHODAS 2.0 in adolescents in China. *Journal of Clinical Nursing*, *21*(17–18), 2438–2451. https://doi.org/10.1111/j.1365-2702.2012.04126.x

Imms, C., Granlund, M., Wilson, P. H., Steenbergen, B., Rosenbaum, P. L., & Gordon, A. M. (2017a). Participation, both a means and an end: A conceptual analysis of processes and outcomes in childhood disability. *Developmental Medicine & Child Neurology*, *59*(1), 16–25. https://doi.org/10.1111/dmcn.13237

Imms, C., King, G., Majnemer, A., Avery, L., Chiarello, L., Palisano, R., Orlin, M., & Law, M. (2017b). Leisure participation-preference congruence of children with cerebral palsy: A children's assessment of participation and enjoyment international network descriptive study. *Developmental Medicine and Child Neurology*, *59*(4), 380–387. https://doi.org/10.1111/dmcn.13302

Jamieson, L., Berry, L., & Lake, L. (2017). *The South African ChildGauge 2017* (L. Jamieson, L. Berry, & L. Lake, Eds.). Children's Institute, University of Cape Town. http://www.ci.uct.ac.za/sites/default/files/image_tool/images/367/Child_Gauge/South_African_Child_Gauge_2017/Child_Gauge_2017_lowres.pdf

Kara, O. K., Turker, D., Kara, K., & Yardimci-Lokmanoglu, B. N. (2020). Psychometric properties of the Turkish version of participation and environment measure for children and youth. *Child: Care, Health & Development*, *46*(6), 711–722. https://doi.org/10.1111/cch.12801

King, G., Imms, C., Palisano, R., Majnemer, A., Chiarello, L., Orlin, M., Law, M., & Avery, L. (2013). Geographical patterns in the recreation and leisure participation of children and youth with cerebral palsy: A CAPE international collaborative network study. *Developmental Neurorehabilitation*, *16*(3), 196–206. https://doi.org/10.3109/17518423.2013.773102

King, G., Law, M., Hurley, P., Petrenchik, T., & Schwellnus, H. (2010). A developmental comparison of the out-of-school recreation and leisure activity participation of boys and girls with and without physical disabilities. *International Journal of Disability, Development and Education*, *57*(1), 77–107. https://doi.org/10.1080/10349120903537988

King, G., Law, M., King, S., Hurley, P., Hanna, S., Kertoy, M., & Rosenbaum, P. (2007). Measuring children's participation in recreation and leisure activities: Construct validation of the CAPE and PAC. *Child: Care, Health and Development*, *33*(1), 28–39. https://doi.org/10.1111/j.1365-2214.2006.00613.x

King, G., Law, M., King, S., Hurley, P., Rosenbaum, P., Hanna, S., Kertoy, M., & Young, N. (2004). *Children's Assessment of Participation and Enjoyment & Preferences for Activities of Children*. Pearson.

King, M., Shields, N., Imms, C., Black, M., & Ardern, C. (2013). Participation of children with intellectual disability compared with typically developing children. *Research in Developmental Disabilities*, *34*(5), 1854–1862. https://doi.org/10.1016/j.ridd.2013.02.029

Landgraf, J. M., Abetz, L., & Ware, J. E. (1996). *Child Health Questionnaire (CHQ): A User's Manual*. Health Institute, New England Medical Center.

Law, M., Anaby, D., Teplicky, R., Khetani, M. A., Coster, W., & Bedell, G. (2013). Participation in the home environment among children and youth with and without disabilities. *British Journal of Occupational Therapy*, *76*(2), 58–66. https://doi.org/10.4276/030802213X13603244419112

Law, M., King, G., Petrenchik, T., Kertoy, M., & Anaby, D. (2012). The assessment of preschool children's participation: Internal consistency and construct validity. *Physical & Occupational Therapy in Pediatrics*, *32*(3), 272–287. https://doi.org/10.3109/01942638.2012.662584

Law, M., King, G., King, S., Kertoy, M., Hurley, P., Rosenbaum, P., Young, N., & Hanna, S. (2006). Patterns of participation in recreational and leisure activities among children with complex physical disabilities. *Developmental Medicine and Child Neurology*, *48*(5), 337–342. https://doi.org/10.1017/S0012162206000740

Longo, E., Badia, M., Orgaz, B., & Verdugo, M. (2014). Cross-cultural validation of the children's assessment of participation and enjoyment (CAPE) in Spain. *Child: Care, Health and Development*, *40*(2), 231–241. https://doi.org/10.1111/cch.12012

Majnemer, A., Shevell, M., Law, M., Birnbaum, R., Chilingaryan, G., Rosenbaum, P., & Poulin, C. (2008). Participation and enjoyment of leisure activities in school-aged children with cerebral palsy. *Developmental Medicine and Child Neurology, 50*(10), 751–758. https://doi.org/10.1111/j.1469-8749.2008.03068.x

Mancini, M. C., Coster, W. J., Amaral, M. F., Avelar, B. S., Freitas, R., & Sampaio, R. F. (2016). New version of the Pediatric Evaluation of Disability Inventory (PEDI-CAT): Translation, cultural adaptation to Brazil and analyses of psychometric properties. *The Brazilian Journal of Physical Therapy*, 1–10. https://doi.org/10.1590/bjpt-rbf.2014.0166

Mehraban, A. H., Hasani, M., & Amini, M. (2016). The comparison of participation in school-aged cerebral palsy children and normal peers: A preliminary study. *Iranian Journal of Pediatrics, 26*(3), 1–8. https://doi.org/10.5812/ijp.5303

Milićević, M. (2020). Home participation of children with and without cerebral palsy in Serbia: An exploratory study. *Disability and Rehabilitation: An International, Multidisciplinary Journal, 42*(25), 3696–3706. https://doi.org/10.1080/09638288.2019.1610506

Morel, P. (2008). *The Delta Screener: Screening Adults at Risk for Learning Disabilities* (pp. 1–15). http://www.disabilityissues.ca/english/Link_docs/DeltaScreener-June 2011 (NonFillable).pdf

Narayan, A., Van der Weide, R., Cojocaru, A., Lakner, C., Redaelli, S., Gerszon Mahler, D., Gupta N. Ramasubbaiah, R., & Thewissen, S. (2018). *Fair Progress? Economic Mobility across Generations around the World*. Creative Commons Attribution CC BY 3.0 IGO. https://doi.org/10.1596/978-1-4648-1210-1

Noreau, L., Lepage, C., Boissiere, L., Picard, R., Fougeyrollas, P., Mathieu, J., Desmarais, G., & Nadeau, L. (2007). Measuring participation in children with disabilities using the Assessment of Life Habits. *Developmental Medicine and Child Neurology, 49*(9), 666–671. https://doi.org/10.1111/j.1469-8749.2007.00666.x

Ozdogan, H., Kasapçopur, O., Ozen, S., Ugurlu, U., Printo, O., & Policlinico Matteo, I. S. (2001). The Turkish version of the Childhood Health Assessment Questionnaire (CHAQ) and the Child Health Questionnaire (CHQ). *Clinical and Experimental Rheumatology, 19*(Suppl 23), 158–162. http://www.medit.it/printo/

Page, M. J., Mckenzie, J. E., Bossuyt, P. M., Boutron, I., Hoffmann, T. C., Mulrow, C. D., Shamseer, L., Tetzlaff, J. M., Akl, E. A., Brennan, S. E., Chou, R., Glanville, J., Loder, W., Mayo-wilson, E., Mcdonald, S., Mcguinness, L. A., Stewart, A., Thomas, J., Tricco, A. C., … & Moher, D. (2021). The PRISMA 2020 statement : An updated guideline for reporting systematic reviews. *PLoS Medicine, 18*(3), 1–15. https://doi.org/10.1371/journal.pmed.1003583

Parkes, J., & Mccullough, N. (2010). To what extent do children with cerebral palsy participate in everyday life situations? *Heath and Social Care in the Community, 18*(3), 304–315. https://doi.org/10.1111/j.1365-2524.2009.00908.x

Piškur, B., Beurskens, A., Jongmans, M., Ketelaar, M., & Smeets, R. (2015). What do parents need to enhance participation of their school-aged child with a physical disability? A cross-sectional study in the Netherlands. *Child: Care, Health and Development, 41*(1), 84–92. https://doi.org/10.1111/cch.12145

Rumrill, P. D., Fitzgerald, S. M., & Merchant, W. R. (2010). Using scoping literature reviews as a means of understanding and interpreting existing literature. *Work, 35*(3), 399–404. https://doi.org/10.3233/WOR-2010-0998

Ruperto, N., Ravelli, A., Pistorio, A., Malattia, C., Cavuto, S., Gado-West, L., Tortorelli, A., Landgraf, J. M., Singh, G., Martini, A., & The Paediatric Rheumatology International Trials, & Organisation (PRINTO). (2001). Cross-cultural adaptation and psychometric evaluation of the Childhood Health Assessment Questionnaire (CHAQ) and the Child Health Questionnaire (CHQ) in 32 countries. Review of the general methodology. *Clinical and Experimental Rheumatology, 19*(Suppl. 23), S1–S9. http://www.medit.it/printo/

Sachdeva, R., & Rao, C. S. (2012). Community participation activities involving money handling skills of children with learning disability as compared to children with typical development aged 10 to 14 years. *Indian Journal of Occupational Therapy, 44*(2), 25–31.

Şahin, S., Kara, Ö. K., Köse, B., & Kara, K. (2020). Investigation on participation, supports and barriers of children with specific learning disabilities. *Research in Developmental Disabilities, 101*, 1–8. https://doi.org/doi.org/10.1016/j.ridd.2020.103639

Samuels, A., Dada, S., Van Niekerk, K., Arvidsson, P., & Huus, K. (2020). Children in South Africa with and without intellectual disabilities' rating of their frequency of participation in everyday activities. *International Journal of Environmental Research and Public Health, 17*(18). https://doi.org/10.3390/ijerph17186702

Sánchez, P. A., Rodríguez, R. de H., & Martínez, R. M. M. (2019). Barriers to student learning and participation in an inclusive school as perceived by future education professionals. *Journal of New Approaches in Educational Research, 8*(1), 18–24. https://doi.org/10.7821/naer.2019.1.321

Schlebusch, L., Huus, K., Samuels, A., Granlund, M., & Dada, S. (2020). Participation of young people with disabilities and / or chronic conditions in low- and middle-income countries : A scoping review. *Developmental Medicine & Child Neurology*, 1–7. https://doi.org/10.1111/dmcn.14609

Schuelka, M. J., Braun, A. M. B., & Johnstone, C. J. (2020). Beyond access and barriers: Inclusive education and systems change. *FIRE: Forum for International Research in Education*, 6(1), 1–7. https://doi.org/10.32865/fire202061198

Shi, L., Granlund, M., Zhao, Y., Hwang, A.-W., Kang, L.-J., & Huus, K. (2021). Transcultural adaptation, content validity and reliability of the instrument "Picture My Participation" for children and youth with and without intellectual disabilities in mainland China. *Scandinavian Journal of Occupational Therapy*, 28(2), 147–157. https://doi.org/10.1080/11038128.2020.1817976

Shields, N., Synnot, A., & Kearns, C. (2015). The extent, context and experience of participation in out-of-school activities among children with disability. *Research in Developmental Disabilities*, 47, 165–174. https://doi.org/10.1016/j.ridd.2015.09.007

Shikako-thomas, K., Shevell, M., Lach, L., Law, M., Schmitz, N., Poulin, C., Majnemer, A., Lach, L., Law, M., Poulin, C., Majnemer, A., The Quala Group, Schmitz, N., Poulin, C., & Majnemer, A. (2013a). Research in developmental disabilities picture me playing: A portrait of participation and enjoyment of leisure activities in adolescents with cerebral palsy. *Research in Developmental Disabilities*, 34(9), 1001–1010. https://doi.org/10.1016/j.ridd.2012.11.026

Shikako-thomas, K., Shevell, M., Schmitz, N., Lach, L., Law, M., Poulin, C., Majnemer, A., & The Quala Group. (2013b). Research in developmental disabilities determinants of participation in leisure activities among adolescents with cerebral palsy. *Research in Developmental Disabilities*, 34(9), 2621–2634. https://doi.org/10.1016/j.ridd.2013.05.013

Solish, A., Perry, A., & Minnes, P. (2010). Participation of children with and without disabilities in social, recreational and leisure activities. *Journal of Applied Research in Intellectual Disabilities*, 23(3), 226–236. https://doi.org/10.1111/j.1468-3148.2009.00525.x

Srinivasan, R., Kulkarni, V., Smriti, S., Teplicky, R., & Anaby, D. (2021). Cross-cultural adaptation and evaluation of the participation and environment measure for children and youth to the indian context: A mixed-methods study. *International Journal of Environmental Research and Public Health*, 18(4). https://doi.org/10.3390/ijerph18041514

Tarakci, E., Yeldan, I., Kaya Mutlu, E., Baydogan, S. N., & Kasapcopur, O. (2011). The relationship between physical activity level, anxiety, depression, and functional ability in children and adolescents with juvenile idiopathic arthritis. *Clinical Rheumatology*, 30(11), 1415–1420. https://doi.org/10.1007/s10067-011-1832-0

The World Bank (2018a). *Atlas of Sustainable Development Goals 2018: From World Development Indicators*.

The World Bank (2018b). *Poverty and Equity Brief South Asia, Bangladesh*. http://databank.worldbank.org/data/download/poverty/33EF03BB-9722-4AE2-ABC7-AA2972D68AFE/Global_POVEQ_SAR.pdf

Twible, R. L., & Henley, E. C. (2000). Preparing occupational therapists and physiotherapists for community based rehabilitation. *Asia Pacific Disability Rehabilitation Journal*, Jan, 113–129. http://search.ebscohost.com/login.aspx?direct=true&db=cin20&AN=2002015858&lang=es&site=ehost-live

Ullenhag, A., Almqvist, L., Granlund, M., & Krumlinde-Sundholm, L. (2012). Cultural validity of the Children's Assessment of Participation and Enjoyment/Preferences for Activities of Children (CAPE/PAC). *Scandinavian Journal of Occupational Therapy*, 19(5), 428–438. https://doi.org/10.3109/11038128.2011.631218

Ullenhag, A., Krumlinde-Sundholm, L., Granlund, M., & Almqvist, L. (2014). Differences in patterns of participation in leisure activities in Swedish children with and without disabilities. *Disability and Rehabilitation*, 36(6), 464–471. https://doi.org/10.3109/09638288.2013.798360

Unicef (1999). *United Nations Convention on the Rights of the Child, 1989*.

Üstün, T. B., Kostanjsek, N., Chatterji, S., & Rehm, J. (Eds.). (2010). *Measuring Health and Disability Manual for WHO Disability Assessment Schedule*. World Health Organisation.

Warschburger, P., Landgraf, J. M., Petermann, F., & Freidell, K. (2003). Health-related quality of life in children assessed by their parents: Evaluation of the psychometric properties of the CHQ-PF50 in two German clinical samples author (s): Petra Warschburger , Jeanne M. Landgraf, Franz Petermann and Klaus Freidel Publ. *Quality of Life Research*, 12, 291–301.

World Health Organisation (2007). *International Classification of Functioning, Disability and Health - Child and Youth Version (ICF-CY)*. World Health Press.

11
PERCEIVED STRENGTHS OF AUTISTIC PEOPLE AND ROADMAP FOR INTERVENTION

Parents and Practitioners' Perspectives

Santoshi Halder*, Susanne Marie Bruyere, and Wendy Strobel Gower

Introduction

Autism Spectrum Disorder (ASD) is defined as a certain set of behaviours that affect a person's ability to connect and communicate with others and affects people to different degrees; hence all autistic populations cannot be generalized to fit in the same profile (Panzano, 2018). ASD, classified as one of the most complex neuro-developmental disorders with a wide range of inter- and intra-autistic variability, is one of the most researched areas that is explored by almost all the disciplines worldwide since the term 'autism' was first coined by Kanner or explained by Asperger as early as in the 1940s (Asperger, 1944; Kanner, 1943). Despite abundant research from various disciplines to date what is known so far about ASD is still not enough for a comprehensive understanding of the autistic population (Panzano, 2018), and hence there remains a gap.

Autism is considered a disorder or disability as per *DSM-5* classification, predominantly highlighting deficits in communication, social interactions, and stereotypical or repeated behaviour (APA, 2013; Bonini, 2017). However, despite the marked atypical behaviours, there are also signs of strengths and abilities according to evidence-based findings as documented in selected literature including biographies and narratives of many world-renowned autistic people (Baron-Cohen et al., 2009; Grandin, 1984; Happé, 2018; Treffert, 2014). Such evidence provides valid bases for researchers around the world to examine under-explored areas of strengths of autistic people in various cultures and countries for a more robust understanding of Autism Spectrum Disorder.

Attention to the underpinning strength focus got more impetus in the last decades when the advocates of the neuro-diversity movement (Blume, 1998) worldwide raised their voices in favour of the acceptance of any sort of differences or deviations and demanded consideration of such differences as normal developmental variability while claiming the need for acceptance and respect for such human diversities (which include Autism, ADHD, learning disabilities, etc.) (Jaarsma & Welin, 2012). Surprisingly, despite their enormous potential, literature on this valuable area of strengths and abilities of autistic people is sparse (Putt, 2019). Small sample in-depth qualitative studies across countries and cultures analysing the foundations and nature of such

---

* santoshi_halder@yahoo.com; shedu@caluniv.ac.in

uniqueness and differences may add valuable information and insights for undertaking large-scale exploration in this direction for broader generalization.

Despite demonstrating multiple strengths and reporting positive feedback from reputed companies and employers around the world on the contribution of autistic adults[1] to the workforce, about 66% to 86% of adults with autism are unemployed or seriously underemployed (Hedley et al., 2016). The Office for National Statistics reports that only 16% of autistic people are in full-time work despite 77% being willing to work (Office for National Statistics, 2016). The growing body of literature evidence that approximately 10% of autistic individuals have some type of exceptional skills, and 50% of individuals with such skills have a diagnosis of ASD (Asperger, 1944; Frith, 1989; Goodman, 1972; Howlin et al., 2009; Kanner, 1971; Meilleur et al., 2015; Rutter, 2011; Treffert, 2010). Kanner noted in his research as early as in the 1940s that the children he studied showed excellent long-term memory for events taking place in the past, as well as excellent rote memory skills (Kanner, 1943).

Moreover, sufficient existing documentation demonstrates evidence of abilities in the autistic population that may be non-exceptional but have a lot of potential for further development through proper nurturance in an appropriate environment (Hagner et al., 2014; O'Callaghan, 2017). The gap between successful employment and the first signs of subtle skills and strengths needs to be closed up through proper interventions as soon as in the early developmental period (Giarelli et al., 2013), and the parents and practitioners (two of the most important groups of people) can play a crucial role.

Paradoxes of Strengths and Atypicalities

Baron-Cohen, through his "empathizing–systemizing" (E-S) Theory (Baron-Cohen, 2002, 2003, 2009) while explaining social and communication difficulties in autism, reported *delays and deficits in empathy*, whilst claiming intact or *even superior skill in systemizing* (i.e., unraveling the rules of a system). Such intense systematizing posits traits like excellent attention to detail (in perception and memory) and excellent understanding of a whole system if given the opportunity to observe and control all the variables in that system. Hence, they may be specifically good at particular subjects aligned with their specific pattern. For decades after finding limitations in cognitive abilities in the autistic population, the reason being the atypical ways of understanding, interpreting, and responding, the clinical neuropsychologist Soulières, based on her collaborative research with colleagues, concluded that some children with autism understand far more than what we expect as their ways of expression may be different hence many such strengths are lost subsequently and sometimes are even mistaken as deficits (Soulières et al., 2010) as also endorsed by other researchers (Zeliadt, 2018).

It is also claimed by researchers that autistic people are more inclined towards local processing than global processing and that their local processing is much enhanced relative to the neuro-typical brain (Mottorn et al., 2003). Researchers also posit that the high end of autism may be largely people who are eccentric geniuses or with splinter skills (often not consistent with skills in other areas of development) (Pring, 2005; de Schipper et al., 2016). Research also reports enhanced processing of information in certain specific patterns (Hudac et al., 2018); hence an autistic brain seems to seek patterns, qualities, and levels that it prefers and avoids those not aligned with it.

Strength Focus Underpinning

There is a growing body of literature that estimates approximately 10% of individuals with ASD to have some type of exceptional skills and 50% of individuals with such skills have a diagnosis of

ASD (Asperger, 1944; Frith, 1989; Goodman, 1972; Kanner, 1971; Meilleur et al., 2015; Rutter, 2011; Treffert, 2010). There are multiple documents showing that children with ASD are often predominantly considered visual learners and have prominent thinking abilities that surely can be considered their strengths (Putt, 2019) if this inclination can be channelized further through a matched teaching-learning context (Halder & Bruyere, 2021).

It is crucial to understand the early markers of strengths at a very early age, strengths that are superior to others and strengths that are superior to a child's own skills (inter and intra) for navigating the right type of intervention based on their traits for further nurturance of the existing skills and abilities. Autism and high IQ share a diverse set of convergent correlates including large brain size, fast brain growth, increased sensory and visual-spatial abilities, enhanced synaptic functions, increased attention focus, more deliberative decision-making etc. (Crespri, 2016; Kohls et al., 2018).

Research exploration through the strengths and ability-focused lens rather than disability or deficits-focused approach may provide valuable prerequisites for ameliorating effective, appropriate personalized early childhood intervention and environment (Mottron et al., 2014). Understanding the strengths and abilities simultaneously with areas that need improvements would be helpful for developing better interventions, access to services, and the desired support needs (Zeliadt, 2018). Henceforth, there is a need to see through a different lens instead of a deficit-based assessment to have a comprehensive understanding of ASD.

Two groups of people who are directly involved with the child's major developmental trajectory are parents and the professionals who work with the child with ASD for a prolonged time in the natural environment at home and school. Acceptance of such strengths by the practice group coupled with appropriate strategies for development may increase the scope of early identification of the markers of strengths and further nurturance for skill development for a more productive, participatory, and independent life for people with ASD. Research in the area of the strength-focused approach is sporadic and more research specifically exploring the same would provide valuable leads towards a more robust understanding of the targeted area (Garbacz et al., 2016).

Need for Qualitative Exploration by Parents and Practitioners

The reports of the parents and practitioners can provide first-hand valuable insights and experiences and bridge the existing gaps between research and practice. Qualitative studies comprising both perspectives together may bring forth interesting insights into the area and help leverage the lacuna. On the other hand, identifying and fostering special interests and abilities can increase self-esteem, opportunities for interaction and appreciation, and employment options for those on the autism spectrum (Happé, 2018). Caregivers, educators, and therapists, if aware and informed on the various spectra of autism, can capitalize on the strength areas most effectively.

Hence the purpose of the study is to explore the perceived strengths and abilities of autistic people as noticed and reported by the parents and practitioners and to analyze the related perspective and concerns.

Research Questions

- What are the perceived strengths and abilities of autistic people noticed by the participants (i.e., parents and practitioners)?
- What are the participants' (i.e., parents and practitioners) perspectives about the potentialities of the strengths and abilities of autistic people?

Methodology

The study is based on 30 participants (16 parents and 14 practitioners). The demographic and personal details of the participants are given in Table 11.1. Participants were recruited from various parts of the USA (viz. 13 from New York, four from California and one each from Nebraska, Indianapolis, and Texas) and ten from India, recruited through purposive sampling pooled through an online recruitment process via the autism support groups. These autism support groups help the parents and stakeholders including the practitioners connect to each other and share relevant information, resources, and services. For the final study, only willing and interested participants who signed the informed consent and fulfilled the inclusion and exclusion criteria based on the semi-structured questionnaires that comprised demographic, relevant personal, and background information were further included for the in-depth one-to-one interview with the researcher.

Participant Recruitment and Data Collection

Participants were recruited through purposive sampling based on initial selection through a semi-structured questionnaire. Inclusion criteria for participant recruitment for parents were:

Table 11.1 Demographic details of the participants

Characteristics	Sub-categories	N = 30 (%)
Parents	Total	16 (53%)
	Mother	12 (40%)
	Father	4 (14%)
Practitioners	Total	14 (47%)
	Males	2 (7%)
	Females	12 (40%)
Location (combined)	India	10 (33%)
	USA	20 (67%)
	New York	13 (43%)
	California	4 (14%)
	Nebraska	1 (3%)
	Indianapolis	1 (3%)
	Texas	1 (3%)
Ethnicity (combined)	White	17 (57%)
	Mixed (one parent American and other Mexican)	3 (10%)
	Asian	10 (33%)
Highest level of Education of participants (combined)	Masters and above	18 (60%)
	Bachelor	12 (40%)
	High School	0 (NA)
Occupation of parents	Special educator/associate/academic advisor	5 (17%)
	Doctor/lawyer/engineer/scientist	5 (17%)
	Clerical/account/insurance/nurse	3 (10%)
	Homemaker	3 (10%)
Practitioners' function/role (worked 5–30 years with 5 to 90 people with ASD)	School counsellor/psychologist	1 (3%)
	Special ed. teacher/clinician	11 (37%)
	Outreach coordinator	1 (3%)
	Student aid/advocate	1 (3%)

(a) parents with children clinically diagnosed with ASD (APA, 2013) prior to the study, or (b) practitioners who have served already diagnosed autistic people for at least five years in a clinical, home or school setting, (c) willing to participate voluntarily, and were (d) proficient enough in the English language to understand and respond to the questions. Details of the participants are presented in Table 11.1.

The final data collection consisted of 30 participants who satisfied the inclusion criteria. The in-depth face-to-face interviews were conducted by the first author, a board-certified behaviour analyst (BCBA) spanning 20 years of experience working with various special needs populations including autistic people (for ten years) in various low-, middle-, and high-income regions and countries of heterogeneous nature.

Interview Questions

The interviews were initiated by providing a brief description and objective of the study and then asking the participants to talk freely about their child (for parents) or the autistic child with whom they have served (for practitioners). Questions were asked to extract and understand the early markers of strengths and abilities in people with Autism, their own perspective and the further scope for nurturance or manifestation of the strengths including the associated challenges.

Compliance with Ethical Standards

The study was ethically approved by the Cornell University IRB board under the human subject exempt category (approval ref: Protocol ID#: 2001009333), which includes data collection procedure, participant recruitment, interview protocols, etc. Written consent was taken from each participant, as per the Declaration of Helsinki. Participation was voluntary; hence no monetary compensation was provided.

Result and Interpretation

Among the parents 12 were mothers and 4 were fathers having autistic ward age spanning from 10 to 35 years at the time of the interview. The parent reporting was based on experiences with their own autistic ward (child or adult), and practitioners' revelation was based on the autistic child or adult they had served in their span of career at schools, clinical settings, or in homebound programmes. Out of the 13 parents, 3 worked in a school in the capacity of special educator or school teacher. Parents had either completed their Masters ($n = 18$) or Bachelors ($n = 12$). Among practitioners 12 were females and 2 were males of age 25 to 50 years with vast experiences of working with autistic populations spanning 5 to 30 years (they had worked with five to 90 autistic people of varied ages). The practitioners worked in various capacities as special educators, psychologists, teacher aid, clinician, school counsellor, and others. Kindly note (^{PR}) denotes quotes by practitioners and (^{PA}) denotes quotes by parents.

Theme 1: Perceived Strengths

Proportion of exceptional skills. Only five parents and three practitioners out of the 30 noticed the existence of considerable abilities in the autistic people they have served so far. One of the practitioners with experience of serving around 80 autistic children or adults (25% of the autistic people she served) reported having found very few instances ($n = 5$) of such striking or exceptional skills. Another practitioner who has more than 30 years of experience and worked with nearly 20 autistic children conveyed to have noticed certain notable exceptional/striking abilities in about five of her autistic children. The revelation set forth valuable information and insights about many important under-searched areas of autistic people.

> I noticed striking abilities in around ten of the thirty-five autistic people I served in my forty years of experience that ranged from attention to detail and/or pattern following, exceptional ability to pick up songs verbatim without much formal training, artistic traits of pencil sketching like caricatures, striking memory like remembering dates of events exceptionally well, etc. (Laura[PR])

Sub-Theme 1.1: Types of Exceptionalities Reported

The abilities reported by participants were not based on any formal clinical assessments and were entirely based on their relative comparison to either the neuro-typical people or their peers of the same age group. The types of perceived strengths (i.e., artistic or creative, music, memory, maths, and in-depth perception) reported by participants in the study are accounted for here.

Artistic and or creative traits. One of the practitioners reported having worked with three such children who demonstrated superior artistic traits including two parents who noticed such similar notable traits in their children.

> *She is very good at drawing, cartoons, doodling & writing and had her artwork exhibited at the Indian Autism Convention, and she serves as a member of her school's student government body. She created a book four years ago (at 6) that demonstrates her abilities. Link: https://www.blurb.com/b/7919521-jackie-and-annie. (Jessica [PA])*

> *I have known 3 separate students who were very gifted visual artists, mostly working with pencil, ink, or pastel. (Laura [PR])*

Striking memory. Striking memory and ease of reproduction manifesting through instances of memorizing movies, bus routes, maps, sports, etc. are some of the related strengths of autistic people, as reported by the study participants.

> *Regarding Geography, she knows a lot of facts or trivia involving numbers, dates, state capitals, their locations (demographic data) for multiple countries/states/cities and schools. For example, she really likes finding out the data or figures, remembers verbatim, and compares schools in our district with others, such as saying the percentage of white students in Northeast elementary school is "x" while in BJM is "y." (Jessica[PA])*

> *One of my students had an exceptional memory, and he enjoyed memorizing information presented visually, for example, the periodic table, course schedules displayed in the room, or important events on a school calendar. Another student could recall days of the week corresponding to specific dates years after the fact, and remembers dates, birthdays, important milestones in his life, etc. (Laura [PR])*

Mathematical ability. One of the parents and one practitioner reported having noticed in their children manifestation of notable skills in mental arithmetic calculations at a level above their age, relatively superior as compared to their peers.

> *My Son is very good in mental maths and achieved significantly well in maths-based subjects all through. (Kathleen [PA])*

Musical ability. Manifestation of absolute pitch or music (viz., identifying the node of a pitch just by listening to it or reproducing a piece of music after hearing it for the first or only a few times) was reported by one of the practitioners.

> *My son has been exceptional in singing since age five without any formal training. Eventually, with formal training he became a renowned professional singer and acquired a name and position in this sphere. (Kathleen [PA])*

In-depth attention to details or visual perception. Two parents in the study reported having noticed exceptional visual perception and attention to detail in their children.

She can draw intricate mythological creatures. As a child he was able to see small insects from a distance of eight feet or more. Once she picked out a 'Dora the Explorer' from a large collection of magazines in seconds. (Michael [PA])

This one child I found can exceptionally follow the detailed patterns in things, features, and environment. (Laura [PR])

Sub-theme 1.2: Perspectives and Nature of Exceptionalities

Perspectives about the existence or non-existence of exceptionalities in autistic people were fraught with differences of opinion, while most practitioners expressed that they do not believe entirely in the *existence of exceptional skills* in autistic people for two reasons: *first*, the proportion of such exceptional abilities in the autistic population is very low. *Second*, they reasoned, based on their experience of many years that such exceptional skills, even if they exist in a few people, lack the potential to be utilized most productively due to their intrapersonal deficits or lack of prerequisites in developmental areas. There were parents who also differed in their opinion and admitted their strong beliefs in the existence of such exceptional abilities even though in small proportions in one or more areas. Furthermore, they expressed that with a proper environment, adult coaches, and consistent efforts such skills do have the potential to be nurtured to a productive and application level. However, there were many participants who did not accept the existence of such skills in autistic people. Hence the overall report was contained with mixed responses on this account.

I felt that even if I did notice my kid's abilities but I felt those cannot be utilized most productively due to deficits in many allied areas. (Laura [PR])

I feel many of these exceptional or non-exceptional abilities can be manifested or trained further in many autistic children but that needs a lot of effort and necessitates a full-fledged collecting effort of the team comprising parents, practitioners, and teachers / special educators to work on the necessary prerequisites to facilitate and nurture the targeted ability. It may take many years to first work on the pre-requisites and needs enormous patience and belief. For e.g., despite having exceptional musical traits, one of the children I worked with took ten years to attain mastery and finally sang a song on stage himself even having deficits in other essential traits. (Laura [PR])

The exceptional skills are definitely strengths. However, it can be difficult to facilitate those abilities into activities that mainstream society values. (David [PR])

Identification; striking and easily noticeable? Most participants (n = 12; both parents and practitioners) in the study reported the existence of multiple skills to be apparent and striking enough to get noticed. However, in a few, it took a while to get recognized after working with them one-to-one in close proximity allowing free choice or taking the child's lead.

The exceptional skills are mostly very striking and pronounced so usually, they are visible to others. (Cynthia [PR])

I noticed as early as at the age of merely 2 years that my child was fond of music and started picking up sections of songs that he liked. (Kathleen [PA])

Out of the 5 autistic people in whom I noticed such exceptional abilities, it took many years for me to really understand their exceptional traits. Even the parents misinterpreted them as a common stereotypical trait without any utility or potentialities. (Cynthia [PR])

Manifestation; whether training is needed? This has assorted with mixed responses. Participants (n = 15) reported they felt such abilities as inherent in the child's repertoire and can feel their own unique ways of processing quite different from the neuro-typical people, though most participants reported no such practice for the manifestation of the exceptional abilities in most children and were able to apply even with minimum or without practice. However, there were parents (n = 3) and practitioners (n=3) who conveyed that despite having these inherent striking abilities, with practice and proper, needful guidance and support attuned to their brain wiring and striking the right match at the right time, many of such abilities flourished extremely well and also became their career and profession later.

Despite much assistance or practice one of my students was able to retain and produce what was taught without even the teacher's coaching, unlike many other students. I was surprised that despite being nonverbal the child was able to answer with a communication device independently. I felt as if it was already there in his repertoire. (Rebecca [PR])

I feel that these exceptional abilities were something that the students engaged in of their own volition, and that they could often be very rigid while a teacher was trying to "co-opt" or shape the ability further towards an end goal that the student may not have in mind. (David [PR])

It is difficult to get an appropriate coach or trainer well apt to train an autistic person. A combination of specific skills and required training to handle autistic people is hard to find. (Angela [PR])

Rigidity and obsession. Parents and practitioners reported extreme obsession of their children with their own self-driven interests and expression that is predominantly comprised with rigidity and inflexibility. Parents reported their child's devotion and engagements in prolonged specific interests and obsessions and their resistance to switchover.

Both my girls (twin) were obsessed about specific things. One was obsessed with supernatural stuff while the other with witchcraft very early. So, I had to search for specific books on those unusual subjects in the market and library and facilitated their interests which might be odd or unusual for mainstream people. (Barbara [PA])

It is sometimes hard to take them out of their unique respective interest or passion. There are certain times when it becomes extremely hard. (Angela [PR])

Serving some intrinsic need or drive. There is still much to know about these exceptional abilities when it comes to autistic people due to the unique brain wiring of autistic minds and the extreme inter- and intra-individual autistic variability. Knowledge about this aspect of abilities and related uniqueness is limited by sporadic explorative studies on the line.

I found these students to be often rigid and inflexible in how they approach these areas of strength like they were some rituals. (David [PR])

They seemed engaged in these repeated activities as if they served some inner need and drive, maybe to self-regulate, out of some sort of distraction from external input or an environment that is overwhelming to them. It seemed like the motivation for these activities was entirely intrinsic (David [PR])

Intra- and interpersonal discrepancy in abilities. Most participants in the study reported to have noticed wide interpersonal differences manifesting discrepancies in specific abilities relative to their general abilities in their child/children. Participants (parents and practitioners both) reported that autistic people are significantly superior to their peers of the same age group in many areas demonstrating stark and markedly incongruous contrast.

She was a very early reader, fluent, and could decode extremely well, spelled words from a group of three words several grade levels above. She showed wide discrepancy/ Intra differences; could read at an M level but could answer questions at a C level. Her math scores were well above the grade level and those for ELA (English Language Arts) were far below. She's ahead of her grade in spelling, grammar, and math while her comprehension and demonstration ability lag behind. (Jessica [PA])

Comfort and preference for online mode. Despite having in-person direct communication challenges, participants reported their wards having certain technology-inclined interests and being relatively exceptionally comfortable in online modes of communication. Some children manifest a combination of their skills and interests (e.g., in drawing cartoon characters with technology) to create extremely valuable and marketable skill sets.

My child loves to be in the company of friends and loves socializing. He has limited in-person friends but quite a good number of online friends through social networking sites and would devote hours with them. (Linda [PA]*)*

He spends hours watching others online and their works and reading comments, responding, and interacting. Something that he did from a very young age. (Jessica [PA]*)*

Sub-theme 1.3: Non-exceptional Strengths and Abilities

Research exploring the non-exceptional abilities of autistic people is limited. It is mostly overshadowed by their deficits and behavioural issues. Almost all of the parents and practitioners (n = 24) reported the existence of multiple potentialities (e.g., cooking, artistic traits, music, knitting, particular interest in science and maths subjects, inclination towards nature, various specific unique interests) in their autistic children. Nevertheless, they expressed their uncertainty on the boundaries of exceptionality and non-exceptionality because there are no clinical assessments to verify their existence. Participants strongly adhered to supporting the existence of immense possibilities of abilities and strengths in the autistic population. Parents reported persistent efforts to capture the levels of such abilities and strengths.

She had good traits like reading, knitting, archaeology, chemistry, and attention to details but she eventually lost interest. I remember one of her teachers said that she can be very good in a lab-based subject and that she follows instructions very well. (Linda [PA]*)*

He has multiple special interests like cooking/baking, computer/gaming, drama-acting, and debates (won 2 medals at his first competition). He's also very good with number puzzles (not genius-level but very good). She has created some puzzles, sudoku-like at a very young age. (Jessica [PA]*)*

My child was good at many traits; poetry, good memory, writing ability, and mental arithmetic calculation apart from his exceptional skill in music. (Kathleen [PA]*)*

I have seen in my daughter multiple skills that may not be exceptional but quite good like she sings really well, takes special interest in drawing, and is good at attention to detail as well. (Angela [PR]*)*

I do believe that many of the non-exceptional skills that I noticed also can be nurtured further with the right environment and strategies but sometimes it is extremely difficult to convince them all. (Anna [PR]*)*

Discussion

A thorough analysis of the participants' reporting summarized the relevant information under the sub-themes extracted from the interviews. The sub-themes (i.e., strengths perceived together with the participants' perspective with regard to the strengths and abilities) led to more in-depth coverage of the study objective. Significant findings are discussed in the subsequent section.

Potentialities of Strengths

Existence of Certain Strengths and Abilities

Parents reported the *existence of certain strengths and abilities* among their autistic wards. Practitioners with multiple years of experience working with autistic children and adults shared their firsthand experiences in relation to the strengths and abilities perceived. To sum up, the range of abilities reported by the participants in the study were memory, math, music, art, and in-depth visual perception. It is apparent that the existence of such exceptionalities cannot be completely denied or refuted, and hence there is need of large sample study across countries on the clinical assessment of such exceptionalities to achieve a true estimate of their nature so that further intervention can be ameliorated (Halder & Bruyere, 2021). It may be critical to outline the criterion for defining exceptional abilities in the autistic population due to inter- and intrapersonal variability. A more robust definition of exceptionality and non-exceptionality would help capture the real proportion or estimation of such exceptional skills along with the various types and nature of the autistic population.

The strengths, as reported by parents and practitioners, need further investigation for a valid foundation and generalization. For instance, the inclination and interest of autistic people for online modes of communication warrants more research to understand whether such responses are due to the inner desire to socialize that is hindered by challenges of in-person interaction and non-rewarding experiences and thus looking for alternative ways or, rather, due to inherent differences in the way autistic peoples' brains are wired and also whether their having a genuine interest in technology is a separate field of investigation altogether (Sigman & McGovern, 2005; Van Hees et al., 2015).

Identifying These Traits as Early as Possible

The study revealed many significant perspectives that came out of the participants' in-depth reporting. Further exploration in this area with empirical findings may provide an extensive understanding of further function-based intervention approaches. It becomes clear that the entire population of autistic people needs to be categorized separately in a *continuum with the exceptional on one hand and non-exceptional on the other hand* with a completely differentiated teaching-learning environment clearly assigning a differential role and function for the facilitators or adult coaches (i.e., parents at home and teacher at school or others). There are accounts of many biographies by world-renowned autistic people that reveal this perspective about autistic strengths that such exceptional traits are extremely striking and get noticed very soon. However, from the study, it appears that there may be a necessity *to identify these traits as early as possible* and that it is not always possible that these traits would get noticed on their own.

Appropriate Training and Environment to Hone the Inner Natural Potentialities

Furthermore, though there are accounts of world-renowned talented autistic people who got the right match mediated by the right kind of environment, this may not be generalized for all. Hence striking the right chord in terms of getting the appropriate *adult coach or guidance, training, and environment to hone the inherent skills might be essential* in many cases. There is exhaustive literature on the line of whether *autistic people have rigidity or creativity*. However, more extensive research is crucial in having a clear line of demarcation with respect to this perspective. There have been many changes in the understanding of the term 'savant' since Down first coined the term in the 1880s (Down, 1887). It is interesting to note that many myths and stereotypes associated with savant skills have been refuted over time through evidence-based arguments or research (Kapur, 1996; Treffert, 2014), but still more clarity would be beneficial. Many practitioners and parents both felt some inner drive behind those manifestations. *It may not be certain whether practice and training can make any difference.* Now, whether their exceptional abilities are also a combined outcome of their self-driven practices or completely steered by intrinsic drives remains a question. Whether it's due to the weak central coherence (Frith, 1989) and a predisposition to repetitive behaviour patterns or as a result of intense concentration and self-driven practice in the absence of teaching may be worth exploring. How much this structural, rule-based knowledge or exceptional skills are driven by inner motive and zeal and have the possibility to be nurtured further by practice mediated through appropriate environments, and to what extent, calls for extensive empirical research on the area.

Non-Exceptional Abilities and Strengths

Furthermore, it is evident from the participants' first-hand accounts that autistic people do have various extensive *non-exceptional abilities and strengths* which may not fulfil the criteria of being called 'exceptional' or superior but may have the potential to be further developed for effective participation, inclusion, independent living and better quality of life. Identifying non-exceptional potentialities may be a challenge, as they are not striking and may not be quite visible on their own. These skills may be flourished and mediated by adult coaches who can help in the identification and development of these skills. The typical deficit-based defining measures based on the conventional autism triad coupled with prior assumptions about autism overridden by the array of behaviours and general deficits seem to impede and overshadow true recognition of the strengths and abilities of many autistic people. Hence it is crucial to inform and educate the general public and masses regarding both sides of the autistic spectrum with evidence-based empirical findings for recognizing their true phenotypes for mapping differential appropriate interventions.

Future Direction

Nurturance of Both; Exceptional and Non-exceptional Autistic Abilities

A pertinent need identified during the conversation with participants was for a tailor-made differential programme for *nurturance of exceptional and non-exceptional abilities for autistic people*. The striking visible exceptionalities call for a resourceful adult coach who is attuned to the needs of the child of relatively superior ability. An adult coach who can guide and regulate the child to support his ability level and progress thereafter through a collective differential programme of acceleration, enrichment, and appropriate mentorships can be of immense importance, while identifying the non-exceptional skills of autistic people may call for continued observation of the child's abilities and interests mediated through a wide variety of exposures coupled with multiple opportunities for practice. This suggests opportunities and facilitation to develop expertise in the subjects of their interest (Liu et al., 2011). Matching their abilities with their interests is evidently essential in both ability groups by allowing maximum freedom of choice and flexibility without enforcing any demand but by free will. Intervention strategies needed to be entirely personalized and calls for treating both exceptional and non-exceptional groups as two different abilities categories. The importance of reward and reinforcement can play a crucial role in nurturing strengths from the very early developmental years. Autistic people, more specifically the ones with exceptional abilities, may be less likely to be driven by external motivation as compared to neuro-typical people; hence they may need alternative strategies for constant regulation for striving for goals, success, or accomplishments.

Enriched and Flexible Environment

The *school and home environment* needs to be full of enrichment, desired support, positive reinforcements, flexibility, ample opportunities to practice, the scope for acceleration, curriculum modifications, trained and enthusiastic teachers, and scope to showcase their talents and abilities in a variety of novel interesting ways (Van Hees et al., 2015). The upsurge of fitting into the mainstream inclusion model of special education with ill-equipped teachers and incapacity to meet the specific needs of autistic people can be devastating (Brown et al., 2013). Teachers need to have a natural urge to understand the individualized needs of their autistic learners to design personalized programmes based on function-based needs and interventions. Parents can offer valuable insight into how teachers can effectively support and nurture their autistic wards. Parents' inquisitiveness is intrinsically driven through the interplay and collective contribution of primary (i.e., studying and observing their own child) and secondary resources (i.e., existing literature; empirical and foundational) to understand the different ways of processing information in autistic people. Trying to understand their way of knowing is very important and a necessary prerequisite for understanding and addressing their needs better and bringing out their true potential. Teachers need to design a tailor-made process of differential, ecological support programme/environment for the child, built on the foundation of the needs of the child (Garbacz et al., 2016) mapped in consultation with the entire team of specialists and parents for an effective outcome.

Strengths of the Study

The study sample consisted of participants of heterogeneous nature in terms of age, gender, and distribution within the autistic population forming a good comprehensive representation of the target population of the study. Conducting in-depth semi-structured interviews and offering the utmost flexibility with no time bindings led to full-fledged free expression of the participants and led to many revelations, direct and indirect insights that produced a rich source of qualitative data and contributed much in-depth understanding of the area under investigation. It is one of few studies that focused on the person-centred first-hand account and perspectives on the under-researched area of autism.

Limitations of the Study

The study was based on purposive sampling, and this limits the generalization aspects of the findings. The study reports certain limitations. *First*, it comprised only 30 autistic adults so the findings may not be a representation of the entire autistic population. *Second*, the participants considered only the already diagnosed autistic population who were all adults and did not cover many non-diagnosed autistic populations. *Third*, the study sample was largely from autistic people residing mostly in the USA and very few from India, so findings cannot be generalized to autistic people in other parts of the world. Cross-cultural research addressing these limitations would yield many more aspects not covered in the present study and could also lead to the generalization of the findings.

Authors' Contributions

SH developed the idea and designed the study, collected data, analysed, interpreted, and wrote the manuscript. While SB assisted at every stage from the beginning, from shaping the thought process, data collection, and also the fine-tuning of the manuscript. WSG assisted in shaping further with valuable comments and suggestions.

Funding

Funding for the first author was supported by the Fulbright Academic and Professional Excellence Fellowship, United States India Education Foundation (USIEF), India, International Institute of Education (IIE), USA.

Ethics Approval (Include Appropriate Approvals or Waivers)

The study is a part of an ethically approved study by the Cornell University IRB board under the Human subject exempt category (approval ref: Protocol ID#: 2001009333).

Conflict of Interest

The author reports no conflict of interest.

Note

1 The term 'autistic adults' will be used all through the chapter as the participants of the study reported here desired this term over the term adults with autism.

References

American Psychiatric Association (2013). *Cautionary statement for forensic use of DSM-5* (5th ed.). American Psychiatric Publishing. https://doi.org/10.1176/appi.books.9780890425596.744053

Asperger, H. (1944). Die "Autistischen Psychopathen" im Kindesalter. [The "Autistic Psychopaths" in Childhood]. *Archiv für Psychiatrie und Nervenkrankheiten, 117*, 76–136. https://doi.org/10.1007/BF01837709

Baron-Cohen, S. (1995). Learning, development, and conceptual change. In *Mindblindness: An essay on autism and theory of mind*. The MIT Press.

Baron-Cohen, S. (2003). *The essential difference: Men, women and the extreme male brain*. London: Penguin.

Baron-Cohen, S. (2002). The extreme male brain theory of autism. *Trends in Cognitive Sciences, 6*, 248–254.

Baron-Cohen, S. (2009). Autism: The empathizing-systemizing (E-S) theory. *Annals of the New York Academy of Sciences, 1156*, 68–80. https://10.1111/j.1749-6632.2009.04467.x

Baron-Cohen, S., Ring, H., Wheelwright, S., Bullmore, E., Brammer, M., Simmons, A., & Williams, S. (1999). Social intelligence in the normal and autistic brain: An fMRI study. *European Journal of Neuroscience, 11*, 1891–1898.

Baron-Cohen, S., Wheelwright, S., Skinner, R., Martin, J., & Clubley, E. (2001). The Autism-Spectrum Quotient (AQ): Evidence from Asperger syndrome/high-functioning autism, males and females, scientists and mathematicians. *Journal of Autism and Developmental Disorder, 31*, 5–17. https://doi.org/10.1023/a:1005653411471

Baron-Cohen, S., Ashwin, E., Ashwin, C., Tavassoli, T., Chakrabarti, B. (2009). Talent in autism: Hyper-systemizing, hyper-attention to detail and sensory hypersensitivity. *Philosophical Transactions of the Royal Society B, 364*, 1377–1383.

Blume, H. (1998). Neurodiversity: On the neurological underpinnings of geekdom, *The Atlantic*.

Bonini, L. (2017). The extended mirror neuron network: Anatomy, origin and functions, *Neuroscientists, 23*, 56–57.

Brown, H. M., Oram-Cardy, J., & Johnson, A. (2013). A meta-analysis of the reading comprehension skills of individuals on the autism spectrum. *Journal of Autism and Developmental Disorders, 43*, 932–955. http://doi.org/10.1007/s10803-012-1638-1

Crespi, B. J. (2016). Autism as a disorder of high intelligence, hypothesis and theory. *Frontiers in Neuroscience*. https://doi.org/10.3389/fnins.2016.00300

DeSantis, L. A., & Ugarriza, D. (2000). The concept of theme as used in qualitative nursing research. *Western Journal of Nursing Research, 22*(3), 351–372. https://doi.org/10.1177/019394590002200308

de Schipper, E., Mahdi, S., de Vries, P., Granlund, M., Holtmann, M., Karande, S., Almodayfer, O., Shulman, C., Tonge, B., Wong, V. V., Zwaigenbaum, L., & Bölte, S. (2016). Functioning and disability in autism spectrum disorder: A worldwide survey of experts. *Autism Research, 9*(9), 959–969. https:// 10.1002/aur.1592. Epub 2016 Jan 8. PMID: 26749373; PMCID: PMC5064728.

Down, J. L. (1887). *On some mental affections of childhood and youth*. Churchill.

Frith, U., & Frith, C. (2003). Development and neurophysiology of mentalizing. *Philosophical Transactions of the Royal Society A, 358*, 459–473.

Furniss, G. J. (September 2008b). Celebrating the artmaking of children with autism. art education, 61(5), 8–12.

Garbacz, S. A., McIntyre, L. L., & Santiago, R. T. (2016). Family involvement and parent-teacher relationships for students with autism spectrum disorders, *School Psychology Quarterly*, *31*(4), 478–490. http://10.1037/spq0000157.

Giarelli, E., Ruttenberg, J., & Segal, A. (2013). Bridges and barriers to successful transitioning as perceived by adolescents and young adults with asperger syndrome. *Journal of Pediatric Nursing*, *28*(6), 563–574.

Goodman, J. (1972). A case study of an autistic-savant: Mental function in the psychotic child with markedly discrepant abilities. *Journal of Child Psychology and Psychiatry, and Allied Disciplines*, *13*, 267–278.

Grandin, T. (1984). My experiences as an autistic child. *Journal of Orthomolecular Psychiatry*, *13*, 144–174.

Hagner, D., Kurtz, A., May, J., & Cloutier, H. (2014). Person-centered planning for transition- aged youth with autism spectrum disorders. *Journal of Rehabilitation*, *80*, 4–10.

Happé, F. (2018). Why are savant skills and special talents associated with autism? *World Psychiatry*, *17*(3), 280–281. httpe://10.1002/wps.20552

Happe, F., & Vital, P. (2009). What aspects of autism predispose to talent? *Philosophical Transactions of the Royal Society B*, *364*, 1369–1375.

Halder, S., & Bruyere, S. M. (2021). Self-reported impediments at home, school, and community: Autistic adults' first-person accounts of their life trajectories and derived pathways. *International Journal of Developmental Disabilities (IJDD)*, 1–13. https://10.1080/20473869.2021.1917111

Hedley, D., Uljarevic, M., Cameron, L., Halder, S., Richdale, A., & Dissanayake, C. (2016). Employment programs and interventions targeting adults with autism spectrum disorder: A systematic review of the literature. *Journal of Autism*, *21*(8), 1–13.

Howlin, P., Goode, S., Hutton, J., & Rutter, M. (2009). Savant skills in autism: Psychometric approaches and parental reports. *Philosophical Transactions of the Royal Society B*, *364*, 1359–1367. https://10.1098/rstb.2008.0328

Hudac, C. M., DesChamps, T. D., Arnett, A. B., Cairney, B. E., Ma, R., Webb, S. J., & Bernier, R. A. (2018). Early enhanced processing and delayed habituation to deviance sounds in autism spectrum disorder. *Brain and Cognition*, *123*, 110–119. https://doi.org/10.1016/j.bandc.2018.03.004

Jaarsma, P., & Welin, S. (2012). Autism as a natural human variation:reflections on the claims of the neurodiversity movement. *Health Care Analysis*, *20*(1), 20–30.

Kanner L. (1943). Autistic disturbances of affective contact. *Nervous Child*, *2*, 217–250.

Kanner, L. (1971). Follow up study of eleven autistic children originally reported in 1943. *Journal of Autism and Childhood Schizophenia*, *1*, 119–145.

Kapur, N. (1996). Paradoxical functional facilitation in brain-behaviour research. A critical review. *Brain*, *119*, 1775–1790.

Kohls, G., Antezana, L., Mosner, M. G., Schultz, R. T., & Yerys, B. E. (2018). Altered reward system reactivity for personalized circumscribed interests in autism. *Molecular Autism*, *9*, 9. https://doi.org/10.1186/s13229-018-0195-7

Liu, M-J., Shih, W-L., & Ma, L-Y. (2011). Are children with Asperger syndrome creative in divergent thinking and feeling? A brief report. *Research in Autism Spectrum Disorders*, *5*, 294–298. https:// 10.1016/j.rasd.2010.04.011

Meilleur, A-A. S., Jelenic, P., & Mottron, L. (2015). Prevalence of clinically and empirically defined talents and strengths in autism. *Journal of Autism and Developmental Disorders*, *45*, 1354–1367. https://10.1007/s10803-014-2296-2

Mottorn, L. (2011). The power of Autism, *Nature*, *479*, 33.

Mottron, L., Burack, J. A., Iarocci, G., Belleville, S., & Enns, J. T. (2003). Locally oriented perception with intact global processing among adolescents with high-functioning autism: Evidence from multiple paradigms. *Journal of Child Psychology and Psychiatry and Allied Disciplines*, *44*, 904–913.

Mottron, L., Belleville, S., Rouleau, G. A., & Collignon, O. (2014). Linking neocortical, cognitive, and genetic variability in autism with alterations of brain plasticity: The Trigger-Threshold-Target model. *Neuroscience & Biobehavioral Reviews*, *47*, 735–752. https://doi.org/10.1016/j.neubiorev.2014.07.012Mottron

Mottron, L., Belleville, S., Stip, E., & Morasse, K. (1998). Atypical memory performance in an autistic savant. *Memory*, *6*(6), 593–607.

O'Callaghan, H. (2017). What they say about temple grandin:The cork autism conference – understanding autism, empowering potential. Irish Examiner. https://www.irishexaminer.com/lifestyle/healthandlife/dr-temple-grandin-focus-on-strengths-rather-than-deficits-in-children-with-autism-456215.html

Office for National Statistics (2016). *Dataset: A08: Labour market status of disabled people*. Office for National Statistics.

Panzano, L. (2018). Five research-based strengths associated with autism. http://blog.stageslearning.com/blog/five-research-based-strengths-associated-with-autism

Pring, L. (2005). Savant talent. *Developmental Medicine & Child Neurology, 47*, 500–503.

Putt, A. (2019). Common strengths in autism. https://supersimple.com/article/common-strengths-in-autism/

Rutter, M.L. (2011). Progress in understanding autism: 2007-2010. *J Autism Dev Disord., 41*(4), 395–404. https://10.1007/s10803-011-1184-2.

Rutter, M. L. (2011). Progress in understanding autism: 2007–2010. *Journal of Autism Developmental Disorder, 41*, 395–404.

Sigman, M., & McGovern, C.W. (2005). Improvement in cognitive and language skills from preschool to adolescence in autism. *Journal of Autism and Developmental Disorders, 35*, 15–23. https://doi.org/10.1007/s10803-004-1027-5

Soulières, I., Hubert, B., Rouleau, N., & Mottron, L. (2010). Superior estimation abilities in two autistic spectrum children. *Cognitive Neuropsychology, 27*(3), 261–276. https://10.1080/02643294.2010.519228

Treffert, D. A. (2010). *Islands of genius: The bountiful mind of the autistic, acquired, and sudden savant*. Jessica Kingsley Publishers.

Treffert, D. A. (2014). Savant syndrome: Realities, myths and misconceptions. *Journal of Autism and Developmental Disorders, 44*, 564–571.

Van Hees, V., Moyson, T., & Roeyers, H. (2015). Higher education experiences of students with autism spectrum disorder: Challenges, benefits and support needs. *Journal of Autism and Developmental Disorders, 45*, 1673–1688. https://doi.org/10.1007/s10803-014-2324-2

Zeliadt, N. (2018). Autism's sex ratio, explained. Retrieved from https://www.spectrumnews.org/news/autismssex-ratio-explained/

12
INCLUSIVE CLASSROOMS AS THINKING SPACES FOR TEACHERS AND STUDENTS

*Sharon Moonsamy**

Introduction

Instructional discourse in classrooms in South Africa includes the learning outcomes (LOs) of listening, speaking, reading, writing and problem-solving and reasoning. Cognitive application is required across all the LOs, when approaching the task at hand. Even though cognitive skills are stipulated in the curriculum and may be implicated in the instruction, explicit teaching of these skills has not been mandated. There is a dearth of studies published on the explicit teaching of cognitive skills in classrooms and more so in inclusive classrooms.

The reason for limited studies on the application of explicit cognitive instruction is frequently a result of educators (teachers, speech-language therapists, learning support therapists and other cognate professionals) assuming that thinking occurs spontaneously and automatically when engaged in tasks (Moonsamy, 2014). Research has shown that effective thinking requires a conscious awareness of cognitive application.

This chapter is, in the main, a conceptual chapter and includes vignettes from students' and teachers' experiences of cognition. The chapter presents qualitative data from studies and from experiences within workshops. Furthermore, the chapter provides theory that guides the text and assumptions that frame the writing. Definitions of concepts that relate to cognitive instruction in teaching and learning in inclusive classrooms are presented so that educators and students can achieve a level of understanding of how to be effective thinkers, how to approach all tasks with motivation and affect, and to choose to be life-long learners. Context is foundational to exploring thinking spaces. For the purpose of this chapter, classrooms will be the context of learning; however with hybrid teaching in the twenty-first century, learning spaces refer to any space conducive to learning and not necessarily only classrooms within school buildings.

South Africa's Educational Context

Following post-1994 – the education system in South Africa adopted the Policy of Inclusion as a principle of basic human rights as enshrined in the new constitution of the Republic of South Africa (Act 108 of, 1996). This was an attempt to redress past inequalities and to provide access

---

* sharon.moonsamy@wits.ac.za

for all children, including children from marginalised communities (Mophosho & Moonsamy, 2021). As Nelson Mandela (former president) said, Education is the most powerful weapon which you can use to change the world. He also stated that education is the key to eliminating social, psychological and emotional ills, including gender inequality, reducing poverty, creating a sustainable planet, preventing needless health matters, eliminating violence but fostering peace (The Borgen Projects Quotable Quotes, 2018). In a knowledge economy, education is the new currency via which nations can maintain economic competitiveness and global prosperity.

Thus, post-1994, students from diverse backgrounds were included in mainstream classrooms, irrespective of race, creed, class or religion. The constitution embodies the rights of all children to receive quality and equal education. Mr. Mandela argued that '*Education is the great engine to personal development. Without education, your children can never really meet the challenges they will face. So it's very important to give children education and explain that they should play a role for their country*' (The Borgen Projects Quotable Quotes, 2018). Children from diverse backgrounds brought their different educational preparation, reflecting their context, to the inclusive classroom.

Differentiated instruction according to the needs of each child (from here on, child/children will be referred to as student/s) was, nonetheless, initially not part of the instruction manual, so equity was not discussed. Many students emerged from backgrounds that lacked resources and were disadvantaged by the system they had been socialised in due to the apartheid policies before 1994. Hence, many of these students experienced barriers to learning. Inclusive Education (IE), as explained in White Paper 6, supported access and participation of all students who experienced barriers in the classroom (Department of Education – DoE, 2001). Barriers to learning and development may arise from both intrinsic and extrinsic factors (DoE, 2001). These terms are elaborated on in subsequent sections.

The constitution of South Africa has embedded in it the importance of critical thinking skills. Frequently, this remains just a concept but if the concepts of *critical thinking skills* are unpacked, it will assist teachers and students in grasping what they need to do in the teaching and learning spaces.

Pre-requisite Skills for Learning

Teachers working with students in classrooms require a sound pedagogic knowledge of learning, which is part of their teacher training. An understanding of formal and epistemological access to learning is essential (Walton et al., 2015). Formal access is a systemic issue, and major focus was placed on this. However, little attention was given to epistemological access, where students' access to knowledge is essential for learning. The following skills to support epistemological access, required for learning, are discussed briefly.

Language skills. To be effective in processing information to learn, students require foundational skills in oral language. Language consists of Form (grammar/syntax, morphology, phonology), Content (meaning, semantics) and Use (social use of language/pragmatics); these domains continue to be refined during the school years (Koutsoftas, 2020). Breakdown at any section of language skills will affect the student's effectual comprehension for classroom success. The level of language competence is also key, as the medium of classroom instruction may not be in the home language of the student or the teacher. Language of Learning and Teaching (LOLT) impacts the processing of the instruction. Differences in LOLT and home languages are frequently an area of debate in South African schools. Many students may therefore experience barriers to learning as a consequence of insufficient competence

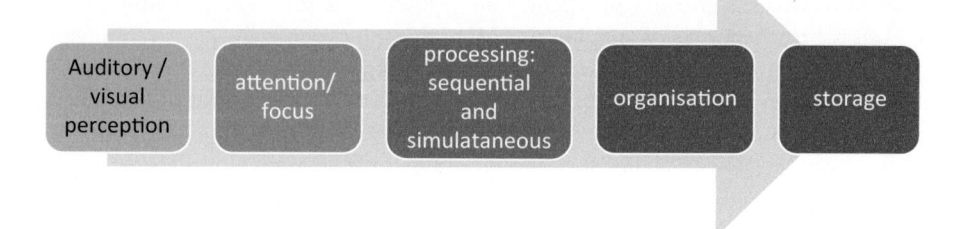

[Auditory / visual perception] → [attention/focus] → [processing: sequential and simultaneous] → [organisation] → [storage]

Figure 12.1 Flow map of cognitive management of information.

in the LOLT. In addition to linguistic competence, the student requires cognitive competence to navigate through scholastic tasks.

Cognition. Cognition occurs parallel to language development and influences language development and vice versa. Cognitive skills also refer to the executive functions, including attention, memory, processing, planning and organisation of information. The student has to attend, receive the information, process the information using their working memory, organise the information and store the information into schemas for easy retrieval when needing to plan and execute a task. This simple description is shown on the flow map in Figure 12.1, which depicts the processing of information from the point of reception to storage. A breakdown at any level of the processing model will result in ineffective use of cognitive resources to complete a task. Figure 12.1 shows the processing of information for effective outcomes.

Motivation. Students' learning is in part related to their motivation to acquire knowledge (Kyriacou, 2001). Motivation occurs at two levels – intrinsic motivation and extrinsic motivation. Intrinsic motivation is the internal drive of the student, whereas extrinsic motivation refers to outside factors that drive the student. As students mature, their intrinsic motivation should energise and drive their learning.

Affect. The students' emotions (affect) influence how students learn. Hence, students who hail from impoverished communities or emotionally broken environments may not be accessible to learning. Thus, the teacher needs to consider the effect that the affect has on the student, as it can create a barrier to learning.

Barriers to Learning

Teaching and learning are affected negatively, when students display barriers to learning. As indicated earlier, these factors may be intrinsic to the student or extrinsic to the student. Other terms for these intrinsic and extrinsic factors are 'distal' and 'proximal' factors. Brittnacher (2014) defines distal factors as those within the student (intrinsic), including their language, cognitive, emotional and behavioural dispositions. Proximal describes factors outside of the student (extrinsic) and includes home and school environment, curriculum, community, among others. Interferences in learning are therefore caused by a number of factors which influence the teacher's and the student's engagement. Distal and proximal factors also reflect the biopsychosocial model of Bronfenbrenner, confirming that subsystems impact the student. Pather (2007) confirms that some factors may not necessarily be within the learner and could be social or within the school and/or curriculum. The student should, therefore, be seen holistically in the learning context.

DoE (2005: 13-14) provides a description of these distal and proximal factors:

1. Factors that relate to students' learning styles and learning needs
2. Factors relating to educators' teaching methodology and attitudes
3. Content of the curriculum
4. Resources required for teaching and learning
5. Physical environment
6. Psychosocial environment in which the students are engaged
7. Factors related to the student's background - different subsystems that influence learning
8. Community and social dynamics which influence the student's learning

Systemic barriers: lack of basic and appropriate learning support materials, lack of assistive devices, inadequate facilities at school, overcrowded classrooms, and lack of mother tongue teachers.

Societal barriers: severe poverty, late enrolment, gangs/violence in neighbourhoods and at home.

Pedagogical barriers: insufficient support of teachers, inappropriate and unfair assessment procedures, and inflexible curriculum.

Medical barriers: sensory disabilities, neurological disabilities, physical disabilities, and cognitive disabilities.

These barriers to learning do not exist all the time but can arise suddenly due to change in circumstances, emotional trauma and a variety of other factors. These barriers need to be understood by the teacher so that they can be mitigated where possible to promote learning. Even though the barriers are highlighted, a deficit approach to teaching and learning, which focuses on the distal factors (intrinsic to the student), must be avoided. Teaching instruction can be one avenue to alleviate these barriers so that students experience success in learning.

Inclusive Education (IE) – in South Africa

UNESCO (1994, p. 6) argues that 'schools should accommodate all children regardless of their physical, intellectual, social, emotional, linguistic or other conditions. This should include children with disabilities and gifted children and children from other disadvantaged or marginalized areas or groups'. IE was long established as a philosophy internationally before it was introduced in South Africa. The philosophy of IE is aligned with the values of human rights justified in the constitution of South Africa (Constitution of South Africa, 1996). A learning environment that supports all students irrespective of their learning style or learning barriers is aligned to inclusive education philosophy. The realisation of the IE philosophy is however dependent on the ethos of the school, the training of the teachers and the support systems required to scaffold the curriculum.

IE as a philosophy has both advantages and limitations for the students, the teachers and the education system. The advantage of IE for students is that they benefit from engaging in classroom discussions, where peer learning and socially constructed knowledge are important for the consolidation of concepts. Peer learning also provides the opportunity for rephrasing of information which allows students the time to process the information. The student with barriers to learning should, therefore, benefit from frequent encounters with the lexicon and consolidate their understanding of information, thereby enhancing their knowledge schemas. Furthermore, students whose barriers to learning are a result of social deprivation will be provided with an opportunity to learn within a supported environment and attempt to bridge gaps in their learning. The teacher would scaffold the learning for these students, employing strategies applicable to individuals. Individual education plans (IEPs) are a part of the teaching and learning framework. Hence, a student whose comprehension breakdown is a result of less than adequate linguistic skills would benefit from a teacher whose aim is to build their vocabulary and language skills through explanations and clarification strategies.

The latter assumption is that teachers are equipped to assist students with barriers to learning. Jali (2014), however, argues that the successful implementation of IE depends on teachers' preparedness to embrace the diversity of students' learning behaviours in their classrooms. In addition, teachers who are insufficiently prepared to manage students with barriers to learning would not provide the necessary and appropriate support students need. The ethos of the school where the philosophy of IE is not embraced would fail to support both the teachers and students with barriers to learning. Furthermore, Bronfenbrenner's systems' theory describes the school as one system within a macro-system which involves the country's education system. Hence, within the larger system, a lack of consensus about what constitutes best practice within inclusive classrooms creates a further hindrance to this philosophy of education (Donohue & Bornman, 2014). Thus, if the education department does not provide support services of multidisciplinary professionals, including SLTS, OTs and psychologists amongst others, the student with barriers to learning and their respective teachers would not have the systems in place that would normally support a student, holistically.

What Do Teachers Need to Teach Effectively in Inclusive Classrooms?

Teachers in mainstream schools need to develop a different skills-set and knowledge in order to deal with learners who experience barriers to learning. Understanding the student as a whole requires the teacher to know the systems that influence learning. Knowledge of Bronfenbrenner's (1979) biopsychosocial theory provides a platform for understanding the different systems that impact the student. Teachers need to understand the importance of a student feeling a sense of belonging, where they feel safe and secure so that learning is accessible. In addition, the teacher should have an understanding of factors that cause barriers to learning and have some knowledge about resources internal and external to the school to minimise these barriers. Factors that create barriers to learning, in addition to those already discussed, would also include the curriculum and the instruction. Teachers need to be selective about the content of the curriculum, as '*coverage of content*' does not ensure learning (Erikson, 2007).

What Do Students Need to Learn Effectively in Inclusive Classrooms?

In addition to skills (language, cognition, motivation and affect), discussed earlier in the chapter, students need to understand their learning styles, the importance of seeking clarification when they are unsure of information, and how to work collaboratively within groups, whilst valuing their independence. Active participation of students is important so that they are part of the lesson.

Cognitive Instruction in the Classroom

Cognitive instruction should be a holistic practice within education, where support is attained from the Department of Education, the ethos of the school, teacher instruction and student

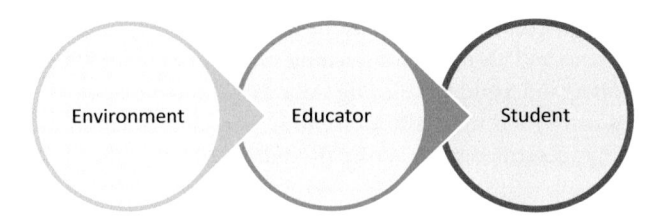

Figure 12.2 Contributing aspects of cognitive instruction

learning. Cognitive education is developmental in its approach, building skills for effective teaching and learning so that epistemological access is attained. In addition, developing thinking attitudes and behaviours in teachers and students should aim towards setting up the student for a future world of work so that they become contributing citizens for a better society and economy.

To create thinking spaces within the classroom requires a discussion of the different aspects that contribute to cognitive instruction. Figure 12.2 delineates three contributing factors: the environment, the educator and the student, among others. The environment is a laboratory of learning, as described by Greenberg (2005), where tasks are set up that create curiosity and inquiry among the students. Knowledge, according to Vygotsky (1978), is socially constructed; therefore the educator should encourage different perspectives when engaging students so that diverse points of view are explored to create understanding. Furthermore, the student needs to feel a sense of belonging so that they are confident and experience the classroom as a safe space to share their perspectives. A sense of belonging is foundational to being accepted before the student can engage in learning (Feuerstein et al., 1980). Students from marginalised populations, be it a result of distal or proximal factors, need to feel accepted.

Educators (teachers, SLPs, OTs, LST) have the responsibility of creating an environment that is stimulating and conducive to learning, more so in an inclusive classroom. Green (2014: 5) states that 'active mediation of thinking by skilled teachers would enable more students to succeed'. Instruction in the classroom therefore needs to consider the student and the task at hand, from the planning phase to the execution. The educator should exercise their metacognitive skills, which include reflection, evaluation and monitoring so that the instruction is at the appropriate level. Evaluating the instruction in tasks, specifically the cognitive demands of each task presented, is essential in building success in students. Hence, instruction must be considered in light of the student. If the instruction is too complex, the student may struggle, if they do not have the schema to draw on, to aid understanding. However, if the instruction is too simple, the cognitive demands would be too low and the student may allocate cognitive resources ineffectively. Wittwer and Renkel (2008) refer to this as '*expertise reversal*', where students who experience information redundancy in classroom instruction appropriate resources incorrectly; thus they have fewer resources available for the cognitive processing of new information (Moonsamy, 2011).

Students process information either sequentially or simultaneously, depending on the content received. They create links and draw on previous knowledge to build their understanding. The effectiveness of students' retrieval strategies will depend on how they stored the content they received previously. Breakdown in any of these areas (processing of information, storage or retrieval of information) creates barriers to learning. It requires a skilled teacher to be alert to these breakdowns and allow students to discover strategies to problem-solve. These strategies can be referred to as '*thinking tools*' to navigate through a problem (Green, 2014: 7).

Problem-solving and reasoning can be done independently or interdependently. Thus, students would need to develop collaborative and co-operative learning strategies to work effectually with other students, whilst developing independent learning skills. How students apply their thinking skills individually, in groups or beyond the classroom will reflect the mediation provided by a more knowledgeable other, as described by Vygotsky (Kozulin, 2004, Kozulin, 2011).

Cognitive Instruction That Creates Thinking Spaces

Cognitive instruction is developmental in its approach. The educator has to be intentional and explicit in their instruction, when encouraging thinking in classroom discourse. If the instruction is not sufficiently intentional, some learners with barriers to learning may miss an opportunity to develop thinking strategies when learning. The following concepts attempt to impart how thinking spaces can promote valuable learning for the educator and for the student. Table 12.1 delineates some of the concepts among others that should be considered to create thinking spaces in inclusive classrooms.

Table 12.1 Creating thinking spaces

#	Topics
1.	Cognitive Map
2.	Mediated Learning Experience (MLE)
3.	Concept Formation
4.	Metacognition
5.	Feedback

Evaluating or analysing the content (what) and the process (how) should provide a deeper understanding of cognitive instruction. Mentis (2008) described the analyses of the cognitive map, where the content can be examined so that it is responsive to the context. She referred to it in the abbreviation of COMAN – C = content or subject matter; O = operations; M = modality; A= abstract; N = Novelty. The following model of analyses can be applied by a teacher in an inclusive classroom (see Table 12.2) so that students with barriers to learning can be accommodated and scaffolded for success.

The quality of the instruction during mediation needs to be monitored and evaluated. How do educators measure the quality of any instruction? Kozulin and Presseisen (1995) explain the Mediated Learning Experience (MLE) as indicated in Feuerstein's Structural Cognitive Modifiability theory. They state that mediation allows the student with the guidance of the more knowledgeable other (educator) to achieve what would not have been achieved without that guidance. This mediation occurs within what Vygotsky describes as the zone of proximal development (ZPD). Feuerstein describes 14 MLE, of which the first three are key to the quality of the instruction (Tzuriel, 2013). These are, first, *intentionality and reciprocity*, second, *meaning* and, third, *transcendence*. The mediator (educator) intentionally frames and focuses the content for the student. A rapport is built between the educator and the student, the content is presented and through discussion using questions and explanations, the meaning of content is demystified. The educator then links the learning from the classroom and allows the student to express how that content or process of learning would apply to other situations outside the immediate learning context, for example, how it relates to the home and to social engagements. Greenberg (2005) refers to this concept of transference as 'bridging'. The new learning is generalised so that deeper understanding

Table 12.2 Cognitive Map: Analyses of Instruction (COMAN)

Cognitive Map	Description	Teacher's response	Student's response
C	Content	The teacher examines the content for a particular grade in the inclusive classroom. The student with the barriers to learning may need revision of previous content before new content can be added.	Student links the old learning with the new learning.
O	Operations	The teacher then looks at the operations, that is, the skills the student would need to do the task, assessing its complexity.	Practice of an easier task requiring the same skills would help the student transfer to new task. Practice consolidates learning.
M	Modality	Which modality would be most appropriate for the content to be presented?	As students have different learning styles, the content can be presented as verbal, written or through creative arts.
A	Abstract	The level of abstraction must be determined so that the student comprehends the task with some mediation.	The student should move from easy to more abstract tasks
N	Novelty	How familiar is the task?	The student with discussion can work towards mastery.

is achieved when a student sees the link between what they learnt and the application to real life. Effective learning occurs when students are able to apply strategies to problem-solve and reason in tasks.

Learning spaces also create the building blocks for concept formation, and with mediation from a more knowledgeable other (educator), it allows the student to tap into their potential to discover new learning. When students are guided into exploring cognitive strategies to navigate a task, they own their learning. Educators guide students through question techniques to reflect on their thinking. The questions including *where, why and how* help students to reason. These higher-order questions draw on the prior experiences of students. Furthermore, oral discussions are opportunities for students to reflect on their thinking, evaluate their understanding of the information, formulate hypotheses, integrate other knowledge bases, make comparisons and draw conclusions (Moonsamy, 2011). In addition to questions that unlock the meaning of concepts, the educator may introduce evidence-based cognitive strategies from programmes, including Thinking Maps (Hyerle, 2014), Cognitive Enrichment Advantage (CEA) (Greenberg, 2005), Instrumental Enrichment (basic or advanced) (Feuerstein et al., 1980; Lomofsky, 2014), among others. These programmes are founded on the principles of Vygotsky and Feuerstein's theories. Moreover, the revised Bloom's Taxonomy is a robust foundational model on which to build cognitive instruction (Anderson & Krathwohl, 2001).

To develop thinking spaces in learning, metacognition must be included. Metacognition refers to the reflection, evaluation and monitoring of one's thinking processes. Teachers need to reflect on their instruction, evaluating its appropriateness in relation to the student. Students reflect on their thinking when approaching a learning experience. One student in a local study said: 'At school we are not generally asked about our thinking' (Moonsamy, 2011). This indicates that metacognition was absent in classroom instruction. Awareness of evaluating and monitoring thinking is essential in order to ensure that the appropriate outcomes are achieved. The teacher and the student who practise metacognition learn about their own thinking processes and thereby improve their application.

Engaging in reflective practice also links to feedback from the teacher to students and vice versa, regarding the content and the thinking processes. Targeted feedback over non-targeted feedback has been found to be valuable (Burnett & Mandel, 2010). However, student preference for effort or ability feedback needs to be considered and this has implications in an inclusive classroom, especially for students with barriers to learning.

The flow diagram (see Figure 12.3) is an example that should guide educators through the process that creates thinking among their students who display barriers to learning. The cognitive strategy of Approach to Task is from CEA (Greenberg, 2005).

When students with barriers to learning are faced with a task that they perceive as difficult, they may be overwhelmed with anxiety. Therefore, working systematically through the cognitive skill of *Exploration*, they can handle their feelings of anxiety. Feelings or emotions of students with barriers to learning should not be underestimated; the teacher should discuss cognitive

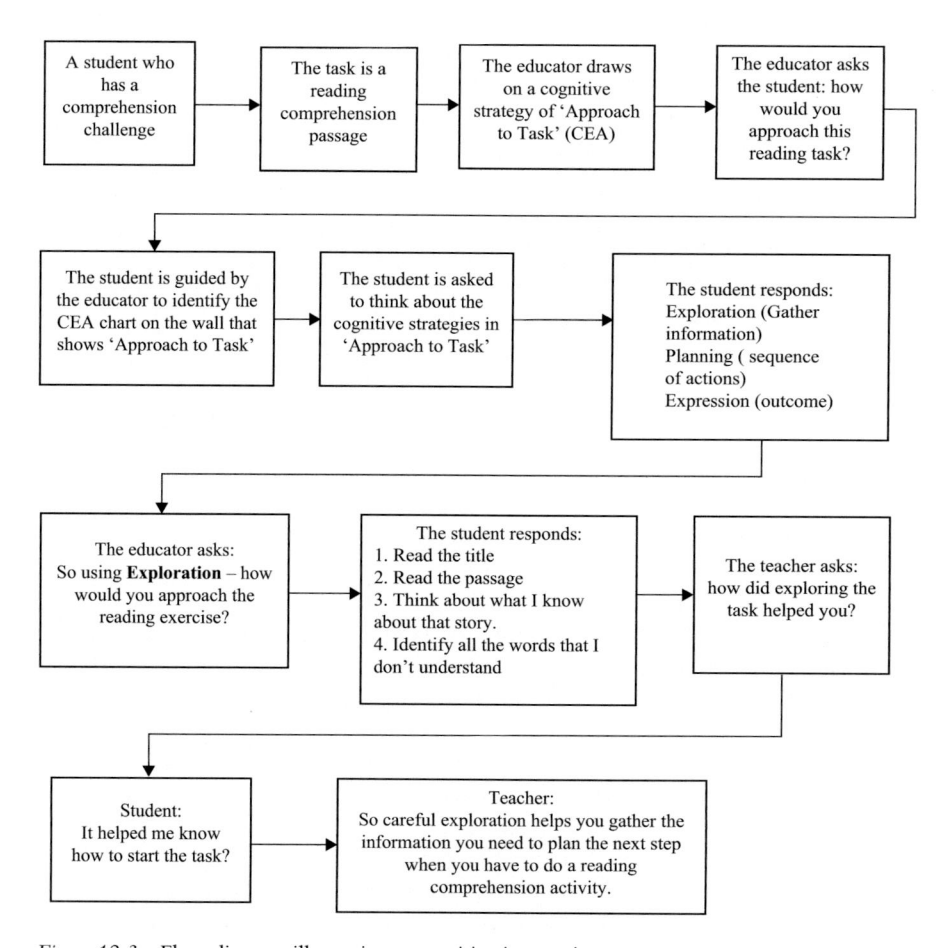

Figure 12.3 Flow diagram illustrating a cognitive instruction

strategies with them so that they manage their tasks in smaller portions. Greenberg (2005) states that students need to search carefully for the information they need before they can plan their next step. Careful gathering of information will avoid impulsive responses. The educator in the above example also used questions to encourage the student to reflect on their actions. The educator's feedback and acknowledgement should motivate the student to build their confidence, when approaching a task.

Conclusion – Way Forward

Cognitive instruction should occur in all learning engagements. One student in a local study said: '*application of thinking skills depended on the subject being learnt, and that mathematics, economic management science and natural sciences were seen as challenging subjects that would require thinking*'. The myth about only exercising thinking strategies in perceived difficult content needs to change, as vital opportunities to learn more successfully would be lost. Explicit cognitive instruction, therefore, would allow educators and students to function more effectively within the inclusive classroom. The strategies imparted would empower teachers to operate within a flexible framework and integrate instruction with their existing knowledge of good mediation practice. The students will be motivated to identify and develop their own learning strategies, building their skills for life-long learning. No specific programme needs to be stipulated, but the principles of quality mediation are foundational for the success of students in the inclusive classroom. Creating thinking spaces does require time and training; hence the curriculum needs to be flexible so that learning outcomes for each student are considered. A collaborative approach among all educators would promote learning across the curriculum. Cognitive instruction is a call for educators to go back to delving deeper into good teaching practice where theory and practice integrate (Greenberg, 2014). Furthermore, cognitive instruction is continually evolving, as thinking is a dynamic process; thus continued research will be needed.

References

Anderson, L. W., & Krathwohl, D. R. (2001). *A taxonomy for learning, teaching and assessing: A revision of Bloom's Taxonomy of educational objectives: Complete edition*. New York: Longman.

Brittnacher, L. (2014). *The role of the personal and contextual factors on emergent literacy skills* (PhD thesis. The University of Wisconsin-Milwaukee, USA).

Bronfenbrenner, U. (1979). *The ecology of human development: Experiments by nature and design*. Cambridge, MA: Harvard University Press.

Burnett, P. C., & Mandel, V. (2010). Praise and feedback in the primary classroom: Teachers' and students' perspectives. *Australian Journal of Educational & Developmental Psychology, 10*, 145–154.

Constitution of South Africa (1996). South Africa. Retrieved from https://www.gov.za/documents/constitution-republic-south-africa-1996

Department of Education (DoE). (2001). *Education white paper 6 (special needs education) building an inclusive education and training system*. Pretoria: Government Printer.

Department of Education (DoE). (2005). *Conceptual and operational guidelines for the implementation of inclusive education: District support teams*. Pretoria: Government Printer.

Donohue, D., & Bornman, J. (2014). The challenges of realising inclusive education in South Africa. *South African Journal of Education, 34*(2), pp. 1–14.

Erickson, H. L. (2007). *Concept-based curriculum & instruction for the thinking classroom*. Thousand Oakes: Corwin Press, Sage Publications Ltd.

Feuerstein, R., Rand, Y., Hoffman, M. B., & Miller, R. (1980). *Instrumental Enrichment . An intervention program for cognitive modifiability*. Baltimore: University Park Press.

Green, L. (2014). *Schools as thinking communities*. Pretoria: Van Schaik's Publications.

Greenberg, K. H. (2005). *The cognitive enrichment advantage. Teacher handbook*. Knoxville, TN, USA: KCD Harris & Associates Press.

Greenberg, K. H. (2014). Cognitive Enrichment Advantage (CEA). In L. Green's (Ed.), *Schools as Thinking Communities* (Chapter 9, pp.141–160). Pretoria: Van Schaik's Publications.

Hyerle, D. (2014), Thinking maps. In L. Green (Ed.), *Schools as Thinking Communities* (Chapter 10, pp. 161–178). Pretoria: Van Schaik's Publications.

Jali, J. S. (2014). *Challenges of teaching in the context of inclusive education: An exploration* (Unpublished MA thesis. University of KwaZulu Natal).

Koutsoftas, A. D. (2020). School-aged language development: Application of five domains of language across four modalities. In N. C. Singleton & B. B. Shulman (Eds.), *Language development: Foundations, processes and clinical applications* (Chapter 11, pp. 223–237). USA, MA, Burlington: Jones & Bartlett Learning.

Kozulin, A. (2004). Vygotsky's theory in the classroom: Introduction. *European Journal of Psychology of Education, XIX*(1), 3–7.

Kozulin, A. (2011). Introduction to Vygotsky's "The Dynamics of the Schoolchild's Mental Development in Relation to Teaching and Learning". *Journal of Cognitive Education and Psychology, 10*(2), 195–197.

Kozulin, A., & Presseisen, B. Z. (1995). Mediated learning experience and psychological tools: Vygotsky's and Feuerstein's perspectives in a study of student learning. *Educational Psychologist, 30*(2), 67–75.

Kyriacou, C. (2001). Teacher stress: Directions for future research. *Educational Review, 53*(1), 27–35. https://doi.org/10.1080/00131910120033628

Lomofsky, L. (2014). Instrumental Enrichment. In L. Green (Ed.), *Schools as Thinking Communities* (Chapter 11, pp.179–200). Pretoria: Van Schaik's Publications.

Lomofsky, L., & Lazarus, S. (2010). South Africa: First steps in the development of an inclusive education system. *Cambridge Journal of Education, 31*(3), 303–317.

Mentis, M. (2008). Instrumental enrichment. Instrumental Enrichment Conference and Workshop, Johannesburg.

Moonsamy, S. (2011). *Effectiveness of metacognitive instruction on reading comprehension among intermediate phase learners: Its link to the PASS theory* (Unpublished PhD Thesis, University of the Witwatersrand).

Moonsamy, S. (2014). Thinking classrooms: How to recognise a thinking classroom. In L. Green (Ed.), *Schools as thinking communities* (Chapter 4, pp. 49–60). Pretoria: Van Schaik's Publications.

Mophosho, M., & Moonsamy, S. (2021). Identification of barriers to learning from ECD to Post-school education. In M. O. Maguvhe, H. R. Maapola-Thobejane, & M. K. Malahlela (Eds.), *Strengthening inclusive education from EDC to post-school education* (Chapter 4, pp. 47–59). Pretoria: Van Schaik's Publishers.

Pather, S. (2007). Demystifying inclusion: Implications for sustainable inclusive practice. *International Journal of Inclusive Education, 11*(5), 627–643.

The Borgen Projects Quotable Quotes (2018). https://borgenproject.org/nelson-mandela-quotes-about-education

Tzuriel, D. (2013). Mediated learning experience and cognitive modifiability. *Journal of Cognitive Education and Psychology, 12*(1), 59–80. https://doi.org/10.1891/1945-8959.12.1.59

UNESCO (1994). *The Salamanca statement and framework for action on special needs education.* Paris: UNESCO.

Vygotsky, L. S. (1978). *Mind in society: The development of higher psychological processes.* Cambridge, MA: Harvard University Press.

Walton, E., Bekker, T., & Thompson, B. (2015). South Africa: The educational context. In S. Moonsamy & H. Kathard (Eds.), *Speech-language therapy in a school context* (Chapter 2, pp. 15–37). Pretoria: Van Schaik.

Wittwer, J., & Renkl, A. (2008). Why instructional explanations often do not work: A framework for understanding the effectiveness of instructional explanations. *Educational Psychologist, 43*(1), (pp. 49–64).

PART III

Identification and Assessment

Identification and assessment of students with disabilities are pivotal for successful and positive outcomes in an inclusive setting. Important aspects and methods of assessment of the diverse needs of learners must be examined and implemented so that successful and effective intervention can be ameliorated. This section discusses the various important aspects of identification and assessment that are considered potent pre-requisites of successful intervention programs.

Part III

Identification and Assessment

13
CONCEPTUAL, IDENTIFICATION AND ASSESSMENT OF STUDENTS WITH DIVERSE NEEDS

*Shakila Dada**

Introduction

The Salamanca Statement states that all children have the right to participate fully in school regardless of their physical, intellectual, social, emotional and linguistic abilities (UNESCO, 1994). The World Report on Disability highlights that approximately 15% of the world's population has disabilities (WHO, 2011). Most young people with disabilities and/or chronic health conditions in the world reside in low- and middle-income countries (Olusanya et al., 2018). It is estimated that Sub-Saharan Africa has the highest incidence of disability, with about 66% of people with disabilities living in Sub-Saharan Africa (McLahan & Schwarts, 2009). The prevalence of disability in South Africa is approximately 13%, with severe disability at approximately 5% (Statistics South Africa, 2013). Communication disabilities in South Africa are estimated to be 6–12%. Accurate and current statistics are however lacking.

The experience of living with disability is dominated by stigma and discrimination (Mall & Swartz, 2012; Mueller-Johnson et al., 2014) and social exclusion (Kijak, 2011; Mpofu et al., 2011). Many children with disabilities in schools in South Africa face discriminatory practices which serve as barriers to receiving an education, according to a recent report (Human Rights Watch, 2015). The barriers include access to education, curriculum, costs and quality of education, increased vulnerability to abusive practices and inadequately trained teachers. This has resulted in the youth with disabilities who leave school lacking basic life skills which are needed to find employment or continue with tertiary education (Human Rights Watch, 2015). Despite progressive policies, the majority of children with disabilities struggle with inequality in education settings and these challenges are exacerbated in children with severe communication disabilities.

The barriers children with disabilities face in terms of accessing education are varied and could possibly be explained by models of disabilities. Whilst models of disability define and shape the self-identity of persons with disabilities, unfortunately, they can also be drivers and reinforcers of prejudice and discrimination against them (Retief & Letšosa, 2018).

Models and Frameworks of Disability

The medical model identifies disability at the level of the person, and as a result disability is viewed at the level of impairment with body function and structure (Marks, 1997). The medical

---

* shakila.dada@up.ac.za
DOI: 10.4324/9781003266068-17

model therefore exclusively focuses on the impairment and on curative or treatment options that medical interventions can offer. It is important to differentiate between an impairment and disability. An impairment arises through dysfunction at the level of the body. A disability on the other hand has a causal effect of limiting human body activity (Carter, 2018). For example, for a child with cerebral palsy, a neurological injury to the brain (body impairment), consequently activities such as walking or talking become difficult (disability). In other words, disability occurs when there is an interaction between the child's impairment and the environment which affects the functioning of the child in a specific domain.

The medical model – it could be argued - does not really consider the environment as it sees impairment as the cause of activity limitations. The medical model's response to disability is aimed at prevention, curing and treatment of the impairment. The medical model also appeared to have implications for education for children with disabilities in that many special schools were focused on specific disabilities e.g. schools for the deaf or for the blind.

The social model of disability emphasizes that disability is determined not by the biological diagnosis but by the organization of the physical and social environment of an individual. The social model of disability is preferred by persons with disabilities as well as disability activists (Whitehead, Kathard, Lorenzo, 2019) as the model argues that society is responsible for disabling a person. Hence, the challenges encountered by children with disabilities in society are attributed to society rather than the physiological, cognitive or functional impairments of the child.

More recently, issues of disability and its impact on the lives of persons with disabilities have been steered by the World Health Organization. The International Classification of Functioning, Disability and Health (ICF), developed by the WHO, is a classification of health and health-related domains (World Health Organization, 2001). The ICF (World Health Organization, 2001) and its extension for children and youth, the ICF-CY (Simeonsson, 2009), was created to provide a universal framework for categorizing and describing disability. These frameworks describe the health and functioning of individuals in for example the school setting. They are utilized as a structure for exploring the commonalities across disabilities and what is considered distinctive about disabilities to develop a shared terminology for educators working in a school setting. The ICF has a "common language" about disability. In this framework, disability has been described as the complex interaction between an individual's health condition and personal factors, and the external factors of an individual, specifically their individual circumstances.

The ICF has its foundations in the concept of person–environment interactions. The environmental factors include physical, social and attitudinal factors. The ICF can document the limitations and environmental barriers. Environmental factors provide insights into how the context may affect the functioning of an individual (WHO, 2007). The ICF therefore describes the participation of a person within the context of the interaction between environmental and personal factors.

The ICF framework is congruent in some ways with the social model of disability. The framework considers disability as the result of the interaction between a person's functional ability and the adaptability and inclusivity of the environment in which they live. Unlike the social model, the person's individual characteristics are not ignored (Shakespeare, 2013). However, a number of critiques have been offered in relation to the ICF. The lack of links to existing disability-related legislation, as well as the deficit views of people with disabilities, has been mentioned (Helander, 2003). While the environment is considered as a dimension in the ICF, the "unpleasant realities" of the environment are possibly not satisfactorily captured or mentioned (Helander, 2003; Kathard & Pillay, 2013). The abuse of people with disabilities, abuse of alcohol and drugs, persons on streets, exploitation are some of the realities of the environments of persons with disabilities that are fully contemplated in the framework (Helander, 2003).

In spite of these critiques, the ICF may still be a useful framework not only for rehabilitation but also for educational provision for persons with disabilities (Castro & Palikara, 2017). For special education, the ICF-CY can provide a common language bridging between disability-focused determinants and education-related knowledge (Simeonsson et al., 2008; Simeonsson & Lee, 2017). These authors suggest that the ICF-CY can provide school nurses, special educators, allied health professionals and psychologists with a common language to document the characteristics of the child and to identify needed interventions and environmental supports. They argue that this may reduce the problem of discipline-specific languages and promote a holistic, integrated view of the child and the support to address child needs.

Definitions of Disability

Disability has been defined as a dynamic multidimensional interaction between the domains of body functions and structures (physiological systems and anatomical parts), activities (execution of tasks and limitations) and participation (involvement in life situations), participation restrictions and contextual factors (WHO, 2001). Disablement is described as a limitation in any one or more of these areas. In this framework, disability is conceptualized as the outcome or result of a complex relationship between an individual's health condition and personal factors and the environmental factors in which the person lives (UNESCO, 2006). In the ICF-CY model, disability is described as an umbrella term that encompasses impairments, activity limitations and participation restrictions, which are affected by barriers in the environment (WHO, 2007). The manner in which disability is defined shows that understanding disability from a biological perspective as an individual problem is insufficient. It implicates the importance of the environment to the development and functioning of a child.

The School Environment

Children's functioning in school can be seen as a process of interaction between the child and the school environment (Jennings, 2003; John-Akinola & Nic-Gabhainn, 2014). In the literature, the school environment is commonly categorized as physical or social. The physical environment is described as legislative policies, supportive resources (e.g. assistive devices), accessibility of school buildings and facilities and availability of school activities, while the social environment is more about teacher–child relationship, peer interaction, attitudes from teachers and peers and teacher's or professional's support (Egilson & Traustadottir, 2009; John-Akinola & Nic-Gabhainn, 2014).

Systems Approach to Assessment

The previous sections of the chapter highlight the importance of the environment to determine functioning for the child with a disability. It is further important to understand that the school environment is a set of nested systems, and therefore the school system is not an isolated system. The school environment is not an isolated system but a subsystem in relation to other systems (i.e. community, state or country). All of these influence the development and functioning of the learners in the school environment.

System theory focuses on the arrangement of relations between the parts of systems. Each part of a system interacts with other parts through ongoing feedback to achieve the balance of the system and to make the system function. Bronfenbrenner's bioecological model looks at human development as an entire ecological system in which growth occurs. The system comprises interactive subsystems that support and guide human growth (Bronfenbrenner, 1994). The microsystem consists of the child's most immediate environment such as home, school, peer and religious groups (Bronfenbrenner & Evans, 2000). The interaction between different parts of the microsystem makes up the mesosystem. The relationship between teacher and parents is one example. The ecosystem consists of settings that influence the development of the child indirectly and would include for example parents' workplace, school boards and planning commissions (Garbarino & Ganzel, 2000). The macrosystem is the sociocultural context that provides values, beliefs and customs in which a child grows up (Bronfenbrenner, 2005).

School is a primary setting in children's microsystem where children participate via interaction with elements in the school environment. The interactions could occur between teacher and child, child and peers, child and professionals, etc. Children develop through this proximal process and the quality of interactions could affect children's participation in school and influence academic outcomes (Reyes et al., 2012).

Assessment

Children often enter school with a medical diagnosis of a disability. Whilst the diagnoses may provide some insight into the child's weaknesses, teachers often do not have information that can help them understand the strengths of the child. Hence, teachers or school-based therapy teams may be involved in assessing the child at the school and in the classroom in order to ascertain the strengths of the particular child. The types of assessment conducted may be influenced by a variety of factors including the availability of professionals in the school-based team, time, expertise and resources available.

The term "assessment" is derived from the Latin word *assidere*, which means to "sit beside" or "to get to know someone". Assessment has been defined by a number of authors in a number of different ways. Hoghugi and Hoghugi (1992 p.1) defined it as "A process of evaluating a person's condition to determine how to deal with the condition". Although this definition attempts to describe the process, guidelines regarding the exact elements are lacking.

Assessment is a complex process (involving many areas of development), a collaborative team process (involving parents and professionals) and an on-going process. Care should be taken when using traditional assessment tools that do not take the school setting into consideration and that do not view the parents, family and community as important members in the assessment process.

Natural assessments, such as interviews and observations of the child, emphasize areas of strength rather than areas of concern (Bagnato et al., 1997). An assessment approach that focuses on areas of strengths may directly lead to suggestions for improved interventions and may enhance the relationship between the professionals and the families that they are working with (Cosden et al., 2006). By identifying capabilities and assets, the family is mobilized to respond to their current challenges (Brun & Rapp, 2001). Parents and professionals form a partnership built on mutual trust and respect. Working together, the team discusses the collection of information, brainstorms possible uses and outcomes of this information, and then comes to a consensus with regard to the intervention plan. "It is the comprehensiveness and richness of the information acquired through assessment that directly affects the quality, utilization, and socio-ecological soundness of the program plan" (LaMontagne & Russel, 1998, p. 208). When parents and families are meaningfully involved in the comprehensive assessment process, they develop a clear picture of the child and their family's strengths and needs, which is empowering and helpful in developing a plan and way forward.

Fundamentally, the transdisciplinary approach is based on systems thinking. Children's development is viewed as interactive and integrated, and intervention happens within the context of the family (Woodruff & McGonigel, 1990) and the school environment. The model implies that the various needs of children are interconnected and that children do not perform skills irrespective of function and environmental demands (Rainforth et al., 1992). The transdisciplinary model of assessment aims to assess functional skills, allow for greater family involvement, promote inclusive educational opportunities, combines strengths and creativity, and support an integrated therapy approach (Linder, 1993). The transdisciplinary model allows for role release and the inclusion of paraprofessionals as part of the team. Paraprofessionals play an important role in the provision of family-centred and culturally relevant service delivery. Paraprofessionals extend the impact of the professional team, assist with direct programming in community-based, inclusive environments, provide on-going support to families, assist families in gaining access to needed resources, and provide respite care (Striffler, 1996). Concerns regarding the transdisciplinary model involve the scheduling of professionals and the length of time required to conduct the assessments and plan intervention (Brink, 2002).

Zoom Lens Approach to Assessment

A zoom lens approach (Van Kleeck & Richardson, 1988) was suggested for the assessment of children with speech language impairment. This approach to assessment may be beneficial for teachers in order to obtain a holistic view of the child and assist teachers with zooming in and focusing on the strengths of the child and supports needed. The teacher can then zoom out and look at the child in the context of the classroom, i.e. participation in the curriculum and the adaptations for testing required. Finally the teacher may zoom further out and look at the school environment in terms of the policies for facilitating children with disabilities' participation in the school. Research about children with disabilities in school has gradually shifted the focus from the individual conditions of the child to the environment they interact with (Sanches-Ferreira et al., 2017) (Figure 13.1).

At the child level the assessment is a complex process which focuses on the evaluation of the individual's capabilities to participate in all his activities by completing a capability assessment. This is the process in which the team gathers information about a child's capabilities in certain areas. The capability assessment indicates the person's current functioning level and points out those skills that currently exist and that can be utilized in the intervention process. The issue is, however, not to assess these abilities in isolation but where they count most, which is functionally in the classroom environment. The interrelated domains to be assessed would include

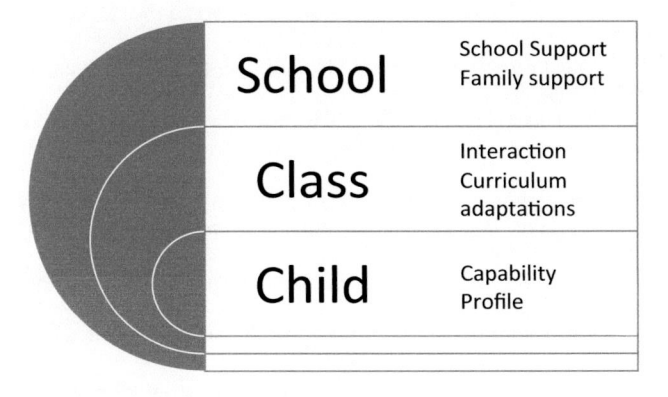

Figure 13.1 A zoom lens approach to assessment for children with disabilities in the school environment

literacy skills, motor skills, cognitive skills, language and communication skills, positioning and seating, sensory skills and socio-emotional behaviour.

At the classroom level, teachers have a significant role in whether a child could actively engage in classroom activities and have pleasant experiences during school time (Egilson & Traustadottir, 2009). Mutually rewarding interactions with peers are a great facilitator for a child to learn and achieve (Falkmer, 2013). A study by John-Akinola and Nic-Gabhainn (2014) shows that children's participation in school is positively associated with the socio-ecological environment of the school and their well-being. The teacher would need to assess the children's ability to interact with the curriculum, teachers and peers. What are the supports and adaptations to the classroom system that are required to facilitate the inclusion of the child? Are there adaptations to the curriculum and testing that need to be made? How can the environment be optimized to facilitate the child's ability to interact with the teacher and their peers?

At the school level, questions should be asked such as what is the overall culture of the school in terms of supporting a child with a disability? Is there a mutually beneficial interaction between family and the school?

Conclusion

This chapter argues that disability cannot be viewed in isolation at the level of the child. It is a complex interaction between the child and the environment. This interaction needs to be understood in relation to understanding the disability as well as the strengths of the child. This understanding should also assist teachers in supporting children with disabilities in their classrooms.

References

Bagnato, S. J., Neisworth, J. T., & Munson, S. M. (1997). *LINKing Assessment and Early Intervention: An Authentic Curriculum-Based Approach*. Baltimore: Paul Brookes.

Brink, M. B. (2002). Involving parents in early childhood assessment: Perspectives from an early intervention instructor. *Early Childhood Education Journal, 29*(4), 251–257.

Brofenbrenner, U. (1994). Ecological models of human development. International Encyclopedia of Education, *3*(2), 1643–1647.

Bronfenbrenner, U. (2005). Making human beings human: Bioecological Perspectives on human development. Thousand Oaks, CA: Sage.

Bronfenbrenner, U., & Evans, G.W. (2000). Developmental science in the 21st century: Emerging questions, theoretical models, research designs and empirical findings. Social Development, *9*(1), 115–125. https://doi.org/10.1111/1467-9507.00114

Brun, C., & Rapp, R. C. (2001). Strength-based case management: Individual's perspectives on strengths and the case manager relationship. *Social Work, 46*(3), 278–288.

Cosden, M., Koegel, L. K., Koegel, R. L., Greenwell, A., & Klein, E. (2006). Strength-based assessment for children with autism spectrum disorders. *Research and Practice for Persons with Severe Disabilities, 31*(2), 134–143.

Carter, S. L. (2018). Impairment, disability and handicap. Department of paediatrics; Emory University School of Medicine website (www.emory.edu). Retrieved from http://www.pediatrics.emory.edu/divisions/neonatology/dpc/Impairment%20MX.html

Castro, S., & Palikara, O. (Eds.). (2017). *An emerging approach for education and care : Implementing a worldwide classification of functioning and disability*. New York: Routledge

Egilson, S. T., & Traustadottir, R. (2009). Participation of students with physical disabilities in the school environment. *American Journal of Occupational Therapy, 63*(3), 264–272.

Falkmer, M. (2013). Participation in mainstream schools for students with autism spectrum disorders. [Video]. Available from https://pingpong.hj.se/courseId/16677/content.do?id=12574192

Garbarino, J., & Ganzel, B. (2000). The human ecology of early risk. In J. P. Shonkoff, & S. J. Meisels (Eds.), *Handbook of early childhood intervention* (2nd ed., pp. 76–93). Cambridge: Cambridge University Press.

Helander. E. (2003). A critical review of the International Classification of Functioning (ICF). Paper presented at Bucharest, Romania. Retrieved from http://www.einarhelander.com/critical-review

Hoghughi, M., & Hoghughi, M. S. (1992). *Assessing Child and Adolescent Disorders: A Practice Manual*. London: Sage.

Human Rights Watch (2015). *"Complicit in Exclusion": South Africa's Failure to Guarantee an Inclusive Education for Children with Disabilities*. Retrieved from https://www.hrw.org/report/2015/08/18/complicit-exclusion/south-africas-failure-guarantee-inclusive-education-children

Jennings, G. (2003). An exploration of meaningful participation and caring relationships as contexts for school engagement. *The California School Psychologist, 8*(1), 43–51. https://doi.org/10.1007/BF03340895

John-Akinola, Y. O., & Nic-Gabhainn, S. (2014). Children's participation in school: A cross sectional study of the relationship between school environments, participation and health and well-being outcomes. *BMC Public Health, 14*(1), 964. https://doi.org/10.1186/1471-2458-14-964

Kathard, H., & Pillay, M. (2013). Promoting change through political consciousness: A South African speech-language pathology response to the World Report on Disability. *International Journal of Speech-Language Pathology, 15*(1), 84–89.

Kijak, R. J. (2011). A desire for love: Considerations and sexuality and sexual education of people with intellectual disability in Poland. *Disability and Sexuality, 29*, 65–74.

LaMontagne, M. J., & Russel, G. W. (1998). Informal and formal assessment. In L. J. Lawrence, M. J. LaMontagne, P. M. Elgas, & A. M. Bauer (Eds.), *Early Childhood Education: Blending Theory, Blending Practice* (pp. 201–232). Baltimore: Paul Brookes.

Linder, T. W. (1993). *Transdisciplinary Play-Based Intervention: Guidelines for developing meaningful curriculum for young children*. Baltimore: Paul Brookes.

Mall, S., & Schawartz, L. (2012). Sexuality disability and human rights: Strengthening health care for disabled people. *South African Medical Journal, 112*, 792–790.

Marks, D. (1997). Models of disability. *Disability and Rehabilitation, 19*(3), 85–91.

McLachlan, M., & Schwartz, L. (2009). *Disability and International Development: Towards Inclusive Global Health*. New York: Springer.

Mpofu, E., Ukasoanya, G., Mupowase, A., Harley, D., Charema, J., & Nthinds, K. (2011). Counseling people with disabilities. In E. Mpofu (Ed), *Counseling People of African Ancestry*. Cambridge: Cambridge University Press.

Mueller-Johnson, K., Eisner, M., & Obsuth, I. (2014). Sexual victimisation of youth with a physical disability: An examination of prevalence rates and risk and protective factors. *Journal of Interpersonal Violence, 29*(17), 3180–3206.

Olusanya, B. O., Davis, A. C., Wertlieb, D., et al. (2018). Developmental disabilities among children younger than 5 years in 195 countries and territories, 1990–2016: A systematic analysis for the global burden of disease study 2016. *Lancet Global Health, 6*, e1100–21.

Retief, M., & Letšosa, R. (2018). Models of disability: A brief overview. *HTS Teologiese Studies/Theological Studies, 74*(1), 1–8.

Rainforth, B., York, J., & MacDonald, C. (1992). *Collaborative Teams for Students with Severe Disabilities: Integrating Therapy and Educational Services*. Baltimore: Brookes.

Reyes, M. R., Brackett, M. A., Rivers, S. E., White, M., & Salovey, P. (2012). Classroom emotional climate, student engagement, and academic achievement. *Journal of Educational Psychology, 104*(3), 700–712. https://doi.org/10.1037/a0027268

Sanches-Ferreira, M., Silveira-Maia, M., Alves, S., & Simeonsson, R. J. (2017). The use of the ICF-CY for supporting inclusive practices in education: Portuguese and Armenian experiences. In *An Emerging Approach for Education and Care*. (pp. 53–70). Routledge.

Shakespeare, T. (n.d.). The social model of disability. In J. L. Davis (Ed.), *The Disabilities Study Reader* (4th ed., pp. 214–220). London: Routledge.

Simeonsson, R .J. (2009). ICF-CY: A universal tool for documentation of disability. *Journal of Policy and Practice in Intellectual Disabilities, 6*(2), 70–72.

Simeonsson, R. J., & Lee, A. (2017). The international classification of functioning, disability and health-children and youth : A universal resource for education and care of children. In *An Emerging Approach for Education and Care*. (pp. 5–22). Routledge.

Simeonsson, R. J., Simeonsson, N., & Hollenweger, J. (2008). The international classification of functioning, disability and health for children and youth: A common language for special education. In L. Florian & M. McLaughlin (Eds.), *Disability Classification in Education: Issues and Perspectives* (pp. 207–226). Thousand Oaks: Corwin Press.

Statistics South Africa (2013). Statistical release P0302: Midyear population estimates 2013. Retrieved from http:// www.statsa.gov.za/publications/P 0302/P 0302 2013.pdf

Striffler, N. (1996). The paraprofessionals role. In D. Bricker & A. Widerstrom (Eds.), *Preparing Personnel to Work with Infants and Young Children and Their Families: A Team Approach* (pp. 231–251). Baltimore: Brookes.

UN General Assembly (13 December 2006). Optional protocol to the convention on the rights of persons with disabilities. A/RES/61/106, Annex II. https://www.refworld.org/docid/4680d0982.html (accessed 29 May 2020).

Van Kleeck, A., & Richardson, A. (1988). Language delay in the child. *Handbook of Speech-Language Pathology and Audiology* (pp. 675–681). Toronto: BC Decker.

UNESCO (1994). The Salamanca Statement and Framework for action on special needs education. Adopted by the World Conference on Special Needs Education; Access and Quality, Salamanca, Spain, 7–10 June 1994. UNESCO.

Whitehead, S., Kathard, H., & Lorenzo, T. (2019). Why disability should be included in the professional education of general practice medical doctors. Preprints 2019, 2019050209. https://doi.org/10.20944/preprints201905.0209.v1

Woodruff, G., & McGonigel, M. J. (1990). Early intervention team approaches: The transdisciplinary model. In J. B. Jordan, J. J. Gallagher, P. L. Huntinger, & M. B. Karnes (Eds.), *Early Childhood Special Education: Birth to Three* (pp. 164–181). Reston: Council for Exceptional Children.

World Health Organisation/World Bank (2011). World report on disability (WRD). Retrieved 2 January 2019. http://www.who.int/ disabilities/world_report/2011/report.pdf). 1–325.

World Health Organization (WHO) (2001). *International Classification of Functioning, Disability, and Health*. Geneva, Switzerland: World Health Organization.

World Health Organization (WHO) (2007). *International Classification of Functioning, Disability, and Health for Children and Youth (ICF-CY)*. Geneva, Switzerland: World Health Organization.

14
ISSUES AND TRENDS IN ASSESSMENT IN EARLY CHILDHOOD INTERVENTION FOR DIVERSE POPULATIONS

Angi Stone-MacDonald*, Serra Acar, Zachary Price, and Ozden Pinar-Irmak

Assessing young children offers a variety of challenges but yields much important information about their skills, strengths, needs, and contextual knowledge within their world. Younger children often do not consistently demonstrate their skills and knowledge across contexts compared to their older peers (National Association for the Education of Young Children [NAEYC], 2009). Children between the ages of zero and five years of age have shorter attention spans, require more direct interactions with adults to collect valid assessment information, and have fewer assessment methods designed for their age groups and characteristics (NAEYC, 2009). In addition, the typical or acceptable developmental range is in the early years, making assessment data harder to interpret within that acceptable range. The definitions of developmental delay and eligibility criteria for early intervention (EI) and early childhood special education (ECSE) services vary from state to state in the United States (US) and around the world (Barger et al., 2019; WHO & World Bank, 2011).

Given the various challenges with assessment for children from birth to age five, educators should use ethically responsible assessment practices (Formosinho & Pascal, 2017). A skillful assessor should choose the specific tools and practices that align with the strengths and needs of the child and family, but they must also conduct each assessment with integrity by adhering to the standards of validity and reliability for that tool. Ethical assessment practices include the ability to choose assessment methods based on their purpose and intent; use assessment methods as tools to improve learning and development; engage families in authentic conversations about the assessment results for their child; and implement a team collaboration approach with other professionals when conducting assessments (Division for Early Childhood [DEC], 2014; NAEYC, 2003; Stone-MacDonald et al., 2018). Providers often struggle with maintaining standardization when using standardized assessment, while at the same time respecting linguistic and cultural differences and implementing the family-centered practices that are at the core of early childhood education and EI (Stone-MacDonald & Silva, 2020).

---

* angi.stone-macdonald@csusb.edu

Overview of the Chapter

In this chapter, we will provide a brief history of early childhood assessment, define assessment, examine current practices for culturally responsive assessment for children in EI/ECSE in the US and describe some common assessment practices in various countries to address early childhood intervention (ECI). The key themes addressed will be: (1) culturally responsive assessment in the US and selected other countries in ECI; (2) challenges faced by practitioners and families with assessment and their connections to the procurement of educational services; (3) current trends in measurement and informal assessment methods used in ECI; and (4) recommendations for educators and researchers to implement best practice in culturally responsive assessment in ECI and meet the needs of diverse populations and their families. For the purpose of this chapter, we define assessment as the ongoing multiple methods and procedures used by trained practitioners to identify the child's individual strengths and needs and the services appropriate to meet those needs. The purpose of the assessment is to gather information about children in order to understand and support their ongoing learning and development deeper and wider. Informal assessments (e.g., naturalistic observations and anecdotal records, language samples, caregiver interviews, portfolios of children's work) and formal assessments with psychometrically sound tools could provide valuable information about a child's strengths and needs.

A Brief History of Early Childhood Assessment

The world of early childhood assessment is full of competing paradigms and ideologies to determine what are considered developmentally appropriate assessment practices for young children. In the past, the early childhood assessment was very different from assessment in K–12 settings because of the different origins of assessment in each setting. Up until the 1800s, formal early childhood settings did not exist in Europe, because it was thought that young children could not learn classic academic subjects such as math or literacy (Henson, 2003; Kamerman, 2007). Early formal assessment methods were predicated on the belief in the innate capabilities that individual children possessed and the need to understand the developmental progressions of those abilities. Usually, assessment at this time for young children used solely qualitative methods, such as observation and documentation of children's learning to understand the complexities of child development in a more profound way (Stone-MacDonald et al., 2018).

Early assessment practices were heavily shaped by the biologist Charles Darwin, developmentalist Jean Piaget, and educators Maria Montessori and Loris Malaguzzi. Piaget's research involved qualitative notetaking and intense study of children to establish the "stages" of development that describe learning across time (Piaget & Inhelder, 1969). The identification of "developmental milestones" to easily assess growth and development as a developmental trajectory is an essential component of early childhood education and assessment still today. Montessori started an educational program in which children manipulated tangible materials in a rich environment that was meant to be easily individualized based on a child's current levels of performance across domains (Montessori, 1995). These concepts were arranged in an order that incrementally increased in difficulty as children moved independently through each skill (Montessori, 1995). In educational settings, a checklist is typically used to document and track the progress of learning over time. Malaguzzi focused on discovery-based learning through a child-centered framework, prioritizing children's individual learning goals and developing a system to monitor them using rigorous observation and documentation procedures (Vakil et al., 2003). Educators using Malaguzzi's system needed to be extremely familiar and practiced in observational assessment with particular attention on observer bias, techniques to obtain myriad types of educational data (e.g., forms, notes, pictures, video), and thorough reflections on the data to support improved teaching and learning (Malaguzzi, 1993). After the work of these pioneers of early childhood education, observation and documentation of learning and development have been central tenets of early childhood practice, assessment, and evaluation. During this same period in the 1800s, early childhood education also started in the US through the influence of the scientific method in the fields of psychology and education (Smuts et al., 2006). As a result, educational assessment in the US began to diverge from the commonly used forms of assessment in Europe. US researchers focused on scientific study, mostly implementing quantitative methodology and psychometric evaluation to develop systematic assessment methods for the field of education.

Current assessment practices for young children blend the collective knowledge and methodologies of child study and educational measurement to create a comprehensive variety of tests and assessment options that can be used for young children. The purpose of the assessment should dictate the tools and techniques used when assessing individual children (NAEYC, 2003). In a seminal report by the National Education Goals Panel, Shepard, Kagan, and Wurtz (1998) identified four distinct purposes for assessment in early childhood: "assessments to promote learning; assessments for identification of special needs; assessments for program evaluation and monitoring trends; and assessments for high-stakes accountability" (p. 7). For each purpose, they laid out standards of practice to ensure that that specific purpose is being met, including specifying distinct processes and recommended assessments geared to that purpose (Espinosa & López, 2007). Educators and researchers should keep intended purposes in mind when selecting assessment methods (NAEYC, 2003; 2009). Therefore, to understand the quality of an assessment and how to administer it with fidelity the purpose of the assessment must be acknowledged and respected when selecting assessment methods for individual children or early childhood settings (Stone-MacDonald et al., 2018).

Considerations for Assessing Culturally and Linguistically Diverse Children

Providing an equitable assessment of culturally and linguistically diverse children presents additional challenges to early childhood and EI practitioners (Stone-MacDonald et al., 2018). Many assessment methods available have been created using a norming process or understanding of a curriculum targeted toward middle-class, white families who speak English at home. This process of assessment development for a stereotypical American middle class has resulted in the failure of these assessment methods to reliably capture the knowledge and strengths of diverse cultural and linguistic groups (Padilla, 2001). Moreover, most early educators are white, middle-class women (Cheruvu et al., 2015). When an educator or the creator, or the region the assessment was developed for, does not align in terms of cultural or linguistic diversity with the child being assessed, it is possible the practitioner may not be able to accurately interpret key pieces of information because of notable cultural or language differences (Espinosa & López, 2007).

Furthermore, few assessment methods were intentionally designed for administration in languages other than English although some have been translated into other languages such as Spanish. Even those assessments translated into Spanish were not created from the ground up in Spanish with a focus on Latinx culture in specific regions. Rather, they are adapted or translated versions of English-based assessment methods. Bilingual assessment or assessment in other languages is more complicated than simply translating the assessment tool. Translation "from English to Spanish neither ensures that the psychometric properties automatically carry over from the English version to the Spanish version nor ensures that the cultural and linguistic characteristics are appropriate for use with any given Spanish-speaking population" (Barrueco et al., 2012, p. 24).

Furthermore, examiners might translate assessment methods into other languages that are not readily available for use with families who come from other cultures or speak other languages outside the few more common such as Spanish, French, or Chinese. A critical issue with translation and interpretation for assessment tools not meant for translation or normed for other cultures means that the process violates standardization and has consequences for validity (Barrueco et al., 2012; Espinosa, 2010; Espinosa & López, 2007). In addition, translation can also fundamentally modify the content of the assessment or inadvertently change its level of difficulty. The issues discussed above regarding the translation of assessment tools also apply to interviewing families using assessment checklists or other common tools such as Routines-Based Interviewing (McWilliam et al., 2009). When interviewing families using a translation, it is still important to maintain the validity and integrity of the assessment so that educators and families know they are getting the intended information from the specific questions.

When assessment methods are not culturally or linguistically appropriate, children and families can suffer because they may not get the services they need. For example, children from diverse cultural, linguistic, and racial backgrounds are especially vulnerable and have often been misidentified or over-identified for special education services (Sullivan, 2011). Consequentially, some linguistically and racially diverse children may receive unnecessary services, while others may not receive the services they need. Current research demonstrates that misidentification is an ongoing issue today (Bal et al., 2014). NAEYC (2009) recommends the use of multidisciplinary teams when making eligibility determinations for early intervention or special education. This team should include a professional knowledgeable about language and second language acquisition, be bilingual in the language of the family, be trained in appropriate assessment techniques, and be active in obtaining information from the family about the child's strengths and needs (NAEYC, 2009; Stone-MacDonald et al., 2018).

Why "Early Childhood Intervention"?

Early childhood intervention (ECI) "is a system of services that provides support to the families of children with developmental delays, disabilities, social-emotional difficulties, or children who may develop delays due to biological or environmental factors" (Vargas-Barón et al., 2019, p. 7). In order to receive these intervention services, children need to be assessed to understand their strengths, challenges, and present level of skills to design an effective intervention program. According to the Global Survey of Inclusive Early Childhood Education and Early Childhood Intervention Programs, "effective ECI systems are: (a) individualized; (b) intensive; (c) family-centered; (d) transdisciplinary or interdisciplinary; (e) team-based; (f) evidence-informed; and (g) outcomes-driven" (Vargas-Barón et al., p. 7). We have chosen to use the term *early childhood intervention*, as opposed to early intervention or inclusive early childhood intervention, because it is more inclusive of programs and services around the world. More countries use the terminology of ECI than other terms that might be more common in the US, such as early intervention. Furthermore, ECI is also more inclusive of services and programs for young children and their families with a variety of special needs that may be defined differently in their countries or contexts. For example, in Tanzania, albinism is considered a disability in the same way as intellectual disability or cerebral palsy. Finally, ECI is also more inclusive of services delivered around the world to children between zero and seven years of age and families from a variety of professions, settings, and organizations, such as hospitals, non-governmental organizations, schools, and rehabilitation centers.

Overview of Current Practices in Culturally Relevant Assessment around the World

For the purpose of this chapter, culturally responsive assessment can be defined as the assessment process whereby practitioners ensure that children's sociocultural, linguistic, racial/ethnic, and other relevant background characteristics are addressed at all stages, including choosing the appropriate assessment tools and methods to document the child's strengths and needs (García & Ortiz, 2006), matching family with the ECI team who could sustain an equal partnership, involving the stakeholders (e.g., translators/interpreters, cultural brokers or liaisons) and interpreting the results so that they are understandable and useful to families (DEC, 2014). For this chapter early childhood settings include any group care settings or classrooms for children from birth to age eight, including but not limited to nurseries, early childhood centers, preschool to second-grade classrooms in public or private primary schools. Early interventions are services provided in home, educational, rehabilitation, or hospital settings to children with delays or disabilities. In the United States, early intervention is typically for children ages zero to three, with some services extending to age five, but in international settings, early intervention can extend to age eight as the first interventions a child or family receives related to concerns around a delay or disability. The increase in the numbers of children and families who are culturally and linguistically diverse in the US requires ECI services to be responsive to the strengths and needs of children and families (Banerjee & Luckner, 2014).

When discussing ECI, it is important to note that providing coordinated EI/ECSE services aims to support a child's strengths and needs as well as family outcomes through supporting participation in education, development, and communities within cultures. Unfortunately, there is an inconsistent understanding of what ECI means in each culture/country and caregivers' definition of EI/ECSE for their child. There is a major need for agreed-upon observation and documentation of a child's strengths and needs, as well as assessment/progress-monitoring measures (Bricker et al., 2020). Worldwide it is estimated that there are 93 million children with disabilities, although this number could be much higher (WHO & World Bank, 2011).

Challenges in Providing Culturally Responsive Assessment Practices

For professionals, the challenges to providing services to children and families who are culturally and linguistically diverse (CLD) can be summarized as (a) difficulties in timely identification of young children who benefit from EI because of a lack of culturally and linguistically responsive standardized assessment tools, (b) limited experience of EI/ECSE practitioners on working with culturally and/or linguistically diverse children with disabilities, (c) limited number of EI/ECSE practitioners who are bilingual and bicultural, (d) the lack of training and personnel preparation programs focusing on working with children and families who are culturally and linguistically diverse (Banerjee & Luckner, 2014; NAEYC, 2005).

Examples from Asia

As a developed country, the US has a remarkable history of early intervention, research, legislation, policies, and training of service providers in early intervention services (Pang & Richey, 2005). The US and some European countries also have successful concepts for child identification, screening, assessment, and service delivery and have influenced the developments of early intervention in underdeveloped and low-income countries (Pang & Richey, 2005). However, intervention models which are imported from the US or Europe mostly raise concerns and problems in developing and implementing culturally responsive early intervention programs in those countries (Pang & Richey).

The World Bank and UNICEF frequently support ECI programs in low- and middle-income countries. According to (Smythe et al., 2021; Srinivasan & Karlan, 1997), India is an example of a culture outside North America with imposed US/European influence on early intervention. Early intervention professionals who are trained in countries such as Great Britain, Germany, or the US return to India and try to implement intervention models and strategies learned in those countries. However, without taking into consideration cultural appropriateness for Indian society, implementing those strategies and models may not be effective. Therefore, the interventionists should consider Indian society's view of children, child-rearing practices within that society, and patterns of interaction between adults and infants (Smythe et al.; Srinivasan & Karlan).

China has also been influenced by the US and European EI/ECSE programs (Xie et al., 2017; Zheng et al., 2015a). According to Ding et al. (2006), US and Western educational programs and services may be beneficial to the development of special education in China, but they need to be culturally sensitive and appropriate for the social values and realities. For example, some diagnostic instruments and tests (e.g., the Stanford-Binet Intelligence Scale IV, the Draw-a-Person Test) that were translated or revised from the US are not culturally appropriate and cultural biases exist in these tests (Deng et al., 2001, Zheng et al., 2015a). Intellectual disability is frequently diagnosed by using a few inaccurately adapted instruments that were created in the US, and this practice contributes to inaccurate diagnoses (Deng et al., 2001). Similarly, due to the differences in the identification of terminology used for disabilities between China and countries in the Global North, some disability categories are not truly recognized in China and the exact number of children under the age of six years with disabilities is not known (Ellsworth & Zhang, 2007; Deng et al., 2001).

The emphasis on collectivism and interdependence in Asian cultures appears to form parents' expectations for their child's development and learning (Acar et al., 2021). For example, in a survey study, more than half of the participating parents reported their child being "obedient" as very important or important (Puckett & McCoy, 2013). In another study, Chinese parents valued their children developing skills in choice making, self-regulation, and engagement within the context of an emphasis on dependence and obedience (Zheng et al., 2015b). EI/ECSE practitioners and US research should take into consideration the effects of culture on parental expectations during EI/ECSE assessment.

Example from Sub-Saharan Africa

The use of measures of US or European origin in the assessment of children is also common in sub-Saharan Africa. According to Matafwali and Serpell (2014), culturally appropriate instruments for children with disabilities are not available in sub-Saharan Africa and importation of US/European-developed assessment tools has resulted in a resource gap for child assessment. Cultural and social factors play a significant role in the development of language, motor, verbal and nonverbal cognitive skills, psychology, and physical growth. The professionals may not distinguish the differences between cultural and linguistic differences and the presence of a disability or potential risk of a disability (McLean, 2001). For example, children lack exposure to staircases in rural African settings so an instrument requiring the child to climb a staircase would be inappropriate (Matafwali & Serpell, 2014). Therefore, cultural factors may give rise to methodological variation in the assessment of children with disabilities and require modifications considering cultural characteristics such as language or parental education (Matafwali & Serpell, 2014). Regarding this fact, a committee of Zambian experts in the fields of child development, special education and psychology worked with a Harvard-based consultant to create the Zambia Child Assessment tool (ZamCAT) for children five to six years old. The purpose of this assessment tool is to develop an instrument that was sensitive to the cultural context and comparable with other international instruments (Matafwali & Serpell, 2014). To norm this assessment tool, it was given to 1,900 children, all six years old. The tool was found to capture development across the domains and provide an assessment of school readiness, as well as to identify children at potential risk for developmental delays (Matafwali & Serpell, 2014).

Examples from the Middle East

Arab countries have also been influenced by the special education and early intervention models used in Western countries (Hadidi and Al khateeb, 2015). Most Arab countries have no clear policies or regulations regarding the early identification and assessment of children with disabilities under three years old (Hadidi and Al khateeb, 2015). There is also a lack of research concerned with disability, and early intervention programs are very limited in the Arab region. The "Portage project" home-based early intervention model is one of intervention programs, which has been implemented in some Arab countries such as Egypt, Yemen, Saudi Arabia, Lebanon, Jordan, United Arab Emirates, Oman, Qatar, Bahrain, Morocco, and Kuwait for more than 25 years (Hadidi and Al khateeb, 2015). The Early Start Denver Model for evidence-based early intervention services for children with autism is another EI model that has recently been used in the Arab region (i.e., Saudi Arabia, Qatar, Kuwait, United Arab Emirates, Oman, and Bahrain) (Hadidi and Al khateeb, 2015). Arab countries face considerable challenges in identification, referral of at-risk children, and providing early intervention and transition services. Therefore, there is a need to promote realistic attitudes, policies, and regulations regarding early intervention and transition services (Hadidi and Al khateeb, 2015).

Assessment with Refugee Children

Refugee children with disabilities are at-risk populations who are the most hidden and neglected and unable to access early intervention programs. Identifying and collecting reliable, accurate data on the number of refugee children with disabilities and types and causes of disability is one of the major needs in the context of displacement and emergency (Simmons, 2010). Scant literature exists on service delivery experiences for refugee children with identified disabilities. The absence of accessible government and service information, the lack of knowledge on available support and benefits of early childhood special education, language barriers, the lack of culturally adaptive practices, and providing culturally sensitive support are the other significant challenges for refugee families with children with disabilities (King et al., 2015; Bešić & Hochgatterer, 2020). Moreover, there is a limited number of assessment tools with strong psychometric properties to use for refugee children with disabilities (Acar et al., 2019). The literature for the assessment of children with refugee backgrounds and disabilities is still limited, and the current assessment tools do not include children with refugee backgrounds in their normative samples; therefore caution must be used when administering the translated and adapted versions of the tools with children having refugee backgrounds and at risk for developmental delays or disabilities. The ECI field needs a comprehensive assessment system that emphasizes collaboration with family members, interpreters, and cultural liaisons/brokers during the assessment process.

Challenges Faced with Finding and Using Appropriate Measures

Assessment tools questionnaires, checklists, or tests with observable items by completed parents or practitioners should be validated, reliable, and culturally and linguistically appropriate. It should be important to note that finding linguistic equivalents for the concepts of disability and developmental progress is challenging. Therefore, it is important to use caution when translating and adapting Western-based assessment tools to other cultures or languages. In the context of EI/ECSE research, it is critically important to promote, facilitate, and disseminate research for and about children with disabilities living in Low and Middle Income (LAMI) countries.

Supporting parental engagement in ECI is critical, but it is also important to remember that in many developing countries caregiving responsibilities of a child with disabilities may fall on mothers, older siblings, and extended family members such as grandparents. It is essential to identify the primary and secondary role players in a child's development and learning and involve all stakeholders to holistically support child and family outcomes. The challenges faced by practitioners and families with assessment and their connections to the procurement of educational services appear to be created by multiple and compounding factors. For instance, some factors may include (1) lack of understanding and knowledge of the causes of disability in LAMI countries (Maulik & Darmstadt, 2007), (2) lack of services and support (Peyton et al., 2020), (3) inadequate funding to develop child find programs (Macy et al., 2014), (4) limited number of trained practitioners to support child and family outcomes (Macy et al., 2014), and (5) limited approaches to collect data in the field (Acar et al., 2019).

Current Trends in Measurement and Informal Assessment

Measurement issues within early childhood are numerous (McCoy et al., 2017). Whether it is through formal or informal assessment methods, validity and reliability issues are seen within many measures when there is a variance between ethnic (e.g. Espinosa, 2005), income (Washington & Craig, 1999), and cultural groups (e.g. Langdon & Cheng, 2002) within the US. As evidenced above, similar issues are seen around the world when researchers try to validate measures created for other contexts. There is a wealth of screening tools available to determine developmental delays for young children (Moodie et al., 2014) (see Table 14.1). Some of the more common in use are the Ages and Stages Questionnaire Third Edition (ASQ-3; Squires & Bricker, 2009), Battelle Developmental Inventory, second edition (BDI-2, Newborg, 2016; Elbaum et al., 2010), and Bayley Third Edition (Bayley, 2005). In a compendium examining 17 different screening tools for children from 0-5 (Moodie et al., 2014), only one assessment, DIAL-4, examined the validity and reliability of their tool in multiple languages. Translating formal assessment methods can be costly since the items need to make sure they still have construct validity. Additionally, each of these translated tools must be normed and validated with the new population.

All these measurement issues have been discussed in previous literature examining the content and construct validity of differing measures. However, recent work has examined how practitioners implement the assessment. In work examining the fidelity to the implementation of the BDI-2 (Newborg, 2016), notable issues were found with how trained assessors were using the BDI-2 to screen children 0-2 for developmental delays (Stone-MacDonald et al., 2018). Some of the behaviors created cues for the parents or children to respond in a certain way. Others included asking the wrong prompt, skipping questions, or even providing the wrong materials. While Stone-MacDonald et al. did not rescore the BDI-2 to see if scores were changed, the

Table 14.1 Summary of the assessment tools

Name	Description	Age range	Time frame	Assessors
Ages and Stages Questionnaire Third Edition (ASQ-3; Squires & Bricker, 2009)	ASQ-3 is a developmental screening tool that pinpoints developmental progress in children.	1 to 66 months	10-15 minutes to complete, 1-3 minutes to score	Parents/caregivers complete questionnaires; early childhood and health care professionals score them
Battelle Developmental Inventory (BDI-2, Newborg, 2016; Elbaum et al., 2010)	BDI-2 is an individually administered, standardized assessment battery, measuring key developmental skills in the following areas: Adaptive, personal-social, communication, motor, and cognitive.	Birth to 7 years, 11 months	1 hour for children younger than 2 and older than 5, and approximately 90 min for children between the ages of 2 and 5	Members of multidisciplinary evaluation teams
Bayley Scales Infant Development Third Edition (Bayley, 2006)	Bayley is an individually administered, norm-referenced tool to assess the developmental functioning of infants and young children on cognitive, language, and motor scales. Information about the child's social-emotional functioning and adaptive behavioral skills is obtained from the child's caregiver.	1 to 42 months	30 to 90 minutes	Trained and qualified professional meeting the requirements of the tool
Carolina Curriculum for Infants and Toddlers with Special Needs (Johnson-Martin et al., 2004)	It is an assessment and intervention program designed for use with young children from birth to five years who have mild to severe disabilities.	Birth to 36 months	60-90 minutes	Early childhood professionals
DIAL-4 (Mardell & Goldenberg, 2011)	Screens all five early childhood areas: motor, language, concepts, plus self-help and social development.	2:6 to 5:11	30-45 minutes	Trained professionals and early childhood practitioners
High/Scope Child Observation Record (COR; Barghaus & Fantuzzo, 2014)	COR aims to track child developments and progress, assist in translating anecdotal reports into a comprehensible language that parents, teachers and administrators can understand, and improve lesson plans and curriculums.	Birth to 6	NA. Ongoing	Early childhood educators and school administrators
Teaching Strategies GOLD (TS-GOLD; Lambert et al., 2015)	The Teaching Strategies GOLD is a teacher rating system (authentic performance assessment) child observation tool designed to measure the ongoing development and learning progress of children across various domains: social-emotional, physical, language, cognitive, literacy, mathematics, and English language acquisition.	Birth through kindergarten	NA. Ongoing	Early childhood educators and teachers

inaccuracy created by departure from prescribed procedures casts doubt on the validity of the outcomes.

Fidelity of implementation of assessment is a newly opened question with regards to understanding the assessment of young children and requires an examination of the structure of formal measurement with an eye towards the difficulty of implementation. Multiple avenues to get the same information, as with BDI-2, can help us to understand the overall complexity of a child's development. However, more options to obtain the data allow the assessor more opportunities to make mistakes, assumptions, or misinterpretations. Other assessment methods such as checklists or observation tools can help to alleviate these issues, but are we sacrificing easy implementation with a less robust understanding of the developmental needs of the children being assessed? On the other hand, non-standardized assessments such as developmental checklists like the *Carolina Curriculum for Infants and Toddlers with Special Needs* (Johnson-Martin et al., 2004) is a useful tool for educators working with children with moderate and severe disabilities for whom a standardized assessment such as the BDI-2 would yield little usable information because of the fine grain of skills assessed in the *Carolina Curriculum* and the opportunity to find splinter skills or skills that are developed closer to the child's chronological age, rather than their developmental age due to the extent of their disabilities.

Reliability and validity are often talked about when it comes to measurement; however we need to be more specific when it comes to how our measurement tools are or are not valid across cultures. Content validity is the assurance that the measurement is actually assessing the underlying behaviors or skills necessary. For our purpose, we must examine not only the assessed content validity but also the method by which the assessment obtains its information. Specifically, the cultural and language context that are inherent within the test.

Strong psychometrics is a strength to using formal assessment tools. It is important to understand that the outcomes obtained from the instruments will be consistent across multiple tests, when or where the test takes place, and even the accuracy of the results. This specificity comes at a cost. Each tool needs to be normed and referenced for the population it is intended to be used with. However, this is rarely the case. ASQ-3 (Squires & Bricker, 2009) is used throughout the US, Canada, and in multiple countries as it has been translated into 13 languages, but there is a struggle to obtain up-to-date validation and normed studies (Marks et al., 2019). Marks et al. noted that the populations in which ASQ-3 is used in the Scandinavian countries differ from how it is used in the US. In the US, ASQ-3 is most often used as an EI screener as was the original intention. However, in Scandinavian countries, ASQ-3 was used to track the developmental differences longitudinally for children receiving intervention services and those who were not. ASQ-3 was used even though there was not acceptable normed data for this population.

There are several alternatives to formal screening tools such as the ones described above. Multiple early childhood curricula also have created assessment tools less focused on psychometrics and more on understanding development across domains. Teaching Strategies GOLD (TS-GOLD; Lambert et al., 2015) and High/Scope Child Observation Record (COR; Barghaus & Fantuzzo, 2014) use anecdotal, photographic, or work sampling to create multiple data points longitudinally. Barghaus and Fantuzzo note that there are problems with the psychometrics of the Preschool COR and similarly Kim, Lambert, and Burts (Kim et al., 2013) found issues with TS-GOLD, and both studies noted issues with the assessment methods when it comes to ELLs and children with disabilities. Kim, Lambert, and Burts suggested that some of the issues with TS-GOLD seem to be similar to other authentic assessment tools, with teacher bias playing a part in the poor psychometrics with these groups. Kim, Lambert, and Burts note that training for the teachers specific to combating these biases may be an effective tool. Like TS-GOLD and COR, other assessment systems specific to an overarching curriculum to create a picture of a child's development can also be useful. If the developmental image of the child shows deficits in certain areas or differences between domains, this can be used as data to form plans to help the child. Additionally, the holistic picture can also help the parents and teachers see new strengths or growth where they previously saw none.

While strong psychometric tools allow for a much more cut-and-dried decision-making process, no formal assessment is perfect. The inclusion of both formal and informal assessment methods should be used throughout ECI. One of the key concepts for the implementation of ECI noted the need not only for the use of formal and informal assessment methods of children but also the gathering of this data across multiple environments (Workgroup on Principles and Practices in Natural Environments & OSEP TA Community of Practice: Part C Settings, 2008). Multiple data sources for assessment become even more needed when the formal assessment methods lack translations or localizations to the populations where they are being used.

We should be cautious about putting too much weight on formal assessment methods, yet it is also true in cases where we do not know how the cultural differences of locality will affect the validity of the measure. Using the formal screening data in different ways from its purpose is also implemented in the field. For instance, in the US, ASQ is mainly used to detect developmental delays in general, which increase early detection and referral to ECI services, whereas in Scandinavian studies ASQ is used to monitor developmental differences in children receiving ECI services (Marks et al., 2019).

Recommendations for Educators and Researchers

Early childhood intervention assessment has developed greatly over the last 150 years, but the field still has a long way to go to be able to effectively and efficiently assess young children from a variety of backgrounds, while taking into account culture, language, context, and family-centered practices. While assessment methods need to be valid and reliable, they also need to reflect the child's language and culture and assess the child within the expected developmental trajectory in that culture and context. With the adoption of the sustainable development goals by the United Nations in 2012, more effort has gone into developing assessment methods to determine the progress of young children as they obtain access to quality early education and care (SDG 4.2) and prepare for primary education around the world (United Nations, n.d.). Nevertheless, most of these assessment methods are designed for group or population use and are not fine-tuned to accurately assess a disability or delay, or if they can assess the delay, the assessment provides a binary decision and does not provide all the additional needed information on strengths, challenges, and developmental trajectory to support that child and family as they continue to grow and develop.

Based on the research reviewed in this chapter, we have four key recommendations for researchers and educators as they continue to work with children and families in early childhood intervention assessment. First, it is critical to think about and use a variety of assessment methods and types of assessment methods when identifying children with delays and disabilities and when assessing their progress. Various assessment methods serve different purposes. For example, psychometrically sound and standardized assessment methods can provide information about eligibility for services and provide a useful comparison of that child and their developmental status compared to their same-age peers. On the other hand, checklists or informal assessment methods that look at developmental trajectories and key skills and content for children in that context can provide useful information for culturally responsive interventions and strategies for educators and families. Checklists are a great way to assess a child's progress at various time points and determine growth and change in different domains. Furthermore, best practices indicate that children should always be assessed using multiple assessment methods to be able to more fully understand the child's strengths and challenges and their delay's impact on daily routines (DEC, 2014). It is critical when assessing a child to gather information from the family and about the family to understand the child and family within their context and daily routines.

Second, researchers should work on developing validated assessment methods for children in a variety of countries, contexts, and languages, but do so with collaboration with local experts to support linguistic and cultural understanding within communities and contexts. We need more validated assessment methods around the world, but particularly in languages that are less common and cultures that are very different from the US or European cultures. Assessment methods cannot be adopted from country to country. Assessment methods need to be developed with the culture and language in mind from the beginning, using a process such as backward mapping for curriculum development. Researchers who are members of languages and cultures less represented in assessment methods can add their cultural, linguistic, and assessment knowledge to the work. Local partners are critical in developing truly accurate and useful assessment tools rather than simply adopting tools or translating tools from English.

Third, as a field, it is very important that we ensure that educators and other professionals working in ECI are trained to implement the assessment methods to fidelity and understand how to use them. While having valid assessment methods is one step, if the professionals giving the assessment methods to young children and their families do not know how to use them to fidelity, or how to use the tool overall, the results will not be valid or reliable and can do more harm than good for the child and family. In addition, educators and other professionals using assessment methods should also know how to explain the assessment process and results to families in an accurate but user-friendly way that avoids jargon.

Finally, as an ECI community, we must think globally about how to work together to improve assessment around the work and in turn ECI services for young children and their families. How can researchers determine the most needed areas of assessment to develop now? How can we engage local partners and educators to support assessment development? How can we better support the ECI needs of special populations such as refugee children? All of these questions will drive the work in ECI and assessment over the next ten years and hopefully help us get closer to or meet SDG 4.2, where all young children have access to quality education and are ready for primary education, including children with delays and disabilities.

Conclusion

Early childhood intervention supports young children with disabilities and delays and their families but also supports young children with various situations or conditions that often locally (e.g. albinism in Tanzania) and globally (e.g. refugees) marginalize them and make participation in early childhood education difficult. Early childhood assessment methods that help to identify children's delays and their developmental strengths and needs should consider the local and the global context. As assessment developers and researchers work to validate more assessment methods, they need to be developed with local educators and interventionists and the assessment methods need to be responsive to local languages and cultures. In addition, local educators, interventionists, and other staff working with the children need to be well trained in how to administer the assessment methods to fidelity and in what they mean and what they are measuring. By better understanding the purpose and outcome of the assessment, examiners can be more purposeful in their use of the assessment and more supportive in describing and explaining the assessment to families and caregivers. Finally, as educators and researchers, we should recognize the balance between standardized formal assessment and informal assessment methods and use both at the right time for a more holistic understanding of the child and their context. Culturally responsive and holistic assessment will guide us to best meet the needs of children and families.

References

Acar, S., Pinar-Irmak, O., & Martin, S. B. (2019). Data needs for children with special needs in refugee populations. *NORRAG Special Issue (NSI), Data collection and Evidence Building to Support Education in Emergencies, 2*, 102–104.

Acar, S., Chen, C. I., & Xie, H. (2021). Parental involvement in developmental disabilities across three cultures: A systematic review. *Research in Developmental Disabilities, 110*, 103861.

Bal, A., Sullivan, A., & Harper, J. (2014). A situated analysis of special education: Disproportionality for systemic transformation in an urban school district. *Remedial and Special Education, 35*(1), 3–14.

Barger, B., Squires, J., Greer, M., Noyes-Grosser, D., Eile, J., Rice, C., Shaw, E., Surprenant, K., Twombly, E., London, S., Zubler, J., & Wolf, R. (2019). State variability in diagnosed conditions for IDEA Part C eligibility. *Infants & Young Children, 32*, 231–244. https://doi.org/10.1097/IYC.0000000000000151

Barghaus, K. M., & Fantuzzo, J. W. (2014). Validation of the preschool child observation record: Does it pass the test for use in Head Start? *Early Education and Development, 25*(8), 1118–1141. https://doi.org/10.1080/10409289.2014.904646

Barrueco, S., López, M., Ong, C., & Lozano, P. (2012). *Assessing Spanish-English bilingual preschoolers: A guide to best approaches and measures*. Brookes.

Banerjee, R., & Luckner, J. (2014). Training needs of early childhood professionals who work with children and families who are culturally and linguistically diverse. *Infants & Young Children, 27*(1), 43–59.

Bayley, N. (2005). *Bayley Scales of Infant and Toddler Development (BSID-III)*. Psychological Corp.

Bešić, E., & Hochgatterer, L. (2020). Refugee families with children with disabilities: Exploring their social network and support needs. A good practice example. *Frontiers in Education, 5*(61). https://doi.org/10.3389/feduc.2020.00061

Bricker, D. D., Felimban, H. S., Lin, F. Y., Stegenga, S. M., & Storie, S. O. M. (2020). A proposed framework for enhancing collaboration in early intervention/early childhood special education. *Topics in Early Childhood Special Education*. https://doi.org/10.1177/0271121419890683

Cheruvu, R., Souto-Manning, M., Lencl, T., & Chin-Calabaquib, M. (2015). Race, isolation, and exclusion: What early childhood teacher educators need to know about the experiences of pre-service teachers of color. *The Urban Review, 47*, 237–265. https://doi.org/10.1007/s11256-014-0291-8

Deng, M., Poon-Mcbrayer, K. F., & Farnsworth, E. B. (2001). The development of special education in China: A sociocultural review. *Remedial and Special Education, 22*(5), 288–298.

Ding, Y., Gerken, K. C., VanDyke, D. C., & Xiao, F. (2006). Parents' and special education teachers' perspectives of implementing individualized instruction in PR China: An empirical and sociocultural approach. *International Journal of Special Education, 21*(3), 138–150.

Division for Early Childhood. (2014). *DEC recommended practices in early intervention/early childhood special education 2014*. http://www.dec-sped.org/recommendedpractices

Elbaum, B., Gattamorta, K. A., & Penfield, R. D. (2010). Evaluation of the Battelle Developmental Inventory, 2nd Edition, screening test for use in states' child outcomes measurement systems under the Individuals with disabilities Education Act. *Journal of Early Intervention, 32*(4), 255–273. https://doi.org/10.1177/1053815110384723

Ellsworth, N. J., & Zhang, C. (2007). Progress and challenges in China's special education development: Observations, reflections, and recommendations. *Remedial and Special Education, 28*(1), 58–64.

Espinosa, L. M. (2005). Curriculum and assessment considerations for young children from culturally, linguistically, and economically diverse backgrounds. *Psychology in the Schools, 42*(8), 837–853. https://doi.org/10.1002/pits.20115

Espinosa, L. M., & López, M. (2007). *Assessment considerations for young English language learners across different levels of accountability*. Retrieved from http://www.first5la.org/files/AssessmentConsiderationsEnglishLearners.pdf

Espinosa, L. (2010). Assessment for young English language learners. In E. García & E. Frede (Eds.), *Young English language learners: Current research and emerging directions for practice and policy* (pp. 123–126). Teachers College Press.

Formosinho, J., & Pascal, C. (Eds.). (2017). *Assessment and evaluation for transformation in early childhood*. Routledge.

García, S. B., & Ortiz, A. A. (2006). Preventing disproportionate representation: Culturally and linguistically responsive prereferral interventions. *Teaching Exceptional Children, 38*(4), 64–68.

Hadidi, M. S., & Al Khateeb, j. M.. (2015). Special education in Arab countries: Current challenges. *International Journal of Disability, Development and Education, 62*(5), 518–530.

Henson, K. (2003). Foundations for learner-centered education: A knowledge base. *Education, 124* (1), 5–16.

Johnson-Martin, N. M., Attermeier, S. M., & Hacker, B. J. (2004). *The Carolina curriculum for infants and toddlers with special needs* (3rd ed.). Brookes.

Kamerman, S. B. (2007). A global history of early childhood education and care. *Background paper for EFA global monitoring report*. Retrieved from https://olcstage.worldbank.org/sites/default/files/3-A_global_history_of_early_childhood_care_and_education_Background_paper_EFAGlobalMonitoringRepo rt2007UNESCO_0_0.pdf.

King, G., Desmarais, C., Lindsay, S., Piérart, G., & Tétreault, S. (2015). The roles of effective communication and client engagement in delivering culturally sensitive care to immigrant parents of children with disabilities. *Disability and Rehabilitation, 37*(15), 1372–1381.

Kim, D.-H., Lambert, R. G., & Burts, D. C. (2013). Evidence of the validity of teaching strategies GOLD® assessment tool for English language learners and children with disabilities. *Early Education and Development, 24*(4), 574–595. https://doi.org/10.1080/10409289.2012.701500

Lambert, R. G., Kim, D.-H., & Burts, D. C. (2015). The measurement properties of the Teaching Strategies GOLD® assessment system. *Early Childhood Research Quarterly, 33*, 49–63. https://doi.org/10.1016/j.ecresq.2015.05.004

Langdon, H. W., & Cheng, L.-R. L. (2002). *Collaborating with interpreters and translators: A guide for communication disorders professionals*. Thinking Publications.

Macy, M., Marks, K., & Towle, A. (2014). Missed, misused, or mismanaged: Improving early detection systems to optimize child outcomes. *Topics in Early Childhood Special Education, 34*(2), 94–105.

Malaguzzi, L. (1993). For an education based on relationships. *Young Children, 49*(1), 9–12.

Marks, K. P., Madsen Sjö, N., & Wilson, P. (2019). Comparative use of the ages and stages questionnaires in the USA and Scandinavia: A systematic review. *Developmental Medicine & Child Neurology, 61*(4), 419–430. https://doi.org/10.1111/dmcn.14044

Matafwali, B., & Serpell, R. (2014). Design and validation of assessment tests for young children in Zambia. *New Directions for Child and Adolescent Development, 146*, 77–96.

Maulik, P., & Darmstadt, G. (2007). Childhood disability in low- and middle-income countries: Overview of screening, prevention, services, legislation, and epidemiology. *Pediatrics, 120*(Supplement1), S1–S55. https://doi.org/10.1542/peds.2007-0043B

McCoy, D. C., Sudfeld, C. R., Bellinger, D. C., Muhihi, A., Ashery, G., Weary, T. E., Fawzi, W., & Fink, G. (2017). Development and validation of an early childhood development scale for use in low-resourced settings. *Population Health Metrics, 15*, 3, 1–18. https://doi.org/10.1186/s12963-017-0122-8

McLean, M. (2001). Conducting culturally sensitive child assessments. In *Serving the underserved: A review of the research and practice in child find, assessment, and the IFSP/IEP process for culturally and linguistically diverse young children. ERIC clearinghouse on disabilities and gifted education, council for exceptional children* (ED 454 640, pp. 11–16). Author.

McWilliam, R. A., Casey, A. M., & Sims, J. (2009). The routines-based interview: A method for gathering information and assessing needs. *Infants & Young Children, 22*(3), 224–233.

Montessori, M. (1995). *The absorbent mind*. Holt.

Moodie, S., Daneri, P., Goldhagen, S., Halle, T., Green, K., & LaMonte, L. (2014). *Early childhood developmental screening: A compendium of measures for children ages birth to five* (OPRE Report 2014-11). Office of Planning, Research and Evaluation, Administration for Children and Families, U.S. Department of Health and Human Services.

National Association for the Education of Young Children. (2003). *Position statement on early childhood curriculum, assessment, and program evaluation*. Author.

National Association for the Education of Young Children. (2005). *Screening and assessment of young English-language learners*. http://www.naeyc.org/positionstatements

National Association for the Education of Young Children. (2009). *Developmentally appropriate practice in early childhood programs serving children from birth through age 8: A position statement of the National Association for the Education of Young Children*. NAEYC.

Newborg, J. (2016). *Battelle developmental inventory TM, second edition normative Update*. Houghton Mifflin Harcourt.

Padilla, A. (2001). Issues in culturally appropriate assessment. In L. A. Suzuki, J. G. Pontcrotto, & P. J. Meller (Eds.), *Handbook of multicultural assessment. Clinical, psychological, and educational applications* (2nd ed., pp. 5–27). Jossey-Bass.

Pang, Y., & Richey, D. (2005). A comparative study of early intervention in Zimbabwe, Poland, China, India, and the United States of America. *International Journal of Special Education, 20*(2), 122–131.

Piaget, J., & Inhelder, B. (1969). *The psychology of the child* (H. Weaver, Trans.). Basic Books.

Peyton, D. J., Acosta, K., Harvey, A., Pua, D. J., Sindelar, P. T., Mason-Williams, L., ... & Crews, E. (2020). Special education teacher shortage: Differences between high and low shortage states. *Teacher Education and Special Education, 44*(1), 5–23. https://doi.org/10.1177/0888406420906618

Puckett, K. S., & McCoy, K. M. (2013). Parents as teachers of children with autism in the Peoples' Republic of China. *Journal of International Special Needs Education, 16*(2), 68–81.

Shepard, L., Kagan, S. L., & Wurtz, E. (Eds.). (1998). *Principles and recommendations for early childhood assessments*. DIANE Publishing.

Simmons, K. B. (2010). Addressing the data challenge. *Forced Migration Review, 35*, 10.

Smuts, A. B., Smuts, R. W., Smuts, R. M., Smuts, B. B., & Chase-Lansdale, P. L. (2006). *Science in the service of children: 1893–1935*. Yale University Press.

Smythe, T., Zuurmond, M., Tann, C. J., Gladstone, M., & Kuper, H. (2021). Early intervention for children with developmental disabilities in low and middle-income countries–the case for action. *International Health, 13*(3), 222–231.

Squires, J., & Bricker, D. (2009). *Ages & stages questionnaires®, third edition (ASQ®-3): A parent-completed child monitoring system*. Paul H. Brookes Publishing Co., Inc.

Srinivasan, B., & Karlan, G. R. (1997). Culturally responsive early intervention programs: Issues in India. *International Journal of Disability, Development and Education, 44*(4), 367–385.

Stone-MacDonald, A., & Silva, S. (2020, January). Raising fidelity: Using early childhood standardized assessment to support young children with developmental delays and disabilities. In Division on Autism and Developmental Disabilities International Conference, Sarasota, FL.

Stone-MacDonald, A., Pizzo, L., & Feldman, N. (2018). *Fidelity of implementation in assessment of infants and toddlers*. Springer International Publishing. https://doi.org/10.1007/978-3-319-74618-0

Sullivan, A. L. (2011). Disproportionality in special education identification and placement of English language learners. *Exceptional Children, 77*, 317–334.

United Nations. (n.d.). *The 17 goals: Sustainable development*. The United Nations. https://sdgs.un.org/goals

Vakil, S., Freeman, R., & Swim, T. J. (2003). The Reggio Emilia approach and inclusive early childhood programs. *Early Childhood Education Journal, 30*, 187–192.

Vargas-Barón, E., Small, J., Wertlieb, D., Hix-Small, H., Gómez Botero, R., Diehl, K., Vergara, P., & Lynch, P. (2019). *Global survey of inclusive early childhood development and early childhood intervention programs*. RISE Institute.

Washington, J. A., & Craig, H. K. (1999). Performances of at-risk, African American preschoolers on the Peabody Picture Vocabulary Test-iii. *Language, Speech, and Hearing Services in Schools, 30*(1), 75–82. https://doi.org/10.1044/0161-1461.3001.75

WHO, & World Bank. (2011). *World report on disability*. https://www.who.int/disabilities/world_report/2011/report.pdf

Workgroup on Principles and Practices in Natural Environments, & OSEP TA Community of Practice: Part C Settings. (2008). *Seven key principles: Looks like /doesn't look like*. http://www.ectacenter.org/~pdfs/topics/families/Principles_LooksLike_DoesntLookLike3_11_08.pdf

Xie, H., Chen, C. I., Chen, C. Y., Squires, J., Li, W., & Liu, T. (2017). Developing a home-based early intervention personnel training program in southeast China. *Topics in Early Childhood Special Education, 37*(2), 68–80.

Zheng, Y., Maude, S. P., & Brotherson, M. J. (2015a). Early childhood intervention in China. *Journal of International Special Needs Education, 18*(1), 29–39.

Zheng, Y., Maude, S. P., Brotherson, M. J., Summers, J. A., Palmer, S. B., & Erwin, E. J. (2015b). Foundations for self-determination perceived and promoted by families of young children with disabilities in China. *Education and Training in Autism and Developmental Disabilities, 50*(1), 109–122.

15
PARADIGM SHIFT IN IDENTIFICATION AND ASSESSMENT OF NEURODIVERSE PEOPLE: TOWARDS A STRENGTH FOCUS LENS

Santoshi Halder*, Susanne Marie Bruyere, and Wendy Strobel Gower

Introduction

In the last few decades there has been an unprecedented increase in the prevalence of autism spectrum disorder (ASD) globally (Maenner et al., 2016). This has prompted researchers to investigate key issues to enhance the understanding of various aspects of ASD for ameliorating promising practices for serving the needs of this rapidly growing population. The *DSM-V* classification (American Psychiatric Association, 2013) attempted to consolidate the definition of autism and its related categories under one umbrella term 'autism spectrum disorder'. However, that does not minimize the complexities of understanding ASD per se. ASD may be one of the most complex and challenging etiologies to be cracked by a single discipline. Thus, effective identification and intervention may require an interdisciplinary, mutually collaborative approach. Understanding both general and specific skills in autistic people has been an area of extensive worldwide research for decades (Clark, 2017; Corrigan et al., 2012; Down, 1887; Happé, 2018; Kanner, 1943). Yet, much remains unknown and as such, increased and detailed understanding is needed.

It has been reported that savant skills are more common in autism spectrum conditions (ASC) (Happé & Vital, 2009; Treffert, 2009). Such claims have driven investigators to explore the underlying bases of such association between ASD and savant skills. Over the years there have been many false beliefs, stereotypes, and even over-generalizations about the existence of such skills in ASD, which resulted in the failure to capture the rich range of phenotypes across the spectrum (Conn, 2012). While there exists a pressing need to have a true estimation of savant skills among the ASD population, there is also the need for a large-scale review of the related studies to improve the understanding of the various aspects of savant skills in the ASD population, including specialized skills. Extensive research from well-established research groups has

---

* santoshi_halder@yahoo.com; shedu@caluniv.ac.in

attempted to understand the underlying phenomenon of the unique range of abilities and the related challenges in people with autism.

Objectives

The chapter analyzes the existing theoretical underpinnings by reviewing the associated literature through a strength-based lens to derive collective input based on a strong foundation for developing a strength-based model of nurturance for people with ASD. It aims to, *first*, understand the basis of the belief in exceptional skills among people on the spectrum, reviewing and analyzing select literature on savant skills and autism. *Second*, to explore the underlying theories in terms of strengths for further skill development. *Third*, to expose the potential and possibilities of strengths regardless of exceptionality and nurturance. *Fourth*, to identify key elements of essential practice for facilitating the strengths of people with ASD. And, *fifth*, to propose pathways to develop specialized skills in people with ASD.

Methodology

Relevant evidence-based published papers irrespective of specific disciplines were reviewed to conduct this unsystematic critical review analysis. By turning a strength-based lens on existing research, the hope was to better understand how educators can support specialized skill development in people with ASD. The crucial points of discussion are presented in the following section under relevant headings and subheadings.

Savant Skills as Documented in the Literature

Typically, and most commonly, savant skills have been defined as an individual's extraordinary ability in a specific area, while having limited ability to express or understand others or demonstrate competency in other areas (Treffert, 2009, 2014). The range of such skills covers splinter skills at one end and prodigious savants at the other, with talented savants in the middle (Rutter 2011). Various terminologies such as '*islets of ability*', '*splinter skills*', or '*savant skills*', which have been frequently and widely used in literature, will constitute 'exceptional skills' in this article.

Various studies have reported the manifestation of such exceptional skills among people with ASD (Crespi, 2016; Treffert, 2014). Table 15.1 provides a complete account of the different types of exceptional skills to date, as reported in ASD literature. Apart from these, some other appealing and many sought-after traits documented repeatedly in literature in relation to ASD are a strong sense of morality, honesty, trustworthiness, simplicity, preference to work on repeated or monotonous tasks, intense spontaneous concentration for longer periods, unique or innovative ideas and problem-solving, high tolerance, and precise technical abilities, among others (Cooney, 2005; Hendricks, 2010; Hillier et al., 2007; Howlin, 2005; Jordan, 1995; Lee et al., 2020). Interestingly, the contrasting characteristics of strengths and deficits across individuals with ASD add to the complexities of understanding the clear picture of abilities in relation to the ASD population. These contrasting skills in people with ASD have interested researchers all over the world as they seek to understand why and how these specialized skills develop in individuals.

Evidently, employers are looking to capitalize on the specialized skills that people with ASD can bring to the workplace. Recent decades have seen an increase in autism-friendly employ-

Table 15.1 Exceptional skills with descriptors and the corresponding researchers and citations

Savant skills	Description	Researchers (e.g.)
Memory	Memorization of films, bus routes, maps, sports, etc.	Hughes et al., 2018; Treffert, 2009
Mathematical ability	Fast mental arithmetic calculations, generation of prime numbers, etc.	Heavey et al., 1999; Kelly & Macaruso, 1997
Calendar calculation	Generate an appropriate day of the week of a given date	Dubischar-krivec et al., 2014; Kennedy & Squire, 2007
Musical ability and or absolute pitch	Identify the node of a pitch at first attempt or play a musical instrument without much practice	Boso et al., 2013; Fung, 2009; Heaton et al., 2008; Sloboda and Hermelin, 1985
Mechanical and spatial abilities	Building, creating, measuring distances	Brink, 1980; Hoffman & Reeves, 1979; Smith & Iadarola, 2015; Stevenson & Gernsbacher, 2013
Art and drawing	Drawing, painting, sculpting	Howlin et al., 2009; Mottron et al., 1998; O'Connor & Hermelin, 1989; Pring & Heavey, 1995
In-depth visual perception	Attention to detail, pattern or truth-detector, understanding a system etc.	Baron-Cohen et al., 2009; de Schipper et al., 2016; O'Riordan & Plaisted, 2001; Pring, 2005

Note. The table has not been used elsewhere.

ers willing to hire people on the spectrum, particularly in countries such as the United States, Australia, Sweden, and Denmark. Many of these are through renowned companies, such as SAP, Microsoft, Freddie Mac, Ernst and Young, Walgreens, Home Depot and CVS Caremark, and AMC. Despite the positive feedback from employers hiring autistic people for the workforce still 66% to 86% remain unemployed or seriously underemployed (Hedley et al., 2017; Lee et al., 2020). It is thus imperative to identify key elements to bridge the gap between potentialities in people with ASD and successful employment opportunities.

Deriving Strength-based Elements from Evidence-based Literature

ASD is characterized by a wide range of diverse and unique characteristics across individuals. Outcomes from neurocognitive sciences and clinical studies can help the practice community to better understand how people with ASD think and learn, and lead to improved interventions for these individuals (Halder & Bruyere, 2021).

This article promotes possible strengths and abilities identified in the review process from the selected existing theories and literature. Among the theories most prominently analyzed in this review are *Enhanced Perceptual Functioning Theory (EPF)* (Mottron et al., 2003), *Intense World Hypothesis (IWH)* (Markram & Markram, 2010), *Weak Coherence Theory (WCC)* (Frith & Happe, 1994; Frith, 1989), *Mind Blindness Theory or Theory of Mind (ToM)* (Baron-Cohen & Leslie, 1985) and *Empathizing-Systemizing (E-S) Theory* (Simon Baron-Cohen, 2009). Additionally, selected talent development theories have been analyzed to identify the possibilities of strengths of people with ASD (Gagné, 2009; Kalat, 2014; Myers, 2009; Spearman 1863–1945; Spearman, 2005; Tannenbaum, 1986, 2003).

Potentialities Deriving from Local versus Global Processing Inclination

Over the years, many theories have highlighted the various function-based justifications for the ASD phenomenon, contributing enormously to the autism literature and the progress in the area. It would be significant to analyze some of the relevant outcomes as reflected by some of the pivotal theories to derive their strengths. One of the revelations of *Weak Coherence Theory (WCC)* (Frith & Happe, 1994; Frith, 1989) is that people on the spectrum are inclined towards local coherence (i.e., commonly referred to as local processing bias), whereas neurotypical people are inclined towards global coherence. *Weak central coherence* refers to a specific cognitive style that encompasses a limited ability to understand wider contexts (Kimhi, 2014). *Executive function* is an umbrella term for cognitive processes that include working memory, inhibition, planning, and shifting (Kimhi, 2014). This suggests that, compared to neurotypical people, individuals with ASD are more locally inclined than globally inclined while processing information.

There is a controversy around autistic global versus local processing ability and inclination or preference with many relevant explanations (Kasirer & Mashal, 2014; Liu et al., 2011). Two important findings emerge from the overview of the relevant research described here. The first is that if people with ASD excel at local processing, why not focus on developing and exploring this skill, rather than pushing them to learn global processing skills? The second is that if global processing may be achieved by people with ASD, what teaching-learning strategies would enhance the development of these skills? Either or both approaches may benefit individuals on the spectrum to navigate their world more effectively, as well as their interactions with others.

Locating Unique Possibilities from Deficits in Mind-Reading

Interestingly, many of the strengths of people with ASD are claimed by some researchers to be beneficial if appropriately used (Baron-Cohen, 2010; Markram et al., 2007). Theories such as the *Mind Blindness Theory or Theory of Mind (ToM)* provide a compelling explanation of the underlying reasons for the deficits in autism, commonly termed as a delay in 'mind reading' or leaving them with degrees of mindblindness (i.e., an inability to attribute opinions, perceptions or attitudes to others) (Baron-Cohen, 1995) – this being a crucial element for success in the social context (Baron-Cohen et al., 2001; Baron-Cohen & Leslie, 1985; Happé & Vital, 2009). In its broader use, the term 'mind reading' refers to the more direct processing of mental-state information, including both verbal and nonverbal cues, and thoughts and feelings (Roeyers & Demurie, 2010). The social communication deficits and the associated social impediments of people on the spectrum have been well documented in the literature (Baron-Cohen et al., 1999; Baron-Cohen, 1992; Sodian & Frith, 1992). Briefly, the ToM hypothesis (Baron-Cohen and Tager-Flusberg, 2000) posits a robust explanation for impairment in the ability to comprehend the mental states (i.e., goals, emotions, and beliefs) and the use of mental-state concepts to interpret and predict one's own and other people's behavior. While the theory of mind, on the one hand, explains (Baron-Cohen, 1995) many impediments in social interaction and communication existing in people with ASD, on the other hand, it also explains the reason for the out-of-the-box innovative thinking and problem-solving ability of autistic people unusual in typical people. As people with autism are unaware of other people's expectations, their responses may not be driven by typical, external social goals. Essentially, the focus should be on harnessing strengths rather than removing differences. This further emphasizes the need to accept, embrace and harness the neurodiverse ways of thinking and facilitating natural expressions rather than regulate them to fit with typical societal expectations.

Possibilities of Skills Development from Intense Systemizing

Baron-Cohen (2009) proposed the E-S or *Empathizing-Systemizing (E-S) Theory* (Baron-Cohen 1995), which classifies individuals with ASD based on their empathic thinking (E) and systematic thinking (S). To explain the underlying phenomenon of the non-social features of ASD exhibited in narrow interests, there exists a need for sameness and attention to detail. According to this conceptualization of abilities, people with ASD have a disproportion of E-S that is reflected in their differences in certain related responses. 'Systemizing' is defined as the drive to analyze or construct any system or identify the rules that govern the system (Baron-Cohen, 2009); such systemizing may be seen as inherent in many people on the autistic spectrum (Jolliffe & Baron-Cohen, 2001; Mottron et al., 2003; Riordan & Plaisted, 2001; Shah, 1993). This corroboration of scientific opinion provides support to Baron-Cohen's argument made in the E-S theory. To some extent, it also counters those promoting the WCC Theory that people with autism will be forever lost in detail and never achieve an understanding of the system as a whole. Baron-Cohen (2009) even argued that, with possibilities of relevant opportunities e.g., intense concentration and practice, this may even lead to scientific truth for some autistic people. This further extends the scope of abilities and stresses the importance of exposing people with ASD to multiple opportunities for practice or intense systemizing. It highlights the crucial role and responsibility of the parents and school in facilitating these exposures in people with ASD, rather than limiting opportunities due to a lack of immediate outcome, working instead on removing such atypical systemizing. Additional research will be required to further test this assumption and scope.

Baron-Cohen (2009) reasoned that the delays and deficits in advanced mind-reading were due to low empathizing and that areas of strength or superior skill (such as attention to detail, scientific truth or pattern detection, prediction of lawful events, etc.) were the result of high and intense systemizing in the ASD population – particularly in males (Baron-Cohen, 2002; Jolliffe & Baron-Cohen, 2001; Mottron et al., 2003; Riordan & Plaisted, 2001; Shah, 1993). Baron-Cohen et al. (2009) explain intense systemizing in people with autism and claims the positive outcomes of such systemizing in cracking the pattern of a system leading to unexplored expositions. This laid important groundwork for educators and other stakeholders to better understand the underlying basis of such skills and may help to identify ways to develop scope in an individual's environment for the functional application of such skills, matched to the specific systemizing. Major systemizing in people with ASD as proposed by Baron-Cohen (see details, Baron-Cohen, 2009) posits the functionality and application of such systemizing: collectible systems (e.g., distinguishing between types of stones or wood), mechanical systems (e.g., a video recorder or a window lock), numerical systems (e.g., a train timetable or a calendar), abstract systems (e.g., the syntax of a language or musical notation), natural systems (e.g., the weather patterns or tidal wave patterns), social systems (e.g., a management hierarchy or a dance routine with a dance partner), and motoric systems (e.g., throwing a frisbee or bouncing on a trampoline). Instances of such specific systemization with common, day-to-day functional skills explained as the outcome of the particular systemization can be the beginning of strong possibilities for further application of the natural inner potentialities (Baron-Cohen et al., 2009). This established and important rationale for the identification of such traits urges that action be taken to ensure that these are matched with appropriate intervention through tailor-made personalized environmental manipulation.

Hence the systemization in people with autism as reported by Baron-Cohen (2009) may provide new leads and insight into a different view of autistic people that may be quite different from the conventional view of autism (de Schipper et al., 2016; Pring, 2005). What is termed a 'stereotypical narrow pattern or interest' of people with ASD, if identified at the right age and facilitated and matched with the appropriate context and activity, can result in people with ASD reaching their potential to excel in areas where they can capitalize on their skills through systemizing (Baron-Cohen et al., 2009). Furthermore, the superiority of people with ASD characterized by enhanced perceptual processing has been accounted for by *Enhanced Perceptual Functioning Theory (EPF)* (Mottron & Burack, 2001; Mottron et al., 2003, 2006), which posits relative peaks of ability in the visual and auditory modalities of people with ASD. The enhanced detection of patterns, as accounted for by the *Enhanced Perceptual Hypothesis* and as supported by others (Dakin, 2005; Samson et al., 2006), may be a basis for higher-level cognitive processes in people with ASD. This may present an array of possibilities for the nurturance of abilities and further skill development matched with strengths surfaced (e.g., in mnemonic, attention, or visuospatial operations), due to their enhanced perceptual focusing. Looking through a neurodiverse lens with the aim to utilize and facilitate the indigenous abilities of autistic people, instead of being overwhelmed by the perceived deficits of people with ASD, may open up new possibilities and leads.

Non-rewarding Social Context and Impediments to Decoding

Understanding the challenges of people on the spectrum in light of the differences in the way their minds work may inform the support team to design intervention effectively. Further, some researchers have identified certain other characteristics of people on the spectrum to engage in repeated, stereotypical behaviors or personal focus areas rather than investing mental energy into social interactions or communication, as accounted for by the *Social Motivation Theory (SMT)* (Stavropoulos, 2014, 2018). Researchers attribute the inclination for preferred focus areas over social interaction and communication to the different reward systems in the brains of people with ASD (Kohls et al., 2018; Stavropoulos, 2014, 2018). People with ASD find engaging in repetitive or "stim" behaviors to be more rewarding than engaging in social interactions that tend to motivate neurotypical people. This is further justified by the *Intense World Hypothesis (IWH)* (Markram & Markram, 2010), which states that because of the presence of too many brain synapses in people with ASD, selectivity is difficult for them. This idea may be further strengthened by the *Theory of Mind (ToM)* (Baron-Cohen, 1995; Baron-Cohen & Leslie, 1985), which posits that people with ASD demonstrate a delay in mind-reading, which may act as an inhibiting factor for rewarding social communication.

Researchers do not know whether the social situation itself is unrewarding for people with ASD or if it is the challenges around the ability to decode the social context of interactions, but many people with ASD prefer their own (possibly isolated) world and avoid social contexts. This may be justified to some extent by the encoding and decoding model of communication, which defines communication as a two-way process that includes simultaneous encoding or decoding (Hall, 1973, 2016). Any successful communication comprises encoding or decoding or translating both verbal and nonverbal forms of communication. Decoding (i.e., obtaining, absorbing, and understanding information) the message is crucial for a successful and rewarding communication experience. In common face-to-face communication, multiple instances of simultaneous coding and decoding occur and are warranted for a successful interaction. This includes understanding the language in which communication is taking place; understanding your communication partner's body language, gestures, eye contact, and expressions; and understanding the tone of voice used to enhance communication. While communicating, a neurotypical person unconsciously attends to and decodes all of this information simultaneously, allowing them to understand and appreciate social interaction. For those on the spectrum, due to ToM claims (Baron-Cohen & Leslie, 1985), completing these tasks may be quite challenging and can lead to limited ability to decode the communication and understand the message of their communication partner (Baron-Cohen, 1995). Generally speaking, people tend to do what seems to be rewarding or reinforcing and avoid doing that which is not rewarding or punishing. As a result, social communication may be non-rewarding or less rewarding, which can lead to interaction or social context avoidance in the ASD population.

The above argument of in-person social avoidance in people with ASD may be further strengthened by the frequent instances of their inclination and comfort in online modes of communication through the internet (Katherine et al., 2019). Despite having in-person social interaction and communication difficulties, select research studies report that people with ASD are exceptionally good at online communication. This includes interacting with online friends. This seems to be especially true for people with ASD who may be sharing their inner social drives through an online medium of communication, which may be more comfortable than in-situ (Benford & Standen, 2009). Understanding the underlying patterns of communication in ASD can contribute greater insight into these efforts and enhance success on the way forward.

Some people on the spectrum are able to effectively navigate social contexts, perhaps because early exposure to social interaction allowed them to develop strategies to decode social interaction. As quoted by Tammet (2007) in his autobiography, '*Peek inside a singular mind*': "I am lucky that the autism I have is mild, and that I was born into a large family and had to learn social skills, so I am able to speak up" (p. xx). Further empirical research into the impact of early social interaction opportunities would provide better evidence of the validity of this statement. These arguments facilitate two valid directions for future research. First, they highlight the need to explore alternative strategies to identify the essentials for facilitating the decoding of social interactions and advanced mind-reading among people on the spectrum. These may further remove the impediments and enhance the participation of people on the spectrum in social interaction, thus making sociability equally rewarding. Second, they necessitate exploring how the internet can be utilized to facilitate various ways of inter-connections between the typical and neurodiverse world.

Reviewing Talent Development Literature for the Nurturance of Strengths

Despite the strengths and abilities of people with ASD, very few finally succeed in showcasing and utilizing their abilities in successful pre- and post-school engagements, as reported in several family studies (Howlin et al., 2009). It would be noteworthy to understand whether people with ASD have the prerequisite skills for further development. There is limited research that explores the possibility of nurturance of talent among people with ASD. Research on talent development in the general population, including the gifted population, is an established field of research with valid results (Olszewski-kubiliu et al., 2015). It has the potential to provide significant insight into talent development for people with ASD. The remainder of this chapter will review the existing literature regarding developing skills in the general population and may pave the way for further exploration of the possibility of nurturance in the ASD population.

Understanding the Prerequisites of Talent Development

Talent Development in the literature has been defined as a process that starts from the early signs of raw skills, strengths, or abilities and undergoes a multi-stage process to assist a child to reach their full potential (i.e., childhood to adulthood) (Tannenbaum, 1986, 2003). The five essential prerequisites for talent development, as proposed by Tannenbaum (1986, 2003), are: (a) general ability; (b) special or domain-specific abilities; (c) non-cognitive factors; (d) environmental supports (e.g., in and outside school); and (e) the positive role of chance (Olszewski-kubiliu et al., 2015). As per Spearman, 'g', or *general ability* influences the performance on all mental tasks, while 's' or *specific ability* influences abilities on a particular task (Kalat 2014; Spearman (1863-1945), n.d.). Spearman concludes that general ability predicts important social outcomes, such as educational and occupational levels, and influences all the specific abilities (Myers, 2009). This lack of general ability may impede or limit the specific ability from being fully functional. Spearman called general abilities "educative" and "reproductive", stating their necessity for performance on all mental tasks, including social outcomes (Spearman, 2005). This implies that the proper functioning of specific abilities needs a certain level of general abilities. People with ASD may fare abysmally in some complex areas, despite having superior specific abilities. How the interaction between general and specific abilities plays out in the ASD population and how far the general abilities can be manifested in them is a crucial target for further exploration.

Creativity is an essential prerequisite for talent development in the later stages of development and has been highlighted by many talent development theorists (Gagné, 2009; Tannenbaum, 1986, 2003). However, it has been much cited in autism literature that people on the spectrum lack flexibility and display rigidity (Geurts, 2009; Jarrold & Boucher, 1996; Lewis, 1991; Poljac, 2012). Contrary to such claims, there are studies, such as those done by Liu et al. (2011), which posit that participants with ASD scored high on originality and low on flexibility. As early as 1944, Asperger (1944) reported the potential for people with ASD to achieve high-level skill development in some areas, which has been scientifically observed by other researchers in more recent times (Fung, 2009; Gillberg, 2002). It has furthermore been argued that people on the spectrum may show extreme rigidity beyond their own passion or interest, but in-depth systemizing in a specific area, field, or activity, and may be able to, if provided the opportunity, make scientific discoveries not previously identified by others (Baron-Cohen et al., 2009). The study by Lui et al. (2011) also brings forth the necessity for multiple opportunities to develop expertise in the matched area of the interests of people with ASD to propagate creative possibilities. Moreover, some researchers, such as Torrance (1974), stressed the essence and necessity of deep passion and enjoyment of the tasks as a crucial prerequisite for creativity where people with ASD may have an advantage (Hetzroni et al., 2019). Mixed reporting regarding the association of creativity, talent development, and the ASD population opens up fertile ground for further exploration.

Importance of Environment and Adult Coaches

Almost all of the talent development models reviewed in this study stressed the importance of an environment that provides ample opportunities for learning and practice (i.e., in and outside home and school), coupled with the crucial role played by facilitators such as adult coaches with sufficient expertise, teachers and parents, to nurture the subtle traits from a very early age (Gagné, 2005, 2009; Kubilius, 2011). Additionally, the identification of raw subtle markers within individuals through providing multiple varied exposures at a neuroplastic age (when their brains are malleable), mediated by knowledgeable adult coaches, parents, and teachers, has been emphasized throughout the literature (Kubilius, 2011). Exposing young minds to varied experiences from an early age, together with assorted activities, and finding the right match in terms of their interests and passion, combined with positive rewards or reinforcements, can play a crucial role (Csikszentmihalyi & Rathunde, 1993). Whether and to what extent this is applicable to the ASD population calls for further empirical research with the specific target population.

Future Directions and Conclusion

Increasing opportunities for people on the spectrum notwithstanding, education and employment participation report very limited accounts of the successful demonstration by the ASD population despite their unique abilities to reach their full potential. Even though 77 percent of people with ASD are willing to work, only 16 percent of autistic adults are in full-time employment (Office for National Statistics 2016). There exists a gap between successful employment and the first signs of subtle skills and strengths that can be overcome by the strength-focused model of nurturance. Essentially, such an effort will need successful and strategic teamwork with parents and teacher-educators through early identification and function-based intervention. The idea is to focus on how best to utilize the strengths-based view of the individual rather than being overpowered or overwhelmed by the deficits. There should be no limit to finding alternative ways of better understanding and serving the needs of people with ASD. This is often due to the lack of acceptance, agreeableness, and understanding, together with a lack of strategic action. Effective pathways for advancing strengths into functional skills from the paradoxes of abilities and strengths remain a challenge. Although researchers who focus on a strengths-based model report challenge encountered in identifying the subtle markers of strengths among people with ASD (Heaton et al., 2008), evidence is building to affirm that with appropriate direction and support, change can occur.

It is crucial to orient and inform the general public regarding the myths, misconceptions, and facts associated with the strengths and challenges of people with ASD and provide an understanding of the underlying phenomenon of differences in autism through evidence-based findings. There is also a need to simultaneously enhance the strengths and supporting deficits for maximum functionality of the specific skills. Among the false beliefs and stereotypes are over-generalizations and over-expectations with regard to people with ASD (Lee and Deng 2020). These expectations need to be validated with empirical evidence. To realize the desired changes, there is a need for an increased understanding of the possibilities of people with ASD, based on both inter-and intra-differences for effective, function-based interventions. This may include people with eccentric genius and necessitates the cultivation of such traits and abilities while simultaneously working on deficits or challenges. There may also be those without such exceptional skills but with equally probable strengths that need to be strategically nurtured within an appropriate environment and with adult support. Effectively educating and preparing autistic people to be successful in a neurotypical world calls for personalization rather than generalization. There is a need to understand the atypicalities of select characteristics of individuals with ASD, rather than seeking typicality, as atypical may capture more accurately the diversity and experience of individuals with ASD for needs-based support (Halder & Bruyere, 2021; Lee & Deng, 2020).

Underestimating or discounting family-based qualitative studies, because they might be seen as lacking technical methodologies or due to limited samples, would mean losing a significant source of information. To better explore the potentialities, differences, and uniqueness of these individuals will require the design and implementation of a process that facilitates appropriate strategies implemented in a symbiotic partnership. Collaboration between basic science and applied researchers, families, and practitioners is furthermore required to realize successful identification and function-based interventions for individuals with ASD.

Author Contributions

SH developed the idea behind the review, analyzed and wrote the manuscript while SB assisted in shaping the thought process and contributed to the fine-tuning of the manuscript throughout. WSG assisted in shaping further through review with valuable comments and suggestions.

Funding

Funding for the first author was supported by the Fulbright Academic and Professional Excellence Fellowship, United States India Education Foundation (USIEF), India, International Institute of Education (IIE), USA.

Ethics Approval (Includes Appropriate Approvals or Waivers)

The study is a part of an ethically approved study by the Cornell University IRB board under the Human subject exempt category (approval ref: Protocol ID#: 2001009333).

Conflict of Interest

The author reports no conflict of interest.

References

Papers of particular interest, published recently, have been highlighted as:
★Of importance
★★Of major importance

Asperger, H. (1944). Die Autistischen Psychopathen" im Kindesalter. *Archiv f. Psychiatrie, 136*(117), 1837709. https://doi.org/10.1007/BF01837709

Baron-Cohen, S. (1992). Out of sight or out of mind? Another look at deception in autism. *Journal of Child Psychological Psychiatry, 33*(7), 1141–1155.

Baron-Cohen, S. (1995). *Mindblindness: An essay on autism and theory of mind (learning, development, and conceptual change)*. https://doi.org/10.1027//0269-8803.13.1.57

Baron-Cohen, S. (2002). The extreme male brain theory of autism. *Trends in Cognitive Sciences, 6*(6), 248–254. https://doi.org/10.1016/S1364-6613(02)01904-6

Baron-Cohen, S. (2009). Autism: The empathizing-systemizing (E-S) theory. *Annals of the New York Academy of Sciences, 1156*, 68–80. https://doi.org/10.1111/j.1749-6632.2009.04467.x

Baron-Cohen, S., & Leslie, A. M. (1985). Does the autistic child have a "theory of mind" ?. *Cognition, 21*, 37–46.

Baron-Cohen, S. (2010). Empathizing, systemizing, and the extreme male brain theory of autism. *Prog Brain Res., 186*, 167–75. https://10.1016/B978-0-444-53630-3.00011-7.

Baron–Cohen S., & Tager–Flusberg H. C. D. (Eds.) (2000). *Understanding other minds: Perspectives from developmental cognitive neuroscience*. Oxford: Oxford University Press.

Baron-Cohen, S., O'Riordan, M., Jones, R., & Stone, V, & P. K. (1999). A new test of social sensitivity. *Journal of Autism and Developmental Disorders, 29*, 407–418.

Baron-Cohen, S., Wheelwright, S., Skinner, R., Martin, J., & Clubley, E. (2001). The Autism-Spectrum Quotient (AQ): Evidence from... *Journal of Autism and Developmental Disorders, 31*(1), 5–17.

Baron-Cohen, S., Ashwin, E., Ashwin, C., Tavassoli, T., & Chakrabarti, B. (2009). Talent in autism: Hyper-systemizing, hyper-attention to detail and sensory hypersensitivity. *Philosophical Transactions of the Royal Society B: Biological Sciences, 364*(1522), 1377–1383. https://doi.org/10.1098/rstb.2008.0337

Benford, P., & Standen, P. (2009). The Internet: A comfortable communication medium for people with Asperger syndrome (0S) and high functioning autism (HFA)?, *Journal of Assistive Technologies 3*(2), 44–53. https://doi.org/ 10.1108/17549450200900015

Boso, M., Forth, J., Bordin, A., Faggioli, R., D'Angelo, E., Politi, P., Barale, F., & Heaton, P. (2013). Transposition ability in a young musician with autism and blindness: Testing cognitive models of autism. *Psychomusicology: Music, Mind, and Brain, 23*(2), 109–116. https://doi.org/10.1037/a0033760

Brink, T. (1980). Idiot savant with unusual mechanical ability. *American Journal of Psychiatry, 137*, 250–251.

Cautionary statement for forensic use of DSM-5. American Psychiatric Association. (2013). Cautionary statement for forensic use of DSM-5. In A. A. P. Publishing (Ed.) (5th edition). Arlington: American Psychiatric Publishing (Vol. 1). https://doi.org/doi.org/10.1176/appi.books.9780890425596.744053.

Clark, T. (2017). *The application of Savant and Splinter skills in the autistic population through an educational curriculum, results of a case study research project*. Sydney, Australia: Autism Association of New South Wales.

Conn R, B. D. (2012). The portrayal of autism in Hollywood films, The portrayal of autism in Hollywood films. *International Journal of Culture and Mental Health, 5*, 54–62.

Cooney, D. H. and B. F. (2005). 'I do that for everybody': Supervising employees with autism. *Focus on Autism and Other Developmental Disabilities, 20*(2), 91–97.

Corrigan, N. M., Richards, T. L., Treffert, D. A., & Dager, S. R. (2012). Toward a better understanding of the savant brain. *Comprehensive Psychiatry, 53*(6), 706–717. https://doi.org/10.1016/j.comppsych.2011.11.006

Crespi, B. J. (2016). Autism As a disorder of high intelligence, hypothesis and theory. *Frontiers in Neuroscience*. https://doi.org/10.3389/fnins.2016.00300

Csikszentmihalyi M, Rathunde K, W. S. (1993). *Talented teenagers: The root of success and failures, New York, Cambridge University Press*. New York: Cambridge University Press.

Dakin S, F. U. (2005). Vagaries of visual perception in autism. *Neuron, 48*, 497–507. https://doi.org/10.1016/j.neuron.2005.10.018

de Schipper, E., Mahdi, S., de Vries, P., Granlund, M., Holtmann, M., Karande, S., Almodayfer, O., Shulman, C., Tonge, B., Wong, V. V. C. N., Zwaigenbaum, L., & Bölte, S. (2016). Functioning and disability in autism spectrum disorder: A worldwide survey of experts. *Autism Research, 9*(9), 959–969. https://doi.org/10.1002/aur.1592

Down, J. L. (1887). Lettsomian lectures on some of the mental affections of childhood and youth. *British Medical Journal, 1*(1360), 149–151. https://doi.org/10.1136/bmj.1.1360.149

Frith, U. (1989). *Autism: Explaining the Enigma*. Oxford: Basil Blackwell.

Frith, U., & Happé, F. (1994). Autism: Beyond theory of mind. *Cognition, 50*, 115–132.

Fung, C. H. M. (2009). Asperger's and musical creativity: The case of Erik Satie. *Personality and Individual Differences, 46*(8), 775–783. https://doi.org/10.1016/j.paid.2009.01.019

Gagné, F. (2005). From gifts to talents: The DMGT as a developmental model. In R. J. Sternberg & J. E. Davidson (Eds.), *Conceptions of giftedness* (2nd ed.). New York: Cambridge University Press.

Gagné, F. (2009). The Differentiated Model of Giftedness and Talent. In J. Renzulli, E. J. Gubbins, K. S. McMillen, R. D. Eckert, & C. L. Little (Eds.), *Systems and models for developing programs for the gifted and talented* (2nd ed.). Mansfield Center: Creative Learning Press.

Geurts, H. M., C. B., & S. M. (2009). The paradox of cognitive flexibility in autism. *Trends in Cognitive Sciences, 13*(2), 74–82. https://doi.org/10.1016/j.tics.2008.11.006.

Gillberg, C de S. L. (2002). Head circumference in autism, Asperger syndrome, and ADHD: a comparative study. *Dev Med Child Neurol, 44*(5), 296–300.

Halder, S., & Bruyere, S. M. (2021). Self-reported impediments at home, school, and community: autistic adults' first-person accounts of their life trajectories and derived pathways, *International Journal of Developmental Disabilities*, 1–13. https://10.1080/20473869.2021.1917111

Hall, S. (1973). *Encoding and Decoding in the Television Discourse. Birmingham: Centre for Contemporary Cultural Studies*. Birmingham: Centre for Contemporary Cultural Studies.

Hall, S. (2016). Encoding/decoding model and the circulation of journalism in the digital landscape Henrik Bødker. *Critical Studies in Media Education, 33*(5), 409–423. http://dx.doi.org/10.1080/15295036.2016.1227862

Happé, F. (2018). Why are savant skills and special talents associated with autism? *World Psychiatry, 17*(3), 280–281. https://doi.org/10.1002/wps.20552

Happé F, & Vital, P. (2009). What aspects of autism predispose to talent? *Philosophical Transactions of the Royal Society B: Biological Sciences, 364*(1522), 1369–1375. https://doi.org/10.1098/rstb.2008.0332

Heaton, P., Williams, K., Cummins, O., & Happé, F. (2008). Autism and pitch processing splinter skills: A group and subgroup analysis. *Autism, 12*(2), 203–219. https://doi.org/10.1177/1362361307085270

Heavey, L., Pring, L., & Hermelin, B. (1999). A date to remember: The nature of memory in savant calendrical calculators. *Psychological Medicine, 29*(1), 145–160. https://doi.org/10.1017/S0033291798007776

Hedley, D., Uljarević, M., Cameron, L., Halder, S., Richdale, A., & Dissanayake, C. (2017). Employment programmes and interventions targeting adults with autism spectrum disorder: A systematic review of the literature. *Autism, 21*(8). https://doi.org/10.1177/1362361316661855

Hendricks, D. (2010). Employment and adults with autism spectrum disorders: Challenges and strategies for success. *Journal of Vocational Rehabilitation, 32*(2), 125–134. https://doi.org/10.3233/JVR-2010-0502

Hetzroni, O., Agada, H., & Leikin, M. (2019). Creativity in Autism: An Examination of General and Mathematical Creative Thinking Among Children with Autism Spectrum Disorder and Children with Typical Development. *Journal of Autism and Developmental Disorders, 49*(9), 3833–3844. https://doi.org/10.1007/s10803-019-04094-x

Hillier, H., Campbell, K., Mastriana, M., et al. (2007). Two-year evaluation of a vocational support program for adults on the autism spectrum. *Career Development for Exceptional Individuals, 30*(1), 35–47.

Hoffman, E. and Reeves, R. (1979). An idiot savant with unusual mechanical ability. *American Journal of Psychiatry, 136*(5), 713–714. https://doi.org/10.1017/CBO9781107415324.004

Howlin, P. (2012). Understanding savant skills in autism. https://doi.org/10.1111/j.1469-8749.2012.04244.x

Howlin, P., Goode, S., Hutton, J., and Rutter, M. (2009). Savant skills in autism: psychometric approaches and parental reports. *Phil. Trans. R. Soc. B., 364*, 1359–1367.

Hughes, J. E. A., Ward, J., Gruffydd, E., Baron-cohen, S., Smith, P., Allison, C., & Simner, J. (2018). *Savant syndrome has a distinct psychological profile in autism* (pp. 1–18).

Jarrold, C., Boucher J, & S. P. K. (1996). Generativity deficits in pretend play in autism. *British Journal of Developmental Psychology, 14*, 275–300.

Jolliffe, T., & Baron-Cohen, S. (2001). A test of central coherence theory: Can adults with high-functioning autism or Asperger syndrome integrate fragments of an object? *Cognitive Neuropsychiatry, 6*(3), 193–216. https://doi.org/10.1080/13546800042000124

Jordan, R.R, E. G. H. P. (1995). *Distance Education Course in Autism (Adults, Module 3, Unit 3)*. Birmingham, UK: University of Birmingham, School of education.

Kalat, J.W. (2014). *Introduction to psychology* (10th ed.). Cengage Learning.

Kanner, L. (1943). Autistic disturbances of affective contact. *Nervous Child, 2*, 217–250.

Kasirer, A., & Mashal, N. (2014). Verbal creativity in autism: comprehension and generation of metaphoric language in high-functioning autism spectrum disorder and typical development. *Frontiers in Human Neuroscience, 11*. https://doi.org/10.3389/fnhum.2014.00615

Katherine, V., Cristian, R., Daniela, Q., & Erick, J. (2019). The impact of technology on people with autism spectrum disorder: A systematic literature review. *Sensors, 1*, 1–22.

Kelly, S. J., & Macaruso, P. S. S. (1997). Mental calculation in an autistic savant: A case study. *Journal of Clinical and Experimental Neuropsychology, 19*(2), 172–184.

Kennedy, D. P., & Squire, L. R. (2007). An analysis of calendar performance in two autistic calendar savants. 533–538. https://doi.org/10.1101/lm.653607.several

Kimhi, Y. (2014). Theory of mind abilities and deficits in autism spectrum disorders. *34*(4), 329–343. https://doi.org/10.1097/TLD.0000000000000033

Kohls, G, Antezana, L, Mosner, M. G., Schultz, R. T., & Yerys, B. E. (2018). Altered reward system reactivity for personalized circumscribed interests in autism. *Molecular Autism, 9*(9). doi: 10.1186/s13229-018-0195-7.

Kubilius P, & W. F. (2011). Subotnik, R. F., Olszewski- Rethinking giftedness and gifted education: A proposed direction forward based on psychological science. Interest. *Psychological Science in the Public, 12*, 1–52. https://doi.org/10.1177/1529100611418056

Lee, J., & Deng, Z. (2020). *Atypical: A novel portrayal of individuals with autism spectrum disorder*. March, 20.

Lewis V, & B. J. (1991). Skill, content and generative strategies in autistic children's drawings. *British Journal of Developmental Psychology, 9*, 393–416.

Lim Lee, E. A. L., Black, M. H., Falkmer, M., Tan, T., Sheehy, L., Bölte, S., & Girdler, S. (2020). We can see a bright future": Parents' perceptions of the outcomes of participating in a strengths-based program for adolescents with autism spectrum disorder. *Journal of Autism and Developmental Disorders*, Feb. https://doi.org/10.1007/s10803-020-04411-9

Liu, M., Shih, W., & Ma, L. (2011). *Research in Autism Spectrum Disorders Are children with Asperger syndrome creative in divergent thinking and feeling ?, A brief report. 5*, 294–298. https://doi.org/10.1016/j.rasd.2010.04.011

Maenner, M. J., Shaw, K. A., Baio, J, et al. (2016). Prevalence of autism spectrum disorder among children aged 8 years, 11 sites, United States, 2016. MMWR Surveill Summ 2020. *Autism and Developmental Disabilities Monitoring Network, 4*(69), 1–12. https://doi.org/10.15585/mmwr.ss6904a1external icon.itle

Markram, H., Rinaldi, T., & Markram, K. (2007). The Intense World Syndrome: An alternative hypothesis for autism. *Frontiers of Neuroscience*, *1*(1), 77–96. https:// 10.3389/neuro.01.1.1.006.2007..

Markram, K., & Markram, H. (2010). The Intense World Theory: A unifying theory of the neurobiology of autism. *4*(December), 1–29. https://doi.org/10.3389/fnhum.2010.00224

Mottron, L., & Burack, J. A. (2001). Enhanced perceptual functioning in the development of autism. In J. A. Burack, T. Charman, N. Yirmiya, & P. R. Zelazo (Eds.), *The development of autism: Perspectives from theory and research*. Lawrence Erlbaum Associates Publishers.

Mottron, L., Montre, Â., Stip, E., Morasse, K., & Montre, Â. (1998). Atypical memory performance in an autistic savant. *6*(6).

Mottron, L., Burack, J. A., Iarocci, G., Belleville, S., & Enns, J. T. (2003). Locally oriented perception with intact global processing among adolescents with high-functioning autism: Evidence from multiple paradigms. *Journal of Child Psychology and Psychiatry and Allied Disciplines*, *44*(6), 904–913. https://doi.org/10.1111/1469-7610.00174

Mottron, L., Dawson, M., Soulières, I., Hubert, B., & Burack, J. (2006). Enhanced perceptual functioning in autism: An update, and eight principles of autistic perception. *Journal of Autism and Developmental Disorders*, *36*(1), 27–43. https://doi.org/10.1007/s10803-005-0040-7

Myers, D. G. (2009). *Psychology: Ninth edition in modules*. Worth Publishers.

Ne'eman, A. (2011). *Talk about Autism Q&A: Ari Ne'eman*. London: Ambitious about Autism.

O'Connor, N., & Hermelin, B. (1989). The memory structure of autistic idiot-savant mnemonists. *British Journal of Psychology*, *80*, 97–111.

O'Riordan, M., & Plaisted, K. (2001). Enhanced discrimination in autism. *Q Journal of Experimental Psychology Sect A Human Experimental Psychology*, *54*, 961–979. https://doi.org/org/10.1080/713756000

Office for National Statistics. (2016). *Dataset: A08: Labour market status of disabled people*.

Olszewski-kubiliu, P., F, S. R., & C, W. F. (2015). Conceptualizations of giftedness and the development of talent: Implications for counselors. *Journal of Counseling & Development*, *93*(April), 143–152. https://doi.org/10.1002/j.1556-6676.2015.00190.x

Poljac E, & B. H. (2012). A review of intentional and cognitive control in autism. *Frontiers in Psychology*, *3*, 436. https://doi.org/doi:10.3389/fpsyg.2012.00436

Pring, L. (2005). Savant talent. *Developmental Medicine and Child Neurology*, *47*(7), 500–503. https://doi.org/10.1017/S0012162205000976

Pring, L., & Heavey, L. (1995). Savants, segments, art and autism. *Journal of Child Psychology and Psychiatry*, *36*(6), 1065–1076. https://doi.org/10.1111/j.1469-7610.1995.tb01351.x

Roeyers, H., & Demurie, E. (2010). How impaired is mind-reading in high-functioning adolescents and adults with autism? *7*(1), 123–134. https://doi.org/10.1080/17405620903425924

Rutter, M. L. (2011). Progress in understanding Autism: 2007–2010. *Journal of Autism Developmental Disorder*, *41*, 395–404.

Samson, F., Mottron, L., Jemel, B., Belin, P., & Ciocca, V. (2006). Can spectro-temporal complexity explain the autistic pattern of performance on auditory tasks? *Journal of Autism Developmental Disorder*, *36*, 65–76. https://doi.org/10.1007/s10803- 005-0043-4

Shah, A. F. U. (1993). Why do autistic individuals show superior performance on the block design task? *Journal of Child Psychology and Psychiatry*, *34*(8), 1351–1364.

Simon, B.-C. (2010). Empathizing, systemizing, and the extreme male brain theory of autism. In *Progress in Brain Research* (Vol. 186). Elsevier B.V. https://doi.org/10.1016/B978-0-444-53630-3.00011-7

Sloboda, J. A., & Hermelin, B. O. N. (1985). An exceptional musical memory. *Music Perception*, *3*, 155–170.

Smith, T., & Iadarola, S. (2015). Evidence base update for autism spectrum disorder. *Journal of Clinical Child and Adolescent Psychology*, *44*(6), 897–922. https://doi.org/10.1080/15374416.2015.1077448

Sodian, B., & Frith, U. (1992). Deception and sabotage in autistic, retarded and normal children. *Journal of Child Psychology and Psychiatry*, *33*, 591–605.

Spearman (1863–1945). (n.d.). In Thomson, G. H. (1947). "Charles obituary notices of fellows of the royal society. *5*(15), 373–385. https://doi.org/10.1098/rsbm.1947.0006.

Spearman, C. (2005). *The Abilities of Man: Their Nature and Measurement*. The Blackburn Press.

Stavropoulos, K. K., & C. L. (2014). Reward anticipation and processing of social versus non-social stimuli in children with and without autism spectrum disorders. *Journal of Child Psychology and Psychiatry*, *55*(12), 1398–1408. https://doi.org/10.1111/jcpp.12270. Epub

Stavropoulos, K. K., & C. L. (2018). Oscillatory rhythm of reward: anticipation and processing of rewards in children with and without autism. *Molecular Autism*, *9*(4). https://doi.org/10.1186/s13229-018-0189-5

Stevenson, J. L., & Gernsbacher, M. A. (2013). Abstract spatial reasoning as an autistic strength. *8*(3). https://doi.org/10.1371/journal.pone.0059329

Tammet, D. (2007). *Born on a Blue Day: Inside the Extraordinary Mind of an Autistic Savant* (Free Press, ed.). https://www.theguardian.com/theguardian/2005/feb/12/weekend7.weekend2

Tannenbaum, A. J. (1986). Giftedness: A psychosocial approach. In R. J. Sternberg & J. E. Davidson (Eds.), *Conceptions of giftedness*. New York: Cambridge University Press.

Tannenbaum, A. J. (2003). Nature and nurture of giftedness. In N. Colangelo & G. A. Davis (Eds.), *Handbook of gifted education* (3rd ed.). New York: Pearson.

Torrance, E. P. (1974). *The Torrance Tests of Creative Thinking: Technical-norms manual*. Bensenville, IL: Scholastic Testing Services.

Treffert, D. A. (2009). The savant syndrome: an extraordinary condition. A synopsis: past, present, future. *Philosophical Transactions of the Royal Society B, 364*, 1351–1357. https://doi.org/10.1098/rstb.2008.0326

Treffert, D. A. (2014). Savant syndrome: Realities, myths and misconceptions. *Journal of Autism and Developmental Disorders, 44*(3), 564–571. https://doi.org/10.1007/s10803-013-1906-8

16
IDENTIFICATION OF POSSIBLE LEARNING PROBLEMS IN CHILDREN WITH INTELLECTUAL DISABILITIES

Patrik Arvidsson*, Tom Storfors and Jenny Wilder

Introduction

What Is Inclusive Education for Children with Intellectual Disabilities?

According to United Nations conventions, all children, including children with intellectual disabilities have the right to education and to be an equal citizen of the society (United Nations, 1989; 2006; UNESCO, 1994). To become an equal citizen of society and education we must raise the question of what is the purpose of education. The purpose of education is not only child learning even though learning is the main part of education. According to Biesta (2015; 2020) and Biesta and van Braak (2020) education contains three domains of educational purpose – qualification, socialization and subjectification – and raises questions about content, purpose and relationships. In short, qualification "is about providing students with knowledge, skills, and understanding that will qualify them to do 'something'" (Biesta, 2015; 2020; Biesta & van Braak, 2020). Socialization concerns the (re)presentation of cultures, traditions and practice and last, but not least, subjectification is the right to exist as subjects of initiative and responsibility (Biesta, 2015; 2020; Biesta & van Braak, 2020). To put it differently, it is about freedom, self-determination and speaking in your own voice. All three domains should be present at all levels in education, including in the classroom setting.

There is a consensus about that there are challenges related to providing optimal and inclusive education to children with intellectual disabilities (Okyere et al., 2019). Thus, inclusive education is a question at a policy level but to really support change in different educational contexts, also the levels closest to the children have to work through the practical implications to really implement an inclusive approach to education (Ainscow, 2005; Schwab et al., 2018). It means that it's hard to talk about inclusive education without also asking questions about what the child should be included in, or what the child is/was excluded from, especially when talking about inclusive education for children with intellectual disability. If the inclusion is considered to be limited to the learning situation at school, the child can still be excluded from other essential life situations that are included in being a citizen of a society. But if inclusive

---

* patrik.arvidsson@regiongavleborg.se

education is rather a means to facilitate children with intellectual disabilities becoming equal citizens of the society we cannot focus only on the learning situation in school or problems that might be related to learning. Then we have to observe facilitative and hindering pre-requisites to inclusion not only in the classroom, we have to widen it up to also include general aspect of the society and, not the least, to the child's preferences to what situations and processes he or she wants to be included in. So endorsing the different policies of the right to education and the right to equal citizenship implies that the information about what is needed for a certain child to be included should be found at least at the level of the individual, the classroom and at a societal or policy level.

In the terms of the International Classification of functioning, disability and health (ICF) the individual level can be considered as the child's body functions and possible problem can be expressed as impairments (WHO, 2001). The participation construct can be seen as the outcome of a person's functioning and interaction in its actual life situation and for example taking *both* the child's intellectual functional level (as well as possible cognitive/intellectual limitations) and facilitating and hindering environmental factors (such the availability of individualized support) into account. Functioning at the classroom level as well as in the societal level can be considered as the participation level and problems can be expressed as participation restriction. Collecting information about the child's perceived participation in, for example, different learning activities and learning processes in the classroom will provide essential information about both possible supportive interventions and the perceived participation can be used as a reflector of the extent to which an intervention is successful or not.

This way of looking at functioning, in different levels and considering participation to be a reflector of both individual and environmental factors, is one main contribution of the interactive bio–psycho–social model of disability in ICF and the suggested interactive model of functioning, disability and health (Arvidsson et al., 2014). Endorsing an interactive model of disability implies that the outcome of for example learning is always a question of both individual and environmental factors, it's the interaction between the child and his/her context, and therefore this interaction should also be the focus for inclusive education. This means that when looking specifically at children with intellectual disabilities in the classroom also societal factors such as wealth, religion, buying habits, caregivers education level, family size and structure and population density etc. are relevant to the study. How to deal with these pure societal factors is not within the aim of this chapter, but it is important to have them in mind, not in relation to the three domains of education purpose - qualification, socialization and subjectification (Biesta, 2015; 2020; Biesta & van Braak, 2020).

Furthermore, there needs to be a discussion about whether inclusive education for children with intellectual disabilities is something different from inclusive education for all children (Cornelius & Balakrishnan, 2012; Okyere et al., 2019). There also has to be a discussion about whether education for children with intellectual disabilities is performed in an integrated or segregated setting and what that comes with in terms of what kind of inclusive education would be possible. Inclusion in school can still be exclusion at the societal level. If the goal is that a child with intellectual disabilities should be included in the society like any other citizen it will entail different challenges to achieve this depending on whether the child is educated in a regular/mainstream school or in a special school for children with intellectual disabilities, or in segregated special groups inside a regular mainstream school (Michailakis & Reich, 2009; Cornelius & Balakrishnan, 2012). There are challenges with both integrated and segregated solutions in relation to inclusive education. Generally, compared to children without intellectual disabilities, children with intellectual disabilities are more dependent on support at different levels, both from peers, teachers and families and from economical resources and societal stakeholders. Thus, in the integrated solution, the main challenges are often related to psychological and physical health (such as problems with peer victimization and corporal punishment) (Cornelius & Balakrishnan, 2012; Okyere et al., 2019). If education is segregated the main challenges are related to excluding effects in relation to the general society such as participation restrictions in work, family, leisure activities etc. (Tideman, 2015). This implies that the pre-requisites for inclusive education for children with intellectual disabilities will differ a lot in relation to, and sometimes also within, different societies and cultures (Okyere et al., 2019). Thus, the development of and approaches to inclusive education will vary between different societal settings, at least between different countries (Michell, 2005; Andersson & Wilder, 2015). As a consequence, inclusive education should receive and use information about not only what a child needs to function better in the learning situation. Inclusive education is, to at least the same extent, a question about receiving and using information about for example what the teacher requires to support the child in a learning situation in an individualized way and what/how the society should be like and/or develop to let all citizens become equal.

One main dilemma for achieving inclusive education in practice is how to identify possible learning problems and the need for support of children with disabilities without stigmatizing the child (Michailakis & Reich, 2009). This dilemma is absolutely not easy to solve: how can a child's needs for support be met without excluding them from society or stigmatizing them? Most often this is not a question about knowledge; it's a question about resources. For example, when there are too many children and too few teachers, the possible adaptations of the classroom will be limited and a specialized setting would therefore often be the better alternative. In such a case, and not least in a low- and middle-income context, it's important to have in mind that the problem with inclusion is then not to be considered as related to the child's functioning or impairment, nor to the competence of the teachers or to the possible lack of policies. The problem is rather related to the lack of resources in relation to what is needed to provide a sufficiently individualized education to each child. Researchers claim that inclusive education is possible for everyone but that a lot of requirements and adaptations have to be made, some related to school settings and classroom environment and some related to child differences in terms of learning styles and need for support (Andersson & Wilder, 2015). A lack of an inclusive approach is highly related to different problems in school but also to other exclusive processes in everyday life such as societal participation (Tideman, 2015). This is valid for children in general and for children with intellectual disabilities in particular. Successful inclusive education is a question of resources in terms of, for example, environmental facilities and numbers of teachers in relation to the group size of children, but it is also a question of having sufficient knowledge about the different children to be able to adapt the learning processes to the children's specific needs (Andersson & Wilder, 2015).

In this chapter we consider inclusive education for children with intellectual disabilities as a tool for supporting learning processes regardless of whether the child is in an integrated or segregated setting, and with a long-term goal that the child should be an equal citizen in the society. In relation to this reasoning, it is important to take into account that the authors' perspective emanates from a Western World context and it would be unwise to be too certain about conclusions in terms of what is the best way for all teachers in all contexts. All learning and education is performed within a context and is thus related to societal and cultural aspects as well as economic resources, political policies and guidelines, attitudes and infra-structure. As such, inclusive education should always be more or less contextualized and based on the present pre-requisites and have to be didactically adapted – thus a question of why, what, who, when, where and how.

Inclusive Education for Children with Intellectual Disabilities at the Individual Level – the Understanding of Problems with Cognitive Functioning

The diagnosis criteria of intellectual disability refer to limitations in both intellectual functioning and in adaptive behaviour that should have originated before the age of 18 (WHO, 1999; APA, 2010). To diagnose intellectual disability standardized tests are provided, but for ecological validity it is also recommended that factors related to societal and cultural environment as well as availability and level of support have to be taken into account (AAIDD, 2010). The recommendation to use a standardized test (with good psychometrical properties) is, however, in practice methodologically difficult to combine with the latter recommendation. This is because the less interaction with the environment a person has and the less support that is allowed during the assessment, the better psychometrical properties the instrument will have. So even if it shouldn't be the case, the core substance in the diagnosis of intellectual disability is the result from the assessment of intellectual functioning that most often is synonymous with a test of intelligence quotient (IQ) (AAIDD, 2010). Furthermore, taking IQ tests that have been developed in one context (e.g. a Western World context) and using them in another context (e.g. in a low- and middle-income context) has also been highly criticized. Another dimension, perhaps an additional explanation to the dilemma described above, is the idea that IQ has a correlate at the body level and thus needs a standardized and valid measurement (Arvidsson & Granlund, 2018; Tiekstra et al., 2009). This idea belongs to a medical approach to function and disability that seek explanations for problems at the body level (Schalock et al., 2018). But the support in everyday life, including learning, needs to endorse an interactive social-ecological approach, and this means seeking explanations for problems in both the body and the environment or in the individual's interaction. This is one of the main reasons why the diagnosis in itself doesn't give any specific information about how inclusive education should be adapted or performed (Arvidsson & Granlund, 2018). At the most, the diagnosis, and thus the information about the specific impairment, can give knowledge that there might be a problem related to learning, but not specifically in what way and not how to intervene with the problems. If IQ really is considered to only be in the body, the approach to support and learning should be to intervene with the body; but we don't. We intervene in the interaction and/or in the environment of the child. Thus, to endorse an interactive bio-psycho-social approach is a requirement for the idea that learning can be supported in any child and not least in children with intellectual disabilities, and this is an absolute pre-requisite for inclusive education approaches in practice.

Looking at difficulties that most children with intellectual disabilities have in the interaction, difficulties that are also related to problems in learning would give better clues to possible inclusive approaches. Compared to children with typical development, children with intellectual disabilities often (but not always and not all children with intellectual disabilities) have problems in at least three cognitive functional areas: abstract thinking, thinking in several steps and handling complex information simultaneously (Piaget, 2001; Räty et al., 2016). Problems regarding abstract thinking include problems in understanding and using abstract symbols (text, numbers, money and time), which is essential in for example communication (in a broader sense) and will of course affect essential activities in relation to education and learning. Problems regarding abstract thinking also include problems in imagining non-experienced things and situations. In a teaching situation in a classroom, problems with abstract thinking can be manifested as a lack of attention and understanding, even leading to feelings of despair (what is happening?). Problems regarding thinking in several steps include problems in understanding multiple-level instructions and other relationships that include connections between cause and effect. In a teaching situation in a classroom, problems in thinking in several steps can be manifested as disorientation and a lack of self-determination (where do I start?). Problems regarding handling complex information simultaneously include difficulties in making nuanced considerations and comparisons, risk considerations and problem solving that manifest in complex social situations. In a teaching situation in a classroom, problems in handling complex information simultaneously can be manifested as frustration and fight/flight defence reactions (I don´t want to be here anymore!).

Inclusive Education for Children with Intellectual Disabilities – Handling Problems with Cognitive Functioning in the Classroom

From an interactive bio-psycho-social understanding of intellectual disabilities possible learning problems should be considered as the outcome of a discrepancy between the abilities of the individual on the one hand and the level, quality and availability of support on the other (Arvidsson et al., 2014; Imms et al., 2017). According to a medical approach to disability and function, the individual's problems with ability can be categorized as impairments (i.e. non-function, dis-ability), but according to an interactive approach the problems have to be described in a context, in terms of interactive limitations, like for example participation restrictions, and thus also include a supportive or hindering environment (Schalock et al., 2018). The outcome, that a child learns or experiences problems in learning, is thus always a result of both individual and environmental factors, and this is also why the diagnosis in itself doesn't provide sufficient information as a foundation for inclusive education.

There are a lot of ways to describe inclusive strategies in a classroom, but in this chapter we focus on two main areas of evident strategies that are found in the research literature: *Optional (self-selected) use of concrete prompting systems* and *Promotion of the development of positive attitudes* (Räty et al., 2016; Beulkeman & Light, 2020). These strategies are, in some way or another, evident to handle some of the possible learning problems related to difficulties in the different cognitive functional areas that have been presented above. But the strategies are, in another way, more general and can handle other possible learning problems as well.

Optional (Self-selected) Use of Concrete Prompting Systems as an Inclusive Strategy in a Classroom

This area focuses on the different kinds of low or high technological aids that can be used to support the learning process for children with intellectual disabilities (Räty et al., 2016; Beulkeman & Light, 2020). It includes any kind of technological aid such as the use of objects, pictures, symbols, videos or voice recordings. The aid can be implemented in different levels of abstraction, from very concrete use of well-known objects, pictures or symbols put in an order to visualize a sequence of events to the use of self-operated tablets for giving feedback and further instructions when the teacher is not available to do it. High technological aids such as tablets (or smartphones, computers and music players) can be successfully used as self-operated prompting systems or for simulated instruction when community-based instruction is not possible. Low technological aids such objects, pictures and symbols may be more successful the more concrete support the child needs to be prompted and are also easier for the teacher to adjust and adapt simultaneously

One main finding that is a key point for the successful use of support in general, is that preventing problems is always better than treating them when they have occurred (Räty et al., 2016; Beulkeman & Light, 2020). In practice this often means that if the teacher is successful in supporting the child to be engaged in a task it will often "automatically" prevent, for example, behaviour problems. But this is of course not easy to achieve; it's always a question of balancing or matching the demands and support to the abilities and needs of the child. The teacher will not be successful in this if their demands or standards are too low or too high; there has to be a sufficient balance/match. For example, if reading expectations for students with moderate intellectual disabilities should be raised it is important to have an appropriate method for assessing the correct level at which the instructions should be implemented. For this the use of standardized assessment methods is often recommended.

Another main finding that is a key point for the successful use of prompting systems, regardless of the level of technology, is to find a system that the child prefers to use (Räty et al., 2016; Beulkeman & Light, 2020). Systems selected by the child are always more efficient than non-self-selected systems. Thus, the teachers should always strive to develop the use of any technological aid together with the child and/or with the caregivers and other teachers/professionals. To increase the likelihood of being successful in this collaboration it's also recommended that supportive content of the system should be based on the child's strengths rather than limitations.

Promotion of the Development of Positive Attitudes as an Inclusive Strategy in a Classroom

This area focuses on different ways to promote inclusive processes related to the child's learning activities and the focus to create a supportive social atmosphere around the child, preferably by encouraging positive attitudes in the closest social network (Räty et al., 2016; Beulkeman & Light, 2020). The main finding also suggests that the most efficient way of achieving positive attitudes around children with intellectual disabilities is to ensure that children with typical development have the opportunity to acknowledge the competence of their peers with intellectual disabilities by social interaction (Schaefer et al., 2016). An essential goal is to increase the number of social situations and activities where children with and without intellectual disabilities can interact and that teachers ensure that students with typical development have the opportunity to both acknowledge any ability of their peers but also to be aware of and explicitly instruct values and behaviours in social interaction. To some extent, the interaction between the children has to take the different levels of cognitive and intellectual functions into account. Although it is more important that children with similar interests and similarities in other characteristics that are not related to different cognitive and intellectual levels meet and play and learn.

There is a lot of evidence that increased experiences of this kind of social interaction are related to increased positive attitudes for both the children with intellectual disabilities and the children with typical development. The literature often also suggests that it is important to have a procedure plan both for the implementation of new situations and activities for social interaction and for following up on how the interaction develops. There are suggestions that these procedures should use methods based on applied behaviour analysis, for example, prompting and instruction for various discrete and chained skills, but there are no explicit suggestions as to how this can be implemented in inclusive settings.

Inclusive Education for Children with Intellectual Disabilities as a Means to General Inclusion in the Society

The Problem with Knowledge Transfer from the Classroom to Other Life Situations

As a consequence of the cognitive functional difficulties, children with intellectual disabilities have difficulties transferring experiences and knowledge from one situation or context to another situation or context (Feuerstein et al., 2004; Räty et al., 2016). This is an overall problem that has to be taken into consideration when implementing inclusive strategies in the classroom. For example, children with intellectual disabilities have more difficulties than children with typical development in using a strategy they have learned to solve one task to also solve an even similar task. When comparing the task itself, where the learning takes place (e.g. different classrooms, inside or outside the school building, other places than at school) as well as the required strategy to get into a learning process, children with intellectual disabilities "tolerate" fewer differences from one situation to another in comparison to children without these cognitive difficulties. This problem with transferring knowledge from one situation to another can be considered the main reason why children with intellectual disabilities need more support in learning and education in comparison to children without intellectual disabilities (Feuerstein et al., 2004; Räty et al., 2016). Hence, it's essential to identify how a child perceives differences between different situations to really understand what the child experience as a too-wide gap. For this, both social support such as peer collaboration and teacher guidance and instructions and technological support such as different types of cognitive aids (e.g. time assistive devices and pictures) can be used to facilitate the transfer of experiences and knowledge between learning situations (Feuerstein et al., 2004; Räty et al., 2016; Palmqvist, 2020). If the goal is inclusion in the society it's really important to facilitate as much knowledge as possible and to identify what works in one situation and which skills the child uses in that situation, which will provide essential clues to what kind of support the child will need to be able to use the same skills in slightly different situations.

Moving Focus from Limitations to Possibilities

If the goal is inclusion in society it is important to be aware of the possible learning problems at different levels and it is important to get knowledge about what the child needs to support transferring knowledge between different learning activities and situations. This means, for instance, that the child's abilities and problems have to be assessed and observed in different contexts, not only in the classroom and with different persons but also for example at different times of the day and when the child has different moods. Information about the child's needs to support knowledge transfer needs to be varied and contextualized, and the assessment should be conducted when the child is involved in any kind of interaction. In school that means that the more the child can be observed *in* situations that include actual interaction (e.g. between the child and what should be learned, between the child and the teacher, and/or between child and peer) the better. This also means that traditional cognitive assessments such as standardized tests will not be sufficient to provide the required information. These tests are most often designed to assess impairment (dis-ability) rather than possible ability and thus strive to rather exclude, or at least control for, effects from contextual and/or interactive factors (Arvidsson & Granlund, 2018; Schalock et al., 2018; Tiekstra et al., 2016). This doesn't mean that the child's cognitive level of functions is not important for learning but rather that the information about the individual level is not sufficient to provide information about how inclusive education should be implemented. If the goal of inclusive education is to provide as supportive an environment as possible and allowing the child to learn "as much as possible" despite the cognitive/intellectual problems, the individual's limitations in cognitive and intellectual functioning can rather be considered as the "possible level" of learning without any support. This pertains to the "floor" of Vygotsky's Zone of Proximal Development (ZPD) (Vygotsky, 1979)). Hence, what's possible for the child to learn with optimal individualized support is the "ceiling" of the ZPD. This also means that whatever the child actually manages to learn with any kind of support, and thus can be observed when the child interacts in any learning situation, can be considered as inside the ZPD and possible to achieve.

By using information about the child's observed performance in different situations, the focus will almost automatically be on something that is possible for the child to perform and not on something the child can't perform, and this is another essential principle for inclusive education. Because if the focus is on limitations (disability rather than ability) it takes away the focus from assessing the individual's strengths and what the child actually needs, in order to adjust and improve the individualized support (Schalock et al., 2018; Tideman, 2015; AAIDD, 2010). Even if cognitive and intellectual functions are essential for learning, enhanced interaction and positive learning outcomes are also (and maybe even more) related to other positive individual factors such as motivation, experiences, interests and mood (Garrels & Arvidsson, 2019; Imms et al., 2017; Räty et al., 2016). This way of relating difficulties with learning to different functions or areas of functions is of course a simplified construction. In real life, difficulties overlap and the causes of the difficulties are often impossible to reduce to one function or even one area of functions. The way difficulties are manifested will also change over time, both in terms of a general change that can be related to the age of the child but also in a more fluctuating change, or variation, within each child (Fagot et al., 2018). For the specific child, this variation is even greater outside school and this variation is very much relatable to individual factors such as motivation, experiences, mood and interest. What is more, these factors are very sensitive for contextual changes such as change of attitudes and availability, resources, support etc. Information about these positive individual factors (e.g. motivation, experiences, interests and mood) and how they contribute to learning and transfer of knowledge for a specific child can be provided by questions like: How can you be motivated? What experiences are needed and desired? What puts you in an emotionally positive mood? What interests do you have, and how can these interests be used as your goals for learning? The questions can be addressed directly to the child but also as questions to for example other teachers, caregivers and/or to other persons in the child's social network. This approach to learning opens up ways of thinking about interventions in terms of *what is possible* rather than "only" focusing on the limitations in intellectual functions, *what is not possible* (Fagot et al., 2018). This approach also ensures that the teachers' expectations of the specific child are not too low. Even if we "only" look at a child's difficulties that generally are related to having an intellectual disability, such as problems with abstract thinking, thinking in several steps and handling complex information simultaneously, it makes sense that these difficulties are much better observed if they are put into the context where the difficulties actually occur and where the possible outcome from an intervention such as implemented or adjusted support, should be recognized.

Conclusion

The focus on possibilities highlights what is possible from the teachers' and the society's point of view, more or less, regardless of the present recourses. To endorse the interactive bio-psycho-social approach to inclusive education will be to focus on the entire learning context around the children, not only the classroom and the school, but in every situation that it is possible for the child to interact with The focus for a teacher is then not only a specific child but rather on getting experience of as many different learning styles and different strengths among the children as possible. The focus should move from thinking about possible learning problems as something related to the specific child to looking for what possible situations there are for the children to be involved in – in the classroom, in the school and elsewhere, together with peers, teachers and others. This also means that the teachers are an essential part of the solutions, and the focus will move towards for example competences, attitudes and possible collaborations among the teachers but also available resources from the stakeholders. Because to allow a universal and creative inclusive learning atmosphere for both the children and the teachers, resources, as well as inclusive policies from the stakeholders, are essential. The stakeholders need to for example provide competence-oriented teacher training as well as facilitate collaboration in the wider school community and also with the families. An inclusive atmosphere also comprises time and resources for ongoing follow-ups where the teachers together can reflect on and evaluate their practice and learn from each other and from the children. To get to this collaborative atmosphere in practice, the knowledge and uses of the inclusive strategies have to involve at least all the children and staff at school, but preferably also the children's families and caregivers (at least to the sense that the approach is endorsed). To really achieve a universal inclusive atmosphere at a school, regardless if the purpose of the education is qualification, socialization or subjectification, there has to be ongoing work and discussion about for example tools and methods that are used to get the best knowledge about possible learning problems as well as possible situations for further inclusion.

To conclude, universal inclusive education has to be based on the point of view that all children have the same right to become equal citizens of the society. Children with intellectual disabilities have difficulties in learning, and they may need support to reach that equality, and for this some extra resources may be needed. However, the most essential part of an inclusive approach to learning is a question of having an attitude, at school and in the society, which focuses on possibilities in learning rather than limitations. The approach seeks present and new ways of providing learning situations where children with intellectual disability can interact with any children and that the interaction is based on common interests and strengths rather than on cognitive level. The most important role for a teacher, related to universal education, is to find ways to support the children in that interaction.

References

AAIDD (American Association on Intellectual and Developmental Disabilities). (2010). *Intellectual Disability: Definition, Classification, and Systems of Supports* (11th ed.). Washington, DC: American Association on Intellectual and Developmental Disabilities.

Ainscow, M. (2005). Developing inclusive education systems: What are the levers for change? *Journal of Educational Change, 6*, 109–124. https://doi.org/10.1007/s10833-005-1298-4

Andersson, A.-L., & Wilder, J. (2015). Swedish classroom communities including learners with mild intellectual disabilities: Lower secondary school. In *Children and Young People in School and in Society* (pp. 111–133). Retrieved from http://urn.kb.se/resolve?urn=urn:nbn:se:mdh:diva-29179

APA (American Psychiatric Association). (2013). *Diagnostic and Statistical Manual of Mental Disorders* (5th ed., Text Revision (DSM-5)). Washington, DC: American Psychiatric Association.

Arvidsson, P., Granlund, M., Thyberg, I., & Thyberg, M. (2014). Important aspects of participation and participation restrictions in people with a mild intellectual disability. *Disability and Rehabilitation, 36*, 1264–1272.

Arvidsson, P., & Granlund, M. (2018). The relationship between intelligence quotient and aspects of everyday functioning and participation for people who have mild and borderline intellectual disabilities. *Journal of Applied Research in Intellectual Disabilities, 31*, e68–e78. https://doi.org/10.1111/jar.12314

Beukelman, D & Light, J. (2020). *Augmentative & Alternative Communication: Supporting Children and Adults with Complex Communication Needs* (5th ed). Baltimore: Paul Brookes Publishing.

Biesta, G. (2015). What is education for? On good education, Teacher Judgement, and Educational Professionalism. *European Journal of Education. 50*(1), 75–81. https://doi.org/10.111/ejed.12109

Biesta, G. (2020). Risking ourselves in education: Qualification, socialisation and subjectification revisited. *Educational Theory, 70*(1), 89–104. https://doi.org/10.1111/edth.12411

Biesta, G., & van Braak, M. (2020). Beyond the medical model: Thinking differently about medical education and medical education. *Teaching and Learning in Medicine, 32*(4), 449–456. http://doi.org/10.1080/10401334.2020.1798240

Cornelius, D and Balakrishnan, J. (2012). Inclusive education for students with intellectual disability. *Disability, CBR & Inclusive Development*, 23(2), 81–93. http://doi.org/10.5463/dcid.v23i2.111

Fagot D, Mella N, Borella E, et al. (2018). Intra-individual variability from a lifespan perspective: A comparison of latency and accuracy measures. *Journal of Intelligence*. 6(1), 16.

Feuerstein, R. Rand, Y., Hoffman, M. B., & Miller, R. (2004). *Instrumental Enrichment: An Intervention Program for Cognitive Modifiability*. Baltimore, MD: University Park Press.

Garrels, V., & Arvidsson, P. (2019). Promoting self-determination for students with intellectual disability: A Vygotskian perspective. *Learning, Culture and Social Interaction*, 22, 100241. https://doi.org/10.1016/j.lcsi.2018.05.006.

Imms, C., Granlund, M., Wilson, P. H., Steenbergen, B., Rosenbaum, P. L., & Gordon, A. M. (2017). Participation, both a means and an end: A conceptual analysis of processes and outcomes in childhood disability. *Developmental Medicine and Child Neurology*, 59, 16–25.

Michailakis, D., & Reich, W. (2009). Dilemmas of inclusive education, *ALTER, European Journal of Disability Research* 3(1), 24–44. doi.org/10.1016/j.alter.2008.10.001.

Mitchell, D. (2005). Introduction: Sixteen propositions on the contexts of inclusive education. In D. Mitchell (Ed.), *Contextualizing Inclusive Education: Evaluating Old and New International Perspectives* (pp. 1–21). Abingdon, Oxfordshire: Routledge.

Okyere, C., Aldersey, H. M., & Lysaght, R. (2019). The experiences of children with intellectual and developmental disabilities in inclusive schools in Accra, Ghana. *African Journal of Disability* 8, a542. https://doi.org/10.4102/ajod.v8i0.542

Palmqvist, L. (2020). *Time to Plan : How to Support Everyday Planning in Adolescents with Intellectual Disability* (PhD dissertation, Linköping University Electronic Press). https://doi.org/10.3384/diss.diva-164916

Piaget, J. (2001). *The Psychology of Intelligence*. London: Routledge.

Räty, L., Kontu, E. K., & Pirttimaa, R. (2016). Teaching children with intellectual disabilities: Analysis of research-based recommendations. *Journal of Education and Learning*, 5(2), 318–336. https://doi.org/10.5539/jel.v5n2p318.

Schaefer, J. M., Cannella-Malone, H. I., & Carter, E. W. (2016). The place of peers in peer-mediated interventions for students with intellectual disability. *Remedial and Special Education*, 37(6), 345–356.

Schalock, R. L., Luckasson, R., Tassé, M. J., & Verdugo, M. A. (2018). A holistic theoretical approach to intellectual disability: Going beyond the four current perspectives. *Intellectual and Developmental Disabilities*, 56(2), 79–89. doi: https://doi.org/10.1352/1934-9556-56.2.79

Schwab, S., Sharma, U., & Loreman, T. (2018). Are we included? Secondary students' perception of inclusion climate in their schools, *Teaching and Teacher Education*, 75, 31–39. https://doi.org/10.1016/j.tate.2018.05.016

Tideman, M. (2015). Education and support for people with intellectual disabilities in Sweden: Policy and practice, *Research and Practice in Intellectual and Developmental Disabilities*, 2(2), 116–125. https://doi.org/10.1080/23297018.2015.1067868

Tiekstra, M., Hessels, M., & Minnaert, A. (2009). Learning capacity in adolescents with mild intellectual disabilities. *Psychological Reports*, 105, 804–814.

Tiekstra, M., Minnaert, A., & Hessels, M. (2016). A review scrutinising the consequential validity of dynamic assessment. *Educational Psychology*, 36, 112–137. doi.org/10.1080/01443410.2014.915930.

United Nations. (1989). *Convention on the Rights of the Child, 44/25 CFR*. New York: United Nations.

United Nations. (2006). *Convention on the Rights of Persons with Disabilities*. New York: United Nations.

UNESCO (United Nations Educational, Scientific and Cultural Organization Ministry of Education and Science. (1994). *The Salamanca Statement and Framework for Action for Special Needs Education*. Paris: UNESCO.

Vygotsky, L. (1979). The genesis of higher mental functions. In J. V. Wertsch (Ed.), *The concept of activity in Soviet psychology* (pp. 144–188). New York: M.E. Sharpe, Inc.

WHO (World Health Organization). (1999). *ICD-10: International Statistical Classification of Diseases and Related Health Problems*. Geneva: World Health Organization.

WHO (World Health Organization). (2001). *International Classification of Functioning, Disability and Health*. Geneva: World Health Organization.

WHO (World Health Organization). (2007). *International Classification of Functioning, Disability and Health – Version for Children & Youth (ICF-CY)*. Geneva: World Health Organization.

17
BRAIN–BEHAVIOUR RELATIONSHIP IN ATTENTION-DEFICIT/ HYPERACTIVITY DISORDER

A Microanalysis

Pritha Mukhopadhyay* and Piya Saha

Introduction

Attention-Deficit Hyperactivity Disorder (ADHD) is a common childhood psychiatric disorder. It is a persistent neurodevelopmental disorder characterized by symptoms of inattention, impulsivity, and hyperactivity. Symptoms of ADHD typically begin in early childhood, which bear a significant negative impact on an array of behaviours and task performance, both at school and at home; it adversely affects their academic performance and social interaction pattern (Wolraich et al., 2019). The conceptualization of ADHD has evolved over the years. With exponential advances in neuroimaging and genetic research on ADHD (Faraone et al., 2015), the present notion should be how to integrate discrete knowledge to understand ADHD in a biopsychosocial framework. ADHD receives clinical attention as it disrupts a child's academic and social life, which has a long-drawn impact throughout his life. The high prevalence of ADHD across the globe to date is a cause of worry for the clinician. A meta-analysis of 41 studies across 27 countries revealed that the worldwide prevalence of ADHD is 3.4% among children and adolescents (Polanczyk et al., 2015). The range of prevalence varies from 4.6% to 9.5% across the globe (Moffitt & Melchior, 2007; Pastor et al., 2015). Many factors may be responsible for a wide range of prevalence rates.

For example, the Diagnostic and Statistical Manual of Mental Disorders (DSM) (American Psychological Association [APA],1994; APA, 2013) makes the diagnosis, when ADHD symptoms meet the criteria of any single dimension of either inattention or hyperactivity (Chinawa & Obu, 2015), as it categorizes ADHD in three sub-groups, namely, inattentive presentation, hyperactive/impulsive presentation and combined type presentation (DSM-IV, APA, 1994; DSM-5, APA, 2013). Co-morbidity does not exclude the diagnosis of ADHD in DSM (Moffitt & Melchior, 2007), but the International Classification of Diseases-10 (ICD-10) (World Health Organisation [WHO], 1993) strictly requires the presence of symptoms in all three dimensions

---

* prithamukhopadhyay@gmail.com

(inattention, hyperactivity, and impulsivity, be it at home or school), for the diagnosis and any co-morbid condition excludes singular ADHD diagnosis. Perhaps it explains the low prevalence rate of ADHD in European countries (4.6%) (Moffitt & Melchior, 2007), where researchers had followed the ICD-10 criteria in comparison to that in North America (6.2%) (Polanczyk et al., 2007), Australia (7.4%) (Lawrence et al., 2015), and Africa (7.47%) (Ayano et al., 2020), where DSM-IV (APA, 1994) is used for case definition. It is evident that in Germany, the prevalence is 5% on DSM-IV (APA, 1994) but 1.0% on ICD-10 (WHO, 1993) (Döpfner et al., 2008).

Variability in prevalence also depends on the areas selected for the study. Maybe, in the urban areas, greater awareness and greater demand for social sophistication and etiquette, greater task demand at school, and less tolerance for socially disapproved behaviour, cause more referrals, with a higher prevalence rate of 57.76% compared to that of 42.0% from rural areas (Arya et al.,2019). Private schools also use their own screening protocols at the time of admission which exclude most of the children with behaviour problems (Suthar et al., 2018) that may explain the lesser prevalence of ADHD in private schools (1.25%) as compared to the government school (1.37%) (Ramya et al., 2017). Greater prevalence in boys, also partially, may be due to their presentation of the features of hyperactivity/impulsivity with externalizing tendency (Cuffe et al., 2015; Katzman et al., 2017), which are inevitably more noticeable to others. Girls with ADHD are more likely to have problems of inattention, with a co-morbid internalizing condition, like anxiety or depression (Tung et al., 2016). Poor diagnosis in females with ADHD often causes greater intellectual impairment in them than in males (Agnew-Blais et al., 2016), highlighting the importance of detailed evaluation for the diagnosis and treatment in time.

To obviate the difficulties of labelling and identification, in addition, it may be necessary to identify the underlying parameters of the psychopathology of ADHD and to correlate it with clinical observation and phenomenological diagnosis.

Methodology

To reach the micro diagnosis of ADHD, the first and foremost, necessity is taking a case history, mental status examination (MSE)/behavioural observation, and building up a genuine rapport with the child. Psychoeducation of the parents and teachers is almost mandatory. Before the assessment, we become cautious to assess ADHD with a judicious selection of reinforcement paradigms and a congenial setting for the child, without which the ADHD child may not feel the urge to initiate and complete any task. One of the major reasons for poor cognitive performance in ADHD is their motivational lag (Johnson et al., 2009), which may be owing to their poor coordination among cognitive processes (including encoding, search, decision, motor organization), effort, and executive system (Karalunas & Huang-Pollock, 2011).

Participants

In our study (Saha et al., 2017a; Saha et al., 2017b; Saha et al., 2017c; Saha et al., 2019), children with ADHD combined type presentation (*DSM-5*) (APA,2013), aged between 8 and 12 years were selected through purposive sampling. The children with ADHD were selected from psychiatric services of R.G. Kar Medical College and Hospital, Kolkata, India. The diagnosis of ADHD was made by both the psychiatrist and the psychologist. A thorough and detailed clinical examination was conducted by a psychologist in the Centre with Potential for Excellence in Particular Area (CPEPA) laboratory, Department of Psychology, University of Calcutta. The ADHD children were on methylphenidate (MPH) for 12 months. The child with a history of any other psychiatric illness, organic brain- or neurological disorders, and sensory impairment was not included in the study.

The healthy participants (HP) that matched with the ADHD group in terms of age and education, and with no history of psychiatric illness, developmental disorders, learning disability, brain injury, or sensory impairment, were selected from the community through the snowballing technique.

Materials

- Binet Kamat Test (Kamat, 1967)
- Devereux Scales of Mental Disorder (Naglieri et al., 1994)
- Child Symptom Inventory-4 (Gadow & Sprafkin, 2002)
- Wechsler Intelligence scale for Children (WISC-IV, Indian Adaptation, Wechsler, 2003)
- Conner's Parent Rating Scale 3rd edition TM (Conners, 2008)
- For Electroencephalography (EEG) and Event-Related Potential (ERP) recording and analysis Brain Electro Scan System (B.E.S.S.) from Axxonet System Technologies was used.

Method for EEG and ERP Recording

In our study (Mukhopadhyay, 2019; Saha et al., 2017a; Saha et al., 2017b; Saha et al., 2017c; Saha et al., 2019), EEG was recorded with B.E.S.S., by Axxonet System Technologies. The 19 active Ag/AgCl electrodes were used following the modified version of the 10-20 system of the American Electroencephalographic Society. Channels were referenced to the left ear. The EEG was sampled at 256 Hz. A Butterworth filter of range 0.05 to 30 Hz was used with a 50 Hz notch filter. The EEG was analyzed in the following six frequency bands: Delta (1-3 Hz), Theta (4-7Hz), Alpha (8-12 Hz), Beta (13-35 Hz), Gamma-1 (35-55Hz), Gamma-2 (55-85Hz).

For ERP, the "2N-Back test" was presented as a visual stimulus; 112 trials were presented for 500 ms with a pre-stimulus of 200 ms and inter-stimulus gap of 4000 ms using the B.E.S.S (Saha et al., 2015). The Latency windows of ERP were designated in the following ranges: 75-150 ms for N1, 120-250 ms for P2, 150-350 ms for N2, and 250-700 ms for P3 (Saha et al., 2015), which was comparable with the protocol of other ERP studies of the ADHD children (Tsai et al., 2012; Voorde et al., 2010).

Test Scoring and EEG Analysis

The scoring of the cognitive test and behavioural measure was done following the standard method of scoring of the respective test.

For EEG analysis, epochs containing artefacts were removed through visual appraisal, maintaining an average of 15 epoch rejections across all subjects, and participants with bad segments were rejected from the analysis. Fast Fourier Transform was performed with 2sec epoch segments (Kitsune et al., 2015). Spectral power was computed for absolute and relative power using B.E.S.S software. The power spectral density measures power per unit of frequency, and the absolute power of a band is the integral of all of the power values within its frequency range. Relative power indices for each band were derived by expressing absolute power in each frequency band as a percentage of the absolute power summed over all the six frequency bands (Amer et al., 2010). Relative delta power, for example, is equal to (absolute delta power/ absolute delta power + absolute theta power + absolute alpha power + absolute beta power + absolute gamma1 + absolute gamma2) * 100. Further, analytic signal representation is done in the complex plane for both ADHD and HP using MATLAB 2016b software (Saha et al., 2017a, 2017b, 2017c).

Procedure

All the participants with IQ ≥ 90 were included in the study. To measure the IQ of the participant Binet Kamat Test was administered. Child symptom Inventory and Devereux Scales of Mental Disorder were administered for screening other psychiatric disorders in ADHD children and HP and to identify the ADHD symptoms in the ADHD children. Conner's Parent Rating Scale was administered to find out the severity of symptoms in ADHD children. To assess the cognitive functions, subtests of digit span (digit forward, digit backward) and the coding, and cancellation task of WICS-IV were administered. The digit span task helped to evaluate sustained attention, freedom from distractibility, and working memory function. The processing speed and visuo-motor coordination were assessed on coding and cancellation tasks. Then, resting-state EEG was recorded for 7 min in the eye-closed resting conditions while seated on a chair, followed by ERP recording, following the standardized protocol. All the caregivers of the participant provided consent to participate in the study, and institutional ethical clearance was obtained.

Computerized cognitive training was done using Captain's Log Brain Train software (Sandford, 2012) in the domain of selective and sustained attention, working memory, processing speed, response inhibition and problem-solving skills. These programmes were presented in a combined visual auditory mode. The cognitive training was given for 36 min twice a week for 35 sessions, i.e., for a period of 4 months (Mukhopadhyay, 2019; Saha et al., 2015).

Rationale

We have observed in our clinical setting that ADHD children suffer from a deficit functioning of persistence that hinders them from meeting the task demands. The congenial ambience makes the cognitive task- demand pleasant to the child, being blended with his/her positive affective state of mind. It creates an intrinsic goal-directed motivation that helps the child to be in a cognitive flow state. It is a state of task absorption. Neither the assessment nor the intervention works for ADHD children unless a congenial ambience is provided to them that facilitates their cognitive flow state in them.

Reason for Difficulty of the ADHD Children Not to Maintain Necessary Cognitive Flow State

We noted that ADHD pathology does not allow cognitive absorption. In a regular environment, with heterogeneous conglomeration of stimuli, when one is bombarded with an array of stimuli, it is necessary to discriminate between the relevant and irrelevant stimuli, depending on the demand of the environment right at that moment for a given person. It is also necessary to screen out the irrelevant ones by adequate bottlenecking of irrelevant information in the information processing system and focussing on the point of interest. The processing of stimuli does not complete cognitive understanding unless the organization of the stimuli makes a meaningful gestalt relating it with other associated experiences to build up a conceptual understanding. Integration between bottom-up and top-down processing is essential to make a decision and develop an adaptive behaviour to the dynamic environment.

The total process requires the maintenance of neural recording of the flow of the events and execution upon it. However, this executive monitoring of information processing is compromised in ADHD pathology. We have noted in our laboratory that owing to their deficit in the basic attention process, including impaired selective attention, easy distractibility, failure in the sustenance of attention, and the inefficiency of working memory, causes the failure in maintaining neural recording of information for its implementation in goal-directed behaviour. It so happens as ADHD easily moves away from any task, being distracted by the appearance of any new bottom-up information in the environment. In addition, their hyperactivity compels them to move from one task to another, one place to another, disabling them to concentrate.

Data Collection

The initial assessment of the children was done through four to five sessions. In the first session, case history, behavioural observation/ MSE were recorded. In the second and third session, cognitive and behavioural measures were obtained with frequent breaks in between the session as ADHD children have difficulty sustaining attention for a long span. To understand the neural underpinning of ADHD psychopathology, we started with obtaining a child's baseline data from the performance in the cognitive tasks, like, digit forward and digit backward tasks from the subtest of WISC-IV to assess the sustained attention, freedom from distractibility, and working memory function. Coding and cancellation tasks of WISC-IV were selected to assess the processing speed of ADHD children. The behavioural measures were assessed in the domains of inattention, hyperactivity, executive function, and aggression using Conner's Parent Rating Scale, which was further corroborated by the behavioural observation of the clinician. Finally, in the fourth session, the child was taken for EEG and ERP recording, which was done following the standard procedure of the CPEPA laboratory (Mukhopadhyay, 2019; Saha et al., 2015; Saha et al., 2017a, 2017b, 2017c; Saha et al., 2019). It is comparable to the methods employed by other researchers (Bashiri et al., 2018; Swartwood et al., 2003). From the fifth session, psychoeducation of the parents followed by cognitive training was initiated. After four months of cognitive training, the same protocol of baseline assessment of cognitive, behavioural, and electrophysiological measures was repeated.

Major Research Findings

We identified two sub-groups of ADHD based on resting-state EEG profiles (Saha et al., 2019). The first group, a predominantly slow-wave oscillatory group (SWO), is characterized by excess slow-wave oscillation of relative delta, theta, and alpha waves and reduced relative fast waves of beta in the frontal and central regions and gamma power in frontal, central, and posterior regions of the brain. The total profile is related to inattention, poor executive function, and poor working memory function.

The other group with predominantly fast-wave oscillation (FWO) is characterized by excess fast-wave oscillation in frontal, central, and posterior regions of the brain, i.e., excess relative gamma- and beta-waves, with reduced relative theta and alpha power, relating predominantly to hyperactivity, impulsivity, aggression, poor executive functioning, and poor working memory. In our sample, a small percentage (18.9%) of children with ADHD was found to belong to the FWO group and 81.1% of ADHD children belonged to the SWO group. However, this distinct EEG profile in ADHD children identifies two sub-groups based on differential brain oscillation patterns.

It is evident that altered neural oscillation of either SWO or FWO is associated with cognitive and behaviour impairment (Saha et al., 2019). Either slow- or fast-wave EEG oscillations are an indication of altered cortical arousal, which is the outcome of the arousal pathology of ascending reticular activating system, indicating ADHD has an inherent deficient condition that interferes with maintaining the necessary optimal level of neural oscillation (Saad et al., 2018; Yu et al., 2019). The excess slow waves indicate under-aroused cortical functioning (Loo & Makeig,

2012), whereas excess fast-wave oscillation denotes unspecific excitation that increases cortical noise to its signal ratio (Lenz et al., 2008).

Predominantly Slow-Wave Oscillatory Group (SWO)

Considering the SWO, the finding of predominant delta waves (1-3 Hz) itself reveals ADHD's difficulty in focussing and sustaining attention, which is a prerequisite for task absorption, owing to its inability to arouse the cortex to an optimal level for processing information. Delta waves have a direct relationship with the activation of the default mode network (Neuner et al., 2014; Rommel et al., 2017), which is involved in internally directed attention, like self-related processing (Buckner et al., 2008).

Effect of Cognitive Tasks on Integrated Activation of Attention Systems

ADHD children have high sensitivity to environmental distraction and find it difficult to attend to the relevant information. To reduce the environmental distraction, the children were attended to in a sound-proof room with no extra visual or auditory distractors. The clinician was the only person in the room. This ambience helps to monitor the ventral attention network and facilitates attentional reorientation to salient and behaviourally relevant external stimuli to focus and perform the task.

The children were then engaged in tasks with active involvement, like computer-based-cognitive training in our laboratory and/or on-hand cognitive training at home, in the domain of sustained attention, selective attention, working memory, processing speed, response inhibition, and problem-solving skills. Further, with successful completion of each task, continuous virtual reinforcement was provided in the form of stars, scores, smiley stickers, or pleasant pictures (Mukhopadhyay, 2019; Saha et al., 2015; Saha et al., 2017a, 2017c). Another important point is that their successful performance itself yielded positive feedback by taking the shape of a flower/design. The child felt that it was intrinsic to his task performance and got motivated to perform. In the case of negative feedback, as it was coming from an impersonal agent, it was non-threatening and it became easier for them to accept their non-performance. The pleasantness of the task motivated the child to engage in goal-directed activity with increased cognitive absorption. This cognitive involvement with positive valence, along with a controlled motor activity to execute the task, facilitates dorsal attention networks with efficient top-down and bottom-up attentional monitoring.

Effect of Cognitive Tasks on Integrated Activation of Frontostriatal Loops

This cognitive intervention in an amiable ambience can facilitate the synergistic interaction among the frontostriatal associative, motor and limbic loops with the optimal secretion of dopamine (DA) that binds these trio-loops together in ADHD. Integration across these loops that carry information about motor, cognitive, and limbic components, through intervention, is associated with processing of goal-oriented behaviour and simultaneous suppression of alternative non-goal-oriented behaviour (Nigg & Casey, 2005; Simonyan, 2019), which modifies ADHD deficit and excess behaviour.

EEG Profile, Default Mode Network (DMN) and Task Positive Network (TPN)

We observed inattention to be directly correlated with the delta wave in the frontoparietal region and the theta wave in the frontotemporal region, which are the substrates for the dorsal and ventral attention network. The finding gets support from the parent's ratings also (Saha et al., 2017a). In the cognitive domain, the frontoparietal delta is inversely correlated with the digit forward task, which is related to sustained and selective attention function and freedom from distractibility. The right frontal delta, however, is inversely correlated with the digit backward task, which is related to the working memory function (Saha et al., 2019). Active engagement in the tasks during cognitive intervention helped them to activate the TPN, which includes the dorsal attention network, ventral attention network, and frontoparietal network (Finc et al., 2020; Simon et al., 2016), necessary for mediating attention during cognitive task engagement, supporting active externally directed orientation of attention during response selection, planning, and executive processing. These tasks have been so designed that they flexibly couple with DMN or the TPN, depending on the attentional demand of the task (Salmi et al., 2020). Regular exposure to the task was provided, for a duration of 3 min pace for each task, with an optimal level of challenge (i.e., neither too difficult nor too easy to make them feel frustrated). Task involvement for a duration of 36 min per session, with a rapid presentation, along with homework, for a prolonged duration of 4 months helped the development of long-term potentiation, which is essential for developing flexible brain connectivity that they lacked due to a neurodevelopmental lag.

Impact of Integrated Approach of Cognitive Training with Positive Ambience along with Pharmacotherapy, on EEG and Cognitive Behaviour Functions

Again, their easy distractibility, an index of vulnerable ventral attentional networks, being mediated by the relatively slow brain waves, was effectively monitored by providing an environment with minimal distraction. It also explains the reason why mild dosage stimulant drugs are administered on SWO. It helps in enhancing the DA availability in the prefrontal cortex (Berridge & Stalnaker, 2002) to integrate the functions of three attention systems. Unless the frontal lobe exerts inhibitory regulation on the information received by the parietal lobe from the extra-personal area, it causes a cacophony of neural noise in the neural circuit that exactly happens in ADHD.

The efficacy of EEG parameters in ADHD for diagnosis is better understood with reference to post-cognitive intervention changes. In the SWO, in post-intervention, excessive slow wave of the relative delta, theta, and alpha power, which are almost EEG signatures of ADHD, is reduced with improvement in sustained and selective attention, working memory, visuo-motor coordination. This indicates that under-aroused cortical functioning is related predominantly to inattention (Mukhopadhyay, 2019; Saha et al., 2019). In our study (Saha et al., 2017a; Saha et al., 2017b), analytic signal representation of the central area (C3, C4 & Cz) of the EEG signals of ADHD and HP (Figure 17.1) reveals that the EEG signals of ADHD (blue signals) have much more scatter with a larger spread from the centre in complex plane than the signal of HP (red signals). The increased surface area of the EEG signals of ADHD is related to the large amplitude oscillation of the analytic signal (Saha et al., 2017a; Saha et al., 2017b). EEG signals of low frequency with high amplitude are associated with hypo-aroused ADHD symptomatology.

Reduction in the surface area of the EEG signals that caused EEG signals (blue signals) moving more towards the centre in the complex plane of ADHD (Figure 17.2) could be the function of reduced amplitude oscillation after cognitive training (Saha et al., 2017a).

Also, our observation from the ERP case study (Saha et al., 2015) revealed decreased latency in the N1 and mostly in P3 components in the frontal and central regions. The findings indicate improved information processing during working memory tasks. Increased amplitude in the N1

Brain–Behaviour Relationship in ADHD

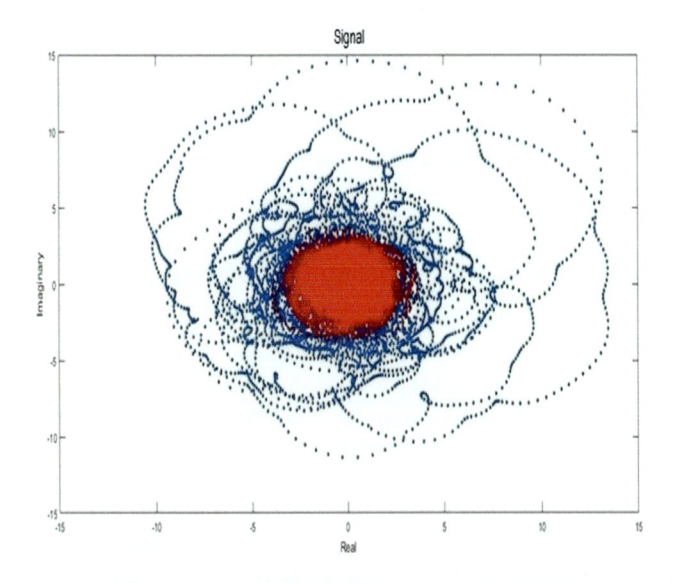

Figure 17.1 Analytic signal representation in the complex plane for both ADHD and HP is shown (ADHD – blue signals, HP – red signals)

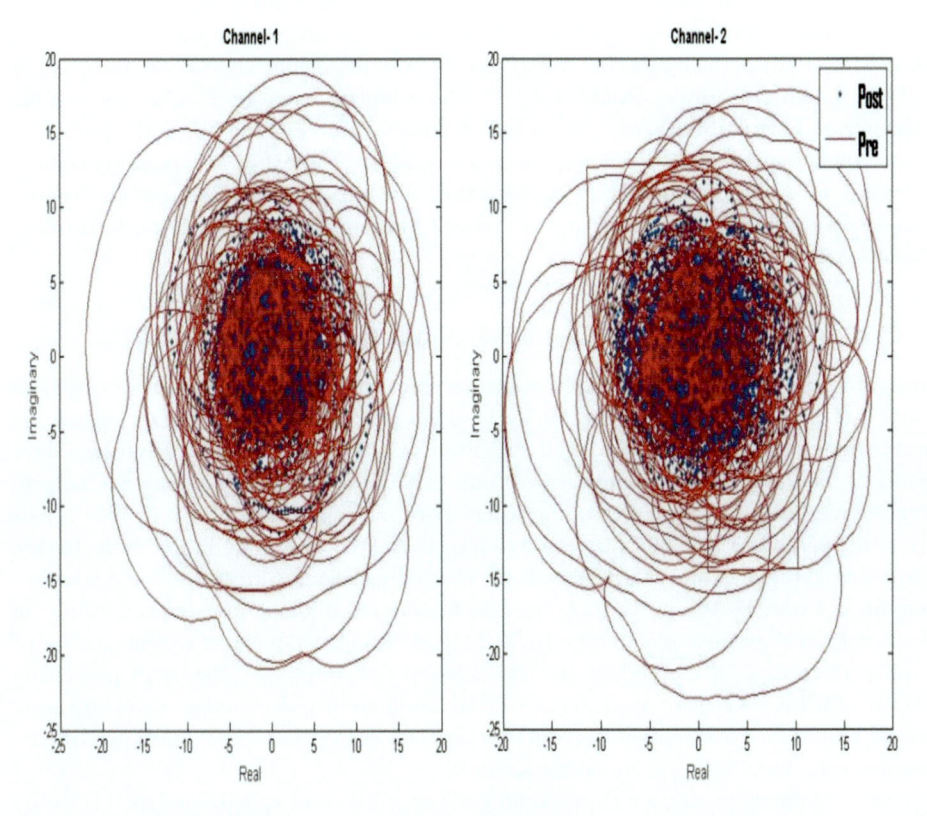

Figure 17.2 Depicting analytic signal representation in the Fp1 and Fp2 channels in the complex plane (pre-intervention – red signals; post-intervention – blue signals)

component in the frontocentral region; P3 component in the central and posterior region was evident post-intervention with improved performance in 2N-Back task that assesses working memory function (this task was presented as a visual stimulus during ERP recording), indicating improved sustained attention and working memory function (Saha et al., 2015), which is associated with better cognitive flow in task performance that justifies that EEG as an efficient measurement in the area of ADHD.

Predominantly Fast-Wave Oscillatory Group (FWO group)

Cortical fast-wave condition, in the FWO group, was also found not to be conducive to cognitive processing (Saha et al., 2019). It has been observed that frontal gamma power was inversely correlated with digit span tasks, which assess sustained attention and working memory function. The frontal beta that correlated with hyperactivity in ADHD children (Saha et al., 2017a) indicates the fast-wave beta and gamma power oscillation in the background of low power theta and alpha oscillation in ADHD is perhaps related to non-specific cortical excitation (Mukhopadhyay, 2019; Saha et al., 2019). Post-intervention reduction in unspecific excitation facilitated filtering of stimuli that increased the signal-to-noise ratio, helping them to engage in goal-directed activity with reduced hyperactivity and impulsivity and improved executive functioning (Mukhopadhyay, 2019). In FWO, a stimulant drug in high dosage is administered that acts upon the DA receptors in the frontostriatal network, targeting the frontostriatal motor loops (Diamond, 2005; Volkow et al., 2002). The stimulant medication by augmentation of extracellular DA helps to improve response inhibition, psychomotor function, and distractibility by acting on the striatum (Vaidya et al., 1998). The DA and norepinephrine (NE) are intrinsically linked via the chemical pathway (Axelrod, 1974). The stimulant medication enhances synaptic DA in the striatum by inhibiting reuptake by DA transporters and DA and NE in the prefrontal cortex by stimulating receptors. Both systems play a modulator role, NE in arousal regulation, DA in reward processing (Pietrzak et al., 2006) in the presence of reward. Both catecholamines target to facilitate executive functioning in ADHD children through neuromodulation of frontostriatal circuits.

Critical Summarizing of Brain-Behaviour Relationship in ADHD

If pharmacotherapy were the endpoint of the treatment of ADHD, the question of cognitive or behavioural intervention could be irrelevant. However, when the ADHD children on pharmacotherapy report to the clinic, their symptom was at a quite elevated level even after 12 months of medication. It prompted us to think that the medicine alone may not help in symptom reduction. The children belonging to either of the sub-groups (SWO or FWO) first reported to the psychologist with a very elevated level of ADHD symptoms in the clinic. In fact, baseline data of all the measures of inattention, hyperactivity, executive functions, and aggression obtained from Conner's Parent Rating Scale indicated behavioural impairment. Also, the performance in the digit forward and digit backward task from the subtests of working memory index and performance in the coding and cancellation task from the subtests of processing speed index of WISC- IV were impaired in ADHD children. It indicates deficits in sustained and selective attention, working memory function, and processing speed with poor visuo-motor coordination, even though they were on medication.

We noted that pharmacotherapy alone could not bring down the symptoms. DA availability that plays a role in volition towards goal-directed behaviour, initiated by medicine, does not become effective, unless an environment is provided that sets a goal and encourages the goal-directed behaviour of the child, rendering a behavioural direction. Neurotransmitters can be activated not by medicine only, but a psychosocial environment could be an important determinant of the release of neurotransmitters, here primarily, DA and /or NE by altering the feeling tone of a given person. DA and NE help in enhancing the signalling value of the given stimulus situation (Arsten, 2007). The associative loop is primarily concerned with the "Cool" executive function, which is higher cognitive functions including, response inhibition, sustained attention, working memory, organizing, planning, problem-solving, decision-making (Pievsky & McGrath, 2018; Rubia, 2011), and is the prime cognitive predictor of academic performance. "Cool" executive function is subserved by the dorsolateral prefrontal cortex, along with the critical neural network, encompassing the thalamus, basal ganglia, hippocampus, and association areas of the neocortex (Zelazo & Mueller, 2011).

The "Hot" executive function is supposed to be mediated predominantly by the frontostriatal limbic loop. "Hot" executive function plays an important role in the cognitive abilities required for motivationally or emotionally salient decision-making and goal-setting (Poon, 2018; Zelazo & Mueller, 2002). "Hot" executive function is subserved by the orbitofrontal and ventromedial regions of the prefrontal cortex, with a neural network including amygdala and limbic system, implicated in emotional processing (Phan et al., 2004). Integration of both systems is necessary for a goal-directed behaviour.

It upholds our observation with the ADHD children, who better responded when they were actively engaged in the task, like, computer-based training and on-hand training for home that they enjoyed more with a keen task involvement. The training had a generalized impact on self-initiation. This cognitive involvement with a positive feeling tone, along with a controlled motor activity to execute the task confirms our notion that the intervention facilitated prefrontal and frontostriatal connectivity, necessary for being in cognitive absorption and in a flow state.

Conclusion

Post-cognitive intervention recovery (Mukhopadhyay, 2019; Saha et al., 2015) suggests that the integration amongst the attention systems in cortical regions and that of the attention systems with the limbic- and associative- loops in the frontostriatal cortex in SWO; and the integration of motor loop with limbic- and associative- loops in the frontostriatal cortex in FWO, can be facilitated with the active involvement of the ADHD child during the task with a suitable goal in an amiable ambience. It enhances the synergistic interaction among the frontostriatal associative, motor, and limbic loops with the optimal secretion of DA (Doya, 2000; Dovis et al., 2015). The intervention binds these trio-loops by best utilizing the neurochemical platform provided by the pharmacological agent for effective adaptive function in consonance with the demand of the environment. This purpose is served by cognitive and behavioural intervention in clinical settings, gradually expanding it to the everyday-life situation of ADHD children. EEG can be considered an important measure for the understanding of the pre- and post-intervention brain dynamics and serve as a diagnostic (whether SWO or FWO) and recovery index.

References

Agnew-Blais, J. C., Polanczyk, G.V., Danese, A., Wertz, J., Moffitt, T. E., & Arseneault, L. (2016). Evaluation of the persistence, remission, and emergence of attention deficit/hyperactivity disorder in young adulthood. *JAMA Psychiatry, 73*(7), 713–720. https://doi.org/10.1001/jamapsychiatry.2016.0465

Amer, D. A., Mona, Y., Rakhawy, M. Y., & Kholy, S. H. E. (2010). Quantitative EEG in children with attention deficit hyperactivity disorder. *The Egyptian Journal of Neurology, Psychiatry and Neurosurgery, 47*(1), 399–406.

American Psychiatric Association. (1994). *Diagnostic and statistical manual of mental disorders* (4th ed.).

American Psychiatric Association. (2013). *Diagnostic and statistical manual of mental disorders* (5th ed.). https://doi.org/10.1176/appi.books.9780890425596

Arnsten, A. F. (2007). Catecholamine and second messenger influences on prefrontal cortical networks of "representational knowledge": A rational bridge between genetics and the symptoms of mental illness. *Cerebral Cortex, 17*(Suppl 1), i6–i15. https://doi.org/10.1093/cercor/bhm033

Arya, S., Jangid, P., Verma, P., & Sethi, S. J. (2019). Psychiatric co-morbidities in attention deficit hyperactive disorder (ADHD): A retrospective clinical chart review from a tertiary hospital in north India. *Journal of Indian Association of Child and Adolescent Mental Health, 15*(1), 39–48.

Axelrod, J. (1974). Regulation of the neurotransmitter norepinephrine. In F. O. Schmitt, & F. G. Worden (Eds.), *The neurosciences: Third study program* (pp. 863–876). MIT Press.

Ayano, G., Yohannes, K., & Abraha, M . (2020). Epidemiology of attention-deficit/hyperactivity disorder (ADHD) in children and adolescents in Africa: A systematic review and meta-analysis. *Annals of General Psychiatry, 19*, 21. https://doi.org/10.1186/s12991-020-00271-w

Bashiri, A., Shahmoradi, L., Beigy, H., Savareh, B. A., Nosratabadi, M. N., Kalhori, S. R., & Ghazisaeedi, M. (2018). Quantitative EEG features selection in the classification of attention and response control in the children and adolescents with attention deficit hyperactivity disorder. *Future Science OA, 4*(5), FSO292. https://doi.org/10.4155/fsoa-2017-0138

Berridge, C. W., & Stalnaker, T. A. (2002). Relationship between low-dose amphetamine-induced arousal and extracellular norepinephrine and dopamine levels within prefrontal cortex. *Synapse, 46*(3), 140–149. doi:10.1002/syn.10131

Buckner, R. L., Andrews-Hanna J. R., & Schacter, D. L. (2008). The brain's default network: anatomy, function, and relevance to disease. *Annals of the New York Academy of Sciences, 1124*, 1–38. https://doi.org/10.1002/syn.10131

Chinawa, J. M., & Obu, H. A. (2015). Epidemiology of attention deficit/hyperactivity disorder. In J. M. Norvilitis (Ed.), *ADHD - New directions in diagnosis and treatment* (pp. 3–14). IntechOpen. http://dx.doi.org/10.5772/61016

Conners, C. K. (2008). *Conners* (3rd ed.): Technical manual. MultiHelath Systems.

Cuffe, S. P., Visser, S. N., Holbrook, J. R., Danielson, M. L., Geryk, L. L., Wolraich, M. L., & McKeown, R. E. (2015). ADHD and psychiatric comorbidity: functional outcomes in a school-based sample of children. *Journal of Attention Disorders, 24*(9), 1345–1354. https://doi.org/10.1177/1087054715613437

Diamond, A. (2005). Attention-deficit disorder (attention-deficit/ hyperactivity disorder without hyperactivity): A neurobiologically and behaviorally distinct disorder from attention-deficit/hyperactivity disorder (with hyperactivity). *Development and Psychopathology, 17*(3), 807–825. https://doi.org/10.1017/S0954579405050388

Döpfner, M., Breuer, D., Wille, N., Erhart, M., Sieberer, R. U., & BELLA Study Group. (2008). How often do children meet ICD-10/DSM-IV criteria of attention deficit-/hyperactivity disorder and hyperkinetic disorder? Parent-based prevalence rates in a national sample-results of the BELLA study. *European Child & Adolescent Psychiatry, 17*(Supplement 1), 59–70. https://doi.org/10.1007/s00787-008-1007-y

Dovis, S., Van der Oord, S., Wiers, R. W., & Prins, P. J. (2015). Improving executive functioning in children with ADHD: training multiple executive functions within the context of a computer game. a randomized double-blind placebo-controlled trial. *PLoS One, 10*(4), e0121651. https://doi.org/10.1371/journal.pone.0121651

Doya, K. (2000). Complementary roles of basal ganglia and cerebellum in learning and motor control. *Current Opinion in Neurobiology, 10*(6), 732–739. https://doi.org/10.1016/s0959-4388(00)00153-7

Faraone, S. V., Asherson, P., Banaschewski, T., Biederman, J., Buitelaar, J. K., Ramos-Quiroga, J. A., Rohde, L. A., Sonuga-Barke, E. J., Tannock, R., & Franke, B. (2015). Attention-deficit/hyperactivity disorder. *Nature Reviews: Disease Primers, 1*, 15020. https://doi.org/10.1038/nrdp.2015.20

Finc, K., Bonna, K., He, X., Lydon-Staley, D. M., Kühn, S., Duch, W., & Bassett, D. S. (2020). Dynamic reconfiguration of functional brain networks during working memory training. *Nature Communications, 11*(1), 2435. https://doi.org/10.1038/s41467-020-15631-z

Gadow, K. D., & Sprafkin, J. (2002). *Child Symptom Inventory-4: Technical manual*. Checkmate Plus.

Johnson, K. A., Wiersema, J. R., & Kuntsi, J. (2009). What would Karl Popper say? Are current psychological theories of ADHD falsifiable? *Behavioral Brain Functions: BBF, 5*, 15. https://doi.org/10.1186/1744-9081-5-15

Kamat, V. V. (1967). *Measuring Intelligence of Indian children (4th ed.)*. Oxford University Press.

Karalunas, S. L., & Huang-Pollock, C. L. (2011). Examining relationships between executive functioning and delay aversion in attention deficit hyperactivity disorder. *Journal of Clinical Child and Adolescent Psychology: The official journal for the Society of Clinical Child and Adolescent Psychology, American Psychological Association, Division 53, 40*(6), 837–847. https://doi.org/10.1080/15374416.2011.614578

Katzman, M. A., Bilkey, T. S., Chokka, P. R., Fallu, A., & Klassen, L. J. (2017). Adult ADHD and comorbid disorders: Clinical implications of a dimensional approach. *BMC Psychiatry, 17*(1), 302. https://doi.org/10.1186/s12888-017-1463-3

Kitsune, G. L., Cheung, C. H., Brandeis, D., Banaschewski, T., Asherson, P., McLoughlin, G., & Kuntsi, J. (2015). A matter of time: The influence of recording context on EEG spectral power in adolescents and young adults with ADHD. *Brain Topography, 28*(4), 580–590. https://doi.org/10.1007/s10548-014-0395-1

Lawrence, D., Johnson, S., Hafekost, J., Haan K. B. D., Sawyer, M., Ainley, J., & Zubrick, S. R. (2015). *The mental health of children and adolescents. Report on the Second Australian Child and Adolescent Survey of Mental Health and Wellbeing* (Online ISBN: 978-1-76007-188-2). Department of Health, Canberra.

Lenz, D., Krauel, K., Schadow, J., Baving, L., Duzel, E., & Herrmann, C. S. (2008). Enhanced gamma-band activity in ADHD patients lacks correlation with memory performance found in healthy children. *Brain Research, 1235*, 117–132. https://doi.org/10.1016/j.brainres.2008.06.023

Loo, S. K., & Makeig, S. (2012). Clinical utility of EEG in attention-deficit/hyperactivity disorder: A research update. *Neurotherapeutics, 9*(3), 569–587. https://doi.org/10.1007/s13311-012-0131z

Moffitt, T. E., & Melchior, M. (2007). Why does the worldwide prevalence of childhood attention deficit hyperactivity disorder matter? *The American Journal of Psychiatry, 164*(6), 856–858. https://doi.org/10.1176/ajp.2007.164.6.856

Mukhopadhyay, P. (2019, December 20–22). Post-intervention neuropsychological efficiency in cardiovascular, stroke and ADHD patients. In M. Mondal, (Chair), *A search for the connectivity between pathophysiology and neurocognitive dysfunctions and its role in formulating intervention* [Symposium]. XXIX Annual Convention of National Academy of Psychology (NAOP) India & International Conference on Making Psychology Deliverable to the Society, Pondicherry University, India.

Naglieri, J., LeBuffe, P., & Pfeiffer, S. I. (1994). *Devereux scales of mental disorders: Technical manual*. PsychCorp.

Neuner, I., Arrubla, J., Werner, C. J., Hitz, K., Boers, F., Kawohl, W., & Shah, N. J. (2014). The default mode network and EEG regional spectral power: a simultaneous fMRI-EEG study. *PLoS One, 9*(2), e88214. https://doi.org/10.1371/journal.pone.0088214

Nigg, J. T., & Casey, B. J. (2005). An integrative theory of attention-deficit/ hyperactivity disorder based on the cognitive and affective neurosciences. *Development and Psychopathology, 17*(3), 785–806. https://doi.org/10.1017/S0954579405050376

Pastor, P., Reuben, C., Duran, C., & Hawkins, L. (2015). Association between diagnosed ADHD and selected characteristics among children aged 4–17 years: United States, 2011–2013. *NCHS Data Brief, 201*, 201.

Phan, K. L., Wager, T. D., Taylor, S. F., & Liberzon, I. (2004). Functional neuroimaging studies of human emotions. *CNS Spectrums, 9*(4), 258–266. https://doi.org/10.1017/s1092852900009196

Pietrzak, R. H., Mollica, C. M., Maruff, P., & Snyder, P. J. (2006). Cognitive effects of immediate-release methylphenidate in children with attention-deficit/ hyperactivity disorder. *Neuroscience & Biobehavioral Reviews, 30*(8), 1225–1245. https://doi.org/10.1016/j.neubiorev.2006.10.002

Pievsky, M. A., & McGrath, R. E. (2018). The Neurocognitive profile of attention-deficit/hyperactivity disorder: A review of meta-analyses. *Archives of Clinical Neuropsychology, 33*(2), 143–157. https://doi.org/10.1093/arclin/acx055

Polanczyk, G. V., Salum, G. A., Sugaya, L. S., Caye, A., & Rohde, L. A. (2015). Annual research review: A meta-analysis of the worldwide prevalence of mental disorders in children and adolescents. *Journal of Child Psychology and Psychiatry, and Allied Disciplines, 56*(3), 345–365. https://doi.org/10.1111/jcpp.12381

Polanczyk, G., De Lima M. S., Horta, B. L., Biederman, J., & Rohde, L. A. (2007). The worldwide prevalence of ADHD: A systematic review and metaregression analysis. *The American Journal of Psychiatry, 164*(6), 942–948. https://doi.org/10.1176/ajp.2007.164.6.942

Poon, K. (2018). Hot and cool executive functions in adolescence: Development and contributions to important developmental outcomes. *Frontiers in Psychology, 8*, 2311. https://doi.org/10.3389/fpsyg.2017.02311

Ramya, H. S., Goutham, A. S., & Pandit, L.V. (2017). Prevalence of attention deficit hyperactivity disorder in school going children aged between 5–12 years in Bengaluru. *Current Pediatric Research, 21*(2), 321–326.

Rommel, A. S., James, S. N., McLoughlin, G., Brandeis, D., Banaschewski, T., Asherson, P., & Kuntsi, J. (2017). Altered EEG spectral power during rest and cognitive performance: a comparison of preterm-born adolescents to adolescents with ADHD. *European Child & Adolescent Psychiatry, 26*(12), 1511–1522. https://doi.org/10.1007/s00787-017-1010-2

Rubia, K. (2011). "Cool" inferior frontostriatal dysfunction in attention-deficit/hyperactivity disorder versus "hot" ventromedial orbitofrontal-limbic dysfunction in conduct disorder: A review. *Biological Psychiatry, 69*(12), e69–e87. https://doi.org/10.1016/j.biopsych.2010.09.023

Saad, J. F., Kohn, M. R., Clarke, S., Lagopoulos, J., & Hermens, D. F. (2018). Is the theta/beta EEG marker for ADHD inherently flawed? *Journal of Attention Disorders, 22*(9), 815–826. https://doi.org/10.1177/1087054715578270

Saha, P., Chakraborty, P., Mukhopadhyay, P., Bandhopadhyay, D., & Ghosh, S. (2015). Computer-based attention training for treating a child with attention deficit/hyperactivity disorder: An adjunct to pharmacotherapy: A case report. *Journal of Pharmacy Research, 9*(11), 612–617.

Saha, P., Mukhopadhyay, P., & Mukundan, C. R. (2019, December 20–22). Distinct executive functioning and oscillatory pattern of EEG in attention deficit hyperactivity disorder children. In M. Mondal, (Chair), *A search for the connectivity between pathophysiology and neurocognitive dysfunctions and its role in formulating intervention* [Symposium]. XXIX Annual Convention of National Academy of Psychology (NAOP) India & International Conference on Making Psychology Deliverable to the Society, Pondicherry University, India.

Saha, P., Mukhopadhyay, P., & Mukundan, C. R. (2017a, December 22–24). Impact of cognitive intervention for treating the children with subtypes of ADHD- A comparative case studies. [Paper presentation]. The 27th Annual Conference of the National Academy of Psychology (NAOP) on Psychology of Millennial, IIT Kharagpur, India.

Saha, P., Mukhopadhyay, P., Chakraborty, P., Poria, S., Mukundan, C. R., Sharma, S., Ghosh, P., Vijay, M., Nath, S., & Ghosh, S. (2017b). Neural oscillations in resting state EEG in ADHD children- A preliminary study. *Journal of Indian Association of Child and Adolescent Mental Health, 13*(3), 180–207.

Saha, P., Mukhopadhyay, P., Chakraborty, P., Poria, S., Mukundan, C. R., Sharma, S., Ghosh, P., Vijay, M., Nath, S., & Ghosh, S. & Bandhopadhyay, D. (2017c, February 10–12). Identifying the distinct pattern of neural oscillations and efficacy of attention training on ADHD children [Poster presentation]. International Conference on Neurodegenerative Disorders: Current and Future Perspective organised by CPEPA, University of Calcutta; Institute of Neuroscience, Kolkata; Institute of Neuroscience, Newcastle University, Newcastle upon Tyne, UK, Kolkata, India

Salmi, J., Soveri, A., Salmela, V., Alho, K., Leppämäki S., Tani, P., Koski, A., Jaeggi, S. M., & Laine, M. (2020). Working memory training restores aberrant brain activity in adult attention-deficit hyperactivity disorder. *Human Brain Mapping, 41*(17), 4876–4891. https://doi.org/10.1002/hbm.25164

Sandford, J. A. (2012). *Captain's log* [Computer Software]. Brain Train, Inc.

Simon, A. J., Skinner, S. N., & Ziegler, D. A. (2016). Training working memory: anatomy matters. *Journal of Neuroscience, 36*(30), 7805–7806. https://doi.org/10.1523/JNEUROSCI.1513-16.2016

Simonyan, K. (2019). Recent advances in understanding the role of the basal ganglia. *F1000 Research, 8*, F1000, Faculty Rev-122. https://doi.org/10.12688/f1000research.16524.1

Suthar, N., Garg, N., Verma, K. K., Singhal, A., Singh, H., & Baniya, G. (2018). Prevalence of attention-deficit hyperactivity disorder in primary school children: A cross sectional study. *Journal of Indian Association of Child and Adolescent Mental Health, 14*(4), 74–88.

Swartwood, J. N., Swartwood, M. O., Lubar, J. F., & Timmermann, D. L. (2003). EEG differences in ADHD-combined type during baseline and cognitive tasks. *Pediatric Neurology, 28*(3), 199–204. https://doi.org/10.1016/s0887-8994(02)00514-3

Tsai, M. L., Hung, K. L., & Lu, H. H. (2012). Auditory event-related potentials in children with attention deficit hyperactivity disorder. *Pediatrics and Neonatology, 53*(2), 118–124. https://doi.org/10.1016/j.pedneo.2012.01.009

Tung, I., Li, J. J., Meza, J. I., Jezior, K. L., Kianmahd, J. S., Hentschel, P. G., O'Neil, P. M., & Lee, S. S. (2016). Patterns of comorbidity among girls with ADHD: A meta-analysis. *Pediatrics, 138*(4), e20160430. https://doi.org/10.1542/peds.2016-0430

Vaidya, C. J., Austin, G., Kirkorian, G., Ridlehuber, H. W., Desmond, J. E., Glover, G. H., & Gabrieli, J. D. E. (1998). Selective effects of methylphenidate in attention deficit hyperactivity disorder: a functional magnetic resonance study. *Proceedings of the National Academy of Sciences of the United States of America, 95*(24), 14494–14499. https://doi.org/10.1073/pnas.95.24.14494

Volkow, N. D., Wang, G. J., Fowler, J. S, Logan, J., Franceschi, D., Maynard, L., Ding, Y. S., Gatley, S. J., Gifford, A., Zhu, W., & Swanson, J. M. (2002). Relationship between blockade of dopamine transporters by oral methylphenidate and the increases in extracellular dopamine: therapeutic implications. *Synapse*, *43*(3), 181–187. https://doi.org/10.1002/syn.10038

Voorde, S. D. V., Roeyers, H., Verté, S., & Wiersema, J. R. (2010). Working memory, response inhibition, and within-subject variability in children with attention-deficit/hyperactivity disorder or reading disorder. *Journal of Clinical and Experimental Neuropsychology*, *32*(4), 366–379. https://doi.org/10.1080/13803390903066865

Wechsler, D. (2003). *Wechsler intelligence scale for children- IV (WISC-IV, Indian Adaptation) Technical manual*. Pearson India.

Wolraich, M. L., Hagan, J. F., Allan, C., Chan, C., Davison, D., Earls, M., Evans, S. W., Flinn, S. K., Froehlich, T., Frost, J., Holbrook, J. R., Lehmann, C. U., Lessin, H. R., Okechukwu, K., Pierce, K. L., Winner, J. D., Zurhellen, W., & Subcommittee on Children and Adolescents with Attention-Deficit/Hyperactive Disorder. (2019). Clinical practice guideline for the diagnosis, evaluation, and treatment of attention-deficit/hyperactivity disorder in children and adolescents. *Pediatrics*, *144*(4), e20192528. https://doi.org/10.1542/peds.2019-2528

World Health Organization. (1993). *The ICD-10 classification of mental and behavioural disorders: Diagnostic criteria for research*. World Health Organization.

Yu, C. L., Chueha, T. Y., Hsieh, S. S., Tsaia, Y. J., Hung, C. L., Huang, C. J., Wu, C., & Hung, M. T. (2019). Motor competence moderates relationship between moderate to vigorous physical activity and resting EEG in children with ADHD. *Mental Health and Physical Activity*, *17*, 100302. https://doi.org/10.1016/j.mhpa.2019.100302

Zelazo, P. D., & Müller, U. (2002). Executive function in typical and atypical development. In U. Goswami (Ed.), *Handbook of childhood cognitive development* (pp. 445–469). Blackwell Publishing. https://doi.org/10.1002/9780470996652.ch20

Zelazo, P. D., & Müller, U. (2011). Executive function in typical and atypical development. In U. Goswami (Ed.), *The Wiley-Blackwell handbook of childhood cognitive development* (2nd ed., pp. 574–603). Wiley-Blackwell.

18
PRENATAL, PERINATAL AND POSTNATAL MATERNAL RISK FACTOR FOR AUTISM SPECTRUM DISORDER

Need to Understand the Genetic–Environment Intersect

*Bappaditya Adak and Santoshi Halder**

Introduction

Autism spectrum disorder (ASD), earlier known as pervasive developmental disorder (PDD), is a complex neurodevelopmental behavioral disorder exhibited in the early years of life with specific medical conditions and characterized by social deformities, uneven behavior patterns, and repetitive and stereotypical interests and/or activities (American Psychiatric Association [APA], 2013). Evidence shows that the prevalence of ASD across the world has increased more than tenfold over the last two decades, due to many factors such as enhanced screening and diagnostic techniques (Gobrial, 2018), more awareness among the common masses, etc. Although ASD is occurring globally, relevant literature shows a more substantial increase in ASD density in high-resource or developed countries; currently, 1 in 54 children in the USA is identified with ASD (Center for Disease Control and Prevention [CDC], 2020) while the percentages of school-aged children (6–15 years) diagnosed with ASD in other countries are 3.5% in the UK (Dillenburger et al., 2015); 2.5% in Sweden (Idring et al., 2015), and 2.3% in Northern Ireland (Department of Health Social Services and Public Safety, 2016); in Japan it is 181 per 10,000 (Kawamura et al., 2008). However, this may not be the real picture as the prevalence estimates from developing countries have also increased in recent times. Mexico has 0.87% of the total population (Fombonne et al., 2016); Brazil has reported 27 in 10,000 (Paula et al., 2011), while Malaysia has reported a 30% increase in the enrolment of children with ASD in recent years (National Autism Society of Malaysia, 2013). In India, the world's second-most populous country, more than 10 million (1–1.3%) children aged between 2 and 9 years have been diagnosed with ASD, as reported by a multicentric community study (Gulati et al., 2014). These findings are important because this increased rate of ASD estimation shows that diagnoses are rapidly rising over time,

---

* santoshi_halder@yahoo.com; shedu@caluniv.ac.in

even in underdeveloped and low-/middle-income countries. Interestingly, ASD is not dependent on race, ethnicity, or socio-economic status (SES); rather, it affects populations across the world and is thus a global concern (Baio, 2014). Due to the unpredictable nature of and recent rapid increase in ASD, more and more researchers around the world are investigating the field of ASD and the possible associative factors.

Contribution to Etiology of Autism: Genetic or Environmental?

Even years after Kanner's description (Kanner, 1943), the causes and contributing factors of ASD remain unrevealed to a large extent (Gardener et al., 2009). In the early days, people believed that parents might somehow be responsible for this disorder, as ASD appeared to be more common in families with higher SES. Gradually, it was clarified that genetics may be an influencing factor though only a small fraction of cases have been found to establish the association. According to studies with fraternal twins, when one identical twin has ASD, the chance of concordance in the other twin is 36–95% times higher than Sibling concordance rates (Ozonoff et al., 2011; Rosenberg et al., 2009). The rate of ASD in monozygotic twins is 90% and in dizygotic twins is 10% (Mendelsohn & Schaefer, 2008). Further studies have revealed that the incidence of gene deletion, genetic anomalies, and gene mutations are all linked with ASD (Sutcliffe, 2008). In some cases, ASD is also associated with chromosome abnormalities (Muhle et al., 2004) and monogenic disorders.

Other researchers have been interested in identifying potential environmental risk factors for ASD and have conducted several studies to explore these factors. A recent study suggests that nearly 55% of the variance in ASD could be attributed to shared environmental factors (Hallmayer et al., 2011). It is well accepted that polygenic and epistatic factors may affect neurological development of the fetus while environmental factors may interact with genetic factors to exacerbate the risk of ASD (Gardener et al., 2009). Additionally, exposure to toxic elements in the environment (such as pollution, insecticides, and thiomersal, or thimerosal in vaccines (Landrigan, 2010) and chemicals such as lead and methyl mercury can impact the development of the human brain in the first trimester of pregnancy (Kenet et al., 2012). Radiation has also been proposed as a possible environmental factor for ASD (Kolevzon et al., 2007). Similarly, environmental exposure to thalidomide (Arndt et al., 2005), misoprostol (Bandim et al., 2003), valproic acid (Snow et al., 2008), and chlorpyrifos has been linked to possible risk factors for ASD (von Ehrenstein et al., 2019). In addition, epidemiological researchers have gradually recognized the influences of maternal prenatal exposures on the development of ASD (Bilder et al., 2009).

Risk Factors during Pregnancy and Childbirth

Recent studies have also considered risk factors during pregnancy and childbirth. A common question posed by parents and scholars is whether complications during pregnancy, labor, and delivery could cause ASD. The response is that ASD may indeed begin during pregnancy and manifest a few months into the child's life. Numerous studies have investigated the significance of pregnancy-related complications in relation to neonatal ASD outcomes (Stein et al., 2006). Studies also show that neonatal deviations (neurological and psychiatric outcomes) and maternal complications have positive associations with ASD (Dean & Davis, 2007; Indredavik et al., 2010).

Prenatal Risk Factors for ASD. No single environmental factor explains the increased prevalence of ASD. Studies on animals have reported that maternal health factors, prenatal complications, and delivery care may lead to long-term neurodevelopmental and behavioral disorders among newborn children (Glover, 2011). A mother with a history of pregnancy-related and/or obstetric complications is more likely to bear a child with ASD than a mother with a normal obstetric history (Lyall et al., 2014). Researchers have continually investigated the association between prenatal incidence and risk of developmental disorders that include several risk factors for ASD such as preeclampsia (Mann et al., 2010), maternal thyroid (Able, 2012; Roman, 2007), gestational diabetes (Lyall et al., 2012), maternal obesity (Stein et al., 2006), congenital malformation (Ozgen et al., 2011), vitamin D deficiency (Cannell, 2008), maternal flu or fever that persists for more than one week (Atladottir et al., 2012), exposure to valproate during pregnancy (Gentile, 2011), prenatal exposure to ultrasound (Rodgers, 2006), history of miscarriage or abortion in the first four months (Robin, 2006), herpes (Magaret & Wald, 2017), mother's infections (Atladottir et al., 2010), mother's addiction to alcohol and tobacco (Butwicka et al., 2017), maternal exposure to smoking (Khalil et al., 2018), prenatal maternal stress, anxiety, and depression (Beversdorf et al., 2005; Kinney et al., 2008a), maternal bleeding (Lyall et al., 2014), malnutrition (Hallmayer et al., 2011), and maternal age (Gardener et al., 2009) etc.

Perinatal Risk Factors for ASD. Every newborn has to overcome or undergo a complex, multi-phased process of growth and development to emerge as a normal well-functioning adult. A retrospective examination of relevant medical records suggests that individuals with ASD have experienced more than one perinatal complication. Such complications, at times called obstetric complications, can be defined as deviations from the expected course of events during pregnancy, labor, delivery, or the first 28 days of life (Burstyn et al., 2010). Earlier studies have established significant associations of neonatal ASD with other factors such as gestational complications (Grossi et al., 2015), nuchal cord (Malla et al., 2017), a cesarean delivery (Nagano et al., 2021), prolonged labor (Maramara et al., 2014), oxygen deprivation or hypoxia (Kolevzon et al., 2007), abnormal gestational age (35 or 42 weeks) (Brimacombe et al., 2007; Larsson et al., 2005), breech presentation, and low APGAR (Appearance, Pulse, Grimace, Activity, and Respiration) scores (Modabbernia et al., 2019).

Postnatal Risk Factors for ASD. Numerous case-control studies endorse the importance of the first 90 days of life for child growth and development. Any kind of deviation from the typical milestones may lead to developmental disabilities, including ASD (Chattopadhyay & Mitra, 2012). Maternal health is also important for the child's survival. Studies have shown that prematurity (Allen et al., 2020), low birth weight (LBW; Halmoy et al., 2012; Losh et al., 2012), neonatal diarrheal disease (Niehaus et al., 2002), neonatal jaundice (Buchmayer et al., 2009; Jangaard et al., 2008), and neonatal brain injury (Singh et al., 2016) are associated with ASD.

Family History. Previous research has not found any single factor that can independently explain the increased prevalence of ASD, though researchers believe that there is a strong association between familial autoimmunity and neonatal ASD outcomes. According to studies focused on families, family members of autistic children were found to exhibit mild symptoms of ASD, including social-communication deficit, cognitive impairment, the sameness of interests, narrow behavioral patterns, and other personality and psychiatric difficulties (Georgiades et al., 2013).

Besides these, several other pregnancy-related factors such as abnormal fetal presentation, fetal distress (Lee et al., 2012), birth injury or trauma (May-Benson et al., 2009), multiple births (Incerpi, 2007), maternal hemorrhage (Langridge et al., 2013), low five-minute APGAR score (Maimburg & Vaeth, 2006), neonatal anemia (El-Baz et al., 2011), neonatal infection (Zebro et al., 2014), weak or no crying, medical intervention in the first month (Gardener et al., 2009), and Rh incompatibility have been hypothesized as potential risk factors of ASD by earlier studies. However, most of these factors have been extensively studied in mothers in well-developed, high-resource regions or countries but there is very little or no epidemiological data from developing countries such as India, which promote maternal health awareness.

Emergence of the Problem and Significance of the Present Study

Even though the number of studies is increasing, the etiology of ASD has not been discerned as yet, though it is believed that its increasing prevalence is beyond any specific cultural, racial, ethnic, or geographic boundaries. There is a dearth of knowledge among professionals and educators regarding the characteristics and etiology of ASD (Barned et al., 2011; Hendricks, 2011; Sansosti & Sansosti, 2012; Segall & Campbell, 2012) and, without proper knowledge and information about the associative factors among the various stakeholders, successful prevention or complete cure is not possible. A thorough examination is thus needed in low-resource regions to establish the factors, such as environmental, which influence the etiology of ASD. Factors such as maternal infections in pregnancy, smoking, and vitamin D deficiency have not been linked to ASD in recent times. Also, the identified risk factors for ASD found in mothers from western countries need to be established from other countries before such findings are generalized. Most findings and biological mechanisms of experiments are based on animal models and researchers assume that these may be generalized to human beings. Within the overarching investigation into associative factors, it is also pertinent to study the contributions of potential risk factors of ASD among Indian mothers. Thereafter, it is vital to reassess these factors among mothers to confirm which one of the factors is not a potential risk factor for ASD. Given that our lifestyles and daily habits do get altered with environmental changes, it is likely that prenatal factors could hold an explanation for the unprecedented increase of ASD worldwide.

Methodology

Objective

The purpose of this study is to identify probable maternal risk factors for ASD. The study calls for a quantitative approach and intends to understand maternal health conditions, various exposures, and related triggers for ASD in order to understand the need for genetic–environmental intersectional factors.

Operational Definition of Probable Maternal Risk Factors of ASD

The term 'probable maternal risk factor for ASD' in this study refers to prenatal, perinatal, and postnatal conditions or factors related to maternal and child health including information regarding mothers and their children with ASD from the beginning of conception through gestation, labor, delivery, and the first 90 days of life.

Nature of Sample

Designed as a case-control type study, this study selected 100 mothers of children with ASD (already diagnosed with ASD) for data collection from 13 special schools in Kolkata. The simple random sampling technique was used to satisfy the study's inclusion and exclusion criteria. The samples comprised 100 mothers with a total of 74 males (74%) and 26 females (26%) with children, aged between 3 and 15 years diagnosed with moderate to severe ASD. In the control group, 100 mothers were selected randomly (maintaining inclusion and exclusion criteria) from three schools in Kolkata and Howrah city having a total of 60 males (60%) and 40 females (40%) with children, aged between 3 and 15 years. Subjects were matched for age, gender, and SES.

Tools Used

(a) General Information Schedule (GIS)

GIS comprised information such as (child's) gender, age, habitat, and religion, diagnosis age, grade in school, school type (according to cascade system), living conditions, and behavioral characteristics, and (parent's) education, occupation, SES, and family structure (joint/nuclear).

(b) Childhood Autism Rating Scale (CARS)

Originally developed and standardized by Schopler, Reichler, and Renner (1986), the Childhood Autism Rating Scale (CARS) is meant to identify the presence of ASD and assess the severity of autism symptoms in children. It rates the child on a seven-point Likert scale, from one to seven categories in each of 15 dimensions relating to people, emotional response, imitation, body use, object use, listening response, fear or nervousness, verbal communication, non-verbal communication, activity level, consistency of intellectual response, adaptation to change, visual response, taste, smell, touch response, and general impression. Ratings from within normal limits to a severely abnormal range are based on observations and parent interviews. The total score, generated from the 15 dimensions, provides a rating in one of three categories: non-autistic, mild to moderately autistic, and severely autistic.

The reliability of CARS (Schopler et al., 1980) was .94, indicating a high degree of internal consistency. Also, the average inter-rater reliability of .71 indicated good agreement between these raters. The test–retest correlation was .88 (p< .01). The criterion-related validity of CARS was determined through a comparison of total scores to clinical ratings obtained during the same diagnostic sessions by a child psychologist and a child psychiatrist. The resulting correlation r = .84 (p< .001) indicates that the CARS scores have high validity when compared with the criterion clinical ratings.

(c) Risk Factors for Autism Spectrum Disorder Interview Schedule (RFASDIS)

This semi-structured interview schedule for parents, to explore the probable maternal risk factors for ASD, is designed based on existing literature and includes factors specific to the Indian context. The schedule consisted of three broad dimensions (prenatal, perinatal, and postnatal) and included family history, comprising 34 subdimensions framed with 138 items designed to retrieve responses following a quantitative approach. The items described events during an infant's gestation, birth, and first six months of life as well as the mother's prenatal history including disease, medication, substance addiction, abortion/miscarriage, bleeding, age, and family history.

After development, the tool was standardized by administering a sample of 40 mothers of children with ASD to estimate its reliability and validity. To ensure the validity of the interview schedule, an inter-rater agreement was attained from five eminent experts and professionals in the field of ASD and developmental disability to rate the items on a three-point scale, namely *agree* = 1, *disagree*= 2, and *doubtful* or *don't know*= 0. The experts were from the fields of special education, psychology, and psychiatry, with over a decade of experience working in proximity with autistic children and their families. Only those items were selected and retained for the final study that were in consensus with all the experts. The overall inter-rater agreement across all categories was 81.76% (range 50–100% for individual categories). To determine the reliability of the test items through Kuder, Richardson-20 shows that the internal consistency of the test was .71 (p < .05), indicating high reliability.

Results and Interpretation

Table 18.1 provides a general description of the nature of the sample.

Table 18.1 provides a general description of the nature of the sample. Most case mothers belonged to urban areas (residing in and around Kolkata), were aged between 25 and 35 years, hailed from high SES, were highly educated, and served as the primary caregivers for their children. The study results show that most of the control group mothers were aged below 30 years, which was also statistically significant ($X^2 = 13.34$; $p = 0.01$). Many factors listed in the section titled 'Method' have zero occurrence in either group; case or control. Only those factors were reported and presented with significant results.

Results of Unadjusted Analyses
Results of Unadjusted Analyses of Prenatal Risk Factors

The results show that, with unadjusted analyses, maternal conditions during pregnancy were found to be significant risk factors for ASD (Table 18.2). In cases where the expected frequency was relatively too small, the Fisher Exact Probability Test was done to bring in close to true probability. The following were identified as probable risk factors of ASD; indigestion, medicines for insomnia, analgesics, antibiotics, medicines for chronic diseases, threatened abortion, skin

Table 18.1 General comparison between cases and controls as regards to some demographic factors

Sample	Cases (N = 100) Number	%	Control (N = 100) Number	%	X^2	Sig level
Child's gender						
Male	74	74	60	60		
Female	26	26	40	40	3.32	0.05*
Mother's age						
Below 30 years	65	65	88	88		
30–40 tears	28	28	12	12		
Above 40 years	7	7	00	00	13.34	0.01*
Socio-economic status						
High	65	65	61	61		
Moderate	23	23	25	25		
Low	12	12	14	14	0.36	NS
Education of mothers						
College and university	74	74	68	68		
High school	24	24	22	22		
Elementary	02	02	10	10	5.68	NS
Occupation of mothers						
Job	22	22	14	14		
Housewife	78	78	86	86	2.8	NS
Marital status						
Married	83	83	94	94		
Separated	12	12	04	04		
Widow	05	05	02	02	5.94	NS

Note. *p<.05; **p< .01.

Table 18.2 Distributions, unadjusted Odd Ratio, and 95% CI for prenatal, perinatal, and postnatal risk factors and family history

	Case N	Control N	OR	95% CI	p
Prenatal condition					
Mother's prenatal disease					
Indigestion					
Yes	11	02			
No	89	98	4.5	1.02, 23.03	0.03
Diabetes (F)					
Yes	09	03			
No	91	97	3.19	0.84, 12.18	0.07
Hypothyroid					
Yes	11	07			
No	89	93	1.64	0.61, 4.42	0.32
Hypertension					
Yes	17	03			
No	83	97	6.62	1.87, 23.39	0.0009
Obesity					
Yes	06	02			
No	94	98	3.13	0.62, 15.89	0.27
Medication of mothers					
Analgesic					
Yes	08	02			
No	92	98	4.26	0.88, 20.59	0.05
Pain killer					
Yes	03	00			
No	97	100	00	00	0.24
Medicines for Insomnia					
Yes	09	02			
No	91	98	4.85	1.02, 23.03	0.03
Antidepressant (F)					
Yes	07	01			
No	93	99	7.45	0.9, 61.73	0.06
Unprescribed Vitamins (F)					
Yes	04	02			
No	96	98	2.04	0.37, 11.41	0.68
Antibiotics (F)					
Yes	08	01			
No	92	99	8.61	1.06, 70.17	0.034
Medicines for chronic disease (F)					
Yes	08	01			
No	92	99	8.61	1.06, 70.17	0.034
Investigation with radiation					
Ultra-sonography (USG)					
Yes	92	90			
No	08	10	1.28	0.48, 3.38	0.62
Intravenous injections					
Yes	08	07			
No	92	93	1.16	0.40, 3.32	0.79

(Continued)

Table 18.2 (Continued)

	Case N	Control N	OR	95% CI	p
Threatened abortion					
Yes	22	08			
No	78	92	3.24	0.37, 7.69	0.005
Maternal infection					
Measles (F)					
Yes	04	02			
No	96	98	2.04	0.37, 11.41	0.68
Chicken pox (F)					
Yes	04	01			
No	96	99	4.13	0.45, 37.57	0.36
Herpes (F)					
Yes	03	00			
No	97	100	00	00	0.24
Skin infections					
Yes	14	03			
No	86	97	5.26	1.46, 18.93	0.05
Urinary infection *E. coli/B. coli* (F)					
Yes	03	01			
No	97	99	3.06	0.31, 29.95	0.62
Substance use during pregnancy					
Alcohol (hard)					
Yes	03	02			
No	97	98	1.52	0.25, 9.27	1
Tobacco (oral) (F)					
Yes	03	00			
No	97	100	00	00	0.24
Tobacco (smoking)					
Yes	06	02			
No	94	98	3.13	0.62, 15.89	0.28
Passive smoking					
Yes	19	19			
No	81	81	1	0.49, 2.03	1
Prenatal psychological environment					
Abusive family and work environment					
Yes	24	08			
No	76	92	3.63	1.54, 8.55	0.002
Mental and physical assortment					
Yes	21	09			
No	79	91	2.69	1.16, 6.21	0.01
Stressful life situation					
Yes	39	24			
No	61	76	2.02	1.10, 3.72	0.02
Any shocking Incidence (F)					
Yes	06	02			
No	94	98	3.13	0.62, 15.89	0.28

(*Continued*)

Table 18.2 (Continued)

	Case N	Control N	OR	95% CI	p
Injury during pregnancy					
Fall from height and stepping					
Yes	17	06			
No	83	94	2.21	1.21, 8.52	0.01
Bleeding					
Yes	14	05			
No	86	95	3.09	1.07, 8.95	0.02
Maternal age					
Above 30 years					
Yes	35	12			
No	65	88	3.94	1.90, 8.19	0.0001
Perinatal condition					
Difficulties during delivery					
Prolonged labor					
Yes	09	02			
No	91	98	4.85	1.02, 23.03	0.03
Nuchal cord					
Yes	07	04			
No	93	96	1.81	0.51, 6.38	0.35
Nature of delivery					
Cesarean					
Yes	76	63			
No	24	37	1.86	1.01, 3.43	0.04
Premature					
Yes	34	09			
No	66	91	5.21	2.34, 11.59	<.0001
Obstetric forceps (F)					
Yes	06	01			
No	94	99	6.32	0.75, 53.48	0.11
Delayed birth cry					
Yes	27	07			
No	73	93	15.59	6.04, 40.26	<.0001
Need for oxygen supplement					
Yes	12	02			
No	88	98	6.68	1.45, 30.69	0.005
Postnatal factors					
Child weight at birth					
Below 2.5 kg					
Yes	16	07			
No	84	93	2.53	0.99, 6.45	0.04
Child's after birth Disease					
Fever					
Yes	10	01			
No	90	99	11	1.38, 87.64	0.005
Diarrhea					
Yes	10	06			
No	90	94	1.74	0.61, 4.99	0.03

(*Continued*)

Table 18.2 (Continued)

	Case N	Control N	OR	95% CI	p
Jaundice					
Yes	10	08			
No	90	92	1.28,	0.48, 3.38	0.62
Pneumonia (F)					
Yes	06	03			
No	94	97	2.06	0.50, 8.49	0.49
Family history					
PDD (F)					
Yes	03	01			
No	97	99	3.06	0.31, 29.95	0.62
Medical/genetic disorder					
Yes	12	01			
No	88	99	13.5,	1.72, 105.94	0.001
Schizophrenia					
Yes	05	02			
No	95	98	2.58	0.49, 13.61	0.44
Depression					
Yes	17	05			
No	83	95	3.89	1.38, 11	0.006
Emotional/behavioral disorder					
Yes	26	06			
No	74	94	5.36	2.09, 13.69	0.0001
Obesity (F)					
Yes	02	00			
No	98	100	00	00	0.49
Hypertension (F)					
Yes	05	00			
No	95	100	00	00	0.05
Mental retardation (F)					
Yes	06	03			
No	94	97	2.06	0.50, 8.49	0.49

Note. F = Fisher Exact Probability Test was used to obtain p values when incidence was relatively small.
*p< .05; **p< .01.

infections/candidiasis abusive family and work environment, stressful life situation, assault, fall leading to injury, maternal prenatal bleeding, and maternal age above 30 years. The odds ratio of all these risk factors were at least two. Table 18.2 lists the frequencies of the number of maternal gestational complications.

The odds ratio (OR) for the 'indigestion' factor was found to be 4.5, 95% Confidence Interval () 1.02 to 23.3 p= *0.03*; thus it may be concluded that the risk of indigestion in the case group was 4.5 times more than in control groups (Table 18.2). The analysis revealed that the odds for persistent prenatal medicines for insomnia in the case group were 4.85 times more than in the control group, and were significant at $p = 0.03$ levels with 95% CI, 1.02 to 23.03. According to unadjusted analyses, Case mothers who took analgesic drugs increased the risk for ASD child to 4.26 times more than control mothers, and it was significant at $p = 0.05$ level with 95% CI

.88 to 20.59. So, there may be a probable link between antigenic affecting neonatal health. The unadjusted odds ratio for antibiotics was found to be 8.61, 95% CI, and 1.06 to 70.17, $p = 0.034$. It may be concluded that the risk for ASD for using antibiotics in the case group was 8.61 times more than in the control group. In case mothers who use medication for chronic diseases, the risk of neonatal ASD is 8.61 times more than in control mothers (8.61, 95% CI, 1.06 to 70.17, $p = 0.034$). The odds ratio shows that threatened abortion in case mothers increases the risk of neonatal ASD 3.24-foldin comparison to control mothers (95% CI 1.37 to 7.69, $p = 0.05$). Case mothers who develop skin infections during pregnancy have a 5.26-fold higher risk of having a child with ASD than control mothers; significant at $p = 0.05$ level with 95% CI 1.46 to 18.93. An abusive family and work environment in case mothers increases the incidence of ASD 3.63 times as compared to control mothers (95% CI 1.54 to 8.55, $p = 0.02$). Stressful life situations of case mothers increased the incidence of ASD twice (OR= 2.02, 95% CI 1.10 to 3.72), and were found to be statistically significant ($p = 0.02$). The mental and physical assault of case mothers was 2.69 times more prevalent than that of control mothers (OR=2.69, 95% CI 1.16 to 6.21), and was found statistically significant ($p = 0.01$). A fall or injury during pregnancy in case mothers increases the incidence of ASD 4.71 times (95% CI 1.21 to 8.52) more than in control mothers, as was found statistically significant ($p = 0.01$). Maternal age above 30 in case mothers increases the chance of ASD 3.94 times more than in control mothers (95% CI 1.90 to 8.19) and was found statistically significant ($p = 0.0001$). All results are indicated in Table 18.2.

Maternal bleeding during pregnancy increases the incidence of ASD 3.09 times more in case mothers than in control mothers (95% CI 1.07 to 8.95) and is found to be statistically significant (0.02). On the other hand, the unadjusted analysis did not show significant associations between ASD and the factors such as mother's obesity, substance addiction, viral infections, and use of analgesics, antidepressants, unprescribed vitamins, and intravenous injections. Other significant associations were observed but the number of exposed controls was small and did not indicate any significant associations (Table 18.2).

Results of Unadjusted Analyses of Perinatal Risk Factors

According to unadjusted analyses, the following five statistically significant factors (Table 18.2) during labor time were identified as risk factors of ASD; prolonged labor, premature birth, cesarean delivery, delayed birth cry, and need for supplementary oxygen. The probability of the observed results under prolonged labor was very small, $p = 0.03$ levels. Thus, it may be concluded that there is a significant relation between prolonged labor and the incidence of ASD. The odds of prolonged labor were significantly greater for case mothers than for control mothers (OR= 4.85, 95% CI 1.02 to 23.03). The odds of premature birth were 5.21 times greater for mothers with autistic children, as compared to mothers in the control group. So, it may be concluded that there is a significant association between premature birth and the incidence of ASD as found statistically significant (95% CI 2.34 to 11.59, $p = .0001$). In response to a cesarean section, case mothers increased the incidence 1.86 times more than control mothers and it was significant at a $p = 0.04$ level with 95% CI 1.01 to 3.43. The inference is that there is a significant association between cesarean delivery and the incidence of ASD.

The incidence of a delayed birth cry was more prevalent in case children with an odds ratio of 15.59 as found statistically significant at $p = 0.0001$ level with 95% CI 6.04 to 40.26. It may be concluded that a delayed birth cry is significantly associated with the incidence of ASD (Table 18.2).

In case mothers, the need for supplementary oxygen during birth was 6.68 times more than in control group mothers, and it was found statistically significant at $p = 0.005$ levels with 95%

CI 1.45 to 30.69. This implies that there might be an association between oxygen supplementation and the incidence of ASD.

Meanwhile, the factors of rounded embolic cord in the neck (7% cases and 4% control) and obstetric forceps or ventouse (6% cases and 1% control) were found statistically insignificant so it may be concluded that there is a low association between the incidence of ASD and cases of nuchal cord and forceps delivery.

Results of Unadjusted Analyses of Postnatal Risk Factors

The factors of LBW, neonatal fever, and neonatal diarrhea were found statistically significant. Table 18.2 also shows that LBW was more prevalent in the case group, with a 2.53-fold increase in the incidence of ASD in comparison to the control group and was statistically significant at $p = 0.04$ levels with 95% CI 0.99 to 6.45.

The prevalence of neonatal fever was much greater in the case group 11 times the incidence of ASD in comparison to control group was statistically significant at $p = 0.005$ levels with 95% CI 1.38 to 87.64. Thus, it may be concluded that there might be an association between neonatal fever and the incidence of ASD.

Also, neonatal diarrhea was more prevalent in the case group with odds of 1.74 in comparison to the control group and was found statistically significant at $p = 0.003$ with 95% CI 0.61 to 4.99. Based on this result, it may be assumed that neonatal diarrhea is associated with the incidence of ASD.

Meanwhile, neonatal jaundice (10% in the case group, 8% in the control group) and pneumonia (6% case, 3% control) were found insignificant as the value crossed 0.05 levels.

Results of Unadjusted Analyses of Family History

The factors of medical/genetic disorders, emotional/behavioral disorders, and hypertension in family members (maternal or paternal) were found statistically significant (Table 18.2). Medical/genetic disorders were found to be statistically significant, with much greater incidences in the case group compared to the control group, indicating a 13.5-fold increase in the incidence of ASD ($p = 0.001$ 95% CI 1.72, 105.94).

The probability of the observed results under emotional/behavioral disorders was very small ($p = 0.0001$). It may be concluded that there is a significant association between emotional/behavioral disorders and the incidence of ASD.

Hypertension among family members of the case group is much higher than in the control group and is statistically significant ($p = 0.05$). Meanwhile, the factors of PDD (3% in case group, 1% in control group), schizophrenia (5% case, 2% control), obesity (2% case, 0% control), and Mental Retardation (MR) (6% case, 3% control) were found statistically insignificant (Table 18.2).

Adjusted Analyses

Adjusted analysis was carried out with an odds ratio for the prenatal, perinatal, and postnatal factors and certain factors were found to be significant, namely history of the family including frequent maternal indigestion, prenatal maternal hypertension, use of antigenic, use of unprescribed medicines, use of antibiotics, abortion, skin infection, injury due to a fall, abusive family environment, mental and physical harms, stressful life situation, vaginal bleeding, maternal age above 30, cesarean delivery, prematurity, delayed birth cry, need for oxygen supplement, LBW, general/medical disease, depression, emotional/behavioral disorder, and hypertension. After

Table 18.3 Adjusted association between autism and risk Factor

	aOR	95%CI	p
Prenatal factors			
Indigestion	1.27	.166, 9.63	.82
Mother's hypertension	2.22	.45, 11.03	.33
Antigenic/analgesic	2.93	.29, 30.09	.36
Unprescribed medicine	.54	.049, 5.99	.62
Antibiotics	2.00	.163, 24.60	.59
Abortion	3.46	1.13, 10.58	.03
Skin infection	3.67	.60, 22.54	.16
Injury from height	3.04	.73, 12.62	.13
Abusive family	3.46	1.09, 11.03	.03
Mental and physical assortment	1.52	.38, 6.007	.55
Stressful life situation	1.47	.57, 3.89	.44
Vaginal bleeding	.72	.137, 3.75	.69
Mother's age above 30 years	5.14	1.93, 13.70	.001
Perinatal risk factors			
Cesarean delivery	1.71	.70, 4.23	.24
Premature child	2.55	.72, 9.07	.15
Delayed cry	4.67	1.35, 16.13	
Need for Oxygen supplement	4.14	.25, 69.21	.32
Postnatal factors			
Birth weight below 2.5 kg	.33	.07, 1.50	.15
Family history			
General/medical disease	17.62	1.86, 166.66	.01
Depression	7.2	1.6, 32.43	.01
Emotional/behavioral disorder	4.60	1.42, 14.95	.01
Hypertension	0.23	.02, 2.67	.23

adjusting the odds ratio the factors significant in the univariate analyses remained significant in multiple logistic regression models (Table 18.3).

The adjusted model thus showed that previous maternal abortion posed a 3.46-fold increased risk of maternal complications during pregnancy relative to control mothers (95% CI, 1.13 to 10.58, $p = .03$), and there were 57% insignificant odds of abortion among case mothers, as compared to control mothers.

Similarly, an abusive family and/or work environment posed a 3.46-fold increased risk of experiencing prenatal complications for case mothers, relative to control mothers (95% CI 1.08 to 11.03 $p = 0.03$), and there were insignificant 59% odds in an abusive family and/or work environment factor among case mothers compared with control mothers.

The results (Table 18.3) show that maternal age had a 5.14-fold increased risk of ASD in case mothers, as compared to the insignificant 50% odds in control mothers (95% CI 1.93 to 13.70, $p = 0.01$). The delayed birth cry had a 4.67-fold increased risk of ASD in case mothers relative to the control group (95% CI 1.35 to 16.13, $p = 0.01$), and there were 63% insignificant odds of delayed birth cry among case children.

In family history, the factor of general and medical disease had a 17.62-fold increased risk of ASD in case mothers relative to the control group (95% CI, 1.86 to 166.66, $p = 0.01$), and there were 59% insignificant odds among case mothers rather than in control mothers (Table 18.3). Depression among family members and relatives had a 5.67-fold increased risk of ASD in case mothers relative to the control group (95% CI 1.60 to 32.43, $p = 0.01$), and there were insignificant 75% odds of depression among the case group compared with the control group.

Similarly, emotional/behavioral disorders in the family had a 4.60-fold increased risk of neonatal ASD (95% CI 1.45 to 14.95, $p = 0.01$), and there were insignificant 60% odds of emotional/behavioral disorders in the family among the case group compared to the control group.

Meanwhile, the probability of the observed results based on the Wald Test at 0.05 level, can be concluded that the association between ASD after adjustment for these factors was not found significant. *The factors* were namely of; indigestion (aOR = 1.27, $p = .82$), maternal hypertension (aOR = 2.22, $p = .33$), use of antigenics (aOR = 2.93, $p = .36$), use of unprescribed medicines (aOR = .54, $p = .62$), use of antibiotics (2.00, $p = .59$), skin infection (aOR = 3.67, $p = .16$), maternal injury (aOR = 3.04, $p = .13$), mental and physical assault (aOR = 1.52, $p = .55$), stressful life situation (aOR = 1.47, $p = .44$), vaginal bleeding (aOR = .72, $p = .69$), cesarean delivery (aOR = 1.71, $p = .24$), prematurity (aOR = 2.5, $p = .15$), need for oxygen supplementation (aOR = 4.14, $p = .32$), LBW (aOR = .32, $p = .15$), and maternal hypertension (aOR = .21, $p = .23$).

Table 18.4 Binary logistic regression model for autism spectrum disorder

Step 1	B	S.E	Wald	df	sig	Exp (B)	95% C.I. for Exp (B) Lower	Upper
Indigestion	.236	1.035	.052	1	.820	1.26	.166	9.633
Mother's hypertension	.797	.819	.947	1	.331	2.218	.446	11.033
Antigenic	1.078	1.187	.824	1	.346	2.938	.287	30.086
Unprescribed medicines	−.609	1.224	.248	1	.619	.544	.049	5.992
Antibiotics	.694	1.280	.294	1	.588	2.001	.163	24.595
Abortion	1.240	.571	4.715	1	.030	3.455	1.128	10.582
Skin infection	1.300	.926	1.969	1	.161	3.669	.597	22.544
Injury from height	1.110	.727	2.332	1	.127	3.035	.730	12.619
Abusive family	1.242	.591	4.421	1	.036	3.463	1.088	11.025
Mental and Physical	.417	.702	.354	1	.552	1.518	.384	6.007
Stressful life	.386	.497	.604	1	.437	1.471	.556	3.893
Bleeding	−.333	.845	.155	1	.694	.717	.137	3.758
Nature of birth	.540	.460	1.378	1	.240	1.716	.697	4.226
Premature	.937	.647	2.096	1	.148	2.552	.718	9.077
Delayed cry	1.541	.632	5.945	1	.015	4.671	1.353	16.125
Need of oxygen	1.420	1.437	.976	1	.323	4.138	.247	69.211
Below 2.5	−1.127	.785	2.061	1	.151	.324	.070	1.509
General/ medical	2.869	1.146	6.263	1	.012	17.620	1.863	166.657
Depression	1.973	.768	6.599	1	.010	7.195	1.596	32.430
Emotional/ Behavioral	1.526	.601	6.440	1	.011	4.600	1.415	14.947
Hypertension	−1.543	1.289	1.433	1	.231	.214	.017	2.673
Mother's age above 30	1.637	.500	10.718	1	.001	5.142	1.929	13.704
Constant	−2.457	487	25.403	1	.000	.086		

Table 18.5 Hosmer and Lemeshow test

Step	Chi-square	df	sig
1	4.298	8	.829

Table 18.6 Omnibus tests of model coefficients

		Chi-square	df	sig
Step 1	Step	105.134	22	.000
	Block	105.134	22	.000
	Model	105.134	22	.000

The following independent significant factors were entered into a logistic regression model; abusive family and/or work environment, diabetes, abortion, frequent indigestion, medicine for insomnia, skin infection, prolonged labor, premature birth, delayed birth cry, depression in family members, and emotional/behavioral disorders. The adequacy of the model was analyzed using the Hosmer-Lemeshow goodness of fit test [$\chi 2$ (5) = 4.30, p= .82], indicating that the model is a good fit and also statistically significant [Omnibus test $\chi 2$ (11) = 105.134, p = 000].

Discussion

This study was conducted to investigate the probable risk factors associated with ASD, and it covered prenatal, perinatal, postnatal, and family history of mothers and children. Its main strength is that information was collected directly from mothers through standardized interview schedules and that its findings were consistent with the observations of earlier researchers.

Prenatal Risk Factors of ASD

Mother's Prenatal Diseases

Mother's prenatal diseases such as diabetes, hypertension, obesity, or thyroxine deficiency have been associated with an increased risk of ASD that might occur at any time during pregnancy. One of the important findings of this study was that there is a higher incidence of *frequent indigestion* among case mothers as compared to control mothers, and the result is consistent with earlier studies (Whitehouse et al., 2018). Such indigestion may occur when the stomach remains empty for hours, leading to feelings of fullness, bloatedness, gas, nausea, and vomiting, which may cause pre-pregnancy weight change, dehydration, ketonuria, electrolyte imbalance, metabolite imbalance, and possible vitamin and mineral deficiencies thereby affecting the neonate's cognitive development (Clark et al., 2012).

This study found that pregnancy hypertension (preeclampsia or essential hypertension) in mothers had a significant association with an increased risk of mild to moderate intellectual disability, including ASD, and this is similar to other studies (Buchmayer et al., 2009; Burstyn et al., 2010). Hypertension or preeclampsia in pregnant women is a major cause of poor placental perfusion and function; is at least partly responsible for damage to fetal development through hypoxia (Ratsep et al., 2016; Brown et al., 2014; Mohaupt, 2015); and may cause poor neurodevelopment through maternal, placental, and fetal pathophysiological mechanisms (Ornoy et al., 2015). Some researchers also rationalize that abnormal trophoblast bilayer folding has been associated with ASD (Walker et al., 2013), which mount suboptimal uteroplacental perfusion during embryogenesis affecting vascular compromise progress at a disparate rate through gestation (Neerhof et al., 2008).

Earlier research has shown that *thyroxine deficiency* in case mothers, between 8 and 12 weeks of pregnancy, has been postulated to produce changes in the fetal brain resulting in ASD (Roman et al., 2013; Getahun et al., 2018). However, this study did not find any positive association between ASD and thyroxine deficit, as also shown by earlier studies (Brown et al., 2015; Lazarus et al., 2012).

Earlier research shows mixed results with regard to *maternal diabetes* as a probable risk factor of ASD (Xiang et al., 2015; Lyall et al., 2012; Buchmayer et al., 2009). This study did not find any significant association between maternal diabetes and neonatal ASD, a result consistent with some recent studies (Buchmayer et al., 2009; Burstyn et al., 2010; Dodds et al., 2011; Guinchat et al., 2012).

Weight gain during pregnancy is an independent risk factor for ASD in the offspring as is well documented and is considered an inflammatory state (Bilder et al., 2009; Krakowiak et al., 2011; Li et al., 2016; Stein et al., 2006). However, pre-pregnancy weight gain and body mass index were not found significant in this study, as consistent with some earlier research findings (Bilder et al., 2013; Suren et al., 2014).

Medication

In this study, the effect of unprescribed maternal medication was found to have a positive association with neonatal ASD, as also endorsed by earlier studies (e.g., Viktorin et al., 2017; Christensen et al., 2013). Although the basis for this suggested association is unclear, it can be assumed that a variety of medications consumed during pregnancy may cross the placenta and affect fetal development. Selective serotonin reuptake inhibitors (SSRIs) and other antidepressants can cross the placenta and harm the fetus and the newborn through breastfeeding mothers (Croen et al., 2011b; Gidaya et al., 2014). A recent population-based retrospective study reported that maternal use of antidepressants (Boukhris et al., 2016), paracetamol (acetaminophen, N-acetylp, and aminophenol), and antiepileptic drugs may increase the risk of ASD (Bauer & Kriebel, 2013; Becker & Schultz, 2010; Liew et al., 2016).

Treatment/Investigation with Radiation

Multiple ultrasound examinations during pregnancy have become a universal norm. However, whether exposure to *ultrasound* is significantly associated with ASD is an ongoing debate among researchers. Several authors have hypothesized that repeated use of ultrasound and neonatal ASD outcomes are interlinked (Rosman et al., 2018; Webb et al., 2016; Williams & Casanova, 2010). However, this study is similar to some other studies, which found no significant association between antenatal ultrasound exposure and risk of neonatal ASD (Grether et al., 2010; Hoglund et al., 2016; Stoch et al., 2012). *Intravenous injection* during pregnancy was also not found significant in this study.

Threatened Abortion

Threatened abortion before 20 weeks of gestation was found to have a positive association with increased risk of ASD in this study, and this is similar to findings of other studies (Zhang et al.,

2010; Langridge et al., 2013; Li et al., 2018). Condition of the uterus, maternal nutritional status, ambient environmental insults on the placenta, fetal genetic defects or structural variants, and overall health conditions of mother and baby are related to the mother's earlier unsuccessful pregnancy (Zhang et al., 2010). Hence, fetal damage during pregnancy may increase the risk of ASD with the probability of impaired brain development (Cunningham et al., 2010).

Infections during Pregnancy

Viral and bacterial infections in the mother during pregnancy can cause several neuropsychiatric disorders in the fetus including neonatal ASD (Adams & McAdams, 2013; Mazina et al., 2015). According to two register-based birth cohort studies, hospitalization of the mother due to maternal viral infection in the first trimester increases the risk of ASD (Atladottir et al., 2012; Lee et al., 2015). In this study, the effects of maternal skin infection rate were found to be higher among case mothers than among control mothers. According to animal studies, prenatal infection with the influenza virus is associated with ASD risk characteristics in the offspring (Shi et al., 2003). The rationale behind these findings was that viruses or bacteria may cross the placenta and disrupt fetal neurodevelopment by cross-reacting with fetal brain antigens via molecular mimicry (Braunschweig & Van de Water, 2012).

Mother's Substance Addiction

It is believed that fewer Indian women, as compared to women in western countries, are addicted to substances owing to socio-cultural ethics and moral taboos of the land. However, this study did not find any significant difference between the case group and the control group with reference to the consumption of substances, and this result is similar to other studies (Burstyn et al., 2010; Lee et al., 2012; Maimburg & Vaeth, 2006). Also, second-hand smoke exposure, as well as alcohol consumption, was found to be rare in both case and control mothers, a result consistent with earlier studies (Daniels et al., 2008).

Unhygienic and Unhealthy Environment

The factors of an abusive family and work environment, mental and physical assault and stressful life situations (causing tensions and manifested as headaches) were found to be statistically significant in the present study. Earlier studies reported that maternal stress or exposure to environmental or social stressors, including family problems, were associated with increased risk of ASD (Beversdorf et al., 2005; Frye et al., 2013; Grizenkoet al., 2012). Zhang et al. (2010) hypothesized that maternal mood swings during pregnancy may increase the levels of adrenal hormones in the mother's body and cause placental vasoconstriction, which may affect fetal cerebral blood flow or fetal hormone levels, with a negative impact on fetal development.

Injury during Pregnancy

In this study, more case mothers have injuries due to a fall from a height than the control group mothers. Road accidents comprise the most common cause of blunt trauma to pregnant mothers (Divekar & Keith, 2004). If there is a fetal limbic area injury involving the amygdala or the frontal lobe, it may lead to ASD diagnosis characteristics such as sensory disintegration, difficulty in concentration, emotional disconnection, and cortical disorganization (Newell et al., 2009).

Higher incidence of maternal bleeding, another severe complication faced by mothers, is believed to be associated with fetal hypoxia and the risk of ASD (Brimacombe et al., 2007; Kolevson et al., 2007). However, this study did not find a significant association between maternal prenatal bleeding and neonatal ASD.

Maternal Age

In this study, higher maternal age has been found to be associated with neonatal risk of ASD, as also endorsed by earlier studies (Bilder et al., 2009; Buchmayer et al., 2009; Burstyn et al., 2010). According to Kolevson et al. (2007), due to the increased risk of chromosomal abnormalities and unstable trinucleotide repeats in ova, advanced maternal age has been found to be associated with an increased risk of obstetric complications. Another proposition was that among older mothers, alteration of hormonal factors affected the utero environment and epigenetic changes also occurred with nucleotide repeat instability (Anello et al., 2009).

Perinatal Risk Factors for ASD
Difficulties during Delivery

A rounded embolic cord may cause a deficiency of blood, oxygen, and nutrition in the fetal brain and damage the neonatal central nervous system, especially in cases of severe or long-lasting deficiency (Zhang et al., 2010). Earlier research has reported that nuchal cord complication is one of the major causes of ASD and associated stereotypes and social-communication deficit (Brimacombe et al., 2007; Chien et al., 2019). This study did not find any significant results regarding nuchal cord complications.

It has been well documented that fetal distress and labor complications are significant factors causing negative impacts on neonatal survival and further development (Singh et al., 2007). Prolonged labor has also been reported to cause asphyxia, resulting in neonatal brain damage (Rodgers, 2020). In this study, case mothers have longer labor periods than control mothers; the result is consistent with earlier studies (Brimacombe et al., 2007). According to Glasson et al. (2004), less than one-hour labor induction increases the risk of ASD. Complications during prolonged labor can increase the extended pressure of traumatic brain injury, which could lead to permanent neonatal brain damage (Juul-Dam et al., 2001).

Nature of Delivery

Owing to social and medical complexities, the prevalence of cesarean sections has increased in recent times (Liphant et al., 2010). Some studies have found a positive association between a cesarean section and risk factors for ASD, but the mechanism is still not known/understood completely and is debatable (Brimacombe et al., 2007; Dodds et al., 2011; Zhang et al., 2010). This study did not find any significant association of cesarean section with ASD risk among case mothers.

However, this study did find a positive association between prematurity and neonatal ASD outcome, as endorsed by some earlier studies (Buchmayer et al., 2009; Dodds et al., 2011; Mann et al., 2010). Prematurity occurs because of placental dysfunction along with intrauterine infections and autoimmunity, which may also contribute to ASD and long-term adverse neurodevelopmental outcomes in the offspring due to anoxia (Elovitz et al., 2011; Vojdani, 2008).

Vacuum-assisted vaginal deliveries and breech presentations can cause significant fetal morbidity including scalp lacerations, subgaleal hematomas, cephalohematomas, intracranial hemorrhage, facial nerve palsies, hyperbilirubinemia, and retinal hemorrhage (Bilder et al., 2009; Burstyn et al., 2010; Maimburg et al., 2008). This study, however, did not detect the associations found in earlier studies (Burstyn et al., 2010; Gregory et al., 2013).

Delayed Birth Cry

It is expected that human life begins with the child's first cry. However, according to this study, most children of case mothers (as compared to those of the control group) started life with a delayed birth cry. These findings are consistent with earlier studies (Bilder et al., 2009; Brimacombe et al., 2007; Glasson et al., 2004; Guinchat et al., 2012; May-Benson et al., 2009; Stein et al., 2006; Zhang et al., 2010). This outcome may be associated with impairment in the delivery of adequate oxygen to the child's organs, including the brain, during critical moments of the delivery. A delayed birth cry induces hypoxic conditions leading to neurological consequences (Low, 2004).

The study found that oxygen deprivation during birth is significantly positively associated with neonatal ASD. Several researchers have demonstrated that perinatal conditions that indicate prolonged or acute hypoxia to the fetus are major risk factors for neuropsychological and neuropsychiatric disturbances (Van Handel et al., 2007; Pin et al., 2009). Neonatal hypoxia is strongly associated with a low APGAR score, cesarean delivery, fetal distress, threatened abortion, and hemorrhage during pregnancy (Kolevzon et al., 2007). It is documented that an APGAR score of 7 is a strong predictor of ASD (Driscoll et al., 2018; Gardener et al., 2009).

Postnatal Factors for ASD

Child's Disease after Birth

Diarrheal diseases, including cholera, comprise the third most common cause of death in low-income countries and are responsible for approximately 1.8 million deaths annually (WHO, 2011). For children under the age of five years, it is the second most common cause of death, after pneumonia (WHO, 2013). Diarrhea and cholera often lead to dehydration, which is a life-threatening condition. The most important clinical factor influencing the pregnancy outcome and the child's health condition in the postnatal period is dehydration related to severe maternal diarrhea (Parisot et al., 2016; Rouphael et al., 2008). Also, neonatal fever was found to be a significant risk factor for ASD in this study, as is consistent with earlier studies (e.g., Maimburg & Vaeth, 2006). The history of neonatal jaundice and pneumonia was found to be statistically insignificant in this study, again as consistent with earlier studies (e.g., Bilder et al., 2009). However, a recent study has discovered a positive association between neonatal jaundice and ASD (Amin et al., 2011).

Family History

This study found that the incidence of medical/genetic disorders, depression, emotional/behavioral disorders, and hypertension were much higher in families of case mothers than those of control mothers. In a recent meta-analysis, researchers have found a positive association between family histories of combined autoimmune diseases and neonatal ASD outcomes (Wu et al., 2015). A family record of psychiatric history may, however, confound the association between perinatal factors and ASD. Anttila et al. (2018) suggested that families of individuals with ASD tend to demonstrate a set of cognitive disorders that are not seen in other families. A large population-based study in Denmark confirmed that infantile ASD was associated with a family history of Type I diabetes, rheumatoid arthritis and fever, and maternal celiac disease (Atladottir et al., 2010). However, no studies are known to have examined whether the association between perinatal factors and ASD disappears when adjusting for parental psychiatric history.

Implications of this Study

The rates of diagnosis of ASD have increased markedly over the last several years. Several explanations have been proposed by the researchers from various parts of the world for this high estimation including modified diagnostic criteria, improved diagnostic instruments, the broader definition of ASD, uses of different research methodologies, cultural differences and greater awareness and recognition of ASD. However, understanding and awareness of the disorder appear to be quite low among the general population, parents of autistic children, and even professionals of various disciplines (Shih et al., 2009). People still harbor several misconceptions about ASD, for instance, the belief that ASD is 'childhood schizophrenia' and caused by vaccination or a 'damaged child-mother relationship' (Ruiz & Bell, 2014; Mitchell & Locke, 2015). Undoubtedly, different religious and cultural groups hold specific sets of values, which shape individual beliefs and attitudes toward the acceptance of people with ASD (Pitten, 2008). As there is no conclusive evidence of the causes of ASD, special educators and primary caregivers develop their own perceptions of it. In a recent study in China, most preschool teachers opined that the etiology of ASD is psychological and that it could be cured with proper diagnosis and treatment (Liu et al., 2016). Studies from Indonesia (Budiyanto et al., 2020), Pakistan (Arif et al., 2013), Singapore (Bin Lian et al., 2007), and Saudi Arabia (Ahmed, 2019) reveal that most primary school teachers are unaware of the basic science of ASD, as cultural beliefs significantly influence their awareness and understanding of ASD. The findings of this study have several implications for teacher educators.

First, the findings can encourage teachers and educators to accept and believe the biomedical maternal risk factors of ASD, including pregnancy-related factors associated with heredity. Accurate and comprehensive knowledge of the disorder will help the teachers in identifying pupils with ASD at an early age and guide them in executing evidence-based interventions (Cohen & Miguel, 2018).

Second, because teachers are the main collaborators in ensuring the successful inclusion of marginalized pupils (WHO, 2011), a clearer understanding of the phenomenon and its various aspects will prompt the teachers to bust many myths around ASD and orient the parents, expectant mothers, and other family members to the various risk factors of ASD and necessary care methods (Epstein, 2005).

Third, as educators are the primary providers of psychosocial support to parents and families, especially those of children with ASD, their sensitization to the risk factors of ASD and interactive gene-environment effects may help parents discard their misconceptions, break through the stigma and fear around ASD, and be better prepared to nurture their autistic child (Kim et al., 2011). With an improvement in the parents' insights into the causes of ASD and knowing about the possible associated risk factors, such outcomes might be prevented to some extent.

Fourth, the study emphasizes the need for a healthy relationship between educators and parents (and families) of children with ASD in enhancing their knowledge toward a scientific understanding of the various causes and removing various myths, and building culturally relevant practices (Yeh et al., 2004) may ensure some possible outcome in this direction.

Fifth, research indicates that people in several well-developed countries such as the USA and Canada still believe that vaccines cause ASD (Bazzano et al., 2012; Castillo et al., 2020; Desmarais et al., 2015). However, research proves that ASD is a neurodevelopmental disorder and suggests the importance of the nexus of genetic and environmental exposures rather than any single factor. The educators could sensitize the parents in this aspect.

Sixth, this empirical study can inform newly pregnant mothers and their families about the various risk factors (prenatal, perinatal, and postnatal) of ASD and advise them on the role of a healthy environment and satisfactory maternal health.

Finally, educators and mental health workers should participate in community education to inform people about the importance of genetic–environmental interactions (Byrne, 2000). Educators should also organize campaigns to remove misconceptions about ASD and to create public awareness through scientifically robust, evidence-based information dissemination. Hence, educating and informing teachers about the importance of their roles in the genetic–environment interaction will have a long-lasting impact on ensuring and promoting a healthy environment for mothers and orienting various stakeholders about ASD. There is a need for further research to identify the exact etiological factors of ASD and the ways to improve the quality of life of children with ASD.

References

Adams, W. K. M., & McAdams, R. M. (2013). Influence of Infection During Pregnancy on Fetal Development. *Reproduction*, *146*(5), R151–R162. https://10.1530/rep-13-0232.

Ahmed, K. (2019). *Teachers' Knowledge on Evidence-Based Practices for Students with Autism Spectrum Disorders in Saudi Arabia* (Doctoral Dissertations. *1701*). https://doi.org/10.7275/15005535.

Allen, L., Leon-Attia, O., Shaham, M., Shefer, S., & Gabis, L.V. (2020). Autism Risk Linked to Prematurity is more Accentuated in Girls. *PLoS ONE*, *15*(8), e0236994. https://doi.org/10.1371/journal.pone.0236994

American Psychiatric Association. (2013). *Diagnostic and Statistical Manual of Mental Disorders* (5th ed.). Washington, DC: American Psychiatric Association.

Amin, S. B., Smith, T., & Wang, H. (2011). Is Neonatal Jaundice Associated with Autism Spectrum Disorders: A Systematic Review? *Journal of Autism and Developmental Disorders*, *41*(11), 1455–1463.

Anello, A., Reichenberg, A., Luo, X., Schmeidler, J., Hollander, E., Smith, C. J., ...Siverman, M. J. (2009). Brief Report: Parental Age and the Sex Ratio in Autism. *Journal of Autism and Developmental Disorders*, *39*(10), 1487–1492.

Anttila,V., Bulik-Sullivan, B., Finucane, H. K., Walters, K. R., Bras, J., Duncan, L., ...Corvin, A. (2018). Analysis of Shared Heritability in Common Disorders of the Brain. *Science*, *360*(6395), 8757. https://10.1126/science.aap 8757

Arif, M. M., Niazy, A., Hassan, B., & Ahmed, F. (2013). Awareness of Autism in Primary School Teachers. *Autism Research and Treatment*. http://dx.doi.org/10.1155/2013/961595

Arndt, T. L., Stodgell, C. J., & Rodier, P. M. (2005). The Teratology of Autism. *International journal of developmental neuroscience*, *23*, 189–199.

Atladottir, H. O., Henriksen, T. B., Schendel, D. E., & Parner, E. T. (2012). Autism after Infection, Febrile Episodes, and Antibiotic Use during Pregnancy: An Exploratory Study. *Pediatrics*, *130*(6), e1447–e1454. https://10.1542/peds.2012-1107

Atladottir, H. O., Thorsen, P., Ostergaard, L., Schendel, D. E., Lemcke, S., Abdallah, M., & Parner, E.T. (2010). Maternal Infection Requiring Hospitalization during Pregnancy and Autism Spectrum Disorders. *Journal of Autism and Developmental Disorders*, *40*(12), 1423–1430.

Baio, J. (2014). Prevalence of Autism Spectrum Disorder among Children Aged 8 Years Autism and Developmental Disabilities Monitoring Network, 11 sites, United States, 2010. *Morbidity and Mortality Weekly Report Surveillance Summaries* (Washington, DC: 2002), *63*(2), 1–21.

Bandim, J. M., Ventura, L. O., Miller, M. T., Almeida, H. C., & Costa, A. E. (2003). Autism and Mobius Sequence: An Exploratory Study of Children in Northeastern Brazil. *Archives of Neuropsychiatry*, *61*(2A), 181–185.

Barned, N. E., Knapp, N. F., & Neuharth-Pritchett, S. (2011). Knowledge and Attitudes of Early Childhood Pre-Service Teachers Regarding the Inclusion of Children with Autism Spectrum Disorder. *Journal of Early Childhood Teacher Education, 32*, 302–321. https://10.1080/10901027.2011.622235

Bauer, A. Z., & Kriebel, D. (2013). Prenatal and Perinatal Analgesic Exposure and Autism: An Ecological Link. *Environmental health, 12*(41). https://10.1186/1476-069X-12-41.

Bazzano, A., Zeldin, A., Schuster, E., Barrett, C., & Lehrer, D. (2012). Vaccine-Related Beliefs and Practices of Parents of Children with Autism Spectrum Disorders. *American Journal on Intellectual and Developmental Disabilities, 117*(3), 233–242. https://doi.org/10.1352/1944-7558-117.3.233

Becker, K. G., & Schultz, S. T. (2010). Similarities in Features of Autism and Asthma and a Possible Link to Acetaminophen Use. *Medical Hypotheses, 74*, 7–11.

Beversdorf, D. Q., Manning, S. E., Hillier, A., Anderson, S. L., Nordgren, R. E., Walters, S. E., ...Bauman, M. L. (2005). Timing of Prenatal Stressors and Autism. *Journal of Autism and Developmental Disorder, 35*(4), 471–8.

Bilder, D., Pinborough-Zimmerman, J., Miller, J., & McMahon, W. (2009). Prenatal, Perinatal, and Neonatal Factors Associated with Autism Spectrum Disorders. *Pediatrics, 123*(5).

Bilder, D. A., Bakian, A. V., Viskochil, J., Clark, S. A. E., Botts, L. e., Smith, R. K.,...Coon, H. (2009). Maternal Prenatal Weight Gain and Autism Spectrum Disorders. *Pediatrics, 132*, e1276-83.

Bilder, D. A., Bakian, A. V., Viskochil, J., Clark, E. A., Botts, E. L., Smith, K. R., Pimentel, R., McMahon, W. M., & Coon, H. (2013). Maternal prenatal weight gain and autism spectrum disorders. *Pediatrics, 132*(5), e1276–e1283. https://doi.org/10.1542/peds.2013-1188

Bin Lian, W., Kah Ying, H. S., Henn Tean, C. S., & Kwai Lin, C. H. (2007). Pre-School Teachers' Knowledge, Attitudes and Practices on Childhood Developmental and Behavioural Disorders in Singapore. *Journal of Paediatrics and Child Health, 44*(4), 187–194.

Boukhris, T., Sheehy, O., Mottron, L., & Berard, A. (2016). Antidepressant Use during Pregnancy and the Risk of Autism Spectrum Disorder in Children. *JAMA Pediatrics, 170*(2), 117–124. https://10.1001/jamapediatrics.2015.3356.

Braunschweig, D., & Van de Water, J. (2012). Maternal Auto Antibodies in Autism. *Archives of Neurology, 69*(6), 693–699.

Brimacombe, M., Ming, X., & Lamendola, M. (2007). Prenatal and Birth Complications in Autism. *Matern Child Health Journal, 11*(1), 73–9.

Brown, A. S., Surcel, H. M., Hinkka-Yli-Salomaki, S., Cheslack-Postava, K., Bao, Y., & Sourander, A. (2015). Maternal Thyroid Autoantibody and Elevated Risk of Autism in a National Birth Cohort. *Progress in Neuro-Psychopharmacology and Biological Psychiatry, 57*, 86–92. https://10.1016/j.pnpbp.2014.10.010

Brown, A. S., Sourander, A., Hinkka-Yli-Salomaki, S., McKeague, I. W., Sundvall, J., Surcel, H. M. (2014). Elevated Maternal C: Reactive Protein and Autism in a National Birth Cohort. *Molecular Psychiatry, 19*(2), 259–264. doi:10.1038/mp.2012.197

Buchmayer, S., Johansson, S., Johansson, A., Hultman, C. M., Sparen, P., & Cnattingius, S. (2009). Can Association between Preterm Birth and Autism be explained by Maternal or Neonatal Morbidity? *Pediatrics, 124*(5), 817–825. https://10.1542/peds.2008-3582.

Budiyanto, B., Sheehy, k., Kaye, H., & Rofiah, K. (2020). Indonesian Educators' Knowledge and Beliefs about Teaching Children with Autism. *Athens Journal of Education, 7*(1), 77–98

Burstyn, I., Sithole, F., & Zwaigenbaum, L. (2010). Autism Spectrum Disorders, Maternal Characteristics and Obstetric Complications among Singletons Born in Alberta, Canada. *Chronic Diseases in Canada, 30*(4), 125–134.

Butwicka, A., Langstrom, N., Larsson, H., Lundstrom, S., Serlachius, E., Almqvist, C., Frisen, L., & Lichtenstein, P. (2017). Increased Risk for Substance Use-Related Problems in Autism Spectrum Disorders: A Population-Based Cohort Study. *Journal of Autism and Developmental Disorders, 47*(1), 80–89. https://doi.org/10.1007/s10803-016-2914-2

Byrne, P. (2000). Stigma of Mental Illness and Ways of Diminishing it. *Advances in Psychiatric Treatment, 6*(1), 65–72.

Cannell, J. J. (2008). Autism and Vitamin D. *Medical Hypotheses, 70*(4), 750–759.

Castillo, A., Cohen, R. S., Miguel, J., & Warstadt, F. M. (2020). Short Report: Perceptions of Causes and Common Beliefs of Autism Spectrum Disorder in the U.S. *Research in Autism Spectrum Disorders, 70*. https://doi.org/10.1016/j.rasd.2019.101472

Centers for Disease Control and Prevention. (2020). Prevalence of Autism Spectrum Disorders among Children Aged 8 Years: Autism and Developmental Disabilities Monitoring Network, 11 Sites, United States, 2010. *Morbidity and Mortality Weekly Report Surveillance Summaries, 69*(4), 1–12.

Chattopadhyay, N., & Mitra, K. (2012). Neurodevelopmental Outcome of High Risk Newborns Discharged from Special Care Baby Units in a Rural District in India. http://creativecommons.org/licenses/by-nc/3.0/.

Chien, Y. L., Chou, M. C., Chou, W. J., Wu, Y. Y., Tsai, W. C., Chiu, Y. N., & Gau, S. S. (2019). Prenatal and Perinatal Risk Factors and the Clinical Implications on Autism Spectrum Disorder. *Autism, 23*(3), 783–791. https:// 10.1177/1362361318772813. Epub 2018 Jun 28. PMID: 29950101.

Christensen, J., Gronborg, T. K., Sorensen, M. J., Schendel, D., Parner, E. T., Pedersen, L. H., & Vestergaard, M. (2013). Prenatal Valproate Exposure and Risk Of Autism Spectrum Disorders And Childhood Autism. *Journal of the American Medical Association, 309*(16), 1696–1703. https://doi.org/10.1001/jama.2013.2270

Clark, S. M., Costantine, M. M., & Hankins, G. D. (2012). Review of NVP and HG and Early Pharmacotherapeutic Intervention. *Obstetrics and Gynecology International*, 252676.

Croen, L. A., Grether, J. K., Yoshida, C. K., Odouli, R., & Hendrick, V. (2011b). Antidepressant Use during Pregnancy and Childhood Autism Spectrum Disorders. *Archives of General Psychiatry, 68*, 1104–1112. https://10.1001/archgenpsychiatry.2011.73

Cohen, S. R., & Miguel, J. (2018). Amor and Social Stigma: ASD Beliefs among Immigrant Mexican Parents. *Journal of Autism and Developmental Disorders, 48*(6), 1995–2009.https://doi.org/10.1007/s10803-017-3457-x

Cunningham, F. G., Leveno, K. J., Bloom, S. L., Hauth, J. C., Rouse, D. J., & Spong, C. Y. (2010). *Williams obstetrics*, (23rd ed). New York. McGraw-Hill.

Daniels, J. L., Forssen, U., Hultman, C. M., Cnattingius, S., Savitz, D. A., Feychting, M., & Sparen, P. (2008). Parental Psychiatric Disorders Associated with Autism Spectrum Disorders in the Off-Spring. *Pediatrics, 121*, e1357-62.

Dean, R., & Davis, A. (2007). Relative Risk of Perinatal Complications in Common Childhood Disorders. *School Psychology Quarterly, 22*(1), 13–25.

Department of Health Social Services and Public Safety (DHSSPS). (2016). *The Prevalence of Autism (Including Asperger's Syndrome) in School Age Children in Northern Ireland 2016.*\

Desmarais, B., Viereck, A., Berfet, S., Newby, D., Jurgensen, L., Goonetilleke, J.,...Rizzolo, D. (2015). Autism Spectrum Disorder and Immunizations. *Journal of the American Academy of Physician Assistants, 28*(10), 1–5. https://doi.org/10.1097/01.JAA.0000470526.19969.83

Dillenburger, K., Jordan, J. A., McKerr, L., & Keenan, M. (2015). The Millennium Child with Autism: Early Childhood Trajectories for Health, Education and Economic Wellbeing. *Developmental Neurorehabilitation, 18*(1), 37–46. https://doi.org/10.3109/17518423.2014.964378

Divekar, P., & Keith, L. G. (2004). Pregnancy Outcome in Motor Vehicle Accidents. *The Female Patient, 29*(2), 11–23.

Dodds, L., Fell, D. B., Shea, S., Armson, B. A., Allen, A. C., & Bryson, S. (2011). The Role of Prenatal, Obstetric and Neonatal Factors in the Development of Autism. *Journal of Autism and Developmental Disorders, 41*(7), 891–902. https://10.1007/s10803-010-1114-8.

Driscoll, J. O. D., Felice, D. V., Kenny, C. L., Boylan, B. G., & O'Keeffe, W. G. (2018). Mild Prenatal Hypoxia-Ischemia Leads to Social Deficits and Central and Peripheral Inflammation in Exposed Offspring. *Brain, Behaviour, and Immunity, 69*, 418–427. https://doi.org/10.1016/j.bbi.2018.01.001.

El-Baz, F., Ismael, A. N., & El-Din, M. N. S. (2011). Risk Factors for Autism: An Egyptian Study. *The Egyptian Journal of Medical Human Genetics, 12*, 31–38.

Elovitz, M. A., Brown, A. G., Breen, K., Anton, L., Maubert, M., & Burd, I. (2011). Intrauterine Inflammation, Insufficient to Induce Parturition, Still Evokes Fetal and Neonatal Brain Injury. *Early Human Development, 87*(4), 253–257.

Epstein, J. L. (2005). Links in A Professional Development Chain: Pre-Service and In Service Education for Effective Programs of School, Family, and Community Partnerships. *The New Educator, 1*(2), 125–141.doi:10.1080/15476880590932201

Fombonne, E., Marcin, C., Manero, C. A., Bruno, R., Diaz, C., Villalbos, M., Ramsay, K., & Benjamin, N. (2016). Prevalence of Autism Spectrum Disorders in Guanajuato, Mexico: The Leon Survey. *Journal of Autism and Developmental Disorders, 46*(5), 1669–1685.

Frye, R. E., Delatorre, R., Taylor, H., Slattery, J., Melnyk, S., Chowdhury, N., & James, S. J. (2013). Redox Metabolism Abnormalities in Autistic Children Associated with Mitochondrial Disease. *Translation Psychiatry, 3*, e273.

Gardener, H., Spiegelman, D., & Buka, S. L. (2009). Prenatal Risk Factors for Autism: Comprehensive Meta-Analysis. *The British Journal of Psychiatry: The Journal of Mental Science, 195*(1), 7–14.

Gentile, S. (2011). Selective Serotonin Reuptake Inhibitor Exposure during Early Pregnancy and the Risk of Birth Defects. *Acta Psychiatrica Scandinavica, 123*(4), 266–275.

Georgiades, S., Szatmari, P., Boyle, M., Hanna, S., Duku, E., Zwaigenbaum, L.,...Thompson, A. (2013). Pathways In ASD Study Team. Investigating Phenotypic Heterogeneity in Children with Autism Spectrum Disorder: A Factor Mixture Modeling Approach. *Journal of Child Psychology, 54*(2), 206–215.

Getahun, D., Jacobsen, S. J., Fassett, M. J., Wing, D. A., Xiang, A. H., Chiu, V. Y., & Peltier, M. R. (2018). Association between Maternal Hypothyroidism and Autism Spectrum Disorders in Children. *Pediatric Research, 83*(3), 580–588. https://10.1038/pr.2017.308. Epub 2018 Jan 3. PMID: 29244797.

Gidaya, N. B., Lee, B. K., Burstyn, I., Yudell, M., Mortensen, E. L., & Newschaffer, C. J. (2014). Inutero Exposure to Selective Serotonin Reuptake Inhibitors and Risk for Autism Spectrum Disorder. *Journal of Autism and Developmental Disorders, 44*(10), 2558–2567. https://10.1007/s10803-014-2128-4.

Glasson, E. J., Bower, C., Petterson, B., de Klerk, N., Chaney, G., & Hallmayer, J. F. (2004). Perinatal Factors and the Development of Autism: A Population Study. *Archives Of General Psychiatry, 61*(6), 618–627. https://doi.org/10.1001/archpsyc.61.6.618.

Glover, V. (2011). Annual Research Review: Prenatal Stress and the Origins of Psychopathology: An Evolutionary Perspective. *Journal of Child Psychology and Psychiatry, 52*(4), 356–367.

Gobrial, E. (2018). The Lived Experiences of Mothers of Children with the autism spectrum disorder in Egypt. *Social Sciences, 7*(133).

Gregory, S. G., Anthopolos, R., Osgood, C. E., Grotegut, C. A., & Miranda, M. L. (2013). Association of Autism with Induced or Augmented Childbirth in North Carolina Birth Record (1990–1998) and Education Research (1997–2007) Databases. *JAMA Pediatrics, 167*(10), 959–966.

Grether, J. K., Li, S. X., Yoshida, C. K., & Croen, L. A. (2010). Antenatal Ultrasound and Risk of Autism Spectrum Disorders. *Journal of Autism and Developmental Disorders, 40*(2), 238.

Grizenko, N., Fortier, M. E., Zadorozny, C., Thakur, G., Schmitz, N., Duval, R., & Joober, R. (2012). Maternal Stress during Pregnancy, ADHD Symptomatology in Children and Genotype: Gene Environment Interaction. *Journal of the Canadian Academy of Child and Adolescent Psychiatry, 21*(1), 9–15.

Grossi, E., Veggo, F., Narzisi, A., Compare, A., & Muratori, F. (2015). Pregnancy Risk Factors in Autism: A Pilot Study with Artificial Neural Networks. *Pediatric Research, 79*(2). https://doi.org/10.1038/pr.2015.222.

Guinchat, V., Thorsen, P., Laurent, C., Cans, C., Bodeau, N., & Cohen, D. (2012). Pre-, Peri- and Neonatal Risk Factors for Autism. *Acta Obstetricia et Gynecologica Scandinavica, 91*(3), 287–300. https://10.1111/j.1600-0412.2011.01325.

Gulati, S., Aneja, S., Juneja, M., Mukherjee, S., Deshmukh, V., & INCLEN Study Group. (2014). Inclen Diagnostic Tool for Neuromotor Impairments (Indt-Nmi) For Primary Care Physician: Development and Validation. *Indian Pediatrics, 51*(8), 613–619. https://10.1007/s13312-014-0463-3.

Hallmayer, J., Cleveland, S., Torres, A., Phillips, J., Cohen, B., Torigoe, T., ...Risch, N. (2011). Genetic Heritability and Shared Environmental Factors among Twin Pairs with Autism. *Archives of General Psychiatry, 68*(11), 1095–1102. https://archgenpsychiatry.2011.76

Halmoy, A., Klungsoyr, K., Skjaerven, R., & Haavik, J. (2012). Pre and Perinatal Risk Factors in Adults with Attention-Deficit/Hyperactivity Disorder. *Biological Psychiatry, 71*(5), 474–81.

Hendricks, D. (2011). Special Education Teachers Serving Students with Autism: A Descriptive Study of the Characteristics and Self-Reported Knowledge and Practices Employed. *Journal of Vocational Rehabilitation, 35*, 37–50. https://doi.org/10.3233/JVR-2011-0552.

HoglundC. L., Saltvedt, S., Anderlid, B. M., Westerlund, J., Gillberg, C., Westgren, M., & Fernell, E. (2016). Prenatal Ultrasound and Childhood Autism: Long-Term Follow-Up after a Randomized Controlled Trial of First *Vs* Second-Trimester Ultrasound. *Ultrasound in Obstetrics & Gynecology, 48*(3), 285–288.

Idring, S., Lundberg, M., Sturm, H., Dalman, C., Gumpert, C., Rai, D., Lee, B. K., & Magnusson, C. (2015). Changes in Prevalence of Autism Spectrum Disorders in 2001–2011: Findings from the Stockholm Youth Cohort. *Journal of Autism and Developmental Disorders, 45*(6), 1766–1773. https://doi.org/10.1007/s10803-014-2336-y

Incerpi, M. H. (2007). Operative Delivery. In DecherneyA. H., & Nathan, L., Editors. Eds. *Current Diagnosis and Treatment Obstetrics and Gynecology* (10th ed., 445–476). New York: McGraw-Hill.

Indredavik, M. S., Vik, T., Evensen, K. A. I., Skranes, J., Taraldsen, G., & Brubakk, A. (2010). Perinatal Risk and Psychiatric Outcome in Adolescents Born Preterm with Very Low Birth Weight or Term Small for Gestational Age. *Journal of Developmental & Behavioral Pediatrics, 31*, 286–294.

Jangaard, K. A., Fell, D. B., Dodds, L., & Allen, A. C. (2008). Outcomes in A Population of Healthy Term and Near-Term Infants with Serum Bilirubin Levels of > or = 325 Micromol/L (>or = 19 Mg/Dl) who were Born in Nova Scotia, Canada, Between 1994 and 2000. *Pediatrics, 122*(1), 119–124.

Juul-Dam, N., Townsend, J., & Courchesne, E. (2001). Prenatal, Perinatal, and Neonatal Factors in Autism, Pervasive Developmental Disorder-Not Otherwise Specified, and the General Population. *Pediatrics, 107*(4), E63.

Kanner, L. (1943). Autistic Disturbance of Affective Contact. *Nervous Child, 2,* 217–250.

Kawamura, Y., Takahashi, O., & Ishii, T. (2008). Revaluating the Incidence of Pervasive Developmental Disorders: Impact of Elevated Rates of Detection through Implementation of an Integrated System of Screening in Toyota, Japan. *Psychiatry and Clinical Neurosciences, 62,* 152–159.

Kenet, T., Orekhova, E. V., Bharadwaj, H., Shetty, N. R., Israeli, E., ...Manoach, D. S. (2012). Disconnectivity of the Cortical Ocular Motor Control Network in Autism Spectrum Disorders. *Neuroimage, 61*(4), 1226–34. https://10.1016/j. neuroimage.2012.03.010.

Khalil, N., Kaur, B., Lawson, A., Ebert, J., & Nahhas, R. (2018). Second-Hand Smoke Exposure Is Associated with Autism Spectrum Disorder in US Males but Not in Females: Results from the National Survey on Children's Health. *Environmental Disease, 3,* 8–17.

Kim, Y. S., Leventhal, B. L., Koh, Y. J., Fombonne, E., Laska, E., Lim, E. C., ...Grinker, R. R. (2011). Prevalence of Autism Spectrum Disorders in a Total Population Sample. *American Journal of Psychiatry, 168*(9), 904–912.

Kinney, D. K., Miller, A. M., Crowley, D. J., Huang, E., & Gerber, E. (2008a). Autism Prevalence Following Prenatal Exposure to Hurricanes and Tropical Storms in Louisiana. *Journal of Autism and Developmental Disorders, 38*(3), 481–488. doi: 10.1007/s10803-007-0414-0.

Kolevzon, A., Gross, R., & Reichenberg, A. (2007). Prenatal and Perinatal Risk Factors for Autism: A Review and Integration of Findings. *Archives of Pediatrics & Adolescent Medicine, 161*(4), 326–333.

Krakowiak, P., Walker, C. K., Bremer, A. A., Baker, A. S., Ozonoff, S., Hansen, R. L., & Hertz-Picciotto, I. (2011). Maternal Metabolic Conditions and Risk for Autism and Other Neurodevelopmental Disorders. *Pediatrics, 129*(5), e1121-8.

Landrigan, P. J. (2010). What Causes Autism? Exploring the Environmental Contribution. *Current Opinion in Pediatrics, 22,* 219–25.

Langridge, A. T., Glasson, E. J., Nassar, N., Jacoby, P., Pennell, C., Hagan, R., ...Stanley, J. F. (2013). Maternal Conditions and Perinatal Characteristics Associated with Autism Spectrum Disorder and Intellectual Disability. *PLoS ONE, 8*(1), e50963. doi: 10.1371/journal.pone.0050963.

Larsson, H. J., Eaton, W. W., Madsen, K. M., Vestergaard, M., Olesen, A. V., ...Mortensen, P. B. (2005). Risk Factors for Autism: Perinatal Factors, Parental Psychiatric History, and Socioeconomic Status. *American Journal of Epidemiology, 161*(10), 916–925.

Lazarus, J. H., Bestwick, J. P., Channon, S., Paradice, R., Maina, A., Rees, R., ...Wald, J. N. (2012). Antenatal Thyroid Screening and Childhood Cognitive Function. *The New England Journal of Medicine, 366,* 493–501.

Lee, B. K., Gardner, R. M., Dal, H., Svensson, A., Galanti, M. R., Rai, D., Dalman, C., & Maqnusson, C. (2012). Brief Report: Maternal Smoking during Pregnancy and Autism Spectrum Disorders. *Journal of Autism and Developmental Disorders, 42*(9), 2000–2005. https://10.1007/s10803-011-1425-4.

Lee, B. K., Magnusson, C., Gardner, R. M., Blomstrom, A., Newschaffer, C. J., Burstyn, I., ...Dalman, C. (2015). Maternal Hospitalization with Infection during Pregnancy and Risk of Autism Spectrum Disorders. *Brain, Behavior, and Immunity, 44,* 100–105. https://10.1016/j.bbi.2014.09.001.

Li, L., Li, M., Lu, J., Ge, X., Xie, W., Wang, Z., ...Yao, P. (2018). Prenatal Progestin Exposure is Associated with Autism Spectrum Disorders. *Frontiers in psychiatry, 9,* 611. https://doi.org/10.3389/fpsyt.2018.00611

Li, M., Fallin, M. D., Riley, A., Landa, R., Walker, S. O., Silverstein, M., ...Wang, X. (2016). The Association of Maternal Obesity and Diabetes with Autism and other Developmental Disabilities. *Pediatrics, 137*(2), e20152206. https://10.1542/peds.2015- 2206.

Liew, Z., Ritz, B., Virk, J., & Olsen, J. (2016). Maternal Use of Acetaminophen during Pregnancy and Risk of Autism Spectrum Disorders in Childhood: A Danish National Birth Cohort Study. *Autism Research, 9*(9), 951–8. https://10.1002/aur.1591.

Liphant, S. S., Jones, K. A., Wang, L., Bunker, C. H., & Lowder, J. L. (2010). Trends over Time with Commonly Performed Obstetric and Gynecologic Inpatient Procedures. *Obstetrics & Gynecology, 116*(4), 926–31. https://doi.org/10.1097/AOG.0b013e3181f38599.

Liu, Y., Li, J., Zheng, Q., Zaroff, C., Hall, B., Li, X., & Hao, Y. (2016). Knowledge, Attitudes, and Perceptions of Autism Spectrum Disorder in a Stratified Sampling of Preschool Teachers in China. *BMC Psychiatry, 16*(1). https://10.1186/s12888-016-0845-2

Losh, M., Esserman, D., Anckarsater, H., Sullivan, P. F., & Lichtenstein, P. (2012). Lower Birth Weight Indicates Higher Risk of Autistic Traits in Discordant Twin Pairs. *Psychological medicine,. 42*(5), 1091–102. https://10.1017/S0033291711002339.

Low, J. A. (2004). Determining the Contribution of Asphyxia to Brain Damage in Neonate. *Journal of Obstetrics and Gynaecology Research, 30*(4), 276–286.

Lyall, K., Schmidt, R. J., & Hertz-Picciotto, I. (2014). Maternal Lifestyle and Environmental Risk Factors for Autism Spectrum Disorders. *International journal of epidemiology, 43*(2), 443–464.

Lyall, K., Pauls, D. L., Speiegelman, D., Ascherio, A., & Santangelo, S. L. (2012). Pregnancy Complications and Obstetric Sub-Optimality in Association with Autism Spectrum Disorders in Children of the Nurses' Health Study II. *Autism Research. 5*(1), 21–30. https://10.1002/aur.228.

Magaret, A. S., & Wald, A. (2017). Autism Link to Herpes Simplex Virus 2 Antibody in Pregnancy Likely to be Spurious. *mSphere, 2*(2), e00106-17. https://doi.org/10.1128/mSphere.00106-17

Maimburg, R. D., & Vaeth, M. (2006). Perinatal Risk Factors and Infantile Autism. *Actapsychiatrica Scandinavica, 114*(4), 257–264. https://10.1111/j.1600-0447.2006. 00805.x

Maimburg, R. D., Vaeth, M., Schendel, D. E., Bech, B. H., Olsen, J., & Thorsen, P. (2008). Neonatal Jaundice: A Risk Factor for Infantile Autism? *Paediatric and Perinatal Epidemiology, 22*(6), 562–568.

Malla, A., Pathak, J., Shrestha, S., Pant, A., Shrivastava, T., Amatya, M. S., & Joshi, S. K. (2017). A Study on Parental Age, Pregnancy Events and Autism Spectrum Disorders. *Journal of Kathmandu Medical College, 6*(1).

Mann, J. R., McDermott, S., Bao, H., Hardin, J., & Gregg, A. (2010). Pre-Eclampsia, Birth Weight, anautism spectrum disorders. *Journal of Autism and Developmental Disorders, 40*, 548–54.

Maramara, A. L., He, W., & Ming, X. (2014). Pre And Perinatal Risk Factors for Autism Spectrum Disorder in a New Jersey Cohort. *Journal of Child Neurology, 29*, 1645–51.

May-Benson, A. T., Koomar, A. J., & Teasdale, A. (2009). Incidence of Pre, Peri, and Post Natal Birth and Developmental Problems of Children with Sensory Processing Disorder and Children with Autism Spectrum Disorder. *Frontiers in Integrative Neuroscience, 3*(31).

Mazina, V., Gerdts, J., Trinh, S., Ankenman, K., Ward, T., Dennis, M. Y., ...Bernier, R. (2015). Epigenetics of Autism-Related Impairment: Copy Number Variation and Maternal Infection. *Journal of Developmental & Behavioral Pediatrics, 36*(2), 61–67. https:// 10.1097/DBP.0000000000000126.

Mendelsohn, J. N., & Schaefer, B. G. (2008). Clinical Genetics Evaluation in Identifying the Etiology of Autism Spectrum Disorders. *Genetics in Medicine, 10*(4), 301–305.

Mitchell, G. E., & Locke, K. D. (2015). Lay Beliefs about Autism Spectrum Disorder Among the General Public and Childcare Providers. *Autism, 19*(5), 553–561.

Modabbernia, A., Sven, S., Gross, R., Leonard, H., Gissler, M., Parner, T. E., ...Reichenberg, A. (2019). Apgar score and Risk of Autism. *European Journal of Epidemiology, 34*. https://10.1007/s10654-018-0445-1.

Mohaupt, M. G. (2015). Creative Protein and its Role in Preeclampsia. *Hypertension, 65*(2), 285–286. https://10.1161/HYPERTENSIONAHA.114.04531

Muhle, R., Trentacoste, S. V., & Rapin, I. (2004). The Genetics of Autism. *Pediatrics, 113*, 472–486.

Nagano, M., Saitow, F., Higo, S., Uzuki, M., Mikahara, Y., Akimoto, T., ...Suzuki, H. (2021). Caesarean Section Delivery as a Risk Factor of Autism-Related Behaviours in Mice. *Scientific reports, 11*, 8883. https://doi.org/10.1038

Neerhof, M. G., Jilling, T., Synowiec, S., Khan, S., & Thaete, L. G. (2008). Altered Endothelin Receptor Binding in Response to Nitric Oxide Synthase Inhibition in the Pregnant Rat. *Reproductive Sciences, 15*(4), 366–373. https://10.1177/1933719107312627.

Newell, C., Newell, M., & Gillespie, B. (2009). A Research Proposal Evaluating the Effectiveness of the Brain Score and Craniosacral Fascial Therapy for Neonates. *The Internet Journal of Pediatrics and Neonatology, 11*(2).

Niehaus, M. D., Moore, S. R., Patrick, P. D., Derr, L. L., Lorntz, B., Lima, A. A., & Guerrant, R. L. (2002). Early Childhood Diarrheal is associated with Diminished Cognitive Function 4 to 7 Years Later in Children in a Northeast Brazilian Shantytown. *The American journal of tropical medicine and hygiene, 66*(5), 590–603.

Ornoy, A., Weinstein-Fudim, L., & Ergaz, Z. (2015). Parental Factors Associated with Autism Spectrum Disorder. *Reproductive Toxicology, 56*, 155–169. https://10.1016/j.reportox.2015.05.007

Ozgen, H., Hellemann, G. S., Stellato, R. K., Lahuis, B., van Daalen, E., Staal, W. G., ...Engeland, V. H. (2011). Morphological Features in Children with Autism Spectrum Disorders, a Matched Case-Control Study. *Journal of Developmental & Behavioral Pediatrics, 41*(1), 23–31.

Ozonoff, S., Young, G. S., Carter, A., Messinger, D., Yirmiya, N., Zwaigenbaum, L.,....Stone, W. L. (2011). Recurrence Risk for Autism Spectrum Disorders: A Baby Sibling's Research Consortium Study. *Pediatrics, 128*(3), e488–95. https://peds.2010-2825

Parisot, M., Jolivet, A., Boukhari, R., & Carles, G. (2016). Shigellosis and Pregnancy in French Guiana: Obstetric and Neonatal Complications. *The American journal of tropical medicine and hygiene*, *95*, 26–30.

Paula, C. S., Ribeiro, S., Fombonne, E., & Mercadante, M. T. (2011). Brief Report: Prevalence of Pervasive Developmental Disorder in Brazil: A Pilot Study. *Journal of Autism and Developmental Disorders*, *41*(12), 1738–1742.

Pin, T. W., Eldridge, B., & Galea, M. P. (2009). A Review of Developmental Outcomes of Term Infants with Post-Asphyxia Neonatal Encephalopathy. *European journal of paediatric neurology*, *13*, 224–234.

Pitten, K. (2008). How Cultural Values Influence Diagnosis, Treatment and the Welfare of Families with an Autistic Child. *River Academic Journal*, *4*(1), 1–5.

Ratsep, M. T., Paolozza, A., Hickman, A. F., Maser, B., Kay, R. V., Mohammad, S., ...Forkert, D. N. (2016). Brain Structural and Vascular Anatomy is Altered in Offspring of Pre-Eclamptic Pregnancies: A Pilot Study. *American Journal of Neuroradiology*, *37*(5), 939–945. doi:10.3174/ajnr.A4640

Robin, B. R. (2006). *Causal Links to Increased Incidence of Children Developing Autism and Related Neurological Dysfunctions*. The Autism Centre.

Rodgers, C. (2020). Continuous Electronic Fetal Monitoring during Prolonged Labor may be a Risk Factor for Having a Child Diagnosed with Autism Spectrum Disorder. *Medical Hypotheses*, *145*. https://10.1016/j.mehy.2020.110339.

Rodgers, C. (2006). Questions about Prenatal Ultrasound and the Alarming Increase in Autism. *Midwifery Today with International Midwife*, *80*, 16–19, 66–17.

Roman, G. C. (2007). Autism: transient in utero hypothyroxinemia related to maternal flavonoid ingestion during pregnancy and to other environmental antithyroid agents. *Journal of the Neurological Sciences*, *262*(1–2), 15–26. doi:10.1016/j.jns.2007.06.023. PMID17651757.

Roman, G. C, Ghassabian, A., Bongers-Schokking, J. J., Jaddoe, V. W., Hofman, A., de Rijke, Y. B., Verhulst, F. C., & Tiemeier, H. (2013). Association of Gestational Maternal Hypothyroxinemia and Increased Autism Risk. *Annals of Neurology*, *74*(5), 733–42. https:// 10.1002/ana.23976. Epub 2013 Aug 13. PMID: 23943579.

Rosenberg, R. E., Law, J. K., Yenokyan, G., McGready, J., Kaufmann, W. E., & Law, P. A. (2009). Characteristics and concordance of autism spectrum disorders among 277 twin pairs. *Archives of pediatrics & adolescent medicine*, *163*(10), 907–14. https://163/10/907

Rosman, N. P., Vassar, R., Doros, G., DeRosa, J., Froman, A., DiMauro, A., ...Abbott, J. (2018). Association of Prenatal Ultrasonography and Autism Spectrum Disorder. *JAMA pediatrics*, *172*(4), 336–344. https://doi.org/10.1001/jamapediatrics.2017.5634

Rouphael, N. G., O'Donnell, J. A., Bhatnagar, J., Lewis, F., Polgreen, M. P., Beekman, S., ...McDonald, C. L. (2008). Clostridium Difficile-Associated Diarrhea: An Emerging Threat to Pregnant Women. *American journal of obstetrics and gynecology*, *198*(635), e1–6

Ruiz, J. B., & Bell, R. A. (2014). Understanding Vaccination Resistance: Vaccine Search Term Selection Bias and the Valence of Retrieved Information. *Vaccine*, *32*(44), 5776–5780.

Sansosti, J. M., & Sansosti, F. J. (2012). Inclusion for Students with High-Functioning Autism Spectrum Disorders: Definitions and Decision Making. *Psychology in the Schools*, *49*(10), 917–931. https://10.1002/pits.21652

Schopler, E., Reichler, R. J., & Renner, B. R. (1986). *The Childhood Autism Rating Scale (CARS): For Diagnostic Screening and Classification of Autism*. New York: Irvington.

Schopler, E., Reichler, R. J., DeVellis, R. F., & Daly, K. (1980). Toward Objective Classification of Childhood Autism: Childhood Autism Rating Scale (CARS). *Journal of Autism and Developmental Disorders*, *10*, 91–103.

Segall, M. J., & Campbell, J. M. (2012). Factors Relating to Education Professionals Classroom Practices for the Inclusion of Students with Autism Spectrum Disorders. *Research in Autism Spectrum Disorders*, *6*, 1156–1167. https://10.1016/j.rasd.2012.02.007

Shi, L., Fatemi, S. H., Sidwell, R. W., & Patterson, P. H. (2003). Maternal Influenza Infection Causes Marked Behavioural and Pharmacological Changes in the Offspring. *Journal of Neuroscience*, *23*(1), 297–302.

Shih, A., Rosanoff, M., Wallace, S., & Dawson, G. (2009). Autism Speaks Global Autism Public Health Initiative: Bridging Gaps in Autism Awareness, Research, and Services around the World. *Beijing Da Xue Xue Bao*, *18*(41), 389–391.

Singh, R., Turner, R. C., Nguyen, L., Motwani, K., Swatek, M., & Lucke-Wold, B. P. (2016). Pediatric Traumatic Brain Injury and Autism: Elucidating Shared Mechanisms. *Behavioural neurology*, *2016*, 8781725. https://doi.org/10.1155/2016/8781725

Singh, U., Singh, N., & Shikha, S. (2007). A Prospective Analysis of Etiology and Outcome of Preterm Labor. *Journal of Obstetrics and gynecology of India*, 57(1), 48–52.

Snow, W. M, Hartle, K., & Ivanco. T. L. (2008). Altered Morphology of Motor Cortex Neurons in the VPA Rat Model of Autism. *Developmental psychobiology*, 50, 633–639.

Stein, D., Weizmen, A., Riing, A., & Barak, Y. (2006). Obstetric Complications in Individuals Diagnosed with Autism and in Healthy Controls. *Comprehensive Psychiatry*, 47(1), 69–75.

Stoch, Y. K., Williams, C. J., Granich, J., Hunt, A. M., Landau, L. I., Newnham, J. P., & Whitehouse, A. J. O. (2012). Are Prenatal Ultrasound Scans associated with the Autism Phenotype? Follow-Up of a Randomised Controlled Trial. *Journal of Autism and Developmental Disorders*, 42(12), 2693–2701.

Suren, P., Gunnes, N., Roth, C., Bresnahan, M., Hornig, M., Hirtz, D., ...Stoltenberg, C. (2014). Parental Obesity and Risk of Autism Spectrum Disorder. *Pediatrics*, 133, e1128-1138.

Sutcliffe, S. J. (2008). Insights into the Pathogenesis of Autism. *Science*, 321(5886), 208–209. https://10.1126/science.1160555.

The National Autism Society of Malaysia (NASOM). (2013). Retrieved from http://www.nasom.com.my/index.php?option=com_content&view=article&id=58&Itemid=54

Van Handel, M., Swaab, H., de Vries, L. S., & Jongmans, M. J. (2007). Long-Term Cognitive and Behavioural Consequences of Neonatal Encephalopathy following Perinatal Asphyxia: A Review. *European journal of paediatric neurology*, 166, 645–654.

Viktorin, A., Uher, R., Reichenberg, A., Levine, S. Z., & Sandin, S. (2017). Autism Risk following Antidepressant Medication during Pregnancy. *Psychological Medicine*, 47(16), 2787–2796. https://10.1017/S0033291717001301.

Vojdani, A. (2008). Antibodies as Predictors of Complex Autoimmune Diseases and Cancer. *International Journal of Immunopathology and Pharmacology*, 21(3), 553–566.

von Ehrenstein, O. S., Ling, C., Cui, X., Cockburn, M., Park., A. S., Yu, F., ... Ritz, B. (2019). Prenatal and Infant Exposure to Ambient Pesticides and Autism Spectrum Disorder in Children: Population Based Case-Control Study. *British medical journal*, 364, l962. https://10.1136/bmj.l962

Walker, C. K., Anderson, K. W., Milano, K. M., Ye, S., Tancredi, D. J., Pessah, I. N., Hertz-Picciotto, I., & Kliman, H. J. (2013). Trophoblast Inclusions are Significantly Increased in the Placentas of Children in Families at Risk for Autism. *Biological Psychiatry*, 74(3), 204–211. https://10.1016/j.biopsych.2013.03.006.

Webb, J. S., Garrison, M. M., Bernier, R., McClintic, M. A., King, H. B., & Mourad, D. P. (2016). Severity of ASD Symptoms and Their Correlation with the Presence of Copy Number Variations and Exposure to First Trimester Ultrasound. *Autism Research*. 10(3), 472–484. https://doi.org/10.1002/aur.1690 provided

Whitehouse, A. J. O., Alvares, G. A., Cleary, D., Harun, A., Stojanoska, A., Taylor, J. L., ...Maybery, M. (2018). Symptom Severity in Autism Spectrum Disorder is related to the Frequency and Severity of Nausea and Vomiting during Pregnancy: A Retrospective Case-Control Study. *Molecular Autism*, 9(37). https://doi.org/10.1186/s13229-018-0223-7

Williams, E. L., & Casanova, M. F. (2010). Potential Teratogenic Effects of Ultrasound on Corticogenesis: Implications for Autism. *Medical Hypotheses*, 75, 53–58.

World Health Organization (2011). *The top ten causes of death*. Available from: http://www.who.int/mediacentre/factsheets/fs310/en/index.html

World Health Organization (2011). *World report on disability*. Valletta, Malta: World Health Organization.

World Health Organization (2013). Global Health Observatory (*GHO*). Available from: http://www.who.int/gho/en/

Wu, S., Ding, Y., Wu, F., Li, R., Xie, G., Hou, J., & Mao, P. (2015). Family History of Autoimmune Diseases is associated with an Increased Risk of Autism in Children: A Systematic Review and Meta-Analysis. *Neuroscience and biobehavioral review*, 55, 322–332. https://10.1016/j.neubiorev.2015.05.004

Yeh, M., Hough, R. L., McCabe, K., Lau, A., & Garland, A. (2004). Parental Beliefs about the Causes of Child Problems: Exploring Racial/Ethnic Patterns. *Journal of the American Academy of Child & Adolescent Psychiatry*, 43, 605–612.

Zerbo, O., Qian, Y., Yoshida, C., Grether, K. J., Warter, V. J., & Croen, A. L. (2014). Maternal Infection during Pregnancy and Autism Spectrum Disorder. *Journal of Autism and Developmental Disorders*, 45(12), 4015–25. https://10.1007/s10803-013-2016-3.

Zhang, X., Lv, C., Tian, J., Miao, R., Xi, W., Hertz-Picciotto, I., & Qi, L. (2010). Pre-natal and Perinatal Risk Factors for Autism in Child. *Journal of Autism and Developmental Disorders*, 40(11), 1311–1321.

Xiang, A. H., Wang, X., Martinez, M. P., Walthall, C. J., Curry, S. E., Page, K., ...Getahun, D. (2015). Association of Maternal Diabetes with Autism in Offspring. *Journal of the American Medical Association*, 313(14), 1425–1434. https://10.1001/jama.2015.2707

19
UTILIZING ASSESSMENT TO BUILD PARTNERSHIP BETWEEN STUDENTS WITH ID, FAMILIES, AND EDUCATORS

Devadrita Talapatra*, Laurel A. Snider, and Gloria E. Miller

For students with intellectual disabilities (ID) and their families, assessments provide diagnostic clarity, access to federal programs and resources, and information for educational planning (Crane et al., 2016). The frequent interface between families, children with ID, and assessment is intended to not only ensure equitable and comprehensive services for individuals who have disabilities but also create a system for collaborative decision-making between families and schools. It is well acknowledged that families play a critical role in predicting students' educational, social, and behavioral success from birth through high school and beyond (Wang & Sheikh-Khalil, 2014). Strong collaborative relationships also decrease the likelihood that families will engage in due process or legal mediation related to special education services (Burke & Goldman, 2014). However, families often describe the assessment process as frustrating, demeaning, stressful, and potentially damaging to the relationships between school-based professionals and themselves (Ryan & Quinlan, 2017).

When reviewing formal complaints to U.S. State Departments of Education, issues related to school-based assessment represent a significant percentage of cases (White, 2014). Families note that written psychoeducational reports are difficult to understand (Hite, 2017), and verbal feedback and planning meetings are barriers to partnership instead of opportunities for teaming (Fish, 2008). In speaking with caregivers, they note that assessments contribute to the deterioration of family-school partnerships due to a "focus on the IQ number," "lack of strengths-based feedback," and "seeing just the disability" (Roach & Talapatra, 2011).

To minimize conflict during the assessment process and make certain that students with disabilities are receiving the best possible educational services, it is imperative that school-based professionals focus on strengthening the family and school collaborations. However, partnership efforts must move beyond what each system (i.e., home, school, community) does in isolation to intentional service integration across all critical contexts where a child lives and learns. With that in mind, this chapter will provide assessment considerations within a family-school-community partnership (FSCP) framework for students with ID that can be utilized by school-based professionals who engage in evaluation and testing in early childhood, middle childhood, and young adulthood.

---

* Devadrita.talapatra@du.edu

Theoretical Frameworks

Before delving into strategies, practice tips, and considerations, theoretical frameworks for this chapter, and related constructs, are presented to promote shared understanding.

Assessment practices. This chapter differentiates *assessment* from the administration of *tests*. Assessment is the clinical process of identifying referral questions, collecting data, conceptualizing student needs, and linking those needs to intervention and other next steps. While certain tests (e.g., measures of intelligence or academic achievement) may be administered during this process, conceptualizing assessment as a wide-spanning clinical practice is one of the first steps to enacting opportunities for family involvement and voice (Sattler, 2008). Within this process, there are four phases that are present across all types of assessment-related decision-making:

(a) *Referral*: process of linking a student to an evaluator to begin assessment; students may be referred for many different reasons, depending on their age, profile, and life trajectory, which informs the components of the next three phases.
(b) *Data collection*: includes norm-referenced methods, interviews, behavioral observations, and informal assessment procedures in order to gather information about the referral question.
(c) *Conceptualization*: involves comparing and contrasting available data to determine whether more information is needed or whether enough is available to answer the referral question; this phase may involve identifying an appropriate diagnosis, placement, or support programming in response to the referral.
(d) *Feedback*: describes the sharing of assessment with stakeholders (e.g., students, families, educators, and other professionals); it may involve both verbal feedback through meetings and discussion and written feedback through reports and other documentation.

Family, school, and community partnerships. FSCP is built on four critical domains that provide a foundation for collaborative assessment and intervention efforts for students with disabilities and their families (Miller et al., in press):

(a) *Strong relationships*: serves as the backbone of all collaborative partnerships; relationships are fostered by respecting the knowledge, expertise, and roles all stakeholders play within a child's life through microskills such as empathic listening, clarification of feelings, and a focus on each person's hopes and dream for the future, which contribute to relational capacity building practices. Strong relationships require responsiveness to and follow-through on family concerns, choices, and resources.
(b) *Welcoming environments*: ensures all partners feel physically and psychologically safe, accepted, and connected and engenders perceptions of wellbeing, cultural relevance, and a sense of community. Customs, traditions, and family support networks that play a role in student development are honored and approached with supportive curiosity (e.g., holding meetings within home and community environments to allow students' strengths and needs to be considered within naturally occurring routines and activities).
(c) *Multidirectional communication*: refers to a reciprocal flow of information between partners. Multidirectional communication is positive, predictable, proactive, and multi-modal, since no single communication system or method will suit everyone's needs or preferences. Deep and empathic listening, nonjudgmental questioning, and conflict resolution strategies are used when sharing information, concerns, and priorities related to a child's development or performance.

(d) *Shared understanding*: refers to an expectation that all partners are informed participants and have mutual expertise in key issues and information required for knowledgeable and shared decision-making. To guarantee all partners (including family members) being on the same foot in terms of collaborative efficacy, meeting structure must be clearly communicated, basic understanding and skills about assessment, data collection, and analysis that have important implications for future educational and career planning must be shared, and opportunities to prioritize, guide, and evaluate the validity of assessment practices must be offered.

Intellectual disability. For the purposes of this chapter, we define ID as a group of disorders characterized by significant limitations in intellectual functioning and adaptive behavior, originating during the developmental period (Schalock et al., 2010). Intellectual functioning refers to the capacity to reason, learn, and problem solve, while adaptive functioning refers to the skills necessary to carry out everyday activities. ID is an umbrella term that encompasses, but is not limited to, autism spectrum disorders, Fragile X syndrome, Down syndrome, and other developmental and neurocognitive disorders. The term *intellectual disabilities* is relatively new, and this population might also be referred to as having a cognitive disability, intellectual and developmental disability, learning disability, or mental retardation. Long-term success for children and youth with ID often hinges on the attainment of skills related to self-determination, or the ability to define one's own goals, to take initiative, to make choices and have access (Shogren & Ward, 2018). Using self-determination as a basis, we have modified the four key roles identified by Rutland & Hall (2013) for families during the assessment process to align with student roles and responsibilities:

(a) *Consumer*: the student is the audience of the information that is being produced and they have a right to receive and understand the information.
(b) *Informant*: the student provides information that guides diagnostic and treatment planning and validity.
(c) *Team member*: the student is an active participant in the assessment and intervention process (e.g., participating in interviews, determining validity of treatment plans, directing evaluation meetings).
(d) *Advocate*: the student must live with the results and subsequent interventions; thus they must have input into the social validity of recommendations.

These roles position the student with ID in the center of the assessment process while honoring the long-stated tenet held by disability activists: "Nothing about us, without us!"

These constructs inform the structure of this chapter. Across the stages of early childhood, middle childhood, and young adulthood, we will discuss school and family-based considerations for the assessment process, FSCP, and individuals with intellectual disabilities.

Early Childhood: Identification

The following section focuses on ages 3 to 9 or preschool through third grade. During these early years, school-based professionals must prioritize partnerships that focus on both the family and child well-being across assessments and interventions. Relationships at this developmental stage establish how families will view the school system moving forward.

Assessment Practices

Referral. Although assessment follows the general structure of referral, data collection, student conceptualization, and feedback at all life stages, the details of these phases vary based on the unique needs that are present in each stage of development. Assessment during the early years is usually driven by the goals of identifying children who may benefit from early intervention, linking children to appropriate early intervention, and monitoring progress within intervention (Benner & Grim, 2013). Early intervention, in particular, has been identified as an opportunity to improve outcomes across multiple developmental domains, making identification and subsequent referral to intervention especially urgent in early childhood. Due to the urgency of facilitating access to early intervention, screening assessments – a brief measure to identify children who may be at risk for developing a disorder or disability – are commonly encountered by families during visits with pediatric providers. Developmental screening measures provide valuable information regarding whether further investigation, or a comprehensive assessment, is warranted (Sattler, 2008).

Data collection. Because of the interdisciplinary nature of the early intervention, early childhood assessment procedures are increasingly "team" or "arena" based (Macy et al., 2016). During a group or arena assessment, multidisciplinary practitioners may all observe a single play-based activity, like throwing a ball, while collecting data that relates to their specific areas of expertise (e.g., gross motor skills, hand–eye communication, or social referencing during play). Assessment in early childhood is much more likely to utilize broad, performance-based measures of development. This type of test gives clinicians standardized physical-sensory, adaptive, language-communication, social-emotional, and cognitive scores.

Young children should be assessed in the context of their families, communities, and broader society (Macy et al., 2019). Multiple sources of information across these environments should be sought out and integrated (e.g., parent interviews, observations of the family at home, performance measures in a clinic setting) and should be used to depict the child's strengths and needs, investigate whether their performance was similar to what they typically demonstrate at home, and validate the assessment as a whole.

Conceptualization. As children progress through development, practitioners are able to increase the confidence with which they deliver diagnoses such as mental health conditions, ID, attention deficit hyperactivity disorder, or others. However, predicting the trajectory of skill development in early childhood can be much more difficult. Due to this, some practitioners may opt to qualify young children for early intervention services under a broader category. For example, in the U.S., *Developmental Delay* includes children who are younger than nine years old and have significant delays in one or more developmental areas.

Feedback. Psychoeducation for families is an important part of feedback during early childhood assessment. During this phase, caregivers often encounter a wide variety of information – such as developmental milestones, psychometric terms, or diagnostic categories – for the first time. Information obtained from the assessment process should be utilized to develop treatment goals and evaluate treatment progress and determine whether conceptualization of student needs and treatment targets is socially valid in settings beyond the clinic or school.

Family-Professional Partnership Strategies

Strong relationships. During the preschool and early elementary school years, families desire and benefit from personal, face-to-face coaching with school staff in the home and community. Positive relationships begin by asking families for information, utilizing family environments, exploring their concerns, and utilizing familiar routines and environments when developing initial diagnoses or interventions. Techniques that allow families to provide critically important information about the child's daily experiences and learning opportunities and families' concerns, priorities, and resources (e.g., *Routines-Based Interviewing and Assessment Strategies*,

McWilliam et al., 2009) and promote active listening and understanding are vital when families are adjusting to a diagnosis or delay for the first time (Turnbull et al., 2021). School-based professionals should view all persons in kinship roles (i.e., providing critical caretaker and emotional support) as 'family' (Trivette & Keilty, 2017).

Welcoming environments. Early FSCP efforts must promote networking between school-based professionals, caregivers, and extended family members (McGinnis et al., 2018). During this period, social networks provide both the relational support families need to overcome experiences of isolation or negative thinking about their child's future but also sources of information regarding referral processes and early screening. Social networks can also help families avoid feeling isolated and can offer opportunities for community engagement, social inclusion, and caregiver respite. Networking through religious communities or social organizations (e.g., Facebook groups; local or international association chapters; government or nonprofit agencies; parenting blogs; or SMS groups), whether in-person or through online forums, can be instrumental in helping young children and family members experience a smoother and effective transition from early intervention services to school-based and adult services (National Council on Disability, 2011).

Multidirectional communication. In the context of early childhood assessment, it is critical that all family members feel comfortable and able to share their ideas, provide input, and elicit and ask questions during all exchanges with school and community personnel. If families are viewed and valued as an integral part of a coordinated team for the child, they become better advocates for comprehensive and integrated services. Establishing trusting, open, two-way communication must take precedence to ensure families become active participants in their children's development and education from the moment they are born. Such communication promotes efficacy and reinforces family members' participation and engagement in their child's early learning and cognitive, social, and emotional development (Dunst et al., 2014).

Shared understanding. In these early stages, families often experience stress and confusion when first learning of their child's disability. School-based professionals can facilitate shared understanding by explaining content, terminology, or assessment information to families; addressing grief and specific anxieties or worries families may have about the future; and providing resources and information on financial or other impacts that can occur. When adapting to the new reality of their child's diagnosis, the mental health of all family members must be considered. This may require more consistent check-ins and awareness of the family system to alleviate stressors that influence the student, such as job loss, financial hardships, or other adversity. Families who have a child with a disability often worry about other siblings or their additional commitments and responsibilities that can damage families' confidence and quality of life. Family, school, and community partnerships at this stage must also consider a family's social and cultural capital to ensure a full understanding of their child's disability and participation in decisions to promote their child's development (Miller et al., in press). Such discussions are likely to be most successful when families can include family members or family friends who are knowledgeable regarding both the school culture and the community culture to help them navigate conversations.

ID Considerations

Consumer. During early childhood, the student's ability to receive information may be limited by family values or school-based professionals' reticence due to assumptions about understanding or timing. Concerningly, many individuals with ID progress into adulthood without developing a disability identity and, thus, are less prepared to emotionally cope with the stigma attached to "ID" (Beart et al., 2005). To counter the disempowering effects of partial or no understanding of ID by people given this identity, school-based professionals must work with families to help them disseminate information to the student about their disability. Children with ID need to understand ID, the strengths that they have, and the challenges that they may face. This is the first step to building self-determination and developing the attitudes and abilities they will need to be autonomous and self-regulating in later ages.

Informant. As part of assessment, even in early childhood, school-based professionals can work with the student to solicit current wishes and future goals to develop the assessment battery (Snider et al., 2020). Navigating discussions between the child, family, and school-based professional may require a systematic approach to communication, which includes asking families and siblings (i.e., natural communication partners) to share their knowledge of the child in the home setting and being open to alternative forms of communication (e.g., pictures, signing, pointing, augmentative devices, eye gaze, proximity, facial expressions, and body language; Bunning, 2009). The inclusion of the child, along with the family, will ensure meaningful assessment and decision-making practices.

Team member. Assessment practices in early childhood often position the child as the subject versus as a team member who has important input for creating the next steps. As a team member, the child can be offered choices of intervention components, asked about short-term objectives and high-preference activities, and observed to determine learning style preferences and strengths that can promote treatment success. By incorporating the child in all aspects of assessment, school-based professionals and families can promote self-determination and help build young students' capacity for choice, decision-making, goal setting, and problem solving (Palmer & Wehmeyer, 2003). Indeed, self-determination can be more fully achieved in adulthood if there is a lifelong cultivation and acquisition.

Advocate. Advocacy in early childhood involves understanding the rights afforded to individuals with disabilities, demanding high expectations from caregivers and school-based professionals, and requesting appropriate methods of assessment and data collection to individualize the focus of assessment. Despite developmental and emotional limitations in young children with ID, families and school-based professionals can foster a child's initial understanding of advocacy. Social stories incorporating pictures from the child's environments, familiar faces, and commonly used phrases can be created to help explain the assessment and planning process and include the child's needs and preferences. Caregivers and professionals can model how to constructively express dissatisfaction *and* contribute to problem solving, how to feel empowered, and how to receive support (Conley Wright & Taylor, 2014). Finally, pictures can be used to explain student rights during educational planning meetings and pictorial rating scales can help discern student satisfaction with assessment and intervention decisions. These efforts ensure assessments capture a child's capacity instead of access skills and lead to realistic aspirational goals (Snider et al., 2020).

Middle Childhood: Goal Development

Middle childhood refers to the later elementary and middle school years (ages 10 through 13). Within these ages, school-based professionals must take into consideration the many changes that occur in the educational context: students face an increased academic load, interact with more teachers, interface with new peers, and foray into more varied community settings. These increased social and academic encounters present new assessment and partnering challenges. The challenges are compounded by approaching puberty (e.g., increasing behavioral and emotional dysregulation) and adolescents' growing desire for independence and autonomy (reduced inclination to ask for help or have family members communicate with educators; Hill & Tyson, 2009). School-based professionals must consider these shifts to ensure effective strategies.

Assessment Practices

Referral. During this stage, there are often requirements that guide school-based assessment and special education programming (e.g., Individuals with Disabilities Education Act [IDEA], 2004 in the U.S.). To receive services, many schools are required to assess whether students who are referred via caregivers or teachers are experiencing barriers to educational attainment due to a suspected disability. While school processes may vary, comprehensive evaluations are periodically conducted to confirm students with disabilities continue to require school-based services in order to access education. Commonly, students may be first referred to assessment for special education following teacher or caregiver concerns regarding their academic, social, cognitive, or emotional development. Depending on family preference and resources, these same referral concerns may be addressed via psychoeducational assessment in private or medical settings. As children continue to receive school-based interventions, periodic (e.g., annual, triannual) special education assessment should be utilized to identify goals, plan interventions, and monitor student progress. Schools may also approach special education assessment from a problem-solving framework, which places emphasis on a concrete series of steps including clearly defining the problem, analyzing the problem, delivering intervention, and monitoring student outcome (Sattler, 2008), rather than simply identifying a disability or diagnosis that explains the referral concern. Finally, referral at this phase should consider the different ages of onset of conditions that can interfere with school performance. For example, while symptoms of developmental disabilities may be observable in early childhood, other diagnostic categories may become more apparent as environmental demands outpace student ability to compensate. Heightened environmental demands related to academics and mental health may also trigger caregiver or teacher concerns during this period.

Data collection. Multi-source, multi-setting data collection is widely acknowledged as best practice (Christ & Arañas, 2014; Benson et al., 2019). Within schools, Wright (2010) characterizes comprehensive data collection as systematic consideration of *Record reviews, Interviews, Observations, and Tests* (RIOT) to assess factors related to *Instruction, Curriculum, the Environment, and the Learner* (ICEL). School-based professionals involved in assessment (e.g., school psychologists) should consider the referral concern and utilize the clinical judgment to design an assessment battery for each student that considers information from standardized tests of intelligence, academics, or social-emotional functioning, and informal data collection methods (e.g., interviews, review of medical and educational records, analysis of work samples, or other documents). While caregivers may be the primary informants during early childhood, elementary-age children are able to participate in interviews, provide their own perspectives of their struggles and strengths, and offer other information that can provide context to quantitative data (Sattler, 2008). Similarly, as students become older and begin to spend more time in settings outside the home, school-based professionals can provide invaluable information related to the student's needs. Progress monitoring data collected by teachers may also be integrated in order to understand how a student is progressing within their current level of support.

Conceptualization and feedback. Conceptualizing can be complicated by discrepancies in the data provided by families, students, and teachers; these discrepancies may represent differences in informer perspectives or true differences in performance across environments (De Los Reyes et al., 2015). For students who were identified as developmentally delayed during early childhood, conceptualization during elementary school may also require qualification under a different special education category. Evaluators may begin to consider whether a student's performance on standardized measures (e.g., IQ) has begun to stabilize across time points or whether certain types of behaviors (e.g., difficulties with executive functioning) have maintained consistency across settings when making this decision during middle childhood.

Different information may be provided to teachers, students, and families during feedback based on parent consent, contextual requirements, and clinical judgment (Shidman, 2015). During verbal feedback in a private or larger school-based meeting, the psychologist or other team members meet with families to review test findings and other data and discuss recommended next steps (Fish, 2008). It is also common for families to receive a formal psychological report that describes the same information in detail. Increasingly, school and community-based providers have worked to make these written documents more useful to families by using a consumer-focused approach (e.g., organizing the report according to referral questions rather than test findings; Brenner, 2003). Practitioners may also opt to provide child-specific feedback via a private verbal discussion or a personalized written fable to support older students' growing personal insight and engagement in the assessment process (Snider et al., 2020).

Family-Professional Partnership Strategies

Strong relationships. Families are not always seen as integral, natural partners in middle childhood, even though home-school communication is still highly needed and desired at this stage (Turnbull et al., 2021). As assessments become more specific to future planning and more closely tied to school curricula, partnerships require greater family engagement in assessment and intervention planning through regular sharing of student's success and challenges. Families of middle school-aged students also appreciate information on how to support effective study habits and time management skills, how to access positive after-school, community activities, and how to request school-based professionals' assistance.

Welcoming environment. Family engagement during this stage of development is most successful if there has been a "bank" of prior affirmative messages through positive telephone calls, electronic mail, and personalized notices (Park et al., 2017). School-based professionals can continue to facilitate a welcoming environment by selecting meeting spaces that facilitate sharing of assessment information. For example, school-based professionals may physically arrange group meetings to confirm that families are seated next to professionals they know and have close relationships with. Conversely, it is important to consider how the type of information shared may influence how families perceive an environment; it may be important to offer small one-on-one meetings to discuss surprising or upsetting test results rather than sharing this information in a group environment.

Multidirectional communication. Due to developmental challenges, increases in academic demands, and the desire for independence, FSCP during middle childhood requires more frequent, individualized, and systematic meetings to modify ongoing educational plans or to deal with new sources of distress. New challenges that arise often require more intense, complex, and comprehensive partnering efforts that address academic and social-emotional learning and development across school, home and community settings.

Shared understanding. During middle childhood, when there are rapid changes within a student, family input becomes more critical and necessary to gain valid information about a student's progress, goals, and next steps for intervening (Hill & Tyson, 2009). Partnerships with families from minoritized cultures whose children with disabilities are entering middle childhood require additional consideration. Significant encounters with racism over time make it critical to discuss how families promote racial identity and set restrictions to ensure their child's

2004), although there is not clear data to indicate the extent to which students are wholly engaged in these meetings (Shogren & Plotner, 2012). To increase engagement, practitioners may consider reviewing the written report in its entirety or offering one-on-one student feedback meetings.

Family-Professional Partnership Strategies

Strong relationships. As students transition towards adulthood, professionals can facilitate conversations about family expectations and desires in light of their student's preferences and needs during school-based decision-making. Families can offer unique input on the types of support that might be needed for themselves and their student. Additionally, school-based professionals should connect families and students with community professionals who can further explain related resources and services available to students who are 18 and older. The majority of families of youth with ID indicate minimal familiarity with work, school, residential, and community activity options for their young adult and adult children (Gilson et al., 2017).

Welcoming environment. As older students reach adulthood, it is important that they feel informed and included in decision-making regarding the type of support that they may seek or require. Hoagwood and colleagues (2010) note several supports that school-based professionals can consider when creating a welcoming space: (1) *Relational support*, or empathic, affirmative, reflective listening that promotes self-worth, belonging, and efficacy; (2) *Instrumental support*, or the provision of concrete aid and services to address emergencies and help overcome food, health, and housing needs and other barriers to effective participation; (3) *Informational support*, or education about school practices, government regulations regarding college or career paths, and community treatment options associated with the disability of concern; (4) *Instructional support*, or the promotion of mental health and wellness, interpersonal and family communication, and community engagement; and, (5) *Advocacy support*, or the understanding of educational rights, entitlements and on negotiation and leadership dispositions and skills that can increase participation in decision-making and systemic change. Environments that ensure comprehensive supports and services are available had better prepare students and families to address inequities or discrimination that may be encountered in the adult world (Hanson & Lynch, 2013).

Multidirectional communication. Families also have important insights to share with vocational or higher education counselors in regard to their student's tolerance of environmental factors, preference for how to handle social demands, or ability to maintain long-term relationships. These considerations are often more challenging than the "hard" skills required by a given job (Talapatra et al., 2019). Families during this stage can provide input on work or school accommodations, outside service needs, and community-based recreation activities. Conversely, school-based professionals can offer helpful insight on behavioral coaching or other strategies that can foster independence at home and in the community, if that is an identified family concern. Multidirectional communication at this stage can help ensure individual priorities, values, and circumstances are considered so that support can be differentiated to promote successful future educational, work and life outcomes.

Shared understanding. Effective partnerships are grounded in a strength-based view of the critical role families play in promoting students' learning, socialization, and career attainment (Kalyanpur & Harry, 2012). Consequently, transition assessment and decision-making practices must be collaboratively and individually designed to be socially valid. Cultural values and customs are especially critical to consider for future post-graduation vocational, career, or college attainment and to disrupt racial and social inequities woven historically into our community and school institutions (Haines et al., 2017).

ID Considerations

Consumer. During this stage of development, youth with ID should be planning for college, career, and community integration. Employment and education goals should be prioritized in the assessment process, and families, school-based professionals and the student should be ensuring that activities of daily living are part of all educational planning. Based on the goals established during middle childhood and early adulthood, family-school-community partnerships should be considering the type of job the student wants or the type and size of college the student wishes to attend. Housing and transportation arrangements, independent living skills (e.g., ability to use the phone, cooking, e-mail), and self-monitoring skills (e.g., personal hygiene, health management) should all be addressed in the assessment process (Talapatra et al., 2018). Students should request resources to community agencies, vocational internships, and federal support systems. Families, schools, and students should also work together to understand the changes in laws governing children with disabilities versus adults.

Informant. Post-school outcomes for students with ID continue to lag behind other students with disabilities (Lipscomb et al., 2017). To ensure quality of life after graduation, students with ID should strive to remain involved in educational planning, goal setting, and action planning (Seong et al., 2015). To check-in with students regarding their involvement, school-based professionals should periodically use The Arc's free *Self Determination Scale* (SDS; Wehmeyer & Kelchner, 1995) to make sure that there is a positive growth trajectory across responses. Students should be sharing their strengths, interests, and preferences with their families and school staff. This includes discussions about community recreational activities, employment opportunities, housing options (e.g., independent, with the family, group homes), vocational skills, and career trajectories.

Team member. Schwartz and colleagues (2000) identified several hallmarks on a person-centered approach toward participation and educational planning that can be modified for current assessment practices: (1) Assessments must work for the student to capture their dreams, interests, preferences, strengths, and capacities so subsequent activities, services and supports are based on meaningful results; (2) the student must be provided opportunities to exercise control and make informed decisions, based on their experiences and personal goals; (3) families and school-based professionals must work cooperatively to identify community supports that align with intervention goals; (4) activities, supports, and services recommended by assessments must foster skills necessary to achieve personal relationships, community inclusion, dignity, and respect; (5) planning is collaborative, recurring, and involves an ongoing commitment to the person, with decisions being frequently revisited and reassessed; and, (6) the student is satisfied with their activities, supports and services and areas of dissatisfaction result in tangible changes to educational and life plans. By acknowledging the student as a core team member who can collaborate in decision-making, we support the development of the youth's agency, independence, self-efficacy, and self-esteem.

Advocate. As a callback to the early years, students, families, and caregivers must continue to work on disability identity. Many individuals with ID feel negatively about the label ascribed to them. This young adulthood stage, more so than any other, sets the student up for entry to the adult world. To negate feelings of shame, embarrassment, discomfort anger, powerlessness and frustration (Logeswaran et al., 2019), students with ID must be given an opportunity to engage with the community, form relationships (both romantic and platonic), and make decisions for themselves. Families, school staff, and students should work in tandem to demand information that will enable the student to negotiate the modern world effectively. Sexual knowledge, health literacy, and digital etiquette and engagement are only some of the facets of everyday adult life.

Students with ID must go beyond the limited expectation and gatekeeping that occur for their disability group and find opportunity to engage. For example, in interviews with individuals with ID who had unfettered access to the internet, they reported using it to maintain relationships and develop social belonging; access information and develop vocational skills; and create and define identity (Chadwick & Fullwood, 2018).

Conclusion

In the last three decades, researchers have developed a deeper appreciation of the important academic and social-emotional benefits students accrue from collaborative partnerships between families, school and community professionals (Global Family Research Center, 2018). These benefits hold true for all children, including those in the ID community. Long-term success, in fact, for this population hinges on the opportunities students with ID have to develop self-determination skills at school, home, and in the community and caregivers and school-based professions have to openly exchange information about independent living, education, employment, and community experiences. However, these content areas are often informed by assessments, which have a storied negative relationship with family-school partnerships. While there is no "one-size fits all" approach for engaging with families in assessment, we hope this chapter offers several suggestions to build positive relationships between families and school-based professionals, all while positioning the child in the center of the assessment process. Schools, families, and communities can all strive toward higher levels of collaboration during the assessment process and work to create a less stressful and more helpful environment.

References

Beart, S., Hardy, G., & Buchan, L. (2005). How people with intellectual disabilities view their social identity: A review of the literature. *Journal of Applied Research in Intellectual Disabilities, 18*(1), 47–56. https://doi.org/10.1111/j.1468-3148.2004.00218.x

Benner, S. M., & Grim, J. C. (2013). *Assessment of Young Children with Special Needs: A Context-Based Approach, Second Edition*. New York: Routledge.

Benson, N. F., Floyd, R. G., Kranzler, J. H., Eckert, T. L., Fefer, S. A., & Morgan, G. B. (2019). Test use and assessment practices of school psychologists in the United States: Findings from the 2017 National Survey. *Journal of School Psychology, 72*, 29–48. https://doi.org/10.1016/j.jsp.2018.12.004

Brenner, E. (2003). Consumer-focused psychological assessment. *Professional Psychology: Research and Practice, 34*(3), 240–247. https://doi.org/10.1037/0735-7028.34.3.240

Bunning, K. (2009). Making sense of communication. In J. Pawlyn & S. Carnaby (Eds.), *Profound Intellectual and Multiple Disabilities: Nursing Complex Needs* (pp. 46–61). Hoboken, NJ: Wiley-Blackwell.

Burke, M. M., & Goldman, S. E. (2014). Identifying the associated factors of mediation and due process in families of students with autism spectrum disorder. *Journal of Autism and Developmental Disorders, 45*(5), 1345–1354.

Carr, G. F. (2011). Empowerment: A framework to develop advocacy in African American grandmothers providing care for their grandchildren. *International Scholarly Research Notices, 2011*, 1–7. https://doi.org/10.5402/2011/531717

Cavendish, W., & Connor, D. (2018). Toward authentic IEPs and transition plans: Student, parent, and teacher perspectives. *Learning Disability Quarterly, 41*(1), 32–43. https://doi.org/10.1177/0731948716684680

Chadwick, D. D., & Fullwood, C. (2018). An online life like any other: Identity, self-determination, and social networking among adults with intellectual disabilities. *Cyberpsychology, Behavior, and Social Networking, 21*(1), 56–64. http://doi.org/10.1089/cyber.2016.0689

Cheung, N. (2013). Defining intellectual disability and establishing a standard of proof: Suggestions for a national model standard. *Health Matrix, 23*(1), 317. https://scholarlycommons.law.case.edu/healthmatrix/vol23/iss1/26

Christ, T. J. & Arañas, Y. A. (2014). Best practices in problem analysis. Best practices in school psychology: Data-based and collaborative decision making. In P. L. Harrison and A. Thomas (Eds.), *Best Practices in School Psychology: Data-based and Collaborative Decision Making* (pp. 87–97). Bethesda, MD: : National Association of School Psychologists.

Conley Wright, A. & Taylor, S. (2014). Advocacy by parents of young children with special needs: Activities, processes, and perceived effectiveness. *Journal of Social Service Research, 40*(5), 591–605. https://doi.org/10.1080/01488376.2014.896850

Crane, L., Chester, J. W., Goddard, L., Henry, L. A., & Hill, E. L. (2016). Experiences of autism diagnosis: A survey of over 1000 parents in the United Kingdom. *Autism, 20*(2), 153–162. https://doi.org/10.1177/136236131557636

De Los Reyes, A., Augenstein, T. M., Wang, M., Thomas, S. A., Drabick, D. A. G., Burgers, D. E., & Rabinowitz, J. (2015). The Validity of the Multi-Informant Approach to Assessing Child and Adolescent Mental Health. *Psychological Bulletin, 141*(4), 858–900. https://doi.org/10.1037/a0038498

deFur, S. H. (2003). IEP transition planning-from compliance to quality. *Exceptionality, 11*(2), 115–128. https://doi.org/10.1207/S15327035EX1102_06

Dunst, C. J., Bruder, M. B., & Espe-Sherwindt, M. (2014). Family capacity-building in early childhood intervention: Do context and setting matter? *School Community Journal, 24*(1), 37–48.

Fish, W. W. (2008). The IEP Meeting: Perceptions of Parents of Students Who Receive Special Education Services. *Preventing School Failure: Alternative Education for Children and Youth, 53*(1), 8–14. https://doi.org/10.3200/PSFL.53.1.8-14

Gilson, C. B., Bethune, L. K., Carter, E. W., & McMillan, E. D. (2017). Informing and equipping parents of people with intellectual and developmental disabilities. *Intellectual and Developmental Disabilities, 55*(5), 347–360. https://doi.org/10.1352/1934-9556-55.5.347

Global Family Research Project. (2018). *Joining Together to Create a Bold Vision for Next Generation Family Engagement: Engaging Families to Transform Education*. Boston, MA: Carnegie Corporation.

Grigal, M., Hart, D., & Migliore, A. (2011). Comparing the transition planning, postsecondary education, and employment outcomes of students with intellectual and other disabilities. *Career Development and Transition for Exceptional Individuals, 34*(1), 4–17. https://doi.org/10.1177/0885728811399091

Haines, S. J., Francis, G. L., Mueller, T. G., Chiu, C. Y., Burke, M. M., Kyzar, K., Shepherd, K. G., Holdren, N., Aldersey, H. M., & Turnbull, A. P. (2017). Reconceptualizing family-professional partnership for inclusive schools: A call to action. *Inclusion, 5*(4), 234–247. https://doi.org/10.1352/2326-6988-5.4.234

Hanson, M. J., & Lynch, E. W. (2013). *Understanding Families: Supportive Approaches to Diversity, Disability, and Risk*. Baltimore, MD: Paul H. Brookes.

Hill, N. E., & Tyson, D. (2009). Parental involvement in middle school: A meta-analytic assessment of the strategies that promote achievement. *Developmental Psychology, 45*(3), 740–763. https://dx.doi.org/10.1037%2Fa0015362

Hite, J. F. (2017). *Parent evaluations of traditional and consumer-focused school psychoeducational reports* (Doctoral dissertation). http://www.proquest.com/en-US/products/dissertations/individuals.shtml

Hoagwood, K. E., Cavaleri, M. A., Olin, S. S., Burns, B. J., Slaton, E., Gruttadaro, D., & Hughes, R. (2010). Family support in children's mental health: A review and synthesis. *Clinical Child and Family Psychology Review, 13*, 1–45. https://doi.org/10.1007/s10567-009-0060-5

Individuals with Disabilities Education Act, 20 U.S.C. § 1400 (2004).

Kalyanpur, M., & Harry, B. (2012). *Cultural Reciprocity in Special Education: Building Family-Professional Relationships*. Baltimore, MD: Paul H. Brookes Publishing Company.

Lipscomb, S., Haimson, J., Liv, A. Y., Burghardt, J., Johnson, D. R., & Thurlow, M. L. (2017). *Preparing for Life after High School: Findings from the National Longitudinal Transition Study 2012. Volume 1: Comparisons with Other Youth: Full Report (NCEE 2017–4016)*. U.S. Department of Education, Institute of Education Services, National Center for Education Evaluation and Regional Assistance.

Logeswaran, S., Hollett, M., Zala, S., Richardson, L., & Scior, K. (2019). How do people with intellectual disabilities construct their social identity? A review. *Journal of Applied Research in Intellectual Disabilities, 32*(3), 533–542. https://doi.org/10.1111/jar.12566

Macy, M., Bagnato, S. J., & Gallen, R. (2016). Authentic assessment: A venerable idea whose time is now. *Zero to Three, 37*(1), 37–43.

Macy, M., Bagnato, S. J., & Weiszhaupt, K. (2019). Family-Friendly Communication via Authentic Assessment for Early Childhood Intervention Programs. *Zero to Three, 40*(2), 45–51. https://www.zerotothree.org/resource/family-friendly-communication-via-authentic-assessment-for-early-childhood-intervention-programs/

Martin, J. E., Marshall, L. H., Maxson, L. M., & Jerman, P. L. (1996). *The Self-Directed IEP*. Longmont, CO: Sopris West.

Martinez, D. C., Conroy, J. W., & Cerreto, M. C. (2012). Parent involvement in the transition process of children with intellectual disabilities: The influence of inclusion on parent desires and expectations for postsecondary education. *Journal of Policy and Practice in Intellectual Disabilities, 9*(4), 279–288. https://doi.org/10.1111/jppi.12000

McGinnis, S., Lee, E., Kirkland, K., Smith, C., Miranda-Julian, C., & Greene, R. (2018). Engaging at-risk fathers in home visiting services: Effects on program retention and father involvement. *Child and Adolescent Social Work Journal*, 1–12. https://doi.org/10.1007/s10560-018-0562-4

McWilliam, R. A., Casey, A. M., & Sims, J. (2009). The routines-based interview: A method for gathering information and assessing needs. *Infants & Young Children, 22*(3), 224–233. https://doi.org/10.1097/IYC.0b013e3181abe1dd

Miller, G. E., Arthur-Stanley, A., & Banerjee, R. (in press). *Advances in Family-School-Community Partnering: A Practical Guide for School Mental Health Professionals and Educators.* London: Routledge.

National Council on Disability. (2011). *National disability policy: A progress report.* Retrieved from: https://ncd.gov/progress_reports/oct312011

National Technical Assistance Center on Transition (2016). *Age Appropriate Transition Assessment Toolkit Fourth Edition.* Charlotte: University of North Carolina. Original by NSTTAC and A. R. Walker, L. J. Kortering, C. H. Fowler, D. Rowe, & L. Bethune. Update by C. H. Fowler & M. Terrell.

O'Brien, J., Pearpoint, J. & Kahn, L. (2010). *The PATH and MAPS Handbook: Person-centered Ways to Build Community.* Toronto: Inclusion Press.

Palmer, S. B., & Wehmeyer, M. L. (2003). Promoting self-determination in early elementary school: Teaching self-regulated problem-solving and goal-setting skills. *Remedial and special education, 24*(2), 115–126. https://doi.org/10.1177/07419325030240020601

Park, S., Stone, S. I., & Holloway, S. D. (2017). School-based parental involvement as a predictor of achievement and school learning environment: An elementary school-level analysis. *Children and Youth Services Review, 82*, 195–206. https://doi.org/10.1016/j.childyouth.2017.09.012

Purser, K., & Sullivan, K. (2019). Capacity assessment and estate planning: The therapeutic importance of the individual. *International Journal of Law and Psychiatry, 64*, 88–98. https://doi.org/10.1016/j.ijlp.2019.02.005

Rizzolo, M. C., Friedman, C., Lulinski-Norris, A., & Braddock, D. (2013). Home and Community Based Services (HCBS) Waivers: A nationwide study of the states. *Intellectual and Developmental Disabilities, 51*(1), 1–21. http://dx.doi.org/10.1352/1934-9556-51.01.001

Roach, A. T., & Talapatra, D. (2011, July). School Psychologists: Friend or Foe [Conference Session], Toronto Summer Institute, Toronto, Canada.

Rutland, J., & Hall, A. H. (2013). Involving Families in the Assessment Process. *Head Start Dialog: The Research-to-Practice Journal for the Early Childhood Field, 16*(4). https://journals.uncc.edu/dialog/article/view/153

Ryan, C., & Quinlan, E. (2017). Who shouts the loudest: Listening to parents of children with disabilities. *Journal of Applied Research in Intellectual Disability, 31*(2), 203–214. doi:10.1111/jar.12343

Sattler, J. (2008). *Assessment of Children: Cognitive Foundations.* La Mesa, CA: Jerome Sattler Publisher, Inc.

Schalock, R. L., Borthwick-Duffy, S. A., Bradley, V. J., Buntinx, W. H., Coulter, D. L., Craig, E. M., ... & Yeager, M. H. (2010). *Intellectual Disability: Definition, Classification, and Systems of Supports.* Washington, DC: American Association on Intellectual and Developmental Disabilities.

Schwartz, A. A., Holburn, S. C., & Jacobson, J. W. (2000). Defining person centeredness: Results of two consensus methods. *Education and Training in Mental Retardation and Developmental Disabilities*, 235–249. https://www.jstor.org/stable/23879646

Segall, M. J., Bohlke, K. H., & Rossbach, K. H. (2017). Transition assessments for adolescents and young adults with ASD. *VEWAA Journal, 14*(2), 14–22.

Seong, Y., Wehmeyer, M. L., Palmer, S. B., & Little, T. D. (2015). Effects of the self-directed individualized education program on self-determination and transition of adolescents with disabilities. *Career Development and Transition for Exceptional Individuals, 38*(3), 132–141. https://doi.10.1177/2165143414544359

Shidman, J. (2015). *Practitioner's beliefs, practices, and training in the provision of psychological and psycho-educational assessment feedback* (doctoral dissertation, Retrieved from ProQuest Dissertation Publishing).

Shogren, K. & Plotner, A. (2012). Transition planning for students with intellectual disability, autism, or other disabilities. Data from the National Longitudinal Transition Study-2. *Intellectual and Developmental Disabilities, 50*, 16–30.

Shogren, K. A., & Ward, M. J. (2018). Promoting and enhancing self-determination to improve the post-school outcomes of people with disabilities. *Journal of Vocational Rehabilitation, 48*(2), 187–196. https://doi.org/10.3233/JVR-180935

Snider, L. A., Talapatra, D., Miller, G., & Zhang, D. (2020). Expanding best practices in assessment for students with intellectual and developmental disabilities. *Contemporary School Psychology, 24,* 429–444. https://doi.org/10.1007/s40688-020-00294-w.

Talapatra, D., Miller, G. E., & Schumacher-Martinez, R. (2019). Improving family-school collaboration in transition services for students with intellectual disabilities: A framework for school psychologists. *Journal of Educational and Psychological Consultation, 29*(3), 314–336. https://doi.org/10.1080/10474412.2018.1495083

Talapatra, D. & Snider, L. (2021). Leveraging policies for college and career planning for students with intellectual disabilities. *Contemporary School Psychology.* https://doi.org/10.1007/s40688-020-00347-0

Talapatra, D., Roach, A. T., Varjas K., Houchins, D. E., & Crimmins, D. B. (2018). Promoting school psychologist participation in transition services using the TPIE model. *Contemporary School Psychology, 22*(1), 18–29. https://doi.org/10.1007/s40688-017-0159-5

Trivette, C. M., & Keilty, B. (Eds.) (2017). *Family: Knowing families, tailoring practices, building capacity.* Division for Early Childhood.

Turnbull, A. P., & Turnbull, H. R. (1996). Group Action Planning as a strategy for providing comprehensive family support. In L. K. Koegel, R. L. Koegel, & G. Dunlap (Eds.), *Community, School, Family, and Social Inclusion Through Positive Behavioral Support: Including People with Difficult Behavior in the Community* (pp. 99–114). Baltimore: Paul H. Brookes.

Turnbull, A. P., Turnbull, R, Francis, G. L., Burke, M., Kyzar, K., Haines, S., Gershwin, T., Shepherd, K., Holdren, N., & Singer, G. H. S. (2021). *Families and Professionals: Trusting Partnerships in General and Special Education* (8th ed.). Pearson Education.

Wang, M., & Huguley, J. (2012). Parental racial socialization as a moderator of the effects of racial discrimination on educational success among African American adolescents. *Child Development, 83*(5), 1716–1731. https://doi.org/10.1111/j.1467-8624.2012.01808.x

Wang, M. T., & Sheikh-Khalil, S. (2014). Does parental involvement matter for adolescent achievement and mental health in high school? *Child Development, 85*(2), 610–625. https://doi.org/10.1111/cdev.12153

Wehmeyer, M. L., & Kelchner, K. (1995). *The Arc's Self Determination Scale.* Arlington, TX: The Arc National Headquarters. https://www.ou.edu/education/centers-and-partnerships/zarrow/self-determination-assessment-tools/arc-self-determination-scale

White, S. E. (2014). Special education complaints filed by parents of students with autism spectrum disorders in the midwestern United States. *Focus on Autism and Other Developmental Disabilities, 29*(2), 80–87. https://doi.org/10.1177/1088357613478830

Wright, J. (2010). The RIOT/ICEL matrix: Organizing data to answer questions about student performance and behavior [PDF document]. www.interventioncentral.org/sites/default/files/rti_riot_icel_data_collection.pdf

PART IV

Evidence-Based Intervention and Strategies

Over the years, evidence-based interventions have been developed through rigorous and sustained research and have been documented through research reports, policy briefs, and practice in diverse settings. Interventions that demonstrate treatment integrity and positive outcomes for students with disabilities in inclusive settings are discussed in this chapter.

20
APPLIED BEHAVIOUR ANALYSIS BASED INTERVENTIONS FOR APPLICATION BY TEACHERS IN ADDRESSING THE BEHAVIOURAL NEEDS OF DIVERSE LEARNERS

*Santoshi Halder**

Introduction

Educational inclusion is an integral part of the right to education and an important condition for social and community participation in all walks of life (UNESCO, 2015; UNICEF, 2011). Worldwide statistics are currently witnessing a sharp peak in the enrolment rate of students with disabilities as never before (U.S. Department of Education, 2021). However, most students with disabilities are experiencing acute challenges in the sphere of education in terms of dropout, low achievement, performance discrepancy, learning needs, behavioural issues, differences in styles of learning, etc., at almost all levels of education. One of the acute challenges of the students with disabilities (SwD) is their behavioural needs as they often exhibit a broad spectrum of challenging behaviours such as self-injury, hyperactivity, aggression, stereotypes, anxiety, or impulsivity three times more frequently than in the general population (Dykens, 2000; Simó-Pinatella et al., 2019). Nicholls et al. (2019) reported students between the ages of three to 19 years mostly engaged in self-injurious behaviour (36.4%), followed by aggressive/destructive behaviour (30.2%), and stereotyped behaviour (25.9%). The behavioural challenges of people with disabilities (PwD) seriously impact the goal of creating an inclusive society as envisioned by almost all of the UN conventions; United Nations Sustainable Development Goals (UNESCO, 2015), the UN Convention on the Rights of the Child (CRC) (United Nations, 1989) and United Nations Convention on the Rights of Persons with Disabilities (UNCRPD) (Collins et al., 2017; UNICEF, 2011; UNCRPD, 2016).

Disruptive behaviours pose challenges not only for their own lives but also for the lives of others around them and increase the risk of social isolation and exclusion (Kates-McElrath & Axelrod, 2008; Kurth et al., 2014) and are a constant source of stress for teachers in the classroom (Amstad & Müller, 2020; Friedman-Krauss et al., 2014; Hastings & Brown, 2002; Lecavalier et

* santoshi_halder@yahoo.com; shedu@caluniv.ac.in

DOI: 10.4324/9781003266068-25

al., 2006). Problem behaviours and other behavioural needs of individuals with disabilities in different contexts, be it at home (Woodman et al., 2015), school (Hastings & Brown, 2002), or other living arrangements (e.g., Mitchell & Hastings, 1998) significantly impact their overall quality of life and well-being.

Teachers and parents, two of the most crucial facilitators of teaching-learning, express their frustration, lack of knowledge, reluctance due to skill deficits, and persistent feelings of helplessness in addressing the behavioural needs of their learners or wards (Fuller et al., 2004; Leyser & Greenberger, 2008; Wysocki, 2018). Lack of definite guidelines, knowledge, awareness, specialized skills and expertise creates additional barriers for the PwD, their families and the teachers. In spite of the differences in ability every child has the potential to learn and progress, if their needs are addressed appropriately with skilled personnel who can take the right decision and implement appropriate strategy at the right time. In an attempt to facilitate positive behavioural outcome various interventions are being practised all over the world to address the behavioural needs including the various skill deficits such as social, communication, daily living, and play skills, through a systematic process whereby teachers create opportunities for children to produce target behaviours through prompts, cues and reinforcers to shape appropriate behaviour. Unfortunately, there is an alarming shortage of people trained or skilled to specifically understand and implement individualized evidence-based behaviour intervention procedures appropriately. Researchers accentuate the importance of skilled teachers who have the knowledge, ability and skills to effectively address the needs of all their learners in the classroom successfully (Carter, 2014; McIntyre, 2009). Hence there is a pertinent need to prepare, train and orient the teachers and other personnel to cater for the behavioural needs of diverse learners and thereby create opportunities for participation and inclusion in all walks of life (Simó-Pinatella et al., 2019).

Addressing Behavioural Challenges and Finding Evidence-based Interventions

Approximately 6.9% of CwD in special education engage in problem behaviour (Amsted & Muller, 2020; Hagopian & Leoni, 2017) that interferes with their appropriate education, performance, social interactions with peers, academic achievement and safety (Crone & Horner, 2003) impeding their overall quality of life, participation and inclusion in mainstream society. Evidence-based interventions are designed and implemented through a systematic methodological process, based on a strong foundation of robust theories and empirical findings and yield effective results. However, there are concerns about the effectiveness of many of the intervention strategies followed worldwide (Crone & Horner, 2003; Kates-McElrath & Axelrod, 2008). Identifying the function of problem behaviour and analysing the environmental components before developing an intervention is extremely essential as this increases the effectiveness of the intervention to a large extent and allows the teacher to manipulate the antecedents and consequences of maintaining the problem behaviour limiting many harmful effects (Iwata & Dozier, 2008). However, teachers with the requisite skills to implement evidence-based strategies and interventions based on the identification of function-based behaviour are sporadic.

Applied Behaviour Analysis (ABA); An Evidence-based Science of Behaviour Analysis

Of the multifarious interventions followed all over the world, Applied Behaviour Analysis (ABA) has gained ground as an evidence-based science of behaviour analysis for bringing about significant behaviour changes in the life of people with diverse needs at all levels (i.e., mild, moderate or severe) and types. *Applied Behaviour Analysis (ABA)*, also called behaviour engineering, is a science dedicated to the study derived from the principles of behaviour to systematically improve socially significant human behaviour through the use of scientific methods; objective description, quantification, and controlled experimentation. The term *'Applied'* stands for 'socially significant behaviour that targets improving the daily life of the individual', *'Behavioural'* stands for 'behaviour being studied that needs to be changed' and *'Analytic'* means experimenter "demonstrates a functional relationship between events and change in a measurable dimension of the targeted behaviour" (Cooper, et al., 2007, 2020).

ABA-based intervention, the pioneers being Lovaas and colleagues (1960), is one of the most empirically validated (Simpson, 2001) evidenced-based sciences of behaviour analysis that have shown significant results in addressing almost all areas of behavioural needs of all learners including people with diverse needs Howlin et al., 2009; Larsson & Wright, 2011). The philosophy of ABA is that human behaviour is learned through the interaction between the individual and his or her environment through a wide range of instructional strategies based on the principles of ABA (e.g., Cooper et al., 2007). Variables maintaining or controlling the behaviour are identified by making evidence-based changes to an environment to affect behaviour positively and systematically followed by experimentation to produce predictable and replicable improvements in behaviour.

ABA-based strategies such as positive reinforcement, stimulus control, and discrimination learning are implemented systematically in order to bring out significant improvements in the individual's wide range of areas such as language and communication skills, social skills, emotional characteristics, language, motor and academic skills by increasing opportunities to access reinforcement in the environment and avoiding punishers to improve socially significant appropriate behaviour and ensure long-lasting meaning for the person concerned as well as others in the environment (Cooper et al., 2007).

ABA is one of the three major interrelated branches of behaviour analysis, namely: (a) *Behaviourism* (or the *philosophy of the science*) that includes *(i) Methodological behaviourism* (Watson, 1924) or *stimulus-response (S-R) psychology;* that considers behavioural events that cannot be publicly observed outside the realm of the science and *(ii) Radical behaviourism*; that attempts to explain all behaviour, including private behaviour, (b) *Experimental analysis of behaviour (EAB)* that focuses on *basic experimental research* and finally (c) *Applied behaviour analysis (ABA)* that refers to the development of a technology for improving behaviour (Cooper et al., 2007). *Radical behaviourism*, the guiding philosophy of Applied Behaviour Analysis, assumes that a mental or "inner" dimension exists that differs from a behavioural dimension and that phenomena in this dimension either directly cause or at least mediate some forms of behaviour (Morris et al., 2005).

Foundational Bases of Applied Behaviour Analysis

ABA is a systematic scientific process with the *basic characteristics of science*, namely description, prediction and control with the defining characteristics as specified in Figure 20.1. ABA is guided by the *philosophical foundation* of scientific attitudes namely: *(a) Determinism:* all events occur lawfully as a result of other events and have causes, *(b) Empiricism:* are objective, observable, describable, and quantifiable, *(c) Experimentation:* based on the systematic manipulation of an Independent Variable (IV), measurement of Dependent Variable (DV) and analysis of their relationship, *(d) Parsimony:* presented through the simplest explanations for a phenomenon, *(e) Philosophical doubt:* continuously questions facts and the willingness to abandon beliefs in the

Technological
Operative procedures are identified and described with sufficient details and clarity for replicability

Effective
Improve the behaviour to an efficient and practical degree

Generalized Outcome
Last overtime

Applied
Enhance and improve people's lives

Conceptual systematic
Procedure for changing behaviour and any interpretation is described in terms of relevant principles from which they are derived

Behavioural
Studies of behaviour not about behaviour

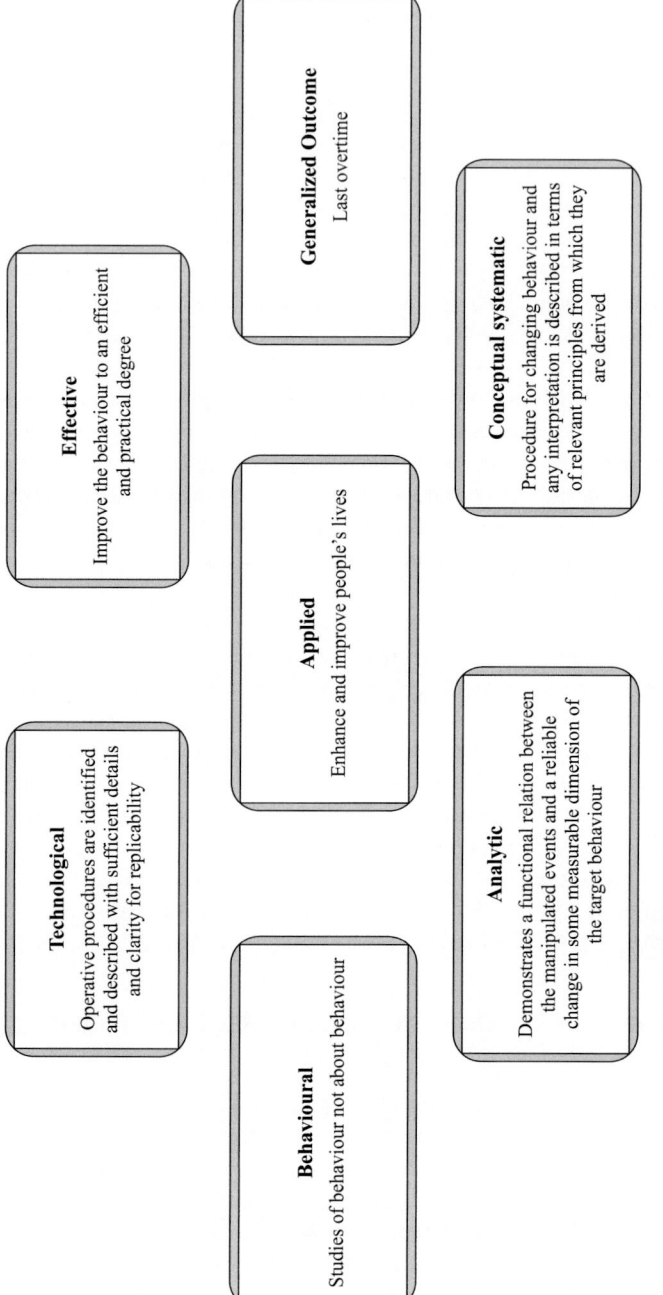

Analytic
Demonstrates a functional relation between the manipulated events and a reliable change in some measurable dimension of the target behaviour

Figure 20.1 Defining characteristics of ABA (Source: Cooper, Heron, & Heward, 2007)

light of new data, *(g) Replication:* increases the credibility of findings through replication of similar studies.

Evolutionary Trajectory of ABA

The beginning of ABA is marked with the two ground-breaking works; (a) first evidence of the application of operant conditioning in human (18-year-old mentally retarded boy) reported by Fuller (1949) whose arm-raising response was successfully conditioned by injecting a small amount of warm sugar-milk solution into his mouth every time he moved his right arm, and (b) second with the publication of series of articles by Lovaas (1965) based on his ground-breaking experimental work on observed behaviours describing antecedents and consequent behaviour maintaining problem behaviour.

Conceptual Shift; Behaviour Modification to Behaviour Analysis

Over the years, the term *behaviour modification* has been replaced with the term *behaviour analysis* based on the changes in the understanding as it shifted from the earlier mere behaviour changes/modification without any analysis to the current focus on systematic in-depth analysis for understanding the function of the behaviour, i.e., analysing antecedents or exploring the reinforcement histories of the antecedent stimuli that emit behaviour popularly known as *operant conditioning* (Skinner, 1930). The core focus of ABA is behaviour modification that focuses on analysing the relevant behaviour-environment interactions after careful assessment of the function of a behaviour and then designing a function-based intervention with replacement by socially significant appropriate behaviour.

Governing Principles of ABA: Three-Term Contingency or the ABC of Behaviour

ABA is concerned with the application of empirical approaches to change behaviour of social significance based on the *basic principles of operant behaviour* (three-term contingency; S-R-S model) rooted in radical behaviourism that is rooted in the experimental work by B.F. Skinner and colleagues (1930-1950). The governing principles of ABA are based on the ABC or three-term contingencies of behaviour; A (Antecedent), B (Behaviour) and C (Consequence). The three-term contingency or ABC of behaviour (see Figure 20.2) illustrates how behaviour is elicited by the environment and how the consequences of behaviour can affect its future occurrence through the various types of temporal and functional relationship between behaviour, antecedents, and consequent variables (Cooper et al., 2007; Vollmer & Hackenberg, 2001). Appendix A20.1 provides ABC (i.e., Antecedent, Behaviour and Consequence) data sheet for recording.

Application of ABA

Behaviour-analytic interventions increase positive behaviour and decrease challenging behaviour through design, implementation, evaluation and modification of treatment programmes to change behaviour of social significance of individuals and groups. Literature is replete with the application of ABA-based intervention strategies (see Figure 20.3) with effective results not only in people with disabilities but also neurotypical people and animal behaviour as well in a wide range of areas; to enhance or develop communication and

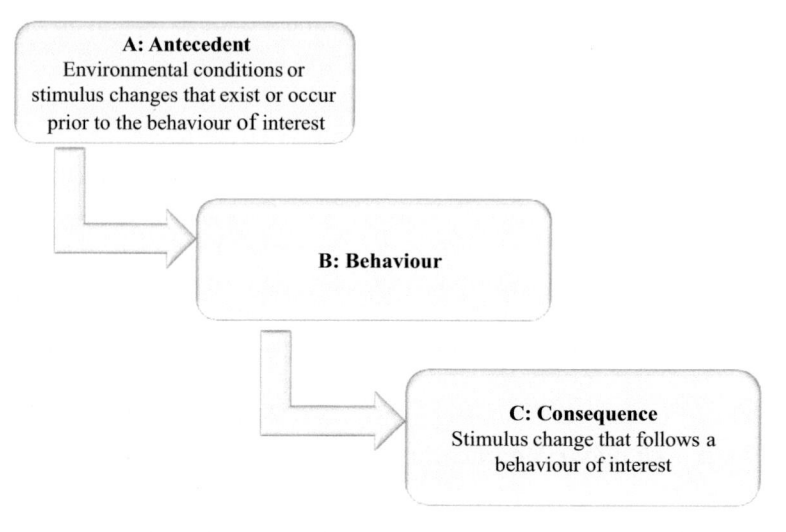

Figure 20.2 Three-term contingencies of behaviour

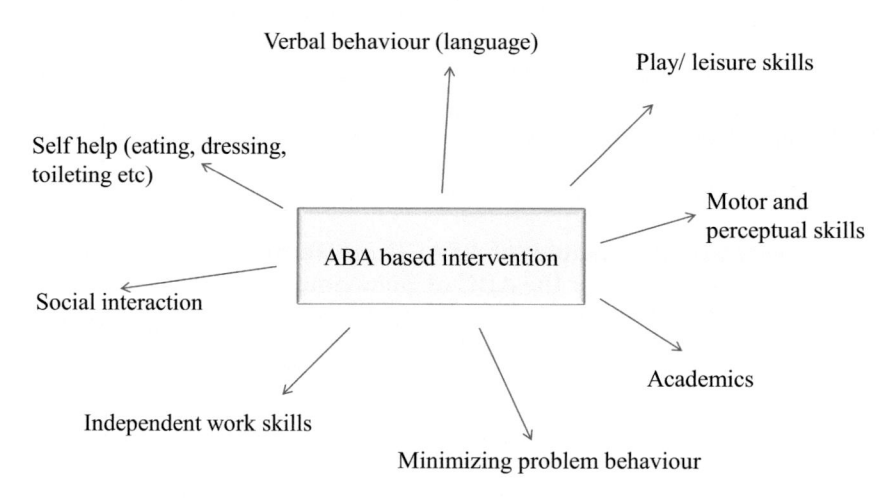

Figure 20.3 Application of behaviour interventions

language, socialization, following instructions, daily living skills, feeding, toilet training, applied animal behaviour, schoolwide positive behaviour support, classroom instruction, structured and naturalistic early behavioural interventions for developmental disabilities, organizational behaviour management etc. (Ardoin, 2016; Martens, Daly, Slocum et al., 2014). The significance and importance of the application of ABA-based principles in effectively addressing the core deficits of autism and other developmental disabilities have been paramount in not only promoting the acquisition and generalization of communication, social, academic, and self-help skills but also in eliminating the occurrence of problematic, inappropriate or challenging behaviours (e.g., Alberto & Troutman, 2005; Halder, 2017; Heflin & Alberto, 2001; Martens et al., 2015). Despite the criticism and controversies by certain groups of people due to the earlier use of punishments, the popularity and impact of interventions based on ABA are immense and unparalleled.

Planning ABA-based Behaviour Intervention

Proper systematic planning for ABA-based intervention is an extremely crucial aspect of the entire process upon which lies the foundation of an effective intervention programme leading to significant outcomes. ABA-based intervention is an extremely systematic, scientific, methodical, technical, analytical, step-by-step process. Taylor (2006) deliberated on a four-phase systematic intervention model; assessment, planning, designing and implementation. The main components of the development plan are (a) gathering, recording and analysing information, (b) setting goals/objectives/directions, (c) developing and writing the intervention plan and (d) implementing and reviewing the intervention plan. The step-by-step assessment process comprising seven crucial aspects is displayed in Figure 20.4.

Assessment for Behaviour Intervention

Assessment means gathering information about a person and his environment and analysing information in order to make necessary decisions about an individual (Wallace et al., 1992). Assessment is necessary for identifying a problem or criteria for achievement, identifying target behaviours, monitoring progress and for follow-up and benefits the researchers, practitioners, and consumers by providing a common means for describing and comparing behaviour with a set of labels having a common meaning. Behaviour assessment is a continuous process that includes pre, during and post-intervention phase and comprises observing, explaining, and predicting human behaviour as a crucial aspect of any intervention plan. Behaviour assessment is

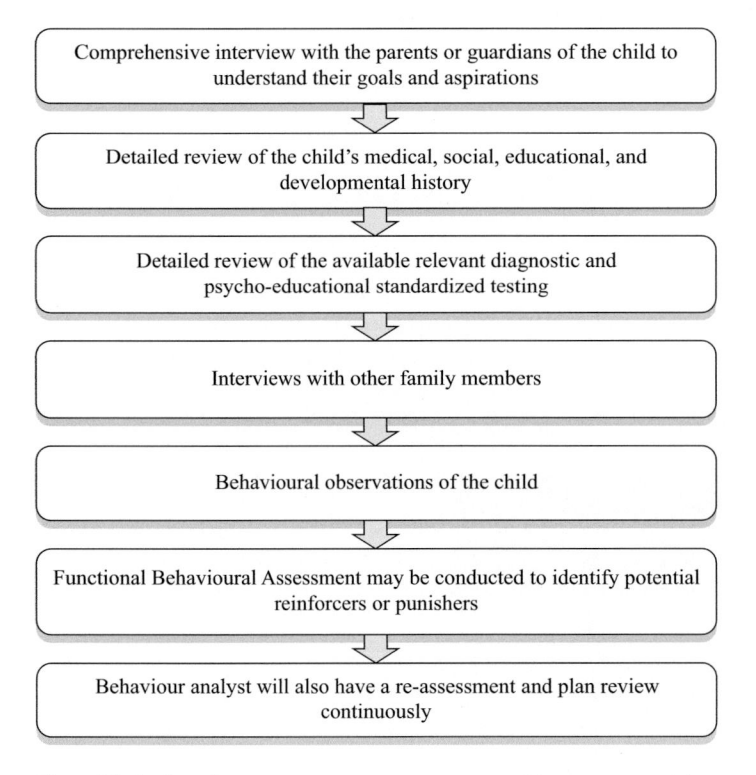

```
┌─────────────────────────────────────────────────────────────────┐
│ Comprehensive interview with the parents or guardians of the    │
│ child to understand their goals and aspirations                 │
└─────────────────────────────────────────────────────────────────┘
                                 ⇩
┌─────────────────────────────────────────────────────────────────┐
│ Detailed review of the child's medical, social, educational,    │
│ and developmental history                                       │
└─────────────────────────────────────────────────────────────────┘
                                 ⇩
┌─────────────────────────────────────────────────────────────────┐
│ Detailed review of the available relevant diagnostic and        │
│ psycho-educational standardized testing                         │
└─────────────────────────────────────────────────────────────────┘
                                 ⇩
┌─────────────────────────────────────────────────────────────────┐
│ Interviews with other family members                            │
└─────────────────────────────────────────────────────────────────┘
                                 ⇩
┌─────────────────────────────────────────────────────────────────┐
│ Behavioural observations of the child                           │
└─────────────────────────────────────────────────────────────────┘
                                 ⇩
┌─────────────────────────────────────────────────────────────────┐
│ Functional Behavioural Assessment may be conducted to identify  │
│ potential reinforcers or punishers                              │
└─────────────────────────────────────────────────────────────────┘
                                 ⇩
┌─────────────────────────────────────────────────────────────────┐
│ Behaviour analyst will also have a re-assessment and plan       │
│ review continuously                                             │
└─────────────────────────────────────────────────────────────────┘
```

Figure 20.4 Step-by-step assessment process comprising seven crucial aspects

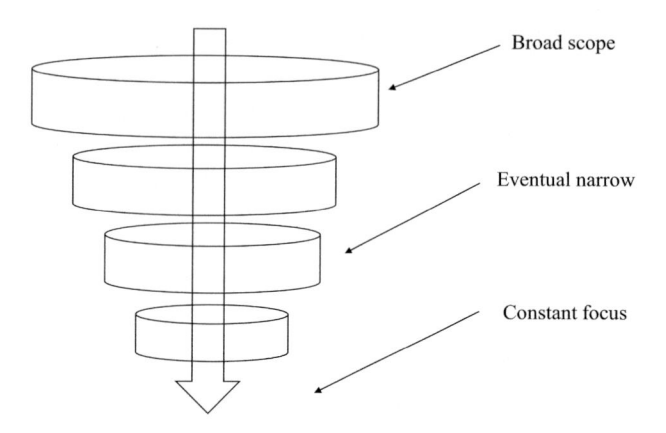

Figure 20.5 Behaviour assessment process as funnel shaped (Hawkins, 1979)

funnel shaped, with an initial broad scope leading to an eventual narrow and constant focus (Hawkins, 1979, see Figure 20.5). Beginning with maximum information about the subject and eventually zeroing down to retrieving in-depth more specific information about the person and his/her behaviours.

Purpose of Assessing Behaviour

A well-planned assessment identifies and defines target behaviour for change including the abilities/strengths and needs and all relevant factors that may inform or impact intervention. Well-constructed thorough behaviour assessment provides a roadmap for understanding and identifying the variables controlling the behaviour; hence it discovers resources, assets, significant others, competing contingencies, maintenance, and generalization factors, including potential reinforcers and/or punishers.

Crucial elements of a well-conceived assessment include consideration of the characteristics of what is being measured, quality, appropriateness of the measurement tools, technical skill of the measurer and how measures will be used. The main components of pre-intervention assessment are listed in Figure 20.6.

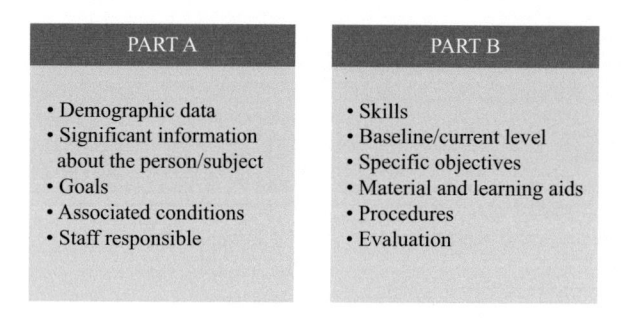

PART A	PART B
• Demographic data • Significant information about the person/subject • Goals • Associated conditions • Staff responsible	• Skills • Baseline/current level • Specific objectives • Material and learning aids • Procedures • Evaluation

Figure 20.6 Main components for pre-intervention assessment

Reviewing Records: Medical, Educational and Historical at the Outset

Exploring medical, educational, and historical records at the outset is one of the most important considerations in behaviour assessment as it guides and provides crucial loops and background understanding essential for ameliorating an effective intervention plan. Prior to conducting an in-depth functional analysis or assessment of behaviour, it is necessary to rule out any *medical, physical, or biological factors* that may impact behaviour. Reviewing records includes medical reports, earlier behaviour support or intervention plans, psychological profiles, individual education or family service plans, information about mental health or well-being, experimental findings, and other specialists' services and their outcomes (e.g., occupational therapy, speech and language therapy, and nursing). *Reviewing medical records* is an essential aspect of any pre-intervention assessment in applied behaviour analysis (Figure 20.7) and may be needed if there are sufficient reasons or the possibility of association of the behaviours under consideration. Biological variables have been found to serve as antecedents as well as establishing operations affecting behaviour and response of an individual by impacting the value of reinforcers and punishers. Thorough reviews of records provide valuable and crucial information about the individuals' medical background, past history including behavioural and academic history, complete picture of a student's problem behaviour or behavioural needs and identify intervention strategies that have been successful or unsuccessful in the past and may discover the environmental settings and elements for successful outcomes.

Literature is replete with various behaviours associated with many common diseases found in people with specific types of disabilities hence such factors need to be ruled out before conducting an in-depth functional analysis or deciding the intervention plan. It is imperative to have a background knowledge by reviewing the existing literature to understand the association of the behaviour with the medical problems or diseases as has been found; such as history of ear or abdominal infections, diabetes, blocked eyes, sight problems, allergies etc. as these have been found commonly in certain disability groups (Bowring et al., 2019; Hyman et al., 2020). Similarly it is necessary to understand the association of mental health problems with anxiety and depression (Hemmings et al., 2013), head banging with Oitis media (Adams et al., 2016),

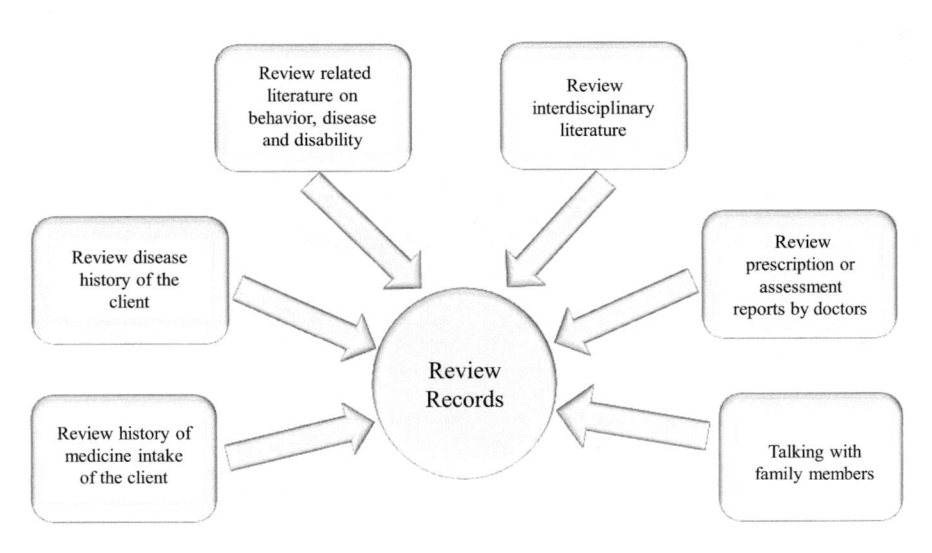

Figure 20.7 Reviewing medical records

incontinence with bladder infection (Niemczyk et al., 2018), aggression with temporal lobe epilepsy (Deb et al., 2020), hyperthyroidism with over-activity (Andersen et al., 2014), dementia with anger (Trahan et al., 2011), anger or aggressive behaviour (David, 2021; Sukhodolsky et al., 2016), with frustration, self-injurious behaviour, etc. (Minshawi et al., 2014). However, reviewing such records should not be taken as the terminal end but such records need to be validated through in-depth further direct and indirect analysis including empirical analysis and observation-based data as they might not present the current status of the individual. Record reviews should be conducted in combination with other indirect assessments and observations for a holistic knowledge of the individual and his/her behaviour in order to increase the quality of the functional assessment and for successful interventions.

Types of Behaviour Assessment Methods

Prior to recommending or developing behaviour-change programmes, it is mandatory to conduct current in-depth properly planned, structured pre-intervention assessments using various methods based on client's needs, consent, environmental parameters, and other contextual variables. The most common assessment methods can be broadly categorised as (a) *indirect assessment,* (b) *direct assessment* and (c) *ecological assessment* (see Figure 20.8).

Indirect Methods

Indirect methods of assessment gather information through indirect ways such as behaviour interviews, behaviour checklists etc. through other important people in the person's environment or life.

Behavioural interviews can be specifically helpful and important in identifying a list of potential target behaviours in order to obtain information about the person concerned that can be further validated by subsequent direct observation. The main purpose of interviews is identifying

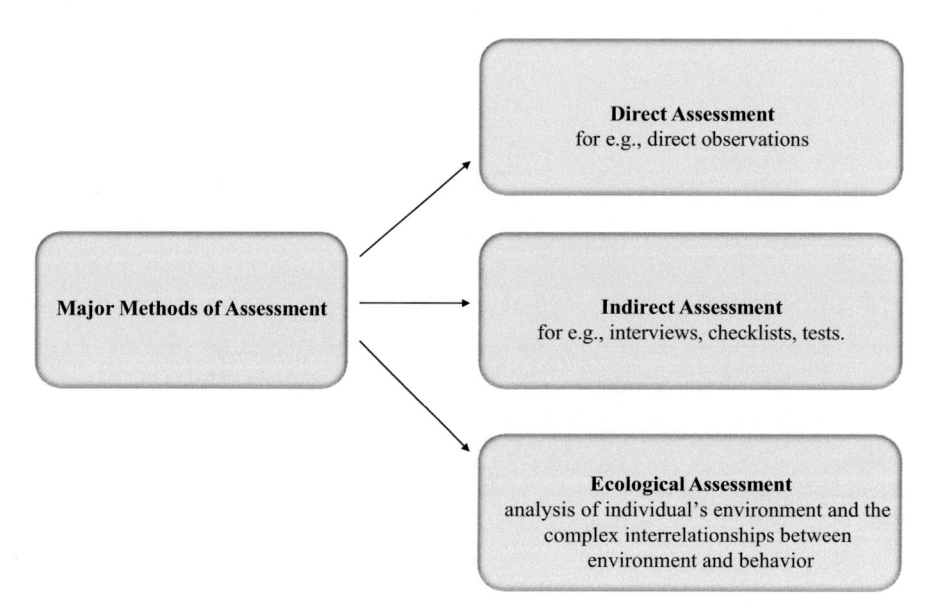

Figure 20.8 Major behaviour assessment methods

Table 20.1 Sample behaviour checklist

Today in class	Needs improvement	Satisfactory	Excellent	Feedback/comment
Whether the child follows teacher instruction?				
Was he/she compliant in the class?				
Did the child listen well?				
Whether the child cooperates with the teacher and others?				
Whether the child sits properly during class?				

variables that occur before, during and/or after the occurrence of a behaviour. Asking WHAT and WHEN questions focusing on the environmental conditions that exist before, during and after a behavioural episode, instead of WHY or HOW questions (to avoid evoking mentalistic explanations that are of little value in understanding the problem) is the key to get the relevant information. Some sample behaviour interview questions to be asked of the teacher to reduce the child's/student's yelling and non-compliant behaviour can be *"Kindly define the problem or target behaviour?"*, *"Can you explain what exactly usually happens just before the behaviour?"*, *"Kindly tell what exactly happens just after the behaviour?"*, *"What do you do or how do you attend the behaviour of the child?"*, *"What is the child's reaction or response when you attend to the child?"* and *"What interventions did you tried to address the behaviour of the child?"*.

Behaviour checklists are descriptions of specific behaviours and conditions under which behaviour occurs that comprise assessing the antecedents and consequences in Likert-type scales. A sample behaviour checklist is given in Table 20.1.

Direct Methods

Indirect methods of assessment need to be supplemented with direct methods of assessment in the natural environment for validation. Some of the widely used direct methods of assessment for behaviour analysis are anecdotal observation, functional assessment etc.

Anecdotal observation is objective, accurate in the form of a narrative or a written short story of the events and describes the incidents or events that are important in a natural environment/context. Anecdotal observation guides future data collection by providing context and information that may not be provided through other assessment methods. *Appendix A20.2* provides a sample Anecdotal recording form for pre-intervention assessment data collection.

Functional Behaviour Analysis (FBA): Understanding Underlying Function of Behaviour

All behaviour occurs for a reason, and one needs to determine that reason scientifically based on data. For a suitable intervention it is pertinent to understand the function of the behaviour (what, why and how of behaviour). The importance and significance of FA has increased with leaps and bounds as evident through the cumulative number of publications which shows a steep increase indicating that FA approaches to assessment have become more widespread and recognized throughout the field of ABA (Bloom et al., 2013; Carr et al. 2009; Kodak et al., 2013; Lambert & Bloom, 2012; Rispoli et al., 2014).

Evidence from research indicates that behaviours desirable or undesirable both are learned and maintained through interaction with the environment of a person, either through positive or negative reinforcement contingencies. All behaviour happens for a reason such as for getting attention, tangible, to avoid or escape from a situation or demand from task, and the aim of functional behaviour analysis is to understand the function by analysing the history of reinforcement contingencies. Extensive research has validated that Functional Analyses (FA) can be an effective method of systematically determining the function of a behaviour (Wilder et al., 2007). There are various types of well-conceived functional analysis (FA) to identify the function of a behaviour and the maintaining variables of problem behaviour exhibited by a child (Iwata & Dozier, 2008; Rispoli et al., 2014).

The development of the FA (Functional Assessment) or FBA (Functional Behaviour Assessment) by Iwata, Dorsey, Slifer, Bauman, and Richman (1982/1994) is considered a milestone and a "gold standard" tool for determining the function of a problem behaviour in applied behaviour analysis. FA has eased down the process of identifying and designing an effective intervention plan. In an FA, putative antecedents and consequences of problem behaviour are arranged within an experimental design and their separate effects on problem behaviour are observed and measured (Cooper et al., 2007). Through a properly conducted FBA the type and source of reinforcement for challenging behaviours is identified based on which an intervention plan is designed to decrease the occurrence of the behaviours through the three strategies (i.e., altering antecedent variables, altering consequent variables, and teaching alternative appropriate or replacement behaviours) (Cooper et al., 2007).

Despite the effectiveness of FA in identifying the function of a behaviour and its immense role in designing an effective intervention plan there are also certain limitations which should be kept in mind during implementation. For example, traditional FA assessment may temporarily strengthen, reinforce or increase the problem behaviour during sessions (Carr et al., 2009), also some behaviours may not be amenable to FA because they occur very infrequently (Kelly et al., 2003), and FA in contrived settings may not take into account variables that increase problem behaviour in a natural environment (Lang et al., 2008) etc. However, many of the limitations can be addressed with a brief trial-based functional analysis that can be effectively implemented in a natural environment (Wilder et al., 2006). A diagrammatic representation of the results of trial-based FA showing test and control conditions on a child with self-injurious behaviour is reported in Figure 20.9.

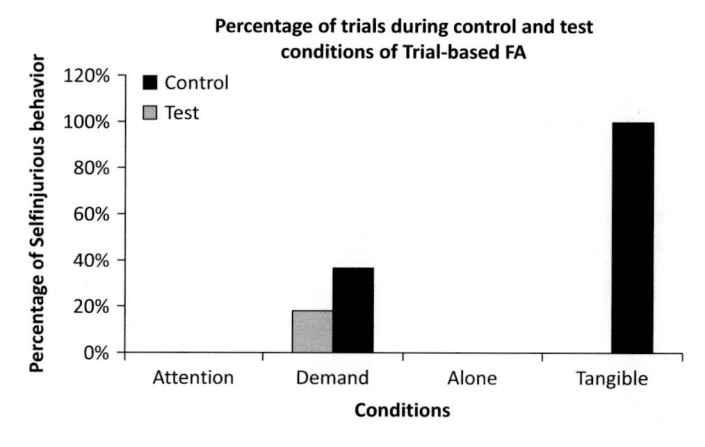

Figure 20.9 Results of trial-based FA on a 7 years child with self-injurious head hitting behaviour shown through percentage of trials during control and test conditions (Source: Halder, 2007)

Note. The vertical axis shows the results of trial-based functional analysis of self-injurious behaviour (Head hitting) of a child with a developmental disability during the control and test conditions in a classroom setting. *The horizontal axis* indicates the four conditions (i.e., attention, demand, alone and tangible) of the FA in control and test conditions.

Behaviour Assessment Scales

Pre-intervention assessment scales have played a crucial role in designing behaviour intervention plans. Some of the most used Indian pre-intervention assessment scales for people with disabilities are: (a) FACP (Myreddi et al., 2004); Functional assessment checklist for programming, (b) BASIC MR (Peshwarayi & Venketesan, 2004); Behaviour assessment scale for Indian children, (c) MDPS (Jeyachandran, 1995, 2000); Madras Developmental Programming System Scale. Some of the most commonly and widely used international pre-intervention assessment scales worldwide are: (a) VB-MAPP (Sundberg, 2008); Verbal Behaviour Milestone assessment and placement programme, (b) EFL (McGreevy et al., 2012); Essential for Learning is designed for verbal and non-verbal children and adults with moderate-to-very-severe disabilities, including autism, and limited skill repertoires.

Ecological Assessment

Ecological assessment refers to the analysis of an individual's learning environment and the complex interrelationships between the environment and behaviour of the person (Cooper et al., 2007). Behavioural change is a complex phenomenon that is influenced by a wide range of an individual's *internal factors;* motivation, skills, abilities, traits, interests etc., as well as the *external factors;* social and physical environment (Michie et al., 2008). Accounting for the internal and external factors in an individual's environment is complex but important consideration for any behaviour intervention plan. Research endorses that interventions considering complex social-cultural context yield more successful/ effective outcomes (Glanz & Bishop, 2010). A well-conceived intervention plan remains incomplete without an adequate understanding of the child and his or her environment, be it internal or external.

An ecological assessment is a *comprehensive process* in which data is collected about how a child functions in different environments or settings and identifies the various factors affecting behaviours of a person, which include physiological conditions, physical aspects of the environment (for e.g., lighting, seating arrangements, noise level), interactions with others, home environment, past reinforcement history, social and cultural environment including auditory, olfactory, and visual environment etc. Some of the *benefits of ecological assessment* are: analysing the resources existing in an individual's environment, discovering and monitoring the current and changing conditions for analysing success or failure, understanding structure and function of ecosystems in order to develop an effective intervention plan, analysing the predictability and/or outcome and consequences of an intervention plan or model beforehand in response to the ecosystems and their interaction so that possible strategies can be designed accordingly considering all factors.

Factors to be Considered in Ecological Assessment

An ecological assessment gathers a great deal of information about the person's environments where he/she lives (Bronfenbrenner, 1979, see Figure 20.10) namely, *microsystem*: the individual, family and friends, *mesosystem*: community, *exosystem:* social systems, and social networks, *mac-

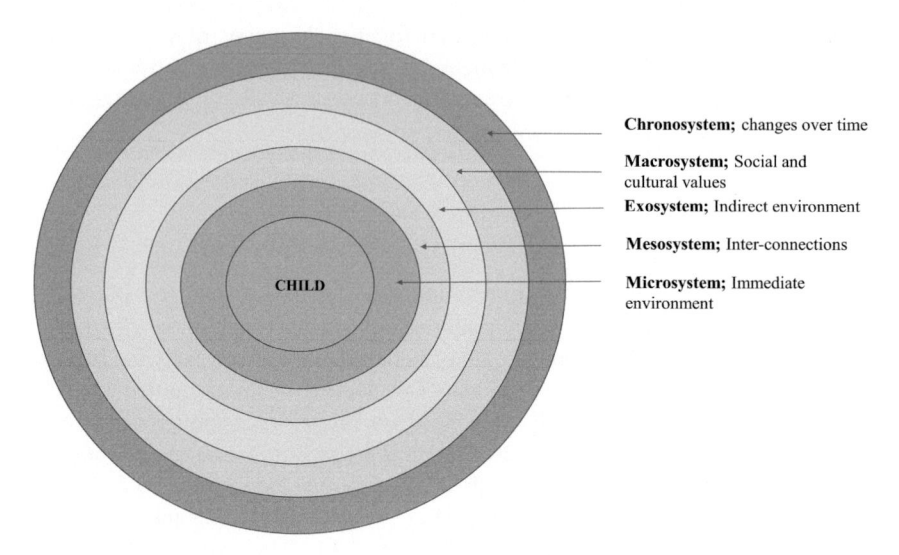

Figure 20.10 Environmental consideration as per the ecological theory (Source: Bronbenfrenner, 1979)

rosystem: laws, beliefs, values and cultural spheres of their respective ecosystem, and *chronosystem:* changes over time. Table 20.2 provides the details of the various factors that need to be considered in the ecological assessment of an individual.

Hence ecological assessment includes a wide range of all possible factors: (a) *physiological or biological factors* such as illness, allergy, fatigue, hunger, medication, pain, time of day, physical activity, sleep deprivation etc.; (b) *physical or environmental factors* such as noise, lighting, size of an area, crowding, high or low activity level, visual distractions, unfamiliar setting, seating arrangements, sequence of activities; and (c) *social or situational factors* such as school holidays, changes in schedule or daily activities, student-teacher or peer interaction, presence or absence of a particular individual, family or home related factors, transitions of an individual etc. (Chandler & Dahlquist, 2002; Cooper et al., 2007). Hence in other words ecological assessment covers *individual characteristics* that influence behaviour change, *interpersonal* – formal and informal social networks and social support systems that influence individual behaviours, *Community:* relationships among organizations and institutions within defined boundaries, *Organizational:* organizations or social institutions with rules and regulations that affect how, or how well, and finally the *Policy/Enabling Environment;* influence of local, state, national and global laws and policies.

Sources of Information for Ecological Assessment

Ecological assessments are conducted at home and/or in the school environment using various procedures such as direct observation, data collection, task analysis, simple statistical analysis, checklists and interviews, and applying them to the ecosystem of the individual and exploring through the various sources of information such as student records, interviews, formal and informal tests, and direct observation. Ecological assessment can be very useful in situations such as when students perform or behave well in some environments but have difficulty in a specific setting. When a student may be peaceful during class time but is upset while travelling. When a student behaves well in all classes but acts inappropriately in one specific class. Some children may be fine at home but depressed or scared in school or social context among peers. A model of ecological assessment is presented in Figure 20.11 (Carroll, 1974).

Table 20.2 Important considerations in ecological assessment (Source: Bronfenbrenner, 1979)

Environments	Explanation	Examples	Key elements
Microsystem	Institutions and groups that most immediately and directly impact the child's development	Constitutes of family, school, religious institutions, neighbourhood, and peers.	Exploring the most basic environmental context by direct or indirect data collection methods.
Mesosystem	Consists of interconnections between the microsystems	Includes interactions between the family and teachers or between the child's peers and the family.	Interviews and checklists to gather information from family members, teachers, peers etc.
Exosystem	Involves links between social settings	Covers a child's experience at home that may be influenced by their parents experiences.	Understanding and exploring the interaction between various members of various environments.
Macrosystem	Describes overarching culture that influences the developing child, as well as the microsystems and mesosystems embedded in those cultures.	Cultural contexts can differ based on geographic location, socioeconomic status, poverty, and ethnicity. Members of a cultural group often share a common identity, heritage, and values that may cause significant influence on the individual.	Explores the effect of various cultural elements or aspects of an individual that include identity, heredity, value system etc.
Chronosystem	Consists of the pattern of environmental events and transitions over the life course, as well as changing socio-historical circumstances.	Impacts of various events and incidents on the child in the course of development.	Explores the long-term impact of a specific culture, historical evolution and the changes and their impact on the individual.

ABA-based Techniques

The most common widely used *ABA-based behaviour techniques are* discrete trial training (DTT), incidental teaching, pivotal response training, fluency building, verbal behaviour training, functional communication training etc. (see Table 20.3); *(a) Discrete Trial Training (DTT);* clear instructions are provided regarding a desired behaviour and the behaviour is reinforced with appropriate reinforcer (Booth & Keenan, 2018); *(b) Incidental Teaching (IT):* utilizes the principle of DTT but the goal is to impart concepts and behaviours through the child's daily experiences instead of emphasizing a particular behaviour (McGee & Daly, 2007), *(c) Pivotal Response Training (PRT):* targets pivotal skills that will lead to related skill development in untrained areas and subsequent application to daily settings (Koegel et al., 2001); *(d) Fluency Building (FB):* involves teaching of a complex behaviour in multiple steps until fluency with appropriate observation, reinforcement, and prompting (Kubina & Yurich, 2009); *(e) Verbal Behaviour Training (VB):* targets to teach language and communication skills by analysing the already existing language skills and developing and reinforcing more helpful and complex skills (Goldsmith et al., 2007),

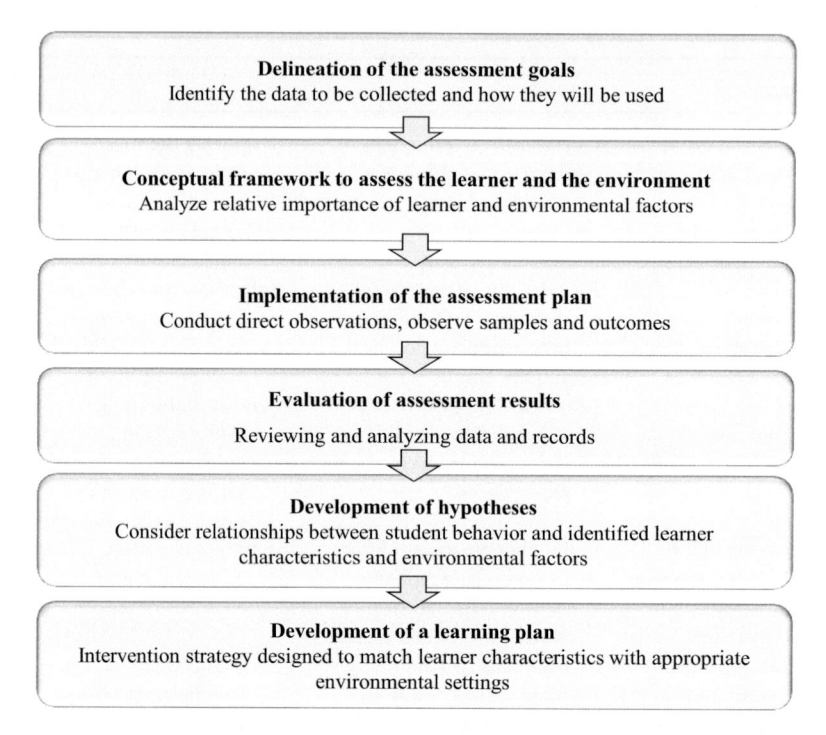

```
┌─────────────────────────────────────────────────────────┐
│           Delineation of the assessment goals           │
│     Identify the data to be collected and how they will be used │
└─────────────────────────────────────────────────────────┘
                            ⇩
┌─────────────────────────────────────────────────────────┐
│   Conceptual framework to assess the learner and the environment   │
│     Analyze relative importance of learner and environmental factors    │
└─────────────────────────────────────────────────────────┘
                            ⇩
┌─────────────────────────────────────────────────────────┐
│           Implementation of the assessment plan         │
│     Conduct direct observations, observe samples and outcomes    │
└─────────────────────────────────────────────────────────┘
                            ⇩
┌─────────────────────────────────────────────────────────┐
│              Evaluation of assessment results           │
│            Reviewing and analyzing data and records     │
└─────────────────────────────────────────────────────────┘
                            ⇩
┌─────────────────────────────────────────────────────────┐
│                Development of hypotheses                │
│  Consider relationships between student behavior and identified learner │
│              characteristics and environmental factors  │
└─────────────────────────────────────────────────────────┘
                            ⇩
┌─────────────────────────────────────────────────────────┐
│              Development of a learning plan             │
│  Intervention strategy designed to match learner characteristics with appropriate │
│                   environmental settings                │
└─────────────────────────────────────────────────────────┘
```

Figure 20.11 Diagrammatic representation of a Model of Ecological Assessment consisting of six steps (Source: Carroll, 1974)

(f) Functional Communication Training (FCT): involves teaching a more appropriate alternative functional communication response (FCR) that results in the delivery of the same reinforcer(s) maintaining problem behaviour (Ghaemmaghami & Hanley, 2021).

Function-based Behaviour Intervention Strategies

Once the function-based pre-interventions assessments are completed, the next step is to identify and design a function-based intervention plan and modify the environment by altering or removing the elements that may increase or trigger problem behaviour or inappropriate behaviour. The ABA strategies can be a remarkable tool for the teachers in classrooms or parents at home to prevent the undesirable behaviour of the children with or without disabilities from occurring by changing the antecedent (i.e., what happened immediately *before*) or consequence (i.e., what happened *after* the behaviour) based on which behaviour interventions can be broadly categorized as: (a) antecedent-based interventions and (b) consequence-based interventions. *Antecedent-based interventions (ABI)* are strategies that involve modifying the environment to reduce undesirable behaviours. Antecedents are the events, action(s), or circumstances that occur immediately before a behaviour. *Consequence-based interventions (CBI)* are those that occur after the behaviour has taken place by minimizing reinforcement for problem behaviour and increasing reinforcement for desirable behaviour. The most used antecedent- and consequence-based intervention strategies based on behaviour-analytic robust research findings are presented in Figure 20.12 and Table 20.3.

Figure 20.13 shows phase-by-phase findings of a completely personalized and individualized combined package intervention plan for a 7-year-old child with developmental disability

Table 20.3 Some widely used ABA-based techniques and strategies

ABA-based techniques and strategies	Short description	Benefits	Citations
a) Discrete Trial Training (DTT)	- small unit of instruction preferably in a 1:1 setting or small groups. - 4 components are taken into account; presentation of a discriminative stimulus, targeted response approximation, delivery of reinforcement, and inter-trial interval.	Enhance, develop or promote communication and speech, stimulus control, academic, social, behaviour, emotional, daily living skills etc.	Abby, 2011; Autism Treatment Info, 2011; Booth & Keenan, 2018; Brown-Chidsey & Steege, 2004; Mosier, 2011; Smith, 2001.
b) Incidental Teaching (IT)	- initially recognized by Hart and Risley in 1978. - uses naturally occurring "incidents" to teach appropriate and important skills. - learning environment is more fun and rewarding (with use of positive reinforcement and rewards) - self-initiated learning in natural environment - learning is natural and no additional materials required.	- increase and improve language, social responses, self-help skills, play skills, etc.	McGee & Daly, 2007.
c) Pivotal Response Training (PRT)	- developed by Dr. Robert L. Koegel and Dr. Lynn Kern Koegel at Stanford University (1970). - also called the Natural Language Paradigm - leads to related development of other behaviours that are not trained. - acquired skills are generalized and applied to new settings.	- development of communication and language skills - increases positive social behaviours - relief from disruptive self-stimulatory behaviours, - enhances communication, socialization and social interactions, - helps in self-regulation or self-management - responds to multiple cues simultaneously - learning is faster - collateral gains in non-targeted areas - addresses challenging behaviour	Koegel, Koegel, & McNerney, 2001; Koegel, & Koegel, 2019;

(Continued)

Table 20.3 (Continued)

ABA-based techniques and strategies	Short description	Benefits	Citations
d) Fluency building (FB)	- teaches complex behaviour - fluency is acquired through step-by-step process with the use of observation, reinforcement, and prompting. - encourages to teach specific elements of behaviour through repetition until fluency is acquired.	- reading skills - interaction with others, daily living skills or any target behaviour that follows a step-by-step approach.	Gist, 2010; Heinicke, et al., 2010; Kubina & Yurich, 2009; Weiss, et al., 2010;
e) Verbal Behaviour Training	- analysis of the existing language skills - targets to develop and reinforce needful complex skills. - teaches language and communication by targeting verbal behaviours proposed by B.F Skinner such as mand, tact, intraverbal, echoic, transcription and textual etc.	- capitalizes on the child's own motivation - teaching the child needful communication. - reduces challenging behaviour - can be combined with other teaching methods such as DTT or Natural Environment Training (NET).	Goldsmith, LeBlanc, & Sautter, 2007; Greer, Ross, 2004; Lowe, Horne, Harris, & Randle, 2002; Heinicke, et al., 2010; Sundberg & Michael, 2001
f) Task Analysis	- breaks complex tasks into a sequence of smaller steps or actions.	- teaches daily living skills (such as brushing teeth, bathing, dressing, variety of household chores, eating in the cafeteria, morning routines, completing assignments etc. - useful in desensitization programmes such as haircuts, sitting in flight, having teeth cleaned, and loud environments etc.	Cooper, Heron, & Heward 2020; Pratt & Steward, 2020

Antecedent-based strategies

(a) Preference and reinforcement assessment	- assessing learner preferences and potential reinforcers. - identify stimuli that function as effective positive reinforcers. - commonly used types of preference assessment are Free Operant Preference Assessments, Single-stimulus (SS), Paired-stimulus (PS), Multiple-stimulus-without replacement (MSWO), Brief Free Operant (FO) etc.	- reduces maladaptive behaviour and increases correct responding. - increase the likelihood of effective interventions. - reduces inappropriate behaviour while increasing the accuracy of responding. - ranks reinforcers in terms of effectiveness	Ciccone, Graff, Ahearn, 2015; Cooper, Heron & Heward, 2007; Cote, Thompson, Hanley, & McKerchar, 2007; Graff & Karsten, 2012; Karsten, Carr & Lepper, 2011; Lecomte, Liberman & Wallace, 2000; Rech, 2012.
(b) Altering the physical environment	- modifying the environment includes many different considerations such as physical structure and visual clarity, visual supports, schedules or routines, enriched environment, altering classroom structure etc.	- help the student to understand what is expected of a task and the steps to complete it - specifies learning goals - removes distractions - facilitates students to focus and express their thoughts	Bullard, 2010; Kremers, Eves, & Andersen, 2012
(c) Using visual supports	- visual representation of routines and expectations visuals schedules	- make abstract concepts more visually concrete - brings in routine, structure, and sequence - hence reduces anxiety of learner - assists in transitions	Cohen & Demchak, 2018; Rutherford, Baxter, Grayson, Johnston, O'Hare, 2020; Hayes, Hirano, Marcu, Monibi, Nguyen, Yeganyan, 2010.
(d) Premack Principle	- commonly known as "Grandma's Rule". - higher probability behaviour reinforces a less probable behaviour. - for e.g., "complete all your homework first if you want to play".	- increases compliance - easily acquires complex responses in the flow of the easy ones.	Azrin, Vinas, & Ehle, 2007; Frey, 2018; Klatt & Morris, 2001; Welsh et al., 1992.
(e) Prompting Procedures	- provide a systematic way of implementing and removing prompts for learner to perform skills independently. - depends on reinforcing correct responses prompted and not prompted both. - most common types are least to most prompting, most to least prompting, verbal prompt, gestural prompt, physical prompt etc.	- increase the probability of correct responding - increases opportunities for positive reinforcement	Cengher, Budd, Farrell, Fienup, 2018; Collins, Park & Haughney, 2018.

(Continued)

Table 20.3 (Continued)

ABA-based techniques and strategies	Short description	Benefits	Citations
(f) Modelling and Video Modelling (VM)	- target based behaviour through a series of scripted actions and or verbalizations - individual watching the video imitates the modelled behaviour resulting modifying existing behaviours or learning new ones.	- acquiring variety of skills; academic, social, vocational and professional, independent living skills, etc.	Ohtake, Takahashi, & Watanabe, 2015; Macpherson, Charlop, & Miltenberger, 2015; O'Handley, et al., 2016.
(g) Imitation	- breaks skills into components - provides the learner with a model of the target behaviour and rewards the learner for responding immediately after the model.	- helps in building a foundation for new skills - learning is fast and efficient - benefits learners of all ages - gain more independence within one's natural environment	Cardon & Wilcox, 2011; Cardon et al., 2015; Ingersoll, 2007; Ingersoll, & Lalonde, 2010; Ishizuka & Yamamoto, 2021; Ledford, & Windsor, 2021; Ledford & Wolery, 2011.
(h) Functional Communication Training (FCT)	- teaching another way to communicate before trying to change a difficult behaviour, so one doesn't need the old behaviour anymore - providing function-based intervention in which an existing behaviour is replaced with an alternative appropriate form of communication resulting in the same reinforcer(s) maintaining the problem behaviour.	- reductions of a variety of different types of problem behaviour - teaching socially appropriate ways of communication that increases access to reinforcers for the person	Harding et al., 2009; Jessel, Ghaemmaghami & Hanley, 2021; Rispoli, Camargo, Machalicek, Lang, & Sigafoos, 2014; Moskowitz, 2015; Tiger et al. 2008.
(i) High Probability Sequence (HPS)	- expected to perform three to five simple tasks that have a high probability of compliance and followed by a direction that has a low probability of compliance. - increase compliance through high-probability request sequences - High-p is used to build behavioural momentum in order for a student to comply with a demand or instruction that has a history of low compliance.	- increases socially appropriate behaviours - decreases defiant behaviour, non-compliance, transition problems and escape-related behaviour relating to task completion etc. - decrease the slowness in responding to low-probability requests. - encourages responding to more difficult, low-p requests.	Bross et al., 2018; Bullock & Normand, 2006; Lane, Menzies, Ennis, & Oakes, 2015

(j) Contriving Motivating Operation (CMO)	- a condition that alters (a) the value of consequences (i.e., reinforcement or punishment), and (b) the probability of behaviours previously associated with such consequences - creates satiation or deprivation states that results in increase or decrease of the effectiveness of reinforcement (i.e., E,O or AO) Establishing Operation (EO) – increases the current effectiveness of some stimulus, object, or event as reinforcement and Abolishing Operation (AO) – decrease the current effectiveness of some stimulus, object, or event as reinforcement.	- alters the effectiveness of the reinforcing value of stimulus, object, or event as a reinforcer - alter the current frequency of all behaviour that has been reinforced in the past by that stimulus, object, or event.	Edwards, Lotfizadeh, Poling, 2019; Endicott & Thomas, Higbee, 2007; Langthorne & McGill, 2009; Lechago, 2019; Simó-Pinatella, Font-Roura, Planella-Morató, McGill, Alomar-Kurz, Giné, 2013.
(k) Choice Making	- offers choices for a sense of environmental control.	- increase compliance in completing work during independent work time.	Howell, Dounavi & Storey, 2019; Martin, Yu, Martin, & Fazzio, 2006; Morgan, 2006; Mintz, Wallace, Najdowski, Atcheson & Bosch, 2007; Shogren, Faggella-Luby, Jik, Wehmeyer, 2004; Sigafoos, & Dempsey, 1992
(l) Chaining Procedures	- teaching a behaviour using behaviour chains. - behaviour chains are sequences of individual behaviours that when linked together form a terminal behaviour. - first step is to complete a task analysis that identifies all of the smaller, teachable units of a behaviour that make up a behaviour chain. - common types are forward chaining, backward chaining and total task chaining.	- gain proficiency in complex, multi-step behaviours such as self-help skills, social skills - helps in breaking down a more complex task	Cooper Heron, Heward, 2007; Jerome, Frantino, Sturmey, 2007; Slocum & Tiger, 2011

(Continued)

Table 20.3 (Continued)

ABA-based techniques and strategies	Short description	Benefits	Citations
	– *Forward chaining*; the behaviour is taught in its naturally occurring order and each step of the sequence is taught and reinforced when completed correctly. – *Backward chaining*; all behaviours identified in the task analysis are initially completed by the trainer, except for the final behaviour in the chain. When the learner performs the final behaviour in the sequence reinforcement is delivered. – *Total task chaining* involves the child learning the task as a whole through each step providing the necessary prompts.		
Consequence-based strategies			
(a) Extinction Procedures (EP)	– discontinues maintaining reinforcement for problem behaviour for decreasing or eliminating occurrences of the negative (or problem) behaviours.	– reduces problem/ dangerous, aggressive, self-injurious behaviour, sleeping/eating problems – reduces dangerous/aggressive behaviours; self-injurious/ others – promotes functional communication – addresses inappropriate social behaviours etc.	Sullivan & Bogin, 2010; Weiss, 2013.

(b) Token Economy	- increase target behaviours and decrease defined undesirable behaviours - reinforces the frequency of a target behaviour - tokens or symbols are provided to the individual when the target behaviour is performed. - tokens can then be exchanged for other types of reinforcement. - reinforcement strategy where generalized reinforcers (tokens) are exchanged for back-up reinforcers - allows sequence of behaviours to be reinforced without any disruption of task	- reinforce skills such as academics, communication, self-help, or prosocial behaviour - reduce the gap between the target behaviour and the back-up reinforcement. - easily allow access to reinforcement - promote maintenance of a skill over longer durations of time when the back-up reinforcement is not accessible. - maintains the value of the back-up reinforcers due to deprivation. - least likely to be affected by satiation. - similar reinforcement can be provided despite the differences in their preference of back-up reinforcer - can be more reinforcing than a single primary reinforcer.	Boniecki & Moore, 2003; Carnett, Raulston, Lang, Tostanoski, Lee, Sigafoos, & Machalicek, 2014; Doll, McLaughlin & Barretto, 2013; Hackenberg, 2009; Matson & Boisjoli, 2008
(c) Differential Reinforcement Strategies	- increases the occurrence of desirable behaviour while simultaneously decreasing undesirable behaviour. - consists of *two components*; a) reinforcing the appropriate behaviour and b) withholding reinforcement of the inappropriate behaviour - most *common types* are; Differential Reinforcement of Incompatible behaviour (DRI), Differential Reinforcement of Alternative behaviour (DRA), Differential Reinforcement of Other behaviour (DRO), Differential Reinforcement of Low Rates (DRL).	- reduce potentially inappropriate or dangerous problem behaviour - increases the rate of existing desired behaviours that occur infrequently - decreasing the rate of appropriate behaviour that occurs too frequently	Athens & Vollmer, 2010; Chowdhury, & Benson, 2011; Petscher, & Bailey, 2008; Vladescu & Kodak, 2010

ABA based intervention

Antecedent based interventions

Occur before the behavior cocurs.
For e.g.:
- Choice
- Prompting
- High-probability sequence
- Non-contingent reinforcement
- Contriving motivating operations

Consequence based intervention

Occur after the behavior cocurs.
For e.g.:
✓ Differential reinforcement
  - Differential reinforcement of alternative behavior (DRA)
  - Differential Reinforcement of Other behavior (DRO)
  - Differential Reinforcement of Incompatible behavior (DRI)
✓ Extinction

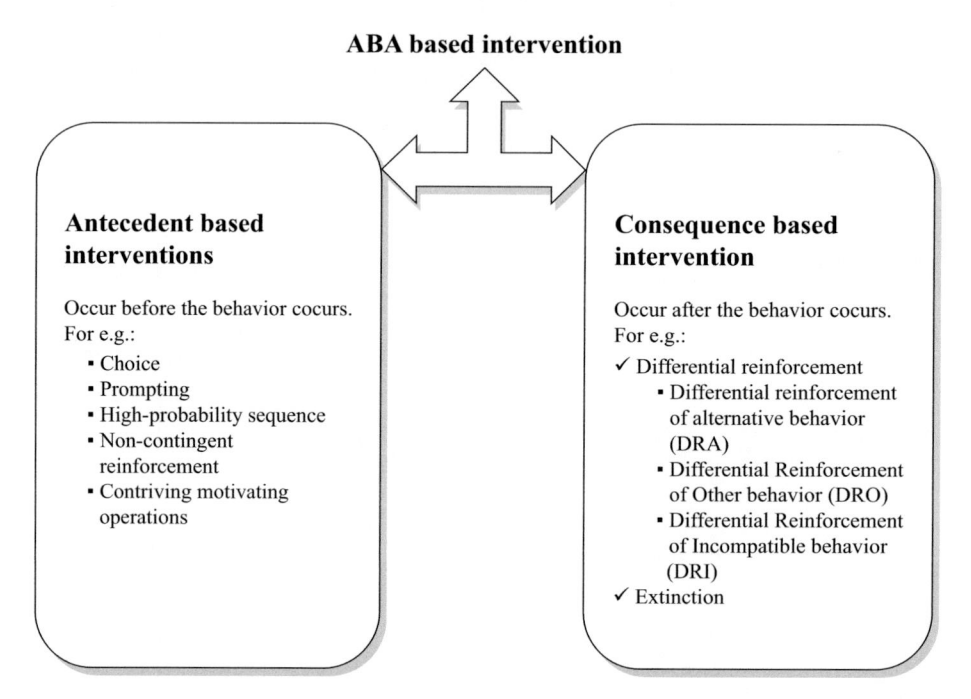

Figure 20.12 Common broad strategies of behaviour interventions (Source: Cooper, Heron & Heward, 2007)

with severe self-injurious behaviour showing effective results. Self-injurious behaviour is seen to reduce substantially with the systematically designed intervention plan. An alternative socially appropriate replacement behaviour is established, including increasing functional communication training that is clearly visible in the result. The targeted self-injurious behaviour is seen to completely drop down as the intervention progresses phase by phase. A behaviour analyst needs

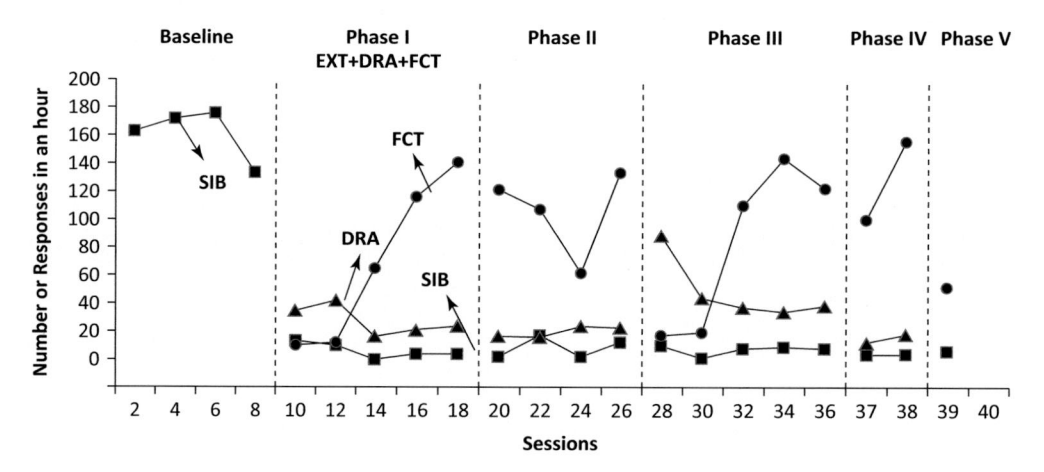

Figure 20.13 Findings of function-based phase by phase, personalized, individualized intervention package of a 7-year-old child with developmental disability targeting self-injurious or inappropriate behaviour (Source. Halder, 2017) *Note*. **FCT** – Functional Communication Training, **EXT** – Extinction, **SIB** – Self-Injurious Behaviour, **DRA** – Differential Reinforcement of Alternative Behaviour.

to be completely alert, with good observing and analytical skills, along with the preparedness and readiness to make necessary alternative modifications to the ongoing or existing intervention plan based on continuous review and analysis of data for effective results.

Table 20.4 summarizes the step-by-step process of ABA-based Intervention Model.

Ethics, Recording, Privacy, and Confidentiality of Data/Records

The Behaviour Analyst (BA) has a *legal and ethical obligation* to accurately observe both appropriate and inappropriate behaviour and all needs to be systematically and appropriately reported

Table 20.4 Summary of step-by-step process of ABA-based Intervention Model

Steps	Details
Conducting pre-intervention Assessments	An initial assessment includes meeting the individual, their parent(s)/guardians, and other important members to find out valuable information to identify the intervention priorities, goals
	Assessment includes various strategies to understand the individuals' strengths, needs unique learning styles etc.
	Complete assessment includes ecological assessment of the learner to understand the behaviours and the learner with respect to the setting, the context, and the environment
	Assessment includes identifying the reinforcement and preference assessments to identify the potential reinforcers of the learners in hierarchy
	Baseline (pre-intervention) measures need to be taken beforehand prior to intervention so as to compare later pre and post data whether or not the intervention is effective after intervention.
Creating Treatment Plans analysing all aspects	Focuses on analysing and managing the learner's environment at the outset.
	Analysing and determining the crucial elements and factors in the various environments of the learner (i.e., home, school, community) that maintains the targeted behaviours.
	Considering what is needed in the environment to teach the alternative socially appropriate replacement behaviour that is meaningful for the individual and the people in his environment.
	Plan an intervention that comprises the best design to implement each part of the intervention plan appropriately for most effective results.
	Deciding the setting/context for intervention, person implementing the intervention and the intensity.
Ongoing Training, Support & Data Collection	Depending on the goals, availability and recommendations deciding the intervention supports needed; other professionals, specialists, materials, aids etc.
	Training parents, family members and other personnel who would implement the plans.
	An effective intervention plan involves a cohesive, collaborative team of professionals.
Implementation of intervention as per plan	Intervention is implemented as per plan and all data are continuously recorded.
Analysis and evaluating the intervention plan	Making sure interventions are working and goals are acquired or progressed as expected.
	Continuous analysis, modification of intervention plan and designing new plans as per the learner ongoing status is necessary for an effective intervention plan.
	All data are recorded and kept for observation and analysis.

and recorded continuously in written form. *Prior written consent* from the client explaining in an easily understandable way is extremely essential at the beginning of any intervention programme. The written document provides a sense of accountability and is an attempt to answer *the questions of Who? What? When? Where? and How?* of the targeted behaviour plan.

Some Quick Tips for Effective Behaviour Interventions

- Prioritizing goals in terms of benefit to the client and social appropriateness is a must.
- Ethical abiding at all steps and informed consent is a must.
- Data keeping and constant and continuous recording of all data.
- Continuous assessment, recording, reviewing, and analysing.
- Continuous revision, modification, and changes to intervention plan.
- A good behaviour analyst should be a good observer and must be constantly analytical.

Conclusion

The ABA-based strategies and interventions come from many years of established evidence-based research since the 1960s with robust findings. ABA is based on the science of learning and behaviour that helps to understand behaviour; how it is influenced by the environment and how learning takes place by increasing appropriate behaviours that are beneficial and decreasing inappropriate behaviours that are harmful by increasing the opportunities to access reinforcement in the person's environment. Numerous people availing the behaviour analytical services through trained and skilled ABA professionals have found significant visible, effective results and benefits all over the world, resulting in meaningful positive changes in the life of the individual and the people in their life or environment for a better quality of life and well-being promoting and ensuring access, participation and hence the inclusion of the people with diverse needs in all walks of life.

Appendices

Appendix A20.1 *Data sheet for ABC (i.e., Antecedent, behaviour and consequence) recording for behaviour assessment*

Date: __/__/__
Name of the person observed_____
Observer: _____
Behaviour(s): _____

Date	Time	Antecedent (What happened immediately before the behaviour)	Behaviour	Consequence (What happened immediately after the behaviour)	Possible functions/comments

Appendix A20.2 *Sample data sheet for Anecdotal recording*

Anecdotal record form
Observer: _____

Date of observation: _____
Time of observation: _____

Name of the person observed: _____

Description of the incident: _____

_____

_____

_____

_____

Description of the setting/context:

_____

_____

Any recommendations/notes:

_____

_____

_____

_____
Signature of the observer

Bibliography

Abby, A. (2011). What is discrete trial teaching? Retrieved on April 3, 2012, from http://www.autism-community.com/what-is-discrete-trial-teaching/

Absoud, M., & Ziriat, M. (2019). Managing challenging behaviour in children with possible learning disability, *BMJ*, *365*, 1663. https://doi.org/10.1136/bmj.l1663.

Adams, D. J., Susi, A, Erdie-Lalena, C.R, Gorman, G., Hisle-Gorman, E., Rajnik, M., Elrod, M., & Nylund, C. M. (2016). Otitis media and related complications among children with autism spectrum disorders. *Journal of Autism and Developmental Disorders*, *46*(5), 1636–42. https://10.1007/s10803-015-2689-x.

Alberto, P. A. & Troutman, A. C. (2005). *Applied Behavior Analysis For Teachers*. Pearson College Division Pub

Ardoin, S. P., Wagner, L., & Bangs, K. E. (2016). Applied behavior analysis: A foundation for response to intervention. In S. R. Jimerson, M. K. Burns, & A. M.VanDerHeyden (Eds.), *Handbook of response to intervention: The science and practice of multi-tiered systems of support* (pp. 29–42). Springer Science + Business Media. https://doi.org/10.1007/978-1-4899-7568-3_3

Amsted, M., & Muller, C. M. (2020). Students' problem behaviours as sources of teacher stress in special needs schools for individuals with intellectual disabilities. *Frontiers in Education*, *4*, 159. https://10.3389/feduc.2019.00159

Andersen, S.L, Laurberg, P., Wu, C. S., & Olsen, J. (2014). Attention deficit hyperactivity disorder and autism spectrum disorder in children born to mothers with thyroid dysfunction: a Danish nationwide cohort study. *BJOG, 121*(11), 1365–74. https://10.1111/1471-0528.12681. Epub 2014 Mar 10. PMID: 24605987.

Azrin, N. H., Vinas, V., & Ehle, C. T. (2007). Physical activity as reinforcement for classroom calmness of ADHD children: A preliminary study. *Child & Family Behavior Therapy, 29*(2), 1–8. https://doi.org/10.1300/J019v29n02_01

Athens, E. S., & Vollmer, T. R. (2010). An investigation of differential reinforcement of alternative behavior without extinction. *Journal of Applied Behavior Analysis, 43*(4), 569–589. https://doi.org/10.1901/jaba.2010.43-569

Autism Academy. (2010). Discrete trial teaching. [PowerPoint slides]. Retrieved on Jun 21, 2010 from http://archives.doe.k12.ga.us/ci_exceptional.aspx?PageReq=CIEXCAutismAc ademy2010

Autism Treatment Info. (2011). What is a discrete trial? Retrieved on April 3, 2012, from http://www.autismtreatment.info/What+Is+a+Discrete+Trial.aspx

Baker, J. C., Hanley, G. P., & Mathews, R. M. (2006). Staff-administered functional analysis and treatment of aggression by an elder with dementia. *Journal of Applied Behavior Analysis, 39*(4), 469–474. https://doi.org/10.1901/jaba.2006.80-05

Bloom, S. E., Lambert, J. M., Dayton, E., & Samaha, A. L. (2013). Teacher-conducted trial-based functional analyses as the basis for intervention. *Journal of Applied Behavior Analysis, 46*(1), 208–18. https://10.1002/jaba.21. PMID: 24114095.

Boniecki, K. A., & Moore, S. (2003). Breaking the silence: Using a token economy to reinforce classroom participation. *Teaching of Psychology, 30*(3), 224–227.

Booth, N., & Keenan, M. (2018). Discrete Trial Teaching: A study on the comparison of three training strategies. *Interdisciplinary Education and Psychology, 2*(2), 3. https://doi.org/10.31532/InterdiscipEduc Psychol.2.2.003

Bowring, D. L., Painter, J. & Hastings, R. P. (2019). Prevalence of challenging behaviour in adults with intellectual disabilities, correlates, and association with mental health. *Current Developmental Disorders Reports, 6*, 173–181. https://doi.org/10.1007/s40474-019-00175-9

Bronfenbrenner, U. (1979). *The Ecology of Human Development: Experiments in Nature and Design*. Cambridge, MA: Harvard University Press.

Bross, L. A., Common, E. A., Oakes, W. P., Lane, K. L., Menzies, H. M., & Ennis, R. P. (2018). High-probability request sequence: An effective, efficient low-intensity strategy to support student success. *Beyond Behavior, 27*(3), 140–145. https://10.1177/1074295618798615

Brown-Chidsey, R., & Steege, M. W. (2004). Discrete trial teaching. In T. S. Watson & C. H. Skinner (Eds.), *Encyclopedia of School Psychology* (pp. 96–97). New York: Springer.

Bullard, J. (2010). *Creating Environment for Learning*, Upper Saddle River: Pearson.

Bullock, C., & Normand, M. P. (2006). The effects of a high-probability instruction sequence and response-independent reinforcer delivery on child compliance. *Journal of Applied Behavior Analysis, 39*(4), 495–499. https://doi.org/10.1901/jaba.2006.115-05

Cardon, T. A., & Wilcox, M. J. (2011). Promoting imitation in young children with autism: A comparison of reciprocal imitation training and video modeling. *Journal of Autism and Developmental Disorders, 41*(5), 654–666.

Cardon, T., Guimond, A., & Smith-Treadwell, A. (2015). Video modeling and children with autism spectrum disorder: A survey of caregiver perspectives. *Education and Treatment of Children, 38*(3), 403–419. Retrieved July 14, 2021, from http://www.jstor.org/stable/44684073

Carnett, A., Raulston, T., Lang, R., Tostanoski, A., Lee, A., Sigafoos, J., & Machalicek, W. (2014). Effects of a perseverative interest-based token economy on challenging and on-task behavior in a child with autism. *Journal of Behavioral Education, 23*(3), 368–377.

Carr, D. C., Wellin, C., & Reece, H. (2009). A review of arts and aging research: Revealing an elusive but promising direction for the era of the third age. *Journal of Aging, Humanities, and the Arts, 3* (3), 199–221.

Carter, A. (2014). *Carter Review of Initial Teacher Training (ITT)*. London: Department for Education.

Carter, P., & Darling-Hammond, L. (2016). Teaching diverse learners. In D. H. Gitomer & C. Bell (Eds.), *Handbook of Research on Teaching* (5th ed., pp. 593–638). Washington, DC: American Educational Research Association.

Carroll, A. W. (1974). e classroom as an ecosystem. *Focus on Exceptional Children, 6*, 1–11.

Cengher, M., Budd, A., Farrell, N., & Fienup, D., (2018). A Review of Prompt-Fading Procedures: Implications for Effective and Efficient Skill Acquisition, *Journal of Developmental and Physical Disabilities, 30*(2), 155–173. https://10.1007/s10882-017-9575-8

Chandler, L. K. & Dahlquist, C. M. (2002). *Functional Assessment: Strategies to Prevent and Remediate Challenging Behavior in School Settings.* Merrill Prentice Hall, 300 pages

Chowdhury, M., & Benson, B. A. (2011). Use of differential reinforcement to reduce behavior problems in adults with intellectual disabilities: A methodological review. *Research in Developmental Disabilities, 32*(2), 383–394.

Ciccone, F. J., Graff, R. B., & Ahearn, W. H. J. (2015). Increasing the efficiency of paired-stimulus preference assessments by identifying categories of preference. *Applied Behavior Analysis, 48*(1), 221–6. https://10.1002/jaba.190.

Cohen, A., & Demchak, M. (2018). Use of Visual Supports to Increase Task Independence in Students with Severe Disabilities in Inclusive Educational Settings. *Education and Training in Autism and Developmental Disabilities, 53*(1), 84–99. Retrieved July 8, 2021, from https://www.jstor.org/stable/26420429

Collins, P.Y., Pringle, B., Alexander, C., Darmstadt, G. L., Heymann, J., Huebner, G., et al. (2017). Global services and support for children with developmental delays and disabilities: Bridging research and policy gaps. *PLoS Med, 14*(9), e1002393. https://doi.org/10.1371/journal.pmed.1002393

Collins, B. C., Lo, Y., Park, G., & Haughney, K. (2018). Response prompting as an ABA-based instructional approach for teaching students with disabilities. *Teaching Exceptional Children, 50*(6), 343–355. https://10.1177/0040059918774920

Conway, P., & Sloane, F. (2005). *International Trends in Post-primary Mathematics Education: Perspectives on Learning, Teaching and Assessment.* Dublin: National Council for Curriculum and Assessment.

Cooper, J. O., Heron, T. E., & Heward, W. L. (2007). *Applied Behavior Analysis* (2nd ed.) Upper Saddle River: Pearson Education

Cooper, J. O., Heron, T.E, & Heward, W. L. (2020). *Applied Behavior Analysis* (3rd Edition). Upper Saddle River: Pearson Education, Inc.

Cote, C. A., Thompson, R. H., Hanley, G. P., & McKerchar, P. M. (2007). Teacher report and direct assessment of preferences for identifying reinforcers for young children. *Journal of Applied Behavior Analysis, 40*, 157–166.

Crone, D. A., & Horner, R. H. (2003). *Building Positive Behavior Support Systems in Schools: Functional Behavioral Assessment.* New York: Guilford Press.

David S. (2021). Treatment of aggression in adults with autism spectrum disorder: A review. *Harvard Review of Psychiatry, 29*(1), 35–80. https://10.1097/HRP.0000000000000282

Deb, S., Akrout Brizard, B., & Limbu, B. (2020). Association between epilepsy and challenging behaviour in adults with intellectual disabilities: Systematic review and meta-analysis. *BJPsych open, 6*(5), e114. https://doi.org/10.1192/bjo.2020.96

Doll, C., McLaughlin, T. F., & Barretto, A. (2013). The token economy: A recent review and evaluation. *International Journal of Basic and Applied Science, 2*(1), 131–149.

Durand, V. M., & Moskowitz, L. (2015). Functional communication training: Thirty years of treating challenging behavior. *Topics in Early Childhood Special Education. 35*(2), 116–126. doi:10.1177/0271121415569509

Dwyer-Moore, K. J., & Dixon, M. R. (2007). Functional analysis and treatment of problem behavior of elderly adults in long-term care. *Journal of Applied Behavior Analysis, 40*(4), 679–683. https://doi.org/10.1901/jaba.2007.679-683

Dykens, E. M. (2000). Annotation: psychopathology in children with intellectual disability. *Journal of Child Psychology and Psychiatry, 41*, 407–417. https://10.1111/1469-7610.00626.

Edwards, T. L., Lotfizadeh, A. D., & Poling, A. (2019). Motivating operations and stimulus control. *Journal of Experimental Analysis of Behaviour, 112*(1), 1–9.

Endicott, K., Thomas, S. & Higbee, T. S. (2007). Contriving motivating operations to evoke mands for information in pre-schoolers with autism. *Research in Autism Spectrum Disorders, 1,* 210–217.

Frey, B. (2018). *The Sage Encyclopedia of Educational Research, Measurement, and Evaluation* (Vols. 1–4). Thousand Oaks: Sage Publications, Inc. https:// 10.4135/9781506326139.

Friedman-Krauss, A. H., Raver, C. C., Morris, P. A., & Jones, S. M. (2014). The role of classroom-level child behavior problems in predicting preschool teacher stress and classroom emotional climate. *Early Educ. Dev., 25*, 530–552. https:// 10.1080/10409289.2013.817030.

Fuller, M., Bradley, A., & Healey, M. (2004). Incorporating disabled students within an inclusive higher education environment. *Disability & Society, 19*(5), 455–468. https://10.1080/0968759042000235307

Ghaemmaghami, M., Hanley, G.P., & Jessel, J. (2021). Functional communication training: From efficacy to effectiveness. *Journal of Applied Behavioural Analysis, 54*(1), 122–143. https://10.1002/jaba.762.

Glanz, K., & Bishop, D. B. (2010). The role of behavioral science theory in development and implementation of public health interventions. *Annu Rev Public Health*, *31*, 399–418 https:// 10.1146/annurev.publhealth.012809.103604. PMID: 20070207.

Graff, R. B. & Karsten, A. M. (2012). Assessing preferences of individuals with developmental disabilities: A survey of current practices, *Behav Anal Pract.*, *5*(2), 37–48. https://10.1007/BF03391822

Gist, C. M. (2010). Building Fluency with Frequency Building and Precision Teaching (Dissertation Presented in Partial Fulfilment of the Requirements for the Degree Doctor of Philosophy in the Graduate School of The Ohio State University, Graduate Program in Educational Studies the Ohio State University).

Goldsmith, T. R., LeBlanc, L. A., & Sautter, R. A. (2007). Teaching intraverbal behavior to children with autism. *Research in Autism Spectrum Disorders*, *1*(1), 1–13. https://doi.org/10.1016/j.rasd.2006.07.001

Greer, R. D. & Ross, D. E. (2004). Verbal behavior analysis: A program of research in the induction and expansion of complex verbal behavior. *JEIBI*, *1*(2), 141.

Hackenberg, T. D. (2009). Token reinforcement: a review and analysis. *Journal of the Experimental Analysis of Behavior*, *91*(2), 257–286. https://doi.org/10.1901/jeab.2009.91-257.

Halder, S (2017). 'Individualized Intervention approach for inclusion of children with diverse behavioural needs'. In the book *'Inclusion, Disability and Culture: An Ethnographic Approach Traversing Abilities and Challenges', Inclusive Learning and Educational Equity Series, 3*. Springer International Publisher. http://www.springer.com/gp/book/9783319552231

Hastings, R. P., & Brown, T. (2002). Coping strategies and the impact of challenging behaviours on special educators' burnout. *Mental Retardation*, *40*, 148–156. https://10.1352/0047-6765(2002)040<0148:CSATIO>2.0.CO;2

Hagopian, L. P., & Leoni, M. (2017). Self-injurious behavior among individuals with intellectual and developmental disabilities. *Acta Psychopathol*, *3*, 70. https://10.4172/2469-6676.100142.

Harding, J. W., Wacker, D. P., Berg, W. K., Lee, J. F., & Dolezal, D. (2009). Conducting functional communication training in home settings: A case study and recommendations for practitioners. *Behavior Analysis in Practice*, *2*(1), 21–33. https://doi.org/10.1007/BF03391734

Hawkins. R. P. (1979). The functions of assessment: Implications for selection and development of devices for assessing repertoires in clinical, educational and other settings. *12*(4), 501–516. https://doi.org/10.1901/jaba.1979.12-501

Hayes, G. R., Hirano, S., Marcu, G., Monibi, M. H., Boyd Nguyen, D. H., & Yeganyan, M. (2010). Interactive visual supports for children with autism. *Personal and Ubiquitous Computing*, *14*, 663–680.

Heflin, L. J., & Alberto, P. A. (2001). ABA and Instruction of Students with Autism Spectrum Disorders: Introduction to the Special Series. *Focus on Autism and Other Developmental Disabilities*, *16*(2), 66–67. https://doi.org/10.1177/108835760101600201

Hemmings, C., Deb, S., Chaplin, E., Hardy, S., & Mukherjee, R. (2013). Review of research for people with ID and mental health problems: a view from the United Kingdom. *J Ment Health Res Intellect Disabil.*, *6*(2), 127–58. https://doi.org/10.1080/19315864.2012. 708100

Heinicke, M. R., Carr, J. E., [...], & Jamie M Severtson (2010). On the use of fluency training in the behavioral treatment of autism: A commentary. *The Behavior Analyst*, *33*(2), 223–229. https://10.1007/BF03392221

Howell, M., Dounavi, K., & Storey, C. (2019). To choose or not to choose?: A systematic literature review considering the effects of antecedent and consequence choice upon on-task and problem behaviour. *Review Journal of Autism Developmental Disororder.*, *6*, 63–84 (2019). https://doi.org/10.1007/s40489-018-00154-7

Howlin, P., Magiati, I., & Charman, T. (2009). Systematic review of early intensive behavioral interventions for children with autism. *American Journal on Intellectual and Developmental Disabilities*, *114*(1), 23–41. https://10.1352/2009.114:23;nd41.

Hyman, S. L., Levy, S. E., & Myers, S. M. (2020). Identification, evaluation, and management of children with autism spectrum disorder, paediatrics, *145*(1), e20193447. https://doi.org/10.1542/peds.2019-3447

Ingersoll, B. (2007). Teaching imitation to children with autism: A focus on social reciprocity. *The Journal of Speech and Language Pathology, Applied Behavior Analysis*, *2*(3), 269.

Ingersoll, B., & Lalonde, K. (2010). The impact of object and gesture imitation training on language use in children with autism spectrum disorder. *Journal of Speech and Language Hear Research*, *53*(4), 1040–51. https://10.1044/1092-4388(2009/09-0043).

Ishizuka, Y. & Yamamoto, J. (2021). The effect of contingent imitation intervention on children with autism spectrum disorder and co-occurring intellectual disabilities, *Research in Autism Spectrum Disorders, 85*, 101783. https://doi.org/10.1016/j.rasd.2021.101783

Iwata, B. A., & Dozier, C. L. (2008). Clinical application of functional analysis methodology. *Behavior Analysis in Practice, 1*(1), 3–9. https://doi.org/10.1007/BF03391714

Jerome, J., Frantino E. P., & Sturmey P. (2007). The effects of errorless learning and backward chaining on the acquisition of Internet skills in adults with developmental disabilities. *Journal of Applied Behavior Analysis., 40*, 185–189.

Jessel, J., Ghaemmaghami, M., & Hanley, G. P., (2021). Functional communication training: From efficacy to effectiveness, *Journal of Applied Behavior Analysis* (Winter), *54*, 122–143.

Jeyachandran, P. V. (1995 and 2000). Madras Developmental Programming System, Vijaya Human Science, 6 Lakhmiperam Street, Chennai–14.

Karsten, A. M., Carr, J. E., & Lepper, T. L. (2011). Description of a practitioner model for identifying preferred stimuli with individuals with autism spectrum disorders. *Behavior Modification, 35*, 347–369.

Kates-McElrath, K., & Axelrod, S. (2008). *Functional assessment in public schools: A tool for classroom teachers.* In S. C. Luce, D. S. Mandell, C. Mazefsky, & W. Seibert. (Eds.), *Autism in Pennsylvania. What Lies Ahead?* Harrisburg, PA: Pennsylvania House of Representatives. Pp. 83–96

Kelly, M. L., Reitman, D., & Noell, G. (2003). Practitioner's Guide to Empirically Based Measures of School Behavior. Available at: https://nsuworks.nova.edu/cps_facbooks/480

Klatt, K. P., & Morris, E. K. (2001). The premack principle, response deprivation, and establishing operations. *The Behaviour Analyst, 24*(2), 173–180.

Kodak, T., Fisher, W. W., Paden, A., & Dickes, N. (2013). Evaluation of the utility of a discrete-trial functional analysis in early intervention classrooms. *Journal of Applied Behavior Analysis, 46*(1), 301–306. https://doi.org/10.1002/jaba.2

Koegel, L. K. & Koegel, R. L. (2019). *Pivotal Response Treatment for Autism Spectrum Disorders* (2nd ed.). Balmore, MD: Paul H Brookes Publishing Co.

Koegel, R. L,, Koegel, L. K., & McNerney, E. K. (2001). Pivotal areas in intervention for autism. *Journal of Clinical Child Psychology, 30*(1), 19–32. https://10.1207/S15374424JCCP3001_4..

Kremers, S. P., Eves, F. F., & Andersen, R. E. (2012). Environmental changes to promote physical activity and healthy dietary behavior. *Journal of Environmental and Public Health, 2012*, 470858. https://doi.org/10.1155/2012/470858.

Kubina, R. M., & Yurich, K. K. L. (2009). Developing behavioral fluency for students with autism: A guide for parents and teachers. *Intervention in School and Clinic, 44*(3), 131–138. https://10.1177/1053451208326054

Kurth, J. A., Morningstar, M. E., & Kozleski, E. (2014). The persistence of highly restrictive special education placements for students with low-incidence disabilities. *Research & Practice for Persons with Severe Disabilities, 39*, 227–239. https://10.1177/1540796914555580

Lambert, J. M., Bloom, S. E., & Irvin, J. (2012). Trial-based functional analysis and functional communication training in an early childhood setting. *Journal of Applied Behavior Analysis, 45*(3), 579–584. https://doi.org/10.1901/jaba.2012.45-579

Langthorne, P., & McGill, P. (2009). A tutorial on the concept of the motivating operation and its importance to application. *Behavior Analysis in Practice, 2*(2), 22–31. https://doi.org/10.1007/BF03391745.

Lang, P. J., Bradley, M. M., & Cuthbert, B. N. (2008). *International Affective Picture System (IAPS): Instruction manual and affective ratings, Technical Report A-8.* Gainesville: The Center for Research in Psychophysiology, University of Florida.

Lane, K. L., Menzies, H. M., Ennis, R. P., & Oakes, W. P. (2015). *Supporting Behavior for School Success: A Step-by-step Guide to Key Strategies.* New York: Guilford Press.

Larsson, E. V., & Wright, S. (2011). O. Ivar Lovaas (1927–2010). *The Behavior Analyst, 34*(1), 111–114. https://www.ncbi.nlm.nih.gov/pmc/articles/PMC3089401/

Lechago, S. A. (2019). A comment on Edwards, Lotfizadeh, and Poling (2019) on motivating operations and stimulus control. *The Journal of the Experimental Analysis of Behavior, 112*(1), 27–31. https://doi.org/10.1002/jeab.536. Epub 2019 Jun 27. PMID: 31243759.

Ledford, J. R., & Windsor, S. A. (2021). Systematic review of interventions designed to teach imitation to young children with disabilities. *Topics in Early Childhood Special Education.* April issue, https://10.1177/02711214211007190

Lecavalier, L., Leone, S., & Wiltz, J. (2006). The impact of behaviour problems on caregiver stress in young people with autism spectrum disorders. *J. Intellect. Disabil. Res., 50*(Pt 3), 172–183. https://10.1111/j.1365-2788.2005.00732.x

Lecomte T., Liberman R. P., & Wallace, C. J. (2000). Identifying and using reinforcers to enhance the treatment of persons with serious mental illness. *Psychiatric Services, 51,* 1312–1314.

Ledford, J. R. & Wolery, M. (2011). Teaching imitation to young children with disabilities: A review of the literature. *Topics in Early Childhood Special Education, 30*(4), 245–255. https://10.1177/0271121410363831

Lerman, D., Iwata, A., & Wallace, M. (1999). Side effects of extinction: prevalence of bursting and aggression during the treatment of self-injurious behaviour. *Journal of Applied Behaviour Analysis, 32,* 1–8.

Lowe, C. F., Horne, P. J., Harris, D. S., & Randle, V. R. L. (2002). Naming and categorization in young children: Vocal tact training. *Journal of the Experimental Analysis of Behavior, 78,* 527–549.

Leyser, Y. & Greenberger, L. (2008). College students with disabilities in teacher education: faculty attitudes and practices, *European Journal of Special Needs Education, 23*:3, 237–251. https://10.1080/08856250802130442

Lovaas, O. I., Schaeffer, B., & Simmons, J. Q. (1965). Building social behavior in autistic children by use of electric shock. *Journal of Experimental Research in Personality, 1*(2), 99–109.

Martens, B. K., Daly, E. J., & Ardoin, S. P. (2015). Applications of applied behavior analysis to school-based instructional intervention. In *Practical Resources for the Mental Health Professional, Clinical and Organizational Applications of Applied Behavior Analysis edited by Henry et al.* (pp. 125–150). Academic Press. https://doi.org/10.1016/B978-0-12-420249-8.00006-X.

Martin, T. L., Yu, C. T., Martin, G. L., & Fazzio, D. (2006). On choice, preference, and preference for choice. *The Behavior Analyst Today, 7*(2), 234–241. https://doi.org/10.1037/h0100083

Matson, J. L. & Boisjoli, J. A. (2008). The token economy for children with intellectual disability and/or autism: A review. *Research in Developmental Disabilities, 30*(2), 240–248. https://10.1016/j.ridd.2008.04.001

McGee, G. G., & Daly, T. (2007). Incidental teaching of age-appropriate social phrases to children with autism. *Research and Practice for Persons with Severe Disabilities, 32*(2), 112–123.

McGreevy, P., Fry, T., & Cornwall, C. (2012). *Essential for Living.* Orlando: McGreevy.

McIntyre, D. (2009). The difficulties of inclusive pedagogy for initial teacher education and some thoughts on the way forward. *Teaching and Teacher Education, 25*(4), 608–613

Mintz, C., Wallace, M. D., Najdowski, A. C., Atcheson, K., & Bosch, A. (2007). Reinforcer identification and evaluation of choice within an educational setting. *Journal of Behavioral Education, 16*(4), 333–341. https://doi.org/10.1007/s10864-007-9045-y.

Minshawi, N. F., Hurwitz, S., Fodstad, J. C., Biebl, S., Morriss, D. H., & McDougle, C. J. (2014). The association between self-injurious behaviours and autism spectrum disorders. *Psychology Research and Behavior Management, 7,* 125–136. https://doi.org/10.2147/PRBM.S44635

Mitchell, G., & Hastings, R. P. (1998). Learning disability care staff's emotional reactions to aggressive challenging behaviours: development of a measurement tool. *Brirish Journal of Clinical Psychology, 37,* 441–449. https://10.1111/j.2044-8260.1998.tb01401.x

Michie, S., Johnston, M., Francis, J., Hardeman, W., & Eccles, M. (2008). From theory to intervention: Mapping theoretically derived behavioural determinants to behaviour change techniques. *Journal of Applied Psychology, 57*(4), 660–680.

Macpherson, K., Charlop, M. H. & Miltenberger, C. A. (2015). Using portable video modeling technology to increase the compliment behaviours of children with autism during athletic group play. *Journal of Autism and Developmental Disorders, 45,* 3836–3845. https://doi.org/10.1007/s10803-014-2072-3

Morgan, P. L. (2006). Increasing task engagement using preference or choice-making. *Remedial and Special Education, 27*(3), 176–187. https://doi.org/10.1177/07419325060270030601.

Morris, K. E., Smith, N. G., & Altus, D. E. (2005). B. R Skinner's contributions to applied behavior analysis. *The Behavior Analyst, 28,* 99–131

Mosier, A. K. (2011). *Applied Behavior Analysis Techniques: Discrete Trial Training & Natural Environment Training.* Research Papers. Paper 226. http://opensiuc.lib.siu.edu/gs_rp/226

Myreddi, V., Narayan, J., Saleem, S., Sumalini, K., & Padma, V. (2004). *Functional Assessment Checklist for Programming (FACP).* Secundrabad: NIMH, Ministry of Social Justice and Empowerment.

Neitzel, J. (2009). *Overview of Antecedent-based Interventions.* Chapel Hill, NC: The National Professional Development Center on Autism Spectrum Disorders, Frank Porter Graham Child Development Institute, The University of North Carolina.

Nicholls, G., Hastings, R. P., & Grindle, C. (2019). Prevalence and correlates of challenging behaviour in children and young people in a special school setting. *European Journal of Special Needs Education 3,* 1–15. https:// 10.1080/08856257.2019.1607659.

Niemczyk, J., Wagner, C., & von Gontard, A. (2018). Incontinence in autism spectrum disorder: A systematic review. *European Child Adolescent Psychiatry*, *27*(12), 1523–1537. https://10.1007/s00787-017-1062-3.

Nuzzolo-Gomez, R. & Greer, R. D. (2004). Emergence of untaught mands or tacts with novel adjective-object pairs as a function of instructional history. *The Analysis of Verbal Behavior*, *24*, 30–47.

Ohtake, Y. Takahashi, A., & Watanabe, K. (2015). Using an animated cartoon hero in video instruction to improve bathroom-related skills of a student with autism spectrum disorder. *Education and Training in Autism and Developmental Disabilities*, *50*(3), 343–355.

O'Handley, R. D., Ford, W. B., Radley, K. C., Helbig, K. A., & Wimberly, J. K. (2016). Social skills training for adolescents with intellectual disabilities: A school-based evaluation. *Behavior Modification*, *40*(4), 541–567. https://10.1177/0145445516629938

Peshwarayi & Venketesan, (2004). *Behavior Assessment Scale for Indian Children (BASIC-MR)*. Secundrabad: National Institute for Mentally Handicapped (NIMH), Government of India, Ministry of Social Justice and Empowerment.

Petscher, E. S., & Bailey, J. S. (2008). Comparing main and collateral effects of extinction and differential reinforcement of alternative behavior. *Behavior Modification*, *32*(4), 468–488.

Pratt, C. & Steward, L. (2020). Applied behavior analysis: The role of task analysis and chaining. https://www.iidc.indiana.edu/irca/articles/applied-behavior-analysis.html.

Rech, H. (2012). *The Origins, Evolution, and Future of Preference Assessments in Applied Behavior Analysis*. Research Papers. Paper 282. http://opensiuc.lib.siu.edu/gs_rp/282

Rispoli, M., Camargo, S., Machalicek, W., Lang, R., & Sigafoos, J. (2014). Functional communication training in the treatment of problem behavior maintained by access to rituals. *Journal of Applied Behaviour Analysis*, *47*(3), 580–593. https://doi.org/10.1002/jaba.130

Rutherford, M., Baxter, J., Grayson, Z., Johnston, L., & O'Hare, A. (2020). Visual supports at home and in the community for individuals with autism spectrum disorders: A scoping review. *Autism*, *24*(2), 447–469. https://10.1177/1362361319871756

Shogren, K. A., Faggella-Luby, M. N., Jik, S., & Wehmeyer, M. L. (2004). The Effect of Choice-Making as an Intervention for Problem Behavior: A Meta-Analysis. *Journal of Positive Behavior Interventions*, *6*(4), 228–237. https://10.1177/10983007040060040401

Sigafoos, J., & Dempsey, R. (1992). Assessing choice making among children with multiple disabilities. *Journal of Applied Behavior Analysis*, *25*(3), 747–755. https://doi.org/10.1901/jaba.1992.25-747

Simó-Pinatella D, Font-Roura J, Planella-Morató J, McGill P, Alomar-Kurz E, & Giné C. (2013). Types of motivating operations in interventions with problem behavior: A systematic review. *Behavior Modification*, *37*(1), 3–38. https://10.1177/0145445512448096

Simó-Pinatella, D., Günther-Bel, C., & Mumbardó-Adam, C. (2021). Addressing challenging behaviours in children with autism: A qualitative analysis of teachers' experiences. *International Journal of Disability, Development and Education*. https://10.1080/1034912X.2020.1870664

Simó-Pinatella, D., Mumbardó-Adam, C., Alomar-Kurz, E., Sugai, G., & Simonsen, B. (2019). Prevalence of Challenging Behaviours Exhibited by Children with Disabilities: Mapping the Literature. *Journal of Behavioral Education*, *28*, 323–343 https://doi.org/10.1007/s10864-019-09326-9 1 3.

Simpson, R. L. (2001). ABA and students with autism spectrum disorders; Issues and considerations for effective practice. *Focus on Autism and Other Developmental Disabilities*, *16*(2), 68–71. https://doi.org/10.1177/108835760101600202

Slocum, T. A., Detrich, R., Wilczynski, S. M., Spencer, T. D., Lewis, T., & Wolfe, K. (2014). The evidence-based practice of applied behavior analysis. *The Behavior Analyst*, *37*(1), 41–56. https://doi.org/10.1007/s40614-014-0005-2

Smith T. (2001). Discrete Trial Training in the Treatment of Autism. *Focus on Autism and Other Developmental Disabilities*. *16*(2), 86–92. https://10.1177/108835760101600204

Sullivan, L. & Bogin, J. (2010). *Steps for Implementation: Extinction*. Sacramento: The National Professional Development Center on Autism Spectrum Disorders, M.I.N.D Institute, University of California at Davis School of Medicine.

Sundberg, M. L., & Michael, J. (2001). The benefits of Skinner's analysis of verbal behavior for children with autism. *Behavior Modification*, *25*(5), 698–724. https://10.1177/0145445501255003. PMID: 11573336.

Sundberg, M. L. (2008). *The Verbal Behavior Milestones Assessment and Placement Program: The VB-MAPP* (2nd ed.). Concord, CA: AVB Press.

Sukhodolsky, D. G., Smith, S. D., McCauley, S. A., Ibrahim, K., & Piasecka, J. B. (2016). Behavioral interventions for anger, irritability, and aggression in children and adolescents. *Journal of Child and Adolescent Psychopharmacology, 26*(1), 58–64. https://doi.org/10.1089/cap.2015.0120.

Slocum, S. K., & Tiger, J. H. (2011). An assessment of the efficiency of and child preference for forward and backward chaining. *Journal of Applied Behavior Analysis, 44*(4), 793–805. https://doi.org/10.1901/jaba.2011.44-793

Trahan, M. A., Kahng, S., Fisher, A. B., & Hausman, N. L. (2011). Behavior-analytic research on dementia in older adults. *Journal of Applied Behavior Analysis, 44*(3), 687–691. https://doi.org/10.1901/jaba.2011.44-687

Taylor, E. W. (2006). The challenge of teaching for change. Special Issue: teaching for change: fostering transformative learning in the classroom. *Spring Issue, 109*, 91–95. https://doi.org/10.1002/ace.211

Tiger, J. H., Hanley, G. P., & Bruzek, J. (2008). Functional communication training: a review and practical guide. *Behavior Analysis in Practice, 1*(1), 16–23. https://doi.org/10.1007/BF03391716

United Nations. (2015). *Transforming Our World: The 2030 Agenda for Sustainable Development*. New York: United Nations General Assembly.

UNESCO. (2015). *Education for All 2000–2015: Achievements and Challenges*. Paris: United Nations Educational, Scientific and Cultural Organization.

UNICEF. (2011). *The Right of Children with Disabilities to Education: A Rights-based Approach to Inclusive Education*. Geneva: UNICEF.

United Nations. (1989). *Convention on the Rights of the Child*. New York: United Nations.

U.S. Department of Education (2021). Office of Special Education Programs, Individuals with Disabilities Education Act (IDEA) database, retrieved February 2, 2021, from https://www2.ed.gov/programs/osepidea/618-data/state-level-data-files/index.html#bcc

UN Committee on the Rights of Persons with Disabilities (CRPD), *General comment No. 4 (2016), Article 24: Right to inclusive education*, 2 September 2016, CRPD/C/GC/4, available at: https://www.refworld.org/docid/57c977e34.html [accessed 10 November 2022]

Vladescu, J. C., & Kodak, T. (2010). A review of recent studies on differential reinforcement during skill acquisition in early intervention. *Journal of Applied Behavior Analysis, 43*(2), 351–355. https://doi.org/10.1901/jaba.2010.43-351

Vollmer, T. R., & Hackenberg. T. D. (2001). Reinforcement contingencies and social reinforcement: Some reciprocal relations between basic and applied research. *Journal of Applied Behaviour Analysis, 34*, 241–253.

Wallace, G., Larsen, S., & Elksnin, L. K. (1978). *Educational Assessment of Learning Problems: Testing for Teaching*. Boston: Allyn and Bacon.

Wallace, G., Larsen, S. C., & Elksnin. L. (1992). *Educational Assessment of Learning Problems: Testing for Teaching* (p. 543). Boston: Allyn and Bacon.

Weiss, M. J. (2013). Extinction procedures. In: Volkmar F. R. (Eds.), *Encyclopaedia of Autism Spectrum Disorders*. New York: Springer. https://doi.org/10.1007/978-1-4419-1698-3_1137.

Weiss, M. J., Pearson, N., Foley, K., & Pahl, S. (2010). The importance of fluency outcomes in learners with autism. *The Behavior Analyst Today, 11*(4), 245–252. http://dx.doi.org/10.1037/h0100704

Welsh, D. H. B., Bernstein, D. J., & Luthans, F. (1992). Application of the Premack Principle of reinforcement to the quality performance of service employees. *Journal of Organizational Behavior Management, 13*(1), 9–32. https://10.1300/J075v13n01_03.

Wilder, D. A., Harris, C., Reagan, R., & Rasey, A. (2007). Functional analysis and treatment of noncompliance by preschool children. *Journal of Applied Behavior Analysis 40*(1), 173–7. https://10.1901/jaba.2007.44-06

Wilder, D.A., Atwell, J., & Wine, B. (2006). The effects of varying levels of treatment integrity on child compliance during treatment with a three-step prompting procedure. *Journal of Applied Behavior Analysis, 39*(3), 369–73. https://10.1901/jaba.2006.144-05

Woodman, A.C., Mawdsley, H.P., Hauser-Cram, P. (2015). Parenting stress and child behavior problems within families of children with developmental disabilities: Transactional relations across 15 years. *Research in Developmental disabilities, 36C*, 264–276. https:// 10.1016/j.ridd.2014.10.011.

Watson, J. B. (1924). The Unverbalized in Human Behavior. *Psychological Review, 31*(4), 273–280. https://doi.org/10.1037/h0071569

Wysocki, C. D. (2018). *Obstacles to Inclusion: One Early Childhood Inclusive Teacher's Perspective*. Open access peer-reviewed chapter. https:// 10.5772/intechopen.80982

21
AUGMENTATIVE AND ALTERNATIVE COMMUNICATION FOR THE CLASSROOM

Kerstin Tönsing* and Shakila Dada

Inclusion and the Role of AAC

In many countries across the world, public education is seen as an important vehicle to equip children with knowledge, skills and values that will enable them to lead fulfilled and autonomous lives as productive members of society. The right to education is enshrined in the Universal Declaration of Human Rights (United Nations, 1948), and also articulated through the Convention on the Rights of the Child (United Nations, 1989). This right extends to all children, including those with disabilities (Convention on the Rights of Persons with Disabilities [CRPD], United Nations, 2006). Children not only have a right to education (fulfilled if schools are available and accessible), but also have rights in education (including an acceptable standard and an education system that is adaptable to the individual needs of all children) (Tomasevski, 1999). Inclusive education therefore requires the use of pedagogies that optimise learning opportunities for all children in the classroom.

Communication plays an important role in classroom learning. Learners receive information represented by others (teachers, peers), and also express their own knowledge and abilities, either for the purpose of assessment or to co-construct knowledge in a dialogic learning approach (Kathard & Pillay, 2015). Much of this classroom communication traditionally takes place via spoken or written language, requiring learners to take on the roles of speakers and listeners, and, later on, also as readers and writers. When children have severe communication disabilities, taking on some or all of these roles can be problematic for a variety of reasons. While children with typical speech and language development have usually had the opportunity to become fluent speakers in the community language by the time they enter formal schooling, children with severe communication disabilities have often received limited support in developing equivalent communication skills using modalities other than speech (Zangari & Van Tatenhove, 2009). As a consequence, the language- and communication-intensive nature of many traditional learning activities presents a significant barrier to their participation within the classroom. This may lead to passivity and/or challenging behaviour, further exacerbating their exclusion, eventually resulting in poor educational outcomes, limited community inclusion and poor prospects for employment and for taking up other valued adult roles in the future.

---

* kerstin.tonsing@up.ac.za

DOI: 10.4324/9781003266068-26

Educators of children with severe communication disabilities are tasked with designing learning opportunities in a way that allows all children, including those with severe communication disabilities, to take part and to reach curriculum goals. One method to achieve this is through the use of augmentative and alternative communication (AAC) – the use of less frequently used modes and means of communication to compensate for limited speech and/or understanding of spoken language, at times also extending to written language (Lloyd et al., 1997). AAC comprises a variety of strategies, techniques, communication symbols, and aids to enhance communication (Beukelman & Mirenda, 2013). A teacher may use manual signs from sign language, for example, to enhance understanding of a learner with Down syndrome in her class. The learner may then acquire the manual signs and use them to answer a question in class as a way of compromising delayed speech development. A learner with cerebral palsy whose speech is unintelligible may be taught to point to picture symbols on a communication board to express herself. Her classmates would need to be taught to interpret the picture symbols in order to understand her. A survey amongst South African special school teachers who had experience implementing AAC showed that teachers rated AAC systems as useful for both supporting learning and supporting classroom interactions (Tönsing & Dada, 2016), underlining the close integration of learning and communication.

In low-resource contexts, AAC may not be implemented in educational contexts for a variety of reasons. Educators may be unfamiliar with AAC strategies. AAC systems and intervention approaches developed in primarily Western high-income contexts may be culturally and linguistically inappropriate to other contexts (Muttiah et al., 2016; Soto & Yu, 2014). Educators and other role players may have negative attitudes towards AAC implementation (Dada, 2019). One reason may be that AAC implementation may be perceived as resource intensive – requiring manpower, trained professionals, and assistive technology that is not available. The literature on best practices in educational inclusion of children who require AAC has primarily been generated in high-resource contexts and is therefore often based on the assumption of the availability of such resources (Calculator, 2009; Calculator & Black, 2009). It is of necessity also situated within a particular educational model based on a specific educational paradigm with implicit assumptions regarding, amongst others, the goal of education; the methods employed; and the roles of teachers, learners, parents, administrators, and other educational personnel (Alexander, 2001). Educators in low-resource settings may perceive many recommendations as unattainable or irrelevant to their context. On the other hand, teachers may be the only intervening professionals for many children with severe communication disabilities residing in low-resource contexts, where there is typically a shortage of speech-language therapists (Singh et al., 2020; Pillay et al., 2020; Wylie et al., 2013). This makes their role all the more important.

There are educational approaches relevant for learners with severe communication disabilities and AAC strategies for classroom contexts that are implementable even in resource-constrained settings. After a brief overview of AAC strategies, a narrative review is provided in the rest of this chapter to describe these approaches, the evidence for their effectiveness, as well as important considerations for classroom implementation.

Augmentative and Alternative Communication: A Brief Overview

According to the American Speech-Language Hearing Association (2020), Augmentative and Alternative Communication (AAC) describes all methods of communication (other than speaking) that we as humans use to express our thoughts, feelings, ideas, and desires. We may use facial expressions to show how we feel about something or use a gesture such as waving or 'thumbs up' to communicate a message over a distance or in a noisy context where speech would not be heard. Many of us use communication technology such as text message functions or email on a smart device or computer to send and receive messages. While all of us use these methods of communication from time to time, persons with severe communication disabilities rely on augmentative and alternative methods more often and sometimes permanently and exclusively to compensate for their limited speech. Some of these methods may develop naturally between the person and their partners – for example, the parents of a child with cerebral palsy and severely unintelligible speech may attribute meaning to the subtle body movements and the way the child directs his/her eye gaze, and these methods may then become methods the child uses to convey messages (Sargent et al., 2013). More formal methods may be introduced within an educational context, for example, the use of pictures to indicate choices. The aim of all AAC strategies, techniques, symbols, and aids is to maximise communication interaction and thereby improve participation of persons with severe communication disabilities in all aspects of life. Use of AAC can scaffold language development, increase social interaction, reduce learnt helplessness and challenging behaviour, and pave the way for literacy acquisition for children with a variety of conditions and diagnoses (Branson & Demchak, 2009; Ganz, 2015; Novak et al., 2013; Shire & Jones, 2015). In some instances, the use of AAC may also foster speech development, specifically in children with autism spectrum disorder (ASD) and in children with developmental apraxia of speech (Brewis, 2015; Millar et al., 2006; Schlosser & Wendt, 2008). It is important to note that the aim of AAC is never to replace speech or inhibit its development but to supplement it in order to enhance communication.

By way of an overview, AAC may be described as consisting of (a) *symbols,* (b) *strategies and techniques,* and (c) *communication aids, displays and devices* (Beukelman & Mirenda, 2013). These can again be divided into *aided* and *unaided* categories. An overview with examples is provided in Figure 21.1.

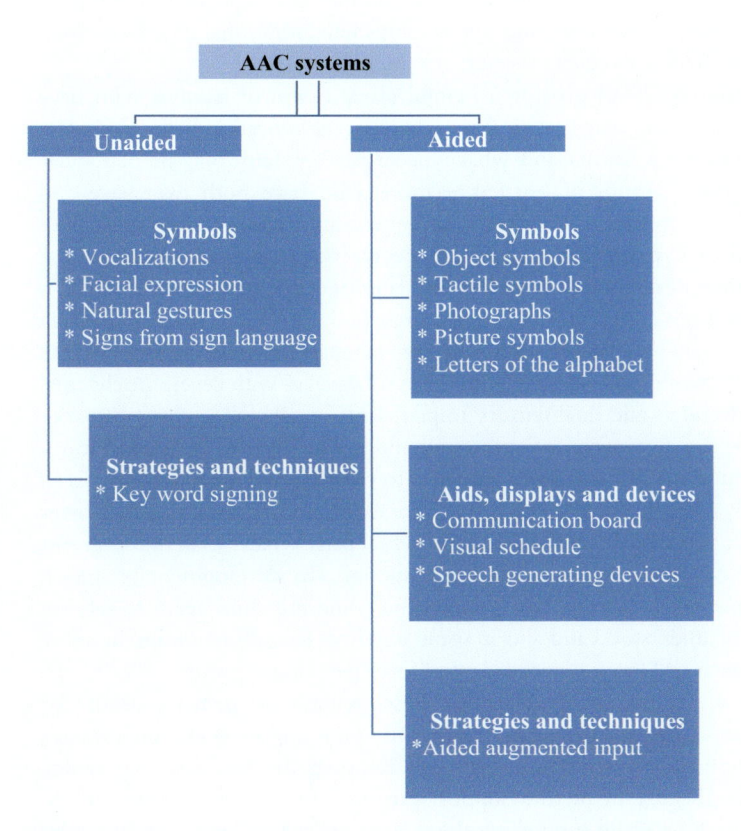

Figure 21.1 An overview of AAC symbols, strategies, aids, displays, and devices.

Learners Who Can Benefit from AAC

AAC strategies were originally conceptualised to provide communication support to learners with severe communication disabilities – learners who cannot use speech adequately to express themselves. As a group, the profiles of these learners vary considerably. While some may have a good understanding of spoken language and require AAC primarily to express themselves, others may struggle to understand spoken language. AAC may then also be required to assist them with comprehension. For some learners, it is likely that speech will never develop to such a level that it will be their primary mode of communication. AAC will therefore be a permanent measure. For others, AAC may be a temporary measure of support while the learner's speech has not yet developed adequately.

A variety of conditions and diagnoses are associated with severe communication disabilities. These include conditions associated with intellectual disability (e.g., genetic syndromes such as Down syndrome and Angelman syndrome), as well as conditions associated with physical disabilities (e.g., cerebral palsy). Learners with autism spectrum disorders (ASD) typically struggle with various aspects of human interaction and communication and often experience a delay in developing speech that is functional. Learners with childhood apraxia of speech have trouble planning and co-ordinating the motor movements for speech – although the speech muscles are not paralysed or weak, the child may have difficulties in planning and co-ordinating the lips and tongue into the right positions to produce speech sounds. Although learners with hearing impairment certainly also have difficulties with spoken language, interventions in the form of sign language, hearing aids, and cochlear implants are often considered as separate to the typical AAC strategies. However, if learners with hearing impairments have additional disabilities such as cerebral palsy or blindness, AAC strategies are often considered.

Von Tetzchner and Martinsen (2000) provide a helpful classification of learners who have severe communication disabilities and may benefit from AAC. This classification helps to explain what the role of AAC may be for a learner and what type of AAC systems may be beneficial. They distinguish between three groups of learners – those who have both expressive and receptive difficulties (i.e., limited speech and limited comprehension of spoken language), those with only expressive difficulties (typically due to a severe speech motor impairment), and those who experience a delay in their development of speech and language. For the first group, AAC is typically necessary to support both comprehension and expression long-term. Speech is unlikely to emerge. These learners will rely on gestures, signs from sign language, and aided forms of AAC to help them understand the world and interact with others. Learners with severe intellectual disability, autism spectrum disorders and dual sensory impairments usually fall in this group. For the second group, AAC is primarily a means of expression and is also likely to be needed long-term. Although speech may improve, it may not be adequate to meet communication needs in all contexts. This group typically relies on aided forms of AAC for expression, because unaided forms require motor skills for production. Learners with severe cerebral palsy typically fall in this group. The third group requires AAC as an interim measure to support the development of speech and language. Speech is expected to emerge, but for the time being the child needs to rely on aided and unaided AAC to be understood and also in some instances to scaffold comprehension. Learners with apraxia of speech or Down syndrome often form part of this group.

Although learners with severe communication disabilities remain the primary group for whom AAC strategies are implemented, enhancing classroom communication and interactions through using multiple methods of communication can improve the learning experience of all learners. For example, the use of picture support during a lesson can help to engage learners visually, and this may also assist in supporting the comprehension of learners whose first language is not the language used in the classroom (Uys & Harty, 2007). Learners who tend to be distractible may benefit from a visual focus. Using multiple methods of communication in the classroom forms one of the principles of Universal Design for Learning (Meyer et al., 2014), an approach that emphasises the design of classrooms and teaching in a way that allows the participation of all learners.

AAC for the Classroom Setting

In the classroom setting, AAC has three primary functions (Shane et al., 2014). First, it may serve to scaffold the comprehension of learners who do not sufficiently benefit from the primarily spoken interactions in the classroom. Second, it may serve as a means of expression for learners whose speech is too limited to meet all their expressive needs. Lastly, AAC in the form of visual aids can assist learners in improving executive function such as sustaining engagement in the learning task and developing self-regulation skills to monitor their understanding, learning, and execution of tasks.

In high-resource contexts, it has been found that teachers seem to relegate the responsibility for supporting communication of learners in need of AAC to the speech therapist and/or educational assistant assigned to the learner (Kent-Walsh & Light, 2003). However, communication cannot be compartmentalised to a skill to be practised in dedicated speech therapy sessions, as it happens in the interactions of daily life. Whether or not support personnel is available, teachers remain key in ensuring that AAC is embedded in classroom interactions to facilitate the full participation of learners with communication challenges (Tönsing & Dada, 2016). In the sections following, augmented input (aided and unaided) will be reviewed as methods to support both comprehension and expression of learners in need of AAC. Thereafter, visual schedules will be reviewed as methods to increase independence and on-task behaviour, facilitate transitions and decrease problem behaviour. For each method, evidence of effectiveness will be summarised, followed by a focus on research to guide classroom implementation in low-resource contexts. Important considerations for classroom implementation will also be highlighted.

Aided Augmented Input

Aided augmented input (also termed 'aided modelling') is an umbrella term describing a variety of approaches developed over the years (Allen et al., 2017; Sennott et al., 2016; Dada et al., 2020). Aided augmented input entails that communication partners (including teachers) supplement their spoken language with the use of aided AAC symbols. In many cases this may be pointing to picture symbols on a communication board or a large facilitator board or activating the cells on the child's speech-generating device while talking to the child. Aided augmented input has been shown to have benefits for both expressive and receptive communication development of children in need of AAC (Allen et al., 2017; Sennott et al., 2016). Sociocultural models of language development emphasise that children need to be immersed in a language community where they see competent partners modelling the use of the communication system (typically speech) that they are expected to acquire and use. Therefore, children who need to make use of aided symbols for expression need to be exposed to communication partners who model this form of communication to them, if they are to learn to use it expressively (Sennott et al., 2016). This augmented input can therefore teach them not only to understand that aided symbols have meaning but also encourage them to imitate this form of communication and to start pointing to or activating symbols in order to express themselves. For children with spoken language comprehension difficulties, aided augmented input is seen as a method of supplementing the spoken input with visual input to support understanding. A visual form of input is added to the auditory input, and learners are hypothesised to benefit from this multimodality (Loncke, 2008). Picture symbols may exploit the iconicity principle where the symbol and the referent share recognisable features, assisting learners to acquire the association between symbol and referent (Stephenson, 2009). For example, a picture of a pen may help the learner understand the concept and also make a link between the spoken word 'pen' and the referent. The aided visual form has the advantage of being permanent and not transient like speech (Schlosser et al., 2020). Furthermore, communication partners tend to slow down their rate of speech when simultaneously pointing to or activating aided AAC symbols, and this further enhances comprehension (Dada & Alant, 2009).

Evidence for the Effectiveness of Aided Augmented Input

A number of reviews attest to the effectiveness of aided augmented input methods to improve both comprehension and expression in children in need of AAC (Allen et al., 2017; Biggs et al., 2018; Sennott et al., 2016). Allen et al. (2017), as well as 52Sennott et al. (2016), reviewed studies that employed aided input provided within naturalistic contexts (i.e., naturally occurring routines or emulated ones performed at the clinic) as the single independent variable. Biggs et al. (2018) also included studies that combined aided augmented input with other teaching methods, such as prompting output or creating communication opportunities. However, Biggs et al. (2018) only included studies that focussed on expressive outcomes.

Aided augmented input has been shown to effectively increase receptive and expressive vocabulary, expressive syntax and morphology, as well as pragmatic skills of children with a variety of diagnoses, such as autism spectrum disorder, intellectual disability, cerebral palsy, Down syndrome, and childhood apraxia of speech. The reviews also show that various communication partners, such as parents, peers, teachers and teaching assistants can be taught to provide aided augmented input.

Implementation in Classroom Contexts

We distinguish in this section between strategies aimed at the whole class that primarily aim to scaffold understanding and build receptive language skills, and those that are aimed at individual children, modelling the use of their personal communication system to encourage them to imitate the use of the system. Whole class strategies typically involve the use of a large facilitator board displaying a number of symbols. This board is positioned in a way that the whole class is able to observe it as the teacher points to symbols on the board while speaking (teaching). Aided language stimulation, although originally described and conceptualised for modelling on the child's personal system (Goossens, 1989), was adapted for use in preschool classrooms (Goossens et al., 1994). In a South African study, Dada and Alant (2009) implemented aided language stimulation with learners with severe communication disabilities aged 8-12 years during naturalistic group teaching activities and measured its effect on learners' acquisition of new vocabulary items. Three large facilitator boards (one each for arts and craft, food preparation and story time activities) with 24 picture symbols each were prepared. These included 16 core words (words that were the same across all three activities) and eight activity-specific words. During the activity, the facilitator pointed to the picture symbols while speaking, ensuring that she co-ordinated the spoken word with the picture at least 70% of the time. She also used more comments than questions (ratio 80:20). The acquisition of novel target vocabulary that was modelled on the board gives evidence that this strategy scaffolds learners' understanding. Naudé et al. (2020) used aided language stimulation in a group teaching situation to teach learners with severe intellectual disabilities how to solve subtraction word problems during group mathematics instructions. They also used a facilitator board with picture symbols that she pointed to during instruction, adhering to the 70% co-ordinated spoken word–picture pointing principle and the 80:20 statement: question ratio. The results of the study showed that this intervention was successful to improve mathematical word problem solving in most of the participants. Uys and Harty (2007) successfully taught South African teachers in inclusive settings to use aided language stimulation during various teaching activities. Classroom observations and teacher self-ratings suggested that teachers increased their use of aided language stimulation and also improved in classroom management skills and skills in fostering learner interactions.

Several characteristics of aided language stimulation make it ideal for the classroom context. The group strategy is compatible with the nature of typical teacher-led classroom interactions. The focus on input from the teacher is also compatible with the didactic nature of most classroom interactions, and the focus on comprehension is compatible with the pedagogical aim of learners acquiring an understanding of a subject matter in class. Only paper-based resources are required, making it easily implementable even in low-resource contexts. However, teachers will require practice to co-ordinate picture pointing with the production of spoken words and to focus on comments rather than questions.

Core vocabulary input/modelling approaches have also been proposed as classroom-based strategies to promote language learning, and specifically early syntactical skills.[1] Core vocabulary consists of those words we reuse frequently across a variety of contexts and partners. In English, this includes words like 'have', 'want' and 'go'. Heel-Beckman et al. (2013) describe the implementation of a core word-based facilitator board across classrooms in a special school in Germany. A large wall chart with 220 core words is mounted in every classroom, and teachers point to these pictures in tandem with spoken input while teaching. In order to minimise the number of core words targeted at a particular time, a number of focus words are selected for a period of six weeks and teachers concentrate particularly on modelling these words during that time. Each symbol also has a removable duplicate on a small card attached to the chart with Velcro. This enables the removal of symbols and the building up of picture-based sentences on a felt surface. Heel-Beckman et al. (2013) give anecdotal evidence of its implementation across various academic and non-academic school activities (e.g. lessons, break time, story reading), and positive effects on learners' communication and sentence building.

Like aided language stimulation, modelling core words using a wall chart only requires paper-based resources and is implementable as a group strategy. However, a core word list in the specific language used in the classroom is required to make the wall chart, and teachers require practice to point to the picture symbols of focus words while teaching.

A number of studies conducted during contextualised classroom activities have investigated the effects of providing augmented input using an individual learner's own AAC system on learners' expressive skills. In these studies, teachers, peers and/or teaching assistants were trained, amongst others, to model the use of a learner's AAC system to them. Most of these studies combined augmented input with augmented output strategies, such as prompting the target learners to use the AAC system. Chung and Carter (2013), for example, showed that augmented input and output strategies implemented by peers and teaching assistants during lessons increased the speech-generating device use and amount of peer interaction of adolescents using AAC in inclusive classrooms. Specific tasks and strategies that teaching assistants and peers were trained to do included programming the device, ensuring that it was available, as well as modelling its use and prompting learners to do the same. McMillan and Renzaglia (2014a,

2014b) trained elementary school teachers to support the use of speech-generating devices in their learners with ASD. Teachers were trained to programme the speech-generating devices, create opportunities for use and prompt use with models, questions and time delay strategies. Learners with ASD increasingly initiated communication using their speech-generating devices. In both studies teachers rated the social validity of the training highly. In a descriptive study of South African special school teachers with experience in teaching learners using aided AAC (Tönsing & Dada, 2016), it was found that teachers reported engaging in many of the tasks on which the participants in the above-mentioned two studies were trained. For example, teachers selected and added vocabulary to learners' AAC systems, ensured that the system was available to the learner, and created opportunities for use. They also rated the implementation of aided systems in the classroom as beneficial to promote learning and classroom communication.

Considerations for Classroom Implementation

Aided augmented input strategies implemented in classroom settings can facilitate comprehension, expression and learning of learners with receptive and expressive difficulties. From the research conducted in the field, a few important considerations for implementation come to the fore:

- Paper-based resources are effective to support aided augmented input, making this a relatively low-cost strategy in terms of required resources (Dada & Alant, 2009; Naudé et al., 2020; Uys & Harty, 2007).
- Teachers benefit from in-situ training and coaching to implement aided augmented input strategies in their classrooms (Chung & Carter, 2013; McMillan & Renzaglia, 2014a; Tönsing & Dada, 2016; Uys & Harty, 2007).
- Preparation of materials, lesson planning with integration of aided augmented input strategies, and self-directed practice and monitoring enhance implementation (McMillan & Renzaglia, 2014a; Uys & Harty, 2007).
- The incorporation of core vocabulary as part of the augmented input allows for generalisation of use across contexts and time (Dada & Alant, 2009; Heel-Beckman et al., 2013).
- Involving additional communication partners such as peers, educational assistants, and where possible, even parents, expands the opportunities for strategy implementation (Chung & Carter, 2013; Tönsing & Dada, 2016).
- Whole-school training seems promising to allow maximum continuity across classes and a full immersion approach (Heel-Beckman et al., 2013).

Unaided Augmented Input: Key Word Signing

Key word signing entails the use of signs from the sign language of the country to supplement spoken words used by the communication partner (Tan et al., 2014). While aided augmented input requires pointing to an aided symbol such as a picture to supplement spoken words, signs from sign language are used during key word signing. For example, a teacher may say, "Today we are going to talk about fruit," and simultaneously sign the words WE, TALK, and FRUIT. Like aided augmented input, this technique has been shown to support both receptive and expressive language of learners in need of AAC, particularly those with autism spectrum disorders, Down syndrome and intellectual disability (Clibbens, 2001; Meuris et al., 2015; Tan et al., 2014; Wendt, 2009). As with aided augmented input, the immersion in an environment where partners use signs and speech simultaneously has been deemed necessary if learners are to acquire signs for expressive use (Meuris et al., 2015). In supporting comprehension, signs have been hypothesised to be easier to process than speech because gestures precede speech developmentally (Vandereet et al., 2011). Like aided symbols, signs add a visual component to the auditory message, potentially benefiting especially children with strengths in visual processing (Loncke et al., 2006). Although manual signs are more transient than aided symbols, they are still less so than spoken language. Signing while speaking tends to slow the speech rate, and the key word approach (signing only key words) furthermore reduces the syntactic complexity of the message (Bowles & Frizelle, 2016).

In comparison to aided methods, unaided methods of communication (such as the use of signs from sign language) have certain advantages and disadvantages. Unaided methods do not require an external aid and are therefore more directly producible by the communicator. They do not require a visual focus outside of the communicator's body. Because they are closer to the behavioural early communication signals children produce with their bodies, they may be experienced as easier and more natural to produce and to incorporate into communication interactions (Cress & Marvin, 2003). The challenge of keeping an external system at hand and updated with relevant vocabulary is also not experienced when using unaided methods. However, two significant drawbacks of key word signing in comparison to aided systems are (1) the motor skills required to produce them, which may be beyond the capacities of children with physical impairments; and (2) that children using manual signs for expression may not be as readily understood by all communication partners as those using aided AAC, especially when the latter is combined with written words and/or speech generation from a device.

Evidence for the Effectiveness of Unaided Augmented Input

Key word signing has a long-standing history in the field of AAC, and early studies demonstrate its effectiveness for improving expressive and receptive communication in adults and children with autism and Down syndrome (Brady & Smouse, 1978; Carr et al., 1978; Launonen, 1996; Remington & Clarke, 1983). Although research on this approach was somewhat eclipsed by the advent of AAC technology, which seemed to draw the focus of many researchers away from key word signing approaches, a steady succession of studies have investigated this approach over the years. Clibbens (2001) provides a narrative overview of the literature on the benefits of combining spoken and signed input to boost the communication development of children with Down syndrome. According to Clibbens (2001), there is evidence from both case studies and larger-scale descriptive and quasi-experimental studies that providing signed input to children with Down syndrome boosts their expressive vocabulary, reduces challenging behaviour, and improves speech intelligibility. In a quasi-experimental longitudinal study, Launonen (1996) compared the expressive vocabularies and various other developmental domains of two groups of children with Down syndrome – a group who had received key word signing interventions between the ages of 0.5 to three years and a group who had not received such intervention. Comparisons were done at ages three, five and eight. At age three, children who had received the intervention had significantly larger vocabularies than those who had not received intervention. The intervention group was also found to be ahead in the domains of language, social skills, motor development, and self-help skills at age five, with better language and social skills persisting up until age eight. A single case experimental design study found that modelling manual signs in tandem with spoken words during naturalistic lay activities increased the expressive skills (signs and words) of young children with Down syndrome (Wright et al., 2013).

Wendt (2009) summarised the evidence of manual sign-based interventions for children with autism aged 1–15 years and found that these interventions were generally effective in promoting expressive communication (sign and speech) as well as speech comprehension. In a relatively recent investigation using a single case design, Tan et al. (2014) found that key word signing was effective in teaching young children with autism to produce signs and generalise their use to novel play situations while also increasing the spoken language skills of some children.

Dada et al. (2020) reported in their scoping review that one study comparing extensive sign training with mediated sign training was deemed as providing conclusive evidence of effectiveness. One study on total communication was found to provide preponderant evidence, and three studies were found to provide suggestive evidence of the positive effects of unaided AAC interventions.

Implementation in Classroom Contexts

In spite of the focus of research on aided approaches in recent years, descriptive studies show that the implementation of key word signing is relatively prevalent in practice, specifically in the school context, as evidenced by a number of more recent publications across countries. Sheehy and Duffy (2009), for example, found that teachers in the UK had overwhelmingly positive attitudes towards the implementation of the key word signing approach that forms part of Makaton, a multimodal AAC implementation package developed in the UK. Similar findings were made by Sheehy and Budiyanto (2014) in Indonesia. Lámh, a key word signing approach developed in Ireland, has been found to be used quite widely in schools for children with intellectual and developmental disabilities in that country (Byrne et al., 2019), and direct support staff including teachers and teaching assistants generally viewed it as beneficial and implementable. In a South African study, McDowell (2019) found that teachers at public and private schools for learners with special educational needs used key word signing and felt positive about doing so. Rombouts et al. (2017) found positive views of key word signing amongst teachers at special schools in Belgium. From these studies, it is apparent that key word signing is implemented in classrooms and regarded as a socially valid teaching approach.

Dolly and Noble (2018) conducted a study to evaluate the effect of a whole-school training approach over the course of one year on communication partners' use of key word signing. All school staff (including administrators) were trained. Five signs were introduced on a fortnightly basis and modelled in isolation in the first week and in different combinations during the second week. Communication partners increased their use of signs from an average of one per sentence to four per sentence at the completion of the year of training. Another study investigating a partner-training approach to increase the use of key word signing in a functional context was conducted by Meuris et al. (2015), although not in a school context. Meuris and colleagues taught support staff to implement key word signing with adults with intellectual disability in a care facility (residential and day facility) and found that the one-year immersion programme resulted in a significant increase in sign use by support staff, and also in a significant increase in communicative functions as expressed during a narrative task by adults with intellectual disability as compared to pre-intervention performance.

The research evidence therefore suggests that key word signing is implementable within the school environment, even in low-resource contexts, and that implementation can have positive effects on the communication of learners with severe communication difficulties. No resources are needed by communication partners to produce signs, although training in signs is required. According to the literature, this can include training workshops, ad-hoc training and support given by competent colleagues (e.g., the speech-language therapist), as well as self-training through sign resources such as paper-based or electronic sign language dictionaries (Byrne et al., 2019; Glacken et al., 2019). Continuous support and a signing 'culture' at the school were found to be beneficial (Dolly & Noble, 2018; Byrne et al., 2019). Teachers' positive attitude towards signing and their willingness to self-monitor implementation also contribute to more consistent use (Rombouts et al., 2017).

Considerations for Classroom Implementation

Unaided augmented input strategies, and in particular, key word signing, can be implemented in classroom settings to facilitate receptive and expressive communication of learners with severe communication disabilities. The research in the field highlights some important considerations for implementation:

- As is the case with aided augmented input, in-situ training and support is beneficial for teachers to learn and continuously use this approach in the classroom (Byrne et al., 2019; Glacken et al., 2019; Rombouts et al., 2017).
- A whole-school training approach can contribute to an organisational culture where signing is accepted and expected as a method of communication (Byrne et al., 2019; Meuris et al., 2015).
- Incremental training focusing on a limited number of signs per training session and building a sign vocabulary slowly over time seems to be a successful strategy to encourage sign retention (Dolly & Noble, 2018; Meuris et al., 2015).
- Focus on core vocabulary can enhance generalisation across contexts (Tan et al., 2014).

Visual Activity Schedules

A visual activity schedule depicts a series of activities or steps within a single activity by means of a series of visual representations, for example, pictures, photographs, written words, or objects (Koyama & Wang, 2011). One aim of an activity schedule is to teach a learner to follow the sequence of activities or steps within an activity independently, thereby avoiding dependency on prompts and instructions from teachers (Banda & Grimmett, 2008). Activity schedules can also orientate learners as to the daily programme, enhance their co-operation during transitions between activities, and better prepare them for any changes in the daily routine. Executive functioning of learners can be enhanced by activity schedules as learners' on-task behaviour and task completion behaviour improves. Since on-task behaviour and task completion correlate with better learning outcomes, visual activity schedules therefore improve learning. Like augmented input strategies, activity schedules provide visual (and therefore more permanent) input, potentially assisting learners with strengths in visual processing, for example, learners with autism spectrum disorders and learners with Down syndrome (Knight et al., 2014). Visual schedules can increase the predictability of the learner's daily environment, leading to a reduction in problem behaviour.

Evidence for the Effectiveness of Visual Activity Schedules

A number of systematic reviews have summarised and evaluated the effectiveness of visual activity schedules to enhance the functioning of persons with disabilities. Banda and Grimmett (2008) and Knight et al. (2014) systematically reviewed the evidence of the effect of visual activity schedules on individuals with autism, with Knight et al. particularly focusing on learners (students). The reviews included 13 and 16 studies, respectively, most of which were conducted within the school environment, including special or general education settings across elementary, middle, and high school grades. In many of these studies, visual activity schedule implementation was facilitated by the teacher. The majority of visual schedules implemented were non-electronic, using photographs or simple pictures. Some used line drawings. A minority made use of electronic platforms, displaying, for example, video schedules. In almost all cases, schedule implementation was supported by training. This included naturalistic teaching strategies such as time delay and prompting. Both reviews found that visual activity schedules were effective to enhance a number of learner outcomes. These included increased on-task behaviour, decreased dependence on prompting, correct task and schedule completion, and improved transition behaviour. Social initiations and social exchanges were also found to be improved. In addition, both reviews found that social validity of visual activity schedules interventions was rated highly by teachers and parents.

Lequia et al. (2012) reviewed the evidence regarding the effect of visual activity schedules on reducing behaviour challenges in children and youth with autism. Based on a review of 18 studies, they found that visual activity schedules were very effective in reducing challenging behaviour, resulting in improvements for 95% of the participants. Once again, most of the studies reviewed were conducted in the classroom context, and teachers were often involved in facilitating implementation. Koyama and Wang (2011) reviewed 23 studies that investigated the effect of visual activity schedules on various behavioural outcomes of persons with intellectual impairment (including but not limited to those with autism spectrum disorders). Most participants were school-aged individuals, and most studies were conducted in the school setting. Similar to the findings in the other reviews, the authors found that visual activity schedules improved engagement and on-task behaviour, decreased challenging behaviour including self-injury, improved task initiation and transition, and taught participants to self-schedule more effectively. Social validity of the interventions was high, although this was only measured in seven studies.

Implementation in Classroom Contexts

It is clear from the preceding summary of the effectiveness of visual activity schedules that a variety of studies have been conducted in the classroom context. Bryan and Gast (2000), for example, taught teachers to implement personal visual schedules (four line-drawn pictures placed in a plastic photo album) with four elementary school-aged learners with autism to enable them to complete and transition independently between four literacy-related tasks. Learners were taught to remove one line drawing from their schedule at a time, move to the relevant activity area, complete the activity, and then place the line drawing in a 'finished task' basket, before removing the next line drawing and moving on to the next activity. The learners' resource room teachers provided learners with manual prompts which faded as learners became more independent in using the schedule. All four participants increased their on-task behaviour and their independence in transitioning from task to task and also generalised their abilities to four novel learning tasks using four novel schedule pictures. The intervention was judged to be socially valid by the learners' general education teachers, teacher assistants and speech-language therapists. A similar study was conducted by Spriggs et al. (2007), whereby four learners with moderate intellectual disabilities aged 12-13 years were taught to independently complete and transition between four activities related to various academic skills (e.g., maths, literacy and computer skills). Using a similar picture schedule and similar procedures as those used by Bryan and Gast (2000), all four learners increased their on-task and independent transitioning behaviour.

Cihak (2011) compared the effect of teaching four elementary school learners with autism to use a photographic versus a video modelling schedule on their ability to independently transition between different activities during their school day. Each learner was taught to make five transitions with the support of a photographic schedule and five transitions using a video modelling schedule. The photographic schedule consisted of five personalised photographs showing the learner engaged in the five activities. Photos were printed and mounted horizontally in sequence of occurrence. The video modelling schedule consisted of five short video clips showing the learner transitioning from one task to the next. The five video clips were displayed on a touch screen windows computer in a horizontal sequence in order of occurrence. Learners could play the video by touching the thumb nail. Teachers used a least-to-most prompting hierarchy to teach learners to use the schedule to facilitate transitions. All learners increase independent transitioning supported by both types of schedules. Three learners reached criterion (100% independent transitions for three consecutive sessions) in the photographic schedule condition, while two reached criterion in the video schedule condition. The author concluded that both types of schedules are effective in promoting independent transitions.

Research on visual activity schedules clearly illustrates that these schedules can be implemented by teachers in classroom settings. The study by Cihak (2011) suggests that paper-based schedules are as effective as electronic ones. Paper-based options may be more easily implemented in low-resource contexts. The procedures to implement visual activity schedules are typically simple, and teachers only require minimal training to learn to implement them.

Considerations for Classroom Implementation

Visual activity schedules are effective in promoting transitions and on-task behaviour, as well as engagement for learners with disabilities. The following aspects need to be considered in classroom implementation:

- The provision of a schedule on its own is typically not enough to bring about behavioural changes in learners (Banda & Grimmett, 2008; Bryan & Gast, 2000; Spriggs et al., 2007). Learners need to be taught to use the schedule. The most commonly used teaching strategies are verbal, physical and gestural prompts. Once learners have understood the use of the schedule, prompts can be faded and independent use of the schedule typically occurs.
- Choice of symbols to be displayed on the schedule should be directed by the learner's symbolic abilities (i.e., whether they can recognise photographs, pictures or line drawings). A variety of formats (e.g. folders where one picture is displayed at a time, versus desk or wall mountings where all symbols are displayed at the same time) were used across studies. Authors suggest that choice of display also be directed by learner abilities. For younger learners or those with more severe disabilities, a one-symbol-per-page format has been suggested to be more effective (Banda & Grimmett, 2008).
- Visual schedules can be easily made and implemented to teach any activity that can be segmented into individual steps, as long as each step is visualised by a separate symbol. Schedules can be used across and within school activities (Banda & Grimmett, 2008).

Conclusion

Overcoming communication barriers that learners with severe communication disabilities experience is an integral step in facilitating their participation in the learning environment. Fulfilling their rights to a meaningful and equitable education requires that they can gain from and can participate in classroom communication and thereby benefit from learning opportunities. AAC can be used to facilitate learners' comprehension, expression, and self-management strategies in the learning environment. The role of the teacher is crucial in implementing AAC within educational contexts.

This review focussed on aided augmented input, unaided augmented input and visual activity schedules as three methods that can improve classroom communication and participation for children with severe communication disabilities. All three methods have been shown to be effective in improving a number of communication skills in learners with severe communication disabilities. For all three methods, the literature also supports the implementation of these techniques in classroom contexts. This chapter therefore presents teachers in inclusive settings with a description and with research evidence that supports the implementation of these strategies in the classroom for the benefit of learners with various communication challenges. These strategies require only simple paper-based resources for the most part, making them more realistically attainable in a variety of contexts, including low-resource contexts. However, teacher training remains an important factor to facilitate implementation (Singh et al., 2020; Tönsing & Dada, 2016). Without adequate and context-sensitive and -relevant training, implementation remains limited (Byrne et al., 2019). In this regard, studies are urgently needed to identify effective training methods for teachers in various low-resource settings.

Note

1 Examples are the Pixon Project kit™ produced by Pretke Romich Company, and the Cologne Communication wallpaper developed by Prof Jens Boenisch.

References

Alexander, R. J. (2001). *Culture and pedagogy: International comparisons in primary education*. Blackwell.

Allen, A. A., Schlosser, R. W., Brock, K. L., & Shane, H. C. (2017). The effectiveness of aided augmented input techniques for persons with developmental disabilities: A systematic review. *Augmentative and Alternative Communication*, *33*(3), 149–159. https://doi.org/10.1080/07434618.2017.1338752

Banda, D. R., & Grimmett, E. (2008). Enhancing social and transition behaviors of persons with autism through activity schedules: A review. *Education and Training in Developmental Disabilities*, *43*(3), 324–333.

Beukelman, D. R., & Mirenda, P. (2013). *Augmentative and alternative communication: Supporting children and adults with complex communication needs* (4th ed.). Paul H. Brookes.

Biggs, E. E., Carter, E. W., & Gilson, C. B. (2018). Systematic review of interventions involving aided AAC modeling for children with complex communication needs. *American Journal on Intellectual and Developmental Disabilities*, *123*(5), 443–473. https://doi.org/10.1352/1944-7558-123.5.443

Bowles, C., & Frizelle, P. (2016). Investigating peer attitudes towards the use of key word signing by children with Down syndrome in mainstream schools. *British Journal of Learning Disabilities*, *44*(4), 284–291. https://doi.org/10.1111/bld.12162

Brady, D. O., & Smouse, A. D. (1978). A simultaneous comparison of three methods for language training with an autistic child: An experimental single case analysis. *Journal of Autism and Childhood Schizophrenia*, *8*, 271–279.

Branson, D., & Demchak, M. (2009). The use of augmentative and alternative communication methods with infants and toddlers with disabilities: A research review. *Augmentative and Alternative Communication*, *25*(4), 274–286. https://doi.org/10.3109/07434610903384529

Brewis, K. (2015). *Comparative effects of two AAC systems on the vocal productions of children with motor speech disorders*. (Unpublished master's thesis). University of Pretoria, Pretoria, South Africa.

Bryan, L. C., & Gast, D. L. (2000). Teaching on-task and on-schedule behaviors to high-functioning children with autism via picture activity schedules. *Journal of Autism and Developmental Disorders*, *30*(6), 553–567.

Byrne, Á., Pyne, J., & Sheehan, V. (2019). Use of key word signing for children and adults with intellectual disability in an Irish context. *Tizard Learning Disability Review*, *24*(3), 113–120. https://doi.org/10.1108/TLDR-07-2018-0023

Calculator, S. N. (2009). Augmentative and alternative communication (AAC) and inclusive education for students with the most severe disabilities. *International Journal of Inclusive Education*, *13*(1), 93–113. https://doi.org/10.1080/13603110701284656

Calculator, S. N., & Black, T. (2009). Validation of an inventory of best practices in the provision of augmentative and alternative communication services to students with severe disabilities in general education classrooms. *American Journal of Speech-Language Pathology, 18*, 329–343.

Carr, E. G., Binkoff, J. A., Koliginsky, E., & Eddy, M. (1978). Acquisition of sign language by autistic children. 1: Expressive labelling. *Journal of Applied Behavior Analysis, 11*, 489–501.

Chung, Y. C., & Carter, E. W. (2013). Promoting peer interactions in inclusive classrooms for students who use speech-generating devices. *Research and Practice for Persons with Severe Disabilities, 38*(2), 94–109. https://doi.org/10.2511/027494813807714492

Cihak, D. F. (2011). Comparing pictorial and video modeling activity schedules during transitions for students with autism spectrum disorders. *Research in Autism Spectrum Disorders, 5*, 433–441. https://doi.org/10.1016/j.rasd.2010.06.006

Clibbens, J. (2001). Signing and lexical development in children with Down syndrome. *Down's Syndrome, Research and Practice : The Journal of the Sarah Duffen Centre / University of Portsmouth, 7*(3), 101–105. https://doi.org/10.3104/reviews.119

Cress, C. J., & Marvin, C. a. (2003). Common questions about AAC services in early intervention. *Augmentative and Alternative Communication, 19*(4), 254–272. https://doi.org/10.1080/07434610310001598242

Dada, S. (2019). A comparison of speaical education teachers' attitudes towards various augmentative and alternative communication systems. In S. Halder & V. Argyropoulos (Eds.), *Inclusion, equity and access for individuals with disabilities* (pp. 153–178). Palgrave Macmillan.

Dada, S., & Alant, E. (2009). The effect of aided language stimulation on vocabulary acquisition in children with little or no functional speech. *American Journal of Speech-Language Pathology, 18*(1), 50–64. https://doi.org/10.1044/1058-0360(2008/07-0018)

Dada, S., Flores, C., Bastable, K., & Schlosser, R. W. (2020). The effects of augmentative and alternative communication interventions on the receptive language skills of children with developmental disabilities: A scoping review. *International Journal of Speech-Language Pathology*, 1–11.

Dolly, A., & Noble, E. (2018). "Lámh signs combined" - investigating a whole school approach to augmentative and alternative communication (AAC) intervention through research in practice. *REACH Journal for Special Needs Eduaiton in Ireland, 31*(1), 53–68.

Ganz, J. B. (2015). AAC interventions for individuals with autism spectrum disorders: State of the science and future research directions. *Augmentative and Alternative Communication, 31*(3), 203–214. https://doi.org/10.3109/07434618.2015.1047532

Glacken, M., Healy, D., Gilrane, U., Gowan, S. H.-M., Dolan, S., Walsh-Gallagher, D., & Jennings, C. (2019). Key word signing: Parents' experiences of an unaided form of augmentative and alternative communication (Lámh). *Journal of Intellectual Disabilities, 23*(3), 327–343. https://doi.org/10.1177/1744629518790825

Goossens, C. (1989). Aided communication intervention before assessment: A case study of a child with cerebral palsy. *Augmentative and Alternative Communication, 5*, 14–26. https://doi.org/10.1080/07434618912331274926

Goossens, C., Crain, S., & Elder, P. S. (1994). *Communication displays for engineered preschool environments. Books I-III.* Mayer Johnson.

Heel-Beckman, C., Bünk, M., Kohnen, M., & Schmidt, C. (2013). Kreativer Umgang mit der Wortschatztafel im Unterricht [Creative interaction with the vocabuary chart during teaching]. In A. Hallbauer, T. Hallbauer, & M. Hüning-Meier (Eds.), *UK kreativ* (pp. 71–85). Loeper.

Kathard, H., & Pillay, M. (2015). A study of teacher–learner interactions: A continuum between monologic and dialogic interactions. *Language, Speech, and Hearing Services in Schools, 46*, 222–241. https://doi.org/10.1044/2015

Kent-Walsh, J., & Light, J. (2003). General education teachers' experiences with inclusion of students who use augmentative and alternative communication. *Augmentative and Alternative Communication, 19*(2), 104–124. https://doi.org/10.1080/0743461031000112043

Knight, V., Sartini, E., & Spriggs, A. D. (2014). Evaluating visual activity schedules as evidence-based practice for individuals with autism spectrum disorders. *Journal of Autism and Developmental Disorders, 45*(1), 157–178. https://doi.org/10.1007/s10803-014-2201-z

Koyama, T., & Wang, H. T. (2011). Use of activity schedule to promote independent performance of individuals with autism and other intellectual disabilities: A review. *Research in Developmental Disabilities, 32*(6), 2235–2242. https://doi.org/10.1016/j.ridd.2011.05.003

Launonen, K. (1996). Enhancing communication skills of childre with Down Syndrome: Early use of manual signs. In S. Von Tetzchner & M. H. Jensen (Eds.), *Augmentative and alternative communication: European perspectives* (pp. 213–231). Whurr.

Lequia, J., MacHalicek, W., & Rispoli, M. J. (2012). Effects of activity schedules on challenging behavior exhibited in children with autism spectrum disorders: A systematic review. *Research in Autism Spectrum Disorders, 6*(1), 480–492. https://doi.org/10.1016/j.rasd.2011.07.008

Lloyd, L. L., Fuller, D. R., & Arvidson, H. H. (1997). Glossary. In L. L. Lloyd, D. R. Fuller, & H. H. Arvidson (Eds.), *Augmentative and alternative communication: A handbook of principles and practices* (pp. 522–543). Allyn & Bacon.

Loncke, F. (2008). Basic principles of language intervention for children who use AAC. *SIG 12 Perspectives on Augmentative and Alternative Communication, 17*(2), 50–55. https://doi.org/10.1044/aac17.2.50

Loncke, F. T., Campbell, J., England, A. M., & Haley, T. (2006). Multimodality: A basis for augmentative and alternative communication—psycholinguistic, cognitive, and clinical/educational aspects. *Disability and Rehabilitation, 28*(3), 169–174. https://doi.org/10.1080/09638280500384168

McDowell, A. C. M. (2019). *The use of unaided augmentative and alternative communication strategies to support learners in South African special schools: A study of teachers' perceptions* (Master's dissertation). Retrieved from University of Pretoria Repository, https://repository.up.ac.za/handle/2263/73057

McMillan, J. M., & Renzaglia, A. (2014a). Supporting speech generating device use in the classroom. Part 1: Teacher professional development. *Journal of Special Education Technology, 29*(3), 31–47. https://doi.org/10.1177/016264341402900303

McMillan, J. M., & Renzaglia, A. (2014b). Supporting speech generating device use in the classroom. Part 2: Student communication outcomes. *Journal of Special Education Technology, 29*(3), 49–61. https://doi.org/10.1177/016264341402900304

Meuris, K., Maes, B., & Zink, I. (2015). Teaching adults with intellectual disability manual signs through their support staff: A key word signing program. *Journal of Speech, Language, and Hearing Research, 24*(2), 545–560. https://doi.org/10.1044/2015

Meyer, A., Rose, D. H., & Gordon, D. (2014). *Universal design for learning: Theory and practice.* CAST.

Millar, D. C., Light, J. C., & Schlosser, R. W. (2006). The impact of augmentative and alternative communication intervention on the speech production of inidviduals with developmental disabilities: A research review. *Journal of Speech, Language and Hearing Research, 49,* 248–264.

Muttiah, N. A., McNaughton, D., & Drager, K. D. R. (2016). Providing instructional support for AAC service delivery in low- and middle-income (LAMI) countries. *International Journal of Speech-Language Pathology, 18*(4), 341–353. https://doi.org/10.3109/17549507.2015.1101154

Naude, T., Dada, S., & Bornman, J. (2020). The effect of an augmented input intervention on subtraction word-problem solving for children with intellectual disabilities: A preliminary study. *International Journal of Disability, Development and Education, Early online,* 1–22. https://doi.org/10.1080/1034912X.2020.1840530

Novak, I., Mcintyre, S., Morgan, C., Campbell, L., Dark, L., Morton, N., Stumbles, E., Wilson, S. A., & Goldsmith, S. (2013). A systematic review of interventions for children with cerebral palsy: State of the evidence. *Developmental Medicine and Child Neurology, 55*(10), 885–910. https://doi.org/10.1111/dmcn.12246

Pillay, M., Tiwari, R., Kathard, H., & Chikte, U. (2020). Sustainable workforce: South African audiologists and speech therapists. *Human Resources for Health, 18*(1), 1–13. https://doi.org/10.1186/s12960-020-00488-6

Remington, B., & Clarke, S. (1983). Acquisition of expressive signing by autistic children: An evaluation of the relative effects of simultaneous communication and sign-alone training. *Journal of Applied Behavior Analysis, 16,* 315–328.

Rombouts, E., Maes, B., & Zink, I. (2017). Beliefs and habits: Staff experiences with key word signing in special schools and group residential homes. *Augmentative and Alternative Communication, 33*(2), 87–96. https://doi.org/10.1080/07434618.2017.1301550

Sargent, J., Clarke, M., Price, K., Griffiths, T. and Swettenham, J. (2013), Use of eye-pointing by children with cerebral palsy: What are we looking at? *International Journal of Language & Communication Disorders, 48,* 477–485. https://doi.org/10.1111/1460-6984.12026

Schlosser, R. W., Shane, H. C., Allen, A. A., Benz, A., Cullen, J., O'Neill, L., … Pasupathy, R. (2020). Coaching a school team to implement the visual immersion system tm in a classroom for children with autism spectrum disorder: A mixed-methods proof-of-concept study. *Advances in Neurodevelopmental Disorders, 4,* 447–470. https://doi.org/10.1007/s41252-020-00176-5

Schlosser, R. W., & Wendt, O. (2008). Effects of augmentative and alternative communication intervention on speech production in children with autism: A systematic review. *American Journal of Speech-Language Pathology, 17*(August), 212–230. https://doi.org/10.1044/1058-0360(2008/021)

Sennott, S. C., Light, J. C., & McNaughton, D. (2016). AAC modeling intervention research review. *Research and Practice for Persons with Severe Disabilities, 41*(2), 101–115. https://doi.org/10.1177/1540796916638822

Shane, H. C., Laubscher, E., Schlosser, R. W., Fadie, H. L., Sorce, J. F., Abramson, J. S., Flynn, S., & Corley, K. (2014). *Enhancing communication for individuals with autism: A guide to the Visual Immersion System.* Paul H. Brookes.

Sheehy, K., & Budiyanto. (2014). Teachers' attitudes to signing for children with severe learning disabilities in Indonesia. *International Journal of Inclusive Education, 18*(11), 1143–1161. https://doi.org/10.1080/13603116.2013.879216

Sheehy, K., & Duffy, H. (2009). Attitudes to Makaton in the ages of integration and inclusion. *International Journal of Special Education, 24*(2), 91–102.

Shire, S.Y., & Jones, N. (2015). Communication partners supporting children with complex communication needs who use AAC: A systematic review. *Communication Disorders Quarterly, 37*(1), 3–15. https://doi.org/10.1177/1525740114558254

Singh, S., Diong, Z. Z., & Mustaffa Kamal, R. (2020). Malaysian teachers' experience using augmentative and alternative communication with students. *Augmentative and Alternative Communication, 36*(2), 107–117. https://doi.org/10.1080/07434618.2020.1785547

Soto, G., & Yu, B. (2014). Considerations for the provision of services to bilingual children Who use augmentative and alternative communication. *Augmentative and Alternative Communication, 30*(1), 83–92. https://doi.org/10.3109/07434618.2013.878751

Spriggs, A. D., Gast, D. L., & Ayres, K. M. (2007). Using picture activity schedule books to increase on schedule and on-task behaviors. *Education and Training in Developmental Disabilities, 42*(2), 209–223.

Stephenson, J. (2009). Iconicity in the development of picture skills: Typical development and implications for individuals with severe intellectual disabilities. *Augmentative and Alternative Communication, 25*(3), 187–201. https://doi.org/10.1080/07434610903031133

Tan, X.Y., Trembath, D., Bloomberg, K., Iacono, T., & Caithness, T. (2014). Acquisition and generalization of key word signing by three children with autism. *Developmental Neurorehabilitation, 17*(2), 125–136. https://doi.org/10.3109/17518423.2013.863236

Tomasevski, K. (1999). *Preliminary report of the Special Rapporteur on the right to education.* United Nations.

Tönsing, K. M., & Dada, S. (2016). Teachers' perceptions of implementation of aided AAC to support expressive communication in South African special schools: A pilot investigation. *AAC: Augmentative and Alternative Communication, 32*(4). https://doi.org/10.1080/07434618.2016.1246609

United Nations. (1948). *Universal declaration of human rights.* UN General Assembly.

United Nations. (1989). *The convention on the rights of the child.* https://doi.org/10.1111/j.1467-9515.1989.tb00500.x

United Nations. (2006). Convention on the rights of persons with disabilities. Author. http://www.un.org/disabilities/convention/conventionfull.shtml

Uys, C. J. E., & Harty, M. (2007). Narrowing the gap: Using aided language stimulation (ALS) in the inclusive classroom. *South African Journal of Occupational Therapy,* November(1), 29–33. https://doi.org/10.1177/000271625932400107

Vandereet, J., Maes, B., Lembrechts, D., & Zink, I. (2011). Expressive vocabulary acquisition in children with intellectual disability: Speech or manual signs? *Journal of Intellectual and Developmental Disability, 36*(2), 91–104.

Von Tetzchner, S., & Martinsen, H. (2000). *Introduction to augmentative and alternative communication* (2nd ed.). Whurr.

Wendt, O. (2009). Research on the use of manual signs and graphic symbols in autism spectrum disorders: A systematic review. In P. Mirenda & T. Iacono (Eds.), *Autism Spectrum Disorders and AAC.* (pp. 83–140). Paul H Brooks.

Wright, C. A., Kaiser, A. P., Reikowsky, D. I., & Roberts, M. Y. (2013). Effects of a naturalistic sign intervention on expressive language of toddlers with Down Syndrome. *Journal of Speech, Language and Hearing Research, 56*, 994–1008. https://doi.org/10.1044/1092-4388(2012/12-0060)994

Wylie, K., McAllister, L., Davidson, B., & Marshall, J. (2013). Changing practice: Implications of the World Report on Disability for responding to communication disability in under-served populations. *International Journal of Speech-Language Pathology, 15*(1), 1–13. https://doi.org/10.3109/17549507.2012.745164

Zangari, C., & Van Tatenhove, G. (2009). Supporting more linguistically advanced communicators in the classroom. In G Soto & C. Zangari (Eds.), *Practically speaking: Supporting langauge, literacy, and academic development for students with AAC needs* (pp. 173–193). Paul H Brookes.

22
INTERVENTIONS FOR THE REMEDIATION OF DYSLEXIA
A Systematic Review of Evidence-Based Practices

*Suparna Nag and Santoshi Halder**

Background Literature

Learning Disability (LD) is an umbrella term that covers a wide range of learning difficulties, including reading disabilities (RDs) or disorders, difficulties in writing, and challenges in arithmetic. Globally 15–20% of the population suffers from LD (Balakrishnan et al., 2015) and among these, 70–80% have been identified diagnosed as dyslexic (Balakrishnan et al., 2015). Several research studies in India report that 10–14% of school-going children are identified with LD (Kamala & Ramganesh, 2015). Developmental dyslexia is a specific type of deficit in reading and reading acquisition, which develops despite average intelligence (IQ), regular schooling, and a regular educational environment; it can be found in the absence of any sensory or psychiatric disorder (115Lallier et al., 2010). Children with lower or very poor reading skills, as compared to average children in their age range, may be described as having 'specific learning difficulties', 'specific reading impairment', or 'developmental dyslexia'. The International Dyslexia Association (2002) states that dyslexia is a specific type of LD and that it is neurobiological in origin (Leon and Chia, 2017). It is characterized by difficulties in accuracy and/or fluency in word recognition and also by poor spelling and decoding abilities. These difficulties typically result from a deficit in the phonological component of language that is often unexpected in relation to other cognitive abilities and the provision of effective classroom instruction. Secondary consequences of having dyslexia may include problems in reading comprehension, resulting in reduced reading, which can impede the growth of vocabulary and background knowledge (adopted by the IDA Board of Directors, 2002; NICHD). Children with dyslexia suffer from a series of impairments, including severe RD, phonological deficit, phonological short-term memory loss, and poor phoneme awareness (Lallier et al., 2010; Vellutino et al., 2004). Ongoing research into dyslexia focuses on the effects of gene structure and neurological risk factors, thus emphasizing that it has a genetic origin and is a neurological LD (Andrade et al., 2015; Peterson & Pennington, 2012; Shaywitz et al., 2008; Vellutino et al., 2004).

People with dyslexia face a wide range of reading challenges, mainly phonological deficit, spelling deficit, problems in fluency, difficulty in decoding and encoding, incorrect pronuncia-

* santoshi_halder@yahoo.com; shedu@caluniv.ac.in

tion, and perceptual problems (Hornickel et al., 2012; Mercer et al., 2000; Papadopoulos et al., 2004; Park et al., 2014;). They also have difficulties in identifying and manipulating words, sound orders, or rhymes, and in learning the sounds of letters. As a result, they have problems in recognizing groups of letters and also, they are confused if the sequence of words is changed. These drawbacks serve to decelerate their academic achievement and adversely affect their daily learning skills. It is vital to remedy these difficulties to catalyze an improvement in daily reading skills and academic achievement of dyslexic students. Jiménez and Defior (2014) have stated: 'Consequently, the difficulty profile will be very important in determining the intervention approach as children with dyslexia should require individualized and customized intervention based on the deficits that have been identified in their assessment'.

Significant trends in the remediation of reading-related disorders, identified from empirical research evidence of intervention programs, teaching strategies, and instructional methods from researchers across the world, have already demonstrated alleviation of identified reading problems. In this review, the focus is to provide a systematic analysis of the evidence of the enrolled evidence approaches mainly applied to children with dyslexia followed by different headings/categories and to identify the best intervention practices for the remediation of RD.

Rationale for the Study

Given the growing volume of systematic reviews in this field, it is evident that the systematic reviews/meta-analysis done on this perspective area is followed by a wide range of reading-related disorders along with multiple treatment approaches in several countries.

The report of a research analysis (Graham & Santangelo, 2014; Wanzek et al., 2015) demonstrates that one of the foremost challenges for a dyslexic child is that of spelling, a difficulty that can be overcome through reading instruction, as per several research outcomes. Recent meta-analyses report that reading strategies have a significant influence on improving reading comprehension (Duff & Clarke, 2011; Scammacca et al., 2015; Swanson et al., 2014).

Earlier reviews on the subject indicated variations with respect to target groups, number and nature of samples (or a number of papers considered), etc. Another meta-analysis done on Tier 2 reading interventions made for K–3 students includes all those papers where the researcher(s) implemented interventions specifically for the target behavior of reading comprehension. The objective was to ascertain the effectiveness of the less extensive and multicomponent reading interventions and observe the relationship between the key features of these interventions and the expected outcomes. Wanzek et al. (2015) selected 72 relevant papers for this meta-analysis and emphasized the response to intervention (RTI) model for the improvement of reading skills. In most research work, this RTI model was structured in three tiers. However, this review focused only on the Tier 2 intervention and attempted to explore its effective outcomes in comparison with those of Tier 3. Similarly, there were other literature reviews targeting specific types of problematic behaviors and related reading intervention strategies.

From the preceding summarization of earlier evidence, it is clear that the studies were mainly focused on different target behaviors and appropriate intervention strategies for the remediation of those particular behaviors. Moreover, the target group in most studies was kindergarten students. Research has shown that adults too can be diagnosed with dyslexia, as there is no age limitation (Berninger et al., 1991; Pinneli, 2014). However, no single systematic review provides an overview of all the intervention strategies for the remediation of the gamut of reading-related problems. It is essential to understand which target group the intervention was focused on and what specific remediation is needed for adults with RD. It is also not clear whether the trends are based on geographical region and the actual condition. This systematic review is an endeavor to gain improved insights into the advantages and limitations of all effective intervention programs implemented thus far. It is also an attempt to review relevant published papers to extract significant themes for analyses and identify research gaps and trends in the field.

Research Questions

This systematic review was conducted to answer the following research questions.

- What are the different types of reading intervention strategies implemented in the cases of students with RD or dyslexia?
- Which intervention program has been found to be the most effective in alleviating RD or dyslexia?
- Is there any region- or location-wise trend identified in the remediation of dyslexic students?
- On which target behavior was the intervention for RD predominantly focused?
- What research designs were adapted and what age of the sample was predominantly considered in the published works?
- Which types of journals published these studies?

Method

Inclusion Criteria

To conduct this systematic review, the following inclusion criteria were established to identify relevant articles. *First*, only peer-reviewed papers written in English were considered. *Second*, studies available through online resources and electronic databases were included. *Third*, only studies focused specifically on RD were included.

Search Procedure

Studies to be reviewed were identified via a search of several electronic databases, based on the pre-set criteria. Electronic databases were searched for peer-reviewed papers published between 1987 and 2020. Only full papers were considered. No hand search journals were included. Figure 22.1 provides an overview of the search process for the systematic analysis. Many articles that did not fulfill the inclusion and exclusion criteria were excluded at the screening stage.

After screening all the studies, several papers were excluded as they did not meet the inclusion criteria. Finally, 80 articles were tabulated into a systematic review table highlighting the key points of each published paper with descriptions of relevant aspects. Each study was analyzed to extract the following information to establish the trends: (a) author, (b) publication year, (c) publication source, (d) geographical location of where the study was conducted, (e) purpose or objective of the study, (f) intervention for dyslexia, (g) target behavior considered in the study, (h) sample size, (i) research design, (j) learning materials, and (k) important outcomes.

Result

After an extensive literature search across electronic databases, 80 papers fulfilled the inclusion criteria and were finally selected for the study.

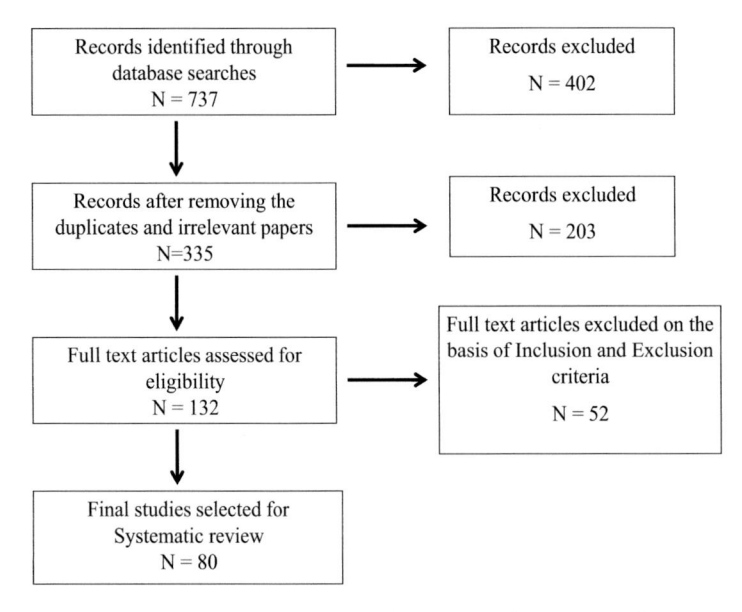

```
┌─────────────────────────┐         ┌─────────────────────────┐
│ Records identified      │         │   Records excluded      │
│ through database        │────────▶│       N = 402           │
│ searches                │         │                         │
│       N = 737           │         └─────────────────────────┘
└───────────┬─────────────┘
            │
            ▼
┌─────────────────────────┐         ┌─────────────────────────┐
│ Records after removing  │         │   Records excluded      │
│ the duplicates and      │────────▶│       N = 203           │
│ irrelevant papers       │         │                         │
│       N = 335           │         └─────────────────────────┘
└───────────┬─────────────┘
            │
            ▼
┌─────────────────────────┐         ┌─────────────────────────┐
│ Full text articles      │         │ Full text articles      │
│ assessed for            │────────▶│ excluded on the basis   │
│ eligibility             │         │ of Inclusion and        │
│       N = 132           │         │ Exclusion criteria      │
│                         │         │       N = 52            │
└───────────┬─────────────┘         └─────────────────────────┘
            │
            ▼
┌─────────────────────────┐
│ Final studies selected  │
│ for Systematic review   │
│       N = 80            │
└─────────────────────────┘
```

Figure 22.1 Systematic review flow diagram specifying stages of inclusion of the papers

Trend based on Publication Year

Most of the papers included in this review study on reading interventions for dyslexia were published between the years 2013 and 2014 (n = 14 out of 80). These journals can be grouped into six categories: special education, psychology and education, interdisciplinary, behavioral science, scientific and technological, and music education. Most papers (43.75%; n = 35) on RD were published in journals under the 'special education' category.

The geographical location or continent-based trends depicted that the area was extensively explored from various parts of the world. The results show that most of the papers were published in North America (n = 33). The rest of the papers were identified as having been published in Europe (n = 29), Asia (n = 15), Australia (n = 2), and Africa (n = 1).

There were variations with respect to subjects and sample sizes. The results indicated that most of the papers had a large sample size (n = 50), fewer papers had a small sample (n = 25), and the frequency of single-subject design-based papers was fairly sporadic (n = 6). There was a variation in the age of the sample, and results indicated that most works were related to children with RD (5 to 12 years) while very few studies were conducted on adults with RD (n = 10). A detailed summary of all the papers also demonstrated that there was diversity in the research designs adhered to, with 92.5% of the papers based on quantitative research, 4.92% on qualitative research, and only 5% on mixed-method research.

Effective Interventions

The main focus of this systematic review was to find which intervention programs were effective for dyslexia. Various intervention strategies were found through the review of identified papers. To make an in-depth analysis of all the intervention strategies, the researcher categorized them under relevant broad subheadings based on treatment approaches. The categories finally extracted were as follows: academic and psychological approach (APA), process training approach (PTA), multisensory approach (MA), cognitive training approach (CTA), self-instruction training approach (SITA), visual reception training approach (VRTA), listening exercise approach (LEA), music training approach (MTA), educational software approach (ESA), and medical-neurological approach (MNA). Results indicated a more or less positive impact of the identified intervention strategies on dyslexic children. Of the 80 papers reviewed, 25 papers (31.25%) followed the PTA, implying that they primarily emphasized the reading approach while 21 papers (27.5%) were based on ESA. Along with these, eight papers (10%) were identified as implementing CTA, seven papers each (8.75%) followed MA and VRTA, and four papers (5%) followed LEA interventions. MTA and SITA were followed by three papers (3.75%). APA interventions were identified in two studies (2.5%). Only one paper (1.25%) was found to have followed interventions based on MNA.

Figure 22.2 describes several remedial interventions for people with dyslexia, and these are grouped under ten broad intervention categories or approaches (see Figure 22.2 and also Tables 22.1–22.5 for details). Earlier systematic reviews focused on the primary objective of exploring the most effective intervention. These studies also identified research works studied from APAs and interventions for reading and spelling challenges (Williams et al., 2016). From the previous studies, it was found that neuroimaging can be significant in relation to dyslexia and has a significant effect on RD; thus, intervention programs specially designed for this field were also explored by researchers (Barquero et al., 2014). This review did not focus on any particular type of reading intervention. Its target, instead, was to analyze and explore all interventions and to identify the effective ones and also the various trends. The findings emphasized three approaches, namely PTA, ESA, and MA. To identify the most effective intervention, all strategies were coded under ten well-known approaches (see Figure 22.2 for details). Results showed that PTA was most frequently used in this specific field of dyslexia (see Figure 22.2 and Table 22.1).

Findings by Intervention Categories

Process Training Approach

In PTA-based interventions, psychological processes are targeted in a bid to resolve specific learning difficulties (Gearheart et al., 1992; Rajkumari et al., 2004). The results indicate that out of all revised studies, 25 papers follow this approach (31.25% of 80).

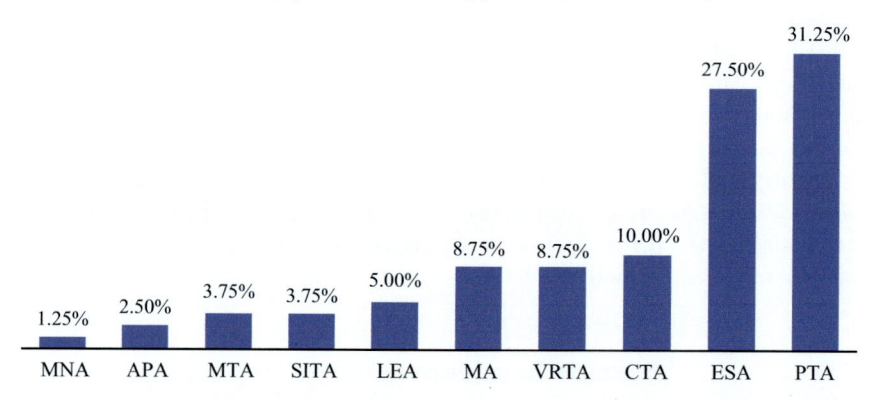

Figure 22.2 Graphical representation of intervention strategies/programs implemented for the remediation of reading difficulty or dyslexia *Note.* Process training based approach Intervention (31.25%), Educational software-based Approach Intervention (27.50%), Cognitive Training Approach Intervention (10%), Visual Reception Training based Approach Intervention & Multisensory Approach based Intervention (8.75%), Listening exercise Approach Intervention (5%), Self-instruction Training based Approach Intervention & Music Training based Approach Intervention (3.75%), Academic and Psychological Approach Intervention (2.5%) and Medical Neurological Approach Intervention (1.25%).

Table 22.1 Summary of intervention studies followed by Process Training approach

Study author and year	Intervention	Region/location	Target behavior	Research design	Target group	Measure	Findings
Duff et al. (2014)	Reading and Language Intervention (RAIL)	Europe	Reading skill	Mixed method	Children (age 6)	Various word reading test	Small to moderate effects on letter knowledge, phoneme awareness and vocabulary.
Park et al. (2014)	The CORE Phonics survey 1*	North America	Reading Fluency	**QR	Children (age 12 years)	Standardized test battery	Significant improvement in reading comprehension and reading speed.
Nelson et al. (2012)	CTOPP 2*	North America	Phonological processing	**QR	First grader (age 5-6)	Standardized Norm Reference Test NRT	Phonological processing had an indirect effect on reading rather on phonological awareness. Effect was moderate.
Ise & Korney (2010)	Orthographic Spelling training	Europe	Spelling training	**QR	Children (age 9-12)	Several exercises from books	Statistical analyses showed significant improvements in reading along with orthographic spelling and it enhanced reading and spelling ability.

(Continued)

Table 22.1 (Continued)

Study author and year	Intervention	Region/ location	Target behavior	Research design	Target group	Measure	Findings
Otaiba et al. (2010)	TAILS 3★	North America	Reading performance	★★QR	KG students (age 4)	Reading activities and speed game	Result indicated greater improvement in reading abilities.
Klubnik & Ardoin (2010)	Fluency-based reading intervention (R–CBM) 4★	North America	Reading performance	★★QR	Second grader (age 7)	Reading passages	After the intervention students gained significant improvements on oral reading skills.
Otterloo & Leij (2009)	Home based pre reading intervention	Europe	Phonological awareness	★★QR	KG children (age 4)	Rhymes, picture of letters, books, chalk and slate	Students benefited positively after the treatment and gained significantly in word reading and spelling.
Pavlidou et al. (2009)	AGL 5★	Europe	Reading ability	Mixed method	Primary school children (age 5–8)	Standardized battery screening test, grammatical items	Students with Dyslexia/ LD can enhance learning potentialities through this instruction.

Cirino et al. (2009)	Proactive reading intervention Lectura proactiva (Spanish language intervention)	North America	Reading performance	Follow-up	First graders (age 5)	Listening comprehensions, letter pictures	Significant influence on spelling, fluency, decoding and comprehension after providing intervention on Spanish and English language students.
Vaughn et al. (2006)	Proactive reading based on direct instruction approach (English intervention) Lectura proactiva (Spanish language intervention)	North America	Reading difficulty	**QR	First grader (age 5/6)	English passage / text, word games, list of syllables	All findings were in favor of intervention group and they made a meaningful progress in reading skills. In Spanish reading the results were also positive. The comparison groups also made significant gains both in English and Spanish.
Papadopoulos et al. (2004)	PASS & PREP 6*	Europe	Early phonological reading skills	*QL	Kindergarten (age 3/4)	Text and rhymes	Significant effect was found in phonological skills.

(*Continued*)

385

Table 22.1 (Continued)

Study author and year	Intervention	Region/ location	Target behavior	Research design	Target group	Measure	Findings
Trout et al. (2003)	Reading mastery, I and Great Leaps Reading Program	North America	Reading skills	★★QR	Kindergarten (age 3/4)	Scripted lessons	Supplementary reading program is very effective for increasing phonemic awareness and basic reading skills.
Uhry & Shepherd, (1997)	Balanced Reading Tutorials	North America	Phonological awareness	★★QR	First and Second grader (age 5/6)	List of Consonant-Vowel-Consonant (CVC) words, wooden blocks, text	Significant growth in ability to read and read words by phonological recoding with correct spelling. Significant gains in phonological awareness.
Guyer, Banks, & Guyer, (1993)	Wilson Reading System (WRS) and Non-Phonetic spelling power/Spelling Power	North America	Spelling ability	★★QR	Adolescent students (age 18–32)	Syllable rules, words with suffix, Sound options in English language, list of words	Significant increase of spelling performance in adults having dyslexia.
Jan et al. (2011)	Multivariate predictive model	Europe	Reading ability	★★QR	Elementary children (age 7–9)	list of isolated words and numbers, complete sentences and specific words	All the reading-related variables positively correlated with each other and a significant relation was found.

The Remediation of Dyslexia

Study	Intervention	Region	Focus	Design	Participants	Materials	Results
Berninger et al. (1991)	Selective reminding technique and written reproduction technique (Study 1)	North America	Orthographic disability	**QR	I, II and III graders (age 5–8)	List of single words item, primary pencil and lined papers	The first one facilitated the process of rapid automatic retrieval of a name code.
	Rosner Auditory Analysis Training Program (Study 2)	North America	Reading ability	Single-subject design	One adult person (age 18)	List of nonsense words and real words, newspaper reading	Significant impairment in phonemic skills may be trained and can develop to some extent.
Mercer et al. (2000)	Great Leaps Reading Program (fluency-based reading intervention)	North America	Reading fluency	**QR	Middle school students (age 10–14)	Reading materials, listed sequenced words, one story, charts	Result indicated significant growth in reading rate and reading level of the target group.
Given et al. (2007)	FFW and SM, Regular Class instruction 7*	North America	Reading and Language disorder	**QR	Middle group school student (age 10–14)	Series of games, list of words and sentences, stories	Significant gains on reading with this intervention.
Wolff, (2014)	Phonemic Decoding and Phonemic Awareness training, Reading Fluency training, Reading comprehension strategies	Europe	Reading skill	**QR	Grade III children	List of consonant letters, nonsense words, short story	Reading skills were significantly enhanced by training program and there was a reciprocal relationship between RAN and reading speed.

(*Continued*)

Table 22.1 (Continued)

Study author and year	Intervention	Region/location	Target behavior	Research design	Target group	Measure	Findings
Leong et al. (2011)	ASA 8★	Asia	Chinese spelling	★★QR	Children (age 8)	One short text, one lesson with several morphemes	Effective influence on orthographic performance after this intervention.
Wrighta et al. (2011)	Sub lexical teaching strategy	Australia	Reading ability and reading comprehension	Single-subject design	One child (age 9)	Reading comprehension test, list of words, memory games	Substantial and significant influence was seen on irregular word reading, phonological skills and text reading accuracy.
Denton et al. (2014)	Guided Reading intervention (GR), Explicit Intervention (EX)	North America	Reading skill and reading comprehension	★★QR	I grader (age 5/6)	Text reading, video clippings, reading books	The two types of training program accelerated reading ability and academic progress.
Bonacina et al. (2015)	RRT 9★	Europe	Reading performance	★★QR	Junior high students (age 11–14)	Computer, list of words, syllables, pseudo-words, phrases	Positive effect on both reading speed and accuracy.
Barth et al. (2016)	Text processing Comprehension intervention	North America	Reading comprehension	★★QR	134 students grade 6–8	WJ iii oral comprehension subtest, Gates-Mac Ginitie Reading Test–Fourth Edition, Word Reading Efficiency-2	Significant effects found on Vocabulary. Moderate effects found on listening comprehension and reading comprehension.

| Rijthoven et al. | Phonics through Spelling intervention | Netherland | Pseudo word reading, word reading, word spelling | **QR | 54 children (37 boys, 17 girls) Age 9 to 11 years | Mnemonic card, flashcards, | Result indicated that pseudoword reading, word reading, and word spelling abilities were significantly improved after the intervention. Positive effects found on both spelling and reading. |

Note.
1★CORE – Consortium on Reading Excellence; 2★CTOPP – Comprehensive Test of Phonological Processing; 3★TAILS – Tutor-Assisted Intensive Learning Strategies; 4★R–CBM – Curriculum-Based reading intervention; 5★AGL – Artificial Grammar Learning task; 6★PASS – Planning, Attention, Simultaneous and Successive processing & PREP – PASS Reading Enhancement Program; 7★FFW – Fast for Word Learning & Fast for Word Learning to Read; SM – Success Maker; 8★ASA – Analytic and Synthetic approach; 9★RRT – Rhythmic Reading Training.
★★QR – Quantitative Research & ★QL – Qualitative Research

Table 22.2 Studies following interventions based on an educational software-based approach

Study author and year	Intervention	Region/ location	Target behavior	Research design	Target group	Measure	Findings
Horowitz-Kraus et al. (2014)	RAP 1*	North America	Reading performance	QR	Early childhood (age 8-12 years)	Reading tests along with number of texts	Significant improvement seen in brain function that is related with reading abilities
Niedo et al. (2015)	RAP software 1*	North America	Silent reading	**QR	Fourth grade children, age limit 9/5-11/1 (n = 14)	Reading tests, passage reading, Questionnaire	Significant improvement leading silent reading rate by using this strategy
Mosanezhad-Jeddi & Nazari, (2013)	NET software 2*	Asia	Working memory	Single-subject design	Children (age 8-10)	Intelligent scale, checklist, computerized task, Electrocap Test battery	Result indicated positive changes in working memory and attention
Kast et al. (2011)	Spelling REF software	Europe	Spelling ability	**QR	Children (age 8-12)		Significantly improve their spelling.
Oakland et al. (1998)	DTP 4*	North America	Reading and spelling skills	**QR	School children (age 11)	Videotape	Students with RD displayed significantly higher reading recognition and comprehension
Pinnelli S., (2014)	Reading training software	Europe	Reading skill	Case study	Adult (age 27)	Series of texts, PC machine	Technological devices/ software seem to be a reliable tool for the remediation of reading speed and accuracy

Predeaux et al. (2005)	Cellfield intervention software	Australia	Multiple deficits	**QR	School children (age 12)	Computer software, test battery	Positive impact on reading skills and oral reading proficiency.
Torgesen et al. (2010)	RWT & LIPS 3★	North America	Early reading difficulties	**QR	I graders (age 5/6)	Story rhyming, digitized speech, colored blocks	Powerfully accelerated the growth of word-level reading skills and reading development. Stronger outcomes are shown in #PS, ##RN, Spelling and reading comprehension
Husni & Jamaludin (2009)	ASR technology 5★	Asia	Reading ability	**QR	Children (age 5–8)	PC machine, microphone, list of words	Immediate intervention led to remediation of reading ability.
Tjus et al. (2004)	Delta messages program	Europe	Reading ability	**QR	Children group (age 9/10)	PC Computer machines, graphics, a different list of sentences, video clippings	This multimedia program improved the reading ability of students with several disabilities.
Saine et al. (2010)	Computer-assisted reading intervention and Classroom instruction	Europe	Reading fluency	**QR	I grader (age 7)	Questionnaire, phonological test, list of letters, PC computers	Reading fluency can be enhanced by using this instruction rather than traditional classroom instruction. CAI is more effective
Gonzalez et al. (2015)	Computer-assisted training program	Europe	Reading performance	**QR	Children (age 8/9)	Several skilled tasks	Children improved substantially in reading and spelling
Park et al. (2016)	TTS software 6★	North America	Reading performance	**QR	134 student's Ninthgraders	GMRT vocabulary and comprehension sub test, Reading comprehension passage	TTS intervention had a significant, positive effect on student reading vocabulary and reading comprehension

(*Continued*)

Table 22.2 (Continued)

Study author and year	Intervention	Region/ location	Target behavior	Research design	Target group	Measure	Findings
Koen et al.	Flash Word (version 2.2) *followed by VHSS Training *7	USA	Reading Fluency	Mixed design	15 students Age 8–19 years (n = 15)	Computer, projector screen, word list	Dyslexic children were able to increase their reading fluency rate after this intervention. Result also indicated high increasing reading rate in contextual text
Rello et al. (2014)	Dyseggxia (technology-based game)	Europe	spelling	**QR	School children (age 6–11)	i-Pad	Significant improvement in spelling skills and let to less writing errors
Elazab Mohamed Elazab Elshazly (2016)	i-Pad intervention program	Asia	Reading, writing, and spelling skills	Mixed method	20 male students 3rd graders	Computer, trans scripter, colored text	Effective results
Svensson et al.	Assistive Technology Training	Sweden	Reading ability, Assimilation, and communication ability	Experimental design	Total of 149 participants (53 girls, 96 boys) Grade 4th – 8th	Local applications through tablets with the speech-to-text facility, question battery	Results indicated a positive impact on reading ability after providing intervention
Balqees Al-dabayba, Shaidah Jusoh	Assistive technology-based tool	Jordan	Reading problems in the Arabic language	Experimental	6 participants Age 7–10 years (n = 6)	Two Arabic Applications	Results indicated a set of usability features (menus, colors, navigation, feedback) are needed to develop to help the dyslexic children

Park et al.	TTS software (Text-To-Speech)	USA	Reading performance, Reading comprehension, Reading vocabulary, Reading rate	Experimental study	Total 164 students from 9th Grade (N = 164)	Self-reported checklist, course textbooks, reading articles, magazines, software tools, electronic text	Result indicated significant influences in reading performance. Highly positive impact found on reading comprehension skills, reading vocabulary, and also in reading rate
Lindeblad et al.	Assistive Technology (AT) application	Sweden	Reading Progression (Text Reading Skill)	Follow-up and Experimental method	Total 137 children and Adolescents Age 10-16 years (n = 137)	Audio Books, Tablets	Research report did not show the positive impact of Assistive technology (AT) on the self-concept and psychological health of children with reading deficit. Moderate impact has been found on reading progression
Bigueras et al.	Mobile Game-Based Learning (LaroLexia Application)	Philippines	Reading performance	Descriptive study	12 children Age range 8-12 years Elementary level	The mobile game, mobile application	Significant differences have been found in reading performance after the intervention. Results considered this game-based learning intervention as a very effective tool for the learning of the Filipino language for dyslexic children

Note.
1★RAP - Reading Acceleration Program; 2★NET - Neurofeedback training;
3★RWT - Read, Write and Type; LIPS - Lindamood Phoneme Sequencing Program for Reading, Spelling, and Speech; 4★DTP - Dyslexia training Program; 5★ASR - Automatic Speech Recognition;
6★TTS - Text-to-speech software. ★7VHSS - Visual Hemisphere-Specific Stimulation
★★QR - Quantitative research★★★GMRT - Gates-MacGinitie Reading Test;
#PS - Phonological skill; ##RN - Rapid naming

Table 22.3 Intervention studies based on the Cognitive Training Approach

Study author and year	Intervention	Region/location	Target behavior	Research design	Target group	Measure	Findings
Rello, L., Subirats, S., & Bigham, J. P. (2016)	Online Chess Game	USA	Classroom performance	**QR	Total of 64 participants, 31 were diagnosed as Dyslexic (N = 64)	Mouse tracking data (Questionnaire), Demographic questionnaire, online chess lesson	Positive impact has been found on dyslexic participants as their cognitive skills (i.e., visuospatial skills) can be trained followed by this intervention
Vaughn et al.	Word and Text-based intervention	USA	Word reading and reading comprehension	**QR	280 participants Grade –4th to 5th	Expository and narrative text, word cards	Result indicated high impact of the intervention on word reading skills and reading comprehension of dyslexic children
Kashyap, D. Kaur, K	Mindfulness-based intervention	India	Reading anxiety	**QR	44 participants Class vi	Reading anxiety tools, intervention modules	Results revealed that dyslexic students are were able to reduce reading anxiety after the intervention
Habib et al.	Cognitive Musical Training (CMT) method	France	Categorical perception and Word metric structure	**QR	12 children age range (8.2 to 11.7) (n = 12)	Piano keyboard, colorful square boxes, audiotape, text reading, etc.	Significant improvement in categorical perception and auditory perception

The Remediation of Dyslexia

Author	Model/Intervention	Country	Focus	Method	Participants	Materials	Results
Irdamurni, Kasiyati, Zulmiyetri, Johandri Taufan (2018)	Mingle model	Indonesia	Reading ability	**QR	23 participants Primary grade	List of words	Results indicated significant improvement of reading skills among dyslexic students
Carol Goldfus	Cognitive processing model	Israel	Metacognitive awareness	Case study research	17-year-old adolescent (n = 1)	Various tests	After this intervention student returned their situation from failure to success
Adubasim, I. (2018)	Brainfeed intervention program	Nigeria	Working Memory, Processing Speed	**QR	Total 24,727 Senior Secondary School students	Stopwatch, A4 paper, Androids, ipads, Laptops	Result indicated a significant effect on the improvement of working memory of dyslexic children
Barth et al.	Text Processing Comprehension Intervention	USA	Language-based skills, Reading Comprehension, Listening Comprehension, Reading Performance	**QR	134 students 6th Grade & 8th Grade (N = 83 N = 51)	Semi scripted lesson, Science text, Audio recorder	Significant effects have been found on reading comprehension skills (e.g., vocabulary skills), Moderate effects have been found on listening comprehension, Effective for middle school struggling readers

Note. **QR – Quantitative Research

Table 22.4 Studies following interventions based on the Multisensory Approach

Study author and year	Intervention	Region/location	Target behavior	Research design	Target group	Measure	Findings
Hwee & Houghton, (2011)	OG instruction 1*	Asia	Reading skill	**QR	Primary readers (age 6–8)	Psycho educational test	Effective changes shown on the development of sentence reading and word recognition and expression skills of RD children
Elkind et al. (1993)	Bookwise computer-based system	USA	Reading skill	**QR	Middle school students (age 10–14)	Synchronized auditory and visual reading material	Results indicated reading comprehension in most of the cases enhanced and can be a valuable reading aid
Stebbins et al. (2012)	Wilson Reading System	North	Reading skill	Mixed method	IV graders (age 10)	Text reading, word cards, list of words, sound cards	Substantial growth was found in reading comprehension skills with this intervention
Cohen et al. (1987)	Language experience approach, (synthetic phonics program)	North America	Reading skill	**QR	Children (age 7–15)	Reading materials	Significant improvement in word recognition skills was demonstrated. No significant trend noted in reading comprehension

Dev et al. (2009)	The Orton-Gillingham technique (reading instruction)	North America	Language skill	**QR	Elementary children (age 6/7)	Numeric symbols, letter-sound	Results denote multisensory techniques can enhance such academic skills for students at risk for reading difficulties
Nourbakhsh et al. (2013)	Multisensory methods and cognitive skills training	Asia	Reading and perceptual abilities	**QR	III graders (age 7/8)	List of words, comprehensions, #RDT and ##BVMGT and ###ROCF	Intervention strategy significantly improves the academic performance of dyslexic students along with their reading and perceptual skills
Crammer et al., (2016)	Dynamic Color Coding (computer-based program)	Canada	Contextual Spelling	Mixed method	9 children from 3rd to 7th Grade (n = 9)	Phono blocks	Result indicated a positive impact on learning of spelling followed by color coding program and it helps dyslexic children to learn contextual spelling rules

*Note.*1*OG – Orthon-Gillingham;
#RDT – Reading and Dyslexic test; ##BVMGT – Bender Visual Motor Gestalt Test; ###ROCF – Rey-Osterrieth Complex Figure test. ** QR – Quantitative research

Table 22.5 Studies following interventions based on the Visual Reception Training Approach

Study author and year	Intervention	Region/location	Target behavior	Research design	Target group	Measure	Findings
Hell et al. (2003)	Visual Dictation training program	Europe	Spelling difficulty	**QR	Children (age 9/10)	Text reading, list of inconsistent words	Results indicated a positive impact on the remediation of spelling difficulties among children with reading disabilities
Meng et al. (2014)	Visual Texture Discrimination Text training	Asia	Reading performance	**QR	IV, V & VI graders (age 8-11)	Text reading, Vocabularies	Reading fluency ability was significantly enhanced and a positive influence on reading performance.
Tressoldi et al. (2007)	Bakker's methodology (Balance model)	Europe	Reading performance	**QR	IV graders (age 13)	Computer technology	Young dyslexic children obtained statistical gain in both accuracy and fluency in comparison with their elder peers.
Edmen Leong and Alexius Chia	The Designed Picture based intervention program	Singapore	Inferential Comprehension skills	Experimental	16 participants Age 11 to 14 years	Short comic strips, page-long comic stories	Result indicated that students improved their understanding of inferential comprehension skills after the intervention

Author	Intervention	Region	Focus area	**QR	Participants	Tools	Results
Lorusso et al. (2006)	VHSS & RT 1*	Europe	Reading performance	**QR	Children (age 7-15)	A set of text, test battery, non-word list, computer	Reading accuracy was significantly improved, memory and phonemic skills of the students were also higher.
Bucci, M. P. (2019)	Visual oculomotor training	France	Reading acquisition (Visual perception, eye movements, semantic and linguistic abilities)	Experimental	Total 36 participants 18 Dyslexic 18 non-Dyslexic (n = 36)	Medical eye tracking device (Mobile EBT), projector, Color filtered lenses	Results indicated positive impact on the reading capabilities of children with dyslexia
Vojoudi et al.	Educational training package followed by visual-spatial abilities	Iran	Reading performance	Experimental	60 students from 3rd, 4th/5th grade	Written short story copies, list of words, beans, play dough, finger dolls	Result reported that a significant effect is found on word reading, word comprehension, and text comprehension. But no significant result is found on rhyming, reading the non-words, marks of letters and words.

Note.
1*VHSS - Visual hemisphere-specific stimulation; RT - Reading focused training program; **QR - Quantitative research

Table 22.1 provides details of all the treatments or interventions based on PTA. Most studies revealed that interventions based on PTA were significant in most cases, excluding a negligible percentage where positive results were not found. The findings revealed that efficacy may not be the outcome of the implementation of any one strategy or approach as much as the result of a combination of strategies. The results also indicated that adults with dyslexic challenges also benefit from such interventions, even if applied at a later stage in life (Berninger et al., 1991; Guyer et al. 1993) (see Table 22.1).

Educational Software Approach

In recent decades, various types of software have been developed to help foster multiple reading skills in dyslexic learners. Much research has already been conducted to find the most effective technology-based intervention for dyslexia. Existing literature suggested a positive impact of multiple software types, mobile games, and multimedia-based interventions on the remediation of various RDs. In this review, results indicate that all the software- or technology-based interventions can be categorized under ESA, which creates a realistic teaching-learning environment such that dyslexic learners can improve their reading skills effectively (Balsara, 2011; Bigueras et al., 2020; Drigas & Dourou 2013; Gearheart et al., 1992; Rajkumari et al., 2004).

Table 22.2 describes various ESAs that have been used for the remediation of RDs. The review noted that several kinds of software, mobile apps, and computer-assisted instructions (CAIs) were also administered as interventions for dyslexia. 26.25% of research works were found to have followed this particular approach (see Table 22.2).

Cognitive Training Approach

CTA-based treatments involve training the cognitive processes that are mainly responsible for reading, writing, and arithmetic skills. Experts suggest that this approach is significant and has positive impacts; eight published papers have been identified as following this specific approach. The results showed significant improvement in the specific problem areas, as a result of CTA interventions. Two experimental studies implemented CTA strategies and found significant improvements. Findings also indicated that a number of reading-related issues can also be enhanced through different CTA-based interventions (i.e., online chess games, word and text-based intervention, mindfulness-based intervention, and others). Another study implemented the cognitive processing model focused on the development of metacognitive awareness in dyslexic children, and its findings suggest significant improvement of the treatment group vis-à-vis the control group (Goldfus, 2012) (see Table 22.3 for details).

Multisensory Approach

In MA, sensory training is emphasized to help the person with RD gain experiences through several senses. In this review, some interventions targeting several sensory processes have been identified.

It was found that seven studies (8.75%) implemented interventions based on MA. The focus was on reading skills, with the results from all the studies indicating significant improvements. Orton-Gillingham-based reading instruction is one of the most popular interventions in MAs. This review found only two studies that followed this specific instruction (Dev et al. 2009; Hwee & Houghton, 2011). Other treatments were also seen to be effective for the remediation of the target behaviors of the participants. In most studies pure quantitative designs were followed; only one study deployed a mixed-method design to explore in-depth the effects of such a strategy over a period of time (Stebins et al., 2012). In fact, the approaches most commonly used in these studies for the development of senses are the visual, the auditory, and the tactual (see Table 22.4 for details).

Visual Reception Training Approach

This systematic review found that only seven papers (8.75%) implemented VRTA for the remediation of RDs. In all of these studies, quantitative designs were followed for implementation. The dependent variables or target behaviors were also similar to previous studies (i.e., Reading performance, Inferential Comprehension skills, Reading acquisition), except for spelling difficulty. The results showed that spelling difficulty can also be eradicated via a visual dictation training program, which is an MA (Hell et al., 2003) (see Table 22.5 for details).

Listening Exercise Approach

Throughout this review, only four papers were identified as following interventions based on the LEA. Results indicated that these had a positive effect on several dyslexic problems as well. An assistive listening device system is an intervention that has yielded positive outcomes in the target population for the development of auditory processing (Hornickel et al., 2012). Another study focused on the development of reading abilities in dyslexic children followed by the implementation of the Rosner auditory analysis training program. A single-subject research design was followed and the result indicated that impairment in phonemic skills may be overcome and reversed to some extent (Berninger et al., 1991). Reading deficiencies such as phonological awareness may also be countered by the application of the Auditory Discrimination program (ADD) which was based on LEAs. Results reported significant gains in phonological awareness and decoding skills in children with RD (Alexander et al., 1991).

Music Training Approach

In this review, only three studies (3.75%) were identified as being based on MTA. The aim was to help dyslexic children read musical notations with the proper correct sound. The results indicate that musical therapy proved to be highly effective for the remediation of dyslexia. One study that implemented such an intervention encompassed the technique of Written Music Instruction for the development of music reading skills (Flach et al., 2014). Results indicated that children with RDs showed significantly higher improvement in music reading skills when compared to children without RDs. In another study, musical training was provided for the improvement of phonological awareness. It was found that MTA could also be effective for the modification of reading and phonological abilities (Flaugnacco et al., 2015). Similarly, a case study where the researcher conducted an in-depth analysis revealed that MTA could be successfully used to train dyslexic children to read out musical notations in the correct order (Geiger, 2015).

Self-Instruction Training Approach

Another type of approach, SITA, was also observed to be effective in the remediation of reading-related difficulties. Two types of interventions were identified in three studies (3.75%) and both had a positive effect on the target behaviors in students with dyslexia (Denton et al., 2020; Hughes et al. 2013; Mason, et al. 2013).

Academic and Psychological Approach

The APA approach-based interventions focused on both academic and psychological problems related to dyslexia. Dyslexic children have severe deficiencies in the academic field. Apart from this, they are also diagnosed with several psychological problems. RTI is a popular approach for the remediation of challenges of dyslexia and LD, as seen all over the world, especially in the USA (Fuchs et al. 2007; Vaughn and Fletcher, 2012). This review identified two published papers following this approach; the results demonstrate significant improvements in the target behaviors of learners with LD or dyslexia (Fuchs, et al. 2007; Vaughn and Fletcher, 2012).

Medical-Neurological Approach

Only one study implemented the MNA, and its results indicated significant improvements in academic achievement and self-esteem among learners with dyslexia (Bull, 2007). It was also found that of all of the approaches identified through this systematic review, those most commonly utilized worldwide are PTA, ESA, MA, and VRTA; these are conducted in several countries across North America, Europe, Asia, and Australia (see Tables 22.1, 22.2, 22.4 and 22.5 for details). While PTAs were identified mostly in several regions of North America, ESAs and MAs-based interventions were predominant in several European countries. This evidence-based review presented various trends specifically on interventions used worldwide as remediation for dyslexia with a focus on specific interventions. It concluded that most of the intervention-based studies on dyslexia were conducted in North America and Europe.

Discussion

The purpose of this systematic review was to identify effective interventions for the remediation of multiple RDs faced by dyslexic children. There are multiple treatments for the remediation of the different reading disorders.

Effectiveness of the Major Treatment Approaches

Periodically, books, research papers, and articles present various approaches for the purpose of providing suitable interventions to children with dyslexia. After reviewing existing literature, two main approaches for reading intervention, namely MNA and APA, were identified. Further categorization led to five further categories under APA (Rajkumari et al., 2004). In the MNA, an LD child is treated as a patient with Minimal Brain Dysfunction (MBD). An important characteristic of LD is hyperactivity. This behavior can be alleviated by the use of psychostimulants and such treatment may improve and be effective for children with LD. However, research findings suggest that there is no proof that these psychostimulants can also be effective for the learning enhancement. Though psychostimulants have a positive impact on a child's classroom behavior one of their limitations is that they render it difficult to observe a child's learning problems and also find remedies for such problems. In such circumstances, a behavioristic approach or an APA can be advantageous in facilitating classroom teaching-learning; in an APA, children with LD are treated not as patients but as learners waiting to be taught in a proper learning environment.

The children are diagnosed with LD through various identification procedures, several tools, and techniques as suggested by psychologists. Further evidence-based interventions are implemented following appropriate diagnosis. The intervention procedures may be provided in a resource room in a regular school or in a clinic or in a special school based on the child's need (Balsara, 2011; Gearheart et al., 1992; Rajkumari et al., 2004). Most of the treatment approaches identified through this review were applied in a natural educational set-up, and the materials available in the natural environments are used. All those interventions were further categorized as different subtypes of APAs (Table 22.1).

Among the APAs, PTA-based interventions were most commonly applied. In PTA, importance is given to the psychological processes required for the learning of academic subjects. An LD or dyslexic child faces difficulties in these psychological processes, which subsequently translate to challenges in reading, writing, arithmetic, etc. Psychologists, clinicians, or special education teachers first teach them several psychological processes, such as visual skills, listening, understanding, memorization, retrieval, etc. (Balsara, 2011; Gearheart et al., 1992; Otaiba et al., 2010; Rajkumari et al., 2004) Otaiba et al. (2010) investigated the efficacy of Tutor-Assisted Intensive Learning Strategies (TAILS) on kindergarten students at high reading disability risk. TAILS were applied for the improvement of several reading parameters, for instance, phonological awareness, fluency, and comprehension. The intervention was planned in a game-like format with sound. In this study, classroom tutoring and instructions were emphasized. Dyslexic children face difficulties in phonological awareness, and that affects their reading acquisition. The study indicated greater improvement in reading skills as a result of the intervention. Dyslexia is a specific disorder that may comprise attention deficit, visuo-attentional deficit, and memory deficit (Jan et al., 2011). Jan et al. (2011) provided a screening model comprising different sets of tasks (reading, spelling, memory, attention, meta-phonological, phonological automatism, visuo-attentional, auditory, etc.) for the improvement of multiple reading skills with significant outcomes. Apart from this, there are many PTA-based intervention programs that show effective results in the remediation of dyslexia. Psychological and cognitive processes have been targeted from multiple directions. PTA-based intervention programs are applicable to all age groups. Though most studies reviewed interventions especially implemented during infancy and/or childhood, one study was conducted on adults (Guyer, Banks & Guyer, 1993). One PTA-based study was identified to evaluate the effect of the Analytic and Synthetic approach to improving Chinese spelling (Leong et al. 2011), and the results showed that it was effective for spelling as well as orthography.

The review indicated that ESA interventions were more effective in the remediation of reading deficits. ESA is another sub-category of APA, fully based on CAI. The main purpose was to provide a real situation and real instruction, such that students could achieve results as per ability and developmental stage, while also proving competitive to non-LD learners. Research has reported that the brain structure of a dyslexic child is not similar to that of a non-dyslexic child. Impairments are also found in their cognitive processes (working memory, attention, etc). Neurofeedback is an effective intervention for the remediation of such deficits (Mosanezhad-Jeddi & Nazari, 2013). The target behaviors are mostly spelling, silent reading, multiple deficits, etc. (see Table 22.2). Most findings reflected significant improvements in all such target behaviors with the implementation of ESAs. Previous systematic reviews (Drigas & Dourou, 2013) reported a varied range of intervention programs that have been effective in the cases of dyslexic learners. Results suggested that certain software- or computer-based tools were very effective for dyslexic learners; these include Phonological Awareness Educational Software (PHAES) for providing phonological instruction; digital media (DTV Digital Television, T-islessia) for performing daily rehabilitation exercises; Magicabra, a highly interactive game; and Interactive Multimedia Learning Object (IMLO). ESA interventions also indicated success in the implementation of multiple treatments for dyslexic children. Three studies were identified emphasizing different target behaviors; multiple deficits (Predeaux et al., 2005), working memory (Mosanezhad-Jeddi & Nazari, 2013), and silent reading (Niedo et al., 2015). Working memory is related to cognitive factors. Children with RD have also impairment in cognitive factors as well. Mosanezhad-Jeddi and Nazari (2013) evaluated the efficiency of neurofeedback training software on working memory and attention and revealed that participants exhibited improvement in their working memory capacity after attending the treatment sessions. In another study, fourth-graders improved their silent reading rate after implementation of the Reading Accelerated Program (RAP) software (Niedo et al., 2015). They used Breznitz's computerized RAP software in different ways. In this study, the authors applied this software followed by three different tasks: word cloze, sentence logic, and paragraph understanding. Results indicated positive changes in working memory and attention. Predeaux et al. (2005) conducted a study for the remediation of multiple deficits of dyslexia, such as phonological to visual and visual to the phonological deficit, followed by the Cellfield intervention program, a computerized intervention including visual, auditory, and phonological processing-based tasks. Results indicated positive impacts on multiple reading skills and oral reading proficiency. Apart from this, one intervention was found to investigate the usability features required for Arabic dyslexic learners (Aldabaybah & Jusoh, 2018). Results indicated a set of features (i.e., menus, colors, navigation, feedback) to help dyslexic children. Apart from these interventions, this review identified several other software- or technology-based treatments that have been used and have been found to be effective.

CTA was the third major intervention approach identified through this review. Children with LD or dyslexia exhibit deficient problem-solving skills and act impulsively, without considering the alternatives available to them. CTA proves to be significantly effective in mitigating such impulsive behavior. Through this technique, the children are trained to slow down before reading words or sentences and to respond to questions very carefully (Balsara, 2011; Gearheart et al., 1992; Rajkumari et al., 2004). There were very few studies that followed CTA-based interventions for dyslexic learners. One study was identified for the remediation of reading anxiety followed by a CTA-based treatment called 'Mindfulness Intervention'. Dyslexic learners are often identified with reading anxiety, as they demonstrate unpleasant emotional feelings and specific phobias at the time of any reading activity (Kashyap & Kaur, 2017). Various cognitive reactions (feeling of helplessness, sense of dread, feeling of low self-esteem, the expectation of public humiliation, etc.) also influence reading ability. Results revealed that dyslexic students were able to manage reading anxiety after the CAT-based intervention (Kashyap & Kaur, 2017). Another CAT-based intervention, e.g. CMT, can be considered effective for the improvement of categorical perception and auditory perception. Habib et al. (2016) evaluated the effectiveness of the Cognitive Musical Training method by targeting cognitive processes. It is a type of musical intervention that has several tasks or components, which stimulate visual, auditory, and sensory-motor processing. A few other intervention programs were also found after this review and studies indicated positive impacts on the remediation of RDs.

A few studies have seen effective results of MA-based interventions. This approach involves sensitive and perceptual organ-based training, which heightens the senses involved in reading and facilitates experiences via several senses. It is based on the assumption that if the children are more involved in sensory training to gather learning experiences from the environment, it will be more significant and more effective for the development of sense-based activities. MA techniques are specifically used for younger children 6 to 10 years old to involve them in an array of sensory modalities (i.e., visual, auditory, kinesthetic, tactile). The inputs through multiple sensory modalities help consolidate the learning process (Balsara, 2011; Gearheart et al., 1992; Rajkumari et al., 2004). Studies included under the MA category have targeted the training of visual or auditory or both types of sense organs (Cramer et al., 2016; Elkind et al., 1993; Hwee & Houghton, 2011; Stebbins et al., 2012). As children with dyslexia face major problems in reading and phonology, they are not quick at sensual and perceptual information processing like other non-dyslexic children are. The results of this review postulate the effectiveness of several PTA interventions for the remediation of dyslexic learners.

A person with dyslexia also faces challenges in gaining sensory experiences (Lorusso et al., 2006). This systematic review identified seven studies that followed VRTA interventions (Table 22.5). The main purpose was to offer proper instruction and assistance so that children with dyslexia could read and enunciate every word and sentence clearly. Through this approach, the children can enhance their visual skills and perceive experiences visually. Following this approach, their perceptual and cognitive skills are also developed or enhanced. The researcher emphasized the development of listening ability in dyslexic children. Assistive learning devices and auditory analysis training programs were also implemented for auditory training (Berninger et al., 1991; Hornickel et al., 2012). The results reported four studies that followed LEA with positive impacts. Some studies have been identified as following these approaches but they are applicable only to the remediation of particular RDs. Accordingly, this review shows that MTA can also be implemented for the remediation of RDs in dyslexic children. Limited studies were identified that followed LEA (5%), SITA and MTA (3.75%), APA (2.5%), and MNA (1.25%). However, the results also indicated positive impacts to counter reading deficits.

Target Behaviors

The review identified different target behaviors considered by the studies for remediation. Results indicated that dyslexic children face difficulties in reading and exhibit an array of reading-related disorders. Dyslexic children face several RDs such as orthographic dysfunction, problems in phonemic awareness (Vliet et al., 2004), word sound problems, impairments in grapheme/phoneme (Nanda, 2012), phonological deficit, spelling deficit, problem in fluency, decoding and encoding, incorrect pronunciation, etc. (Hornickel et al., 2012; Mercer, et al., 2000; Papadopoulos et al., 2004; Park et al., 2014; Sandra et al., 2009). After scanning all the selected studies, 21 types of target behaviors/problems were identified for remediation in this review. Results indicated that 23 papers targeted the remediation of reading skills/ abilities of children with dyslexia. Reading performance, reading fluency, spelling, etc. were also considered. A few studies undertook other target behaviors for remediation, including working memory, perceptual abilities, orthography, metacognitive awareness, silent reading, and reading anxiety.

Conclusion

Delimitation

This chapter is a systematic review of interventions for the remediation of dyslexia. The researcher included peer-reviewed papers published from 1987 to 2020. The objective was to systematically identify and analyze all studies on interventions for dyslexia. Many papers were not accessible from university databases, and hence could not be included. Hence, the systematic review was executed on the basis of 80 related and accessible studies on RD interventions.

Future Directions

For further investigations, it may be suggested that instead of focusing on best practices for the remediation of dyslexia, research may also be conducted by selecting various target behaviors and intervention strategies usually implemented for the remediation of that particular behavior, as mentioned above. Based on this systematic review, the following suggestions can be made for future research:

- Future prospects may be to conduct a systematic review of types of assistive technologies used for the remediation of dyslexia.
- Systematic review can be undertaken to investigate the best approaches for the remediation of working memory and perceptual abilities.
- Research can be undertaken to explore various MTAs and their effects as these form part of the most recent intervention approaches for remediation and have yielded effective results.

References

Adubasim, I. (2018). Brainfeed intervention programme: An alternative approach for supporting people living with dyslexia. *Journal of Education & Entrepreneurship*, 5(2), 124–143. https://doi.org/10.26762/jee.2018.40000018

Alex, J. (2013). Learning disabilities: Assessment and intervention. *Indian Journal of Research*, 2(2), 2013.

Aldabaybah, B., & Jusoh, S. (2018). *Usability Features for Arabic Assistive Technology for Dyslexia*. IEEE (Institute of Electrical and Electronics Engineers). https://10.1109/icsgrc.2018.8657536

Alexander, A. W., Andersen, H. G., Heiltnan, P. C., Voeller, K. K. S., & Torgeseti, J. K. (1991). Phonological awareness training and remediation of analytic decoding deficits in a group of severe dyslexies. *Annals of Dyslexia*, 41. http://www.jstor.org/stable/23768524

Andrade, O.V. C. A., Andrade, P. E., & Capellini, S. A. (2015). Collective Screening tools for early identification of dyslexia. *Frontiers in Psychology*, 5, https://doi.org/10.3389/fpsyg.2014.01581

Balakrishnan, B., Chong, H. B., Idris, M. Z., Othman, A. N., Wong, M. F., & Azman, M. N. A. (2015). Improving the English literacy skills of Malaysian dyslexic children: The case of culturally responsive mobile multimedia tool. *Malaysian Journal of Society and Space*, 11(13), 49–59.

Barquero, L. A., Davis, N., & Cutting, L. E. (2014). Neuroimaging of Reading Intervention: A Systematic Review and Activation Likelihood Estimate Meta-Analysis. *PLoS One*, 9(1). https://journals.plos.org/plosone/article?id=10.1371/journal.pone.0083668

Barth, A. E., Vaughn, S., Capin, P., Cho, E., Stillman-Spisak, S., Martinez, L., & Kincaid, H. (2016). Effects of a text-processing comprehension intervention on struggling middle school readers. *Top Lang Disorders*, 36(4), 368–389.

Berninger, V. W., Lester, K., Sohlberg, M. M., & Mateer, C. (1991). Interventions based on the multiple connections model of reading for developmental dyslexia and acquired deep dyslexia. *Archives of Clinical Neuropsychology*, 6, 375–391.

Bigueras, R. T., Arispe, M. C. A., Torio, J. O., & Maligat, D. E. (2020). Mobile game-based learning to enhance the reading performance of dyslexic children. *International Journal of Advanced Trends in Computer Science and Engineering*, 9(1.3). https://doi.org/10.30534/ijatcse/2020/5191.32020

Bonacina, S., Cancer, A., Lanzi, P. L., Lorusso, M. L., & Antonietti, A. (2015). Improving reading skills in students with dyslexia: The efficacy of a sublexical training with rhythmic background. *Frontiers in Psychology*, 6(1510). https://doi.org/10.3389/fpsyg.2015.01510

Bucci, M. P. (2019). Visual training could be useful for improving reading capabilities in Dyslexia. *Applied Neuropsychology: Child* https://doi.org/10.1080/21622965.2019.1646649

Bull, L. (2007). Sunflower therapy for children with specific learning disability (dyslexia): A randomised, controlled trial. *Complementary Therapies in Clinical Practice*, 13, 15–24. https://10.1016/j.ctcp.2006.07.003

Cirino, P. T., Vaughn, S., Linan-Thompson, S., Cardenas-Hagan, I., letcher, J., & Rancis, D. J. (2009). One-year fouow-up outcomes of Spanish and English interventions for English language learners at risk for reading problems. *American Educational Research Journal*, 46(3), 744–781. https://doi.org/10.3102/0002831208330214

Cohen, M., Krawiecki, N., & Durant, R. H. (1987). The neuropsychological approach to the remediation of dyslexia. *Archives of Clinrcal Nampsycholoby, 2*, 163–173.

Cramer, E. S., Antle, A. N., & Fan, M. (2016). *The Code of Many Colours: Evaluating the Effects of a Dynamic Colour-Coding Scheme on Children's Spelling in a Tangible Software System* (pp. 473–485). https://www.researchgate.net/publication/305726784_The_Code_of_Many_Colours_Evaluating_the_Effects_of_a_Dynamic_Tangible_Software_System

Denton, C. A., Fletcher, J. M., Taylor, W. P., Barth, A. E., & Vaughn, S. (2014). An experimental evaluation of guided reading and explicit interventions for primary-grade students at-risk for READING DIFfiCULTIES. *Journal of Research on Educational Effectiveness, 7*, 268–293. https://doi.org/10.1080/19345747.2014.906010

Denton, C. A., Montroy, J. J., Zucker, T. A., & Cannon, G. (2020). Designing an intervention in reading and self-regulation for students with significant reading difficulties, including dyslexia. *Learning Disability Quarterly*, 1–13. https://doi.org/10.1177/0731948719899479

Dev, P. C., Doyle, B. A., & Valente, B. (2009). Labels needn't stick: "at-risk" first graders rescued with appropriate intervention. *Journal of Education for Students Placed at Risk (JESPAR), 7*(3), 327–332. https://doi.org/10.1207/S15327671ESPR0703_3

Drigas, A., & Dourou, A. (2013). A Review on ICTs, E-Learning and Artificial Intelligence for Dyslexic's Assistance. *International Journal of Emerging Technologies in Learning, 8*(4). https://online-journals.org/index.php/i-jet/article/view/2980

Duff, F. J., & Clarke P. J. (2011). Practitioner review: Reading disorders: What are the effective interventions and how should they be implemented and evaluated? *Journal of Child Psychology and Psychiatry, 52*(1), 3–12. https://doi.org/10.1111/j.1469-7610.2010.02310.x

Duff, F. J., Hulme, C., Grainger, K., Hardwick, S. J., Miles, J. N. V. & Snowling, M. J. (2014). Reading and language intervention for children at risk of dyslexia: A randomised controlled trial. *Journal of Child Psychology and Psychiatry, 55*(11), 1234–1243. https://doi.org/10.1111/jcpp.12257

Elkind, J., Cohen, k., & Murray, C. (1993). Using computer-based readers to improve reading comprehension of students with dyslexia. *Annals of Dyslexia, 43*, 238–259. http://www.jstor.org/stable/23768424

Flach, N., Timmermans, A., & Korpershoek, H. (2014). Effects of the design of written music on the readability for children with dyslexia. *International Journal of Music Education*, 1–13. https://doi.org/10.1177%2F0255761414546245

Flaugnacco, E., Lopez, L., Terribili, C., Montico, M., Zoia, S., & Schon, D. (2015). Music training increases phonological awareness and reading skills in developmental dyslexia: A randomized control trial. *PLoS ONE, 10*(9). https://doi.org/10.1371/journal.pone.0138715

Fuchs, L. S., Bryant, J., & Davis, G. N. (2007). Making "secondary intervention" work in a three-tier responsiveness-to-intervention model: findings from the first-grade longitudinal reading study of the National Research Center on Learning Disabilities. *Read & Write, 21*, 413–436. https://doi.org/10.1007/s11145-007-9083-9

Gearheart, B. R., Weishahn, M. W., & Gearheart, C. J. (1992). *Teaching Students with Learning Disabilities in the Exceptional Student in the Regular Classroom* (pp. 300–340). New York: Merrill.

Geiger, O. (2015). Musical notation reading versus alphabet reading - comparison and implications for teaching music reading to students with dyslexia. *International Journal of Social, Behavioral, Educational, Economic, Business and Industrial Engineering, 9*(8).

Given, B. K., Wasserman, J. D., Chari, S. A., Beattie, K., & Eden, G. F. (2007). A Randomised, Controlled study of computer-based intervention in middle school struggling readers. *Brain and Language, 106*, 83–97. https://doi.org/10.1016/j.bandl.2007.12.001

Goldfus, C. (2012). Intervention through metacognitive development: A case study of a student with dyslexia and comorbid attention deficit disorder (ADD). *Journal of Language and Culture, 3*(3), pp. 56–66. https://doi.org/10.5897/JLC11.042

Gonzalez, G. F., Zaric, G., Tijms, J., Bonte, M., Blomert, L., & Molen, M. W. V. (2015). A randomized controlled trialon the beneficial effectsof training letter-speech sound integrationon reading fluencyin children with dyslexia. *PLoS ONE, 10*(12), https://doi.org/10.1371/journal.pone.0143914

Graham, S., & Santangelo, T. (2014). Does spelling instruction make students better spellers, readers, and writers? A meta-analytic review. *Reading and Writing, 27*, 1703–1743.

Guyer, B. P., Banks, S. R., & Guyer, K. E. (1993). Spelling improvement for college students who are dyslexic. *Annals of Dyslexia, 43*, 186–193.

Habib, M., Lardy, C., Desiles, T., Commeiras, C., Chobert, J., & Besson, M. (2016). Music and dyslexia: A new training method to improve reading and related disorders. *Frontiers in Psychology,* 7(26), https://doi.org/10.3389/fpsyg.2016.00026

Hell, J. G. V., Bosman, A. M. T., & Bartelings, M. C. G. (2003). Visual dictation improves the spelling performance of three groups of dutch students with spelling disabilities. *Learning Disability Quarterly,* 26, 239–255.

Hornickel, J., Zecker, S. G., Bradlow, A. R., & Kraus, N. (2012). Assistive listening devices drive neuroplasticity in children with dyslexia. Proceedings of the National Academy of Sciences of the United States of America, *109*(41), 16731–16736. https://doi.org/10.1073/pnas.1206628109

Horowitz, K. T., Vannest, J. T., Kadis, D., Cicchino, N., Wang, Y. Y., & Holland, S. K. (2014). Reading acceleration training changes brain circuitry in children with reading difficulties. *Brain and Behaviour,* 4(6), pp. 886–902. https://doi.org/10.1002/brb3.281

Hughes, J. A., Phillips, G., & Reed, P. (2013). Brief exposure to a self-paced computer-based reading programme and how it impacts reading ability and behaviour problems. *PLOS ONE,* 8(11). https://doi.org/10.1371/journal.pone.0077867

Husni, H., & Jamaludin, Z. (2009). ASR technology for children with dyslexia: Enabling immediate intervention to support reading in Bahasa Melayu. *US-China Education Review,* 6(6).

Hwee, N. C. K., & Houghton, S. (2011). The effectiveness of Orton-Gillingham-based instruction with Singaporean children with specific reading disability (dyslexia). *British Journal of Special Education,* 38(3). https://doi.org/10.1111/j.1467-8578.2011.00510.x

Ise, E., & Korne, S. G. (2010). Spelling deficits in dyslexia: Evaluation of an orthographic spelling training. *Annals of Dyslexia,* 60(1), 18–39. https://10.1007/sl 1881-010-0035-8

Irdamurni, I., Kasiyati, K., Zulmiyetri, Z., & Taufan, J. (2018). The effect of mingle model to improve reading skills for students with dyslexia in primary school. *Journal of ICSAR,* 2(2). https://doi.org/10.17977/um005v2i22018p167

Jan, G. L., Bouquin-Jeannès, R. L., Costet, N., Troles, N., Scalart, P., Pichancourt, D., Faucon, G. & Gombert, J. E. (2011). Multivariate predictive model for dyslexia diagnosis. *Annals of Dyslexia,* 61, 1–20. https://doi.org/10.1007/s11881-010-0038-5

Jiménez-Fernández, G., & Defior, S. (2014). Developmental dyslexia intervention framework for speech therapists. *Revista de Investigación en Logopedia,* 4, 48–66. https://www.redalyc.org/pdf/3508/350833942003.pdf

Kamala, R., & Ramganesh, E. (2015). Difficulties in identifying the dyslexics in multilingual context. *International Journal of Humanities and Social Science Invention,* 4(1), pp. 18–22. http://www.ijhssi.org/papers/v4(1)/Version-2/C0412018022.pdf

Kashyap, D., & Kaur, K. (2017). Effect of Mindfulness based intervention on reading anxiety among students with dyslexia, *International Journal of Education,* 8. http://ijoe.vidyapublications.com

Kast, M., Baschera, G. M., Gross, M., Jäncke, L., & Meyer, M. (2011). Computer-based learning of spelling skills in children with and without dyslexia. *Annals of Dyslexia,* 61, 177–200. https://10.1007/s11881-011-0052-2

Kirk, S. A. (September, 1981). Learning disabilities: A historical note. Retrieved from http://psycnet.apa.org/psycinfo/1982-01467-001

Klubnik, C., & Ardoin, S. P. (2010). Examining immediate and maintenance effects of a reading intervention package on generaliation materials: Individual verses group implementation. *Journal of Behavioural Education,* 19(1), 7–29. https://10.1 007/s 1 0864-009-9096

Koen, B. J., Hawkins, J., Zhu, X., Jansen, B., Fan, W., & Johnson, F. (2017). The location and effects of visual hemisphere-specific stimulation on reading fluency in children with the characteristics of dyslexia. *Journal of Learning Disabilities,* 1–17. https://us.sagepub.com/en-us/journals-permissions

Lallier, M., Donnadieu, S., Berger, C., & Valdois, S. (2010). A case study of developmental phonological dyslexia: Is the attentional deficit in the perception of rapid stimuli sequences amodal? *Cortex,* 231–241. https://www.sciencedirect.com/science/article/abs/pii/S0010945209001415

Leong, C. K., Loh, K. Y., Ki, W. W., & Tse, S. K. (2011). Enhancing orthographic knowledge helps spelling production in eight-year-old Chinese children at risk for dyslexia. *Ann. of Dyslexia,* 61, 136–160. https://10.1007/sl 1881-011-0051-3

Leong, E., & Chia, A. (2017). Reading with pictures for inferential understanding: Strategies for adolescent learners with dyslexia. *Asia Pacific Journal of Developmental Differences,* 4(1), 113–122. https:// 10.3850/S2345734117000079

Lindeblad, E., Nilsson, S., Gustafson, S., & Svensson, I. (2019). Self-concepts and psychological health in children and adolescents with reading difficulties and the impact of assistive technology to compensate and facilitate reading ability. *Cogent Psychology, 6*(1).https://doi.org/10.1080/23311908.2019.1647601

Lloyd, J. W., & Hallahan, D. P. (2005). Going forward: How the field of learning disabilities had and will contribute to education. *Learning Disability Quarterly, 28,* (133–136). https://10.2307/1593612

Lorusso, M. L., Facoetti, A., Paganini, P., Pezzani, M., & Massimo, M. M. (2006). Effects of visual hemisphere-specific stimulation versus reading-focused training in dyslexic children. *Neuropsychological Rehabilitation, 16*(2), 194–212. https://doi.org/10.1080/09602010500145620

Mason, L. H., Kaplansky, M. H., Hedin, L., & Taft, R. (2013). Self-Regulating Informational Text Reading Comprehension: Perceptions of Low-Achieving Students, Exceptionality: *A Special Education Journal, 21*(2), 69–86. https://10.1080/09362835.2012.747180

Meng, X., Lin, O., Wang, F., Jiang, Y., & Song, Y. (2014). Reading performance is enhanced by visual texture discrimination training in Chinese-speaking children with developmental dyslexia. *PLoS ONE, 9*(9). https://10.1371/journal.pone.0108274

Mercer, C. D., Campbell, K. E., Miller, M. D., Mercer, K. D., & Lane, H. B. (2000). Effects of a Reading Fluency Intervention for middle scholars with specific learning disorder. *Learning Disabilities Research & Practice, 15*(4), 179–189.

Mohamed, E., & Elshazly, E. (2016). A case study of an intervention program for studentswith dyslexia in a primary school in the UAE. *Education Commons, 355.* https://scholarworks.uaeu.ac.ae/all_theses

Mosanezhad, J. E., & Nazari, M. A. (2013). Effectiveness of EEG-biofeedback on attentiveness, working memory and quantitative electroencephalography on reading disorder. *Iran Journal of Psychiatry Behavioural Science,* 7.

Nanda, B. (Ed.). (2012). *Challenged Children: Problems and Management.* Kolkata: Ankush Prakashan.

Nelson, J. M., Lindstrom, J. H., Lindstrom, W., & Denis, D. (2012). The structure of phonological processing and its relationship to basic reading. *Exceptionality: A Special Education Journal, 20*(3), 179–196. https://10.1080/09362835.2012.694612

Niedo, J., Lee, Y. L., Breznitz, Z., & Berninger, V. (2015). Computerized silent reading rate and strategy instruction for fourth graders at risk in silent reading rate. *Learning Disability Quarterly, 37*(2), 100–110. https://10.1177/0731948713507263

Nourbakhsh, S., Mansor, M., Baba, M., & Madon, Z. (2013). The effects of multisensory method and cognitive skills training on perceptual performance and reading ability among dyslexic students in Tehran-Iran. *International Journal of Psychologicl Studies, 5*(2). https://10.5539/ijps.v5n2p92

Oakland, T., Black, J. L., Stanford, G., Nussbaum, N. L., & Balise, R. R. (1998). An evaluation of the dyslexia training program: A multisensory method for promoting reading in students with reading disabilities. *Journal of Learning Disabilities, 31*(2), 140–147.

Otaiba, S. A., Schatschneider, C., & Silverman, E. (2010). Tutor-assisted intensive learning strategies in Kindergarten: How much is enough? *Exceptionality: A Special Education Journal, 13*(4), 195–208. https://10.1207/ s15327035ex1304_2

Otterloo, S. G. V., & Leij, A. V. D. (2009). Dutch home-based pre-reading intervention with children at familial risk of dyslexia. *Annals of Dyslexia, 59,* 169–195. https://10.1007/s 11881 -009-0030-0

Palchick, O. O., & Gaab, N. (2016). Tackling the 'dyslexia paradox': Reading brain and behaviour for early markers of developmental dyslexia. *WIREs Cogn Sci 2016.* https://www.researchgate.net/publication /292949158

Papadopoulos, T. C., Charalambous, A., Kanari, A., & Loizou, M. (2004). Kindergarten cognitive intervention for reading difficulties: The PREP remediation in Greek. *European Journal of Psychology of Education, 19*(1), 79–105.

Park, Y., Benedict, A. E., & Brownell, M. T. (2014). Construct and predictive validity of the CORE phonics survey: A diagnostic assessment for students with specific learning disabilities. *Exceptionality: A Special Education Journal, 22*(1), 33–50, https://10.1080/09362835.2013.865534

Park, H. J., Takahashi, K., Roberts, K. D., & Delise, D. (2016). Effects of text-to-speech software use on the reading proficiency of high school struggling readers. *Assistive Technolog, 29,* 146–152.

Pavlidou, E. V., Williams, J. M., & Kelly, L. M. (2009). Artificial grammar learning in primary school children with and without developmental dyslexia. *Annals of Dyslexia, 59,* pp. 55–77. https://10.1007/ s11881-009-0023-z

Peterson, R. L., & Pennington, B. F. (2012). Developmental dyslexia. *Lancet, 379*(9830). https://www.ncbi.nlm.nih.gov/pmc/articles/PMC3465717/

Pinnelli, S. (2014). Dyslexia and young adults. A case study: From assessment to intervention with Reading Trainer software. *ICT in Higher Education and Lifelong Learning*, 84–93.

Predeaux, L. A., Marsh, K. A., & Caplygin, D. (2005). Efficacy of cellfield intervention for reading difficulties: An integrated computer-based approach targeting deficits associated with dyslexia. *Australian Journal of Learning Disabilities*, *1*, 51–62.

Rajkumari, M. A., Sudari, R. S., & Rao, B. D. (2004). *Learning Disability in the Special Education* (pp. 203–242). New Delhi: Discovery Publishing House (DPH).

Rello, L., Otal, Y., Pielot, M., & Bayarri, C. (2014). A computer-based method to improve the spelling of children with dyslexia. http://arxiv.org/pdf/1508.04789.pdf

Rello, L., Subirats, S., & Bigham, J. P. (2016). *An Online Chess Game Designed for People with Dyslexia* (pp. 11–13). USA: Association for Computing Machinery. https://www.cs.cmu.edu/~jbigham/pubs/pdfs/2016/dyslexia-chess.pdf

Rijthoven, R. V., Kleemans, T., Segers, E., & Verhoeven, L. (2020). Response to phonics through spelling intervention in children with dyslexia. *Reading & Writing Quarterly*. https://10.1080/10573569.2019.1707732

Saine, N. L., Lerkkanen, M. K., Ahonen, T., Tolvanen, A., & Lyytinen, H. (2010). Predicting word-level reading fluency outcomes in three contrastive groups: Remedial and computer-assisted reading intervention and mainstream instruction. *Learning and Individual differences*. https://10.1016/j.lindif.2010.06.004

Scammacca, N. K., Roberts, G., Vaughn, S., Stuebing, k. k. (2015). A Meta-Analysis of Interventions for Struggling Readers in Grades 4–12: 1980–2011. *Journal of Learning Disabilities*, *48*(4). https://doi.org/10.1177/0022219413504995

Shaywitz, S. E., Escober, M. D., Shaywitz, B. A., Fletcher, J. M., & Makuch, R. (1992). Evidence that dyslexia may represent the lower tail of a normal distribution of reading ability. *New England Journal of Medicine*, *326*(3), 145–150. http://refhub.elsevier.com/S0042-6989(13)00285-X/h0350

Shaywitz, S. E., Morris, R., & Shaywitz, B. A. (2008). The Education of Dyslexic Children from Childhood to Young Adulthood. *The Annual Review of Psychology*, *59*, 451–475. https://www.annualreviews.org/doi/abs/10.1146/annurev.psych.59.103006.093633

Stebbins, M. S., Stormont, M., Lembke, E. S., Wilson, D. J., & Clippard, D. (2012). Monitoring the effectiveness of the wilson reading system for students with disabilities: One district's example. *Exceptionality: A Special Education Journal*, *20*(1), 58–70. https://10.1080/09362835.2012.640908

Sun, Z., Zou, L., Zhang, J., Mo, S., Shao, S., Zhong, R., Ke, J., Lu, X., Miao, X., & Song, R. (2013). Prevalence and associated riskfactors of dyslexic children in a middle-sized city of China: A cross sectional study. *PLoS ONE*, *8*(2), e56688. https://10.1371/journal.pone.0056688

Svensson, I., Nordström, T., Lindeblad, E., Gustafson, S., Björn, M., Sand, C., Bäck, A. G., & Nilsson, S. (2019). Effects of assistive technology for students with reading and writing disabilities. *Disability and Rehabilitation: Assistive Technology*. https://10.1080/17483107.2019.1646821

Swanson, E., Hairrell, A., Kent, S., Ciullo, S., Wanzek, J. A., & Vaughn, S. (2014). A synthesis and meta-analysis of reading interventions using social studies content for students with learning disabilities. *Journal of Learning Disabilities*, *47*(2), 178–195. https:// 10.1177/0022219412451131

Swanson, H. L. (2001). Research on interventions for adolescents with learning disabilities: A meta-analysis of outcomes related to higher-order processing. *The Elementary School Journal*, *101*(3), 331–348.

Tjus, T., Heimann, M., & Nelson, K. (2004). Reading acquisition by implementing a multimedia intervention strategy for fifty children autism or other learning and communication disabilities. *Journal of Cognitive and Behvioural Psychotherapies*, *4*(2), 203–221.

Torgesen, J. K., Wagner, R. K., Rashotte, C. A., Herron, J., & Lindamood, P. (2010). Computer-assisted instruction to prevent early reading difficulties in students at risk for dyslexia: Outcomes from two instructional approaches. *Annals of Dyslexia*, *60*(1), 40–56. https://10.1007/s 11881 -009-0032-y.

Tressoldi, P. E., Lorusso, M. L., Brenbati, F., & Donini, R. (2007). Fluency remediation in dyslexicchildren: Does age make a difference? *DYSLEXIA*, *14*, 142–152. https:// 10.1002/dys.359

Trout, A. L., Epstein, M. H., Mickelson, W. T., Nelson, J. R., & Lewis, L. M. (2003). Effects of a reading intervention for kindergarten students at risk for emotional disturbance and reading deficits. *Behavioral Disorders*, *28*(3), 313–326. http://www.jstor.org/stable/23889199

Uhry, J. K., & Shepherd, M. J. (1997). Teaching phonological recoding to young children with phonological processing deficits: The effect on sight-vocabulary acquisition. *Learning Disability Quarterly*, *20*(2),104–125. http://www.jstor.org/stable/1511218

Vaughn, S., Cirino, P. T., Linan-Thompson, S., Mathes, P. G., Carlson, C., Hagan, E. C., Pollard, U. S., Fletcher, J. M., & Francis, D. J. (2006). Effectiveness of a Spanish intervention and an English intervention for

English-language learners at risk for reading problems. *American Educational Research Journal, 43*(3), 449–487. https://doi.org/10.1177/00222194060390010601

Vaughn, S., & Fletcher, J. M. (2012). Response to intervention with secondary school students with reading difficulties. *Journal of Learning Disabilities, 45*(3), 244–256. https://10.1177/0022219412442157

Vaughn, S., Roberts, J. G., Miciak, J., Taylor, P., & Fletcher, J. M. (2019). Efficacy of a word- and text-based intervention for students with significant reading difficulties. *Journal of Learning Disabilities, 52*(1), 31–44. https:// 10.1177/0022219418775113.

Vellutino, F. R., Fletcher, J. M., Snowling, M. J., & Scanlon, D. M. (2004). Specific reading disability (dyslexia): what have we learned in the past four decades? *Journal of Child Psychology and Psychiatry, 45*(1), 2–40. https://acamh.onlinelibrary.wiley.com/doi/full/10.1046/j.0021-9630.2003.00305.x

Vliet, E. C., Miozzo., M., & Stern, Y. (2004). Phonological dyslexia: A test case for reading models. *Psychological Science, 15*, 583–590. https://10.1111/j.0956-7976.2004.00724.x https://journals.sagepub.com/doi/abs/10.1111/j.0956-7976.2004.00724.x

Vojoudi, K., Tafti, A. M., & Ashkzari, M. K. (2017). The effectiveness of educational package based on visual- spatial processing in reading performance of dyslexic students. *Avicenna Journal of Neuropsycho Physiology, 4*(3), 79–86. https://doi.org/10.32598/ajnpp.4.3.79

Wanzek, J., Vaughn, S., Scammacca, N., Gatlin, B., Walker, M. A., & Philip, C. (2015). Meta-analyses of the effects of tier 2 type reading interventions in grades K-3. *Educational Psychological Review.* https://10.1007/s10648-015-9321-7

Werts, M. G., Culatta, R. A., & Tompkins, J. R. (2011). *Students with Learning Disabilities in the Fundamentals of Special Education: What Every Teachers need to Know* (pp. 118–146). New Delhi: PHI Learning.

Williams, K. J., Walker, M. A., Vaughn S., & Wanzek J. (2016). A synthesis of reading and spelling interventions and their effects on spelling outcomes for students with learning disabilities. *Journal of Learning Disabilities*, 1–12. https://10.1177/0022219415619753

Wolf, U. (2014). RAN as a predictor of reading skills, and vice versa: Results from a randomised reading intervention. *Ann. of Dyslexia, 64*, 151–165. https://10.1007/s11881-014-0091-6

Wright, C., Conlonb, E., Wrighta, M., & Dyckb, M. (2011). Sub-lexical reading intervention in a student with dyslexia and Asperger's Disorder. *Australian Journal of Educational & Developmental Psychology, 11*, 11–26.

Zhao, H., Zhang, B., Chen, Y., Zhou, X., & Zuo, P. (2016). Environmental risk factors in Han and Uyghur children with dyslexia: A comparative study. *PloS One, 11*(7), https://10.1371/journal.pone.0159042.

23
THE EFFICACY OF LITERACY INTERVENTIONS FOR STUDENTS WHO USE AUGMENTATIVE AND ALTERNATIVE COMMUNICATION

Cissy (Cheng) Cheng* and Tiffany Chavers

No student is too good at anything to be able to read and write.

David Yoder, ISAAC (2000)

Introduction

One of the most fundamental skills students learn in school is literacy (i.e., reading and writing; Bailey et al., 2011; Erickson & Clendon, 2009). Literacy fosters cognitive development and advances learning; increases participation in the educational curriculum; promotes access to employment opportunities; enhances social relationships; and supports the use of mainstream technology (Beukelman & Light, 2020; Koppenhaver et al., 1991; Light & McNaughton, 2009; Light et al., 2008).

Unfortunately, not everyone is given the same opportunity to acquire literacy skills. There are individuals who have little to no functional speech due to developmental disorders such as autism spectrum disorders (ASD), cerebral palsy (CP), and dual sensory impairments, among others. Many of them rely on augmentative and alternative communication (AAC) systems to communicate. AAC is an area of clinical and educational practice that aims to support the communication of individuals who require adaptive support and assistance for speaking and/or writing (Koul & Chavers, 2019). For instance, instead of verbally saying the word *apple*, individuals who rely on AAC may communicate by pointing to an apple, pointing to a picture of an apple, or touching an icon that represents an apple on a speech-generating device (SGD). SGDs are communication aids that produce synthetic or digitized speech upon the selection of a message (Koul, 2011).

A national survey conducted by Andzik et al. (2018) investigated how students with limited to no functional speech were supported in the classroom. Results indicate that the majority of

---

* ccheng@austin.utexas.edu

students with disabilities using AAC are not proficiently communicating, exerting a negative impact on communication, language, and literacy outcomes. Specifically, research also suggests that students who rely on AAC usually struggle with literacy learning (Kurth et al., 2020; Yorke et al., 2020) as they are provided with fewer opportunities to participate in literacy instruction and limited access to a desired mode of communication during literacy activities (Beck 2002; Kent-Walsh, & Light, 2003; Koppenhaver, 1993; Light & Kelford-Smith 1993; Smith, 2005). Most students who rely on AAC communicate at the semantic level (i.e., word meaning). However, traditional literacy instruction requires students to participate by orally saying letter sounds, syllables, blending words, or reading out loud (Machalicek et al., 2010; Ruppar et al., 2011; Stahl & Murray, 1994; Stanovich et al., 1984). Therefore, without adaptation to literacy instruction and individualization on AAC systems, these students will have limited opportunities to participate in literacy activities in inclusive settings (Kent-Walsh et al., 2010; Light et al., 1994; Wilkins & Ratajczak, 2009).

In this chapter, we will first provide an overview of AAC methods, strategies, and technologies. Then, we will summarize empirical evidence for adapting traditional literacy intervention to teach literacy skills. Specifically, literacy interventions that target phonological awareness, letter–sound correspondence, decoding skills, and sight word recognition will be addressed. We suggest that teachers collaborate with school speech-language pathologists (SLPs) and other professionals to form interprofessional teams to support literacy learning in students using AAC in inclusive settings. We hope to bridge the gap between empirical evidence and practice in literacy intervention to help these students develop adequate literacy skills and broaden their horizons.

Augmentative and Alternative Communication Systems

There are many AAC options available to accommodate individuals with various linguistic, cognitive, and motor needs. AAC options can be categorized into technology-based and no-technology-based intervention approaches. The technology-based AAC intervention approaches include the use of dedicated speech-generating devices (SGDs; e.g., Tobii Dynavox Indi™) and/or software applications to produce digitized or synthetic speech upon selection of a message (Koul, 2011). In contrast, no-technology-based AAC intervention approaches do not involve the production of speech upon selection of a message. No-technology-based AAC intervention approaches include picture communication boards, spelling boards, gestures and signs, and tangible objects.

AAC interventions can be further categorized into symbol-based AAC and text-based AAC options. Symbol-based AAC interventions include line drawings and/or photographs that are organized in a grid display or visual scene display (VSD). A grid display (Figure 23.1) organizes symbols in a logical sequence (e.g., syntactic structure and/or semantic hierarchy), whereas a VSD (Figure 23.2) presents an activity, place, or a situation using photographs, places, or virtual environments in integrated scenes (i.e., fewer screens; Koul & Chavers, 2019). Students who use symbol-based communication often have not developed literacy skills and must rely on others to provide symbols to represent language concepts they wish to express (Beukelman & Light, 2020). However, students who rely on AAC and acquire literacy skills can formulate their own messages using text-based AAC systems that contain traditional orthography (e.g., English alphabets and/or pre-stored parts of speech). Unlike symbol-based AAC systems, text-based AAC systems provide students who rely on AAC the opportunity to independently generate novel messages to express ideas, thoughts, and feelings.

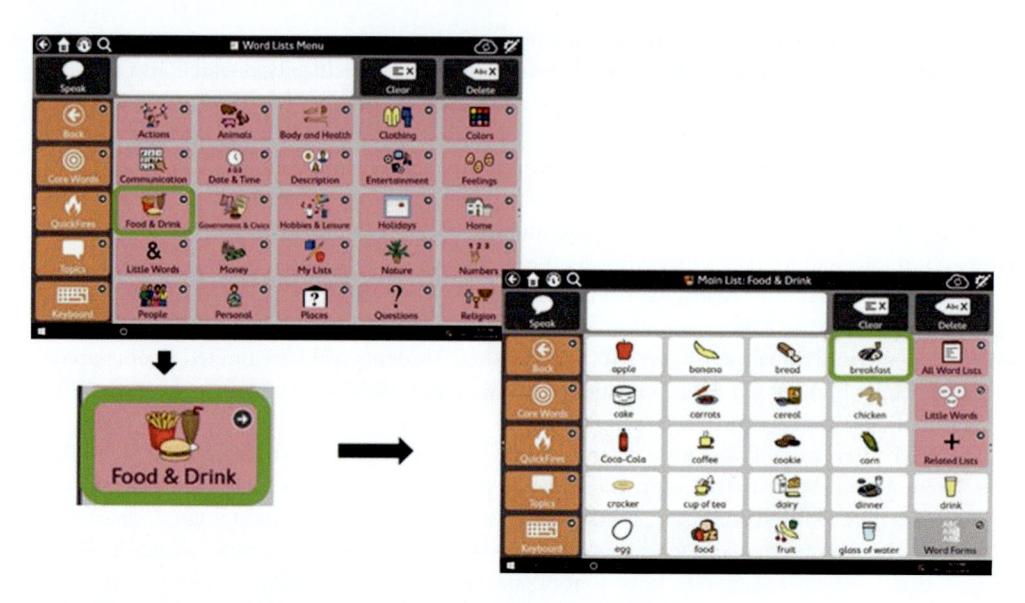

Figure 23.1 An example of a grid display on Tobii Dynavox I-13®

Figure 23.2 An example of a visual scene display (VSD) on Tobii Dynavox I-13®

Evidence-Based AAC Intervention Strategies to Teach Basic Reading Skills

Development of reading and writing skills is dependent upon the integration of knowledge and skills across various domains (National Institute of Child Health and Human Development, [NICHD], 2000). Components of literacy instruction include phonological and phonemic awareness, letter–sound correspondence, decoding skills, and sight word recognition. Each of these skills is discussed below with an emphasis on evidence-based interventions for individuals who rely on AAC.

Phonological and Phonemic Awareness

Studies indicate that phonological awareness is one of the most important predictors of reading outcomes (Ehri et al., 2001; Stanovich, 1994). Phonological awareness is an umbrella term that refers to the ability to attend to and manipulate sounds at different linguistic levels, namely sentence, syllable, word and phoneme levels (Torgesen et al., 1994). An example of a basic level of phonological awareness could be knowing that a sentence consists of words; an example of an advanced level of phonological awareness could be knowing that a word consists of individual phonemes (i.e., the smallest units of sound). The ability to attend to and manipulate the phonemes of words refers to phonemic awareness. With phonemic awareness, an individual can match, isolate, blend, segment, and substitute sound(s) in a word. For instance, an individual who has phonemic awareness may understand that the word *cat* is comprised of three individual phonemes - /k/, /æ/, and /t/. The individual can also blend the three phonemes to generate the word *cat*.

In traditional literacy activities, students are asked to produce verbal responses to answer questions. For students with limited to no functional speech, literacy instructions should be adapted to bypass the need for oral responses (Light & McNaughton, 2013), and students' AAC systems can be individualized to contain all the possible responses. Research indicates that severe speech impairments do not impede students' acquisition of phonological awareness skills if adaptive instruction and systematic scaffolding are utilized (Benedek-Wood et al., 2016; Light et al., 2009; Mandak et al., 2018).

Sound blending, which is the ability to combine individual sounds to form words, is pivotal for reading. In order to read words, students must be able to know the sounds for the letters and put the sounds together to identify the word. Light, McNaughton, and Fallon (2009) suggested the following instructional procedures to teach sound blending. First of all, the teacher says the word "mom" slowly by holding each sound for one to two seconds (e.g., "mmmmooom-mmm"). Then, the student listens to the sounds and mentally blends them together to determine the word. At last, the student says the word out loud or uses AAC strategies such as signing or selecting a picture for "mom".

Like sound blending, conventional segmentation tasks require a student to produce verbal responses as well. For instance, students are asked to segment the initial phoneme from a word or segment the entire word into individual phonemes. An adapted instruction could be presenting them with a spoken word and then asking them to select the symbols on their AAC systems that have the same initial sounds; also, students could be instructed to select the target letter for the initial sound on their AAC systems (Light et al., 2009). In addition, students can be taught to segment the entire word into individual phonemes by having a teacher pronounce one phoneme at a time; the students are then instructed to map each letter onto the individual phoneme (Coleman-Martin et al., 2005; Heller et al., 2002).

In Ahlgrim-Delzell et al. (2016), researchers investigated the efficacy of a phonics-based reading curriculum where students participated in conventional literacy tasks using an iPad-based application called *GoTalk Now* (GTN; the Attainment Company, n.d.). Participants were K–8th Grade students diagnosed with ASD, intellectual disability, or developmental delay. They did not have access to traditional reading instruction due to the use of AAC for communication. Participants were randomly assigned to a treatment group (n = 17) or a control group (n

= 14). In the treatment group, participants received phonics-based intervention, which involves explicit instruction in the phonemes and their association with the letters. They were instructed to use the GTN application to perform tasks such as segmenting, decoding sight words, and comprehending a short passage. Intervention for both groups includes time delay and systematic prompts. Auditory cueing was programmed in the GTN application, which allowed participants to press icons to voice phonemes or words for review before the final selection of their answer. Participants could select a series of phonemes to hear them voiced as a blended word. Verbal approximations (i.e., using their voice) of the words were also encouraged. In the control group, participants were instructed to use the application to learn sight words or read-aloud stories. They answer questions by identifying vocabulary words and pictures on the iPad. No phonics-based intervention procedures were involved.

Data were analyzed using a repeated-measures ANOVA comparing pre-test and post-test scores in the treatment group and control group. Results suggest that participants in both groups improved their ability to identify phonemes, blending sounds to identify words and decoding for picture-word matching. The average of the total score for the three subtests was 34.29 (SD = 14.5) in the pre-test and 54.12 (SD = 18.91) in the post-test for the treatment group; the average of the total score was 32.86 (SD = 17.48) in the pre-test and 37 (SD = 19.60) in the post-test. Cohen's d (Cohen, 1988) at post-test was .89 for the total score, indicating a large effect. There were statistically significant interaction effects between two intervention groups in phoneme identification, $F(1, 7) = 3.23, p < .01, \eta^2 = .12$; decoding for picture-word matching, $F(1, 7) = 3.81, p < .01, \eta^2 = .12$, and total score of the three subtests $F(1, 7) = 7.09, p < .01, \eta^2 = .21$. The results indicated that participants in the treatment group outperformed the students in the control group in these phonics tasks. There was no significant between-group difference in blending sounds to identify words, $F(1, 7) = .88, p = .53, \eta^2 = .03$.

The researchers concluded that students with intellectual disability, developmental delay, or ASD who rely on AAC could benefit from phonics-based instruction in conjunction with systematic prompts. An iPad-based application (i.e., GTN) with phonemes, words, and pictures programmed in it and the text-to-speech function could allow students to produce individual phonemes and blend phonemes to words. Therefore, students can use their iPad to participate in phonics-based literacy tasks, such as identifying sounds in words and reading words to select pictures. The researchers also discussed the challenges of modifying traditional phonics-based tasks and AAC systems to accommodate students' communication needs. One challenge is that learning phonological awareness skills imposes high demands on students' auditory processing and working memory (Ahlgrim-Delzell et al., 2016; Light & McNaughton, 2013). For instance, in a blending task, participants must process the sounds in sequence, identify each sound, and hold the sounds in working memory in the correct sequence to blend them together to determine the target word from highly similar distractors. Ahlgrim-Delzell and colleagues (2016) suggested that modifications are needed to reduce the cognitive resources and provide participants with opportunities to listen to each letter and use the technology to voice the word before selecting it.

Letter–Sound Correspondence

In order to read and write, individuals who rely on AAC must understand the concept of letter–sound correspondence (LSC). LSC includes both the knowledge of the sounds represented by letters of the alphabet and the knowledge of letters used to represent sounds (Light & McNaughton, 2012). Instructions for teaching children who rely on AAC the concept of LSC involves the instructor saying a phoneme or sound followed by the learner selecting the letter corresponding to the sound from an array of letters provided for the instructional task or from a keyboard (Beukelman & Light, 2020).

Multiple studies have investigated the effects of instruction on the acquisition of LSC by individuals who rely on AAC (e.g., Benedek-Wood, et al., 2016; Blischak et al., 2004; Fallon et al., 2004; Johnston et al., 2009; Light et al., 2008; Millar et al., 2004). For instance, Benedek-Wood et al. (2016) implemented a multiple probe design across participants to investigate the effectiveness, efficiency, and social validity of literacy activities on the acquisition and maintenance of LSC skills. Participants included three children with ASD who have limited speech. Six LSCs (i.e., o, t, r, l, u, p) were targeted in the intervention sessions. Each intervention session consisted of five phases: (1) introducing the LSC; (2) modeling the task; (3) providing guided practice; (4) providing independent practice; and (5) providing an extension activity. To introduce the LSC, the researcher presented a letter card, pointed to the letter, and said its sound. Next, the researcher showed the participants a series of picture cards containing the targeted sound and emphasized the target sound. After introducing the LSC, the researcher began modeling the task. To model the task, the researcher showed the participants two letter cards: one contained the target letter and the other contained a nontargeted letter. The researcher instructed the participants to look at both letter cards and point to the letter that match the targeted sound. During each model, the researcher presented one of the five nontargeted letters and varied the location of the targeted letter. After modeling the task, the researcher provided the participant with guided practice. Guided practice began with the researcher stating the sound and waiting 3 to 5 s before prompting. If the participant did not initiate a response, the researcher would restate the targeted sound and model the correct response. After providing the correct response, the researcher prompted the participant to touch the letter independently. To support correct methods of responding, instructional scaffolding was introduced. Instructional scaffolding included: (a) starting with a smaller number of response options; (b) pausing and looking for an expectant response; (c) reaching for (but not selecting) the correct response and/or (d) lightly lifting the hand of participant to indicate that a response was expected. If the participant provided an incorrect response, the researcher provided immediate corrective feedback which included (a) modeling the correct response, (b) prompting the participant to select the targeted letter with the researcher, and (c) telling the participant to select the targeted letter independently. After the participant independently selected the targeted letter two consecutive times, the researcher gradually reduced scaffolding support by increasing the length of the pause and increasing the field size of options by adding one foil letter card until the participant could select the target letter out of a field of six letters. Once the participant began to demonstrate increased accuracy with the recently introduced LSC, other previously learned LSCs were presented in random order. After the participant selected the targeted LSC from a field of six choices for three consecutive trials with minimal support, the participant began the independent practice phase of instruction. Independent practice included ten trials of the recently targeted LSC and five trials of any previously learned LSC. During independent practice, no prompts were provided, and response options were in a field of six-letter cards. LSCs were considered acquired when the participant reached a criterion of at least 80% accuracy in two consecutive independent practice sessions. After the participant demonstrated acquisition of the targeted LSC, the researcher introduced a new LSC. Intervention sessions ended with an age-appropriate activity that provided participants the opportunity to practice learned LSCs (e.g., I-Spy, color-and-paste task).

Results indicated that all three participants learned new LSCs, maintained their knowledge of LSCs after instruction was completed, and generalized learned skills to modified tasks. Additionally, effect sizes were calculated using non-overlap of all pairs (NAP; Parker & Vannest, 2009). All participants demonstrated effects that were between .88 (medium effect) to .99

(strong effects) across participants. This study provides evidence that adapting reading instruction for children with ASD and little to no functional speech can be an effective, efficient, and appropriate method of instruction for teaching LSCs.

Decoding Skills

After an individual acquires sound-blending skills and demonstrates knowledge of a few letter–sound correspondences, he or she has the fundamental skills to learn how to decode written words (Aarnoutse et al., 2001). Decoding involves an individual looking at letters in a targeted word, identifying the sounds of the letters in the targeted word, and blending sounds together to determine the target word (Beukelman & Light, 2020). Most decoding or word identification strategies involve students saying words or parts of a word and a teacher providing feedback on the students' responses. However, these decoding strategies are ineffective for students who use AAC because the student is not able to produce a verbal response. Therefore, the teacher is unable to hear the student read aloud and determine the type of reading errors the student is making (Swinehart-Jones & Heller, 2009).

Multiple studies have investigated an alternate approach called Nonverbal Reading Approach (NRA) to teach decoding skills to students who rely on AAC (Coleman-Martin et al., 2005; Hanser & Erickson, 2007; Heller et al., 2002). NRA implements a decoding method that utilizes internal speech (e.g., silently speaking oneself) along with diagnostic distracter arrays, error analysis, and additional instruction (Coleman-Martin et al., 2005). Diagnostic distracter arrays are a written or verbal list of choices provided to the student that are implemented to evaluate a student's acquisition of targeted words. Students' incorrect responses from the diagnostic distractor array can be analyzed to help the teacher select correction strategies (Heller et al., 2002).

To determine the efficacy of NRA in students who use AAC, Swinehart-Jones and Heller (2009) conducted a study to examine the use of NRA with the addition of a motoric indicator. A motoric indicator (e.g., touching a word card, tapping a finger) was used to verify that participants attended to a word. The study implemented a changing-criterion design to analyze the casual relationship between NRA with motoric indicators and the accuracy of students' word identification. In a changing-criterion design, the researcher implements intervention and successively changes the criterion in gradual steps from baseline levels to a desired terminal level. If the behavior changes successively at the target criterion levels, the researcher could conclude that the changes are due to intervention but not other factors (Hall & Fox, 1977). In this study, the step-wise criterion was two words per each subphase in the intervention phase. The criterion for changing subphases involved reaching 100% on all targeted words taught in the current and preceding subphases.

Four participants with cerebral palsy and severe dysarthric speech were recruited for the study. The participants first completed a word selection pre-test to determine which ten words would be targeted during intervention. The intervention phase began with a guided-practice component. Guided practice for each targeted word began with the researcher stating, "Let's look at this word. Let's sound it out together. I'll say the sounds slowly while you say it with me in your head". The researcher would then display the targeted word typed on a notecard but conceal it with a blank notecard. Next, the researcher would slowly reveal the initial letter and then instruct the participant to say the corresponding sound in his or her head. The researcher then provided a model of the sound (e.g., "cccc") and continued guided practice for the remainder of the sounds in the targeted word. After completing guided practice for all the sounds in the targeted word, the researcher instructed the participant to say all the sounds together in their head without stopping between the sounds. A model then would be provided by the researcher (e.g., "ccccaaaaatttt"). The last step of guided practice consisted of the researcher instructing the participant to say the sounds fast in their head followed by the researcher saying the targeted word out loud as it would be pronounced when reading text (e.g., "cat"). To monitor whether the participants were performing the three-step decoding strategy, a specific motor movement or motoric indicator for each student was established. The presence of the movement served as indicator that the participant was using internal speech to complete the decoding steps. Examples of motoric indicators included thumb or finger movements, leaning forward from the waist, or leaning his or her head forward.

Two hours after the guided practice sessions, each participant's decoding skills were evaluated using words from the word selection pre-test. The evaluation process began with the researcher presenting a target word in written form, pausing for the participant to implement the three-step decoding strategy with motoric indicators, and then verbally providing distractor arrays for the targeted word. Diagnostic distractor arrays consisted of one target word and three distractor words that were similar to the target word. The participants signified their selection from the distractor array by using their most reliable means of response (e.g., orally stating "yes", using eye gaze to select a yes card, using AAC devices to select a yes message, etc.). If the participants selected the wrong target words, they were taught the word through the decoding strategy implemented in the guided practice. If participants did not implement their motoric indicator during the evaluation process, they were corrected and instructed to sound out the word. After the participants completed the evaluation process, the participants' errors were analyzed to determine error patterns. If an error pattern was identified, corrective instruction was given to target the specific errors.

After the participants received criteria on all ten of their words, a generalization phase of the study was conducted to determine whether the participant independently used the decoding strategy with motoric indicators when reading unknown words in connected text. Observation of a participant independently performing a motoric indicator during classroom instruction implied that the participant had internalized and generalized the decoding strategy to reading connected text.

Data were analyzed and interpreted within and across phases for all participants for the dependent variable (the number of words read correctly) using level (i.e., the data points around the vertical axis), trend (i.e., the direction of the overall data points), and immediacy (i.e., the latency in change of level, trend, and variability after conditional change; Barton et al., 2018). Intervention data for all four participants indicated a change in level compared to baseline data, a change in trend to a positive trend, and low variability. Additionally, visual analysis revealed a functional relationship between the number of words correctly identified and the use of NRA with a motoric indicator was demonstrated for all four students. The authors concluded that the three-step decoding strategy with motoric indicators can be an effective method for teaching word identification. The successful implementation of motoric indicators in this study is consistent with other reading strategies and methods that implemented motor movements as a part of the instruction on word identification (Cohen et al., 2008; Fernald 1988; Gillingham & Stillman, 1970).

Sight Word Recognition

When approaching a written word, rather than sounding it out, an individual can also recognize it on sight, which is referred to as sight word recognition skills. To become a competent reader, an individual must be able to recognize both regular words (i.e., words that are decodable using knowledge of LSCs, such as "fish") and irregular words (i.e., words that are not decodable based on common LSC rules, such as "steak") on sight. These skills allow individuals to read longer texts accurately and efficiently (Mandak et al., 2018; Mandak et al., 2019). In addition, the ability to read sight words also helps an individual with vocabulary building. A larger vocabulary promotes reading comprehension and facilitates further vocabulary expansion (Light et al., 2008; Mandak et al., 2019).

Instruction in sight word recognition skills is most effective when incorporating systematic instruction and prompting (Boyle et al., 2020; Caron et al., 2020; Mandak et al., 2018). Also, students should be provided with appropriate instructional materials tailored to their communication needs and competences to practice sight word recognition skills such as matching a target written word to a picture, photograph, or other AAC symbols (Light & McNaughton, 2009; Mandak et al., 2019).

Mandak et al. (2019) used iPad-based digital books with visual scene display (VSD), dynamic text, and speech output to train three preschoolers with ASD to recognize sight words. Training materials included the pages of the book *Brown Bear, Brown Bear, What Do You See?* (Martin & Carle, 1984) and ten written words (e.g., bear, cat, sheep, etc.). An image (e.g., the bear) was a "hotspot" on a page. When a hotspot was touched by a participant, the dynamic text feature would be activated – the associated written word appeared on the screen, grew larger, and then faded away. There was also speech output paired with the appearance of the written to support phonological processing. In the baseline phase, participants were asked to read all ten target words and match each word to the colored images from the book, given a field of four options. The words were presented in a random order with no feedback provided. In the intervention phase, participants listened to researchers read through the stories twice, activated hotspots to see the dynamic text and listened to speech output under systematic instruction and prompting. Procedures of the first and second read through are described in Tables 23.1 and 23.2. In the generalization phase, participants read the ten trained words and matched each word to the correct image from a field of four real photos. The maintenance phase was identical to the generalization phase, except the pictures were illustrations in the book but not real photos.

Results suggest that the first participant matched words to picture with an average of 26% accuracy at baseline and acquired all ten target words after 2 hours and 10 minutes of intervention. He demonstrated a gain of 74% accuracy from baseline and a Tau-U score (Parker et al., 2011) of 0.63, indicating a large effect. The second participant performed with an average of 28% accuracy at baseline and acquired nine target words after 55 minutes of intervention. He demonstrated a gain of 68% from baseline and a Tau-U score of 0.76, suggesting a large effect. The third participant

Table 23.1 Description of the researcher, participants, and training materials during the first read-through

Researcher, participants, and training materials	Description
Researcher	- Read the story to participants page by page on the VSD app - Paused after each page and encouraged participants to activate the hotspot - Provided verbal prompt if participants did not activate the hotspot
Participants	- Listened to the story read by the researcher, viewed book pages on the VSD app and activated the hotspot on each page
Target word pairs	- Dynamic text and speech output upon activation of hotspots - Two exposures
Nontargeted word pairs	- Speech output only after activation of hotspots - Two exposures

Table 23.2 Description of the researchers, participants, and training materials during the second read-through

Researcher, participants, and training materials	Description
Researcher	- Read the story to participants page by page on the VSD app - Went back to the pages with the targeted words - Encouraged students to activate hotspots and gave prompt if necessary
Participants	- Listened to the story read by the researcher and viewed book pages on the VSD app - Went back to the pages with targeted words and activated hotspots for three times
Target word pairs	- Dynamic text and speech output upon activation of hotspots - Three exposures
Nontargeted word pairs	- vNot directed with attention nor activation of hotspots - Not revisited by the researcher or the participants

performed with an average of 24% accuracy at baseline and acquired ten target words in 2 hours and 15 minutes of intervention. He demonstrated a gain of 76% from baseline and a Tau-U score of 0.41, indicating a moderate effect. Furthermore, the first and the third participants achieved 100% accuracy with the generalization probes in the intervention phase and maintenance phase.

In summary, three pre-literature preschoolers with ASD successfully learned to read words using digital books with dynamic text paired with speech output. The participants were also able to demonstrate maintenance of the target sight words and generalize the sight words to new representations (i.e., real photographs rather than the illustrations used during intervention). The researchers explained the training results could be due to: (1) the dynamic text was able to attract participants' attention to the orthography of the target word; (2) the presentation of the text upon selection of the hotspot supported learning of the association between the image and text, resulting in comprehension of the text; (3) speech output was paired with the dynamic text, which promoted the development of phonological awareness that facilitated reading skills. It is worth noting that the author argued that their sight word training is not meant to replace formal literacy instruction. They would consider incorporating instruction in decoding skills in future research to maximize literacy outcomes.

Conclusion

Literacy skills play a very important role in the successful participation in academic and social activities for students who rely on AAC. Sufficient literacy skills promote students' language development, knowledge acquisition, social relationship building, and so forth.

Despite the importance of literacy skills, students who rely on AAC face numerous challenges that need to be addressed to promote AAC users' participation in inclusive settings. Evidence shows that students with disabilities using AAC are not proficiently communicating, exerting a negative impact on communication, language, and literacy outcomes. Furthermore, special educators are generally not sufficiently trained to support students who rely on AAC. Therefore, it is critical to bring evidence-based practices to inclusive settings to support literacy learning for students who use AAC. In this chapter, we summarized current research that provides guidance to adapt conventional reading activities to meet the communication needs and skills of students with little to no functional speech. These research studies provided empirical evidence showing that these students can acquire literacy skills with adapted instruction, systematic prompting, and individualized AAC methods, strategies, and techniques.

We suggest that school speech-language pathologists (SLPs), classroom teachers, special educators, and other professionals form interprofessional teams to implement evidence-based practices to adapt traditional literacy intervention and individualize AAC strategies for these students. When the students develop sufficient literacy skills, it will empower them to achieve the maximum potential in their educational and social life.

Though all the studies discussed in this chapter were conducted in the United States, the idea of promoting participation behind these literacy interventions can be utilized in other countries as well. We encourage teachers to collaborate with SLPs and other professionals to form interprofessional teams to support literacy skills in students who rely on AAC. Furthermore, many of the aforementioned studies utilized visual support to teach literacy skills. We suggest that teachers and other professionals also utilize visual aids (e.g., picture cards, symbols) when teaching literacy skills to individuals who rely on AAC. Lastly, teachers should be vigilant and patient when providing literacy instruction to individuals who rely on AAC as their learning trajectory may differ from typically developing children.

Resources for Teachers

American Speech-Language-Hearing Association: Evidence Maps: https://www2.asha.org/evidence-maps/

Assessment of Phonological Awareness and Reading (APAR): http://elr.com.au/apar

Center for Literacy and Disability Studies at the University of North Carolina-Chapel Hill: http://www.med.unc.edu/ahs/clds

DyslexiaHelp at the University of Michigan: http://dyslexiahelp.umich.edu/professionals

Literacy Instruction for Individuals with Autism, Cerebral Palsy, Down Syndrome and Other Disabilities at the Pennsylvania State University: https://aacliteracy.psu.edu/index.php/page/show/id/1/index.html

PrAACticalAAC: Loving Literacy Resources: https://praacticalaac.org/praactical/loving-literacy-resources/

Tobbi Dynavox: Accessible Literacy Learning (ALL): https://us.tobiidynavox.com/products/accessible-literacy-learning

References

Aarnoutse, C., Van Leeuwe, J., Voeten, M., & Oud, H. (2001). Development of decoding, reading comprehension, vocabulary and spelling during the elementary school years. *Reading and Writing*, 14(1–2), 61–89. https://doi.org/10.1023/A:1008128417862

Ahlgrim-Delzell, L., Browder, D. M., Wood, L., Stanger, C., Preston, A. I., & Kemp-Inman, A. (2016). Systematic instruction of phonics skills using an iPad for students with developmental disabilities who are AAC users. *The Journal of Special Education*, 50(2), 86–97. https://doi.org/10.1177/0022466915622140

Andzik, N. R., Schaefer, J. M., Nichols, R. T., & Chung, Y. C. (2018). National survey describing and quantifying students with communication needs. *Developmental neurorehabilitation*, 21(1), 40–47. https://doi.org/10.1080/17518423.2017.1339133

Bailey, R. L., Angell, M. E., & Stoner, J. B. (2011). Improving literacy skills in students with complex communication needs who use augmentative/alternative communication systems. *Education and Training in Autism and Developmental Disabilities*, 46(3), 352–368.

Barton, E. E., Lloyd, B. P., Spriggs, A. D., & Gast, D. L. (2018). Visual analysis of graphic data. In J. R. Ledford, & D. L. Gast (Eds.), *Single-case research methodology: Applications in special education and the behavioral sciences* (pp. 179–214). Routledge. https://doi.org/10.4324/9781315150666

Beck, J. (2002). Emerging literacy through assistive technology. *Teaching Exceptional Children, 35*(2), 44–48. https://doi.org/10.1177/004005990203500206

Benedek-Wood, E., McNaughton, D., & Light, J. (2016). Instruction in letter-sound correspondences for children with autism and limited speech. *Topics in Early Childhood Special Education, 36*(1), 43–54. https://doi.org/10.1177/0271121415593497

Beukelman, D. R., & Light, J. C. (2020). *Augmentative & alternative communication supporting children and adults with complex communication needs* (5th ed.). Paul H. Brookes Publishing.

Blischak, D. M., Shah, S. D., Lombardino, L. J., & Chiarella, K. (2004). Effects of phonemic awareness instruction on the encoding skills of children with severe speech impairment. *Disability and Rehabilitation, 26*(21–22), 1295–1304. https://doi.org/10.1080/09638280412331280325

Boyle, S., McNaughton, D., Light, J., Babb, S., & Chapin, S. E. (2020). The effects of shared e-book reading with dynamic text and speech output on the single-word reading skills of young children with developmental disabilities. *Language, Speech, and Hearing Services in Schools*, 1–10. https://doi.org/10.1044/2020_LSHSS-20-00009

Caron, J., Light, J., & McNaughton, D. (2020). Effects of an AAC app with transition to literacy features on single-word reading of individuals with complex communication needs. *Research and Practice for Persons with Severe Disabilities, 45*(2), 115–131. https://doi.org/10.1177/1540796920911152

Cohen, E. T., Heller, K. W., Alberto, A., & Fredrick, L. (2008). Using a three-step decoding strategy with constant time delay to teach word reading to students with mild and moderate mental retardation. *Focus on Autism and Other Developmental Disabilities, 23*(2), 67–78. https://doi.org/10.1177/1088357608314899

Cohen, J. (1988). *Statistical power analysis for the behavioral sciences*. Routledge Academic

Coleman-Martin, M. B., Heller, K. W., Cihak, D. F., & Irvine, K. L. (2005). Using computer-assisted instruction and the nonverbal reading approach to teach word identification. *Focus on Autism and Other Developmental Disabilities, 20*(2), 80–90. https://doi.org/10.1177/10883576050200020401

Ehri, L. C., Nunes, S. R., Willows, D. M., Schuster, B. V., Yaghoub-Zadeh, Z., & Shanahan, T. (2001). Phonemic awareness instruction helps children learn to read: Evidence from the National Reading Panel's meta-analysis. *Reading Research Quarterly, 36*(3), 250–287. https://doi.org/10.1598/RRQ.36.3.2

Erickson, K. A., & Clendon, S. A. (2009). Addressing the literacy demands of the curriculum for beginning readers and writers. *Practically speaking: Language, literacy, and academic development for students with AAC needs*, 195–215. Paul H. Brookes.

Fallon, K. A., Light, J., McNaughton, D., Drager, K., & Hammer, C. (2004). The effects of direct instruction on the single-word reading skills of children who require augmentative and alternative communication. *Journal of Speech, Language, and Hearing Research, 47*(6), 1424–1439. https://doi.org/10.1044/1092-4388

Fernald, G. M. (1988). *Remedial techniques in basic school subjects* (Lorna Idol, Ed.). Pro-Ed.

Gillingham, A., & Stillman, B. (1970). *Remedial training for children with specific disability on reading, spelling, and penmanship*. Educators Publishing Service.

Hall, R. V., & Fox, R. G. (1977). Changing-criterion designs: An alternative applied behavior analysis procedure. In Etzel, B. C., LeBlanc, J. M., & Baer, D. M. (Eds.), *New developments in behavioral research: Theory, method, and application* (pp. 151–166). Lawrence Erlbaum.

Hanser, G. A., & Erickson, K. A. (2007). Integrated word identification and communication instruction for students with complex communication needs: Preliminary results. *Focus on Autism and Other Developmental Disabilities, 22*(4), 268–278. https://doi.org/10.1177/10883576070220040901

Heller, K. W., Fredrick, L. D., Tumlin, J., & Brineman, D. G. (2002). Teaching decoding for generalization using the nonverbal reading approach. *Journal of Developmental and Physical Disabilities, 14*(1), 19–35. https://doi.org/10.1023/A:1013559612238

Johnston, S. S., Buchanan, S., & Davenport, L. (2009). Comparison of fixed and gradual array when teaching sound-letter correspondence to two children with autism who use AAC. *Augmentative and Alternative Communication, 25*(2), 136–144. https://doi.org/10.1080/07434610902921516

Kent-Walsh, J., & Light, J. (2003). General education teachers' experiences with inclusion of students who use augmentative and alternative communication. *Augmentative and Alternative Communication, 19*(2), 104–124. https://doi.org/10.1080/0743461031000112043

Kent-Walsh, J., Binger, C., & Hasham, Z. (2010). Effects of parent instruction on the symbolic communication of children using augmentative and alternative communication during storybook reading. *American Journal of Speech-Language Pathology, 19*, 97–107. https://doi.org/10.1044/1058-0360

Koppenhaver, D. A., & Yoder, D. E. (1993). Classroom literacy instruction for children with severe speech and physical impairments: What is and what might be. *Topics in Language Disorders, 13*(2), 1–15. https://doi.org/10.1097/00011363-199302000-00003

Koppenhaver, D., Evans, D., & Yoder, D. (1991). Childhood reading and writing experiences of literate adults with severe speech and motor impairments. *Augmentative and Alternative Communication, 7*(1), 20–33. https://doi.org/10.1080/07434619112331275653

Koul, R. K. (Ed.). (2011). *Augmentative and alternative communication for adults with aphasia*. Brill.

Koul, R., & Chavers, T. (2019). Augmentative and alternative communication. In T. Marquardt & Gillam, R. (Eds.), *Communication Sciences and Disorders: From Science to Clinical Practice*, (pp. 211–226). Jones & Bartlett Learning.

Kurth, J. A., Miller, A. L., & Toews, S. G. (2020). Preparing for and Implementing Effective Inclusive Education with Participation Plans. *Teaching Exceptional Children, 53*(2), 140–149. https://doi.org/10.1177/0040059920927433

Light, J., Binger, C., & Smith, A. K. (1994). Story reading interactions between preschoolers who use AAC and their mothers. *Augmentative and alternative communication, 10*(4), 255–268. https://doi.org/10.1044/1058-0360

Light, J., & Kelford-Smith, A. (1993). Home literacy experiences of preschoolers who use AAC systems and their nondisabled peers. *Augmentative and Alternative Communication, 9*, 10–25. https://doi.org/10.1080/07434619312331276371

Light, J., & McNaughton, D. (2009). *Accessible literacy learning: Evidence-based reading instruction for learners with autism, cerebral palsy, Down syndrome and other disabilities*. Mayer-Johnson.

Light, J., & McNaughton, D. (2012). Literacy instruction for individuals with autism, cerebral palsy, down syndrome, and other disabilities. Retrieved from http://aacliteracy.psu.edu/index.php/page/show/id/1/index.html.

Light, J., & McNaughton, D. (2013). Putting people first: Re-thinking the role of technology in augmentative and alternative communication intervention. *Augmentative and Alternative Communication, 29*(4), 299–309. https://doi.org/10.3109/07434618.2013.848935

Light, J., McNaughton, D., & Fallon, K. A. (2009). Sound blending. In J. Light & D. McNaughton (Eds.), *Accessible Literacy Learning (ALL): Evidence-based reading instruction for learners with autism, cerebral palsy, Down syndrome, and other disabilities*, (pp. 105–118). Mayer-Johnson.

Light, J., McNaughton, D., Fallon, K. A., & Millar, D. (2009) Phoneme segmentation. In J. Light & D. McNaughton (Eds.), *Accessible Literacy Learning (ALL): Evidence-based reading instruction for learners with autism, cerebral palsy, Down syndrome, and other disabilities*, (pp. 75–85). Mayer-Johnson.

Light, J., McNaughton, D., Weyer, M., & Karg, L. (2008). Evidence-based literacy instruction for individuals who require augmentative and alternative communication: A case study of a student with multiple disabilities. *Seminars in speech and language, 29*(2), 120–132. https://doi.org/10.1055/s-2008-1079126

Machalicek, W., Sanford, A., Lang, R., Rispoli, M., Molfenter, N., & Mbesaha, M. K. (2010). Literacy interventions for students with physical and developmental disabilities who use aided AAC devices: A systematic review. *Journal of Developmental and Physical Disabilities, 22*(3), 219–240. https://doi.org/10.1007/s10882-009-9175-3

Mandak, K., Light, J., & Boyle, S. (2018). The effects of literacy interventions on single-word reading for individuals who use aided AAC: a systematic review. *Augmentative and Alternative Communication, 34*(3), 206–218. https://doi.org/10.1080/07434618.2018.1470668

Mandak, K., Light, J., & McNaughton, D. (2019). Digital books with dynamic text and speech output: Effects on sight word reading for preschoolers with autism spectrum disorder. *Journal of Autism and Developmental Disorders, 49*(3), 1193–1204. https://doi.org/10.1007/s10803-018-3817-1

Martin, B., & Carle, E. (1984). *Brown bear, brown bear, what do you see?* Henry Holt.

Millar, D. C., Light, J. C., & McNaughton, D. B. (2004). The effect of direct instruction and writer's workshop on the early writing skills of children who use augmentative and alternative communication. *Augmentative and Alternative Communication, 20*(3), 164–178. https://doi.org/10.1080/07434610410001699690

National Institute of Child Health and Human Development. (2000). *Report of the National Reading Panel. Teaching children to read: An evidence-based assessment of the scientific research literature on reading and its implications for reading instruction: Reports of the subgroups*. U.S. Government Printing Office.

Parker, R., & Vannest, K. (2009). An improved effect size for single-case research: Nonoverlap of all pairs. *Behavior Therapy, 40*(4), 357–367. https://doi.org/10.1016/j.beth.2008.10.006

Parker, R. I., Vannest, K. J., Davis, J. L., & Sauber, S. B. (2011). Combining nonoverlap and trend for single-case research: Tau-U. *Behavior Therapy, 42*(2), 284–299. https://doi.org/10.1016/j.beth.2010.08.006

Ruppar, A. L., Dymond, S. K., & Gaffney, J. S. (2011). Teachers' perspectives on literacy instruction for students with severe disabilities who use augmentative and alternative communication. *Research and Practice for Persons with Severe Disabilities, 36*(3–4), 100–111. https://doi.org/10.2511/027494811800824435

Smith, M. M. (2005). The dual challenges of aided communication and adolescence. *Augmentative and Alternative Communication, 21*(1), 67–79. https://doi.org/10.1080/10428190400006625

Stahl, S. A., & Murray, B. A. (1994). Defining phonological awareness and its relationship to early reading. *Journal of Educational Psychology, 86*(2), 221–234. https://doi.org/10.1037/0022-0663.86.2.221

Stanovich, K. E. (1994). Annotation: Does dyslexia exist? *Journal of Child Psychology and Psychiatry, 35*(4), 579–595. https://doi.org/10.1080/23273798.2017.1325509

Stanovich, K. E., Cunningham, A. E., & Cramer, B. B. (1984). Assessing phonological awareness in kindergarten children: Issues of task comparability. *Journal of Experimental Child Psychology, 38*(2), 175–190. https://doi.org/10.1016/0022-0965(84)90120-6

Swinehart-Jones, D., & Heller, K. W. (2009). Teaching students with severe speech and physical impairments a decoding strategy using internal speech and motoric indicators. *The Journal of Special Education, 43*(3), 131–144. https://doi.org/10.1177/0022466908314945

Torgesen, J. K., Wagner, R. K., & Rashotte, C. A. (1994). Longitudinal studies of phonological processing and reading. *Journal of Learning Disabilities, 27*(5), 276–286. https://doi.org/10.1177/002221949402700503

Wilkins, J., & Ratajczak, A. (2009). Developing students' literacy skills using high-tech speech-generating augmentative and alternative communication devices. *Intervention in School and Clinic, 44*(3), 167–172. https://doi.org/10.1177/1053451208326050

Yoder, D. (2000). DJI-AbleNet literacy lecture. ISAAC. (Found in Farrall, J., balanced literacy instruction: Writing for real reasons. Retrieved from https://isaac-online.org/balanced-literacy-instruction-writing-for-real-reasons/).

Yorke, A. M., Caron, J. G., Pukys, N., Sternad, E., Grecol, C., & Shermak, C. (2020). Foundational Reading Interventions Adapted for Individuals Who Require Augmentative and Alternative Communication (AAC): a Systematic Review of the Research. *Journal of Developmental and Physical Disabilities*, 1–46. https://doi.org/10.1007/s10882-020-09767-5

24
MUSIC PUZZLE

A Game to Support the Sound Environment of the Deaf and Hard of Hearing Students

*Rumi Hiraga**

Introduction

There are several types of sounds around us - speech, environmental sounds, and music. Naturally, we sometimes listen to inconsequential noises, but I concentrate on meaningful sounds in this chapter. Sound for Deaf and Hard of Hearing (DHH) people most likely indicates "speech." However, speech has several meanings; one requires the ability to understand articulate sounds.

Focusing on "articulate sounds," speech understanding is the most important way to obtain information around us with finer granularity or specification than listening to other types of sounds, namely non-verbal sounds. With speech, we can not only obtain information by learning or communicating but also experience affective and emotional states.

Are these communication or affective experiences generated only by speech? We obtain information from non-verbal sounds also - experience changes in seasons from the singing of birds, stopping driving a car when hearing an ambulance siren, recalling a city in a foreign country from a song, etc. We will be able to obtain the same amount of information from language for non-verbal sounds, for example,

- This sound is frogs singing in a chorus.
- This sound is a mosquito's wings flapping.
- An ambulance is coming.
- This is a song I listened to in Mexico City.

We can see that the same amount of information gives you different impressions depending on the media (sound or text) through which you obtain the information, especially if you read an independent sentence just to obtain information.

If we just hear a frog chorus, then that could have an affective meaning - say, "Oh, it's already the rainy season. How fast the time goes by." On the other hand, when we read the sentence "This sound is frogs singing in chorus," other sentences will be required, such as to specify the time or the place of the sound. In that sense, non-verbal sounds can sometimes have richer meaning than language (and speech).

---

* rhiraga@a.tsukuba-tech.ac.jp

DHH and Speech

It might not be appropriate to classify all people with hearing impairments as "Deaf and Hard of Hearing" when we think of speech and DHH. Some do not use sound including speech - they have their language without sound. From here, "DHH" people refer to those who acquire sound or try to use sound.

DHH people, especially if they are congenitally deaf or lose their hearing before language acquisition, go through speech training by speech therapists who have nationally recognized qualifications in Japan.

Even though I understand that my students went through speech training, I find it quite surprising and even miraculous and forget their hardness of hearing when

- I can verbally communicate with them and/or
- they talk to me quite fluently,

because some of them are profoundly deaf.

On the other hand, sometimes their speech is quite difficult to understand even though their hearing acuity measured by an audiogram is not bad. This can be due to the individual characteristics of how DHH people speak - the same as hearing people; some speak unnecessarily loudly, some comfortably, some flatly, etc. The examples above are described from the viewpoint of hearing people.

DHH and Non-verbal Sounds

Thinking of our everyday life in terms of sounds: if we are alone somewhere, do we listen to the speech? Yes, when we turn on a TV or radio, we will most likely hear speech. How about going shopping? Going walking? Having lunch? There are lots of opportunities for us to be surrounded by sounds other than speech.

We may listen to background music at a shopping mall, birds chirping in the woods, or our own chewing when having lunch. While hearing people may be able to notice these sounds, they can acquire these sounds passively. DHH people, however, cannot easily acquire sounds around them, or even if they notice sounds, they have difficulty identifying the source of the sounds because they lack the hearing experience to judge the sounds they acquire.

These sounds hearing people unintentionally obtain are difficult for DHH to recognize. Besides, these are sounds that hearing aids/cochlear implants may not be designed to acquire as their main purpose is to improve speech recognition. In other words, sounds other than speech are eliminated by noise canceling. In that sense, environmental sounds and music are noise. *Therefore, DHH people have far less experience in listening to non-verbal sounds than hearing people do.*

Music has more affective meaning than other environmental sounds. Some environmental sounds such as an earthquake or tsunami alerts have direct meanings (e.g., evacuate urgently). Hearing people understand the relationship between a sound and its meaning from their everyday experiences and so take actions in response to specific sounds. On the other hand, there is no curriculum and little training at school for DHH people to understand or learn environment sounds. In most cases, learning environmental sounds is completely left to the individual.

DHH and Music

In Japan, music classes are given during elementary school and junior high school regardless of whether students have hearing impairments or not. Besides the classes, some DHH students have personal music lessons - such as piano lessons. Some students grow up in families that play or listen to music - they listen to music often.

At elementary or junior high schools that offer special education for DHH, the way to teach music is completely left up to the teachers. Besides the instruments commonly used in music classes, such as recorders and pianos, many DHH schools have Wadaiko, a big Japanese drum. Wadaiko generates sounds with high energy at low frequency and strong vibrations that are recognizable for profoundly deaf children. Music classes are given by each teacher on the basis of their not necessarily rich experience of teaching music, particularly to DHH children, and there has been *no research to accumulate knowledge or experience or analyze these music classes.*

National University Corporation Tsukuba University of Technology (NTUT)

I have been teaching DHH undergraduates and postgraduates at the National University Corporation Tsukuba University of Technology (NTUT) (Tsukuba University of Technology, n.d.) for about 25 years. NTUT is one of the few universities worldwide that is dedicated to students with hearing impairments or visual impairments. DHH students study engineering or design here at NTUT. There are 50 students per grade. I teach classes related to computer sciences such as algorithms, software engineering, computer architecture, and operating systems. Some like writing software source codes (programs) very much, but others do not care about writing programs - similar to students of computer science courses at other universities.

Students are not uniform in their hearing loss and hearing acuity, for example.

- The time when they were found to have difficulties in hearing - some are congenitally deaf, some found out in their teens.
- Their education until high school - some experienced only integrated education, some special education.
- Their hearing levels are from 60 dBs to over 120 dBs.
- Their home environment - from deaf families to being the only DHH member of a family.
- Their attitudes toward sounds - from not using sounds at all to having interest in sounds.
- Their use of hearing support devices - hearing aids, cochlear implants, or nothing.
- Their use of sign language - from very fluent to not using sign language.

Since there are far fewer students per grade than other university courses, teachers support not only students academically but sometimes also physically and mentally.

Although we refer to students as "Deaf and Hard of Hearing," their communication ways vary - some use Japanese sign language (JSL) without using sound at all, some use sign language as well as speech, some listen to sound with visual information such as lip movements, and some even make phone calls.

We understand Japanese and JSL are different languages, but still hearing teachers use their voices by facing the students when we talk, using pidgin sign expressions, presenting terms in sign expressions, and all kinds of visual aids. No sign language interpreters attend the classes except for non-full-time teachers, and no notes are taken. Therefore, DHH students are taught differently from hearing students. DHH undergraduate students understand my talk from pidgin sign expressions and mainly verbal expressions, and most of them read my lips. This means that they have to look at several things - class materials (whiteboard or class presentation material), a textbook, a notebook, and the teacher's face and hands - to compensate for the sound information. The teacher looks at students' faces to judge whether they understand the contents or might like to ask questions. In this sense, classes with DHH students more naturally become two-way interactive classes than classes with many hearing students.

This way of giving them interactive classes is the same as when we have given classes online in response to the COVID-19 pandemic. In online classes, some teachers add captions generated by automatic speech recognition (ASR). However, although the technology of speech recognition is marvelous and is now used daily, ASR is not yet good enough to produce correct captions for classes, because it does not accurately recognize technical terminology and does not meet the requirement of high precision to be used for captions in classes.

NTUT students tend to enjoy music very much. Some of them like to participate in music activities - singing at karaoke, playing music games either on a tablet, on a PC, or at an arcade, or dancing. Since I had been playing the piano and other musical instruments before joining NTUT, it was an unexpected joy for me.

Computer Music Class

I proposed giving a computer music class for DHH students in the late 1990s when I was a temporary lecturer at Tsukuba College of Technology. It was difficult to make a syllabus for the class - first of all, what should be taught in a computer music class? What I knew was that some students, independent of their degree of impairment, liked to play music games.

The contents of a computer music class for hearing students could vary: music notations for a computer, musical expressions generated by a computer, etc. On the other hand, these are not suitable for DHH students, because these contents are based on the tacit understanding that people are able to listen to music. Usually, music is defined as sounds (vocal, instrumental, or both); sometimes it has the expression of emotion.

In accordance with this definition, listening to sound is necessary for enjoying music. On the other hand, DHH students like music games not necessarily because of the sound of the music itself. Thinking of this, I decided the contents of the computer music class for DHH students must include the following;

- maintain students' interest in music (with fewer sounds),
- use computer-related music,
- music not necessarily in the sense of conventional songs.

Finally, I presented a brand-new musical instrument in those days and asked them to play it. The instrument was Miburi by Yamaha Corporation, Japan. Miburi is an electronic wearable musical instrument, which a player puts on and plays by moving their body parts - acceleration sensors are attached to a suit at the shoulders, elbows, wrists, toes, and heels. Several types of sounds including sound effects were provided by the Miburi system. Students put on the suit, chose the sound, and moved. Then sounds were generated that they could notice. Once they decided what to present, they practiced playing the Miburi.

Some played air-Taiko. One student played a set of Taiko in front of her and to her right by just moving her arms as if she were playing Taiko drums with drumsticks (Figure 24.1). Another produced a short piece by making signs with sound effects like dog barks or thunder. This way

Figure 24.1 Playing Taiko with Miburi

of using Miburi was so astonishing that even Yamaha never expected it. The videos of their performances are my treasure now (Hiraga & Kawashima, 2006).

Students' Research

With the efforts of both students and teachers, some students conducted brilliant research on non-verbal sounds. Some of their performances at domestic conferences were awarded, and some performed at international conferences by themselves. Some went on to study "sounds" with computer science at the graduate school of NTUT, and some even went on to doctoral courses at other universities (there are no doctoral courses at NTUT).

Working with DHH students on sounds gave me many insights into the relationship between DHH people and non-verbal sounds. They could provide inquiries to DHH people from their experiences.

Towards Improving Hearing Ability for Environmental Sounds

A student felt that she could not sufficiently understand environmental sounds because little or no time was dedicated to learning environmental sounds at her DHH school. Anxious to understand environmental sounds by listening, she developed a system to learn environmental sounds. The sounds involved in the system were selected from the results of a questionnaire on "necessary sounds in everyday life at home and at school" given to DHH students of NTUT (Hiraga et al., 2016).

Finding the Best Musical Instruments for Music Classes for DHH Children

Another research theme was to find out what musical instruments are suitable for DHH children in music classes in elementary school and junior high school (Nakahara et al., 2018). "Good" involves "ease of listening." To find such instruments, she conducted a beat-tapping experiment with 20 musical instruments. In the tapping experiment, participants were asked to tap along with the regular sound of the musical instruments. If participants could tap along with the sound, then it indicated that they could listen to that instrument's sound. The experiment was completely designed by the student. The results revealed DHH students' likes and dislikes and ease of listening to the timbres of instruments.

The following are the difficult parts for me to design such an experiment.

- Choosing musical instruments. As a deaf student who went through music classes and knew the music well, she could choose musical instruments on the basis of her experience.
- Making subjective inquiries. She gave four questions for each musical instrument, including the question, "Was the sound high?" This is because all sounds were supposed to have the same pitch from a single musical score that had only C4 sound. Hearing people presume that the pitch of sounds from a single score must be the same. Since the actual pitch has an important meaning for DHH people, the question was necessary for DHH people.

Her experiment taught me that timbre for DHH people means ease of listening and pitch, which hearing people are less conscious of when they think about timbre. Hearing people tend to express timbre differences in quite subjective and qualitative terms, such as brilliant or sharp.

Music Training for Improving Hearing Ability

For some DHH students, music is essential to their lives – everyday life without music is unexpected and unacceptable. It does not depend on their hearing acuity. They just like music.

From my experience of having been with DHH students at NTUT, I was able to find out many are passionate and enthusiastic about listening to non-verbal sounds. Here sounds mainly involve non-verbal sounds – environmental sounds and music, which led me to research ways for DHH youth to improve their hearing abilities for non-verbal sounds. The point is that *there are differences between hearing acuity which is measured by an audiogram and hearing ability to understand, enjoy, and appreciate the sound.* Although I am, with my background in computer science, not able to improve their hearing acuities like otolaryngologists who perform operations for cochlear implanting, I assumed I could create an environment for DHH youth to improve their hearing abilities. *My hypothesis is* hearing abilities could be improved by listening to music a lot – *being exposed to music, being bathed in music.*

Ways DHH People Enjoy Music

As I mentioned previously, many DHH people are enthusiastic about music - they like to listen to music, dance to music, sing at karaoke, etc. At the same time, they worry whether what they listen to is different from what hearing people listen to and are eager to enjoy music more.

There are three possible ways for DHH people to enjoy music.

1. Using other senses as substitutes for hearing, such as touch or sight through some devices,
2. Changing musical instruments so that DHH can listen to them,
3. Training their hearing ability so that they can listen to non-verbal sounds by themselves.

DHH students who like music have their own opinion about music, and their opinions are not directly related to their degrees of hearing impairment: their passion for music is not related to understanding and/or speaking well (i.e., verbal communication). The following are some of their opinions.

- a. Music with vibrations is nice to experience.
- b. Visual images give me supportive information of music.
- c. I can see a child dancing along to a performer's movements.
- d. I like to "listen to" music.

DHH people who have had little experience in obtaining sounds find it fun to interact with music through vibrations (a). A regular concert series with body sonic systems is a good way for DHH people to experience music. (a) and (b) above are mentioned by DHH people who enjoy music through substitute senses (1). A profoundly deaf student said (c) when he attended a live percussion performance. (c) is a type of (1) but the DHH listener generates the substitute sound cues. (d) (I like to "listen to" music) indicates that the DHH listener is not content with experiencing music through vibrations or visual images. One such person was a student I described previously who researched the timbres of musical instruments. For this way of enjoying music, hearing ability is important. Therefore, training to improve hearing ability is necessary (3).

Music Training

Music training can be analytic or synthetic. Analytic training (bottom-up training) focuses on a single music element such as a melody contour. In synthetic training (top-down training), music is presented as-is. In the sense of human intervention, music training is conducted by music specialists or without a supervisor.

Music therapy is a type of music training conducted usually by music therapists who are music specialists and sometimes by speech therapists who know music well in order to increase the quality of life for those who have difficulties in language understanding or daily life. Speech therapists help DHH students who were diagnosed as having hearing loss either congenitally or at an early age, including intervention to support language acquisition. It is not usual for DHH students to see music therapists in Japan. Music therapists use methods involving music, and typically their clients have no hearing impairment. However, there are cases where music therapy is conducted with DHH people, for instance with person-to-person activities (Gfeller et al., 2011; Looi et al., 2012; Torppa & Huotilainen, 2019) or in school settings (Darrow & Gfeller, 1991; Petersen et al., 2015). Music training with human intervention provides synthetic training – music is presented as it is, not divided into elements.

Pros in music therapy are as follows:

- music used in a session is interactively chosen
- a session is interactive and communicative

Cons are as follows:

- restricted resources in terms of time, place, and therapists.

Computer-based music training is a kind of computer-based auditory training (CBAT). CBAT enables users to practice auditory training with a computer or a tablet. Thus, they can do the training anytime, anywhere, and by themselves, which overcomes the restrictions of training given by a specialist. As with the expectation of lower cost and more convenience than music therapy, the results of efficacy through CBAT are not robust, including programs that have been developed for DHH people. So far, the purpose of all CBAT for DHH people has been to improve recognition of verbal information, such as listening and communication enhancement, not to improve the hearing ability of non-verbal sounds.

Most *computer-based music training* (CBMT) designs are analytic – for instance, listening to short melodies and determining whether they were the same or not. Fuller et al. compared their own analytic music training with the synthetic training of music therapy (Fuller et al., 2018).

By listening repeatedly to the same melodies (analytical training), participants discriminated between different melody contours. Though both types of training showed a small improvement in listening ability, Fuller et al. were not sure of their effectiveness. Looi et al. reviewed music perception and training for cochlear implantees (Looi et al., 2012). Although they also pointed out the need to further research music training for DHH people, they noted a relationship between music training and speech comprehension by DHH people. Torppa and Huotilainen pursued speech improvement with music training (Torppa & Huotilainen, 2019). In general, so far, the efficacy of CBMT has not been as consistent or robust as that of CBAT.

Assessment of Music Ability for DHH People

The effectiveness of music training cannot be determined without an effective assessment method. Therefore, the development of an assessment method is actually not only another research topic but also required when we propose a training method.

Several music assessment methods have been proposed for hearing people. Usually, assessments consist of answering questions after listening to music stimuli. The musical aptitude profile by Gordon has long been widely used in the United States to measure understanding of music elements (melody, harmony, tempo, meter, phrasing, balance, and style) by listening to music stimuli (Gordon, 1967). The Timbre Perception Test by Lee and Müllensiefen asks participants to generate the timbre resembling a given timbre by controlling one of the audio profiles (Lee & Müllensiefen, 2020). The Goldsmith Musical Sophistication Index (Müllensiefen et al., 2014) gives a set of inquiries to see how a person understands and describes music not only by a listening test but also by choosing the frequency of music activities in everyday life. There is a test for identifying congenital amusia (Vuvan et al., 2018). The participants of all of these tests do not have hearing loss. In this sense, we can say hearing acuity that is shown by an audiogram and clinical assessment and hearing ability to understand or appreciate music are different.

There are not many music tests for cochlear implantees. Roy et al. proposed the Music in Children with Cochlear Implants (MCCI) battery that measures music perception by children with cochlear implants by discrimination tests in each music element (rhythm, pitch, melody, harmony, and timbre) (Roy et al., 2014). Appreciation of Music in Cochlear Implantees (AMICI) is another test of music for cochlear implantees (Cheng, Spitzer, Shafiro, Sheft, & Mancuso, 2013). The contents of the test are different from those of MCCI.

Generally speaking, because of the sound processing of cochlear implants or digital hearing aids, DHH people with those hearing aids are good at recognizing temporal cues but not spectral cues. This leads to DHH people appreciating rhythm in music but not melody, harmony, or timbre. NTUT students' passion for dance or Wadaiko can be explained by the understanding of a time-dependent music element (tempo, beat, rhythm). Not only MCCI or AMICI, but the target people of many studies of music and DHH people are also restricted to cochlear implantees.

Restriction of participants for music and DHH research to only cochlear implantees clarifies the sounds they obtain. Even in this case, the researchers have to consider other factors in investigating music and DHH: the age of hearing loss, the age of starting to use cochlear implants, music experience, etc. Though DHH people's past music experience is hard to quantify, it has quite a large effect on music appreciation.

Since our research participants are students of NTUT, not only are their music-listening profiles diverse but also their hearing aids are not only cochlear implants. Nonetheless, we hope to improve their hearing ability by giving them opportunities for active music listening. Thus, we conducted an experiment using a music game for training.

Music Training with Music Puzzle

Besides its cost efficiency and convenience, another advantage of CBMT is to keep users incentivized and motivated – just like the music games that DHH people are willing to play regardless of their hearing loss. Despite all this, and as far as we can judge from published material, no CBMT for DHH has been designed to be fun to use. Is a strong will required to bear going through monotonous training to improve music appreciation? No!

There is a shortage of music games that can be used for training and improving hearing abilities with the goal to increase the enjoyment of non-speech sounds (music and environmental sounds). Thus, we present an attempt at providing DHH people with an enjoyable CBMT for acquiring music and environmental sounds through active listening.

I used an original music game named Music Puzzle (MP), which was developed in collaboration with a researcher in Sweden for music training (Hansen et al., 2013). In short, MP is an audio version of a jigsaw puzzle. The goal is to reconstruct an original sound (Figure 24.2) from several randomly ordered sound particles (Figure 24.3). Players listen to sound particles with

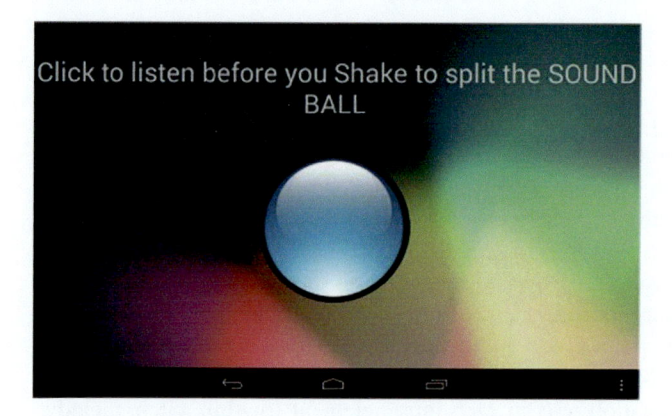

Figure 24.2 Original sound with the interface of a large ball

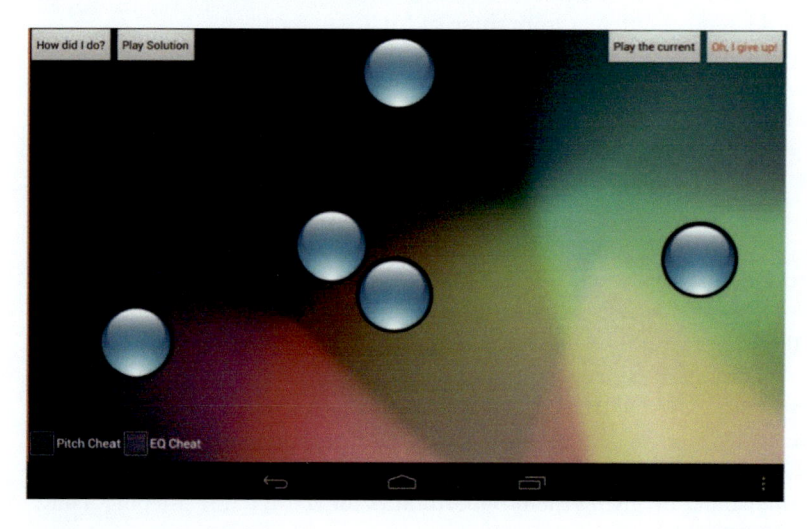

Figure 24.3 Sound particles

modified timbre and pitch, correct them, and then place them in order horizontally from left to right to construct the original sound.

In a previous experiment involving DHH students and MP, I found that many of them were interested in playing MP (Hiraga et al., 2015). From the results, we found that even a profoundly deaf person played MP very well if he/she has had plenty of music experience, especially actively listening to music. Moreover, we found that this type of music game was appreciated by many of the DHH participants. Therefore, we tried to use MP to improve hearing ability and conducted an experiment (Hiraga & Falkenberg, 2020).

Using MP as a training tool, we conducted an experiment to see the effect of hearing ability of using MP for four weeks. Since we did not have an appropriate battery to measure the effect of the training, we had our own evaluation methods.

MP Experiment

This was a preliminary experiment to find out whether:

- MP is effective at improving hearing ability, and
- the assessment method is appropriate for measuring the effect of MP.

The experiment was approved by the ethical committee of NTUT.

Experiment Design

- Period: four weeks.
- Time: playing MP at least 30 minutes per day, 5 days per week.
- Difficulty level: increased each week

Assessment Method

Since MP playing is synthetic training, not targeting a single ability to be improved, we used the items as a test set: speech recognition, beat recognition (Afreth, 2017), melody discrimination (Gordon, 1967), environmental sound identification (open-set), harmony preference (Hiraga & Matsubara, 2014), and an easy game of MP. The whole test took about 30 minutes to complete. Contents of my past experiments were used for some of the test items.

Participants

Two participants, P1, hard of hearing (male, 22, 90 dB hearing acuity), and P2, profoundly deaf (female, 23, 115 dB hearing acuity), participated. Their music experiences were private piano lessons when they were elementary school students besides music classes in elementary school and junior high school. P1 listened to music three hours a day, and P2 listened to it for one hour per day. They mostly listened to music with lyrics.

Results and Discussion

After playing MP for four weeks, the participants did not show an obvious improvement in hearing ability. From the results of the experiment, we could obtain the following points to continue the research of music training for DHH people.

- The design and implementation of the assessment to measure DHH people's ability to hear music. Since we pursue synthetic training, there is no clear correspondence even when we measure participants' ability to recognize music elements.
- The selection of sound material used in the music training. Even if the sound material is easy in the sense of music context, DHH people may not be able to "listen to" it because of their hearing characteristics. If participants of the training cannot obtain sound in the training, the training has less meaning.
- Time and period. Though the time of using MP (30 minutes per day, 5 days per week) was sufficient, the period of four weeks was not. On the other hand, the longer the period, the more difficult it will be to determine the effect of playing MP even if the hearing ability is improved because the improvement could be due to the time effect of exposure to other sounds.

Conclusion

I have described the sounds around us, listening to non-verbal sounds, the fondness Deaf and Hard of Hearing (DHH) people have for music, the unexplored research of improving DHH people's ability to listen to non-verbal sounds, and our approach to using a computer-based music game to derive active listening that leads to improving hearing ability. So far, I have not provided a set of music training methods and an assessment method, so my future objective is to propose a fun music training system that will be beneficial to NTUT students.

References

Afreth, J. (2017). The BEAT test: Training fundamental temporal perceptual motor skills. International Conference for Music Perception and Cognition.

Cheng, M.-Y., Spitzer, J. B., Shafiro, V., Sheft, S., & Mancuso, D. (2013). Reliability measure of a clinical test: Appreciation of Music in Cochlear Implantees (AMICI). *Journal of the American Academy of Audiology*, 24(10), 969–979.

Darrow, A.-A., & Gfeller, K. (1991). A study of public school music programs mainstreaming hearing impaired students. *American Music Therapy Association. Journal of Music Therapy* 28(1), Oxford Press. https://doi.org/10.1093/jmt/28.1.23

Fuller, C. D., Galvin, J. J., Maat, B., Başkent, D., & Free, R. H. (2018). Comparison of two music training approaches on music and speech perception in cochlear implant users. In *Trends in Hearing*. SAGE.

Gfeller, K., Driscoll, V., Kenworthy, M., & VanVoorst, T. (2011). Music therapy for preschool cochlear implant recipients. In *American Music Therapy Association. Music Therapy Perspectives*. Oxford University Press.

Gordon, E. (1967). The musical aptitude profile. *Music Educators Journal* 53(6).

Hansen, K. F., Hiraga, R., Li, Z., & Wang, H. (2013). Music puzzle: An audio-based computer game that inspires to train listening abilities. *LNCS 8253*. Springer International Publishing.

Hiraga, R., & Falkenberg, K. (2020). Computer-based music training with hearing impairments: Lessons from an experiment. In Proceedings of Sound and Music Conference 2020.

Hiraga, R., & Kawashima, M. (2006). Performance visualization for hearing-impaired students. *Journal of Systemics, Cybernetics and Informatics* 3(5).

Hiraga, R., & Matsubara, M. (2014). Appreciating Harmony-differences between the hearing-impaired, musically inexperienced, and musically experienced. In IEEE International Conference on Systems, Man, and Cybernetics (SMC).

Hiraga, R., Hansen, K. F., Kano, N., Matsubara, M., Terasawa, H., & Tabuchi, K. (2015). Music perception of hearing-impaired persons with focus on one test subject. In IEEE International Conference on Systems, Man, and Cybernetics (SMC).

Hiraga, R., Kato, Y., Matsubara, M., Terasawa, H., & Tabaru, K. (2016). A Learning System for Environmental Sounds on Tablets: Toward a teaching resource for deaf and hard of hearing children. In Linz: Proceedings of the Conference Universal Learning Design.

Lee, H., & Müllensiefen, D. (2020). The Timbre Perception Test (TPT): A new interactive musical assessment tool to measure timbre perception ability. *Attention, Perception, & Psychophysics, 82*, 3658–3675. Springer.

Looi, V., Gfeller, K., & Driscoll, V. (2012). Music appreciation and training for cochlear implant recipients: A review. *Semnars in Hearing, 33*(4), Thieme Medical Publishers, Inc. https://10.1055/s-0032-1329222

Müllensiefen, D., Gingras, B., Musil, J., & Stewart, L. (2014). The musicality of non-musicians: An index for assessing musical sophistication in the general population. *PLOS ONE*.

Nakahara, Y., Hiraga, R., & Kato, N. (2018). A subjective evaluation of music beat recognition with different timbres by hearing-impaired people. *Springer LNCS 10896*, Springer International Publishing. https://doi.org/10.1007/978-3-319-94277-3_34

Petersen, B., Weed, E., Sandmann, P., Brattico, E., Hansen, M., Sorensen, D. S., & Vuust, P. (2015). Brain responses to musical feature changes in adolescent cochlear implant users. *Frontiers in Human Neuroscience*. https://doi.org/10.3389/fnhum.2015.00007

Roy, A. T., Scattergood-Keepper, L., Carver, C., Jiradejvon, P., Butler, C., & Limb, C. J. (2014). Evaluation of a test battery to assess perception of music in children with cochlear implants. *JAMA Otolaryngol. Head Neck Surg. 140*(6).

Torppa, R., & Huotilainen, M. (2019). Why and how music can be used to rehabilitate and develop speech and language skills in hearing-impaired children. *Hearing Research, 380*, Elsevier. https://doi.org/10.1016/j.heares.2019.06.003

Tsukuba University of Technoogy. (n.d.). NTUT Tsukuba University of Technology. Retrieved November 2020, from https://www.tsukuba-tech.ac.jp/english/index.html

Vuvan, D. T., Paquette, S., Goulet, M. G., Royal, I., Felezeu, M., & Peretz, I. (2018). The Montreal protocol for identification of Amusia. *Behavior Research Methods, 50*, Springer.

25
VIDEO MODELING INTERVENTIONS AT SCHOOLS
A Guide for Teachers and Practitioners

*Christos K. Nikopoulos**

Introduction

The Individuals with Disabilities Act (IDEA, 2004) suggests that efforts need to be maximized so that students with disabilities are educated alongside their non-disabled peers in mainstream educational settings. Indeed, research has moved positively towards that direction, since evidence-based practices are systematically explored in inclusive school settings (e.g., Cardon, Wangsgard & Dobson, 2019; Sam, Odom, Tomaszewski et al., 2021).

The use of video technology in a form of video modeling has been empirically suggested as an effective and evidence-based method for developing many skills in diverse behavioral and clinical populations (e.g., Bilias-Lolis, Bray, & Howell, 2017; Nikopoulos & Keenan, 2006; Tereshko, MacDonald, & Ahearn, 2010; Wang, Cui, & Parrila, 2011). Conceptually, video modeling is based on observational learning or learning through modeling that occurs when the observer responds to the contingencies as a function of observing the effects of contingencies on the behavior of a model (Greer, 2002). This method is not only an effective strategy, but it can also be a practical and efficient tool that is well-suited to the school environment (Buggey, 2005; Plavnick et al., 2013; Wilson, 2013). Indeed, either in an individual or group format, video modeling at schools might focus on:

- Increasing academic performance across a number of subjects;
- Responding according to the feelings that someone shows;
- Paying attention to others' instructions;
- Trying to make others feel better;
- Taking turns in conversation in a consistent way;
- Starting conversations with peers;
- Resolving disagreements with teachers and peers in an appropriate and calm way;
- Making new friends;
- Interacting appropriately with peers and within the context each time;
- Introducing oneself to others;
- Responding to criticism without getting upset;

---

* christosnikopoulos@hotmail.com

- Showing concern for others;
- Inviting others to join in activities or joining activities that have already started;
- Avoiding withdrawing him/herself from others; or
- Reducing the presence of inappropriate behaviors.

What follows is a concise presentation of a few examples as derived from the literature with a view of identifying pertinent VM methodologies and making practical suggestions. In that way, goals such as the above ones and others could become targets for a VM intervention. Most of these examples come from autism literature, only because most research has targeted this clinical population. Nevertheless, most students, with or without autism (e.g., neurodevelopmental disorders or intellectual and developmental disabilities), enjoy watching videos (Wang & Koyama, 2014). The chapter has been organized across the following sections: 1. Academic Performance; 2. Social-communication Performance at School; 3. Presence of Challenging Behaviors in the Classroom; 4. Video Modeling and Practitioner Training; and 5. Suggestions for Making Video Modeling an Effective Procedure.

Academic Performance

a) Following basic classroom rules. A video can be constructed to teach students to stay in their assigned area; or to do what the teacher says; or to keep their hands to themselves, as was investigated in the Lang et al. study (2009). In a form of discrimination training, the students were shown a video, which depicted them breaking a particular rule, and were asked whether they had done something incorrectly. Prompting was provided accordingly not only for helping them provide the correct response (i.e., state the rule), but also for acting out that correct response. This was video-recorded and students were praised for stating the respective rule that was followed. This form of video-based intervention is called video self-modeling (VSM), which has gained a lot of attention and popularity within the merits of school practice (Bilias-Lolis et al., 2017; Hitchcock et al., 2003; Kwolek et al., 2019). It provides individuals with the opportunity to view themselves as performing a task beyond their present functioning level. Students' behavior is being recorded over time and then, the parts showing inappropriate behaviors are erased (e.g., Collier-Meek et al., 2012; Gelbar et al., 2012; Tsui & Rutherford, 2014). Alternatively, students perform the target behavior with the provision of verbal prompting and they watch themselves behaving appropriately in a video, in which the verbal prompting had been erased (e.g., Buggey, 2012; Dowrick, 2012).

b) Teaching transitions between locations and activities. For such behaviors, it is important that students watch a video presenting the appropriate behaviors from their own perspective, as focus on the essential aspects of the required behaviors is facilitated. This is accomplished when the video recording is made by holding the camera at eye level, forming the Point-of-View (POV) video modeling procedure. In that way, students do not watch any models, but rather the environment exactly as they would see it in reality (Gardner & Wolfe, 2013; Mason, Davis, Boles, & Goodwyn, 2013). For example, with the use of a portable device, students can watch videos of lining up with classmates, walking in the hallway, entering the next location, or transferring from one activity to another, just before each respective transition takes place (Cihak et al., 2010).

c) Responding appropriately to teacher's questions. During classroom instruction, a relatively common scenario is when a student may ask questions completely irrelevant to the task at hand and s/he would rarely pose any correct response to the teacher's questions, at least, in the absence of any prompting. Since the student has to initiate a verbal behavior, it is more than likely that a verbal prompt will be provided. This is when the use of VSM seems to be the ideal option, as the student's correct response can be captured and shown in the video, but the verbal prompting can be easily erased! Such brief videos that highlight the desired behavior (i.e., correct, unprompted, academic responses to each of the teacher's questions) can be presented to the student during class time on a portable device (Hart & Whalon, 2012).

d) Solving mathematical problems. A further illustration of the appropriate use of VSM can be when students are taught to solve real-life problems based on mathematical manipulations. This complex skill may require solving functional multistep math problems, converting between mathematical forms, and using mental computation and estimation. A video will depict the teacher providing the essential prompting to the student in order that s/he read the steps of the math problems and solves the story problems. An edited version of the video in which the teacher prompts have been eliminated can be available to the student on a portable device. Whilst students watch the video before or during the task, s/he can also pause it, fast-forward, or rewind it as necessary to solve the same problem on paper (Burton, Anderson, Prater et al., 2013).

It needs to be highlighted that any form of video modeling intervention stands as a prompting strategy and therefore, it needs to be systematically faded out. Thus, in the above scenario, when the student solves successfully each problem after having watched all steps, the fading procedure requires him/her to complete a novel problem without having previously watched a video model. This is exactly what was done in Burton and colleagues' (2013) study, where they replaced the videos with visual prompts; the steps were listed on the worksheets, giving the students the opportunity to independently prompt themselves.

Within this topic, POV video modeling has also been successfully examined for teaching mathematics problem-solving process involving mixed fractions (Yakubova et al., 2015) as well as mathematics concepts (Yakubova et al., 2016). During the intervention, students watched a video presenting the teacher's hands either solving a fraction word problem using paper and a marker or using manipulatives and a worksheet to solve the problem; the teacher was also verbally describing the process of the problem solving. Problems represented word stories applicable to functional skills of everyday life. After having watched the video, students practiced using a similar problem-solving checklist, as derived from the video. This procedure continued until students were able to solve a similar problem or how to use manipulatives, without having previously watched any respective video. A similar approach was successfully employed by Hughes (2019) for teaching simplifying fractions to middle school students with mathematics learning disabilities (MLD).

e) Promoting reading fluency. Another example of the effective use of VSM can be when students have got the ability to demonstrate skill of reading, for example; however, they may lack fluency and consistency. Teaching involves watching themselves reading more fluently and at a quicker pace than normal, with the support of the verbal promotion of the teacher, who sits outside of the video frame. Afterward, they practice reading aloud from a written text, what they have just watched (i.e., Edwards & Lambros, 2018; Wu et al., 2018).

f) Facilitating word recognition and pronunciation. The most common type of video modeling explored in the literature is the third-person perspective. This basically involves the video presentation of someone (or more) completing a task from beginning to the end (i.e., whole task presentation). Learning through this type is extremely important as it enhances the skills for observational learning – observing and imitating the behaviors of others based on the consequences of their behavior – in the natural environment (Catania, 1998). During teaching, irrelevant elements of the modeled behavior can be removed so that the student will focus primarily on the essential aspects of critical behaviors (e.g., Tereshko et al., 2010).

In the task of word recognition and pronunciation, the observer should focus on the face and mouth of the teacher. In the training, videos may initially present the models from the waist-up, saying the respective word. Afterward, the videos may show a close-up of the model's mouth, stating the word again, whilst the word may also appear written on a card, at the bottom of the screen. This is exactly how Morlock and colleagues (2015) successfully taught three adolescents with ASD, who were talking in short sentences and had adequate attention and imitation skills.

g) Drawing simple figurines. Tasks that require a number of steps to be followed in a specific order for their successful completion may be taught with the use of another type of video modeling; video prompting (VP) (e.g., Kellems & Edwards, 2015; Sigafoos, O'Reilly, Cannella et al., 2005). The student does not watch the entire task sequence in the video, but one step at a time until all of the steps have been mastered (e.g., Bennett, Gutierrez, & Honsberger, 2013; Cannella-Malone, Fleming, Chung et al., 2011).

In a combined version of POV and VP, Akmanoğlu and Pektaş-Karabekir (2020) taught young children with ASD the skill of drawing a six-part person. As it was expected, the videos were showing only the hands of the model. Moreover, each child viewed the video of the first step on a portable device before practicing it in vivo. Then, s/he viewed the second step and so on. In general terms, whenever training of a subsequent step was initiated, the child viewed first the video of each of the previous steps, and afterward, s/he was assessed to complete the respective step.

h) Improving geometry skills. Similar to VP, an additional variation is the instructional video modeling. This approach usually adopts a third-person perspective by presenting a step-by-step walk-through of each target skill (Shipley-Benamou et al., 2002). The process of making the video is facilitated following a prior analysis of the target task. A task analysis is completed in order to break down rather complex task sequences into constituent elements in an effort to tailor the demands of the task to the individual needs of each child. In other words, a rather difficult scenario is made easier by allowing children to experience selected parts from it. Once the required behaviors in these parts are identified they can be taught to the child individually and then reconstructed into a larger sequence (Stokes, Cameron, Dorsey, & Fleming, 2004). A narrator may also be included in such videos.

Cihak's and Bowlin's study (2009) stands as an excellent example of this type of VM. Teacher's step-by-step instructions on how to solve geometry problems (e.g., the perimeter of squares, triangles or various polygons) were recorded. Students were able to watch them as many times as necessary in a mobile device, when they were doing their homework assignments. In that way, students were provided with more opportunities to learn and revise the more difficult instructional content that was being delivered in class. This is a challenging task to be undertaken by a teacher who has to teach in a heterogeneous class with at least 25 students.

Social-communication Performance at School

a) Answering simple questions. A third-person perspective video modeling can be successful in teaching children to answer questions from their teachers as initially demonstrated by Sherer and colleagues (2001). Students were watching videos in which the teacher asked a question, a peer-model responded, then, s/he asked the teacher the same question, who replied as required. After watching this video sequence, they practiced in vivo in the presence of the same teacher. The same procedure can be followed when VSM is used instead; however, the peer model should be replaced by the student observer and any verbal prompting is erased in the video as appropriate.

b) Increasing communicative interactions. Another kind of video modeling can also be effective for promoting communicative initiations; priming video modeling (Cihak, Smith, Cornett et al., 2012). Priming video modeling involves the recording of future events so that they can become more predictable when a student previews them (Schreibman, Whalen, & Stahmer, 2000). These videos can be filmed from either a first- (i.e., POV) or third-person perspective. Children watch a short video-recorded scenario, just before they experience the same situation.

c) Sharing material and cooperative play. A school setting provides a wide range of models, as pupils can freely imitate each other. Therefore, peers can also serve as models for the construction of videos. Typically, they need to undergo some very basic training in order to learn the basics of video modeling and the target behaviors. This is exactly what happened in Cardon et al.'s study (2019), wherein two typically developing peers were taught a brief script (e.g., "let's play", "can I have a piece") to correspond with the actions of sharing (puzzles), engaging in cooperative play (woodblocks), and transitioning between centers. During the intervention, the participants, who had been diagnosed with ASD, watched a series of videos in which the two peers were interacting with each other and demonstrating the social–communication skills being targeted.

d) Promoting conversational turn-taking. On most occasions, video modeling is structured in such a way that the observer is required to imitate specific behaviors emitted by a specific model. However, it may also happen that the observer may imitate any behavior emitted by more than one model in a video, as in the case of a conversation between two or more people. Third-person perspective videos can be utilized which present adults engaged in a conversation, whilst a narrator may discuss the key features for each skill, as occurred in Mason et al.'s (2012) study.

In that study, a series of conversation topics were recorded, which were unscripted and consisted of spontaneous exchanges on topics such as homework, plans for the weekend, and summer holidays. Arrows, text, and boxes had been embedded in the video to further highlight key communication features such as eye contact, body orientation, and facial expressions. Following video viewing, unscripted conversation between the facilitators and the participants took place and recording of the occurrence of the target behaviors was occurring.

Ezzeddine and colleagues (2020) used a very similar approach (third-person perspective) to teach children with ASD in dyads to comment during leisure activities, with the main exception that the children with ASD were also the conversational partners! The dyads were structured in a way that children were similar in age, attended the same school, and demonstrated mastery of similar leisure activities.

In the videos, two familiar adults were shown to interact appropriately across some play activities and to engage in a reciprocal conversation across a number of conversational exchanges. These exchanges included a social initiation, compliment, assertive statement, and statement of activity termination. Children watched each video on a tablet once, before having practice in vivo.

e) Delivering compliments. The effectiveness of a third-person perspective video modeling intervention for enhancing a skill, frequently used in schools (i.e., delivering compliments) was examined a few years ago (Macpherson, Charlop, & Miltenberger, 2015). Participants were aged 9-11 years with ASD, who attended a mainstream educational setting and demonstrated little or no complementary behaviors towards peers.

During the intervention, children viewed short videos of a familiar adult on an iPad, demonstrating three pairs of verbal compliments (i.e., "Wow, that went far!", "That was a great kick!" & "That was a nice job") and their respective compliment gestures (i.e., Thumbs-up, Fist pump & Clapping). The model faced the camera and modeled the phrases and gestures at an exaggeratedly slow pace (e.g., Charlop & Milstein 1989; Charlop et al., 2010). The first time the video was introduced, the child watched it twice; thereafter, the video was shown only once. Then, s/he was given the opportunity to practice what was previously watched. The session continued until each child had a minimum of five opportunities to demonstrate compliment behaviors. Once a child demonstrated a compliment during four out of five such opportunities, another session was conducted without showing the video (i.e., fading out process).

f) Enhancing school-based social skills. Joining an activity and requesting materials; offering assistance to others and asking for information about others; showing something to a peer and directing an open-ended comment toward a peer are all skills that are so important for any student to be able to demonstrate in a school setting. It seems reasonable to suggest that such complex social skills should be taught in a group format, utilizing video-based group instruction (VGI). Indeed, students can watch a range of such behaviors emitted by all members of a group in an effort to imitate some of those in the natural contingencies. Typically, a series of different group-based videos are structured, adopting a third-person perspective, which students watch multiple times during the day (e.g., Plavnick et al., 2013; Plavnick et al., 2015).

g) Promoting social initiations. The study by Nikopoulos and Keenan in 2003 was the first to examine the effectiveness of the third-person perspective video modeling to promote a critical skill within the social-communicative domain; social initiation. The use of child-social initiations has been repeatedly identified as a key pivotal behavior for any effective training program in order to increase children's learning opportunities (Koegel, Koegel, & Carter, 1999). Several studies have demonstrated that such engagement directly affects other behaviors even when these behaviors are not significantly targeted by the teaching program. For example, in verbal children, both the frequency of language used and the development of novel vocabulary have been demonstrated to increase along with increases in social engagement (e.g., Krantz & McClannahan, 1993; Stahmer, 1995; Thorp, Stahmer, & Schreibman, 1995). Also, inappropriate behaviors have been shown to decrease during periods of active social engagement (Lee & Odom, 1996). Moreover, while children with ASD can learn to respond to social initiations by others, they may face major difficulties in initiating complex social behaviors and as a result, initiating simple conversation remains at low levels (Pierce & Schreibman, 1995). Thus, social engagement and particularly child-social initiations appear to be skills that lead directly to increased attainment of other important skills without the need for direct programming (Rogers, 2000). Social skills are related to the long-term adjustment of and prognosis for both typically and atypically developing children, and therefore, their development constitutes an integral part of any school curriculum (Charlop-Christy & Daneshvar, 2003; Hwang & Hughes, 2000).

The vast majority of research outputs concern studies employing third-person perspective video modeling. Further examples within the social domain in a school environment include the research presented by (a) Charlop, Dennis, Carpenter, and Greenberg (2010) to promote appropriate verbal comments, intonation, gestures, and facial expressions during social interactions of three children with ASD; (b) Rudy and colleagues (2014) to teach children with ASD to initiate bids for joint attention by orienting toward the object, emitting a vocal statement, and shifting eye gaze toward unique objects in the environment); (c) Alzyoudi et al. (2014) to teach five children with ASD to complete a social task such as social initiation (e.g., asking to sit with someone, etc.), conversation (e.g., responding to others' comments, etc.), appropriate non-verbal communication (e.g., identifying others' non-verbal cues, etc.) or answering/asking informational questions (e.g., what is your name, etc.); or (d) Green et al., (2017) to enhance the peer social interaction skills of 3 preschool children.

In all the above studies, a third-person perspective video modeling was utilized! This is extremely important as the use of VM, or modeling in general, should not be viewed only as a procedure for teaching a set of skills based on imitation; rather, enhancement of observational learning in the natural environment in the absence of a specific training should be targeted. Observational learning, modeling, and imitation are three terms that in common language are used interchangeably. However, from a behavioral analytic viewpoint, there are some distinctions between them. For example, Catania (1998) suggests that imitation cannot be used synonymously with observational learning, because it does not imply that the observer has learned something about contingencies. In general, observational learning is one of the most important influences on personality development. Whether used therapeutically for training or occurring spontaneously, this process refers to a behavioral change that is influenced by the observation of others engaged in similar actions (Bandura, 1986). This vital learning is better promoted by this type of video modeling.

h) Following teacher directions. Third-person perspective video modeling can further be used for the purposes of discrimination training by including error models. That is, students will need to discriminate the examples from non-examples modeled by typically developing peers in the video clips. Afterward, they can participate in group activities with peers without disabilities, and assessment for skill acquisition will take place. This video modeling intervention can produce rapid gains in the performance of the targeted skills, leading to self-monitoring and most importantly in the natural environment (Simpson, Langone, & Ayres, 2004).

i) Initiating greetings and a conversation. Although the effectiveness of VM as a "stand-alone" intervention strategy has well been established, there have also been some reports in which video modeling has been combined with other strategies. In one of them (Kocaoz, Little, & Gallup, 2019), a treatment package comprising video modeling and Skill streaming was demonstrated as effective in teaching greetings and initiation of conversation. Following the steps of the Skill streaming curriculum, initially, a series of third-person perspective videos were created for modeling the target skills. After having viewed the video, students reviewed and discussed the content with their teacher, and finally, they role-played the target skills with their teacher. Such an instructional package may be helpful for older students whose profile is relatively more advanced, as it contains elements frequently found within typical educational classrooms.

j) Using the online library catalog. Another demonstration of the use of video modeling as a component of a treatment package was made by Markey and Miller (2015). They taught students how to search for information in a school library by employing instructional video modeling and least-to-most prompting. The peer model demonstrated how to search for a book using book titles, authors, and subjects or keywords. The video had been located as a thumbnail icon on their computer and the students were instructed to watch the video and follow the directions given by the peer model in the video. They were allowed to stop and replay the video whenever they found the directions difficult to follow. In case they were still making mistakes, then, least-to-most prompting was provided by the teacher. Again, the whole approach has been very close to typical educational practices. A very similar approach was adopted by Taber-Doughty and colleagues (2013) to teach a series of novel skills to students with moderate intellectual disabilities within school and community settings

Presence of Challenging Behaviors in the Classroom

A common co-varying group of behaviors exhibited by pupils with ASD and other neurodevelopmental disorders is those called challenging behaviors. Such behaviors can become physically dangerous to others and themselves and undoubtedly can impede learning and access to normal activities, interfering with the quality of their life (Emerson, 2003; Murphy et al., 2005). Furthermore, disruptive, dangerous, inappropriate, and socially undesirable behaviors even in a form of noncompliance present major difficulties for developing meaningful relationships within the family and in the wider community (Shane and Albert, 2008). A general definition of challenging behavior may be:

> *Culturally abnormal behavior(s) of such an intensity, frequency or duration that the physical safety of the person or others is likely to be placed in serious jeopardy or behavior which is likely to seriously limit or deny access to and use of ordinary community facilities.*
>
> *(Emerson, 2001)*

Within the autistic spectrum and other neurodevelopmental disorders, behaviors that could be described as challenging include: *self-injury, physical aggression, verbal aggression, noncompliance, property destruction, inappropriate vocalizations, disruptions/tantrums, and stereotypies* (e.g., Matson & Nebel-Schwalm, 2007). Most of these behaviors are easily noticeable by other people since their rate of appearance can be rather high. However, there are individuals who present less severely challenging behaviors, particularly in a school environment, and hence, it would rather be essential if Qureshi's definition was also considered:

> *People are said to display challenging behavior if they: Had, at some time, caused more than minor injuries to themselves or others, or destroyed their immediate living environment.* Or *Showed behavior, at least weekly, that required intervention by more than one member of staff to control or remove them from physical danger, or caused damage that could not be rectified by immediate care staff or caused at least one hour's disruption.* Or *caused more than a few minutes disruption at least daily.* (1994)

Research on video modeling has been extended for increasing a variety of adaptive skills; however, just very few reports have concentrated on the management of challenging behaviors. For example, a video priming procedure has been used to reduce challenging behaviors of students with ASD that are associated with transition situations (Schreibman et al., 2000). Students were shown videos, which depicted the transition from one environment to another as they would see it, making the upcoming transition predictable to them. In another study (Nikopoulos and Panagiotopoulou, 2015), VSM was explored for reducing vocal stereotypy in children with ASD, when engaging in play activities. They watched videos of themselves "playing quietly", as verbal and gestural prompts had been used for the creation of the videos, which subsequently were erased. A similar approach was also adopted by Ohtake et al. (2013) and Sadler (2019) for successfully reducing task avoidance behaviors and modifying aggressive behaviors in students with ASD.

Critically, the literature on video modeling in this area is still limited but emerging. More studies will be developed and effective procedures are explored when potential reasons for the emission of the challenging behaviors are identified and carefully considered and included in the construction of the videos; *a function-based video modeling intervention!* The term "function-based intervention" refers to the development of behavior change strategies that are directly linked to information and data gathered during the functional behavioral assessment (FBA) procedure (e.g., Bachmeyer et al., 2009; Delfs & Campbell, 2010; Manente et al., 2010; Matson & Wilkins, 2009; Matson & Minshawi, 2007).

A functional behavioral assessment (FBA) is a precise description of behavior, its context, and its consequences, with the intent of better understanding the behavior and those factors influencing it. The typical format includes three approaches to assessment:

i. *Indirect Assessment* consisting of structured interviews and checklists which have been developed to solicit information about situations in which problem behavior occurs;
ii. *Direct Descriptive Assessment,* involving direct observation of behavior and the environmental situations in which it occurs. Opportunities are scheduled to observe and describe the target behavior across a broad sample of environments and occasions with a focus on identifying functional relations between the target behavior and the environment based on the A-B-C recording form (A - antecedent, B - behavior, C - consequence). That is, an observer enters data whenever problem behavior occurs: time and setting, problem behavior, and events occurring immediately prior to and following the target behavior. The data collected from

these observations are analyzed and one should look for trends in the occurrences of that behavior, for stimuli that may be evoking it or the needs that the individual is attempting to fill by exhibiting this behavior; and

iii. Finally, *experimental functional analysis* involves the systematic manipulation of environmental conditions in an artificial setting, to identify the variables that control and maintain challenging behaviors. Experimental control is deemed to be evident when a change in condition brings an associated change in behavior (e.g., Harvey et al., 2009). Although generally considered superior to other functional assessment methods, experimental functional analysis has known practical limitations and therefore it may be used only when data from the other two approaches are insufficient for the creation of reliable hypotheses.

Hence, the content of each scenario in any video clip will be determined by the results from the FBA with respect to the sources of environmental reinforcement for the challenging behavior(s) of each individual. Hence, strategies selected based on the FBA will be successful because they address the antecedents and consequences that influence and maintain behavior. However, the process of linking interventions to assessment results can be complicated and difficult. In a hypothetical example, FBA has suggested that the function of a student's verbal aggression is to get attention from a member of school staff during lunch. Based on this suggestion, in the video, the model will be shown performing an appropriate behavior (verbal or gestural) in order to get the attention of the member of the school staff and the student will be trained to follow the model's behavior instead of being reprimanded for engaging in the inappropriate behavior.

Video Modeling and Practitioner Training

Although beyond the scope of this chapter to provide extensive guidance on practitioner training (some useful resources, however, have been included at the end), there is accumulating support for video modeling in training practitioners to implement varied assessment and instructional methods. These applications are important to highlight given the practical advantages of video modeling for training purposes. For example, training videos can cover many areas, demonstrate desired skills in relevant contexts, standardize training protocols, and accommodate practitioners performing at different competency levels (Catania et al., 2009; Rosales, Gongola, & Homlitas, 2015).

Rosales et al. (2015) incorporated video modeling with embedded instructions for training three teachers of children with autism to conduct preference assessments. The teachers viewed a video that illustrated three assessment modalities with supplemental (inserted text) written instructions. After viewing the videos, the teachers performed simulated assessments with a confederate. The video modeling training was highly effective with each teacher, increasing their moderate baseline performance to near 100% accuracy.

Training practitioners to conduct discrete trial instruction (DTI) has also been approached through video modeling. Catania et al. (2009) developed a video of two experimenters simulating a teacher-student dyad during a 10-step DTI session. Within 10-min of viewing the video, three direct-care staff at a school for children with autism independently carried out a DTI session with a confederate. During video modeling training all of the staff achieved 85-98% implementation accuracy. Vladescu, Carroll, Paden, and Kodak (2012) also trained three early intervention staff in DTI with video modeling that featured a voiceover script and explanation of each instructional step. These staff learned to accurately conduct DTI with a confederate and with children who had developmental disabilities.

Teaching the variety of different approaches of functional analysis (FA) methodology can also be facilitated by the use of video modeling. Moore and Fisher (2007) constructed a video in which a practitioner modeled multiple exemplars constituting a conventional FA. Through video modeling, three practitioners were able to conduct FA sessions at a mastery level and they performed better when compared to lecture-based training and viewing a video that showed only a few exemplars.

As seen in the preceding examples, the basis of video modeling for care-provider/teacher training is comparable to the advantages of video modeling as an instructional strategy for children. That is, care-provider/teacher training can proceed efficiently by having standardized videos that concentrate on defined competencies and work-related expectations. Compared to traditional training protocols (Luiselli, 2015), the ease of viewing, visual effects, and multiple practice opportunities with video modeling may also appeal more to care providers/teachers (Luiselli, Bass, & Whitcomb, 2010).

Suggestions for Making Video Modeling an Effective Procedure

Videos for the implementation of video modeling should be carefully structured in consideration of the specific characteristic features of modeling. Thus, the model's behavior should be one or two steps ahead of the observer's present level of competence, as it is less likely to perform a similar behavior when this is several steps ahead without extensive practice (Baldwin & Baldwin, 1986). Further, the attending skills of the observer (e.g., staying seated, keeping hands on a table, looking at the material, etc.) should have been thoroughly established (Miltenberger, 2015). Also, the motivation of the observer to imitate the model's behavior increases if the positive consequences of the model are also depicted in the video (Ross, 1981). Nevertheless, people tend to do what works for them independently of whether it worked for a model (Chance, 1999). Finally, extensive practice with similar videos should be arranged, particularly during the initial stages, in order to build an imitative repertoire. This is because past reinforcement for imitating a particular model or type of behavior increases the probability of performing the modeled behavior when the contexts are similar to those wherein reinforcement occurred in the past (Leslie & O'Reilly, 1999).

From a practical perspective, preferably one model should be used at the initial efforts, and simple behaviors by the model are demonstrated, lasting 30-40 seconds maximum. The setting viewed in the video may be the same as the setting in which the student will demonstrate imitative behavior. Videos show a close-up of the action the student will imitate, who must be given multiple initial opportunities to respond (Nikopoulos & Keenan, 2006).

An example of the basic video modeling process for a child - let's call him Bryan - to teach him how to tact (name) everyday objects is illustrated below:

a) *Choose a behavior to target.* During the initial phase of investigating how Bryan learns, the target behavior will be a verbal one, especially, "tacting" (naming).
b) *Gather the correct equipment.* A smartphone, a tablet or any other hand-held device that records video can be used to record the video. It has become clear that Bryan is familiar with the technology to be used.
c) *Plan the video recording.* One of the peers will act as the model. The "script" will be as follows:

   The teacher/teacher assistant holds an everyday object and asks the peer: What is this?

The peer answers in a clear and a slower pace voice: [Name of the item]; and
The teacher/teacher assistant gives a reinforcer to the peer.
d) *Record the video.* The above script is used to record 10 same scenes with the use of 10 different everyday objects. The "cameraman" makes sure that:
Both people are shown in the camera all the time;
Slightly turns the camera towards the person who talks each time;
Zooming the object slightly when the peer says the name of the item; and
The scene ends with the teacher/teacher assistant praising enthusiastically the peer and giving a reinforcer *(something that Bryan likes)*.
e) *Show the video.* The teacher/teacher assistant shows Bryan the video concerning the first everyday object in the same room (prompting may be provided as needed to keep attention). When Bryan has finished watching the video, the teacher/teacher assistant tells him "Let's do the same".
The teacher/teacher assistant holds the same object, as shown in the video, and asks: "What is this?"
If Bryan says the name of the object, then, the teacher/teacher assistant provides reinforcement in a very enthusiastic way!
- The same occurs with the video concerning the second object. Again, if Bryan says the name of the object, the teacher/teacher assistant provides reinforcement in a very enthusiastic way!
- Then, the teacher/teacher assistant does the same with the video concerning the first object again. If Bryan says the name of the object, reinforcement is provided and the teacher/teacher assistant does the same with the video concerning the second object again.
- In one session (max 10 mins), the teacher/teacher assistant will have tried (alternatively) to practice 3 different objects for 3 trials each. NO more!
Whenever Bryan does not say the name of the object within 3-5 secs, further "extra" prompting is NOT provided. Instead, Bryan is shown the video again and the instruction "Let's do the same".
- If Bryan names the object, then, the procedure continues as above.
- If Bryan does not name the object, then, he is shown the video again and at the end, the teacher/teacher assistant says "Let's do the same".
- If Bryan names the object, then, the procedure continues as above.
- If not, then, the entire video modeling process starts about 20 minutes later.
f) *Collect data to monitor progress.* Continue collecting data on this tacting behavior using the provided data collection form *(please see below an example)* (Table 25.1).

However, if video modeling does not produce direct results, then, the following arrangements make take place: (i) models may perform at a slow, exaggerated pace; (ii) occasional reinforcement may be used during video viewing and performing; (iii) different models can be used for each video to ensure that specific model characteristics do not influence the performance of the student; or (iv) the videos can be edited to include an opening title and a closing screen with text and several visual symbols or animated favorite video segments can also be embedded (e.g., Jowett, Moore, & Anderson 2012).

Video modeling constitutes a prompting strategy and hence, it needs to be faded out. Fading refers to gradually reducing the strength of a prompt. In essence, the use of video modeling should not be used anymore, when the target behavior(s) are mastered. Certainly, the process of fading videos should be gradual and may involve one or more of the following:

Table 25.1 Data collection Form for video modeling

Video no: _____

The only prompt, which is used, is the video presentation. After *Bryan* has watched the video he is instructed, "Let's do the same".

Data collection

✔ = Correct response
x = Incorrect response
p = Prompt used (only video)
0 = No response

Date	Trials									Comments

i. *Delaying start/premature stop.* By delaying the start of the video or ending it before it is over, less of the video is shown. When the amount of the video is gradually decreased, the learner sees less of the video. This procedure is maintained if the learner continues to use the target behavior successfully. At a certain point, the video can be stopped entirely.
ii. *Error correction.* This procedure can be used if a learner continues to make mistakes with certain parts of the target behavior. Only the particular scene where the mistake has been occurring is played for the learner to re-watch and practice.
iii. *Scene fading.* This technique involves gradually removing scenes or parts of the task from the video that the learner has mastered.

Finally, a list of suggested useful resources appears below:
- A Module on Video Modeling from the National Professional Center on Autism Spectrum Disorder https://autismpdc.fpg.unc.edu/new-afirm-module-video-modeling.
- Video Modeling. Association for Science in Autism Treatment (ASAT): https://asatonline.org/for-parents/learn-more-about-specific-treatments/applied-behavior-analysis-aba/aba-techniques/video-modeling/
- How to Create Video Models:
  - http://www.autisminternetmodules.org

- https://afirm.fpg.unc.edu/video-modeling/
- http://home.edweb.net/practical-application-using-video-models-students-autism/
- Apps of Professionally Designed Video Models:
  - Going Places
  - Everyday Skills
  - Responding Social Skills
- Apps for Creating Video Models:
  - AutisMate 365
  - VideoTote
  - iModeling
  - iMovie
  - Pinnacle Studio
  - ReelDirector
  - Visual Impact

Conclusion

Video modeling is an evidence-based teaching strategy that may help students with ASD and other neurodevelopmental disorders develop or improve several communication and socialization skills when implemented systematically. Video modeling interventions may be more cost-efficient for teachers, because they could use the strategy not only with the target student, but also with other students who display similar skill deficits.

This approach has been so favorable to researchers, clinicians, teachers or parents, because (a) videos are broadly used by neurotypical children for leisure and educational purposes and therefore they are perceived as socially acceptable forms of support; (b) visual support can be very effective for learners who face difficulties in processing print materials or verbal instructions; (c) changes in behavior can be produced in a remarkably short period of time, after just a few video-only presentations; (d) video recording of a model's actions could reduce the cost of live models employed in training programs; or (e) videos can be recorded in a variety of real-world environments and then be successfully presented in a training set. Video modeling is not only a promising intervention strategy for students with disabilities, but it is also a practical tool that may be well-suited to the school setting (Wilson, 2013).

References

Akmanoğlu, N., & Pektaş-Karabekir, E. (2020). The effectiveness of video prompting in teaching children with autism the skill of drawing a six-part person. *Journal of Developmental and Physical Disabilities, 32*, 617–631. DOI: 10.1007/s10882-019-09709-w.

Alzyoudi, M., Sartawi, A., & Almuhiri, O. (2014). The impact of video modeling on improving social skills in children with autism. *Journal of the American Academy of Special Education Professionals*, 219–230. DOI: 10.1111/1467-8578.12057.

Bachmeyer, M.H., Piazza, C.C., Fredrick, L.D., Reed, G.K., Rivas, K.D., & Kadey, H.J. (2009). Functional analysis and treatment of multiply controlled inappropriate mealtime behavior. *Journal of Applied Behavior Analysis, 42*(3), 641–658. DOI: 10.1901/jaba.2009.42-641.

Baldwin, J.D., & Baldwin, J.D. (1986). *Behavior principles in everyday life*. Englewood Cliffs, NJ: Prentice-Hall.

Bandura, A. (1986). *Social foundations of thought and action. A social cognitive theory*. Englewood Cliffs: Prentice-Hall.

Bennett, K. D., Gutierrez, A., & Honsberger, T. (2013). A comparison of video prompting with and without voice-over narration on the clerical skills of adolescents with autism. *Research in Autism Spectrum Disorders*, 7, 1273–1281. DOI: 10.1016/j.rasd.2013.07.013.

Bilias-Lolis, E., Bray, M., & Howell, M. (2017). Exploring public self-consciousness as an unconsidered behavioral change pathway to video self-modeling: implications for school practice. *School Psychology Forum: Research in Practice*, 11(2), 63–75.

Buggey, T. (2005). Video self-modeling applications with students with autism spectrum disorder in a small private school setting. *Focus on Autism and Other Developmental Disabilities*, 20, 52–63. DOI:10.1177/10883576050200010501.

Buggey, T. (2012). Effectiveness of video self-modeling to promote social initiations by 3-yearolds with autism spectrum disorders. *Focus on Autism and Other Developmental Disabilities*, 27(2), 102–110. DOI:10.1177/1088357612441826.

Burton, C. E., Anderson, D. H., Prater, M. A., & Dyches, T. T. (2013). Video self-modeling on an iPad to teach functional math skills to adolescents with autism and intellectual disability. *Focus on Autism and Other Developmental Disabilities*, 28(2), 67–77. DOI: 10.1177/1088357613478829.

Cannella-Malone, H., Fleming, C., Chung, Y., Wheeler, G. M., Basbagill, A. R., & Singh, A. H. (2011). Teaching daily living skills to seven individuals with severe intellectual disabilities: A comparison of video prompting to video modeling. *Journal of Positive Behavior Interventions*, 13, 144–153. DOI: 10.1177/1098300710366593.

Cardon, T., Wangsgard, N., & Dobson, N. (2019). Video modeling using classroom peers as models to increase social communication skills in children with ASD in an integrated preschool. *Education and Treatment of Children* 42(4), 515–536. DOI: 10.1353/etc.2019.0024.

Catania, A.C. (1998). *Learning*. (4th ed.). Upper Saddle River, NJ: Prentice-Hall.

Catania, C. N., Almeida, D., Liu-Constant, B., & DiGennaro Reed, F. D. (2009). Video modeling to training staff to implement discrete trial instruction. *Journal of Applied Behavior Analysis*, 42, 387–392. DOI: 10.1901/jaba.2009.42-387.

Chance, P. (1999). *Learning and behavior*. Pacific Grove: Brooks/Cole.

Charlop-Christy, M.H., & Daneshvar, S. (2003). Using video modeling to teach perspective taking to children with autism. *Journal of Positive Behavior Interventions*, 5, 12–21. DOI: 10.1177/10983007030050010101.

Charlop, M. H., & Milstein, J.P. (1989). Teaching autistic children conversational speech using video modeling. *Journal of Applied Behavior Analysis*, 22(3), 275–285. DOI: 10.1901/jaba.1989.22-275.

Charlop, M.H., Dennis, B., Carpenter, M.H., Greenberg, A.L. (2010). Teaching socially expressive behaviors to children with autism through video modeling. *Education and Treatment of Children*, 33(3), 371–393. DOI: 10.1353/etc.0.0104.

Cihak, D.F., & Bowlin, T. (2009). Using video modeling via handheld computers to improve geometry skills for high school students with learning disabilities. *Journal of Special Education Technology*, 24(4), 17–29. DOI: 10.1177/016264340902400402.

Cihak, D., Fahrenkrog, C., Ayres, K.M., & Smith, C. (2010). The use of video modeling via a video iPod and a system of least prompts to improve transitional behaviors for students with autism spectrum disorders in the general education classroom. *Journal of Positive Behavior Interventions*, 12(2), 103–115.

Cihak, D.F., Smith, C.C., Cornett, A., & Coleman, M.B. (2012). The use of video modeling with the Picture Exchange Communication System to increase independent communicative initiations in preschoolers with autism and developmental delays. *Focus on Autism and Other Developmental Disabilities*, 27(1), 3–11. DOI: 10.1177/1088357611428426.

Collier-Meek, M. A., Fallon, L. M., Johnson, A. H., Sanetti, L. M. H., & Del Campo, M. A. (2012). Constructing self-modeling videos: Procedures and technology. *Psychology in the Schools*, 49, 3–14. DOI:10.1002/pits.20614.

Delfs, C., & Campbell, J. M. (2010). A quantitative synthesis of developmental disability research: The impact of functional assessment methodology on treatment effectiveness. *Behavior Analyst Today*, 11(1), 4–19. DOI: 10.1037/h0100685.

Dowrick, P. W. (2012). Self-modeling: Expanding the theories of learning. *Psychology in the Schools*, 49(1), 30–41. DOI:10.1002/pits.20613.

Edwards, N.M & Lambros, K.M. (2018). Video self-modeling as a reading fluency intervention for dual language learners with disabilities. *Contemporary School Psychology*, 22, 468–478. DOI: 10.1007/s40688-018-0207-9.

Emerson, E. (2001). *Challenging behavior: Analysis and intervention in people with intellectual disabilities* (2nd Ed.). Cambridge: Cambridge University Press.

Emerson, E. (2003). Prevalence of psychiatric disorders in children and adolescents with and without intellectual disability. *Journal of Intellectual Disability Research, 47*, 51–58. DOI: 10.1046/j.1365-2788.2003.00464.x.

Ezzeddine, E.W., DeBar, R.M., Reeve, S.A., & Townsend, D.B (2020). Using video modeling to teach play comments to dyads with ASD. *Journal of Applied Behavior Analysis, 53*(2), 767–781. DOI: 10.1002/jaba.621.

Gardner, S., & Wolfe, P. (2013). Use of video modeling and video prompting interventions for teaching daily living skills to individuals with autism spectrum disorders: A review. *Research & Practice for Persons with Severe Disabilities, 38*(2), 73–87. DOI: 10.2511/027494813807714555.

Gelbar, N. W., Anderson, C., McCarthy, S., & Buggey, T. (2012). Video self-modeling as an intervention strategy for individuals with autism spectrum disorders. *Psychology in the Schools, 49*(1), 15–22. DOI:10.1002/pits.20628.

Green, V.A., Prior, T., Smart, E., Boelema, T., Drysdale, H., Harcourt, S., Roche, L., & Waddington, H. (2017). The use of individualized video modeling to enhance positive peer interactions in three preschool children. *Education & Treatment of Children, 40*(3), 353–378. DOI: 10.1353/etc.2017.0015.

Greer, R.D. (2002). *Designing teaching strategies. An applied behavior analysis systems approach.* San Diego: Academic Press.

Hart, J. E., & Whalon, K. J. (2012). Using video self-modeling via ipads to increase academic responding of an adolescent with autism spectrum disorder and intellectual disability. *Education and Training in Autism and Developmental Disabilities, 47*(4), 438–446.

Harvey, S.T., Boer, D., Meyer, L.H., Evans, I.M. (2009). Updating a meta-analysis of intervention research with challenging behavior: Treatment validity and standards of practice. *Journal of Intellectual & Developmental Disability, 34*(1), 67–80. DOI: 10.1080/13668250802690922.

Hitchcock, C.H., Dowrick, P.W., & Prater, M.A. (2003). Video self-modeling intervention in school-based settings: A review. *Remedial and Special Education, 24*(1), 36–45. DOI: 10.1177/07419325030 2400104

Hughes, E.M. (2019). Point of view video modeling to teach simplifying fractions to middle school students with mathematical learning disabilities. *Learning Disabilities: A Contemporary Journal, 17*(1), 41–57.

Hwang, B., & Hughes, C. (2000). The effects of social interactive training on early social communicative skills of children with autism. *Journal of Autism and Developmental Disorders, 30*, 331–343. DOI: 10.1023/A:1005579317085.

Jowett, E.L., Moore, D.W., & Anderson, A. (2012). Using an iPad-based video modeling package to teach numeracy skills to a child with an autism spectrum disorder. *Developmental Neurorehabilitation, 15*(4), 304–312.

Individuals with Disabilities Education Act, 20 U.S.C. § 1400 (2004).

Kellems, R.O., & Edwards, S. (2015). Using video modeling and video prompting to teach core academic content to students with learning disabilities. *Preventing School Failure*, 1–8. DOI: 10.1080/1045988X.2015.1067875.

Koegel, R.L., Koegel, L.K., & Carter, C.M. (1999). Pivotal teaching interactions for children with autism. *School Psychology Review, 28*, 576–594. DOI: 10.1080/02796015.1999.12085986.

Kocaoz, O.E., Little, M.E., Gallup, J. (2019). Impact of video modeling combined with Skillstreaming teaching procedures on the social interaction skills of middle school-aged children with ASD. *Education and Training in Autism and Developmental Disabilities*, 2019, *54*(3), 237–248.

Krantz, P.J., & McClannahan, L.E. (1993). Teaching children with autism to initiate to peers: Effects of a script-fading procedure. *Journal of Applied Behavior Analysis, 26*, 121–132. DOI: 10.1901/jaba.1993.26-121.

Kwolek, H.A., Bray, M., DeLeyer-Tiarks, J., Gammie, L., & Root, M.M. (2019). Video self-modeling: Research to practice for school psychologists. *Communique, 47*(8), 4–8.

Lang, R., Shogren, K. A., Machalicek, W., Rispoli, M., O'Reilly, M., Baker, S., & Regester, A. (2009). Video self-modeling to teach classroom rules to two students with Asperger's. *Research in Autism Spectrum Disorders, 3*, 483–488. DOI: 10.1016/j.rasd.2008.10.001.

Lee, S., & Odom, S.L. (1996). The relationship between stereotypic behavior and peer social interaction for children with severe disabilities. *Journal of Association of Severely Handicapped, 21*, 88–95.

Leslie, J.C., & O'Reilly, M.F. (1999). *Behavior analysis. Foundations and applications to psychology.* Amsterdam: Harwood.

Luiselli, J. K. (2015). Performance management and staff preparation. In F. D. Reed & D. D. Reed (Eds.), *Bridging the gap between science and practice in autism service delivery*. New York: Springer.

Luiselli, J., Bass, J.D., & Whitcomb, S.A. (2010). Teaching applied behavior analysis knowledge competencies to direct-care service providers: outcome assessment and social validation of a training program. *Behavior Modification, 34*(5), 403–14. DOI: 10.1177/0145445510383526.

Macpherson, K., Charlop, M.H., & Miltenberger, C.A. (2015). Using portable video modeling technology to increase the compliment behaviors of children with autism during athletic group play. *Journal of Autism and Developmental Disorders, 45* (12), 3836–45. DOI: 10.1007/s10803-014-2072-3.

Manente, C. J., Maraventano, J. C., LaRue, R. H., Delmolino, L., & Sloan, D. (2010). Effective behavioral intervention for adults on the autism spectrum: best practices in functional assessment and treatment development. *Behavior Analyst Today, 11*(1), 36–48. DOI: 10.1037/h0100687.

Markey, P.T., & Miller, M.L. (2015). Introducing an information-seeking skill in a school library to students with autism spectrum disorder: using video modeling and least-to-most prompts. *School Library Research, 18*, 1–31.

Mason, R.A., Rispoli, M., Ganz, J.B., Boles, M.B., & Orr, K. (2012). Effects of video modeling on communicative social skills of college students with Asperger syndrome. *Developmental Neurorehabilitation, 15*(6), 425–434. DOI: 10.3109/17518423.2012.704530.

Mason, R.A., Davis, H.S., Boles, M.B., & Goodwyn, F. (2013). Efficacy of point-of-view video modeling: A meta-analysis. *Remedial and Special Education, 34*(6), 333–345. DOI: 10.1177/0741932513486298.

Matson, J., & Minshawi, N. (2007). Functional assessment of challenging behavior: Toward a strategy for applied settings. *Research in Developmental Disabilities, 28*(4), 353–361. DOI: 10.1016/j.ridd.2006.01.005.

Matson, J.L., & Nebel-Schwalm, M. (2007). Assessing challenging behaviors in children with autism spectrum disorders: A review. *Research in Developmental Disabilities, 28*, 567–579. DOI: 10.1016/j.ridd.2006.08.001.

Matson, J. L., & Wilkins, J. (2009). Factors associated with the questions about behavior function for functional assessment of low and high rate challenging behaviors in adults with intellectual disability. *Behavior Modification, 33*(2), 207–219. DOI: 10.1177/0145445508320342.

Miltenberger, R.G. (2015). *Behavior modification. Principles and procedures* (6th Ed.). Pacific Grove: Brooks/Cole.

Moore, J. W., & Fisher, W. W. (2007). The effects of videotape modeling on staff acquisition of functional analysis methodology. *Journal of Applied Behavior Analysis, 40*, 197–202. DOI: 10.1901/jaba.2007.24-06.

Morlock, L., Reynolds, J.L., Fisher, S., & Comer, R.J. (2015). Video modeling and word identification in adolescents with Autism Spectrum Disorder. *Child Language Teaching and Therapy, 31*(1), 101–111. DOI: 10.1177/0265659013517573.

Murphy, G.H., Beadle-Brown, J., Wing, L., Gould, J., Shah, A., & Holmes, N. (2005). Chronicity of challenging behaviors in people with severe intellectual disabilities and/or autism: A total population sample. *Journal of Autism and Developmental Disorders, 35*, 267–280. DOI: 10.1007/s10803-005-5030-2.

Nikopoulos, C. K., & Keenan, M. (2003). Promoting social initiation in children with autism using video modeling. *Behavioral Interventions, 18*(2), 87–108. DOI: 10.1002/bin.129

Nikopoulos, C.K., & Keenan, M. (2006). *Video modelling and behaviour analysis: A guide for teaching social skills to children with autism*. Jessica Kingsley Publishers.

Nikopoulos, C.K & Panagiotopoulou, I.E. (2015) Video self-modeling for reducing vocal stereotypy in children with autism spectrum disorder (ASD). *European Journal of Behavior Analysis, 16*(2), 322–337, DOI: 10.1080/15021149.2015.1094886.

Ohtake, Y., Kawaib, M., Takeuchic, A., & Utsumid, K. (2013). Effects of video self-modeling interventions on reducing task avoidance behaviors of students with autism spectrum disorders. *International Journal of Disability, Development and Education, 60*(3), 225–241. DOI:10.1080/1034912X.2013.812186.

Pierce, K. & Schreibman, L. (1995). Increasing complex social behaviors in children with autism: Effects of peer-implemented pivotal response training. *Journal of Applied Behavior Analysis, 28*, 285–295. DOI: 10.1901/jaba.1995.28-285.

Plavnick, J.B., Kaid, T., & MacFarland, M.C. (2015). Effects of a school-based social skills training program for adolescents with autism spectrum disorder and intellectual disability. *Journal of Autism and Developmental Disorders, 45*(9), 2674–90. DOI: 10.1007/s10803-015-2434-5.

Plavnick, J.B., Sam, A.M., Hume, K., & Odom, S.L. (2013). Effects of video-based croup instruction for adolescents with autism spectrum disorder. *Exceptional Children, 80*(1), 67–83. DOI: 10.1177/001440291308000103.

Qureshi, H. (1994). The size of the problem. In E. Emerson, P. McGill & J. Mansell (Eds.) *Severe learning disabilities and challenging behaviours: designing high quality services*. London: Chapman & Hall.

Rogers, S.J. (2000). Interventions that facilitate socialization in children with autism. *Journal of Autism and Developmental Disorders, 30*, 399–409. DOI: 10.1023/a:1005543321840.

Rosales, R., Gongola, L., & Homlitas, C. (2015). An evaluation of video modeling with embedded instructions to teach implementation of stimulus preference assessments. *Journal of Applied Behavior Analysis, 48*, 209–214. DOI: 10.1002/jaba.174.

Ross, A.O. (1981). *Child behavior therapy. Principles, procedures, and empirical basis*. USA: John Wiley.

Rudy, N.A., Betz, A.M., Malone, E., Henry, J.E., & Chong, I.M. (2014). Effects of video modeling on teaching bids for joint attention to children with autism. *Behavioral Interventions, 29*, 269–285. DOI: 10.1002/bin.1398.

Sadler, K.M. (2019). Video self-modeling and functional behavior assessment to modify aggressive behaviors in students with autism spectrum disorder and intellectual disabilities. *Education and Training in Autism and Developmental Disabilities, 54*(4), 406–419.

Sam, A. M., Odom, S. L., Tomaszewski, B., Perkins, Y., & Cox, A. W. (2021). Employing evidence-based practices for children with autism in elementary schools. *Journal of Autism and Developmental Disorders, 51*, 2308–2323. DOI: 10.1007/s10803-020-04706-x

Schreibman, L., Whalen, C., & Stahmer, A.C. (2000). The use of video priming to reduce disruptive transition behavior in children with autism. *Journal of Positive Behavior Interventions, 2*, 3–11. DOI: 10.1177/109830070000200102.

Shane, H. C., & Albert, P. D. (2008). Electronic screen media for persons with autism spectrum disorders: Results of a survey. *Journal of Autism and Developmental Disorders, 38*, 1499–1508. DOI:10.1007/s10803-007-0527-5.

Sherer, M., Pierce, K. L., Paredes, S., Kisacky, K. L., Ingersoll, B., & Schreibman, L. (2001). Enhancing conversational skills in children with autism via video technology. Which is better, "self" or "other" as a model? *Behavior Modification, 25*(1), 140–158. DOI: 10.1177/0145445501251008.

Shipley-Benamou, R., Lutzker, J. R., & Taubman, M. (2002). Teaching daily living skills to children with autism through instructional video modeling. *Journal of Positive Behavior Interventions, 4*(3), 166–177. DOI: 10.1177/10983007020040030501

Sigafoos, J., O'Reilly, M., Cannella, H., Upadhyaya, M., Edrisinha, C., Lancioni, G.E., Hundley, A., Andrews, A., Garver, C., & Young, D. (2005). Computer-presented video prompting for teaching microwave oven use to three adults with developmental disabilities. *Journal of Behavioral Education, 14*(3), 189–201. DOI: 10.2307/41824353.

Simpson, A., Langone, J., & Ayres, K.M. (2004). Embedded video and computer based instruction to improve social skills for students with autism. *Education and Training in Developmental Disabilities, 39*(3), 240–252.

Stahmer, A.C. (1995). Teaching symbolic play skills to children with autism using pivotal response training. *Journal of Autism and Developmental Disorders, 25*, 123–141. DOI: 10.1007/BF02178500.

Stokes, J., Cameron, M., Dorsey, M., & Fleming, E. (2004). Task analysis, correspondence training, and general case instruction for teaching personal hygiene skills. *Behavioral Interventions, 19*, 121–135. DOI: 10.1002/bin.153.

Taber-Doughty, T., Miller, B., Shurr, J., & Wiles, B. (2013). Portable and accessible video modeling: teaching a series of novel skills within school and community settings. *Education and Training in Autism and Developmental Disabilities, 2013, 48*(2), 147–163.

Tereshko, L., MacDonald, R., & Ahearn, W. H. (2010). Strategies for teaching children with autism to imitate response chains using video modeling. *Research in Autism Spectrum Disorders, 4*(3), 479–489. DOI: 10.1016/j.rasd.2009.11.005.

Thorp, D.M., Stahmer, A.C., & Schreibman, L. (1995). Effects of sociodramatic play training on children with autism. *Journal of Autism and Developmental Disorders, 25*, 265–282. DOI: 10.1007/BF02179288.

Tsui, G.H.H., & Rutherford, M.D. (2014). Video self-modeling is an effective intervention for an adult with autism. *Case Reports in Neurological Medicine*, 425897, 6 page. DOI: 10.1155/2014/425897.

Vladescu, J. C., Carroll, R., Paden, A., & Kodak, T. M. (2012). The effects of video modeling with voiceover instruction on accurate implementation of discrete trial instruction. *Journal of Applied Behavior Analysis, 45*, 419–423. DOI: 10.1901/jaba.2012.45-419.

Wang, H-T., & Koyama, T. (2014). An analysis and review of the literature and a three-tier video modeling intervention model. *Research in Autism Spectrum Disorders, 8*, 746–758. DOI: 10.1016/j.rasd.2014.03.010.

Wang, S-Y., Cui, Y., & Parrila, R. (2011). Examining the effectiveness of peer-mediated and video-modeling social skills interventions for children with autism spectrum disorders: A meta-analysis in single-case research using HLM. *Research in Autism Spectrum Disorders, 5,* 562–569. DOI: 10.1016/j.rasd.2010.06.023.

Wilson, K.P. (2013). Incorporating video modeling into a school-based intervention for students with autism spectrum disorders. *Language Speech and Hearing Services in Schools, 44*(1), 105–117. DOI: 10.1044/0161-1461.

Wu, S., Gadke, D.L., & Stratton, K.K. (2018). Using video self-modeling as a small group reading fluency intervention for elementary school students. *Journal of Applied School Psychology, 34*(4), 297–315. DOI: 10.1080/15377903.2018.1443984.

Yakubova, G., Hughes, E.M., & Hornberger, E. (2015). Video-based intervention in teaching fraction problem-solving to students with autism spectrum disorder. *Journal of Autism & Developmental Disorders, 45,* 2865–2875. DOI: 10.1007/s10803-015-2449-y.

Yakubova, G., Hughes, E.M., & Shinaberry, M. (2016). Learning with Technology: Video modeling with concrete-representational-abstract sequencing for students with Autism Spectrum Disorder. *Journal of Autism & Developmental Disorders, 46,* 2349–2362. DOI 10.1007/s10803-016-2768-7.

26
INCLUSION OF CHILDREN WITH PHYSICAL RESTRICTIONS IN OUT-OF-THE-CLASSROOM ACTIVITIES

Karin Bertills*

Introduction

School is an arena for learning and interaction. Current inclusion legislation and policies are striving towards free, equitable, and quality education for all as envisioned in the UN Sustainable Development Goals 2030. Inclusive mainstream schooling has become common practice in many countries, and although intentions are inclusive there is a tension between policy and practice (Wermke et al., 2020). Increasing student heterogeneity places demands on teachers to adequately differentiate their instructions to meet the needs of diverse learners (Pozas et al., 2019). A collaborative team approach, in which support is provided both to colleagues and students, has been identified as one successful factor for inclusion (Lyons et al., 2016). One barrier to inclusion is attributed to the tension between addressing educational needs while at the same time teaching for academic achievement (Jordan et al., 2010). Transitioning into secondary school means students need to adapt to a new environment with higher educational demands. This transition concurs with individual factors connected to biological changes and socio-cognitive growth (Vaz, 2010), which affect adolescents' overall autonomy (Eriksson et al., 2007), functioning, development and identity (Steinberg, 2016). Learners are diverse, and participatory gains from out-of-the-classroom activities may be more important than academic gains to students who are less successful in typically academic subjects. Activities outside the classroom mainly take place during recess and in more practical school subjects, for example Physical Education (PE). Regular physical activity in school-aged individuals with disabilities can decrease the risks of developing health-related issues connected to sedentary behaviors (e.g. overweight, diabetes, depression) (Rimmer et al., 2007). Restricted opportunities to participate in extracurricular physical activities for students with disabilities (Kang et al., 2014) make school-based PE an important context for these students to gain and share the benefits of physical activity with their peers (Block & Obrusnikova, 2007). School-based PE provides an opportunity for social interaction (Jespersen & He, 2015). Interactions that are positive, frequent, meaningful, and where equal status relationships are formed benefit not only students with disabilities but also those without (Qi & Ha,

---

* Karin.Bertills@ju.se

2012). However, school-based PE has been criticized for fostering normative values (Rekaa et al., 2019) and traditional views of physical ability and "a fit body" (Fitzgerald, 2012), which makes inclusion in this environment challenging. A large body of research about inclusion in school-based PE practices has concluded that successful inclusion is largely dependent on teacher attitudes towards inclusion (Hutzler et al., 2019; Qi & Ha, 2012). PE teachers are generally positive to inclusion but identified barriers to successful inclusion in PE are perceived competence, a lack of adapted equipment, lack of knowledge about various disabilities, and lack of skills on how to adapt and modify their teaching (Block & Obrusnikova, 2007; Tant & Watelain, 2016).

Participation

Placement in a setting of inclusive mainstream secondary school does not guarantee feelings of "being included". According to the International Classification of Functioning, Disability and Health for Children and Youth, ICF-CY (World Health Organization, 2007) the definition of participation is "Involvement in a life situation". Conceptualizing participation there are two key elements; attendance and involvement (Imms et al., 2017). There are environmental and personal dimensions of participation that facilitate or hinder a person from full participation. Physical attendance is a prerequisite for participation and concerns the frequency of attendance. Intensity, in terms of how engaged a person is while attending, is yet another element that affects perceived participation (Maxwell et al., 2018). Meaningful experiences of increased participation in leisure activities for persons with disabilities are often targeted in interventions since they are presumed to affect the future quality of life, healthy lifestyles, and emotional psychosocial well-being (Kang et al., 2014). School attendance is often, but not always, mandatory, which places demands of environmental adaptations on schools to provide opportunities for participation for persons with disabilities. These environmental aspects can be described in five dimensions, the five A's: availability, accessibility, accommodability, affordability and acceptability (Maxwell et al., 2018).

- Availability – Is attendance possible, is there a school?
- Accessibility – Is access to school facilities possible?
- Accommodability – Can adaptations be made to meet the specific needs of the child?
- Affordability – Is it worth the effort, in terms of time and money?
- Acceptability – Do values and common beliefs allow for diversity?

Providing opportunities for experiences of "full participation" can be seen as an expression of inclusion. Teachers' dual task to teach and to foster their students to prepare them for future life includes creating optimal environments for learning and social interaction. Current inclusion legislation and policies focus more on making learning situations available, accessible, and affordable, but there is also a need to bring in and focus more on accommodations and acceptability (Maxwell et al., 2018). The focal point is how to increase participation in physical out-of-the-classroom activities, more specifically exemplified by learning situations for students with functional restrictions in a setting of inclusive school-based Physical Education (PE). Physical functional restrictions may vary, and different barriers can be perceived independently of whether a disability is diagnosed (e.g. cerebral palsy, developmental coordination disorder, spina bifida) or not (e.g., overweight, long-term health conditions such as asthma). Both environmental and personal factors act as facilitators/barriers to participation in physical activities; physical impairments may inhibit the ability or desire to be physically active. Participatory gains rather than perceived health benefits motivate the attendance in physical activity of students with physical disabilities (Shimmell et al., 2013). Limitations to physical activity reported by students with physical disabilities include physical restrictions, pain, and other people's negative attitudes (Kang et al., 2007).

Inclusion in Physical Education

Despite increasing diversity, the situation of students with disabilities is a largely overlooked issue in school-based research (Haegele & Hodge, 2017). If students with disabilities are not studied as a separate group, their voices will not be heard. Students with disability participate less in school activities (both unstructured and structured by adults) than their typically developing peers, but the type and degree of disability is not strongly related to participation (Eriksson et al., 2007). The mere fact that you have functional restrictions is a first barrier to the participation in activities outside the classroom for students with disabilities. Experienced competence is questioned by these students themselves, who reported six times less likelihood to perceive high PE-specific self-efficacy compared to their typically developing high-functioning peers at the beginning of secondary school (Bertills et al., 2018). Although physical, social, cognitive and affective educational benefits of school-based PE have been claimed (Bailey et al., 2009), a strong discourse of physical ability and performance prevails (Fitzgerald, 2012). In addition, the allocation of special educational resources is primarily directed toward typically academic subjects, and the ability of learning support assistants to facilitate inclusion in PE has been questioned, since they have not received PE-specific training (Maher, 2014). Friendship and positive peer interaction can be experienced in school-based PE, if students experience actions of encouragement, reinforcement, help and guidance (Seymour et al., 2009). Positive experiences are described by students with physical disabilities when they feel a sense of belonging, their participation is appreciated as skillful, and where they share benefits. Social isolation, when their competence is questioned and when participation is restricted are examples of negative experiences (Goodwin & Watkinson, 2000). Students with disability were more sensitive to environmental factors such as the classroom climate than their typically developing peers, which affected their perceived self-efficacy and their aptitude to participate (Bertills et al., 2018). They may need support to improve their social position (Pijl et al., 2008). Daily physical activity and adapted motor skills training during nine years of compulsory school showed not only better motor skills in students with disabilities but also improved general school performance (Ericsson, 2011). More inclusive teaching strategies include creativity to adapt methods, equipment and environment, knowledge sharing in collaborative networks, attempts to enhance social inclusion, extra attention and support when needed, and constant evaluation and revision (Pocock & Miyahara, 2018). Physical activities need to be perceived as meaningful, and although students with disabilities enjoy PE lessons they have questioned the appropriateness of activities (Coates & Vickerman, 2010). Competitive activities like relays where performance before effort is promoted and traditional team games with set rules have been shown to be exclusive (Smith, 2004). Activities like swimming, dance, and gymnastics were easier to adapt (Morley et al., 2005) but do not always carry the same status and value for students with disabilities as for example traditional team games (Coates & Vickerman, 2010). Teachers can facilitate participation by for example creating a welcoming PE environment (Haegele & Sutherland, 2015) that promotes open communication and positive interaction (Wilhelmsen et al., 2019). Other participation-enhancing actions are modification and adaptation of equipment and traditional team games and providing optional activities at appropriate skill levels (Tant & Watelain, 2016). Being offered a choice between participating either within or segregated from ordinary classroom activity may also promote PE participation (Bredahl, 2013). Concluded from research to date is that there is an on-going change (Rekaa et al., 2019), but teachers need further training on inclusive practices and differentiated teaching to appropriately accommodate students with disabilities in PE (McLennan & Thompson, 2015). Drawing on educational research about inclusion, this chapter aims to identify environmental aspects that may facilitate/hinder the participation of students with physical functional restrictions in activities outside the classroom. Dimensions of environmental aspects, the five A's (availability, accessibility, accommodability/adaptability, affordability and acceptability) (Maxwell et al., 2018) will be used to structure the findings.

Methodology

The findings from observations (Bertills et al., 2019) and focus interviews (Bertills & Björk, 2021) are framed in a setting of compulsory inclusive mainstream secondary school education. In Sweden, there is a national curriculum with knowledge requirements and a fixed set of grading criteria. The grading scale is criterion-referenced, the degree to which a student has achieved knowledge and skills in relation to knowledge requirements is to be assessed. School achievement is high-stakes in the sense that final grades from compulsory school determine access to further education. All subjects, academic as well as practical, are equally important and summed into a final grade mean score (The Swedish National Agency for Education, 2018). Support is to be supplied in case the student faces the risk of failing to achieve a passing grade. The knowledge requirements apply to all students, but the rule of exception may be applied when functional restrictions, due to disability or a long-term health condition, make specific requirements unattainable (Swedish Statute Book [SFS], 2010:800).

A time-sampling method was used in structured observations of 40 PE lessons. Individual, contextual, and environmental aspects of student participation and teacher actions were scored. The observer repeatedly took short visual "snapshots" of on-going activities, i.e. the target students and teachers were "caught in action". Observed actions were coded into sets of variables (e.g. proximity, interaction, engagement, type of activity, materials used, focus) constructed to be summed into frequency of observations. Student engagement was a subjective judgement of the intensity of engagement. Frequencies and intensity of student engagement were compared between groups of students with disabilities (n=23), and students with high grades (n=44) and with low grades (n=27). Level of instruction, affective tone when instructing and aligning curriculum content into teacher instructions were used as quality indicators of high/low teaching skills. Nine of the teachers (n=21) participated in focus interviews to further investigate how to best include students with disabilities in regular school-based PE. The research question is: How can the participation of students with functional restrictions be facilitated in out-of-the-classroom activities?

Results and Discussion

Strategies to Successful Inclusion of Persons with Physical Disabilities in Out-of-the-Classroom Activities

Mobility restrictions limit participation in out-of-the-classroom activities that are physical. Tag games and relays are examples of strategies used by any teacher to sharpen students' focus, concentration, attention, and engagement. However, students' diverse prerequisites in an inclusive setting require differentiated teaching. A challenge that is placed on teachers, who commonly report inadequate training as a barrier to successful inclusion. Effects of inclusion legislation and policies are limited in inclusive education when support is insufficient (Pocock & Miyahara, 2018). Competitive activities that are neither adapted nor modified to student functioning may cause negative effects on student participation and social interaction. There are environmental factors that teachers can affect and others that are out of their control. Indicators of inclusive education suggested by Lancaster (2014) include pedagogies, curriculum differentiation, teacher language and processes to communicate student progress, teacher self-efficacy, and actual classroom practice. Regarding participation as an expression of inclusion *the five A's* (availability, accessibility, accommodability, affordability, and acceptability) offer a useful strategy to map environmental aspects of inclusiveness in accordance with the ICF-CY (Maxwell et al., 2018). School obligations include the organizing of curricular activities to guarantee availability, accessibility, and affordability, whereas teachers may be in control of accommodability and acceptability issues. In a perspective of students with physical disability Table 26.1 shows an example of factors to consider in order to make participation in out-of-the-classroom possible.

Availability concerns the physical environment. School-based physical activities arranged outside the classroom may take place outdoors or may need activity-specific facilities such as swimming pools, sport arenas designed for ball- or racket sports, or facilities with music systems. Due to school location or resources such facilities may not be available.

Accessibility refers to participation in specific activities that may take place within or outside the school area. Outdoor physical activities in for example forests, or on gravel-yards, and indoor gym facilities with changing rooms and showers keep different standards for a variety of environmental reasons. Accessibility may be problematic to students with physical disabilities. Transportation, elevators, lifts, or technical aides may be required for participation in activity-specific areas or facilities.

Affordability means the least restrictive environment needs to correspond to the financial or effort cost invested in the activity. For full participation, i.e. when the two environmental dimensions of attendance and involvement (Imms et al., 2017) are attained, activities must be perceived as meaningful for the student. Out-of-the-classroom activities may require special arrangements with attributes of safety, comfort and social cohesion that cause obstacles for participation to be valuable and worthwhile (Petrenchik & King, 2011). In mutual teacher-student understanding, the planning of special solutions tailored to fit the person's abilities can create meaningful activities. Out-of-the-classroom activities, especially if they are competitive and require physical ability, may be insurmountable. For students with physical disabilities, who in

Table 26.1 The five A's applied to prerequisites for the participation of students with physical disability in out-of-the-classroom activities

	Referring to	*Example*
Availability	Is the activity offered?	Physical environment, curricular intentions, scheduling, equipment, etc. makes the activity available
Accessibility	Can you access the activity-specific facility?	Elevators, transportation, technical aides make various physical activities accessible
Affordability	Is it worth the money or energy?	Individual financial or effort investment to participate in activity is worthwhile
Accommodability/ adaptability	Is the activity adapted and/or equipment modified?	Modified equipment, alternative pathways, assistance when needed, etc. make the activity adapted to individual ability and special needs
Acceptability	Is your presence accepted by self or others?	Student diversity is considered to contribute to the activity

such conditions may experience feelings of *being a burden* (Fitzgerald, 2005; Fitzgerald & Stride, 2012), optional physical activity segregated from the class may offer opportunities to practice individually adapted training programs.

Accommodability/adaptability calls for attention since innovative solutions in contextual learning situations are key to the participation of students with physical disabilities. Support provided by school is primarily academic. As advocated by inclusive legislation and policies, communication between stakeholders is needed to also support student participation in out-of-the-classroom activities. Instructional and curricular adaptations may need to be made, as well as modification of equipment and activities. Students with disabilities participate less in school activities than their typically developing peers but more in activities structured by adults than in unstructured activities e.g. recess (Eriksson et al., 2007). Classroom placement near the exit, and prospects of leaving the classroom a few minutes earlier than typically developing peers are examples of time-providing actions that facilitate attendance in activities outside the classroom (Giangreco et al., 1997). Cooperative learning, i.e. when peers help each other in the learning process has shown promising results of increasing student engagement (Grenier et al., 2005). Appointing peers to assist when support was needed increased physical activity not only for students with physical disabilities, but also for the assisting peer (Klavina et al., 2013).

Acceptability refers to the social environment. Including students in need of special support into mainstream schooling remains a challenge for teachers and there is no key to successful inclusion. However, there are indicators of inclusive education that refer to acceptability. Teacher attitudes affect the school environment, and good teacher-student relationships affect peer to peer attitudes positively (Falkmer, 2013). Teachers need to embrace student diversity and make adjustments that relieve the student from the sole responsibility of adapting learning style to the teaching offered (Coates, 2012). Students perceived that there were lower levels of friction in classroom environments where teachers held more positive attitudes towards inclusion. They also reported such classroom environments to be more satisfactory and cohesive and less competitive and difficult (Monsen et al., 2014). Collaboration is required from teachers to problem-solve and find novel solutions that facilitate participation, and teachers need assistance to develop and implement such teaching strategies. Approaches such as *explicit teaching* and *cooperative learning* are used for successful teaching in inclusive classrooms. In *explicit teaching*, intended learning outcomes are clear to the student, achievable sub-goals are set to promote student progress, and students are continually being monitored and given feedback. In *cooperative learning* students are responsible for their own learning and work in small groups to achieve group success (Lancaster, 2014). A mastery climate with performance approach goals in out-of-the-classroom activities, i.e. emphasizing effort before competition, shows a range of positive student motivational outcomes e.g. perceived competence in sport and physical activity (Harwood et al., 2015), improved physical self-concepts (Hagger et al., 2001), and motor skills (Valentini & Rudisill, 2004). Mastery-oriented and autonomy-supportive climates have been shown to promote social inclusion in PE (Wilhelmsen et al., 2019).

Inclusion in Physical Education – Best Practice

Observations of compulsory PE lessons in year 8 of Swedish compulsory inclusive mainstream secondary school showed that students enjoy PE, and all student groups were equally highly engaged in PE, but differences were seen (Bertills et al., 2019). Students with disabilities were significantly less frequently on-task. There was also a tendency that they socialized less with peers and were more alone than their typically functioning peers, who could perform physical activities and chat with friends simultaneously. All students were generally more engaged when teachers had better teaching skills. The teachers' ability to adapt and modify activities is important and differences were seen in how teachers accommodate students. Accommodations can be described in terms of structure, complexity, and instruction, and proximity, differentiation, and efficiency.

Structure, Complexity, and Instruction

Long- and short-term planning prepares the students for up-coming activities, enables student-teacher communication to find alternative solutions beforehand, and provides the student with an opportunity to feel in control of the situation (Bertills et al., 2018). Observations showed that simple self-sustaining activities facilitate participation, i.e. activities familiar to the student with set rules and established expectations. Students with disabilities were observed more frequently and to be more engaged in whole-group formats with simple activities. The primary source of support in PE was the teacher. Compared to their peers, students with disabilities were more often seen close to the teacher, either for clarification of instructions, or because the teacher ascertained additional support by placement nearby students in need of special support. Sufficient support seemed to be inadequate in small-group formats, causing disengagement in students with physical functional restrictions (diagnosed and undiagnosed). Complex activities that contain a combination of motor skills, strategy, technique, or certain drills require more and clear instructions. Visual cues, white-board drawings, signs, pictures, demonstrations by peers or teachers, complement oral or written instructions.

Proximity, Differentiation, and Efficiency

Differentiation affects student engagement. Significantly more instructions were used in conditions where teachers were observed to show high teaching skills, implying that lessons were more complex. The setting was also provided with established routines well known and accepted by the students. Relevant teaching materials were set-up strategically to ascertain lesson flow. More equipment was available, balls and music for practicing specific drills were for example more commonly used. Health-related content was more often integrated with physical practice, which increased engagement in students with disabilities. Lessons were more efficiently organized offering a choice of activities, utilizing gym space effectively. Alternative pathways to avoid queues, activities modified to challenge students at different levels of performance, and quick transitions between activities were successful strategies used to maintain high student activity and engagement levels. Students were observed to be more on-task, practicing skills, since they knew the purpose of the activity, what was expected from them, where to go, and what to do. PE teachers' closer communicative proximity to all students implies that these teachers moved about in the classroom to supply students with performance-enhancing feedback and support to encourage and empower individuals' engagement. The more commonly occurring whole-group formats indicate that teachers prefer this structure to ensure high student activity when assistance is inadequate; teacher assistance is rare in PE. Simple self-sustaining activities in whole-group formats may be used as a solution for teachers to allocate themselves as resources into activities in smaller groups aiming at practicing more advanced exercises, e.g., motor skills or certain drills.

Focus interviews of PE teachers in a setting of compulsory inclusive mainstream secondary school that is *available* and *accessible* to all students (Bertills & Björk, 2021) support that PE teachers generally are positive toward inclusion (Tant & Watelain, 2016). Differences are revealed in how systematically PE teachers work with inclusion. The students' willingness to participate in physical activities seems to be crucial to how far teachers are willing to adapt their teaching. If the students themselves want to participate, i.e. they are willing to invest effort, time, and energy into participating in specific activities (*affordable*), and suggest how adaptations can be applied, teachers are also willing to make required adjustments. On the other hand, teachers who embrace diversity relieve the students from the sole responsibility of adapting to the PE that is being taught by actively and continuously communicating with the student. Targeting inclusion, teacher, student, parents, personal assistant, and other professionals work collaboratively to plan activities that are adapted to increase participation (*adaptable*). A mastery climate, emphasizing effort before competition, promotes pedagogical and social inclusion (Wilhelmsen et al., 2019) in which diversity is valued as an asset (*acceptable*).

The following quote is one teacher's example of how to include a girl, aged 13, with profound physical restrictions (cerebral palsy) in ordinary PE class:

*I read in her blog that she is in pain after PE class (laughter), so then I talked to her to work out a plan on how we should work. As a result she now has a different lesson content. Now she swims in one of the lessons and in the other I structure the lesson so that she can participate on her own capacity level half of the lesson, and the other half she works on her training program that she composed herself. So, she has adapted lessons and works together with her personal assistant, but she is within the same facilities as her peers, and I keep myself informed all the time. I ask her how she is doing, and I ask the assistant. The other day we played volleyball, and I, well I **try** to make her feel included. She used balloons instead of volleyballs and she hit that balloon in different ways. And I asked the assistant "What's in it for her?", really, because I mean, I don't feel like this exercise did any good, and the assistant replied, "It makes her feel that she can participate". There may not be any physical benefits, but the fact that she attends and that she is involved, well then it feels like … (silence)… it works!*

Conclusion

This chapter highlights for teachers in an inclusive classroom various teaching strategies and environmental aspects to consider that facilitate the participation and interaction of students with disabilities in out-of-the-classroom activities. Furthermore, quantitative time-sampling methods to observe student engagement in relation to teaching behaviours in regular school-based out-of-the-classroom activities give novel information about successful inclusive teaching practices. The five A's (availability, accessibility, accommodability, affordability, and acceptability) can be used to map and explore environmental aspects of inclusion.

References

Bailey, R., Armour, K., Kirk, D., Jess, M., Pickup, I., & Sandford, R. (2009). The educational benefits claimed for physical education and school sport: An academic review. *Research Papers in Education*, *24*(1), 1–27. https://doi.org/10.1080/02671520701809817

Bertills, K., & Björk, M. (2021). Facilitating Physical Education for optimal participation of students with disabilities. (manuscript).

Bertills, K., Granlund, M., Dahlström, Ö., & Augustine, L. (2018). Relationships between physical education (PE) teaching and student self-efficacy, aptitude to participate in PE and functional skills: With a special focus on students with disabilities. *Physical Education and Sport Pedagogy*, *23*(4), 387–401. https://doi.org/10.1080/17408989.2018.1441394

Bertills, K., Granlund, M., & Augustine, L. (2019). Inclusive teaching skills and student engagement in physical education. *Frontiers in Education*, *4*(74). https://doi.org/10.3389/feduc.2019.00074

Block, M. E., & Obrusnikova, I. (2007). Inclusion in physical education: A review of the literature from 1995–2005. *Adapted Physical Activity Quarterly*, *24*(2), 103–124.

Bredahl, A.-M. (2013). Sitting and watching the others being active: The experienced difficulties in PE when having a disability. *Adapted Physical Activity Quarterly 30*(1), 40–58.

Coates, J. K. (2012). Teaching inclusively: Are secondary physical education student teachers sufficiently prepared to teach in inclusive environments? *Physical Education and Sport Pedagogy, 17*(4), 349–365. https://doi.org/10.1080/17408989.2011.582487

Coates, J. K., & Vickerman, P. (2010). Empowering children with special educational needs to speak up: Experiences of inclusive physical education. *Disability and Rehabilitation, 32*(18), 1517–1526. https://doi.org/10.3109/09638288.2010.497037

Ericsson, I. (2011). Effects of increased physical activity on motor skills and marks in physical education: An intervention study in school years 1 through 9 in Sweden. *Physical Education & Sport Pedagogy, 16*(3), 313–329.

Eriksson, L., Welander, J., & Granlund, M. (2007). Participation in everyday school activities for children with and without disabilities. *Journal of Developmental and Physical Disabilities, 19*(5), 485–502. https://doi.org/10.1007/s10882-007-9065-5

Falkmer, M. (2013). *From Eye to Us Prerequisites for and levels of participation in mainstream school of persons with Autism Spectrum Conditions* [Dissertation, Jönköping University, School of Education and Communication, Swedish Institute for Disability Research].

Fitzgerald, H. (2005). Still feeling like a spare piece of luggage? Embodied experiences of (dis)ability in physical education and school sport. *Physical Education and Sport Pedagogy, 10*(1), 41–59. https://doi.org/10.1080/1740898042000334908

Fitzgerald, H. (2012). 'Drawing' on disabled students' experiences of physical education and stakeholder responses. *Sport, Education and Society, 17*(4), 443–462. https://doi.org/10.1080/13573322.2011.609290

Fitzgerald, H., & Stride, A. (2012, 2012/09/01). Stories about physical education from young people with disabilities. *International Journal of Disability, Development and Education, 59*(3), 283–293. https://doi.org/10.1080/1034912X.2012.697743

Giangreco, M. F., Edelman, S. W., Luiselli, T. E., & MacFarland, S. Z. C. (1997). Helping or hovering? Effects of instructional assistant proximity on students with disabilities. *Exceptional Children, 64*(1), 7–18. https://doi.org/10.1177/001440299706400101

Goodwin, D. L., & Watkinson, E. J. (2000). Inclusive physical education from the perspective of students with physical disabilities. *Adapted Physical Activity Quarterly, 17*(2), 144–160.

Grenier, M., Dyson, B., & Yeaton, P. (2005, 2005/08/01). Cooperative learning that includes students with disabilities. *Journal of Physical Education, Recreation & Dance, 76*(6), 29–35. https://doi.org/10.1080/07303084.2005.10608264

Haegele, J. A., & Hodge, S. (2017). Current practices and future directions in reporting disability in school-based physical education research. *Quest, 69*(1), 113–124. https://doi.org/10.1080/00336297.2016.1165122

Haegele, J. A., & Sutherland, S. (2015). Perspectives of students with disabilities toward physical education: A qualitative inquiry review. *Quest, 67*(3), 255–273. https://doi.org/10.1080/00336297.2015.1050118

Hagger, M. S., Chatzisarantis, N., & Biddle, S. J. H. (2001, 2001/01/01). The influence of self-efficacy and past behaviour on the physical activity intentions of young people. *Journal of Sports Sciences, 19*(9), 711–725. https://doi.org/10.1080/02640410152475847

Harwood, C. G., Keegan, R. J., Smith, J. M. J., & Raine, A. S. (2015). A systematic review of the intrapersonal correlates of motivational climate perceptions in sport and physical activity. *Psychology of Sport and Exercise, 18*, 9–25. https://doi.org/10.1016/j.psychsport.2014.11.005

Hutzler, Y., Meier, S., Reuker, S., & Zitomer, M. (2019, 2019/05/04). Attitudes and self-efficacy of physical education teachers toward inclusion of children with disabilities: A narrative review of international literature. *Physical Education and Sport Pedagogy, 24*(3), 249–266. https://doi.org/10.1080/17408989.2019.1571183

Imms, C., Granlund, M., Wilson, P. H., Steenbergen, B., Rosenbaum, P. L., & Gordon, A. M. (2017). Participation, both a means and an end: A conceptual analysis of processes and outcomes in childhood disability. *Developmental Medicine and Child Neurology, 59*(1), 16–25. https://doi.org/10.1111/dmcn.13237

Jespersen, E., & He, J. (2015). The embodied nature of autistic learning: Implications for physical education. *Physical Culture and Sport: Studies and Research, 65*(1), 63–73. https://doi.org/10.1515/pcssr-2015-0012

Jordan, A., Glenn, C., & McGhie-Richmond, D. (2010). The Supporting Effective Teaching (SET) project: The relationship of inclusive teaching practices to teachers' beliefs about disability and ability, and about their roles as teachers. *Teaching and Teacher Education: An International Journal of Research and Studies, 26*(2), 259–266. https://doi.org/10.1016/j.tate.2009.03.005

Kang, L.-J., Palisano, R. J., King, G. A., & Chiarello, L. A. (2014). A multidimensional model of optimal participation of children with physical disabilities. *Disability and Rehabilitation*, *36*(20), 1735–1741. https://doi.org/10.3109/09638288.2013.863392

Kang, M., Zhu, W., Ragan, B. G., & Frogley, M. (2007, 2015-02-03). Exercise barrier severity and perseverance of active youth with physical disabilities. *Rehabilitation Psychology*, *52*(2), 170–176. https://doi.org/10.1037/0090-5550.52.2.170

Klavina, A., Jerlinder, K. K., Hammar, L., & Soulie, T. (2013). Cooperative-oriented learning in inclusive physical education. *European Journal of Special Needs Education*, *29*(2), 1–16.

Lancaster, J. (2014). School and classroom indicators of inclusive education. In C. Forlin & T. Loreman (Eds.), *Measuring Inclusive Education* (Vol. 3, pp. 227–245). Emerald Group Publishing Ltd. https://doi.org/10.1108/s1479-363620140000003027

Lyons, W. E., Thompson, S. A., & Timmons, V. (2016, 2016/08/02). 'We are inclusive. We are a team. Let's just do it': Commitment, collective efficacy, and agency in four inclusive schools. *International Journal of Inclusive Education*, *20*(8), 889–907. https://doi.org/10.1080/13603116.2015.1122841

Maher, A. J. (2014). Special educational needs in mainstream secondary school physical education: Learning support assistants have their say. *Sport, Education and Society*, 1–17. https://doi.org/10.1080/13573322.2014.905464

Maxwell, G., Granlund, M., & Augustine, L. (2018). Inclusion through participation: Understanding participation in the international classification of functioning, disability, and health as a methodological research tool for investigating inclusion. *Frontiers In Education*, *3*(41). https://doi.org/10.3389/feduc.2018.00041

McLennan, N., & Thompson, J. (2015). *Quality physical education (QPE): Guidelines for policy makers*. UNESCO publishing. http://unesdoc.unesco.org/images/0023/002311/231101E.pdf

Monsen, J. J., Ewing, D. L., & Kwoka, M. (2014, 2014/04/01). Teachers' attitudes towards inclusion, perceived adequacy of support and classroom learning environment. *Learning Environments Research*, *17*(1), 113–126. https://doi.org/10.1007/s10984-013-9144-8

Morley, D., Bailey, R., Tan, J., & Cooke, B. (2005). Inclusive physical education: teachers' views of including pupils with special educational needs and/or disabilities in physical education. *European Physical Education Review*, *11*(1), 84–107. https://doi.org/10.1177/1356336X05049826

Petrenchik, T. M., & King, G. A. (2011). Pathways to positive development: Childhood participation in everyday places and activities. In *Mental health promotion, prevention, and intervention in children and youth: A guiding framework for occupational therapy*, 71–94.

Pijl, S., Frostad, P., & Flem, A. (2008). The social position of pupils with special needs in regular schools. *Scandinavian Journal of Educational Research*, *52*(4), 387–405. https://doi.org/10.1080/00313830802184558

Pocock, T., & Miyahara, M. (2018, 2018/07/03). Inclusion of students with disability in physical education: A qualitative meta-analysis. *International Journal of Inclusive Education*, *22*(7), 751–766. https://doi.org/10.1080/13603116.2017.1412508

Pozas, M., Letzel, V., & Schneider, C. (2019). Teachers and differentiated instruction: Exploring differentiation practices to address student diversity. *Journal of research in special educational needs*, *20*(3), 217–230. https://doi.org/10.1111/1471-3802.12481

Qi, J., & Ha, A. S. (2012). Inclusion in physical education: A review of literature [Article]. *International Journal of Disability, Development & Education*, *59*(3), 257–281. https://doi.org/10.1080/1034912X.2012.697737

Rekaa, H., Hanisch, H., & Ytterhus, B. (2019). Inclusion in physical education: Teacher attitudes and student experiences. A systematic review. *International Journal of Disability, Development and Education*, *66*(1), 36–55. https://doi.org/10.1080/1034912X.2018.1435852

Rimmer, J. H., Rowland, J. L., & Yamaki, K. (2007). Obesity and secondary conditions in adolescents with disabilities: Addressing the needs of an underserved population. *Journal of Adolescent Health*, *41*(3), 224–229. https://doi.org/10.1016/j.jadohealth.2007.05.005

Seymour, H., Reid, G., & Bloom, G. A. (2009). Friendship in inclusive physical education. *Adapted Physical Activity Quarterly*, *26*(3), 201–219. https://doi.org/10.1123/apaq.26.3.201

Shimmell, L. J., Gorter, J. W., Jackson, D., Wright, M., & Galuppi, B. (2013, 2013/11/01). "It's the Participation that Motivates Him": Physical activity experiences of youth with cerebral palsy and their parents. *Physical & Occupational Therapy in Pediatrics*, *33*(4), 405–420. https://doi.org/10.3109/01942638.2013.791916

Smith, A. (2004). The inclusion of pupils with special educational needs in secondary school physical education. *Physical Education and Sport Pedagogy*, *9*(1), 37–54. https://doi.org/10.1080/1740898042000208115

Steinberg, L. D. (2016). *Adolescence* (11th ed.). New York : McGraw-Hill.
Swedish Statute Book [SFS]. (2010:800). *Skollagen [Education Act]*. Utbildningsdepartementet.
Tant, M., & Watelain, E. (2016, 11//). Forty years later, a systematic literature review on inclusion in physical education (1975–2015): A teacher perspective. *Educational Research Review, 19*, 1–17. https://doi.org/10.1016/j.edurev.2016.04.002
The Swedish National Agency for Education. (2018). *Curriculum for the compulsory school, preschool class and school-age educare.* Retrieved April 30 from https://www.skolverket.se/publikationer?id=3984
Valentini, N. C., & Rudisill, M. E. (2004). An inclusive mastery climate intervention and the motor skill development of children with and without disabilities. *Adapted Physical Activity Quarterly, 21*(4), 330–347. https://doi.org/10.1123/apaq.21.4.330
Vaz, S. M. A. (2010). *Factors affecting student adjustment as they transition from primary to secondary school: A longitudinal investigation* [Dissertation, Curtin University of Technology, School of Occupational Therapy and Social Work, Centre for Research into Disability and Society].
Wermke, W., Höstfält, G., Krauskopf, K., & Adams Lyngbäck, L. (2020). 'A school for all' in the policy and practice nexus: Comparing 'doing inclusion' in different contexts. Introduction to the special issue. *Nordic Journal of Studies in Educational Policy: A School for all, 6*(1), 1–6. https://doi.org/10.1080/20020317.2020.1743105
Wilhelmsen, T., Sørensen, M., & Seippel, Ø. (2019). Motivational pathways to social and pedagogical inclusion in physical education. *Adapted Physical Activity Quarterly, 36*(1), 19–41. https://login.e.bibl.liu.se/login?url=https://search.ebscohost.com/login.aspx?direct=true&AuthType=ip,uid&db=edsnor&AN=edsnor.11250.2595920&site=eds-live&scope=site
World Health Organization. (2007). *International classification of functioning, disability and health: Children and youth version.* World Health Organization.

27
GETTING THE WORD OUT
How Teachers Can Recognise and Support Children with Developmental Language Disorder in an Inclusive Classroom

Duana Quigley* and Martine Smith

Introduction

Think back to the last time you were in a primary school classroom. What did you hear? What did you say? What were the daily routines and regular activities of the classroom you observed or participated in? Make a quick note of the first things that come to mind.

Now consider how many of your notes relate to children **talking**, such as answering a question, contributing to a class discussion, asking for help, sharing stories, using new vocabulary, engaging in group work with peers, giving advice or break time banter. How many of your reflections relate to children **understanding someone else who has spoken**, such as following a teacher's instructions, grasping new curricular material and concepts, comprehending the words in textbooks and stories, or laughing at a joke shared by a peer?

Language ability comprises our ability to talk and express ourselves (i.e., expressive language skills) and our capacity to understand what others are saying (i.e., receptive language skills). A pupil's competence in receptive and expressive language is integral to all components of school curricula and mediates their capacity to participate in multiple activities at home and in their community (Deary et al., 2007; Nagy & Townsend, 2012). Bowen and Snow (2017, p. 175) consider our language ability to be "our most human characteristic" and describe language as:

> *a learned code that lets us think about our world; generate, remember, share and understand information; appreciate knowledge, ideas, literature, science and the arts; enjoy leisure pastimes; express political and religious convictions, humour and emotion; reveal our personalities and needs; and survive in today's society.*

This chapter aims to *get the word out* about a common hidden disability – developmental language disorder (DLD). It summarises key theories on how children learn language and outlines the nature of DLD and the potential impact of language difficulties in a classroom environment. The chapter draws on the International Classification of Functioning, Disability and Health (ICF; World Health Organization [WHO], 2001), promoting an inclusive, holistic perspective

---

* QUIGLED1@tcd.ie

DOI: 10.4324/9781003266068-32

that considers multi-faceted interactions between child-internal and external factors. The ICF supports the reader in considering the impact of DLD on a child's ability to understand and construct words and sentences to communicate with others (i.e., internal body functions and structures), alongside the possible impact on a child's functioning and participation at home, school, and in society (i.e., external activities, participation and environmental factors) (Dempsey & Skarakis-Doyle, 2010). We conclude by outlining ways of recognising and supporting pupils with DLD to help them reach their communicative potential in an inclusive classroom.

Language Development

Although learning to speak and understand words and sentences expressed by others is considered a major life achievement, for many children the acquisition of language occurs effortlessly (Reilly et al., 2015). Theories of how children develop language skills typically refer to two distinct forces at work: nature and nurture. On the nature end of the continuum, the nativist perspective, led by Chomksy, suggests that all children have an innate species-specific capacity for language acquisition (Chomsky, 1965). As children are exposed to their native language, a process of parameter setting begins, whereby rules specific to the child's language are set (Bohannon & Bonvillian, 2009), thus accounting for the extraordinary diversity of languages that exist. On the opposite end of the continuum, the empiricist perspective, advocated by prominent researchers such as Skinner, suggests that children learn language primarily through processes of imitating the adults around them (Foster, 1996) and subsequent reinforcement from those adults (Bohannon & Bonvillian, 2009). Bridging the nature-nurture divide, the social interactionist perspective and the emergentist perspective lie somewhat in the middle of this theoretical continuum. The social interactionist approach recognises the role of language input and the social environment. It emphasises the social-communicative functions that language plays and the importance of explicitly mediated interactions with more knowledgeable conversational partners as essential development mechanisms (Justice & Kaderavek, 2002; Tomasello, 2003). An emergentist approach, described as a fusion of the social interactionist and nativist perspectives (Hollich et al., 2000), views language as "*a product of the interaction of the inside learning capabilities of the child and the outside language environment*" (Poll, 2011, p. 581). Children are born with a genetic predisposition to attend to particular kinds of behaviours, and they are immersed in social worlds where the unwritten 'rules' of communication and social interaction play out. Current prevailing theories of language acquisition recognise the need for **both** nature (e.g., human capacity to develop language skills, cognitive abilities, neurological competencies, perceptual and motor skills) and nurture (e.g., environmental experiences and exposures to adequate quantity and quality of communicative interactions) (Ambridge & Lieven, 2011; Tomasello, 2003).

When there is an impairment or fragility in the essential foundations that nature or nurture provide, children may struggle to develop language skills in line with age expectations. Language difficulties may affect receptive and expressive domains or impact one or all aspects of language. A child may experience difficulties with semantics (e.g., poor vocabulary knowledge), morphology (e.g., confusing grammatical markers such as past tense), syntax (e.g., problems constructing longer or complex sentences), auditory processing (e.g., struggling to remember all the details of a spoken instruction), narrative (e.g., difficulty in telling a coherent story) and/or pragmatics (e.g., not understanding the rules of conversation or humour and jokes) (Bishop, 2016; Reilly et al., 2015). Each element of language is highly integrated and co-dependent (Dollaghan, 2011). For example, a pupil who has difficulty understanding concepts of size (e.g., semantic concept of 'narrow') may also have difficulty understanding syntactic structures or idioms containing those concepts (e.g., "put the book back on the *narrow* shelf"; "the giant had a *narrow escape*"). However, it is difficult to predict what the precise presentation of a pupil with language difficulties in the classroom may be; each child is unique and each profile of language strengths and challenges is individual.

Developmental Language Disorder (DLD): The Hidden Disability

Given the many different presentations that can occur, it is not surprising that many different terms are used to describe a child who presents with language difficulties (Bishop, 2016). Speech Language and Communication Needs (SLCN) is an umbrella term describing children with a wide range of communication difficulties, and it is estimated that up to one-in-ten children may have some level of SLCN (Law et al., 2001). Sometimes, SLCN occurs in association with disabilities such as Intellectual Impairment or autism spectrum disorder. However, the term 'Developmental Language Disorder' (DLD) describes a particular group of children, those *"who are likely to have language problems enduring into middle childhood and beyond, with a significant impact on everyday social interactions or educational progress"*, where there is no known associated condition that might 'explain' the language difficulties (Bishop et al., 2017, p. 3). Estimates suggest that 7% of children may present with DLD (Law et al., 2000). On this basis, two children in any class of 30 pupils may experience language difficulties severe enough to impede their academic progress or social interactions (Norbury et al., 2016). Aligned with the theories of language acquisition described above, environmental factors such as socio-economic status have been recognised as risk factors for DLD (Bishop et al., 2017). The prevalence of language difficulties amongst children growing up in areas of low SES has been found to be as high as 55.6% (almost eight times higher than the prevalence reported in the general population) (Locke et al., 2002).

The prevalence rate of DLD is similar to that of dyslexia, and current estimates suggest it is up to five times more prevalent than autism. Nonetheless, many professionals and families appear to be far less familiar with DLD as a construct (Kamhi, 2011). This led Bishop (2017) to describe DLD as *"the most common childhood condition you've never heard of"*. Low levels of awareness of DLD may stem from the fact that it is often a hidden disability with no overt physical or acoustic characteristics (McGregor, 2020). Children who are struggling to master speech sounds (i.e., those who have articulation difficulties) may be easily identified, but behaviours arising from language difficulties are often misinterpreted as shyness, laziness or disinterest (Komesidou & Summy, 2020). In addition, children's problems understanding others can be masked by subtle scaffolding provided by communication partners through gestures, pictures, or context (e.g., pupil puts the book on the same shelf as their classmate and so it goes unnoticed that they don't understand the concept of 'narrow'). Children with expressive language difficulties can blend in and remain undetected if they sound the same as their peers, manage to communicate their basic, everyday wants and needs effortlessly, make similar errors in their expressive language to those heard from younger children or those learning English as an additional language, or if there are limited opportunities for their language skills to be heard, expanded or evaluated (Archibald, 2019). In many countries standardised assessments of pupils' written language competencies are administered annually. However, pupils' verbal language abilities are frequently not routinely assessed or monitored, thus reinforcing the challenges in identifying children with DLD. For instance, the average pupil utterance in the literacy hour in the UK was three words (English et al., 2002). Consequently, this hidden disability may only become noticeable over time or as a result of its broader and extensive impact on other areas of a pupil's performance and functioning.

Impact of DLD

In addition to the direct impact of DLD on children's ability to express themselves and understand what others have said, the effects may be all encompassing, negatively impacting upon academic achievement and associated with social, emotional and behavioural problems that can have pervasive consequences (Lindsay et al., 2002; Myers & Botting, 2008; Paradice et al., 2007; Stothard et al., 1998; Tomblin & Nippold, 2014). Stothard et al. (1998) completed a 10-year follow up of a cohort of children identified with DLD at 5:6 years of age, and 70% of participants continued to have difficulties at age 15 years. Likewise, children who scored −1.25 standard deviations below the mean on a language assessment (i.e., mild/moderate difficulties) in preschool continued to be at risk of poor long-term outcomes when followed up at 16 years of age (Tomblin & Nippold, 2014). The long-term impact is confirmed by a recent study which showed children presenting with DLD at age seven years still performed poorly on formal language and literacy assessments when followed up at age 24 years (Botting, 2020). In relation to academic achievement, as outlined above, language mediates learning of curricular subjects and a pupil's ability to verbally contribute to all aspects of the curriculum; therefore reduced language ability can negatively affect educational outcomes (Alexander, 2008). The potential negative effect of poor verbal learning, auditory memory and language processing difficulties commonly reported in DLD extends beyond English and other languages to other subject areas (Donlan et al., 2007; Kopenen et al., 2006; Matson & Cline, 2012).

DLD is also associated with literacy difficulties, compounding the possible negative impact on academic achievement (Myers & Botting, 2008). It is estimated that half of children with DLD also have dyslexia or difficulties decoding words (McArthur et al., 2000). Snow's (2020) 'language house' in the Science of the Language and Reading (SOLAR) provides a useful analogy to highlight the links between language development and literacy development. In the same way that a well-constructed house requires solid foundations, Snow (2020) argues that literacy success is dependent on solid foundations of robust receptive and expressive language skills that emerge from a supportive social and emotional context for language use. Akin to building walls of a house on sound foundations to effectively support a sheltering roof, the walls of Snow's language house are constructed of language and literacy environments at home and in school to firmly support social-emotional and behavioural well-being, academic success, vocational achievement and full engagement in society. Importantly, much like a house has a load-bearing wall, Snow (2020) emphasises that a classroom with a language- and literacy-rich instructional environment will sustain reciprocity between language development and literacy development, as strides in one area will promote gains in the other. There is robust evidence that if a child's language difficulties continue until the time that they are beginning to learn to read, then reading difficulties are highly likely (Bishop & Adams, 1990; Nathan et al., 2004). For instance, poor vocabulary skills have been correlated with poor reading comprehension skills, as pupils who struggle to understand the meanings of words in a text may also struggle to understand the meaning of the text as a whole (Lyons et al., 2013; Ouellette, 2006; Snow, 2002). Furthermore, as children progress through the primary and secondary school years, their vocabulary learning largely occurs through their written language experiences, so that the relationship between oral and written language skills becomes increasingly intertwined. Consequently, DLD and possible associated literacy difficulties have been demonstrated to negatively impact educational attainment (McLeod et al., 2014; Spencer et al., 2017).

From a personal and social perspective, language skills provide the means for children to establish and maintain relationships and regulate their emotions (Snow et al., 2014; Snow & Powell, 2011). As a result, children with DLD frequently score lower on measures of social competence and higher on measures of behavioural problems than their peers who have typical language development (Botting & Conti-Ramsden, 2000; Stanton-Chapman et al., 2007). From a quality of life perspective, children with DLD have been reported to score poorly relative to their peers on indicators of 'mood and emotions' and 'social exclusion and bullying'

(Ravens-Sieberer et al., 2005) and to demonstrate higher levels of peer problems and greater pro-social difficulties (Lindsay et al., 2011). As children grow older, anxiety, social phobias, and social isolation have been documented (Brinton et al., 2007; Conti-Ramsden & Botting, 2008; Voci et al., 2006). Moreover, longitudinal studies of individuals with a history of DLD have shown that, as adults, many may struggle with independent living, present with difficulties forming and sustaining relationships, have unsatisfactory employment histories, and may be more likely to experience mental health problems (Clegg, et al., 2005; Clegg et al., 2012; Whitehouse et al., 2009).

However, through early identification and the right supports, many children with DLD avert multiple possible negative trajectories and go on to achieve positive learning outcomes, well-adjusted social skills, and satisfactory life outcomes (Snowling et al., 2006). Teachers, in particular, are a key discipline for supporting school-aged children with DLD through child-focused or environment-focused approaches because of their regular contact with children, the strong relationships they build with children, their in-depth knowledge of their pupils, and the potential to integrate language enrichment into curricular objectives (Glover et al., 2015; Squires et al., 2013). The multi-dimensional nature of the International Classification of Functioning, Disability and Health (ICF) (WHO, 2001) provides a framework for teachers to help identify and support children with DLD in an inclusive classroom.

Using the ICF Framework to Identify and Support Children with DLD in the Classroom

The ICF framework (WHO, 2001) and its subsequent paediatric version, ICF–Children and Youth (ICF-CY; WHO, 2007), propose five main components that interact when a child has a disability: Body Functions and Structures (e.g., anatomical features and physiological and psychological functions), Activity and Participation (e.g., performance of tasks and involvement in social situations), and Contextual Factors (e.g., the physical, social and attitudinal environment; personal–individual traits). The ICF framework supports the conceptualisation of the nature, impact, and potential support for a pupil with DLD holistically by describing a child's level of functioning as an intricate interaction between his/her language difficulties, the unique impact and consequences for that specific child, distinct personal factors, and a child's particular environment. Rosenbaum and Gorter (2012) relate each ICF category to an "F-word": 'fitness' (body functions and structures); 'function' (activity); 'friendships' (participation); 'family' (environment); and 'fun' (personal). In addition, a sixth 'F-word' highlights the potential impact of a child's condition on his/her 'future'. The wrap-around conceptualisation of DLD through an ICF lens can help guide educators in identifying and supporting pupils with DLD in a way that will be effective in recognising and improving both their language ability and functioning in important everyday events now and into the future (Dempsey & Skarakis-Doyle, 2010; Washington, 2007; Westby, 2007). The ICF considers the effects on a child's body functions and structures (e.g., auditory memory) alongside subsequent broader impacts that any impairment may have on limiting activities (e.g., speaking out in class, telling a story to a classmate) or restricting participation (e.g., forming friendships, joining an after-school club). In addition, contextual factors are put under the spotlight such as potential barriers and facilitators in the child's environment (e.g., visual supports in the classroom to support comprehension, societal attitudes that children with DLD are immature or less intelligent) as well as personal factors (e.g., child's coping mechanisms). Importantly, the bidirectional influence of each component means it is possible that any element can impact and interact with another (Dempsey & Skarakis-Doyle, 2010). For example, impaired syntactic ability to form a question may hinder a child's ability to ask to have a turn of a classmate's game, and the inverse is also possible where a child's lack of experience engaging in such games may result in limited opportunities for peer conversations and intensify expressive language difficulties. Furthermore, it recognises that these are dynamic interactions that evolve and change over time. Consequently, a more comprehensive and systematic assessment of a pupil with DLD is promoted which enables diverse barriers to be documented and addressed, and supportive strategies, facilitators and interventions to be planned and implemented in the classroom.

Identification and Assessment of DLD in the Classroom

Through holistic consideration of each component of the ICF lens, a comprehensive and systematic assessment of language ability and its impact on functioning may include:

(i) **Specialised Language Assessments That Examine Body Functions, Body Structures and Activities**

This may entail formal, standardised assessments of a pupil's language ability by a speech and language therapist or educator to diagnose and determine the nature and severity of any language impairment. Commonly used standardised assessments include: Clinical Evaluation of Language Fundamentals-5 (CELF-5; Wiig et al., 2013); British Picture Vocabulary Scales III (BPVS; Dunn et al., 2009); Test for Auditory Comprehension of Language–4 (TACL; Carrow-Woolfolk, 2014); and Test of Language Development-Primary 4 (TLD; Newcomer & Hammill, 2008). Frequently, school-based literacy assessments will have an oral language dimension too (e.g., vocabulary scores of the Drumcondra Primary Reading Test – Revised, 2006). There have been calls for school-based universal language assessments to support the early identification of children with DLD (Adlof & Hogan, 2019; Komedidou & Summy, 2020). The above impairment-based assessments provide valuable information about a child's strengths and areas yet to develop in numerous linguistic domains. However, they are administered in a controlled, testing context and not focused on how a child uses those language skills when they are participating in daily classroom tasks or extracurricular activities (Westby & Washington, 2017). Impairment-based assessments also ignore the child's communicative environment and how this may be facilitating or hindering language ability and functioning, and so additional assessment measures that examine these factors are recommended.

(ii) **Checklists, Rating Scales, Interviews and Questionnaires That Examine Participation**

Teachers' astute classroom observations of a pupil in his/her education context are central to an assessment of the ICF component of participation. In addition, there are several assessment tools that support a broader evaluation of a child's language ability in context across numerous ICF components, including their participation in school, home and society. For example, Focus on the Outcomes of Children Under Six (FOCUS; Thomas-Stonell et al., 2010) examines a child's activity capacity and participation performance through 7-point Likert scales of 50 items. It is also available in a streamlined version of 34 items (i.e., FOCUS-34) and its reliability has been documented (Oddson et al., 2019). Other useful assessment tools that enable teachers and parents to evaluate a pupil's participation in familiar contexts include the CELF-5 Pragmatics Profile and the CELF-5 Observation Rating Scale (Wiig et al., 2013). The former scale explores social and academic communication, while the latter evaluates how a child manages classroom interactions. Both assessments can be completed with information provided by teachers.

In addition, the Pragmatic Language Observation Scale (PLOS; Newcomer & Hammill, 2009) consists of 30 items that teachers can complete to measure pupil's participation in numerous language-based classroom interactions. It is norm-referenced, thereby facilitating comparisons with peers and scores achieved on standardised assessments of language ability.

(iii) **Classroom Observation Tools That Examine Context**

Three useful assessment tools that specifically support an analysis of the communicative barriers and facilitators in a child's educational context are the Communication Supporting Classrooms Observation Tool (CSCOT) (Dockrell et al., 2015), Classroom Assessment Scoring System (CLASS) and its accompanying Language Modelling and Literacy Focus scales (Justice et al., 2008; Pianta et al., 2008); and the Classroom Practices Checklist (Quigley, 2018). The CSCOT facilitates reflection and discussion on enablers and barriers to supporting pupils' communication in the classroom, capturing good practice and providing a means to set goals for changing educator practices if necessary (Law et al., 2019). It is divided into three sections: language learning environments including opportunities for children to communicate with their peers and adults; language learning opportunities such as group work and story book engagement; and language learning interactions with adults in the classroom through for example structured conversations (Dockrell et al., 2015). Likewise, CLASS (Pianta et al., 2008) places an emphasis on optimal classroom environments and focuses on teacher-student interactions including emotional support, classroom organisation, and instructional support. The discrete Language Modelling scale that accompanies CLASS includes an evaluation of language facilitating behaviours such as asking open-ended questions, extending and recasting children's utterances and conversations, and modelling advanced vocabulary (Justice et al., 2008). The Classroom Practices Checklist (Quigley, 2018) draws on teacher expertise and empirical evidence to extend the Self Evaluation of Teacher Talk (SETT) framework published by Walsh (2006). This checklist includes 23 items that help examine the presence of communication facilitating features in the classroom environment including teacher talk, resources, actions and organisational settings.

(iv) **Other Observations and Evaluations That Examine Personal Factors**

Educators can also consider individual personal factors that may be barriers or facilitators to a child's language development (e.g., languages spoken at home, cognitive ability, temperament) (Westby & Washington, 2017). For example, dynamic assessment can determine a child's language learning potential through test-teach-retest processes (Karpov & Tzuriel, 2009). Moreover, asking a child to self-rate what they perceive may help or hinder them in their ability to express themselves and understand others may provide valuable information (Hughes et al., 2009). This has been achieved successfully with children with DLD using the Pediatric Quality of Life Inventory (PedsQL) (Varni et al., 1999) and more informally through structured arts-based activities (Thomas-Stonell et al., 2009; Roulstone et al., 2012). The Speech Participation and Activity of Children assessment tool (SPAA-C; McLeod, 2004) is intended for children with speech impairment but the child-friendly self-rating Likert scales are broad enough to provide useful and relevant information about children with DLD and their insights into their language ability (e.g., 'how do you feel when your teacher asks you a question'?).

The diverse and valuable information gleaned from the assessments above can help educators plan relevant interventions and support for an inclusive classroom.

Language Enrichment Interventions and Supports for Children with DLD in an Inclusive Classroom

Careful attention to the ICF framework can ensure interventions and supports are integrated and balanced between those that address the impairment and directly develop language skills (e.g., expand pupil's vocabulary), those that focus on compensation (e.g., use visual aids to aid pupil's comprehension), or target social language performance (e.g., facilitate pupil to communicate adequately with peers), and those that concentrate on educational achievement (e.g., support pupil's reading comprehension skills), dismantle environment barriers (e.g., alter negative societal attitudes towards children with DLD) and/or tackle policy restrictions (e.g., expand services beyond those for children with severe difficulties only) (Dempsey & Skarakis-Doyle, 2010: Westby & Washington, 2017). On a daily basis, through routine curricular objectives and activities, all teachers are "directly and intimately involved with language" and its development (Love, 2009, p.558). However, challenges to robust language enrichment in the classroom have been documented. For example, language support may be presumed to occur through literacy and curricular content objectives rather than being explicitly addressed in lesson plans (Rice, 2020). In addition, teachers may hold the communicative floor in classrooms for a much greater proportion of time than their pupils, thereby reducing opportunities for verbal participation or limiting scaffolding and extension of pupil's language contributions (Dockrell et al., 2015; Fisher, 2011; Hayes & Matusov, 2005). There are also many examples of good practice, where more explicit and direct language support is provided. Explicit language enrichment interventions in an inclusive classroom may focus on both receptive and expressive language abilities or may hone attention on a specific area of language competence such as "conversation skills (discourse and narrative), forming sentences (syntax), learning grammatical rules (morphology), inferring information, understanding figurative language and other literary devices, using pragmatic language skills, developing vocabulary (semantics), word retrieval skills" (Bowen & Snow, 2017, p. 177). Aligned with a holistic view of disability, language enrichment interventions may encompass working directly with the child to change language behaviours (i.e., child-focused approaches) or working to change the context in which the child's behaviour takes place (i.e., environment-focused approaches) (Pickstone et al., 2009), or both.

Child-Focused Language Enrichment Interventions

Child-focused approaches often address the ICF components of body functions/structures, activity and personal factors. They emphasise the active engagement of pupils in their own learning, supporting children to develop the linguistic knowledge, skills, and strategies needed to access curricular content (Wallach, 2014). For instance, a child-focused language enrichment intervention to develop vocabulary knowledge may aim to increase exposure to the target vocabulary, highlight semantic relationships with other known words, provide multiple opportunities to discuss and meaningfully engage with the meaning of a word in a variety of contexts, and scaffold opportunities to practise using the vocabulary (Beck et al., 2002). Better still, when such targeted supports are implemented universally to all pupils in an inclusive classroom, the language skills of all the children in the classroom are supported at the one time, interventions are embedded in the school curriculum, and challenges related to selection criteria or timetabling for individual sessions are avoided (Spencer et al., 2017). Providing language interventions to a whole class of pupils may avoid any potential stigma associated with a child receiving individualised specialist help, which may differentiate children from their peers and undermine their sense of belonging and well-being (Lyons & Roulstone,

2016). The recommendation for more universal classroom language interventions is especially relevant for children from low SES backgrounds considering the escalated risk and increased prevalence of DLD reported amongst this population. There are a number of organisations that aim to raise awareness of DLD and provide useful, practical resources for educators to choose from: DLDandMe (www.dldandme.org), Raising Awareness of Developmental Language Disorder (RADLD; www.radld.org), and National Association of Professionals concerned with Language Impairment in Children (NAPLIC; www.naplic.org). Table 27.1 also provides a sample of readily available child-focused language enrichment programmes for an inclusive classroom.

It is important to highlight that taking a language enrichment intervention 'off the shelf' to implement in the classroom is often insufficient for children with DLD, unless there is adequate professional development, coaching, and safeguarded time to maximise its potential benefits (Joyce & Showers, 2002). For instance, drawing on manualised interventions provided through consultancy has been reported as less effective than direct intervention by SLTs or SLT assistants, mainly due to inconsistencies in regular and systematic delivery (McCartney et al., 2011). However, a randomised controlled trial demonstrated that indirect language intervention by *trained and supported* learning support assistants was as effective as direct intervention by an SLT for expressive language difficulties (Boyle et al., 2009). Positive relationships have been reported between teachers' attendance at professional development workshops and quality of language instruction (Justice et al., 2008). The importance of combining training with manualised interventions, to be delivered consistently and regularly, was stressed by Botting et al. (2016) who reported gains for school-aged children when both were provided. Appropriate training and fidelity to the programme were also pinpointed as key factors in positive outcomes of school-based language enrichment interventions in a recent systematic review (Sedgwick & Stothard, 2018). The former conclusions emphasise the benefits of inter-professional practice between SLTs and teachers in an inclusive classroom (McCartney et al., 2010). Transfer of knowledge and expertise between teachers and SLTs can lead to more creative solutions, a more holistic approach to addressing children's language needs, and an increased sense of personal and professional support (Korth et al., 2010; Quigley, 2018; Wright & Kresner, 2004; Wright et al., 2008), for child-focused and environment-focused language enrichment interventions (Law et al., 2019).

Environment-Focused Language Enrichment Interventions

In parallel to child-focused interventions, and regularly implemented in tandem, environment-focused interventions seek to address the ICF components of participation and environment. Principles of an inclusive classroom characterise this approach, such as acceptance and promotion of equality, diversity, care and responsiveness (Black-Hawkins, 2010; Danforth & Naraian, 2015). Interventions may be broad and general, aiming to be facilitative, such as increasing awareness and promoting positive attitudes towards pupils with DLD (Howe, 2008). More specifically, environment-focused language enrichment interventions in the educational context frequently focus on fine-tuning the everyday practices of teachers and educational support staff and the resources available to the child (Pickstone et al., 2009). In the evaluation of over 100 classrooms in the UK based on the CSCOT tool described earlier, structured language learning environments were evident in many classrooms (e.g., learning areas, classroom displays, educational resources), but opportunities for language learning to scaffold and advance children's language abilities were frequently areas for development (e.g., interactive book reading, structured conversations, small and inclusive group work) (Dockrell et al., 2015).

Table 27.1 Examples of child-focused language enrichment interventions

Name of intervention	Author	Language domain targeted
Time to Talk: A Programme to Develop Oral and Social Interaction Skills for Reception and Key Stage One (https://www.sociallyspeaking.co.nz/product/time-to-talk/)	Schroeder	Expressive Language Social Communication
Language Therapy Manual (https://pureportal.strath.ac.uk/en/publications/language-therapy-manual)	McCartney	Expressive Language Receptive Language
Talk Boost (https://ican.org.uk/training-licensing/i-can-programmes/talk-boost-ks1/)	ICAN & The Communication Trust UK	Expressive Language Receptive Language
Narrative Enrichment Programme (https://www.city.ac.uk/people/academics/victoria-joffe#profile=publications)	Joffe	Vocabulary
Vocabulary Enrichment Programme (https://www.city.ac.uk/people/academics/victoria-joffe#profile=publications)	Joffe	Vocabulary
Talk Time (https://curriculumonline.ie/getmedia/7238be9f-5c5e-416b-a494-41eac6cb1505/OL_TalkTime_1.pdf?ext=.pdf)	Quigley	Vocabulary
Word Aware: Teaching vocabulary across the day, across the curriculum (http://thinkingtalking.co.uk/word-aware/)	Parsons & Branagan	Vocabulary
Supporting new word learning in secondary schools website (https://adolescentvocabulary.wordpress.com/)	Spencer	Vocabulary
Word Generation (https://www.serpinstitute.org/wordgen-elementary)	Snow & Donovan	Vocabulary
Dialogic Reading to Teach Morphologic Structures (https://journals.sagepub.com/doi/10.1177/1525740114525657)	Maul & Ambler	Morphology

Therefore, environment-focused language enrichment interventions often focus on creating classroom environments that support language development to be "organized so that they afford high quality language learning experiences, where children have regular and structured opportunities to develop their language through their interactions with both peers and adults, and adults talk with children in ways that enhance receptive and expressive language skills" (Dockrell et al., 2015, p. 273). Practical advice and recommended strategies for environment-focused language enrichment interventions are shared in the useful "*Classroom Adjustments: DLD*" podcast, including: give students more time to process and answer questions; consider seating configurations and background noise; and aid comprehension through concrete examples, visual/written prompts, repeating key information, breaking down concepts and relating them to students' experience (https://podcasts.apple.com/au/podcast/classroom-adjustments-developmental-language-disorder/id1452120534). Further suggestions are for teachers to create natural contexts for high-quality verbal input, enhance adult responsiveness and develop understanding through expansions and recasts, create opportunities for pupils to produce language development targets, and employ strategies such as open-ended and challenging questions (Dickinson et al., 2014; Dockrell et al., 2010; Ellis Weismer & Robertson, 2006; Huttenlocher et al., 2010). Two useful resources for an inclusive classroom are the *Supporting Spoken Language in the Classroom* knowledge exchange programme, which promotes a whole school approach to language awareness, use, support and development (SSLIC; https://www.ucl.ac.uk/ioe/departments-centres/centres/centre-for-inclusive-education/supporting-spoken-language-in-theclassroom) and the '*Communication Friendly Environments*' programme that provides ideas and strategies to support language development and involves assistance from a 'coach' to help develop an action plan for the classroom (Crosskey & Vance, 2011).

Conclusion

We hope this chapter has helped to *get the word out* about a common hidden disability, DLD, including its potential multi-faceted impact on pupils in a classroom environment. We have put forward recommendations for a holistic, multi-dimensional assessment of language ability that draws on all components of the WHO (2001) ICF framework and described suggestions for interventions that are both child- and environment-focused. We have stressed the importance of inter-professional practice between SLTs and teachers to support pupils with DLD. We are confident that this wrap-around perspective of DLD in an inclusive classroom will ensure the individual needs of pupils are recognised and supported, and they will be assisted to reach their potential in school, home and society.

References

Adlof, S., & Hogan, T. (2019). If we don't look, we won't see: Measuring language development to inform literacy instruction. *Policy Insights from the Behavioural and Brain Sciences*, 6(2), 210–217. https://doi.org/10.1177/2372732219839075

Alexander, R. (2008). *Towards Dialogic Teaching: Rethinking Classroom Talk*. York: Dialagos.

Ambridge, B., & Lieven, E. (2011). *Child Language Acquisition: Contrasting Theoretical Approaches*. Cambridge: Cambridge University Press.

Archibald, L. (2019). *Why is DLD Hard to Recognize?* [online]. Available from: https://dldandme.org/recognizing-dld/. Accessed 28/10/2020.

Beck, I., McKeown, M., & Kucan, L. (2002). *Bringing Words to Life: Robust Vocabulary Instruction*. London: The Guilford Press.

Bishop, D. (2016). CATALISE: A multinational and multidisciplinary Delphi consensus study. Identifying language impairments in children. *PLOS ONE*, 11(7), 1–26. https://doi.org/10.1371/journal.pone.0168066

Bishop, D. (2017). *DLD: A Deeper Understanding with Dorothy Bishop*. [online]. Available from: http://blog.ican.org.uk/2017/10/dorothy-bishop-dld-understanding/. Accessed 28/10/2020.

Bishop, D., & Adams, C. (1990). A prospective study of the relationship between specific language impairment, phonological disorders and reading retardation. *Journal of Child Psychology & Psychiatry*, 31(7), 1027–1050. https://doi.org/10.1111/j.1469-7610.1990.tb00844.x

Bishop, D., Snowling, M., Thompson, P., & Greenhalgh, T. (2017). Phase 2 of CATALISE: A multinational and multidisciplinary Delphi consensus study of problems with language development: Terminology. *Journal of Child Psychology and Psychiatry*. https://doi.org/10.1111/jcpp.12721

Black-Hawkins, K. (2010). The framework for participation: A research tool for exploring the relationship between achievement and inclusion in schools. *International Journal of Research and Method in Education*, 33, 21–40. https://doi.org/10.1080/17437271003597907

Bohannon, J., & Bonvillian, J. (2009). Theoretical approaches to language acquisition. In J. Berko Gleason & N. Bernstein Ratner (Eds.), *The Development of Language* (7th ed., pp. 227–284). London: Pearson.

Botting, N. (2020). Language, literacy and cognitive skills of young adults with developmental language disorder (DLD). *International Journal of Language and Communication Disorders*, 55(2), 255–265. https://doi.org/10.1111/1460-6984.12518

Botting, N., & Conti-Ramsden, G. (2000). Social and behavioural difficulties in children with language impairment. *Child Language Teaching & Therapy*, 16(2), 105–120. https://doi.org/10.1177/026565900001600201

Botting, N., Gaynor, M., Tucker, K., & Orchard-Lisle, G. (2016). The importance of natural change in planning school-based intervention for children with Developmental Language Impairment (DLI). *Child Language Teaching and Therapy*, 32(2), 159–177. https://doi.org/10.1177/0265659015595444

Bowen, C., & Snow, P. (2017). *Making Sense of Interventions for Children with Developmental Disorders*. Croydon, UK: J&R Press Ltd.

Boyle, J., McCartney, E., O' Hare, A, & Forbes, J. (2009). Direct versus indirect and individual versus group modes of language therapy for children with primary language impairment: Principal outcomes from a randomised controlled trial and economic evaluation. *International Journal of Language and Communication Disorders*, 44(3), 826–846. https://doi.org/10.1080/13682820802371848

Brinton, B., Spackman, M., Fujiki, M., & Ricks, J. (2007). What should Chris say? The ability of children with specific language impairment to recognise the need to dissemble emotions in social situations. *Journal of Speech, Language, and Hearing Research*, 50(4), 798–811. https://doi.org/10.1044/1092-4388(2007/055)

Carrow-Woolfolk, E. (2014). *TACL-4: Test for Auditory Comprehension of Language-Fourth Edition*. London: Pearson.

Chomsky, N. (1965). *Aspects of a Theory of Syntax*. Cambridge, MA: MIT Press.

Clegg, J., Hollis, C., Mawhood, L., & Rutter, M. (2005). Developmental language disorders: A follow-up in later adult life. Cognitive, language and psychosocial outcomes. *Journal of Child Psychology & Psychiatry*, 46(2), 128–149. https://doi.org/10.1111/j.1469-7610.2004.00342.x

Clegg, J., Ansorge, L., Stackhouse, J., Donlan, C., Nippold, M. A., & Reichle, J. (2012). Developmental communication impairments in adults: Outcomes and life experiences of adults and their parents. *Language, Speech & Hearing Services in Schools*, 43(4), 521–535. https://doi.org/10.1044/0161-1461(2012/11-0068)

Conti-Ramsden, G., & Botting, N. (2008). Emotional health in adolescents with and without a history of specific language impairment. *Journal of Child Psychology & Psychiatry*, 49(3), 516–525. https://doi.org/10.1111/j.1469-7610.2007.01858.x

Crosskey, L., & Vance, M. (2011). Training teachers to support pupils' listening in class: An evaluation using pupil questionnaires. *Child Language Teaching and Therapy*, 27(1), 165–182. https://doi.org/10.1177/0265659010397249

Danforth, S., & Naraian, S. (2015). This new field of inclusive education: Beginning a dialogue on conceptual foundations. *Intellectual and Developmental Disabilities*, 53(1), 70–85. https://doi.org/10.1352/1934-9556-53.1.70

Deary, I., Strand, S., Smith, P., & Fernandes, C. (2007). Intelligence and educational achievement. *Intelligence*, 35(1), 13–21. https://doi.org/10.1016/j.intell.2006.02.001

Dempsey, L., & Skarakis-Doyle, E. (2010). Developmental language impairment through the lens of the ICF: An integrated account of children's functioning. *Journal of Communication Disorders*, 43, 424–437. https://doi.org/ 10.1016/j.jcomdis.2010.05.004

Dickinson, D., Hofer, K., Barnes, E., & Grifenhagen, J. (2014). Examining teachers' language in head start classrooms from a systemic linguistics approach. *Early Childhood Research Quarterly*, 29(3), 231–244. https://doi.org/10.1016/j.ecresq.2014.02.006

Dockrell, J., Stuart, M., & King, D. (2010). Supporting early oral language skills for English language learners in inner city preschool provision. *British Journal of Educational Psychology*, 80(4), 497–515. https://doi.org/10.1348/000709910X493080

Dockrell, J., Bakopoulou, I., Law, J., Spencer, S., & Lindsay, G. (2015). Capturing communication supporting classrooms: The development of a tool and feasibility study. *Child Language Teaching and Therapy*, 31(3), 271–286. https://doi.org/10.1177/0265659015572165

Dollaghan, C. (2011). Taxometric analyses of specific language impairment in 6-year-old children. *Journal of Speech, Language, and Hearing Research*, 54, 1361–1371. https://doi.org/10.1044/1092-4388(2011/10-0187)

Donlan, C., Cowan, R., Newton, E., & Lloyd, D. (2007). The role of language in mathematical development: Evidence from children from specific language impairments. *Cognition*, 103(1), 23–33. https://doi.org/10.1016/j.cognition.2006.02.007

Dunn, L., Dunn, L., & Styles. (2009). *British Picture Vocabulary Scale (BPVS-III)* (3rd ed.). Windsor: NFER-Nelson.

Ellis Weismer, S., & Robertson, S. (2006). Focussed stimulation approach to language intervention. In R. McCauley & M. Fey (Eds.), *Treatment in Language Disorders in Children: Conventional and Controversial Approaches* (pp. 175–202). Baltimore: Brookes.

English, E., Hargreaves, L., & Hislam, J. (2002). Pedagogical dilemmas in the national literacy strategy: Primary teachers' perceptions, reflections and classroom behaviour. *Cambridge Journal of Education*, 32(1), 9–26. https://doi.org/10.1080/03057640220116409

Fisher, A. (2011). Creating an articulate classroom: Examining pre-service teachers' experiences of talk. *Language & Education: An International Journal*, 25(1), 33–47. https://doi.org/10.1080/09500782.2010.519775

Foster, S. (1996). *The Communicative Competence of Young Children*. London: Longman.

Glover, A., McCormack, J., & Smith Tamaray, M. (2015). Collaboration between teachers and speech and language therapists: Services for primary school children with speech, language and communication needs. *Child Language Teaching and Therapy*, 31(3), 363–382. https://doi.org/10.1177/0265659015603779

Hayes, R., & Matusov, E. (2005). Designing for dialogue in place of teacher talk and student silence. *Culture & Psychology*, 11(3), 339–357.

Hollich, G., Hirsh-Pasek, K., & Golinkoff, R. M. (2000). II. The emergentist coalition model. *Monographs of the Society for Research in Child Development*, 65(3), 17. https://doi.org/10.1111/1540-5834.00092

Howe, T. (2008). The ICF Contextual Factors related to speech-language pathology. *International Journal of Speech-Language Pathology*, 10(1–2), 27–37. https://doi.org/10.1080/14417040701774824

Hughes, D., Turkstra, L., & Wulfeck, B. (2009). Parent and self-ratings of executive function in adolescents with specific language impairment. *International Journal of Language and Communication Disorders*, 44(6), 901–916. https://doi.org/10.1080/13682820802425693

Huttenlocher, J., Waterfall, H., Vasilyeva, M., Vevea, J., & Hedges, L. (2010). Sources of variability in children's language growth. *Cognitive Psychology*, 61(4), 343–365. https://doi.org/10.1016/j.cogpsych.2010.08.002

Joyce, B., & Showers, B. (2002). *Student Achievement Through Staff Development* (3rd ed.). Alexandria: Association for Supervision and Curriculum Development.

Justice, L., & Kaderavek, L. (2002). Using shared book reading to promote emergent literacy. *Teaching Exceptional Children*, 34(1), 8–13. https://doi.org/10.1177/004005990203400401

Justice, L., Mashburn, A., Harare, B., & Pianta, R. (2008). Quality of language and literacy instruction in preschool classrooms serving at-risk pupils. *Early Childhood Research Quarterly*, 23(1), 51–68. https://doi.org/10.1016/j.ecresq.2007.09.004

Kamhi, A. (2011). Balancing certainty and uncertainty in clinical practice. *Language, Speech and Hearing Services in Schools*, 42(1), 88–93. https://doi.org/10.1044/0161-1461(2009/09-0034)

Karpov, Y., & Tzuriel, D. (2009). Dynamic assessment: Progress, problems, and prospects. *Journal of Cognitive Education and Psychology*, 8(2), 228–237. https://doi.org/10.1891/1945-8959.8.3.228

Komedidou, R., & Summy, R. (2020). Developmental language disorder: Considerations for implementing school-based screenings. *Clinical Psychology and Special Education*, 9(3), 34–47. https://doi.org/10.17759/cpse.2020090303

Korth, B., Sharp, A., & Culatta, B. (2010). Classroom modeling of supplemental literacy instruction. *Communication Disorders Quarterly*, 31(2), 113–127. https://doi.org/10.1177/1525740109333239

Kopenen, T., Mononen, R., Rasanen, P., & Ahonen, T. (2006). Basic numeracy and literacy in children with specific language impairment: Heterogeneity and connections to language. *Journal of Speech, Language, and Hearing Research*, 49(1), 58–73. https://doi.org/10.1044/1092-4388(2006/005).

Law, J. (2000). Intervention for Children with Communication Difficulties. In L. J. A. Parkinson, & R. Tamhne (Eds.), *Communication Difficulties in Childhood: A Practical Guide* (pp. 135–152). Oxon: Radcliffe Medical Press Ltd.

Law, J., Lindsay, G., Peacey, N., Gascoigne, M., Soloff, N., Radford, J., & Band, S. (2001). Facilitating communication between education and health services: The provision for children with speech and language needs. *British Journal of Special Education*, 28(3), 133–234. https://doi.org/10.1111/1467-8527.00212

Law, J., Tulip, J., Stringer, H., Cockerill, M., & Dockrell, J. (2019). Teachers observing classroom communication: An application of the communicating supporting classroom observation tool for children aged 4–7 years. *Child Language Teaching and Therapy*, 35(3), 203–220. https://doi.org/10.1177/0265659019869792

Lindsay, G., Soloff, N., Law, J., Band, S., Peacey, N., Gascoigne, M., & Radford, J. (2002). Speech and language therapy services to education in England and Wales. *International Journal of Language & Communication Disorders*, 37(3), 273–288. https://doi.org/10.1080/13682820210137204

Lindsay, G., Dockrell, J., Law, J., & Roulstone, S. (2011). *Better Communication Research Programme.* second Interim Report. London: Department for Education.

Locke, A., Ginsborg, J., & Peers, I. (2002). Development and disadvantage: Implications for the early years and beyond. *International Journal of Language & Communication Disorders*, 37(1), 3–15. https://doi.org/10.1080/13682820110089911

Love, K. (2009). Literacy pedagogical content knowledge in secondary teacher education: Reflecting on oral language and learning across the disciplines. *Language & Education: An International Journal*, 23(6), 541–560. https://doi.org/10.1080/09500780902822942

Lyons, R., & Roulstone, S. (2016). Labels, identity and narratives in children with primary speech and language impairments. *International Journal of Speech-Language Pathology*, 19(5), 503–518. https://doi.org/10.1080/17549507.2016.1221455.

Lyons, R., Fives, A., Kearns, N., Canavan, J., Devaney, C., & Eaton, P. (2013). Exploring the utility of the simple view of reading in Irish children attending schools in areas designated as socially disadvantaged. *Journal of Education and Training Studies*, 1(1), 204–220. https://doi.org/10.11114/jets.v1i1.107

Matson, G., & Cline, T. (2012). The impact of specific language impairment on performance in science and suggested implications for pedagogy. *Child Language Teaching and Therapy*, 28(1), 25–37. https://doi.org/10.1177/0265659011414276

McArthur, G., Hogben, J., Edwards, V., Heath, S., & Mengler, E. (2000). On the "specifics" of specific reading disability and specific language impairment. *Journal of Child Psychology and Psychiatry, and Allied Disciplines*, 41(7), 869–874. https://doi.org/10.1111/1469-7610.00674

McCartney, E., Boyle, J., Ellis, S., Bannatyne, S., & Turnbull, M. (2011). Indirect language therapy for children with persistent language impairment in mainstream primary schools: Outcomes from a cohort intervention. *International Journal of Language and Communication Disorders*, 46(1), 74–82. https://doi.org/10.3109/13682820903560302

McCartney, E., Ellis, S., Boyle, J., Turnbull, M., & Kerr, J. (2010). Developing a language support model for mainstream primary school teachers. *Child Language Teaching and Therapy*, 26(3), 359–374. https://doi.org/10.1177/0265659010369306

McGregor, K. (2020). How we fail children with developmental language disorder. *Language, Speech, and Hearing Services in Schools*, 1(1), 1–12. https://doi.org/10.1044/2020_LSHSS-20-00003

McLeod, S. (2004). Speech pathologists' application of the ICF to children with speech impairment. *International Journal of Speech-Language Pathology*, 6(1), 75–81. https://doi.org/10.1080/14417040410001669516

McLeod, S., McAllister, L., McCormack, J., & Harrison, L. (2014). Applying the world report on disability to children's communication. *Disability and Rehabilitation*, 36(18), 1518–1528. https://doi.org/10.3109/09638288.2013.833305

Myers, L., & Botting, N. (2008). Literacy in the mainstream inner-city school: Its relationship to spoken language. *Child Language Teaching & Therapy*, 24(1), 95–114. https://doi.org/10.1177/0265659007084570

Nagy, W., & Townsend, D. (2012). Words as tools: Learning academic vocabulary as language acquisition. *Reading Research Quarterly*, 47(1), 91–108. https://doi.org/10.1002/RRQ.011

Nathan, L., Stackhouse, J., Goulandris, N., & Snowling, M. (2004). The development of early literacy skills among children with speech difficulties: A test of the "critical age hypothesis". *Journal of Speech, Language, and Hearing Research*, 47(3), 377–391. https://doi.org/10.1044/1092-4388(2004/031)

Newcomer, P., & Hammill, D. (2009). *Pragmatic Language Observation Scale*. London: Proed.

Newcomer, P. L., & Hammill, D. D. (2008). *Test of Language Development–Primary* (4th ed.). Austin, TX: PRO-ED.

Norbury, C., Gooch, D., Wray, C., Baird, G., Charman, T., Simonoff, E., ... Pickles, A. (2016). The impact of nonverbal ability on prevalence and clinical presentation of language disorder: Evidence from a population study. *The Journal of Child Psychology and Psychiatry*, 57(11), 1247–1257. https://doi.org/10.1111/jcpp.12573

Oddson, B., Thomas-Stonell, N., Robertson, B., & Rosenbaum, P. (2019). Validity of a streamlined version of the focus on the outcomes of communication under six: Process and outcome. *Child: Care, Health and Development*, 45(4), 600–605. https://doi.org/10.1111/cch.12669

Ouellette, G. (2006). What's meaning got to do with it? The role of vocabulary in word reading and reading comprehension. *Journal of Educational Psychology*, 98(3), 554–566. https://doi.org/10.1037/0022-0663.98.3.554

Paradice, R., Bailey-Wood, N., Davies, K., & Solomon, M. (2007). Developing successful collaborative working practices for children with speech and language difficulties: A pilot study. *Child Language Teaching & Therapy*, 23(2), 223–236. https://doi.org/10.1177/0265659007076295

Pianta, R. C., La Paro, K. M., & Hamre, B. K. (2008). *Classroom Assessment Scoring System™: Manual K-3*. Baltimore: Paul H Brookes Publishing.

Pickstone, C., Goldbart, J., Marshall, J., Rees, A., & Roulstone, S. (2009). A systematic review of environmental interventions to improve child language outcomes for children with or at risk of primary language impairment. *Journal of Research in Special Educational Needs*, 9(2), 66–79. https://doi.org/10.1111/j.1471-3802.2009.01119.x

Poll, G. (2011). Increasing the Odds: Applying Emergentist Theory in Language Intervention. *Language, Speech & Hearing Services in Schools*, 42(4), 580–591A. https://doi.org/10.1044/0161-1461(2011/10-0041)

Reilly, S., McKean, C., Morgan, A., & Wake, M. (2015). Identifying and managing common childhood language and speech impairments. *British Medical Journal*, 350(h2318), 1–10. https://doi.org/10.1136/bmj.h2318

Sedgwick, A., & Stothard, J. (2018). A systematic review of school-based, mainstream, oral language interventions for key stage 1 children. *Support for Learning*, 33(4), 360–387. https://doi.org/10.1111/1467-9604.12225

Snow, C. (2002). *Reading for Understanding: Toward a Rand Programme in Reading Comprehension*. Santa Monica: RAND Corporation.

Spencer, S., Clegg, J., Stackhouse, J., & Rush, R. (2017). Contribution of spoken language and socio-economic background to adolescents' educational achievement at age 16 years. *International Journal of Language & Communication Disorders*, 52(2), 184–196. https://doi.org/10.1111/1460-6984.12264

Quigley, D. (2018). *Inter-Professional Practice to Support Effective Language Enrichment in Primary School Classrooms: An Action Research Inquiry*. [Unpublished doctoral dissertation]. Trinity College Dublin.

Ravens-Sieberer, U., Gosch, A., Rajmil, L., Erhart, M., Bruil, J., Duer, W., ... Czemy, L. (2005). KIDSCREEN: 52 quality of life measures for children and adolescents. *Expert Review of Pharmacoeconomics and Outcomes Research*, 5(3), 353–364. https://doi.org/10.1586/14737167.5.3.353

Rice, M. (2020). Advances in specific language impairment research and intervention: An overview of five research symposium papers. *Journal of Speech, Language, and Hearing Research*, 63, 3219–3223. https://doi.org/10.1044/2020_JSLHR-20-00504

Rosenbaum, P., & Gorter, J. (2012). The 'F-words' in childhood disability: I swear this is how we should think! *Child: Care, Health and Development*, 38(4), 457–463. https://doi.org/ 10.1111/j.1365-2214.2011.01338.x

Roulstone, S., Coad, J., Ayre, A., Hambly, H., & Lindsay, G. (2012). The preferred outcomes of children with speech, language and communication needs and their parents. [online]. Available at https://www-gov-uk.elib.tcd.ie/government/publications/the-preferred-outcomes-of-children-with-speech-language-and-communication-needs-and-their-parents (Accessed 3/11/2020).

Stothard, S., Snowling, M., Bishop, D., Chipchase, B., & Kaplan, C. (1998). Language-impaired preschoolers: A follow-up into adolescence. *Journal of Speech, Language & Hearing Research*, 41(2), 407–418. https://doi.org/10.1044/jslhr.4102.407

Snow, P. (2020). SOLAR: The science of language and reading. *Child Language Teaching and Therapy*, 1–12. https://doi.org/10.1177/0265659020947817

Snow, P., & Powell, A. (2011). Oral language competence in incarcerated young offenders: Links with offending severity. *International Journal of Speech-Language Pathology*, 13(6), 480–489. https://doi.org/10.3109/17549507.2013.845691

Snow, P., Eadie, P., Connell, J., Dalheim, B., McCusker, H., & Munro, J. (2014). Oral language supports early literacy: A pilot cluster randomized trial in disadvantaged schools. *International Journal of Speech-Language Pathology*, 16(5), 495–506.

Snowling, M., Bishop, D., Stothard, S., Chipchase, B., & Kaplan, C. (2006). Psychosocial outcomes at 15 years of children with a preschool history of speech-language impairment. *Journal of Child Psychology & Psychiatry*, 47(8), 759–7765. https://doi.org/10.1111/j.1469-7610.2006.01631.x

Squires, K., Gillam, S., & Reutzel, D. (2013). Characteristics of children who struggle with reading: Teachers and speech-language pathologists collaborate to support young learners. *Early Childhood Education Journal*, 41(6), 401–411. https://doi.org/ 10.1007/s10643-013-0577-6

Stanton-Chapman, T., Justice, L., Skibbe, L., & Grant, S. (2007). Social and behavioural characteristics of preschoolers with specific language impairment. *Topics in Early Childhood Special Education*, 27(2), 98–109. https://doi.org/10.1177/02711214070270020501

Thomas-Stonell, N., Oddson, B., Robertson, B., & Rosenbaum, P. (2009). Predicted and observed outcomes in preschool children following speech and language treatment: parent and clinician perspectives. *Journal of communication disorders*, *42*(1), 29–42. https://doi.org/10.1016/j.jcomdis.2008.08.002

Thomas-Stonell, N., Oddson, B., Robertson, B., & Rosenbaum, P. (2010). Development of the FOCUS (focus on the outcomes of communication under six), a communication outcome measure for preschool children. *Developmental Medicine & Child Neurology*, 52(1), 47–53. https://doi.org/10.1111/j.1469-8749.2009.03410.x

Tomasello, M. (2003). *Constructing a Language: A usage-based theory of language acquisition*. Cambridge: Harvard University Press.

Tomblin, B., & Nippold, M. (2014). Features of language impairment in the school years. In B. Tomblin & M. Nippold (Eds.), *Understanding Individual Differences in Language Development Across the School Years* (pp. 79–116). New York: Psychology Press.

Varni, J., Seid, M., & Rode, C. (1999). The PedsQL: Measurement model for the pediatric quality of life inventory. *Medical Care*, 37(2), 126–39. https://doi.org/10.1097/00005650-199902000-00003

Voci, S., Beitchman, J., Brownlie, E., & Wilson, B. (2006). Social anxiety in late adolescence: The importance of early childhood language impairment. *Journal of Anxiety Disorders*, 20(7), 915–930. https://doi.org/10.1016/j.janxdis.2006.01.007

Wallach, G. (2014). Improving clinical practice: A school-age and school-based perspective. *Language, Speech and Hearing Services in Schools*, 45(2), 127–136. https://doi.org/10.1044/2014_LSHSS-14-0016

Walsh, S. (2006). *Investigating Classroom Discourse*. London: Routledge.

Washington, K. (2007). Using the ICF within speech-language pathology: Application to developmental language impairment. *International Journal of Speech-Language Pathology*, 9(3), 242–255. https://doi.org/10.1080/14417040701261525

Westby, C. (2007). Application of the ICF in children with language impairments. *Seminars in Speech and Language*, 28, 265–272. https://doi.org/10.1055/s-2007-986523

Westby, C., & Washington, K. (2017). Using the international classification of functioning, disability and health in assessment and intervention of school- aged children with language impairments. *Language, Speech, and Hearing Services in Schools*, 48(2), 137–152. https://doi.org/10.1044/2017_LSHSS-16-0037

Whitehouse, A., Watt, H., Line, E., & Bishop, D. (2009). Adult psychosocial outcomes of children with specific language impairment, pragmatic language impairment and autism. *International Journal of Language & Communication Disorders*, 44(4), 511–528. https://doi.org/10.1080/13682820802708098

Wiig, E., Semel, E., & Secord, W. (2013). *Clinical Evaluation of Language Fundamentals–Fifth Edition*. London: Pearson Press.

World Health Organization (WHO). (2001). *International Classification of Functioning, Disability and Health (ICF)*. Geneva, Switzerland: WHO.

World Health Organization (WHO). (2007). *Classification of Functioning, Disability and Health–Children and Youth Version (ICF-CY)*. Geneva, Switzerland: WHO.

Wright, J., & Kresner, M. (2004). Short-term projects: The standards fund and collaboration between speech and language therapists and teachers. *Support for Learning*, 19(1), 19–23. https://doi.org/10.1111/j.0268-2141.2004.00313.x

Wright, J., Stackhouse, J., & Wood, J. (2008). Promoting language and literacy skills in the early years: Lessons from interdisciplinary teaching and learning. *Child Language Teaching and Therapy*, 24(2), 155–171. https://doi.org/10.1177/0265659007090292

28
A FRAMEWORK FOR THE SELECTION OF ASSISTIVE TECHNOLOGY FOR THE CLASSROOM

Karin van Niekerk*, Shakila Dada, and Kerstin Tönsing

Introduction

Learners with disabilities experience a multitude of barriers to learning. Access to education remains a significant barrier in South Africa (Donohue & Bornman, 2014) and around the world, with high numbers of children with disabilities being out of school (United Nations Department of Economic and Social Affairs, 2018). However, ensuring that children are in school does not guarantee access to the curriculum and learning in the classroom.

The provision of assistive technology (AT) for learners with disabilities may be a powerful way to facilitate access to learning within the classroom environment. The use of AT is a method to adapt the environment of the learner. The focus in education has shifted in recent years from providing services such as therapy to individual learners that experience barriers to learning to attempting to remove barriers to learning through environmental or social intervention (McKenzie, 2020). AT is one such intervention that aims to adapt the environment in order to facilitate participation and learning in education (Haq & Elhoweris, 2013; Lyner-Cleophas, 2019), as in all other spheres of life (Henderson et al., 2008).

An assistive product has been described as "any product (devices, equipment, instruments and software), either specially designed and produced or generally available, whose primary purpose is to maintain or improve an individual's functioning and independence and thereby promote their wellbeing" (Khasnabis et al., 2015, p. 2229).

Appropriate AT selection contributes to increased user satisfaction, long-term use, and cost effectiveness of AT (Friederich et al., 2010). Within a low-resourced context this is particularly important, as limited budgets imply that the best use should be made of available resources.

Several barriers exist in the provision of appropriate AT for use in classrooms. These include limited or inconsistent funding for the purchase of AT (Karlsson et al., 2018; Matter et al., 2017; O'Sullivan et al., 2021; Visagie et al., 2019). However, the challenges tend to run much deeper than the funding required to purchase the AT initially. AT is typically recommended by healthcare professionals, such as occupational, speech-language and physiotherapists. The availability of these professionals may be a significant barrier to the provision of AT products – particularly

* karin.vanniekerk@up.ac.za

DOI: 10.4324/9781003266068-33

in low-resourced contexts. Rural communities (that often have limited resources) may face additional difficulties in accessing rehabilitation services (Davis et al., 2013; Ned et al., 2017; Wegner & Rhoda, 2015), such as AT. Furthermore, professionals that are available may not have the required expertise to provide AT services (Karlsson et al., 2018).

This may necessitate teachers – who are typically not trained to provide AT services - to step into this role in order to facilitate the learning of students in their classes (Alkahtani, 2013).

Several principles have been suggested to guide the appropriate provision of AT to children (Malcolm MacLachlan et al., 2018; World Health Organisation & UNICEF, 2015). These are aimed at ensuring the appropriateness of AT for a specific child and include availability, accessibility, affordability, adaptability, acceptability and quality. The availability and accessibility of AT remains challenging in low-resourced contexts Matter et al., 2017; Visagie et al., 2016; Schlünz et al., 2017; Tönsing et al., 2018; Van Niekerk & Tönsing, 2015). Eide and Øderud (2009) estimate that only 5–15% of people within low and middle income contexts have access to the AT they require. Service providers often have to balance the availability and affordability of AT with its acceptability to the user as well as its quality when selecting AT.

AT selection for children can be challenging, even for experienced service providers (Niekerk et al., 2019). Due to the multitude of factors that have to be considered, the challenge often lies in weighing up the importance of the different influencing factors for a specific child within a specific context (Webb et al., 2019). For teachers, who are typically not trained to perform this role and may not be comfortable in providing inclusive education services to begin with (e.g. Nel et al., 2016), selecting AT has been shown to be a particularly daunting task (Alkahtani, 2013; Karlsson et al., 2018; O'Sullivan et al., 2021).

Theory is successfully used in various disciplines to guide practice (see e.g. Higgs, 2013; Wong, 2018; Younas & Quennell, 2019). A theoretical framework could provide professionals, including teachers, with guidance regarding aspects to consider during the AT provision process.

Several such frameworks exist, including the Assistive Technology Device (ATD) Selection Framework (Scherer et al., 2007), the Human Activity Assistive Technology (HAAT) model (Cook & Polgar, 2008) as well as the Matching Person and Technology Model. Unfortunately, none of the frameworks were developed for use in a low-resourced context or with children specifically, and do not include detailed factors to indicate individual factors that influence AT provision.

It is important that theory should continuously develop as new research becomes available and additional applications of the theory become possible. This should be reflective of our continuous striving towards evidence-based practice, that has been defined as the "integration of best and current research evidence with clinical/educational expertise and relevant stakeholder perspectives, in order to facilitate decisions about assessment and intervention that are deemed effective and efficient for a given direct stakeholder" (Schlosser & Raghavendra, 2004, p. 3). Therefore, the authors endeavoured to adapt a theoretical framework to guide professionals towards current evidence-based practice.

This chapter aims to share the results of a multi-phased study that aimed to adapt the ATD Selection Framework (Scherer et al., 2007) for use in the South African context, specifically with young children. Although this framework was adapted specifically for use by rehabilitation professionals, the results of this project will be described in relation to its application to teachers potentially in a position to recommend or implement AT services at their schools.

Method

Design

Phase 1 of adapting the framework entailed conducting a systematic review. Systematic reviews are an important way in which results from different studies can be combined as part of the process to establish evidence-based practice (Godshall, 2015). The review was aimed at identifying factors that rehabilitation professionals perceive to influence the provision of AT to children as found in published literature.

A further important aspect required to establish an evidence-based framework to guide practice was to include "clinical/educational expertise and relevant stakeholder perspectives" (Schlosser & Raghavendra, 2004, p. 3). For Phase 2 of the study, two asynchronous online focus groups were conducted. Each online focus group had eight participants (total n=16).

Participants

Participants in the online focus groups were occupational therapists, physiotherapists, speech-language therapists and speech-language therapists and audiologists (dually qualified), registered with the Health Professions Council of South Africa. Registration with this regulatory body is compulsory in order to practice in the country. All participants were experienced in providing AT to young children, had access to the internet and were able to communicate in written English. Participants provided services in diverse contexts, for example in schools, and private or public healthcare settings. They worked in large metropolitan areas as well as rural communities.

Data analysis

In Phase 1 (systematic review) the results section of identified papers were analysed deductively according to the ATD Selection framework (Scherer et al., 2007). All existing aspects of the ATD Selection framework were confirmed, and newly identified factors (identified during a process of inductive analysis) were synthesised into the existing framework. For comprehensive details on the review see van Niekerk et al. (2018).

The analysis of data gathered during Phase 2 entailed deductive (theoretical) thematic analysis of the transcripts, again utilising a pre-existing coding framework (Braun & Clarke, 2006), the ATD Selection Framework (Scherer et al., 2007). This was followed by inductive analysis of the data to create sub themes based on patterns in the data (Braun & Clarke, 2006). Again, the existing components were confirmed (although somewhat adapted) and newly identified factors were synthesised into the framework. For comprehensive details on this process see van Niekerk et al., (2019).

Results

The results from Phases 1 and 2 were integrated into the Adapted ATD Selection framework. For comprehensive details of this process please see van Niekerk et al. (2021) and van Niekerk (2019). This adapted framework can be viewed in Figure 28.1.

Application

The factors included in the framework will be described and aspects highlighted that teachers should focus on when considering AT for use within their classroom. Reference will also be made to further supporting literature.

Environmental Factors: Cultural Context

Culture has been defined as "a system of learned patterns of behaviour" (Krefting & Krefting, 1991) and is shared by members of a group. Teachers should consider the value that the learner's

Karin van Niekerk et al.

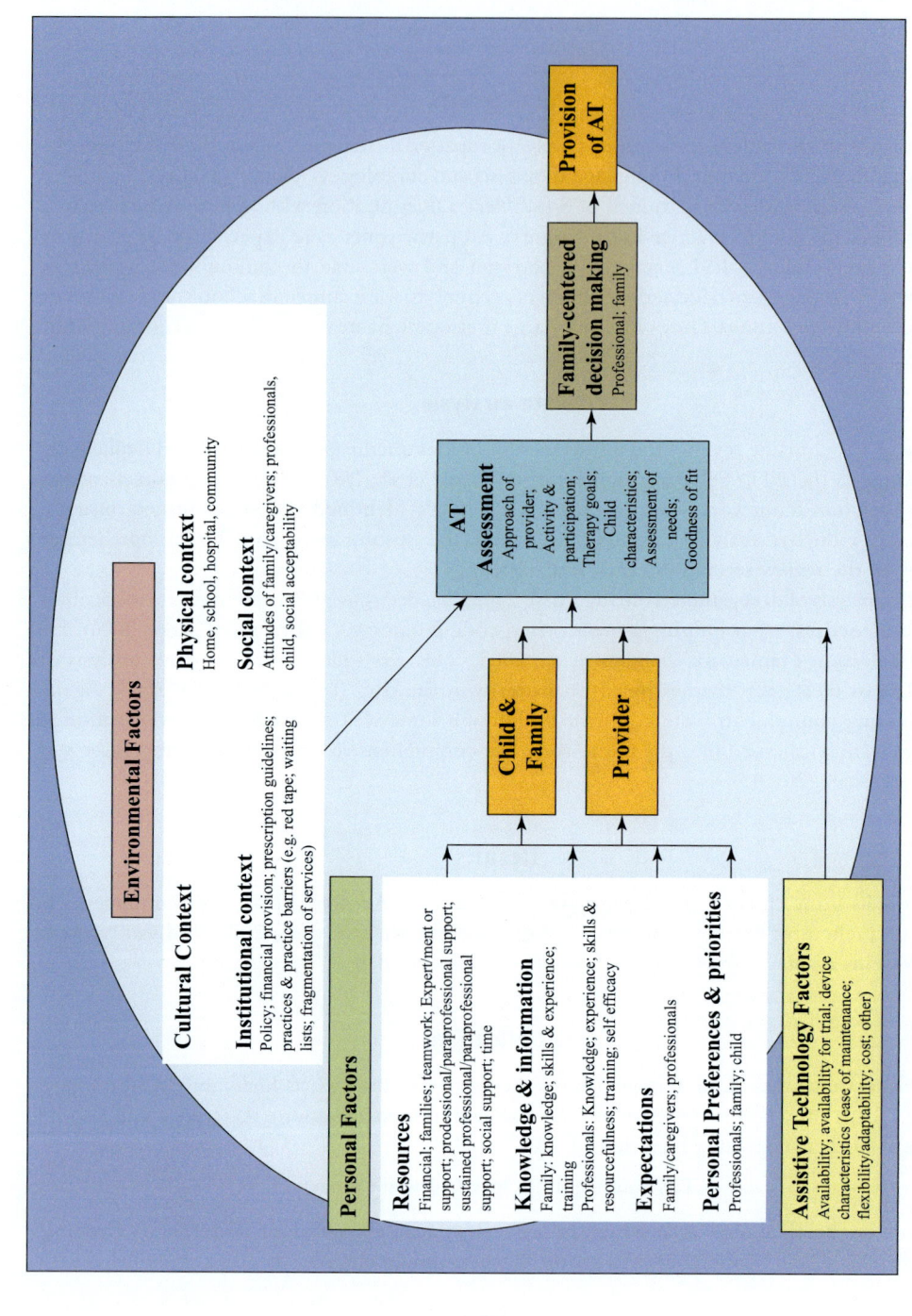

Figure 28.1 Adapted framework

culture gives to independence when AT is recommended. In a context where independence is not highly valued, families and other team members may not be as interested in pursuing AT that increases their child's independence. Furthermore, the cultural beliefs pertaining to the cause of the child's disability may also be influential.

Environmental Factors: Social Context

The social context refers to persons with whom the learner interacts within his/her environment (Cook & Polgar, 2008). Attitudes towards AT and the social acceptability of the AT are to be considered. The attitude of the learner is viewed as very important and any service provider tasked with recommending AT should determine the learner's attitude before making any recommendations. The motivation of the learner may be much higher to use the recommended device if he/she had some input into the selection (Satsangi et al., 2019).

Furthermore, the attitudes of the family towards AT should be determined. This may be difficult if teachers do not have regular contact with family/caregivers. Partnering with the family is vital in order to ensure the successful implementation of AT (see e.g. Delarosa et al., 2012; Perfect et al., 2019), however challenging this may be.

The attitudes of professionals, including teachers, were also identified as influential (van Niekerk et al., 2019). Teachers may need to reflect on their own attitudes towards AT before attempting/expanding the use thereof in their classrooms as their attitudes are thought to influence the experience of learners in their class (Ahmed, 2018). The expansion in available technology options has left many professionals feeling overwhelmed by the options (Davis et al., 2013). Facilitating a positive attitude towards AT in school and throughout the education system should be the goal.

The social acceptability of the AT should not be overlooked. School-going children are often concerned about the opinions of their peers (Satsangi et al., 2019). Socially acceptable or even appealing technology may contribute to the motivation of the learner to use the AT.

Environmental Factors: Institutional Context

The institutional context refers to "larger organisations in society" (Cook & Polgar, 2008). Factors to consider within the institutional context would be, for example, the policies of national or local Departments of Education pertaining to AT in classrooms.

It is important that teachers familiarise themselves with the procedures and policies pertaining to the provision of AT in their school and wider district/school community (O'Sullivan et al., 2021).

Fragmentation of services has been identified as a barrier to the provision of AT services (Niekerk et al., 2019). Appropriate selection and implementation of AT in the classroom is facilitated by good intra- and interagency collaboration, for example, between different teachers in the school (intra-agency) or between the health and education departments (interagency). For example, services and resulting learning can be disrupted when a learner transitions to a new class and there is a lack of communication and collaboration between the previous and new teacher (Karlsson et al., 2018).

Current intervention/education practices in the school are also an influencing factor. Teachers may easily comprehend the importance of selected AT being able to "fit" into the classroom practices where it will be used. An example of this may be using an adapted keyboard if learners are encouraged to type, while preferring a splint or adapted grip if learners are encouraged to practice their handwriting.

Environmental Factors: Physical Context

The physical context refers to the physical characteristics of a specific environment (Cook & Polgar, 2008). Teachers should determine the space requirements of the technology that they are considering. Certain AT may require a large space for set-up, for example, specialised mounting or a power wheelchair. Additional considerations in the physical context may include lighting (e.g., light may cause glare from screens), temperature (e.g., computers may overheat in hot classrooms) or access to electricity (e.g., to charge devices). The crime rate in the community was also mentioned by South African professionals (van Niekerk et al., 2019). Teachers should ensure that recommended AT can be secured and will not place learners at risk (e.g., when taking expensive devices home).

Personal Factors: Knowledge and Information

The knowledge and information of the recommending professional was identified as an influential consideration when selecting AT. Authors from around the world have reported that teachers do not typically have the knowledge to select AT (Alkahtani, 2013; O'Sullivan et al., 2021) and lack competence related to AT (Onivehu Adams et al., 2017). Teachers who are interested in selecting AT for their classrooms should inform themselves about the different options available. Training of teachers has been described as essential in order to facilitate the implementation of AT services in schools (Karlsson et al., 2018; Onivehu Adams et al., 2017). Teachers are advised to contact their respective Departments of Education pertaining to training possibilities regarding AT for the classroom. In addition to training teachers how to operate different types of AT, training should be designed to train teachers how to integrate AT into their lessons. Teachers have also indicated that training in how to collaborate with others regarding AT was needed (Coleman et al., 2015), as well as training specifically in the selection of AT (Davis et al., 2013).

All persons at school that would interact with the learner should also receive training (Dukes & Smith, 2007) in order to ensure that they are able to support the implementation of AT with the learner in order to foster increased participation.

Personal Factors: Resources

In terms of resources, access to financial resources is obviously important. However, the most costly solutions are not necessarily the best or only options that may be effective (van Niekerk et al., 2019). Examples of this may include paper-based Augmentative and Alternative Communication systems that may be used instead of high-technology devices and Adapted Paper Technology that may be used to fabricate seating equipment. Teachers may have to initiate fundraising campaigns to contribute the finances needed. Importantly, networking between different stakeholders, including non-profit organisations, corporate sponsors, as well as individuals, may be needed. Resources provided by the family should not be overlooked.

As the recommendation and implementation of AT is such a complex matter, it is recommended that teachers provide and implement AT services as part of a team (Davis et al., 2013; Karlsson et al., 2018). Teachers should advocate for ongoing professional support at the school, as this will assist in the selection and implementation of the AT (Karlsson et al., 2018). Having team members physically present during assessment and implementation may be very challenging. Online teaming may provide an excellent alternative to face-to-face meetings (Anderson et al., 2015). This may also eliminate the barrier faced by teachers employed in rural communities with limited access to support services. Good communication between different members of the team (i.e. the family and professionals) is essential (Garcia et al., 2016).

Ideally, teachers selecting and implementing AT should have access to guidance and support from an experienced professional (Karlsson et al., 2018). Teachers should aim to establish a relationship with a mentor in order for guidance and reflection on the process and progress made.

Importantly, teachers should be aware of the considerable time requirements of AT (van Niekerk et al., 2019) – therefore the availability of time should be considered when selecting devices.

Personal Factors: Expectations, Preferences and Priorities

The learner, family, teacher and other professionals each bring expectations to the AT selection process. All parties will have their own preferences and priorities. It is crucial that the recommending professional/s determine the expectations, preferences and priorities of the learner and family during a team meeting. Learners tend to gravitate towards AT that they have had good experiences with (Satsangi et al., 2019). The recommended professional/s should also reflect on their own expectations, preferences and priorities to make sure that they are clear and can be communicated to the family and learner.

Assessment

During the actual assessment of a learner for AT, a collaborative process between multiple professionals, the child and family should be followed as far as possible (Copley & Ziviani, 2005). The presence of an experienced and knowledgeable professional is recommended (Karlsson et al., 2018) to lead this process. If such an individual is not available within the school, the use of telepractice may be investigated to create opportunities to involve additional professionals in assessments.

During the assessment the current abilities of the learner should be determined, together with their needs and wants. Importantly, the activities in which the learner needs to or wants to participate as well as those in which the family wants the child to participate should be considered. The teacher is expertly qualified to highlight the school environment and the activities in which the learner is required to participate within the particular educational setting. The recommending professionals should use their knowledge on available AT to determine the most appropriate match for the learner. The most appropriate AT would aim to optimise the participation of the learner by incorporating the abilities of the learner and the activities they want to/have to perform, all while considering the unique home, school and community environment.

AT

Any service provider who wants to be competent in the recommendation of AT should familiarise themselves with the characteristics of the available AT. Aspects such as the weight of AT (e.g. if it has to be carried by the user), the power requirements and the ease of maintenance are important considerations.

A very important additional consideration is the ability of the AT to "grow with the child". This refers to the adaptability of the AT for future use by the same user. The availability of various options of AT for trial by the learner makes it much easier for the service provider to make a recommendation (Karlsson et al., 2018). Therefore, it is recommended that schools build up a library of resources to ensure that different pieces of AT are available for trial.

Conclusions

This chapter has described the adaptation of the ATD Selection framework for application to children in multiple contexts. The framework was explained with application to teachers who may be tasked with selecting AT within their school contexts. By becoming aware of the multitude of factors that influence AT selection, teachers can more consciously address and consider those factors when selecting and using AT with the learners in their classrooms. Importantly, due to the complexity of AT recommendation, it should be recommended as part of a team as far as possible. Although support from and collaboration with other team members, including the family and other professionals, may be challenging, innovative methods including telepractice should be explored to maximise the selection of relevant AT as a basis for increased participation of learners with disabilities in the classroom.

References

Ahmed, A. (2018). Perceptions of using assistive technology for students with disabilities in the classroom. *International Journal of Special Education, 33*(1), 129–139.

Alkahtani, K. D. F. (2013). Teachers' knowledge and use of assistive technology for students with special educational needs. *Journal of Studies in Education, 3*(2), 65–86. https://doi.org/10.5296/jse.v3i2.3424

Anderson, K. L., Balandin, S., & Stancliffe, R. J. (2015). Alternative service delivery models for families with a new speech generating device: Perspectives of parents and therapists. *International Journal of Speech-Language Pathology, 17*(2), 185–195. https://doi.org/10.3109/17549507.2014.979876

Braun, V., & Clarke, V. (2006). Using thematic analysis in psychology. *Qualitative Research in Psychology, 3*(2), 77–101. https://doi.org/10.1191/1478088706qp063oa

Coleman, M. B., Cramer, E. S., Park, Y., & Bell, S. M. (2015). Art educators' use of adaptations, assistive technology, and special education supports for students with physical, visual, severe and multiple disabilities. *Journal of Developmental and Physical Disabilities, 27*(5), 637–660. https://doi.org/10.1007/s10882-015-9440-6

Cook, A. M., & Polgar, J. M. (2008). *Cook & Hussey's assistive technologies* (3rd ed.). Mosby Elsevier.

Copley, J., & Ziviani, J. (2005). Assistive technology assessment and planning for children with multiple disabilities in educational settings. *British Journal of Occupational Therapy, 68*(12), 559–566.

Davis, T. N., Barnard-Brak, L., & Arredondo, P. L. (2013). Assistive technology: Decision-making practices in public schools. *Rural Special Education Quarterly, 32*(4), 15–23. https://doi.org/10.1177/875687051303200403

Delarosa, E., Horner, S., Eisenberg, C., Ball, L., Renzoni, A. M., & Ryan, S. E. (2012). Family impact of assistive technology scale: Development of a measurement scale for parents of children with complex communication needs. *Augmentative and Alternative Communication, 28*(3), 171–180. https://doi.org/10.3109/07434618.2012.704525

Donohue, D., & Bornman, J. (2014). The challenges of realising inclusive education in South Africa. *South African Journal of Education, 34*(2), 1–14. https://doi.org/10.15700/201412071114

Dukes, C., & Smith, M. (2007). *Working with parents of children with special educational needs*. SAGE Publications.

Eide, A. H., & Øderud, T. (2009). Assistive technology in low-income countries. In M. MacLachlan & L. Swartz (Eds.), *Disability & international development: Towards inclusive global health* (pp. 149–160). Springer.

Friederich, A., Bernd, T., & De Witte, L. (2010). Methods for the selection of assistive technology in neurological rehabilitation practice. *Scandinavian Journal of Occupational Therapy, 17*(4), 308–318. https://doi.org/10.3109/11038120903377082

Garcia, M. E., Frunzi, K., Dean, C. B., Flores, N., & Miller, K. B. (2016). Toolkit of resources for engaging families and the community as partners in education: Part 3: Building trusting relationships with families and the community through effective communication. *Regional Educational Laboratory Pacific*, September. https://files.eric.ed.gov/fulltext/ED569112.pdf

Godshall, M. (2015). Introduction to evidence-based practice. In *Fast facts for evidence-based practice in nursing, second edition : Implementing EBP in a nutshell* (pp. 1–17). Springer Publishing Company.

Haq, F., & Elhoweris, H. (2013). Using assistive technology to enhance the learning of basic literacy skills for students with learning disabilities. *International Journal of Social Sciences and Education, 3*(4), 880–885.

Henderson, S., Skelton, H., & Rosenbaum, P. (2008). Assistive devices for children with functional impairments: Impact on child and caregiver function. *Developmental Medicine and Child Neurology, 50*(2), 89–98. https://doi.org/10.1111/j.1469-8749.2007.02021.x

Higgs, L. G. (2013). Theory in educational research and practice in teacher education. *Bulgarian Comparative Education Studies, 11*, 105–111.

Karlsson, P., Johnston, C., & Barker, K. (2018). Influences on students' assistive technology use at school: The views of classroom teachers, allied health professionals, students with cerebral palsy and their parents. *Disability and Rehabilitation: Assistive Technology, 13*(8), 763–771. https://doi.org/10.1080/17483107.2017.1373307

Khasnabis, C., Mirza, Z., & MacLachlan, M. (2015). Opening the GATE to inclusion for people with disabilities. *The Lancet, 386*(10010), 2229–2230. https://doi.org/10.1016/S0140-6736(15)01093-4

Krefting, L. H., & Krefting, D.V. (1991). Cultural influences on performance. In C. Christiansen & C. Baum (Eds.), *Occupational therapy*. SLACK.

Lyner-Cleophas, M. (2019). Assistive technology enables inclusion in higher education: The role of higher and further education disability services association. *African Journal of Disability, 8*, 1–6. https://doi.org/10.4102/ajod.v8i0.558

MacLachlan, Malcolm, Banes, D., Bell, D., Borg, J., Donnelly, B., Fembek, M., Ghosh, R., Gowran, R. J., Hannay, E., Hiscock, D., Hoogerwerf, E. J., Howe, T., Kohler, F., Layton, N., Long, S., Mannan, H., Mji, G., Odera Ongolo, T., Perry, K., ... & Hooks, H. (2018). Assistive technology policy: A position paper from the first global research, innovation, and education on assistive technology (GREAT) summit. *Disability and Rehabilitation: Assistive Technology, 13*(5), 454–466. https://doi.org/10.1080/17483107.2018.1468496

Matter, R., Harniss, M., Oderud, T., Borg, J., & Eide, A. H. (2017). Assistive technology in resource-limited environments: A scoping review. *Disability and Rehabilitation: Assistive Technology, 12*(2), 105–114. https://doi.org/10.1080/17483107.2016.1188170

McKenzie, J. (2020). Intellectual disability in inclusive education in South Africa: Curriculum challenges. *Journal of Policy and Practice in Intellectual Disabilities*, 1–5. https://doi.org/10.1111/jppi.12337

Ned, L., Cloete, L., & Mji, G. (2017). The experiences and challenges faced by rehabilitation community service therapists within the South African primary healthcare health system. *African Journal of Disability, 6*, 1–11. https://doi.org/10.4102/ajod.v6i0.311

Nel, N. M., Tlale, L. D. N., Engelbrecht, P., & Nel, M. (2016). Teachers' perceptions of education support structures in the implementation of inclusive education in South Africa. *Koers, 81*(3), 1–14. https://doi.org/10.19108/KOERS.81.3.2249

O'Sullivan, K., McGrane, A., Long, S., Marshall, K., & Maclachlan, M. (2021). Using a systems thinking approach to understand teachers perceptions and use of assistive technology in the republic of Ireland. *Disability and Rehabilitation: Assistive Technology*, 1–9. https://doi.org/10.1080/17483107.2021.1878297

Onivehu Adams, O., Ohawuiro Onyiyeche, E., & Oyeniran Bunmi, J. (2017). Teachers' attitude and competence in the use of assistive technologies in special needs schools. *Acta Didactica Napocensia, 10*(4), 21–32. https://doi.org/10.24193/adn.10.4.3

Perfect, E., Hoskin, E., Noyek, S., & Davies, T. C. (2019). A systematic review investigating outcome measures and uptake barriers when children and youth with complex disabilities use eye gaze assistive technology. *Developmental Neurorehabilitation*, 1–15. https://doi.org/10.1080/17518423.2019.1600066

Satsangi, R., Miller, B., & Savage, M. N. (2019). Helping teachers make informed decisions when selecting assistive technology for secondary students with disabilities. *Preventing School Failure, 63*(2), 97–104. https://doi.org/10.1080/1045988X.2018.1483314

Scherer, M., Jutai, J., Fuhrer, M., Demers, L., & Deruyter, F. (2007). A framework for modelling the selection of assistive technology devices (ATDs). *Disability and Rehabilitation: Assistive Technology, 2*(1), 1–8. https://doi.org/10.1080/17483100600845414

Schlosser, R. W., & Raghavendra, P. (2004). Evidence-based practice in augmentative and alternative communication. *Augmentative and Alternative Communication, 20*(1), 1–21. https://doi.org/10.1080/07434610310001621083

Schlünz, G., Gumede, T., Wilken, I., Van Der Walt, W., Moors, C., Calteaux, K., Tönsing, K., & Van Niekerk, K. (2017). Applications in accessibility of text-to-speech synthesis for South African languages: Initial system integration and user engagement. *ACM International Conference Proceeding Series*, Part F1308. https://doi.org/10.1145/3129416.3129445

Tönsing, K. M., van Niekerk, K., Schlünz, G. I., & Wilken, I. (2018). AAC services for multilingual populations: South African service provider perspectives. *Journal of Communication Disorders*, *73*(March 2017), 62–76. https://doi.org/10.1016/j.jcomdis.2018.04.002

United Nations Department of Economic and Social Affairs. (2018). Disability and development. In *Disability and development report*. https://doi.org/10.4337/9781847202864.00035

Van Niekerk, K. (2019). *Perspectives of rehabilitation professionals on assistive technology provision for young children with disabilities in South Africa*. University of Pretoria.

van Niekerk, K., Dada, S., & Tönsing, K. (2019). Influences on selection of assistive technology for young children in South Africa: Perspectives from rehabilitation professionals. *Disability and Rehabilitation*, *41*(8), 912–925. https://doi.org/10.1080/09638288.2017.1416500

van Niekerk, K., & Tönsing, K. (2015). Eye gaze technology: A South African perspective. *Disability and Rehabilitation: Assistive Technology*, *10*(4), 340–346. https://doi.org/10.3109/17483107.2014.974222

van Niekerk, K., Dada, S., & Tönsing, K. (2021). Perspectives of rehabilitation professionals on assistive technology provision to young children in South Africa : A national survey Perspectives of rehabilitation professionals on assistive technology. *Disability and Rehabilitation: Assistive Technology*, 1–8. https://doi.org/10.1080/17483107.2021.1892842

van Niekerk, K., Dada, S., Tönsing, K., & Boshoff, K. (2018). Factors perceived by rehabilitation professionals to influence the provision of assistive technology to children: A systematic review. *Physical and Occupational Therapy in Pediatrics*, *38*(2), 168–189. https://doi.org/10.1080/01942638.2017.1337661

Visagie, S., Eide, A. H., Mannan, H., Schneider, M., Swartz, L., Mji, G., Munthali, A., Khogali, M., van Rooy, G., Hem, K.-G., & MacLachlan, M. (2016). A description of assistive technology sources, services and outcomes of use in a number of African settings. *Disability and Rehabilitation: Assistive Technology*, 1–8. https://doi.org/10.1080/17483107.2016.1244293

Visagie, S., Matter, R., Kayange, G., Chiwaula, M., Harniss, M., & Kahonde, C. (2019). Perspectives on a mobile application that maps assistive technology resources in Africa. *African Journal of Disability*, *8*, 1–9. https://doi.org/10.4102/ajod.v8i0.567

Webb, E. J. D., Lynch, Y., Meads, D., Judge, S., Randall, N., Goldbart, J., Meredith, S., Moulam, L., Hess, S., & Murray, J. (2019). Finding the best fit: Examining the decision-making of augmentative and alternative communication professionals in the UK using a discrete choice experiment. *BMJ Open*, *9*(11), 1–12. https://doi.org/10.1136/bmjopen-2019-030274

Wegner, L., & Rhoda, A. (2015). The influence of cultural beliefs on the utilisation of rehabilitation services in a rural South African context: Therapists' perspective. *African Journal of Disability*, *4*(1), 1–8. https://doi.org/10.4102/ajod.v4i1.128

Wong, M. E. (2018). Guiding teachers of students with visual impairments to make assistive technology decisions: Preliminary experience using the Wisconsin assistive technology initiative. *Support for Learning*, *33*(4), 429–439. https://doi.org/10.1111/1467-9604.12228

World Health Organisation, & UNICEF. (2015). *Assistive technology for children with disabilities: Creating opportunities for education, inclusion and participation*. A discussion paper.

Younas, A., & Quennell, S. (2019). Usefulness of nursing theory-guided practice: An integrative review. *Scandinavian Journal of Caring Sciences*, *33*(3), 540–555. https://doi.org/10.1111/scs.12670

PART V

Practice-Based Consideration

Developing and implementing educational programs in inclusive classrooms is an extremely important and crucial aspect of an inclusive classroom/educational institution. Important consideration needs to be undertaken and kept in mind while implementing interventions to increase the effectiveness of any intervention. This section covers some of the most important practice-based considerations for teachers in inclusive classroom and or educational settings.

29
STRATEGIES FOR IMPLEMENTING AUGMENTATIVE AND ALTERNATIVE COMMUNICATION IN CLASSROOM SETTINGS IN LOW- AND MIDDLE-INCOME COUNTRIES

Nimisha Muttiah*, Kathryn D.R. Drager and Inoka S. Samarasingha

Introduction

Globally it is estimated that about 1–2% of people experience significant communication difficulties (Bunning, Gona, Newton, & Hartley, 2014). The prevalence of disability in low-income countries is higher than in high-income countries (World Health Organization and The World Bank, 2011), although worldwide prevalence numbers for individuals with specific disabilities such as communication disabilities is scare, especially from low- and middle-income countries (LMICs) (Olusanya, Ruben, & Parving, 2006). As Kieling and colleagues point out, the developmental needs of children in LMICs remain an area that requires more attention (Kieling et al., 2011).

Augmentative and alternative communication (AAC) methods and approaches can supplement or replace speech to benefit individuals with severe communication disabilities (Romski & Sevcik, 1997). AAC includes both low-technology (low-tech) systems such as printed communication boards, communication books and other uses of pictures, as well as high-technology (high-tech) systems such as the use of communication apps on tablet devices. Using AAC on mainstream mobile devices has created access for many individuals with developmental disabilities who may otherwise not have been able to afford expensive speech-generating devices (McNaughton & Light, 2013). This is particularly relevant for individuals from LMICs to access AAC via mobile technology. However, despite mobile technology making access to AAC easier, many individuals in LMICs are still unable to access these types of devices. Therefore, in

* nimisha@kln.ac.lk

many situations the most feasible option for individuals with complex communication needs in LMICs is to rely on low-tech AAC.

This chapter will focus on low-tech AAC as a viable option for children with complex communication needs living in LMICs and for individuals living in any country who may have limited financial resources. The focus of this chapter will be on AAC systems and partner communication strategies that help to build social engagement and communication in preschool and school-age individuals with complex communication needs.

Augmentative and Alternative Communication in LMICs

AAC has the potential to enhance communication, language, and learning for individuals with communication disabilities and significantly impact social and educational outcomes (Drager et al., 2010). Providing access to AAC enables students to fully participate in their classrooms (Calculator, 2009). Most research in the field of AAC, however, has been conducted in high-income countries. The challenges to providing AAC services in LMICs are different to those in high-income countries. Unfortunately, we only have a limited understanding of AAC service provision in LMICs due to insufficient research on this area in these contexts (Srinivasan, Mathew, & Lloyd, 2011). Kieling and colleagues (2011) highlighted this as the 90-10 phenomenon, where although 90% of the world's children and adolescents with disabilities live in LMICs, only 10% of health research funding is used to address the difficulties in these contexts. Therefore, it is essential to consider AAC systems and partner communication training that is specific to LMIC contexts.

We will first discuss low-tech AAC systems and approaches, some of which have been implemented in LMICs and others that have not but could readily be adapted to use in other contexts. Next, we will talk about partner communication training and strategies that have specifically focused on training conducted in LMICs and places with low resources, as these could be applicable to other broader contexts as well.

Low-Tech Visual Scene Displays (VSDs)

A visual scene display (VSD) is an image, usually a photograph that shows a meaningful event or situation that has occurred in the life of the individual with complex communication needs (Babb et al., 2019). The vocabulary relevant to that event is embedded as "hotspots" within the visual scene itself. For example, in a visual scene display of a birthday party the display could be a picture of the cake cutting, and the potential hotspots in this scene could be the birthday cake, balloons, and grandma. The rationale behind using VSDs with children is that they facilitate rich, context-supported and event-based learning essential for young children learning language (Drager et al., 2003; Wilkinson & Light, 2011). In typically developing children, social-interactive contexts have been found to support language acquisition universally across cultures and languages (Snow, 1999). VSDs provide similar contexts by embedding language concepts within visual scenes that are familiar to the child, providing a visual form to support the learning of concepts (Wilkinson, Light, & Drager, 2012). Therefore, current research suggests that VSDs may be a more appropriate option than grid displays for infants, toddlers, young preschoolers and beginning communicators (Light et al., 2012).

Traditionally, VSDs have been used with children and young adults with complex communication needs on high-tech systems (e.g., Drager et al., 2019; Holyfield et al., 2018). However, creating and using VSDs on low-tech systems may have several advantages for children with complex communication needs, particularly if high-tech systems are not accessible. One main advantage of using low-tech VSDs is the low cost involved in their development. They can also be used in environments where high-tech systems cannot be used, such as in or near water and sand. It is also possible that presenting visual scenes in low-tech form can incorporate components in the scenes that make them more prominent than when they are presented on computerized devices. The hotspots on the VSDs can be made more salient by presenting them in a way that makes them "pop" out of the scene, creating a 3D effect. As McCarthy et al. (2006) argued, it is essential to make the items available for selection explicit to young children. Although their arguments were related to scanning, this same reasoning can be applied to making the hotspots on VSDs more salient (from the rest of the scene) as well. Additional cues such as motion can also be incorporated into interactions with the VSDs. If the hotspots on the low-tech scenes were moveable, both the communication partners and children with complex communication needs can take advantage of motion while interacting with the VSDs and hotspots. Making the hotspots moveable would also allow a child to make a selection not just by pointing to a hotspot, but also by pulling the hotspot off the scene. Jagaroo and Wilkinson (2008) reported on the benefits of using movement as a cue: motion draws attention to stimuli, helps children discriminate between stimuli and improves memory for a specific stimulus.

Construction of Low-Tech VSDs

Low-tech VSDs are developed by first printing out two copies of color photos; hotspots are cut out from one of the photos and protected with contact paper. These hotspots are then attached with transparent Velcro onto the original photo. Therefore, even when the hotspots are removed the original photo still retains the context as the scene remains visible underneath the transparent Velcro. As can be seen in Figures 29.1 and 29.2, objects and individuals of interest (including the children themselves) are chosen as hotspots in the VSDs. The hotspots in the Figures below are circled in black.

Limited evidence exists on the use of low-tech VSDs with young children who are beginning communicators. Muttiah et al. (2019) investigated the effectiveness of a treatment package combining a low-tech VSD AAC system with partner modeling. Three pre-school-aged children with complex communication needs participated. All three children were beginning communicators with less than 50 expressive vocabulary words. A single-subject multiple probe across participants design was used. The independent variable was an intervention combining low-tech VSDs and aided modeling provided during naturalistic, social communication situa-

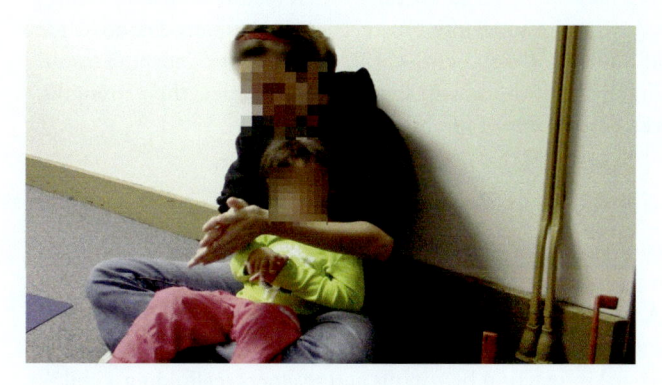

Figure 29.1   A VSD showing 1 large hotspot

Figure 29.2 A VSD showing multiple hotspots

tions. The dependent variables were the number of communication turns taken and the number of unique semantic concepts expressed by young children with complex communication needs. The intervention was conducted at their pre-school and two of the children's paraprofessionals participated in the study as well.

All three children demonstrated significant increases in the number of communication turns taken after introduction of the intervention. The children appeared to enjoy seeing themselves and their communication partners in the scenes, which may have resulted in increasing their motivation and interest to look at and touch the VSDs. This study demonstrated positive results for three young children who had differing diagnoses and who were mainly at a pre-symbolic level of communication. This intervention is a low-cost option for low-resource communities that may not have access to high technology or computers. These low-tech VSDs can be developed easily and incorporated into social communication contexts by speech language pathologists, teachers and parents.

Adapted Books

Another low-tech tool that aims to support communication development and social interaction is the use of adapted books. Adapted books refers to modifying the text in a book, providing access to tactile objects, visual support by adding picture icons to a page, and textured surfaces to the book (Mims, 2009; Mucchetti, 2013). These types of adapted books can be easily implemented in inclusive classrooms targeting universal learning for all children. Shared reading of adapted books allows for repeated exposure to adapted materials in a structured context for children with complex communication needs (Mucchetti, 2013). These types of adapted books in particular could be useful for individuals on the autism spectrum as it targets their strengths, specifically the visual and interactive components of the books.

Shared Book Reading

Shared book reading has been documented as providing an ideal context for communication interactions between children with complex communication needs and their communication partners (Liboiron & Soto, 2006). A majority of children are first exposed to the world of literacy by participating in book reading activities with adults (Gilkerson et al., 2017). Shared book reading is an activity that promotes social interaction by parents and teachers scaffolding a child's language development (Milburn et al., 2014).

Shared book reading refers to an adult reading a book aloud to a child while also interacting with the child by discussing the text, by asking questions, responding to the child's interests, relating the story to the child's life experiences and reinforcing the child's correct responses (Boyle et al., 2019). The advantage of shared book reading is that it provides repeated exposure to rich language that is beyond the child's language level and many opportunities for partners to build on the child's language (Yorke et al., 2018). Best practices for shared book reading include, (a) having an adult read to the child, (b) repeated reading of the book with explanations of word meanings, and (c) interactive instruction (McKeown & Beck, 2014). In addition, just reading the text to implicitly teach vocabulary has been found to not be as effective as direct teaching during shared book reading experiences (Beck et al., 2013).

Mims and colleagues (2012) implemented shared book reading of adapted books with two students with significant intellectual impairments and visual impairments in the United States. The specific adaptations made to the books were the stories were shortened, pages were laminated, objects (nouns) were velcroed directly onto the pages, and repeated storylines were added. The students were asked comprehension questions based on the stories. Both of the students showed increases in comprehension across the three books that were read to them.

Muchetti (2013) conducted a shared book reading study using adapted books specifically targeting four children diagnosed with autism spectrum disorder with complex communication needs in the United States. The intervention was carried out by teachers of the children. The books were adapted by simplifying the text, providing visual support by adding picture symbols corresponding to the text on each page, and by adding tactile objects to some pages highlighting salient objects in the story. The teachers asked comprehension questions related to the story. All four students showed increased comprehension and task engagement following intervention when compared to baseline.

Samarasinghe and colleagues (2018) conducted a similar shared book reading intervention with three children diagnosed with autism spectrum disorder who presented with complex communication needs. This study expands on previous research as it was conducted in an LMIC, Sri Lanka. In addition, the specific focus of the study was to increase receptive vocabulary skills by using a direct instruction strategy. The target vocabulary consisted of nouns, verbs and adjectives. The books that were chosen for the study were all by the same author. All the books contained the following elements, (a) interesting to pre-school-age children, (b) had large fonts, (c) were colorful, (d) contained photos of vocabulary that could be easily represented, and (e) had simple language. The adapted book was created by obtaining two identical storybooks, cutting out the vocabulary from one of the books, and then laminating the original book as well as the cut-out vocabulary elements. It was determined to be more economical to purchase two storybooks instead of making color photocopies of the pages of one of the books. The cut-out elements were then fixed back on to the original book using transparent Velcro. The cut-out elements created a 3-D effect (see Figure 29.3). The advantages of the cut-out vocabulary were similar to the moveable hotspots on the low-tech VSDs. The motion in the cut-out elements helped to engage the children and made the shared book reading activity more interactive. In addition, the motion facilitated learning verbs such as "fly" and "fall" because the interventionist could actually remove the owl from the page and use movement to simulate flying (Figure 29.4).

The direct intervention strategy that was used was a mnemonic instruction strategy. In this strategy, the interventionist uses both the targeted and non-targeted vocabulary words to interact with each other to aid in the child's comprehension of the targeted words. All three children in the study showed improved comprehension of the target vocabulary words. Furthermore, the comprehension of these words was maintained a month after the conclusion of the study.

Figure 29.3 Cut-out elements

Both of these interventions, low-tech VSDs and adapted books, are types of AAC approaches that can facilitate the communication and language development of children with complex communication needs in a school-based setting. They are relatively low-cost approaches that require a minimum of materials, and may be adapted for use in any context in which resources are constrained. However, providing appropriate AAC systems alone does not guarantee the ability to communicate successfully (Schepis & Reid, 2003). It is also important that communication partners for children with complex communication needs in inclusive settings are able to support them and provide an appropriate context.

Communication Partner Training

Children with complex communication needs often require assistance from their communication partners to communicate effectively using AAC (Binger, Kent-Walsh, Ewing, & Taylor, 2010). Similarly, students with the most significant disabilities require a high level of support from educators in order to participate actively in inclusive education settings (Kent-Walsh & Light, 2003). These educators require training on communication partner strategies to better facilitate the students' communication. There have been many positive outcomes as a result of training communication partners: increased knowledge and skills in AAC (Bornman et al., 2007; McConachie & Pennington, 1997; Patel & Khamis-Dakwar, 2005), provision of increased number of opportunities for communication (Binger et al., 2010; Bingham, Spooner, & Browder,

Figure 29.4 Showing action verb flying

2007; Douglas et al., 2014; Kent-Walsh, Binger, & Hasham, 2010; Rosa-Lugo & Kent-Walsh, 2008), improved communication with individuals with CCN (Douglas et al., 2014), and increased positive attitudes regarding AAC (Patel & Khamis-Dakwar, 2005). The positive outcomes reported were not only for communication partners but also for students with complex communication needs. For example, they have increased access to the general education curriculum, improved use of AAC in the classroom and increased social participation (Calculator, 2009).

Communication partners of children with complex communication needs may not intuitively know how to provide opportunities for communication (Binger & Kent-Walsh, 2012). In fact, communication partners have been reported to exhibit less than ideal partner communicative behaviors. These include: (a) dominating interactions; (b) asking predominantly yes or no questions; (c) taking a majority of conversational turns; (d) providing fewer opportunities for individuals who use AAC to respond; (e) interrupting; (f) focusing on the technology or technique being used rather than the individual; and, (g) not always confirming the content of the message. Caregivers of children with developmental delays tend to be more directive, as compared to the caregivers of typically developing children (Tannock, Girolametto, & Siegel, 1992). As a result, children who use AAC are passive communicators, only responding when required and infrequently initiating during interactions with their caregivers (e.g., Bornman, Alant, & Meiring, 2001; Light and Kelford-Smith, 1993). In contrast, evocative communication opportunities provide the child an opportunity to play a more active role (Whitehurst et al., 1988). An evocative communication opportunity can be defined as: (a) an open-ended question (excluding yes/no questions), comment, or choice; (b) provision of some means of aided AAC for the child to respond; and (c) wait time of 5 s or more (adapted from Douglas et al., 2014; Light, Collier, and Parnes, 1985; Whitehurst et al., 1988).

Communication Partner Training in LMICs

There is a growing recognition and need to train communication partners in LMICs. In places with a limited number of speech and language therapists (SLTs), and an even smaller number of SLTs who have sub-specialized in AAC (e.g., Fuller, Gray, Warrick, Blackstone, & Pressman, 2009) it is all the more vital to train communication partners to take on the responsibility of providing AAC supports. Despite this urgent need, we currently have only a limited understanding of how to go about training communication partners living in these contexts. Muttiah and colleagues (2014) conducted a focus group study exploring best practices when conducting AAC training in LMICs. The authors urged trainers to consider the following four factors:

1. Investigate learner needs: to understand the trainee learning needs prior to conducting the training. This was to be able to conduct a training program that was customized to the participants.
2. Provide contextually relevant instructional content: The content and materials used in training should be relevant to trainees' contexts. This is especially important when considering the differences between high-income and low-income contexts.
3. Use engaging instructional activities: The training activities should be learner-centered. For example, learners should be actively engaged and conducting hands-on activities during training.
4. Assess the impact of instructional activities: Both the short-term and long-term impact of the training should be evaluated. The evaluation is important to make sure learners have understood what was taught, able to implement strategies accurately and in order to promote sustainability and continued use of AAC.

Muttiah, Drager, McNaughton and Perera (2018) implemented these best practices when conducting a training for a group of nine special education teachers in Sri Lanka. The researchers initially investigated learners' needs by conducting a pre-training questionnaire as part of a needs analysis to understand what teachers wanted to learn more about. They provided contextually relevant instructional content by specifically providing communication strategies and activities based on the individual students the teachers worked with using locally available, inexpensive material. Engaging instructional activities were implemented during the training by providing teachers with opportunities to develop their own AAC materials and to role-play using these. The impact of the training was assessed by observing learners demonstrate providing communication opportunities and by conducting a satisfaction survey. The training consisted of one group training, which was between 3.5 and 4 hours and three individual follow-ups with each teacher in their own classrooms that were between 20-30 minutes. A repeated measures ANOVA mixed effects model was used to evaluate differences between the number of teacher-provided communication opportunities during the pre-training, post-training and follow-up phases. The main effect for the pre-post-follow-up variable was statistically significant. Teachers provided a statistically significant higher number of evocative communication opportunities in the post-training and follow-up conditions than in the pre-training condition. The calculated effect size for the pre-post comparison was large.

A repeated measures ANOVA mixed effects model was used to evaluate differences between the number of communication turns taken by students during the pre-training, post-training and follow-up phases. The main effect for the pre-post-follow-up variable was statistically significant. The students took a statistically significant higher number of communication turns in the post-training and follow-up conditions than in the pre-training condition. The calculated effect size for the pre-post comparison was large.

All the teachers stated that they would participate in a similar training program if given another opportunity to do so. Additionally, all of them said that they would recommend this training program to other teachers. All teacher participants reported a noticeable change in the students they worked with. This relatively quick training in a context with limited resources resulted in positive outcomes for both the teachers and the students they worked with.

Low-Tech VSDs and Paraprofessionals Training

Paraprofessionals provide educational support to individuals with complex communication needs throughout the day. However, paraprofessionals may not necessarily have received specific training on communication strategies that would facilitate communication with individuals who have communication difficulties. Schepis and Reid (2003) argue that effective use of AAC systems depends significantly on the level of support from staff and other communication partners; in turn, their ability to support individuals with complex communication needs will depend on their level of training (Kent-Walsh and Light, 2003).

The best practices when conducting AAC training in LMICs were extended to a high-income context when Muttiah, Drager, and Hall (2016) conducted a study training six paraprofessionals on the use of low-tech VSDs in the United States. The training consisted of a group training and three individual follow-ups with each paraprofessional-student dyad in their classrooms. During the training paraprofessionals were taught to: (a) provide evocative communication opportunities, (b) provide a means for the students to respond via the low-tech VSDs, and (c) wait for a response. Paraprofessionals were involved in developing personalized low-tech VSDs for each student they worked with. During the group training they were shown how to construct the VSDs, how to decide on the hotspots for each scene, and how to present evocative communication opportunities (see Figure 29.5). Using the low-tech VSDs was made user-friendly by writing the appropriate evocative communication opportunity corresponding to that particular VSD on the back of it. The most salient hotspots were also written on the back of the VSDs. Therefore, when the paraprofessional held up the VSD in front of the child he/

Figure 29.5 Training for paraprofessionals

Figure 29.6 Example VSD

Figure 29.7 Example VSD

she knew exactly what to say and where on the VSDs they should be pointing to or modeling. See Figures 29.6 and 29.7 for examples of VSDs that were constructed by the paraprofessionals. All the paraprofessionals in the study provided a higher number of evocative communication opportunities to the students following the training. In addition, all the students in the study demonstrated increased communication by taking a higher number of communication turns following the training for their paraprofessionals. Conventionally, research conducted in Western countries is extended to LMICs; however, in this instance research conducted first in an LMIC was transferred to a high-income context and remained applicable. There is a need for more research to be conducted in LMICs so that this type of transactional learning between LMICs and high-income countries can take place.

Conclusion

This chapter discussed low-tech AAC systems and partner communication strategies that are appropriate for low-resource contexts. This chapter provides teachers in inclusive classrooms with information on low-tech VSDs and adapted books. In addition, it talks about how both these low-tech tools can be implemented in inclusive classrooms. Although these tools were specifically discussed as being applicable in low-resource contexts they could be effective in high-income countries as well. Teachers will also be able to identify key principles when conducting training for communication partners from LMIC contexts. The AAC systems discussed and the partner communication strategies can be easily implemented by teachers, clinicians and parents globally.

References

Babb, S., Gormley, J., McNaughton, D., & Light, J. (2019). Enhancing independent participation within vocational activities for an adolescent with ASD using AAC video visual scene displays. *Journal of Special Education Technology, 34*, 120–132.

Beck, I. L., McKeown, M. G., & Kucan, L. (2013). *Bringing words to life: Robust vocabulary instruction.* Guilford Press.

Bingham, M. A., Spooner, F., & Browder, D. (2007). Training paraeducators to promote the use of augmentative and alternative communication by students with significant disabilities. *Education and Training in Developmental Disabilities, 42*, 339–352. www.jstor.org/stable/23879627

Binger, C., & Kent-Walsh, J. (2012). Selecting skills to teach communication partners: Where do I start? *SIG 12 Perspectives on Augmentative and Alternative Communication, 21*, 127–135. doi:10.1044/aac21.4.127

Binger, C., Kent-Walsh, J., Ewing, C., & Taylor, S. (2010). Teaching educational assistants to facilitate the multisymbol message productions of young students who require augmentative and alternative communication. *American Journal of Speech-Language Pathology, 19*, 108–120. doi:10.1044/1058-0360(2009/09-0015)

Bornman, J., Alant, E., & Lloyd, L. L. (2007). A beginning communication intervention protocol: In-service training of health workers. *Education and Training in Developmental Disabilities, 42*, 190.

Bornman, J., Alant, E., & Meiring, E. (2001). The use of a digital voice output device to facilitate language development in a student with developmental apraxia of speech: A case study. *Disability and Rehabilitation, 23*, 623–634. doi:10.1080/09638280110036517

Boyle, S. A., McNaughton, D., & Chapin, S. E. (2019). Effects of shared reading on the early language and literacy skills of children with autism spectrum disorders: A systematic review. *Focus on Autism and Other Developmental Disabilities, 34*, 205–214. doi:10.1177/1088357619838276

Bunning, K., Gona, J. K., Newton, C. R., & Hartley, S. (2014). Caregiver perceptions of students who have complex communication needs following a home-based intervention using augmentative and alternative communication in rural Kenya: An intervention note. *Augmentative and Alternative Communication, 30*, 344–356. doi:10.3109/07434618.2014.970294

Calculator, S. N.. (2009). Augmentative and alternative communication (AAC) and inclusive education for students with the most severe disabilities. *International Journal of Inclusive Education, 13*, 93–113. doi:10.1080/13603110701284656

Douglas, S. N., McNaughton, D., & Light, J. (2014). Online training for paraeducators to support the communication of young students. *Journal of Early Intervention, 35*, 223–242. doi:10.1177/1053815114526782

Drager, K., Light, J., & McNaughton, D. (2010). Effects of AAC interventions on communication and language for young children with complex communication needs. *Journal of Pediatric Rehabilitation Medicine, 3*, 303–310.

Drager, K. D. R., Light, J. C., Speltz, J. C., Fallon, K. A., & Jeffries, L. Z. (2003). The performance of typically developing 2 1/2-year-olds on dynamic display AAC technologies with different system layouts and language organizations. *Journal of Speech, Language and Hearing Research, 46*, 298–312. doi:10.1044/1092-4388(2003/024)

Drager, K. D., Light, J., Currall, J., Muttiah, N., Smith, V., Kreis, D., Nilam-Hall, A., Parratt, D., Schuessler, K., & Wiscount, J. (2019). AAC technologies with visual scene displays and "just in time" programming and symbolic communication turns expressed by students with severe disability. *Journal of Intellectual & Developmental Disability, 44*, 321–336. doi:10.3109/13668250.2017.1326585

Fuller, P., Gray, C., Warrick, A., Blackstone, S., & Pressman, H. (2009). Setting up AAC services in emerging AAC areas. *Communication Matters, 23*, 13–16.

Gilkerson, J., Richards, J. A., & Topping, K. J. (2017). The impact of book reading in the early years on parent–child language interaction. *Journal of Early Childhood Literacy, 17*, 92–110. doi:10.1177/1468798415608907

Holyfield, C., Caron, J. G., Drager, K., & Light, J. (2018). Effect of mobile technology featuring visual scene displays and just-in-time programming on communication turns by preadolescent and adolescent beginning communicators. *International Journal of Speech-Language Pathology*, *21*, 201–211. doi:10.1080/17549507.2018.1441440

Jagaroo, V., & Wilkinson, K. (2008). Further considerations of visual cognitive neuroscience in aided AAC: The potential role of motion perception systems in maximizing design display. *Augmentative and Alternative Communication*, *24*(1), 29–42. doi:10.1080/07434610701390673

Kent-Walsh, J., & Light, J. (2003). General education teachers' experiences with inclusion of students who use augmentative and alternative communication. *Augmentative and Alternative Communication*, *19*, 104–124. doi.org/10.1080/0743461031000112043

Kent-Walsh, J., Binger, C., & Hasham, Z. (2010). Effects of parent instruction on the symbolic communication of students using augmentative and alternative communication during storybook reading. *American Journal of Speech-Language Pathology*, *19*, 97–107. doi:10.1044/1058-0360(2010/09-0014)

Kieling, C., Baker-Henningham, H., Belfer, M., Conti, G., Ertem, I., Omigbodun, O., ... & Rahman, A. (2011). Child and adolescent mental health worldwide: Evidence for action. *The Lancet*, *378*(9801), 1515–1525. doi.org/10.1016/S0140-6736(11)60827-1

Liboiron, N., & Soto, G. (2006). Shared storybook reading with a student who uses alternative and augmentative communication: A description of scaffolding practices. *Child Language Teaching and Therapy*, *22*, 69–95. doi.org/10.1191/0265659006ct298oa

Light, J., Collier, B., & Parnes, P. (1985). Communication interaction between young nonphysically disabled students and their primary caregivers: Part I-discourse patterns. *Augmentative and Alternative Communication*, *1*, 74–83.

Light, J., & Kelford-Smith, A. (1993). Home literacy experiences of preschoolers who use AAC systems and of their nondisabled peers. *Augmentative and Alternative Communication*, *9*, 10–25. doi:10.1080/07434619312331276371

Light, J., Drager, K., & Wilkinson, K. (2012). Designing effective visual scene displays for young children with complex communication needs. Presented at the Biennial Conference of the International Society of Augmentative and Alternative Communication, Pittsburgh.

McCarthy, J., Light, J., Drager, K., McNaughton, D., Grodzicki, L., & Parkin, E. (2006). Re-designing scanning to reduce learning demands: The performance of typically developing 2-year-olds. *Augmentative and Alternative Communication*, *22*, 269–283. doi:10.1080/00498250600718621

McConachie, H., & Pennington, L. (1997). In-service training for schools on augmentative and alternative communication. *International Journal of Language & Communication Disorders*, *32*(Spec No), 277–288. doi:10.1080/13682829709177101

McKeown, M. G., & Beck, I. L. (2014). Effects of vocabulary instruction on measures of language processing: Comparing two approaches. *Early Childhood Research Quarterly*, *29*, 520–530. doi:10.1016/j.ecresq.2014.06.002

McNaughton, D., & Light, J. (2013). The iPad and mobile technology revolution: Benefits and challenges for individuals who require augmentative and alternative communication. *Augmentative and Alternative Communication*, *29*, 107–116. doi:10.3109/07434618.2013.784930

Milburn, T. F., Girolametto, L., Weitzman, E., & Greenberg, J. (2014). Enhancing preschool educators' ability to facilitate conversations during shared book reading. *Journal of Early Childhood Literacy*, *14*, 105–140. doi:10.1177/1468798413478261

Mims, P. J. (2009). *The effects of the system of least prompts on teaching comprehension skills during a shared story to students with significant intellectual disabilities* [Doctoral Dissertation, The University of North Carolina at Charlotte]. www.uncc.edu

Mims, P. J., Hudson, M. E., & Browder, D. M. (2012). Using read-alouds of grade-level biographies and systematic prompting to promote comprehension for students with moderate and severe developmental disabilities. *Focus on Autism and Other Developmental Disabilities*, *27*, 67–80. doi:10.1177/1088357612446859

Mucchetti, C. A. (2013). Adapted shared reading at school for minimally verbal students with autism. *Autism*, *17*, 358–372.

Muttiah, N., Drager, K., & Hall, L. (2016, August). Effects of training paraprofessionals to use low-tech visual scene displays (VSDs). Paper presented at the International Society of Augmentative and Alternative Communication (ISAAC), Toronto, Canada.

Muttiah, N., McNaughton, D. B., & Drager, K. D. (2014). Providing instructional support for AAC service delivery in low and middle-income countries. *International Journal of Speech-Language Pathology*, *18*, 341–353. doi:10.3109/17549507.2015.1101154

Muttiah, N., Drager, K. D. R., McNaughton, D., & Perera, N. (2018). Evaluating an AAC training for special education teachers in Sri Lanka, a low- and middle-income country. *Augmentative and Alternative Communication, 34,* 276–287. doi:10.1080/07434618.2018.1512651

Muttiah, N., Drager, K. D. R., Beale, B., Bongo, H., & Riley, L. (2019). The effects of an intervention using low-tech visual scene displays and aided modeling with young children with complex communication needs. *Topics in Early Childhood Special Education, 42,* 91–104. doi.org/10.1177/0271121419844825

Olusanya, B. O., Ruben, R. J., & Parving, A. (2006). Reducing the burden of communication disorders in the developing world: An opportunity for the millennium development project. *JAMA, 296,* 441–444.

Patel, R., & Khamis-Dakwar, R. (2005). An AAC training program for special education teachers: A case study of Palestinian Arab teachers in Israel. *Augmentative and Alternative Communication, 21,* 205–217. doi:10.1080/07434610400011638

Romski, M. A., & Sevcik, R. A. (1997). Augmentative and alternative communication for children with developmental disabilities. *Mental Retardation And Developmental Disabilities Research Reviews, 3,* 363–368. doi:10.1002/(sici)1098-2779(1997)3:4<363::aid-mrdd12>3.0.co;2-

Rosa-Lugo, L. I., & Kent-Walsh, J. (2008). Effects of parent instruction on communicative turns of Latino students using augmentative and alternative communication during story book reading. *Communication Disorders Quarterly, 30,* 49–61.

Samarasinghe, S. I. S., & Muttiah, N. (2018). *Effectiveness of share book reading to increase receptive vocabulary skills of 3–4 year old children with autism* [Undergraduate Thesis, The University of Kelaniya].

Schepis, M., & Reid, D. (2003). Issues affecting staff enhancement of speech-generating device use among people with severe cognitive disabilities. *Augmentative and Alternative Communication, 19,* 59–65. doi:10.1080/0743461032000056469

Snow, C. E. (1999). Social perspectives on the emergence of language. In B. MacWhinney (Ed.), *The emergence of language* (pp. 257–276). Mahwah: Lawrence Erlbaum Associates.

Srinivasan, S., Mathew, S. N., & Lloyd, L. L. (2011). Insights into communication intervention and AAC in South India: A mixed-methods study. *Communication Disorders Quarterly, 32,* 232–246. doi:10.1177/1525740109354775

Tannock, R., Girolametto, L., & Siegel, L. B. (1992). Language intervention with students who have developmental delays: Effects of an intervention approach. *American Journal on Mental Retardation, 97,* 145–160.

Whitehurst, G. J., Falco, F. L., Lonigan, C. J., Fischel, J. E., DeBaryshe, B. D., Valdez-Menchaca, M. C., & Caulfield, M. (1988). Accelerating language development through picture book reading. *Developmental Psychology, 24,* 552–559.

Wilkinson, K. M., & Light, J. (2011). Preliminary investigation of visual attention to human figures in photographs: Potential considerations for the design of aided AAC visual scene displays. *Journal of Speech, Language and Hearing Research, 54,* 1644. doi:10.1044/1092-4388(2011/10-0098)

Wilkinson, K. M., Light, J., & Drager, K. (2012). Considerations for the composition of visual scene displays: Potential contributions of information from visual and cognitive sciences. *Augmentative and Alternative Communication, 28*(3), 137–147. doi:10.3109/07434618.2012.704522

World Health Organization, & The World Bank. (2011). *World report on disability.* Geneva: World Health Organization.

Yorke, A. M., Light, J. C., Gosnell Caron, J., McNaughton, D. B., & Drager, K. D. (2018). The effects of explicit instruction in academic vocabulary during shared book reading on the receptive vocabulary of children with complex communication needs. *Augmentative and Alternative Communication, 34,* 288–300. doi:10.1080/07434618.2018.1506823

30
SUICIDE IDEATION AND PREVENTION IN STUDENTS WITH INTELLECTUAL DISABILITIES

Amy K. McDiarmid*, Jillian Talley and Devadrita Talapatra

Suicide was the fourth leading cause of death for 15–29-year-olds worldwide in 2019 and remains the second leading cause of death in the United States for individuals between the ages of 10 and 24 (Centers for Disease Control and Prevention, National Center for Health Statistics [CDC], 2020 & WHO, 2021). In recent years, the suicide rates for this age range have nearly tripled (Curtin & Heron, 2019). Although these rates are inclusive of youth with and without disabilities, to better serve school-aged youth, it is imperative that school mental health providers (e.g., school psychologists, school counselors, special educators, and school social workers) understand the unique risks and challenges faced by the distinct disability populations they serve. One group that has long been absent in prevention and intervention discussions of suicide, suicidal ideation, crisis, and trauma are students with intellectual disabilities (ID); Merrick et al., 2012; Razza et al., 2014; Ricciardi, 2013). Despite being neglected in this topic area, these individuals experience the same suicide rate as their peers without disabilities (Merrick et al., 2012). School-based mental health providers have the skills and the opportunity to create systems and modify current practices to support students with ID in addressing suicide within this population (National Association of School Psychologists [NASP], 2020b).

Intellectual Disabilities and Mental Health

ID is an umbrella term that encompasses several disorders, such as autism spectrum disorders, Fragile X syndrome, Down syndrome, and other developmental and neurocognitive disorders. Several characteristics define this population. The American Association on Intellectual and Developmental Disabilities (AAIDD), along with the Diagnostic and Statistical Manual of Mental Disorders (DSM–5), states that an individual with ID must have significant limitations in intellectual *and* adaptive functioning that originated during the developmental period and continue throughout the lifespan; these significant impairments in communication, self-care, social skills, community use, self-direction, health and safety, and functional academics negatively impact daily functioning (AAIDD, n.d.; Gargiulo & Bouck, 2018). These limitations that individuals with ID experience have impacted how mental health providers understand and identify the suicide risk of an individual with ID.

* amy.mcdiarmid@du.edu

There is a persistent myth that individuals with ID cannot feel grief (Dodd et al., 2008) and do not experience trauma (Talapatra et al., 2020), but the reality is that youth with ID have similar rates of suicidal ideation and suicide attempts as their neurotypical peers (Dickerson Mayes et al., 2015). Students with ID often have their mental health concerns "overshadowed" by their diagnosis (Merrick et al., 2012; Razza et al., 2014). Many mental health providers discount symptoms of mental health distress in individuals with ID; instead, they attribute any changes to current presentation and functioning to the primary disability condition, which leads to the underdiagnosing of co-morbid conditions that may increase the likelihood of suicidal ideation (Merrick et al., 2012; Razza et al., 2014; Trauma and Intellectual/Developmental Disability Collaborative Group, 2020). Consequently, individuals with ID are less likely to be referred for suicidal behavior, even though these individuals have thought, attempted, and died by suicide (Ludi et al., 2012). This lack of knowledge and misunderstanding by mental health providers is reflected in the limited research concerning individuals with ID and trauma, let alone suicidal ideation (Razza et al., 2014; Talapatra et al., 2020). This (lack of) data indicates that a call to action must be made for school-based mental health providers to engage in training about this specific population of individuals so that they are able to more readily differentiate between behaviors that may be a manifestation of ID and behaviors that may indicate suicidal ideation and tendencies.

Suicide Risk Assessment

When examining processes for suicide risk assessment, a variety of terminology is utilized. In an effort to provide context and consistency throughout this chapter, important terms related to suicide assessment are defined in Table 30.1.

Table 30.1 Definitions of terminology related to suicide risk assessment

Term	Definition	Citation/Website
Suicide	act of deliberately killing oneself	World Health Organization. (2014). *Preventing suicide: A global imperative executive summary.* Geneva, Switzerland: Author.
Suicidal Ideation	Thinking about, considering, or planning suicide	National Institute of Mental Health. (2021, January). Suicide. Retrieved from https://www.nimh.nih.gov/health/statistics/suicide.shtml
Mental Health Screening	An evaluation of a population of students or a subset of a population of students to determine whether they may be at risk for a mental health concern	Substance Abuse and Mental Health Services Administration. (2019). *Ready, Set, Go, Review: Screening for Behavioral Health Risk in Schools.* Rockville, MD: Office of the Chief Medical Officer.
Suicide Risk Assessment	Formal process/tool to determine the level of risk and appropriate actions to ensure the immediate and long-term health of a student.	National Association of School Psychologists. (2015a). *Preventing Suicide: Guidelines for Administrators and Crisis Teams.* Bethesda, MD, USA.

To assess for suicidality within the general population, school-based mental health providers typically rely on written screeners or verbal interviews.

Many standardized screeners related to characteristics of suicidality such as *Patient Health Questionnaire-9* (Kroenke et al., 2001), *Beck Depression Inventory* (Beck et al., 1996) and *Ask Suicide-Screening Questions* (Horowitz et al., 2012) are developed to meet a sixth grade or higher reading level, and students with ID may be unable to access these measures appropriately. Often, the screener or interview contains complex sentence structure and vocabulary within prompts or question items. They may contain items written in the past tense and response options of four or more choices (Ludi et al., 2012). The complexity of the prompts can limit the capacity of students with ID to understand the question or concept (Ludi et al., 2012), while complicated response formats can be confusing given that youth with ID perform better with fewer and consistent choice options (Masi et al., 2012). Furthermore, in modifying screeners and assessments (e.g., reading self-report screeners aloud), school mental health providers break standardization of the assessment, which can influence the validity and reliability of response interpretation. These limitations create barriers to accurately assessing the suicide risk exhibited within students with ID.

Suicide Prevention and Assessment of Students with an Intellectual Disability

Although there is limited data related to students with ID and suicidal ideation, as noted above, research concludes that suicide risk is present within this population (Ludi et al., 2012). The importance of screening for suicidal ideation and behaviors in youth as a method of prevention and early detection is evident. Suicide risk assessment is arguably one of the most difficult aspects of a school mental health provider's role, but also one of the most critical (Erps, Ochs, & Myers, 2020). School mental health providers can provide access to mental health supports that students might not otherwise receive and thus play a vital role in determining a student's suicide risk (Weir, 2019). Indeed, assessing children and adolescents for risk of suicide is an essential component of school psychology practice. Although rates of suicidal ideation tend to peak in middle school, the rates of suicide attempts and deaths continue to grow through high school (Singer et al., 2019). The following sections review risk and protective factors, a tiered approach to suicide screening, and adaptations that can be used in suicide risk assessments for youth with ID.

Suicide Risk Factors for Individuals with Intellectual Disability

We believe school mental health providers must be aware of both the heightened risk factors and the depressed protective factors that encapsulate the ID population. Several studies suggest that individuals with ID have poor mental health, self-harm, suicidal thinking, and suicidal attempts (Giannini et al., 2010; Gilmore & Cuskelly, 2014; King et al., 2019; Ludi et al., 2020). Knowledge of these factors is critical for mental health providers so they may correctly interpret screeners, assessments, and interviews for suicide risk.

High prevalence risk factors. A myriad of risk factors increases suicidal ideation, such as having a psychiatric disorder, experiencing bullying, family dysfunction, bereavement, and a history of physical or sexual abuse (see Figure 30.1; Borowsky et al., 2013; Giannini et al., 2010).

Individuals with ID experience these risk factors at rates similar to or higher than their neurotypical peers (Giannini et al., 2010; Ludi et al., 2012; Mollison et al., 2014; Razza et al., 2014). Notably, individuals with mild ID were shown to have the highest rates of risk factors

| Students with ID are more likely to experience trauma | Students with ID have higher comorbidity rates with psychiatric | Students with ID are more likely to have stronger negative | Mental health providers are more likely to designates previous | Mental health providers are more likely to dismiss suicidal |

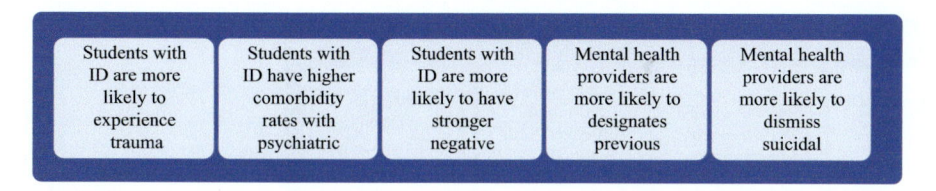

Figure 30.1 Overview of increased suicide risk factors for individuals with any severity ID

when comparing between the severity ranges for ID (Giannini et al., 2010; Ludi et al., 2012). For example, when comparing the rates of psychiatric disorders such as anxiety, depression, and psychosis in children and adolescents with mild ID to children and adolescents without ID, individuals with mild ID are four to six times more likely than their neurotypical peers to have a co-morbid mental health or psychiatric disorder (Enfield et al., 2011; Giannini et al., 2010; Ricciardi, 2013). Additionally, these rates may underestimate the prevalence of psychiatric disorders in individuals with ID because these individuals often have difficulty in expressive and receptive communication (Razza et al., 2014).

One particular risk that is significantly higher for individuals with ID are the higher rates of victimization. Individuals with ID experience sexual abuse and other forms of victimization at a significantly higher rate (1.5 to 10 times) than their neurotypical peers (Brown-Lavoi et al., 2014; Stevens, 2012; Sobsey & Doe, 1991). This is concerning considering that individuals with ID who expressed suicidal ideation or manifested suicidal behaviors, also have experienced high rates of physical abuse (46%), sexual abuse (10.5%), or both (26%; Ludi et al., 2012). As with any reporting in the ID community, abuse is also likely to be underreported, which only exacerbates the likelihood of crimes committed against them (Whittle & Butler, 2018). Further, these traumatic events may lead to changes in independence, care providers, educational settings which can impact symptoms related to trauma (Talapatra et al., 2020). Additionally, in the ID population it is seen that a cumulation of smaller upsetting events can lead to a suicide attempt more often than in the neurotypical population (Bardon, 2020). Practitioners could dismiss one small event and not realize the gravity of the domino effect from the previous unfortunate small events particularly those when a person feels powerless that lead to a suicide attempt (Bardon, 2020).

A history of previous suicide attempts also serves as a significant risk factor for future suicide completion (Mollison et al., 2014). Individuals with mild ID who attempt suicide tend to use more opportunistic methods, which in turn, can lead to mental health providers mistaking a suicide attempt as self-harm or as accidental (Mollison et al., 2014). These attempts require an understanding of that individual's culture because what is available is culture dependent. This incorrect evaluation of the individual's actions may lead to missed opportunities for intervention and dire consequences for these individuals.

The final risk factor that must be considered is the attitude of the mental health community. Some clinicians believe that this population is unable to understand death due to their cognitive abilities, and thus do not take suicidal comments as seriously (Razza et al., 2014; Ricciardi, 2013). This pattern of thought can have grim consequences. Although suicidal behavior is most common among persons with mild ID, the behavior is found at all levels of functioning for individuals with ID (Giannini et al., 2010). Persons with ID tend to use methods linked to opportunity, such as jumping off high structures, hanging, firearms, running into traffic, poisoning, drowning, and stabbing or slashing (Giannini et al., 2010; Merrick et al., 2012). These methods rarely include elaborate planning as a precursor and may seem impulsive in nature making

Lower Protective Factors

- Students with ID have less connection to others
- Students with ID have less self-determination
- Students with ID have more difficulties with Emotion Regulation
- Students with ID often have poor communication skills

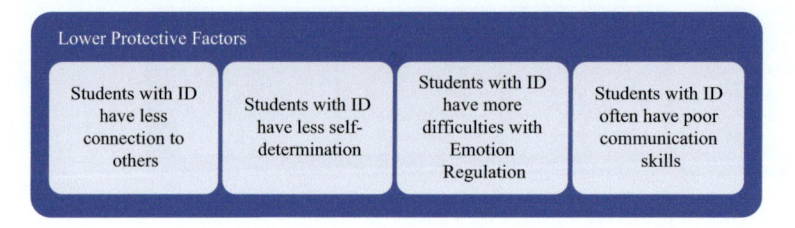

Figure 30.2 Overview lower protective against suicide factors in individuals with ID for all severity levels

it even more difficult to predict (Bardon, 2020; Merrick et al., 2012; Razza et al., 2014). This further supports the need for school-based mental health providers to pay attention to individuals with ID who may be demonstrating symptoms indicative of a psychiatric disorder or poor coping after a stressful event, such as a death.

Lower prevalence protective factors. Protective factors are variables that are specific to the individual that serve as safeguards against suicidal ideation and attempts. Often these protective factors found in the general population maintain lower prevalence or are absent for individuals with ID at all severity levels (Borowsky et al., 2013 see Figure 30.2).

One protective factor that has been shown to be consistent across cultures and individuals is feeling connected to family, friends, or a community (Giannini et al., 2010; Fowler, 2012; Mollison et al., 2014). In schools, this can look like a student having a trusted adult to talk to or having a close peer group. Trusted people not only support, encourage, and increase the likelihood that their friends seek out mental health services and community agencies, but also serve as a person who can alert the school mental health provider that a student is experiencing suicidal ideation (Lieberman et al., 2014). Unfortunately, youth with ID have more difficulty creating close friends (Tipton, et al., 2013). Further, these youth more often experience low-quality friendships than their peers without ID (Tipton et al., 2013). Consequently, students with ID often experience isolation and loneliness (Gilmore & Cuskelly, 2014). Further, families often feel emotionally overwhelmed and incompetent in their role of parenting a child with ID (Widmer et al., 2008). This happens more often if the family only perceives medical staff as their sole support system (Widmer et al., 2008). Connection to someone within the school can serve as a protective factor, unfortunately this connection does not often exist for individuals with ID.

A more recently studied protective factor is self-determination, or the ability to make choices and decisions independently, problem-solve, self-monitor/self-regulate, set goals, and improve their quality of life by pursuing their dreams (Tucker & Wingate, 2014; Wehmeyer, 2005). Self-determination is a skill often difficult for individuals with ID to comprehend and apply due to poor cognitive reasoning and limited explicit instruction in this area (Wehmeyer, 2005). As a result, coping skills, emotional regulation, and mental flexibility – all of which are needed to problem-solve in difficult situations – are compromised.

Lastly, if a student can communicate about their suicidal ideation, then a school mental health provider can intervene (Page et al., 2013). This ability to utilize verbal and non-verbal communication can serve as a protective factor. However, an intellectual disability typically negatively impacts expressive communication and thus affects how well a person with ID can relay messages and express intent, particularly regarding their need for help (Mollison et al., 2014).

School-Based Suicide Risk Assessment Practices

A lack of measures designed for youth with ID presents challenges in screening and assessment for suicide risk. Specifically, designed suicide prevention programming and screening measures for youth with ID do not exist. In addition, youth with ID vary in levels of cognitive and adaptive functioning. However, several measures used to assess the general population can be adapted for students with ID at the universal (Tier 1), targeted (Tier 2) and intensive (Tier 3) level. Within a multi-tiered framework, it is critical that schools have policies and procedures in place to prevent, assess risk, and intervene and respond to youth suicidal behavior (American Foundation for Suicide Prevention, American School Counselor Association, NASP & The Trevor Project, 2019; Singer et al., 2019).

Universal Practices. Schools can embed general suicide prevention curricula into their programming at the universal level; this involves training adults and students within the school community on warning signs and interventions and suicide screeners that allow school mental health personnel to determine which students may need additional suicide risk assessment and intervention. Early detection and assessment training are crucial in suicide prevention and intervention for youth; it ensures staff can act quickly to safeguard the student. School-based suicide prevention programs are one strategy that has proven to be successful in educating school staff on suicide, screening for suicide risk, reducing ideation, decreasing suicide attempts, and increasing coping skills (Aseltine et al., 2007). Many suicide prevention programs aim to educate students on the symptoms of depression and warning signs of suicide. In addition, suicide prevention programs instruct students on how to support peers or themselves when facing a crisis and considering suicide (Schilling et al., 2014). A key component of suicide prevention programming focuses on how to seek help for themselves or peers and whom to approach for help. Although there is not specific programming designed for students with ID, these universal suicide prevention programs can be modified to serve this population. Modifications might include video modeling, social stories, direct teaching, and behavioral rehearsal. These strategies are common practices in teaching social skills to students with ID (Gül, 2016; Talapatra et al., 2020).

Many commonly implemented curriculums for suicide prevention within schools focus on peer response to students in distress. These suicide prevention programs are well researched and registered as evidenced-based programs (Aseltine et al., 2004; Schilling et al., 2014; Substance Abuse and Mental Health Services Administration, 2011). Participants in suicide prevention programming have demonstrated increases in knowledge about depression and suicidal thoughts when compared to a control group (Aseltine, et al., 2004; Aseltine et al., 2007; Schilling et al., 2014). Suicide prevention programming exists for middle school through high school, and encompasses trainings for educators, caregivers, and peers to ensure encouraging and supportive relationships for students. These prevention programs raise awareness of depression in yourself and others while emphasizing the importance of seeking out help from an adult. Universal-level suicide prevention programs that can be adapted for use with students with ID are listed in Table 30.2.

At the universal level, school personnel must make all efforts to identify youth at-risk for suicide as youth do not often refer themselves for evaluation and treatment (Lieberman et al., 2014). Students with ID display many of the common warning signs of suicide exhibited within neurotypical youth, but with more ambiguity. The level of lethality associated with the warning sign for a student with ID is not always an accurate indicator of their suicidal ideation (Bardon, 2020). In practice, this might mean that students with ID may *possess unexpressed thoughts of suicide* and *express less lethal methods within their threats of suicide* but *have a high risk for suicide*. Common warning signs exhibited by youth with mild or moderate ID include threats of suicide (verbal or written); a plan, method and means to commit suicide; discussing death more often; drawings representing a violent act, a suicidal act, pain, symbols related to death (e.g., crosses, caskets, deadly weapons); miming cutting or strangling oneself; previous suicide attempts; making final arrangements (in person or

Table 30.2 ID adaptation of a selected suicide prevention curriculum for middle school and high school students (Gül, 2016; Jacobs, 2013; Talapatra et al., 2020)

Key Component	Goal	Activity	ID Adaptations
Warning Signs of Depression	Students understand and recognize the warning signs of depression	Video presentation	Simplify language and provide visuals to define the signs
Responding to Distressed Friend	Students learn how to respond to a friend in distress and learn mnemonics to remember how to respond	Video vignettes and scripted discussion	Pause the video vignettes to discuss each interaction to slow the pace and reinforce understanding. Role play each response step. Breaking down the components and utilizing supplemental resources to reinforce understanding
Screening for Support	Identify through self-referral students in distress	Written Exit Ticket	Limit wording on exit tickets; use color codes or a yes/no response system to identify students; consider nonverbal response formats

on social media); aggressive behavior towards oneself (e.g., trying to push an object through skin, swallowing substances without knowing their level of actual danger, trying to strangle oneself or hold one's breath); and, displaying symptoms of depression (Bardon, 2020; Lieberman et al., 2014). For students with ID these warning signs can manifest differently depending on the severity of their disability. For students with ID at all severity levels, early warning signs may also include changes in behavior related to sleep problems, sadness, irritable mood, agitation, motor regression, and loss of interest (Sturmey, 2007). Although students with ID at risk for suicide often go unnoticed, they all typically display warning signs that indicate they are considering suicide (Lieberman et al., 2014). It is imperative that staff, parents, and peers are trained in suicide prevention that encompasses the ability to detect warning signs of suicide within a student (see Table 30.3).

Targeted practices. For a more targeted approach to suicide prevention, school mental health providers often conduct a suicide risk assessment with a student. A student might be identified via a suicide screening tool, might be referred by a school staff member or student due to concerns around the student's safety, or self-referred when a student discloses their suicidal ideation to a mental health provider. The suicide risk assessment utilizes an interview format to identify suicidal ideation, including the student's intent and plan, to determine the likelihood of a student harming themselves in the near future (Erbacher et al., 2014). As school mental health providers assess the risk of suicide through active listening, they themselves must develop a plan for intervention (Lieberman et al., 2014).

When working with students with ID, school mental health providers must ask the assessment interview questions *directly* and *contextualize* the student's current responses and actions based on the risk and protective factors and available and perceived resources. For each student with ID, their comprehension of the finality of death may vary (Bardon, 2020). Thus, for each student, it is important to include questions that assess a student's understanding of death and allow the student to provide their own examples and visualizations. A more structured inter-

Table 30.3 Possible manifestations of warning signs for students with ID (Bardon, 2020; Lieberman et al., 2014)

Warning Sign	Possible Manifestation for Students with ID
Unexpressed Thoughts	Not observable, thoughts of one's own death; seeing oneself dead; visualizing relatives' reactions to one's death
Symptoms of Distress	Sadness, mood swings, increased anxiety, fears, somatization, difficulties with sleep, appetite, regression in adaptive functioning, treatment refusal, self-depreciation
Threat of Suicide – Verbal Direct communication	"I want to die", "I want to kill myself"
Threat of Suicide – Verbal Indirect Communication	"I want to go far away and not come back", "I want to join my grandfather at the cemetery"
Threat of Suicide – Written	Drawings of self-harm, death, objects to commit suicide and written words, phrases, notes
Threats of Suicide – Nonverbal	Miming suicide, swallowing non-toxic substances, choking oneself with hands, holding breath, physically harming self with non-lethal objects
Plan	Spontaneous, opportunistic, unstructured thoughts or verbal and nonverbal expressions of method
Previous Suicide Attempts	Swallowing toxic substances, cutting, strangle or hanging, jumping from a high place or out a window, jumping in front of vehicle or running into traffic

view may be helpful. Initial questions within the suicide risk assessment interview establish the student's current feelings specifically around levels of depression, hopelessness, and helplessness. The school mental health provider can use pictures, short stories, and other tools to elicit the student's feeling (Talapatra et al., 2020). They can also read screener items aloud and record responses instead of having the student read and write.

The assessment interview also examines the student's thoughts of suicide currently and any previous suicide attempts to determine the present level of risk. The suicide risk assessment interview incorporates questions to determine if the student has a plan for suicide, including a method, a timeframe, and if the individual has initiated any final preparations. When working with students with ID, this should involve reaching out to the adults that the student trusts (e.g., family members, family friends, peer buddies, and school professionals) to determine the student's present level of risk. Students may not be able to articulate a specific plan or recall previous attempts, so utilizing drawings, pictures and other projective measures may be useful in establishing the depth of suicidal ideation (Hurley et al., 1998).

Additionally, the risk assessment interview should examine the student's perceptions of their current support system. This examination allows school staff to assess the level of protective factors a student perceives in their environment. Understanding the student-identified protective factors and current systems of support enables the school mental health provider to utilize a strengths-based perspective for safety planning and intervention. This strengths-based perspective allows for the mental health provider to use the student's own strengths and resiliency to build a plan that can be safe and successful. For students with ID, this might require observations of the student in their classroom, home, and community environments as well as interviews of caregivers and teachers to determine a change in the student's behavior (Sturmey, 2007). Adaptations to suicide risk assessment can be found in Table 30.4.

Table 30.4 Proposed adaptations to suicide risk assessment based on information from Bardon, 2020; Masi et al., 2012; Talapatra et al., 2020

Process to Assess Suicide Risk	Current Practices for Individuals without ID	Adaptations for Individuals with Mild ID	Adaptations for Individuals with Moderate ID
Presentation of Suicide Risk Assessment	Attitude: Empathetic and Serious; use clinical judgement to determine distress	Attitude: Empathetic, serious, adapt language to match their communication level; can use visual supports; use observations; use clinical judgement to determine distress	Empathetic, serious, adapt language to match their communication level, consider using assistive technology, consider using yes/no questions with yes/no papers for the student to point to; use clinical judgement to determine distress
Understanding the concept of death	Currently not assessed	Ask questions about what death is – some examples: • What does being dead mean? • What happens when you die? • Has anyone you know died? Ask questions about the finality of death • Can you see your friends after you die?	Ask concrete questions • Has anyone you know died? • Is death the only way to end pain? • Is death forever? • Has anyone you know killed themselves?
Indicators of suicidal ideation	Threats of suicide (verbal or written); a plan, method and means to commit suicide; previous suicide attempts; making final arrangements (in person or on social media); displaying symptoms of depression	Additional Indicators: • discussing death more often • drawings representing a violent act, a suicidal act, pain, symbols related to death e.g., crosses, caskets, deadly weapons. • miming cutting or strangling oneself. • aggressive behavior towards oneself e.g., trying to push an object through skin, swallowing substances without knowing their level of actual danger, trying to strangle oneself or hold one's breath.	Additional Indicators: • Chronic Powerlessness • Expectations either being too high or too low for what they feel they can do.

(*Continued*)

Table 30.4 (Continued)

Process to Assess Suicide Risk	Current Practices for Individuals without ID	Adaptations for Individuals with Mild ID	Adaptations for Individuals with Moderate ID
Asking about passive Suicidal Ideation	There are no standard questions, but some common ones are: • Do you ever think about going to sleep and not waking up? • Have you thought about just not wanting to be alive?	There are no standard questions, try to stay concrete and ask about past, present and future thoughts. Be direct. • Do you ever want to go away and never come back?	
Asking about active Suicidal Ideation	Has a focus on intent. • Have you thought about killing yourself? • Do you have a plan? Or how would you kill yourself?	Continue to focus on concrete. Try to avoid suggestions • Do you think about killing yourself? • In the past have you thought about killing yourself? • How would you kill yourself? • Talk to trusted adults if the individual has mentioned wanting to kill themselves	Continue to focus on concrete. Try to avoid suggestion • Do you think about killing yourself? • Focus more on distress than intent • Connect with trusted adults about changes in behavior or various ways the individual could communicate distress
Ask about protective factors	Ask about factors that could stop someone from killing themselves e.g. What do you have to live for? Why would you not want to kill yourself?	Focusing on the concrete: • What do you hope to do in the future? Talk to trusted adults about ways the individual can connect to the community	Focusing on concrete: • What do you hope to do in the future? Talk to trusted adults about ways the individual can connect to the community

(Continued)

Table 30.4 (Continued)

Process to Assess Suicide Risk	Current Practices for Individuals without ID	Adaptations for Individuals with Mild ID	Adaptations for Individuals with Moderate ID
Determining Risk	Actual lethality and danger based on plan and method correlates to risk e.g., high lethality, specific plan leads to high risk	Perceived lethality correlates to risk e.g., if the person fully believes they can die by swimming with whales, then it is a higher risk and consider long term risk factors	Perceived lethality correlates to risk e.g., if the person fully believes they can die by jumping from 2nd floor window, then it is a higher risk and consider long term risk factors

Areas of Intervention for School Based Mental Health Providers

Bolstering protective factors can be an effective way for school mental health providers to intervene. The first area of intervention can be creating stronger family-school partnerships. As previously stated, when families and individuals with ID feel connected to the school this decreases the risk of suicidal ideation (Shaw & Jankowska, 2018). School mental health providers can help to create the partnership and connect families with additional resources in the community. This can further enhance a family's ability to support their child with ID and help a parent feel more confident parenting a child with ID. Family-school partnerships can not only increase verbal communication and connection, but also can help with understanding nonverbal communication. Family members may notice changes in the communication or behavior of a student with ID that can help a school mental health provider determine suicide risk. Further, if the student is working with a speech and language pathologist, multidisciplinary collaboration can help to understand the way the student communicates best.

Teaching individuals with ID aspects of self-determination is another area that school mental health providers can actively strengthen through interventions (Field et al., 2003). For example, the ability to self-regulate emotions, a skill youth with mild/moderate ID often struggle to learn, impacts youth's ability to make friends (Gilmore & Cuskelly, 2014). At the individual level, school mental health providers can instruct students with ID to pay attention to their body's responses to emotions to help them identify what emotion they are experiencing and build a coping skill to handle that emotion (Talapatra et al., 2020). At the group level, social-emotional learning groups and social skills groups may be useful for teaching students with ID ways to regulate their emotions and make and maintain meaningful friendships (NASP, 2015b; Talapatra et al., 2020). At the community level, working with other educators in the building and families to create opportunities for practicing self-determination skills (e.g., communication skills, decision-making, and goal setting) can be just as beneficial as partnering with them to notice changes in behavior.

Focusing on Collaboration to Address Mental Health Needs

Students with ID often interact with multiple educators and mental health providers, but their signs of distress are overlooked due to the lack of research and training on ways these individuals display severe distress. This untreated distress can lead to suicidal ideation and behaviors. School

Caregivers	Educators	School Mental Health Providers	Students with ID
Attend Suicide Prevention Training Provide Cultural Context for Curriculum Talk with Their Student about Suicide Prevention Have Open Communication with School Personnel	Attend Suicide Prevention Training Collaborate to Adapt Suicide Prevention Curriculum Co-Host Suicide Prevention Training for Students Continue to Practice Suicide Prevention Skills in Class	Facilitate Suicide Prevention Training for Caregivers and Educators Collaborate to Adapt Suicide Prevention Curriculum Co-host Suicide Prevention Training for Students	Participate in Suicide Prevention Training Practice the Suicide Prevention Skills Notice Warning Signs in Friends and Alert Adults

Figure 30.3 Model of suicide prevention for students with ID

mental health providers are well poised to support these students due to their training in mental health assessment, promoting safe and supportive schools, creating equitable practices for diverse student populations, and utilizing research and evidence-based practices (NASP, 2020a). In collaboration, educators and school mental health providers can provide a suicide prevention curriculum to students with ID that supports their well-being. The administration of suicide prevention curriculum for students with ID involves a collaboration between caregivers, educators, school mental health providers, and students to ensure the universal curriculum is understood, and its concepts are integral components within the classroom (see Figure 30.3).

Caregivers and educators. One critical aspect of suicide prevention programming relies on recognizing changes in baseline for students with ID. Given the limitations of screening measures and structured interviews, the importance of caregiver and teacher input integrated with a comprehensive understanding of the youth is essential to determining suicide risk (Ludi et al., 2012).

Caregivers must be viewed as experts on their child, and their narratives must be taken seriously, documented, and sought out (Talapatra et al., 2020). Information gathered from caregivers and educators in the student's life will aid in recognizing differences in a student's baseline and detect the warning signs of suicide in youth with ID. Many school mental health providers have limited experience assessing and treating youth with ID and therefore fail to recognize the differences in warning signs that youth with ID may exhibit; caregivers can guide school mental health providers. Often, caregivers recognize important changes in baseline behavior regarding indicators of distress (sleeping, regression, sadness, somatization, and mood swings) in their children. Caregivers can provide school mental health providers with information regarding patterns of behaviors, warning signs displayed at home or concerns around student distress to aid in determining the level of suicide risk for their student. Understanding changes in behavior is critical because youth with ID are more likely to communicate through their behavioral indicators instead of verbal expression (Trauma and Intellectual/Developmental Disability Collaborative Group, 2020). Open communication within this partnership will aid in overcoming communication barriers with the student. Caregivers can provide important guidance and information around cultural considerations and understand their child's skills and learning style. School mental health providers should adopt the roles of facilitator and collaborator and recognize caregiver expertise.

The observations and information that educators possess is essential in the process of assessing a student with ID for suicide risk. A suicide risk assessment for students with ID requires adaptations to the school protocols and procedures to accommodate the student's comprehension and communication levels. Educators are the experts in understanding the student's skill level and pattern of behavior that aid in detecting changes in behavior indicative of student distress. To be effective, school mental health providers must incorporate multiple sources of information in assessing youth with ID for suicide risk. Weaving together caregivers' and educators' expertise around the student's patterns of behavior and communication level with the school mental health provider's knowledge of suicide risk provides a comprehensive process for determining a student with ID's level of distress and potential suicide risk (Bardon, 2020).

Community. School mental health providers can also advocate for community suicide prevention resources to provide inclusive supports for students with ID. The American Association of Suicidology recently released information for crisis support hotlines specific to suicide risk and other mental health concerns for the Autism Spectrum community with notable modification for warning signs, communication, and relationships (Morgan, 2018). Similar development of prevention program modifications designed to support students with ID is necessary for community collaboration and inclusive practices for students with ID. For example, in crisis plan development, essential components are prevention and preparedness for psychological trauma (Brock et al., 2016). To do so, this requires creating crisis plans that consider *all* student populations within a school (Brock et al., 2016). Students with ID are more vulnerable to psychological trauma than their peers without ID (Giannini et al., 2010; Ludi et al., 2012; Merrick et al., 2012). Thus, special consideration should be included for these populations to prevent unnecessary psychological trauma, which can in turn lead to suicidal ideation or behaviors.

Conclusions

To have an effective approach to suicide prevention in youth with ID, one method, one source is not appropriate or reliable. Instead, a model of risk assessment that is inclusive of caregiver, educators, and school mental health providers is necessary (see Figure 30.4).

Caregivers	Educators	School Mental Health Providers	Students With ID
Report Behavior Changes Provide Cultural Context Notice Warning Signs	Provide an Understanding of Students' Communication Ability Provide Undertanding of Students' Comprehension Level Report Behavior Changes Notice Warning Signs	Assess Risk Levels by Using the Data/Information Provided by Educators and Caregivers Assess Risk Levels by Using the Behaviors and Language the Student Expresses Adapt School's Protocols for Suicide Risk to Accommodate Student's Communication and Comprehension	Engage With Trusted Adults about Distress Participate in the Assessment

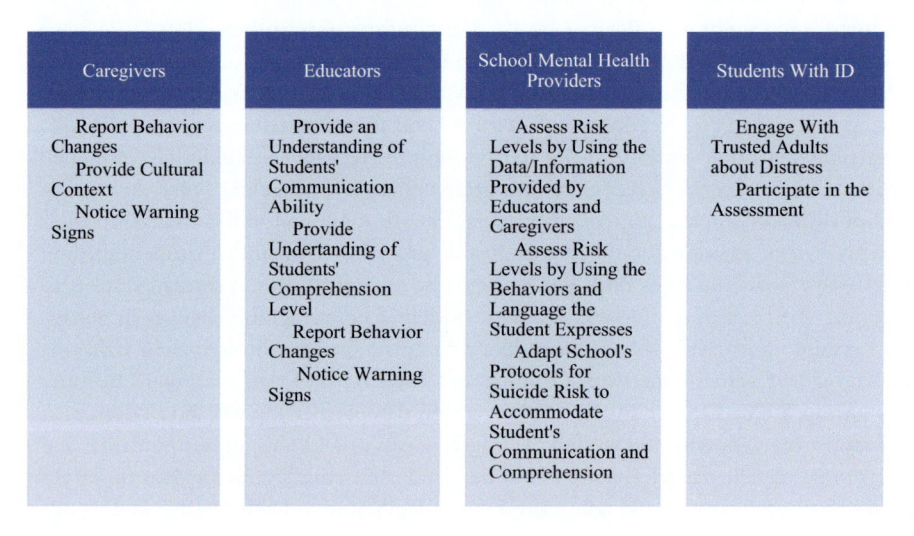

Figure 30.4 Model of suicide risk assessment for students with ID

Ultimately, school mental health providers, educators, and caregivers must increase their knowledge and attention to the distress signals of students with ID. The importance of understanding the warning signs of youth suicide, risk factors, and protective factors is critical in promoting prevention, conducting accurate suicide risk assessments, and providing appropriate intervention. In partnership school mental health providers, educators, and caregivers understand how disability can alter the manifestation of mental health disorders and this collaboration is essential in evaluating suicidal ideation in students with ID.

References

American Foundation for Suicide Prevention, American School Counselor Association, National Association of School Psychologists & The Trevor Project (2019). *Model School District Policy on Suicide Prevention: Model Language, Commentary, and Resources* (2nd ed.). American Foundation for Suicide Prevention.

Aseltine, R. H., & Demartino, R. (2004). An outcome evaluation of the SOS suicide prevention program. *American Journal of Public Health, 94*, 446–451.

Aseltine, R.H., James, A., Schilling, E.A. & Glanovsky, J. (2007). Evaluating the SOS suicide prevention program: A replication and extension. *BMC Public Health, 7*(161). Retrieved from http://www.biomedcentral.com/1471-2458/7/161.

Bardon, C. (2020, March 05). *Understanding and Preventing Suicide in People with IDD: Experiences Learned from a Collaborative Research Project* [Webinar]. AAIDD's Psychology Interest Network, Online. https://www.aaidd.org/education/event-details/2020/03/05/default-calendar/understanding-and-preventing-suicide-in-people-with-idd-experiences-learned-from-a-collaborative-research-project

Beck, A.T., Steer, R.A., & Brown, G.K. (1996). *Manual for the Beck Depression Inventory-II*. Psychological Corporation.

Borowsky, I. W., Taliaferro, L. A., & McMorris, B. J. (2013). Suicidal thinking and behavior among youth involved in verbal and social bullying: Risk and protective factors. *Journal of Adolescent Health, 53*(1, Supplement), S4–S12. https://doi.org/10.1016/j.jadohealth.2012.10.280

Brock, S., Nickerson, A. B., Reeves, M. A., Conolly, C. N., Jimerson, S. R., Pesce, R. C. & Lazzaro, B. R. (2016). *School Crisis Prevention and Intervention: The PREPaRE Model*. National Association of School Psychologists.

Brown-Lavoie, S. M., Viecili, M. A., & Wiess, J. A. (2014). Sexual knowledge and victimization in adults with Autism Spectrum Disorders. *Journal of Autism and Developmental Disorders, 44*(9), 2185 –2196. doi: 10.1007/s10803-014-2093-y

Centers for Disease Control and Prevention, National Center for Health Statistics (2020). *Underlying Cause of Death 1999–2018*. CDC WONDER Online Database. http://wonder.cdc.gov/ucd-icd10.html

Curtin, S. C., & Heron, Melonie. (2019). Death rates due to suicide and homicide among persons aged 10–24: United States, 2000–2017. *NCHS Data Brief, 352*, 8.

Dickerson Mayes, S., Calhoun, S. L., Baweja, R., & Mahr, F. (2015). Suicide ideation and attempts in children with psychiatric disorders and typical development. *Crisis, 36*(1), 55–60. https://doi.org/10.1027/0227-5910/a000284

Dodd, P., Guerin, S., McEvoy, J., Buckley, S., Tyrrell, J., & Hillery, J. (2008). A study of complicated grief symptoms in people with intellectual disabilities. *Journal of Intellectual Disability Research, 52*(5), 415–425. https://doi.org/10.1111/j.1365-2788.2008.01043.x

Enfield, S. L., Ellis, L. A., Emerson E. (2011). Comorbidity of intellectual disability and mental disorder in children and adolescents: A systematic review. *Journal of Intellectual and Developmental Disabilities.* 36(2):137–43.

Erbacher, T., Singer, J., & Poland, S. (2014). *Suicide in Schools: A Practitioner's Guide to Multi-level Prevention, Assessment, Intervention, and Postvention*. (School-based practice in action series) (Erbacher) Routledge. https://doi.org/10.4324/9780203702970.

Erps, K. H., Ochs, S., & Myers, C. L. (2020). School psychologists and suicide risk assessment: Role perception and competency. *Psychology in the Schools, 57*(6), 884–900. https://doi.org/10.1002/pits.22367

Field, S., Sarver, M., & Shaw, S. (2003). Self-determination: A key to success in postsecondary education for students with learning disabilities. *Remedial and Special Education, 24*, 339–349.

Fowler, J. C. (2012). Suicide risk assessment in clinical practice: Pragmatic guidelines for imperfect assessments. *Psychotherapy, 49*(1), 81–90. https://doi.org/10.1037/a0026148

Gargiulo, R.M, & Bouck, E.C. (2018). Individuals with intellectual disability. In *Special education in contemporary society: An introduction to exceptionality* (6th ed., pp. 159–206). Sage Publications, Inc.

Giannini, M. J., Bergmark, B., Kreshover, S., Elias, E., Plummer, C., & O'Keefe, E. (2010). Understanding suicide and disability through three major disabling conditions: Intellectual disability, spinal cord injury, and multiple sclerosis. *Disability and Health Journal, 3*(2), 74–78. https://doi.org/10.1016/j.dhjo.2009.09.001

Gilmore, L., & Cuskelly, M. (2014). Vulnerability to loneliness in people with intellectual disability: An explanatory model. *Journal of Policy and Practice in Intellectual Disabilities, 11*(3), 192–199. https://doi.org/10.1111/jppi.12089

Gül, S. O. (2016). The combined use of video modeling and social stories in teaching social skills for individuals with intellectual disability. *Educational Sciences: Theory and Practice, 16*(1), 83–107.

Horowitz, L. M., Bridge, J. A., Teach, S. J., Ballard, E., Klima, J., Rosenstein, D. L., Wharff, E. A., Ginnis, K., Cannon, E., Joshi, P., & Pao, M. (2012). Ask Suicide-Screening Questions (ASQ): A brief instrument for the pediatric emergency department. *Archives of Pediatrics & Adolescent Medicine, 166*(12), 1170–1176. https://doi.org/10.1001/archpediatrics.2012.1276

Hurley, A., Tomasulo, D. J., & Pfadt, A. G. (1998). Individual and group psychotherapy approaches for persons with intellectual disabilities and developmental disabilities. *Journal of Developmental and Physical Disabilities, 10*, 365–386.

Jacobs, D. (2013). *SOS Signs of Suicide Middle School Program: Procedure Manual.* Screening for Mental Health, Inc.

King, T. L., Milner, A., Aitken, Z., Karahalios, A., Emerson, E., & Kavanagh, A. M. (2019). Mental health of adolescents: Variations by borderline intellectual functioning and disability. *European Child & Adolescent Psychiatry, 28*(9), 1231–1240. https://doi.org/10.1007/s00787-019-01278-9

Kroenke, K., Spitzer, R. L., & Williams, J. B. W. (2001). The PHQ-9. *Journal of General Internal Medicine, 16*(9), 606–613. https://doi.org/10.1046/j.1525-1497.2001.016009606.x

Lieberman, R., Poland, S., & Kornfeld, C. (2014). Best practices in suicide prevention and intervention. In P. Harrison & A Thomas (Eds.), *Best Practices in School Psychology: Systems Level Services* (pp. 273–288). National Association of School Psychologists.

Ludi, E., Ballard, E. D., Greenbaum, R., Pao, M., Bridge, J., Reynolds, W., & Horowitz, L. (2012). Suicide risk in youth with ID: The challenges of screening. *Journal of Developmental & Behavioral Pediatrics, 33*(5), 431–440. https://doi.org/10.1097/DBP.0b013e3182599295

Masi G, Brovedani P, Mucci M, Favilla L. (2012). Assessment of anxiety and depression in adolescents with mental retardation. *Child Psychiatry and Human Development, 32*(3):227–237.

Merrick, J., Merrick, E., Lunsky, Y., & Kandel, I. (2012). Intellectual disability and suicidal behavior. In A. Shrivastava, M. Kimbrell, & D. Lester (Eds.). *Suicide from a Global Perspective Vulnerable Populations and Controversies* (pp. 55–64). Nova Science.

Mollison, E., Chaplin, E., Underwood, L., & McCarthy, J. (2014). A review of risk factors associated with suicide in adults with intellectual disability. *Advances in Mental Health and ID, 8*(5), 302-308. https://doi.org/10.1108/AMHID-05-2014-0021.

Morgan, L. (2018). *Crisis Supports for the Autism Community.* American Association of Suicidology.

National Association of School Psychologists. (2015a). *Preventing Suicide: Guidelines for Administrators and Crisis Teams.* Retrieved June 23, 2021, from https://www.nasponline.org/resources-and-publications/resources-and-podcasts/school-climate-safety-and-crisis/mental-health-resources/preventing-youth-suicide/preventing-suicide-guidelines-for-administrators-and-crisis-teams

National Association of School Psychologist. (2015b). *Preventing Youth Suicide.* National Association of School Psychologists (NASP). https://www.nasponline.org/resources-and-publications/resources-and-podcasts/school-climate-safety-and-crisis/mental-health-resources/preventing-youth-suicide

National Association of School Psychologists. (2020a). *NASP 2020 Domains of Practice.* National Association of School Psychologists (NASP). Retrieved November 11, 2020, from https://www.nasponline.org/standards-and-certification/nasp-2020-professional-standards-adopted/nasp-2020-domains-of-practice

National Association of School Psychologist. (2020b). *NASP 2020 Professional Standards Adopted.* National Association of School Psychologists (NASP). https://www.nasponline.org/standards-and-certification/nasp-2020-professional-standards-adopted

National Institute of Mental Health. (2021, January). Suicide. Retrieved from https://www.nimh.nih.gov/health/statistics/suicide.shtml

Page, R. M., Saumweber, J., Hall, P. C., Crookston, B. T., & West, J. H. (2013). Multi-country, cross-national comparison of youth suicide ideation: Findings from Global School-based Health Surveys. *School Psychology International, 34*(5), 540–555. https://doi.org/10.1177/0143034312469152

Razza, N. J., Laura, S. D., Tomasulo, D., & Ballan, M. S. (2014). Intellectual disability and mental health: Is psychology prepared? *Advances in Mental Health and ID, 8*(6), 381–389. https://doi.org.du.idm.oclc.org/10.1108/AMHID-04-2014-0010

Ricciardi, J. N. (2013). Co-occurring psychiatric disorders in individuals with intellectual disability. In D. D. Reed, F. D. DiGennaro Reed, & J. K. Luiselli (Eds.), *Handbook of Crisis Intervention and Developmental Disabilities* (pp. 213–243). Springer. https://doi.org/10.1007/978-1-4614-6531-7_13

Schilling, E. A., Lawless, M., Buchanan, M., & Aseltine, R. (2014). "Signs of Suicide" Shows Promise as a Middle School Suicide Prevention Program. *Suicide and Life-Threatening Behavior, 44*(6), December, 653–667.

Shaw, S. R., & Jankowska, A. M. (2018). Bridging the Divides Among Healthcare Delivery, Family, and Educational Settings. In S. R. Shaw & A. M. Jankowska (Eds.), *Pediatric Intellectual Disabilities at School: Translating Research into Practice* (pp. 115–136). Springer International Publishing. https://doi.org/10.1007/978-3-030-02992-0_5

Singer, J. B., Erbacher, T. A., & Rosen, P. (2019). School-based suicide prevention: A framework for evidence-based practice. *School Mental Health*, (11), 54–71. https://doi.org/10.1007/s12310-018-9245-8

Sobsey, D., & Doe, T. (1991). Patterns of sexual abuse and assault. *Sexuality and Disability, 9*(3), 243–259.

Stevens, B. (2012). Examining emerging strategies to prevent sexual violence: Tailoring to the needs of women with intellectual and developmental disabilities. *Journal of Mental Health Research in ID, 5*(2), 168–186.

Sturmey, P. (2007). Psychopathology: Depression, Anxiety, and Related Disorders. In J. Matson (Ed.), *Handbook of Assessment in Persons with Intellectual Disability* (vol. 34, pp. 197–226). London: Elsevier Academic Press.

Substance Abuse and Mental Health Services Administration. (2019). *Ready, Set, Go, Review: Screening for Behavioral Health Risk in Schools*. Rockville, MD: Office of the Chief Medical Officer.

Substance Abuse and Mental Health Services Administration. (2011). SAMHSA's national registry of evidence-based programs and practices: SOS signs of suicide. Retrieved February 19, 2021, from https://www.samhsa.gov/resource-search/ebp

Talapatra, D., Parris, L., & Snider, L., (2020). Considerations for implementing school-based trauma informed care for individuals with intellectual and developmental disabilities. *Research and Practice in the Schools, 7*(1), 86–103. https://www.txasp.org/assets/docs/tasp-journal/Volume%207%20Issue%201_Complete%20Issue.pdf

Tipton, L. A., Christensen, L., & Blacher, J. (2013). Friendship quality in adolescents with and without an intellectual disability. *Journal of Applied Research in Intellectual Disabilities, 26*(6), 522–532. https://doi.org/10.1111/jar.12051

Trauma and Intellectual/Developmental Disability Collaborative Group. (2020). *The Impact of Trauma on Youth with Intellectual and Developmental Disabilities: A Fact Sheet for Providers*. Los Angeles, CA, and Durham, NC: National Center for Child Traumatic Stress.

Tucker, R. P., & Wingate, L. R. (2014). Basic need satisfaction and suicidal ideation: A self-determination perspective on interpersonal suicide risk and suicidal thinking. *Archives of Suicide Research, 18*(3), 282–294. https://doi.org/10.1080/13811118.2013.824839

Wehmeyer, M. (2005). Self-determination and individuals with severe disabilities: Reexamining meanings and misinterpretations. *Research and Practice for Persons with Severe Disabilities, 30*, 113–120.

Weir, K. (2019). Better ways to prevent suicide. *Monitor on Psychology, 50*(7), 32.

Whittle, C., & Butler, C. (2018). Sexuality in the lives of people with ID: A meta-ethnographic synthesis of qualitative studies. *Research in Developmental Disabilities, 75*, 68–81. https://doi.org/10.1016/j.ridd.2018.02.008

Widmer, E. D., Kempf-Constantin, N., Robert-Tissot, C., Lanzi, F., & Carminati, G. G. (2008). How central and connected am I in my family: Family-based social capital of individuals with intellectual disability. *Research in Developmental Disabilities, 29*(2), 176–187. https://doi.org/10.1016/j.ridd.2007.02.005

World Health Organization. (2014). *Preventing Suicide: A Global Imperative Executive Summary*. Geneva, Switzerland: Author.

World Health Organization. (2021). *Suicide Worldwide in 2019: Global Health Estimates*. Genva, Switzerland: Author.

31
FUNCTIONAL POSITIONING FOR CLASSROOM PARTICIPATION

Kitty Uys*

Introduction

We can change our position quickly when we are getting stiff or uncomfortable, but children with physical disabilities or mobility impairments cannot transition into different positions easily or at all. This negatively affects their ability to participate in activities and tasks required in the classroom. If children do not have the ability to adjust their posture to meet the requirements of the activity, they need postural support. Traditionally, an anatomical approach to seating was followed, which was restricting movements and participation. To provide the child with physical disabilities an opportunity towards accomplishing tasks, optimal participation and performance in school, a functional approach to seating was introduced (Morress, 2006). This approach is merged with a child-centered approach where the individual treatment and education plan with individual outcomes, are considered. It takes navigation through a multifaceted process to optimize functional seating and positioning so that the child can participate in meaningful and purposeful activities. This chapter will focus on the benefits of functional seating and positioning, how to screen for seating and positioning problems, and lastly identifying guidelines to address problem areas. The outcome of implementing the guideline is to improve children with disabilities' optimal performance in a classroom setting. In a classroom, sitting upright is the best posture for academic learning and therefore detailed discussions about the seated position will be presented. However, children with physical disabilities also require a variety of positions during the day, similar to typical developing children. The chapter will conclude with examples of positioning equipment that can successfully be used in the school context.

Attainment of functional seating and positioning fosters a child's independence and productivity, but it takes a multidisciplinary team to coordinate the process. Consider the following types of children who are commonly identified with seating and mobility problems: cerebral palsy, spina bifida, spinal cord injuries, traumatic brain injuries. The most common diagnosis in early childhood is neurodevelopmental disorders, including cerebral palsy. Approximately 40% of children with CP are not ambulatory and they are unable to sustain a sitting or standing posture (Himmelmann, Beckung, Hagberg, & Uvebrant, 2007). Keeping these children in mind, consider the following problems that they may experience in the classroom: inability to access the table or working surface, poor balance, fatigue, inability to write or to access a device like a com-

---

* kitty.uys@up.ac.za

Functional Positioning

```
                    ┌─────────────────────┐
                    │  Health condition   │
                    │   Cerebral Palsy    │
                    └─────────────────────┘
```

┌───────────────────────────┐   ┌───────────────────────────────┐   ┌───────────────────────────┐
│ Body Structure and Function│   │   Activity (Limitation)   │   │ Participation (Restriction)│
│ Abnormal muscle tone   │   │ Activities of Daily Living   │   │ Poor social interactions with│
│ Movement,   │   │ Instrumental Activities of Daily│ │   peers   │
│ sensation, cognition,   │   │   Living   │   │ Cannot participate in sport│
│ communication, perception │   │ Reach, grasp, manipulate   │   │ Cannot access the device to do│
│ and/or a seizure disorder │   │   objects   │   │   academic work   │
│   │   │   Transfer positions   │   │   │
└───────────────────────────┘   └───────────────────────────────┘   └───────────────────────────┘

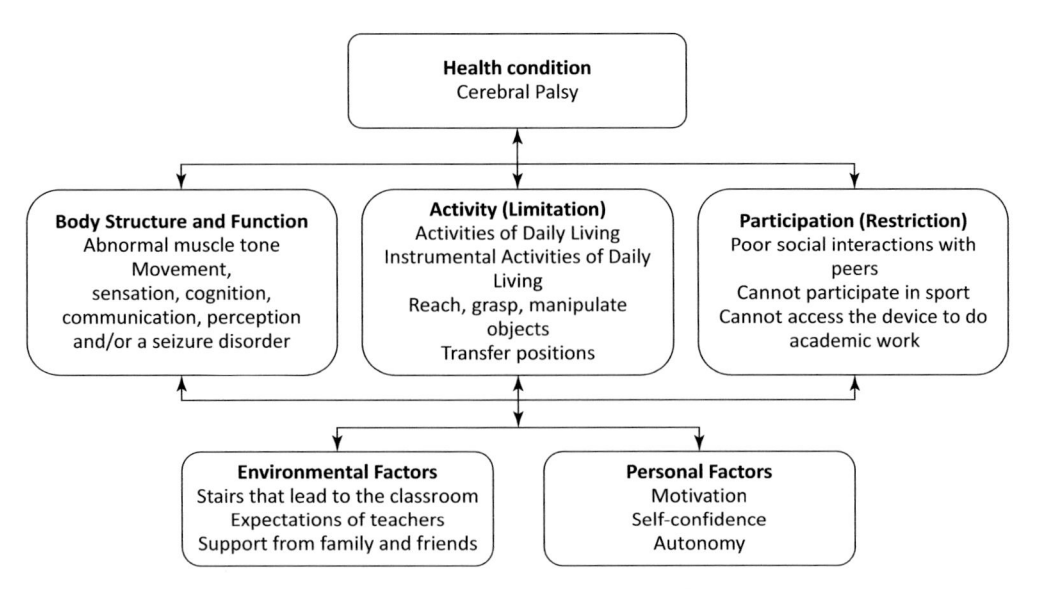

        ┌─────────────────────────────────┐   ┌───────────────────────────┐
        │   Environmental Factors   │   │   Personal Factors   │
        │ Stairs that lead to the classroom│   │   Motivation   │
        │   Expectations of teachers   │   │   Self-confidence   │
        │   Support from family and friends│   │   Autonomy   │
        └─────────────────────────────────┘   └───────────────────────────┘

Figure 31.1 ICF related to cerebral palsy

puter, unable to pay attention to the academic activities in the classroom, inability to sit upright, inability to focus on the educator or the blackboard, inability to work with other children in the classroom. Implementation of functional seating could bring around change in the above-mentioned areas. There should be a match between the child's activity and the seating equipment.

The World Health Organization's (WHO) International Classification of Functioning Disability and Health (ICF) combined the medical and social models of disability into a bio-psycho-social model. The ICF considers the holistic individual who must be able to function within his or her context. The person's activity limitations and participation are viewed within an environmental context. Participation, according to ICF, is a person's involvement in all life situations e.g., going to school and participating in the classroom. In Figure 31.1, the ICF is explained in relation to a child with cerebral palsy who needs to participate in classroom activities.

Cerebral palsy (CP) describes a group of disorders of the development of movement and posture causing activity limitations that are attributed to non-progressive disturbances that occurred in the developing fetal or infant brain. The motor disorders of cerebral palsy are often accompanied by disturbances of sensation, cognition, communication, perception and/or a seizure disorder (Bax, Goldstein, Rosenbaum et al., 2005). According to the ICF, body structure and functioning includes the abnormal muscle tone the CP child presents with. This can be either increased muscle tone or spasticity, decreased muscle tone, or dyskinesia. Abnormal muscle tone advances the development of movement disorders, which contribute to activity limitations and restrictions in participation in the classroom. Here the child indicates problems in amongst others, communication, interaction, social interaction in group activities, academic learning, and sports activities. The external environment like inaccessible buildings, expectations of educators, and support from family friends and community, can either be a barrier or facilitator towards academic learning. Similarly, the internal environment, namely the personal factors of the child, can also be a barrier or facilitator as these include for instance level of motivation, confidence, self-esteem, and autonomy. Using the ICF as indicated in Figure 31.1 clearly shows the impact of CP on participation. One way of making a positive change to these children's level of participation is to address their functional seating.

Factors Impacting Functional Seating

Abnormal muscle tone and the presence of primitive postural reflexes are always present in children with CP. Both factors impact negatively on performance in functional activities. The reflexes most commonly present include the asymmetric tonic neck reflex (ATNR), symmetric tonic neck reflex (STNR), tonic labyrinthine reflexes (TLR) and positive support reaction. Muscle tone is classified as spastic, dyskinetic, ataxic, or a mixture. Most children diagnosed with spastic quadriplegia (all four limbs involved) have high muscle tone in the four extremities with a low muscle tone in the trunk. Sitting may be compromised by weakness of those muscles which should stabilize the trunk and pelvis (Engström, 2011). We can observe a change in muscle tone as a result from participating in a functional activity. If a CP child reaches out to the keyboard of the computer, abnormal muscle tone causes uncoordinated movement and accurately finding the correct key on the keyboard is impaired. And, if a child with an ATNR turns his head to look to the left, there will be an increase in extensor muscle tone of the left upper limb and an increase in flexor muscle tone of the right upper limb. This position is difficult to release, and children can get "stuck" here with head and arms not in the midline and not being able to focus on learning activities in the front of the class.

Gravity is the most influential force when we are seated. Typically developing children do not sit still for extended periods of time as their bodies need to exert sufficient force against gravity to keep them upright. To move against gravity, they need sufficient muscle tone and muscle strength. Children with abnormal muscle tone, reflex activity, and poor muscle strength are not able to change their postures against the influence of gravity. Gravity continues to pull them down and fatigue and discomfort set in. Children with CP are commonly more affected on one side of the body, forcing them into asymmetrical postures (de Mare, de Groot, de Koning et al., 2021). When gravity is outside their base of support (seat), balance is compromised, and it is difficult for them to move back into an upright position due to poor muscle strength and abnormal muscle tone.

Muscle contractures and deformities can therefore develop over time. Contractures are a permanent shortening and hardening of muscles and tendons leading to deformity and rigidity of joints. Spasticity also contributes to this condition. Progressive fixed musculoskeletal deformities like scoliosis and kyphosis of the spine, pelvic obliquity, hip extension contracture, and upper limb flexion contractures aggravate functional seating solutions.

Benefits of Proper Seating

The benefits of functional seating are numerous. Authors such as Strobl (2013) Colangelo, & Shea (2010) and Stier, Chieu, Howell, & Ryan, (2017) identified the following benefits of proper seating postures. It reduces the influence of abnormal muscle tone, reduces the influence of abnormal reflexes, reduces, or accommodates for anatomical deformities, improves comfort, stability and safety, improves autonomic functions like respiratory, oral intake and digestion, improves gastrointestinal tract functions, prevents pressure sores and aids skin and tissue integrity, increases social interactions and improvement of upper limb function like reaching, grasping and manipulating objects. Costigan and Light (2011) presented a summary of research findings on the positive effects of functional seating for school-age children with CP. The findings indicated benefits on body structure and function, activities and participation levels, according to the ICF.

Screening to Identify Possible Problem Areas in Seating

During a screening process for functional seating and positioning, the educator is evaluating the presence of possible problem areas. This process can be done with the assistance of a multidisci-

Table 31.1 Screening for functional seating

Observe the child while seated on a chair (ordinary or wheelchair)	Y	N

1. Does the child need help to keep his head in midline?
2. Does the child need help to transition into a sitting position?
3. Does the child need external support to stay upright sitting (such as a backrest, armrests, lateral support, lap tray or table)?
4. Look at the child from the front:
    a) Does the child's head tilt to the side (to the right or to the left)?
    b) Does the child have an asymmetrical posture?
    c) Do the child's knees spread too far apart?
    d) Do the child's knees pull tightly toward the middle?
    e) Do the child's knees both point to one side?
    f) Can the child bring his/her arms forward?
    g) Can the child move his/her arms independently?
    h) Are the child's feet always turned inward?
    i) Are the child's feet always turned outward?
    j) Are the child's feet always pointing to one side?
5. Look at the child from both sides:
    a) Is the child's head tilted too much to the front or to the back?
    b) Is the child's back arched (bend backwards)?
    c) Is the child's back rounded (C-curve, bend forwards)?
    d) Is the child sitting more on the backbone than in the buttocks?
    e) Is the child sliding down and out of the chair?
    f) Does the child need help to bend or straighten his hips?
    g) Does the child need help to bend or straighten his knees?
6. Does the child have difficulty to look around or visually attend to tasks?
7. Does the child have difficulty in breathing, eating, drinking, or making sounds?
8. Does the child have difficulty in reaching for, grasping, or manipulating an object?
9. Does the child fatigue easily?
10. Does the child prefer to sit in a chair?
11. Does the child prefer to sit on the floor?

(Colangelo, & Shea, 2010; Cook, Polgar, & Encarnação, 2020; Costigan, & Light, 2011; Pope, 2007).

plinary team, as well as the primary caregiver of the child. The benefit of doing screening with a team will facilitate a shared vision for the child's individualized education plan. Table 31.1 outlines the questions to be asked during the screening process. This screening form requires the educator to indicate yes or no if certain problems were identified in the classroom and this will give an indication to the multidisciplinary team how to address assessment further. A specific number of "yes" ticks do not indicate a referral to professionals like occupational and physical therapists who could assist with an in-depth seating assessment. One "yes" tick can impact on the child's function in the class, and is indicative of a referral.

Guidelines to Solve the Functional Seating Problems in Class

There is no "one-size-fits-all" strategy towards solving functional seating and not enough research evidence is available to produce a set of rules that can consistently be successfully implemented for every child with CP (Barton et al., 2020; Costigan & Light, 2011; Robertson, Baines, Emerson, & Hatton, 2018).). The following guidelines can be implemented on an individualized basis to work towards better functional seating. Sitting remains dynamic and the traditional view of an upright posture is now suggested to be non-functional and difficult to maintain over time (Pontes, de Miranda Luzo, da Silva, & Lancman, 2019; Engström, 2002; Neville & Quigg, 2005). Functional seating therefore requires a balance between an upright posture, pelvis mobility, and the ability to function. Posture can be defined as the position of one or many body segments in relation to one another and their orientation in space (Colangelo, & Shea, 2010). A body segment can be any one of the following: head, trunk, pelvis, upper and/or lower limbs. The ability to move the upper limbs independently to allow for distal function of the hands depends on stable proximal body structures like the pelvis, shoulders, and trunk. From a neurophysiological and developmental perspective, normal posture depends on the development of postural control, which is influenced by the neuromotor, somatosensory, vestibular, and musculoskeletal systems (Nichols, 2002). Postural control requires developmental milestones to be achieved and includes the development of postural reactions (righting, protective and equilibrium reactions), integration of primitive reflexes, and normal muscle tone (Wandel, 2000).

Guidelines for Adjusting the Child
Anterior-Posterior Pelvis Tilt

Functional seating and positioning start with the pelvis. The pelvis is considered the anatomical foundation of seated positions (Costigan & Light, 2011; Cook, Polgar, & Encarnação, 2020) and should be stable yet there must be some room for movement. The pelvis can tilt posterior and anterior, influencing the curvature of the spine (Figure 31.2). Neither extremes of posterior and anterior pelvis tilt are appropriate and will contribute to poor functional seating. A posterior tilt of the pelvis will force the spine into a C-curve (kyphosis), which can cause the child to slide out of the chair. A slight posterior tilt can be adopted during rest, as less energy is then used to maintain functional seating. A severe anterior pelvis tilt will force the spine into lordosis at the lumbar region (hollow back), causing secondary hip flexion. A slight anterior tilt produces back extension and it also occurs when the trunk is moving forward with weight supported on the arms. This is an active learning position

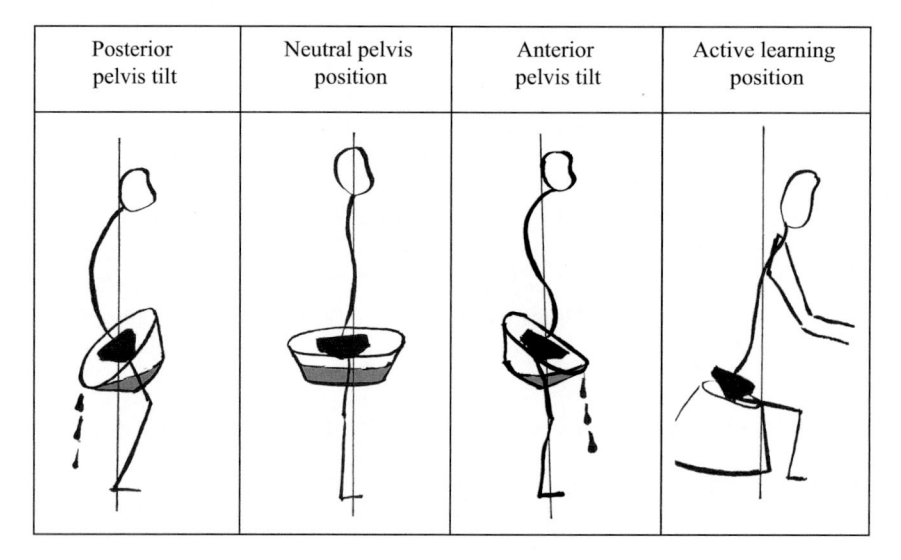

Figure 31.2 Position of the pelvis

which has been described by Strobl (2013) and Costigan and Light (2011) as a functional task position. The knees are bent slightly more than 90°, the feet remain symmetrically on the floor, the trunk is slightly forward, and this offers a more dynamic support structure for the upper body, arms and hands to engage in an activity. Most children in the classroom assume this active learning position. These postures can be seen in Figure 31.2 where the pelvis is compared to a bucket of water to make the abstract concept of posterior and anterior tilt more concrete. If the pelvis is tilted posteriorly the water will drop out behind the person. When the pelvis is tilted anteriorly the water will drop out in front of the person. But when there is a good angle between a neutral and a slight anterior tilt this will force the spine into more extension, creating an active learning position. A stable base will improve postural control, head control, and upper limb function.

These postures will be used interchangeably during the day, as one seating option is not appropriate for all tasks or environments (Kangas, 2000; Kangas, 2003; Livingstone & Field, 2014).

Body Alignment

A well aligned body that is symmetrical with minimal curvature of the spine and tilt of the pelvis will allow for optimal functional seating. Always ensure that the buttocks make good contact with a backrest and enough lateral support is provided on each side of the pelvis for stability, prevention of deformities and maximal respiratory function (de Mare et al., 2021).

Lateral Tilt and Rotation of the Pelvis

The pelvis has the ability to tilt from side to side, relative to the midline, or rotate around the midline (Cook, Polgar, & Encarnação, 2020). A neutral position of the pelvis will optimize upper body function. Symmetry is the golden rule. Side supports or a hip strap is used to maintain the pelvis in a neutral position. Hip straps should always be attached at a 45° angle to prevent the child from sliding out of the chair when extensor patterns of the lower limbs occur.

Legs and Feet

After the pelvis has been stabilized, the next body structure to consider is the feet. Support under the feet has a positive effect on the rest of the lower limbs, pelvis, and trunk. The height of the foot support should provide a gap of 1cm below the thigh, as this would improve blood circulation and prevent skin lesions. Weight should be through the heels of the feet not on the ball of the feet as this would elicit the positive support reaction. Therefore, the knees should be in at least 90° flexion.

Guidelines for Adjusting Equipment to Fit the Child

Not all children with disabilities have the opportunity for expensive custom-made functional seating or positioning. Therefore, the multidisciplinary team should ensure that equipment fits the child. Functional seating requires us to look at the seat, the backrest, and tilt in space.

Seat

The dimensions of the seat should be adapted to fit the child. The width of the seat should have a 2 cm clearance between the widest part of the hips and the armrests or sides of the chair. If the seat is too wide, you can add lateral side supports, like foam rubber or a cushion between the hips and the sides of the chair. The length of the seat should be 1cm shorter as measured from

Figure 31.3 Measuring the seat to fit the child

the buttocks to the back, when the knees are bent (see Figure 31.3). If the seat is a bit longer, you can add a cushion behind the child's back. A hip strap, angled at 45°, is essential for those children who have excessive extensor patterns in the lower limbs. The angle is important as the child will slide out of the chair if the strap is secured perpendicular to the seat. Velcro attachments to the strap ensure that the amount of support can be individualized. Straps should be at least 6cm wide to prevent it from cutting into the skin of the child. Foam rubber lining the straps is an extra padding to prevent injuries from occurring.

Backrest

The height of the backrest becomes important for those children who do not have good head control. Children with poor head control require a higher backrest and in some cases extensions

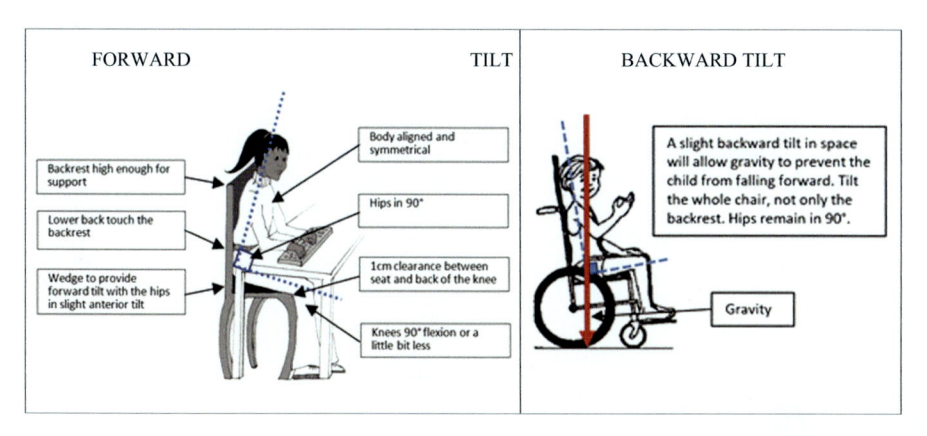

Figure 31.4 Tilt in space

next to the head are required to prevent the head from tilting to the sides. Always support the head with a soft surface. Shoulder or trunk straps can prevent the child from falling forward but care should be taken that the straps (1) do not hurt or choke the child, and (2) do not prevent the ability to move or shift weight.

Tilt in Space

Figure 31.4 explains how tilt in space can be accomplished. As indicated previously, gravity can be of positive assistance. When a child has poor head and trunk control, tilting the whole chair backwards – not more than 10° – prevents the child from falling forwards. To obtain a forward tilt for a functional task position or an active learning position, add a wedge to the seat – with the wide side to the back of the chair. In both cases the hips should remain in 90°, except if the backward tilt position is required for resting.

Equipment That Can Be Used in the Classroom

In the next section specific guidelines are discussed for functional seating and positioning equipment. Checklists provided (Table 31.2), will assist the educator to improve the performance of the child with disabilities in the classroom. The checklist contains the guidelines in summary, so that the educator can use this as a quick check if the child is positioned correctly. As indicated before, a variety of positioning options should be available for the duration the child spends at school. Positions on the floor, on the chair, and standing will be discussed. As a summary, the following general principles are applied in all of the positions below: Symmetry of all the body parts; head in midline to prevent eliciting of reflexes; align anatomical structures; proximal stability for distal function; positive use of gravity; comfort; frequent changes.

Lying in Prone (on Tummy)

Table 31.2a illustrates this position. Symmetry should be maintained and this can be done by adding a weighted blanket over the hips. Space should be provided for the toes so that the ankles are not forced into dorsi flexion (when you stand on the tip of your toes or when the toes point downward). Enough space should be provided for the upper limbs to support the child

Table 31.2 Checklist of criteria for each position

Position	Criteria to incorporate	Check
a) Prone lying 	Body symmetrical Arms forward in midline, bilateral Visual function Active work against gravity Weight shift towards pelvis	
b) Side lying 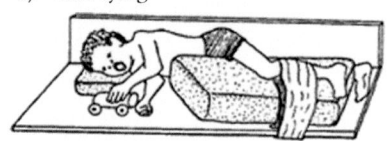	Head supported in midline Symmetrical posture Whole body is supported Tone inhibiting pattern Arms in midline Functional vision Hands free for play	
c) Sitting on an adult's lap 	Back and head supported Shoulders stable, slightly forward Hands are free Symmetrical Pelvis dynamic Feet supported	
d) Using a corner chair when sitting on the floor 	Sit independently with legs crossed Long-sitting creates a wide base of support when hips are in abduction (wide apart) Buttocks in the corner Shoulders pushed a bit forward Hands are free	
e) Cross legged sitting 	Hips in abduction Pelvis in neutral or slight anterior tilt Pelvis stable Wide base of support Hands free for play	

(Continued)

Table 31.2 (Continued)

Position	Criteria to incorporate	Check
f) Sitting on a chair 	A stable postural base – the position of the pelvis is important Postural Control and Alignment Postural Head Control Symmetrical Pommel between knees Sit upright, back straight, head in midline Hips in 90° Buttocks in the back of the chair Lap strap tightened firmly at a 45° angle Support the feet Shoulders slightly forward Hands in front of body to play/engage Tilted or elevated work surface	
g) Elevated and/or slanted work surface 	Extension of the back Arms forward and supported Hands free Elevated surface Slanted surface Slightly higher work surface to support arms	
h) Standing 	Trunk symmetrical Support hips with straps, if necessary Ankle not more than 90° plantar flexion AFOs (Ankle-Foot-Orthotics) Weight through the heel not the ball of the foot Hip extension, not internal rotation, bit abduction Knees in extension Arms forward onto the working surface Working surface should be at about nipple height It is good to push on arms for support	

as well as to participate in an activity. A wedge can be used, with a narrow edge at the feet and the wide end under the shoulders. A cushion can be inserted between the knees for abduction of the hips. This will prevent the lower limbs from going into the typical scissor position. This position allows for the weight to be shifted towards the pelvis to free the arms to come forward in midline and for bilateral hand use. Head control and functional vision are encouraged by structuring the activity in front of the child. This position can be incorporated during circle time, leisure time and outside play.

Side Lying

Side lying is one position in which the child can totally relax and therefore it is often used for sleeping or resting. This position allows for the whole body to be supported and the head should be supported by a cushion. Table 31.2b shows that the head should be supported in midline to prevent any tonic reflex activity (e.g. ATNR and STNR). The lower limbs are dissociated by extending the bottom leg and flexing or bending the top leg. A cushion between the legs would prevent the typical extension and scissor patterns from occurring. As the arms are positioned to the front, the child can now focus on the activity placed within the visual field. It is important to note that the position should be altered between the two sides.

Sitting on an Adult's Lap

This position provides comfort for a young child that might be emotionally distressed. Table 31.2c indicates that the adult's trunk provides support for the child's back and head and keeps the child's posture symmetrical. The adult can sit on various equipment which can contribute to the outcomes the child requires. When the adult is long sitting on the floor, the child can sit between his or her legs, facing towards or away from the adult. An older adult can sit on a chair while the child is positioned across her lap with the child's hips and knees flexed and the head can be supported by the adult's arm. Social interaction between the adult and the child can be enhanced this way. Another position for the adult is to sit across a bench or roller which is just big enough for the child's feet to be supported by the floor. The child sits in front of the adult, facing the same way as the adult. The supporting surface for the feet, as well as the abduction at the hips, provides stability of the pelvis and lower limbs which creates a stable backdrop against which the upper limbs can move and function. The adult can provide extra stability by helping the child to bear weight through the heels of the feet. Care should be taken that the child does not lean against the adult, creating a passive sitting posture. This position can be used during circle time and/or small group sessions.

Corner Chair

A corner chair is a small piece of equipment that could be easily used in a classroom. This chair has a 90° angle at the back in which the child's buttocks and back fits (Table 31.2d). If necessary, the child's hips can be strapped to prevent the child from sliding down. This chair allows the child to create a wide base of support by abducting the hips. A pommel, which is a projecting part of the chair in front of the child, prevents the lower limbs from going into the abnormal, typical scissor position. The angle of the back support pushes the shoulders slightly forward, allowing the arms to move to mid-position and into the visual range. Due to the proximal support of the shoulders, the child's hands are free to function. During circle time, small group work, or play, the child can sit independently and securely, but on the same eye level as the peers which will also improve social interaction.

Cross Leg Sitting

Cross leg sitting is an alternative for a child who tends to sit in a W-sitting position. Although W-sitting gives a wide base of support for a child who has difficulty in maintaining balance while sitting on the floor, this position is harmful to the anatomical structures of the hips and knees. It also contributes to the shortening of the hip adductor muscles that produces the abnormal scissor pattern. Cross leg sitting also provides a wider base of support with the added benefit of hip abduction and flexion. The pelvis is in a more neutral position which facilitates trunk extension and head control. The pelvis can be externally supported to maintain the neutral position (Table 31.2e).

Sitting on a Chair

This position is the optimal position for a child to function in a classroom. Later in this chapter the design of a chair to fit the child will be discussed as each child has different needs that need to be supported by the chair. A chair can be a wheelchair, an ordinary school chair, or a purposely built chair. This chair should provide a stable base of support on which the child will feel in control of his posture and balance. As the hips easily tend to go into extension and adduction, a pommel, and hip strap at a 45° angle can be used to secure the hips in a flexed position. The chair should be narrow enough to keep the child's body symmetrical and aligned (Table 31.2f).

The backrest should be high enough for head support if needed. The angle of the backrest and seat can be varied according to the needs of the child or the activity participation. The seat can be tilted in space to allow gravity to push the child backwards when the child tends to flop into flexion. A fully upright backrest can be applied when a child needs to pay attention to the educator in the front of the class, but an active learning position should be assumed when the child has to work on a table or lap tray. Knees should be at the 90° angle or slightly less. It is important for the child to bear weight through the heels of both feet to prevent the positive support reaction from being elicited. Feet should always be supported by the floor surface or the wheelchair's footrests. Supported feet provide postural stability. If the feet are not supported, the child will always slide down the chair to seek that external support. The pelvis will tilt posteriorly and the lower limbs will extend and adduct. This spiraling unsafe position can be prevented by providing support below the feet.

When a child is slumping forward into flexion, the work surface can either be elevated or slanted. Both guidelines will facilitate the strong back extensors to be activated, getting the child into a more upright position. To elevate the work surface, the front legs of the table can be extended or alternatively, bricks or books could be added underneath as it will have the same effect as illustrated in Table 31.2g.

Standing

Standing helps to build or maintain bone density due to the compression on the joints where the growth plate is situated. As independent standing might be difficult for a child with CP, standing frames or standers can support the child in partial or full upright positions (Table 31.2h). Gravity assists with improving the function of the gastro-intestinal tract and therefore, bladder and bowel function. Upright standing will therefore work against constipation and urinary tract infections as the bladder can empty fully. The improvement in trunk control and core muscle strength will have a positive effect on the cardiopulmonary function.

Conclusion

Working with children with disabilities forces all professionals to adopt practical measures to obtain their optimal functioning and move beyond their hidden potential. Functional seating and positioning are one solution to improve participation in class. The consistent implementation of postural support equipment in the correct manner, enhances children's motor, socio-emotional, cognitive and communication behavior, but it remains complex and multifaceted and requires the input of the multi-professional team. The primary focus of achieving individual outcomes makes functional seating and positioning part of a child-centered approach. Positioning remains an ongoing process as many external and internal variables influence the child's appearance. Therefore, educators should be informed to implement adaptations and modifications to match the child to the equipment for optimal functioning. Educators play a key role in the school-age child's day and when a child with disabilities is positioned correctly during the school hours, learning will become more enjoyable as the child will be able to participate optimally.

References

Barton, C., Buckley, J., Samia, P., Williams, F., Taylor, S. R., & Lindoewood, R. (2020). The efficacy of appropriate paper-based technology for Kenyan children with cerebral palsy. *Disability and Rehabilitation. Assistive Technology*, 1–11. https://doi.org/10.1080/17483107.2020.1830442

Bax, M., Goldstein, M., Rosenbaum, P., Leviton, A., Paneth, N., Dan, B., Jacobsson, B., & Damiano, D. (2005). Proposed definition and classification of cerebral palsy, April 2005. *Developmental Medicine and Child Neurology*, 47(8), 571–576. https://doi.org/10.1111/j.1469-8749.2005.tb01195.x

Colangelo, C.A., & Shea, M. (2010). A biomechanical frame of reference for positioning children for function. In P. Kramer, & J. Hinojosa. (Eds.). *Frames of reference for pediatric occupational therapy* (3rd ed.). Wolters Kluwer Health/Lippincott Williams & Wilkins.

Cook, A. M., Polgar, J. M., & Encarnação, P. (2020). *Assistive technologies: Principles & practice*. (5th ed.). Mosby.

Costigan, F. A., & Light, J. (2011). Functional seating for school-age children with cerebral palsy: an evidence-based tutorial. *Language, Speech, and Hearing Services in Schools*, 42(2), 223–236. doi.org/10.1044/0161-1461(2010/10-0001)

de Mare, L., de Groot, B., de Koning, F., Geers, R., & Tetteroo, D. (2021). The influence of a contoured seating base on pressure distribution and discomfort. *Disability and Rehabilitation. Assistive Technology*, 1–7. https://doi.org/10.1080/17483107.2021.1892841

Engström, B. (2002). *Ergonomic Seating: A True Challenge: Seating and Mobility for the Physically Challenged Risks & Possibilities when Using Wheelchairs/Bengt Engstrom*. Posturalis Books.

Engström, B. (2011). *Ergonomic seating: A true challenge wheelchair weating and mobility for the physically challenged: risks and possibilities: when using wheelchairs*. Posturalis Books.

Himmelmann, K., Beckung, E., Hagberg, G., & Uvebrant, P. (2007). Bilateral spastic cerebral palsy—prevalence through four decades, motor function and growth. *European Journal of Paediatric Neurology*, 11(4), 215–222. https://doi.org/10.1016/j.ejpn.2006.12.010

Kangas, K. M. (2000). The task performance position: Providing seating for accurate access to assistive technology. *Technology Special Interest Section Quarterly*, 10(3), 1–3.

Kangas, K. M. (2003). Powered mobility training for children. In 18th International Seating Symposium. Vancouver, BC, USA; 2002: 1–5. Available from: http://www.seatingandmobility.ca/PowerMobility/pm_PowerMobilityIntro.aspx (accessed 26 January 2021).

Livingstone, R. & Field, D. (2014). Systematic review of power mobility outcomes for infants, children and adolescents with mobility limitations. *Clinical Rehabilitation*, 28(10):954–64. doi-org.uplib.idm.oclc.org/10.1177/0269215514531262

Morress, C. (2006). Bottom-up or top-down? An occupation-based approach to seating. *OT Practice*, 11, 12–16.

Neville, L. & Quigg, J. (2005). *The fundamental principles of seating and positioning in children and young people with physical disabilities*. Thesis. University of Ulster.

Nichols, D.S. (2002). Development of postural control. In J. Case-Smith (Ed.), *Occupational therapy for children*. Mosby.

Pontes, F.V., de Miranda Luzo, M.C., da Silva, T.D., & Lancman, S. (2019). Seating and positioning system in wheelchairs of people with disabilities: a retrospective study. *Disability and Rehabilitation. Assistive Technology*, 1–6. doi.org/10.1080/17483107.2019.1684580

Pope, P. (2007). *Severe and complex neurological disability: management of the physical condition*. Elsevier, Butterworth-Heinemann.

Robertson, J., Baines, S., Emerson, E., & Hatton, C. (2018). Postural care for people with intellectual disabilities and severely impaired motor function: a scoping review. *Journal of Applied Research in Intellectual Disabilities, 31* Supplement 1, 11–28. doi.org/10.1111/jar.12325

Stier, C. D., Chieu, I. B., Howell, L., & Ryan, S. E. (2017). Exploring the functional impact of adaptive seating on the lives of individual children and their families: a collective case study. *Disability and Rehabilitation. Assistive Technology, 12*(5), 450–456. doi.org/10.3109/17483107.2016.1139634

Strobl, W. M. (2013). Seating. *Journal of Children's Orthopaedics, 7*(5), 395–399. https://doi.org/10.1007/s11832-013-0513-8

Wandel, J.A. (2000). Positioning and handling. In J.W. Solomon (Ed.). *Pediatric skill for occupational therapy assistants.* Mosby.

32
THE ROLE OF INCLUSIVE TEACHING AND CREATING LEARNING EXPERIENCES FOR CHILDREN WITH VISUAL IMPAIRMENTS AND MULTIPLE DISABILITIES

Andrea Hathazi and Vassilios Argyropoulos*

Introduction

Visual Impairments and Multiple Disability (MDVI) constitutes a unique, severe, and complex condition that is difficult to capture in all characteristics; for this, there is not an unambiguous definition but a descriptive context, which includes many elements and characteristics (Argyropoulos et. al., 2020; Argyropoulos & Gentle, 2019). Hence, children with MDVI have unique needs and face unique challenges and they can present multiple difficulties including severe or profound learning difficulties (Douglas et al., 2009). The combination of vision and hearing impairment has also a multiplicative nature (Anthony, 2016; Argyropoulos et al., 2020; Brabyn et al., 2007; Bruce & Borders, 2015). Some researchers and authors held the view that the deafblind population is forced to confront great challenges in this modern society, where the information is mainly visual-hearing centered and aspects such as accessibility and communication are very much at stake (Simcock, 2017). Douglas et al. (2009) estimated that 50% of visually impaired children between 0 and 16 years of age have disabilities in addition to their visual impairment. The above authors state that children with MDVI are accounting for approximately 30% of the visually impaired population.

The "Mechanics" of MDVI in Everyday Life

Vision constitutes a major sense which formulates channels of conveying information from the environment into the perceptual system of the individual. The sense of vision is characterized as a "remote sense" because it tells us about distant parts of our environment by receiving waves. One of the main capacities of the light waves is the huge amount of information that can be transferred from outer space (environment) to the inner space (individual). Theoretically, the

---

* ahathazi@yahoo.com

number of the stimuli is infinite, but practically the number of the inserted stimuli, which is received and elaborated, is very limited and incorporates many subjective elements. There are many models which interpret the process of elaborating a message, and most of them converge on the same components. More analytically every communication or perception model usually incorporates the following characteristics: (a) source of the message, (b) the message, (c) mediators, and (d) interpretation.

The above characteristics formulate concomitantly the factors on which clarity and stability of the interpreted message depend. This generic model combines elements mainly of two theoretical underpinnings. First, from the spontaneous interaction theory, the word "mediators" embodies the importance of the context and the general reference organization within which the message is interpreted. The term "mediators" includes the experience of the subjects, conditions in which the subjects interact, their surroundings of them (social and cultural elements), language issues, and anything which can influence one's mental operation named perception. Secondly, from the cognitive theory perspective, interpretation, and higher cognitive operations (memories, assumptions, and decisions) are used in this model, because they are complex mental activities and not just sensory information (Ward et al., 2015). Besides, at this point, Hell (1983) stressed the fact that perception is fundamentally cognitive but at the same time, he does not exclude non-cognitive or sensational parameters. Characteristically, he mentioned that: "Perception depends on two things. Sensory endowment and cognitive equipment" (p. 216).

Hence, the above-simplified model of perception lays the foundations for communication. Communication is one of the most complex bidirectional mental operations because it consists of many levels, which operate simultaneously. The basic conceptual functions are: (a) collection of the data (b) organization of the data, (c) coding and decoding, and (d) interpretations. It is evident that communication depends upon perception and perception depends upon senses; therefore, it may be argued that when there are deficits in sensory functions then potential malfunctions may take place in communication, daily living, and quality of life in general (Pinto et al., 2017). This situation may lead to a discontinuous domain of development which in turn may limit the dynamics of communication between the transmitter and the receiver creating a combining set of barriers, such as psychological, emotional, physical, attitudinal barriers, and so on (Argyropoulos et al., 2020; Kyriacou et al., 2015). Therefore, most children with MDVI experience various behavioral, social, attitudinal, and psychological limitations due to their difficulties in communicating (Ayyildiz et al., 2016). The holistic approach of a student with MDVI is again underlain with teachers focusing on specific areas of development and learning in interdependency with the areas of development. Intervention in communication is considered a priority as it enables access and participation, learning and progress, understanding and expressiveness.

To conclude, it may be argued that the common denominator in all cases that may be characterized as "multiple disability" is the combination or interaction of disabilities and the effect of these factors on development (Argyropoulos & Thymakis, 2014; McLinden, 1999). Emphasis is placed on the cooperative and multiplier effect of multiple disabilities, which goes beyond the context of each disability by combining sensory, mental, and physical disabilities (Erin, 2000). Disabilities vary widely in their nature and their impact on the child, with the result that children themselves may exhibit abilities and weaknesses in their cognitive, sensory, and social abilities. Children with MDVI face difficulties in obtaining sufficient information from their environment to learn (Argyropoulos & Thymakis, 2014). The information received through the haptic modality assumes particular significance for these children (McLinden & McCall, 2010). The limited information, which is usually available through their visual sense, often in combination with additional disability results in "reduced capacity to detect; interpret and interact with people and items" (Goold & Hummell, 1993, p. 8). Hence, it is inevitable that children with

MDVI usually end up with limited range of experiences in exploration and understanding the world (McLinden, 2012).

Implications of MDVI on Development, Communication, and Learning

The implications on intervention and education that need to be acknowledged and taken into consideration when developing and implementing programs for students with MDVI refer to:

- policies and methodologies that support inclusion and access to curriculum according to the learning and developmental profiles of the students;
- working in a multidisciplinary team and cooperation with parents;
- complex assessments, using not only standardized tests, developmental scales, or curriculum-based measures, but also functional assessments with various inventories and checklists based on a structured and systematic observation;
- use of the results of the assessment in the development of the individualized educational plans (IEPs) in which objectives, strategies, and methods, content, and modalities of monitoring and evaluation are determined;
- specific interventions such as individualized intervention and differentiated instruction; prompts and feedback, routines, and natural environments;
- increased knowledge and working skills regarding various forms of communication, implications of nonverbal communication, assessment of communication development, development of communication and language abilities;
- use of resources that facilitate participation and engagement in the learning tasks and activities;
- management of the inclusive contexts, facilitating peer-interaction and support, planning transition activities;
- use of assistive technology and various alternative and augmentative systems of communication;
- continuous professional development to acquire competencies in assessment and intervention, class management, working in multidisciplinary teams, developing documents and resources;
- teachers' competencies development and engagement in a professional community.

Functioning of people with multiple disabilities is the result of the interaction of various factors within five independent dimensions, each of the limitations in one dimension influencing the other, but also results and abilities of one dimension are interconnecting with the other dimensions (Petry & Maes, 2006), supporting thus the importance of implementing a holistic approach of a child's needs and abilities. It is stated that supports are resources and strategies that enhance human functioning (Thompson et al., 2009).

A detailed presentation of the model of five dimensions is made by Petry and Maes (2006) as follows:

1. Cognitive skills refer to reasoning, planning, problem-solving, abstract thinking, comprehension of complex ideas, rapid learning, and learning from own experience.
2. Adaptive behavior includes conceptual, social, and practical abilities which are acquired with the aim of daily functioning.
3. Participation, interaction, and social roles are determined by observing the engagement of individuals in daily experiences.

4. Health conditions such as a complex physical, mental and social state, well-being, and quality of life.
5. Context of personal, family, and social environment.

When considering assessment and intervention for MDVI children, there is a need to use approaches which are taking into consideration the combination and associations of existing impairments and disorders, but also their level of severity and complexity, with a need to understand the impact on the quality of access to information and interaction, level of participation in the environment, way of understanding cues and nonverbal communication behaviors, development of anticipatory abilities in activities and tasks.

Characteristics of Assessment

As mentioned in the introduction, MDVI entails a complexity of needs such as diverse educational, social, and medical needs. Therefore, the involvement of experts and professionals from different disciplines is necessary in order to conduct clinical as well as functional evaluations covering all developmental stages of the child who has MDVI. In essence, all assessments and diagnoses need to be made by an interdisciplinary team that will be based on the child's history consisting of medical information, clinical information, information from a psychologist and social worker, information on the child's development, as well as information on the child's cognitive development and learning development (Anderzen-Carlsson, 2017; Gilliam et al., 2005). Family's needs and family's situation, in general, could not be absent from a holistic assessment procedure. Hence, any evaluation should consider not only the child's needs, but also the needs related to the child's family environment (Hathazi, 2014; Riggio et al., 2004). According to evidence-based practices and relevant research, a holistic-oriented assessment should incorporate the following guidelines:

- Use informal and formal methodologies (standardized tests, observations, interviews, reflective logs, etc.) in order to obtain views and perspectives from the child during its activities.
- Conduct the assessment during a typical day for the child. Avoid laboratory conditions because they are not always suitable conditions for valid results.
- Take into account information and reflection from various professionals and staff involved with the child and family.
- Utilize a variety of methods and techniques to communicate with the child.
- Conduct frequent assessments, revise educational decisions and enhance effective teaching interventions.
- Inform the family on a constant basis of the progress of their child and invite them to be part of the team.
- Take into account family's needs and concerns and discuss them with them (Hathazi, 2014; Riggio et al., 2004).

The complexity of MDVI may have a severe impact on the development of children, making the process a "continuous and up-to-date flow of information". It is common that many educators make use of non-standard tools in the evaluation of children with MDVI which may lead to the synthesis of an incomplete image of the child. Because of this situation, teachers or therapists may not be able to trace and effectively describe the potential knowledge and skills that the child with MDVI occupies or is about to develop (i.e., readiness). This results in the difficulty of designing an effective plan regarding the usage of the most appropriate way in which the educational and therapeutic needs of the children could be met. Assessments must be comprehensive, continuous, and systematic, aiming to set realistic objectives according to the educational, social, or medical needs of the child.

Relevant research from a psycho-pedagogical aspect underlines the importance of early detection and intervention in preschool. It is evident that the sooner the screening and tracing take place the better, the more effectively an early intervention program may be implemented. (Njoroge & Bernhart, 2011). Because of the complexity of multiple disability situations, experts and professionals need time to assess, verify and design appropriate educational and therapeutic interventions that meet the child's needs. Hence, if the situation of a child who has MDVI is traced and studied in preschool, it would be easier for the child to adjust, respond and excel through the implementation of early intervention programs.

A support model should approach the relation between the abilities and the demands within individualized programs, leading to improved personal outcomes (Thompson et al., 2009). The same researchers state that the focus of educational and habilitation service systems should be based on understanding people by their types and intensity of support needs, instead of by their limitations and lack of abilities. This approach should be acknowledged from the beginning when including learners with MDVI in inclusive contexts, sometimes the common practice of focusing on limitations and difficulties, starting with assessment and continuing with the intervention being used by teachers.

Access to the Curriculum in an Inclusive Context: Educational Practices and Methods

Due to the implications of MDVI on development, learning, and communication, great importance must be given to the educational setting and the curriculum that is followed so that participation, motivation, curricular access, acquisitions, and results are supported and acquired. The increase of opportunities and access, development of sequential learning and systematic instruction implementing routines supporting initiatives and behaviors, teaching functional skills, increase of use of natural contexts, and development of a responsive and supporting environment need to be taken into consideration (Hathazi, 2020). Education in an inclusive setting may be challenging due to the characteristics and developmental, learning and communication profiles of learners with MDVI, the limited training of teachers, the criteria and standards in the evaluation and access to the general curriculum, difficulties in class management, and peer interactions. One of the recommendations referring to the decrease of differences between students with severe disabilities and nondisabled peers suggests keeping activities, settings, and instructional materials age-appropriate (Sailor et al., 1988). Rozalski et al. (2011), suggests the need for placing a child with a disability (MDVI included) in the least restrictive environment, which is the general education environment, all the other alternatives (general education classes with accommodations, separate classes, separate schools, home instruction, hospital, and residential institutions) being considered more or less restrictive.

In a study of learners with blindness and autistic spectrum disorder (ASD), de Verdier et al. (2018) state that the students experience difficulties in handling the surrounding stimuli and approaching situations of confusion. Challenges in handling the surrounding stimuli may refer to various distractions such as noise, crowded and dynamic space, sudden stimuli without any signaling, fast rhythm of presenting stimuli and not enough time being given to interpret and respond. Situations of confusion may refer to using visually based language in descriptions and presentations of teachers and peers, unstructured tasks and high expectations in solving them independently, fast rhythm in teaching and learning tasks, missing information that is considered to be known or to be implicit, teachers neglecting the need to assure that the learners understand and present the skills. Without systematic or direct instruction, some learners will encounter great barriers in learning and acquiring new skills (Storey & Miner, 2011).

Various curricular options were used over time to organize instruction for children with MDVI (Smith & Levack, 1996). Starting with the medical model with the self-contained special education classrooms, moving toward a functional curriculum and creating nowadays inclusive contexts within the general education curriculum together with non-disabled peers, though still being of benefit to the value of the individualized educational plan, where specific support is noted and followed, with the respect of the characteristics and the specific needs of the student with MDVI. Spooner et al. (2006) state that when working with schools, the following key features should be taken into consideration: family, community, and school partnerships, ongoing teacher training, performance standards for students, aligned curricula, school accountability for all students and school accountability systems with a very well described set of policies and practices. Teaching functional skills should remain a priority though, in the context of inclusive education and access to the general curriculum, those skills can become unapproached (Storey & Miner, 2011). Functional teaching activities refer to skills with immediate usefulness and resources that are real (Storey & Miner, 2011); this way the learner is able to associate significance to the activity and become aware of the immediate practicality of the acquired information or skill.

Wehmeyer (2006) further highlights the evaluation of success only through testing and the narrowing of the general education curriculum which refers only to core academic content. The author recommends the extension of research regarding instructional strategies that work to teach students core literacy, numeracy, science facts, knowledge, and skills, but also the need to have access to universally designed materials. Focus on progress and not only access, research to intervention actions, focus on student-learning and self-determination are also key aspects presented by Wehmeyer (2006). Regarding self-determination, Agran et al., (2006) suggest that curriculum augmentation strategies are adequate so that learners manage, direct and regulate their own learning, having the opportunities to implement problem-solving strategies.

There is also a need to implement differentiated instruction according to various student backgrounds, readiness levels, languages, interests, developmental, and learning profiles. Tomlinson (2001) defines differentiated instruction as a philosophy of teaching that is based on the premise that students learn best when their teachers accommodate the differences in their readiness levels, interests, and learning profiles. Differentiated instruction represents an educational approach that uses a child-centered strategy that allows adaptation to the various learning needs of children. Even if the teachers are aware of the different learning needs, only a part of them will include these differences in their teaching (Avramidis & Norwich, 2002; Scruggs & Mastropieri, 1996).

Differentiated instruction and individualized support need to be applied in the educational contexts, embedding these strategies in the wider child-adult-environment interaction and context, both with a dyadic and holistic approach. One of the models that present this approach of the necessity of considering for successful instruction and inclusion three elements, that is student, adult, and environment is the Tri-Focus Model developed by Siegel-Causey and Wetherby (2000), a model that refers to the understanding of the child, the role of the adults and the context of the environment, but these must be understood not only with a separate view but in various interactions and influences in a dynamic way.

Spooner et al. (2011) state the importance of implementing systematic instruction with strong evidence of effectiveness. The authors refer to systematic instruction as developing socially meaningful skills, identifying skills that are observable and measurable, gathering data of results proving the effectiveness of the intervention, using behavioral principles, and determining behavior change. Systematic instruction includes antecedent and consequence manipulations, cues, prompts and assistance to the student, direct and ongoing measurement (Storey & Miner, 2011).

When considering the characteristics of learning and the process of planning for a student with MDVI, teachers need to understand how the student is learning, why he or she is learning and the modalities in which learning can be supported. According to Collins (2012) there are four basic phases of learning: (i) acquisition, (ii) fluency, (iii) maintenance, and (iv) generalization. The author states that acquisition is the initial learning of a new behavior, fluency is how well a learner masters the specific behavior, maintenance refers to performing a behavior over time and generalization is the ability to perform a behavior in various conditions and contexts. It is of great importance for teachers not only to prioritize acquisition and fluency, but to give extra consideration to maintenance and specifically to generalization of information, concepts and abilities. It is also important to understand the characteristics of each stage in learning, to know the modalities in which learning can be best facilitated and supported, meaning that teachers not only should approach each stage in learning but need to have the competencies to support the transition from one phase to another with the aim of generalization and independent use and practice of the acquired knowledge and skills. Children with MDVI may present difficulties in maintaining abilities over time whenever there are no prompts and reinforcers within one-to-one instruction and intervention and generalization is even more difficult as sometimes there is a tendency for reduced opportunities to practice in various contexts, at different moments in time, with different people, with different resources. The following strategies for skill generalization can be implemented: verbal or written instructions, adequate feedback, re-teaching, positive practice, rewards, and peer-tutoring (Mastropieri & Scruggs, 1984). Other best practices to be used in the classroom are individually appropriate learning standards and programs; structuring and manipulation of space, use of various materials, management of the class and peer groupings; using of principles of universal design for learning; use of natural supports, facilitating communication, working with families within multidisciplinary teams, and access to assistive technology (Argyropoulos & Ravenscroft, 2019; Bruce, 2011). Janssen et al. (2004) propose further adaptations that can be implemented in intervention the following: offering communication aids and choices, implementing routine-based approaches, using adequate materials, taking use of the child's sensory and motor abilities, supporting interactions.

One of the essential components of developing and implementing education programs for students with MDVI is to formulate objectives. Collins (2012) considers that each behavioral objective should include the characteristics of the learner, the description of the behavior that will be acquired, the contexts in which the behaviors will be put in action and the criteria that are used to assess whether the behavior is mastered. Creating meaningful learning experiences represents a priority in the planning and implementation of educational and intervention activities. Meaningful activities determine participation, but also the development of a sense of belonging and increased motivation. Structured routines embedded in the educational programs throughout the day support a level of anticipation and control, but also an integrated approach and real opportunities for concept development and object engagement (Smith et al., 2020) which is an important ability for sustained participation in the activity and maintaining attention. Engagement in the activity in meaningful contexts also develops semantic knowledge, the function of objects, relationships, and the use of language to name and refer to them (Smith et al., 2020).

The routine-based approach and instruction are based on the idea that teaching the skills in the environment that the children will need and use are highly important (Jung, 2007). The ability to anticipate while participating in the context of a familiar series of steps reduces stress and enhances memory function (Smith et al., 2020). It is shown that repetition of consistent patterns of electrical activity generated during specific experiences strengthens neural networks in the brain, thus increasing the speed and efficiency of information processing (Kolb & Whishaw, 2009). Learning takes place within interaction and action in the environment, making experiences significant and with immediate pragmatic use. The student needs to understand and anticipate the consequence of his or her behaviors and actions within natural environments. A natural environment is defined as everyday routines, experiences, and activities as part of the family and community life, where children learn behavior that is considered meaningful by adults and where activities are child-initiated and interest-based (Raab & Dunst, 2004). Natural environments are contexts in which collaborative interaction, intersubjectivity, assisted performance, and learning occurs (Dunst et al., 2001, p.72). The authors suggest the use of activity setting as a situation-specific experience or opportunity in which the child interacts with people and objects and supports the development of self-awareness of their own abilities. Teachers need to understand the importance of creating meaningful environments so that students with MDVI make use of their knowledge and abilities, interact for the purpose of learning, integrate experiences in development, can take decisions in a secure context with responsive adults, and obtain the reinforcers that promote participation and enable understanding.

The Importance of Specific Professional Competencies of Teachers. Issues of Teacher Training

Inclusion of students with various backgrounds, communication and learning experiences, family and social contexts, students with disabilities, students from diverse cultural identities, and students with high achievements determine the necessity for teachers to rethink their teaching and instructional practices (Subban, 2006). Regarding the education of children with visual impairment, there is an increased need to have trained professionals with specialist expertise, especially within mainstream school placements (Douglas et al., 2009).

Brandenburg (2008) considers that

> teacher education should focus not only on knowledge for teaching but knowledge in and knowledge of teaching. When teachers consider the modifications and accommodations in the curriculum for learners with disabilities, they should not think of these changes as the only ones that characterize the learners and should be the only ones developed and implemented, along with the extra time and work needed.
>
> (p. 19)

In this view, recommendations are that the curriculum should be flexible and address from the beginning various needs, not only for children with specific impairments and characteristics (Baglieri & Shapiro, 2017).

The Association for Teacher Education in Europe (2006, 7) refers to teaching as a "profession that entails reflective thinking, continuing professional development, autonomy, responsibility, creativity, research, and personal judgments". Teaching is a complex and cognitively demanding activity, both for teachers who are at the beginning of their career but also for experienced teachers (Westerman, 1991). This leads to the necessity to invest in teacher training programs that will develop teachers' competencies and improve their experiences addressing the various needs of children. The seven characteristics of effective professional development refer to focus on content, active learning, collaboration within job-embedded context, model and modeling, coaching, reflection, and sustained duration. Teacher training programs as professional development consist of various modalities to develop specific knowledge and techniques (Hathazi, 2020), including participation in projects that are based on expertise and strategic partnerships between organizations and institutions.

Planning future interventions is an essential component of the educational process, and it always needs to take into consideration the results of the evaluations, the needs of the individual and the anticipation of the implemented intervention. Mutton et al. (2011) refer to planning as being mostly informal, occurring at different levels, creative, knowledge based, allowing flexibility, carried out in a practical and ideological context. The authors refer to the need of teachers to develop a reactive teaching, which is characterized by the teacher's willingness to adjust learning objectives to accommodate student interests and intentions.

Previous studies revealed that in order to identify if some teaching strategies are working or not, it is highly important to self-reflect on the teaching process (Argyropoulos and Nikolaraizi, 2009). Reynolds (1992) mentioned that systematic evaluation and keeping track of thoughts and feelings can be useful methods for improving the teaching process.

Teachers need to address more and more diversity within the school population, especially in settings with children with special needs. Challenges that teachers face in assessment, education and intervention must be approached within teacher training programs that aim to develop professional competences in understanding, thinking and practice. Even though teachers may have the competences and apply successful strategies, most of them consider they lack training as adapting methods and materials are considered time and effort consuming (de Verdier et al., 2018).

Many teacher training programs have been evaluated with the idea of understanding their efficiency and impact, trying to identify the one or ones that support the aim and make the difference in teacher training with consistency and for a longer period of time. Teachers are willing to attend training programs and they learn best whenever they can see the value of what has been presented to them, and they can use immediately in a concrete and a specific educational situation the knowledge and the working skills. Kroll (2017) states that

> the characteristics that are needed for teachers to undergo professional development refers to an intrinsic interest in the activity, openness to learning, commitment to participation, accepting vulnerability, availability in sharing and accepting difficulties and willingness to support others. Teachers need to look for answers to the following questions: what I can do to facilitate understanding, meaning and learning, how can I support better the initiatives of the students, what the behavior of the child means, how and why he communicates and why he learns, what he or she understands form my initiatives, interaction, communication, behavior and attitude.
>
> (p. 87)

Stremel and Schutz (1995) state that the general structure of the intervention within interactions is based on strategies of control of activities and complexity of answers and behaviors, techniques of facilitating communication and understanding of natural consequences. Intervention is based on one to one, behaviors that are significant, language that is functional and spontaneously used and interpreted by both partners. Janssen et al. (2004) propose an educator-oriented intervention program which aimed for the development of qualitative interactions between the educators and the children. Teachers develop competencies to respond more adequately to children's initiatives, interactions and observe the children's signals and cues, but also, they are trained to adapt the interactional context so that the child's communication is supported. As a consequence of the development of these competencies of teachers, the results of the study show an increase of development of adequate and independent child behaviors.

Janssen et al. (2010) propose the Diagnostic Intervention Model that is developed for the specialist-child dyad and it is based on several principles: recognizing individual cues, synchronizing the behaviors of adult and child, adapting the context of interaction. The Diagnostic Intervention Model consists of a five-step intervention protocol and the steps are determination of the question, clarification, interaction analysis, implementation of the intervention, and evaluation (Janseen et al., 2010, p. 16). The intervention aims include eight categories of behaviors such as initiatives, confirmations for the observed initiatives in terms of approving and disapproving, alternative roles focusing attention on the communication partner, managing intensity and affective involvement, followed by independent action.

Conclusions

Considering the above, it seems that there is a great need to design and implement training programs for professionals involved in the education and rehabilitation of students with MDVI and opportunities for professional development (Alkahtani, 2013; Papazafiri & Argyropoulos, 2018; Silberman & Sacks, 2007). Instruction of learners with MDVI requires specific professional competencies in assessment and intervention. There is a need to understand the implications of MDVI for development and learning, to best support the needs and the characteristics, to acknowledge the specificity of development profiles, the importance of communication and the various forms of communication of learners. Teachers need to identify the most adequate methods and resources which enables the learner to engage in the learning experiences, such as the use of assistive technology (AT) which constitutes an extremely promising field to enhance the independence of people with MDVI, through support devices in the field of autonomy, communication, and social interaction in general. Nevertheless, despite the development of technology and the production of supportive devices and software, relevant studies show reduced use of AT (Ajuwon et al., 2016; Papazafiri & Argyropoulos, 2018).

Professional development methods should be based on best practices and research as they are the foundation for promoting effective implementation of educational programs for students with disabilities. It is worth mentioning that many European projects – especially Erasmus + projects – conduct systematic needs assessments studies in the area of special education and in turn based on these needs they develop intensive training and learning events. The content of these training events is extremely useful because they incorporate experiential learning, face to face methods coupled with hands-on opportunities and practical work (Argyropoulos et al., 2020). The roles of professionals working with students with MDVI constantly evolve. Learning and teaching methods are changing rapidly at national and international level. Students have the capacity to learn in a wider range of settings with the advent of new technologies opening new ways of teaching and supporting them (Argyropoulos & Ravenscroft, 2019). There is a great need to develop programs in higher education that meet the needs of professionals working with students with MDVI to address the skills and tools needed to serve these students. It is essential for the professionals working with MDVI students to acquire more specialized skills to meet the complex needs of these students (Argyropoulos et al., 2020; McLinden et al., 2006; Papazafiri & Argyropoulos, 2018; Silberman & Sacks, 2007).

References

Agran, M., Cavin, M., Wehmeyer, M., & Palmer, S. (2006). Participation of students with moderate to severe disabilities in the general curriculum: the effects of the self-determined learning model of instruction, *Research and Practice for Persons with Severe Disabilities, 31*(3), 230–241, https://doi.org/10.1177/154079690603100303

Ajuwon, M.P., Kalene Meeks, M., Griffin-Shirley, N., & Okungu, A.P. (2016). Reflections of teachers of visually impaired students on their assistive technology competencies. *Journal of Visual Impairment and Blindness, 110*(2), 128–134. http://dx.doi.org/10.1177/0145482x1611000207

Alkahtani, K. D. F. (2013). Teachers' knowledge and use of assistive technology for students with special educational needs. *Journal of Studies in Education, 3*(2), 65–86. https://doi.org/10.5296/jse.v3i2.3424

Anderzen-Carlsson, A. (2017). A qualitative evaluation of the National Expert Team regarding the assessment and diagnosis of deafblindness in Sweden. *Scandinavian Journal of Disability Research, 19*(4), 362–374. https://doi.org/10.1080/15017419.2016.1268972

Anthony, T. L. (2016). Early identification of infants and toddlers with deafblindness. *American Annals of the Deaf, 161*(4), 412–423. http://www.jstor.org/stable/26235292

Argyropoulos, V., & Gentle, F. (2019). Formal and non-formal education for individuals with vision impairment or multiple disabilities and vision impairment. In J. Ravenscroft (Ed.), *The Routledge Handbook of Visual Impairment* (pp. 118–142). Routledge.

Argyropoulos, V., & Nikolaraizi, M. (2009). Developing inclusive practices through collaborative action research. *European Journal of Special Needs Education, 24*(2), 139–153. https://doi.org/10.1080/08856250902793586

Argyropoulos V., & Ravenscroft J. (2019). Assisting People with Vision Impairments through Technology. In A. Tatnall (Ed.), *Encyclopedia of education and information technologies* (pp. 141–150). Springer Nature.

Argyropoulos, V., & Thymakis, P. (2014). Multiple disabilities and visual impairment: An action research project. *Journal of Visual Impairment and Blindness, 108*(2), 163–167. https://doi.org/10.1177/0145482X1410800210

Argyropoulos, V., Kanari, C., Hathazi, A., Kyriakou, M., Papazafiri, M., & Nikolaraizi, M. (2020a). Children with vision impairment and multiple disabilities: issues of communication skills and professionals' challenges. In M. Carmo (Ed.), Proceedings of the International Conference on Education and New Developments (pp. 271–275). inScience Press. https://10.36315/2020end058

Argyropoulos, V., Kanari, C., Papazafiri, M., & Nikolaraizi, M. (2020b). Effective Communication for Individuals with vision impairment and multiple disabilities: the case of the PrECIVIM project. In M. Mira Tzvetkova-Arsova & M. Tomova (Eds), Proceedings of the 7th ICEVI Balkan Conference (pp. 143–149). ICEVI-Europe.

Argyropoulos, V., Nikolaraizi, M., & Papazafiri, M. (2020c). Alternative routes toward literacy for individuals with deafblindness: The role of assistive technology. In S. Easterbrooks & H. Dostal (Eds.), *The Oxford handbook of deaf studies in literacy* (pp. 371–383). Oxford University Press.

Association for Teacher Education in Europe (2006), The quality of teachers, recommendations on the development of indicators to identify teacher quality. Policy paper. Brussels—Portoroz: ATEE http://www.atee.org/policy/policypaper.pdf

Avramidis, E., & Norwich, B. (2002). Teachers' attitudes towards integration / inclusion: a review of the literature, *European Journal of Special Needs Education, 17*(2), 129–147. https://doi.org/10.1080/08856250210129056

Ayyildiz, E., Akçin, N., & Güven, Y. (2016). Development of preverbal communication skills scale for children with multiple disabilities and visual impairment. *Journal of Human Sciences, 13*(2), 2668–2681. https://10.14687/jhs.v13i2.3718

Baglieri, S., & Shapiro, A. (2017). *Disability studies and the inclusive classroom: Critical practices for embracing diversity in education*. Routledge.

Brabyn, J. A., Schneck, M. E., Haegerstrom-Portnoy, G., & Lott, L. A. (2007). Dual sensory loss: Overview of problems, visual assessment, and rehabilitation. *Trends in Amplification, 11*(4), 219–226, https://doi.org/10.1177/1084713807307410

Brandenburg, R. T. (2008). *Powerful pedagogy: Self-study of a teacher educator's practice* (Vol. 6). Springer Science & Business Media.

Bruce, S. M. (2011). Severe and multiple disabilities. In J.M. Kauffman, & D.P. Hallahan (Eds.) *Handbook of special education* (pp. 291–303). Routledge

Bruce S. M., & Borders C. (2015). Communication and language in learners who are deaf and hard of hearing with disabilities: theories, research, and practice. *American Annals of the Deaf, 160*(4), 68–84. doi: 10.1353/aad.2015.0035

Collins, B. C. (2012). *Systematic instruction for students with moderate and severe disabilities*. Paul H. Brookes Publishing Co.

de Verdier, K., Fernell, E., & Ek, U. (2018). Challenges and successful pedagogical strategies: Experiences from six Swedish students with blindness and autism in different school settings. *Journal of Autism and Developmental Disorders, 48*(2), 520–532.

Douglas, G., McCall, S., McLinden, M., Pavey, S., Ware, J., & Farrell, A. M. (2009). *International review of the literature of evidence of best practice models and outcomes in the education of blind and visually impaired children.* National Council for Special Education.

Dunst, C. J., Bruder, M. B., Trivette, C. M., Hamby, D., Raab, M., & McLean, M. (2001). Characteristics and consequences of everyday natural learning opportunities. *Topics in Early Childhood Special Education, 21*(2), 68–92.

Erin, J. E. (2000). Students with visual impairments and additional disabilities. In A. J. Koenig & M. C. Holbrook (Eds.). *Foundations of education, Vol. II, Instructional strategies for teaching children and youths with visual impairments* (pp. 720–748). AFB Press.

Gilliam, W., Meisels, S., & Mayes, L. (2005). Screening and surveillance in early intervention systems. In M. Guralnick (Ed.), *The developmental systems approach to early intervention* (pp. 73–97). Paul H. Brokes Publishing Co.

Goold, L., & Hummell, J. (1993). *Supporting the receptive communication of individuals with significant multiple disabilities: Selective use of touch to enhance comprehension (Monograph series No. 4).* North Rocks Press and Royal Institute for Deaf and Blind Children.

Hathazi, A. (2014). Interaction – based intervention programs in multiple disabilities. *International Journal of Humanities and Social Science, 4*(12), 135–139.

Hathazi, A. (2020). Support programs for developing competences of teachers as an essential factor for successful inclusive education. *Revista Educação e Cultura Contemporânea, 17*(51), 10–27.

Hell, J. (1983). *Perception and cognition.* University of California Press.

Janssen, M. J., Riksen-Walraven, J. M., & van Dijk, J. P. (2004). Enhancing the interactive competence of deafblind children: Do intervention effects endure?, *Journal of Developmental and Physical Disabilities, 16*(1), 73–94, https://doi.org/10.1023/B:JODD.0000010040.54094.0f

Janssen, M. J., Riksen-Walraven, J. M., van Dijk, J. P., & Ruijssenaars, W. A. (2010). Interaction coaching with mothers of children with congenital deaf-blindness at home: Applying the diagnostic intervention model. *Journal of Visual Impairment & Blindness, 104*(1), 15–29, https://doi.org/10.1177/0145482X1010400106

Jung, L. A. (2007). Writing SMART objectives and strategies that fit the ROUTINE, *Teaching Exceptional Children, 39*(4), 54–58. https://doi.org/10.1177/004005990703900406

Kolb, B., & Whishaw, I. Q., (2009). *Fundamentals of human neuropsychology* (6th ed.). Worth.

Kroll, J. (2017). Requisite participant characteristics for effective peer group mentoring. *Mentoring & Tutoring: Partnership in Learning, 25*(1), 78–96. https://doi.org/10.1080/13611267.2017.1308096

Kyriacou, M., Pronay, B., & Hathazi, A. (2015). *Report of the mapping exercise carried out by the commission of persons with visual impairment and additional disabilities.* EBU document. Retrieved from http://www.icevi-europe.org/files/2015/additional-disabilities.pdf

Mastropieri, M. A., & Scruggs, T. E. (1984). Generalization: Five effective strategies. *Academic Therapy, 19*(4), 427–431, https://doi.org/10.1177/105345128401900407

McLinden, M. (1999). Hand on: haptic exploratory strategies in children who are blind with multiple disabilities. *British Journal of Visual Impairment, 17*, 23–9 https://doi.org/10.1177/0145482X0409800210

McLinden, M. (2012). Mediating haptic exploratory strategies in children who have visual impairment and intellectual disabilities. *Journal of Intellectual Disability Research, 56*(2), 129–139, https://doi.org/10.1111/j.1365-2788.2011.01430.x

McLinden, M., & McCall, S. (2010). The role of touch in the learning experiences of children who have PMLD and visual impairment. *PMLD Link Summer*, 17–21.

McLinden, M., & McCall, S., Hilton, D., & Weston, A. (2006). Participation in online problem based Learning: Insights from postgraduate teachers studying through open and distance education. *Distance Education, 27*(3), 331–353, https://doi.org/10.1080/01587910600940422

Mutton, T., Hagger, H., & Burn, K. (2011). Learning to plan, planning to learn: the developing expertise of beginning teachers, *Teachers and Teaching, 17*(4), 399–416, https://doi.org/10.1080/13540602.2011.580516

Njoroge, W. F. M., & Bernhart, K. P. (2011). Assessment of behavioral disorders in preschool aged children. *Current Psychiatry Report, 13*, 84–92, https//doi.org/10.1007/s11920-011-0181-7

Papazafiri, M., & Argyropoulos, V. (2018). Assistive Technology and special education teachers: the case of students with multiple disabilities and vision impairment. *Proceedings of EDULEARN18 Conference* (pp. 5485–5492). doi: 10.21125/edulearn.2018.1323

Petry, K., & Maes, B. (2006), Identifying expressions of pleasure and displeasure by persons with profound and multiple disabilities, *Journal of Intellectual and Developmental Disability*, *31*(1), 28–38. https://doi.org/10.1080/13668250500488678

Pinto, J. M., Wroblewski, K. E., Huisingh-Scheetz, M., Correia, C., Lopez, K. J., Chen, R. C.,... & Kern, D. W. (2017). Global sensory impairment predicts morbidity and mortality in older U.S. adults. *The American Geriatrics Society*, *65*, 2587–2595.

Raab, M., & Dunst, C. J. (2004). Early intervention practitioner approaches to natural environment interventions. *Journal of Early Intervention*, 27, 15–26, https://doi.org/10.1177/105381510402700102

Reynolds, A. (1992). What is competent beginning teaching? A review of the literature. *Review of Educational Research*, *62*(1), 1–35.

Riggio, M., Heydt, K., Allon, M., Edwards, S., Clark, M., & Cushman, C. (2004). *Perkins activity and resource guide: A handbook for teachers and parents of students with visual and multiple disabilities*. Perkins School for the Blind.

Rozalski, M., Miller, J., & Stewart, A. (2011). Least restrictive environment. In J. Kauffman, & D. Hallahan (Eds.), *Handbook of special education* (pp. 107–120). Routledge.

Sailor, W., Gee, K., Goetz, L., & Graham, N. (1988). Progress in Educating Students with the Most Severe Disabilities: Is There Any? *Journal of the Association for Persons with Severe Handicaps*, *13*(2), 87–99. https://doi.org/10.1177/154079698801300205

Scruggs, T. E., & Mastropieri, M. A. (1996). Teacher perceptions of mainstreaming inclusion, 1958–1995: A research synthesis. *Exceptional Children*, *63*, 59–74, https://doi.org/10.1177/001440299606300106

Siegel-Causey, E., & Wetherby, A. (2000), Nonsymbolic communication. In M. Snell & F. Brown (Eds.), *Instruction of students with severe disabilities* (5th ed., pp. 400–450). Merrill/Prentice-Hall.

Silberman, R. & Sacks, S. (2007). *Expansion of the role of the teacher of students with visual impairments: Providing for students who also have severe/multiple disabilities. A position paper of the Division on Visual Impairments Council on Exceptional Children*. Council for Exceptional Children.

Simcock, P. (2017). One of society's most vulnerable groups? A systematically conducted literature review exploring the vulnerability of deafblind people. *Health & Social Care in the Community*, *25*(3), 813–839, https://doi.org/10.1111/hsc.12317.

Smith, M., Chambers, S., Campbell, A., Pierce, T., McCarthy, T., & Kostewicz, D. E. (2020). Use of routine-based instruction to develop object perception skills with students who have visual impairments and severe intellectual disabilities: two case studies. *Journal of Visual Impairment & Blindness*, *114*(2), 101–113, https://doi.org/10.1177/0145482X20910826

Smith, M., & Levack, N. (1996). *Teaching students with visual and multiple impairments: A resource guide*. Texas School for the Blind and Visually Impaired.

Spooner, F., Browder, D. M., & Mims, P. J. (2011). Evidence-based practice. In D. M. Browder & F. Spooner (Eds.), *Teaching students with moderate and severe disabilities* (pp. 92–124), Guilford.

Spooner, F., Dymond, S. K., Smith, A., &Kennedy, C. H. (2006). What we know and need to know about accessing the general curriculum for students with significant cognitive disabilities, *Research and Practice for Persons with Severe Disabilities*, *31*(4), 277–283, https://doi.org/10.1177/154079690603100401

Storey, K., & Miner, C. (2011). *Systematic instruction of functional skills for students and adults with disabilities*. Charles C Thomas Publisher.

Stremel, K., &Schutz, R. (1995). Functional communication in inclusive settings for students who are deaf-blind. In N. Haring & L. Romer (Eds.), *Welcoming students who are deaf-blind into typical classrooms: s: Facilitating school participation, learning, and friendships* (pp. 197–229). Paul H. Brookes.

Subban, P. (2006). Differentiated instruction: A research basis. *International Education Journal*, 7, 935–947.

Thompson, J. R., Bradley, V. J., Buntinx, W. H., Schalock. R. L., Shogren, K. A., Snell, M. E., ...Yeager, M. H., (2009). Conceptualizing supports and the support needs of people with intellectual disability, *Intellectual and Developmental Disabilities*,47(2), 135–146. https//doi.org//10.1352/1934-9556-47.2.135

Tomlinson, C. (2001). *How to differentiate instruction in mixed-ability classrooms* (2nd ed.). Association for Supervision and Curriculum Development.

Ward, M. O., Grinstein, G., & Keim, D. (2015). *Interactive data visualization: Foundations, techniques, and applications* (2nd ed.). A K Peters/CRC Press.

Wehmeyer, M. L. (2006). Beyond access: Ensuring progress in the general education curriculum for students with severe disabilities. *Research and Practice for Persons with Severe Disabilities*, *31*(4), 322–326. https://doi.org/10.1177/154079690603100405

Westerman, D. A. (1991). Expert and novice teacher decision making, *Journal of Teacher Education*, *42*(4), 292–305. https://doi.org/10.1177/002248719104200407

33

THE USE OF TELEPRACTICE TO SUPPORT TEACHERS IN FACILITATING LEARNING FOR CHILDREN WITH COMMUNICATION DISORDERS

A South African Proposal

Khetsiwe Masuku*, Ben Sebothoma, Nomfundo Moroe, Munyane Mophosho and Katijah Khoza-Shangase

Inclusive Education in South Africa

South Africa's rise to democracy in 1994 birthed one of the world's most progressive constitutions and policies (Murungi, 2015). Since then, there has been progressive transformation of the apartheid government policies with the aim of providing services to all South Africans on an equitable basis (Dalton et al., 2012). One such change is in the provision of education for learners with disabilities and the development of the inclusive education system based on the Constitution of the Republic of South Africa, Act no. 108 of 1996 (Republic of South Africa, 1996). Section 29 of the Bill of Rights states that (i) all citizens have a right to a basic education, including adult and further education, (ii) the State must progressively provide and ensure availability and access to reasonable accommodation; and (iii) the State may not discriminate directly or indirectly against anyone on one or more grounds, including disability. Internationally, in the early 1900s, the Human Rights Framework purported that all children, including those with disabilities, have a right to free and compulsory education (Human Rights Watch, 2015). Due to the slow implementation and uptake of this United Nations position, in 2000 at the World Education Forum, the "Education for All" initiative was launched, with a commitment of achieving this initiative by year 2015 (Human Rights Watch, 2015).

Despite the universal Human Rights Framework on education and the post-apartheid government's policies having the best intentions for facilitating access to education for all, South Africa continues to experience one of the most disproportionate schooling systems in the world (Human Rights Watch, 2015; Dalton et al., 2012; Khoza-Shangase et al., 2021a). As recently as 2015, the South African Department of Basic Education identified challenges in the provision-

---

* Khetsiwe.Masuku@wits.ac.za

DOI: 10.4324/9781003266068-39

ing of quality education. These barriers include "inadequate school infrastructure, insufficient curriculum coverage and delivery, poor retentions, inadequate retrieval and usage of learner and teacher support resources, poor assessments, as well as inadequate quality, efficiency and accountability nationally" (Khoza-Shangase et al., 2021a, p. 223). Beyond these listed barriers, implementation of efficient inclusive education is further negatively influenced by insufficient and/or non-existing collaboration between existing interprovincial and inter-governmental structures to facilitate linkages between policies, programmes and resources to impact on quality improvement in the South African basic education system (Department of Basic Education, 2015).

Although poor implementation of inclusive education has disadvantaged children with disabilities from accessing free and compulsory education (Department of Education, 2001), in some regard, South Africa has made progress in broadening access to education regardless of race, gender, social standing and disability (Donohue & Bornman, 2014). However, the unlevelled schooling system persists through all educational contexts, and it is further compounded in access to education for learners with disabilities, particularly those with communication disorders, indicating a fundamental breach of human rights for these learners with special needs (Pillay & Agherdien, 2021). Donohue and Bornman (2014) lament that in 2014, 70% of children of school-going age with disabilities were out of school, and of those who did attend school, most were still in schools for learners with special educational needs. According to Human Rights Watch (2019), approximately 600,000 children with disabilities were not in school and in 2015, 121,500 learners with disabilities were in 'ordinary schools' and over 119,500 were enrolled in special schools. In 2017, close to 11,500 children with disabilities were on the waiting list to enrol in special schools. Furthermore, Human Rights Watch (2019) lamented that education in South Africa is not yet free for the majority of children with disabilities as local laws do not by default guarantee the right to free education despite the Constitution purporting free education.

Added to these challenges, is the teachers' lack of knowledge and skills on the design and presentation of the curriculum in ways that can meet the diverse needs of learners in their classrooms (Dalton et al., 2012; Mulovhedzi & Mudzielwana, 2021). This speaks to the need for support for teachers in planning, implementing, assessing and monitoring the (Khoza-Shangase et al., 2021a).

The Role and Needs of Teachers of Learners with Communication Disorders

Teaching is the most complex profession in the development of learners (Mahlo, 2017; Snowman et al., 2009). As such, inclusive education has placed a significant amount of stress on teachers who are expected to teach learners irrespective of race, gender, language, class, religion, disability, HIV/AIDS status, and culture, without the benefit of being trained to teach accordingly (Phasha et al., 2013).

Avramidis and Kalyva (2007) argue that teachers are the gatekeepers of the classroom climate and activities. Their role includes identifying barriers to learning, adapting the curriculum and education materials, and collaborating with other professionals to facilitate inclusive education (Department of Education, 2001; Forlin et al., 2008). Inclusive education caters for the diverse needs of learners within the same classroom regardless of their capabilities (Mulovhedzi & Mudzielwana, 2021) putting undue pressure on both the learners and the educators. While the pressure may be good for learners who do not present with educational needs, it may pose a challenge for learners with educational needs, particularly communication disabilities (Mophosho & Masuku, 2021). Communication plays a significant role in the early development of children and in their educational and vocational prospects (Moroe, 2021), and impaired communication negatively influences the outcomes of these children at school (Maluleke et al., 2019a; 2019b). Learning and development occurs through our senses (Kátai et al., 2008; Moroe 2021) and language is the basis of communication (Rabiah, 2012), and literacy is strongly linked to language and communication abilities (Roth et al., 2006); communication disorders may be a barrier to academic success if the schooling environment does not cater to the needs of the learner with a communication disorder (Mophosho & Masuku, 2021; Khoza-Shangase et al., 2021a; Pillay & Sebothoma, 2021; Bezuidenhout et al., 2021). Literacy skills and education in general cannot be underestimated as they undergird an individual's holistic functioning healthwise, socially, psychologically and economically (Mophosho & Moonsamy, 2021). Khoza-Shangase (2021) argues that children with communication disorders are at greater risk for academic success as most do not receive early intervention to prepare them for academic success. Most children with communication disabilities reportedly do not have access to Early Childhood Development (ECD) programmes for stimulation and therefore often enter the schooling system without the necessary language development that facilitates learning (Maluleke et al., 2019a; 2019b; Parliamentary Monitoring Group, 2013 in Khoza-Shangase, 2021).

These communication disorders are often diagnosed and managed by speech-language therapists and audiologists (SLTAs), who have an important role to play in the facilitation of learning outcomes through collaborating with the parents and teachers.

Teachers are often not adequately prepared for the diverse needs of the learners (Khoza-Shangase, 2021a; Manga & Masuku, 2020), and this is compounded in the presence of communication disorders (Mophosho & Masuku, 2021). Specifically, teachers lack training and awareness on the diverse nature of disabilities learners present with, practical training on the specific individual needs of each learner, and adequate basic education to address the task of teaching learners with communication disorders (Khoza-Shangase et al., 2021a; Manga & Masuku, 2020). Evidence suggests that 80% of teachers in schools for the Deaf (Parliamentary Monitoring Group, 2013 in Khoza-Shangase, 2021) and teachers in schools of learners who are deafblind (Manga & Masuku, 2020) are not adequately prepared to teach learners with disabilities. In balancing the demands of teaching and performance on the part of the learners, teachers tend to place fewer demands on learners, leading to reduced communication opportunities and little motivation to develop more effective communication skills (Beukelman & Mirenda, 2005). Additionally, the teaching environment itself is a challenge due to the high teacher-to-learner ratios and the lack of adequate physical, financial, and human resources (Manga & Masuku, 2020). A limited number of schools, where available, are poorly resourced, mostly located in urban areas, and do not promote the principles of inclusive education (Khoza-Shangase, 2021; Parliamentary Monitoring Group, 2013).

Several studies highlight the need for teacher training and provision of skills to facilitate learning in diverse contexts (Adewumi & Mosito, 2019; Dreyer et al., 2012; Manga & Masuku, 2020; Nel et al., 2016). For instance, Dreyer et al. (2012) found that 65% of mainstream teachers did not have a formal initial teacher education qualification that included training in how to respond within mainstream classrooms, and to diverse learning needs. These teachers were either trained only for general mainstream education or for the so-called "specialised education" in separate educational settings. This was also observed by Oswald (2007) who argues that historically, the teacher training curriculum covered either general education or special education, resulting in gaps in training and experience on teaching learners with disabilities

The lack of training for teachers to accommodate children with communication disorders, and the limited number of SLTAs in the provision of services to support learners with communication disorders, mean that there is a call for collaboration between these professionals. Collaborative teamwork between educators and therapists contributes towards inclusive education. SLTAs are trained in the assessment and management of communication and are better placed to guide teachers in developing individualised educational plans for learners with communication disorders (Chhabra et al., 2010). The benefits of early communication intervention need to be stressed as they facilitate academic performance, social and communicative functioning; achievement of developmental milestones; positive parent–child interactions, as well as a supportive family environment (Guralnick, 2005; Khoza-Shangase, 2021; Rossetti, 2004).

In an ideal world, SLTAs would work with learners with communication disabilities in the educational context; however this is not possible in the South African context due to existing documented demand versus capacity challenges (Khoza-Shangase & Kanji, 2021). There is a global shortage of healthcare professionals (Wilford et al., 2018), with an extreme shortage of SLTAs in South Africa (Pillay et al., 2020), which negatively affects the implementation of SLH services nationally. The shortage of SLTAs is more pronounced in educational settings where communication disorders are common (McKinnon et al., 2007; Oyono et al., 2018; Khoza-Shangase et al., 2021a). The shortage of SLTAs and frozen posts in the healthcare sector due to the current economic challenges, ongoing lack of prioritisation of posts in the education sectors, the mismatch between language and culture of SLTAs to that of the South African majority clients requiring SLH services (Khoza-Shangase, 2021), lead the current authors to rethink the feasibility and sustainability of a face-to-face model of delivering training and support to educators, and re-imagine increasing access and success through alternative models such as the use of information and communication technologies (ICT).

Telepractice as the Potential Answer to Teacher-Support

The American Speech-Hearing-Association (ASHA, n.d) defines telepractice as the 'application of ICT to the delivery of SLH professional services at a distance by linking clinician to client or clinician to clinician for assessment, intervention, and/or consultation'. Over the last two-three decades, SLTAs in several nations have engaged in telepractice (Khoza-Shangase et al., 2021b). Sufficient evidence exists on the usefulness of telepractice in the assessment and management of hearing, speech, language, voice, and fluency impairments in various age groups (Boisvert et al., 2010; Khoza-Shangase & Moroe, 2020; Khoza-Shangase et al., 2021b). Furthermore, telepractice has been validated and proven to be successful by several professional bodies (ASHA, 2014; Edwards et al., 2012; Health Professions Council of South Africa-HPCSA, 2020; South African Speech Language and Hearing Association – SASLHA, n.d), their value has been enhanced by the advent of the Covid-19 pandemic which has caused significant disruptions to the delivery of SLH services globally (Khoza-Shangase et al., 2021b)

Telepractice can be delivered asynchronously (store and forward), real-time synchronously, and via a hybrid method (blended approaches) (Rushbrooke, 2016, Coco, 2020; Khoza-Shangase & Moroe, 2020; Khoza-Shangase et al., 2021b). While research has found all models of delivery efficient, the choice of models depends on several contextual factors. For example, in countries such as South Africa, a synchronous method of delivering SLH services, particularly in schools, may not be feasible due to infrastructural challenges such as internet connectivity problems, electricity problems, etc. (Khoza-Shangase et al., 2021a; 2021b). Despite this, telepractice has been shown to be an effective method in this context, and authors of this chapter argue that this method can be used to support teachers of learners with communication disorders.

Potential Benefits of Telepractice

Regina Molini-Avejonas et al. (2015) maintain that telepractice is useful for delivering services in areas that do not have adequate SLH services. Telepractice has been proposed as an alternative modality to bridge the demand versus capacity gap in low- to middle-income countries (LMICs), and as a vehicle to deliver SLH services to underserved communities. Khoza-Shangase et al. (2021b) recently argued that the use of telepractice can remediate barriers to learning, and facilitate empowerment, inclusivity and equality in the education context. Khoza-Shangase et al. (2021b) further assert that there is a need to accelerate the focus on telepractice and teletraining methods in order to increase access for students and patients in LMICs. Current authors believe that telepractice may be the better option, particularly in LMICs to support teachers in schools.

Practical Application of Telepractice in the Classroom

In their scope of practice, the role of STAs is both preventive and curative. In the preventive arm, STAs screen for communication disorders among other conditions. In the curative arm, they identify, assess, and manage communications disorder. Within the field of audiology, this is referred to as Early detection (Identification) to and intervention (EDI). This usually focused on hearing disorders; however Moroe (2021) argue that this should include deafblindness as this currently not a routine practice.

Telepractice can be utilised in the screening, assessment and appropriate placement of learners with communication disorders as well as provide tele-training for teachers. Muñoz et al. (2020) have through telepractice explored tele-assessment in the identification of communication disorders, while Monica et al. (2017) assessed the feasibility of using synchronous tele-hearing screening in India for identifying hearing and other otologic disorders in school aged children using a teacher as a facilitator and compared it to in-person assessment. Monica et al. (2017) found a high agreement between conducting an in-person DPOAE and tele-DPOAE (83.87%), otoscopy and tele-otoscopy (96.4%), and pure tone audiometry (PTA) and tele-PTA (80.64%). These findings support the benefits of using telepractice in resource constrained context.

Recent technological developments in telepractice, including smartphone applications in particular, have been developed as screening tools to assist in identifying hearing loss and other communications disorders (Du Toit et al., 2020; Manus et al., 2021; Potgieter et al., 2016). These applications have been shown to be valid, reliable, easy to use, and can be operated by paraprofessionals such as volunteers or/and community health workers (Manus et al., 2021).

While screening in schools is crucial for early identification and intervention (EDI), and to reduce the potential impacts of communication disorders in school aged children (ISHP, 2012), for children who fail screening tests, a diagnostic assessment is required. Telepractice can thus be used for the diagnosis of communication disorders. However, diagnostic assessment requires a control environment in order to increase the accuracy of results. For example, a sound treated room with minimum ambient noise is required to obtain to conduct a diagnostic hearing assessment. However, South African schools do not have adequate infrastructure suitable for diagnostic assessments. Some of the schools are located closer to noisy places such as airports (Seabi et al., 2013), highway roads (Santika et al., 2017), while others generally have noisy classrooms with poor classroom acoustics (Sebothoma et al., 2022; in press), which will make diagnostic assessment difficult.

Despite these challenges, Eikelboom and Swanepoel (2016) demonstrated assessment feasibility through the use of specially designed headsets that occlude sounds, used in automated audiometry system (Eikelboom & Swanepoel, 2016). These automated systems have been shown to be valid and reliable and can be used in school settings (Govender & Mars, 2018). Although diagnostic assessment of communication disorders requires qualified therapists, diagnostic assessment can be performed asynchronously, where the therapists can make the diagnosis of the communication disorder at a later stage, with the assistance of a paraprofessional or facilitator

(Biagio et al., 2013). In South Africa, where task-shifting seems to be the viable solution for demand versus capacity challenge, technological tools such as smartphone applications will be extremely useful in school context.

For children whose communication disorders already exist and were identified through diagnostic assessment, intervention is needed to improve their communication skills, and provide them with the opportunity to succeed in schools. Tanner et al. (2020) reported that telerehabilitation is an acceptable and feasible method and can be used with children. del Carmen Pamplona and Ysunza (2020) found a significant improvement for severe compensatory articulation after using tele practice. A pre-post study conducted by Dean et al. (2021) used an information communication technology called the Virtual Reading Gym (VRG) to explore the impact of an online, partner-supported reading intervention in school aged children. Their findings indicated that an online reading intervention facilitated by a speech language therapist was associated with reading accuracy and comprehension, which ultimately improves literacy skills for school aged children.

With regard to rehabilitation, tele-rehabilitation can be used to remotely fit patients with hearing aids, programme cochlear implants, provide remote follow up consultations (Tao et al., 2020) and provide auditory training (Ratnanather et al., 2021). In their study, Eikelboom et al. (2014) found no statistical difference between face-to-face and remote programming of cochlear implants in patients with hearing loss. Therefore, in a school setting, tele-rehabilitation can be used with children who have a hearing loss and candidates of amplification.

Additionally, tele-training can be used to train teachers to identify communication disorders and to make them aware of the differences between communication disorders versus normal speech and language development in various language and cultures. This is particularly important considering that in South Africa, communication disorders are compounded by the diversity of students who speak different languages and come from different cultural and religious backgrounds, and the lack of linguistically and culturally appropriate assessment (Khoza-Shangase & Mophosho, 2018; Khoza-Shangase & Mophosho, 2021; Mdlalo et al., 2019). Therefore, tele-training of teachers to contribute towards achieving the goals of inclusive education and provide support, tele-mentoring, facilitated by speech language therapists and/or audiologists. Psarros and McMahon (2016) argue that technology can be used for professional up-skilling, training, mentoring, and supervision. Rushbrooke (2016) further reported that training is essential for the success of telepractice. Therefore, current authors believe that tele-training should form an important part of telepractice to support teachers in schools. Tele-training should also be used to effectively train community workers or volunteer individuals who can provide health education and other tasks that can shifted.

Consideration for the Implementation of Telepractice in Schools

While telepractice is useful and can be used to support teachers of children with communication disorders, there are certain considerations that must be met. Snograss et al. (2017) reported that telepractice requires good internet connection and devices such as the computer, tablet and smartphones to be implemented. Swanepoel et al. (2010) also noted that the implementation of telepractice may be affected by technical, infrastructural and socio-cultural factors. Given that many schools in countries such as South Africa do not have the appropriate infrastructure for technology, which include access to reliable electricity, government and other stakeholders may need to provide schools with these resources. It is the belief of current authors that if the requirements for telepractice are provide, children with communication disorders may be assisted and teachers will be supported.

Conclusion

The implementation of inclusive education is key to achievement of the right to education for learners with disabilities. Teachers are essential to the realisation of inclusive education and ultimately the right to education for all. It is however evident that there are gaps in the training and skills of teachers necessary for the management of learners with communication disorders which contributes towards the slow pace of implementing inclusive education especially for this population in South African schools. A collaborative approach between teachers and professionals who specialise in communication disorders may mitigate most of the training and skills gaps that teachers experience when teaching learners with communication disorders ultimately making education accessible for these learners. In light of the current Covid-19 climate, the general shortage of SLTAs in SA, and the shortage of SLTA posts in the department of education, face to face one on one contact between SLTAs and teachers may not be possible. Therefore, telepractice is proposed as a method of delivering SLTA support services to teachers to alleviate some of the challenges that they experience when they attempt to make the curriculum accessible to learners with communication disorders.

References

Adewumi, T. M., & Mosito, C. (2019). Experiences of teachers in implementing inclusion of learners with special education needs in selected Fort Beaufort District primary schools, South Africa. *Cogent Education*, 6(1), 1703446.

American Speech-Hearing-Association (n.d.). *Telepractice*. https://www.asha.org/practice-portal/professional-issues/telepractice/#collapse_4

Avramidis, E., & Kalyva, E. (2007). The influence of teaching experience and professional development on Greek teacher's attitudes towards inclusion. *European Journal of Special Needs Education*, 22(4), 367–389.

Beukelman, D., & Mirenda, P. (2005). *Augmentative and alternative communication: Management of severe communication impairments* (3rd ed). Brookes.

Bezuidenhout, J. K., Khoza-Shangase, K., De Maayer, T., & Strehlau, R. (2021). Outcomes of newborn hearing screening at an academic secondary level hospital in Johannesburg, South Africa. *South African Journal of Communication Disorders*, 68(1), 741.

Biagio, L., Swanepoel, D. W., Adeyemo, A., Hall, J. W. & Vinck, B. (2013). Asynchronous Video-Otoscopy with Telehealth Facilitator. *Telemedicine and E-Health*, 19(4), 252–258

Boisvert, M., Lang, R., Andrianopoulos, M., & Boscardin, M. L. (2010). Telepractice in the assessment and treatment of individuals with autism spectrum disorders: A systematic review. *Developmental Neurorehabilitation*, 13(6), 423–432.

Chhabra, S., Srivastava, R., & Srivastava, I. (2010). Inclusive education in Botswana: The perceptions of school teachers. *Journal of Disability Policy Studies*, 20(4), 219–228.

Coco, L. (2020). Teleaudiology: Strategies, considerations during a crisis and beyond. *Hearing Journal*, 73(5), 26–29.

Dalton, E. M., Mckenzie, J. A., & Kahonde, C. (2012). The implementation of inclusive education in South Africa: Reflections arising from a workshop for teachers and therapists to introduce Universal Design for Learning. *African Journal of Disability*, 1(1), 1-7.

Dean, J., Pascoe, M., & le Roux, J. (2021). Pilot evaluation of a partner-supported online reading intervention for Grade 3–6 children. *Child Language Teaching and Therapy*, 37(3), 337–354.

del Carmen Pamplona, M., & Ysunza, P. A. (2020). Speech pathology telepractice for children with cleft palate in the times of COVID-19 pandemic. *International Journal of Pediatric Otorhinolaryngology*, 138, 110318.

Department of Education (2001). Education White Paper 6. *Special needs education: Building an inclusive education and training system*. Department of Education.

Department of Education (2008). National reading strategy. Department of Education. Pretoria. https://www.education.gov.za/Portals/0/DoE%20Branches/GET/GET%20Schools/National_Reading.pdf?ver=2009-09-09-110716-507.

Department of Basic Education. (2015). *Action Plan to 2019 Towards the Realisation of Schooling 2030: Taking forward South Africa's National Development Plan 2030*. https://www.education.gov.za/Portals/0/Documents/Publications/Action%20Plan%202019.pdf.

Donohue, D., & Bornman, J. (2014). The challenges of realising inclusive education in South Africa. *South African Journal of Education, 34*(2), 1–14.

Dreyer, L., Engelbrecht, P., & Swart, E. (2012). Making learning support contextually responsive. *Africa Education Review, 9*(2), 270–288.

du Toit, M. N., van der Linde, J., & Swanepoel, D. W. (2020). mHealth developmental screening for preschool children in low-income communities. *Journal of Child Health Care, 25*(4), 573–586.

Edwards, M., Stredler-Brown, A., & Houston, K. T. (2012). Expanding use of telepractice in speech-language pathology and audiology. *Volta Review, 112*(3), 227–242.

Eikelboom, R. H., Jayakody, D. M., Swanepoel, D. W., Chang, S., & Atlas, M. D. (2014). Validation of remote mapping of cochlear implants. *Journal of Telemedicine and Telecare, 20*(4), 171–177.

Eikelboom, R. H., & Swanepoel, D. W. (2016). Remote diagnostic hearing assessment. *Telepractice in Audiology*, 123–139.

Forlin, C., Keen, M., & Barrett, E. (2008). The concerns of mainstream teachers: Coping with inclusivity in an Australian context. *International Journal of Disability, Development and Education, 55*(3), 251–264.

Govender, S. M., & Mars, M. (2018). Validity of automated threshold audiometry in school aged children. *International Journal of Pediatric Otorhinolaryngology, 105*, 97–102.

Guralnick, M. (2005). *The developmental systems approch to early intervention*. Paul H. Brookes Publishing.

Health Professions Council of South Africa – HPCSA. (2020). *Guidelines on telemedicine in South Africa*. https://www.hpcsa.co.za/Uploads/Press%20Realeses/2020/Guidelines_to_telemedicine_in_South_Africa.pdf.

Human Rights Watch Report (2015). "Complicit in Exclusion": South Africa's Failure to Guarantee an Inclusive Education for Children with disabilities. https://www.hrw.org/report/2015/08/18/complicit-exclusion/south-africas-failure-guarantee-inclusive-education-children.

Human Rights Watch Report (2019). South Africa: Events of 2018. https://www.hrw.org/world-report/2019/country-chapters/south-africa

Intergrated School Health Policy. (2012). Integrated school health policy. https://serve.mg.co.za/content/documents/2017/06/14/integratedschoolhealthpolicydbeanddoh.pdf

Kátai, Z., Juhász., K., & Adorjáni, A. K. (2008). On the role of the senses in education. *Computers and Education, 51*(4), 1707–1717.

Khoza-Shangase, K., & Mophosho, M. (2018). Language and culture in speech language and hearing professions in South Africa: The dangers of a single story. *South African Journal of Communication Disorders, 65*(1), a594. https://doi.org/10.4102/sajcd.v65i1.594

Khoza-Shangase, K., & Moroe, N. (2020). South African hearing conservation programmes in the context of tele-audiology: A scoping review. *South African Journal of Communication Disorders, 67*(2), 1–10.

Khoza-Shangase, K. (2021). Confronting realities to early hearing detection in South Africa. In K. Khoza-Shangase & K. Kanji (2021). *Early detection and intervention in audiology: An african perspective*, 66–68. Wits University Press.

Khoza-Shangase, K., & Mophosho, M. (2021). Language and culture in speech-language and hearing professions in South Africa: Re-imagining practice. *South African Journal of Communication Disorders, 68*(1), a793. https://doi.org/10.4102/sajcd.v68i1.793

Khoza-Shangase, K., Sebothoma, B., & Moroe, N. F. (2021a). Teleaudiology as part of efforts to enhance inclusivity and equality through ICT in South African Schools. In M. Maghuve, R. S. Mphahlele & S. Moonsamy (2021). *Empowering students and maximising inclusiveness and equality through ICT* (pp. 223–243). Brill.

Khoza-Shangase, K., & Kanji, A. (2021). Best practice in South Africa for early hearing detection and intervention. *Early Detection and Intervention in Audiology: An African Perspective, 264*.

Khoza-Shangase, K., Moroe, N., & Neille, J. (2021b). Speech-language pathology and audiology in South Africa: Clinical training and service in the era of COVID-19. *International Journal of Telerehabilitation, 13*(1), 1–31. https://doi.org/10.5195/ijt.2021.6376.

Mahlo, D. (2017). Teaching learners with diverse needs in the foundation phase in Gauteng Province South Africa. *SAGE Open, 7*(1), 1–9.

Maluleke, N. P., Khoza-Shangase, K., & Kanji, A. (2019a). Communication and school readiness abilities of children with hearing impairment in South Africa: A retrospective review of early intervention preschool records. *South African Journal of Communication Disorders, 66*(1), 1–7.

Maluleke, N. P., Khoza-Shangase, K., & Kanji, A. (2019b). Hearing impairment detection and intervention in children from centre-based early intervention programmes. *Journal of Child Health Care*, 23(2), 232–241.

Manga, T., & Masuku, K. P. (2020). Challenges of teaching the deaf-blind learner in an education setting in Johannesburg: Experiences of educators and assistant educators. *South African Journal of Communication Disorders*, 67(1), 1–7.

Manus, M., van der Linde, J., Kuper, H., Olinger, R., & Swanepoel, D. W. (2021). Community-based hearing and vision screening in schools in low-income communities using mobile health technologies. *Language, Speech, and Hearing Services in Schools*, 52(2), 568–580.

McKinnon, D. H., McLeod, S., & Reilly, S. (2007). The prevalence of stuttering, voice, and speech-sound disorders in primary school students in Australia. *Language, Speech, and Hearing Services in Schools*, 38, 5–15.

Mdlalo, T., Flack, P. S., & Joubert, R. W. (2019). The cat on a hot tin roof? Critical considerations in multilingual language assessments. *South African Journal of Communication Disorders*, 66(1), a610. https://doi.org/ 10.4102/sajcd.v66i1.610.

Molini-Avejonas, D. R., Rondon-Melo, S., Amato, C. A. H., & Samelli, A. G. (2015). A systematic review of the use of telehealth in speech, language and hearing sciences. *Journal of Telemedicine and Telecare*, 21(7), 367–376.

Monica, S. D., Ramkumar, V., Krumm, M., Raman, N., Nagarajan, R., & Venkatesh, L. (2017). School entry level tele-hearing screening in a town in South India–Lessons learnt. *International Journal of Pediatric Otorhinolaryngology*, 92, 130–135.

Mophosho, M., & Masuku, K. (2021). The uses of augmentative and alternative communication technology in empowering learners overcome communication barriers to learning. In *Empowering students and maximising inclusiveness and equality through ICT* (pp. 203–222). Brill Sense.

Mophosho, M., & Moonsamy, S. (2021). Identification of barriers to learning from ECD to post-school education. In Maguvhe, M. O., Thobejane-Maapola, H. R., & Malahlela, M. K. (2021). *Strengthening inclusive education from ECD to post-school education*. Van Schaik Publishers.

Mophosho, M., & Masuku, K. P. (2021). The uses of augmentative and alternative communication technology in empowering learners overcome barriers to learning. In Maguvhe, M., Mphahlele, R. S., & Moonsamy, S. (2021). *Empowering students and maximising inclusiveness and equality through ICT*. Brill Publishing.

Moroe, N. F. (2021). Sensory impairments in early hearing detection and intervention. In K. Khoza-Shangase & K. Kanji (2021). *Early detection and intervention in audiology: An African perspective* (Vol. 177). Wits University Press.

Mulovhedzi, S. A., & Mudzielwana, N. P. (2021). Early identification of barriers to learning as the first step in the inclusion process. In *Empowering students and maximising inclusiveness and equality through ICT* (pp. 40–56). Brill Sense.

Muñoz, K., Nagaraj, N. K., & Nichols, N. (2020). Applied tele-audiology research in clinical practice during the past decade: A scoping review. *International Journal of Audiology*, 60(sup1), S4–S12.

Murungi, L. N. (2015). Inclusive basic education in South Africa: Issues in its conceptualisation and implementation. *Potchefstroom Electronic Law Journal*, 18(1), 3160–3195.

Nel, N. M., Tlale, L. D. N., Engelbrecht, P., & Nel, M. (2016). Teachers' perceptions of education support structures in the implementation of inclusive education in South Africa. *Koers*, 81(3), 1–14.

Oswald, M. (2007). Training teachers to become inclusive professionals. In Engelbrecht, P & Green, L. (2007). *Responding to the challenges of inclusive education in Southern Africa*. Pretoria. Van Schaik.

Parliamentary Monitoring Group. (2013). *Disabled people's employment and learning challenges: Deputy Minister Women, Children & People with Disabilities*. Departments of Public Service and Basic Education Briefings. Retrieved from https://pmg.org.za/committee-meeting/15545

Phasha, N., Mahlo, D., & Maseko, N. (2013). Developing inclusive grade R classrooms. In Davin, R. J. (Ed.), *Handbook for grade R teaching*. Pearson Education.

Pillay, R., & Agherdien, N. (2021). Inclusivity, equality and equity: Student (Em) Power (ment) through ICT Mediated Learning. In *Empowering students and maximising inclusiveness and equality through ICT* (pp. 11–26). Brill Sense.

Pillay, D., & Sebothoma, B. (2021). Educational audiology within the classroom: The use and importance of information and communication technologies. In *Empowering Students and Maximising Inclusiveness and Equality through ICT* (pp. 244–259). Brill Sense.

Pillay, M., Tiwari, R., Kathard, H., & Chikte, U. (2020). Sustainable workforce: South African audiologists and speech therapists. *Human Resources for Health*, 18(1), 1–13.

Potgieter, J. M., Swanepoel, D. W., Myburgh, H. C., Hopper, T. C., & Smits, C. (2016). Development and validation of a smartphone-based digits-in-noise hearing test in South African English. *International Journal of Audiology*, 55(7), 405–411.

Psarros, C., & McMahon, C. M. (2016). Evaluating the Benefits of a Telepractice Model. In E. Rushbrooke, & K. T. Houston (ed). *Telepractice in Audiology* (pp 47–90). Plural Publishing

Regina Molini-Avejonas, D., Rondon-Melo, S., de La Higuera Amato, C. A., & Samelli, A. G. (2015). A systematic review of the use of telehealth in speech, language and hearing sciences. *Journal of Telemedicine and Telecare*, 21(7), 367–376.

Rabiah, S. (2012). Language as a tool for communication and cultural reality discloser. In The 1st International Conference on media, communication and culture. Muhammadiyah Yogyakarta University, Indonesia.

Republic of South Africa. (1996). *The Constitution Act No. 108 of 1996*. Government Printer.

Ratnanather, J. T., Bhattacharya, R., Heston, M. B., Song, J., Fernandez, L. R., Lim, H. S., ... & Koo, J. W. (2021). An mHealth App (speech banana) for auditory training: App design and development study. *JMIR mHealth and uHealth*, 9(3), e20890.

Rossetti, L. (2004). *Communication intervention: Birth to three* (2nd ed.). Delmar Centage Learning.

Roth, F. P., Paula, D. R., & Pierotti, A. (2006). *Lets talk: For the people with special communication needs*. American Speech-Language-Hearing Association (ASHA). http://asha.org/public/speech/emergent-literact

Rushbrooke, E., & Houston, K. T. (2016). *Telepractice in Audiology*. San Diego: CA: Plural publishing

Santika, B. B., Indrawati, S., & Yahya, E. (2017). Noise evaluation of traffic flows and its effect to concentration capability of the students in one of private school in Surabaya. *Procedia Engineering*, 170, 274–279.

Seabi, J. (2013). An epidemiological prospective study of children's health and annoyance reactions to aircraft noise exposure in South Africa. *International Journal of Environmental Research and Public Health*, 10(7), 2760–2777.

Sebothoma, B., de Andrade, V., & Galvaan, N. (2022; in press). Management of classroom acoustics by teachers at two special needs schools in Johannesburg, South Africa. *South African Journal of Education*, 42(2), 1–7, https://doi.org/10.15700/saje.v42n2a2073.

Snodgrass, M.R., Chung, M.Y., Biller, M.F., Appel, K.E., Meadan, H., & Halle, J.W. (2017). Telepractice in Speech-Language Therapy: The Use of Online technologies for Parent Training and Coaching. *Communication Disorders Quarterly*, 38(4), 242–254

Snowman, J., McCowan, R., & Biehler, R. F. (2009). *Psychology applied to teaching*. Houghton Mifflin.

South African Speech Language and Hearing Association – SASLHA. (n.d.). *Telepractice*. https://cdn.ymaws.com/saslha.co.za/resource/collection/06D0702F-65E6-4515-8467-50E3DECD3DD4/saslha_info_on_telepractice.pdf.

Swanepoel, D. W., & Hall, J. W. (2010). A Systematic Review of Telehealth Applications in Audiology. *Telemedicine and e-Health*, 16(2), 181–200.

Tanner, K., Bican, R., Boster, J., Christensen, C., Coffman, C., Fallieras, K., ... & Marrie, J. (2020). Feasibility and acceptability of clinical pediatric telerehabilitation services. *International Journal of Telerehabilitation*, 12(2), 43.

Tao, K. F., Moreira, T. D. C., Jayakody, D. M., Swanepoel, D. W., Brennan-Jones, C. G., Coetzee, L., & Eikelboom, R. H. (2020). Teleaudiology hearing aid fitting follow-up consultations for adults: single blinded crossover randomised control trial and cohort studies. *International Journal of Audiology*, 60(sup1), S49–S60.

Tchoungui Oyono, L., Pascoe, M., & Singh, S. (2018). The prevalence of speech and language disorders in French-speaking preschool children from Yaoundé (Cameroon). *Journal of Speech, Language, and Hearing Research*, 61(5), 1238–1250.

Wilford, A., Phakathi, S., Haskins, L., Jama, N. A., Mntambo, N., & Horwood, C. (2018). Exploring the care provided to mothers and children by community health workers in South Africa: Missed opportunities to provide comprehensive care. *BMC Public Health*, 18(1), 171.

34
INCLUSION OF STUDENTS WITH A HEARING LOSS IN THE CLASSROOM

Faheema Mahomed Asmail*, Estienne Havanga, and Lidia Pottas

Introduction

Action is required to ensure that those who present with a hearing loss (HL) can reach their full potential through rehabilitation, education and empowerment. Some of these aspects could be achieved by providing inclusive education. Inclusive education can take two forms: (i) attending schools specialized for teaching students with a hearing loss or (ii) attending mainstream schools and learning with hearing students in an inclusive classroom setting (World Education Forum, 2010). The first option focuses on developing a culture of including those with hearing loss in education, with the second associated to mainstream participation of students with hearing loss (World Education Forum, 2010). South Africa (SA) supports the latter with a policy of inclusive schooling, striving to accommodate all children, including those with disabilities, in mainstream schools (Department of Education, 2001). The concept of inclusive education embodies the biopsychosocial model of care, which values and involves the practice of including everyone irrespective of talent, disability, socio-economic background or cultural origin. It involves changing the structure of the parallel systems of special education and general education to a single system in order to provide similar broad educational outcomes for all (Grenot-Scheyer et al., 2001).

To understand the effects of a hearing loss on a child and the support required to ensure they meet the set outcomes, a biopsychosocial model of care that describes the number of factors that influence them needs to be understood. The International Classification of Functioning, Disability and Health Framework (ICF) developed by the World Health Organization (WHO, 2007), is an all-encompassing biopsychosocial approach that can be used to describe the experience of an individual in terms of body functions, body structures, activities and participation, while also taking into account the influence of contextual factors (environmental and personal). Figure 34.1 provides a graphic example of the ICF framework and the factors that may influence a child with hearing loss in the mainstream classroom.

In terms of the health condition, in this case a hearing loss, any degree and type of HL would constitute a barrier to learning. The presence of a HL causes a distortion or weakening of certain sounds which limits the child's ability to accurately hear and effectively understand spoken language. The nature and degree of HL significantly influence the specific developmental and

---

* faheema.mahomed@up.ac.za

DOI: 10.4324/9781003266068-40

```
                        Health condition
                         Hearing loss
```

Body structures and functions
One or both ears, degree and type of hearing loss; difficulties in other areas; pragmatics, cognitive, language and speech.

Activities
Difficulty understanding speech in a quiet background; frequently unaware, misunderstanding directions.

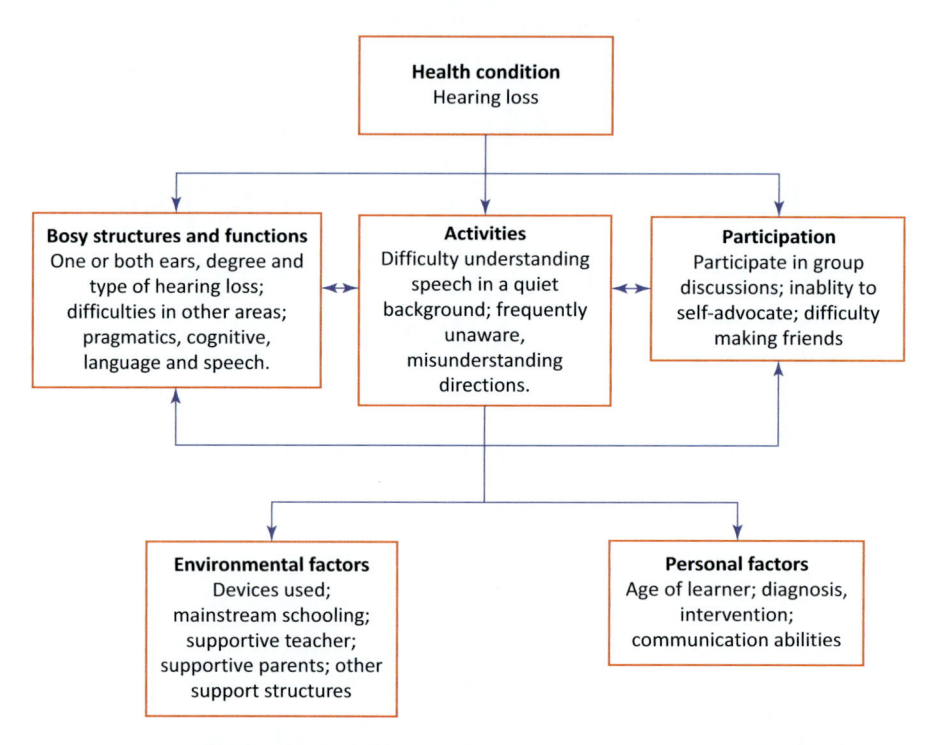

Participation
Participate in group discussions; inablity to self-advocate; difficulty making friends

Environmental factors
Devices used; mainstream schooling; supportive teacher; supportive parents; other support structures

Personal factors
Age of learner; diagnosis, intervention; communication abilities

Figure 34.1 ICF framework of a child with a Hearing Loss *Note.* Example drawn from clinical experience of the authors

educational needs of the child, which in turn determines the intervention and service required by the child (Tye-Murray, 2020). Within the framework, it is clear that the child's difficulty is not always primarily confined to the HL but can extend to unique problems in the learning process. These include activity limitations, participation restrictions as well as environmental factors. The classroom, being an acoustic-verbal environment in which the child is normally expected to spend majority of the day on listening activities, underlines the fact that hearing is crucial to academic achievement. The high noise levels and reflection of sound, known as reverberation, as well as weak lighting and visual distraction in the classroom can be detrimental to academic development (Iglehart, 2016). Students with HL may thus struggle (Figure 34.1) with difficulty understanding speech; they may misunderstand or miss instructions, resulting in limited participation within the classroom and an inability to self-advocate. This in turn also results in speech problems due to the inability to hear the acoustic cues during the period of time when phonemes or language forms are emerging (Tye-Murray, 2020). Additionally, these students will experience problems in monitoring their own speech through auditory feedback and have to use their visual, tactile and kinaesthetic senses to a greater degree than normal hearing children (personal factors). As a result of these factors, the speech of a child with a HL may sound unintelligible to the normal hearing individual (DeConde Johnson & Seaton, 2021).

A child with a HL may also be unable to develop the same competent and intuitive grasp of the language as do their normal hearing peers (Tye-Murray, 2020). As these children receive only fragments of an intended message, they struggle to synthesize it into a meaningful message (Tomblin et al., 2015). This results in expressive and receptive language problems characterized by aspects such as errors in morphology and syntax, limited vocabulary etc. (Tye-Murray, 2020). A restricted language system leads to literary deficits, resulting in typical errors in reading and writing. Thus, the correct functioning, use and maintenance of the child's hearing devices, as well as the adaptation of the listening and acoustic environment, are all important when creating an optimal learning environment.

Furthermore, children with a HL often have trouble fitting into their social surroundings (Batten et al., 2014) caused by personal, environmental and participation restrictions. These children have a low or even negative self-image as a result of not being accepted by their normal-hearing peer group and the community because of social inabilities. Although inclusion in the mainstream classroom provides valuable opportunities for interaction between them and the peer group, it is no guarantee of their successful socializing or social integration (Cambra, 2002).

Finally, there are a large number of external factors that may play a role in the education of children with a HL, which emphasizes the multilevel nature of the problem and implies that simple solutions are not always possible (Pottas, 2015). Parents, families, caregivers and communities can also exert influences that will determine the outcome of the entire educational process of children with a HL (DeConde Johnson & Seaton, 2021). Ultimately, the progress of a student with HL in a mainstream classroom setting needs to be monitored vigorously. If all supportive elements are in place and the child with a HL is achieving sub-optimal outcomes, placement in a school for learners with special needs should be considered. This chapter will focus on the student with hearing loss in an inclusive mainstream classroom in a low- to middle-income country like South Africa (SA).

Methodology

This chapter followed an Evidence Based Practice (EBP) approach in order to provide guidelines on the inclusion of students with hearing loss within the mainstream classroom. The process involved utilizing clinical perspectives and knowledge of the authors as well as research evidence. In terms of research evidence, secondary data that already exists in recently published national and international books, journals and online sources were utilized. The following questions were posed:

- What are the basic descriptors used to define hearing loss (in terms of degree, type and configuration) and the associated symptoms?
- What is the latest evidence-based practice (EBP) and resources available to assist educators to identify a student with a HL in the classroom?
- How can the mainstream classroom environment be adapted to enhance the inclusion of a student with a HL?

Results and Discussion

This section aims to discuss the information obtained in order to answer the research questions.

What Are the Basic Descriptors Used to Define Hearing Loss (in Terms of Degree, Type and Configuration) and the Associated Symptoms?

With the ICF framework in mind (Figure 34.1) and in order to fully realize the ramifications of the unique characteristics of the child as a result of a HL, the descriptions of the various aspects of a HL must be understood. They can thus be used to form the frame of reference against which the barriers to learning can be identified and handled.

Causes of Hearing Loss

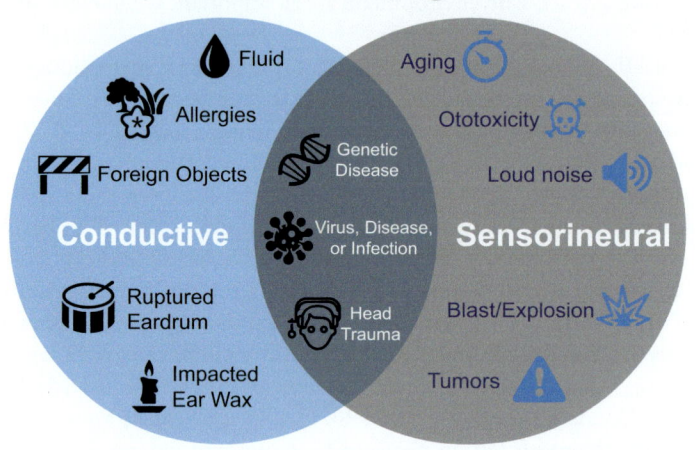

Figure 34.2 Causes and type of hearing loss *Note*. (From "What causes hearing loss," by Hough EAR Institute, 2017 (https://houghear.org/bhsm/). Copyright 2017 by Hough EAR Institute. Reprinted with permission.

Hearing loss can develop at any age and can be caused by many different factors affecting any part of the hearing pathway. In many cases, the cause of hearing loss remains unknown. In the pediatric population, hearing loss can be (i) congenital due to genetic factors, maternal health, etc.; or (ii) acquired after birth due to prenatal risks, ear infections, noise, HIV, etc. The cause of the HL will result in a specific type of HL (Figure 34.2).

A conductive hearing loss indicates an obstruction to the flow of sound energy from the atmosphere to the inner ear (Becker, 1969). A pathology causing conductive HL results in a block of the natural transduction of energy through the external ear canal and middle ear (Swanepoel & Laurent, 2019). Many types of conductive hearing loss are reversible through appropriate intervention by an Ear, Nose and Throat specialist or Audiologist. Children with this type of HL generally have rapid progress in development of skills in audition, speech, language, cognition and communication once the HI has been treated.

Sensorineural HL occurs as a result of a pathology located in the cochlea and/or in the auditory nerve and central nervous system auditory structures (retrocochlear) (Swanepoel & Laurent, 2019). Expected progress with appropriate intervention varies and is influenced by age of onset of the HL, age of identification/diagnosis of HL, age when intervention was started, environment (e.g. access to services) and the degree of HL (Sininger et al., 2010). Mixed HL may occur when a sensorineural HL is compounded by conductive HL or may be related to developmental abnormalities affecting both the middle ear and cochlea. Here intervention would include first addressing the conductive component with medical or surgical care and then providing appropriate hearing devices for the sensorineural component.

Auditory Neuropathy is a type of HL which can be considered a subgroup of sensorineural HI, the inner ear successfully detects sound, but a problem occurs with sending sound from the ear to the brain (Swanepoel & Laurent, 2019). Recommendations on treatment options in the literature range from no amplification at all to Frequency Modulating systems (FM systems) and hearing aid (HA) fittings up to the provision of cochlear implants (CI) (De Siati et al., 2020).

The degree of a HL is usually quantified according to the lowest intensity at which a signal is just audible to a person (measured in decibel or dB) across several frequencies (measured in

Hertz or Hz). HL may range from a mild loss that causes minor problems up to a total loss of sensory function. Most children with a HL have residual hearing and may be able to learn through the auditory sense, depending on how much, how early and how successfully hearing can be amplified.

The configuration, or shape, of the HL refers to the degree and pattern of the HL across frequencies (tones) as illustrated in a graph called an audiogram (ASHA, 2011). Table 34.1 provides a definition of the various degrees and configurations of HL as well as the observable characteristics one should look out for within the classroom.

There is currently a range of different hearing technologies available suited for the varying types and degrees of hearing loss, all of which should be monitored by educators and audiologists to ensure optimal hearing in the classroom setting. These devices include air conduction hearing aids, which are battery-operated devices which are fitted by an audiologist to improve hearing abilities in individuals with mild, moderate or severe hearing loss. This device consists of a microphone that picks up sound, an amplifier, which amplifies the sound, and a receiver which sends the amplified sound through to the ear canal and further along the hearing pathway. Hearing aids are available in different sizes and styles and display a variety of features (ASHA, n.d.).

Another type of device that can be provided includes a bone conduction hearing aid. This is an alternative to a regular hearing aid for those with problems in their outer or middle ears. It transfers sound through bone vibration directly to the cochlea, bypassing the outer and the middle ear. This means it is useful for conductive and mixed hearing losses. A bone conduction hearing device relies on a working cochlea to send sound to the brain (Liu et al., 2017).

There are also a number of surgically implantable devices that can be fitted to improve an individual's hearing; these include Cochlear Implants, Auditory Brainstem Implants and Middle Ear Implants. These devices include an electronic prosthetic device designed to improve hearing for individuals with a hearing loss who do not receive sufficient benefit from hearing aids due to the nature of the loss or severe damage of the cochlea or auditory nerve. These devices provide electrical stimulation directly to the auditory pathway, bypassing the damaged components of the hearing system. The internal component is surgically implanted with the external portion fitted behind-the-ear or as a body-worn device (ASHA, n.d.).

Students may also benefit from hearing assistive technologies that can be coupled to hearing devices to enable them to hear more optimally across a distance or in noisy or reverberating environments. An example of a hearing assistive technology is a Frequency Modulation System (FM System) (Nelson et al., 2013). An FM system transmits sound from a microphone that is usually worn or used by an educator or parent directly to the student's receiver using radio frequency waves (Nelson et al., 2013).

What Are Some of the Latest Evidence-based Practices (EBP) and Resources Available to Assist Educators to Identify a Student with a HL in the Classroom?

The earlier a child with a HL is identified and fitted with an appropriate hearing device, the more readily they can enter mainstream education and the better their potential of closing the gap in their performance relative to their normal hearing peers (Thibodeau & DeConde Johnson, 2005). As universal newborn hearing screening is not fully implemented in South Africa, school-based hearing screening (as a type of universal screening) has become an essential component of our education system to identify HL or hearing-related problems as early as possible and to reverse the adverse effects thereof (Mahomed-Asmail et al., 2016). The universal

Table 34.1 Hearing loss and associated characteristics observable in the classroom

Classification	Audiological description	Observable characteristics within the classroom
Degree of hearing loss		
Slight	16–25 B HL	The student may display difficulty hearing faint or whispered speech and can miss up to 10% of what is said if the educator is at a distance greater than three feet. Furthermore, the student may be unaware of subtle conversational cues and will struggle to hear the complete message whenever there is background noise present. Due to extra effort needed for understanding speech it may result in the student experiencing auditory fatigue.
Mild	26–40 B HL	The student can miss up to 50% of class discussion, particularly if the speaker speaks softly, or outside the line of vision of the student, or in the presence of background noise. They also experience problems with hearing certain consonants (such as /t/, /p/, /k/ and /s/ sounds), particularly in the case of a high frequency HL. They may also have difficulty with early literacy skills such as letter-sound associations. In terms of speech production they often present with normal speech and display no difficulties in pragmatics, discourse and language processing. The student may have minimal difficulties with figure-ground tasks as well as socializing and integrating with peers in typical educational/social environments.
Moderate	41–55 dB HL	This degree of HL may affect language development, interaction with peers and self-esteem as it can lead to 50 – 75% and 80 – 100% loss of what is being said by the educators/peers. The student may display language difficulties including limited vocabulary, disordered syntax, faulty speech production, and flat voice quality.
Moderate-to-severe	56–70 dB HL	Conversation must be very loud to be heard without amplification as the student can lose up to 100% of the speech signal. The HL increases distinct problems with verbal communication (one-to-one and groups) in the school environment. They have delayed speech and language development when compared to their peers and their speech production may be unintelligible with a toneless voice quality.
Severe	71–90 B HL	The student can only hear loud sounds ± 10 cm from the ear and most conversational speech is not heard and subtle conversation cues might not be understood. The student will struggle to keep up with fast-paced communicative interactions and will display difficulties in pragmatics, discourse and language processing. They may be able to discriminate vowel sounds, but not all consonants.
		If the HL is pre-lingual (before language develops), the students' speech and language will not develop spontaneously or slow speech and language development is exhibited. If the HL is post-lingual (after language develops) deterioration of speech and language abilities will be observable. On a social level they display moderate difficulties with socializing and integrating with peers in typical educational/social environments.

(Continued)

Table 34.1 (Continued)

Classification	Audiological description	Observable characteristics within the classroom
Profound	>91 dB HL	The student may perceive loud sounds as vibrations and thus responds more to vibrations than to sound. The student will have limited speech and language development if not fitted with hearing technology. Speech production and quality of voice may be variable. Students with this degree of loss are visually rather than auditorily inclined with regard to communication (e.g. lip-reading). Speech and language do not develop spontaneously and a rapid deterioration of speech and language abilities in the case of a post-lingual hearing impairment will be noted. Students will have difficulties with socializing and integrating with peers in typical educational/social environments.
Configuration of HL		
Low frequency hearing loss	Affects 250-500 Hz (lower speech sounds)	The student displays a weak voice quality which may sound breathy and high-pitched. Their speech may result in voiced consonant deletions ("b", "m", "n", "ing", "d"), for example saying "ca" instead of "can". The student may also experience vowel confusions ("oo" vs "ee"), for example, hearing "two" instead of "tea". They may also experience nasal/plosive confusions ("m" vs "b"), for example, hearing "mad" instead of "bad". Lastly the student may experience voiced/voiceless consonant confusions ("p" vs "b"), for example, hearing "cup" instead of "cub".
Mid frequency hearing loss	Affects 1000 Hz (mid-frequency speech sounds)	The student will have difficulty controlling and monitoring vocal volume or intensity which may present with poor vocal pitch control. One will hear omission of unstressed vowels in words, omission of unstressed words in sentences and neutralization of vowels (e.g. saying "pen" instead of "pan").
High frequency hearing loss	Affects 2000-5000Hz (high-frequency speech sounds)	The student may display confusion of voiceless consonants ("p","t","k"), for example, hearing "cap" instead of "cat". They may further display poor production of high-frequency consonants ("s", "th", "f"), for example, pronouncing "sun" as "shun" or "tun". They may also experience vowel confusions ("oo" vs. "ee"), for example, hearing "too" instead of "tea". Lastly, the student may display omission of final consonants in words and omission of linguistic markers for plurals (e.g. "cars") and tenses (e.g. saying "play" instead of "played").

Note. Adapted from: Anderson & Matkin, 1991, DeConde Johnson & Seaton, 2021)

goal of screening is to identify children with a significant HL in order to allow for further diagnosis assessment and to determine appropriate intervention (American Academy of Audiology, 2011; American Speech Hearing Association, 1997).

A suggested service delivery model for school-based screening in South Africa has been proposed (Mahomed-Asmail, 2015). The objective of this model is to serve as a working document to complement the Integrated School Health Policy (ISHP, 2012) in the form of contextual, evidence-based recommendations and proposed infrastructure. Based on the model, screening should be conducted annually on all children in grade one (ISHP, 2012) and on all chil-

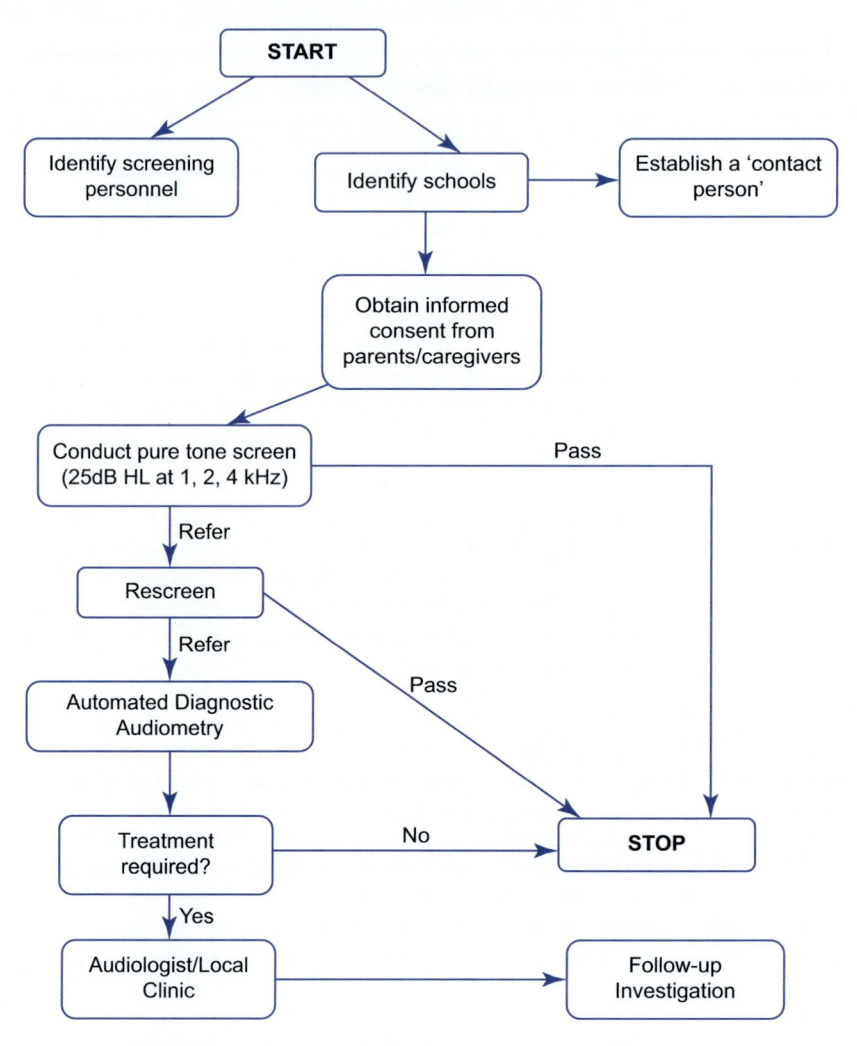

Figure 34.3 Proposed service delivery model *Note.* Obtained from previous work of the first author (Mahomed-Asmail, 2015)

dren at risk for academic failure or children whose parent/caregiver/educators have concerns regarding the student's hearing, speech, language, or learning ability (AAA, 2011; ISHP, 2012). Furthermore, all children with previous or ongoing ear disease should be screened. Figure 34.3 depicts the service delivery model proposed.

The implementation of school-based hearing screening for early detection of hearing loss needs to include a transdisciplinary/multidisciplinary team approach. The primary role players include audiologists, screening personnel (school health nurses or community health workers or educators), team manager, educators and caregivers/parents. It is the responsibility of the audiologist to train the school-health nurses (ISHP, 2012) on how to conduct pure tone screening and facilitate automated diagnostic audiometry. A team manager should ensure all equipment is calibrated prior to testing, establish contact with the school and implement and supervise the screening program (ASHA, 1997).

Once contact with the school has been established, an individual from the school should be nominated who will assist in the screening at the school level and be the *contact person* throughout the screening program at that school. It is the responsibility of the *contact person* to assist in ensuring the informed consent letters have been signed by parents/caregivers of children that need to be screened. Once informed consent from parents/caregivers is provided (AAA, 2011; ASHA, 1997) screening can commence.

The screening personnel should conduct the pure tone screen at 25 dB HL across 1, 2 and 4 kHz, using a device that is light, battery-operated and includes quality control and data management. The hearScreen™ is an example of such a device; it is an application loaded onto a smartphone coupled with calibrated headphones. It makes use of pre-specified screening protocols which utilize automated sequences to be employed by non-specialist personnel (Mahomed-Asmail et al., 2016; Yousuf Hussein et al., 2016). Thus with minimal training, educators or generalist healthcare workers can operate the device (Dawood, Mahomed Asmail, Louw, & Swanepoel, 2020). The test makes use of tones present across the frequencies; the child is required to respond to the tone by raising a hand. If the child passes the pure tone screen no further investigation is needed. If a child 'refers' at any frequency a rescreen should be conducted (AAA, 2011); if a 'refer' is obtained on the rescreen, the child could receive automated diagnostic audiometry. The automated diagnostic audiometry results should be interpreted by an audiologist who will provide further recommendations. The child-specific data and results collected on the smartphone application can be uploaded to a centralized cloud-based server for management, surveillance and to determine appropriate referrals by an Audiologist (Dawood, Mahomed Asmail, Louw, & Swanepoel, 2020; Yousuf Hussein et al., 2018).

Another smartphone application that could be used is the digits in noise test (hearZa™); this screening test can also be embedded into a webpage (hearDigits™). The device should then be coupled to a headphone or earphones to be administered. The test is fully automated, and it can be conducted in a few minutes. It utilizes highly familiar spoken words, digit-triplets, as speech material presented in noise (Potgieter et al., 2016). The child is required to listen and identify digit-triplets randomly presented in the presence of broadband masking noise to both ears, while the phase of the speech stimuli is altered for each ear (i.e. a 180° phase shift) (De Sousa et al., 2020). This allows the test to detect varying types of hearing sensitively in either ear. It determines the level (speech recognition threshold; SRT) at which an individual identifies 50% of the digit-triplets correctly in the presence of changing levels of masking noise (Potgieter et al., 2016, 2018). The SRT can be used to determine if a referral for further diagnostic intervention is required.

If a child refers to either test protocol and presents with a mixed or conductive hearing loss, a referral to a local clinic for medical treatment will be required, whereas children presenting with a sensorineural loss will receive intervention from an audiologist. All referrals should be sent to parents/caregivers of the child through the established *contact person*. Furthermore, it is advisable that all referrals be documented and sent to the school body for their records and to ensure that each child who is referred is followed-up. All screening and automated diagnostic results should be stored on a server for reference purposes or comparison at follow-up assessments. This may further aid in the effective management of the screening program.

If a HL is suspected and the screening protocol (Figure 34.3) cannot be followed or if a student has been fitted with hearing devices, there are several other educator and caregiver questionnaires that may be used to determine if the child requires further adaptation or support. Table 34.2 provides details on some of the questionnaires available.

Table 34.2 Questionnaires for educators or caregivers to utilize in school or home settings

Questionnaire	Description	Applicable age range	Administered by	Availability
Auditory Behavior in Everyday Life (ABEL)	This questionnaire was developed to assess parental perceptions of their children's auditory behavior. It consists of a 49-item questionnaire which intends to assess auditory communication, environmental awareness, functional independence, and social/communication skills (Purdy et al, 1995).	4 to 14 years old	To be completed by parents/caregivers	There are numerous translations into Hebrew, Arabic, Persian, Portuguese. Available for purchase at https://teachertoolstakeout.com/0560-checklists
Children's Auditory Processing Performance Scale (CHAPPS)	It consists of 36 questions that are answered by a teacher comparing the listening ability of a child with that of their classmates (Smoski et al., 1998). It has 6 subscales that assess listening in noise, in quiet, in ideal conditions, and against multiple inputs, auditory memory/sequencing and auditory attention span.	7 to 14 years old	To be completed by the educator	Available in English at the following link https://torontoaudiology.com/wp-content/uploads/2020/11/childrens-auditory-processing-performance-scale-chapps.pdf
Children's Home Inventory for Listening Difficulties (C.H.I.L.D.)	Used to monitor a child's listening skills in various settings within the home environment	3 to 12 years old	To completed by the parent/caregiver for children aged 3 to 12 years. Can be self-administered by the student of 7 years and older.	Available in English at the following link https://successforkidswithhearingloss.com/wp-content/uploads/2011/08/CHILD_pgs3-4.pdf

Listening Inventory For Education – Revised (LIFE-R)	The LIFE-R consists of three inventories, one for the student and two for the educator. The Student Appraisal of Listening Difficulty is intended to be used in a pre- and post-test format in order to document changes following intervention. It has 15 test items that are picture cards depicting different common listening situations in the classroom. The Teacher Appraisal of Listening Difficulty is designed to be given after intervention and consists of 16 questions related to specific areas of improvement in either behavior or communication.	Ages 7 years and older	To be completed by the student and the educator.	Translations in English, Dutch, Arabic, French, Hebrew. It can be downloaded at: https://successforkidswithhearingloss.com/for-professionals/listening-inventory-for-education-revised-life-r/
Screening Instrument for Targeting Educational Risk (SIFTER)	The SIFTER is made up of 15 items and covers five content areas: academics, attention, communication, class participation, and school behavior. It is a screening tool that can be used to identify and track students with a HL	Two versions available: Preschool (ages 3 years to kindergarten), secondary students (ages 12 to 18 years)	To be administered by the educator.	Available in English at the following link https://successforkidswithhearingloss.com/wp-content/uploads/2017/09/Secondary_SIFTER.pdf Can also be purchased in French.
Teachers' Evaluation of Aural/Oral Performance of Children (TEACH)	To record functional hearing and communication ability of the student fitted with a hearing device.	3 to 7 years old	To be completed by the educator	Available in English at the following link: https://www.outcomes.nal.gov.au/teach

How Can the Mainstream Classroom Environment Be Adapted to Enhance the Inclusion of a Student with a HL?

As students with a HL form part of a heterogeneous population, individual differences regarding language and communication development may be present. It is thus important that all educators involved with the student are receptive to having a child with a HL in the classroom.

Table 34.3 Facilitating strategies suggested for the inclusive classroom

Dimension	Facilitating strategies
Acoustic environment	Favorable listening conditions with relatively low background noise levels (good signal-to-noise ratio) should be ensured. This can be achieved by having carpets and curtains to cover reflecting surfaces in order to avoid reverberation. Absorbent panels, such as pressed wood or soft board can be used in the back of the class to prevent echoes and further reduce reverberation. To reduce shuffling noises of classroom furniture, absorbent tips can be placed on chairs, table and desk legs. One should also ensure that fans, heating systems and air conditioners are operating properly to avoid unwanted motorized noise. The child should wear their appropriately fitted hearing aids and their assistive listening devices, such as an FM-system, if available. If unavoidable noise is present the student should be seated away from noise source/s.
Setting	The student should be in a relatively small class size, allowing for individual attention. The student should be seated at a desk that allows him/her to see and hear optimally allowing maximum visibility and audibility.
Visual aspects	The educator should ensure they maintain a full-face presentation, well lighted away from glare during board writing and demonstration. They can also make use of visual cues to indicate that someone is talking during class discussions. An increased and deliberate use of visual aids to compensate for auditory limitations of the hearing loss e.g. television, slides, video, pictures, photographs, writing on the board, etc. is advisable.
Support services	Appropriate support services should be readily available, these may include: educator support in terms of all the educational aspects of HL and workable teaching techniques; academic support, speech-language intervention and audiological support for the student; a team approach ensuring participation of all parties (including the parents) in planning, implementing and evaluating an individualized educational plan for the child through collaboration and consultation.
Classroom management	Educators should provide copies of their notes, written material of the key concepts, questions, vocabulary, and facts when introducing new material. The student may also benefit from the use a 'buddy-system' whereby another student can help the child with a HI with aspects like instructions, etc.
	The educator can assist the student with appropriate strategies for handling communication breakdown, e.g. request direct repetition or clarification. In terms of assessment the educator can allow more time to complete assignments, alternatives to oral presentations such as written responses, provide extra time to complete tests, allow test items to be read to the learner (amanuensis). In order to avoid auditor fatigue the educator should allow for breaks from listening.

Note. Compiled from: Dodd-Murphy & Mamlin, 2002; De Conde Johnson & Seaton, 2021; Luckner & Denzin, 1998; Nelson & Soli, 2000, p. 356; Pottas, 2015; Ross et al., 1991, Tye-Murray, 2020)

In order to ensure the students success and to reduce the educator's frustration it is important that one is willing to make modifications in teaching style, make use of an FM system, allow time for in-service training, work closely with support personnel and have appropriate expectations regarding the student's functional level. Table 34.3 provides facilitating strategies that should be utilized if a child with a HL is included in one's inclusive classroom, with Table 34.4 providing additional resources available for educators to utilize.

Table 34.4 Website resources for educators

Resource Name	Description	Website
Hands and Voices	A parent-driven organization dedicated to providing support to families of children with hearing loss. Online articles focus on aspects such as classroom acoustics and classroom modifications.	http://handsandvoices.org
Make a difference: Tips for teaching students Who are Deaf or Hard of hearing (Downs, Owen & Vammen, n.d)	A handbook providing useful strategies that can be implemented in the classroom in order to support a child with a hearing loss.	https://www.umaryland.edu/media/umb/oaa/campus-life/disability-services-/documents/Tips-for-Teaching-Students-Who-Are-Deaf-or-Hard-of-Hearing.pdf
Education Resources for Teachers of Deaf/Hard of Hearing students (University of Minnesota, 2021)	A helpful resource for students and teachers in various educational settings. It provides useful suggestions for research-based practices, strategies and resources.	http://www.cehd.umn.edu/dhh-resources/
Info to Go- Educational Resources. (Gallaudet University, 2017)	This website includes resources focusing on accommodations and instructional practices to be used in the education of students who have hearing loss	https://www3.gallaudet.edu/clerc-center/info-to-go.html
Deaf and Hard of hearing resources for Educators (Columbia Regional program, n.d.)	A website providing useful resources and video links to support the teacher of the child with a hearing loss.	https://www.crporegon.org/Page/91
Resources for Teachers (Mill Neck International, 2021)	The linked web page provides an extensive collection of online resources on how to teach students with hearing loss hard of hearing	https://millneckinternational.org/resources/resources-for-teachers
Deaf, deaf and hard of hearing (Deakon University, 2021)	A range of resources that can help create inclusive education environments for children with hearing loss	https://allplaylearn.org.au/primary/teacher/deaf/

Conclusion

Educational reform is fundamental to ensure the inclusion of students with a HL into mainstream classrooms across South Africa. As a fair amount of variation may occur between children who present with a HL, it is necessary to develop an individualized program for each student, based on their specific needs and unique characteristics. The individualized educational program should be supervised and monitored vigorously by a team, which includes the parents/caregivers, educators, audiologist, speech-language therapist, Ear- Nose- and Throat Specialist and other therapists where necessary. Thus a significant shift in the way mainstream schools are organized and deliver educational services is necessary to be able to respond to the demands of the student with a HL and society. By understanding the various factors that affect a child with a HL and utilizing the resources and strategies provided in this chapter, an educator may find it possible to include and accommodate a student with a hearing loss within the mainstream classroom.

References

American Academy of Audiology (AAA). (2011). *Clinical practice guidelines childhood hearing screening. Specifications for audiometers.* http://www.cdc.gov/ncbddd/hearingloss/documents/aaa_childhood-hearingguidelines_2011.pdf

American Speech-Language-Hearing Association (ASHA). (1997). *American Speech-Language-Hearing Association Guidelines for audiologic screening.* http://www.asha.org/policy/GL1997-00199/

American Speech-Language-Hearing Association (ASHA). (2011). Audiology information series: Type, degree, and configuration of hearing loss. *ASHA, 7976*(16), 1–2.

American Speech-Language-Hearing Association (ASHA). (n.d.a). *Hearing aids.* Retrieved June 28, 2021, from https://www.asha.org/public/hearing/hearing-aids/

American Speech-Language-Hearing Association (ASHA). (n.d.b). *Cochlear Implants.* Retrieved June 28, 2021, from https://www.asha.org/practice-portal/professional-issues/cochlear-implants/batten

Anderson, K. L., & Matkin, N. D. (1991). Relationship of degree of long-term hearing loss to psychosocial impact and educational needs. *Educational Audiology Association Newsletter, 8,* 17–18.

Batten, G., Oakes, P. M., & Alexander, T. (2014). Factors associated with social interactions between deaf children and their hearing peers: A systematic literature review. *Journal of Deaf Studies and Deaf Education, 19*(3), 285–302. https://doi.org/10.1093/deafed/ent052

Becker, W. (1969). *Atlas of Otorhinolaryngology and Bronchoesophagology.* Saunders.

Cambra, C. (2002). Acceptance of deaf students by hearing students in regular classrooms. *American Annals of the Deaf,* 38–45. https://www.jstor.org/stable/44393494

Columbia Regional Program. (n.d.). Deaf and hard of hearing resources for educators. Retrieved October 10th, 2020, from https://www.crporegon.org/Page/91

Dawood, N., Mahomed Asmail, F., Louw, C., & Swanepoel, D. W. (2020). Mhealth hearing screening for children by non-specialist health workers in communities. *International Journal of Audiology, 60*(sup1), S23–S29.

Deakon University. (2021). Deaf, deaf and hard of hearing. Retrieved October 10th, 202, from https://allplaylearn.org.au/primary/teacher/deaf/

De Siati, R. D., Rosenzweig, F., Gersdorff, G., Gregoire, A., Rombaux, P., & Deggouj, N. (2020). Auditory neuropathy spectrum disorders: From diagnosis to treatment: Literature review and case reports. *Journal of Clinical Medicine, 9*(4), 1074. https://doi.org/10.3390/jcm9041074

De Sousa, K. C., Swanepoel, D. W., Moore, D. R., Myburgh, H. C., & Smits, C. (2020). Improving sensitivity of the digits-in-noise test using antiphasic stimuli. *Ear and Hearing, 41*(2), 442–450. https://doi.org/10.1097/AUD.0000000000000775

DeConde Johnson, C., & Seaton, J. B. (2021). *Educational Audiology Handbook* (3rd ed.). Plural Publishing. https://www.pluralpublishing.com/publications/educational-audiology-handbook

Department of Education. (2001). *Education White Paper 6: Special needs education: Building an inclusive education and training system.* South Africa: Government Gazette. https://www.vvob.org/files/publicaties/rsa_education_white_paper_6.pdf

Dodd-Murphy, J., & Mamlin, N. (2002). Minimizing minimal hearing loss in the schools: What every classroom teacher should know. *Preventing School Failure: Alternative Education for Children and Youth, 46*(2), 86–92. https://doi.org/10.1080/10459880209603352

Downs, S., Owen, C. & Vammen, A.N. (n.d.). *Make a difference : Tips for teaching students who are deaf or hard of hearing*. Retrieved October 10th, 2020, from https://www.umaryland.edu/media/umb/oaa/campus-life/disability-services-/documents/Tips-for-Teaching-Students-Who-Are-Deaf-or-Hard-of-Hearing.pdf

Gallaudet University. (2017). Info to go: Educational resources. https://www3.gallaudet.edu/clerc-center/info-to-go.html

Grenot-Scheyer, M., Fisher, M., & Staub, D. (2001). A framework for understanding inclusive education. In M. Grenot-Scheyer, M. Fisher, & D. Staub (Eds.), *At the end of the day – Lessons learned in inclusive education* (pp. 1–18). Paul H Brookes Publishing. https://psycnet.apa.org/record/2001-18916-000

Hough Ear Institute (2017). *What causes hearing loss*. Retrieved on October 10th, 2020, from https://houghear.org/bhsm/

Iglehart, F. (2016). Speech perception in classroom acoustics by children with cochlear implants and with typical hearing. *American journal of audiology, 25*(2), 100–109. https://doi.org/10.1044/2016_AJA-15-0064

Integrated School Health Policy (ISHP). (2012). Department of Basic Education and Department of Health.

Liu, C.C., Livingstone, D., & Yunker, W. K. (2017). The role of bone conduction hearing aids in congenital unilateral hearing loss: A systematic review. *International Journal of Pediatric Otorhinolaryngology, 94*, 45–51. https://doi.org/10.1016/j.ijporl.2017.01.003

Luckner, J. & Denzin, P. (1998). Adaptations for students who are deaf and hard of hearing. *Perspectives in Deafness and Education, 17*(1). http://clerccenter.gallaudet.edu/Products/Perspectives/sep-oct98

Mahomed-Asmail, F. (2015). *School-based hearing screening and diagnosis using automated and mobile health technologies* (Doctoral dissertation, University of Pretoria).

Mahomed-Asmail, F., Swanepoel, D. W., Eikelboom, R. H., Myburgh, H. C., & Hall, J. (2016). Clinical validity of hearScreen™ smartphone hearing screening for school children. *Ear and hearing, 37*(1), e11–e17. https://doi.org/10.1097/AUD.0000000000000223

Mill Neck International. (2021). Resources for teachers. https://millneckinternational.org/resources/resources-for-teachers

Nelson, P. B., & Soli, S. (2000). Acoustical barriers to learning: Children at risk in every classroom. *Language, Speech. and Hearing Services in Schools, 31*(4), 356–361. https://doi.org/10.1044/0161-1461.3104.356

Nelson, L. H., Poole, B., & Muñoz, K. (2013). Preschool teachers' perception and use of hearing assistive technology in educational settings. *ASHA Language, Speech, and Hearing Services in Schools, 44*(3), 239–251. https://doi.org/10.1044/0161-1461(2013/12-0038)

Potgieter, J. M., Swanepoel, D. W., Myburgh, H. C., Hopper, T. C., & Smits, C. (2016). Development and validation of a smartphone-based digits-in-noise hearing test in South African English. *International Journal of Audiology, 55*(7), 405–411. https://doi.org/10.3109/14992027.2016.1172269

Potgieter, J. M., Swanepoel, D. W., Myburgh, H. C., & Smits, C. (2018). The South African English smartphone digits-in-noise hearing test: Effect of age, hearing loss, and speaking competence. *Ear and Hearing, 39*(4), 656–663. https://doi.org/10.1097/AUD.0000000000000522

Pottas, L. (2015). Audiology in the educational setting. In S. Moonsamy & H. Kathard (Eds.), *Speech-language therapy in a school context principles and practices*. Van Schaik Publishers.

Purdy, S. C., Chard, L. L., Moran, C. A., & Hodgson, S. A. (1995). Outcomes of cochlear implants for New Zealand children and their families. *The Annals of Otology, Rhinology & Laryngology. Supplement, 166*, 102–105. https://europepmc.org/article/med/7668593

Ross, M., Brackett, D., & Maxon, A. B. (1991). *Assessment and management of mainstreamed hearing-impaired children. Principles and practices*. Pro-Ed.

Sininger, Y. S., Grimes, A., & Christensen, E. (2010). Auditory development in early amplified children: Factors influencing auditory-based communication outcomes in children with hearing loss. *Ear and Hearing, 31*(2), 166–185. https://doi.org/10.1097/AUD.0b013e3181c8e7b6

Smoski, W. J., Brunt, M. A., & Tannahill, J. C. (1998). Children's auditory performance scale (CHAPS). Educational Audiology Association. https://www.phonakpro.com/content/dam/phonakpro/gc_hq/en/resources/counseling_tools/documents/child_hearing_assessment_childrens_auditory_performance_scale_chaps_2017.pdf

Swanepoel, D.W., Laurent, C. (2019). Classification of hearing loss. Open access guide to audiology and hearing aids for otolaryngologists. https://vula.uct.ac.za/access/content/group/27b5cb1b-1b65-4280-9437-a9898ddd4c40/Classification%20of%20hearing%20loss.pdf

Thibodeau, L. M., & DeConde Johnson, C. (2005). Serving children with hearing loss in public school settings. *The ASHA Leaders*. https://doi.org/10.1044/leader.FTR2.10132005.6

Tomblin, J. B., Harrison, M., Ambrose, S. E., Walker, E. A., Oleson, J. J., & Moeller, M. P. (2015). Language outcomes in young children with mild to severe hearing loss. *Ear and Hearing, 36*(1) Supplement 1, 76S. https://doi.org/10.1097/AUD.0000000000000219

Tye-Murray, N. (2020). *Foundations of aural rehabilitation: Children, adults, and their family members*. Plural Publishing.

University of Minnesota. (2021). Education resources for teachers of Deaf/Hard of Hearing students. Retrieved on October 10, 2020, from http://www.cehd.umn.edu/dhh-resources/

World Health Organization. (2007). *International classification of functioning, disability, and health: Children & youth version: ICF-CY*. World Health Organization.

World Education Forum. (2010). *Inclusion in education: the participation of disabled learners*. France: UNESCO.

Yousuf Hussein, S., Wet Swanepoel, D., Biagio de Jager, L., Myburgh, H. C., Eikelboom, R. H., & Hugo, J. (2016). Smartphone hearing screening in mHealth assisted community-based primary care. *Journal of Telemedicine and Telecare, 22*(7), 405–412. https://doi.org/10.1177/1357633X15610721

Yousuf Hussein, S., Swanepoel, D. W., Mahomed, F., & Biagio de Jager, L. (2018). Community-based hearing screening for young children using an mHealth service-delivery model. *Global Health Action, 11*(1), 1467077. https://doi.org/10.1080/16549716.2018.1467077

35
COMMUNICATION INTERVENTION STRATEGIES FOR CHILDREN WITH PROFOUND INTELLECTUAL DISABILITIES

What Do We Know and How Can We Use It?

Juliet Goldbart*

Before I start this chapter, we need to establish a point of principle; *communication is a human right*.

This position is supported by Article 19 of the Universal Declaration of Human Rights, by academics (e.g. Sen, 2015), by researchers and practitioners (e.g. McLeod, 2018) and by people with communication disabilities and their supporters (e.g. Murphy et al., 2018). In practice, however, many children with profound intellectual disabilities (ID) have not been able to exercise this right, because they have not had the opportunity to develop or use their communication skills. This chapter aims to provide the background knowledge and skills to enable practitioners, family members and others to support the communication development of all children with profound ID.

Who are Children with Profound ID?

In order to describe and discuss the communication of children with profound ID, it is necessary to define whom we are talking about. It is quite challenging to do this from a Social Model perspective, because, as Lyons and Arthur-Kelly (2014 p.445) state, children with profound ID "present with a diversity of intellectual, physical, sensory and communicative impairments." As well as a level of cognitive development that is very low or untestable (Bellamy et al., 2010), these additional difficulties frequently include visual impairment (Gogate et al., 2011; van Splunder et al. 2006), motor impairment (van Timmeren et al., 2016), hearing impairment (Kerr et al., 2003), and multiple health problems including epilepsy (van Timmeren et al., 2017). They also experience significant challenges in communication, with limited or no comprehension of speech, and communication at pre-symbolic or proto-symbolic levels (e.g. Dhondt et al., 2020; Iacono et al., 2009). It is not surprising, then, that children with profound ID are regarded as

---

* j.goldbart@mmu.ac.uk

having the highest support needs (Lyons & Cassebohm, 2010) or that they frequently experience chronic pain (McGuire et al., 2010). In both the Global North (e.g. Gray et al., 2014) and the Global South (e.g. McKenzie et al., 2021) community participation for children and adults with profound ID and their families is limited, to a greater extent than for those with lesser degrees of intellectual disability.

In much of the Global North, children with profound ID attend school although they are less likely than many other children with disabilities to be in regular (inclusive) classrooms (Lyons & Cassebohm, 2010). In England, where I live and work, the pattern of educational provision is very varied, with far more children with profound ID attending specialist (76%) than inclusive schools (Public Health England, 2020) though the pattern across England is uneven. They are also at much greater risk of missing education due to poor health (Hatton, 2018). It is unclear whether the limited participation of children with profound ID results from social barriers, such as the attitudes of other parents (e.g. de Boer & Munde, 2015) or more practical issues relating to the educational curriculum and skilled teaching these children need (Lacey & Scull, 2015; McKenzie, 2021) and the challenges of their medical needs. See Colley (2020) and McKenzie (2021) for interesting critical reviews.

How Do We Communicate?

The focus of this chapter is communication, so it will be helpful for us to have a shared understanding of this concept. To achieve this, we are going to start with an activity.

What Different Ways of Communicating Can You Think of?

Your answer might include any of the following: speech, writing, emails, facial expression, tone of voice, gestures, pictures, sign language, symbols, objects, body movements, Morse code, Braille, and no doubt many others.

What is important here is that there are many ways we all use to communicate that do not require speech or language. The American Speech and Hearing Association have reinforced this point in their definition of communication (www.asha.org/policy/GL1992-00201.htm)

Inclusive Definitions of Communication

They state that "Communication may be intentional or unintentional, may involve conventional or unconventional signals, may take linguistic or non-linguistic forms, and may occur through spoken or other modes." We will return to the first point, about "intentionality" later in this chapter.

Sometimes, communication is seen as one person formulating a message that they encode in some way then send to another person who receives and decodes the message, and acts on it. With children and adults with profound ID, this definition is too limited. They may not be able to formulate or encode a message and are likely to find it difficult to decode other people's messages, if they are even aware of them.

Helpfully, we have a definition from Bunning (2009 p. 48): "Communication is about two or more people working together and coordinating their actions in an ongoing response to each other and the context." According to this inclusive definition, the communication partner supports the person with a profound ID, working with them, interpreting their behaviour and co-constructing a message.

This allows us to see communication as a joint effort, and to regard *all children and adults as communicators.* The roles of 'sender' and 'receiver' are blurred and we can see the importance of the communication context.

Development of Communication

Children and adults with profound ID are functioning at early stages of development. By looking at the way communication develops in typical children aged from birth to about 12 months of age, we can recognise and value the small steps learners with profound ID might take as they develop their communication skills. We will also be able to identify opportunities and strategies for children or adults with profound ID and their communication partners (see Figure 35.1).

On the right-hand side of this diagram, we see the child's cognitive development, as the complexity of the ways they interact with objects increases. This engagement with objects is important because it allows the learner to learn about the world around them. On the left-hand side of the diagram, we can see the role that communication partners play in the child's development of social interaction.

From around four to six months, a very important series of concepts are acquired; contingency awareness, intentionality and intentional communication. Contingency awareness refers to the learner's awareness of an association between two events in the environment. This could be something unrelated to the child's own actions, for example the door opening and the mother coming into the room. Through repeated experiences, the learner builds up a recognition that these events are linked in a contingent, or "IF-THEN" relationship.

Around four months in typical development, infants associate their own actions with consequences. This might be realising, when lying in their cot, that kicking their legs is associated with making a mobile, positioned above the cot, move. Raab et al. (2009) report the pleasure children show when they realise they can make something happen, and we call this recognition that you can make something happen – and how to do it - "intentionality."

I am going to suggest that intentionality is the most important thing we ever learn! This is for several reasons; the first is that it is the start of goal directed behaviour. The second, which follows, is that once the child realises they can make something happen, they can start the process of learning to make something happen through another person. For example, rather than reaching for, and getting, a cup, the learner waves their arms and looks towards a cup and towards their father, who brings them the cup. This is intentional communication, the deliberate sending of a message to another person.

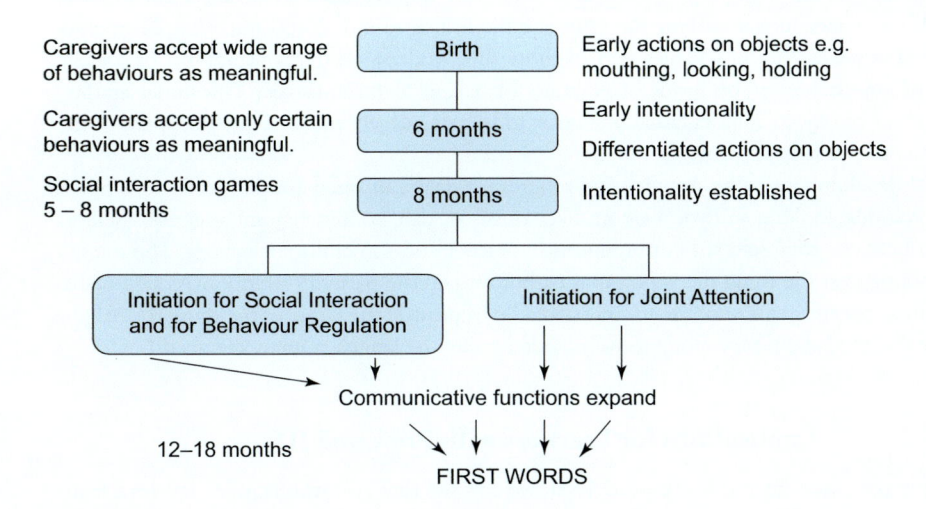

Figure 35.1 The development of early communication

The third reason why intentionality is so important relates to what happens if we do not learn it. If we do not acquire intentionality, if we do not learn that we can affect the world around us, we are at risk of the opposite, learning that nothing we do has any effect. This failure to acquire intentionality is sometimes called 'secondary motivational impairment' or 'learned helplessness.'

This failure to connect actions and their consequences can result in fewer and fewer attempts to engage with objects and people, and may be associated with increased self-stimulatory behaviour and possibly self-injurious behaviour. Learned helplessness or secondary motivational impairment causes considerable difficulties in education and therapy as it is hard to get past the self-stimulatory behaviour and provide alternative, enjoyable experiences of making things happen that are as immediate and stimulating as the self-stimulation.

Returning to the development of communication, in the first few months of the baby's life, caregivers accept a wide range of behaviours as communicating meaning. This leads to rich and enjoyable interactions between baby and caregiver, where the caregiver talks to the baby and accepts any action, a hiccup, kicking legs or wriggling, as the baby's turn in their 'conversation.'

Around four to six months (the time where contingency awareness, and then intentionality, are being acquired) caregivers start to become more selective in their responses, focusing on facial expressions, direction of gaze, hand movements and the sounds the baby makes. They also treat babies as though their (now intentional) actions on objects were intentional communication. For example, the baby is sitting in a highchair and a sibling walks past eating a banana. The baby looks at the banana and makes excited sounds and movements with her arms. The mother treats this as the baby asking for some banana and gives a piece to the baby. Within about two months, the baby has learned that his behaviours affect other people's behaviour, so allowing the baby to achieve his aims indirectly. This is intentional communication.

During this time, the baby has also learned to use smiling, looking and arm movements to initiate social interaction with people around them. For example, the baby looking over the father's shoulder smiles at the person standing behind in a queue. This person smiles back and perhaps waves at the baby.

From around nine or ten months, alternate looking between a person and the desired object, sounds and open-handed reaching gestures are used to get others to provide things the baby wants. Following Seibert et al. (1982), we call this Initiation for Behaviour Regulation.

In terms of cognitive development, the baby has progressed through generic actions such as mouthing, looking and holding objects, to actions which are differentiated according to the physical properties of the object, such as shaking objects that rattle, rolling round objects and crumpling tissues or cloth. By around ten months, babies start to show they understand the conventional or socially agreed use of objects; hats go on heads, brushes are for hair or teeth, and so on. This understanding of the properties of objects is an essential precursor to learning object names, which happens in the following two to five months onwards.

The final development to be noted is the progression from an open-handed reach to a point. Babies use pointing, looking and vocalisations like "ooh" or "dah" to initiate joint attention (Seibert et al., 1982) between themselves, a communication partner and something of interest. The infant's aim here is not to get the thing she is pointing to, but to gain the partner's attention. As supportive communication partners, our response to this would be to provide the name of the thing the baby is interested in. So, the baby is prompting us to provide exactly the language input she needs.

Implications for Learners with Profound ID

What can we conclude from this account? First, we can see that communication develops from both cognitive and social routes, so teaching approaches that focus on developing cognitive skills and/or social skills are likely to be useful.

This account has identified some of the small, but important steps in communication development, and that these steps can be negatively affected by different disabilities. Within this, the development of intentionality and then intentional communication are particularly significant steps. Cioni et al. (1993) compared the cognitive development of young children with cerebral palsy (CP) with typically developing and pre-term peers. Children with CP performed worse than expected, confirming that motor impairments have an effect on cognition, perhaps because it is harder for these children to explore their environment. Children with severe visual impairment, who have limited visual feedback from their actions, are at risk of delayed acquisition of intentionality. Not learning to act external to their own bodies leaves them at risk of developing self-stimulatory behaviours.

The importance of the social origins of communication emphasises the role of communication partners and the communication environment. We will take each of these issues in turn when we look at ideas for communication teaching and therapy.

Assessment of Early Communication

There are several freely available approaches to communication assessment, which will enable us to identify our learners' strengths and needs, and to target our teaching or therapy most appropriately. There are a few points about assessment we need to consider.

First, if we are assessing *pre-verbal* communication, does the language of the assessment, e.g. Gujarati, isiXhosa, English, matter? We would argue that up to the development of the understanding of first words, the linguistic origin of the assessment probably has little impact. Therefore, we will consider assessments from different countries.

Second, because our learners' responses can be idiosyncratic, a familiar person, such as a parent or carer or familiar teacher or therapist should be involved in the assessment. This will have the advantage of giving these different people a common perspective on the learners' stage of development.

Finally, because the responses of learners with profound ID can be very variable, due to the effects of, for example, pain, fatigue, medication or arousal level, we should assess each behaviour or response on more than one occasion.

Routes for Learning (Welsh Government, 2020) assesses the small steps involved in the early development of cognition and communication. A "routemap," the full assessment, with detailed guidance, including background theory and research are available online. Items on the assessment are illustrated by video. The assessment was designed for use in schools and the 2020 version is a thorough revision of the earlier version which was widely used in the U.K. and several other countries.

Affective Communication Assessment (ACA, Coupe et al., 1985): Freely available at http://complexneeds.org.uk/modules/Module-2.4-Assessment-monitoring-and-evaluation/All/m08p020b.html (slides 1-7). The ACA focuses only on preintentional stages and the transition into intentional communication. It uses observation, with video if possible, of the learner's response to a range of stimuli (e.g., smells, tastes, sounds, touches and movements), events and experiences. Familiar people record how the learner responds to each of these stimuli using a form that asks about the learner's facial expression, eye movements, hand and body movements, and vocalisations. The observers interpret what the learner feels about each of these experiences, typically at these early stages of development; is the learner liking, disliking, wanting or rejecting the stimulus?

The patterns of behaviours on which familiar people base their interpretations are hypotheses which are then tested out using a second set of both similar and different, stimuli, events etc. The aim is to identify small sets of behaviours that can be reasonably reliably interpreted by familiar people as showing basic emotional responses, such as like, dislike, wanting and rejecting. So, for example, we can say that when Juliet leans towards the stimulus, smiles and twirls her hands, she LIKES it. When she turns away, stiffens and says "uh uh uh!" she does NOT like it.

You are encouraged to view the ACA assessment of Alice, a child with profound ID (see web link above). The ACA recording sheets can be downloaded from slide 7 on the website above or Couple-O'Kane & Goldbart (1998). You can ask yourself the following question: (a) What does Alice think about the drink of milk? How do you know? (b) What does Alice think about the noise? How do you know? (c) What other stimuli or experiences should we try?

We can use the information from the ACA to provide systematic opportunities for learners to influence our behaviour. We give them more of something we interpret that they like and take away things they seem not to like. In time, we expect learners will come to use these behaviours intentionally (on purpose) to communicate with us.

Communication Matrix (Rowland, 2011, 2013) available either free or at low cost (for multiple use) online at https://www.communicationmatrix.org/ The Communication Matrix is also designed for children with profound ID and the assessment is based on a key question: How does the learner express each of four communicative functions? How do they refuse things, obtain things, engage in social interaction and give or seek information? Responses are allocated to one of seven levels from birth to 24 months developmental level:

Level I Pre-Intentional Behaviour
Level II Intentional Behaviour
Level III Unconventional Communication (pre-symbolic)
Level IV Conventional Communication (pre-symbolic)
Level V Concrete Symbols
Level VI Abstract Symbols
Level VII Language

Comprehension (understanding) is not assessed. Jean Ware and I have suggested parallel levels for the first six on the Matrix (Goldbart & Ware, 2015), but these are based on theory and experience, rather than being evidence based.

1. Responds to emotional tone in voice.
2. Extracts meaning from intonation and facial expression.
3. Understands nonverbal communication and contextually cued language.
4. Understands some single words and abstract symbols without contextual support.
5. Not part of typical development, so we do not know what learners at this stage understand, probably a range of single words, signs and/or symbols.
6. Understands short phrases without a supporting context.

From Assessment to Intervention

From our account of early development, we can see that we use both cognitive and social interaction routes to support communication. Both routes offer opportunities for intervention that have some level of evidential support and, using assessment data, teachers can determine approaches appropriate to the children they teach.

Developing Communication through Social Interaction

Learners with profound ID need to experience responsive, enjoyable interactions with others (Goldbart & Caton, 2010; Hostyn & Maes, 2009). In a busy classroom, it may be difficult to find time to make this happen. Fortunately, communication partners do not have to be paid professionals, but, rather, anyone who has time to learn about an individual with a profound ID and to develop enjoyable interactions with them. This might be parents or other family members such as siblings or grandparents (Nijs et al., 2016), or familiar carers, also teachers, therapists, social workers and professionals. There are other people who may have time and would welcome this opportunity, such as students on placement or wanting experience, volunteers, community members, retired professionals, and peers (Kamstra et al., 2019). Developing these interactions with learners with profound ID takes time, so we may want to build time for them into daily routines, such as on arrival/greeting and leaving times.

Intensive Interaction https://www.intensiveinteraction.org/

One more formalised approach to developing interaction and communication is Intensive Interaction (e.g., Hewett and Nind 1998; Nind, 1996; Nind & Hewitt, 2006). It is based on the highly responsive, individualised interactions between babies and their caregivers and has a developing evidence base.

Intensive Interaction is described as a way of building up enjoyable interactions between people with complex communication needs and significant others in their lives. Through training and reflection, the aim is to promote social communication and enjoyment of interaction, and enhance the learner's sense of agency. The focus is on very fundamental aspects of communication, e.g. taking turns, sharing personal space, understanding and using eye contact, facial expression, physical contact, nonverbal communication and vocalisation (sounds).

Intensive Interaction does need a commitment to several sessions a week with each child or adult, but it is likely that the training will increase staff members' responsiveness outside sessions as well; giving benefits to all children or adults they work with.

Examples of Intensive Interaction in practice can be seen at:

https://www.bing.com/videos/search?q=intensive+interaction+video+clips&view=detail&mid=73FADE1FB5A800BF3AFD73FADE1FB5A800BF3AFD&FORM=VIRE

https://www.youtube.com/watch?v=qkJKktBaTRY

Because of the individualised nature of this intervention and its many components, it is challenging to evaluate. One rigorous study was carried out by Nind (1996); she presents a detailed multiple baseline evaluation of the efficacy of Intensive Interaction, demonstrating gains in communication, sociability and in ability both to initiate and maintain social contact. Another good study found that care staff can learn to use Intensive Interaction, but find it hard to embed in their daily routine (Samuel et al., 2008).

In the UK, the approach is used quite widely (Goldbart et al, 2014), leading to many case studies in the professional literature. A systematic review (Hutchinson & Bodicoat, 2015), however, suggested that more evidence is needed before we can be completely certain of its effectiveness.

Developing Communication through Developing Cognition

The account of early development presented above has demonstrated the importance of cognition, with emphasis on the fundamental role of contingency awareness, leading to intentionality; the realisation that one's actions have consequences, that you can make things happen.

Promoting the Development of Intentionality

In order to learn intentionality, learners need opportunities for affecting and controlling their environment. We can provide these experiences through low or no tech activities and through activities requiring high tech resources, and there is good evidence that these learning experiences are both effective (e.g. Lancioni et al., 2006a & 2006b; 2009, Roche et al., 2015) and pleasurable (Raab et al., 2009).

Simple and inexpensive low or no tech approaches to contingency awareness and intentionality include any activity that gives the learner immediate feedback from very easy actions. For example, playing with water or other responsive media, making a mobile that you have positioned within easy reach, moving, hitting a drum or gong, pushing over a "Bobo" doll. All of these activities are likely to need support or prompting from an adult initially, but eventually the learner will gain pleasure from their sense of control, and act intentionally and independently to make things happen.

There are also plenty of technology-based ways to give learners experience of affecting and controlling their environment. Mainstream tablet technologies offer opportunities for experience of controlling the environment on, for example, piano keyboard apps or the Sensory light box app, which starts with teaching cause and effect, but with options for small onward steps (see, e.g. www.youtube.com/watch?v=ioYkK_i6XDo or www.youtube.com/watch?v=ihMSw8BIXF4)

If you have access to specialist technology, simple microswitches can be used to play music or operate toys or a fan, or other events that the learner is interested in. A BigMack switch can be programmed with a message, enabling the learner to initiate social contact or participate in group activities.

Communication Interventions and Therapies

Drawing on and integrating cognition and social development, there is a range of specific communication interventions which are used with learners with profound ID (Goldbart & Caton, 2010; Goldbart et al., 2014). They have varied levels of evidence to support their effectiveness, but are quite commonly used in schools and adult services in Europe. See https://e-space.mmu.ac.uk/198309/1/Mencap%20Comms_guide_dec_10.pdf

Objects of Reference

"Objects of reference" are objects which are used to represent people, situations or events for the purpose of supporting communication. This approach comes originally from work with people with dual sensory impairments (McLarty, 1995, 1997). The aim is to make use of existing associations between objects and people, activities, etc., and to build on these associations. In the earliest stage, Objects of Reference can be used to signal to someone with little or no comprehension what is about to happen. For example, we might give someone a bar of soap before taking them for a bath, then give them a piece of towel before we take them out of the bath.

For some learners, especially those with visual impairments, sensory cues such as smells and sounds may also help them make sense of what is happening around them (Murdoch et al., 2014). For example, we would always want to allow a learner to smell a spoonful of food before we feed it to them. The smell of toothpaste would tell a learner we were about to brush their teeth.

Objects of Reference can be hung up on a classroom wall, for example, as a visual and tactile timetable, and specific objects can be associated with activities and events. For example, cups and snack time, spoons and lunch time, coats and going home time. Initially, the objects are used by the staff member or parent, but the aim is that the learner will eventually come to use the objects to convey their own needs and wishes, leading towards more formal use of augmentative and alternative communication.

There are only two formal evaluations of Objects of Reference (Harding et al., 2011; Jones et al., 2002). Both studies had mixed findings, with some positive results. Despite this rather limited evidence, it is a popular approach in UK schools (Goldbart et al., 2014), and there are many examples of use of Objects of Reference on the internet.

Park (1997) has described a sequence of four steps of increasing complexity in use of Objects of Reference, which allows us to increase demands on the learner as their skills and understanding develop.

- Index: the objects are a key part of the activity they refer to and play a functional role in the activity. This might be a cup, initially the learner's own cup, that they use at snack time.
- Icon: the object functions as a sign because it has a visual, physical or tactile similarity to the thing it stands for, but is not a functional part of it. This could be a piece of webbing similar to the learner's car seat or seat belt, or an empty juice carton.
- Symbol: there is an arbitrary or conventionally agreed link between the symbol and the object or event. This could be part of a published symbol set, such as Boardmaker, or one devised locally.
- Qualifiers: represent abstract concepts such as yes and no

Schools and services will need to choose whether they have a standard set of objects for use with all appropriate learners in each setting or individualized objects according to personal interests and abilities. Further guidance is available at https://www.oxfordhealth.nhs.uk/oxtc/good-advice/objects-of-reference/

Readers could consider what objects could be objects of reference for their learners? Think about their daily activities and the objects that might be associated with them.

Creative Arts-based Approaches

Both music and story-based approaches are used with children and adults with profound ID (Goldbart et al., 2014). Musicians and music therapists often work in ways that are quite similar to Intensive Interaction (Warner, 2007). The parallels between music and language/communication, in terms of intonation patterns and turn taking, have been used to support communication (Graham, 2004; Perry, 2003) and we have used the Gamelan as a group activity to support interaction (Swindells et al., 2015). There is only limited evidence for the effectiveness of music-based approaches to communication, but they are valued by families (Goldbart & Caton, 2010).

Multisensory stories aim to provide the learning opportunities and pleasure of engaging with a story, without the need to understand language. Multisensory props are used to construct and support the narrative. There have been a few small-scale evaluations of multisensory stories (Mitchell and van der Gaag, 2002; Penne et al., 2012). There is evidence that learners show increased attention during multisensory stories (Young et al., 2011). Bag Books (evaluated by Preece and Zhao, 2014, http://nectar.northampton.ac.uk/6658/7/Preece20146658.pdf) Story Sacks and similar resources provide large format books and multisensory resources for multisensory storytelling and there are several books (e.g. Grove, 2009) which support this approach.

Can you suggest a folk story or a well-known children's book with a simple but strong narrative and scope for repetition that would be a good multisensory story?

Communication Passports

Communication Passports (Millar, 2003) are a way of collecting, organising and sharing information on individual children or adults, including on their communication. The focus on the child or adult as an individual and the information is presented from his or her perspective. Several passport templates, additional guidance and examples of how to complete them are available at http://www.communicationpassports.org.uk/About/

We can think of Communication Passports as an intervention, for two reasons. First, because the process of developing a passport will result in parents and staff members having a shared view of the learner's communication which they can respond to in consistent ways. Second, because the information gathered should allow people to give the learner appropriate communication opportunities and experiences.

A basic passport will give information on the way the person communicates, things they enjoy, things they find difficult and what helps them. It includes basic information about the person, from their own perspective and details on the best ways to communicate with them. It is designed to be a quick way to get to know a person and their communication. A full Communication Passport, however, could comprise as many as 20 pages.

Passports should be completed by people who know the individual well, discussing information, sharing examples and reaching a consensus that can be clearly described in the passport. Even if a family member cannot be involved in developing the passport, they should be asked for permission for it to be developed where possible. There is limited formal evaluation of Communication Passports, but they are reported to be valued by families and staff (e.g. Sajith et al., 2018).

Readers might wish to develop a passport for one of their learners, in conjunction with a family carer.

Conclusions

The most important message to take from this chapter is that *everyone can communicate*.

To answer our research question: Can we enhance the communication and interactions of children with profound intellectual disabilities – and if so, how? We have seen that evidence-based approaches are available for developing very early communication, supporting both cognitive development and social interaction. Beyond this, there are several approaches which draw on both cognition and social development, but for which the evidence base is still limited. A recent paper (Maes et al., 2021) discusses some of the challenges of research with this client group.

As well-informed practitioners, drawing on background theory and assessment data, you can make informed decisions on the best approach for your learners. Finally, we recommend the use of Communication Passports for sharing information about your learners with profound ID, supporting their inclusion, their communication and their wellbeing.

Resources

Many links are provided within the chapter; some additional sources of information are:

- The online training course http://complexneeds.org.uk
- PMLD Link magazine; their back copies and other accessible and useful information are available at http://www.pmldlink.org.uk/

References

Bellamy, G., Croot, L., Bush, A., Berry, H., & Smith, A. (2010). A study to define: Profound and multiple learning disabilities (PMLD). *Journal of Intellectual Disabilities, 14*(3), 221–235.

de Boer, A., & Munde, V. (2015). Parental attitudes toward the inclusion of children with profound intellectual and multiple disabilities in general primary education in the Netherlands. *Journal of Special Education, 49*(3), 179–187.

Bunning, K. (2009). Making sense of communication. In J. Palwyn & S. Carrnaby (Eds.), *Profound Intellectual Multiple Disabilities* (pp. 46–61). Oxford: Wiley-Blackwell.

Cioni, G., Paolicelli, P., Sordi, C., & Vinter, A. (1993). Sensorimotor development in cerebral palsied infants assessed with the Uzgiris-Hunt scales. *Developmental Medicine and Child Neurology, 35*, 1055–1066.

Colley, A. (2020). To what extent have learners with severe, profound and multiple learning difficulties been excluded from the policy and practice of inclusive education? *International Journal of Inclusive Education, 24*(7), 721–738.

Coupe, J., Barton, L., Collins, L., Levy, D., & Murphy, D. (1985). *The Affective Communication Assessment*. Manchester: M.E.C. and http://complexneeds.org.uk/modules/Module-2.4-Assessment-monitoring-and-evaluation/All/m08p020b.html

Coupe-O'Kane, J., & Goldbart, J. (1998). *Communication before Speech: Development and Assessment*. London: David Fulton.

Dhondt, A., Van keer, I., van der Putten, A., & Maes, B. (2020). Communicative abilities in young children with a significant cognitive and motor developmental delay. *Journal of Applied Research in Intellectual Disabilities, 33*(3), 529–541.

Gogate, P., Soneji, F., Kharat, J., Duleri, H., Deshpande, M., & Gilbert, C. (2011). Ocular disorders in children with learning disabilities in special education schools of Pune, India. *Indian Journal of Ophthalmology, 59*(3), 223–228.

Goldbart, J., & Caton, S. (2010). *Communication and People with the Most Complex Needs: What Works and Why This Is Essential*. London: Mencap. https://e-space.mmu.ac.uk/198309/1/Mencap%20Comms_guide_dec_10.pdf (accessed 27. 10. 2020).

Goldbart, J., & Ware, J., (2015). Communication. In P. Lacey, H. Lawson, & P. Jones (Eds.), *Educating Learners with Severe, Profound and Multiple Learning Difficulties*. London: Routledge.

Goldbart, J., Chadwick, D., & Buell, S. (2014). Speech and language therapists' approaches to communication intervention with children and adults with profound and multiple learning disability. *International Journal of Language & Communication Disorders, 49*, 687–701.

Graham, J (2004). Communication with the uncommunicative: Music therapy with preverbal adults. *British Journal of Learning Disabilities, 32*, 24–29.

Gray, K., Piccinin, A., Keating, J., Taffe, J., Parmenter, T., Hofer, S., Einfeld, S., & Tonge, B. (2014). Outcomes in young adulthood: Are we achieving community participation and inclusion? *Journal of Intellectual Disability Research, 58*(8), 734–745.

Grove, N. (2009). *Learning to Tell; a Handbook for Inclusive Storytelling*. Kidderminster: BILD.

Harding, C., Lindsay, G., O'Brien, A., Dipper, L., & Wright, J. (2011). Implementing AAC with children with profound and multiple learning disabilities: A study in rationale underpinning intervention. *Journal of Research in Special Educational Needs, 11*(2), 120–129.

Hatton, C. (2018). School absences and exclusions experienced by children with learning disabilities and autistic children in 2016/17 in England. *Tizard Learning Disability Review, 23*(4), 207–212.

Hewett, D., & Nind, M. (Eds.) (1998). *Interaction in Action*. London: Fulton.

Hostyn, I., & Maes, B. (2009). Interaction between persons with profound intellectual and multiple disabilities and their partners: A literature review. *Journal of Intellectual & Developmental Disability, 34*(4), 296–312.

Hutchinson, N., & Bodicoat, A. (2015). The effectiveness of intensive interaction: A systematic literature review. *Journal of Applied Research in Intellectual Disabilities, 28*, 437–454.

Iacono, T., West, D., Bloomberg, K., & Johnson, H. (2009). Reliability and validity of the revised Triple C: Checklist of Communicative Competencies for adults with severe and multiple disabilities. *Journal of Intellectual Disability Research, 53*(1), 44–53.

Jones, F., Pring, T., & Grove, N. (2002). Developing communication in adults with profound and multiple learning difficulties using objects of reference. *International Journal of Language and Communication Disorders, 37*, 173–184.

Kamstra, A., van der Putten, A., Maes, B., & Vlaskamp, C. (2019). Exploring spontaneous interactions between people with profound intellectual and multiple disabilities and their peers, *Journal of Intellectual & Developmental Disability, 44*(3), 282–291.

Kerr, A. M., McCulloch, D., Oliver, K., McLean, B., Coleman, E., Law, T., Beaton, P., Wallace, S., Newell, E., Eccles, T., & Prescott, R. J. (2003). Medical needs of people with intellectual disability require regular assessment, and the provision of client and carer held reports. *Journal of Intellectual Disability Research*, 47, 134–145.

Lacey, P., & Scull, J. (2015). Inclusive education for learners with severe, profound and multiple learning difficulties in England. In E. West (Ed.), *Including Learners with Low-Incidence Disabilities (International Perspectives on Inclusive Education, Vol. 5)*. Bingley, UK: Emerald Group.

Lancioni, G., O'Reilly, M., Singh, N., Oliva, D., Baccani, S., Severini, L. & Groeneweg, J. (2006a). Micro-switch programmes for students with multiple disabilities and minimal motor behaviour: Assessing response acquisition and choice. *Developmental Neurorehabilitation*, 9(2), 137–143.

Lancioni, G., O'Reilly, M., Singh, N., Sigafoos, J., Didden, R., Doretta, O., & Severini, L. (2006b). A microswitch-based program to enable students with multiple disabilities to choose among environmental stimuli. *Journal of Visual Impairment and Blindness*, 100(8), 488–493.

Lancioni, G., O'Reilly, M., Singh, N., Sigafoos, J., Didden, R., Doretta, O., et al., (2009). Persons with multiple disabilities accessing stimulation and requesting social contact via microswitch and VOCA devices: New research evaluation and social validation. *Research in Developmental Disabilities*, 30(5), 1084–1094.

Lyons, G., & Arthur-Kelly, M. (2014). UNESCO inclusion policy and the education of school students with profound intellectual and multiple disabilities: Where to now? *Creative Education*, 5, 445–456. https://doi.org/10.4236/ce.2014.57054

Lyons, G., & Cassebohm, M. (2010). Life satisfaction for children with profound intellectual and multiple disabilities. In R. Kober (Ed.), *Enhancing the Quality of Life of People with Intellectual Disabilities: From Theory to Practice* (Social Indicators Research Series, Vol. 41, pp. 183–204). Dordrecht: Springer.

Maes, B., Nijs, S., Vandesande, S., van Keer, I., Arthur-Kelly, M., Dind, J., Goldbart, J., Petitpierre, G., & van der Putten, A. (2021). Looking back, looking forward: Methodological challenges and future directions in research on persons with profound intellectual and multiple disabilities. *Journal of Applied Research in Intellectual Disabilities*, 34(1):250–262. https://doi.org/10.1111/jar.12803

McGuire, B. E., Daly, P. & Smyth, F. (2010). Chronic pain in people with an intellectual disability: Under-recognised and under-treated? *Journal of Intellectual Disability Research*, 54, 240–245.

McKenzie, J. (2021). Intellectual Disability in Inclusive Education in South Africa: Curriculum Challenges. *Journal of Policy and Practice in Intellectual Disabilities*, 18(1), 53–57. https://doi: 10.1111/jppi.12337

McKenzie, J. A., Kahonde, C., Mostert, K., & Aldersey, H. M. (2021). Community participation of families of children with profound intellectual and multiple disabilities in South Africa. *Journal of Applied Research in Intellectual Disabilities*, 34(2), 525–536. https://doi.org/10.1111/jar.12818

McLarty, M. (1995/2018). Objects of reference. In D. Etheridge (Ed.), *The Education of Dual Sensory Impaired Children: Recognising and Developing Ability*. London: David Fulton/Taylor & Francis.

McLarty, M. (1997). Putting objects of references in context. *European Journal of Special Needs Education*, 12, 12–20.

McLeod, S. (2018). Communication rights: Fundamental human rights for all. *International Journal of Speech-Language Pathology*, 20(1), 3–11.

Millar, S. (2003). *Personal Communication Passports: Guidelines for Good Practice*. Edinburgh: Call Centre.

Mitchell, J., & van der Gaag, A. (2002). Through the eye of the Cyclops: Evaluating a multi-sensory intervention programme for people with complex disabilities. *British Journal of Learning Disabilities* 30, 159–165.

Murdoch, H., Gough, A., Boothroyd, E., & Williams, K. (2014). Adding scents to symbols: Using food fragrances with deafblind young people making choices at mealtimes. *British Journal of Special Education*, 41(3), 249–267.

Murphy, D., Lyons, R., Carroll, C., Caulfield M., & de Paor, G. (2018). Communication as a human right: Citizenship, politics and the role of the speech-language pathologist, *International Journal of Speech-Language Pathology*, 20(1), 16–20.

Nijs, S., Vlaskamp, C., & Maes, B. (2016). Children with PIMD in interaction with peers with PIMD or siblings. *Journal of Intellectual Disability Research*, 60, 28–42.

Nind, M. (1996). Efficacy of intensive interaction; Developing sociability and communication in people with severe and complex learning difficulties using an approach based on caregiver- infant interaction. *European Journal of Special Educational Needs*, 11(1), 48–66.

Nind, M., & Hewett, D. (2006). *Access to Communication* (2nd ed.). London: David Fulton.

Park, K. (1997). How do objects become objects of reference? A review of the literature on objects of reference and a proposed model for the use of objects in communication. *British Journal of Special Education, 24*, 108–114.

Penne, A., ten Brug, A., Munde, V., van der Putten, A., & Vlaskamp, C. (2012). Staff interactive style during multisensory storytelling with persons with profound intellectual and multiple disabilities, *Journal of Intellectual Disability Research, 56*(2), 167–178.

Perry, M. R. (2003). Relating improvisational music therapy with severely and multiply disabled children to communication development. *Journal of Music Therapy, 40*, 227–246.

Preece, D., & Zhao, Y. (2014). An evaluation of Bag Books multi-sensory stories. Northampton: The University of Northampton. (Unpublished). http://nectar.northampton.ac.uk/6658/7/Preece20146658.pdf

Public Health England (2020). Education and children's social care. In *People with Learning Disabilities in England* Chapter 1 https://www.gov.uk/government/publications/people-with-learning-disabilities-in-england/chapter-1-education-and-childrens-social-care-updates (accessed 09.10.2020).

Raab, M., Dunst, C. J., Wilson, L. L., & Parkey, C. (2009). Early contingency learning and child and teacher concomitant social–emotional behavior. *International Journal of Early Childhood Special Education, 1*(1), 1–14.

Roche, L., Sigafoos, J., Lancioni, G., O'Reilly M., & Green, V. (2015). Microswitch technology for enabling self-determined responding in children with profound and multiple disabilities: A systematic review. *Augmentative and Alternative Communication, 31*(3), 246–258

Rowland, C. (2011). Using the Communication Matrix to assess expressive skills in early communicators. *Communication Disorders Quarterly, 32*, 190–201.

Rowland, C. (2013). *Communication Matrix.* https://www.communicationmatrix.org/

Sajith, S., Tao, Y., & Ling, C. (2018). Development and introduction of "communication passport" in an adult inpatient psychiatric unit for persons with intellectual disabilities: A brief report from Singapore. *Journal of Policy and Practice in Intellectual Disabilities, 15*(2), 166–170.

Samuel, J., Nind, M., Volans, A., & Scriven, I. (2008). An evaluation of Intensive Interaction in community living settings for adults with profound intellectual disabilities. *Journal of Intellectual Disabilities 12*(2), 111–126.

Seibert, J. M., Hogan, A. E., & Mundy, P. C. (1982). Assessing interactional competencies: The early social-communication scales. *Infant Mental Health Journal, 3*, 244–258.

Sen, A. F. (2015). Communication and human rights. *Procedia - Social and Behavioral Sciences, 174*, 2813–2817. https://internationalcommunicationproject.com/profile/communication-basic-human-right/

Swindells, R., Hawley, R., Fisher, M., & Goldbart, J. (2015). Finding our common pulse. *PMLD Link, 27*(3), 16–18.

Van Splunder, J., Stilma, J. S., Bernsen, R. M. D., & Evenhuis, H. M. (2006). Prevalence of visual impairment in adults with intellectual disabilities in the Netherlands: Cross-sectional study. *Eye, 20*(9), 1004.

van Timmeren, E. A., van der Putten, A. A. J., van Schrojenstein Lantman-de Valk, H. M., van der Schans, C. P., & Waninge, A. (2016). Prevalence of reported physical health problems in people with severe or profound intellectual and motor disabilities: A cross-sectional study of medical records and care plans. *Journal of Intellectual Disability Research, 60*, 1109–1118.

van Timmeren, E. A., van der Schans, C. P., van der Putten, A. A. J., Krijnen, W. P., Steenbergen, H. A., van Schrojenstein Lantman-de Valk, H. M. A., & Waninge, A. (2017). Physical health issues in adults with severe or profound intellectual and motor disabilities: A systematic review of cross-sectional studies. *Journal of Intellectual Disability Research, 61*(1), 30–49.

Warner, C (2007). Challenging behaviour: Working with the blindingly obvious. In T. Watson (Ed.), *Music Therapy with Adults with Learning Disabilities* (pp 47–57). Hove: Routledge.

Welsh Government (2020). *Routes for Learning Curriculum for Wales.* https://hwb.gov.wales/curriculum-for-wales/routes-for-learning#:~:text=Routes%20for%20Learning%20materials%20support,their%20interaction%20with%20the%20environment (accessed 27.10.2020).

Young, H., Fenwick, M., Lambe, L. & Hogg, J. (2011). Multi-sensory storytelling as an aid to assisting people with profound intellectual disabilities to cope with sensitive issues: A multiple research methods analysis of engagement and outcomes. *European Journal of Special Needs Education, 26*(2), 127–142.

PART VI

Transitions, Vocation, and Independent Living Support

Transition after education to vocational life or to community and independent living is a crucial aspect of successful inclusive education. The overall aim or goal is to have overall healthy well-being and good quality of life. The goal is to have a function-based independent living. Independent living can be extremely challenging for people with diverse needs. The important aspects of independent living are successful transitions from various settings and training and orientation accordingly beforehand for developing the utmost adaptability. The ultimate goal is to finally be able to live an independent and contented community life. This section covers the various issues and aspects of successful and effective transitions for people with diverse needs.

36
SCHOOL-BASED TRANSITION PROGRAMMING TO IMPROVE EMPLOYMENT OUTCOMES FOR YOUTH WITH DISABILITIES

Andrew R. Scheef[*]

> Work has a central location in many people's lives – one that frequently intersects with other life roles and that can have an immense impact on one's overall quality of life.
>
> *(Brown & Lent, 2013, p. 2).*

In many ways, people are defined by their employment. The frequency with which children ponder potential careers shows us the extent to which it is in human nature for one to work and have a career. Consider a common conversation one might begin when meeting someone for the first time. It is not uncommon for a conversation starter to include some variation of the question "what line of work are you in?" If this unfamiliar individual explains that they are a doctor, for example, certain assumptions (correct or otherwise) about this individual may be made. Many people both define themselves and are defined by others based on their work or career.

Although employment can be a fundamental life component for all individuals, it can be particularly important to those who experience disability. Wehman (2011) described reasons why work is especially valuable for individuals with disabilities. First, like all individuals, people with disabilities work to earn income. Lack of financial independence can be a significant barrier for many individuals with disabilities wishing to live independently and gainful employment can assuage this obstacle. Second, work is a common experience in which many citizens engage. As such, employment provides an opportunity for individuals with disabilities to have the same kinds of experiences as peers without disabilities. Finally, employment can lead to positive self-image and self-dignity. As many individuals with disabilities may receive pity from others, they may have limited opportunities to show their skill and abilities to fellow community members in an authentic way. Employment contributes to self-identity and allows individuals with disabilities to see themselves as productive members of the community.

Saunders and Nedelec (2014) identified similar benefits of employment, but also identified social benefits. Noting that all employees have the opportunity to benefit from social experiences at work, it may be particularly important for individuals with disabilities who may be more prone to social isolation. Employment provides natural opportunities to engage with

[*] ascheef@uidaho.edu

than those with physical disabilities (Gewurtz et al., 2016). Employers interviewed by Kaye et al. (2011) admitted that workplaces do discriminate against job candidates with disabilities because of an assumption that they will not be able to complete job tasks. These perceptions of individuals with disabilities can also lead to employer concerns about employee safety and uncertainty regarding employee discipline should any issues arise (Houtenville & Kalargyrou, 2012). Copeland et al. (2010) explained "Increased attention to promoting awareness of negative attitudes toward individuals with disabilities in the workplace is critical to eliminating barriers to employment" (p. 433).

Although employers may have interest in employing individuals with disabilities, they may have concerns about meeting legal obligations that are designed to protect workers. Legislation designed to promote employment opportunities for individuals with disabilities may have the opposite effect by producing fear in potential employers (Gewurtz et al., 2016). Employers may be reluctant to actively seek out more employees with disabilities due to concerns related to legal protections (e.g., those related to the Americans with Disabilities Act; Erickson et al., 2013). These may include concerns related to the perception that employers may be unable to fire or discipline employees with disabilities due to legal protections (Kaye et al., 2011). Even simply the time it may take for employers to become familiar with legal protection for workers with disabilities may be a barrier for employers (Gewurtz et al., 2016). Additionally, employers have concerns related to legally mandated accommodations. Although the cost of offering accommodations is generally minimal, the perceived high cost of providing these for employees with disabilities that are required by law is a concern of employers (Erickson et al., 2013; Gewurtz et al., 2016).

Preparing Youth with Disabilities for Competitive Employment

Recognizing the existence of significant barriers, school-based special education personnel are tasked with supporting the post-school employment goals of students with disabilities. A description of a key component found in comprehensive school-based transition programs to support employment goals for youth with disabilities is beyond the scope of this chapter. However, recommendations for programming in three broad areas to help youth with disabilities attain goals related to employment are described below. These include recommendations to: (a) develop specific skills that increase the capacity for students to find and maintain work, (b) provide work-based learning opportunities, and (c) make connections with stakeholders outside of school.

Developing Student Skills

In addition to supporting the academic needs of their students, secondary special education teachers are tasked with providing instruction and services to support the post-school goals of their students. Kohler et al., (2016) includes Student Development as one of five domains in the Taxonomy for Post-Secondary Transition Planning. The following are recommendations to improve the skills students need to find and maintain employment.

Soft Skills

Soft skills is a term used to describe "skills, abilities, and traits that pertain to personality, attitude, and behavior rather than to formal or technical knowledge" (Moss & Tilly, 1996, p. 253). Although some of these may be more personal attributes than something that can, or perhaps should, be taught (e.g., personality traits), school-based personnel can promote the development of many of these skills with their students.

Employers may be looking for workers with strong soft skills. As part of their annual Job Outlook report, the National Association of Colleges and Employers (NACE) provided a ranking of attributes that employers hope to see on the resumés of prospective employees. A recent report showed that seven out of the top 10 attributes were associated with soft skills (NACE, 2019). Employers may feel that they can predict the fit of a potential employee based on the soft skills they exhibit in their interview (Lindsay et al., 2014). Ju et al. (2012) polled employers to identify which skills they find most valuable for entry-level employees both with and without disabilities. The four most valued skill areas were the same for both groups and included "demonstrating personal integrity/honesty in work," "ability to follow instructions," "ability to show respect for others," and "ability to be on time" (p. 35). These findings show both the value of soft skills and the fact that employers have similar expectations for workers with disabilities.

From an instructional perspective, a benefit of teaching soft skills is the fact that they are universally applicable. School-based employment training should also consider instruction in job-specific tasks and skills, however the acquisition of these may be meaningless if the soft skills of the students are not strong (Robles, 2012). Regardless of the career interests of the student, basic soft skill instruction has the potential to improve post-school outcomes (Mazzotti et al., 2021; Test et al., 2009).

School-based practitioners can deliver soft skills training for youth with disabilities through a variety of methods. Some of the recommendations provided by Rowe et al. (2015) include: (a) delivering pre-designed curricular activities designed to increase social skills, (b) providing opportunities to develop problem-solving skills, (c) administering ecological assessments to better understand soft skill needs in a variety of settings, (d) implementing self-evaluation opportunities to help students better understand their personal needs, and (e) providing opportunities for students to develop skills in inclusive settings. Using peer mediated instruction may also provide both structured and unstructured opportunities for students to develop social skills (Scheef et al., 2019). School-based practitioners may also consider the use of video modeling for employment-related soft skill development for students with disabilities (Park et al., 2020).

Teaching Job-Specific Skills

When a student has a strong interest in a specific job or job area, instructional programs should teach those skills associated with the position. During their teacher training, special education teachers learn a variety of tools to support the learning of students with disabilities, many of which can also be used to teach job-specific skills. Although learning these skills in the authentic setting (i.e., job site) may be ideal, students can also learn to complete work-related tasks in the school environment with the goal of being able to generalize to other settings. Some instructional tools that may be effective include direct instruction, simulation, and peer-mediated instruction strategies (Gilson et al., 2017).

Additionally, the use of technology can support the acquisition of job-specific skills for youth with disabilities (Gilson et al., 2017). Many job-specific tasks require chaining (i.e., tasks that require multiple steps to fully complete), which may be difficult for individuals with disabilities, especially those with intellectual disabilities. As such, school-based personnel should consider using video self-modeling, which may be effective in improving chained task completion, with or without feedback (Goh & Bambara, 2013). Handheld electronic devices (e.g., smart phone) may also be effective in delivering prompts to assist with job skills development and task completion (Goo et al., 2019). It may also be effective to deliver task-specific prompts to students in real time by using in-ear audio prompting from a job coach observing at a distance (Allen et al., 2012). Teachers who are especially interested in technology may consider the use of augmented reality, which may be an effective means to teach job-specific skills to students with disabilities (Chang et al., 2013).

Technology Training

Although technology can be used in teaching job skills, students also can learn to use electronic devices to support their success at the job site. In an update of the predictors of positive outcomes identified by Test et al. (2009), Mazzotti et al. (2021) identified technology skills (e.g., computer competence) as one of three new predictors. In today's world, employees need to be comfortable with technology and understand how it can support their success in the workplace. Assistive technology tools may be able to assist workers with disabilities by increasing productivity through improved time management and task completion (e.g., wearable technology, portable electronic devices; Morash-Macneil et al., 2018). Location-based technology tools can support employment by aiding in community navigation, including getting to work (McMahon et al., 2015). Training youth to use these tools before they enter the workplace can aid in students achieving their employment goals.

Providing Work-Based Learning Experiences

It is perhaps not surprising that programs to support the post-school employment goals of youth with disabilities would include work-based learning (WBL) components. WBL is an instructional strategy that augments classroom-based employment training by making direct connections with the workplace. In addition to providing opportunities at a job site, WBL includes opportunities for students to increase knowledge and understanding of these experiences by making connections in the classroom (U.S. Department of Education, n.d). As such, in order to better prepare individuals with disabilities for success in the workplace, WBLs should be included as a key component of school services for youth who receive special education services in high school (Kohler et al., 2016; Rowe et al., 2015). The following includes a description of some of the many WBL opportunities that can support the achievement of employment goals for youth with disabilities, including: one-shot experiences, school-based opportunities, and community-based internships and paid work experiences. As the latter may require the most buy-in from employers, an overview of strategies for developing job sites has also been included. Table 36.1 includes a description of no-cost tool kits developed by the National Technical Assistance Center on transition that involve WBL opportunities.

One-Shot WBL Experiences

Work-based learning experiences have the potential to aid in career exploration, allowing youth with disabilities an opportunity to better understand job interests and preferences. Many of these one-shot (i.e., not reoccurring) opportunities can make a significant impact on youth who are unsure what kinds of careers may be a good fit for them. Cease-Cook et al. (2015) described ideas for field career exploration activities, including touring local job sites and facilitating opportunities for students to interview different employers and employees at various businesses. As a follow-up, students should have structured opportunities to reflect upon and discuss the experience with others (Rowe et al., 2015).

Table 36.1 No-cost toolkits developed by NTACT to support employment-related services for youth with disabilities

Toolkit Name and URL	Description
Competitive Integrated Employment Tool Kit https://transitionta.org/cietoolkit	This toolkit is designed to improve transition services to increase the likelihood of competitive integrated employment (CIE) for youth with disabilities. The toolkit includes four sections: (1) description of why CIE is a desirable outcome, (2) overview of school-based and vocational rehabilitation services, (3) illustration of effective interagency collaboration, and (4) recommendations for collaborative professional development.
Interagency Agreement Toolkit https://transitionta.org/interagencytoolkit	This toolkit provides guidance for school-based practitioners and vocational rehabilitation personnel interested in formalizing their relationship to provide employment-related services and training to youth with disabilities
School-Based Enterprise Toolkit https://transitionta.org/schoolbasedtoolkit	Schools interested in developing opportunities for youth with disabilities to develop job skills within their building should consult this toolkit. It provides detailed information for all phases including planning and developing, implementing the business, and evaluating the model. Examples of successful school-based enterprises are also included.
Transition Fair Toolkit https://transitionta.org/toolkitfair	Organizing a transition fair to connect students and families with resources and services can be daunting. This toolkit provides guidance to interested parties by detailing requisite steps though the process, from pre-planning (6 to 12 months prior to the event) to post-fair evaluation.

School-based personnel may also consider leading efforts to plan a local or regional transition fair. These events may include an opportunity for students with disabilities and their families to learn about services to support post-school transition, but it can also be an opportunity for youth to learn about potential careers. The National Secondary Transition Technical Assistance Center (NSTTAC, currently known as the Technical Assistance Center on Transition [NTACT]) offers a comprehensive Transition Fair Toolkit to assist those interested in providing this opportunity for youth in their schools and community (NSTTAC, 2014). Organizing a career-focus panel discussion with successfully employed people with disabilities (as part of a transition fair or a stand-alone event) may also help students better understand personal career interests, preferences, and goals (Bellman et al., 2014)..

Although they could potentially occur multiple times, many job shadowing opportunities are completed for an extended time during a single day (e.g., a career mentoring day). Job shadowing involves an individual spending time alongside an employee at a workplace to gain a greater understanding of the scope of the work involved with that particular position (Luecking, 2020). In addition, students may have the opportunity to learn first-hand about the kinds of training required to obtain work in a particular career and understand if it is a good fit for them. Recognizing that classroom follow-up is an essential component of WBL, students should be given opportunities to engage in activities following the job shadow experience. These may include delivering presentations, exploring training options, understanding the job availability and forecast for that particular position, and considering opportunities for additional related field experiences.

School-Based WBL Opportunities

Although work on authentic job sites may increase the authenticity of WBL experiences, these may not always be possible. Developing school-based WBLs may alleviate barriers, such as transportation and lack of opportunities. As school personnel are dependent on local businesses to provide opportunities for work-based learning experiences at authentic job sites, developing opportunities within the school may be appropriate. In addition, students who are developing appropriate work-place social skills and behaviors may also benefit from the comfort of learning job skills in a familiar environment. Cease-Cook et al. (2015) provided examples of school-based experiences, including: (a) food preparation in the cafeteria, (b) campus landscaping, (c) secretarial skills in the school office, (d) non-sensitive data entry, and (e) providing organizational support for extra-curricular activities. To increase the authenticity of these experiences, it may be appropriate to have school staff members complete job performance evaluations for students completing WBL tasks (Rowe et al., 2015).

School-based enterprises (SBEs) are another option to develop student job skills when community-based options are not possible. Sometimes referred to as microenterprises, SBEs involve students in a school operating as a small business to produce goods or provide services to earn money (NTACT, 2018). Schools considering developing SBEs should consider the inclusiveness of the activity from the start; without involvement of peers without disabilities, an SBE can become a school-based sheltered workshop. Through SBEs, students with disabilities have genuine opportunities to learn work skills, practice appropriate work-place behaviors in a safe setting, and increase self-determination (NTACT, 2018).

Community-Based Internships and Paid Work Experiences

Student work experience at authentic job sites is one of a handful of WBL strategies schools may feature to support the capacity of students to find and maintain employment. Engagement in work experience while in high school is a predictor of positive post-school outcomes for individuals with disabilities (Mazzotti et al., 2021; Test et al., 2009). Unlike most other educational opportunities students experience during their academic career, community-based internships and paid work experiences are dependent on personnel outside of the school community being willing to provide opportunities. As such, practitioners who seek to develop job sites must have an understanding of how to work with employers. Below are broad and general recommendations for both recruiting employer partners as well as maintaining the relationships to allow for continued opportunities. Those interested in more detailed information should consider recommendations provided by Luecking (2020).

Recruiting Employer-Partners. Job developers may struggle to find employers willing to offer internships or paid work experiences for students with disabilities. Due to the barriers to employment for individuals with disabilities described earlier in this chapter, employers may have concerns or disinterest in providing these opportunities.

Although employers may hire workers with disabilities for the greater good of society, their willingness to participate and subsequent sustained involvement is likely dependent on financial rather than charitable factors (Luecking, 2020). As such, focusing on pity and providing a service for an individual with a disability is an undesirable strategy for finding business partners. One employer explained, "If this is strictly a training program…we wouldn't be interested in the program. We want to invest in our future employees and give them a great opportunity to learn a skill with a great company that provides great benefits" (Riesen & Oertle, 2019, p. 30). Instead, job developers should find opportunities to learn about the business and explain how the student can be of value to the employer. Conducting informational interviews with a knowledgeable person in the business may glean valuable information about their needs and demonstrate the job developer is truly interested in finding a way to help the business (Luecking, 2020). When done effectively, this approach has the potential to move past the idea that hiring a person with a disability is not only *possible*, but *desirable*.

Owens and Young (2008) described networking as an essential practice for job developers looking to build relationships with potential employers. The authors suggest that it is necessary for professionals to build a relationship with potential employers before a job is needed in order to get access to the "hidden job market" (p. 6). In order to build these potentially productive relationships with employers, the authors suggested job developers: (a) be formal and sincere with introductions; (b) listen and ask questions to show interest; (c) not immediately ask for something, but rather focus on relationship building; (d) maintain promises; (e) self-introduce rather than waiting for someone else to make introductions; and (f) find a memorable way to thank the employer for their time. Job developers can improve employer relations by under-promising and over-delivering (Luecking, 2020).

In order to secure work experience positions for students, job development specialists must also be ready to present an *elevator speech*, which Owens and Young (2008) defined as "a 30 second commercial for yourself or your company" (p. 3). This brief description of a work experience program must be presented in a way that highlights the program and makes the listener want to learn more. Luecking (2020) listed the basic rules for an elevator speech as being "keep it short, keep it concise, and keep it positive" (p. 110). When proposing the partnership, job developers should also be prepared to describe to employers the benefits associated with employing individuals with disabilities. Table 36.2 describes some of these benefits, as identified by Lindsay et al. (2018) who conducted a review of 20 years of research on the topic.

Maintaining Employer-Partners. Job developers must recognize the importance of providing ongoing support to employers who offer on-site work-based learning opportunities for youth with disabilities. An employer who responded to the survey by Riesen and Oertle (2019) described a lack of communication and support from a school district when a student was placed for work-based learning. The employer said, "That experience made me totally unwilling to work with the schools here ever again. They are really putting these children at risk and the business owners [as well]" (p. 32). Strategies to maintain positive relationships with employers, thus promoting continued partnerships include: (a) developing and following through with a written agreement detailing expectations and responsibilities, (b) soliciting feedback on service from employers and making adjustments based on this information, (c) providing information and support regarding accommodations, (d) modeling desirable interactions with students for employers, and (e) offering continued support to the employer, or service after the sale (Luecking, 2020; Riesen & Oertle, 2019).

Job Developers should also consider supporting work opportunities for students by offering training to the employer; forced training may result in weary employers, however knowing that these options exist may strengthen partnerships (Luecking, 2020). These can be designed to support individual students, or include broader topics, such as disability awareness or accommodations. In addition, finding opportunities to train job coaches (or other support personnel employed by the school) so that they understand essential job functions can improve employer partnerships (Gewurtz et al., 2016; Riesen & Oertle, 2019). Schools should also consider inviting employers to school events, so they feel a greater connection to the community, potentially resulting in additional opportunities for students (Scheef et al., 2017).

Table 36.2 Benefits of hiring people with disabilities (as identified by Lindsay et al., 2018)

Profitability	Hiring people with disabilities can be cost-effective and result in increased profits for the business as well as economic benefits for the community.
Low Turnover, Loyalty, High Retention	Individuals with disabilities are likely to remain loyal to employers who offer opportunities, resulting in a reduced need to hire and train new employees.
Reliability, Punctuality, and Work Ethic	Many individuals with disabilities appreciate routine, and as such may be more dependable workers who arrive on-time and take fewer sick days. Employers may be pleased with the high levels of work ethic displayed by employees with disabilities.
Company Image	Although job developers may want to avoid charitable appeals when seeking work opportunities, employers may feel hiring people with disabilities improves their company image.
Diverse Workforce and Customers	Employees recognize the benefits of a diverse workplace, which includes individuals with disabilities. In addition to improved workplace environments, hiring individuals with disabilities may find increased business from diverse customers
Innovation	Individuals with disabilities may have different ways of viewing the world. These unique perspectives may lead to innovation in the workplace and new ideas to improve products and services.
Productivity and Safety	Although stereotypes may lead some to think otherwise, individuals with disabilities are productive and have strong safety records.
Dis/Ability Awareness	Society may view individuals with disabilities as needy and a liability in the workplace. Opportunities to work with people with disabilities may improve employer perspective about the abilities of this population.

Note: This represents a broad overview of the findings; see Lindsay et al. (2018) for more specific details about each of these items.

Making Connections Outside the School

Although schools are required to support post-school employment goals for students who receive special education services through IDEA (2004), they do not have to be the only party involved with these initiatives. Two of the five domains presented in Kohler et al.'s Taxonomy of Transition Planning (2016) represent the notion that the weight of supporting student employment goals is not solely on the shoulders of school-based personnel (Interagency Collaboration and Family Engagement). The following sections describe the importance of involving family, community partners, and other agencies in supporting student post-school employment goals.

Shared Responsibility with the Family

Because parent expectations of employment for youth with disabilities are a predictor of positive post-school outcomes (Mazzotti et al., 2021), gaining the support of family is crucial. However, significant barriers to family involvement in transition planning are numerous, and include: (a) general stress, (b) lack of resources, (c) limited cultural capital, (d) racism and discrimination, (e) a belief that school personnel did not want to genuinely empower family members, and (f) insufficient or inappropriate transition planning by the school (Hirano et al., 2018). To emphasize the importance of the family, who will continue to be involved after the student is no longer receiving IDEA services, school personnel may consider shifting from the idea of *parent involvement* to a more comprehensive *shared responsibility* (Luecking, 2020). The school is one player in a team with the common goal of supporting post-school employment.

In order to increase family interest in the notion of shared responsibility, school-based personnel should consider a variety of strategies. Gleaning information from the family about activities in the home can help the circle of supporters better understand the student's strengths and preferences as they relate to potential employment environments. This information can help job developers consider potential job placements that they may not have considered. Working directly with families can also help school-based personnel better understand the potential of job placement options that may be available due to existing networks of friends and relatives. Family members may also be able to help identify potential accommodation needs or other potential barriers to employment (e.g., transportation, family commitments). School personnel can help connect families with resources related to disability-related income supports so that they more fully understand how employment may impact benefits (Luecking, 2020). When considering work experience placements, schools may consider bringing parents to view the worksite so they have a better understanding of the work environment. It may also be possible to arrange meetings that include both employers and parents to help make connections that support sustainability (Scheef et al., 2017). The cultural background of the family must be considered throughout the process of building family involvement, empowerment, and preparation (Kohler et al., 2016).

Community Connections

The ability for individuals with disabilities to find and maintain employment benefits their entire community. Recognizing this, school personnel should consider soliciting support from the broad community to increase employment opportunities for individuals with disabilities. School personnel may consider inviting stakeholders to a community conversation focused on employment opportunities. These events provide a structured platform to identify localized solutions to a pressing community need, provide greater context and understanding of the problem, allow for networking and resource mapping, identify individuals with disabilities as an underutilized resource, and support the notion that there is shared responsibility across the community (Carter & Bumble, 2018). School-based practitioners interested in planning a community conversation should consult Schutz et al., 2021, who provide step-by-step recommendations for leading these efforts.

There may also be value in exploring how existing business networking entities can support the efforts to increase employment options for individuals with disabilities. For example, a local Chamber of Commerce may allow school-based practitioners to tap into business networks. Local Chambers of Commerce may view supporting youth employment as part of their mission, but may be less receptive if such opportunities are presented as being disability-specific (Carter et al., 2009). With this in mind, approaching these kinds of entities without focusing on pity (in a similar manner as previously described when approaching employers), is perhaps the most effective route. Other networking opportunities may exist through other community organizations, such as the Rotary Club or Kiwanis Club (Carter et al., 2009).

Working with Vocational Rehabilitation

School-based practitioners in the US looking to improve employment training for youth with disabilities should be working directly with Vocational Rehabilitation (VR). Although they provide supports to improve employment opportunities for adults with disabilities of any age, the reauthorization of the Workforce Innovation and Opportunity Act (WIOA; 2014) included a mandate that state VR offices spend at least 15 percent of their funding on school-age youth. These are known as pre-employment transition services and include training related to five domains, including (a) job exploration counseling, (b) work-based learning experiences, (c) workplace readiness training to develop appropriate social skills, (d) transition counseling regarding post-secondary education and comprehensive programs, and (e) self-advocacy instruction. In order to increase opportunities for collaboration with school-based personnel, WIOA does not require that students be enrolled in VR services; they need only to have a disability that causes a barrier to obtaining or maintaining employment.

Because school-based special education teachers may have skills and knowledge related to supporting the academic needs of students with disabilities, VR personnel may be able to supplement what is currently being done in the classroom. VR counselors and transition specialists may have greater understanding of the supports necessary to coordinate services and increase employability for individuals with disabilities (Plotner et al., 2017). This perhaps explains why students who work with VR while in high school are more likely to obtain post-school employment than peers with disabilities who did not (Poppen et al., 2017). In addition, students who work with employment support agencies, like VR, are more likely to have accommodation requests approved by employers (McDonnall et al., 2014). Scheef and McKnight-Lizotte (in press) provide recommendations for school-based personnel interested in improving collaboration with VR.

Conclusion

Individuals with disabilities may struggle to find and maintain work and as a result may not have the opportunity to experience the many benefits associated with employment. School-based special educators, who are tasked with supporting the post-school goals of youth with disabilities, can improve transition programming to increase the likelihood of students achieving their individual employment goals. Practitioners can improve services by understanding barriers to employment and designing services to address these concerns. Although effective transition planning is detailed and comprehensive, school-based practitioners should ensure that transition services include training to improve student employability skills, provide work-based learning opportunities, and feature collaboration with other stakeholders.

References

Allen, K. D., Burke, R. V., Howard, M. R., Wallace, D. P., & Bowen, S. L. (2012). Use of audio cuing to expand employment opportunities for adolescents with autism spectrum disorders and intellectual disabilities. *Journal of Autism and Developmental Disorders, 42*(11), 2410–2419.

Bellman, S., Burgstahler, S., & Ladner, R. (2014). Work-based learning experiences help students with disabilities transition to careers: A case study of University of Washington projects. *Work, 48*(3), 399–405.

Brown, S. D., & Lent, R. W. (2013). *Career development and counseling: Putting theory and research to work* (2nd Edition). John Wiley & Sons.

Bush, J. H. W. (1990). *Remarks of President George H. W. Bush at the signing of the Americans with Disabilities Act.* https://www.ada.gov/ghw_bush_ada_remarks.html

Carter, E. W., & Bumble, J. L. (2018). The promise and possibilities of community conversations: Expanding opportunities for people with disabilities. *Journal of Disability Policy Studies, 28*(4), 195–202.

Carter, E. W., Owens, L., Swedeen, B., Trainor, A. A., Thompson, C., Ditchman, N., & Cole, O. (2009). Conversations that matter: Engaging communities to expand employment opportunities for youth with disabilities. *Teaching Exceptional Children, 41*(6), 38–46.

Cease-Cook, J., Fowler, C., & Test, D. W. (2015). Strategies for creating work-based learning experiences in schools for secondary students with disabilities. *Teaching Exceptional Children, 47*(6), 352–358.

Chang, Y. J., Kang, Y. S., & Huang, P. C. (2013). An augmented reality (AR)-based vocational task prompting system for people with cognitive impairments. *Research in Developmental Disabilities, 34*(10), 3049–3056.

Copeland, J., Chan, F., Bezyak, J., & Fraser, R. T. (2010). Assessing cognitive and affective reactions of employers toward people with disabilities in the workplace. *Journal of Occupational Rehabilitation, 20*(4), 427–434.

Erickson, W. A., von Schrader, S., Bruyère, S. M., & VanLooy, S. A. (2013). The employment environment: Employer perspectives, policies, and practices regarding the employment of persons with disabilities. *Rehabilitation Counseling Bulletin, 57*(4), 195–208.

Erickson, W. A., Lee, C., & von Schrader, S. (2019). *2017 Disability status report: United States*. Cornell University Yang-Tan Institute on Employment and Disability (YTI).

Gewurtz, R. E., Langan, S., & Shand, D. (2016). Hiring people with disabilities: A scoping review. *Work, 54*(1), 135–148. https://doi.org/10.3233/WOR-162265

Gilson, C. B., Carter, E. W., & Biggs, E. E. (2017). Systematic review of instructional methods to teach employment skills to secondary students with intellectual and developmental disabilities. *Research and Practice for Persons with Severe Disabilities, 42*(2), 89–107.

Goh, A. E., & Bambara, L. M. (2013). Video self-modeling: A job skills intervention with individuals with intellectual disability in employment settings. *Education and Training in Autism and Developmental Disabilities, 48*(1), 103–119.

Goo, M., Maurer, A. L., & Wehmeyer, M. L. (2019). Systematic review of using portable smart devices to teach functional skills to students with intellectual disability. *Education and Training in Autism and Developmental Disabilities, 54*(1), 57–68.

Hirano, K. A., Rowe, D., Lindstrom, L., & Chan, P. (2018). Systemic barriers to family involvement in transition planning for youth with disabilities: A qualitative metasynthesis. *Journal of Child and Family Studies, 27*(11), 3440–3456.

Houtenville, A., & Kalargyrou, V. (2012). People with disabilities employers' perspectives on recruitment practices, strategies, and challenges in leisure and hospitality. *Cornell Hospitality Quarterly, 53*(1), 40–52.

Individuals with Disabilities Education Improvement Act of 2004 (IDEA). Pub.L.No.108-446, 118 Stat. 2647 (2004) [Amending 20 U.S.C. §§ 1400 et seq.].

Jahoda, A., Kemp, J., Riddell, S., & Banks, P. (2007). Feelings about work: A review of the socio-emotional impact of supported employment on people with intellectual disabilities. *Journal of Applied Research in Intellectual Disabilities, 21*, 1–18.

Ju, S., Zhang, D., & Pacha, J. (2012). Employability skills valued by employers as important for entry-level employees with and without disabilities. *Career Development and Transition for Exceptional Individuals, 35*(1), 29–38.

Kaye, H. S., Jans, L. H., & Jones, E. C. (2011). Why don't employers hire and retain workers with disabilities? *Journal of Occupational Rehabilitation, 21*(4), 526–536.

Kiernan, W. E., Hoff, D., Freeze, S., & Mank, D. M. (2011). Employment first: A beginning not an end. *Intellectual and Developmental Disabilities, 49*(4), 300–304.

Kumin, L., & Schoenbrodt, L. (2016). Employment in adults with Down syndrome in the United States: results from a national survey. *Journal of Applied Research in Intellectual Disabilities, 29*(4), 330–345.

Kohler, P. D., Gothberg, J. E., Fowler, C., & Coyle, J. (2016). *Taxonomy for transition programming 2.0: A model for planning, organizing, and evaluating transition education, services, and programs*. Western Michigan University.

Lindsay, S., Adams, T., Sanford, R., McDougall, C., Kingsnorth, S., & Menna-Dack, D. (2014). Employers' and employment counselors' perceptions of desirable skills for entry-level positions for adolescents: How does it differ for youth with disabilities? *Disability & Society, 29*(6), 953–967.

Lindsay, S., Cagliostro, E., Albarico, M., Mortaji, N., & Karon, L. (2018). A systematic review of the benefits of hiring people with disabilities. *Journal of Occupational Rehabilitation, 28*(4), 634–655.

Luecking, R. G. (2020). *The way to work: How to facilitate work experiences for youth in transition* (2nd ed.). Brookes Publishing Co.

May-Simera, C. (2018). Reconsidering sheltered workshops in light of the United Nations Convention on the Rights of Persons with Disabilities (2006). *Laws, 7*(1), 6.

Mazzotti, V. L., Rowe, D. A., Kwiatek, S., Voggt, A., Chang, W.-H., Fowler, C. H., Poppen, M., Sinclair, J., & Test, D. W. (2021). Secondary transition predictors of postschool success: An update to the research base. *Career Development and Transition for Exceptional Individuals, 44*(1), 47–64. https://doi.org/10.1177/2165143420959793

McDonnall, M. C., O'Mally, J., & Crudden, A. (2014). Employer knowledge of and attitudes toward employees who are blind or visually impaired. *Journal of Visual Impairment & Blindness, 108*(3), 213–225.

McFarlane, F. R., & Guillermo, M. (2020). Work-based learning for students with disabilities. *Policy analysis for California education, PACE*. https://files.eric.ed.gov/fulltext/ED605115.pdf

McMahon, D., Cihak, D. F., & Wright, R. (2015). Augmented reality as a navigation tool to employment opportunities for postsecondary education students with intellectual disabilities and autism. *Journal of Research on Technology in Education, 47*(3), 157–172.

Morash-Macneil, V., Johnson, F., & Ryan, J. B. (2018). A systematic review of assistive technology for individuals with intellectual disability in the workplace. *Journal of Special Education Technology, 33*(1), 15–26.

Moss, P., & Tilly, C. (1996). Soft skills and race: An investigation of black men's employment problems. *Work and Occupations, 23*(3), 252–276.

National Association of Colleges and Employers. (2019). *Job outlook 2020*. Author.

National Council of Disability. (2017). *National disability policy. A progress report*. https://ncd.gov/progressreport/2017/national-disability-policy-progress-report-october-2017

National Secondary Transition Technical Assistance Center. (2014). *Transition fair toolkit*. https://transitionta.org/system/files/toolkitfair/Transition_Fair_Toolkit.pdf

National Technical Assistance Center on Transition. (2018). *Developing a school-based enterprise toolkit* (K. A. Clark, D. E. Rusher, A. P. Voggt, & D. W. Test, Eds.). National Technical Assistance Center on Transition

Owens, L., & Young, P. (2008). You're hired! The power of networking. *Journal of Vocational Rehabilitation, 28*, 1–6.

Park, J., Bouck, E. C., & Duenas, A. (2020). Using video modeling to teach social skills for employment to youth with intellectual disability. *Career Development and Transition for Exceptional Individuals, 43*(1), 40–52.

Plotner, A., Rose, C., Stinnett, C. V., & Ivester, J. (2017). Professional characteristics that impact perceptions of successful transition collaboration. *Journal of Rehabilitation, 83*(2), 43–51.

Poppen, M., Lindstrom, L., Unruh, D., Khurana, A., & Bullis, M. (2017). Preparing youth with disabilities for employment: An analysis of vocational rehabilitation case services data. *Journal of Vocational Rehabilitation, 46*, 209–224.

Reichard, A., Stransky, M., Brucker, D., & Houtenville, A. (2019). The relationship between employment and health and health care among working-age adults with and without disabilities in the United States. *Disability and Rehabilitation, 41*(19), 2299–2307.

Riesen, T., & Oertle, K. M. (2019). Developing work-based learning experiences for students with intellectual and developmental disabilities: A preliminary study of employers' perspectives. *Journal of Rehabilitation, 85*(2), 27–36.

Robles, M. M. (2012). Executive perceptions of the top 10 soft skills needed in today's workplace. *Business Communication Quarterly, 75*(4), 453–465. https://doi.org/10.1177/1080569912460400

Rowe, D. A., Alverson, C. Y., Unruh, D. K., Fowler, C. H., Kellems, R., & Test, D. W. (2015). A Delphi study to operationalize evidence-based predictors in secondary transition. *Career Development and Transition for Exceptional Individuals, 38*(2), 113–126. https://doi.org/10.1177/2165143414526429

Saunders, S. L., & Nedelec, B. (2014). What work means to people with work disability: A scoping review. *Journal of Occupational Rehabilitation, 24*(1), 100–110.

Scheef, A. R., & McKnight-Lizotte, M. (in press). Utilizing vocational rehabilitation to support post-school transition for students with learning disabilities. *Intervention in School and Clinic, 57*(5), 316–321.

Scheef, A. R., Barrio, B. L., & Poppen, M. I. (2017). Developing partnerships with businesses to support job training for youth with disabilities in Singapore. *Career Development and Transition for Exceptional Individuals, 40*(3), 156–164.

Scheef, A. R., Hollingshead, A., & Voss, C. (2019). Peer support arrangements to promote positive post-school outcomes. *Intervention in School and Clinic, 54*(4), 219–224. https://doi.org/10.1177/1053451218782430

Schutz, M. A., Carter, E. W., Gajjar, S. A., & Maves, E. A. (2021). Strengthening transition partnerships through community conversation events. *TEACHING Exceptional Children*. https://doi.org/10.1177/0040059920987877

Test, D. W., Mazzotti, V. L., Mustian, A. L., Fowler, C. H., Kortering, L., & Kohler, P. (2009). Evidence-based secondary transition predictors for improving postschool outcomes for students with disabilities. *Career Development and Transition for Exceptional Individuals, 32*(3), 160–181. https://doi.org/10.1177/0885728809346960

United States Bureau of Labor Statistics. (2020). Persons with a disability: Labor force characteristics summary. https://www.bls.gov/news.release/disabl.nr0.htm

United States Department of Education. (n.d.). Work-based learning tool kit. https://cte.ed.gov/wbltoolkit/

Wehman, P. (2011). Employment for persons with disabilities: Where we are now and where do we need to go? *Journal of Vocational Rehabilitation, 35*(1), 145–151.

Wehman, P., Taylor, J., Brooke, V., Avellone, L., Whittenburg, H., Ham, W., ... & Carr, S. (2018). Toward competitive employment for persons with intellectual and developmental disabilities: What progress have we made and where do we need to go. *Research and Practice for Persons with Severe Disabilities, 43*(3), 131–144.

Workforce Innovation and Opportunity Act of 2014, Pub. L. 113–128, 128 STAT 1632, §40

Zappella, E. (2015). Employers' attitudes on hiring workers with intellectual disabilities in small and medium enterprises: An Italian research. *Journal of Intellectual Disabilities, 19*(4), 381–392.

37
EMPOWERING INCLUSION IN HIGHER EDUCATION

The Case of a Multidimensional Peer Support Model for Students with Disabilities

Magda Nikolaraizi*, Maria Papazafiri and Vassilios Argyropoulos

Introduction

During the last decades, a growing number of students with disabilities attend higher education institutions (HEIs). The increasing number of students with disabilities in HEIs democratizes the academy and indicates an inclusive movement (Moola & Orozco, 2021). However, inclusive education is not a simple task. Inclusive education is an ongoing process that supports the right of all students to participate in education. In practice, students with disabilities face several barriers which are pertinent to their physical, communication, and academic access. For example, in many universities, there are several impediments such as lack of lifts, ramps, inaccessible educational material, high noise levels, and lack of sign language interpreters (Fuller, Bradley & Healey, 2004; Holloway, 2001; Hopkins, 2011, Skinner & Lindstrom, 2003). Additional barriers are associated with the attitudes of lecturers who may not be aware of the learning needs of students with disabilities or may find it challenging and be reluctant to address the students' needs through a range of adjustments (Kowalsky & Fresko, 2002; Holloway, 2001; Scott & Gregg, 2000; Shevlin, Kenny & McNeela, 2004). Furthermore, peers' relationships can pose several barriers, because students with disabilities may not be easily accepted as friends, have poor opportunities to interact with their peers, and in general feel rejected (Burgstahler & Cronheim, 2001).

Within the scope of inclusive education, several countries and organizations have developed regulations, frameworks, and policies that support the development and provision of services and practices which enhance the access and participation of students with disabilities in higher education (Moriña & Orozco, 2021). One of these services concerns volunteering peer support, peer-assisted or peer-mediated programs, widely known as peer-tutoring or peer-mentoring programs. Although different terms usually have different characteristics and meanings, they also share many similarities. Specifically, peer-assisted programs usually refer to a relationship in which persons who may be experienced or knowledgeable in a particular area support and facilitate other persons with whom they share some common characteristics (e.g., age, culture, studies), in order to enhance their skills and their potentials (Colvin, 2007; Gilman, 2006; Topping, 1996).

* magdanikolaraizi@gmail.com

Peer Support Programs for Students with Disabilities: The Role of Volunteers

Peer support programs vary depending on the aims, the content and the focus of support, the duration of the programs, the characteristics of the persons that participate, and the criteria based on which these persons are selected (Carter et al., 2019). Furthermore, peer support services may be face-to-face, fully online, or blended. Online or blended peer tutoring has been in use for many years (see Evans & Moore, 2013) and recently has become a common practice, due to the COVID-19 pandemic (Aznam, Perdana, Jumadi, Nurchahyo & Wiyatmo, 2020; Pérez-Jorge, Rodríguez-Jiménez, Arino-Mateo , 2020).

Regardless of the diverse characteristics of these programs, peer-mediated support programs entail benefits for the peers involved. Although in the past the emphasis was placed mostly on the benefits for the ones who received the support, gradually research indicated that the peer-assisted relationship is a reciprocal one and entails several various benefits both for the ones who give as well as the ones who receive the support (Colvin, 2007; Lassegrad, 2008; Mead, 2003). Peer-tutoring empowers communication and enhances social, critical, problem solving, academic, meta-cognitive, collaborative as well as self-determination skills. Also, peer-tutoring can improve self-esteem and self-concept, increasing motivation to learn (Alrahi & Aldharfi, 2015; Colvin, 2007; Falchikov, 2003; Kalkowski 1995; Beasley 1997; Mynard & Arlarzouqi, 2006).

Furthermore, peer-mediated approaches provide structured opportunities for the promotion of peer interactions, social relationships, and social engagement within and beyond the classroom and contribute to the creation of a social network of peers and a community of learners (Hochman, Carter, Bottema-Beutel, Harvey & Gistafson, 2015; Tinto, 2010). This is of major importance for many students who may face challenges in interacting, communicating, and forming relationships. Such needs may be not covered by services in HEIs and many students and in particular students with disabilities feel social anxiety and loneliness (Ames, McMorris, Alli & Bebko, 2016). Peer-tutoring creates a less threatening context, in which students feel less anxious and less stressed. Because they share the same educational venues and clubs, usually they have common experiences with their peers and they feel more comfortable and confident to ask and make mistakes (Alrahi & Aldharfi, 2015; Topping, 2005).

An important factor in the success of a peer support service is associated with the role-knowledge, and skills of the students involved, both the ones who provide as well as the ones who receive the services (Agarwal, Heron, Naseh & Burke, 2021). Several concerns have been expressed regarding the fact that students lack the expertise, knowledge, and skills to understand and address the needs of their peers with disabilities (see Hall, Serafin & Lundgren, 2020; Vogel, Fresko & Wertheim, 2007). Another concerning issue is that in many cases the students who provide the services are volunteers and because their role is very challenging, there is a great need to be motivated in order to engage and retain themselves effectively in their volunteer role (Alfes, Shantz & Bailey, 2015; Studer & Schnurbein 2013). Furthermore, apart from the concerns regarding the role of the volunteer students, there are also concerns about the role of the students who receive the services, who often lack soft skills such as self-advocacy and self-determination skills to identify, describe and communicate their needs to their peers. These challenges point out the need that everybody involved in a peer-assisted relationship requires training and support that will enable them to develop role-specific knowledge and skills (Agarwal et al., 2021; Vogel, Fresko & Wertheim, 2007).

Based on the above, peer support programs in HEIs entail several benefits but also challenges. The aim of the following section is to describe a multidimensional peer support program in an HEI which aims to enhance the access and inclusion of students with disability.

This program is provided under the umbrella of the accessibility centre of the University of Thessaly, called "PROSVASI" (in English "ACCESS"), (http://prosvasi.uth.gr/index_en.html). A description is provided of the framework that underpins the operation of the peer-assisted program and the services that are provided. Also, the emphasis is placed on the important role of training and supporting the volunteers in the effectiveness of the peer-assisted program.

The Case of a Multidimensional Volunteering Peer-support Program in Higher Education

The Role and the Network of PROSVASI

The main goal of the accessibility center PROSVASI is to enhance the spatial, academic, social and digital access of students with disabilities at the University of Thessaly. The core element in all tasks and activities of "PROSVASI" is to act towards the development of an accessible and inclusive environment for students with disabilities at the University of Thessaly, informing and raising awareness about the rights of students with disabilities. A range of services is provided that primarily address students with disabilities as well as the university staff, including lecturers and administrative staff. Additionally, PROSVASI organizes actions, often in collaboration with other organizations, to raise awareness regarding disability and accessibility in higher education.

The peer-support program for students with disabilities is among the oldest and most important services provided by PROSVASI. More analytically, the peer-support program is a service that is provided by the volunteering network of PROSVASI. The volunteers involve students with and without disabilities, while students who receive the services involve only students with disabilities. The volunteering network operates through an interactive sector system that has an intensive collaborative character. Three volunteering groups (see Figure 37.1) with discrete tasks are the main pillars of the volunteer network, which interacts on a constant basis with the scientific group (i.e., it is the fourth group).

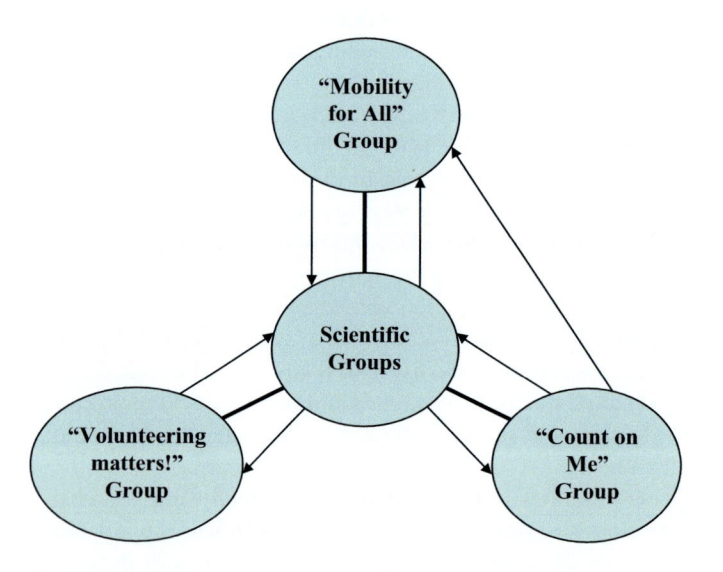

Figure 37.1 The interactive sectors of the PROSVASI's volunteer network

1) The "Volunteering matters!" Group; one or two volunteers from each department participate in this group by forming a coordinating team that contributes to the following actions:
   - Matching volunteers and students who ask for services.
   - Monitoring the collaboration between volunteers and students who receive services.
   - Organizing volunteer meetings.
   - Making suggestions regarding the needs of the volunteers.
2) The "Mobility for All" Group, which contributes to the following actions:
   - Searching for volunteers.
   - Organizing training events for volunteers and students with disabilities.
   - Organizing and participating in awareness and information actions within and outside the University of Thessaly.
3) The "Count on me!" group provides services to students with disabilities in order to enhance their spatial and administrative access, and their academic, social and digital access.

   A representative list of these services is provided below (see Table 37.1). Although these services often address specific aspects of access, such as academic or spatial access, the boundaries are not strict. Therefore, some services may be beneficial for spatial and academic and social access.
4) The "Scientific" Group consists of the coordinator, the members of the Board, and the staff of PROSVASI. The coordinator and the staff of PROSVASI have diverse backgrounds and expertise in relation to disability and accessibility education, while the members of the Board are academics that represent all faculties of the university. The Scientific Group has a coordinating and supportive role and has multiple roles and responsibilities. In relation to the peer-support program, they are informed on a regular basis regarding the progress and the challenges of all groups, they run individual and group meetings to train and support students that participate in the peer-assisted program and also, they take decisions and implement actions to address the needs and challenges.

The Profile of the Volunteers: The Significant Others

As mentioned above, peer support is provided by students who want to provide their services on a volunteer basis, in order to enhance the access of their peers with disabilities. A range of students

Table 37.1 A representative list of PROSVASI's services

Spatial access	• Guiding students to the university space
	• Escorting students within the university space
Academic access	• Note-taking
	• Explaining difficult concepts
	• Communicating with lecturers and peers
	• Audio and video description
	• Studying and management skills
	• Differentiated instruction and assessment
Social Access	• Acquaintance with fellow students
	• Participating in group activities
	• Participation in university and local community events
Digital Access	• Lending assistive technology devices
	• Training on the use of assistive technology devices
	• Training on the use of applications and software

Table 37.2 The diverse characteristics of volunteers

Academic	• Systematic attendance
	• Literacy skills (reading, writing, braille code)
	• Good knowledge of the department's curriculum
Communication	• Ability to communicate with the academic, the administrative staff and their peers
	• Knowledge of Greek Sign Language
Technology	• A friendly attitude towards the use of technology
	• Knowledge and use of several applications
	• Knowledge of video recording and editing
Collaboration	• Teamworking skills
	• Listening
Other characteristics	• Patience
	• Flexibility
	• Consistency
	• Confidentiality
	• Empathy

participate in this program as volunteers and provide a range of services depending on their profile, their preferences, their potential, and the needs of the students who ask for these services. One of the most important elements is that volunteers may be students with or without disabilities. Therefore, a student with a disability may receive but also provide a service. This role empowers students with disabilities, enables them to exploit their potentials and strengths and feel active and vital contributors, enhances their self-esteem, and helps them to feel positive and motivated as also supported based on the model of positive psychology (Krisi & Nagar, 2021; Seligman, 2002).

The volunteer is an active student at the University of Thessaly, regardless of age, gender, political or religious orientation, regardless of economic, cultural, and social origins who freely decides to offer his/her time, work, skills, creativity, and often his or her specialized knowledge in order to enhance the access of students with disabilities. Volunteers have diverse profiles, characteristics, and skills, which are useful and important depending on their role in the peer-assisted program and the services they provide (see Table 37.2).

The Roadmap of Volunteer Training and Supporting

To be a peer supporter for students with disabilities in university is a big challenge (Kelley & Westling, 2013). Therefore, it is important to identify the supportive organizational factors that will promote volunteer motivation, engagement, and willingness to retain the volunteer work (Alfes, Shantz & Bailey, 2015; Studer & Schnurbein 2013). Volunteers who are engaged in their volunteer roles are fulfilled and have better performance (Huynh et al., 2012; Shantz, Saksida & Alfes. 2014). The training of volunteers is critical both for the support of the students as well as for motivating and expanding the voluntary program (Lukovenko, Kalugina, Sorokin, & Bulavenko, 2021). Peer volunteers are not expected to be professionals or experts in accessibility and disability issues. Some of them may have the knowledge and many skills because they attend the Department of Special Education at the University of Thessaly or because they participate often in many voluntary actions that involve persons with disability. However, many of them may not have relative background knowledge and they may, also, have no prior experience as volunteers. Therefore, they need to develop knowledge and skills in many topics. Finally, it is important to note that training may operate as a motive for students' involvement in volunteering work as they want to learn, acquire experience and also use this knowledge for later employment (Cuskelly, Taylor, Hoye & Darcy, 2006; Rao, 2017; Volunteering SA Inc. 2006).

Furthermore, apart from the important role of volunteers' training, the success of a volunteering relationship, as mentioned earlier, requires that both volunteers as well as the ones who receive the services have a good role-knowledge as well as the required skills (Alfes, Shantz, & Bailey, 2016). Therefore, in PROSVASI, a range of actions take place, that have as their target groups both sides within the peer-assisted relationship, including the ones who provide as well as the ones who receive the services aiming to support them at a scientific and emotional level and help them develop a good understanding of their role, manage any challenges that they face and, in the end, feel satisfied.

More analytically, structured or less structured training courses - either individually or in groups - face-to-face or distance coaching, supportive or mentoring services are provided. The content of the structured training programs depends on the needs that arise at any given time. Indicatively, some topics that are important and are regularly covered concern: (a) volunteering relationship, such as the roles, the rights, and responsibilities of the ones who are involved in a volunteering project, the boundaries of this relationship, as well as teamwork principles, (b) disability issues, such as getting familiar with persons with disabilities, models, and myths regarding disability, (c) accessibility aspects, such as differentiated instruction, communicating with deaf or hard of hearing persons, escorting students who have a visual disability, usage of assistive technology devices, (d) self-advocacy, enabling students who receive the services to identify and communicate their needs in relation to their access in the university to their peers.

Apart from structured training programs, ongoing tailor-made training takes place which also ensures ongoing monitoring of the peer-assisted services. This may be "training on the go" (Argyropoulos et al., 2020), which in the case of PROSVASI refers to the training of volunteers while they are providing peer-assisted services. An example of such training in PROSVASI is when the peers provide written explanations and clarifications to students who are deaf. Last year, this service was provided by distance due to COVID restrictions via the use of several platforms and applications that both students and the scientific staff had access to. The students and members of the scientific staff were both attending the lectures and while the peer volunteers were writing their explanations and the students who received this service were asking questions, the scientific staff were demonstrating and guiding the volunteers.

Additionally, both volunteer students as well as the ones who receive the services participate in mentoring, coaching, and supporting meetings with the members of the scientific staff on a regular basis. Group or individual meetings take place during which scientific and emotional support is provided based on the needs and challenges that emerge during the peer-assisted program. Group meetings may be challenging to address certain individual needs, which may be discussed individually, but groups encourage students to express themselves, be more creative and discuss important topics. This process gives the opportunity to develop a culture of teamwork and enhances self-awareness and learning, as well as improving the effectiveness of the volunteer (Worrall, Schweizer, Marks, Yuan, Lloyd, & Ramjan, 2018; Volunteer Now, 2012). Often, there is a need for individual meetings depending on the students' preferences and their needs. During the meetings the members of the scientific staff train and supervise volunteers to develop specific skills and abilities in order to maximize their performance; hence, they may guide, share ideas, facilitate, listen, encourage students to reflect, provide emotional support, take immediate actions to deal with a challenge and help them to take decisions, which are widely used in training, volunteering and mentoring programs (Brudney, & Meijs, 2014; Hillier et al., 2018; Kelley, & Westling, 2013; Rose & Jones, 2007).

Finally, it is important to note that all the above services take place face-to-face or by distance, which is very important at the University of Thessaly because there are 37 Departments and 8 faculties in five cities. Furthermore, distance services became a necessity during the two last years because of COVID. While there was a high risk for the students with disabilities to get isolated and become excluded, the peer-assisted services that were offered via face-to-face were adjusted accordingly and continued to be provided online to enhance the access of students with disabilities. A wide range of media and applications were used for communication, such as phone, email, zoom, WhatsApp, messenger or other chat applications ensuring communication accessibility and flexibility so that the needs of students were met (Butler, Whiteman, & Crow, 2013; Carvin, 2011; Wilbanks, 2014).

Conclusion

In conclusion, a volunteering peer-assisted service in higher education for students with disabilities is a dynamic and multidimensional service that can contribute to the access and inclusion of students with disabilities. Additionally, it entails academic, social, and emotional benefits for all students with and without disabilities, both the ones who provide the services as well the ones who receive these services.

However, a volunteering student peer-assisted service in higher education is quite challenging. Training and support are required to ensure that volunteers as well as students who receive their services know their roles and their responsibilities and feel satisfied during the whole duration of the peer-assisted service.

In PROSVASI training and support are highly valued and provided through structured training courses and through many less structured opportunities. A range of tailor-made, individual or group, face-to-face, or distance meetings is carried out among the PROSVASI's scientific staff and the students that participate in the peer-assisted program, which aim to address the needs of all students that provide and receive services with and without disabilities and ensure the smooth operation of the peer-assisted service.

Therefore, in addition to the professional services that HEIs offer to enhance the access and inclusion of students with disabilities, it is required also to organize volunteering peer-assisted services, provided that they are well monitored and coordinated with the support of scientific staff with knowledge and expertise in issues of disability and accessibility.

Finally, it may be argued that the "inclusive element" in higher education, needs empowerment and consolidation by active networks consisting of the scientific staff with expertise in disability and accessibility issues, from students with and without disabilities and also academic members and administrative staff. Given the growing number of students with disabilities at universities, collaborative networks need to be set up, to ensure their successful integration at all levels. It seems that peer-support programs which are based on volunteering networks "convey" many promising benefits for all sides and especially for students with and without disabilities, strengthening the element of inclusion through fruitful mutual interactions.

References

Agarwal, R., Heron, L., Naseh, M., & Burke, S. L. (2021). Mentoring students with intellectual and developmental disabilities: Evaluation of role-specific workshops for mentors and mentees. *Journal of Autism and Developmental Disorders, 51*, 1281–1289. https://doi.org/10.1007/s10803-020-04599-w

Alfes, K., Shantz, A., & Bailey, C. (2015). Enhancing volunteer engagement to achieve desirable outcomes: What can non-profit employers do? *Voluntas: International Journal of Voluntary and Nonprofit Organizations, 27*, 595–617. Retrieved from http://www.jstor.org/stable/43923195

Alrajhi, M. N., & Aldhafri, S. (2015). Peer tutoring effects on Omani students English Self-Concept. *International Education Studies, 6*, 184–193.

Ames, M., McMorris, C., Alli, L., & Bebko, J. (2016). Overview and evaluation of a mentoring program for university students with ASD. *Focus on Autism and Other Developmental Disabilities, 31*, 27–36.

Argyropoulos, V., Kanari, C., Hathazi, A., Kyriacou, M., Papazafiri, M., & Nikolaraizi, M. (2020). Children with vision impairment and multiple disabilities: Issues of communication skills and professional's challenges. In M. Carmo (Ed.), Proceedings of International Conference of Education and New Developments (pp. 271–275). Zagreb, Croatia.

Aznam, N., Perdana, R., Jumadi, J., Nurcahyo, H., & Wiyatmo, Y. (2020). The implementation of blended learning and peer tutor startegies in pandemic era: A systematic review. *Proceedings of the 6th International Seminar on Science Education, 541*, 906–914.

Beasley, C. (1997). Students as teachers: The benefits of peer tutoring. In R. Pospisil & L. Willcoxson (Eds.), *Learning Through Teaching* (pp. 21–30). Proceedings of the 6th Annual Teaching Learning Forum, Murdoch University, February 1997. Perth: Murdoch University. Retrieved from http://lsn.curtin.edu.au/tlf/tlf1997/beasley.html

Brudney, J. L., & Meijs, L. (2014). Models of volunteer management: Professional volunteer program management in social work. *Human Service Organizations: Management, Leadership & Governance, 38*, 297–309. Retrieved from file:///C:/Users/user/Desktop/%CE%B4%CE%B7%CE%BC%CE%BF%CF%83%CE%AF%CE%B5%CF%85%CF%83%CE%B7%20%CE%B5%CE%B8%CE%B5%CE%BB%CE%BF%CE%BD%CF%84%CE%B9%CF%83%CE%BC%CF%8C%CF%82/BrudneyandMeijsContingenciesofVolunteerAdministrationforSocialWorkPublished.pdf

Burgstahler, S., & Cronheim, D. (2001). Supporting peer–peer and Mentor–Protégé relationships on the internet. *Journal of Research on Technology in Education, 34*, 59–74.

Butler, A., Whiteman, R., & Crow, G. (2013). Technology's role in fostering transformational educator mentoring. *International Journal of Mentoring and Coaching in Education, 2*, 233–248. https://doi.org/10.1108/IJMCE-06-2013-0037

Carter, E. W., Gustafson, J. R., Mackay, M. M., Martin, K. P., Parsley, M. V., Graves, J., Day, T. L., McCabe, L. E., Lazarz, H., McMillan, E. D., Schiro-Geist, C., Williams, M., Beeson, T., & Cayton, J. (2019). Motivations and expectations of peer mentors within inclusive higher education programs for students with Intellectual Disability. *Career Development and Transition for Exceptional Individuals, 42*(3), 168–178. https://doi.org/10.1177/2165143418779989

Carvin, B. N. (2011). The hows and whys of group mentoring. *Industrial and Commercial Training, 43*, 49–52. DOI 10.1108/00197851111098162

Citizens Information Abroad (n.d.). *Managing volunteers. A good practice guide.* Retrieved from https://www.citizensinformationboard.ie/downloads/training/Managing_Volunteers_08.pdf

Colvin, J. W. (2007). Peer tutoring and social dynamics in higher education. *Mentoring & Tutoring: Partnership in Learning, 15*, 165–181. https://doi.org/10.1080/13611260601086345

Cuskelly, G. Taylor, T., Hoye R., & Darcy, S. (2006). Volunteer management practices and volunteer retention: A human resource management approach. *Sport Management Review, 9*, 141–163.

Evans, M., & Moore, J. (2013). Peer tutoring with the aid of the internet. *British Journal of Educational Technology, 44*, 144–155.

Falchikov, N. (2003). *Improving assessment through student involvement. Practical solutions for aiding learning in higher and further education.* London: Routledge.

Fuller, M., Bradley, A., & Healey, M. (2004). Incorporating disabled students within an inclusive higher education environment. *Disability & Society, 19*, 455–468.

Gillman, D. (2006). *The power of peer mentoring.* Waisman Center. University of Wisconsin-Madison. Retrieved from https://www2.waisman.wisc.edu/cedd//pdfs/products/family/PPM.pdf

Hall, B., Serafin, J., & Lundgren, D. (2020). The benefits of academically oriented peer mentoring for at-risk student populations. *Teaching & Learning Inquiry, 8*, 184–199. https://doi.org/10.20343/teachlearninqu.8.2.12

Hochman, J. M., Carter, E. W., Bottema-Beutel, K., Harvey, M. N., & Gustafson, J. R. (2015). Efficacy of peer networks to increase social connections among high school students with and without autism spectrum disorder. *Exceptional Children, 82*, 96–116. https://doi.org/10.1177/0014402915585482

Holloway, S. (2001). The experience of higher education from the perspective of disabled students. *Disability & Society, 16*, 597–615.

Hopkins, L. (2011). The Path of least resistance: A voice-relational analysis of disabled students experiences of discrimination in English universities. *International Journal of Inclusive Education, 15*, 711–727.

Huynh, J.-Y., Metzer, J., & Winefield, A. (2012). Engaged or connected? A perspective of the motivational pathway of the job demands–resources model in volunteers working for nonprofit organizations. *VOLUNTAS: International Journal of Voluntary and Nonprofit Organizations, 23*, 870–898.

Kalkowski, P. (1995). *Peer and cross-age tutoring. School improvement research series.* North West Regional Educational Laboratory. Retrieved from http://www.nwrel.org/scpd/sirs/9/c018.html.

Kelley, K. R., & Westling, D. L. (2013). A focus on natural supports in postsecondary education for students with intellectual disabilities at Western Carolina University. *Journal of Vocational Rehabilitation, 38*, 67–76. doi: 10.3233/JVR-120621.

Kowalsky, R., & Fresko, B. (2002). Peer tutoring for college students with disabilities. *Higher Education Research & Development, 21*, 259–271.

Krisi, M., & Nagar, R. (2021). The effect of peer mentoring on mentors themselves: A case study of college students. *International Journal of Disability, Development and Education*, 1–13. doi.org/10.1080/1034912X.2021.1910934

Lassegard, J. P. (2008). The effects of peer tutoring between domestic and international students: The tutor system at Japanese universities. *Higher Education Research & Development, 27*, 357–369.

Lukoyenko, T., Kalugina, N., Sorokin, N., & Bulavenko, O. (2021). Accompanying persons with disabilities at university: Skills development among volunteers. *International Journal of Instruction, 14*, 935–952. https://doi.org/10.29333/iji.2021.14253a

Mead, S. (2003). *Defining peer support.* Retrieved from http://www.mentalhealthpeers.com/pdfs/DefiningPeer Support.pdf

Moriña, A., & Orozco, I. (2021). Spanish faculty members speak out: Barriers and aids for students with disabilities at university. *Disability & Society, 36*, 159–178.

Mynard, J., & Almarzouqi, I. (2006). Investigating peer tutoring. *ELT Journal, 60*, 13–22.

Pérez-Jorge, D. Rodríguez-Jiménez, M., Arino-Mateo, E., & Barragán-Medero, F. (2020). The effect of COVID-19 in University tutoring models. *Sustainability 2020, 12*, 8631. https://doi.org/10.3390/su12208631

Rao, M. S. (2017). Innovative tools and techniques to ensure effective employee engagement. *Industrial and Commercial Training, 49*, 127–31.

Rose, R., & Jones, K. (2007). The efficacy of a volunteer mentoring scheme in supporting young people at risk. *Emotional and Behavioural Difficulties, 12*, 3–14. https://doi.org/10.1080/13632750601135873

Scott, S., & Gregg, N. (2000). Meeting the evolving education needs of faculty in providing access for college students with LD. *Journal of Learning Disabilities, 33*, 158–167.

Seligman, M. E. P. (2002). Positive psychology, positive prevention and positive therapy. In C. R. Snyder & S. J. Lopez (Eds.), *Handbook of positive psychology* (pp. 3–7). New York: Oxford University Press.

Shantz, A., Saksida, T., & Alfes, K. (2014). Dedicating time to volunteering: Values, engagement, and commitment to beneficiaries. *Applied Psychology. An International Review, 63*, 671–697.

Shevlin, M., Kenny, M., & McNeela, E. (2004). Participation in higher education for students with disabilities: An Irish perspective. *Disability & Society, 19*, 15–30.

Skinner, M. E., & Lindstrom, B. D. (2003). Bridging the gap between high school and college: Strategies for the successful transition of students with learning disabilities. *Preventing School Failure, 47*, 132–137.

Studer, S., & Schnurbein, G. (2013). Organizational factors affecting volunteers: A literature review on volunteer coordination. *VOLUNTAS: International Journal of Voluntary and Nonprofit Organizations, 24*, 403–440.

Tinto, V. (2010). Classrooms as communities: Exploring the educational character of student persistence. *Journal of Higher Education, 68*, 599–623.

Topping, K. J. (1996). The effectiveness of peer tutoring in further and higher education: A typology and review of the literature. *Higher Education, 32*, 321–345. http://dx.doi.org/10.1007/BF00138870

Topping, K. J. (2005). Trends in peer learning. *Educational Psychology, 25*(6), 631–645. https://doi.org/10.1080/01443410500345172

Vogel, G., Fresko, B., & Wertheim, C. (2007). Peer tutoring for college students with learning disabilities perceptions of tutors and tutees. *Journal of Learning Disabilities, 40*, 485–93. https://doi.org/10.1177/00222194070400060101

Volunteer Now (2012). *Providing volunteers with the management they deserve. Workbook two attracting and selecting volunteers*. Retrieved from https://www.volunteernow.co.uk/app/uploads/2018/10/As-Good-As-They-Give-Workbook-2-Attracting-and-Selecting-Volunteers.pdf

Volunteering SA Inc. (2006). *Standardisation of volunteer training project*. unpublished report to Office for Volunteers, Department of Primary Industries and Resources of South Australia, Adelaide. Retrieved from https://www.volunteeringaustralia.org/resources/national-standards-and-supporting-material/#/

Wilbanks, J. E. (2014). E-Mentoring: Examining the feasibility of electronic, online, or distance mentoring. *Journal of Higher Education Theory and Practice*, *14*(5), 24–28. Retrieved from http://www.na-businesspress.com/JHETP/WilbanksJE_Web14_5_.pdf

Worrall, H., Schweizer, R., Marks, E., Yuan, L., Lloyd, C., & Ramjan, R. (2018). The effectiveness of support groups: A literature review. *Mental Health and Social Inclusion*, *22*(2), 85–93. https://doi.org/10.1108/MHSI-12-2017-0055

38
EDUCATIONAL ENVIRONMENT FOR STUDENTS WITH VISUAL IMPAIRMENT IN COMPUTER SCIENCE DEPARTMENT AT JAPANESE UNIVERSITY

Makoto Kobayashi[*]

Background of the University

National University Corporation Tsukuba University of Technology (NTUT) is a higher educational institute in Japan that accepts only Blind and Low Vision (BLV) students and Deaf and Hard of Hearing (DHH) students. This special university has two faculties, i.e., the Faculty of Health Sciences for BLV students and the Faculty of Industrial Technology for DHH students. The Faculty of Health Sciences is composed of three departments, the Department of Acupuncture and Moxibustion, the Department of Physical Therapy, and the Department of Computer Science. The Faculty of Industrial Technology is composed of the Department of Industrial Information and the Department of Synthetic Design. These departments were established around 1990, and the reason the founder selected these fields as departments was that sensory-impaired students can more easily find jobs in these fields (Ohnuma, 2005). The total enrollment capacity is 90 per year, and it shows NTUT is the smallest of the 86 national universities in Japan.

Because of the fact that the undergraduate faculty of NTUT accepts only BLV and DHH students, this university is considered an institute of segregated education in the Japanese higher education system. On the other hand, inclusive education is practiced in regular schools and universities even in Japan, of course, and a large number of BLV and DHH students who would like to attend common universities can do so. However, as there remain several issues concerned with inclusion (Mithout, 2016) and some students have various kinds of difficulty with inclusive education, then such students still require a segregated educational environment. NTUT is one of the options for such impaired students who cannot fit into integration. Actual statistical data shows that at least 887 BLV students and 1,980 DHH students studied in various universities in Japan in the fiscal year 2019 (JASSO, 2020), and 128 BLV students and 193 DHH students studied at NTUT campuses in the same year (NTUT, 2019). We can say that over 10% of sensory-impaired students selected segregated education.

---
[*] koba@cs.k.tsukuba-tech.ac.jp

Since the author belongs to the Department of Computer Science at NTUT, and this field is expected to have educational effects on BLV students (Stefik, Hundhausen, & Smith, 2011), this chapter introduces this department and its studying environment, special equipment, educational system, and how to support to find jobs for students.

Computing Environment in Department of Computer Science

In this section, the lecture rooms and computing environment (hardware and software) in the department are introduced. Basically, four lecture rooms are prepared for each academic year's students. These rooms have 15 computers, and each computer is properly set on each desk and fixed to the desk using Velcro tape to avoid falling on the floor when the earthquake comes. For BLV students, changing the studying environment may cause small problems such as seating mishaps or commonly used items going missing. To prevent such problems, every student is assigned a certain seat in the lecture rooms and keeps that seat for the entire school year. We assign seats for blind students as nearer the doors for easy access, and seats for students who use a magnifying CCTV on the far side of the lecture room, to provide space for the CCTV. Every seat is equipped with a small desktop computer mentioned above and 24-inch LCD monitor. Students can use these computers freely, not only for programming or Internet searching but for reading educational materials, taking notes, etc. When a student requests to use special support software or special equipment such as braille displays, trackballs, and touch panels, then these devices can be set up for the student.

Computer Network

The department prepares a Windows Server machine in the server room connected to all client computers in the lecture rooms. Students can log on to the client computers to use their Windows desktop by placing their school identity card on the card reader. Compared with a normal Windows network system at other common universities, students do not need to input their passwords before logging on. The identity card has encrypted password information, and students can use the computer immediately after putting the card on the card reader. This procedure is not considered safe enough from the viewpoint of security; however, inputting a password using a keyboard might be difficult for blind beginners who are not accustomed to operating the keyboard. This log-on procedure helps such students.

After logging on, students can use several types of network drives. The basic setting of these drives is similar to that at regular universities, as they can access the read-only public drive to acquire educational electrical materials and store their data in their private drive. There are also submission and sharing drives. To submit report files or completed examinations, they use the submission drive, which can only be accessed by teaching staff and the appropriate student. The sharing drive is open to every student, and they can save their programs, photos, etc., for sharing.

The unique point with our network drives is the manner to give a name to a folder in the drives. If a folder is labeled only with Japanese characters, the student will not be able to access the folder by directly inputting one character with the keyboard because inputting Japanese character needs Input Method Editor. Instead, they must use the arrow keys to find a certain folder or file. To prevent such time-consuming operation, we label all folders and important files starting with an alphabetical letter or a number followed by Japanese characters.

Screen-Reading Software

Japanese screen-reading software called PC-Talker (Kochi System Development, 2021) and free screen-reading software used globally called NVDA (NVDA Japanese Team, 2021) is installed on all computers in the lecture rooms. PC-Talker was developed by Kochi System Development, Inc., and is widely used in special schools for the blind in Japan; thus, most blind students have experience in using it before entering university. We also have enough licenses for JAWS, the most well-known screen-reading software, which is provided by Freedom Scientific Corporation. The number of JAWS users in Japan is not large because of the high cost of this software, but after graduating, students sometimes request to use JAWS at their companies.

LCD Monitors

Some low vision students need to move their head position closer to the computer display to acquire more precise visual information during the lecture. To meet this need, all Liquid Crystal Display (LCD) monitors in the lecture rooms are connected to two-links display arms. The two-links structure allows students to control the position of the LCD monitor anywhere they want; hence they do not have to move their heads to the monitor. When students want to use another additional monitor, we prepare more monitors and a two-links arm to connect his/her computer. The dual display environment is useful for some low-vision students. For example, a setting such as one monitor for zooming and the other monitor for taking a glance at the entire desktop can be realized using an appropriate software like ZoomText. It helps them to understand where they magnify on the desktop, and to prevent missing notifications by the computer. On the other hand, in case the eye disease makes narrow eye-field and the eye-power is still in good condition, the size of LCD monitor can be changed to a smaller one, instead of the 22 inches of usual size.

Braille Displays and Refreshable Tactile Graphic Displays

Braille displays are individually set up for students who prefer to use braille when they read materials. The department provides a braille display called "BT-46" by KGS Corporation. The overview of the braille display is shown in Figure 38.1. It is composed of 46 braille cells and

Figure 38.1 Braille display equipped with forty-six cells

connected to the computer via a USB cable, which also supplies power. These braille cells are controlled by the screen-reading software, but they can be used without any speech output. The braille display can show more information than speech output, such as text indentations. Text indentation is important when editing programming code, especially the code of python. Students understand the structure of a code by reading text indentations shown on the braille display.

The department also prepares the most unique piece of equipment at our university. It is a refreshable tactile graphic display called "DV-2," which is also made by KGS Corporation. In Japan, several research projects of tactile display had been conducted before DV-2 came to the market around 2004 and such projects continue even after it (Kobayashi & Watanabe, 2002; Shimada, Murase, Yamamoto, Uchida, Shimojo, & Shimizu, 2010). I think this phenomenon comes from the character of nationalities and language which has a graphical oriented background. Japanese tends to understand things through pictures. As a result, such a device was produced, and blind students can use it to learn the graphical part of lectures. Although we could buy the product, there are only five DV-2 at the university due to their high cost and we set them up mainly in the lecture room where students learn graphical programming. If students in another lecture room would like to use DV-2, one of the devices can be moved to that other lecture room. DV-2 is equipped with 1536 tactile pins, arranged in a grid of 46 by 32 pins, and the pins are placed at 2.4-mm intervals. This unique device can show the entire Windows desktop or window area of any software program individually. The resolution of the display is rough, though the displayed area for these tactile pins can be magnified up to 1:1, to acquire precise information. Using this tactile device, blind students can understand the alignment of components, e.g., graph expressions of Microsoft Excel like bar graphs, line graphs, pie charts, or text alignment of Microsoft Word by zooming up and down. There are several alignments such as "left," "right," "centered," and "justify." Screen-reading software explains the alignment information but cannot show how it is seen by sighted people, only by speech output. Tactile information complements such image information. Figure 38.2 shows that DV-2 displays a bar graph of Microsoft Excel.

The reaction speed of these 1536 pins is fast enough, the minimum refresh time of all pins is 0.1 sec. This allows students to touch these tactile pins and to feel an animation effect of PowerPoint slides or a GIF animation graphics on web pages. Teachers can conduct a variety of lectures by using this device. As mentioned above, this device is mainly used for graphical programming; thus, many graphical interactive programs have been developed by blind students.

Bone Conducted Headphones

In general, students who use screen-reading software use headphones or earphones to listen to the speech output. They might have a problem in a real lecture room, in that it is difficult to listen to the reading voice and explaining voice by a teacher in the room at the same time because the headphone covers their ears. To solve the problem, we prepare bone-conducted headphones for all computers in the lecture room. It allows students to listen to these two voices.

Educational Materials

All educational materials must be accessible for BLV students. We have translated all textbooks required in the lecture into braille and prepared several patterns of enlarged versions to fit various visual impairments. All students can use any of these materials before starting each lecture.

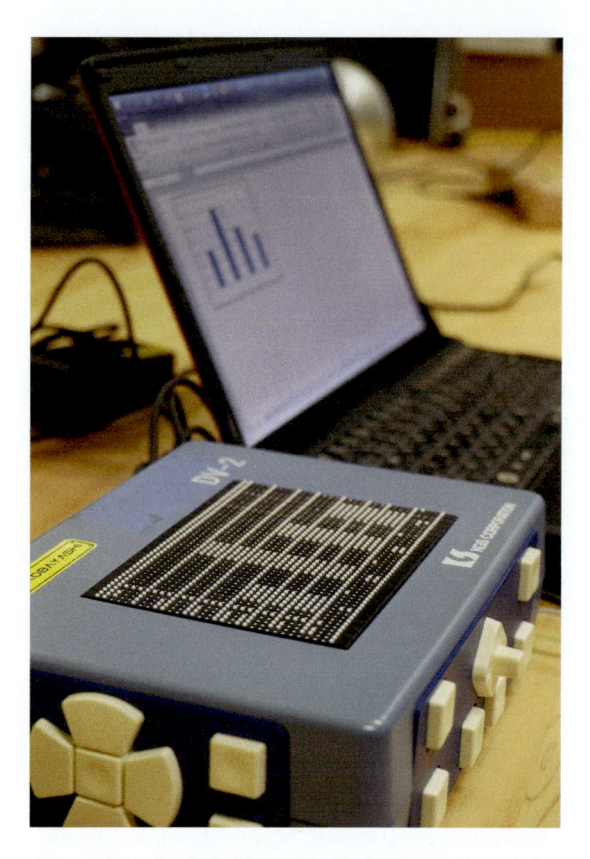

Figure 38.2 Refreshable tactile display, DV-2 shows a bar graph of Microsoft Excel

Braille Textbooks

Braille textbooks are of course important educational materials for blind students. They allow active reading and two-dimensional free access to information, which cannot be done through sound information of screen-reading software. In our department, all printed textbooks used in lectures are translated into braille. This translation is done by a special translation team in the support center of our university.

However, because braille textbooks are thick and heavy, they are inconvenient to carry. One normal printed book might have to be divided into five or more braille textbooks. To address this issue, we provide a borrowing system and prepare storage space in each lecture room. Students can take only one braille book for each lecture when it starts. After finishing the first book, they can borrow a new one and return the first one if they do not need it anymore. If they would like to keep it, they can store it in the storage space.

Digital Materials

Digital educational materials are also important resources not only for blind students but also for other low vision students. Several types of digital files are produced in the translating process of braille textbooks. At first, printed textbooks are scanned, and then pdf files are produced. After that, text format files are created by optical character recognition. The team then creates braille files from the text format files. Finally, these three types of digital files, pdf, text, and braille code files are available. The pdf files are suitable for magnifying and useful for low vision students. The text format files are valuable for screen-reader users. They can use them when they fulfill conditions that the publisher showed for educational use. In addition to these pdf and text files, we also can prepare Digital Accessible Information System (DAISY) format. However, the number of DAISY files is not so large because our students do not often use them these days.

Concerning the digital materials, I would like to mention the unique translation process from text format to braille format in Japan. In most alphabetic languages, there is a one-to-one relationship between each letter and each braille character and vice versa. Although there are grade-2 or grade-3 for braille systems to save spaces, basically it can be seamlessly converted from the original text to the braille text. The translation from alphabetic sentences to braille sentences is very simple and can be an automatic process using computer software. Translation from Japanese sentences into Japanese braille sentences, however, is quite complicated compared with the case in the alphabetical language country. Firstly, Japanese sentences have no spaces between each word. The translator program inserts spaces in appropriate positions, and this process is difficult solely with computer software. Professional translating staff must check all space positions in braille sentences. In addition, one Japanese character has several pronunciations depending on the context. Therefore, the translation process must involve finding the correct pronunciation. Because of these reasons, the translation from printed Japanese sentences to braille sentences is not reversible and it takes more cost.

Tactile Materials

Tactile materials are created using several methods in our department. One of the most popular methods is using a Braille embosser. It embosses small dots (Braille) onto thick paper. Most graphical pages in braille textbooks are made with the embosser. To make them, Japanese software called "EDEL" is used. Advantages of this method are its easiness to copy the material and its inexpensiveness. A disadvantage is that the tactile resolution is not high enough. Because lines are constructed with many dots, it is difficult to recognize connecting points and precise shapes of curves, etc.

The second method is using a swell touch paper. To make this tactile material, a drawing or a graphical expression in monochrome format is printed with a normal laser printer at first. Then, copy the printed sheet to a sheet of Swell Touch Paper using a copying machine and heat the swell paper with special heating equipment. After heating, this paper swells along specified black lines. Since this process is easy and fast, this method is used for making temporal tactile materials. The disadvantage is that it is not very durable, and is more fragile than embossed paper. The surface of the swelled lines might disappear from excessive touching.

The third method is using the brand-new tactile printer, EasyTactix. It can produce tactile material with much higher resolution and precise tactile information. Conventional swell touch paper absorbs thermal energy into the designated black lines, which are swelled. On the other hand, EasyTactix has a moving thermal head like an inkjet printer. Owing to the thermal head resolution and its structure, it produces tactile graphics that have a resolution of 300 dpi. The disadvantage of EasyTactix is that it takes a long time, approximately two minutes for one sheet as for now.

In addition to these two-dimensional tactile graphics or drawings, three-dimensional models are valuable for lectures these days. Recently, the three-dimensional printer has been closer to our life and the price of the printer became lower and lower. Utilizing these models as teaching material is a matter of course; teaching how to use the printer might be a part of the lecture for our BLV students. However, the level of accessibility of designing software is not high enough, and teaching how to design models and how to use the printer to blind students may be difficult. It should be solved in the future.

Support in Finding Jobs for Students

The final section of this chapter covers the topic of finding jobs for BLV students. In Japan, all students in higher educational institutes including universities start looking for jobs almost one year before graduation and fix a job about six months before graduation (Uosaki, 2014). The school year is from April to March, so they look for a job through the spring and summer, and there is a job offer ceremony held for each company on the 1st of October. Students must take part in only one ceremony, and it is a kind of contract. The main reason this custom still exists is the fact that most Japanese companies still offer lifetime employment. Many employees retire at the end of March, and the company must employ new graduates in April. To follow this custom, university students create their CVs and send them to many companies to acquire an opportunity for a job interview during the first semester of their fourth year, and after passing the competitive interview and examinations, they make an informal contract with one company before the ceremony in October. After all, they join the company without any gap year after their graduation.

To support this job-hunting activity, our department has a special system for the BLV students. The Japanese labor market has been gradually changed to be more acceptable for students with disabilities (Hasegawa, 2015), but some difficulties and prejudices remain. We conduct programs like teaching how to prepare outfits, have successful job interviews, write effective CVs are provided for students and various advice to students are prepared for the feedback. All materials of each program are fit for visual impairments.

The usual first step in finding a job involves students taking part in a joint job fair where many companies have booths to conduct job interviews. Students who take part in this event must wait in a queue in front of a booth, and after finishing an interview, they must wait again in another queue. Of course, our students also participate in such job fairs, which have the advantage of being able to contact many companies. However, searching for the end of a queue is difficult for students with severe visual impairment and it is difficult for them to show their ability to use a computer. To solve these problems, we invite job recruiters to interview soon-to-be graduates directly to our campus then ask the person to make a presentation about their company and conduct job interviews in one of our lecture rooms. Our students can then demonstrate how they can operate a computer using assistive technology such as a screen reader or braille display.

The percentage of employees with disabilities that a company must hire was 2.2% in 2020 and the government plans to increase this to 2.3% in 2021. This means that a company that hires 45.5 persons must hire one person with a disability. Because of this law, large companies want to hire persons with disabilities. The significant advantage of our department is that recruiters can meet at least ten impaired students who have computer and information technology skills. I believe this is another advantage of segregated education.

Summary

This chapter introduced how the Department of Computer Science at NTUT supports blind and low vision students. Although basic methods and materials are the same as in other countries, there are some difficulties due to unique cultural issues. Our department will continue to address such difficulties.

References

Hasegawa, T. (2015). Reasonable accommodation for persons with disabilities in Japan. *Japan Labor Review*, *12*(1), 21–37.

Japan Students Services Organization (JASSO). (2020). *The report of actual condition survey of supporting impaired students to study in fiscal year 2019*. Retrieved from JASSO website: https://www.jasso.go.jp/gakusei/tokubetsu_shien/chosa_kenkyu/chosa/__icsFiles/afieldfile/2020/04/02/report2019_0401.pdf

Kobayashi, M., & Watanabe, T. (2002). A tactile display system equipped with a pointing device: MIMIZU. *Computers Helping People with Special Needs. Lecture Notes in Computer Science*, *2398*, 527–534. Springer. https:// 10.1007/3-540-45491-8_100

Kochi System Development, Inc. (n.d.). *Screen reader: PC-Talker*. Retrieved From the Kochi System Development, Inc. website: https://www.aok-net.com/screenreader/

Mithout, A. (2016). Children with disabilities in the Japanese school system: A path toward social integration? *Contemporary Japan*, *28*(2), 165–184. https:// 10.1515/cj-2016-0009

National University Corporation Tsukuba University of Technology (NTUT). (2019). *Outline of Tsukuba University of Technology 2019–2020*.

NVDA Japanese Team. (n.d.). *NVDA Japanese Version*. Retrieved From the NVDA Japanese Team website: https://www.nvda.jp/

Ohnuma, N. (2005). The impact Tsukuba College of Technology made on Japanese Higher Special Education and the role in Future. *TCT Education of Disabilities*, *4*(1), 1–4.

Shimada, S., Murase, H., Yamamoto, S., Uchida, Y., Shimojo, M., & Shimizu, Y. (2010). Development of directly manipulable tactile graphic system with audio support function. *Computers Helping People with Special Needs. Lecture Notes in Computer Science*, *6180*, Springer, 451–458. https:// 10.1007/978-3-642-14100-3_68

Stefik, M. A., Hundhausen, C., & Smith, D. (2011). On the design of an educational infrastructure for the blind and visually impaired in computer science, *Proceedings of the 42nd ACM technical symposium on Computer science education*, 571–576. https:// 10.1145/1953163.1953323

Uosaki, N. (2014). Study on how career support for international students could be enhanced. *Departmental Bulletin Paper of Osaka University*, *18*, 11–21. https:// 10.18910/50833

39
PERSONS WITH CEREBRAL PALSY AND WORKFORCE PARTICIPATION

*Shanti Raghavan and Jeeja Ghosh**

Introduction

Ashwin has been working for over ten years in the open labor market in different IT companies and supports his family with the salary he earns. He recently progressed in his career by becoming a manager. Ashwin is a person with cerebral palsy, travels many kilometers to work and uses a powered wheelchair for his mobility. Though his team understands his speech, it takes effort for a newcomer to understand the same. He needs support for his personal needs. Ashwin is part of a growing number of persons with disability, especially cerebral palsy, who are economically independent and their inclusion in mainstream society is paving the way for many more persons with disability to join the workforce.

Challenges Due to the Complex Nature of Cerebral Palsy

Economic independence is one of the quintessential elements in shaping the personality and personhood of any individual. Means of livelihood, however, still remain an opaque area for persons with disabilities. The barriers to enter into the realm of sustainable means of livelihood are plenty for persons with disabilities. The foremost impediment lies in their opportunity to receive education and training. This is reflected in the report of the National Sample Survey (NSS) of 2018. The report states that 2.2% of India's population consists of persons with disabilities. The data points out that only 19.3% of the disabled population received higher education (high secondary and above). The employment among persons with disabilities is low – with the majority of them engaged in the unorganized sector. According to the report:

- Among persons with disabilities of age 15 years and above, Labour Force Participation Rate in usual status was 23.8%.
- Among persons with disabilities of age 15 years and above, Worker Population Ratio in usual status was 22.8%.
- Among persons with disabilities of age 15 years and above, Unemployment Rate in usual status was 4.2%.

---

* jeeja.ankur@gmail.com

The interesting aspect of disability is its heterogeneous profile. Each disability group is characterized by its unique sets of limitations and more importantly within the same impairment groups, the limitations can vary. Cerebral palsy (CP) is a group of disorders that affect movement and muscle tone or posture. It's caused by damage that occurs to the immature brain as it develops, most often before or during birth. Cerebral palsy's effect on function varies greatly. Some affected people can walk; others need assistance. Some people show normal or near-normal intellect, but others have intellectual disabilities. Epilepsy, blindness, or deafness also might be present

Economic independence and social integration are themes that rank highly among people with CP as long-term objectives for rehabilitation. Employment is very often the way in which individuals define themselves in society and is an important means of participating in society. As the life expectancy and functional capacity of people with Cerebral Palsy increases, so does the need for inclusion in the workforce.

CP is a complex condition usually affecting multiple body functions, which are traditionally classified according to the motor symptoms type and disorder localization. According to the symptom type it is divided into spastic, athetoid, and atastic, and according to the localization into hemiplegia, diplegia, and tetraplegia (quadriplegia). CP is primarily associated with a wide range of motor disorders, which in some cases significantly disrupt everyday life activities.

Difficulties in the domain of speech-language development, associated with poor muscle control and intellectual disability additionally aggravate adaptive functioning and can be found in one- to two-thirds of persons with CP. Social participation of people with CP depends on the severity of motor disorders and intellectual abilities, as well as on the psychosocial capacity of the environment – family and school, public services, socio-economic background, etc.

Many young people with CP have difficulties in achieving full independence in various spheres of life. Although people with CP have the right to education, work, economic independence, and social integration, discrimination and employment availability represent fundamental restrictive factors in the labour market. People with CP in many instances are dependent on caregiver support as they have difficulties in achieving self-dependence in various spheres of life.

Several studies dealing with the education and employment of young people with CP (19-26 years of age) in developed countries (U.S.A., Finland, Sweden) indicate that between 24% to 50% of people with CP are full-time employees, while a certain number of them have flexible employment or are employed in a sheltered workshop. (Andersson & Mattsson, 2001; Kokkonen et al., 1991; Murphy, Molnar & Lankasky, 2000; O'Grady, Crain & Kohn, 1995; Sestic et al., 2012). As generally seen, people with mild degrees of cerebral palsy have greater chances of being inducted into the workforce. In some cases, people with CP may have difficulties in social interaction, mostly as an outcome of limited exposure. Social interaction is a critical aspect of employability and may act as an additional impediment in the work environment.

The significant source of information on obstacles in employment and strategies to overcome them is the experience of people with CP, which has identified a wide spectrum of barriers to obtaining and retaining employment. Some of them are limited abilities with regard to workplace requirements, lack of education and preparedness for the job, architectural barriers, negative attitudes, transportation problems, and technological and communication restrictions. Some people with CP have uncoordinated movements of limbs and body jerks. These tend to further alienate their social participation as they are commonly associated with the manifestation of behavioral or psychosocial disorders.

People with CP sometimes may have uncontrolled drooling due to weak muscle coordination, thus posing a socially awkward situation and limiting social interactions. Impairments in speech may also lead to the social isolation of persons with CP. People with speech impairment, especially those using augmentative and alternative modes of communication (AAC) often become silent listeners and mere spectators with few opportunities of expressing their views. Thus, the above discussion can be interpreted that the complex nature of impairments tends to place persons with CP in a more vulnerable position, hindering their social and economic inclusion leading to subsequently leading to further isolation.

It took Enable India about a year to find the ideal job for Sundar, a person with cerebral palsy who had done his MCA. He was given the job of a software tester in a company where his limited hand mobility would not be a barrier. Instead, his intellect and analytical capability would be used well by the company. Post-employment, Sundar developed vision impairment and was not able to learn the workplace solutions to function effectively in his job with his vision issues. He eventually resigned from the job. The purpose of this article is to discuss the effect of employability training which has enabled persons with disability, especially persons with cerebral palsy, to participate in the workforce just like anybody else.

Theoretical Underpinnings

Before entering into the actual discussion on the modalities of the employability training it is perhaps worthwhile to focus our attention on the core areas the training envisages addressing. The conceptual frameworks discussed in this section will serve as a baseline for analyzing the data. It is a general trend that society has low expectations of persons with disabilities. This becomes more pronounced with the severity of the disability (people with high support needs). Family and society usually garner low expectations regarding the abilities of disabled people. This is especially relevant in the Indian context where people with disabilities are viewed as objects of charity – some in need of lifelong care and protection. Thus, there are in general low expectations from a child or an adult with a disability.

Internalized Oppression

> I was supposed to just find a job. At that point, I thought, even if I find a job where I don't have to work hard, my family is going to be happy only. Why go for training, or get a big, difficult job? It would not make a difference.
> – Govind (person with a physical disability)

The above quote from a study conducted by Enable India reflects on the diminished estimation of one's abilities. This can be interpreted in the light of the psycho-emotional aspects of disability. Initially coined by the feminist writer, Carol Thomas, who argued that the social model of disability greatly undermines the personal experience of disability by putting the emphasis solely on the materialistic and environmental agencies in the disabling society (Thomas, 1999). In her opinion, this is the psychological aspect of disability oppression or disablism. According to her, disablism defines disability as "a form of social oppression involving the social imposition of restrictions of activity on people with impairments and the socially engendered undermining of their psycho-emotional well-being". Thus, for Thomas "the personal is political". (Thomas)

This social relational definition of disability, hence, takes into account the external and the internal aspects of disability oppression (Reeve, 2006). Reeve contends that this dialectical relationship of social oppression due to disability has helped illuminate the economic and social disadvantages disabled people confront. Therefore, an extended social relational definition of disability includes both barriers "out there" and those that operate "in here". The "out there"/public social forces do not exist in isolation from the "in here"/private forces – the personal is political – of disability oppression. Both the "out there" and "in here" dimensions of disability oppression are enveloped by the "cultural representations and disabling images" in society about people with disabilities. The dialectic between the internal and external disabling mechanisms has resulted in internalized oppression by people with disabilities. Thus, Govind's response towards getting "a job" can be enumerated as a consequence of his internalized oppression that puts a limit on his expectation of himself which in turn may act as a barrier towards striving to do better in life.

Self-efficacy

Another conceptual framework that is potentially critical while engaging with the employability of persons with disabilities is self-efficacy, also intrinsically linked to internalized oppression and self-concept. Self-efficacy refers to an individual's belief in his or her capacity to execute behaviors necessary to produce specific performance attainments (Bandura, 1977, 1986, 1997). Self-efficacy reflects confidence in the ability to exert control over one's own motivation, behavior, and social environment. These cognitive self-evaluations influence all manner of human experience, including the goals for which people strive, the amount of energy expended towards goal achievement, and the likelihood of attaining particular levels of behavioral performance.

On a similar plain, self-concept represents the subjective assessment serving as a basis for personal identity formation and based on personal and social experience, i.e., explicit and implicit learning. It is formed on the basis of judgment, perceptions, and emotions people have of themselves and their positions related to others. Thus, it is a subjective idea, the development of which is under the considerable influence of the signals coming from the environment. The process of self-picture development begins in childhood, continues throughout life, and crucially influences one's behavior. According to the social-cognitive theory (Bandura, 1991), the behavior is conditioned by a compound, interactive relationship between the belief of possessing, and the real presence of personal abilities (motivation, self-regulation, self-efficacy) on one side, and social reactions to which a person is subjected, on the other. The theory of self-efficacy can be analyzed through the lenses of Govind's example once more. In his case, his siblings were employed in companies. However, he was content with a job in a telephone stand and did not feel the need or take the challenge to look for better options.

Another example can be cited in the same study by Enable India. As Anand, a person with a physical disability says: *"My family is very supportive ... but, they want me to stay at home. They want to be able to do everything for me, so I don't have to work."* This low expectation from the family in turn is likely to have a ripple effect on the self-motivation of persons with disabilities and limit their chances to succeed in the arena of employment as well as in other facets of life.

Employability Training – How Was It Conceived?

Enable India was founded in 1999 for the economic independence and dignity of persons with disability. In the early years, it became very clear that neither the person with a disability nor the family was ready for the hardship required in getting ready for a job or the rigors of performing and retaining in a job. Initially, it was puzzling that the same disabled person (and families) who were desperate for a job were reluctant to go for almost any job. Every aspect of the job from the travel, the responsibility, the working hours, shift, and salary was turned into an excuse on why it was not possible. It slowly dawned on the practitioners at Enable India that the family and person with a disability were very often hoping for a job on charitable grounds. There were no expectations that the disabled person will and can perform the job successfully. The fundamental values of Enable India are the belief in the potential of every person and what they can offer to the company and nation. This unshakeable belief in the change-making capacity of a person with a disability led to action-based research with candidates via employability training. Some of the observations regarding candidates with a disability were the tendency to give up easily, excuses given due to disability, social awkwardness, inability to have small talk, very little exposure and experience, a theoretical understanding of the job, and more. Enable India adopted a human-centered design approach which led to insights into understanding the real problem underpinning the observations. One significant insight was the lack of expectation by self and family.

"What do I do all day? I watch TV" – a person with a mild disability from a poor family where each household member is working hard to earn a living. *"I am not expected to earn money for my family. My brothers are reminded on a daily basis of their duty to our parents but nothing is expected from me."*

This led to the person with a disability never having had much responsibility or done many chores at home and consequently not having had much exposure or a range of experiences out in the world. This had a ripple effect on the disabled person never getting constructive criticism or feedback while doing chores and not having experienced failure in doing a task wrongly and then learning to do it right. The lack of expectation also led to the disabled person never taking ownership of their life and hence not learning to solve problems posed by the barriers due to disability or otherwise. The lack of self-efficacy posed a significant barrier to employment and this "conditioning" was hard-baked into the individual.

> Today is the first time I have chosen the thing that I want to have. I have never done this at home with my family. Usually, they will give me something of their choice, they have never asked me
>
> > Rachna*, a person with a disability after she was asked by the trainer at Enable India what her preference was regarding juices when they were at the juice shop

Very often such individuals have never made a decision for themselves or expressed their choices or views. This contributes negatively to the self-picture development of self, in turn, decreasing self-expectations and self-efficacy! When such a person wants to get a job, the chances of success are near nil given the complete lack of exposure and lack of decision making on a daily basis

> I was doing a job for some months. I had some problems with the job and I left the job. I am at home now.
> I had to travel far away for my job. So, I left my job.
> My parents do not want me to work the second shift where I had to work from 2 pm to midnight. Hence, I left my job. Now I am without a job.

The second significant insight was that even if the person and family had reasonable expectations and hence lesser challenges of self-efficacy being evident, the everyday barriers and challenges posed by the disability, environment and society and the labor market erode into the self-confidence and willpower of the person and at some point, the person with disability and family just give up and stop doing actions leading to gainful employment.

The above two insights led to the realization that the person with a disability will need to have better self-expectation and cultivate a larger vision for himself or herself with the right self-development tools. The vision will drive the person with a disability to overcome everyday barriers. The self-development tools will enable the sustainability of the vision. The self-expectation will ensure that the person with a disability will build their problem-solving ability which will hold him or her in good stead over the years where challenges will abound not only in the workplace but in their personal life. This gave rise to the principle of "vision and attitude" as a significant component in the development of a person with a disability.

The third insight was that in the process of overcoming everyday barriers and challenges, the family and the person with a disability don't realize what a long way they have come and what they have achieved. Rather than focusing on what has worked (and using the behavior of appreciative inquiry), they tend to see what has not happened and stop in their journey of finding solutions from a disability point of view.

> Because I have to use a crutch, every morning my family heats the water in the kitchen and then carries the bucket of hot water to the bathroom for me
>
> *Rashid*, a person with disability.*

*anonymous

If Rashid can't do daily activities and has never found solutions or workarounds where he can work on his own, this will permeate into his work environment where his inabilities will get amplified and he will have "excuses" on why he can't do something. Work environments are tough places where work needs to get done.

> At Enable India, when I was doing my internship, I was given feedback that you are not taking notes. How can we believe that you will remember everything? That's when I thought of using a recorder. At every stage, the expectation or question pushed me to find solutions. It took three years to find a job but I have grown in my career and am a leader in my company
>
> *a person with a severe disability who has no motor function except her finger. She uses joystick and speech recognition to work on the computer*

This led to the insight into disability and to the second principle in the employability framework called "disability specific skills" which enable the person with disability to work on disability related issues that affect their integration into the open labor market or any kind of livelihoods.

The disability specific skills ensure that the person with disability is able to see themselves as equals to others. When they are able to relate to persons without disabilities, their self-image changes. When they realize that every person has abilities and inabilities and that every person has had a journey in their life to work on the barriers and overcome their limitations or inabilities. When a person with a disability learns to talk about their journey, they are able to make themselves and others comfortable with their disability.

A fundamental insight is that the disabled person who works on building their "includability" competency and the competency of "includability" in others is the most successful in the workplace.

> Though I have done my MBA from the premier institute in the country (Indian Institute of Management) with good results, it took me time to get a job. With Enable India's help, I used the peer sensitization module to make my colleagues feel comfortable with me. They understood how I feel about my disability, I shared funny

things that have happened due to my disability, what solutions I use, and understood my journey to overcome my challenges. Today, they laugh, yell, shout, oppose, fight, enjoy and do normal things with me which usually people never did before! The module just helped normalize differences!

> Sanat*, a person with vision impairment, talking
> about the disability-specific skill he developed to make
> others comfortable with him and made them more
> includable with him

Includability is a competency framework developed by Enable India which helps a manager or person maximize value from all people (especially persons with disability). The framework helps normalize differences and work on changing expectations by pushing the boundary of expectations and using the abilities of people and co-creating solutions for the challenges. The framework enables people to create a level playing field for people with diverse backgrounds.

Another insight was that educational qualifications do not automatically translate to efficacy in the job due to the low exposure and experience, not knowing what is needed in a job or being comfortable working with targets and getting performance feedback. This is coupled with the problem of many employers who are hesitant to give performance feedback to a person with a disability. Hence the principle of "Resilient job skills" addresses these issues.

When a multinational company had 30 positions (contract hiring) during the recession of 2008, Enable India fielded 14 deaf candidates. All of them got selected. After some months, the deaf employees were sharing their experiences on how they were overachieving their targets. They mentioned that the job simulations of account assistants, HR executives, and more conditioned them to understand domain requirements, follow work procedures, and find efficient techniques of working where they learned how to increase their productivity. This helped them to outperform their hearing counterparts who, unfortunately, did not have the benefit of working on such simulations. The contract work of two years finished earlier thanks to their productivity. Many of the deaf were taken on permanent rolls of the company.

Another insight gained is regarding workplace readiness for the person with a disability. A workplace is a place not only where a person has to perform their job but it is a place where each person has to manage perceptions of others, learn to bond with a team, learn to work within the hierarchy and company rules, learn how to develop a career, learn to develop a network and be social and so on.

> He just sits at his desk and stares at space
>
> a sighted colleague, who did not understand that
> his visually impaired colleague was working on the
> computer using a screen-reader and hence did not need
> to look at the screen.

As shown in the above example, if the visually impaired person were to sit like the other colleagues and have a similar posture and look towards his or her screen, the wrong perception can be avoided. Hence workplace readiness includes managing perceptions, ensuring team bonding, and being one with the team

> She kept SMS-ing me because I had interviewed her. I am not her team leader or manager
>
> a senior manager, of a deaf woman who did not
> realize the hierarchy of her team.

As shown in the above example, if the concept of team hierarchy had been known to the deaf person, this issue could have been avoided. With limited exposure or communication persons with disability (in this case deaf persons) will have to overcompensate and learn what persons without disabilities (hearing persons) learn through osmosis of hearing their family and friends talk of office issues and so on.

> There are persons with disabilities in our company and we find many of them are not ambitious to grow. Some of them are interested but do not network or socialize and keep to themselves. Due to this they rarely find growth opportunities. There are others who are quite satisfied where they are and have been in the same job for years. Unfortunately, with dynamic work environments, they cannot be static in their job since many jobs are getting cut, or changing or many roles are combined and the company always expects you to do more every day
>
> *HR manager of an MNC company which has a significant number of disabled and a very inclusive culture.*

Workplace readiness is a factor of learning on the job, networking and finding the next opportunity by socializing. These are hard skills for a person with a disability who has the additional responsibility of understanding the job more to know if there are barriers posed by his disability that have to be overcome.

Components of the Employability Frameworks & Process of Training

The insights over the years led to the employability framework of Enable India which has four guiding principles and 15 practices. The framework can be applied via various formats. Formats such as employability training in batches are done onsite in durations ranging from 45 days to three months or more depending on the disability or batch. Other shorter formats serve as vehicles of awareness for the person with a disability on specific principles and practices which are needed for them to succeed in the workplace. More importantly, the format where the candidate who cannot come for training can evaluate themselves with Enable India's help on the principles and see what applies to them and then develop their path to progress. This enables them to be in their own local area and work on their path at their own pace. This increasingly is a model which will enable reaching a lot of persons with disability across geographies.

The insights over the years gathered while sensitizing, training, coaching, and mentoring company leaders, employees, parents and other stakeholders are of equal importance. It gave rise to the includability framework which enables stakeholders including persons with disability to maximize value. The framework has three principles and six practices.

Framework with Three Principles and Six Practices

Workforce Participation of Persons with Cerebral Palsy

Among all the disabilities that Enable India works with, there are some unique challenges for persons with cerebral palsy. It starts with the first impression that people get due to the unusual gait in walking or their posture in the wheelchair, the uncontrollable or jerky movements of the head or hands, the voice modulation which can appear different than the adult voice modulation. Hence apart from the insights gained on what it takes to make a person with a disability truly ready for mainstream, there are specific learnings on what needs special focus for a person with cerebral palsy.

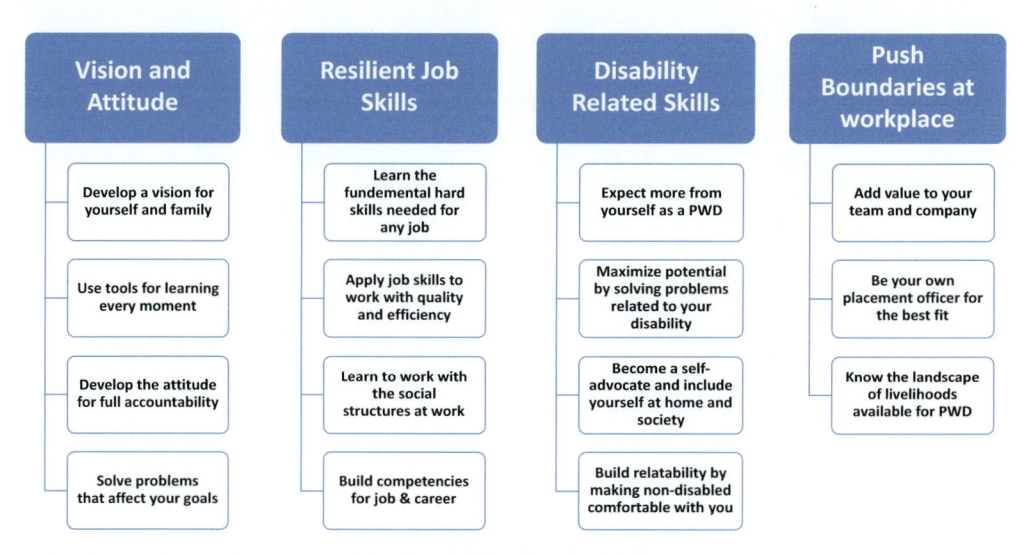

Figure 39.1 (Enable India, 2016) Employability Framework

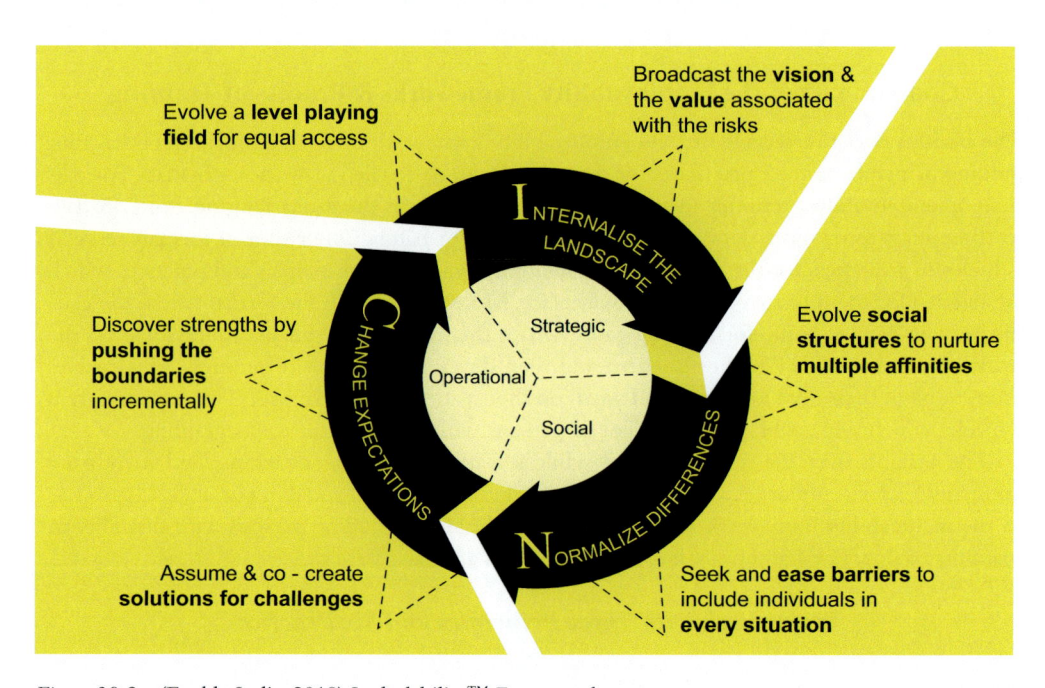

Figure 39.2 (Enable India, 2018) Includability™ Framework

It had been four years since I returned to India at the time and I was not very confident about interacting with people here. My social life was very limited in my hometown. This has impacted my self-confidence a lot. The training at Enable India reinforced my social skills and my confidence in making friends. This led to increasing self-belief when I started working as well that I have good interpersonal skills required for working along with others and maintaining a cordial working relationship.

Shwetha, a person with cerebral palsy.

The focus on social interaction, integration, and exposure is one of the most critical components, especially for a person with cerebral palsy. The training at Enable India does not teach social skills but treats people with disability as adults and provides accelerated opportunities to develop social skills via different project work, volunteer work, and more. More importantly, enables them to develop their social capital.

> I feel I was not ready to face life with confidence. In short, I was an introvert. Definitely, I am not someone who mingles with people around me easily. It was a feel-good factor undergoing employability training. Started talking to people, paying visits to the corporates, Assistive technology demos, interactions. It was all fun.
>
> *Pratap, a person with cerebral palsy, who has had a career across multinational banks in finance roles.*

Each of these time-bound activities to be done in a group where the candidates have to interact with the external world helps them to face their fears, and challenges and develops their ability to solve problems with respect to social skills in a real-time environment. The time-bound nature, coupled with the challenge and interest of reaching the goal of the project, especially the community project, enables candidates to accelerate their growth in social skills and problem-solving, leading to greater self-confidence and self-efficacy.

Some years ago, we had a collaborative internship with a multinational for a batch of 10 candidates with profound disabilities including cerebral palsy. Only candidates with more than severe disability with mobility, speech, and more were chosen. As part of the internship, the candidates did community service. One candidate spread awareness regarding accessibility while others gave tuition to kids and one helped their neighbours to get daily groceries from the shop. The community project requires candidates to do any community service of their liking which also increases their social capital in society.

> Personally, understanding and finally accepting my disability was a huge outcome of the training. This changed the way I spoke about myself to myself and others. It changed how I talked about myself in my resume
>
> *Shwetha, a person with cerebral palsy, speaking about the transformation after the employability training which garnered her a job at a multinational bank.*

Across all persons with cerebral palsy, the development of self-confidence was the number one impact of the training. This is also a testament to the includability of the trainer as well who has learned to relate to a person with cerebral palsy and sees the "person" and gives responsibilities during the training, targets, performance feedback, and more as part of the training.

> When Pratap was the IT manager in our training, his responsibility was to help the trainer to get the equipment ready such as connecting the laptop charger to the power supply, connecting laptop to the projector, and so on. I remember distinctly that I purposely moved away when he was helping me so that he had the "space" and "time" to do this activity. Due to his jerky hands, the tendency of anybody is to either help

him or stare at him or not give him time to do the activity or feel sorry for him. My moving away sends a powerful signal that 'I expect you that will do It'

Employability Trainer of Prathap

No Rocket Science

In the course of this essay, concepts like self-efficacy and internalized oppression have been discussed at some length as also the role of employability training in addressing these gaps and being the preparatory ground for inclusion, particularly in the arena of employment. However, in the way of drawing a conclusion to the chapter we want to emphasize that employability training is not rocket science. It involves simple steps which can be reinforced within the family to enhance the self-efficacy and confidence of persons with disabilities. Hence in the concluding section, we would like to highlight strategies that can be easily adopted in the family and woven into the process of socialization and discipline. What does this imply? As discussed earlier low expectations from the family play a critical role in developing the self-image of persons with disabilities. Thus, one can rightly ask "what needs to be the parenting style for children with disabilities?" A straight answer is to treat them in a similar way as you would treat your non-disabled children. This may sound like an absurd proposition for many parents and families and quite rightly so. Here lies the scope of innovative thinking. The first major task involves assessing your child. What does this imply? This calls for close observation of the child's strengths and weaknesses. This would help the parents to focus on the positive aspects which would in turn help in raising the confidence of the child. What do we mean by this – say the child has limitations in hand functioning then look for alternatives to identify the better hand. Insist the child uses that hand in activities of daily living. Alternatively, observe if the child is more proficient in using his/her feet to do the task. The behavior science of Appreciative Inquiry says that "whatever you focus on grows", and hence the skill of focusing on the strengths of the child will automatically make that strength grow. Some basic tips if kept in mind could be potential catalysts in enhancing this process. These are; Acceptance of disability: This is a critical area on the part of the parents as well as the child. Learning to accept the disability of the child by parents and family members is a major step forward toward building the self-image of the disabled child. This also involves accepting limitations and embracing strengths.

a. **Finding solutions:** This is perhaps the crux that touches the core aspect of disability inclusion. The art of innovating solutions is to perform any activity which a person with a disability otherwise finds difficulty in carrying out. An example of this would be someone who has difficulties in using any of his/her limbs and uses a head-pointer to operate the computer.
b. **Accepting positive criticism and feedback:** This if followed rigorously during the initial stages of socialization both by the parents and schools can be considered the foundation of the employability training. This teaches the person to make constructive use of the feedback to improve performance instead of holding this feedback negatively.
c. **Building relationships:** This is perhaps a grey area for many persons with disabilities especially those with Cerebral Palsy with their extra challenges in communication and social interaction. Establishing workable relationships is once again an important aspect of employability. Similarly, if initiated in the family it has better scope to be reinforced through the employability training.

Today, the above traits for parents have been summed up in the competency of includability. Hence, the parent needs to consciously develop their knowledge, skill, and attitude to get the best out of their child.

One might rightly ask why we chose to introduce these attributes to self-development in the concluding section. But, if one takes a closer look at the earlier discussion on employability, no new concepts were actually introduced in this section. The concluding section rather highlights that actually the employability training (or whatever nomenclature one chooses to give it) needs to begin much earlier in life and is a part of the socialization process, which is likely to address issues like self-efficacy and internalized oppression. This would automatically reduce the responsibilities of the vocational training centers who can now focus more on job related skills if the foundation of the employability training is already laid.

References

Bandura, A. (1977, 1986, 1987). https://www.apa.org/pi/aids/resources/education/self-efficacy

Bandura, A. (1991). Social cognitive theory of self-regulation. *Organizational Behavior and Human Decision Processes, 50*(2), 248–287. https://doi.org/10.1016/0749-5978(91)90022-L

Enable India (2016), Employability Framework

Enable India (2018), Includability™ Framework

Marina, S. R., Milica, G., & Milanovic, D. B. (2012). Problems of Employment and Job Accommodation for persons with Cerebral Palsy, University of Belgrade - Faculty of Special Education and Rehabilitation. *Serbia*. 256–257. https://www.researchgate.net/publication/269130748_Problems_of_employment_and_job_accommodation_of_persons_with_cerebral_palsy

Mission 1000. https://www.enableacademy.org/Mission1000/

National Sample Survey, 76th Round, July-December (2018). Government of India, Ministry of Statistics and Programme Implementation, Statement-35, Persons with Disabilities in India. http://mospi.nic.in/sites/default/files/publication_reports/Report_583_Final_0.pdf

Reeve, D. (2006). Towards a psychology of disability: The emotional effects of living in a disabling society, in D. Goodley, & R. Lawthom (eds) *Disability and Psychology: Critical Introductions and Reflections*. London: Palgrave, 94–107.

Samrudhi, S. (2016). *Great Expectations: Impact of Expectations on Persons with Disabilities*. Enable India Publications, 4–40.

Svelana, K., Gordana, O., & Bojan, D. (2012). Self Esteem of Individuals with Cerebral Palsy, University of Belgrade - Faculty of Special Education and Rehabilitation, Siberia, 187–189. https://www.researchgate.net/publication/268585768_Self-esteem_of_individuals_with_cerebral_palsy

Thomas, C, T. (1999). Female Forms: experiencing and understanding disability, 16–17.

40
INCLUSION OF INDIVIDUALS WITH DISABILITIES IN VOCATIONAL TRAINING IN SOUTH AFRICA?

*Refilwe Elizabeth Morwane**

Introduction

The literature highlights vocational training as a predictor of the successful employment of persons with disabilities (Lindsay et al., 2015; Wehman et al., 2015). Vocational training provides an opportunity for persons with disabilities to be work-ready (Pereira et al., 2016). Furthermore, vocational training programmes provide training in job-related skills, enhance independence, and are also linked to improved well-being (Engelbrecht et al., 2017). In various countries, vocational training has been utilised as a tool for economic growth and independence for unemployed youth with or without disabilities (ILO, 2013).

Persons with disabilities in low- and middle-income countries experience challenges in accessing education as well as skills training. This population is likely to be excluded from school, training opportunities, or participating in employment (Mitra and Sambamoorthi, 2014). Many leave school with limited education and limited employable work-related skills (Tripney et al., 2019; Sefotho et al., 2019). Given the importance of education and skills to enable economic participation, the economic inactivity of individuals with disabilities places them at risk of living in poverty (Banks et al., 2017; Groce et al., 2011).

It is estimated that there are approximately 3 million people living with some form of disability in South Africa. This population has been found to be amongst the poorest in the country (Visagie et al., 2017). More particularly individuals with disabilities who live in rural communities where disability prevalence rates are higher (Loeb et al., 2008; Saloojee et al., 2007). Although unemployment rates overall are at an all-time high in South Africa (32.6%), numbers are higher for individuals with disabilities (Statistics South Africa, 2021). No exact statistics exist; however, unemployment rates are estimated to be 80–90% (Black & de Matos-Ala, 2016). The estimates are supported by the latest Commission for Employment Equity (CEE) (2019-2020). The report indicates a representation of only 0.9% of individuals with disabilities in competitive employment (SA DoL, 2020).

The South African government is committed to improving the lives of individuals with disabilities by facilitating participation in education, training, and employment activities. This

* refilwe.morwane@wits.ac.za

is seen in its adoption of international legislation and initiatives such as the United Nations Conventions on the Rights of Persons with Disabilities (United Nations, 2006), the Sustainable Development Goals (United Nations, 2016), and the African Decade of Persons with Disabilities (2009-2019) (African Union, 2012). Provisions have thus been made with regard to legislation and policy in South Africa on the vocational training programmes of learners with disabilities. The realisation of inclusive vocational training programmes for persons with disabilities is far from being realised in South Africa.

Currently, various vocational training models are available in South Africa; however, most are exclusionary of individuals with disabilities (Lorenzo & Cramm, 2012; Lorenzo, van Niekerk & Mdlokolo, 2007). This is due to access barriers that exist, related to attitudinal barriers, inaccessible physical spaces, inaccessible learning material, and unavailability of skilled trainers and teachers (Ntombela, 2019; SA DoL, 2015; ILO, 2013). Access to vocational training opportunities is particularly challenging for individuals with disabilities in rural and remote areas (Morwane et al., 2021; Tripney et al., 2019). There are limited studies that provide data on the vocational training of individuals with disabilities in South Africa (Soeker, 2020; Soeker et al., 2018; Van Niekerk et al., 2011). In this chapter, four types of vocational training programmes available in South Africa are discussed and barriers in accessing these programmes by individuals with disabilities are highlighted.

Literature Review

Children with disabilities in South Africa, compared to their peers, tend to start their schooling at an older age (Philpott & McLaren, 2011). A report by the Department of Education (DoE) indicated that approximately over half a million children with disabilities were not in school, 67% of which included children with disabilities. Saloojee et al. (2007) explored the education and health needs of 156 children with disabilities from a township in the Gauteng Province. They found that 50% of the children were not in school, and only 30% of the children were receiving the required intervention (that is, speech-language therapy, occupational therapy, and physiotherapy). Even more concerning, assistive technology required by the children such as wheelchairs were not allocated. The lack of assistive technology negatively impacted the children's functioning, and, ultimately, their participation. Due to prevailing negative beliefs regarding disability, a large proportion of persons with disabilities have not completed their schooling or have never been in school, resulting in most being illiterate or semi-literate (Maart et al., 2019). Similarly, the 2014 Census report indicated that 23.8% had no formal education, 24.6% had some primary education, while only 5.3% had attained higher education (Statistics SA, 2014). The lack of education thus adversely impacts accessing education, training, and employment opportunities.

In addition to many challenges in accessing education in South Africa, basic education for children with disabilities is primarily of poor quality with most public special schools in a dire state (Human Rights Watch, 2015). The quality of education for the population with a disability is thus inadequate and of poor quality (DSD, DWCPD & UNICEF, 2012). In an effort to support the inclusion of persons with disabilities in education, the South African government introduced White Paper 6 on inclusive education in 2001 (SA DoE, 2001). This was in response to the number of children with disabilities, estimated to be 280,000, who were at the time not in school (Armstrong et al., 2011). The main goal was therefore to move towards an inclusive education and training system free of barriers to learning and thus accommodative of all learners with special learning needs (Engelbrecht et al., 2016).

The South African government following global trends envisioned a move from segregated school systems (that is special schools vs. mainstream schools) to an inclusive schooling system where all learners despite the presence or absence of disability can be accommodated (Donohue & Bornman, 2014). There were however notable barriers to achieving inclusive education such as poor knowledge in the implementation of inclusive education, lack of teacher support, insufficient facilities and resources such as assistive technologies and adapted curriculum (Nel et al., 2016; Swart et al., 2002). Almost three decades after democracy, children with disabilities are still in 'segregated' schools with the available full-service schools which are supposed to be inclusive of children with disabilities, ill-resourced with teachers lacking the skills and knowledge to educate learners, particularly those with disabilities (Bornman, 2017; Mophosho & Dada, 2015). A negative consequence of the lack of quality education is the lack of advancement of persons with disabilities to post-primary and higher education. A report from the Department of Higher Education (2014) indicated that quite a small number of students, approximately 1% of the total enrolment in 22 out of 26 public universities accounted for students with disabilities. Ramaahlo, Tönsing, and Bornman (2018) explored policies of tier 1 research-intensive universities to determine their role in facilitating the admission of students with disabilities. The lack of inclusiveness in terms of accessibility, availability, adaptability, and affordability contributes to the lack of access to these institutions of higher learning (Ramaahlo et al., 2018).

Legal Framework Related to Vocational Training in South Africa

The following legislation and policies aim to facilitate the economic participation of persons with disabilities in South Africa.

White Paper on the Rights of Persons with Disabilities

The White Paper on the Rights of Persons with Disabilities (WPRPD) (Department of Social Development, 2015) advocates for the removal of discriminatory barriers to accessing education (which includes vocational education), health services, and employment opportunities. The WPRPD was developed from an integration of the National Disability Strategy of 1997, obligations outlined in the CRPD (United Nations, 2006), provision of the Continental Plan of Action for the African Decade of Persons with Disabilities (2009-2019), and the South African legislation and policy frameworks, as well as the National Development Plan 2030. It is envisioned the WPRPD will be escalated to fulfill domestication of the CRPD. As it stands to date, the WPRPD is not enforceable by law and the South African government cannot be held accountable for the lack of implementation of the goals outlined.

White Paper on Post-school Education and Training (DHET, 2013)

The Department of Higher Education and Training (DHET) introduced the National Plan for Post-School Education and Training, which outlined its vision for Continuing Education and Training, Technical and Vocational Education, and Training (TVET), and Higher Education at universities. The document also outlines vocational training for persons with disabilities in both formal education (TVET and universities) and informal training institutions (community colleges). A plan to collaborate with business and government initiatives such as the Expanded Public Works Programme in an effort to facilitate participation in employment following completion of training programmes is also envisioned. To aid the facilitation of participation of persons with disabilities in post-school education and training, the *Strategic Policy Framework on Disability for the Post-School Education and Training System* was developed by DHET. The framework outlines legislation, policies, and guidelines in the implementation and improvement of access to post-school education.

White Paper 6 on Special Needs Education: Building an Inclusive Education and Training System (2001)

As previously highlighted the White Paper 6 on inclusive education describes plans to eradicate barriers to accessing education by learners with disabilities. Various steps are detailed on how the realisation of inclusive education can be reached. These steps include the development of enabling educational structures (i.e. schools) and systems, implementation of teaching methodologies that cater to the learning needs of learners with diverse disabilities, from diverse economic backgrounds, language groups, and cultures. Quite a number of other documents have been introduced to support the implementation of the White Paper 6 on inclusive education which includes the National Strategy on Screening, Identification, Assessment and Support (2008); and guidelines for full service and inclusive schools (2010).

Strategies and Policies Aimed at Skill Development

The Skills Development Act No. 97 of 1998 provides a framework for improving the skills of the SA workforce through national and local workplace strategies. This is conducted by providing various education and training opportunities. The Sector Education and Training Authorities (SETAs) play a role in identifying training opportunities within various sectors and developing the programmes. The South African Qualifications Authority (SAQA) as an Education and Training Quality Assurance body accredits the SETAs the training programmes and ensures compliance with the National Qualification Framework (NQF) (SAQA, 2020; SETA-Training, 2013). Persons with disabilities are offered opportunities to acquire skills and qualifications through a wide range of learnerships designed to enable transition into the labour market and to gain entrepreneurial skills. Funding is received from the National Skills Fund. The Skills Development Levies Act (1999) mandates employers to contribute 4% of employees' earnings to the National Skills Fund.

Types of Vocational Training

There are different models of vocational training programmes followed in South Africa. These include four main types of vocational training programmes, namely, vocational training in schools, in TVET colleges, apprenticeship, on-the-job training, and supported and sheltered workshops. Various government departments have a role in facilitating vocational training of persons with disabilities. Vocational training in schools falls under the Department of Basic Education (DoE), while vocational training post-school falls under the jurisdiction of the Department of Higher Education and Training (DHET). Informal training programmes provided in sheltered and supported employment programmes are managed by the Department of Social Development (DSD). It should be noted that the economic empowerment of persons with disabilities is more of the DSD's secondary mandate (SA DoL, 2015). The certification and qualification acquired through training are facilitated by SETAs and SAQA.

Figure 40.1 outlines the government department responsible for the vocational training programmes offered in South Africa.

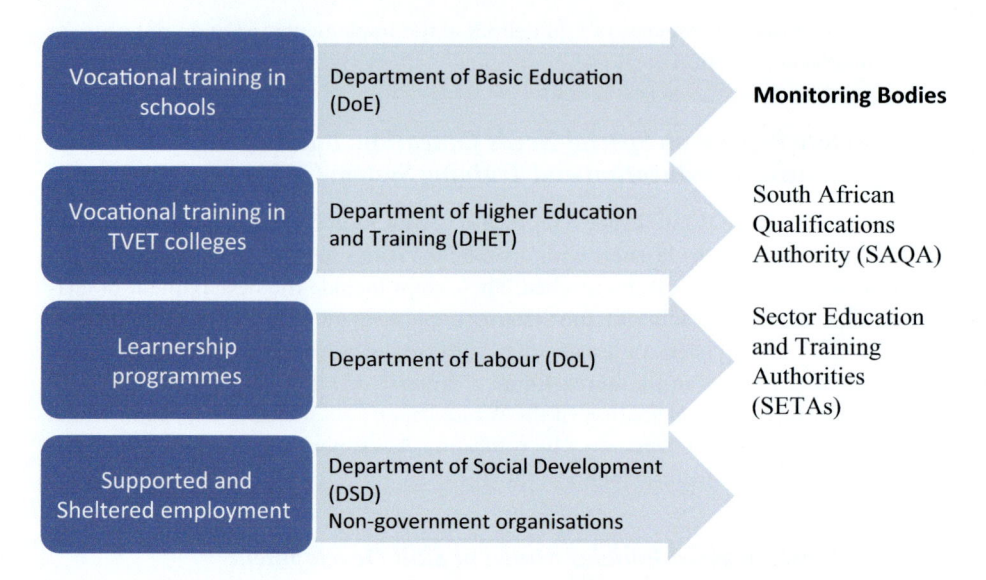

Figure 40.1 Government department responsible for vocational training programmes in South Africa

Vocational Training in Schools

In mainstream schools, vocational training is offered as part of school curricula from Grade 9 to Grade 12. The learners are offered vocational education within the school, where they acquire work-related skills, entrepreneurial skills, and skills in carpentry, tiling, sewing, etc. Completion of such training results in qualifications certified by the SETAs and in compliance with SAQA. In special schools, vocational education is facilitated by the Department of Basic Education. Despite the DoE's recognition of the importance of vocational training for learners with disabilities, implementation is still not in full effect. Special schools currently follow the National Curriculum which is adapted for the special needs of learners with disabilities. Although a limited number of schools have well-developed vocational training programmes, most schools in South Africa lack resources, and trained personnel to carry out skills training (Soeker, 2020; Van Niekerk et al., 2011). A focus in the schools is on the adaptation of curricula in order to ensure formal qualifications are attained at the end of their schooling (Steyn & Vlachos, 2011). This is due to schools being assessed by DoE based on academic performance and how many learners complete their Matriculation (Grade 12). The Human Rights Watch (2015) reported that learners in special schools are subjected to school subjects and assessments that are not suitable for their capabilities and needs. Special schools that offer skills training lack resources such as adapted learning material, assistive technology, and skilled teachers to facilitate vocational training (Human Rights Watch, 2015). This is concerning given that children with disabilities are more likely to require accommodations in order to participate in the training. However, many special schools operate with limited resources (Human Rights Watch, 2015).

Vocational Training in Colleges

Training is also offered at a Technical and Vocational Education and Training (TVET) college which may be at a government or private institution. The TVET colleges offer a variety of courses in study fields such as education, agriculture, engineering, business studies, building, construction, and many more (ILO, 2013). The courses are also accredited by the SAQA and certified by SETA. Completion, of course, emanates from a qualification (NQF level 4 to 6). TVET colleges form part of the post-school training initiatives by the government to get the youth equipped for the open labour market. To qualify to study at these colleges you need Grade 9-12 school qualification. Students who have completed their vocational training in school can continue to gain theoretical knowledge and practical skills in a TVET college.

Despite the availability of policy, representation of persons with diverse disabilities in TVET is low. Individuals with disabilities lack the required qualifications to enrol in programmes offered in the TVET colleges. Most have never been to school and present with poor literacy skills which is a barrier to registering for the enlisted courses (Siwela, 2017). Ntombela explored barriers to accessing TVET colleges in KwaZulu-Natal. She found that access to TVET colleges for persons with disabilities is hindered by the lack of trained lecturers/facilitators, lack of resources and necessary assistive technology (Ntombela, 2019). More concerning is the lack of accessible buildings and spaces for students who use wheelchairs. There is also a lack of rehabilitative professionals who may advise and support the learning of students with disabilities in the colleges, such as occupational therapists and speech therapists (Ntombela, 2019). Furthermore, attitudinal barriers were also identified as a major barrier in the poor inclusion of persons with disabilities in TVET colleges.

Apprenticeship

Apprenticeships involve training through mentoring and guidance of skilled professionals within the workplace (Agyei-Quartey, 2020). In South Africa, apprenticeship is offered through learnership and internship programmes. In the Skills Development Act (No. 97 of 1998; Amended 2003) learnership programmes are described as comprising vocational education and training. They therefore combine theoretical learning and practical work experience (Schneider & Nkoli, 2011). The learnership programmes accommodate persons with disabilities with a qualification of Grade 9-12. Important to note is that most programmes require individuals to have completed their Grade 12 schooling. Upon successful completion of a learnership programme, an individual receives a qualification that is registered on the National Qualifications Framework (NQF). This indicates vocational competence and qualification in a specific specialization (SA Qualification Association [SAQA], 2020). These programmes also result in formal certification by SETA (often NQF level 2-5). As an incentive to companies that provide these apprentice programmes, the South African government provides subsidies for these learnership programmes, and thus companies receive tax-related incentives for employing persons with disabilities (Visser & Kruss, 2009).

These learnership programmes are created to accommodate different levels of academic qualifications and not only for those who have completed Grade 12 (SA DoL, 2015). The learnership programmes have however been problematic as employers fail to create job positions designed for individuals with no Grade 12 qualifications. Furthermore, age restrictions are imposed on these programmes, whereby individuals are required to be 35 years and younger. More concerning is that these learnership programmes are often in insignificant positions that offer poor remuneration, result in low certification that does not advance one to a higher-level qualification, and are also temporary in nature. It should be noted that individuals with disabilities stand to lose the disability grant should they be formally employed. Most are hesitant to do so as it takes a long period to apply and be approved for the disability social grant again should one no longer be employed (Kidd et al., 2018). Plus, not only do disability social grants come with free medical care benefits, but in most families, they are the only source of income

(Lygnegård et al., 2013). To limit the challenge of persons with disabilities losing their disability social grant due to being employed, learnerships stipends are designed to not exceed a certain income level. Although this strategy is implemented with the hope of preventing the loss of a disability social grant, this results in learnership positions created being temporary in nature and of poor remuneration (i.e., under $270 monthly).

In order to be appointed in an internship programme different from a learnership programme, individuals are required to have at least a Diploma or Bachelor's degree. Internship programmes can be in fields such as engineering, information technology, and administrative positions. These programmes are therefore inaccessible to a population like those with disabilities who often present with no work-related skills, poor literacy, and no formal qualifications. These programmes offer employment positions following the completion of the programme. Furthermore, the appointed individuals receive a higher remuneration and have opportunities for advancement in their careers. Important to note that both the learnership and internship programmes are offered in urban areas and not in rural areas (Visagie et al., 2017).

On-the-job Training

Other training models include on-the-job training programmes which are an initiative to improve the skills of those who enter the workplace with limited work experience and require support or enhancement of current skills. Depending on the skills development programme, formal certification may be generated. Also, experience obtained from on-the-job training adds value and weight for future employment prospects as it indicates the acquisition of skills in a specific work area. These types of training are offered within job positions and may thus also be offered within learnerships programmes. On-the-job training is linked to the Skills Development Act No. 97 of 1998 and Skills Development Levies Act (1999). This model aids individuals with disabilities in acquiring training within their job position and thus increases access to future employment positions.

Due to the presence of attitudinal barriers, this vocational training option is often inaccessible to most individuals with disabilities. A scoping review by Morwane et al. (2021) explored factors that facilitate and hinder the employment of persons with disabilities in low- and middle-income countries. They found that employers' misconceptions regarding the capability of persons with disabilities hindered the hiring of employees with disabilities. On-the-job training, on the other hand, was considered a facilitator to employment (Morwane et al., 2021). In order to access these training opportunities, individuals with disabilities first need to be appointed. However, as indicated in the scoping review, individuals with disabilities experience marginalisation in accessing competitive employment (Morwane et al., 2021).

Supported and Sheltered Employment

Supported and sheltered employment provides an inclusive environment where individuals with disabilities can engage in economic activities. Supported and sheltered employment is reported in the literature to provide training in job-related skills, enhance independence, prepare individuals with disabilities for competitive employment, and be linked to improved well-being (Banks et al., 2010). These training programmes are however underdeveloped in South Africa (Lorenzo & Cramm, 2012; Lorenzo et al., 2007). Currently, these types of vocational training programmes are supported by the Department of Social Development, with quite a significant number being run by non-government organisations. The white paper on education and training, outlined programmes to be implemented which cater to individuals who require extensive support in participating in competitive employment. The programmes were described to be in the form of community colleges. This is with the aim of the DHET housing all forms of training within its department.

Supported employment refers to vocational training that prepares and supports individuals with disabilities to transition into competitive employment (Wehman et al., 2014). The programmes provide job-seeking and placement services, skills training, and exposure to work experiences to gain knowledge of the business world as well as connect with employers. Ongoing support is provided once placed in employment (Jang et al., 2014). Programmes of this nature are offered by private recruitment agencies and non-government organisations who form partnerships with various businesses and link individuals with disabilities to employment opportunities. Individuals with disabilities are more likely to be employed through this model. This is due to specialised recruitment agencies or rehabilitative professionals involved in supporting their placement. The professionals work closely with employers in ensuring the retention of individuals with disabilities in employment. A study by Van Niekerk et al. (2011) explored supported employment as a potential strategy to facilitate the employment of persons with disabilities into competitive employment in South Africa. The study found that supported employment programmes were underfunded, limited in South Africa, and required inter-departmental collaboration in order to be successful. Nevertheless, the model was found to be an effective strategy not only for individuals with disabilities but for youth who lacked skills and other marginalised members of society who require job-seeking support (Van Niekerk et al., 2011).

Sheltered employment offers segregated work programmes for people with disabilities who are not able to work in a competitive employment setting. Oftentimes individuals with severe disabilities are found within these types of vocational training programmes. Economic activity occurs under supervision and support from trained personnel and professionals such as occupational therapists and community workers. These informal training centres which are located within communities offer low-level skills training and short-term training programmes (Ebrahim et al., 2020). The programmes offered are not aligned with the skills required in the country, resulting in poor transition to employment (Schneider & Nkoli, 2011). Important to note that these informal centres operate with limited resources and rely on funding from private donors (Schneider, 2006). Tinta et al. (2020) investigated barriers experienced by persons with disabilities participating in a vocational training facility in South Africa. They found that these facilities lacked resources and also lacked material and equipment that accommodated the skills of persons with disabilities. Furthermore, the training facilities did not provide diverse training opportunities which were stimulating. When vocational training programmes are developed, beneficiaries are not consulted on the type of activities they would like to engage in. Another study explored the experiences and perceptions of individuals with disabilities in a South African sheltered workshop (Soeker et al., 2018). The participants reported support from the trainers in the workshop, however, felt they engaged in monotonous activities that were not motivating. Nonetheless, the participants also mentioned training and support from the sheltered workshop prepared them for competitive employment (Soeker et al., 2018).

Conclusions

Individuals with disabilities in South Africa continue to experience barriers to participation in vocational training programmes. Barriers to inclusion in the four types of vocational training models require urgent attention from the government in order to improve the livelihood of an individual with disabilities. Importantly, the issues that impede participation are multi-factorial and require a collaborative effort from various government departments. For instance, the

Department of Basic Education is responsible for the provision of education which is required in order to gain access to post-school qualifications. Similarly, the department of higher education and training has an obligation to provide accessible vocational training programmes in colleges and institutions of higher learning. Be it so, individuals also require support for such a transportation and necessary infrastructure and rehabilitative care. This therefore also includes collaboration with the department of health, public works, and transportation. Given that the department of labour monitors the employment of individuals with disabilities, monitoring of equitable representation of individuals with diverse disabilities including those with disabilities is imperative.

Currently, the department of higher education is responsible for post-school education; however, provisions have yet to be made for vocational skills training of individuals with disabilities. From the discussion of vocational training programmes, removal of barriers can facilitate the participation of individuals with disabilities.

Acknowledgements

The author declares that there are no financial or personal relationships that may have inappropriately influenced the writing of this chapter.

References

African Union Commission Department of Social Affairs. *Continental plan of action for the african decade of persons with disabilities 2010–2019*. https:/:au.int/sites/default/ files/pages/32900-file-cpoa_handbook. _audp.english_-_copy.pdf

Agyei-Quartey, J. (2020). Study to assess the inclusion of youth with disabilities in TVET and among selected companies in the Ghanaian tourism and hospitality sector. https://www.ilo.org/wcmsp5/ groups/public/ed_emp/ifp_skills/documents/publication/wcms_754220.pdf

Armstrong, D., Armstrong, A. C., & Spandagou, I. (2011). Inclusion: By choice or by chance? *International Journal of Inclusive Education*, *15*(1), 29–39. https://doi.org/10.1080/13603116.2010.496192

Banks, L. M., Kuper, H., & Polack, S. (2017). Poverty and disability in low- and middle-income countries: A systematic review. *PLOS ONE*, *12*(12), e0189996. https://doi.org/10.1371/journal.pone.0189996

Banks, P., Jahoda, A., Dagnan, D., Kemp, J., & Williams, V. (2010). Supported employment for people with intellectual disability: The effects of job breakdown on psychological well-being. *Journal of Applied Research in Intellectual Disabilities*, *23*(4), 344–354. https://doi.org/10.1111/j.1468-3148.2009.00541.x

Black, D. R., & de Matos-Ala, J. (2016). Building a more inclusive South Africa: progress and pitfalls in disability rights and inclusion. *Third World Thematics: A TWQ Journal*, *1*(3), 335–352.

Bornman, J. (2017). Developing inclusive literacy practices in South African Schools. In M. Milton (Ed.), *Inclusive principles and practices in literacy education*. United Kingdom: Emerald.

Department of Education (DoE). (2010). *Guidelines for full-service/inclusive schools 2010*. Pretoria: Government Printers.

Department of Education (DoE). (2008). *National strategy on screening, identification, assessment and support*. Pretoria: Government Printers.

Department of Education (DoE). (2001). *Education White paper 6: Special needs education: Building an inclusive education and training system*. Pretoria: DoE.

Department of Labour. (2020). *Commission for employment equity annual report 2019/2020*. Pretoria: Government Printer.

Department of Higher Education and Training (DHET). (2014). *White paper for post-school education and training*. Pretoria: Government Printer.

Department of Social Development (DSD). (2015). *White paper on the rights of persons with disabilities*. Pretoria: Government Printer.

Department of Social Development, Department of Women Children and People with Disabilities, & UNICEF (2012). *Children with disabilities in South Africa: A situation analysis: 2001–2011*. Pretoria:

Department of Social Development/Department of Women, Children and People with Disabilities/ UNICEF.

Donohue, D., & Bornman, J. (2014). The challenges of realising inclusive education in South Africa. *South African Journal of Education, 34*(2), 1–14.

Ebrahim, A., Botha, M., Brand, D., & Mogensen, K. F. (2020). Reimagining rehabilitation outcomes in South Africa. *South African Health Review, 164*, 163–169.

Engelbrecht, P., Nel, M., Smit, S., & Van Deventer, M. (2016). The idealism of education policies and the realities in schools: The implementation of inclusive education in South Africa. *International Journal of Inclusive Education, 20*(5), 520–535.

Engelbrecht, M., Shaw, L., & Van Niekerk, L. (2017). A literature review on work transitioning of youth with disabilities into competitive employment. *African Journal of Disability, 6*(0), a298. https://doi.org/10.4102/ajod.v6i0.298

Groce, N., Kembhavi, G., Wirz, S., Lang, R., Trani, J.-F., & Kett, M. (2011). Poverty and Disability A critical review of the literature in low and middle-income countries. 31. www.ucl.ac.uk/lcccr/.../WP16_Poverty_and_Disability_review.pdf

Human Rights Watch. (2015). *Complicit in exclusion: South Africa's failure to guarantee an inclusive education for children with disabilities.* New York: Human Rights Watch.

International Labour Organization (ILO). 2013. *Inclusion of people with disabilities in vocational training: A practical guide.* Geneva: ILO, International Labour Office, Gender, Equality and Diversity.

Jang, Y., Wang, Y. T., & Lin, M. H. (2014). Factors affecting employment outcomes for people with disabilities who received disability employment services in Taiwan. *Journal of Occupational Rehabilitation, 24*(1), 11–21. https://doi.org/10.1007/s10926-013-9433-1

Kidd, S., Wapling, L., & Bailey-athias, D. (2018). *Social protection and disability in South Africa.* http://www.developmentpathways.co.uk/wp-content/uploads/2018/07/Social-protection-and-disability-in-South-Africa-July-2018.pdf

Krainski, D. J. (2021). Sheltered employment. In *Encyclopedia of autism spectrum disorders* (pp. 4344–4345). Cham: Springer International Publishing.

Lindsay, S., McDougall, C., Menna-Dack, D., Sanford, R., & Adams, T. (2015). An ecological approach to understanding barriers to employment for youth with disabilities compared to their typically developing peers: Views of youth, employers, and job counselors. *Disability and Rehabilitation, 37*(8), 701–711. https://doi.org/10.3109/09638288.2014.939775

Loeb, M., Eide, A. H., Jelsma, J., Toni, M. K., & Maart, S. (2008). Poverty and disability in Eastern and Western Cape Provinces, South Africa. *Disability and Society, 23*(4), 311–321. https://doi.org/10.1080/09687590802038803

Lorenzo, T., van Niekerk, L., & Mdlokolo, P. (2007). Economic empowerment and black disabled entrepreneurs: Negotiating partnerships in Cape Town, South Africa. *Disability And Rehabilitation, 29*(5), 429–436.

Lorenzo, T., & Cramm, J. M. (2012). Access to livelihood assets among youth with and without disabilities in South Africa: Implications for health professional education. *South African Medical Journal, 102*(6), 578–581. https://doi.org/10.7196/SAMJ.5675

Lygnegård, F., Donohue, D., Bornman, J., Granlund, M., & Huus, K. (2013). A systematic review of generic and special needs of children with disabilities living in poverty settings in low-and middle-income countries. *Journal of Policy Practice, 12*(4), 296–315.

Maart, S., Amosun, S., & Jelsma, J. (2019). Disability prevalence-context matters: A descriptive community-based survey. *African Journal of Disability, 8*, 1–8. https://doi.org/10.4102/ajod.v8i0.512

Mitra, S., & Sambamoorthi, U. (2014). Disability prevalence among adults: Estimates for 54 countries and progress toward a global estimate. *Disability and Rehabilitation, 36*(11), 940–947. https://doi.org/10.3109/09638288.2013.825333

Mkabile, S., & Swartz, L. (2020). 'I waited for it until forever': Community barriers to accessing intellectual disability services for children and their families in Cape Town, South Africa. *International Journal of Environmental Research and Public Health, 17*(22), 8504.

Mophosho, M., & Dada, S. (2015). Role of speech- language pathologists in implementing AAC in schools. In S. Moonsamy & H. Kathard (Eds.), *Speech-language therapy in a school context: Its principles and practices* (1st ed., pp. 197–214). Pretoria: Van Schaik Publishers.

Morwane, R. E., Dada, S., & Bornman, J. (2021). Barriers to and facilitators of employment of persons with disabilities in low-and middle-income countries: A scoping review. *African Journal of Disability, 10*, 12. https://doi.org/10.4102/ajod.v10i0.833

Nel, N. M., Tlale, L. D. N., Engelbrecht, P., & Nel, M. (2016). Teachers' perceptions of education support structures in the implementation of inclusive education in South Africa. *Koers, 81*(3), 1–14.

Ntombela, G. N. N. (2019). *The dynamics of inclusive education in further education and training in South Africa: A case study of two technical and vocational education and training colleges in Pietermaritzburg* (Doctoral dissertation).

Pereira, E., Kyriazopoulou, M., & Weber, H. (2016). Inclusive vocational education and training (VET)– Policy and practice. In *Implementing inclusive education: Issues in bridging the policy-practice gap*. Emerald Group Publishing Limited.

Philpott, S., & McLaren, P. (2011). *Hearing the voices of children and caregivers: Children with disabilities in South Africa; A situation analysis* (pp. 2001–2011). Pretoria: Department of Social Development, Republic of South Africa/UNICEF.

Ramaahlo, M., Tönsing, K. M., & Bornman, J. (2018). Inclusive education policy provision in South African research universities. *Disability and Society, 33*(3), 349–373. https://doi.org/10.1080/09687599.2018.1423954

Saloojee, G., Phohole, M., Saloojee, H., & Ijsselmuiden, C. (2007). Unmet health, welfare and educational needs of disabled children in an impoverished South African peri-urban township. *Child: Care, Health and Development, 33*(3), 230–235. https://doi.org/10.1111/j.1365-2214.2006.00645.x

Samuels, A., Slemming, W., & Balton, S. (2012). Early childhood intervention in South Africa in relation to the developmental systems model. *Infants and Young Children, 25*(4), 334–345.

Saran, A., White, H., & Kuper, H. (2020). Evidence and gap map of studies assessing the effectiveness of interventions for people with disabilities in low-and middle-income countries. *Campbell Systematic Reviews, 16*(1), e1070.

Schneider, M. (2006). *Strategies for skills acquisition and work for people with disabilities, A report (for South Africa) submitted to the ILO, Geneva, by Thabo Mbeki Development Trust for People with disabilities, People with disabilities South Africa, and Human Sciences Research Council*. Geneva: ILO, December 2006. www.hsrc.ac.za/en/research-data/ktree-doc/1335

Schneider, M., & Nkoli, M. I. (2011). Affirmative action and disability in South Africa. *Transformation: Critical Perspectives on Southern Africa, 77*(1), 90–106. https://doi.org/10.1353/trn.2011.0041

SECTION 27. (2022). Fix the forgotten schools. *SECTION27 takes education authorities to court for suspending infrastructure projects at Limpopo schools during Covid-19*. Retrieved from https://section27.org.za/2022/10/fix-the-forgotten-schools/ [Accessed 08 November 2022].

Sector Education and Training Authorities. (2013). *SETA-Training*. https://seta-training.co.za//seta-training.html

Sefotho, M. M., Morwane, R. E., & Bornman, J. (2019). Inclusive employment plight of youth with complex communication needs. In *Inclusion, equity and access for individuals with disabilities* (pp. 281–296). Singapore: Palgrave Macmillan.

Siwela, S. (2017). *An exploratory case study of the experiences of students with disabilities at a TVET college: Factors that facilitate or impede their access and success* (Doctoral dissertation).

Soeker, M. S., De Jongh, J. C., Diedericks, A., Matthys, K., Swart, N., & Van Der Pol, P. (2018). The experiences and perceptions of persons with disabilities regarding work skills development in sheltered and protective workshops. *Work, 59*(2), 303–314. https://doi.org/10.3233/WOR-172674

South African qualifications Authority (SAQA). (2020). *NQF implementation framework 2015–2020*. https://www.saqa.org.za/sites/default/files/2019-11/NQF%20Implementation%20Framework%202015-2020.pdf

Statistics South Africa. (2021). *Unemployment rates. Quarter Labour Force Survey (QLFS)*. https://www.statssa.gov.za/publications/P0211/Media%20release%20QLFS%20Q1%202021.pdf

Statistics South Africa. (2014). *Census 2011: Profile of persons with disabilities*. Pretoria: Statistics South Africa. http://www.statssa.gov.za/?p=3180

Steyn, G. M., & Vlachos, C. J. (2011). Developing a Vocational Training and Transition Planning Programme for Intellectually Disabled Students in South Africa: A Case study. *Journal of Social Sciences, 27*(1), 25–37. https://doi.org/10.1080/09718923.2011.11892903

Swart, E., Engelbrecht, P., Eloff, I., & Pettipher, R. (2002). Implementing inclusive education in South Africa: Teachers' attitudes and experiences. *Acta Academica, 34*(1), 175–189.

Tripney, J., Hogrebe, N., Schmidt, E., Vigurs, C., & Stewart, R. (2019). Employment supports for adults with disabilities in low- and middle-income countries: A Campbell systematic review. *Research on Social Work Practice, 29*(3), 243–255. https://doi.org/10.1177/1049731517715316

United Nations. (2016). *Disability in the SDGs indicators.* http://www.un.org/ disabilities/documents/20 16/SDG-disability-indicators- march-2016.pdf

United Nations. (2006). Convention on the Rights of Persons with Disabilities and Optional Protocol. http://www.un.org/disabilities/ docu ments/convention/convoptprot-e.pdf

United Nations Flagship Report. (2018). *Disability and development report 2018: Realizing the sustainable development goals.* https://www.un.org/development/desa/disabilities/publication-disability-sdgs.html

Van Niekerk, L., Coetzee, Z., Engelbrecht, M., Hajwani, Z., Landman, S., Motimele, M., & Terreblanche, S. (2011). Supported employment: Recommendations for successful implementation in South Africa. *South African Journal of Occupational Therapy, 41*(3), 85–90.

Vergunst, R., Swartz, L., Hem, K. G., Eide, A. H., Mannan, H., MacLachlan, M., … Schneider, M. (2017). Access to health care for persons with disabilities in rural South Africa. *BMC Health Services Research, 17*(1), 1–8.

Vergunst, R., Swartz, L., Hem, K.-G., Eide, A. H., Mannan, H., MacLachlan, M., … Schneider, M. (2017). Access to health care for persons with disabilities in rural South Africa. *BMC Health Services Research, 17*(1), 741. https://doi.org/10.1186/s12913-017-2674-5

Visagie, S., Eide, A. H., Dyrstad, K., Mannan, H., Swartz, L., Schneider, M., Mji, G., Munthali, A., Khogali, M., Rooy, G. van, Hem, K. G., & MacLachlan, M. (2017). Factors related to environmental barriers experienced by persons with and without disabilities in diverse African settings. *PLoS ONE, 12*(10), 1–14. https://doi.org/10.1371/journal.pone.0186342

Visser, M., & Kruss, G. (2009). Learnerships and skills development in South Africa: A shift to prioritise the young unemployed. *Journal of Vocational Education and Training, 61*(3), 357–374.

Wehman, P., Chan, F., Ditchman, N., & Kang, H. J. (2014). Effect of supported employment on vocational rehabilitation outcomes of transition-age youth with intellectual and developmental disabilities: A case control study. *Intellectual and Developmental Disabilities, 52*(4), 296–310.

Wehman, P., Sima, A. P., Ketchum, J., West, M. D., Chan, F., & Luecking, R. (2015). Predictors of successful transition from school to employment for youth with disabilities. *Journal of Occupational Rehabilitation, 25*(2), 323–334.

CONCLUSION

41
BEING PUSHED AND PULLED
Making Sense of Inclusive and Exclusive Forces

*Garry Squires**

Introduction

Lay people assume that teaching is straightforward. You turn up at school, teach the class, go home, mark and prepare the next lesson and then repeat. Yet the reality is quite different. The underlying assumption that the 'class' is taught is incorrect. The class consists of around thirty very different individual learners. They all learn in different ways and at different rates. Some learners are good at one subject, others are good at another subject and some seem to struggle with everything. Some learners are well adjusted emotionally; others have experienced trauma, difficult relationships, challenging family relationships, or developmental pathways that make emotional regulation difficult. The classroom may consist of children from different linguistic backgrounds, different cultural backgrounds, and different religious backgrounds. There may be some learners with sensory or physical disabilities in the classroom; some may have hidden disabilities such as dyslexia or autism or ADHD. These are just to name a few of the differences that make each learner unique and remind us that the 'class' is not a homogenic group that can all be taught in the same way and have the same outcomes.

One ideological stance is that effort is focused on those children who will succeed the most and achieve the highest qualifications and to place them together to create high-achieving homogenic classes. In England during the 1940s, this involved setting up grammar schools that creamed off the best performing 11-year-olds. These children received the best education and were destined to go onto well-placed jobs and leadership roles. A second tranche of children were placed in secondary modern schools and received a general education that focused on them joining the mass workforce. There was a third group who had been previously deemed to be ineducable who now went to special schools and hospital schools (Squires, 2012). In one sense, this positioning assumes that children can be neatly divided up at age eleven and receive an education that is somehow suited to them but with different outcomes. It is argued that this approach would lead to the more able learners achieving better qualifications and then as adults, contributing to the economy and through taxation provide the health, social care, and welfare that less able or other vulnerable groups may need. My view is that this ideology is immoral in that it sacrifices some individuals' quality and length of life in favour of a privileged few. It restricts the agency, engagement, and participation of vulnerable individuals in wider society

---

* garry.squires@manchester.ac.uk

and ultimately leads to increased social division and the marginalization of those least likely to benefit from a selective and elitist system. It fails to take into account how children develop as learners, how wider social factors determine their starting points in education and the impact of education on later life chances. It maintains a scenario where those that have more to start with in life, get more later in life, thereby enhancing social division and inequity.

For a truly socially inclusive society in which all people are valued and their participation is enabled and desired, we must think about the roles that education and teaching have to play and to a large extent this shift in thinking is evident in the different educational reforms that have taken place in England. Successful engagement in education and completion of education should be seen as a human right (UN, 1989). There is a moral imperative, for not doing so leaves vulnerable young people disadvantaged throughout their lives. They have fewer opportunities for employment (Bäckman & Nilsson, 2016; Przybylski, 2014; Schwabe & Charbonnier, 2015; Snieskaa, Valodkieneb, Daunorienec, & Draksaited, 2015), poor health outcomes (Christle, Jolivette, & Nelson, 2007; Gallagher, 2011), and wider social exclusion (Bäckman & Nilsson, 2016; Christle & Yell, 2008; Jahnukainen & Järvinen, 2005; Wilkins & Huckabee, 2014). Learners who have been identified as having special educational needs or disabilities (SEND) are more vulnerable and at greater risk of poor psychosocial outcomes (Humphrey, Barlow, Wigelsworth, & Squires, 2013) and three times more likely to leave school early compared to their peers without SEND (Limbach-Reich & Powell, 2016; Squires, 2017, 2019; Squires & Dyson, 2017; Squires & Kefallinou, 2019). Those learners who are identified as having emotional, behavioural, or mental health difficulties are even more likely to experience the poor transition to adulthood and lifelong difficulties (Kern et al., 2015). It is not surprising, therefore, that as we have seen in earlier chapters, there have been repeated calls for societies to move toward a more inclusive education system with an aspiration that all children will be educated in mainstream schools by 2030 (UNESCO, 1994a, 1994b, 2000, 2015a, 2015b; UNESCO & UNICEF, 2015; World Bank, 2015).

The role of teaching in an inclusive education system is discussed in Chapter 1. Inclusive teaching is demanding and requires a range of skills from the teacher to give attention to all the individual learners in the classroom. The more diverse the group of learners, the more the teacher has to think about how best to include all of the learners so that they all receive a good quality of education. Sometimes, I hear teachers complain that the role of the teacher is not what they thought it was, "I didn't sign up to be a social worker" (responding to supporting children from challenging home backgrounds; "I am not a psychiatrist" (responding to supporting emotional wellbeing and mental health); "I wasn't trained for this!" (responding to diversity in the classroom). The teachers commenting feel as though they are being pushed and pulled in different directions. Additionally, external pressures exist that favour one group of learners over others. This in turn adds to the tension between inclusion on the one hand and segregation on the other hand that pulls teachers in one direction and then in the other. While this is challenging for a primary school teacher with up to 30 learners in their class, it is almost impossible for secondary teachers who may have ten or twelve classes a week to remember the individual needs of all 300–360 learners. So perhaps there is a need to move from thinking about individuals to thinking about systems such as the classroom, the school, the education system or even how society itself is structured. As I move through this chapter, I am going to start to look at the different forces at play, present a model for thinking about these forces at the individual level, class level, school level and then finally consider how Universal Design for Learning might help in supporting inclusion.

What Do We Mean by Forces and How Do They Work?

I have used the term force because it is easy to visualize a teacher who is being pushed in one direction or pulled in the opposite direction. It really means all those things that help schools

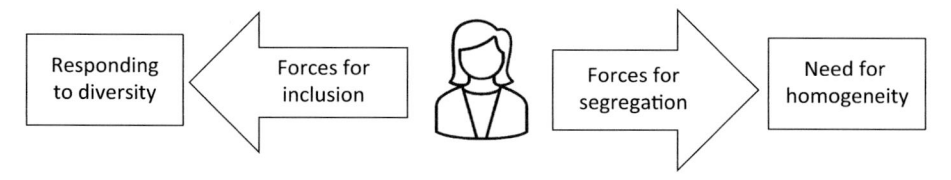

Figure 41.1 Simple force field analysis

become more inclusive and respond to diversity (one direction) versus those things that lead to some children being excluded or marginalized or undervalued and the need for homogeneity.

We can imagine that there is a dimension running from total inclusion through varying degrees of inclusion across to having separate provision for different groups of learners and classes that are largely homogenous (see Figure 41.1). Individual teachers can place themselves anywhere on this dimension; some teachers favour inclusion, while others want more similarity within their teaching class. The forces are really the things that lead teachers to position themselves where they do, and individual teachers will feel themselves pulled or pushed towards one end of the dimension or the other. Kurt Lewin provided a way of thinking about this and introduced how the different forces can be approached through a process called Force Field Analysis (Lewin, 1943, 1947). Force Field Analysis enables us to explore the forces at play, decide where we are positioned on the inclusion-segregation dimension and then see how the strength of particular forces can be adapted and moderated so that we can shift our position. Looked at in this way, we can start to see that individual teacher positions on inclusion are malleable and can shift in either direction, depending on the balance of forces acting on the teacher in question (Squires, 2019). One such force has been identified in the introduction. It is the two opposing ideologies around how education benefits society as a whole. Segregation leads to one group of learners doing well who then support another group of learners throughout their lifetime. Inclusion aims to benefit all learners by allowing them to develop academically, emotionally, and socially and all to then participate and engage in society with reduced need for state support on leaving school. On the one hand there is a belief that different types of children need different types of education; while on the other hand, is the belief that all children should be taught together in the local neighbourhood school. This tends to be summarized as segregated education versus inclusive education. It is important to recognize that these positions are not fixed and that other forces can shift and move the balance point in either direction.

Special schools were first introduced in England to meet the needs of a few children who were unable to attend their local primary school and were a step towards inclusion. The 1870 Education Act had set up compulsory education for all children aged between 5 years and 10 years, but there were some children who were exempt because they might not be able to benefit from the education provided. These children were referred to as 'uneducable'; that is there was something about the child that would mean that they could not be educated. A change in thinking started to emerge that viewed it as a problem of the education system not being able to teach the child. There were some children who needed something more than could be offered by the mass teaching available in mainstream schools. The first special schools for blind and deaf children opened in 1893 followed by special schools for physically impaired children in 1899 (Living Heritage, 2010). Over the years that followed, the number of special schools extended to include those for children with moderate learning difficulties and those with severe learning difficulties. Legislation formalized the placement of children into special schools away from their mainstream peers and required that such children were assessed and diagnosed with one of eleven labels that matched the school in which they would be placed (HMSO, 1944 see Section 34). This approach started to build up expertise in special schools to deal with very specific needs that had originally been considered to be severe medical needs but were slowly starting to extend to children with other types of problems. While the original motivation had been noble in that it provided access to some kind of education for all children, it had started to drift towards a system in which some children were now being moved out of mainstream schools and into special schools. The Warnock report in 1978 started to question the use of the diagnostic labels as a means for determining school placement and the need for special schools for special children. It commented on the rising numbers of children in special schools which had increased from 12,060 in 1947 to 22,639 with another 27,000 waiting for placement in 1955 (Warnock, 1978). The Warnock report took a different view that most children with SEND would be educated in mainstream schools and as many as one in five children would be considered to have SEND at some stage of their education. This is often incorrectly quoted as 20% of children will have special needs rather than seeing special needs as a transitory state and one that might apply at some point to a learner and then not apply. The report set out an expectation that the majority of learners would be educated in their local mainstream school, so long as additional support was made available. The provision of additional support was not tightly specified and was later interpreted as involving the 'efficient use of resources'. This last phrase made the whole concept of inclusion particularly slippery. A head teacher who did not want a particular child in their school could always argue that the school was unable to meet the child's needs, or placement in mainstream would lead to inefficient use of resources. The argument developed that centralized special schools that dealt with particular types of children would have economies of scale in the deployment of resources that could not be achieved in mainstream schools. So, the forces arising around special schools are twofold. First, they helped to get children into education and special schoolteachers became more proficient at teaching children with severe needs. Second, the expertise also involved including other professionals and the development of specialist equipment and resources. Economies of scale were possible by centralizing support in a special school. However, this led to more demand to move children from mainstream to special schools and in turn led to deskilling of mainstream teachers. It also added to the perception that special educational needs were something to do with the child rather than resulting from the way that education was organized.

Since 1981 there have been different reforms in education, special education was reformed in 1994, 2001 and again in 2014. The number of children with support at school or through an official decision leading to an Education Health Care Plan (EHCP) is slightly lower than the 20% quoted by Warnock. However, the number of special schools has increased and in 2021 there were 131,933 children in special schools, and it seems as if more children are being pushed out of mainstream schools over time. Yet the majority of children (another 1,241,867 children) with SEND are in mainstream schools (DfE, 2021). The percentage of children identified as having special educational needs is increasing year on year and now stands at 15.9% of all pupils (DfE, 2021). There is a question then about understanding the more subtle forces that explain why more children are being identified as having special educational needs, this is not something that has arisen purely out of the SARS Cov-2 pandemic and schools being closed, the pattern was emerging from 2016 onwards (see Table 41.1). Warnock commented that the role of Statements (which were the process by which additional help was provided and subsequently replaced by EHCPs in 2014) had expanded beyond the original intention of ensuring that those children with the most severe needs were addressed. They are now being used with a range of children with very mild needs that could be addressed through teaching that recognized individual differences. Between the inception of Statements which were intended for around 2% of children to the chapter written in 2005, the number of children receiving statements had risen

Table 41.1 Percentage of children with SEND over time derived from government statistics (DfE, 2021)

Year	% of children with SEND
2015–16	14.4
2016–17	14.4
2017–18	14.6
2018–19	15.0
2019–20	15.4
2020–21	15.9

dramatically (Warnock & Norwich, 2005, p. 12), and currently this now stands at 3.7%, or almost twice as many as intended (DfE, 2021).

One set of forces is apparently arising from government education policy that adjusts expectations of how teachers can respond to diversity in the classroom. Part of the reason for the increase in children being identified as having special educational needs and requiring additional support has been an emphasis on academic achievement within a narrow curriculum focus (reading, writing and numeracy) and a mistrust of teachers to get on with the task of educating children. In 1988, the government introduced a national curriculum to be used in all schools in England. It moved away from teachers being free to decide the content and pace of teaching to one in which content was broadly determined by central government. The pace was set by dividing the content up into chunks to be covered by the end of Year 4, Year 6, Year 9 and Year 11 of schooling (called Key Stages). It reinforced the idea that all children should be treated the same by having the same curriculum content. The testing at each of the Key Stages led to the pace of the curriculum being determined by content to be covered, rather than the learning mastered by the children. This leads to teaching moving on too quickly for some learners, and arguably, if learning has not taken place, then it could be said that the teaching was not adequate or appropriate. This was summed up in 2005 by Warnock, who had come to the conclusion that education was being hindered by an underlying assumption that on the one hand all learners must be treated the same, while on the other hand teachers must respond to meet the needs of all learners (Warnock & Norwich, 2005). A good thing about the introduction of the national curriculum was that children in special schools who had previously followed a different curriculum to those in mainstream were also expected to follow the national curriculum. This potentially would allow children to move from special schools to mainstream.

The national curriculum set expectations of the standards of learning to be achieved by children and implied that *all* children should reach these standards. To ensure that this happened tests were introduced to allow schools to be compared and schools were inspected to see if the teaching was good enough. Alongside centralized inspection of schools and national testing, the results for each school were published in what the press referred to as league tables, because it introduced a notion of competition similar to that of football clubs in the football league. The purpose was to drive up educational standards by allowing parents to see how their local schools performed and then to choose which school to send their children to. It introduced quasi-market forces based on the principles of Keynesian theory in which demand for good places in one school would be met by shifting supply of places from another school. Good schools would thrive, and poor schools would close. The expected standards, school assessment and inspection regimes increased pressure on teachers to try and get all children to the same level of academic performance. This adds pressure on teachers to only have children who will perform well academically in their classroom or school. These children will perform well in the national tests despite the teaching and the school will be well placed in the league tables. Whereas those children who needed good teachers to achieve well compared to themselves as individuals (ipsative progress) but who would not achieve well compared to their peers (relative progress), tended to be rejected. When this was not possible, simply because there is natural variation between children and some children would never reach the standard, teachers started to think about these children as needing more support or even to go to different schools. The unified national curriculum acted as a potential force for inclusion, while the inspection regime and standards agenda became a strong force to label more children as having SEND and to move children to segregated provision. There is pressure on services to assess children who do not match the political aspirational demands of the national curriculum and to prove that the children are somehow deficient in their learning or ability and needing additional support or placement in a special school. The tension between opposing forces here then is between the inclusion agenda which promotes greater diversity in the classroom and the achievement agenda which assumes that all children should achieve the same outcome on a standardised curriculum if all teachers are equally good. There is a temptation to think about school improvement in terms of developing strategies that would lead to more children achieving the expected standard *because the teaching would be better*. However, the school could look better, not by making changes to its approach, environment or teaching, but by simply being less inclusive. Instead, school improvement could be framed in terms of the inclusion agenda and ensuring that all children make good ipsative progress, rather than all children achieving the same limited academic outcomes. Fundamental to this the question has to be asked about what is meant by education? What is its purpose? Is it simply about children reaching academic standards in a minimalistic curriculum or is it about producing good citizens who can enjoy, engage and participate in society more widely?

What Other Forces Are Operating That Impact on Teaching and earning?

The government data on special educational needs (DfE, 2021) can be interrogated further and this shows that three times as many boys have SEND as girls, the peak age for being classified as having SEND is aged 10, there is a greater percentage of primary aged children classified as having SEND than secondary (14:7% compared to 13.5%), and, just over a third of children with SEND are from poorer backgrounds. What are the forces then that lead to these statistics and how do teachers come to identify children as having SEND or not? Why are more children being moved out of mainstream schools into special schools? Can schools reverse these processes and become more inclusive? To answer these types of questions we need to start to move away from thinking about within-child factors that lead to comparing children and their relative progress (what is sometimes referred to as the medical model) and to consider what children are capable of and how education can enhance these capabilities so that children make ipsative progress (referred to as the capabilities model (Sen, 1985)). The way in which social structures are organized can enable or disable people (referred to as the social model) and therefore leads to us also needing to think about the assessment of the learning environment. We also need to consider how factors in the lives of children or in the way that schools create a learning environment contribute to success (or otherwise) and how wider societal influences impact on the work of the school (sometimes referred to as the ecosystemic model, (Bronfenbrenner, 1986, 1999, 2005)). We also need to understand the interactions between what the child brings in terms of their biology and psychology and what is happening around them in terms of the social environment (referred to as the biopsychosocial model (Engel, 1977) and forming the basis of the International Classification of Functioning).

The importance of the wider social context has been highlighted through both the inspection regime and by comparing schools using national test data. Generally speaking, schools in poorer areas tended to do less well in the tests than schools in more affluent areas. The very place where a child lived was contributing to lower academic performance. This can be attributed to social inequality. Poor housing for instance leads to greater childhood illness and less time spent in school. Poor job prospects for parents or lower paid jobs leads to poorer nutrition for children and this has an impact on brain development and subsequent cognitive ability and academic performance. Parents who are employed might have to work shifts or have several part-time jobs and this distracts from their energy and time to interact with their children, resulting in lower opportunities for learning even before reaching school age. More children attending schools in areas of social deprivation tend to be identified as having SEND than those living in more affluent areas. Schools in these areas were perceived of as being failing schools, however, most of these factors initially appear to be outside the control of the school themselves. Some schools started to trial interventions to tackle some of the social determinates. Breakfast clubs were set up to improve nutrition. The government introduced free school meals for children from poorer families. Additional funding started to be attached to these children for the school to use to provide support directly, initially as Social Priority Funding and now replaced with the Pupil Premium. There is a gradual shift from compensatory approaches of providing money through EHCPs to address needs after they have arisen, to approaches that prevent the needs arising in the first place by trying to deal with the underlying causes. There is a push towards social inclusion through the development of various social policies and this then impacts on educational inclusion by making it more likely that teachers can meet the needs of children in their classroom.

The push towards inclusion is further enhanced by thinking about how the support that occurs in the classroom can be provided so that teachers can respond to increasing diversity (although as we saw earlier, the diversity was always there, but now it is starker because of the increasingly wider use of the SEND label). A code of practice for SEND was originally introduced in 1994 with revisions in 2001 and again in 2015. The principles remain much the same across the revisions. Most children identified with SEND will attend mainstream schools. At the heart of all learning is Quality First Teaching and this must be in place for all children. Quality First Teaching is a term that was introduced to mean that all teachers should have high expectations for all of the children in their class. The teacher makes use of ongoing curriculum-based assessment to see what learning that has taken place in response to the teaching provided. This is then used to plan the next round of teaching by knowing what every child has achieved, mastered or struggled with, in the previous round of teaching. Teachers are encouraged to use differentiation in their teaching which can include strategies such as:

- Using different learning tasks developed for different groups within the classroom (differentiation by task)
- Having different outcomes for different learners (differentiation by outcome)
- Arranging support during the lesson (differentiation by support) which could be peer support through different group work activities, direct support from the teacher in passing around the classroom, adult support from a teaching assistant.
- Scaffolding support for example through the use of writing frames for literacy; backward and forward chaining to teach independent living skills; the use of rules and routines and drill and rehearsal for teaching expected behaviour.

- Explicit instruction in which the teacher provides a detailed explanation then guides the whole class through a practice of the skill and then allows independent practice and repetition
- Flexible groupings within the classroom in which children work in different groups for different types of tasks or different subjects.
- Use of technology to support some children to work individually e.g., using speech to text software; children recording their ideas or responses using short videos or voice comments
- Cognitive strategies such as metacognition (getting children to think about their learning and thinking strategies); supporting memory by bridging from one activity to the next or from one lesson to the next; chunking information to aid storage in memory; use of visual strategies to aid recall and learning. Feuerstein argued that cognitive skills are modifiable and the teacher's role is to act as a mediator to improve cognitive functions by developing Mediated Learning Experiences at the right level for each child (Feuerstein, Feuerstein, & Falik, 2010).
- Teaching different approaches to problem solving such as thinking hats (De Bono, 1999) or developing positive attitudes to learning such as positive mindsets (Dweck, 2017).

However, acting against this is the pace of the national curriculum and some children will not be able to learn at the rate dictated by the curriculum. For these children additional support is offered through small group teaching. This is sometimes referred to as an interventionist strategy and is discussed further in Part IV of this book. A few children need very individualized support, and this is sometimes referred to a compensatory approach. In England, these three levels of responding to learning needs were referred to as Wave 1 or Quality First Teaching, Wave 2 or School Support and Wave 3, SEND Support (DfE & DoH, 2015). Similar tiers of support are found in other countries with different labels being used: in Ireland the terms used are whole school and classroom support 'for all', school support 'support for some' and 'school support plus' (DES, 2020); in the USA terms such as universal support, selective support and indicated or targeted support are used; in Cyprus the terms are generalised support, intensified support and specialised support (Republic of Cyprus, 2021). These models all have a common expectation that the teacher meets the learning needs of all children in the class by focusing their teaching on what is needed either by reducing barriers to learning (social model) or by focusing on what children can already do as a result of previous learning (capabilities model). The models quickly move the focus to within child factors (medical model) through interventionist approaches and at the higher tier with compensatory approaches to providing support. The compensatory approaches are often protected in law which further promotes the use of the medical model by allocating educational approaches to addressing individual needs through the allocation of additional funds and an Education Health and Care plan. In England this is not so straightforward. The achievement agenda leads to expectations about children that may not match their development level. Younger children in the class tend to be more likely to be identified with SEND by teachers, yet when a more complex assessment is undertaken the month of birth effect disappears. This means that teachers are over-identifying younger children in the class with SEND and not taking developmental levels into account (Squires, Humphrey, & Barlow, 2013; Squires, Humphrey, Barlow, & Wigelsworth, 2012).

The Code of Practice for SEND asks teachers to think more about areas of need rather than about diagnostic labels. Four areas are identified that map onto potential barriers for inclusion: communication and interaction; cognition and learning; social, emotional and mental health; and sensory or physical needs. Teachers are then encouraged to think about how to differentiate their teaching or approaches to help children learn, engage with and participate in their education (for example see Edwards, 2016). Yet at the same time, the government collects data about the type of SEND that each child has through its pupil level survey and this forces teachers to categorize children and effectively diagnose a condition. Teachers are not very good at doing this and for very good reasons; the category labels often require a multi-professional assessment, yet the census is completed by teachers who are rightly concerned with teaching not diagnosis. Most children who are not reaching the expected levels of academic performance are placed in the category moderate learning difficulties (Humphrey & Squires, 2011a, 2011b). OFSTED were more critical and said that the SEND label was being used when children simply needed better teaching (OFSTED, 2010). There is a temptation for some teachers to say that once a child has been given the label of moderate learning difficulties they should go to a school designated for such children and that their needs would be better met. However, a report that compared the outcomes for children identified as having moderate learning difficulties found that educational outcomes were the same or better in mainstream schools than in special schools (OFSTED, 2006). So then, do these children need more adult support? The research evidence suggests that more and more teaching assistants are being employed to support children in mainstream classes, however, this can have an adverse effect and lead to lower outcomes compared to similar children who were not supported by a teaching assistant (Farrell, Alborz, Howes, & Pearson, 2010; Webster et al., 2010). It seems that once a teacher knows that there is a teaching assistant in the classroom to work with a particular child, they no longer focus on that child, and they concentrate on teaching the rest of the class. The child who needs the expertise of the teacher is then left to work in isolation with support from often a less qualified adult. This is not educational inclusion, but a form of integration in which the child is in the same location but not really part of the class. There is also a danger that the child becomes over-dependent on the teaching assistant (OFSTED, 2021) and a degree of learned helplessness follows. To be inclusive, the teacher needs to think about all of the children in the classroom and to have good communication with support staff so that teaching objectives can be consistent across whole class teaching, small group work and individually supported work (Squires & McKeown, 2006). Alternatively, the teaching assistant could lead the class while the teacher works with those children who need the teaching matched to their zone of proximal development. In this model, the teacher who is trained in pedagogy and curriculum design, plans the content and delivery for the teaching assistant, while then being able to adapt teaching flexibly for small group and individual learning.

The over-emphasis on the within-child model is in part compounded by the legal system that is designed to protect and ensure that those children with the most severe needs can be supported. Those children that need the most support have a multi-professional assessment that leads to an Education Health and Care plan that specifies how the needs of the individual child can be met and what resources need to be allocated to do this. The focus is on individual difference and deficit rather than exploring the ways in which the environment is inadequate or could be changed. This leads to thinking about children as having needs that are so complex that they cannot possibly be met in a mainstream school and therefore some specialist provision is required. It is an approach that is described as a compensatory approach – different provision compensates for the inadequacies of what is on offer to the majority. This argument is further compounded in England by the way that SEND is defined in a vague manner, such that it can encompass anyone who is not making the aspirational level of progress with the educational resources deployed for this purpose. This then leads to the assumption that to 'close the gap' in learning or to enable learners to 'catch-up', additional resources are needed. If these resources can be allocated to the child in mainstream school, then the child remains there. If, however, the school argues that they cannot meet the child's needs, or it would lead to an inefficient use of resources, then alternative specialist provision is required. There is no question about the meaning of catch-up – catch up to what? To the aspirational target is often taken to be the assumption, however, a child who learns slower than their peers is unlikely to go even faster than their peers in order to catch up. Catching up only works when a child is a quick learner and some essential teaching has been missed that can be put in place quickly. The same is true of the term 'close the gap'; natural variation and a normal distribution in learning is to be expected, consequently all children cannot be 'average' and at the same level of learning. An alternative way of assessing would be to consider both the child's abilities and any impairments and how the environment responds to ensure a better learner-environment fit. A better way of thinking about the impact of interventionist approaches is to consider how much progress the child was making before the intervention and then to see if the child makes more progress with the intervention. The intervention does not need to be one that attempts to fix a deficit within the child (medical model) but could be one that requires a change in the learning environment. The Equality Act (2010) requires employers and public bodies to make use of 'reasonable adjustments' which can include the use of additional adult support or changes to the learning environment or examination processes for those that have a disclosed disability (HMSO, 2010). The Equality Act does move away from the medical model in that it asks organizations to take anticipatory measures. This means to acknowledge that disability and special educational needs are widespread, and it is very likely that service users will have needs that can be mitigated by adopting a preventative strategy. In this sense, school improvement means thinking about all of the children in the neighbourhood and identifying potential barriers to their access and participation in school and then thinking about how to remove these barriers *in advance* of the children attending the school.

Some of the approaches in helping schools to become more inclusive develop this idea further and school improvement focuses on issues that are going to be common to a wide group of learners in attempt to remove barriers to engagement, learning, and participation. The starting point acknowledges that the way that the school operates leads to organization or attitudinal barriers to inclusion and it also acknowledges that individual teachers may think that they do not have the knowledge or skills to be able to respond to greater diversity in the classroom. Inevitably the process starts by asking the school to audit where they are in terms of inclusion and perceived barriers. This then leads to the development of an action plan that usually involves some form of training for the school staff and consideration of ways to improve teaching and the learning environment. A school might want to become more inclusive in a general sense or they may want to take a more cautious approach to change by focusing on a specific target group e.g., children with autism, children with dyslexia, improving mental well-being etc. One such approach was developed with the British Dyslexia Association and called Dyslexia Friendly schools. This was introduced to a local authority where I was the lead psychologist for dyslexia and we had a two-phase approach in which during phase 1, the schools undertook the audit and had specialist awareness training for the whole school staff, they then developed an action plan. Phase 2 involved coaching by specialist teachers and help to implement their development plan over the next year. All schools in England have to submit their attainment data in maths, English and science to the government and they do this through the local authority and this provided us with an opportunity to evaluate how well the Dyslexia Friendly school initiative was working. Those schools that had undertaken both phases had better outcomes than those who had undertaken only phase 1 of the project and these were better than schools that had not engaged with the project (see Figures 41.2 and 41.3).

At first glance, it looks like the whole school improvement approach to inclusion is beneficial to *all* of the learners in the school (Squires, 2010). However, it could be argued that those schools that were most likely to have the capacity to act in a way to develop, would be the ones

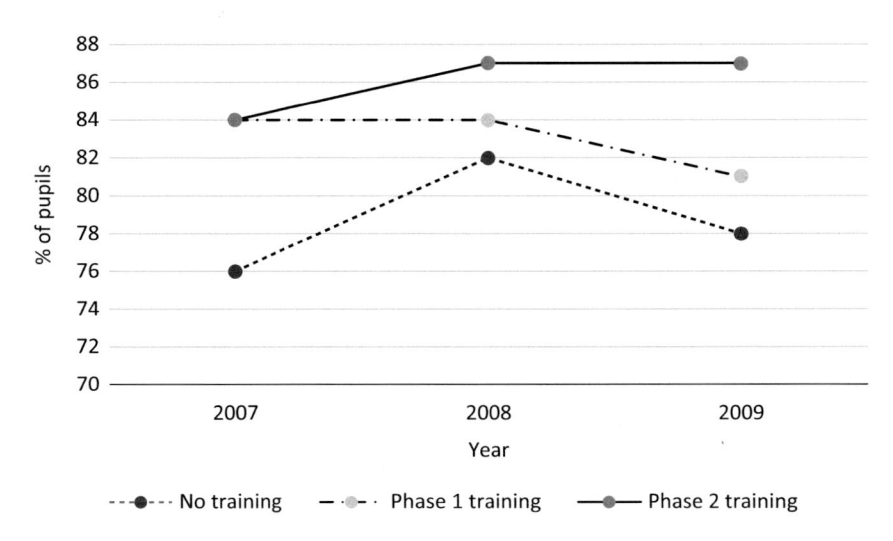

Figure 41.2 Pupils achieving aspirational standards in English in primary schools

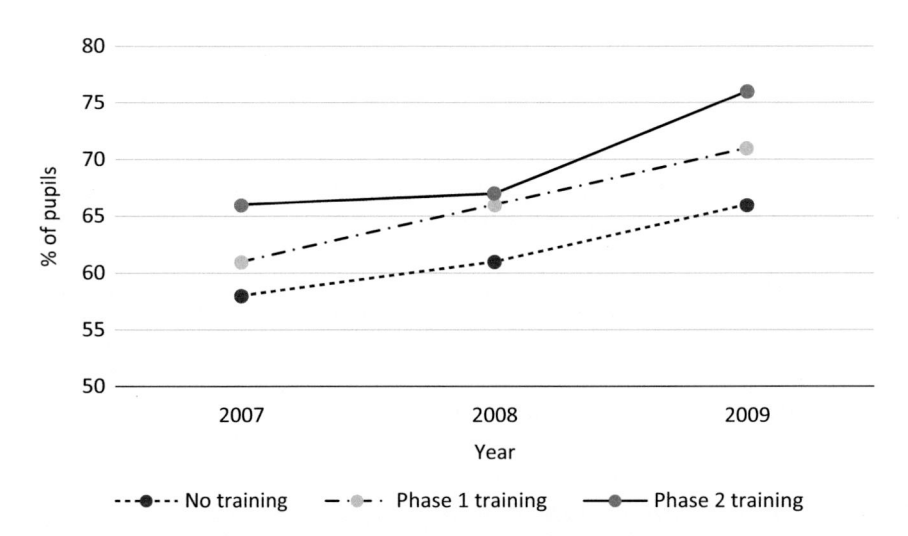

Figure 41.3 Pupils achieving good grades in secondary schools

most able to take on the initiative – or more simply, good schools do better. Perhaps these were already the most reflective and most inclusive schools.

A quasi-experimental design presented itself a few years after this project as the government wanted to pilot a school improvement approach to see if the academic outcomes and wider outcomes for children with SEND could be improved. Four hundred and fifty schools were recruited in ten different local authorities across England and a small number of comparison schools were used with data from the national pupil data base (Humphrey & Squires, 2010, 2011a, 2011b). The results from this study were promising. Over the two-year period of the project, teachers became more certain about how to identify children with SEND and consequently identified fewer children as needing additional support. Those children with SEND made good progress and more than their equivalent peers in the matched comparison schools.

It seemed as though allowing mainstream teachers to talk and reflect about SEND with their colleagues in other schools helped them to get a better understanding of what was normal progress and at what level the child's progress would cause concern. They also shared ideas about teaching and differentiating work. The schools developed better monitoring and tracking processes so that they knew exactly where each child was up to and what level of skill each learner had so that teaching could be adapted more readily. Importantly, the schools involved parents much more in discussions about their children, and both teachers and parents learnt together how best to build on each child's strengths and promote positive engagement and participation in school (Humphrey, Squires, Barlow, Lendrum, & Wigelsworth, 2012; Lendrum, Humphrey, & Squires, 2012). The pilot project was heavily funded and supported by local networks and much of this disappeared in the years that followed with a reduction in spending by local government and then the global banking crisis which reduced spending on education even further through austerity measures. The project rolled out nationally under these tighter fiscal conditions, and schools were invited to buy into the project as it became administered by a charity using the same principles. The initial pilot can be thought of as an efficacy trial because the schools were undertaking changes under ideal conditions (lots of additional funding, lots of technical support from outside, schools co-located and working in networks to promote local learning, single focus for school development), whereas the final rolled-out project was being done under real world conditions (no additional funding, limited technical support, schools isolated from each other, competing demands on development time). We were asked to evaluate the project under these conditions in what is termed an effectiveness trial. Schools were invited to join a randomized control trial in which they would either be part of the intervention arm (receiving the project) or part of the control arm (not receiving the project but allowed to carry on as normal). The control arm is important because schools do not stand still, they continue to strive to improve and follow new initiatives and, in our study, we wanted them to do just that. This allowed us to see if the project was better than what schools would normally do. The results showed that although children made progress in both arms of the study, progress was greater in the control arm than the intervention arm (Humphrey, Squires, Choudry, Byrne, & Demkowicz, 2019; Humphrey et al., 2021). Without all the additional benefits that schools received in the pilot study, the schools trying to follow the same principles did less well than those that simply reviewed where they were up to and made their own plan. This suggests that inclusion can be best supported by ensuring adequate amounts of educational funding to schools, encouraging the development of networks for teachers to learn from each other, having appropriate technical support available when needed, and engaging parents as equal partners.

How Might Universal Design for Learning Help Us to Develop More Inclusive Education Systems?

An alternative would be to use a social model to ask why the education system as a whole is not working for an individual or group of individuals and what can be done to address this? This latter question is starting to be asked with several policy solutions being offered. These include recognizing that areas of poverty lead to a higher incidence of school failure. This then leads to increasing the funding through the setting up of social priority funding or attaching money such as the Pupil Premium in England to children identified as having greater social needs, through proxy indicators such as entitlement to free school meals. This money goes directly to schools and can be spent on preventative measures, or intervention measures. However, we could go a lot further and think about the way the education system is set up and redesign it to accommodate the needs of all learners. If this was taken to its extreme, then the term 'special educational needs and disabilities' would be redundant.

One influential thinker who considered how people were disabled by poor design and how this could be addressed by trying to make the design more suited to the needs of all was Ronald Mace. Mace had contracted polio as a child and this had left him needing a wheelchair. He went on to become a leading architect and champion of the rights of people with disability. He applied his experiences to start to address how buildings could be designed to make them more accessible to a wider group of users and introduced the term Universal Design (Mace, 1988). This fits well within the social model of disability and when applied to education, we can start to think about how schools operate and how they can be improved to make them more accessible to wider and wider groups of learners. This will inevitably start with knowing where the school is in terms of physical, structural, organizational, and attitudinal barriers to inclusion. The importance of school leadership is central to changing attitudes and removing attitudinal barriers so that teachers can respond flexibly to needs as they arise (Humphrey & Squires, 2010, 2011a, 2011b; Humphrey et al., 2019; Humphrey et al., 2021; Squires, Kalambouka, & Bragg, 2016). The school leadership will also be responsible for the deployment of resources including personnel. Within the school, the way that resources are used can be managed in such a way that there is an emphasis on prevention of problems, rather than using them as an afterthought to intervene or compensate learners who have been failed by the education system. At the most simplistic level it is about redesigning schools in a way that allows for flexible learning environments and learning spaces. It focuses on the learner as being central to the process of teaching and goes further than differentiation and reasonable accommodations by having different ways of engaging learners, allowing different modes of representation and expression at its heart. It may present learners with choices of how they learn and how they are assessed. It will include the use of technology to support learners in a way that enables them to become independent learners, rather than learning to be helpless or dependent on others. It replaces teacher centred learning with approaches that focus on enabling a diverse group of learners to participate and can be applied at any stage of education including university level (Squires, 2018). Universal Design for Learning (UDL) is one approach that builds on the general principles of Universal Design (Gordon, Meyer, & Rose, 2014; Rose & Meyer, 2002). UDL is a classroom focused approach and uses the UDL framework for learning (CAST, 2021) which is discussed in Sundeen and Banerjee's chapter and in more detail in Korniyenko's chapter. There has been development of a reliable tool to allow teachers to evaluate the extent to which they are implementing the framework so that UDL can be part of a continuous improvement cycle within the school (Basham, Gardner, & Smith, 2020). We might argue that this is a soft interpretation of UDL and does not start with the design of the whole system but mediates between what is and what could be. It is a pragmatic approach. If, however, we are to take UDL to its extreme, then we need to step beyond the limits of the school and think about how the whole curriculum is constructed, taught, assessed and what content is considered to be important. In essence, what is education about? How does this function in the local community? How does it address the needs of all learners in the neighbourhood? How do educational policies fit with social services, health and employment policies? Thinking in this way helps us to imagine what education could look like in a way that takes us beyond barrier free inclusion (that is removing barriers to engagement and participation) and reliance on assistive technology (or making reasonable adjustments). Other sets of principles for instructional design exist that focus on preventing school failure (Bost & Riccomini, 2006) and these can be mapped onto those of Rose and Meyer (2002). Educators are asked to consider these principles in designing learning:

- How can learning be made stimulating and interesting to motivate all learners to encourage social and academic success?
- How can content and knowledge be presented in different ways to develop resourceful and knowledgeable learners? Moonsamy's chapter discusses how teachers can think about this from the perspective of cognitive psychology.
- How can learners express what they know in a range of different ways and formats that develop strategic and goal directed learners?

This includes questions such as: how to find ways to increase opportunities to learn content and to generalize learning; considering alternative groupings to allow different kinds of support such as: whole class teaching, team teaching, small group teaching, peer tutoring etc. It also needs to focus on how learners can recognize their own learning and become more successful learners such as: teaching how to learn rather than what to learn; teaching how the same knowledge can be applied across the curriculum; addressing both procedural and declarative knowledge; scaffolding instruction to ensure that the learner is successful in the task etc.

There are some challenges to address that arise from individual differences when to help one learner we might inadvertently create difficulties for another learner. For example, a learner with ADHD needs a fast paced, stimulating environment, while a learner with autism might need an environment that is predictable and where stimulation is reduced. Another example might be a learner with visual impairment who needs high contrast materials to read, while a learner with dyslexia finds that high contrast leads to interference patterns and disrupts reading. The solutions to these kinds of dilemmas may be different in different schools and driven by context. One school with large classrooms may choose to zone the classroom so there is a busy area and a quiet area. Another school may make use of workstations with screens to reduce stimulation or allow headphones with relaxing music to reduce noise distraction. As children get older, some of the responsibility can be passed to them, so that if content is presented in a way in which the student can change the contrast easily or select the format of presentation, then it is likely to be more accessible to a wider group of learners. Perhaps the end result is a blended system in which there is an attempt to design the education system so that it will be accessible to as many learners as possible, with ongoing audits to allow teachers to reflect and remove barriers to learning and engage in problem solving with individuals in mind. Castro-Kemp's chapter describes a similar approach to monitoring of daily targets based on the International Classification of Functioning model applied to how statutory guidance is applied in England.

Conclusion

The earlier sections of this chapter looked at some of the forces that are acting on teachers to move them in one direction or the other with respect to inclusion or segregation. These forces can operate at the level of society, government policy around assessment, school inspection regimes, the extent to which the curriculum is centralized, poverty and social inequity in the neighbourhood, the school and how it is organized, teacher attitudes and beliefs, availability of alternative placements other than mainstream, school leadership, deployment of resources in either a preventative, interventionist or compensatory way, etc. The idea of force field analysis is that it enables schools to look at all of the forces at play and to see how they can be changed to allow the school to become more inclusive. How can pro-inclusive forces be enhanced and how can forces that act towards segregation be reduced? How can we involve all stakeholders in the process and understand the different forces that might be operating for each group? For example, Shurr and Minuk discuss the role of parents as advocates in their chapter. It also

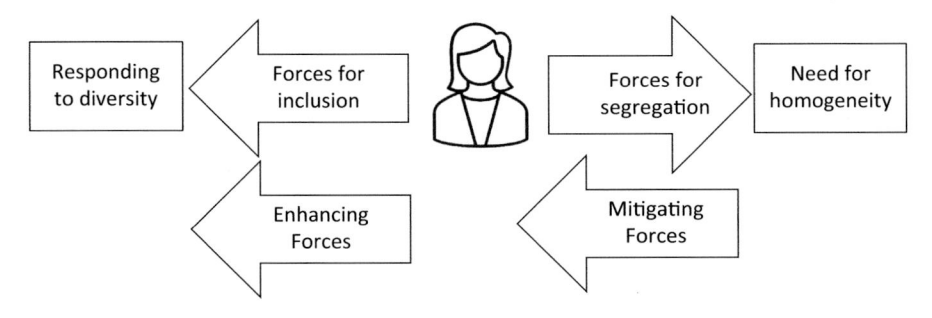

Figure 41.4 Force Field analysis to identify actions (forces) that lead to greater inclusion

requires us to understand the myriad of forces acting on the teacher. These occur at the societal level, the locality level, the school level, the classroom level, the curricular level and within the child. For each of these forces we can draw up a simple diagram to which we can add forces that enhance inclusion and forces that mitigate against segregation (Figure 41.4). We can imagine mapping all of the possible forces into a complex map for a particular school with particular children in mind, and from this we end up with a set of actions that can then form part of a school development plan.

Can we include all learners in mainstream schools? This is a question that I continually return to in my thinking. The starting point is really to ask why are we seemingly not including as many children now as we once did and why are we expanding our special schools? Why are more people being identified as having a disability rather than acknowledging individual differences? This suggests that more children could be included in mainstream and that the line between who is included and who is not is a moveable line. If we take that view then we might accept that the children with the most extreme needs, those who need 24-hour care, tube feeding, have profound and multiple learning difficulties or have extreme behavioural difficulties or extreme mental health problems, *might* need some kind of specialist or segregated provision. Not every mainstream primary school can have a hydrotherapy pool for instance, whereas a large number of pupils who need hydrotherapy can attend a school purposefully built with one. Does that school have to be a special school though, or could each locality have one of its schools with the specialist provision that is then open to all neighbouring schools? Can we reconfigure services such as occupational therapy and physiotherapy to being more community based rather than based in special schools? How far can we move the line on inclusion towards the 2030 agenda of having all children in their local mainstream schools? From time to time, I come across a school that is really pushing their position from the status quo towards greater inclusion. One mainstream primary school that I encountered had a child with profound and multiple learning difficulties in a specialist wheelchair in a classroom with age related peers. Teachers arranged for daily occupational therapy and physiotherapy to take place in the school with the professional providing training to the teachers in what to do between visits. Teachers worked on extending the child's communication skills – so effectively that he was receiving the same as he would if he had attended the local special school. His developmental outcomes would be no different to him attending a special school. His academic outcomes would not be anywhere near the aspirational targets set by the government for children of his age. For him, it appeared to make no difference to his developmental targets where he was educated, just that his needs were met. Teachers worked hard to involve him with support in the main theme for the lesson, albeit in a very modified form and often involving other children in presenting experiences to him. This also enriched his social experience beyond what would have been possible in a special school setting. A great learning experience was also presented for his class peers, who did their best to interact with him, and who came to accept very severe disability as being something normal in society rather than something hidden away and marginalized. His peers learnt about caring and about responsibility and what it is that makes us good human beings with respect for all of our peers. They also learnt about very nuanced behaviours that communicate intent and how best to respond to this communication, effectively giving this pupil a voice that would otherwise have been denied. This primary school was inspirational in their approach and showed that when you re-think education and how it is delivered, you can start to do this in a way that is consistent with universal design for learning.

In becoming more inclusive and striving towards the 2030 agenda, we need to rethink what education is about and to start to consider how all learners can be included, engaged, and supported to participate in their learning and then in wider society. The authors in the previous chapters have raised important considerations that all fit into a myriad of forces felt by individual actors and different stakeholders. The challenge is on recognizing this field of forces and then through analysis, finding ways of moderating some of the forces acting away from inclusion, and enhancing others that push towards inclusion. The goal is to ultimately increase the fit between the educational provision and the capabilities of all learners.

References

Bäckman, O., & Nilsson, A. (2016). Long-term consequences of being not in employment, education or training as a young adult. Stability and change in three Swedish birth cohorts. *European Societies, 18*(2), 136–157. doi:10.1080/14616696.2016.1153699

Basham, J. D., Gardner, J. E., & Smith, S. J. (2020). Measuring the implementation of UDL in classrooms and schools: Initial field test results. *Remedial and Special Education, 41*(4), 231–243. doi:10.1177/0741932520908015

Bost, L. W., & Riccomini, P. J. (2006). Effective instruction an inconspicuous strategy for dropout prevention. *Remedial and Special Education, 27*(5), 301–311.

Bronfenbrenner, U. (1986). Ecology of the family as a context for human development: Research perspectives. *Developmental Psychology, 22*(6), 723–742.

Bronfenbrenner, U. (1999). Environments in developmental perspective: Theoretical and operational models. In S. L. Friedman & T. D. Wachs (Eds.), *Measuring environment across the life span: Emerging methods and concepts* (pp. 3–28). Washington, DC: American Psychological Association Press.

Bronfenbrenner, U. (2005). The bioecological theory of human development. In U. Bronfenbrenner (Ed.), *Making human beings human: Bioecological perspectives on human development* (pp. 3–15). Thousand Oaks: Sage.

CAST. (2021). *Universal design for learning guidelines.* Center for Applied Special Technology. https://www.cast.org/impact/universal-design-for-learning-udl

Christle, C. A., & Yell, M. L. (2008). Preventing youth incarceration through reading remediation: Issues and solutions. *Reading & Writing Quarterly, 24*(2), 148–176.

Christle, C. A., Jolivette, K., & Nelson, C. M. (2007). School characteristics related to high school dropout rates. *Remedial and Special Education, 28*(6), 325–329.

De Bono, E. (1999). *Six thinking hats.* London: Penguin Life.

DES. (2020). *Guidelines for Post-Primary Schools: Supporting Students with Special Educational Needs in Mainstream Schools.* Dublin Department for Education and Science Downloaded from https://www.education.ie/en/The-Education-System/Special-Education/Guidelines-for-Post-Primary-Schools-Supporting-Students-with-Special-Educational-Needs-in-Mainstream-Schools.pdf

DfE. (2021). Special educational needs in England. Retrieved from https://explore-education-statistics.service.gov.uk/find-statistics/special-educational-needs-in-england

DfE, & DoH. (2015). *SEND code of practice: 0 to 25 years.* London: Department for Education & Department for Health. https://www.gov.uk/government/publications/send-code-of-practice-0-to-25

Dweck, C. (2017). *Mindset.* New York: Robinson.

Edwards, S. (2016). *The SENCO survival guide* (2nd ed.). London: David Fulton.

Engel, G. (1977). The need for a new medical model: A challenge for biomedicine. *Science, 196*, 129–136. doi:10.3109/13561828909043606

Farrell, P., Alborz, A., Howes, A., & Pearson, D. (2010). The impact of teaching assistants on improving pupils' academic achievement in mainstream schools: A review of the literature. *Educational Review, 62*(4), 435–448.

Feuerstein, R., Feuerstein, R. S., & Falik, L. H. (2010). *Beyond smarter: Mediated learning and the brains capacity for change*. New York: Teachers College Press.

Gallagher, E. (2011). The second chance school. *International Journal of Inclusive Education, 15*(4), 445–459. doi:10.1080/13603110903131705

Gordon, D., Meyer, A., & Rose, D. (2014). *Universal design for learning: Theory and practice*. Wakefield, MA: CAST Professional Publishing.

HMSO. (1944). *Education act 1944*. London: His Majesty's Stationery Office.

HMSO. (2010). *Equality act 2010*. London: Her Majesty's Stationery Office.

Humphrey, N., & Squires, G. (2010). *DfE RR 028 achievement for all evaluation: Interim report (May 2010)*. London: Department for Education.

Humphrey, N., & Squires, G. (2011a). *DFE-RR176: Achievement for all: National evaluation*. Final report. London: Department for Education.

Humphrey, N., & Squires, G. (2011b). *DfE RR 123. Achievement for all. National evaluation*. London: Department of Education.

Humphrey, N., Squires, G., Barlow, A., Lendrum, A., & Wigelsworth, M. (2012). Improving outcomes for learners with special educational needs and disabilities (SEND): National evaluation of the Achievement for All (AfA) programme. A 90 min workshop. Paper presented at the 10th Annual Hawaii International Conference on Education, Honolulu, Hawaii.

Humphrey, N., Barlow, A., Wigelsworth, M., & Squires, G. (2013). The role of school and individual differences in the academic attainment of learners with special educational needs and disabilities: A multi-level analysis. *International Journal of Inclusive Education, 17*(9), 909–931. doi:10.1080/13603116.2012.718373

Humphrey, N., Squires, G., Choudry, S., Byrne, E., & Demkowicz, O. (2019). *Achievement for all (AfA) effectiveness trial: Report and executive summary*. London: Education Endowment Foundation.

Humphrey, N., Squires, G., Choudry, S., Byrne, E., Troncoso, P., Demkowicz, O., & Wo, L. (2021). *Achievement for all (AfA) effectiveness trial: Adendum report*. London: Education Endowment Foundation.

Jahnukainen, M., & Järvinen, T. (2005). Risk factors and survival routes: Social exclusion as a life-historical phenomenon. *Disability and Society, 20*(6), 669–682. doi:10.1080/09687590500249090

Kern, L., Evans, S. W., Lewis, T. J., State, T. M., Weist, M. D., & Wills, H. P. (2015). CARS Comprehensive intervention for secondary students with emotional and behavioral problems: Conceptualization and development. *Journal of Emotional and Behavioral Disorders, 23*(4), 195–205. doi:10.1177/1063426615578173

Lendrum, A., Humphrey, N., & Squires, G. (2012). Developing positive school-home relationships through structured conversations with parents of learners with special educational needs and disabilities (SEND). Paper presented at the 10th Annual Hawaii International Conference on Education, Honolulu, Hawaii.

Lewin, K. (1943). Defining the 'field at a given time'. *Psychological Review, 50*(2), 292–310.

Lewin, K. (1947). Frontiers in group dynamics: Concept, method and reality in social science; social equilibria and social change. *Human Relations, 1*, 5–41. doi:10.1177/001872674700100103

Limbach-Reich, A., & Powell, J. J. W. (2016). *Supporting young adults with special educational needs (SEN) in obtaining higher qualifications: NESET Ad hoc question No 6*, October2016. Retrieved from http://nesetweb.eu/en/library/supporting-young-adults-with-special-educational-needs-sen-in-obtaining-higher-qualifications/

Living Heritage. (2010). *Going to school: The 1870 act*. Retrieved from http://www.parliament.uk/about/living-heritage/transformingsociety/livinglearning/school/overview/1870educationact/

Mace, R. L. (1988). Designing for the 21st Century: An International Conference on Universal Design. Paper presented at the Hofstra University, Hempstead, New York.

OFSTED. (2006). *Inclusion: Does it matter where pupils are taught? Provision and outcomes in different settings for pupils with learning difficulties and disabilities*. London: OFSTED.

OFSTED. (2010). *The special educational needs and disability review: A Statement is not enough*. Manchester: OFSTED.

OFSTED. (2021). *Supporting SEND*. Online at https://www.gov.uk/government/publications/supporting-send/supporting-send#implications: OFSTED.

Przybylski, B. K. (2014). Unsuccessful in education: Early school leaving. In D. Eißel, E. Rokicka, & J. Leaman (Eds.), *Welfare state at risk: Rising inequality in Europe*. London: Springer.

Republic of Cyprus. (2021). *The inclusive education (support structures) law of 2021*. Cyprus.

Rose, D., & Meyer, A. (2002). *Teaching every student in the digital age: Universal design for learning*. Alexandria, VA: ASCD.

Schwabe, M., & Charbonnier, É. (2015). What are the advantages today of having an upper secondary qualification? In *Education Indicators in Focus – August 2015*. Retrieved from http://www.oecd-ilibrary.org/docserver/download/5jrw5p4jn426.pdf?expires=1442825774&id=id&accname=guest&checksum=CB9A0EA7EBA7D0E7B51D17AFC14B26A8

Sen, A. (1985). *Commodities and capabilities*. Amsterdam and New York: North-Holland.

Snieskaa, V., Valodkieneb, G., Daunorienec, A., & Draksaited, A. (2015). Education and unemployment in European Union economic cycles. *Procedia - Social and Behavioral Sciences*, 213, 211–216.

Squires, G. (2010). Analysis of local authority data to show the impact of being dyslexia friendly on school performance. *Parents in the Know*, 13, 5. Retrieved from http://www.staffordshire.gov.uk/NR/rdonlyres/E44E1F3B-8502-4E84-9145-7CCA0CA9F98B/142062/ParentsintheKnownewsletterSept2010.pdf

Squires, G. (2012). Historical and socio-political agendas around defining and including children with special educational needs. In D. Armstrong & G. Squires (Eds.), *Contemporary issues in special educational needs: Considering the whole child* (pp. 9–24). London: Open University/Mc Graw-Hill Education.

Squires, G. (2017). *Early school leaving and learners with special educational needs and/or disabilities: Final summary report*. Odense, Denmark: European Agency for Special Needs and Inclusive Education.

Squires, G. (2018). Educational psychologists working with universities. In B. Apter, C. Arnold, & J. Hardy (Eds.), *New frameworks and perspectives: Applied educational psychology with young people 16 to 25*. London: UCL IOE Press.

Squires, G. (2019). A European consideration of early school Leaving as a process running through childhood: A model for inclusive action. *Education 3-13: International Journal of Primary, Elementary and Early Years Education*. Retrieved from https://www.tandfonline.com/doi/full/10.1080/03004279.2019.1664412

Squires, G., & Dyson, A. (2017). *Early school leaving and learners with disabilities and/or special educational needs: To what extent is research reflected in European Union policies?* Odense, Denmark: European Agency for Special Needs and Inclusive Education.

Squires, G., & Kefallinou, A. (2019). *Preventing school failure: A review of the literature*. Odense, Denmark: European Agency for Special Needs and Inclusive Education.

Squires, G., & McKeown, S. (2006). *Supporting children with dyslexia* (2nd ed.). New York: Continuum.

Squires, G., Humphrey, N., Barlow, A., & Wigelsworth, M. (2012). The identification of Special Educational Needs and the month of birth: Differential effects of category of need and level of assessment. *European Journal of Special Needs Education*, 27(4), 469–481. doi:10.1080/08856257.2012.711961

Squires, G., Humphrey, N., & Barlow, A. (2013). Over-identification of special educational needs in younger members of the age cohort: Differential effects of level of assessment and category of need. *Assessment and Development Matters*, 5(1), 23–26.

Squires, G., Kalambouka, A., & Bragg, J. (2016). *A study of the experiences of post primary students with special educational needs. Research report 23*. Dublin: The National Council for Special Education.

UN. (1989). *Convention on the rights of the child*. New York: United Nations.

UNESCO. (1994a). *Final report: World conference on special needs education: Access and quality*. Paris: United Nations Educational, Scientific and Cultural Organization.

UNESCO. (1994b). *The Salamanca statement and framework for action on special needs education*. Salamanca, Spain: United Nations Educational, Scientific and Cultural Organization.

UNESCO. (2000). *The Dakar framework for action. Education for all: Meeting our collective commitments*. Paris, France: United Nations Educational, Scientific and Cultural Organization.

UNESCO. (2015a). *Education 2030. Incheon declaration: Towards inclusive and equitable quality education and lifelong learning for all*. Paris, France: United Nations Educational, Scientific and Cultural Organization.

UNESCO. (2015b). *Relationship between sustainable development goal 4 and the education 2030 framework for action*. Paris, France: United Nations Educational, Scientific and Cultural Organization.

UNESCO, & UNICEF. (2015). *Fixing the broken promise of education for all: Findings from the global initiative on out-of-school children*. Montreal: UIS. UNESCO Institute for Statistics.

Warnock, M. (1978). *Special educational needs: Report of the committee of enquiry into the education of handicapped children and young people*. London: Her Majesty's Stationery Office.

Warnock, M., & Norwich, B. (2005). *Special educational needs: A new look*. London: Continuum.

Webster, R., Blatchford, P., Bassett, P., Brown, P., Martin, C., & Russell, A. (2010). Double standards and first principles: Framing teaching assistant support for pupils with special educational needs. *European Journal of Special Educational Needs, 25*(4), 319–336.

Wilkins, J., & Huckabee, S. (2014). *A literature map of dropout prevention interventions for students with disabilities*. Clemson, SC: National Dropout Prevention Center for Students with Disabilities, Clemson University.

World Bank. (2015). *Incheon declaration: Education 2030 - towards inclusive and equitable quality education and lifelong learning for all* (English). Washington, DC: World Bank Group.

INDEX

absolute power 268
abstract systems 246
academic and psychological approach 381, 382, 402
academic disciplines 78, 88; academic performance 439; academic skills 70, 329, 372, 397
accessibility 47; accessibility audits 49; accessible transportation 47; online accessibility 53
accommodation 36, 46, 462; reasonable accommodation 125
acupuncture and moxibustion 618
adaptive behavior 58, 310, 317, 540
adjusted analysis 291
advocacy groups 28, 29, 31; disability advocates 28
aesthetics 46
Affective Communication Assessment 581, 587
Agenda for Sustainable Development 21, 23, 24, 30, 33, 360
Ages and Stages Questionnaire 234, 235
aging population 53
Air Carrier Access Act of 1986 and 2009 46
alpha power 268, 270, 272; alpha waves 270
alternative teaching-learning opportunities 150
ambience 269, 271, 272, 275; amiable ambience 271, 275; congenial ambience 269
American Electroencephalographic Society 268
Americans with Disabilities Act 46, 54, 594
amplitude 272
amygdala 275, 296
analytic signal representation 10, 268, 272, 273
ancestry search 59
anecdotal observation 337
animal models 283; animal studies 296
Anterior-Posterior Pelvis Tilt 528
Anti-Defamation League 27, 28, 41
Applied Behaviour Analysis (ABA) 328, 329; Antecedent-based interventions (ABI) 342; behavioural interviews 336; behaviour checklists 336, 337; behaviour modification 331; functional analyses (FA) 337, 338, 447; functional behavior assessment 454; functional communication training (FCT) 342, 346; function-based behaviour 328, 342; function-based video modeling 445
appreciative inquiry 631, 636
apprenticeships 643
appropriate measures 234
architectural barriers 46, 627; Architectural Barriers Act of 1968 46
arousal regulation 274
ascending reticular activating system 270
assessment: direct assessment 336, 355; ecological assessment 339–341; ethical assessment practices 227; indirect assessment 336, 445; informal assessments 228; misidentification 230; systems approach to assessment 221
assistive technology (AT) 393, 483, 547; assistive listening device(s) 50, 401, 407, 572; assistive technology assessment 490; assistive technology factors 486; assistive technology training 392; role of AAC (Augmentative and alternative communication) 361, 364
The Association for Teacher Education 545
atastic 627
athetoid 627
Attention-Deficit/Hyperactivity Disorder (ADHD) 276; ADHD combined type presentation 267
auditory analysis training 387, 401, 405; auditory discrimination program 401; auditory processing 34, 401, 416, 468, 570
autism: autism spectrum conditions (ASC) 242; autism spectrum disorder (ASD) 98, 191; autistic users 49; etiology of autism spectrum disorders 305

balanced reading tutorials 386
Bandura, A. 450, 637
basal ganglia 275, 276, 278
Bates, C. 55
Battelle Developmental Inventory, 2nd Edition 239
Bayley Third Edition 234
beta power 268; beta-waves 270
bilingual 229–231, 239, 377; bilingual assessment 229
Binet Kamat Test 268, 269
biological mechanisms 283
biopsychosocial framework 266; biopsychosocial model 103, 208, 561, 659
body structure and function 73, 526
bone conducted headphones 621
bottom-up and top-down processing 269; bottom-up information 270; top-down and bottom-up attentional monitoring 271
braille: braille embosser 623; braille textbooks 622, 623
brain dynamics 275
Brain Electro Scan System (B.E.S.S) 268
brain waves 272; frequency bands 268
Brief Questionnaire for Adolescents on Attitudes towards Persons with a Disability (CBAD-12A) 77
butterworth filter 268

Cameron, M. 454
Canadian Charter of Rights and Freedoms 130
cancellation task 269, 274
capabilities model 35–37, 658, 660
Captain's Log Brain Train Software 269
case-control studies 282
case law 28; *Board of Education of the Hendrick Hudson School District v. Rowley (1982)* 32; *Brown v. Board of Education* (1954) 28, 29; *Endrew F. v. Douglas County School District RE-1* (2017) 38
categorical perception and word metric structure 394
causes and contributing factors 281
child-centered pedagogy 33
child-focused language enrichment interventions 14, 474, 476
Childhood Autism Rating Scale (CARS) 284, 306
childhood psychiatric disorder 266
child needs and family desires and expectations 59, 64, 66; children's needs and strengths 10, 92, 97, 98, 101; children's views 96, 97
Children and Families Act (2014) 92–96
child symptom inventory 268, 269, 276; *see also* assessment
Chinese spelling 388, 403
Cihak, D.F. 375, 423, 451, 606
civic life 47
classroom engagement 53; classroom implementation 362, 365, 368, 371, 373; classroom observations 367, 472; classroom participation 8, 354, 524; classroom settings 8, 140, 368, 371, 373, 495; classroom strategies 21, 97
closed captioning 46, 53
cognition 208, 581; cognitive absorption 269, 271, 275; cognitive differences 54; cognitive disabilities 34, 50, 70, 209, 507, 550; cognitive flow state 269; cognitive functioning 259, 260; cognitive functioning in the classroom 260; cognitive impairment(s) 54, 282, 605; cognitive intervention 271, 272, 278, 409; cognitive management of information 10, 208; cognitive map 14, 212, 213; cognitive processes 245, 247, 267, 400, 403, 404; cognitive theory 450, 539, 637; cognitive training approach (CTA) 381; computerized cognitive training 269; task absorption 269, 271
collaborative teamwork 553; collectible systems 246
communication assessment 581, 587; communication boards 106, 413, 495; communication competence 13, 110, 113, 114; communication interventions 32, 375, 584; communication matrix 582, 589; communication partner training 500, 502; communication passports 586, 588; communicative environment 54, 472
comorbidity 276, 278, 511, 521
compensation 119, 195, 474; compensatory 556, 659–661, 666
compliance officers 47, 48
computer music class 429; computer-assisted reading intervention 410; computer-assisted training program 391
Conner's Parent Rating Scale 268–270, 274
contextual spelling 397
continuous virtual reinforcement 271
Convention on the Rights of Persons with Disabilities *see* United Nations Conventions
cool executive function 275, 277
co-teaching 30, 61, 62, 69
Council for Exceptional Children (CEC) 39
course load 50
COVID-19 pandemic 31, 429, 554, 557, 609
creative arts-based approaches 585
cross leg sitting 534
curriculum: *Carolina Curriculum for Infants and Toddlers with Special Needs* 235, 236, 240; curriculum design 46, 661; specialized curriculum 28

deaf and hard of hearing (DHH) 436, 618
decoding skills 401, 413, 415, 418, 419, 421
default mode network 271, 277
deficit discourse 66
definitions of disability 221

delta power 268; delta waves 271
dementia 54, 336, 354, 360
design process 10, 45, 46, 52, 53
determinism 329
developing communication 583, 587
developmental delay(s) 227, 311, 314; developmental disability (disabilities) 310, 509; developmental language disorders 478
Devereux Scales of Mental Disorder 268, 269
diagnosis 34, 220, 259, 299; diagnostic intervention model 547, 549; micro diagnosis 267
Diagnostic and Statistical Manual of Mental Disorders (DSM) 266; DSM-V classification 242
differentiated instruction 207, 543; differentiation 462
Digital Accessible Information System (DAISY) 623
digit span 269, 274; digital divide 53, 115, 117; digital infrastructure 53; digit backward 269, 270, 272, 274; digit forward 269, 270, 272, 274; dignity 21, 41, 139, 141, 319, 629
diplegia 627
disability: definition 27, 31; disability specific skills 631; disablism 628
Discrete Trial Training (DTT) 341, 343
display arms 620
disruptive behaviours 327
The Division for Early Childhood (DEC) 38
dorsal attention network(s) 271, 272
dorsolateral prefrontal cortex 275

early childhood 227; early communication 12, 369, 554, 579, 581, 586; early intervention 227; early phonological reading skills 385; early reading difficulties 391, 410
EasyTactix 623
economic independence 626, 627, 629
economic justification 29, 37
EDEL 623
educational content 62; educational placement 59; educational programs 23, 232, 544, 547; educational services and supports 59, 61, 67; educational software approach 382, 400
Education for All (EFA) goals 30
Education Health Care Plan (EHCP) 656
electrodes 268
electrophysiological measures 270; electroencephalography (EEG) 409; Event Related Potential (ERP) 268
Emerson, E. 452, 522, 537
emotional and behavioral disorders 119
empathic thinking 246
"Empathizing–Systemizing" (E-S) Theory 192
engagement practices 53
Enhanced Perceptual Functioning Theory (EPF) 244, 247; Enhanced Perceptual Hypothesis 247

environment-focused language enrichment interventions 475, 476; environmental problems 55
epilepsy 27, 43, 336, 355, 577, 627
epochs 268
Equality Act, The 662
equitable design 55; inequality 21, 43, 56, 207, 219, 659
Erasmus + projects 547
Evidence-Based Practices 39, 565
exam accommodation 50
executive system 267
Experimental analysis of behaviour 329
externalizing tendency 267

face-to-face interaction 53
facilitating strategies 15, 572, 573
factors impacting functional seating 526
Fair Housing Act Amendment of 1988 46
family-centered decision making 486; family engagement 59, 315, 321, 602; family of participation-related constructs 157
fast wave oscillation (FWO) 270
feedback: assessment 317, 322; strengths-based 308; verbal 308, 309, 315; written 309
fluency building (FB) 341, 344
force field analysis 12, 655, 666, 667
free and appropriate public education (FAPE) 28
freedom from distractibility 269, 270, 272
frontal lobe 272, 296; frontoparietal network 272; frontoparietal region 271; frontostriatal cortex 275; frontotemporal region 271
fundamental right 4, 41, 126, 135

gender-related 86, 87
generalised support 660
genetic research 266
gestalt 269, 397
global coherence 245; global concern 281; global pandemic 50, 51, 53
goal-directed behaviour 270, 274, 275; goal-directed activity 271, 274
grading 50, 51, 55, 459
guided reading intervention 388

hard of hearing 427–428
healthy participants (HP) 268
hearing acuity 427, 428, 431, 433, 435
hemiplegia 627
High/scope Child Observation Record 235, 236
high incidence disabilities 38, 58, 69, 119
high-leverage practices 39, 41, 43
holistic application 53
home based pre reading intervention 384, 409
homogeneity 655, 667
hot executive function 275

Index

identities-disability identity 312, 319; cultural context 233, 485, 486, 519, 520; cultural identities 17, 545; racial identity 315
image narration 46
impersonal agent 271
impulsivity 266, 267, 270, 274, 327
Incheon Declaration (2015) 4
incidental teaching (IT) 341, 343
inclusion justification: economic justification 29, 37; educational justification 29, 37; social justification 29, 37
inclusion xvii, 4, 5; inclusion as a process 32; inclusion in physical education 458, 461, 463, 465, 466; inclusion in society 76, 124, 262; inclusive activities 12; inclusive education 5; inclusive strategies 260, 262, 264; trends in inclusion practices 36
individuality 141, 150
individualized education program (IEP) 102, 322; individualized educational plans (IEPs) 540; individualized support 135, 257, 262, 263, 543, 660
Individuals with Disabilities Act 438; Individuals with Disabilities Education Act (IDEA) of 1975 46
inductive open-coding 59
information processing 269, 272, 404, 545
innovative approaches 6, 18, 19
in-service teachers 7, 10, 152
institutional context 486, 487
instruction: definition 14, 38–40, 62, 207, 211–215, 401, 462; improving geometry skills 441; instructional discourse 206; instructional materials 8, 10, 54, 62, 420, 542; instructional practices 37, 38, 62, 545, 573; instructional strategies 50, 70, 329, 543, 549; instructional video modeling 441, 444, 454; using the online library catalog 444
intellectual disability (disabilities) definition 310; diagnosis 259
intense world hypothesis (IWH) 244, 247
intention 17, 30, 33, 47, 236, 656
interactional 546, 589
internal ableism 50
internalized oppression 628, 629, 636, 637; internalizing condition 267
International Classification of Diseases-10 (ICD-10) 266
International Classification of Functioning, Disability and Health (ICF) 94, 220, 257, 471, 482, 525
International Dyslexia Association 378
intrapersonal 177, 181, 197, 200, 464
intuitive 47, 48, 562
isolated environments 53
iterative process 47

Jean Piaget 228
Job Access With Speech (JAWS) 620; *see also* assistive technology (AT)

Keenan, M. 302, 354, 453
KGS corporation 620, 621
Koegel, L.K. 224, 357, 452
Koegel, R.L. 224, 323, 357, 452

labour market 205, 254, 627, 641, 643
landmark legislation 66; landmarks 54
Lang, R. 354, 359, 424, 452, 557
latency 265, 268, 272, 419
LCD (Liquid Crystal Display) monitor 619, 620
learning and engagement 47, 49, 53; learning materials 47, 53, 380; learning space(s) 53, 206, 207, 213, 665; learning styles 14, 209, 210, 213, 258, 263, 351
least restrictive environment (LRE) 28, 31
letter-sound correspondence(s) 413, 415, 416, 418, 423
life skills 28, 62, 66, 182, 219; living environment 53, 445
lifetime employment 624
Likert scale(s) 77, 110, 112, 284, 472, 473
limbic system 275
linguistic diversity 229
literacy instructions 415
live transcription 53; local coherence 245; long–term-potentiation 272
Low and Middle Income (LAMI) countries 234, 376
low incidence disabilities 58, 70, 357, 588
low vision 37, 618, 620, 622–624

magnifying CCTV 619
marginalization 13, 653
Maria Montessori 228
maternal risk factors of ASD (Autism Spectrum Disorder) 283, 299
MATLAB 2016b software 268
measurement issues 234
mechanical systems 246
mediated learning experiences 660
medical model of disability 34–36
medical-neurological approach 382, 402
mental health screening 509
metacognitive awareness 395, 400, 405
Middle East 37, 233
mindblindness 203, 245, 251; mindfulness-based intervention 394, 400
mind reading 245–248, 254
minorities 17, 18
Mission 1000 637
mobile applications 53; mobile game-based learning 393, 406; mobile technologies 116
moderate learning difficulties 155, 655, 661
modified curriculum 64; adapted 640
motivation 208; motivational lag 267; Social Motivation Theory 247
motor loop(s) 274, 275; motoric systems 246; motor organization 267

multiculturalism 22; democracy 551, 640; multilingual 408, 492, 559
multidirectional communication 309, 312, 315, 318
multiple deficits 391, 403, 404; multiple disability 538, 539, 542
multisensory approach 14, 381, 382, 396, 400

2N-Back test 268
National Association for the Education of Young Children (NAEYC) 227
National Centre for Education Statistics (NCES) 3, 4
National Education Goals Panel 229
National Technical Assistance Center on transition 598
natural systems 246
neighborhood schools 64
neocortex 275; catecholamines 274; dopamine 271, 276, 279; neural circuit 272; neural network(s) 275, 303, 545; neural oscillation(s) 270, 278; neural underpinning 270; neurotransmitter(s) 275, 276; neutral sensory environment 49; norepinephrine 274, 276; orbitofrontal 275, 278; parietal lobe 272
network drives 619
neuro-developmental disorders 191; neurocognitive 244, 277, 278, 310, 508; neurodevelopmental disorders 304, 376, 439, 444, 445, 450, 524; neurodevelopmental lag 272; neurodivergent 53; neurodiverse 7, 15, 36, 242, 245, 247, 248; neurodiverse movement 15; neuro-diversity movement 191; neuroimaging 266, 277, 382; neuro-typical(s) 146, 192, 196, 197, 201
No Child Left Behind 4, 21
noise to its signal ratio 271; cacophony of neural noise 272
non-compliance 54
normalization 47
notch filter 268
note-taking assistance 49, 50
NonVisual Desktop Access (NVDA) 620, 625
numerical systems 246

observational learning 438, 440, 443
odd ratio 14, 286
Odom, S.L. 41, 452–454
Office for National Statistics 192, 205, 250, 254
Ohtake, Y. 359, 453
online accommodation 53; online modes 198, 200, 248; online technologies 53, 560
on-the-job training 641, 644
operant conditioning 331
orthographic disability 387; orthographic spelling training 383, 408
over-stimulating 54

paraprofessionals training 503
parking spaces 54
parsimony 329
participatory 35, 139, 193, 456, 457
partnership(s): collaborative partnerships 27, 309, 320; family, school, community partnerships (FCSP) 309, 312, 319; family-school partnerships 308, 320, 518
PC-Talker 620, 625
Pearson's correlations 82
peer interactions 105, 117, 375, 452, 542, 609; peer-mediated instruction and intervention 40
people with disabilities (PwD) 76, 146, 327
performance-related feedback 58
personalized support 5, 6, 148; personhood 626; personnel support 62
personal spaces 48
pervasive developmental disorder 280, 304, 306
pharmacotherapy 272, 274, 278; methylphenidate 267, 277–279; neurochemical platform 275; pharmacological agent 275
philosophical doubt 329
phonological and phonemic awareness 415
physical infrastructure 53, 127; physical therapy 189, 618
Pivotal Response Training (PRT) 341, 343
Point-of-View (POV) video modeling 439; teaching transitions 439
positive reinforcement(s) 201, 329, 343, 345
possible associative factors 281
potential environmental risk factors 281
power spectral density 268; spectral power 268, 277
predictable elements 54
prefrontal cortex 272, 274–276
pre-requisite skills for learning 207
preservice teacher education 20
prevalence of ASD 280–282
priming video modeling 441
principle of low physical effort 48
problem-solving skills 14, 269, 271, 404, 597
processing speed 269–271, 274, 395
productive 193, 197, 361, 593, 601, 602
progressive outlook 9
progress monitoring 100, 231, 314, 317
prompting system(s) 260, 261, 605
psycho-emotional aspects of disability 628; psychoeducation 267, 270, 311; psychometric tools 237; psychopathology 267, 270, 276, 277, 303, 355, 523; psychosocial outcomes 30, 478, 481, 482, 654
public spaces 53
punishers 329, 333–335
purposive sampling 109, 142, 194, 202, 267

Qualitative research: focus groups 485; qualitative methodologies 61, 65, 228; quantitative methodologies 65; surveys 22, 27, 59, 65, 523

Index

quality first teaching 659, 660
quiet spaces 49

radical behaviourism 329, 331
reading acquisition 378, 399, 401, 403, 410; assimilation and communication ability 392; eye movements 399, 581; reading and language disorder 387; reading difficulty 11, 382, 385; semantic and linguistic abilities 399; visual perception 197, 199, 244, 252, 399
reading problems in the Arabic language 392
reading progression 393; reading vocabulary 391, 393
referrals 267, 569
reflexes 526, 528, 531
refreshable tactile graphic display(s) 620, 621; refugees 4, 17, 18, 23, 238; refugee children 19, 233, 238
Rehabilitation Act of 1973 46
reinforcement paradigms 267
relative power 268
reliability and validity 187, 236, 284, 587; reliable internet connection 49, 53
resilient job skills 632, 634
respite care 67, 223
response inhibition 269, 271, 274, 275, 279
retrospective examination of relevant medical records 282
reward 201, 204, 247, 253, 254, 274
Right to Education 3, 31, 124–135
role of teachers 90
routes for learning 32, 581, 589
Routines-Based Interviewing 230, 311

Salamanca Statement 6, 29, 123; educational justification 29, 37; Policy and Practice in Special Needs Education 29; Salamanca Statement on Principles 29; social justification 29, 37
school support 223, 660; school-based evaluation 359
Schreibman, L. 453, 454
screening tools 234, 236, 406, 555
seating problems 527
Section 508 of the Rehabilitation Act 46
segregated education 125, 618, 624, 655
selective support 660
self-contained placements 66
self-injury 327, 372, 445
self-instruction training approach 381, 401
semi-structured interviews: semi-structured questionnaire 142, 144, 194
sensory accommodation 46; sensory functions 539; sensory over-responsivity 54; sensory training 400, 404
severe learning difficulties 655
Shane, H.C. 374, 376, 377, 454

sight word recognition 413, 415, 419, 420
significant support needs 37, 64
slow-wave oscillatory group (SWO) 270, 271
SMART outcomes 96, 99, 101, 102
social exclusion 32, 106, 219, 65, 470
social model of disability, definition 35; critique for the social model of disability 35
Social Motivation Theory (SMT) 247
social networks 40, 66, 312, 339, 340
social participation 163, 187, 501, 627; social-cognitive theory 629; socialisation 264; social systems 246, 339; socio-pedagogical mediator 151
spastic 526, 536, 627
specialised language assessments 472
specialised support 660
specially designed instruction 38
speech training 427; speech-language development 627
spelling ability 383, 386, 390
splinter skills 192, 236, 243, 252
stereotyping 27, 46; stereotypy 8, 445, 453
strategies and policies 641
streamlining 16
strengths-based approaches 15, 19
striatum 274
students with special needs 5, 7, 13, 90, 141
suicide 508; intervention 518; prevention 510; risk assessment 509; warning signs 515
supplemental notes 50; supplementary aids and services 4, 38
supported and sheltered employment 642, 644
Sustainable Development Goals (SDGs) 30; sustained attention 269–271, 274, 275
swell touch paper 623
synchronous learning 53
systemization 246

tactile clues 47; tactile material 623
targeted support 660
task positive network 271
teacher support 18, 152, 552, 640; teacher specialization 12, 14, 30, 38, 61, 643; teacher training programs 545, 546; teaching-learning strategies 7, 149, 245; each basic reading skills 414; teaching methods 29, 54, 344, 366, 547
Teaching Strategies GOLD 235, 236, 240
technological and communication restrictions 627
telepractice 489, 551; application of telepractice 555; benefits of telepractice 554; telepractice in schools 556
tetraplegia (quadriplegia) 627
text processing comprehension intervention 388, 395
Theory of Mind (ToM) 244, 245, 247
theta power 268; theta waves 271
thinking classroom 215, 216

Index

third-person perspective video modeling 441, 442, 443, 444; answering simple questions 441; conversational turn-taking 442; delivering compliments 442; following teacher directions 444; initiating greetings and a conversation 444; sharing material and cooperative play 442; social initiations 372, 443, 451; word recognition and pronunciation 440
three-dimensional printer 623
time extension(s) 50
Title II of the ADA 47
Title III 47
tolerance for error 48, 51
trained professionals 235, 362, 545
transcribing 50
transition 115, 316, 439, 540, 593; post-secondary transition planning 596; transition assessment 317
translating statutory guidance 6, 92
translation of policy 31
transportation problems 627
Tri-Focus Model 543
triggers 54, 283
trio-loops 271, 275; frontostriatal associative 271, 275; frontostriatal limbic loop 275; frontostriatal loops 271; motor and limbic loops 271
Tsukuba University of Technology (NTUT) 38, 153, 154, 428, 618, 625

unadjusted analysis 290
UN conventions 124, 327
uncoordinated movements 627
undergraduates 77, 87, 107, 117, 428
unemployed 192, 244, 594, 638, 649
United Nations Children's Fund (UNICEF) 36, 123, 232
United Nations Conventions 30, 93, 256; United Nations Convention on the Rights of Persons with Disabilities (CRPD) 124; United Nations Convention on the Rights of the Child (CRC) (1989) 30, 44, 140, 190
The United Nations Educational Scientific and Cultural Organization (UNESCO) 23, 24, 29, 155, 156
United Nations Sustainable Development Goals 4, 327
universal design (UD); universal design for learning (UDL) 40, 46, 150, 665; universal design typology 45

Universal Design for Learning (UDL) 40, 46, 150, 665
universal support 660; universality 45, 47; universal technology 53

ventral attention network 271, 272
ventromedial regions 275
verbal behaviour training (VB) 341
video-based group instruction (VGI) 443; school-based social-skills 442, 453
video modeling: definition 438; practitioner training 439, 446; resources of 16, 151, 617; social-communication performance 439, 441
video prompting (VP) 441
video self-modeling (VSM) 439; following basic classroom rules 439; promoting reading fluency 440; responding appropriately to teacher's questions 439; solving mathematical problems 440
visual reception training approach 14, 398, 401; visuo-motor coordination 272, 274
vocational training in schools 641, 642
volition 198, 274

wayfinding 10, 47, 49, 54
web design 53, 57
Wechsler Intelligence scale for Children (WISC-IV) 268, 279
welcoming environments 309, 312
western-based assessment tools 234
White Paper on the Rights of Persons with Disabilities 640, 646
word and text-based intervention 394, 410
word reading and reading comprehension 394, 480
workplace solutions 628
The World Bank 72, 158, 190, 232, 495, 507
World Declaration on Education for All 29; *see also* The United Nations Educational Scientific and Cultural Organization (UNESCO)
World Education Forum (WEF, 2015) 4
World Health Organization 27, 46, 72, 98; World Health Organization Disability Schedule 2.0 182

zone of proximal development 212, 262, 661
zoom lens 10, 29, 223